Street by Street

WEST YORKSHIRE
Enlarged areas BRADFORD, HALIFAX, HUDDERSFIELD, KEIGHLEY, LEEDS, WAKEFIELD
Plus Barnsley, Castleford, Holmfirth, Ilkley, Littleborough, Penistone, Skipton, Tadcaster, Wetherby

3rd edition April 2006
© Automobile Association Developments Limited 2006

Original edition printed May 2001

Ordnance Survey® This product includes map data licensed from Ordnance Survey® with the permission of the Controller of Her Majesty's Stationery Office. © Crown copyright 2006. All rights reserved. Licence number 399221.

Published by AA Publishing (a trading name of Automobile Association Developments Limited, whose registered office is Fanum House, Basing View, Basingstoke, Hampshire RG21 4EA. Registered number 1878835).

Mapping produced by the Cartography Department of The Automobile Association. (A02548)

A CIP Catalogue record for this book is available from the British Library.

Printed and bound by Leo, China

Ref: MX16y

Key to map pages	ii-iii
Key to map symbols	iv-1
Map pages - 1:10,000	2-15
Map pages - 1:17,500	16-271
Index – towns & villages	272-273
Index – streets	274-330
Index – featured places	330-337
Acknowledgements	337

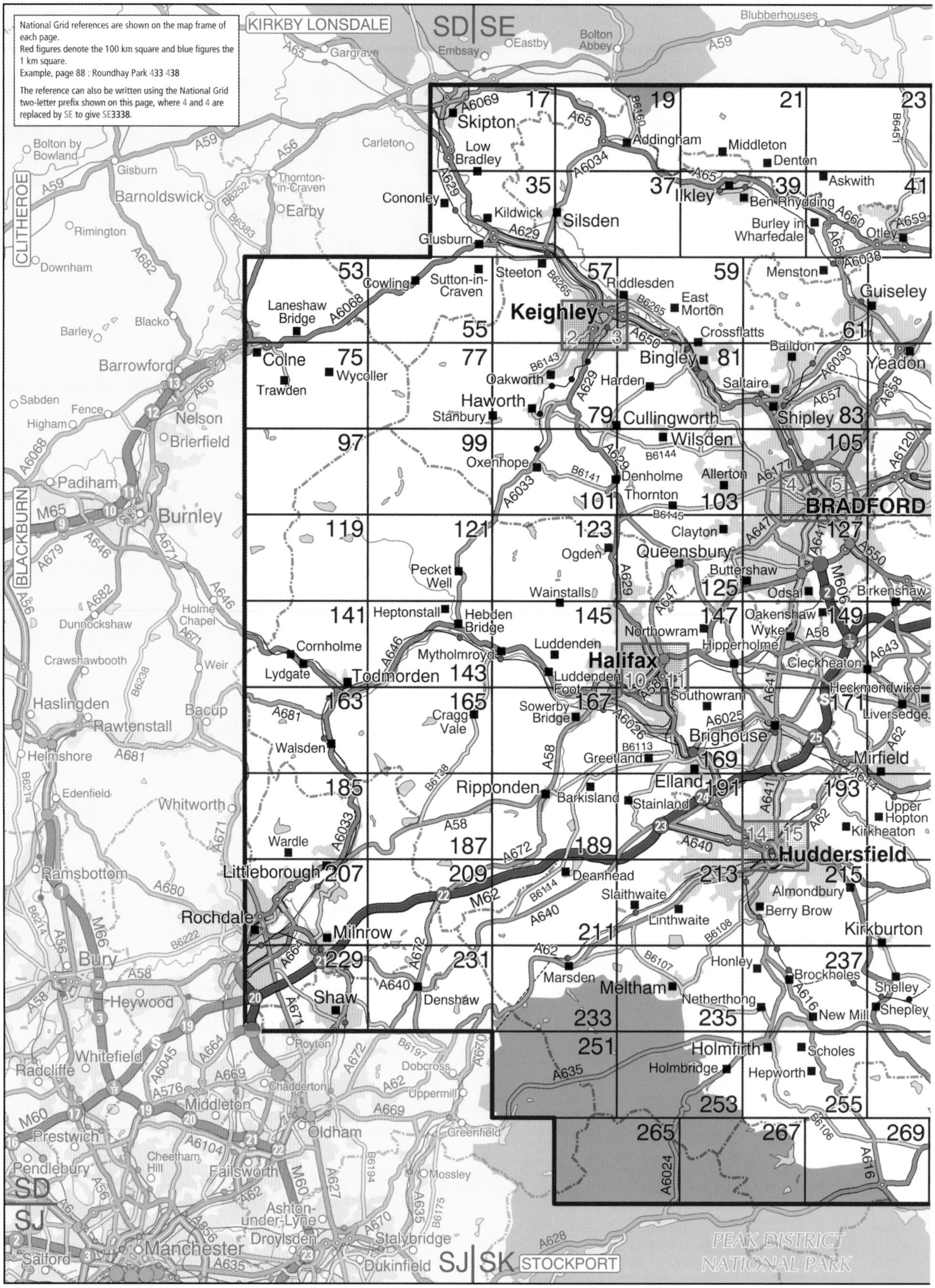

National Grid references are shown on the map frame of each page.
Red figures denote the 100 km square and blue figures the 1 km square.
Example, page 88 : Roundhay Park 433 438

The reference can also be written using the National Grid two-letter prefix shown on this page, where 4 and 4 are replaced by SE to give SE3338.

KIRKBY LONSDALE

SD | SE

Blubberhouses

CLITHEROE

Bolton by Bowland
Gisburn
Barnoldswick
Rimington
Earby
Downham
Barley
Blacko
Barrowford
Sabden
Fence
Higham
Nelson
Brierfield
Colne
Wycoller
Trawden
Padiham
Burnley
BLACKBURN
Dunnockshaw
Crawshawbooth
Holme Chapel
Weir
Haslingden
Rawtenstall
Bacup
Helmshore
Edenfield
Whitworth
Wardle
Ramsbottom
Bury
Heywood
Littleborough
Rochdale
Milnrow
Shaw
Whitefield
Radcliffe
Royton
Chadderton
Middleton
Prestwich
Pendlebury
Salford
Manchester
Droylsden
Dukinfield
Stalybridge
Cheetham Hill
Failsworth
Oldham
Uppermill
Dobcross
Greenfield
Mossley
Ashton-under-Lyne

SD
SJ

SJ | SK STOCKPORT

PEAK DISTRICT NATIONAL PARK

Skipton
Low Bradley
Carleton
Cononley
Gargrave
Thornton-in-Craven
Glusburn
Kildwick
Silsden
Steeton
Cowling
Sutton-in-Craven
Laneshaw Bridge
Keighley
Riddlesden
East Morton
Crossflatts
Bingley
Harden
Saltaire
Oakworth
Haworth
Stanbury
Cullingworth
Wilsden
Oxenhope
Denholme
Thornton
Allerton
Addingham
Middleton
Denton
Ilkley
Ben Rhydding
Burley in Wharfedale
Askwith
Otley
Menston
Guiseley
Baildon
Yeadon
Shipley
BRADFORD
Clayton
Queensbury
Buttershaw
Odsal
Birkenshaw
Oakenshaw
Wyke
Ogden
Wainstalls
Heptonstall
Hebden Bridge
Luddenden
Northowram
Halifax
Hipperholme
Cleckheaton
Heckmondwike
Liversedge
Cornholme
Mytholmroyd
Luddenden Foot
Southowram
Lydgate
Todmorden
Sowerby Bridge
Brighouse
Cragg Vale
Greetland
Elland
Mirfield
Walsden
Ripponden
Barkisland
Stainland
Upper Hopton
Kirkheaton
Pecket Well
Huddersfield
Deanhead
Slaithwaite
Almondbury
Berry Brow
Kirkburton
Linthwaite
Denshaw
Marsden
Meltham
Honley
Brockholes
Shelley
Shepley
Netherthong
New Mill
Holmfirth
Scholes
Holmbridge
Hepworth

17 19 21 23
35 37 39 41
53 57 59
55 61
75 77 81
79 83
97 99 105
101 103 127
119 121 123 125
141 145 147 149
143 171
163 165 167 169 191 193
185 187 189 213 215
207 209 211 237
229 231 233 235
251 253 255
265 267 269

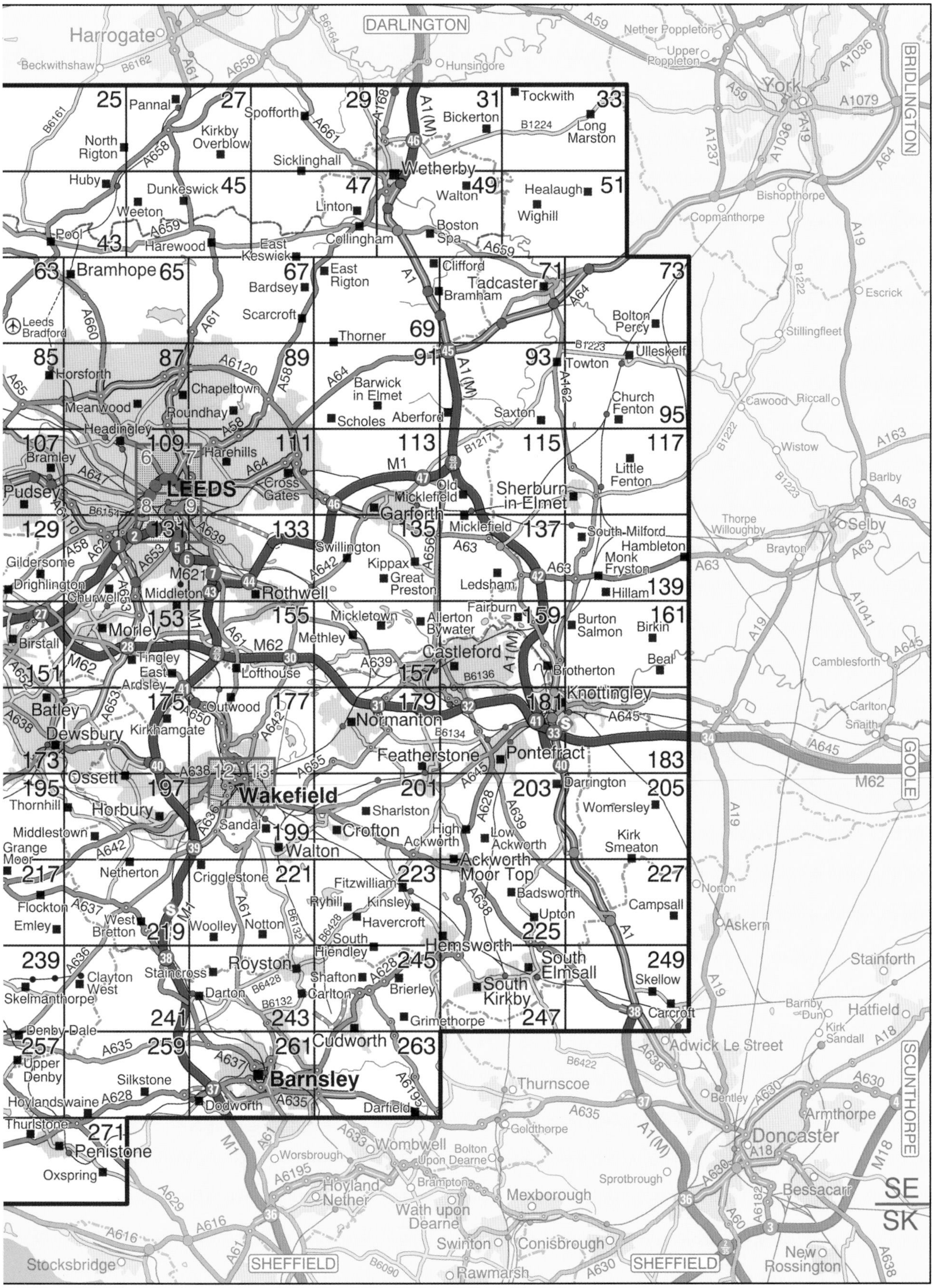

Harrogate
Beckwithshaw
B6162
A61
A658
B6164
DARLINGTON
Hunsingore
A59
Nether Poppleton
Upper Poppleton
BRIDLINGTON
York
A1036
A1079
A59
A19
A64
A1237
Bishopthorpe
Copmanthorpe
25
Pannal
27
Spofforth
29
A168
A1(M)
31
Bickerton
Tockwith
33
B1224
Long Marston
B6161
North Rigton
A658
Kirkby Overblow
A661
Sicklinghall
46
Wetherby
Huby
Dunkeswick
45
47
49
Walton
Healaugh
51
Weeton
Linton
Wighill
A659
Pool
43
Harewood
East Keswick
Collingham
Boston Spa
A659
63
Bramhope
65
67
East Rigton
Bardsey
A1
Clifford
Tadcaster
71
73
Bramham
A64
Leeds Bradford
A660
A61
Scarcroft
Bolton Percy
B1222
Escrick
Stillingfleet
Thorner
69
B1223
Ulleskelf
85
Horsforth
87
A6120
89
A58
A64
91
45
A1(M)
93
Towton
A162
A65
Chapeltown
Barwick in Elmet
Church Fenton
Cawood
Riccall
Meanwood
Roundhay
Scholes
Aberford
Saxton
95
Headingley
A58
107
Bramley
109
Harehills
111
113
B1217
115
117
Wistow
A163
6
7
A64
M1
48 44
Little Fenton
Barlby
Pudsey
A647
LEEDS
Cross Gates
47
Old
Sherburn in Elmet
B1223
A610
B6154
8
9
46
Micklefield
Garforth
A63
129
A58
131
A639
133
135
Micklefield
137
South Milford
Thorpe Willoughby
Selby
A62
1
2
5
A653
A6110
Swillington
A656
A63
Hambleton
Brayton
A63
Gildersome
6
A642
Kippax
Monk Fryston
A63
Drighlington
A653
M621
7
44
Great Preston
Ledsham
42
A63
139
Churwell
Middleton
43
Rothwell
Hillam
A1041
27
153
M1
155
Mickletown
Allerton Bywater
Fairburn
159
Burton Salmon
161
Birkin
Birstall
Morley
Methley
A19
28
Tingley
A61
M62
30
Castleford
A1(M)
A645
A62
151
M62
29 42
A639
157
B6136
Brotherton
Beal
Camblesforth
East Ardsley
Lofthouse
41
Batley
A653
175
A650
Outwood
177
31
179
32
181
Knottingley
Carlton
A638
Kirkhamgate
A642
Normanton
41
A645
33
Snaith
Dewsbury
B6134
34
A645
GOOLE
173
40
A638
12
13
A655
Featherstone
Pontefract
40
183
M62
195
Ossett
197
Wakefield
201
A645
203
Darrington
205
Thornhill
Horbury
Sharlston
A628
A639
Womersley
A19
A636
Middlestown
Sandal
199
Crofton
High Ackworth
Low Ackworth
Kirk Smeaton
Grange Moor
A642
39
Walton
Ackworth Moor Top
217
Netherton
Crigglestone
221
Fitzwilliam
223
227
Norton
Flockton
A637
A61
Ryhill
Kinsley
A638
Badsworth
Campsall
Emley
West Bretton
S
M1
219
Woolley
Notton
B6132
B6428
Havercroft
Upton
225
A1
Askern
South Hiendley
Hemsworth
239
A636
Clayton West
38
Staincross
Royston
Shafton
A628
245
South Elmsall
249
Skellow
Stainforth
Skelmanthorpe
Darton
B6428
Carlton
Brierley
South Kirkby
A19
B6132
243
247
38
Carcroft
Barnby Dun
Hatfield
Denby Dale
241
Grimethorpe
Kirk Sandall
257
A635
259
261
Cudworth
263
A638
Adwick Le Street
A18
Upper Denby
A637
B6422
SCUNTHORPE
Barnsley
A6195
Thurnscoe
A630
Silkstone
Hoylandswaine
A628
37
Dodworth
A635
Darfield
Bentley
A630
37
4
A635
Armthorpe
Thurlstone
271
A633
Goldthorpe
Penistone
M1
A61
Wombwell
Bolton upon Dearne
A1(M)
Doncaster
A18
M18
Worsbrough
Oxspring
A6195
Hoyland Nether
Brampton
Sprotbrough
A630
A6182
Bessacarr
A629
Mexborough
36
SE
SK
36
Wath upon Dearne
A60
3
A616
A616
Swinton
Conisbrough
A61
Stocksbridge
SHEFFIELD
B6090
Rawmarsh
A630
SHEFFIELD
New Rossington
A638

3.6 inches to 1 mile **Scale of main map pages 1:17,500**

0 1/2 miles 1

0 1/2 1 kilometres 1 1/2 2

Junction 9	Motorway & junction		_LC_	Level crossing
Services	Motorway service area		•—•—•—•—•	Tramway
	Primary road single/dual carriageway		- - - - - - - - - -	Ferry route
Services	Primary road service area		··············	Airport runway
	A road single/dual carriageway		—·—·—·—	County, administrative boundary
	B road single/dual carriageway		＼＼＼＼＼＼＼	Mounds
	Other road single/dual carriageway		**93**	Page continuation 1:17,500
	Minor/private road, access may be restricted		**7**	Page continuation to enlarged scale 1:10,000
← ←	One-way street			River/canal, lake
	Pedestrian area			Aqueduct, lock, weir
- - - - - - - - -	Track or footpath		465 ▲ Winter Hill	Peak (with height in metres)
■■■■■■■■ ■■■■■■■■	Road under construction			Beach
[─ ─ ─ ─ ─]	Road tunnel			Woodland
P	Parking			Park
P+🚌	Park & Ride		✝✝✝✝✝ ✝✝✝✝✝	Cemetery
🚌	Bus/coach station			Built-up area
	Railway & main railway station		▰	Industrial building
	Railway & minor railway station		▰	Leisure building
⊖	Underground station		▰	Retail building
⊖	Light railway & station		▰	Other building
++++++++	Preserved private railway		**IKEA**	IKEA store

ᴍᴍᴍᴍᴍ	City wall		♆	Castle
A&E	Hospital with 24-hour A&E department		⌂	Historic house or building
PO	Post Office		Wakehurst Place NT	National Trust property
📖	Public library		Ⓜ	Museum or art gallery
i	Tourist Information Centre		♞	Roman antiquity
i	Seasonal Tourist Information Centre		⊥	Ancient site, battlefield or monument
⛽ ⛽	Petrol station, 24 hour Major suppliers only		⛭	Industrial interest
†	Church/chapel		✳	Garden
🚻	Public toilets		◉	Garden Centre Garden Centre Association Member
♿	Toilet with disabled facilities		❀	Garden Centre Wyevale Garden Centre
PH	Public house AA recommended		♣	Arboretum
◑	Restaurant AA inspected		🛒	Farm or animal centre
Madeira Hotel	Hotel AA inspected		🦌	Zoological or wildlife collection
🎭	Theatre or performing arts centre		🦅	Bird collection
🎥	Cinema		🐋	Nature reserve
⚑	Golf course		🐟	Aquarium
▲	Camping AA inspected		Ⅴ	Visitor or heritage centre
🚐	Caravan site AA inspected		♈	Country park
▲🚐	Camping & caravan site AA inspected		⌒	Cave
🎢	Theme park		🎯	Windmill
⛪	Abbey, cathedral or priory		🛢	Distillery, brewery or vineyard

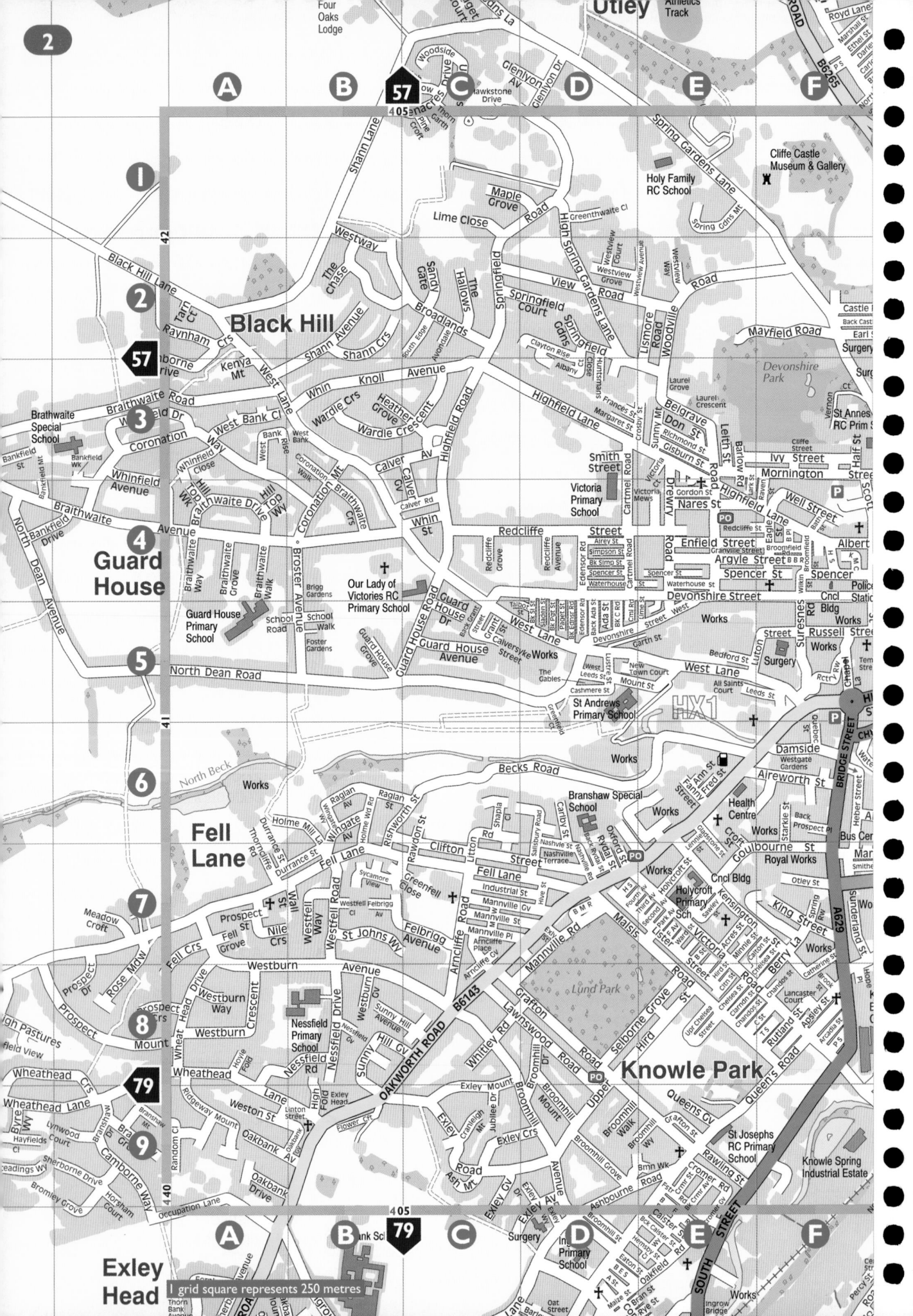

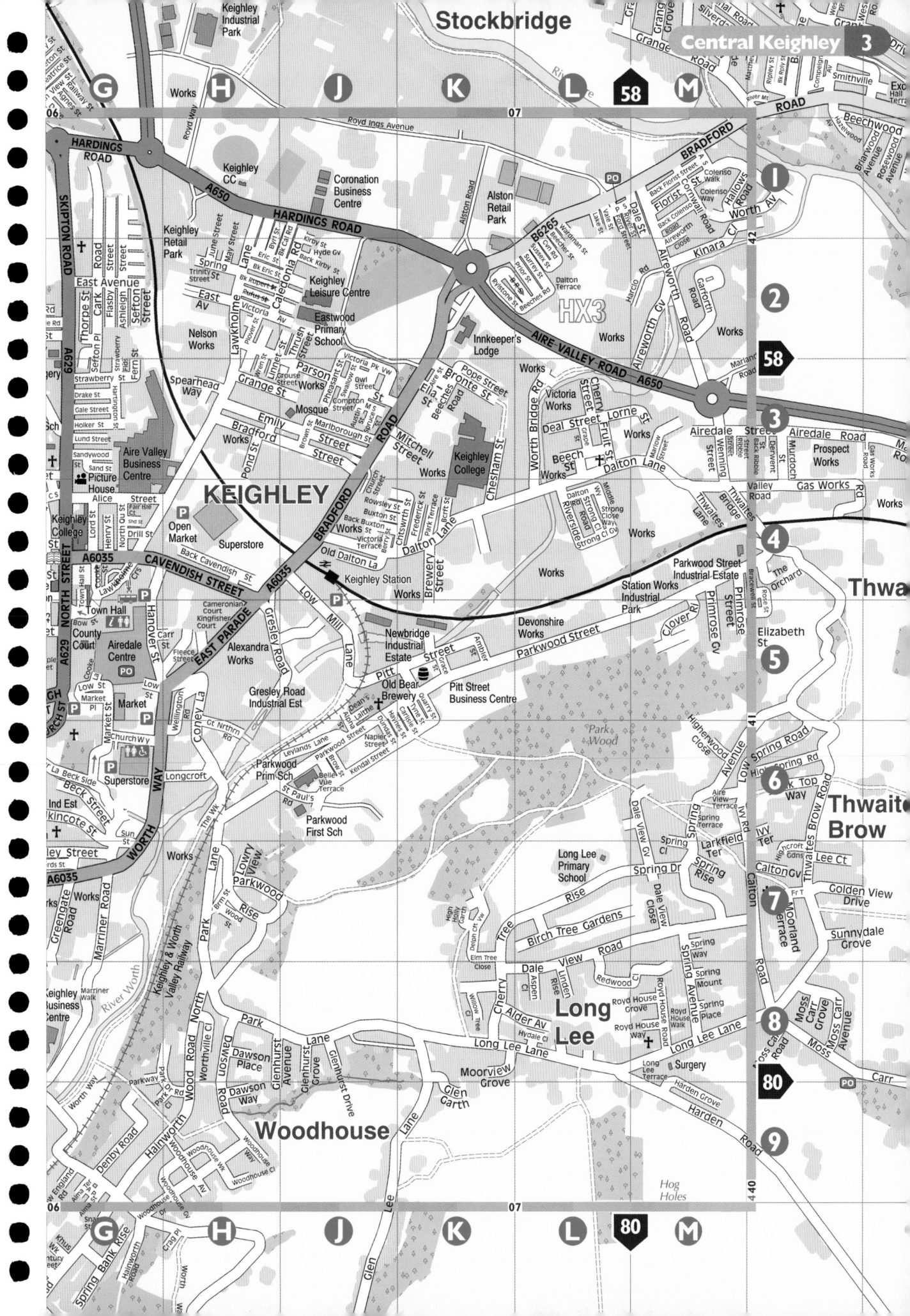

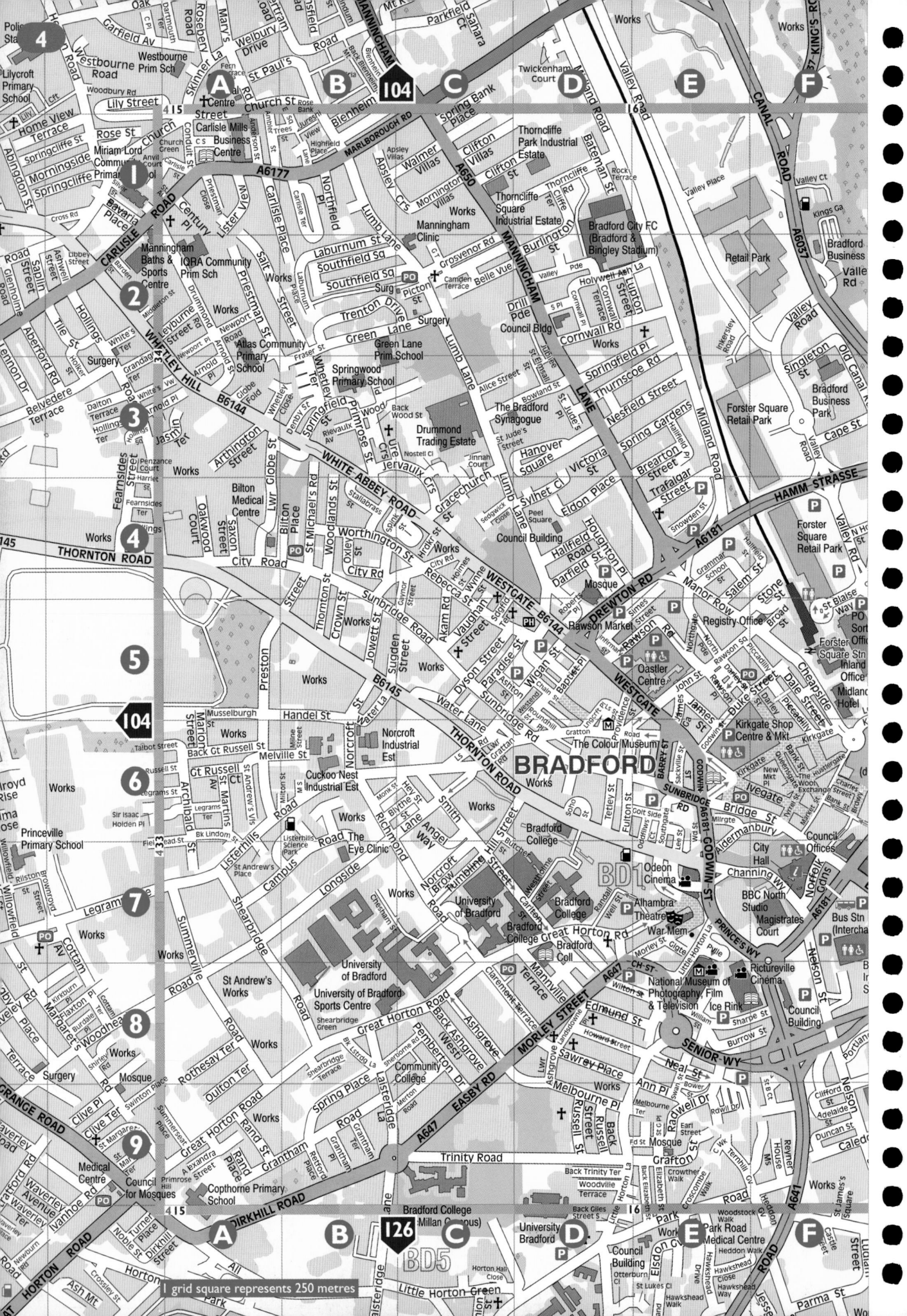

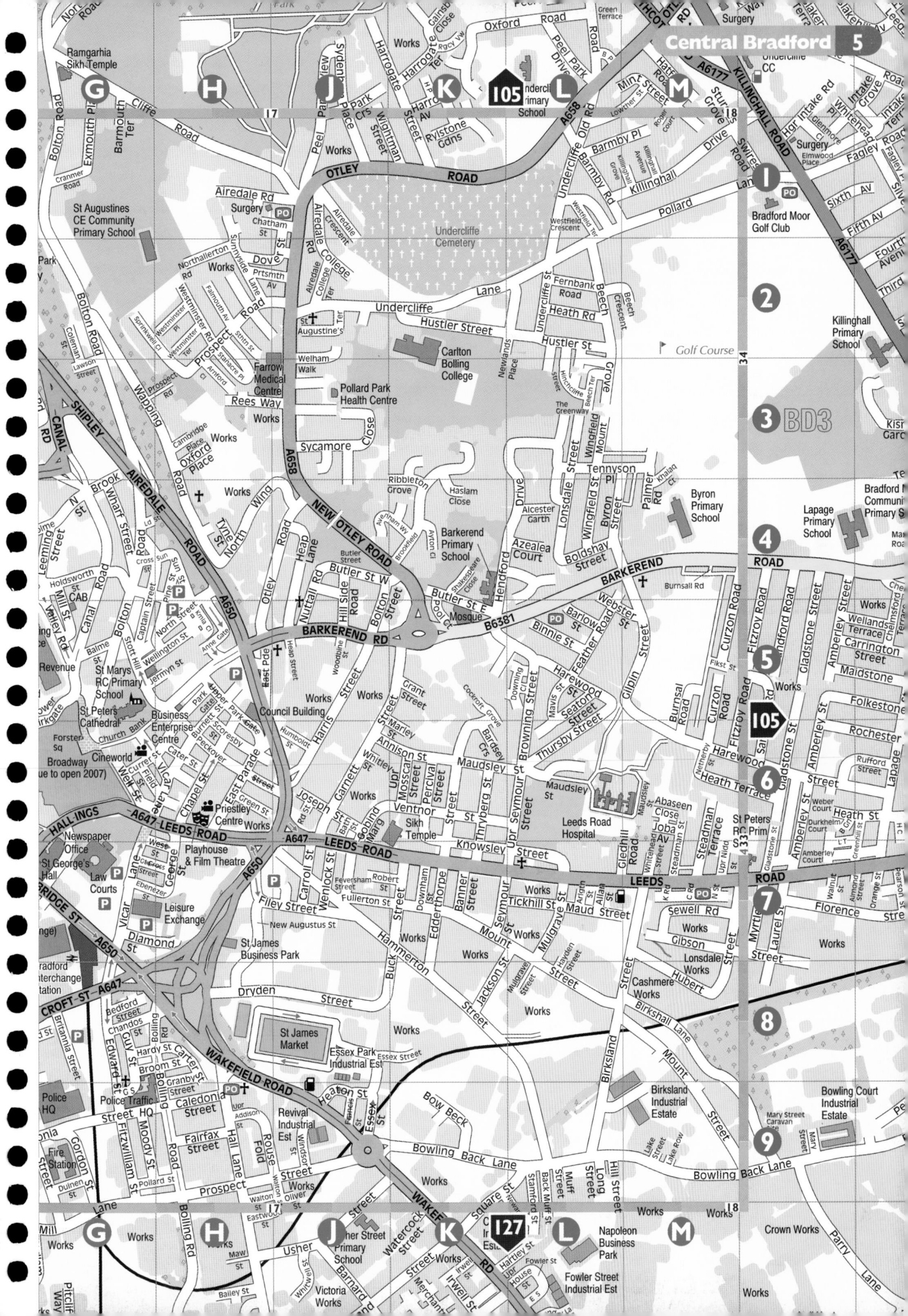

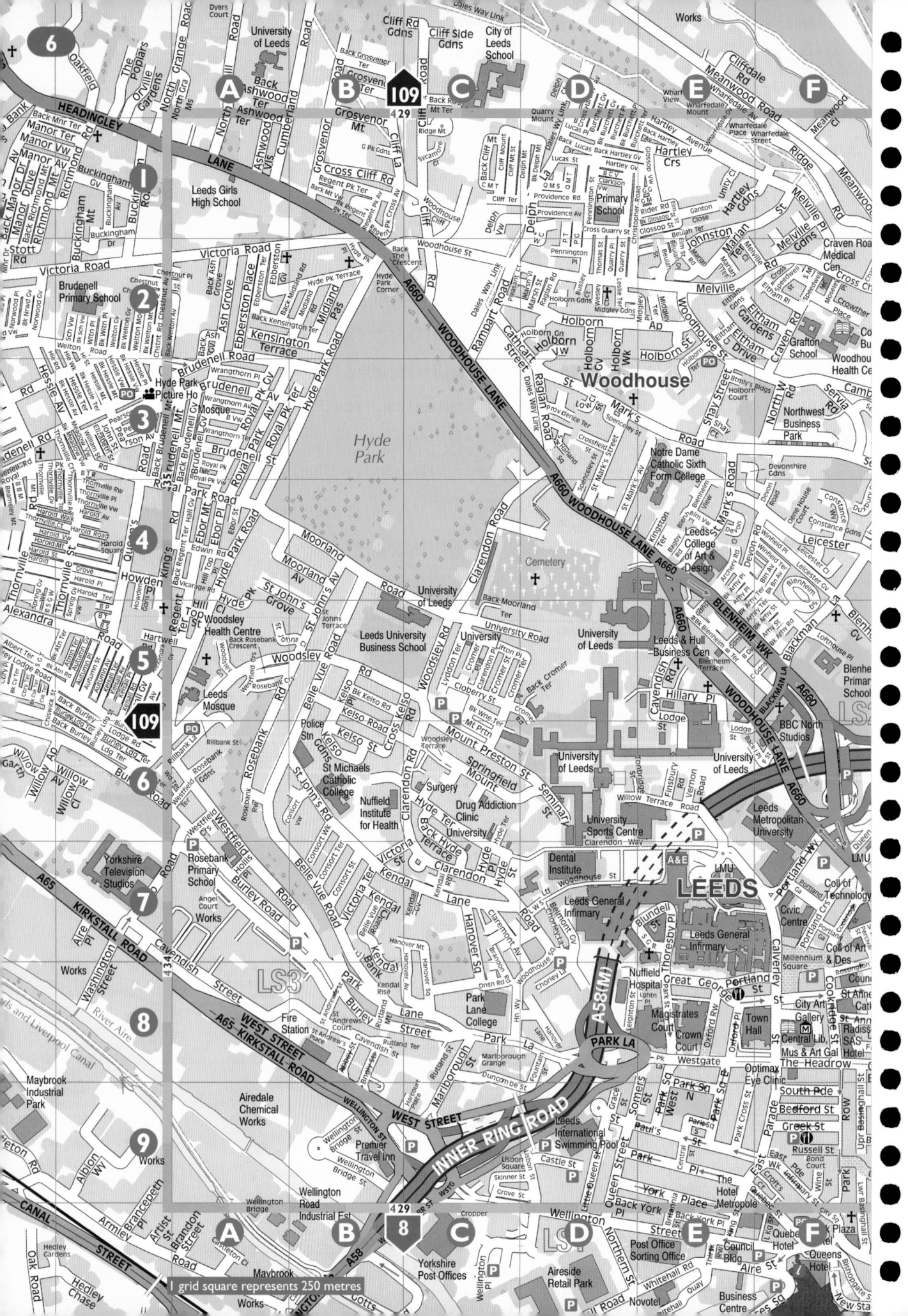

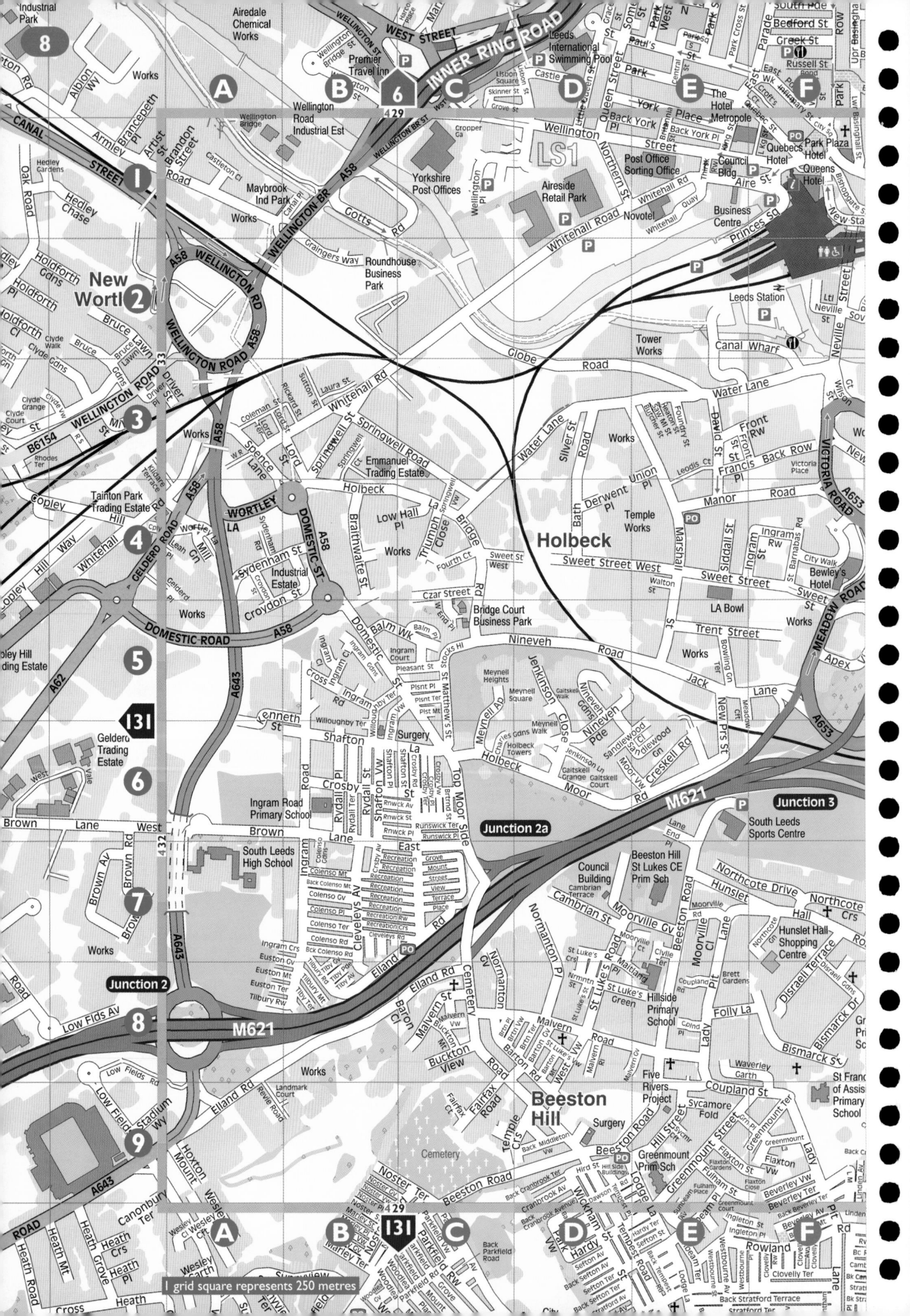

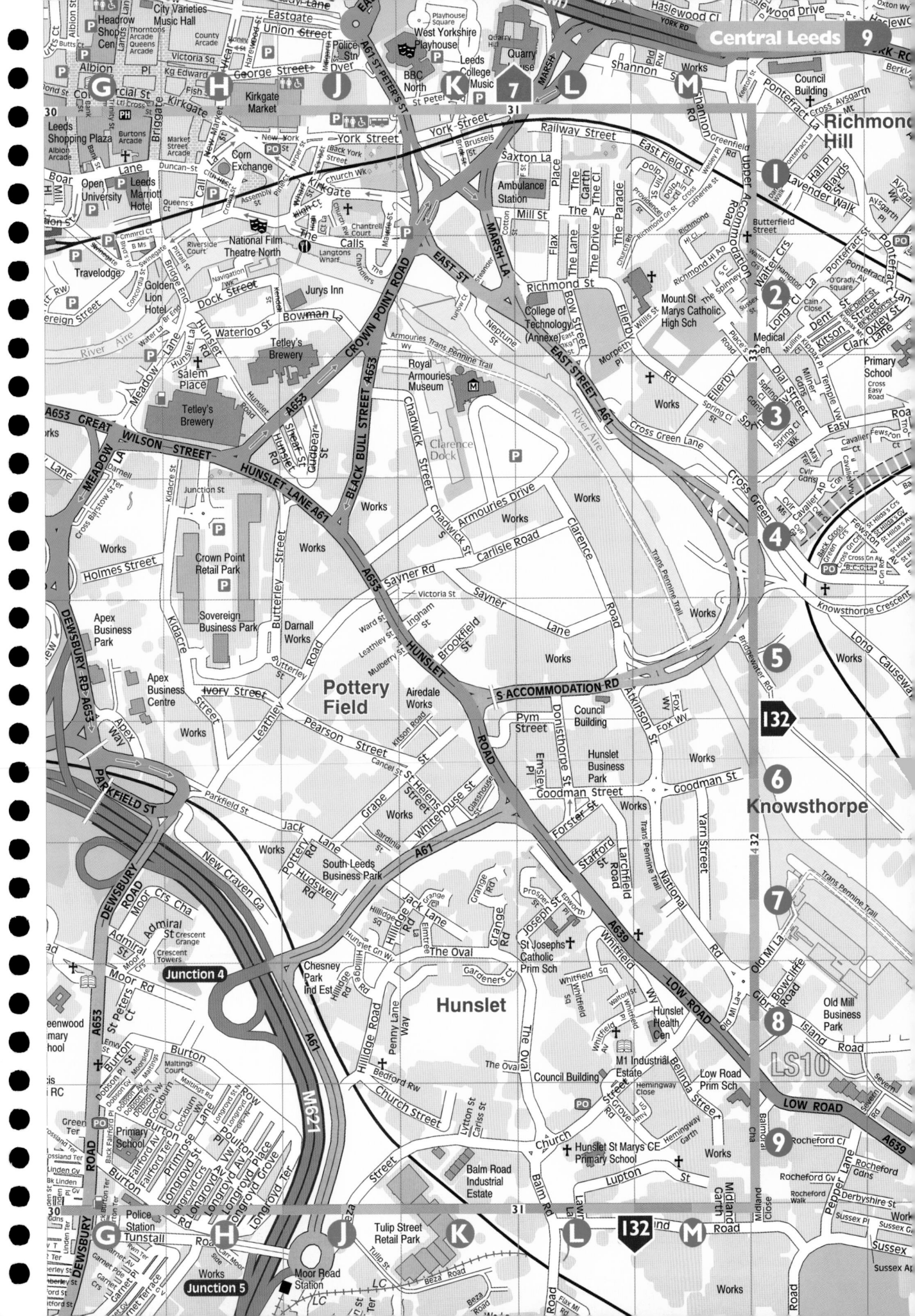

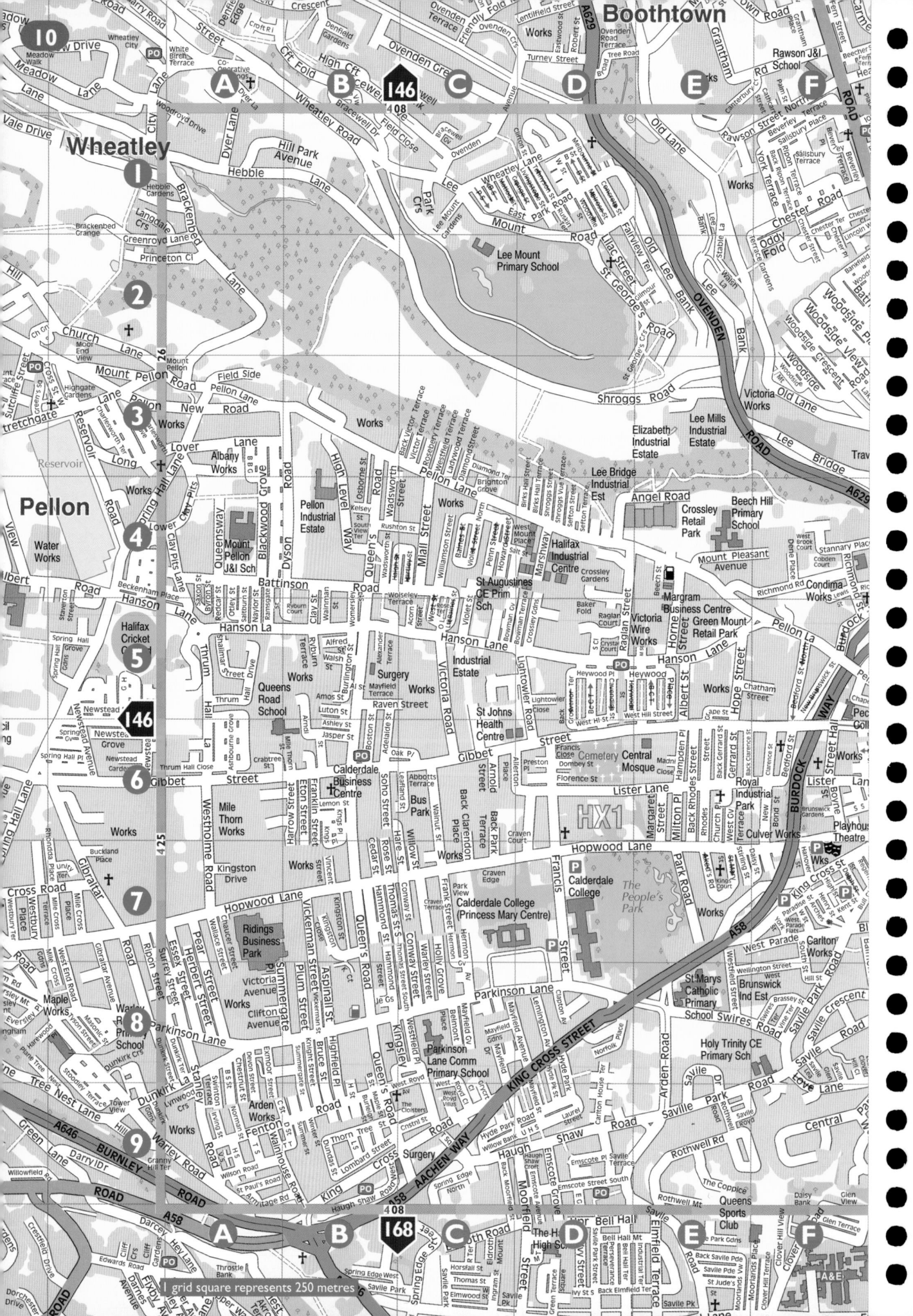

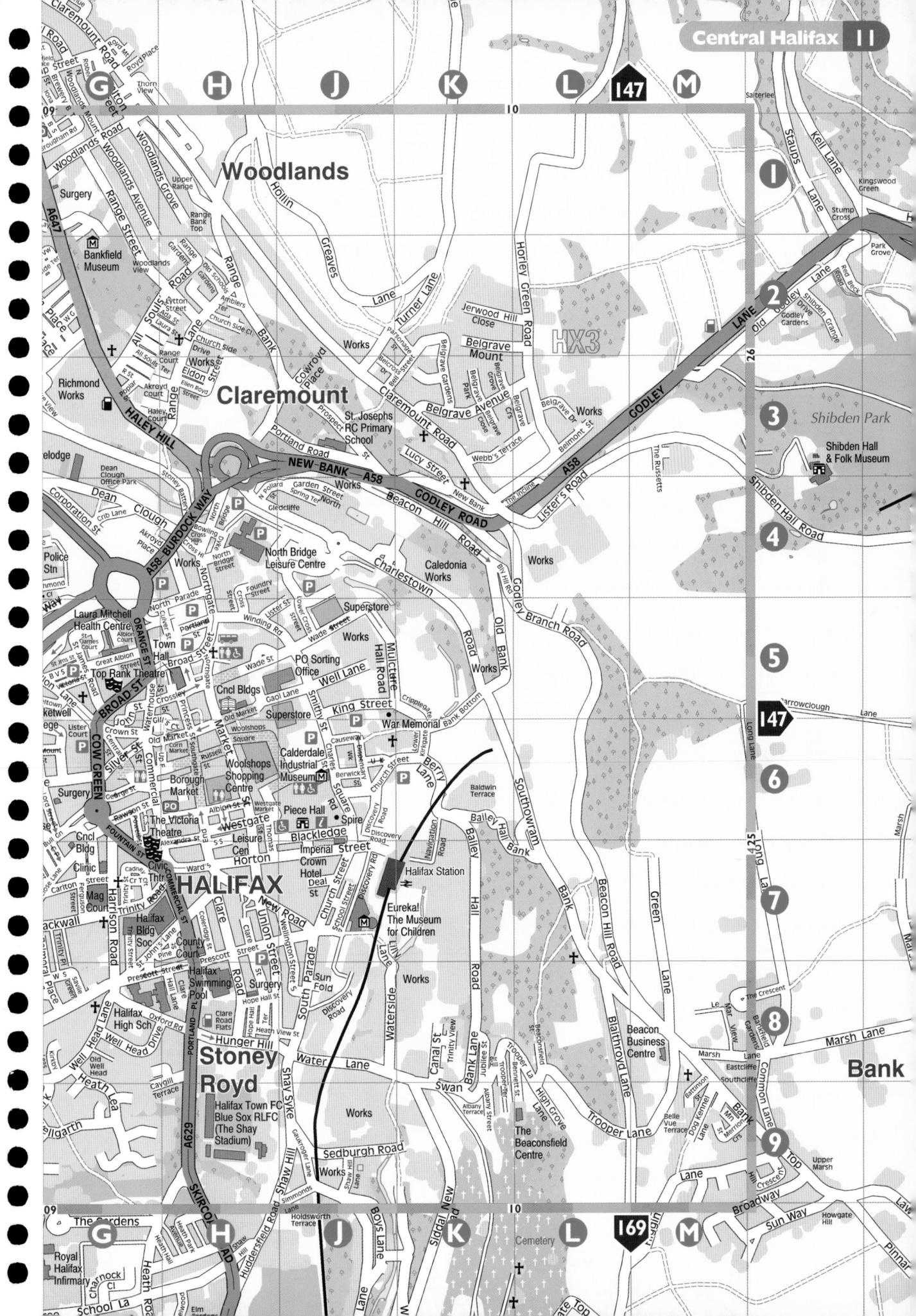

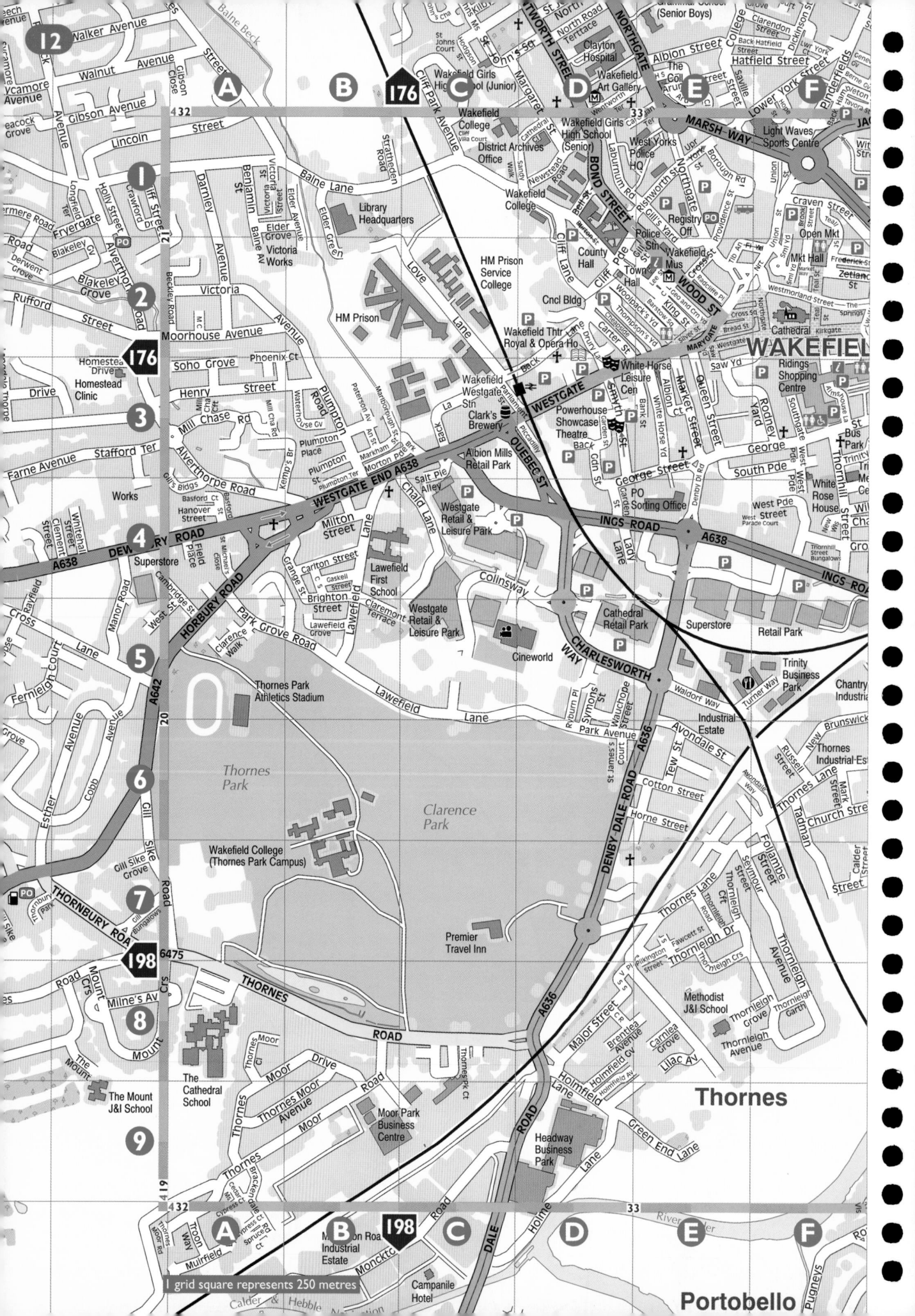

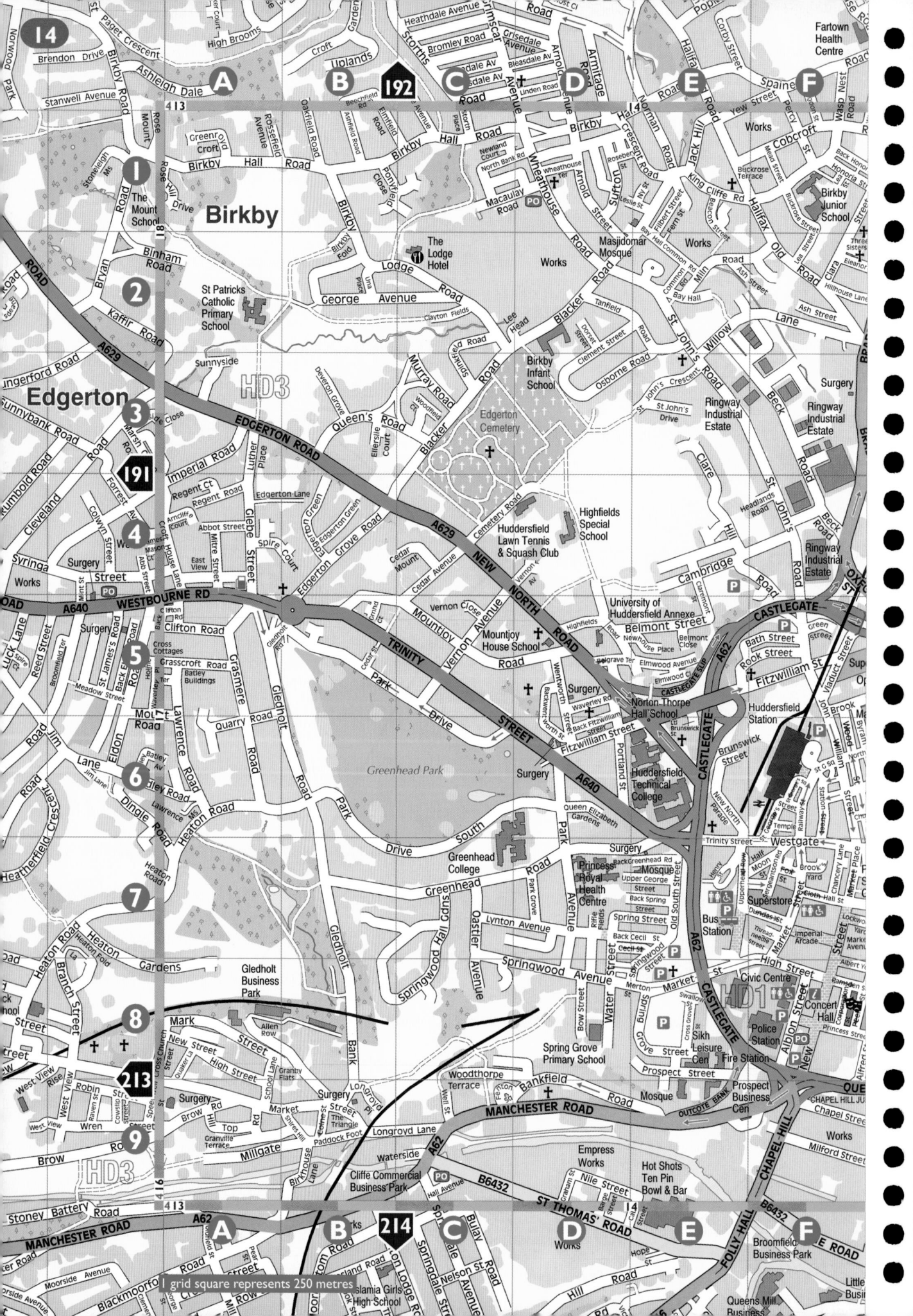

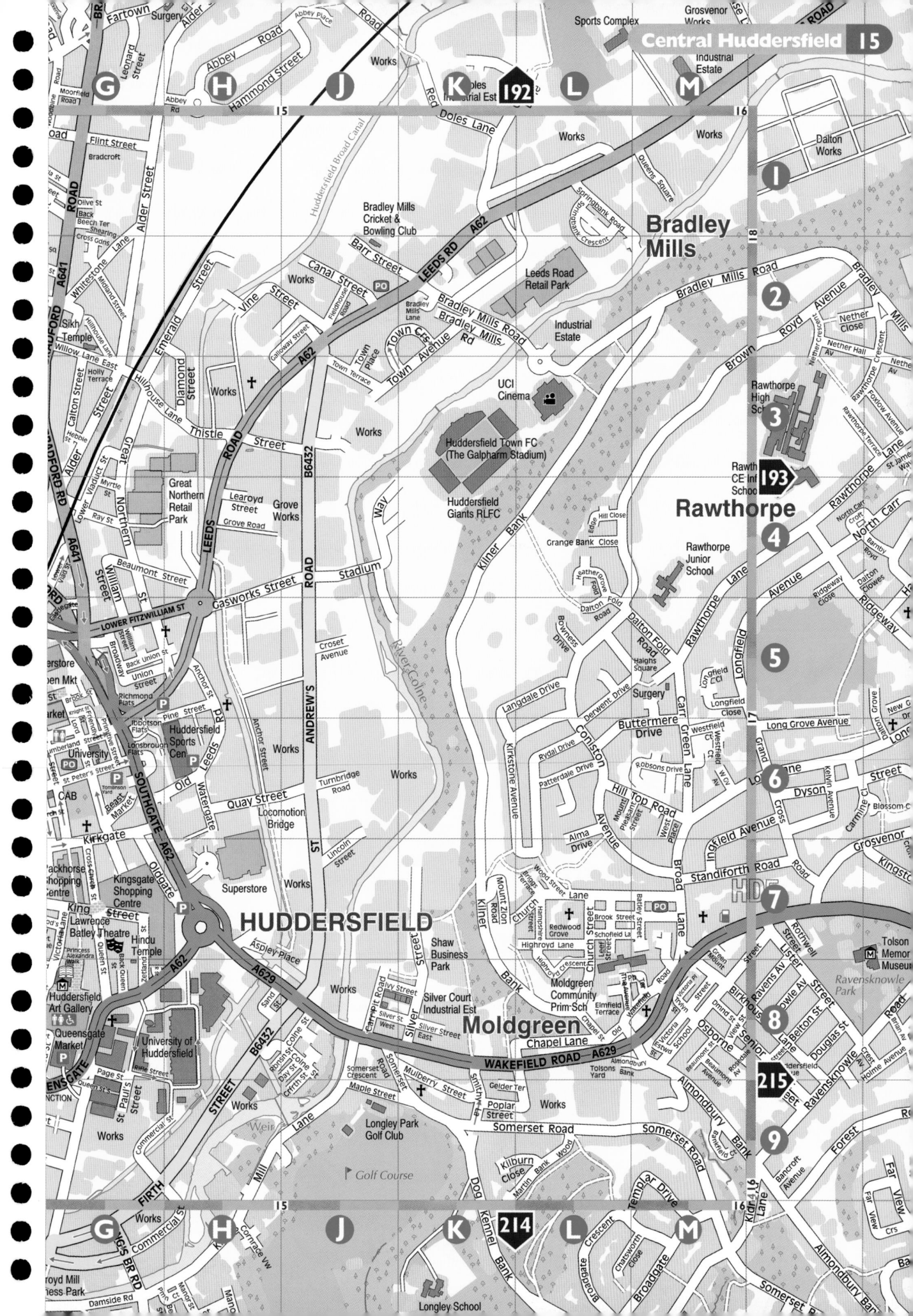

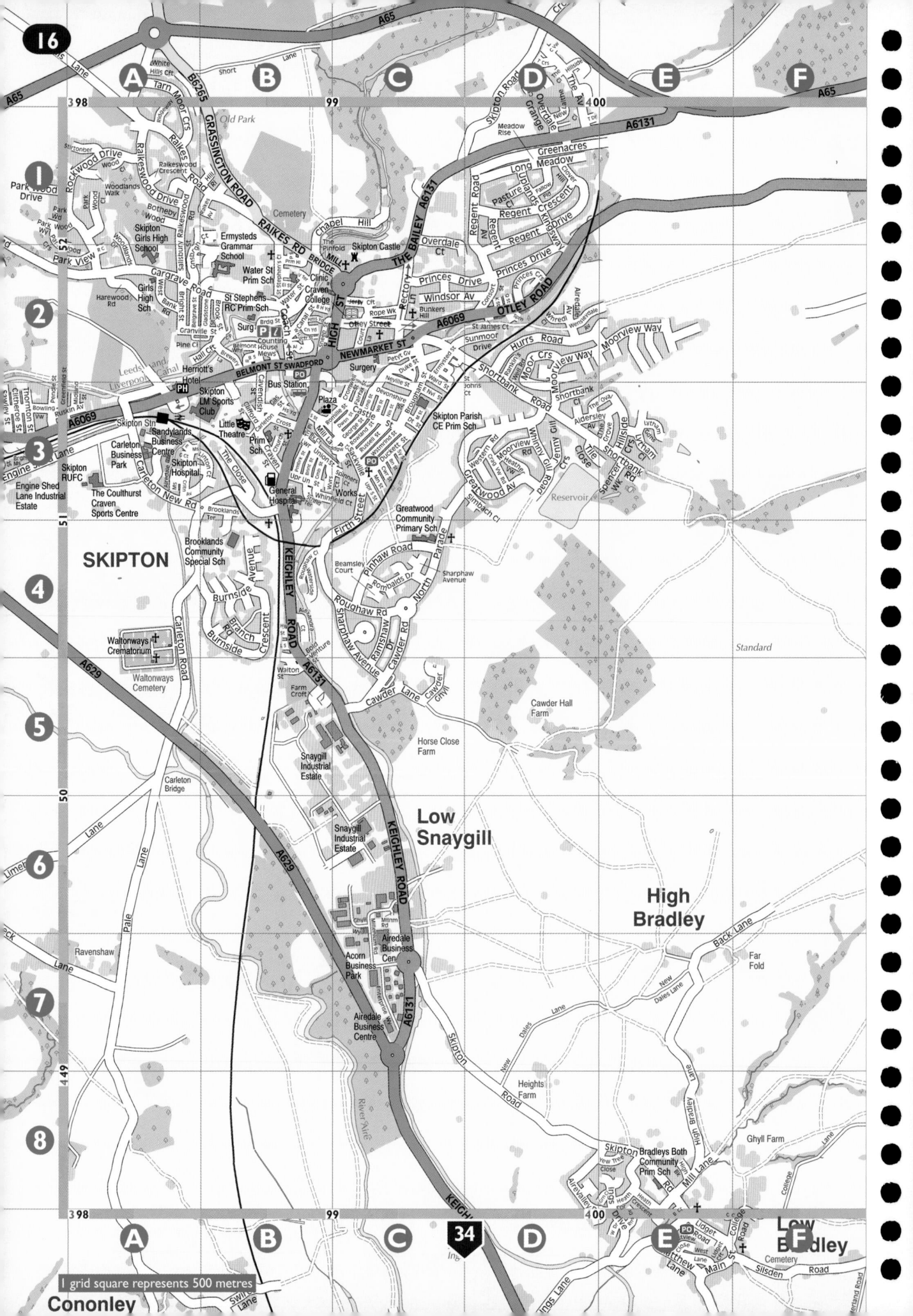

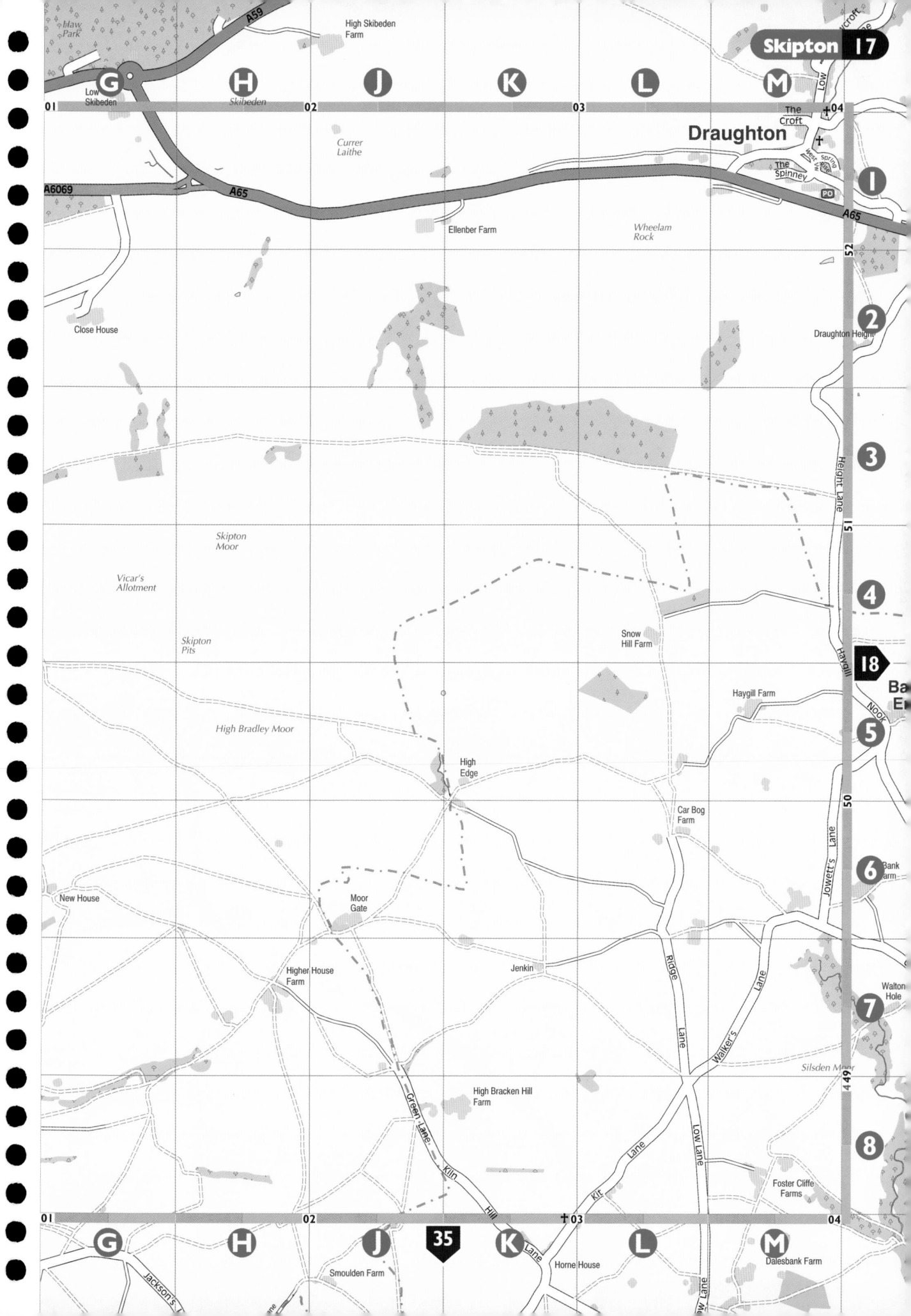

G H J K L M

01 02 03 04

Haw Park

Low Skibeden

Skibeden

High Skibeden Farm

Currer Laithe

Draughton

The Croft

West Spring

The Spinney

PO

A59

A6069

A65

A65

Ellenber Farm

Wheelam Rock

Close House

Draughton Height

52

1

2

3

51

Height Lane

Skipton Moor

Vicar's Allotment

Skipton Pits

Snow Hill Farm

Haygill Farm

4

18

5

Haygill

Nook

Ba
E

High Bradley Moor

High Edge

Car Bog Farm

Jowett's Lane

50

6

Bank Farm

New House

Moor Gate

Jenkin

Ridge Lane

Walker's Lane

Walton Hole

Silsden Moor

7

449

Higher House Farm

High Bracken Hill Farm

Green Lane

Kiln Hill Lane

Kirk Lane

Low Lane

Foster Cliffe Farms

8

Jackson's

Smoulden Farm

Horne House

Dalesbank Farm

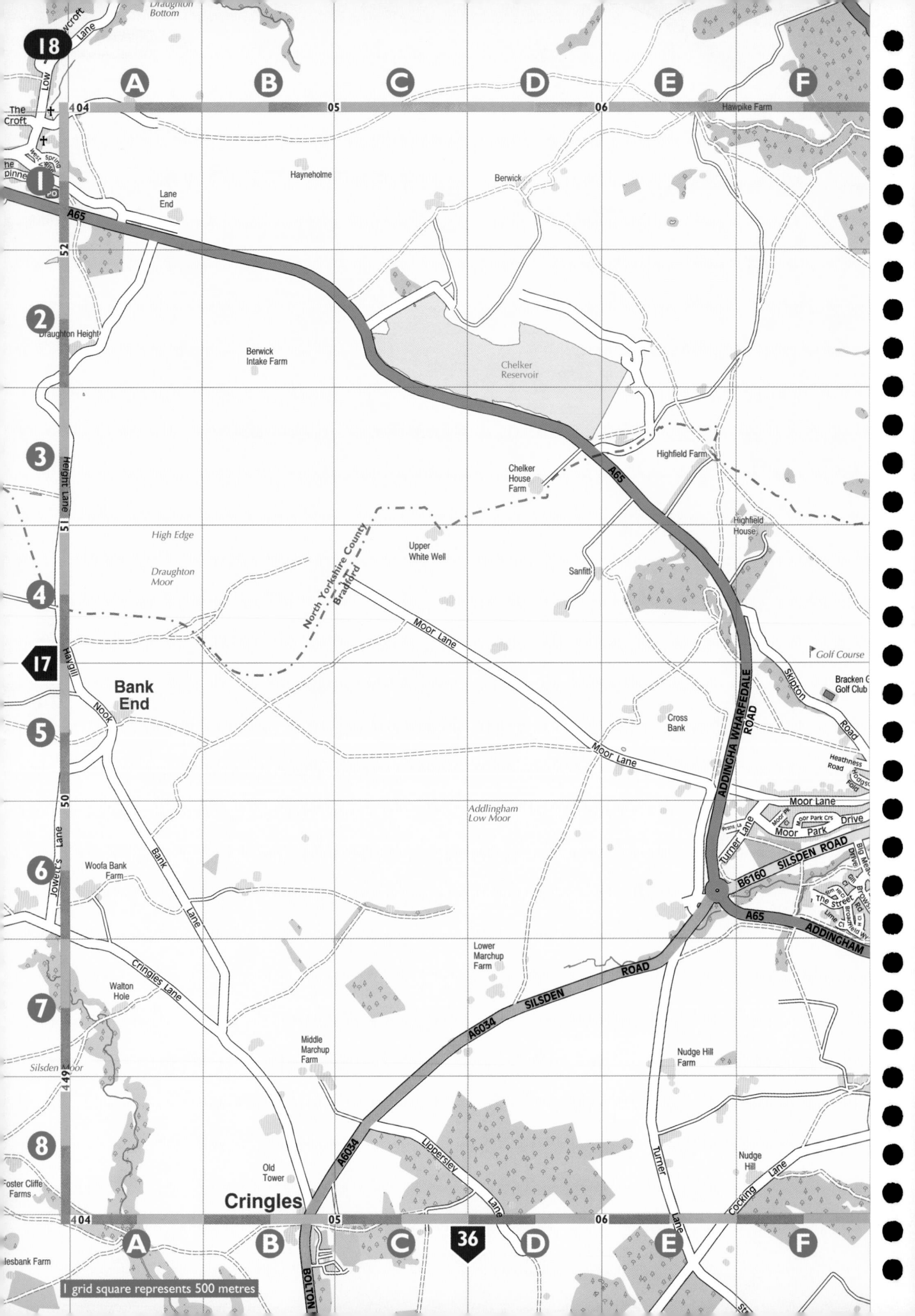

A B C D E F

404 05 06

The Croft

Hawpike Farm

Hayneholme

Berwick

Lane End

1

A65

52

2

Draughton Height

Berwick Intake Farm

Chelker Reservoir

3

Chelker House Farm

Highfield Farm

51

High Edge

Upper White Well

Highfield House

Draughton Moor

Sanfitt

North Yorkshire County. Bradford

Moor Lane

Golf Course

17

Bank End

Addlingham Low Moor

Addingha Wharfedale Road

Skipton Road

Bracken G Golf Club

5

Moor Lane

Cross Bank

Heathness Road

50

Moor Lane

Turner Lane

Moor Park Drive

Moor Park

Height Lane

Haw Gill

Nook

Towers Lane

Bank Lane

Woofa Bank Farm

B6160 SILSDEN ROAD

6

A65

ADDINGHAM

Lower Marchup Farm

Cringles Lane

Walton Hole

Middle Marchup Farm

SILSDEN ROAD

A6034

7

Nudge Hill Farm

449

Silsden Moor

A6034

Uppersley Lane

Turner Lane

Nudge Hill

8

Foster Cliffe Farms

Old Tower

Cocking Lane

esbank Farm

Cringles

404

05

06

BOLTON

A B C D E F

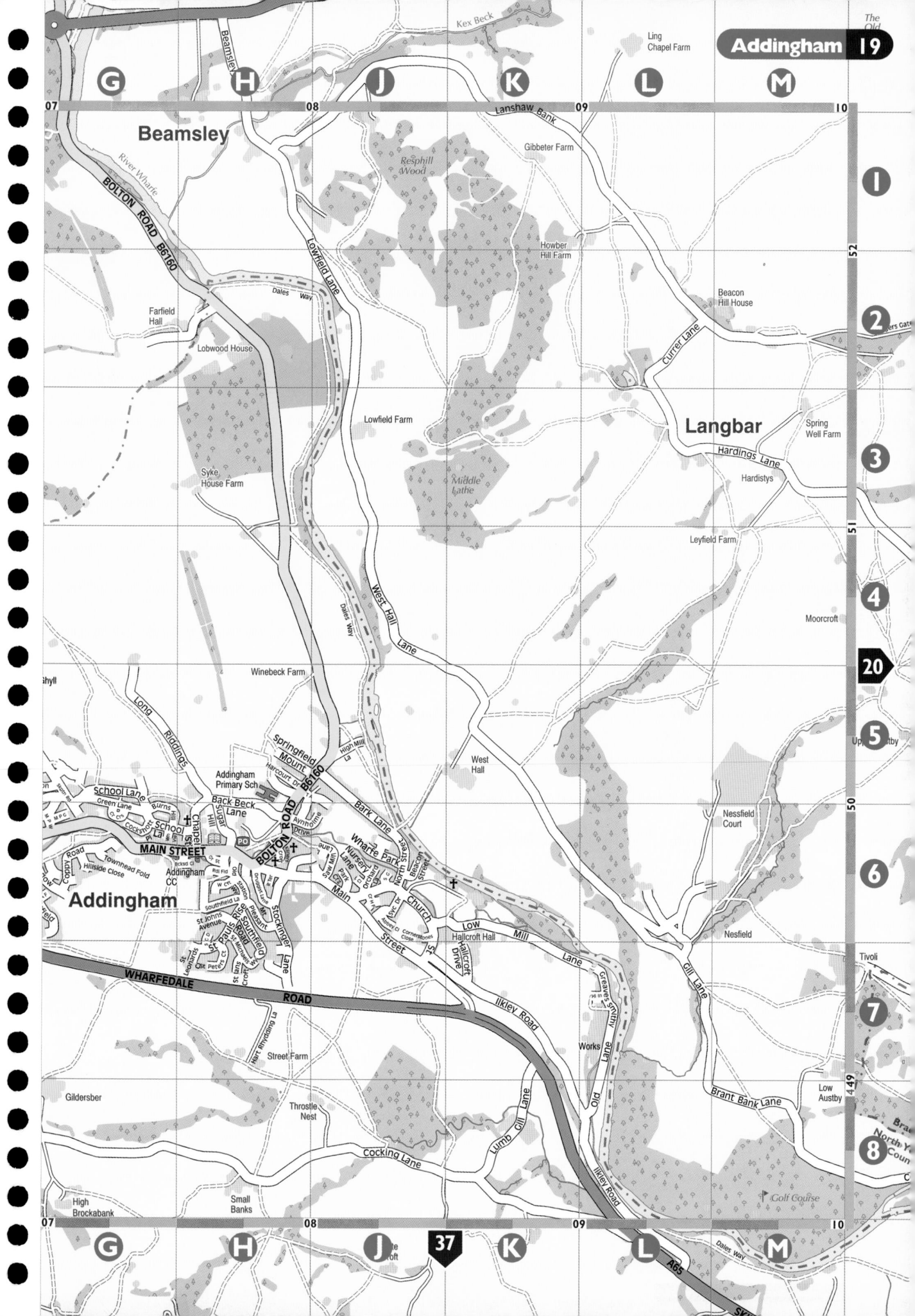

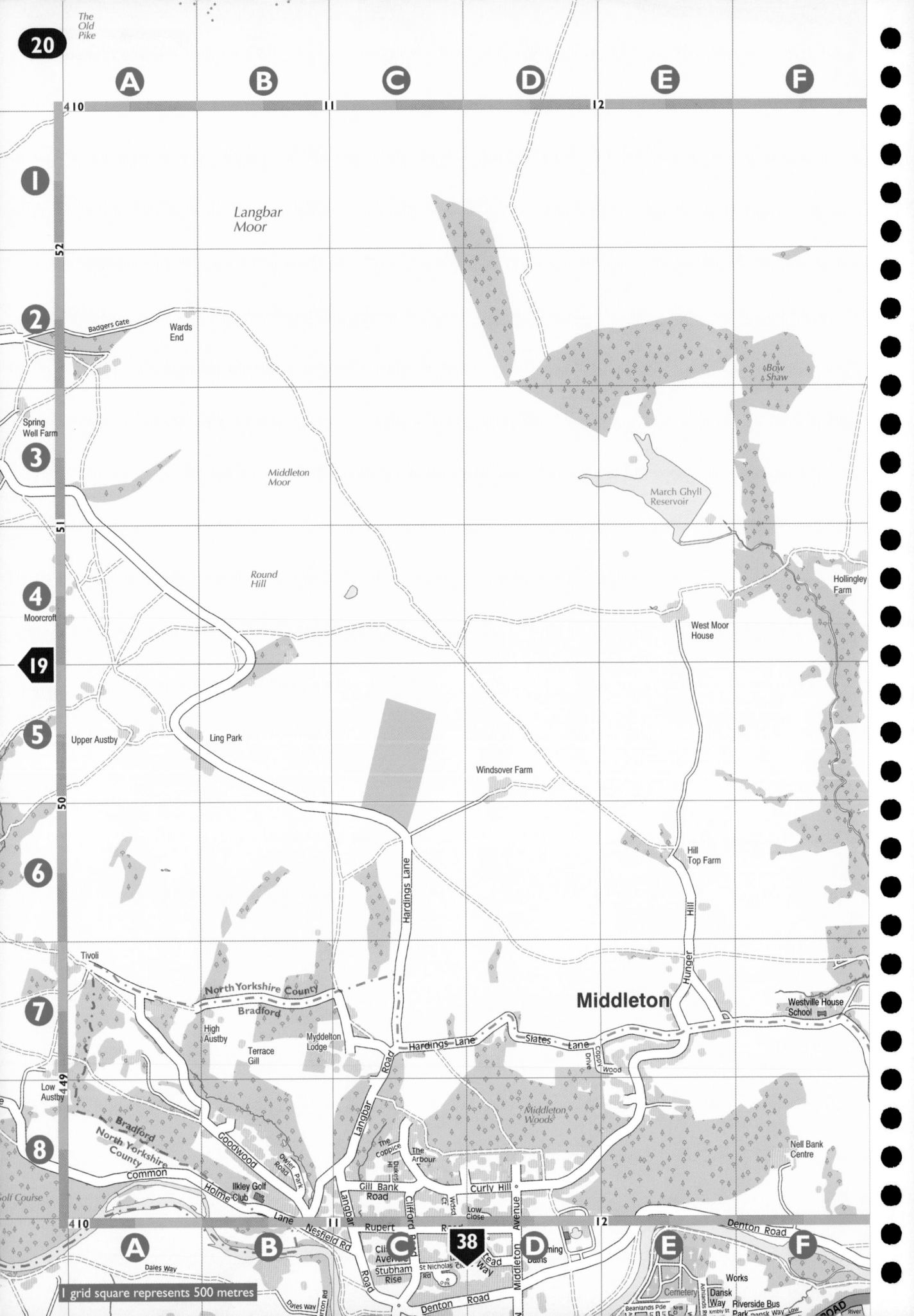

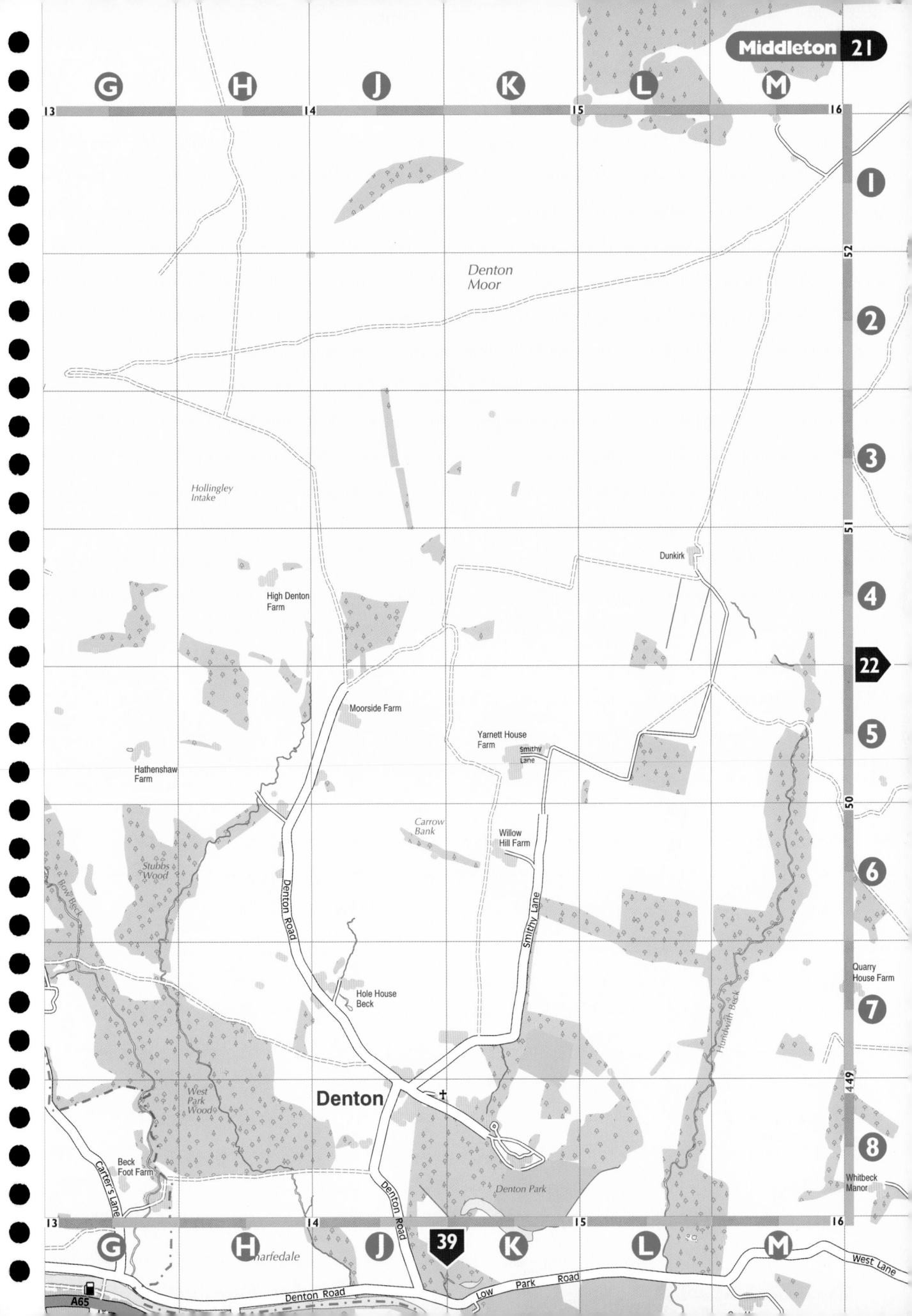

G H J K L M

13 14 15 16

I

52

2

Denton
Moor

3

51

Hollingley
Intake

Dunkirk

4

22

High Denton
Farm

5

Moorside Farm

Yarnett House
Farm

Smithy
Lane

50

Hathenshaw
Farm

Carrow
Bank

Willow
Hill Farm

6

Stubbs
Wood

Bow Beck

Denton Road

Smithy Lane

Hundwith Beck

Quarry
House Farm

7

A 49

Hole House
Beck

West
Park
Wood

Denton

✝

8

Beck
Foot Farm

Carter's Lane

Denton Park

Whitbeck
Manor

13 14 15 16

Wharfedale

Denton Road

39

Low Park Road

West Lane

A65

Denton Road

Timble

A B C D E F

416 17 18

52

1

2

51

3

Askwith
Moor

Timble Gill Beck

Shaw Hall

Low Snowden

Snowden Crags

Carr Farm

4

21

5

50

Snowden
Carr

Snowden Carr Road

Dob
Park

6

Brick House
Farm

Weston
Moor

Weston Moor Road

Quarry
House Farm

Scales
House Farm

Moorside Farm

Moorside

Lane

Hobb Nook Lane

Whin
Castle Farm

Moor Lane

7

449

Moor
Plantation

8

Whitbeck
Manor

Hall Lane

Town
Head

Askwith Lane

East Beck

Grassgarth Farm

Lane Head
Farm

416 17 18

A B 40 D E F

West Lane

E Beck Court

Askwith Community
Primary School

Lane

Covey Hall
Farm

1 grid square represents 500 metres

Askwith

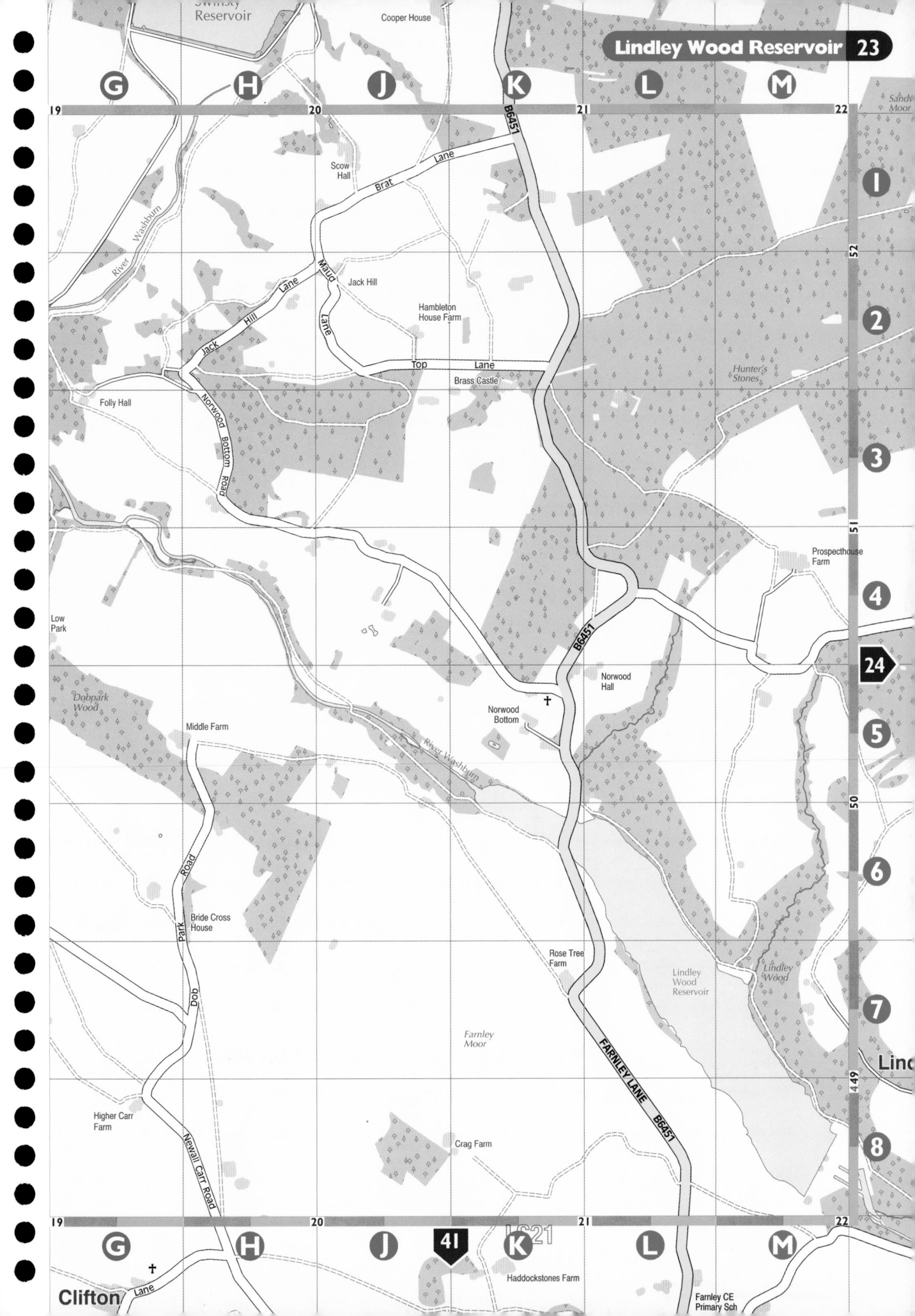

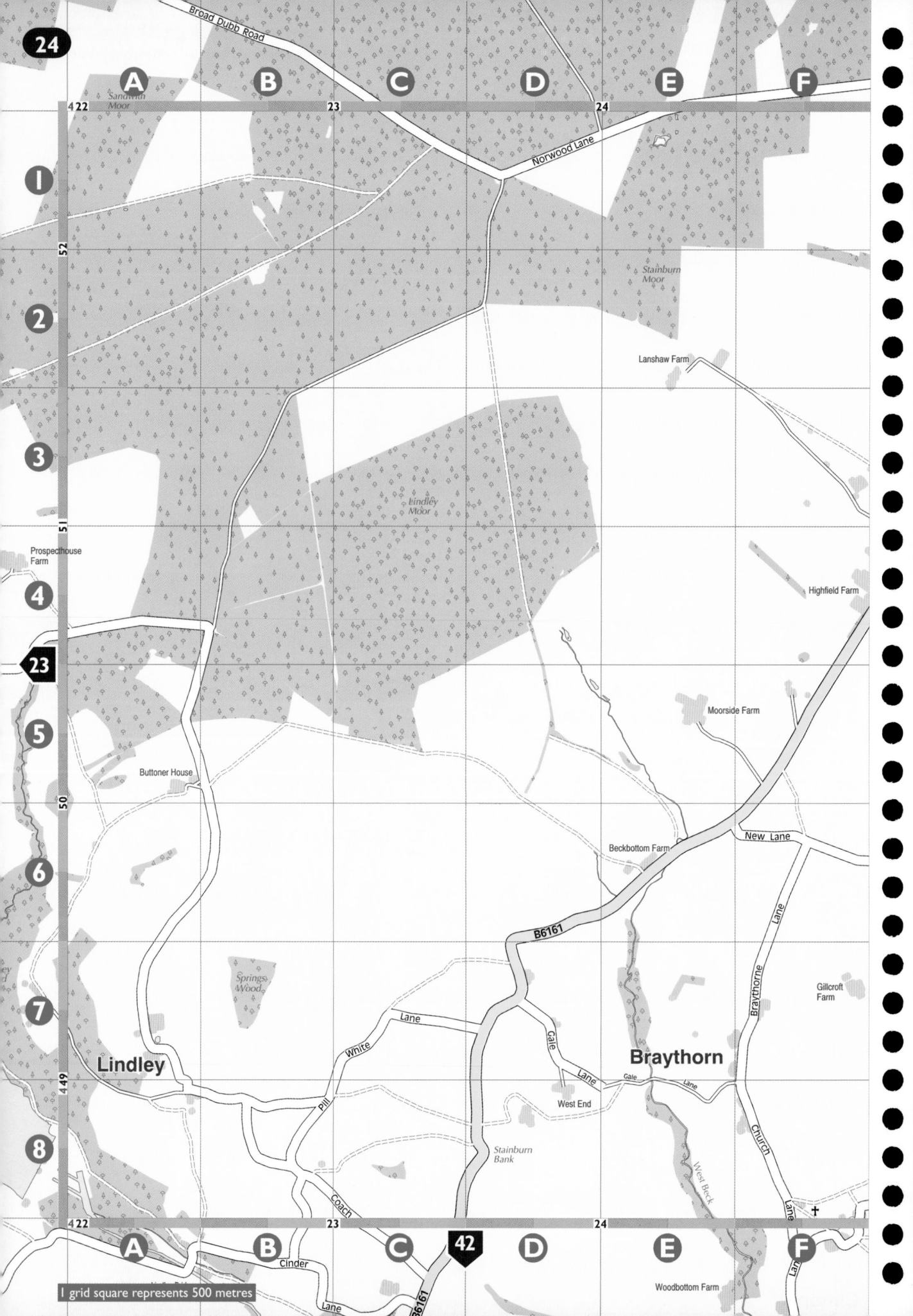

24

A   B   C   D   E   F

4 22   23   24

Broad Dubb Road

Sandwith Moor

Norwood Lane

Stainburn Moor

1

52

2

Lanshaw Farm

3

51

Lindley Moor

Prospecthouse Farm

Highfield Farm

4

23

Moorside Farm

5

50

Buttoner House

New Lane

Beckbottom Farm

6

B6161

7

Springs Wood

White   Lane

Lindley

Gale   Lane

Braythorn

Braythorne Lane

Gillcroft Farm

Pill

West End

Gale   Lane

Church   Lane

8

449

Stainburn Bank

West Beck

4 22   23   24

A   B   Cinder   C   42   D   E   F

B6161

Woodbottom Farm

Coach   Lane

1 grid square represents 500 metres

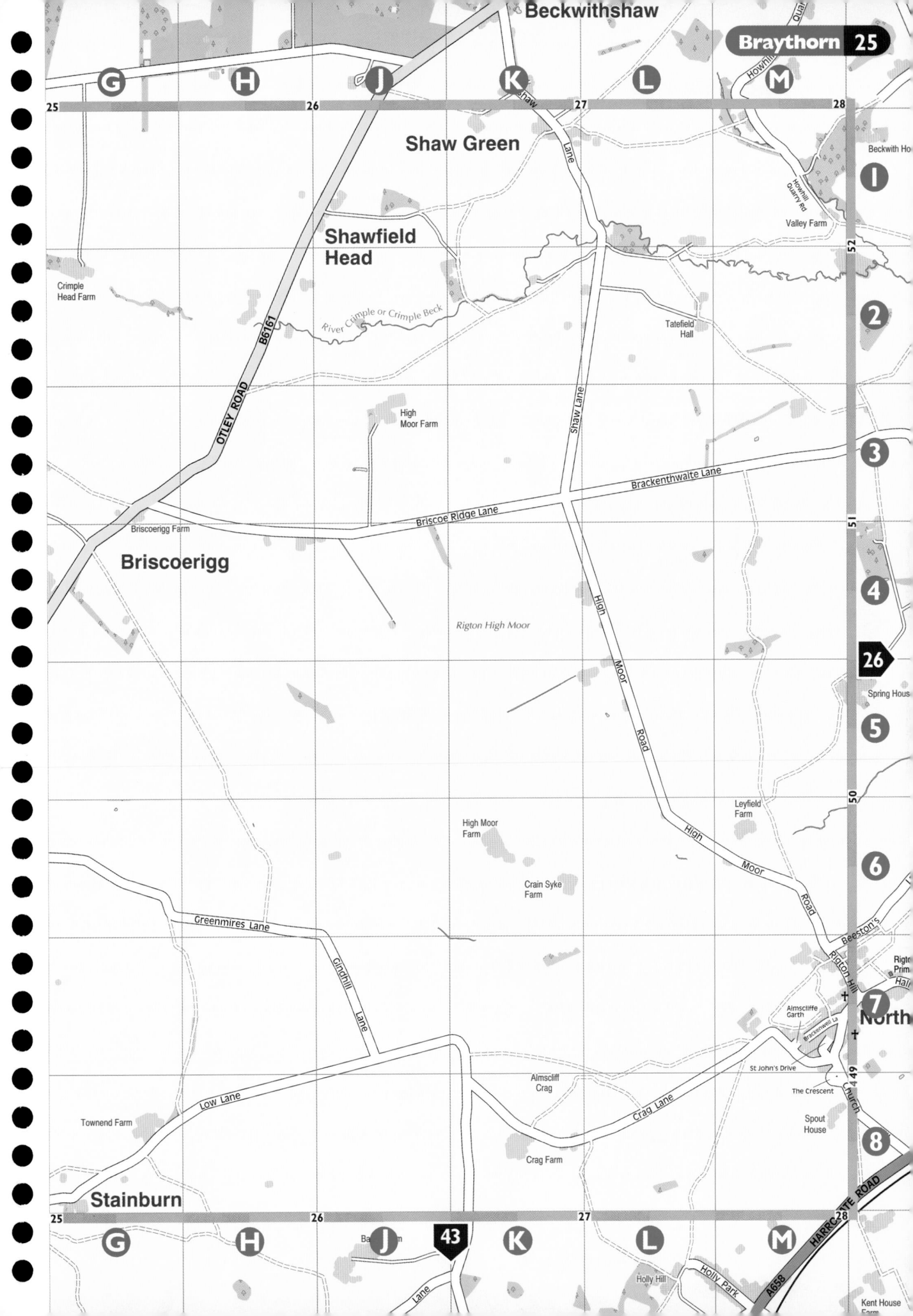

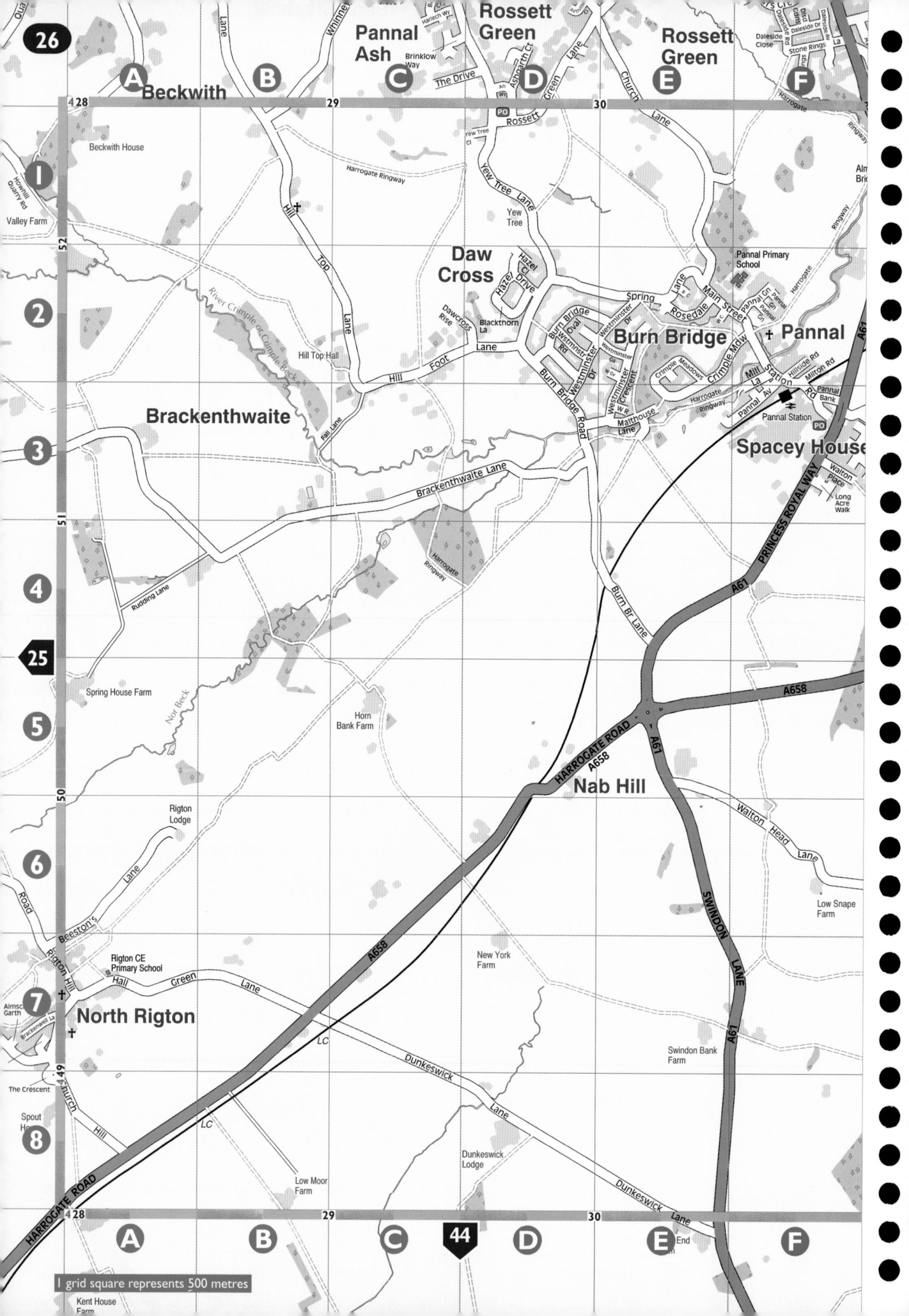

Kirkby Overblow

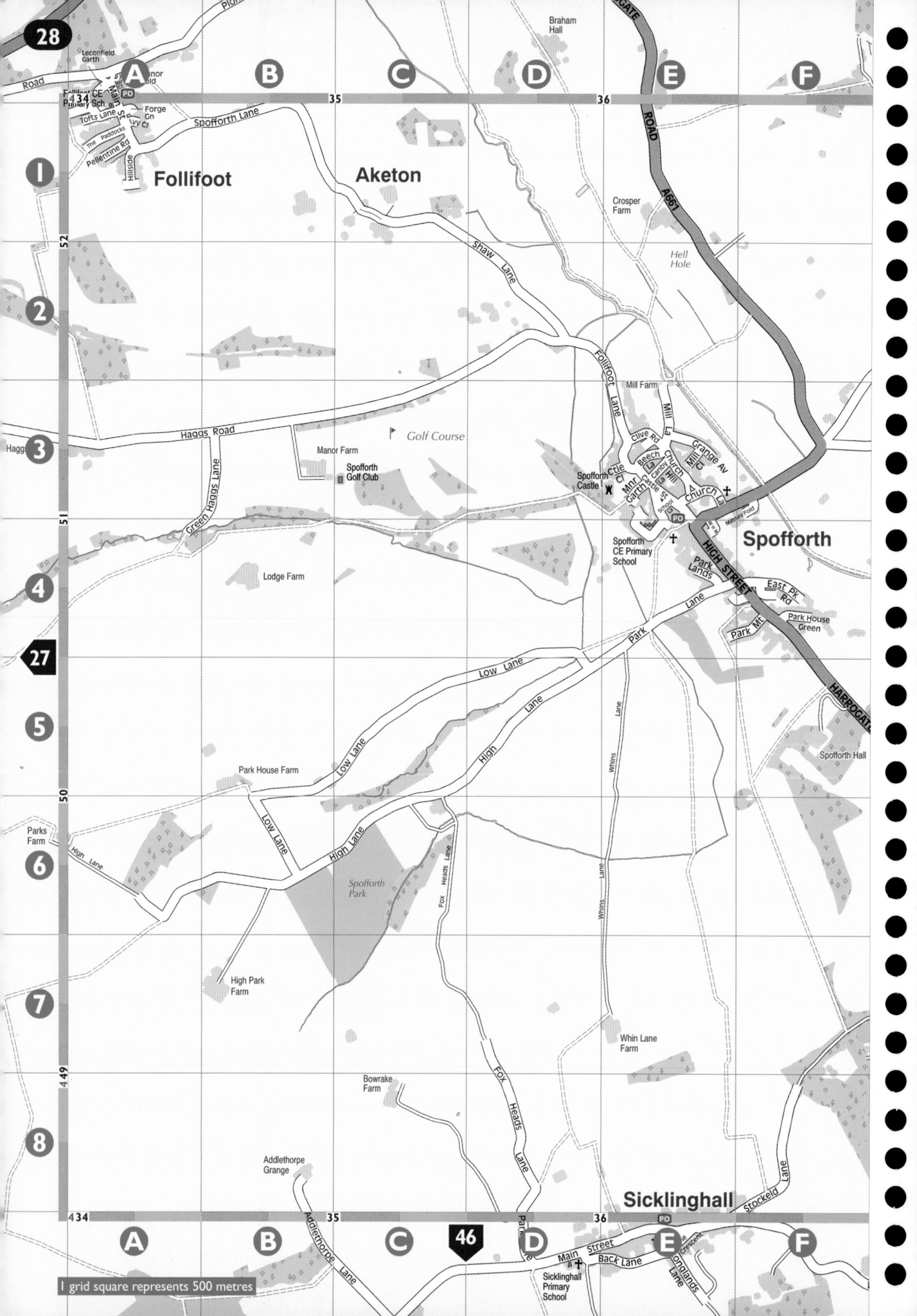

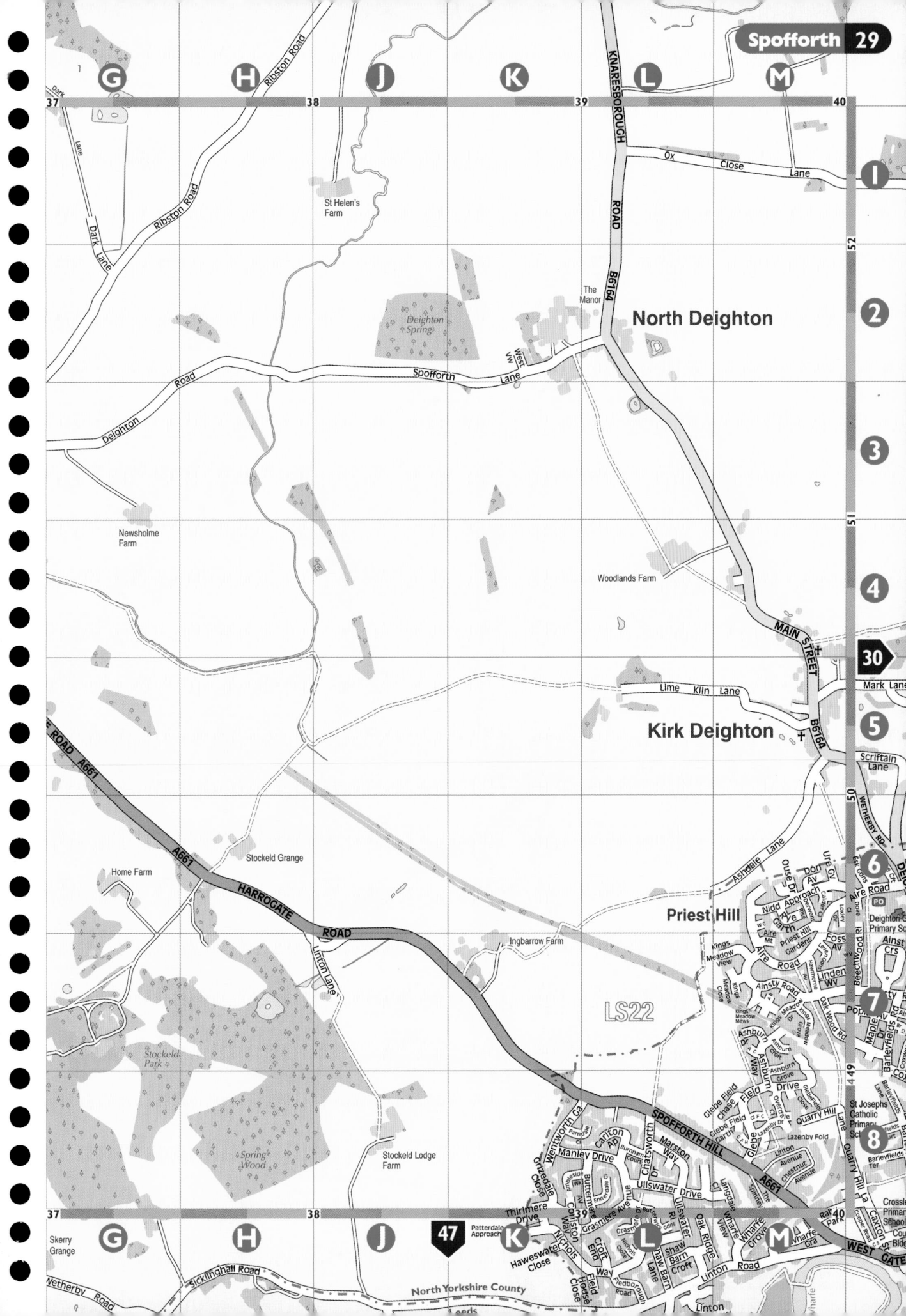

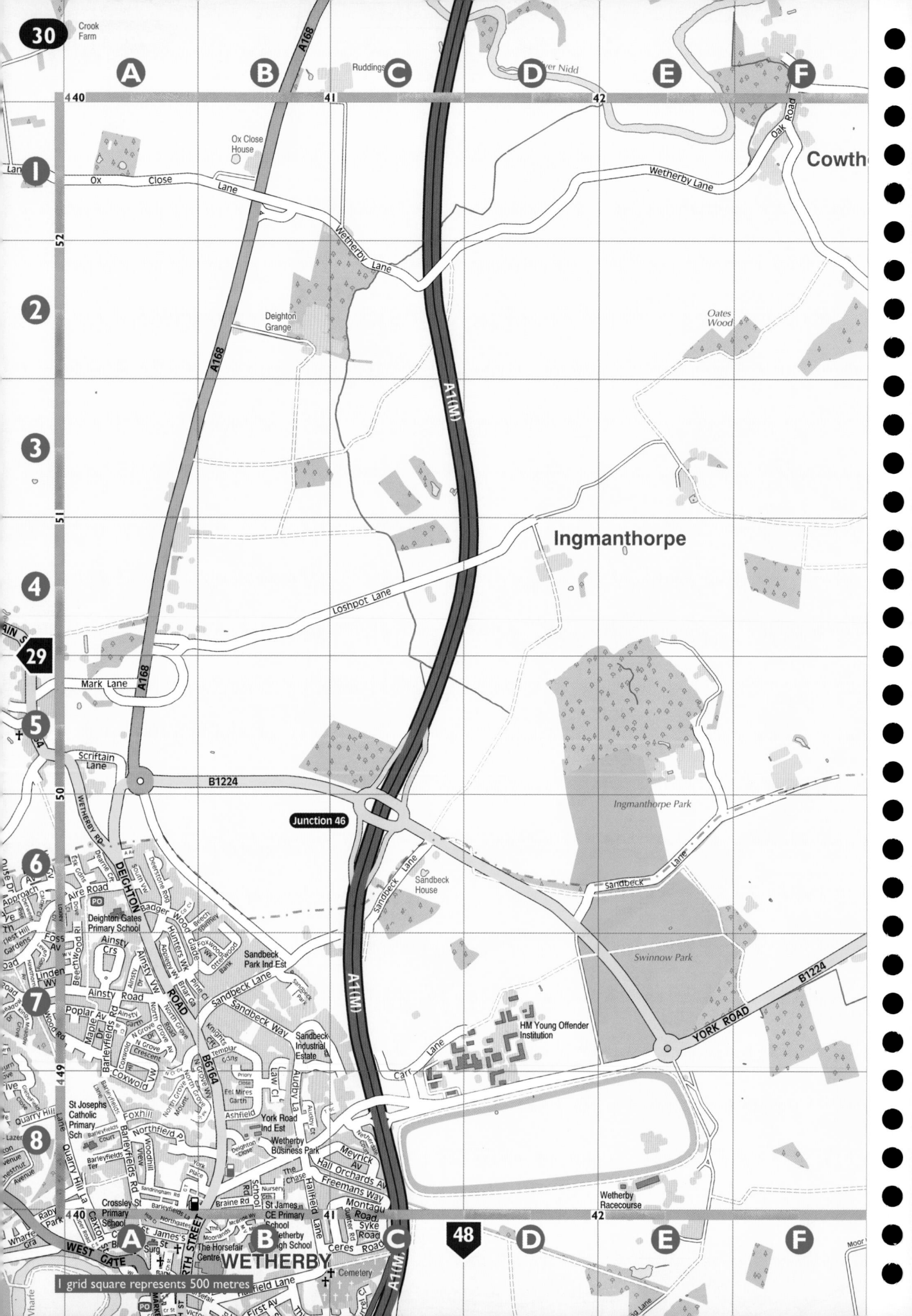

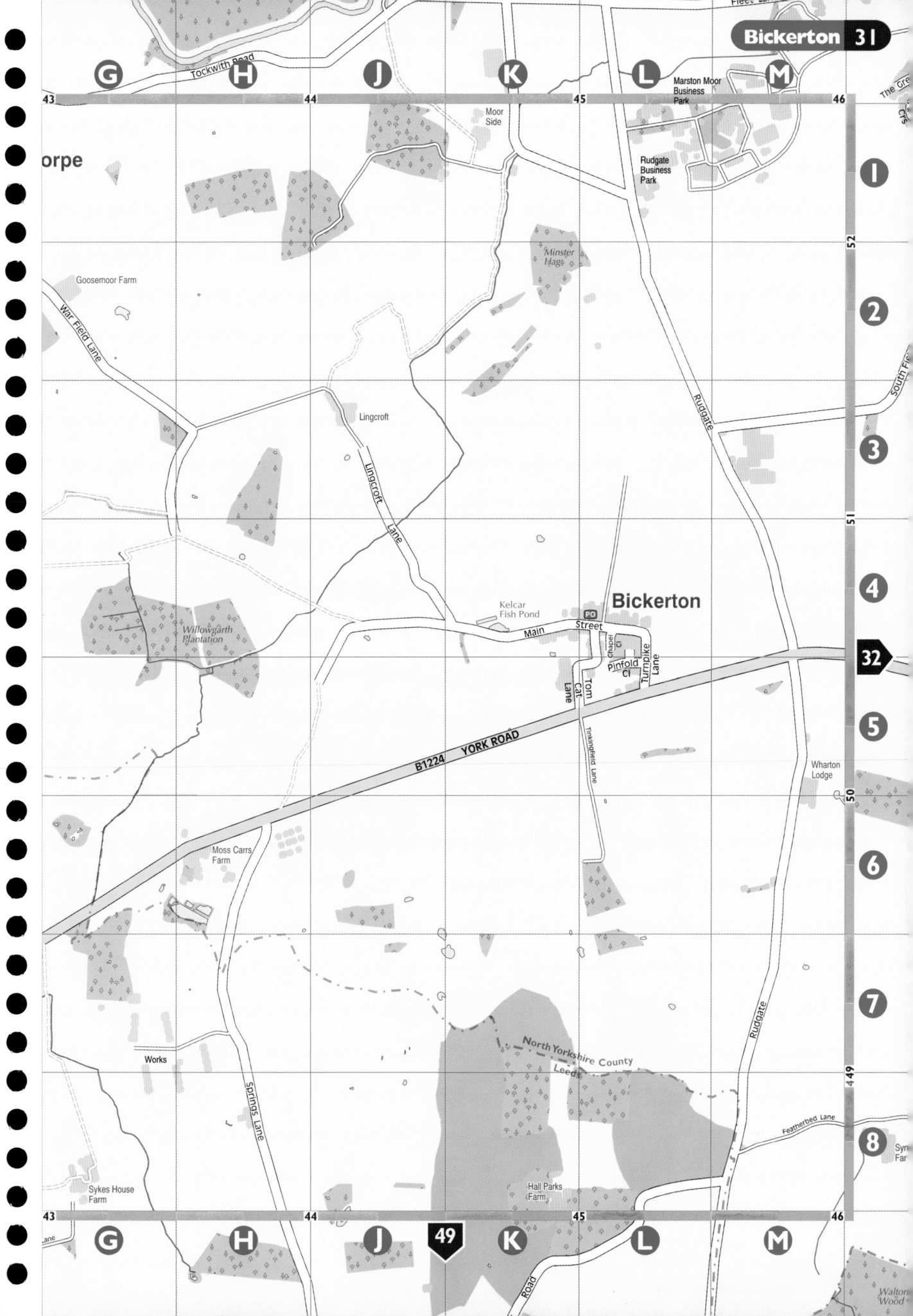

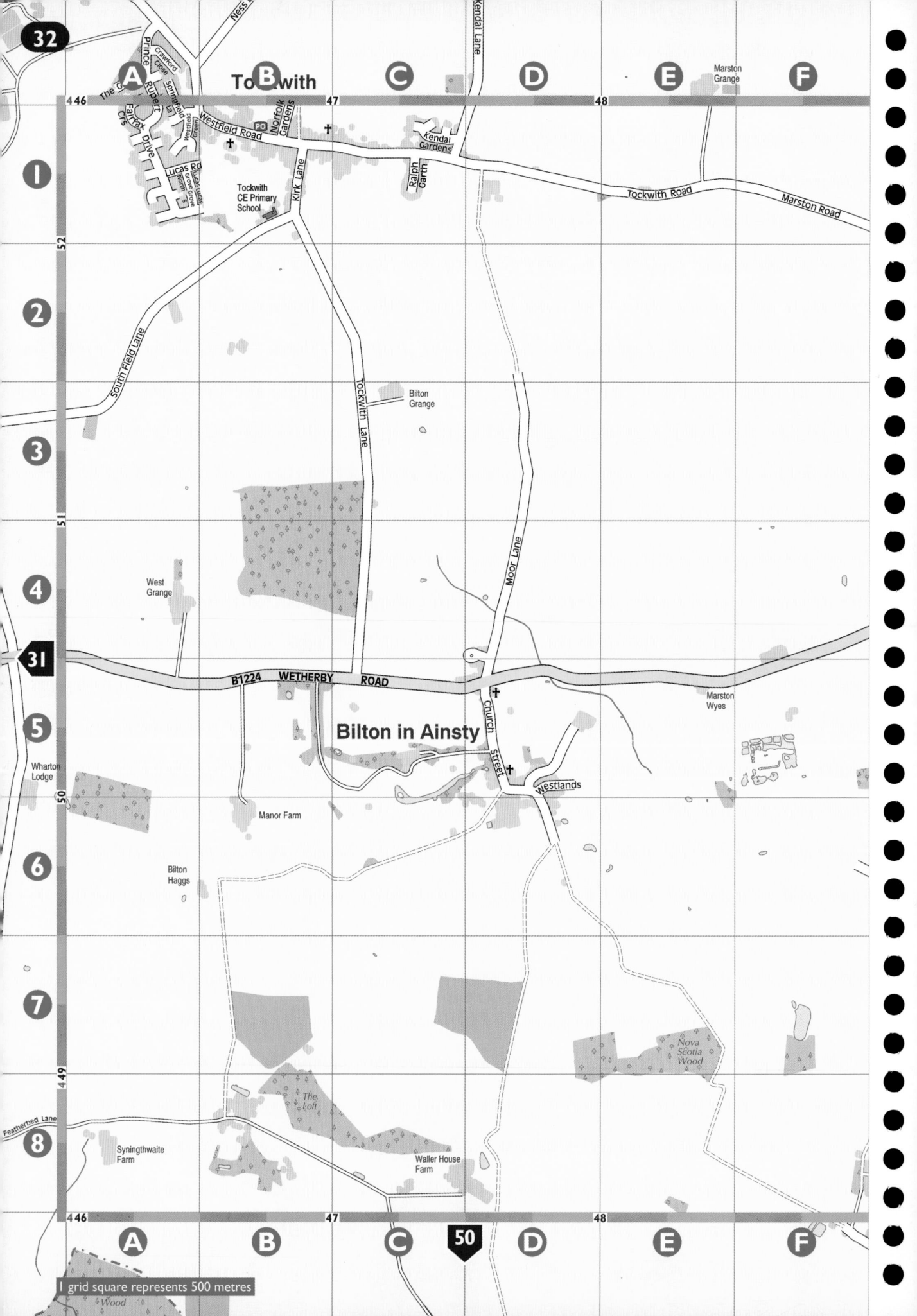

To **B**with

A B C D E F

Marston Grange

4 46 47 48

52

Ness

Prince
Crawford Close
Springfield La
Rupert
The G
Fairfax
Crs
Drive
Westfield Road
PO
Norfolk Gardens
Kendal Lane
Kendal Gardens

Lucas Rd
West
Grove
Lucas
Grove
Grove

Kirk Lane
Ralph Garth

Tockwith
CE Primary
School

Tockwith Road

Marston Road

1

2

South Field Lane

Tockwith Lane

Moor Lane

Bilton Grange

51

3

West Grange

4

31

B1224 **WETHERBY** **ROAD**

Marston Wyes

Church Street

Bilton in Ainsty

5

Wharton Lodge

50

Manor Farm

Westlands

6

Bilton Haggs

7

Nova Scotia Wood

4 49

Featherbed Lane

8

Syningthwaite Farm

The Loft

Waller House Farm

4 46 47 48

A B C D E F

50

Wood

I grid square represents 500 metres

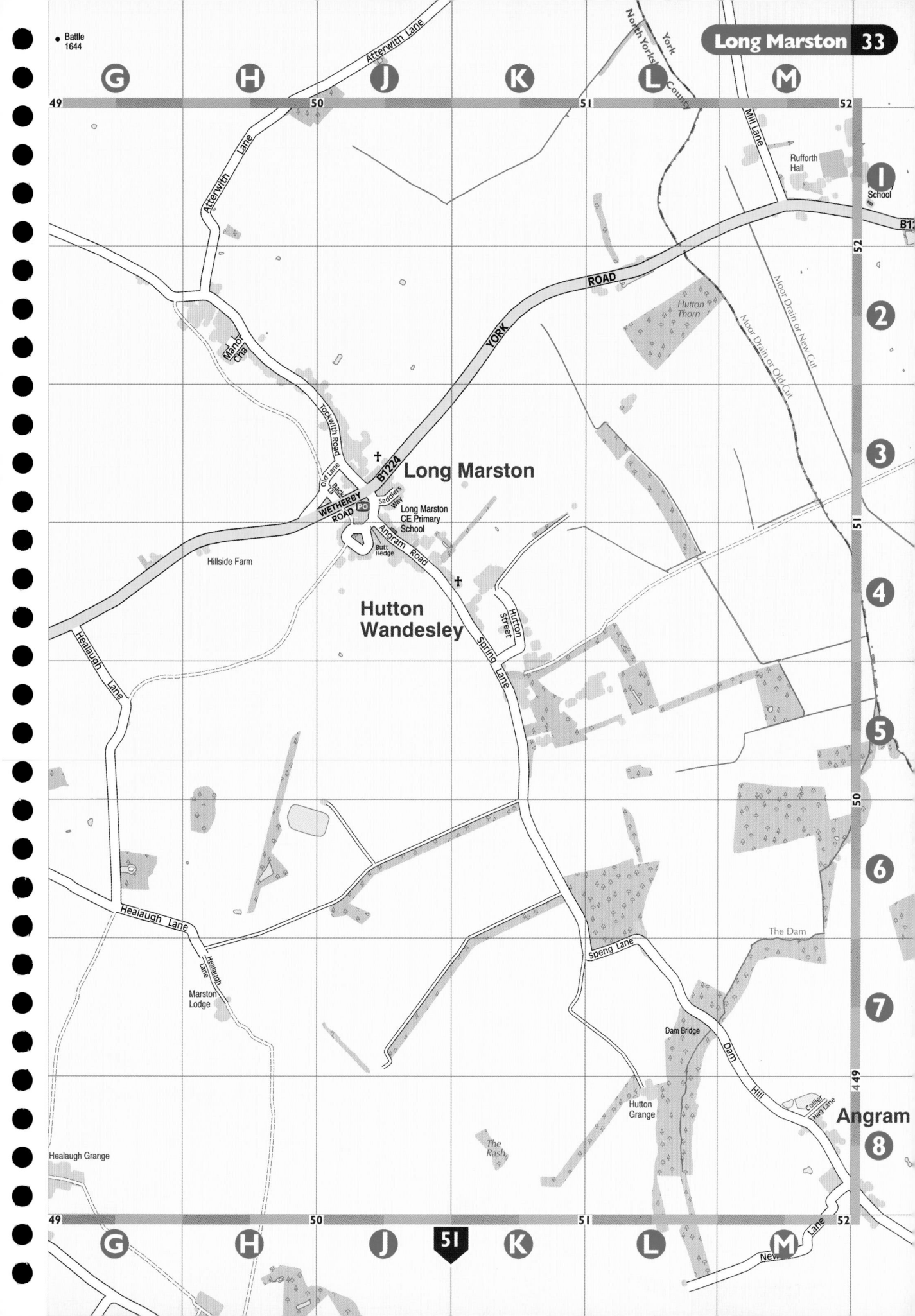

Battle 1644

G H J K L M

Atterwith Lane

Atterwith Lane

North Yorks/County

York

Mill Lane

Rufforth Hall

School

B1

49 50 51 52

York Road

Moor Drain or New Cut

Moor Drain or Old Cut

Hutton Thorn

Manor Cha

Tockwith Road

Old Lane

WETHERBY ROAD PO

B1224

Saddlers Way

Long Marston

Long Marston CE Primary School

Hillside Farm

Angram Road

Butt Hedge

Hutton Wandesley

Hutton Street

Spring Lane

Healaugh Lane

Healaugh Lane

Healaugh Lane

Marston Lodge

Healaugh Grange

Speng Lane

The Dam

Dam Bridge

Dam Hill

Collier Hag Lane

Hutton Grange

The Rash

Angram

New Lane

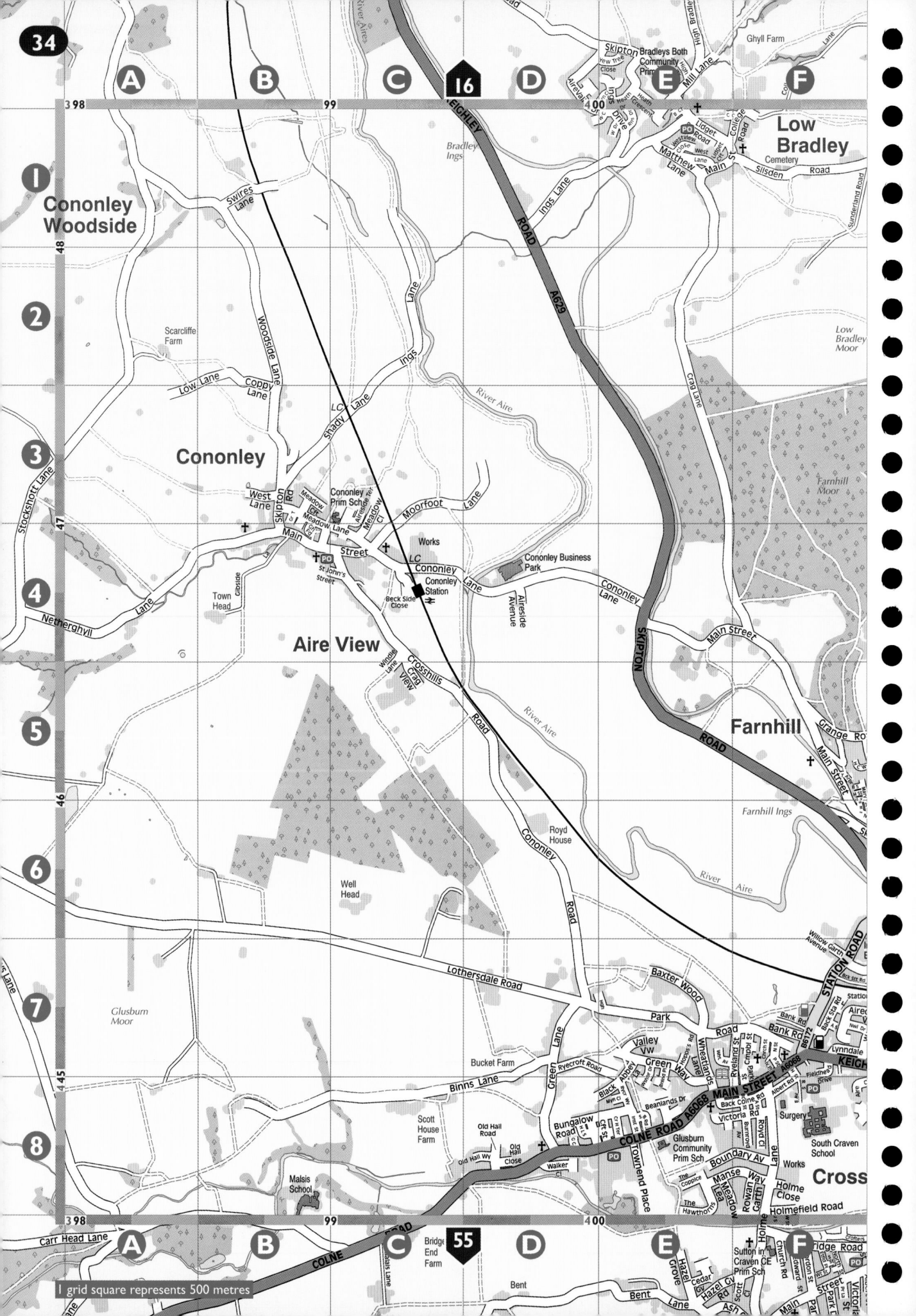

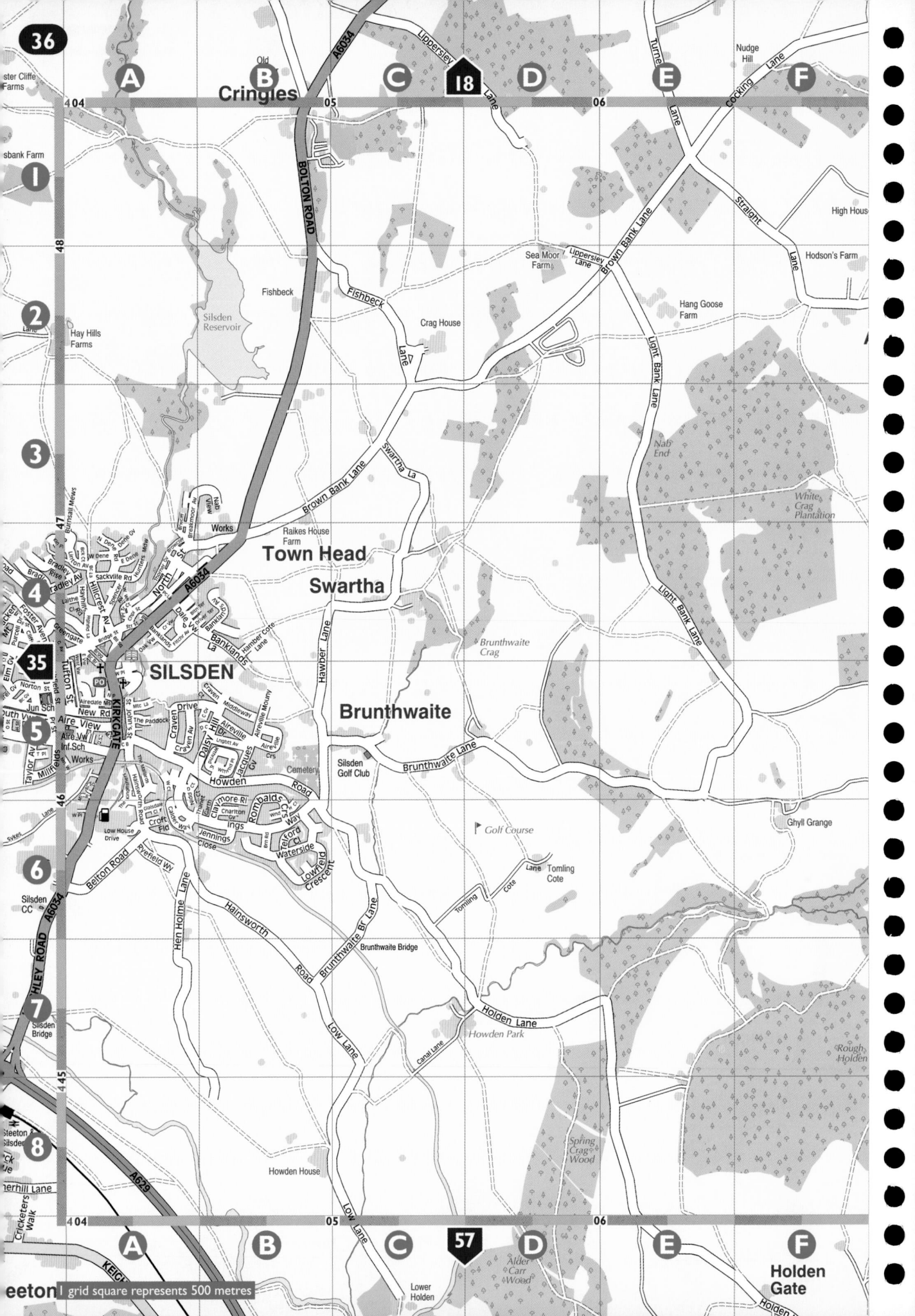

36

A   B   C   **18**   D   E   F

Cringles

Old

Nudge Hill

404   05   06

I

ster Cliffe Farms

sbank Farm

High Hous

Hodson's Farm

Lippersley Lane

Turner Lane

Cocking Lane

Brown Bank Lane

Straight Lane

2

Hay Hills Farms

Lane

Silsden Reservoir

Fishbeck

Fishbeck

Crag House

Sea Moor Farm

Lippersley Lane

Hang Goose Farm

3

Lane

Brown Bank Lane

Swartha La

Light Bank Lane

Nab End

White Crag Plantation

Works

Nab View

Breathmoor Av

Raikes House Farm

Town Head

Swartha

4

Hamber Cote Lane

Hawber Lane

Brunthwaite Crag

Light Bank Lane

35

Jun Sch

SILSDEN

Brunthwaite

Silsden Golf Club

5

Aire View

Inf. Sch

Works

Howden Road

Cemetery

Brunthwaite Lane

Ghyll Grange

Low House Drive

Jennings Close

Telford Way

Waterside

Lowfield Crescent

Golf Course

Lane

Tomling Cote

6

Silsden CC

A6034

Belton Road

Hen Holme Lane

Hainsworth

Cote

Tomling

7

HLEY ROAD

445

Silsden Bridge

Low Lane

Brunthwaite Br Lane

Brunthwaite Bridge

Holden Lane

Howden Park

Rough Holden

Canal Lane

8

Steeton & Silsden

ck

erhill Lane

A629

Cricketers Walk

Howden House

Spring Crag Wood

404   05   06

A   B   C   **57**   D   E   F

Alder Carr Wood

Holden Gate

Lower Holden

eeton | 1 grid square represents 500 metres

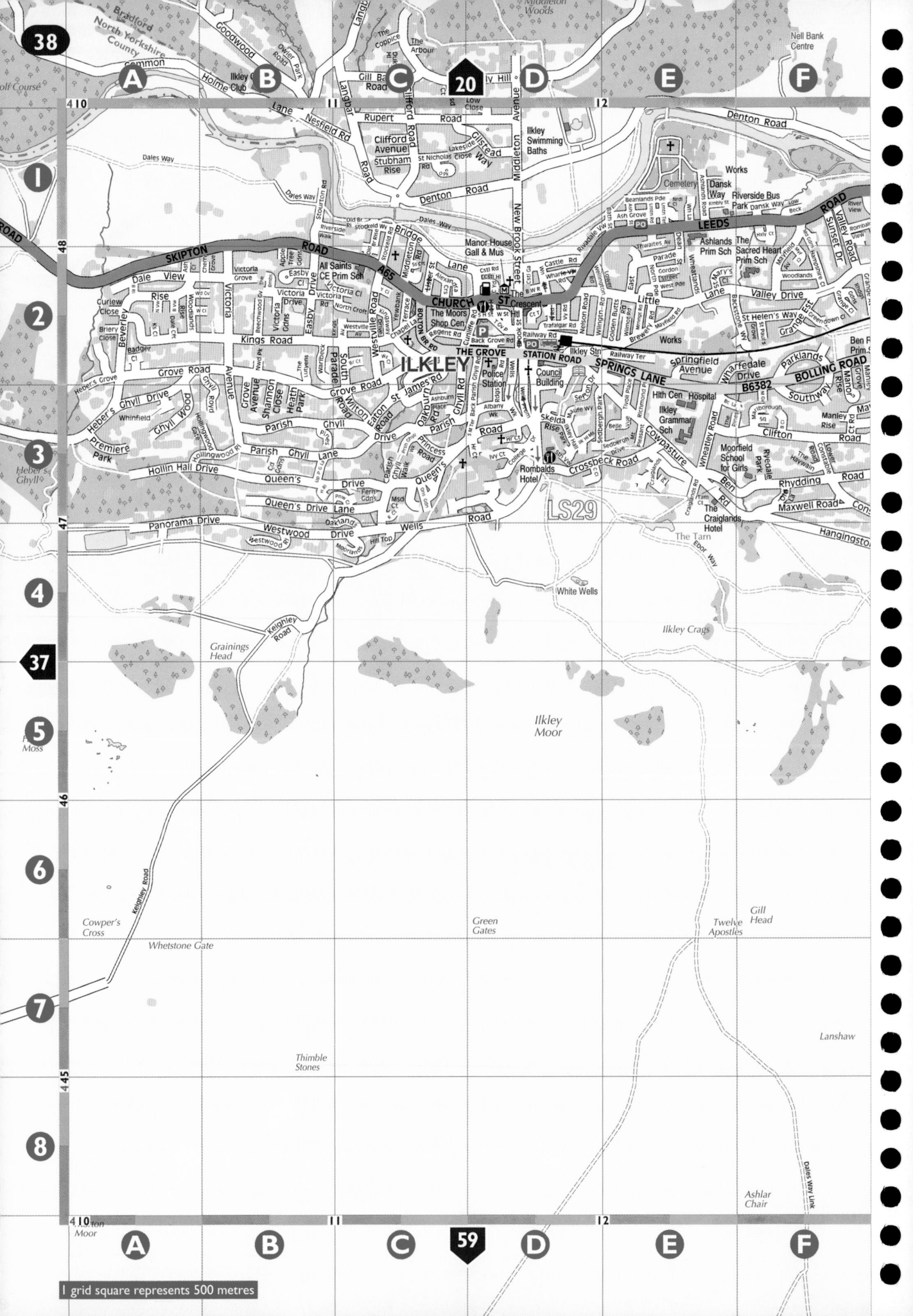

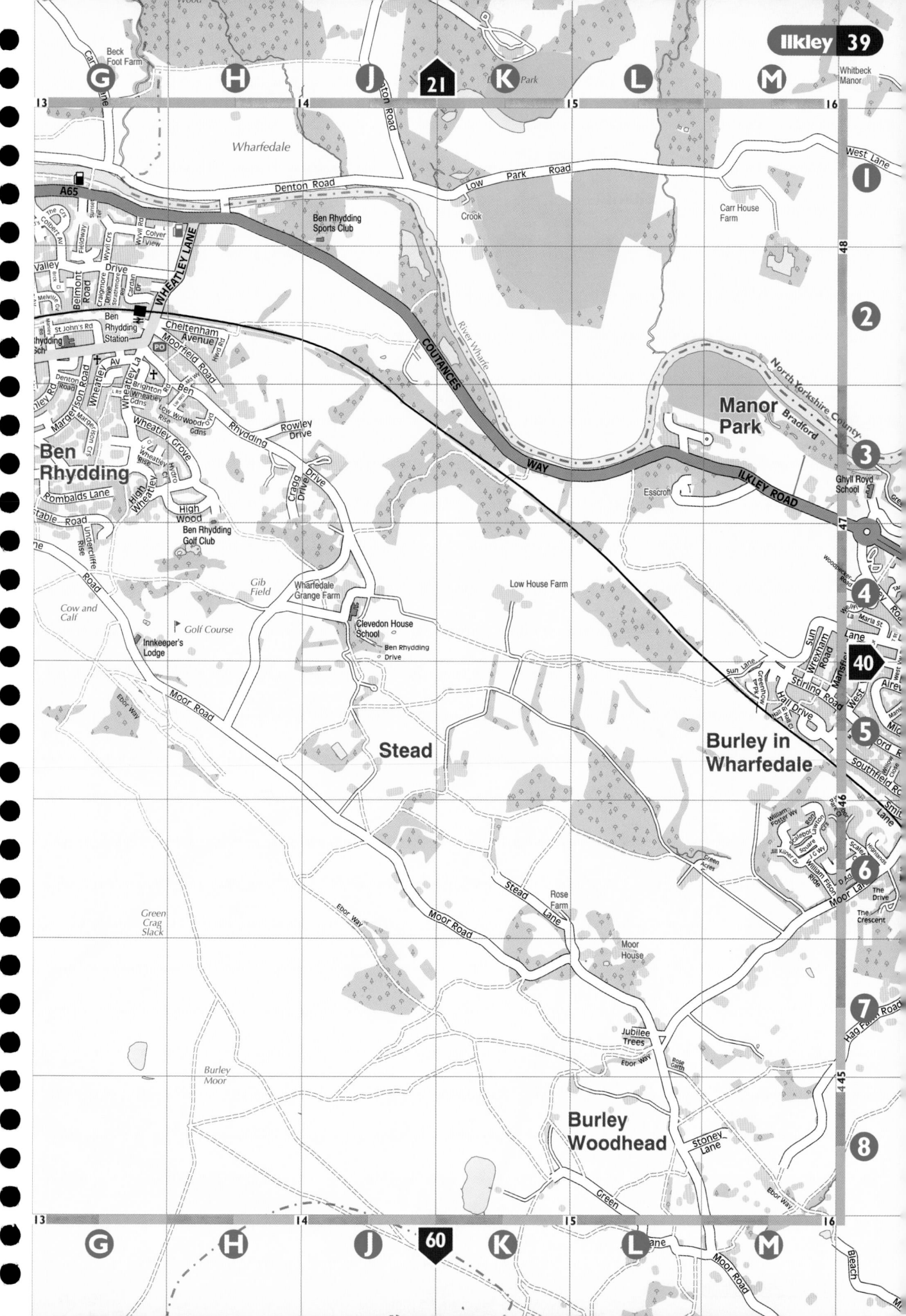

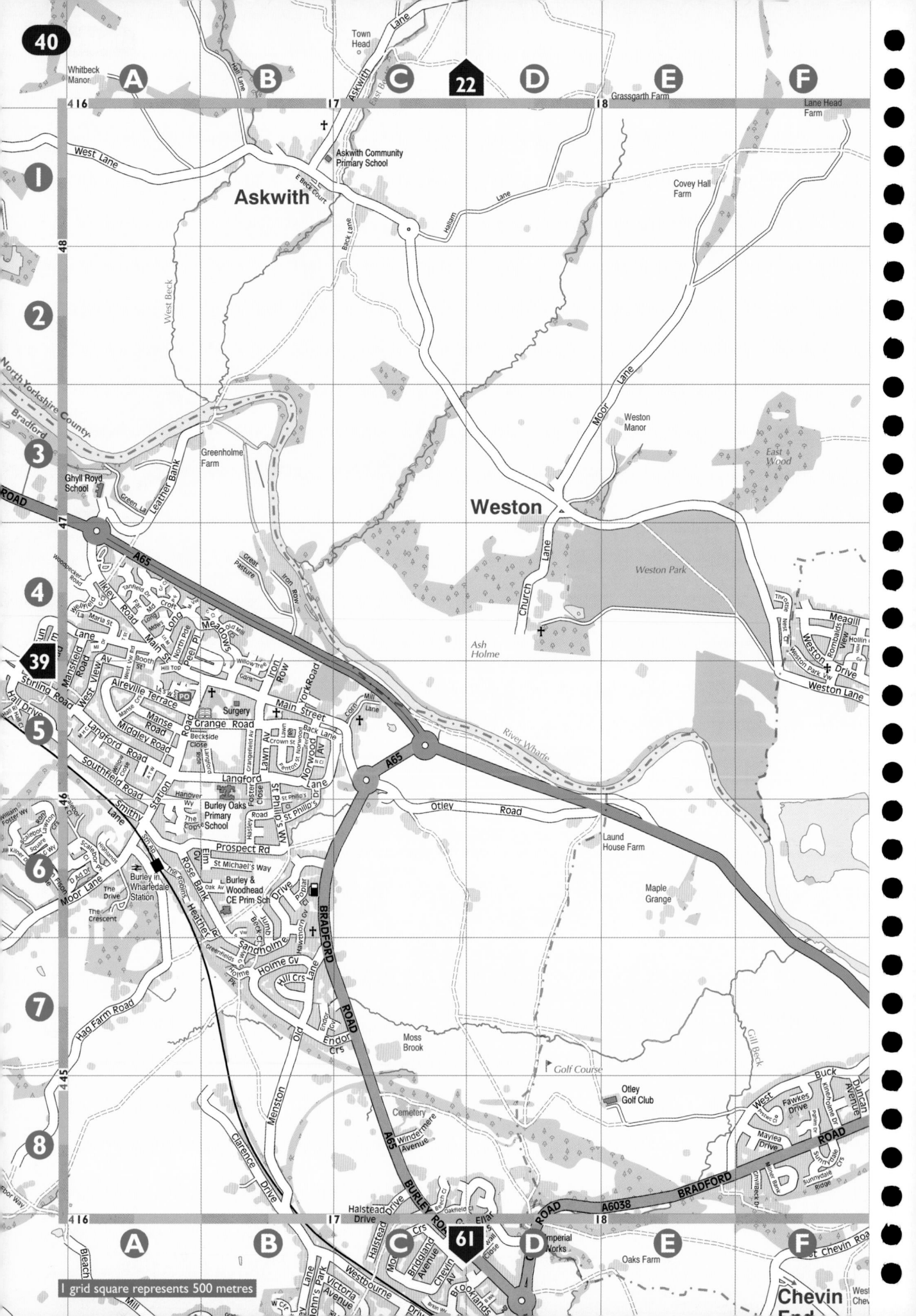

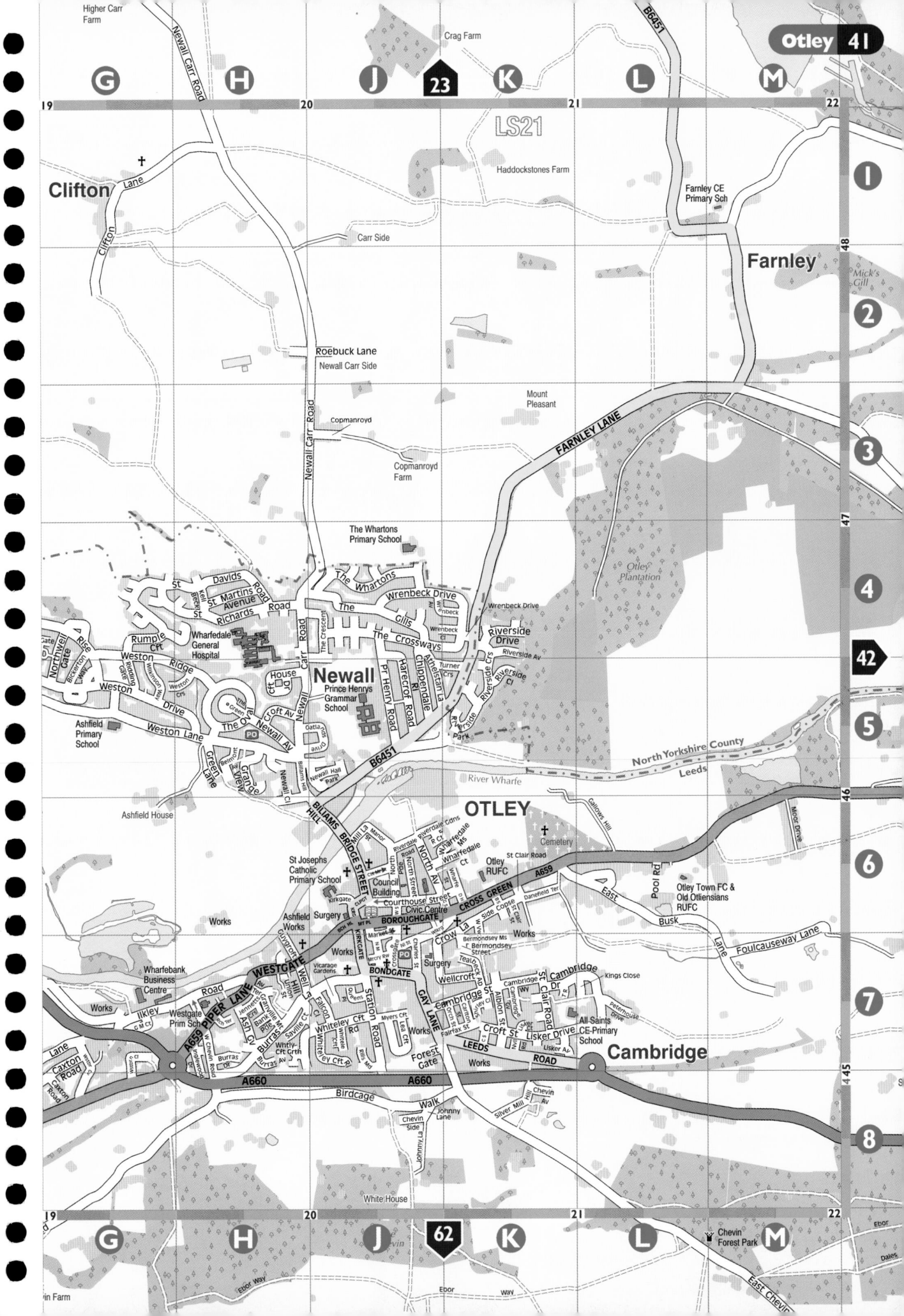

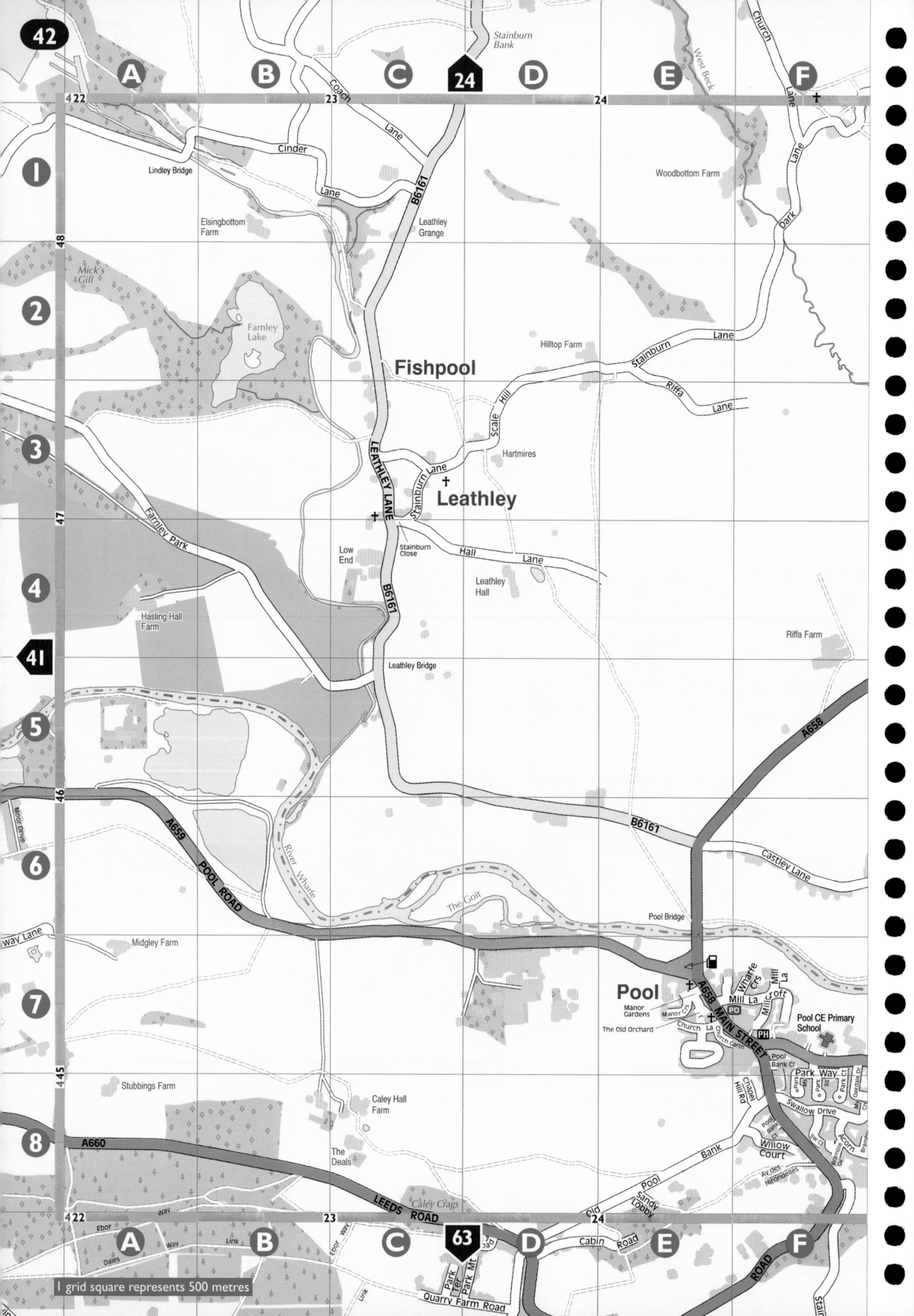

42

A   B   C   **24**   D   E   F

4 22   23   24

Stainburn Bank

West Beck

Church Lane

1

Lindley Bridge

Cinder Lane

Coach Lane

B6161

Leathley Grange

Woodbottom Farm

Dark Lane

48

Elsingbottom Farm

2

Mick's Gill

Farnley Lake

Hilltop Farm

Stainburn Lane

Riffa Lane

Fishpool

3

47

Farnley Park

LEATHLEY LANE

Stainburn Lane

Scale Hill

Hartmires

Leathley

Low End

Stainburn Close

Hall Lane

4

Hasling Hall Farm

B6161

Leathley Hall

Riffa Farm

41

5

Leathley Bridge

A658

46

Moor Drive

A659 POOL ROAD

River Wharfe

B6161

Castley Lane

6

Way Lane

Midgley Farm

The Goit

Pool Bridge

7

Pool

Manor Gardens

The Old Orchard

Manor Ct

Church La

A658 MAIN STREET

Wharfe Crs

Mill La

Mill Croft

PO

PH

Pool CE Primary School

Park Way

Swallow Drive

Pool Bank Ct

Chapel Hill Rd

Acorn

445

8

A660

Stubbings Farm

Caley Hall Farm

The Deals

Pool Bank

Old Sandy Lobby

Willow Court

Av. des Hirondelles

4 22   23   24

LEEDS ROAD

Caley Crags

Cabin Road

STAIR ROAD

A   B   **63**   C   D   E   F

Ebor Way

Dales

Link Way

Ebor Way

Quarry Farm Road

Park Ter

Park Mt

I grid square represents 500 metres

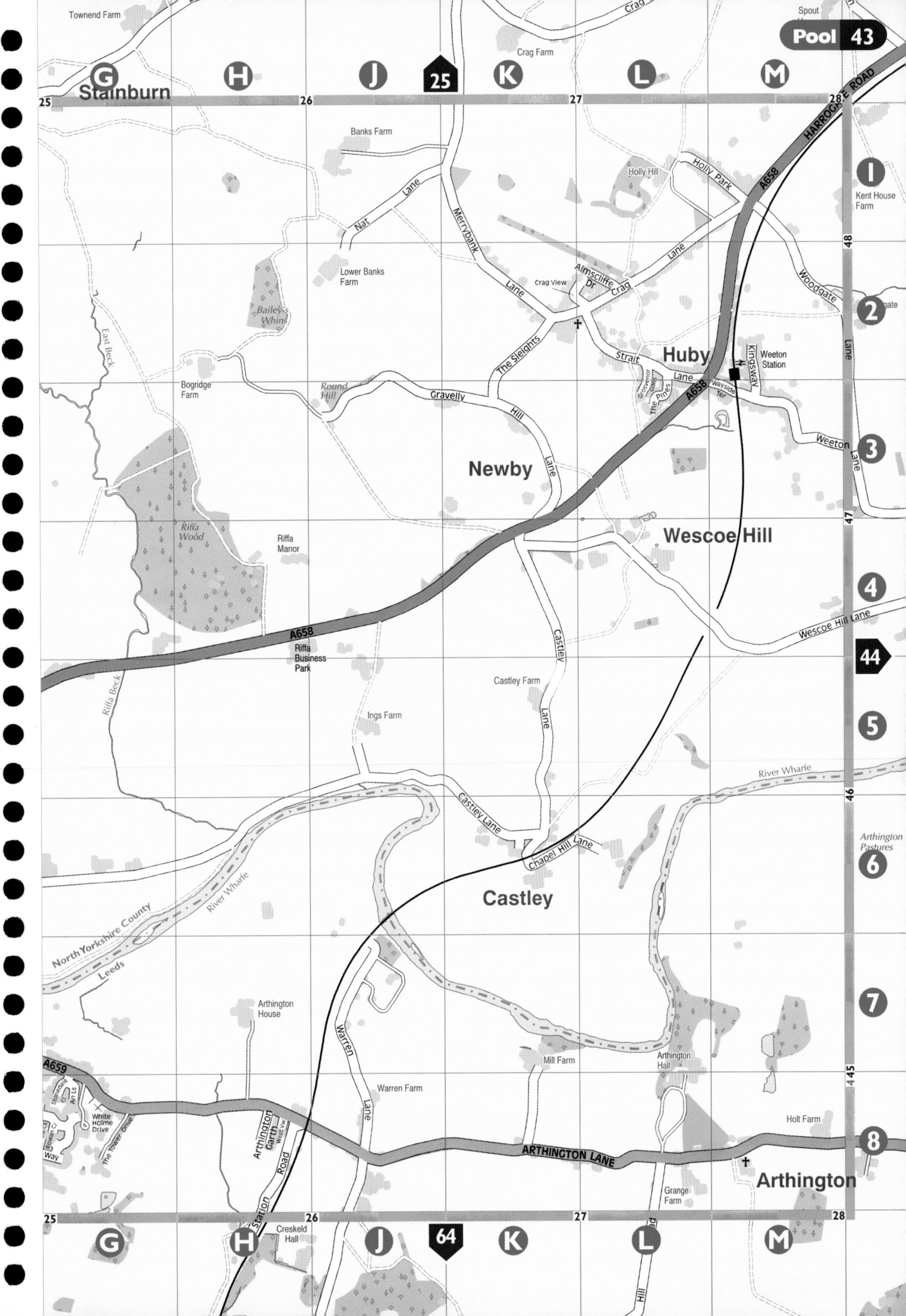

G H J 25 K L M

25   26   27   28

Stainburn

Townend Farm

Crag

Spout

Crag Farm

HARROGATE ROAD

I
Kent House Farm

Banks Farm

Holly Hill

Holly Park

A658

48

Nat Lane

Merrybank Lane

Lane

Crag View

Almscliffe Dr

Crag

Lane

Woodgate

gate

2

Lower Banks Farm

Bailey's Whins

The Sleights

Lane

Huby

Strait Lane

Grosvenor Gdns

The Pines

Kingsway

Wayside Ter

Weeton Station

Weeton Lane

3

East Beck

Bogridge Farm

Round Hill

Gravelly

Hill

Lane

Newby

A658

Wescoe Hill

47

Riffa Wood

Riffa Manor

Castley Lane

4

Wescoe Hill Lane

A658

Riffa Business Park

Castley Farm

44

Riffa Beck

Ings Farm

5

River Wharfe

46

River Wharfe

Castley Lane

Arthington Pastures

6

North Yorkshire County

Leeds

River Wharfe

Chapel Hill Lane

Castley

7

Arthington House

Warren Lane

Mill Farm

Arthington Hall

45

A659

Stonedale Ct

LN LS

Bowran Cl

Way

White Holme Drive

The Power Drive

Arthington Garth

West Vw

Station Road

Warren Farm

Grange Farm

Holt Farm

8

ARTHINGTON LANE

Arthington

25   26   27   28

G H 64 J K L M

Creskeld Hall

Hill Lane

LS17

I grid square represents 500 metres

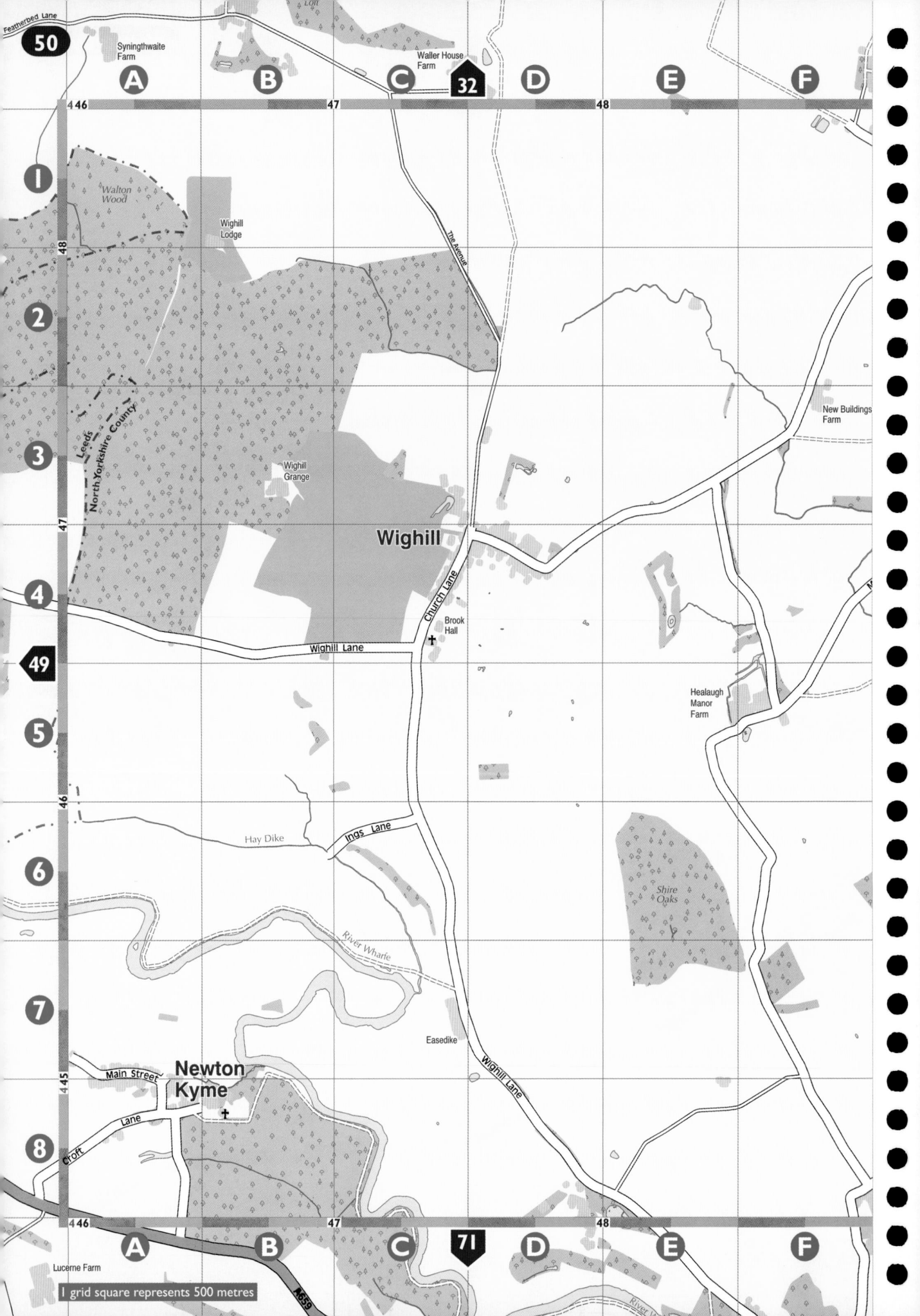

50

A   B   C   32   D   E   F

446   47   48

I

Walton Wood

Wighill Lodge

The Avenue

Syningthwaite Farm

Waller House Farm

48

2

47

3

Leeds
North Yorkshire County

Wighill Grange

Wighill

Church Lane

New Buildings Farm

4

Brook Hall

49

Wighill Lane

Healaugh Manor Farm

5

46

Hay Dike

Ings   Lane

6

Shire Oaks

River Wharfe

7

Easedike

Wighill Lane

445

Main street

Newton Kyme

8

Croft   Lane

446   47   48

A   B   C   71   D   E   F

Lucerne Farm

A659

River W

1 grid square represents 500 metres

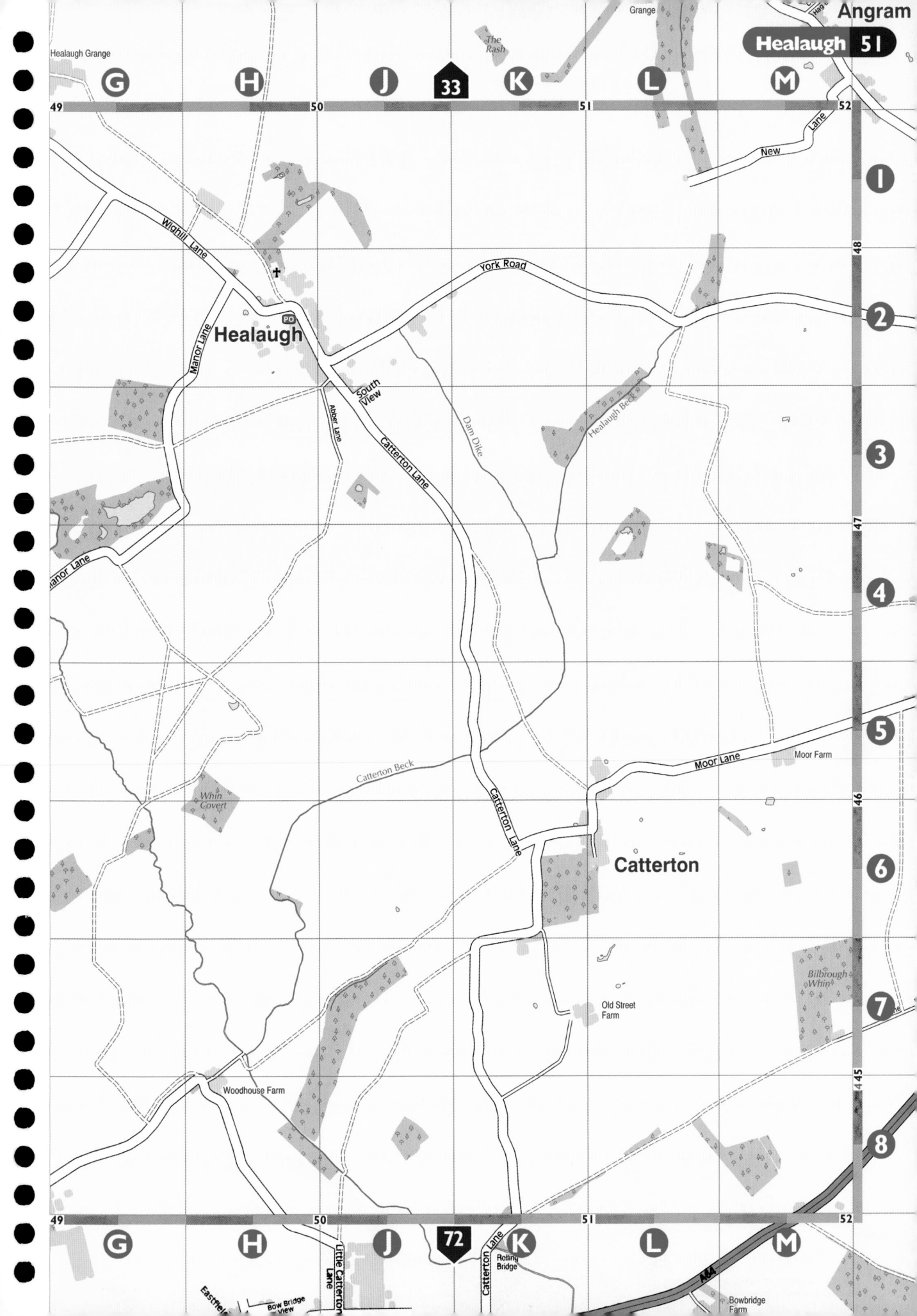

Angram

G   H   J   33   K   L   M

49   50   51   52

Healaugh Grange

The Rash

Grange

New Lane

1

48

Wighill Lane

York Road

2

† Healaugh PO

Manor Lane

Abber Lane

South View

Catterton Lane

Dam Dike

Healaugh Beck

3

47

4

Manor Lane

5

Catterton Beck

Moor Lane

Moor Farm

46

Whin Covert

Catterton Lane

Catterton

6

Bilbrough Whin

7

Old Street Farm

445

Woodhouse Farm

8

49   50   51   52

G   H   J   72   K   L   M

Little Catterton Lane

Catterton Lane

Rotting Bridge

A64

Eastfield

Bow Bridge View

Bowbridge Farm

Kelbrook

Kelbrook Prim Sch

Great Hague

Old Stone Trough

Cob Lane

Thick Bank

Roger Moor

Hague House

Oxenards

Earl Hall

Great Edge

Accornlee Hall

Trent Farm

Works

Noyna Bottom

Flass Bent

Foulridge

Lower Broach

Bent Laithe

Archery Av

Alma Avenue

Noyna Hall

Cock Hill

Salter Syke

St Michaels & All Angels CE Primary School

The Manor

Cockhill Lane

Golf Course

Flass

Foulridge Upper Reservoir

Colne Golf Club

Skipton Old Road

Lane Head

Blue Bell

Castle Road

Hill Lane

Heyroyd

Laneshawbridge Primary School

Park High School

Snellens Gv

Venables Rd

Sheridan Road

Castle Road

Belgrave Avenue

Thorn Gv

Fern Street

Bent Lane

A6068

KEIGHLEY

Langroyd Rd

Skipton Road

Colne CC

74

Christ Church Primary School

Standroyd Drive

North Valley Retail Park

WINDSOR ST

LANGROYD RD

Keighley

Ing Heys

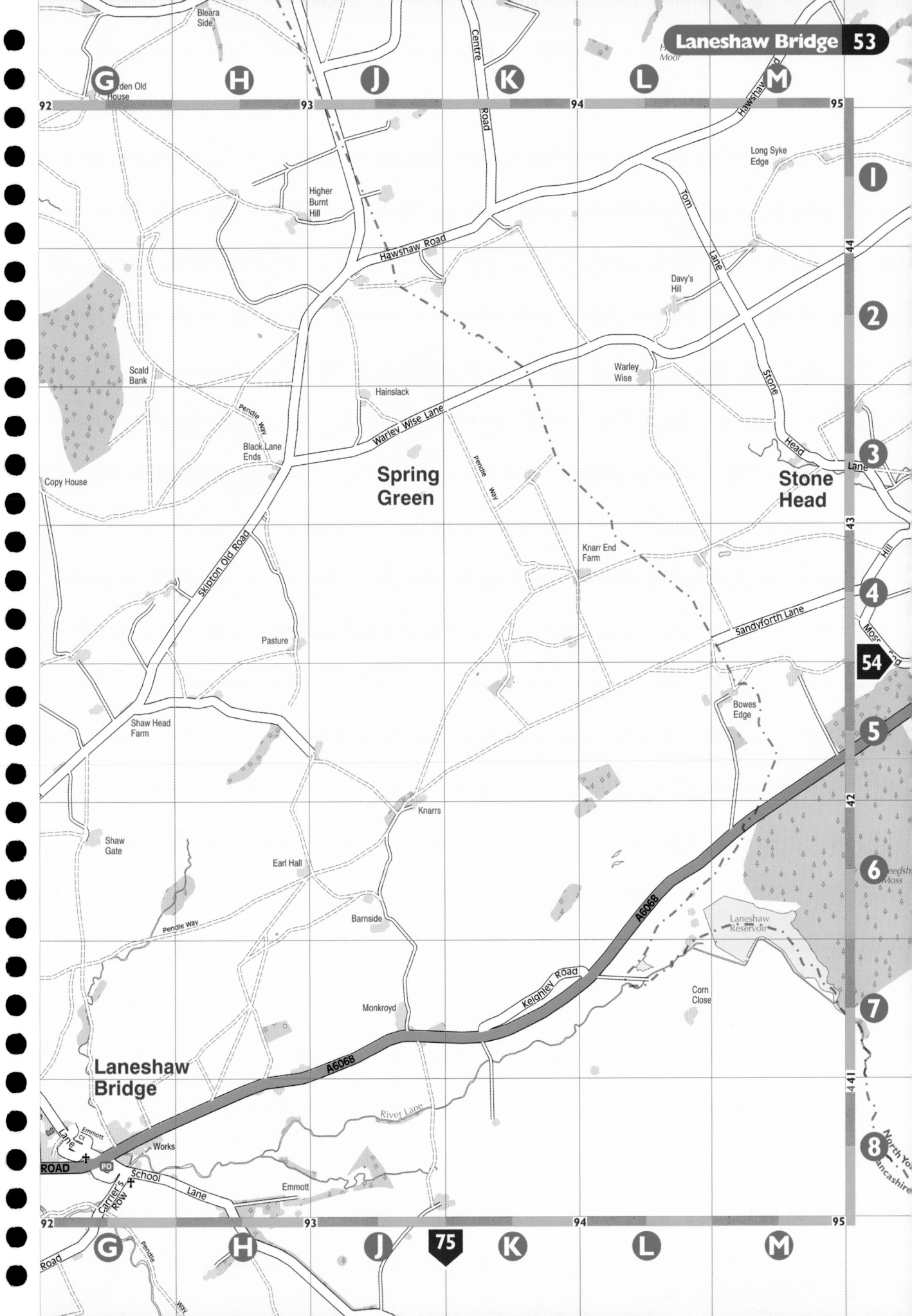

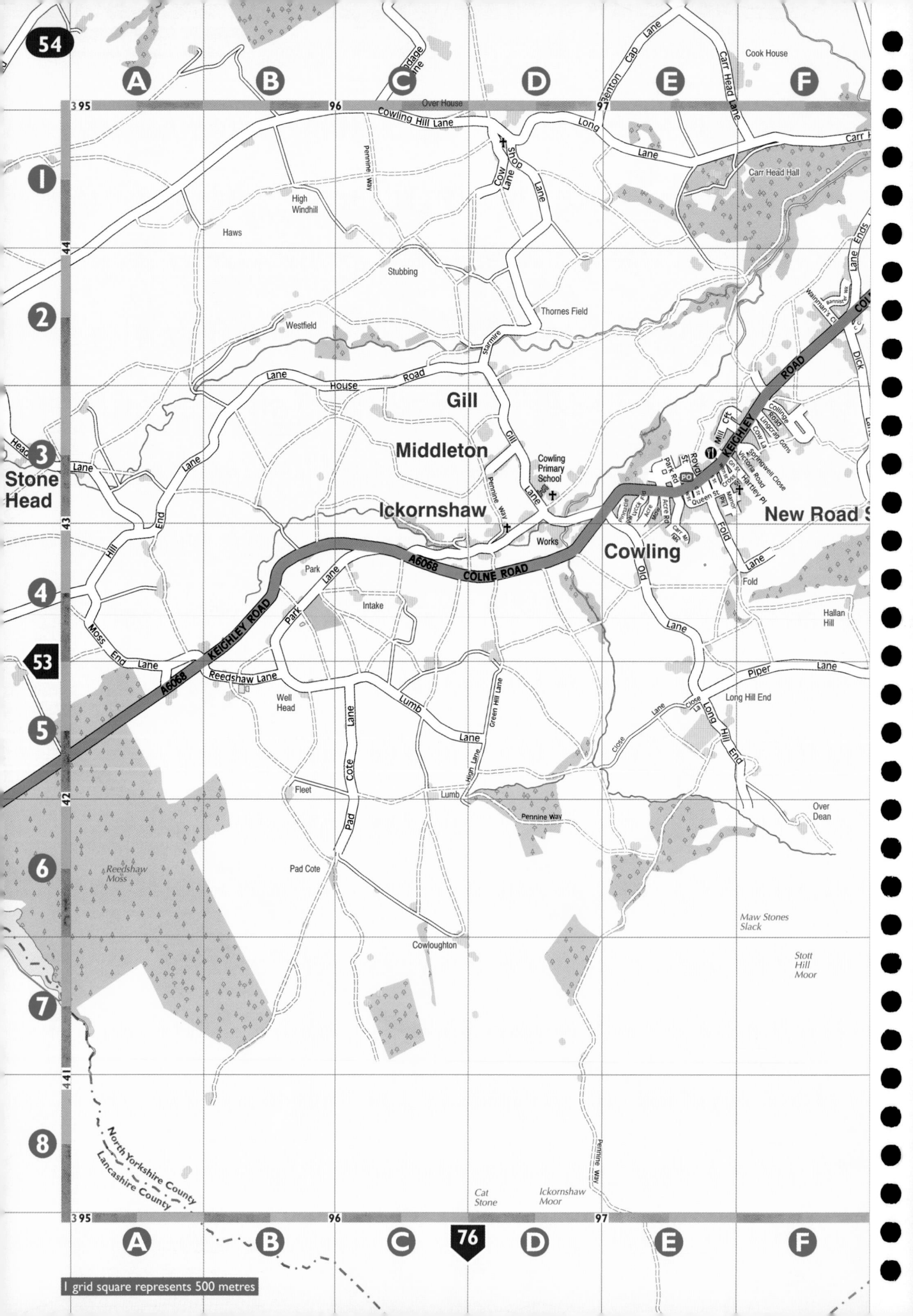

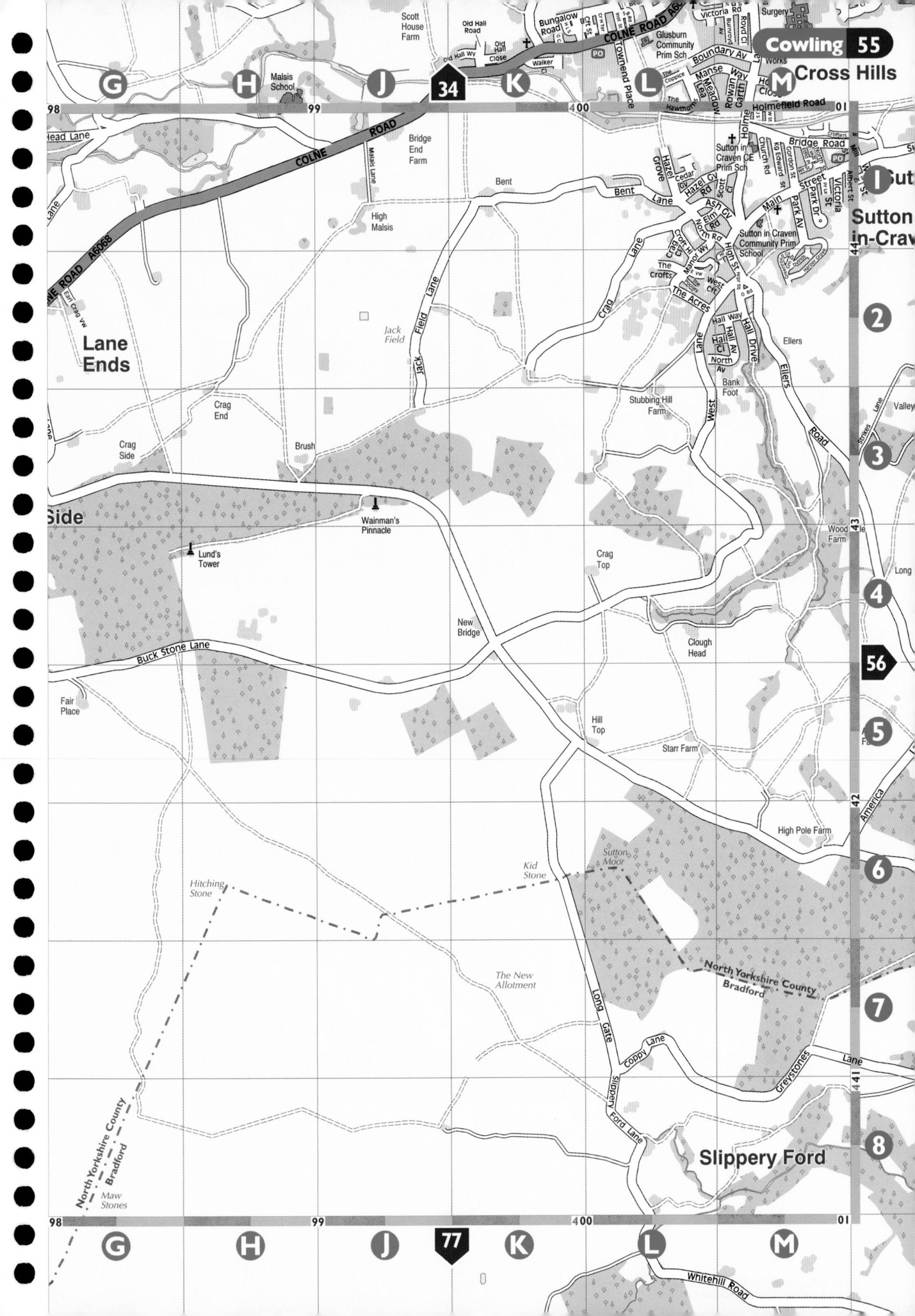

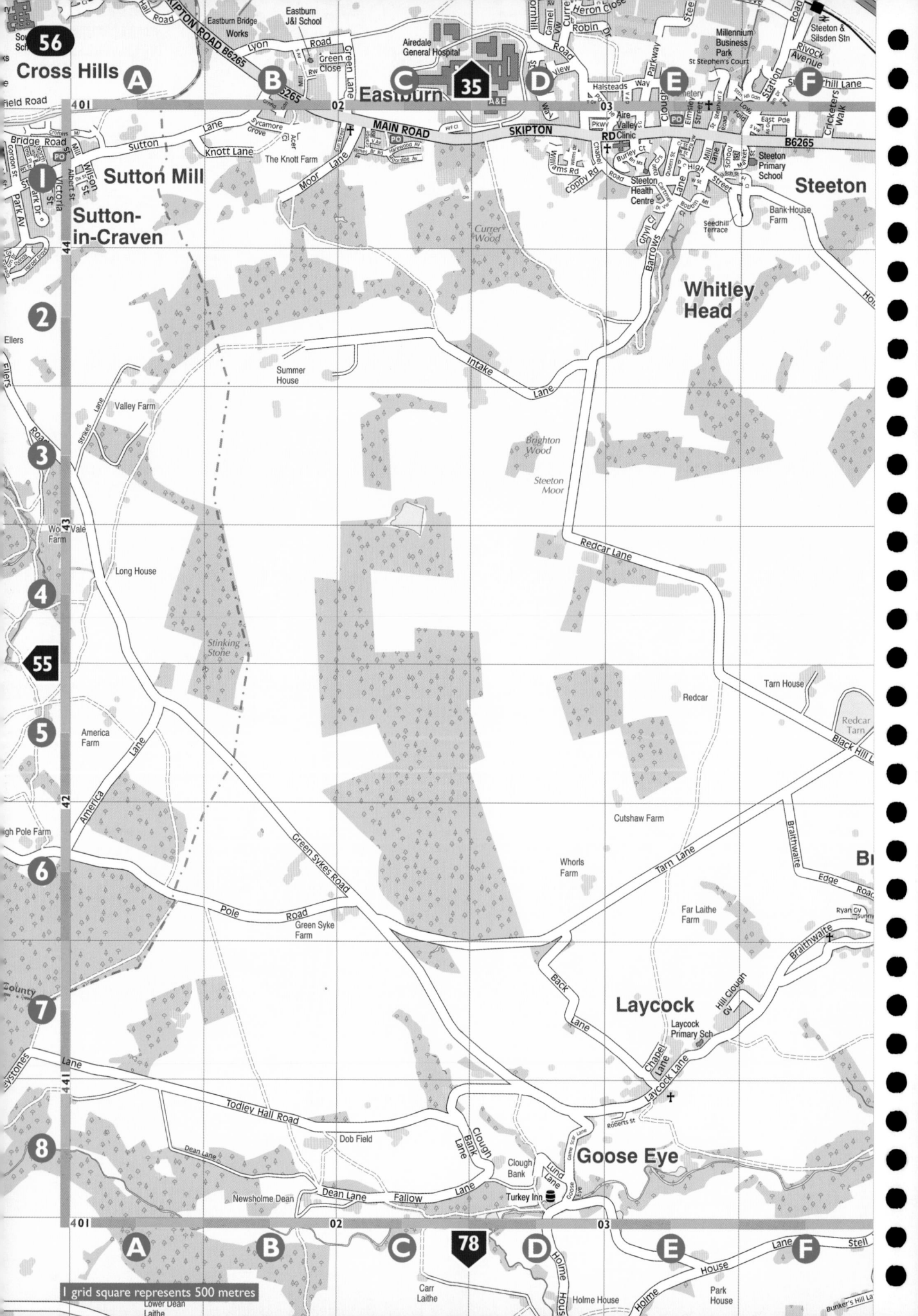

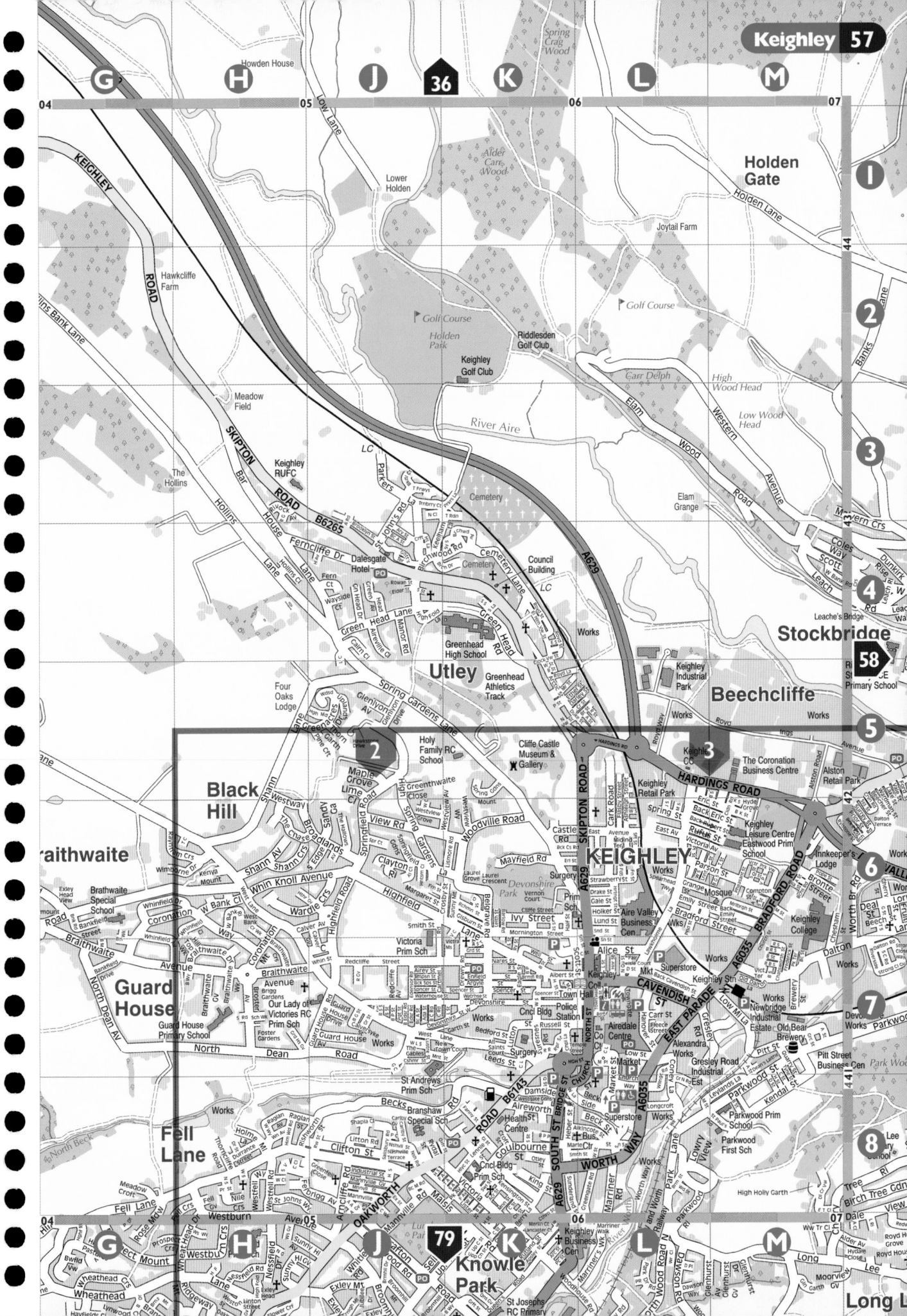

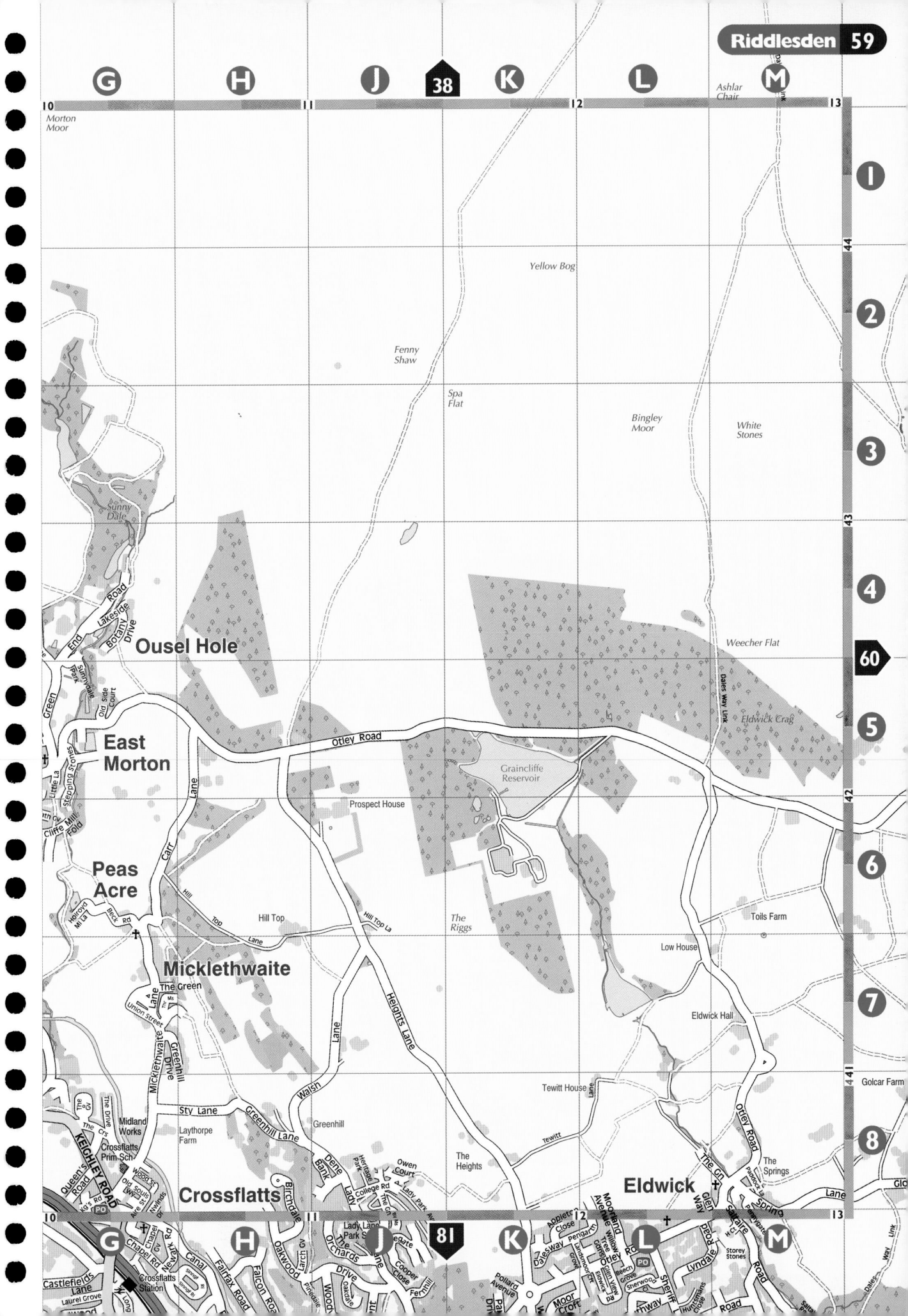

Morton
Moor

Yellow Bog

Fenny
Shaw

Spa
Flat

Bingley
Moor

White
Stones

Sunny
Dale

Weecher Flat

Ousel Hole

Eldwick Crag

Otley Road

**East
Morton**

Graincliffe
Reservoir

Prospect House

**Peas
Acre**

Toils Farm

Hill Top

The
Riggs

Low House

Micklethwaite

The Green

Eldwick Hall

Tewitt House

Golcar Farm

Midland
Works

Greenhill Lane

Laythorpe
Farm

Greenhill

Tewitt

Eldwick

The
Springs

Crossflatts

Crossflatts
Prim Sch

The Heights

Owen
Court

Castlefields
Lane

Crossflatts
Station

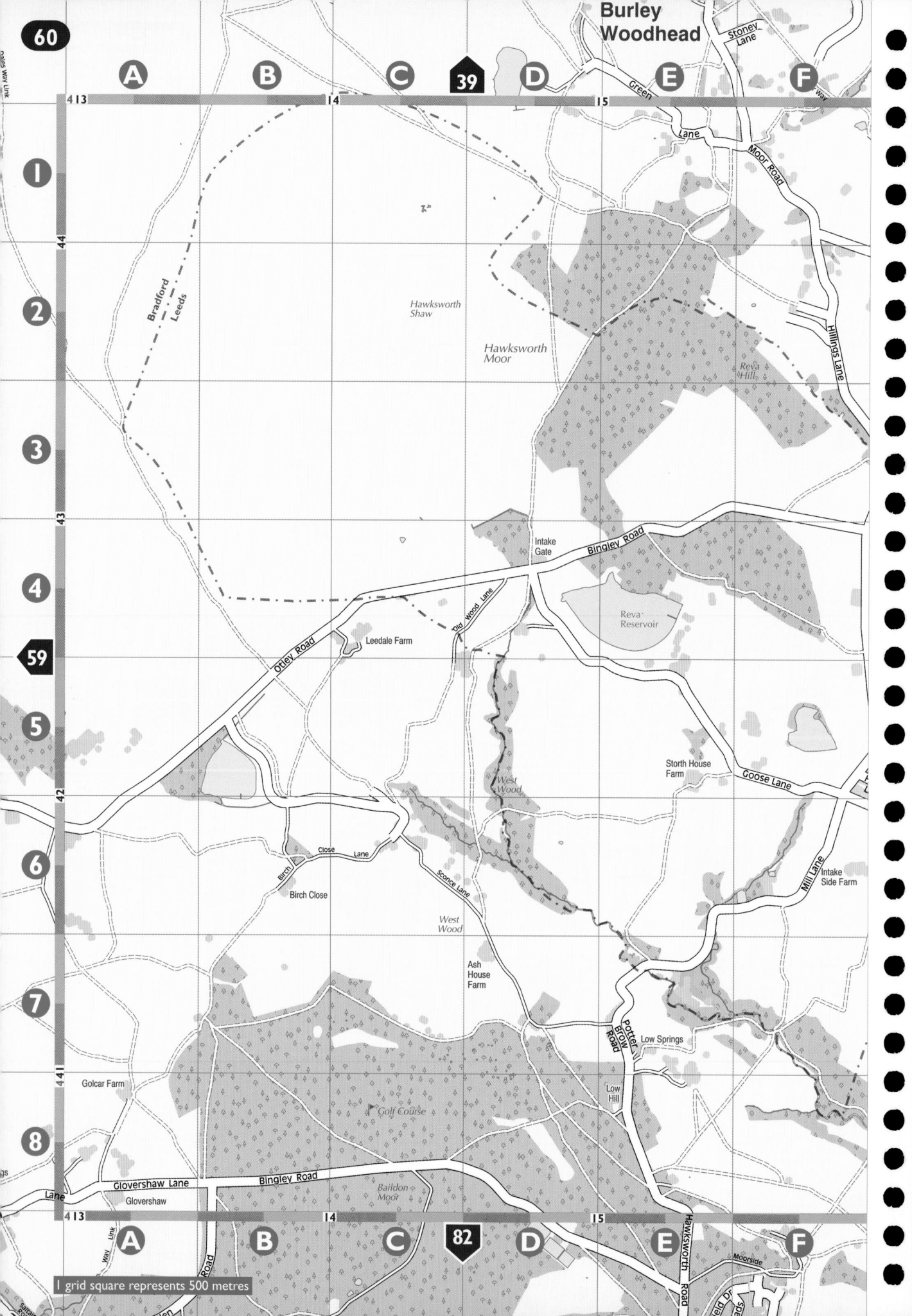

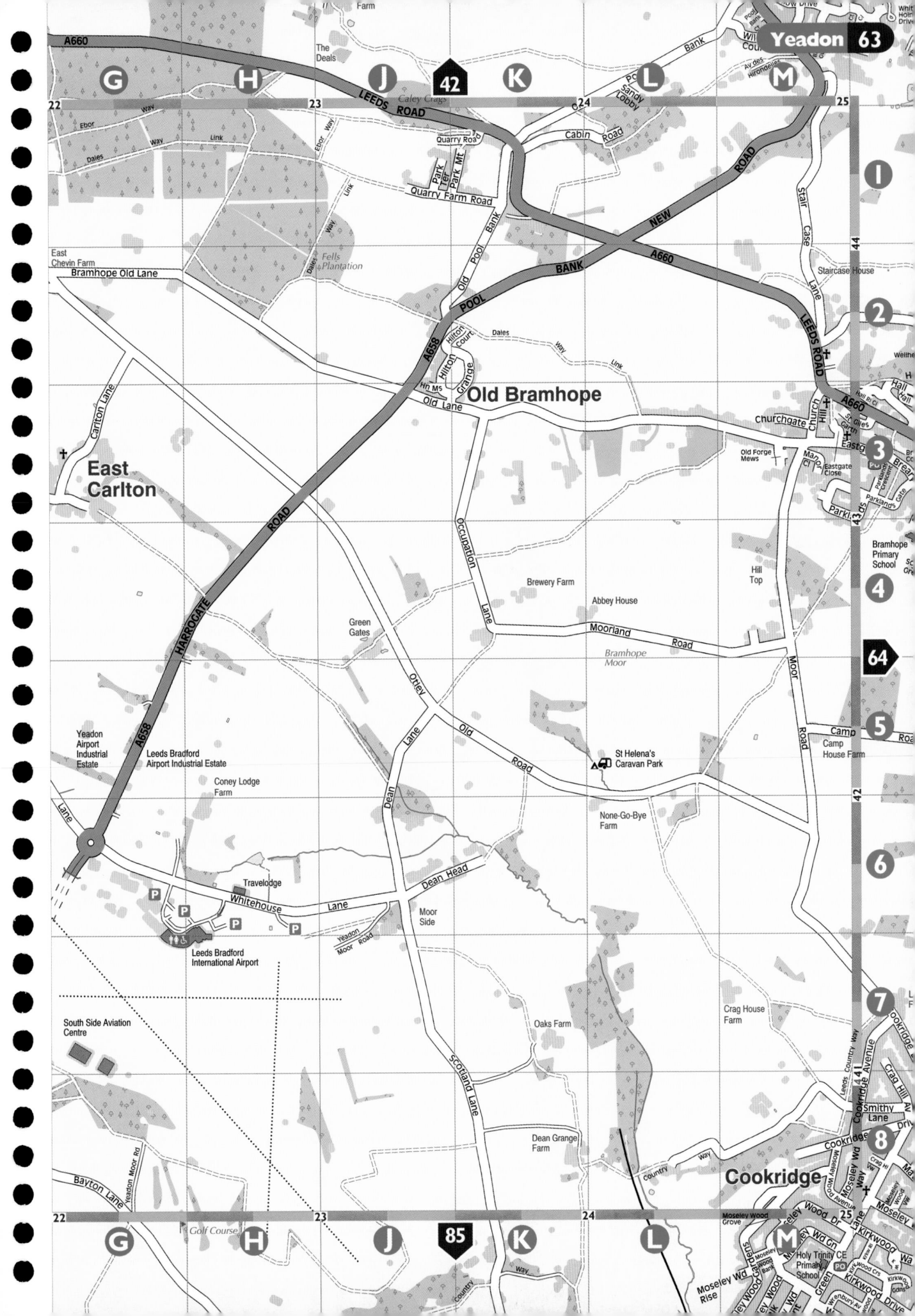

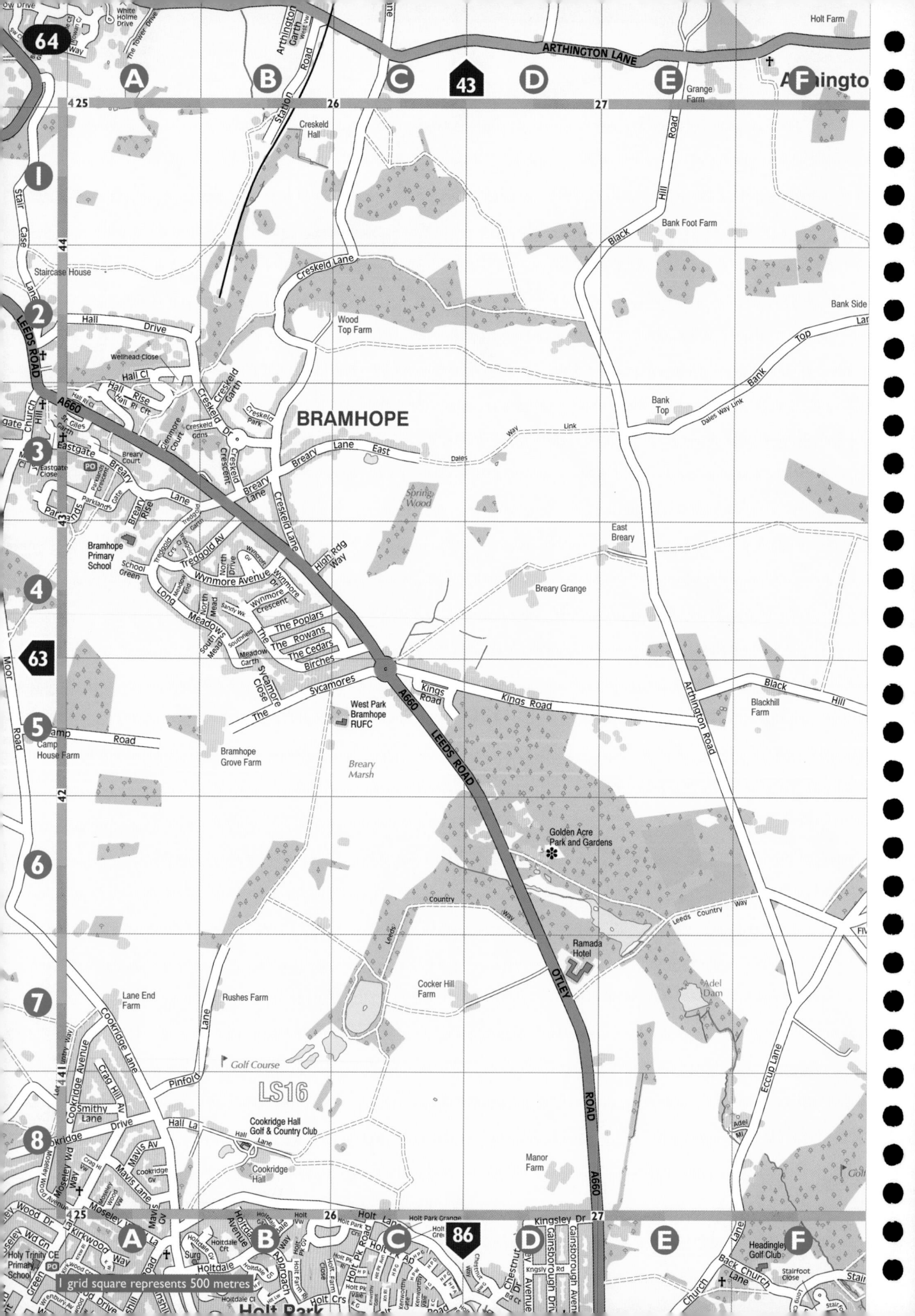

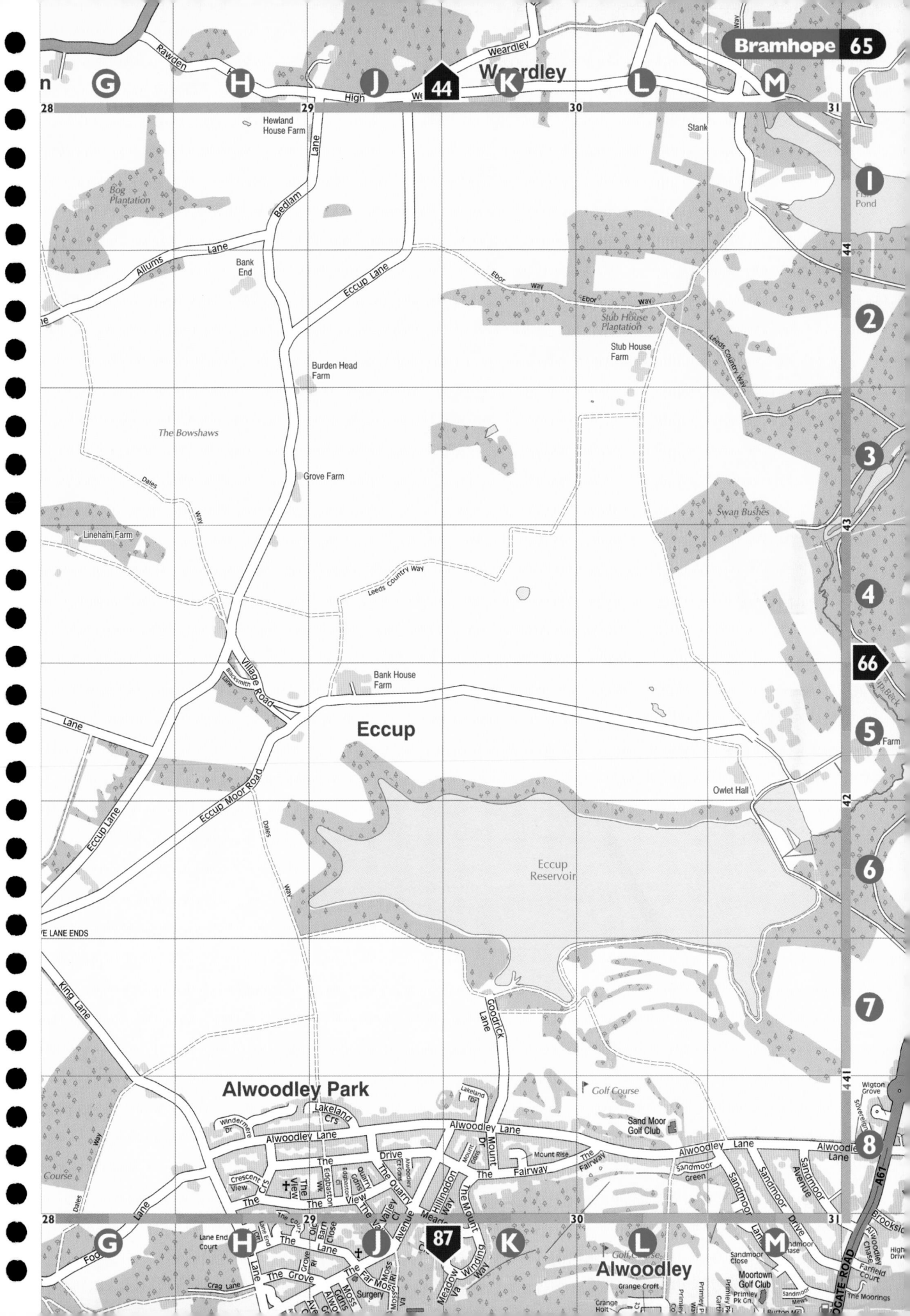

TADCASTER

Stutton

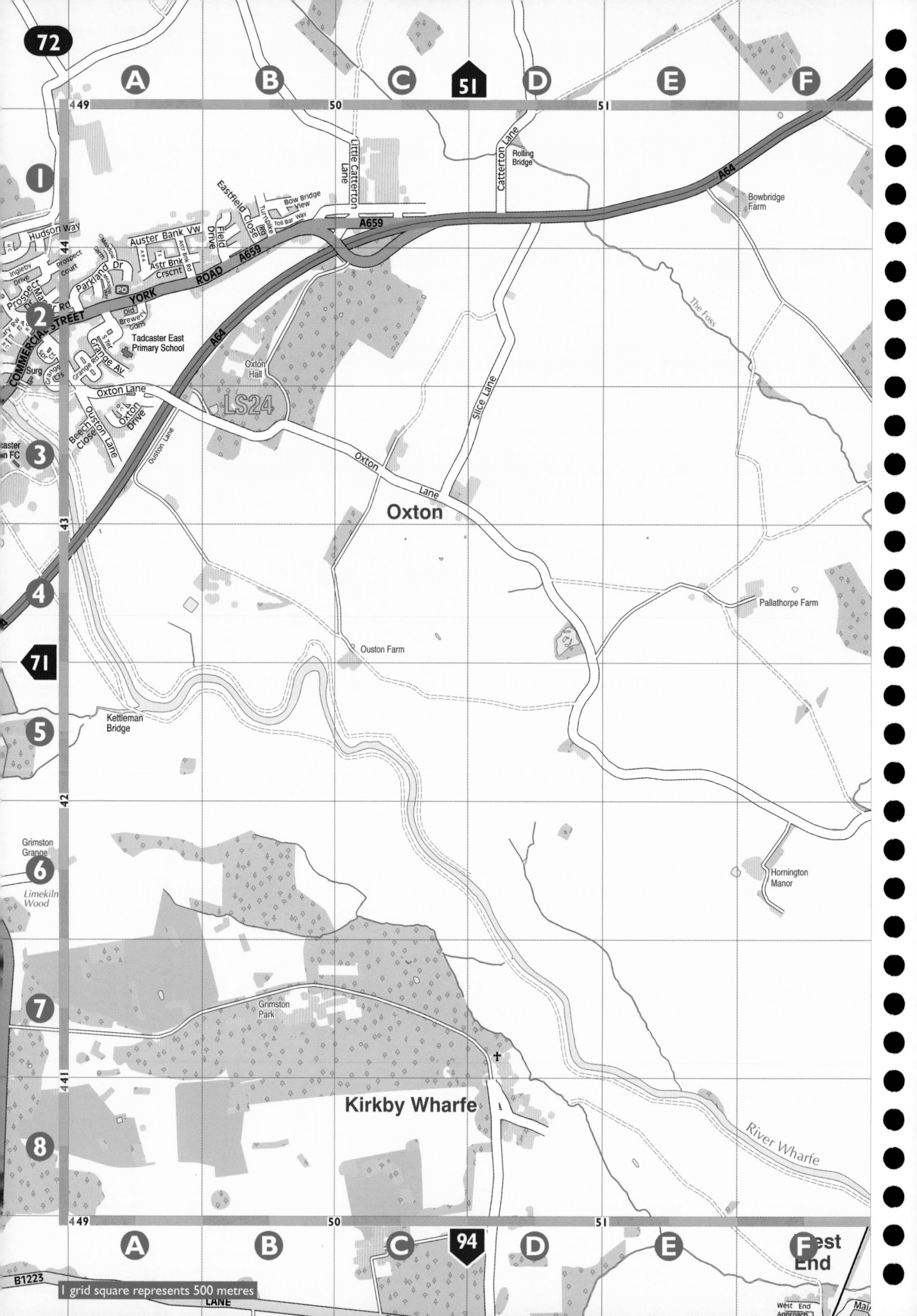

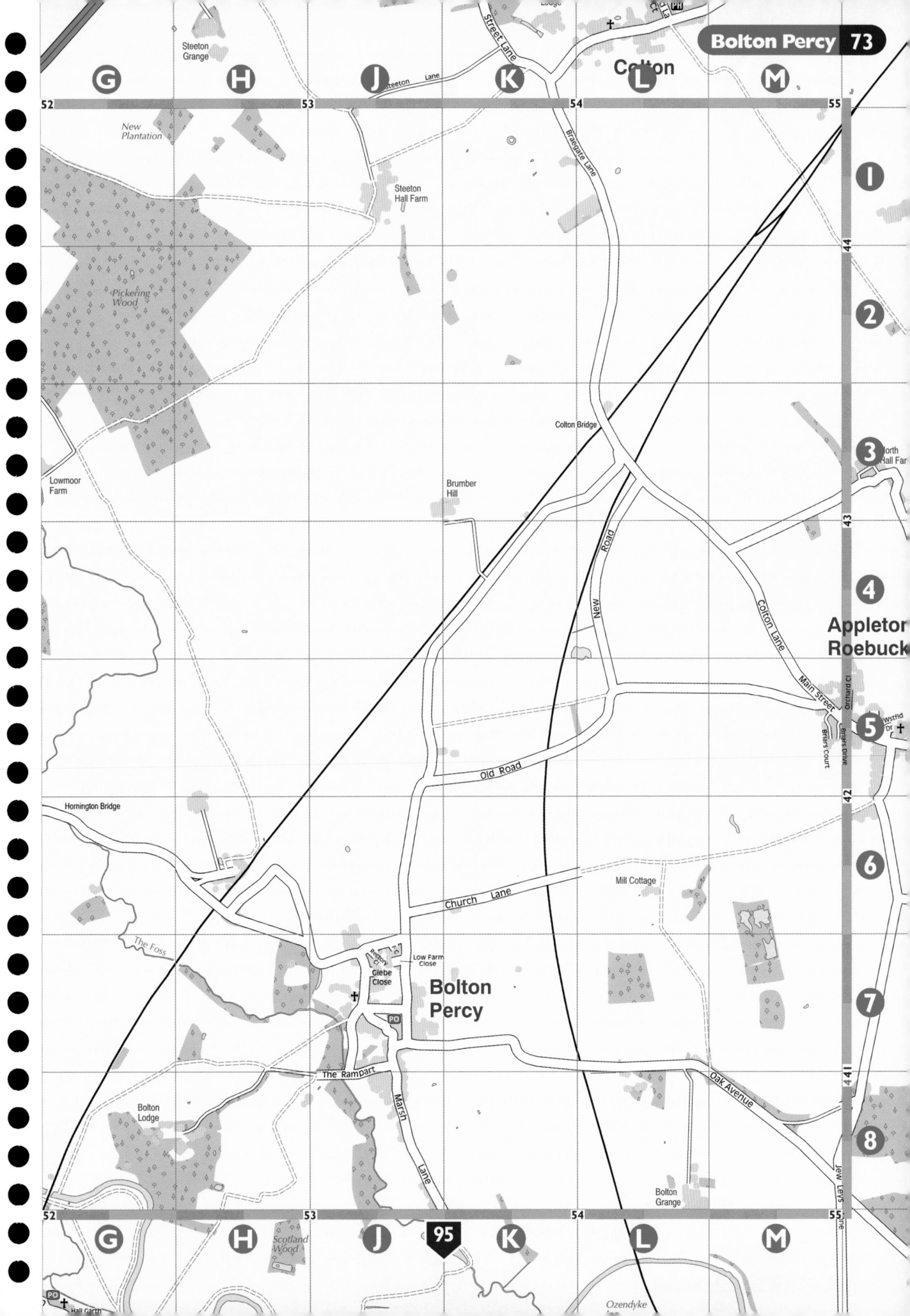

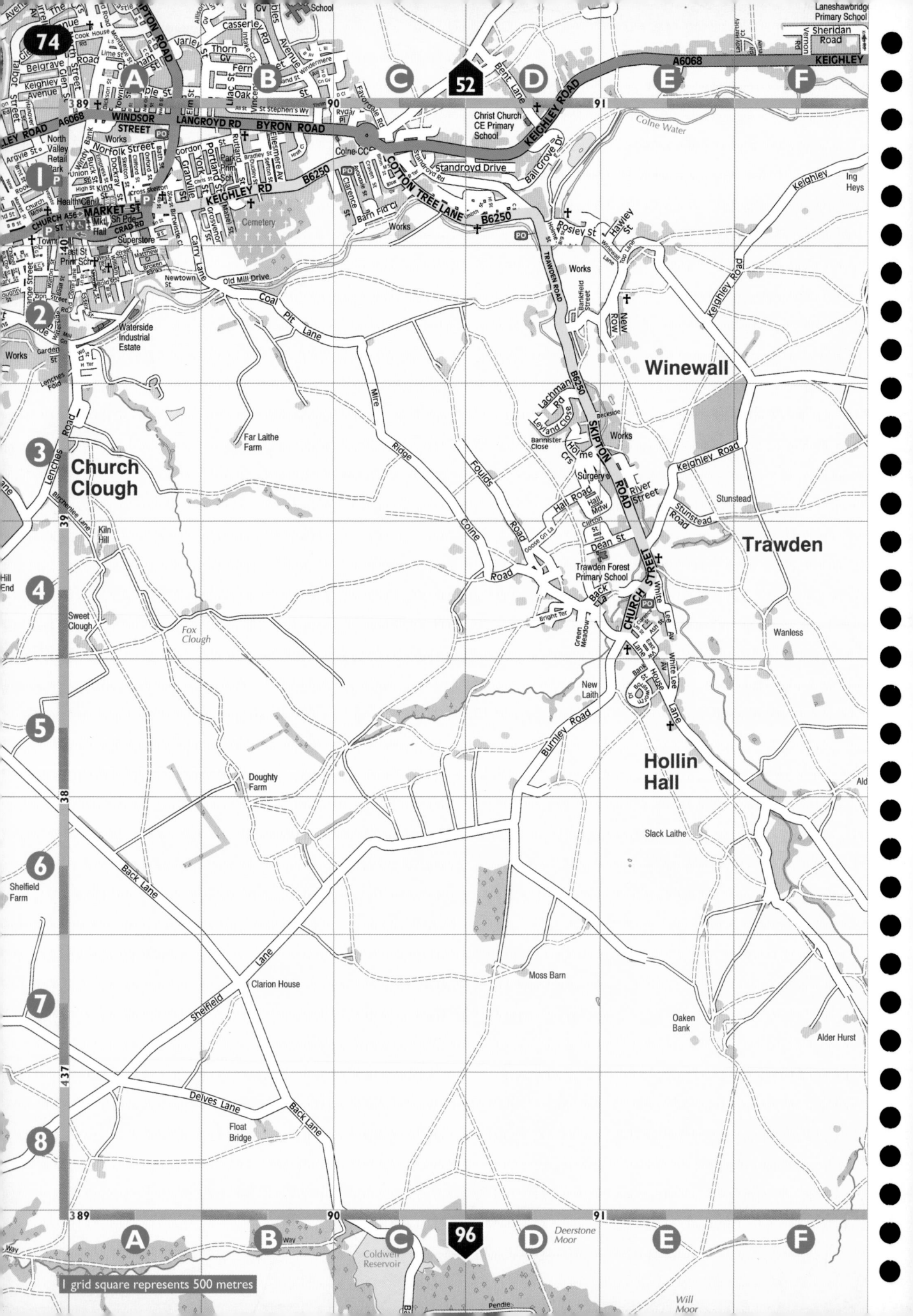

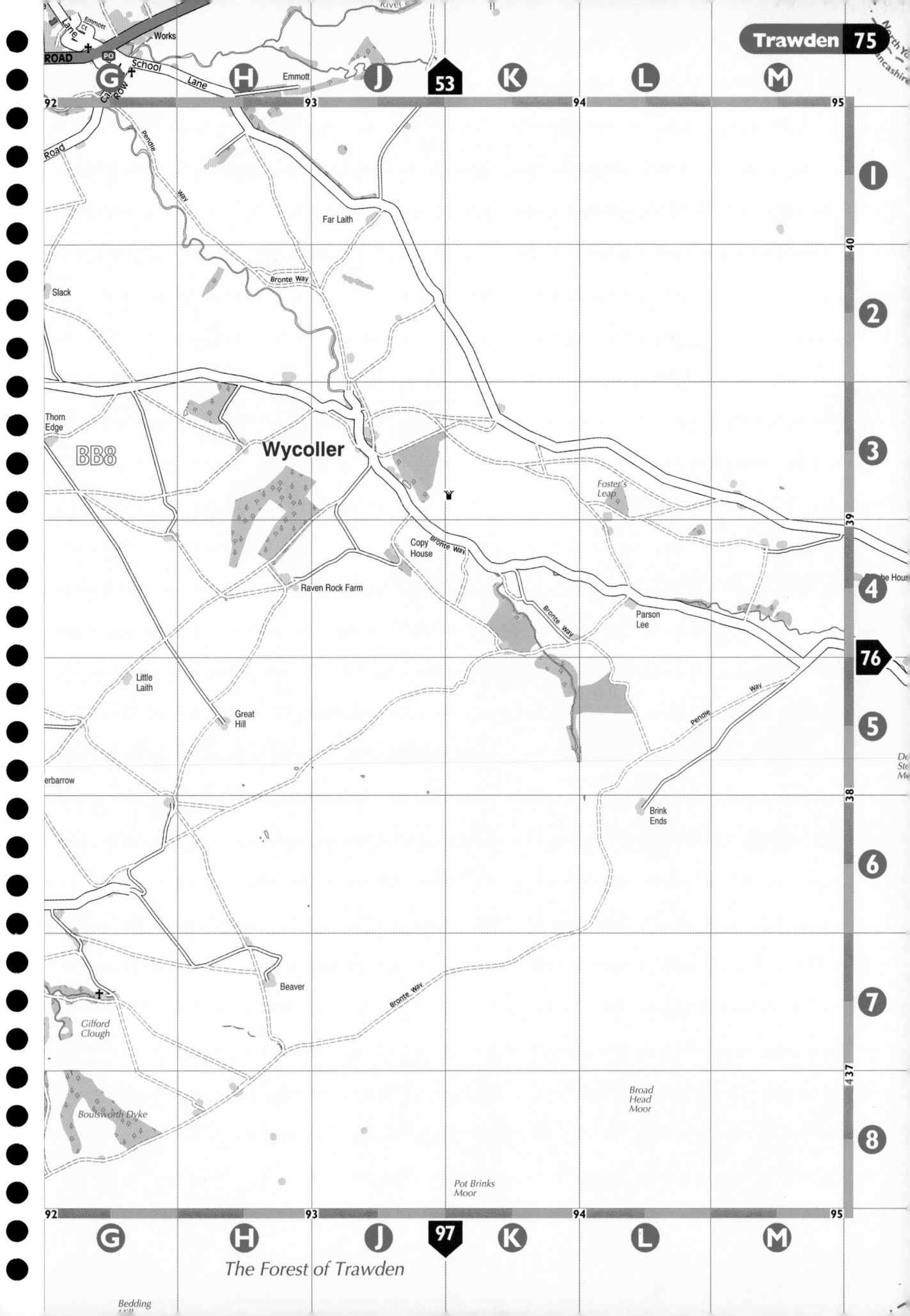

ROAD

Emmott
Ct
Lane

Works

PO
School Lane

Emmott

Car Row

Pendle Way

Far Laith

Bronte Way

Slack

Thorn
Edge

BB8

Wycoller

Foster's
Leap

Copy
House

Bronte Way

Raven Rock Farm

Bronte Way

Parson
Lee

Little
Laith

Great
Hill

Brink
Ends

erbarrow

Beaver

Bronte Way

Gilford
Clough

Broad
Head
Moor

Boulsworth Dyke

Pot Brinks
Moor

Bedding

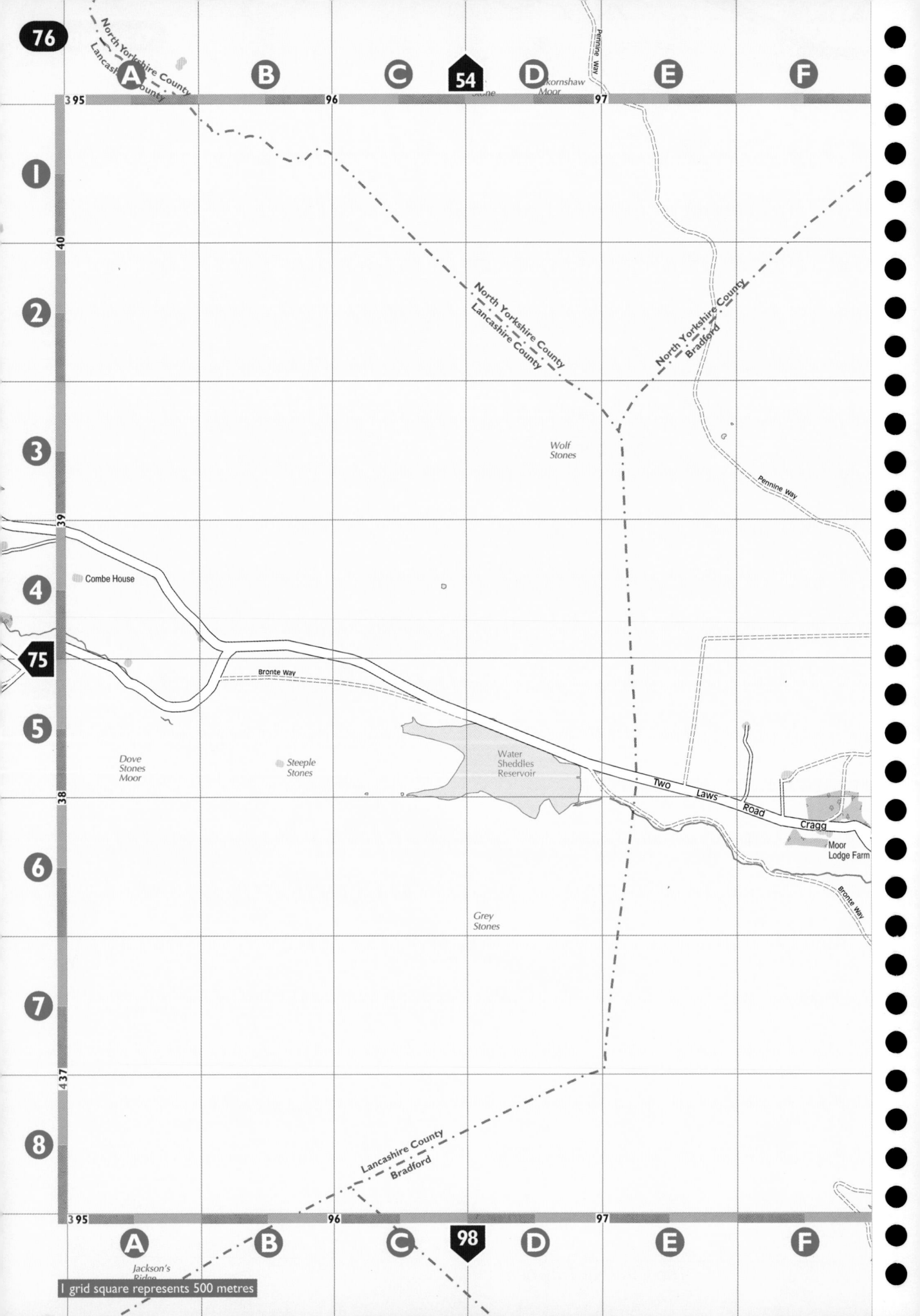

A   B   C 54   D   E   F

3 95   96   97

I

40

2

North Yorkshire County
Lancashire County

North Yorkshire County
Bradford

3

Wolf
Stones

Pennine Way

39

Combe House

4

75

Bronte Way

Dove
Stones
Moor

Steeple
Stones

Water
Sheddles
Reservoir

Two Laws Road

Cragg

38

5

Grey
Stones

Moor
Lodge Farm

Bronte Way

6

7

4 37

8

Lancashire County
Bradford

3 95   96   97

A   B 98   D   E   F

Jackson's
Ridge

1 grid square represents 500 metres

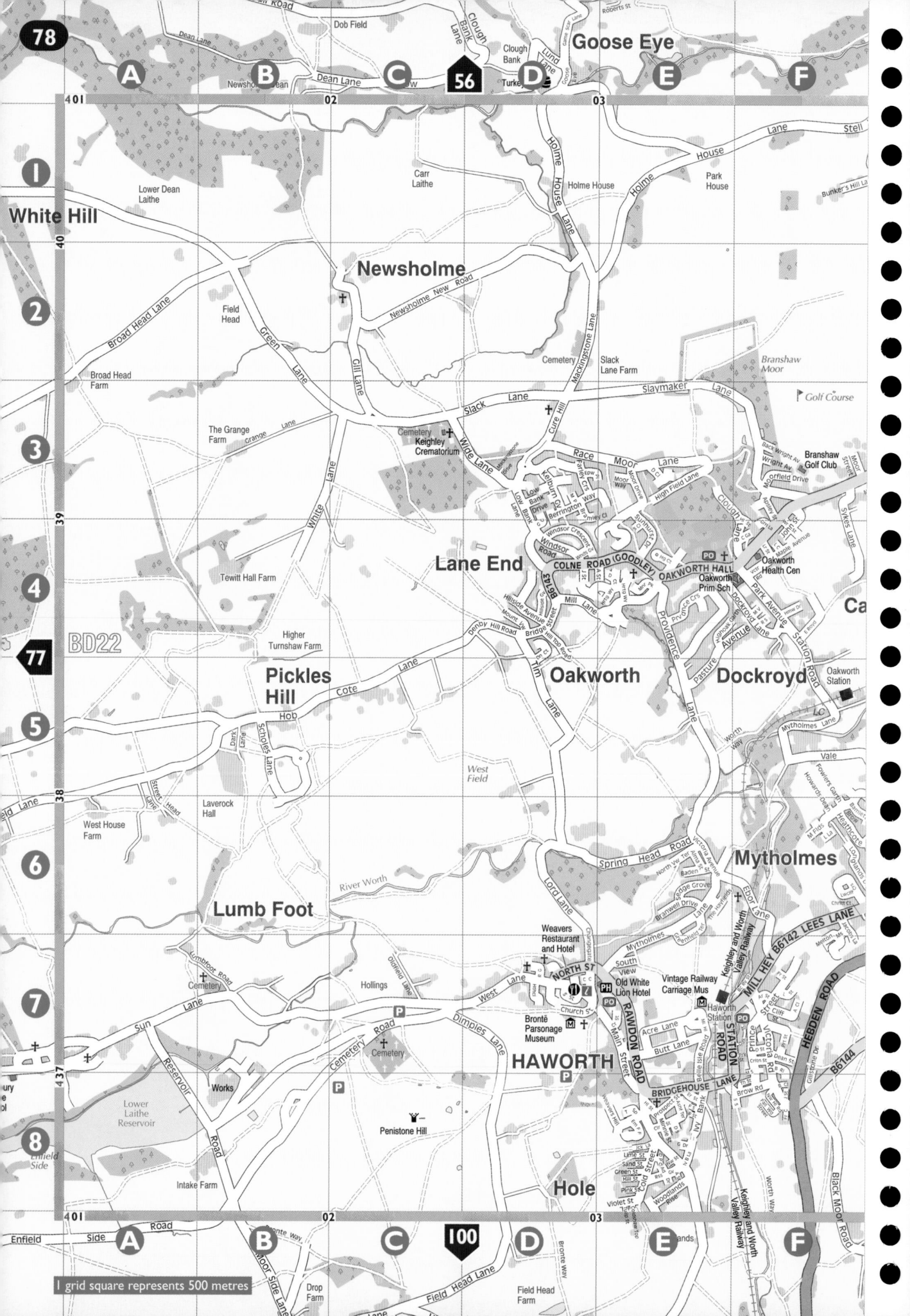

A   B   C   56   D   E   F

401   02   03

Goose Eye

1

White Hill

Lower Dean
Laithe

Carr
Laithe

Clough
Bank

Lung
Lane

Turke

Holme
House Lane

Holme House

Holme
Lane

House

Park
House

Bunker's Hill La

40

2

Broad Head Lane

Field
Head

Newsholme

Newsholme New Road

Dob Field

Dean Lane

Dean Lane

Newsholme Dean

Mackingstone Lane

Cemetery

Slack
Lane Farm

Branshaw
Moor

Golf Course

Broad Head
Farm

Green Lane

Gill Lane

39

3

The Grange
Farm

Grange Lane

Cemetery
Keighley
Crematorium

Slack   Lane

Wide Lane

Cure Hill

Race   Moor   Lane

Slaymaker   Lane

Farley

Back Wright Av
Wright Av

Branshaw
Golf Club

Moorfield Drive

Moor
Street

Sykes Lane

4

White   Lane

Tewitt Hall Farm

Hillside Avenue

Denby Hill Road

Berrington

Windsor
Road

COLNE ROAD (GOODLEY

Bridge Hill

OAKWORTH HALL

Mill   Lane

Providence

Pasture

Park   Avenue

Oakworth
Prim Sch

Oakworth Health Cen

Dockroyd Lane

Station   Road

Oakworth
Station

Ca

77   BD22

Lane End

Oakworth

Dockroyd

LC

38

5

Higher
Turnshaw Farm

Pickles
Hill

Cote   Lane

Hob

Scholes Lane

Dark   Lane

Street   Head

Laverock
Hall

Tim   Lane

West
Field

Worth   Way

Mytholmes Lane

Vale

6

West House
Farm

Lumb Foot

River Worth

Spring Head Road

Mytholmes

Enfield
Side

7

Sun   Lane

Lumbfoot Road

Cemetery

Hollings

Reservoir   Road

Oldfield Lane

Cemetery   Road

Dimples Lane

West   Lane

Lord Lane

Weavers
Restaurant
and Hotel

Mytholmes

NORTH ST

Old White
Lion Hotel

PH

Brontë
Parsonage
Museum

Church   St

RAWDON   ROAD

Vintage Railway
Carriage Mus

Haworth
Station

Keighley and Worth
Valley Railway

MILL HEY   B6142 LEES LANE

Victoria   Rd

STATION   ROAD

HEBDEN   ROAD

437

8

Lower
Laithe
Reservoir

Works

Penistone Hill

HAWORTH

Main Street

Butt Lane

BRIDGEHOUSE LANE

Hole

Keighley and Worth
Valley Railway

Black Moor Rd

401   02   03

Enfield   Side   Road

A   B   C   100   D   E   F

Moor Side Lane

Drop
Farm

Bronte Way

Field Head Lane

Field Head
Farm

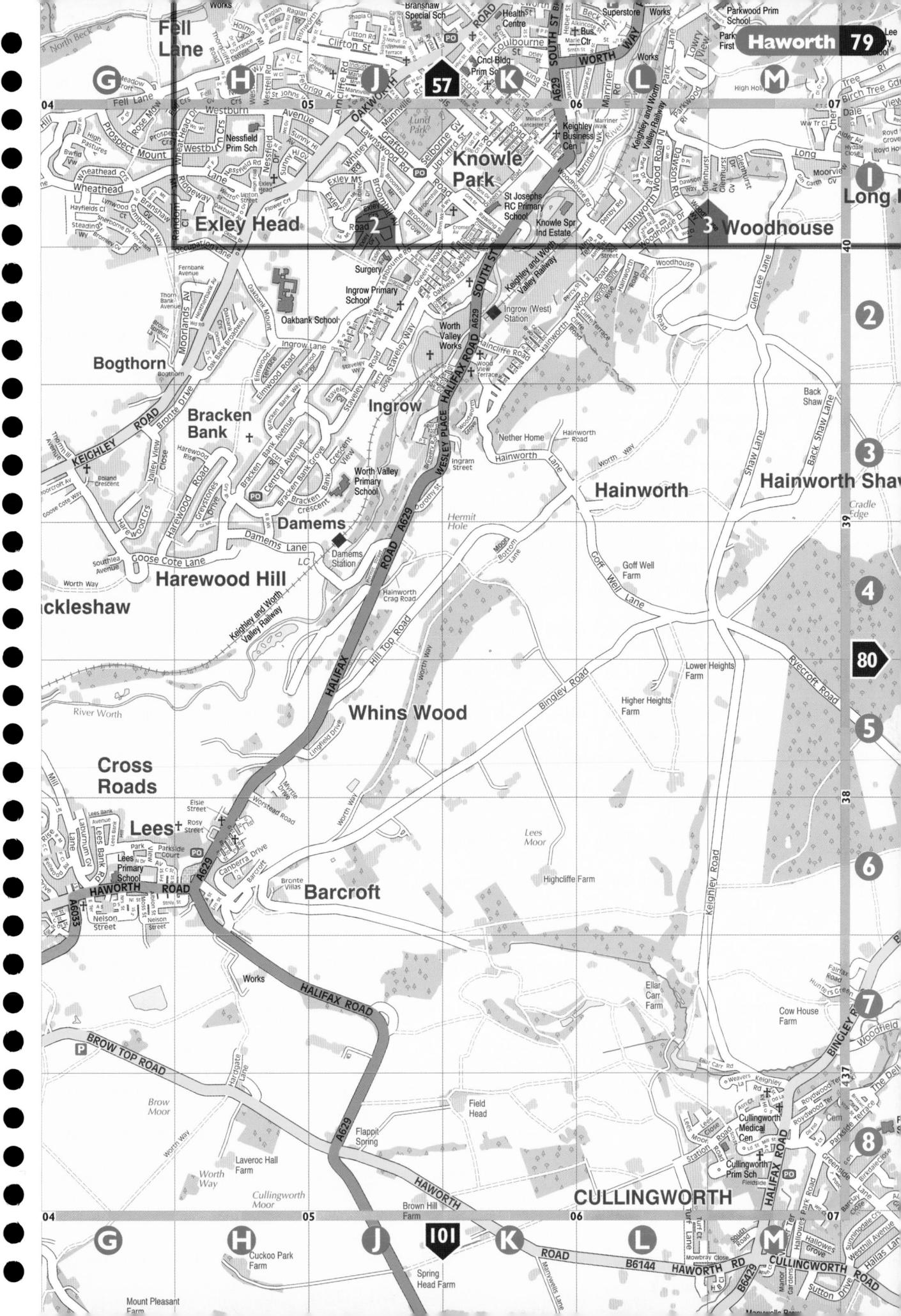

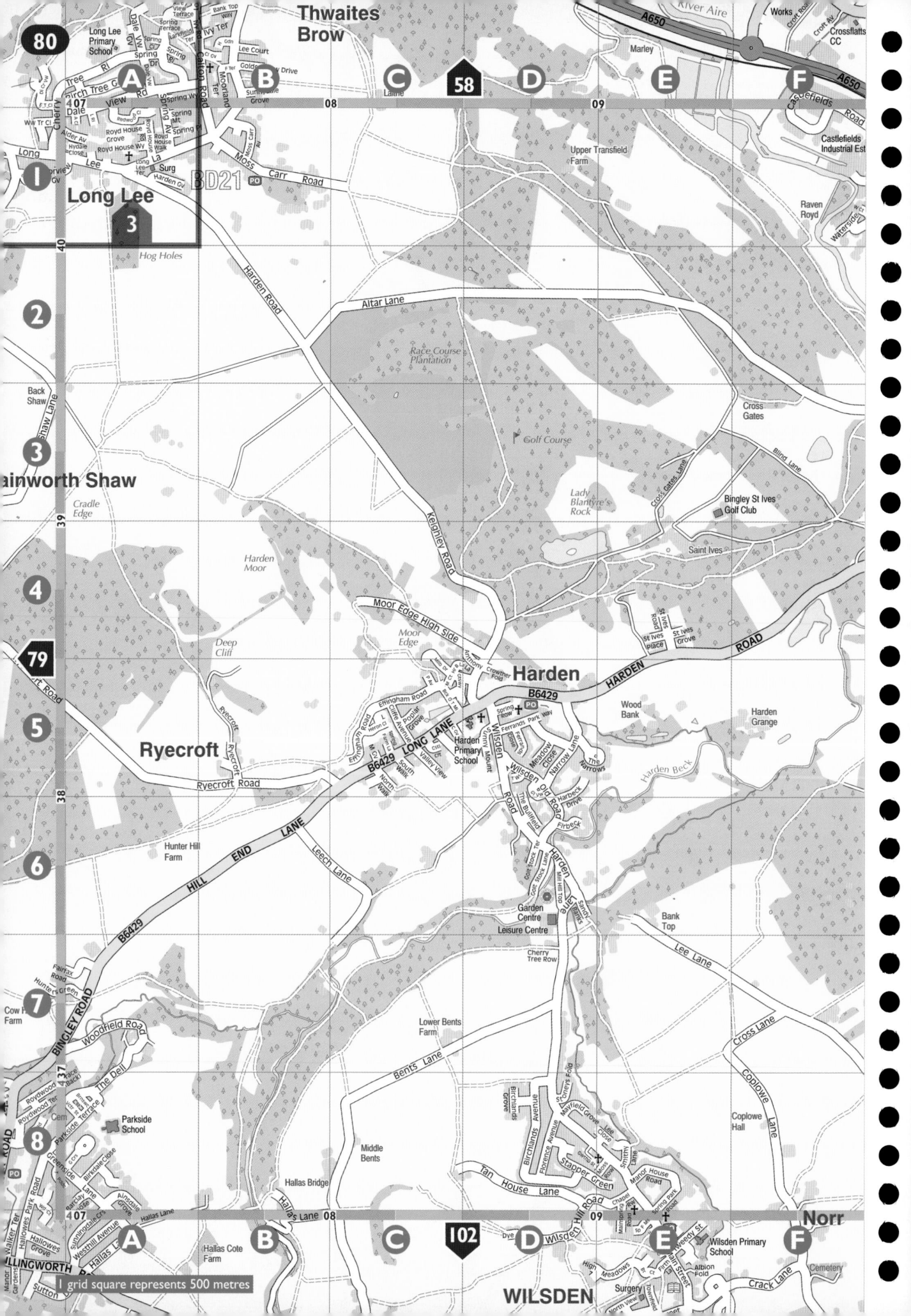

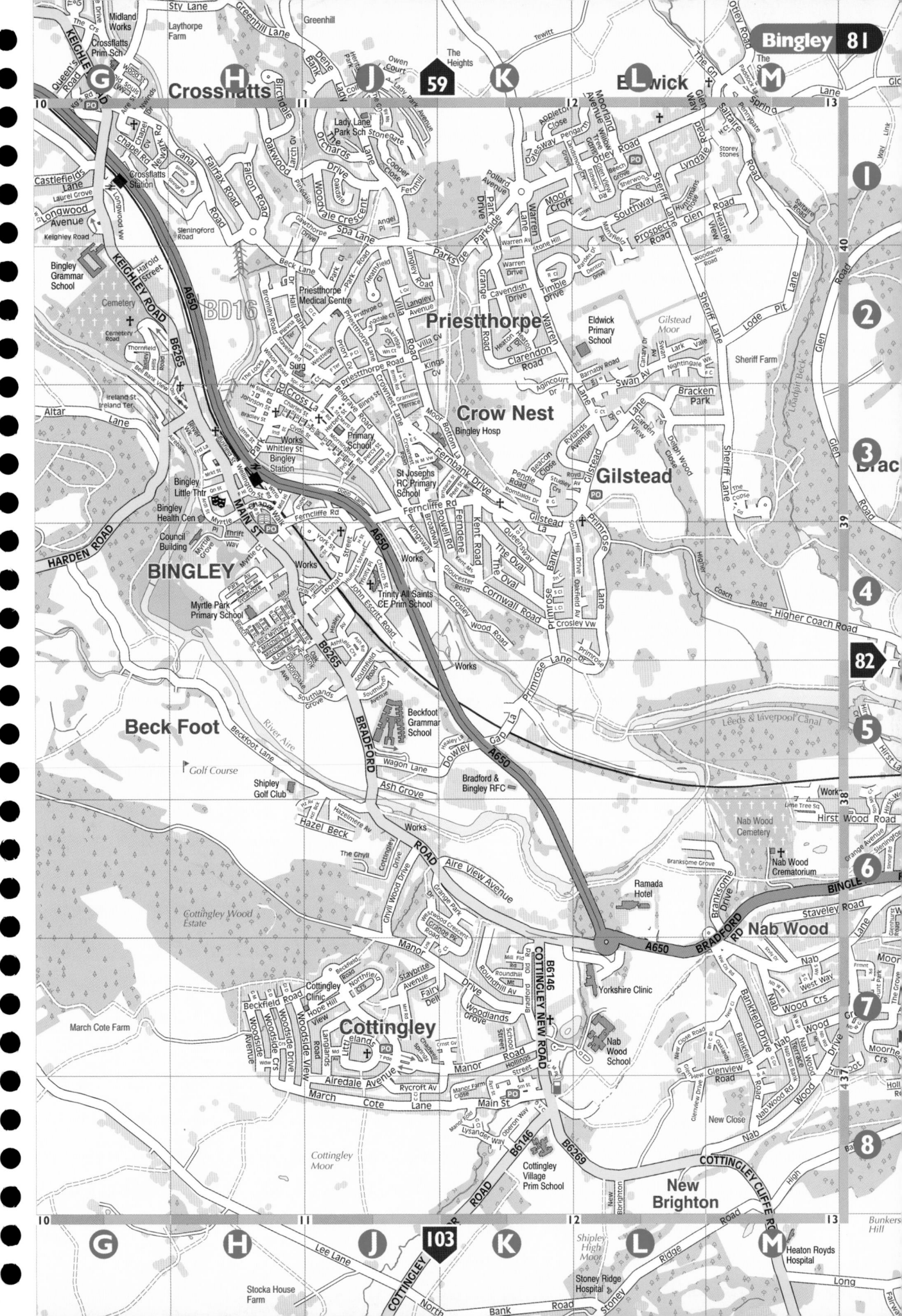

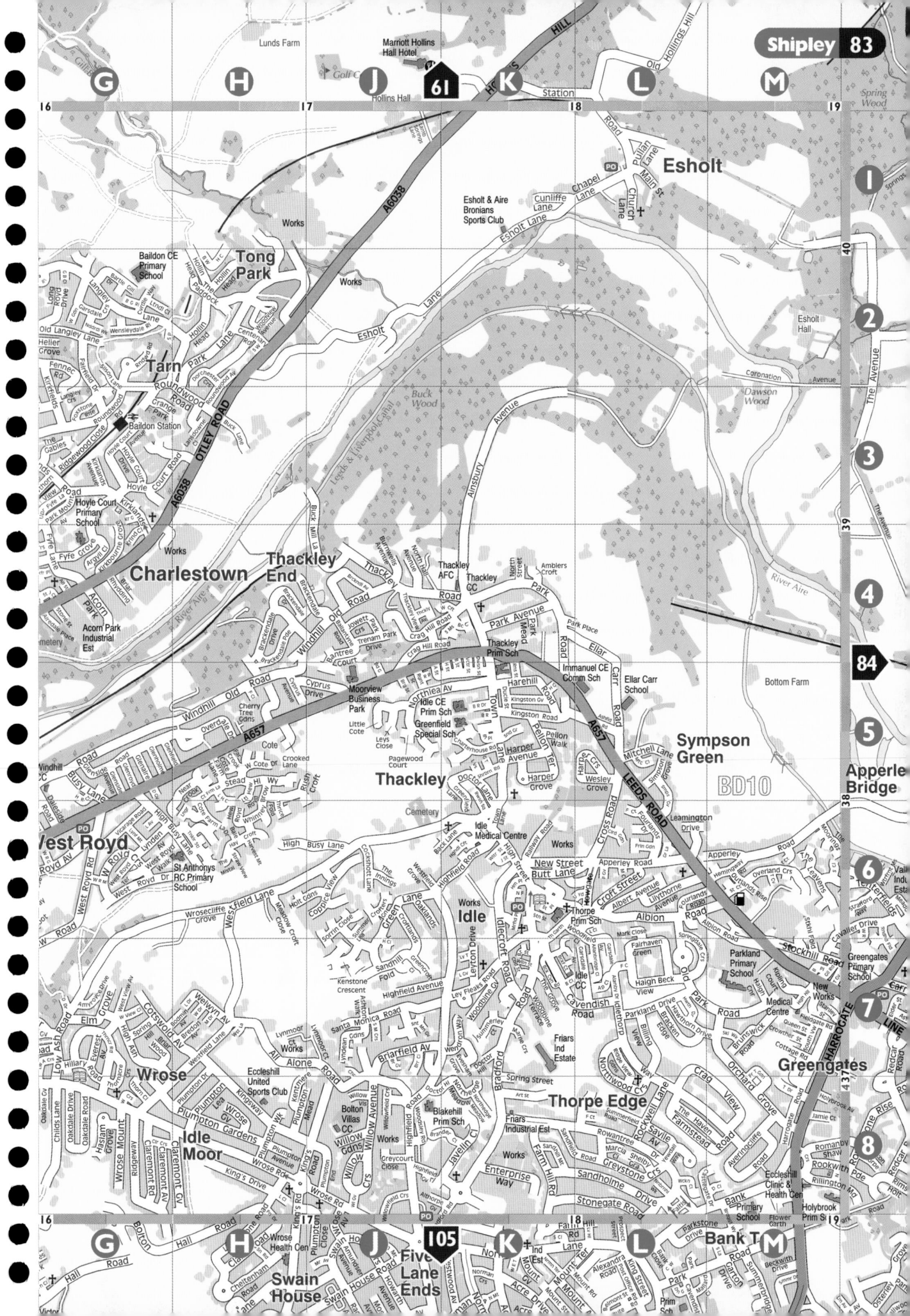

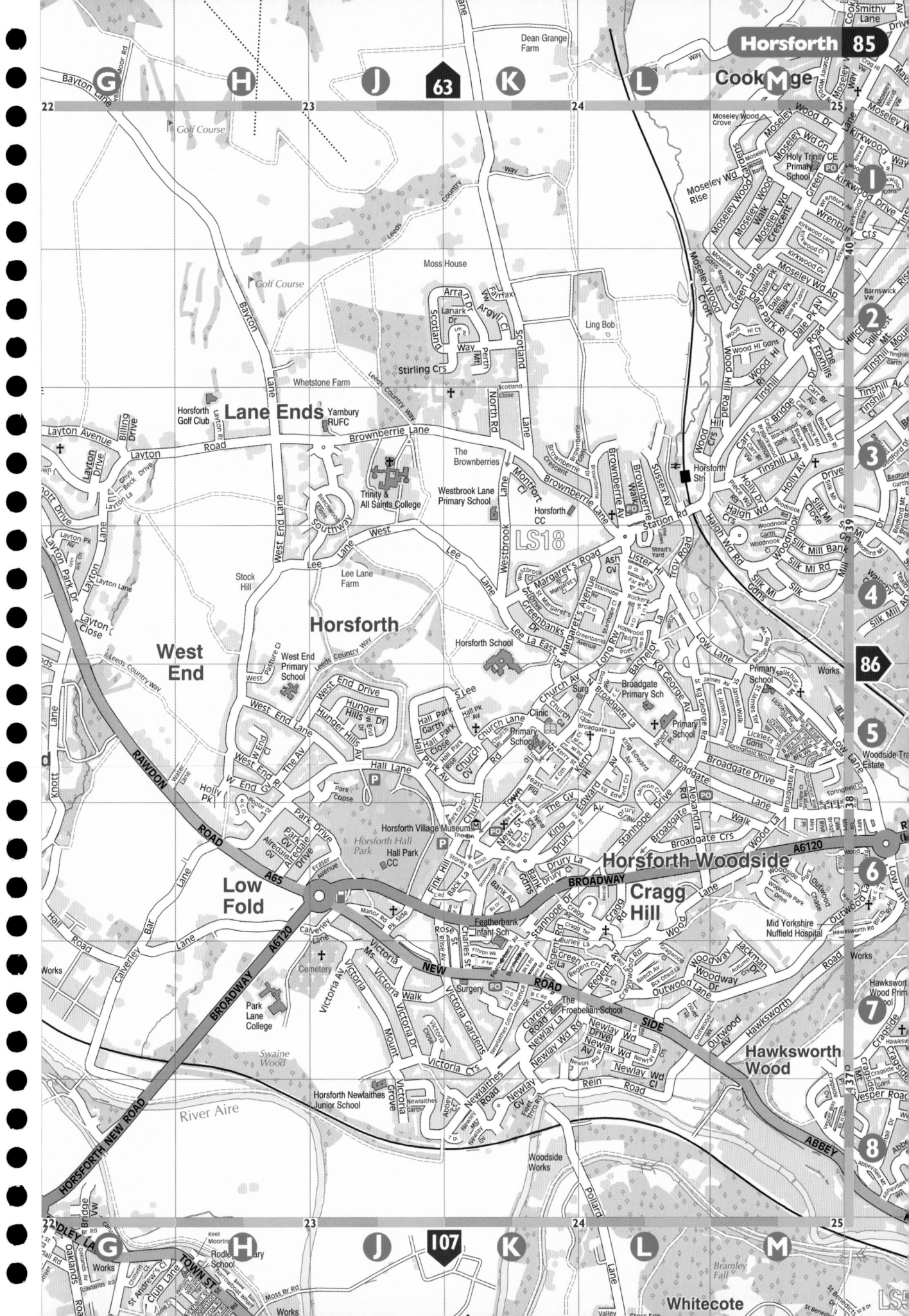

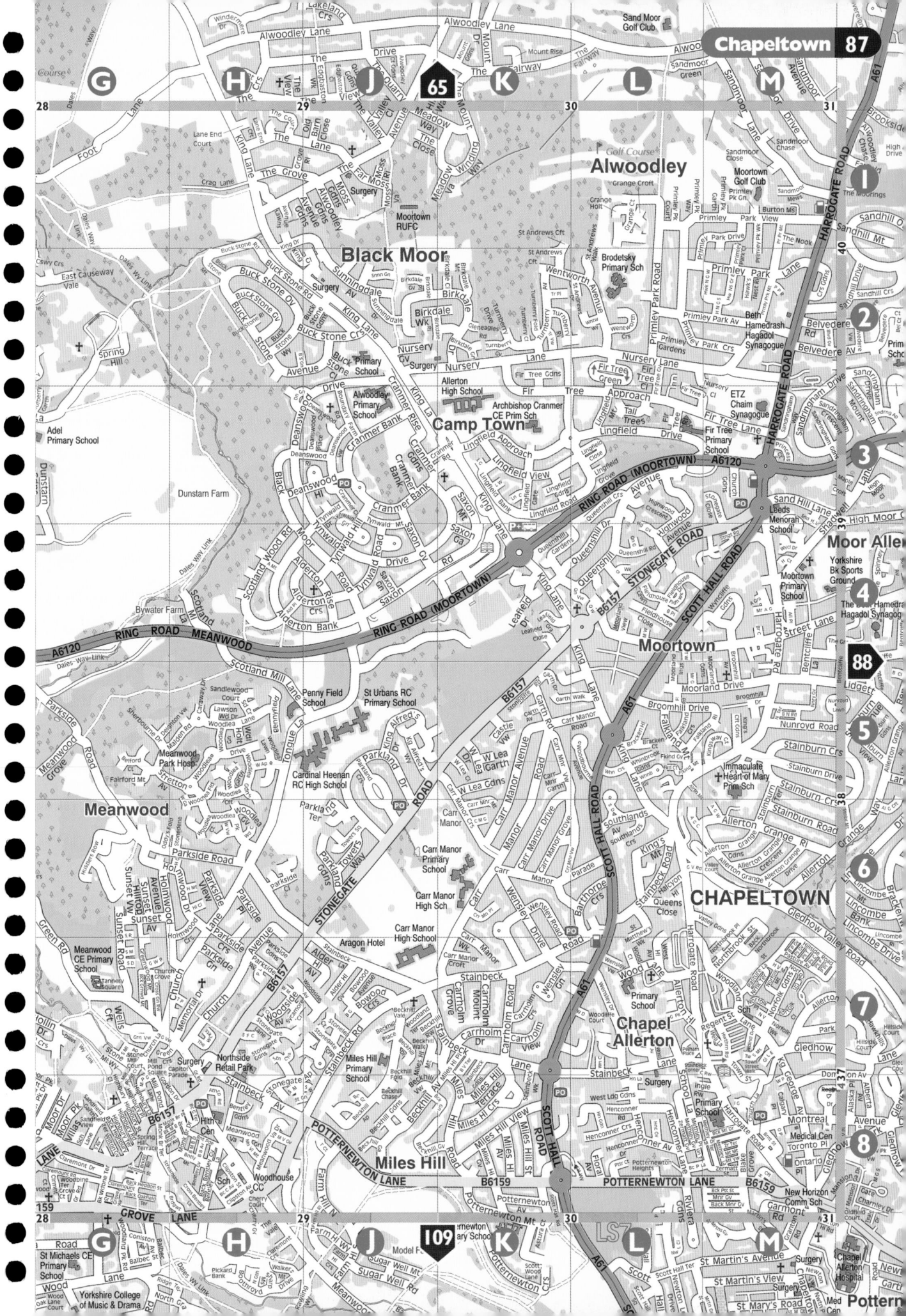

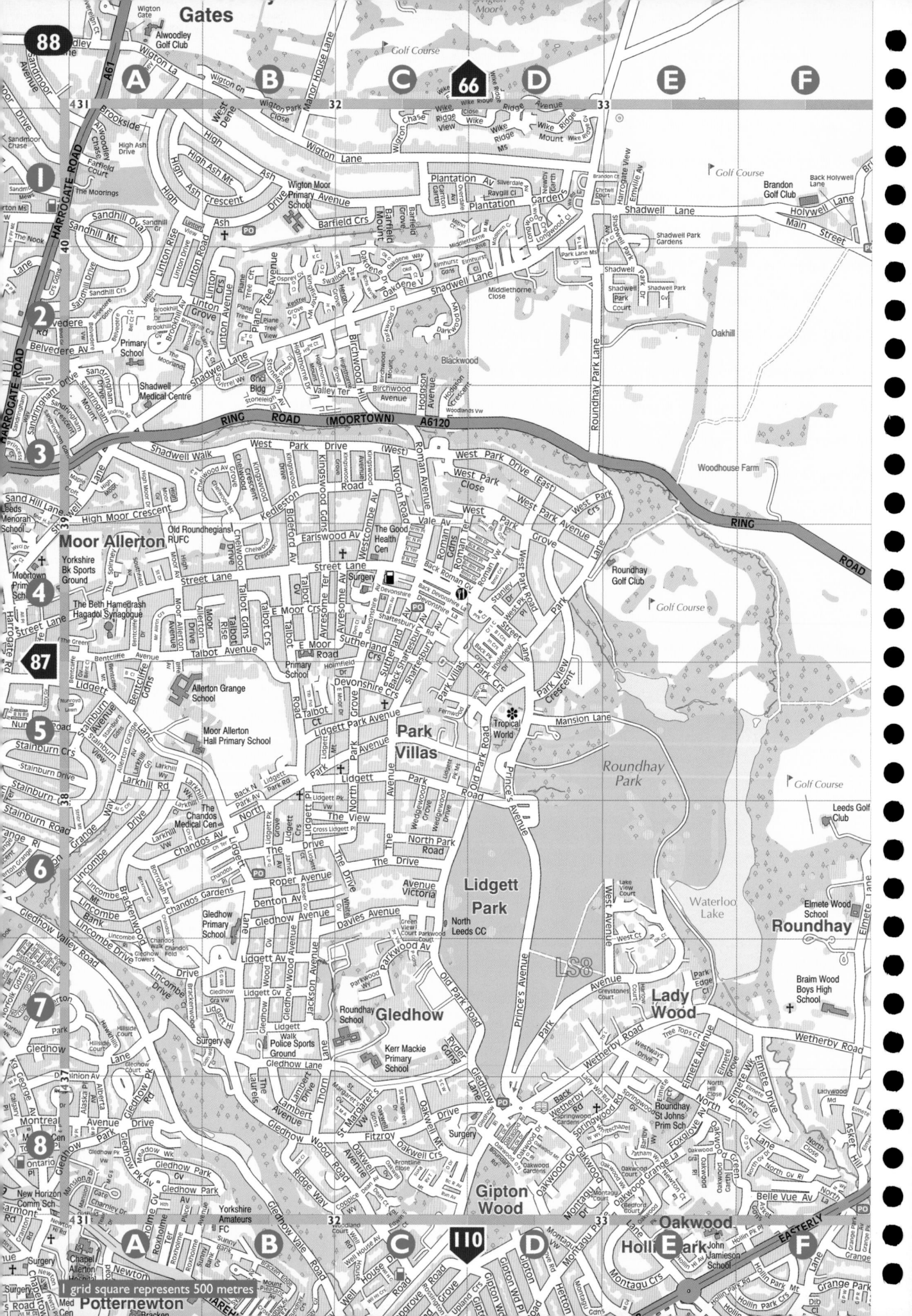

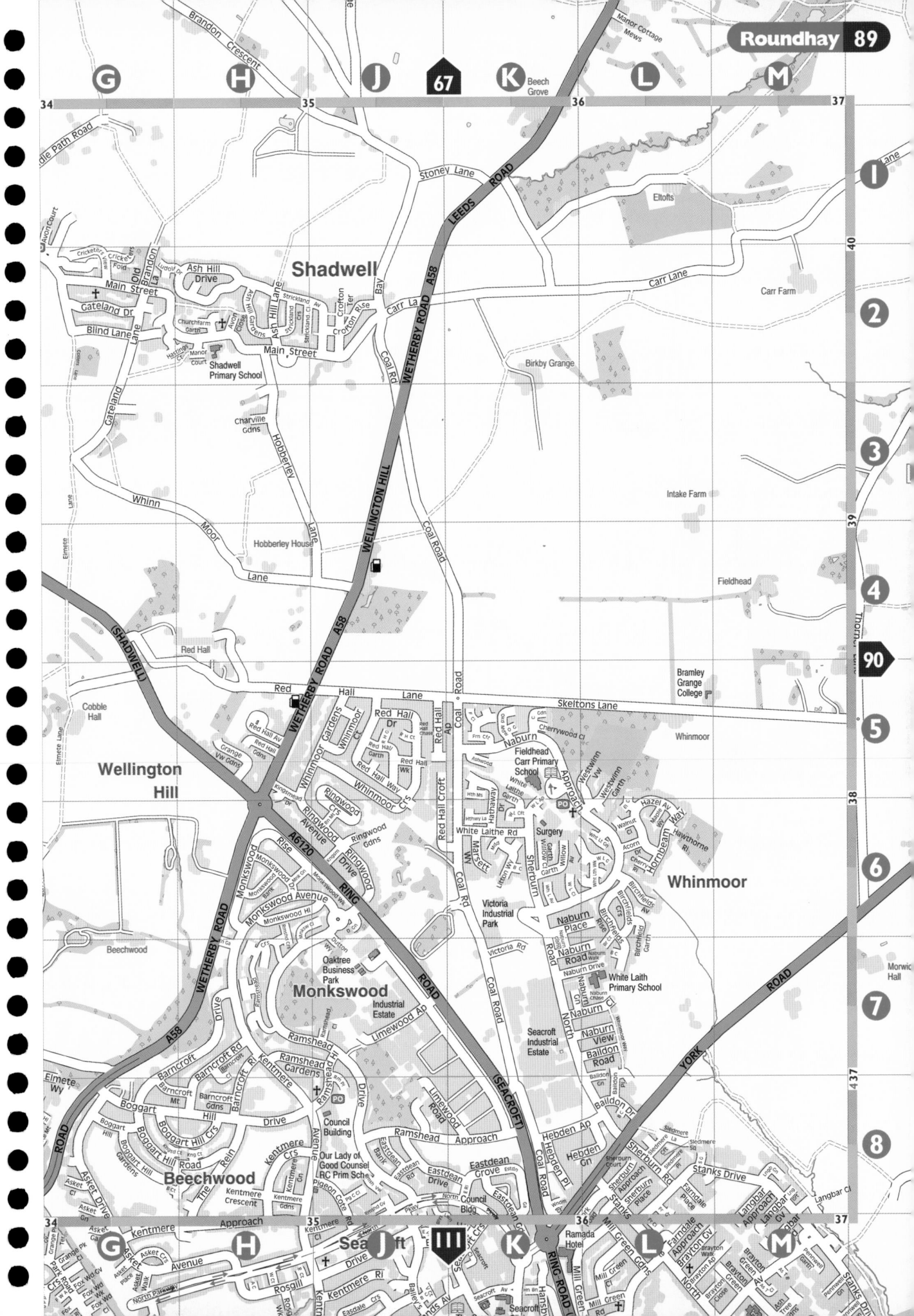

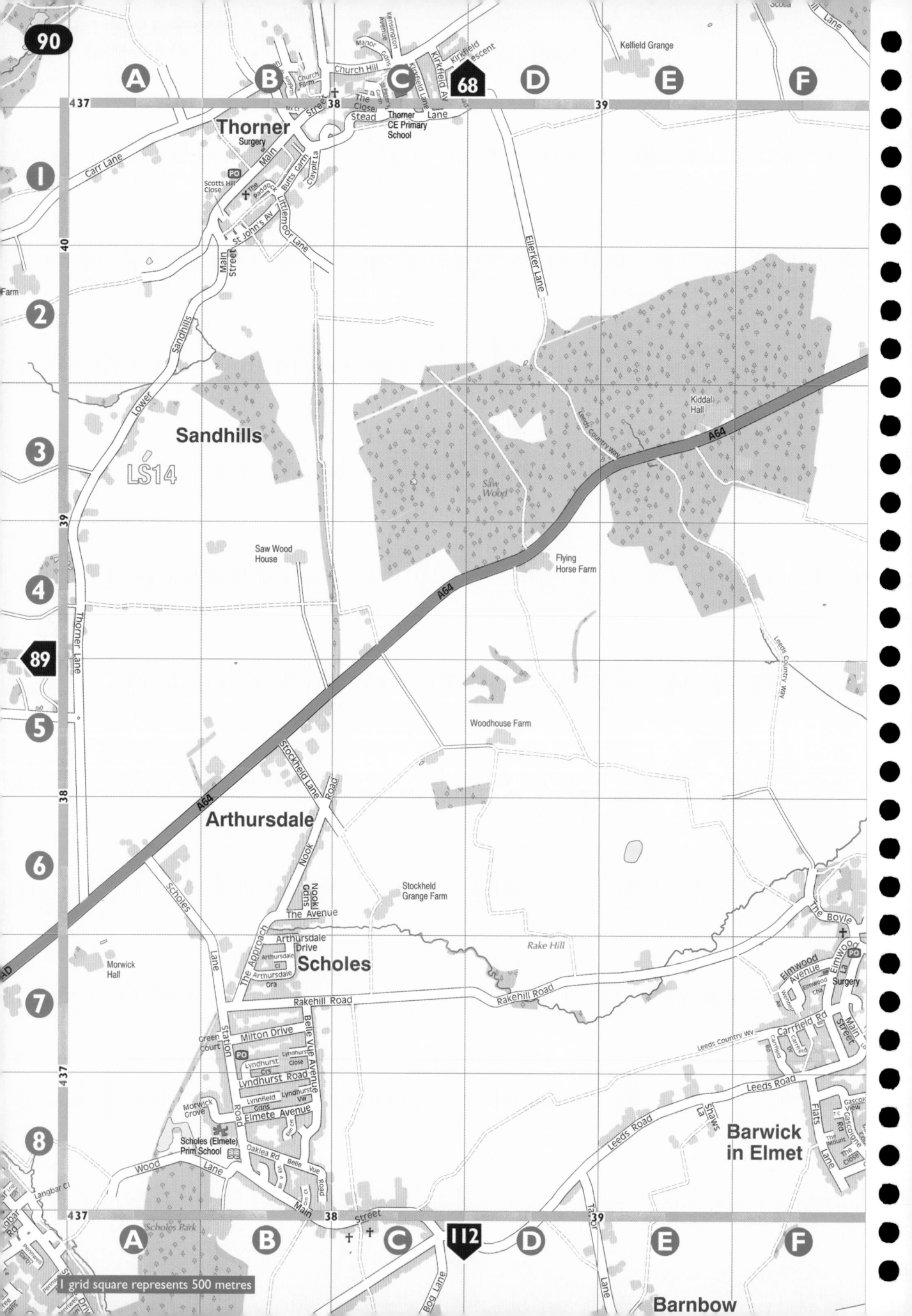

G H J **69** K L M

Junction 45

Windsor Farm

Whitewell Farm

A64

A64

A64

Occupation Lane

Woodlands Farm

Kiddal Lane End

Potterton

Kiddal Lane

Potterton Lane

Mary Lane

Cowthwaite Plantation

Becca Hall

Becca Home Farm

92

St Joh

Cufforth House

Potterton Bridge

Cock Beck

Becca Lane

Leyfield Farm

Fieldhead Drive

Cattle Lane

Cattle Lane

Aberfor

Aberford Road Works

Barwick In Elmet CE Primary School

Richmondfield Garth

Richmondfield Lane

Richmondfield Avenue

Parlington Meadow

Beck Meadow

Elmet Road

Welfare Ave

Chapel Lane

Long Lane

Beech View

Aberford Primary School

A1(M)

I

2

3

4

5

6

7

8

G H J **113** K L M

Highfield Farm

Home Farm

Highfield Lane

Highfield Lane

A   B   C   70   D   E   F

443   44   45

Leeds
North Yorkshire County

Junc 5

Junction 45

A64

Home Farm

Paradise Lane

Crossroads Farm

Chantry Lane

Hazlewood Castle Hotel

Lowpark Farm

North Approach

South Approach

Lodge Farm

Black Horse Farm

South Approach

Hayton Wood

Bullen Wood

91

Hayton House

St John's

Cufforth House

Greystone Park

Haverthwaites Dr

Greystones

St John's Ct

St John's Garth

The Dale

Pinfold Rd

Field Lane

Cock Beck

Rein Closet

Pool

Hayton View

Green Hill

Becca Lane

Highfield Rd

Abbott's Cl

Raper

North Yorkshire County

Leeds

Woodhouse Grange

The Rein

Aberford

Cattle Lane

Parlington Villas

Beech View

Parlington

Field La

Main Street

Aberford CE Primary School

School La

Windmill Rd

Young's Cl

Parlington Lane

ABERFORD BY-PASS A1(M)

Stocking Lane

Stocking Lane

Lotherton Lane

B1217

A   B   C   114   D   LOTHERTON   Lotherton Lane   E   F

443   44   45

Bunk Hill

Hicklam House

B1217

Copley

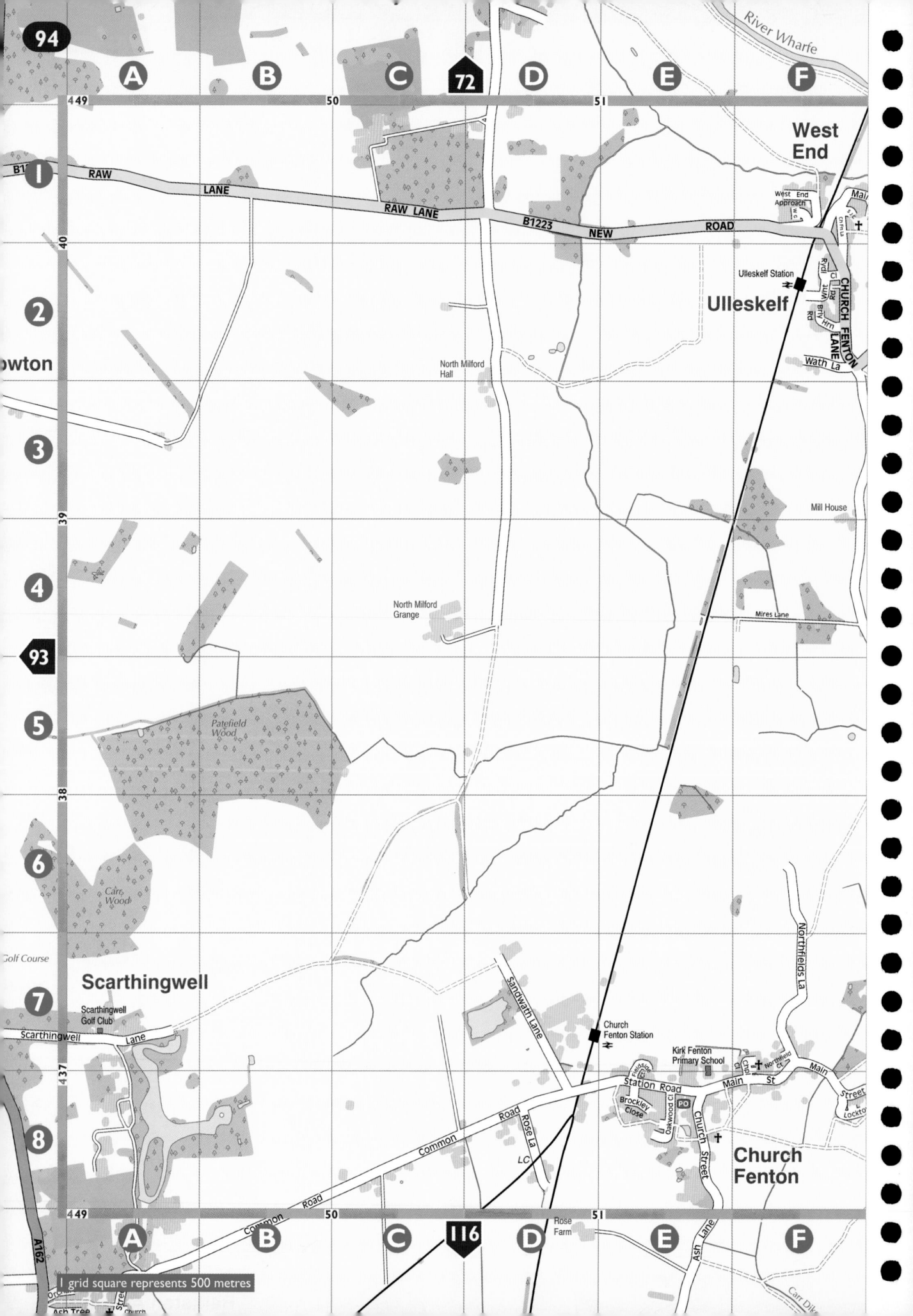

94

A   B   C **72** D   E   F

449   50   51

West End

B1... RAW LANE   RAW LANE   B1223 NEW ROAD

West End Approach

I

40

Ulleskelf Station

Ulleskelf

owton

Wath La

2

North Milford Hall

Mill House

39

3

North Milford Grange

Mires Lane

4

93

Patefield Wood

5

38

6

Carr Wood

Golf Course

Scarthingwell

7

Scarthingwell Golf Club

Sandwath Lane

Church Fenton Station

Kirk Fenton Primary School

Northfields La

Scarthingwell Lane

437

Brockley Close

Station Road   Main   St

Oakwood Cl

PO

Church Street

Main Street

Locktor

8

Common   Road

Rose La

LC

Church Fenton

449   50   51

A   B   C **116** D   Rose Farm E   F

Ash Lane

A162

1 grid square represents 500 metres

Ash Tree   Street

River Wharfe

CHURCH FENTON LANE

Carr Dike

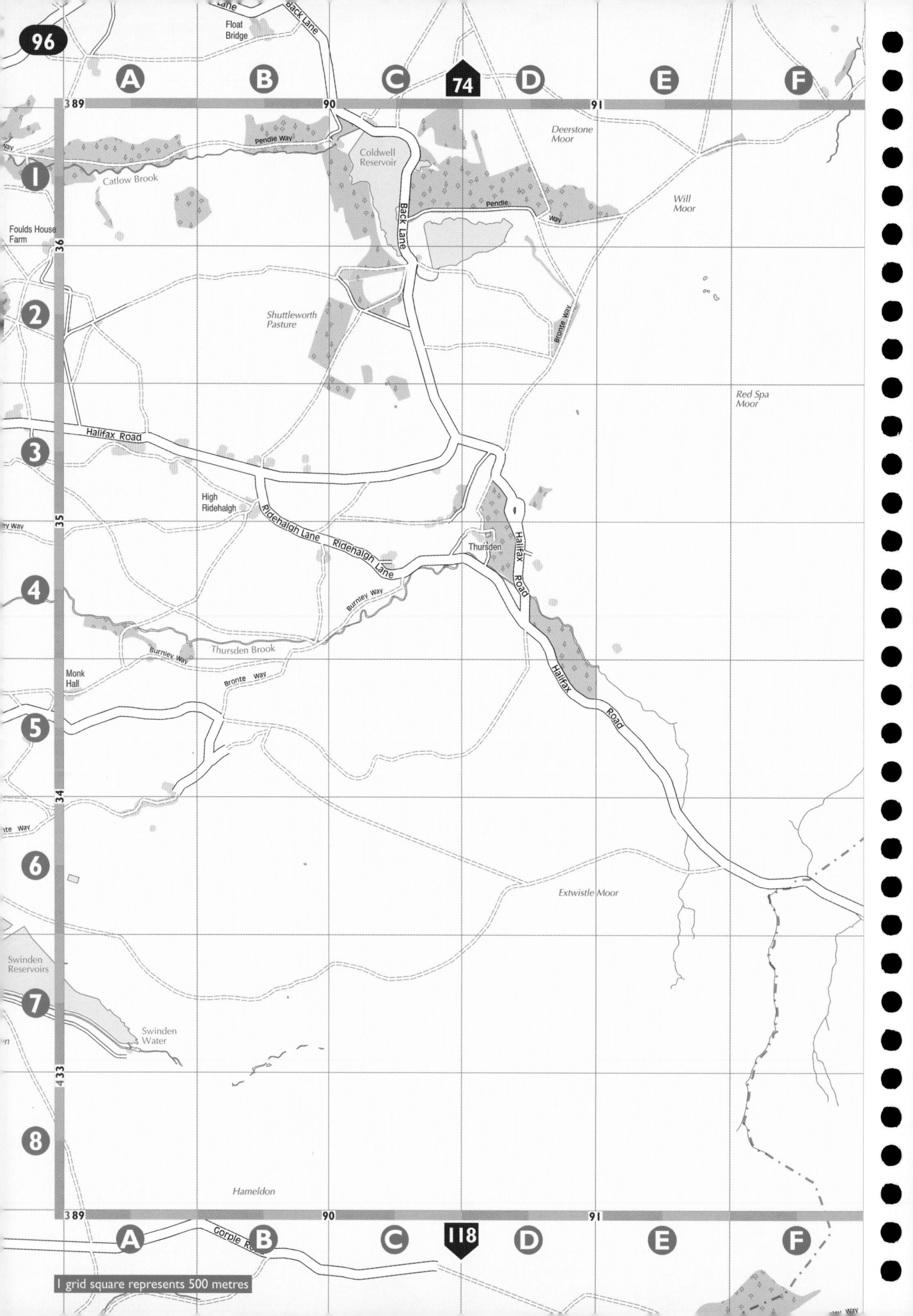

A   B   C   74   D   E   F

3 89   90   91

Deerstone
Moor

Coldwell
Reservoir

Will
Moor

Catlow Brook

Pendle Way

1

Foulds House
Farm

36

Pendle   Way

Back Lane

Shuttleworth
Pasture

2

Red Spa
Moor

Bronte Way

Halifax   Road

3

35

High
Ridehalgh

Ridehalgh Lane

Ridehalgh Lane

Thursden

Halifax   Road

Burnley Way

4

Burnley Way

Thursden Brook

Monk
Hall

Bronte   Way

5

34

Halifax   Road

Extwistle Moor

6

nte   Way

Swinden
Reservoirs

7

Swinden
Water

4 33

8

Hameldon

3 89   90   91

A   B   C   118   D   E   F

Float
Bridge

Back Lane

Lane

Gorple Rd

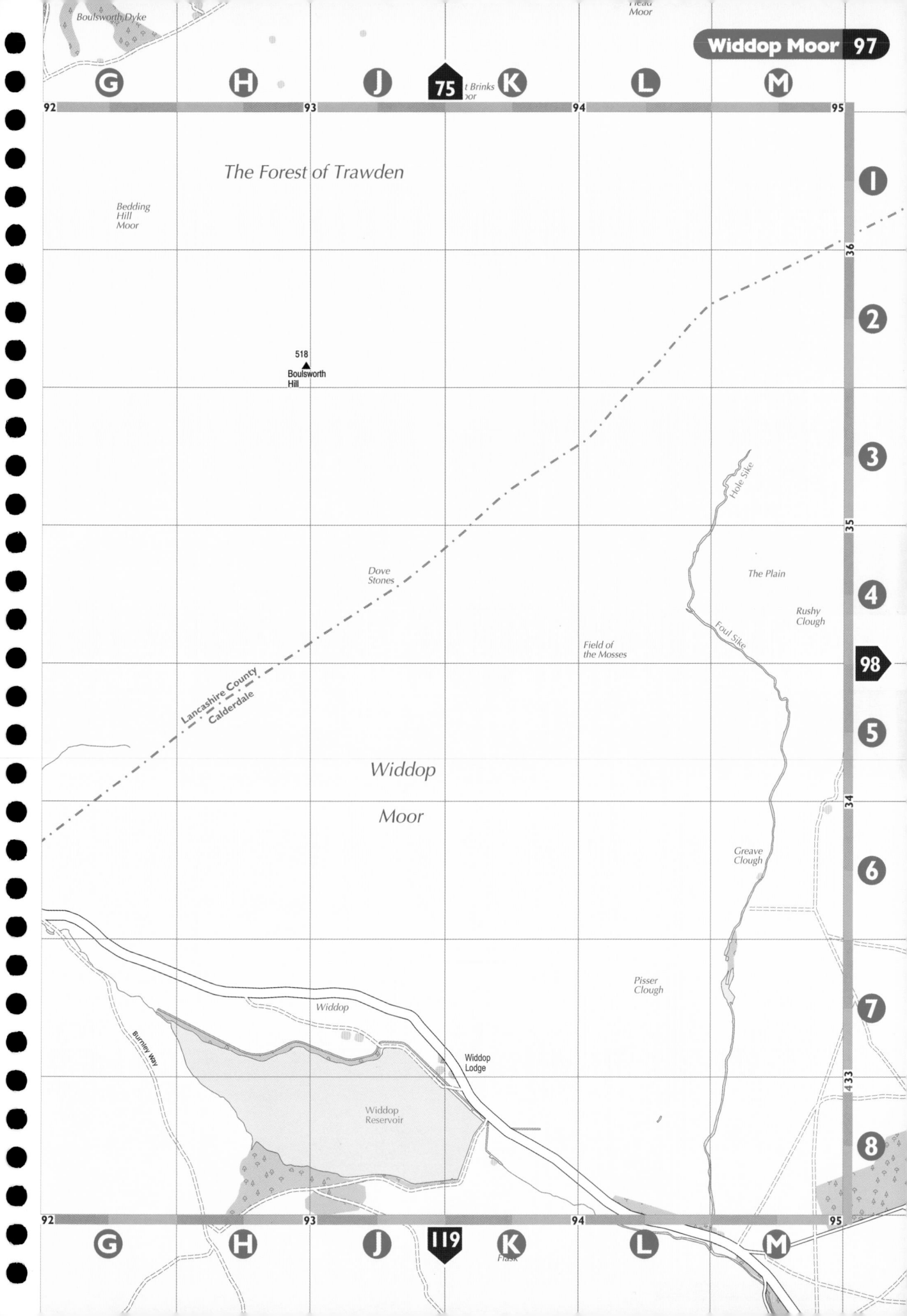

Boulsworth Dyke

G H J K L M

92 75 93 94 95

t Brinks
oor

The Forest of Trawden

Bedding
Hill
Moor

518
▲
Boulsworth
Hill

Dove
Stones

The Plain

Rushy
Clough

Hole Sike

Field of
the Mosses

Foul Sike

98

Lancashire County
Calderdale

Widdop

Moor

Greave
Clough

Pisser
Clough

Burnley Way

Widdop

Widdop
Lodge

Widdop
Reservoir

I
2
3
4
5
6
7
8

36
35
34
33

92 93 94 95

G H J K L M

119

Flask

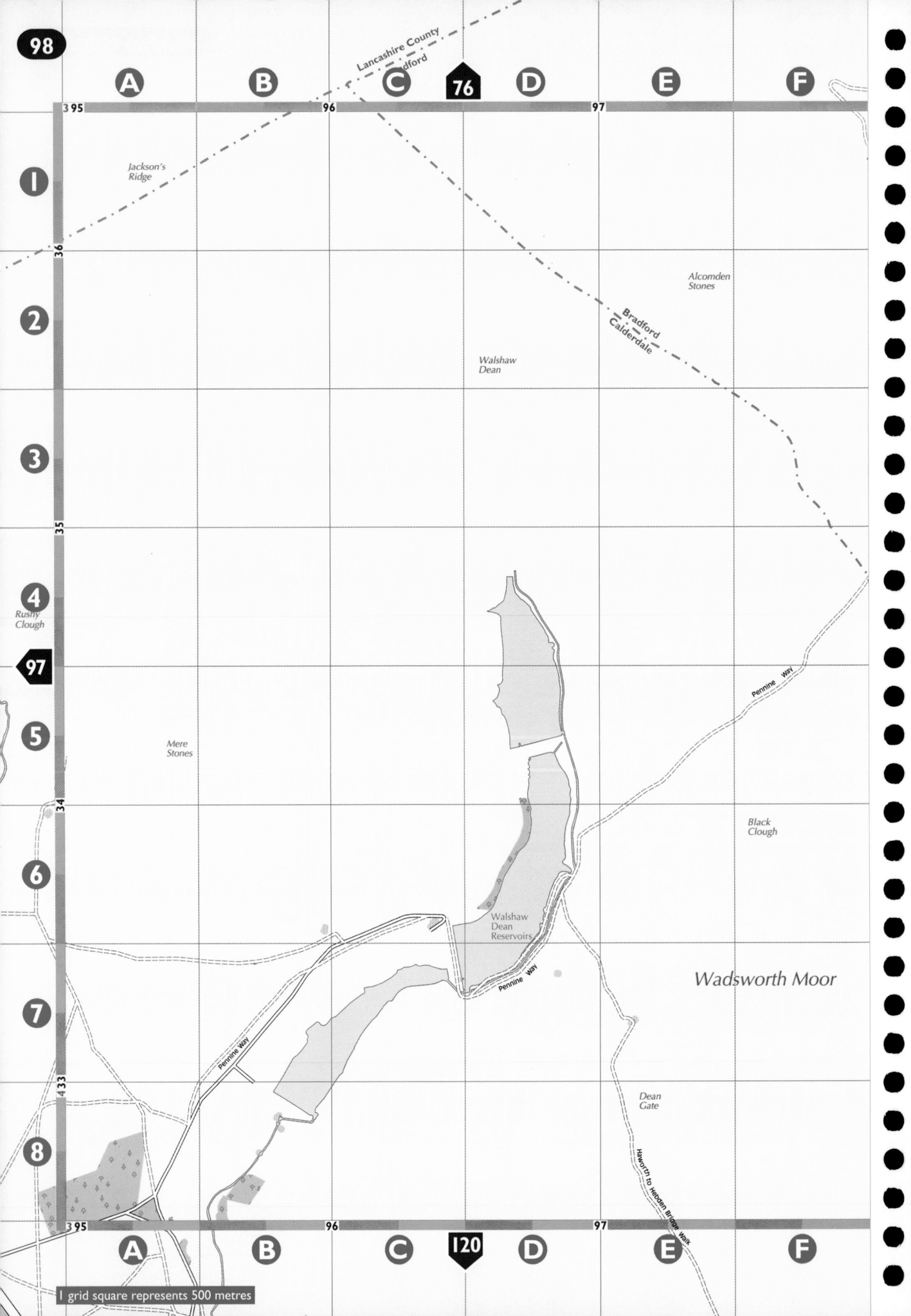

A   B   C   **76**   D   E   F

3 95   96   97

Jackson's
Ridge

Lancashire County
dford

I

36

Alcomden
Stones

2

Bradford
—
Calderdale

Walshaw
Dean

3

35

4
Rushy
Clough

97

5
Mere
Stones

Pennine Way

34

Black
Clough

6

Walshaw
Dean
Reservoirs

Wadsworth Moor

Pennine Way

7

Pennine Way

4 33

Dean
Gate

8

Haworth to Hebden Bridge Walk

3 95   96   **120**   97

A   B   C   D   E   F

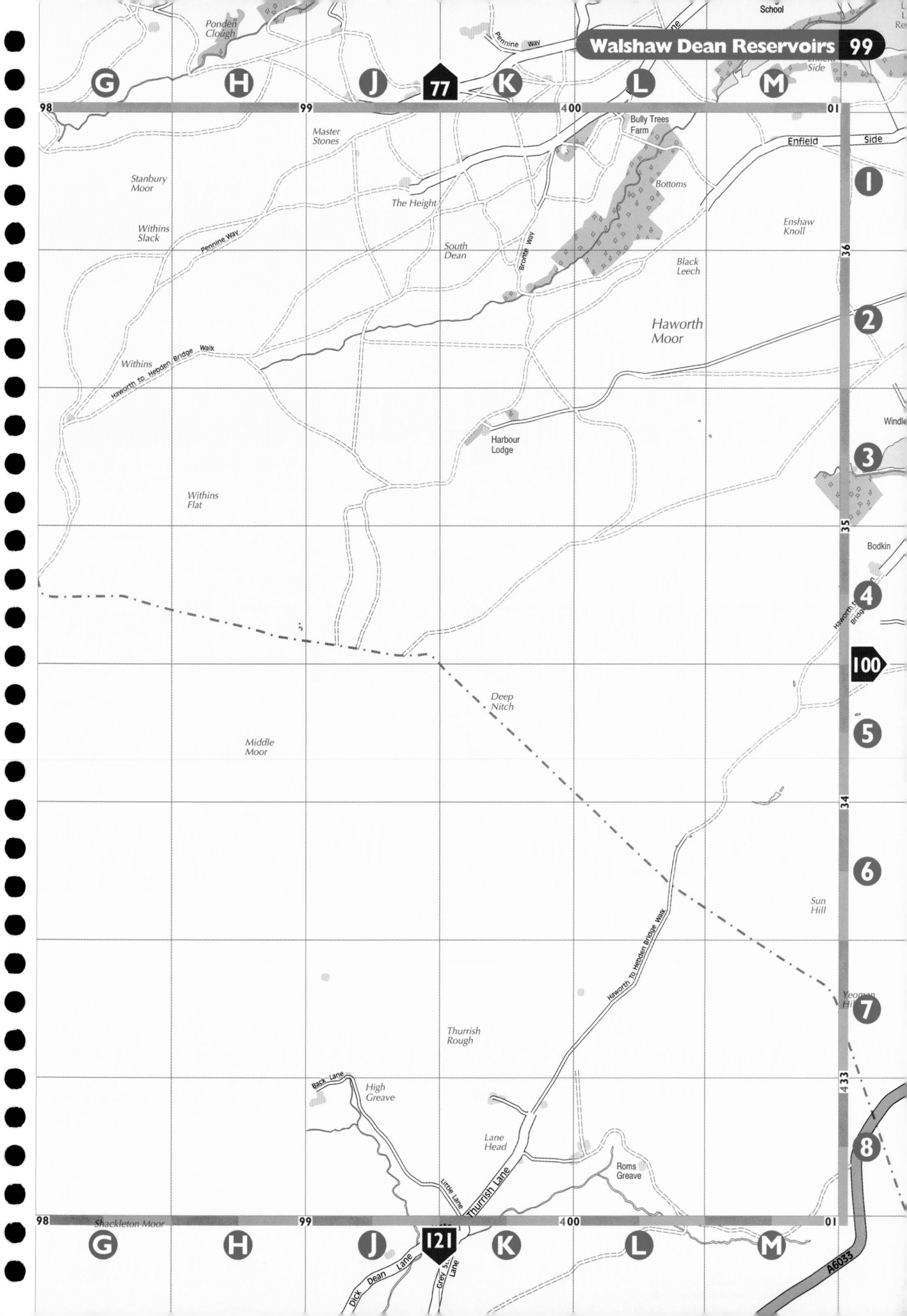

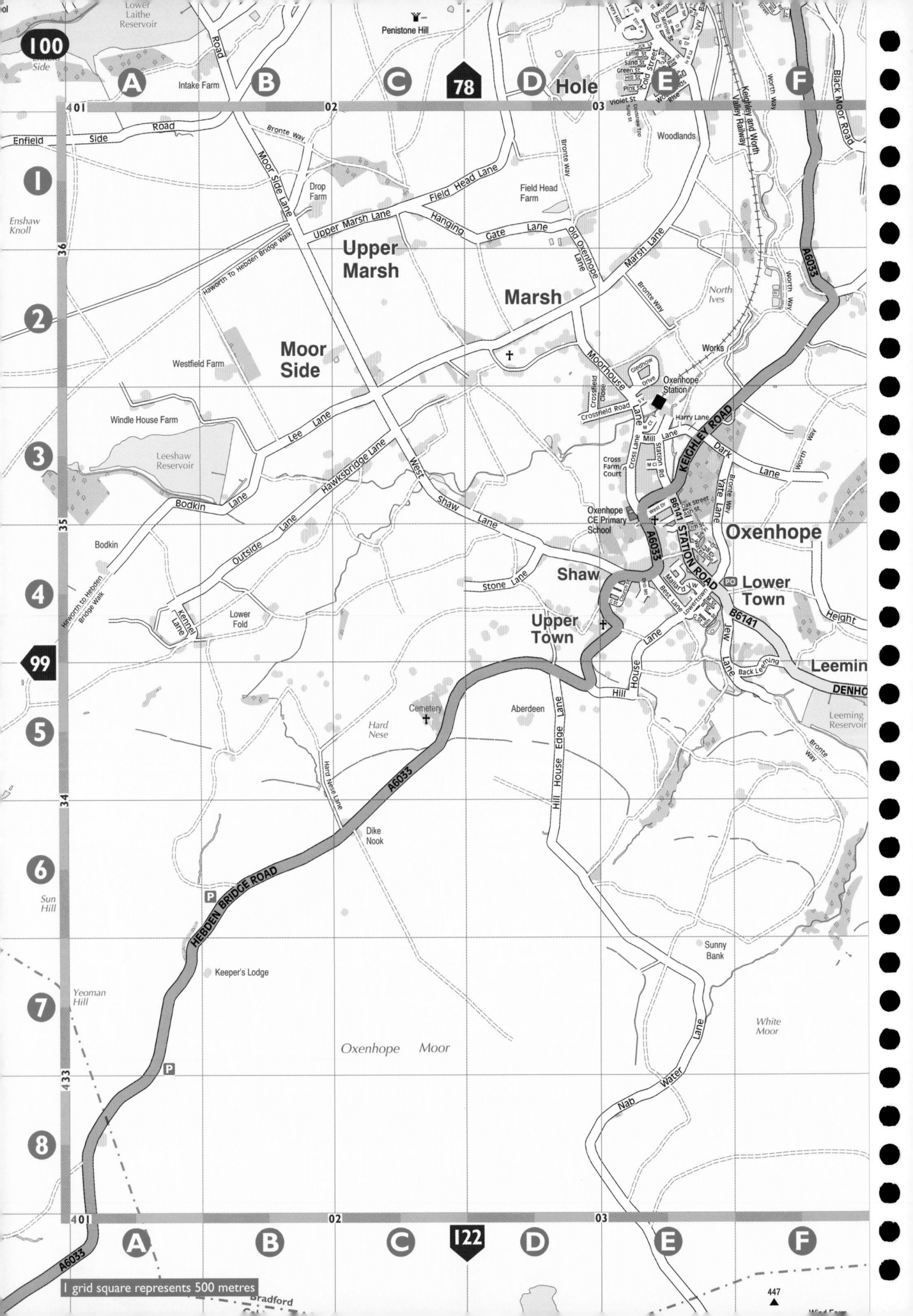

100

A   B   C   78   D Hole   E   F

Lower Laithe Reservoir
Penistone Hill

Enfield Side

1

Enshaw Knoll

Enfield   Side   Road

Bronte Way

Intake Farm

Moor Side Lane

Drop Farm

Field Head Lane

Field Head Farm

Upper Marsh Lane

Hanging   Gate   Lane

Upper Marsh

Haworth To Hebden Bridge Walk

Old Oxenhope Lane

Bronte Way

Marsh Lane

Woodlands

Keighley and Worth Valley Railway

Worth Way

A6033

2

Moor Side

Westfield Farm

Marsh

North Ives

Bronte Way

Works

Worth Way

3

Windle House Farm

Lee   Lane

Hawksbridge Lane

West   shaw   Lane

Leeshaw Reservoir

Bodkin   Lane

Moorhouse Lane

Giddow Drive

Oxenhope Station

Crossfield Close

Crossfield Road

Harry Lane

Keighley Road

Dark   Lane

Worth Way

Bodkin

Outside   Lane

Cross Lane

Station Rd

Mill   Lane

Cross Farm Court

Oxenhope CE Primary School

West Dr

B6141

Oak Street

Bronte Lane

Yate Lane

Oxenhope

4

Haworth to Hebden Bridge Walk

Kennel Lane

Lower Fold

Stone Lane

Shaw

A6033

Station Rd

Lowertown

PO

Lower Town

Height

99

Upper Town

Hill House Edge Lane

House   Lane

Back Leeming

Leemin

DENHO

5

Hard Nese

Cemetery

Aberdeen

Hill   Lane

Jew   Lane

Leeming Reservoir

6

Sun Hill

Hard Nese Lane

A6033

Dike Nook

P

HEBDEN BRIDGE ROAD

Sunny Bank

7

Yeoman Hill

Keeper's Lodge

Oxenhope   Moor

White Moor

8

433

P

Water   Lane

Nab   Lane

A6033

A   B   C   122   D   E   F

1 grid square represents 500 metres

447

G H J **79** K L M

Brow Moor

Field Head

Flappit Spring

Worth Way

Laveroc Hall

Worth Way

Cullingworth Moor

Brown Hill Farm

CULLINGWORTH

Cuckoo Park Farm

Spring Head Farm

HAWORTH RD

ROAD B6144

HAWORTH RD

B6429

CULLINGWORTH

Manywells Lane

Mount Pleasant Farm

Manywells Brow Industrial Estate

West Manywells Farm

Manywells Crescent

MANYWELLS BROW

Royd House

Manywells Height

I

Upwood Farm

Crumack Lane

Black Moor

Hallas Rough Park

Manywells Height

Black Moor Road

Trough Lane

MANYWELLS BROW

KEIGHLEY ROAD

2

3

Beech Avenue

Buck Park

Whalley Lane

Lane Bottom

Booth House

Heatherlands Av

Ogden Lane
Ogden Crescent

Carr Lane

4

102

g

ILME ROAD

Black Moor Road

ROAD

Trough Lane

LONG

CAUSEWAY B6141

Pit Lane

Pit Lane

Clock Lane

Denholme Edge

Hill Crest Road
Hill Crest Mt

Denholme Primary School

Clnc
Surgery
Longlands
Avenue

Longlands Avenue

Foster Road

A629

PO

5

Sawood

Sawood Road

Cobling Farm

Sawood Lane

Denholme

Longhouse Drive

MAIN ROAD

Works

Fairfield

6

Nan Scar

Bronte Way

Works

Thornton Moor Road

Tunnel St
Well St

NEW ROAD

Pit Road

Stubden Reservoir

HALIFAX ROAD A629

7
Works

Thornton Moor Reservoir

Black Edge Lane

SMITHY
John Court

8

A629

Thornton Moor

Foreside Lane

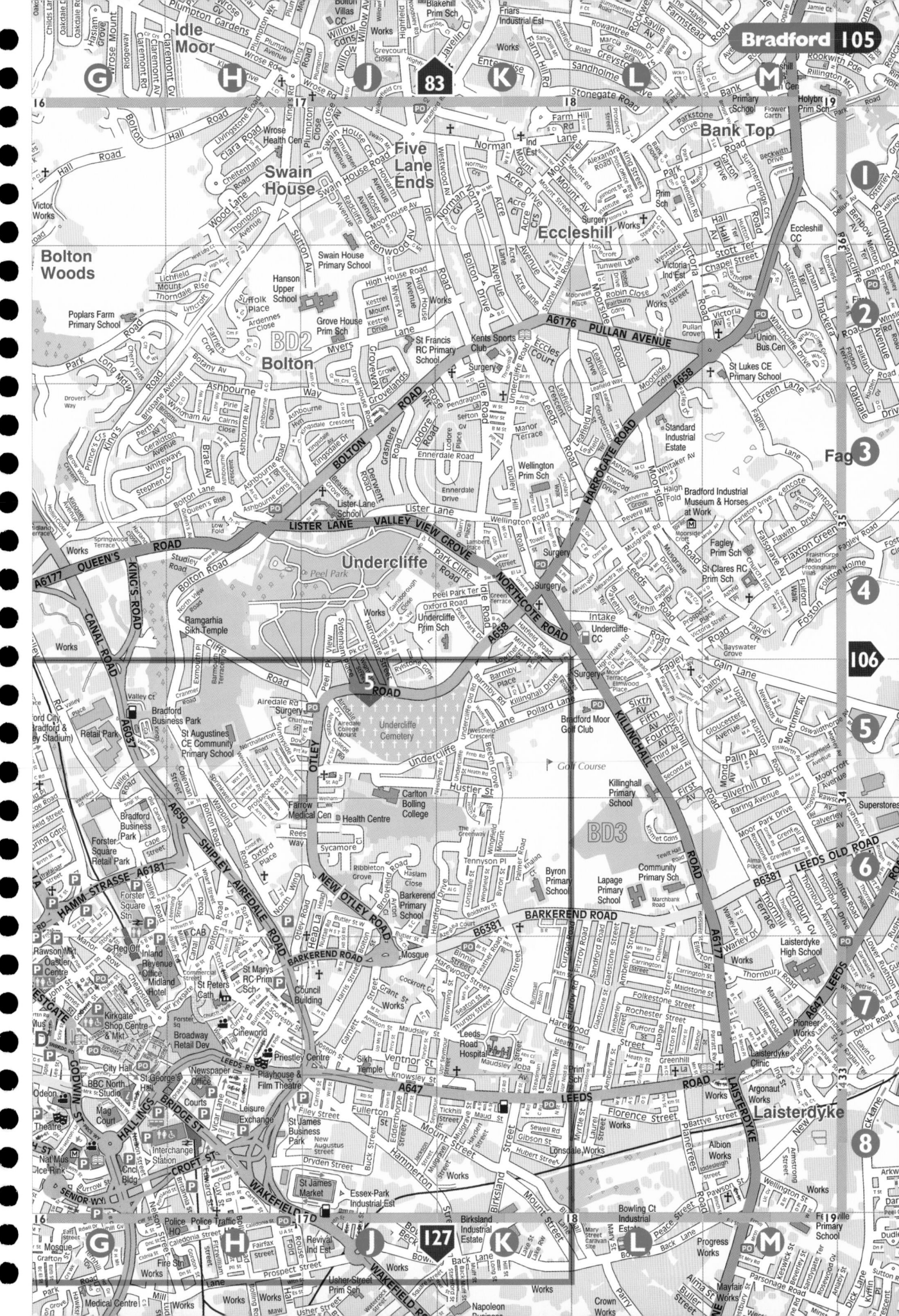

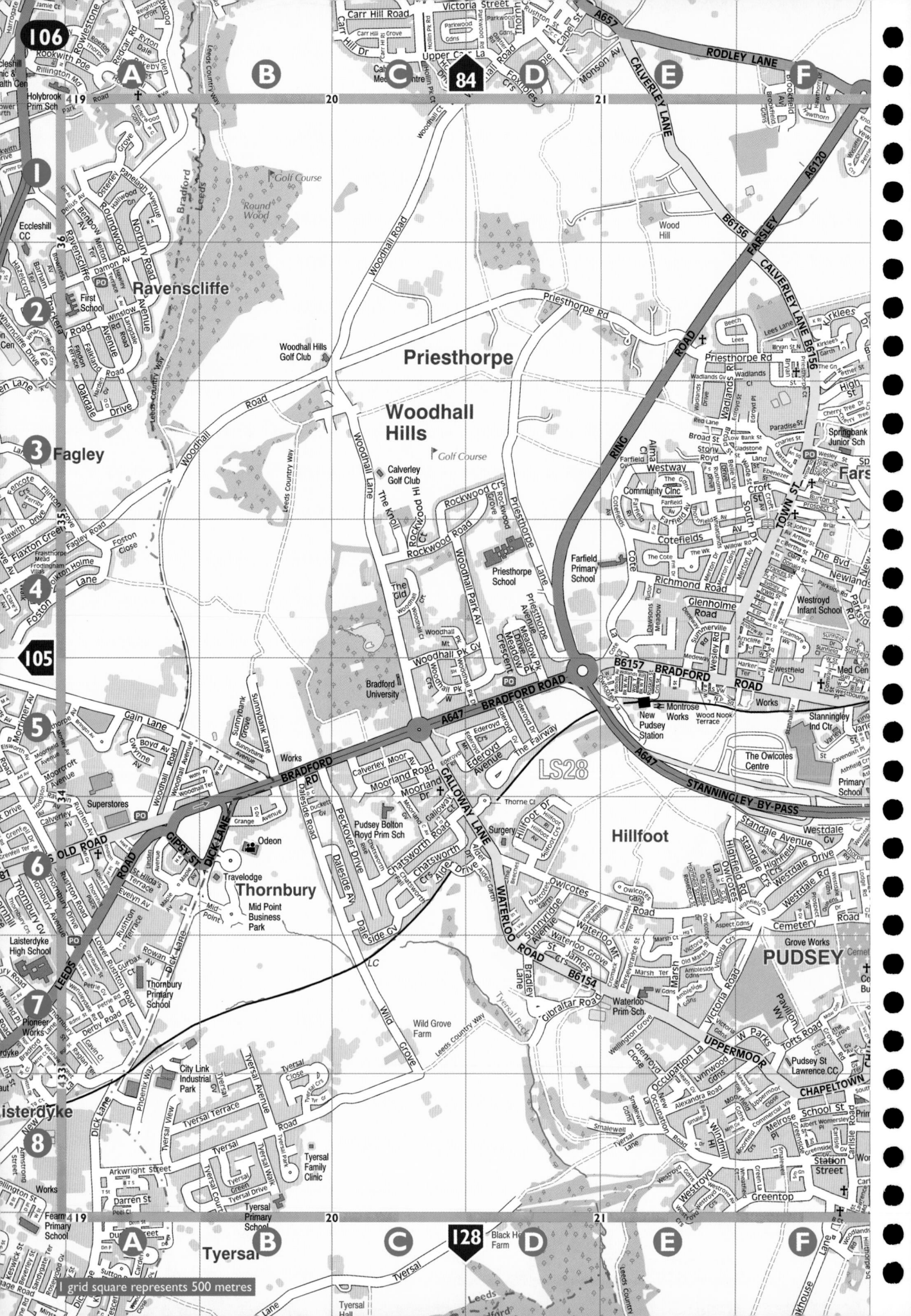

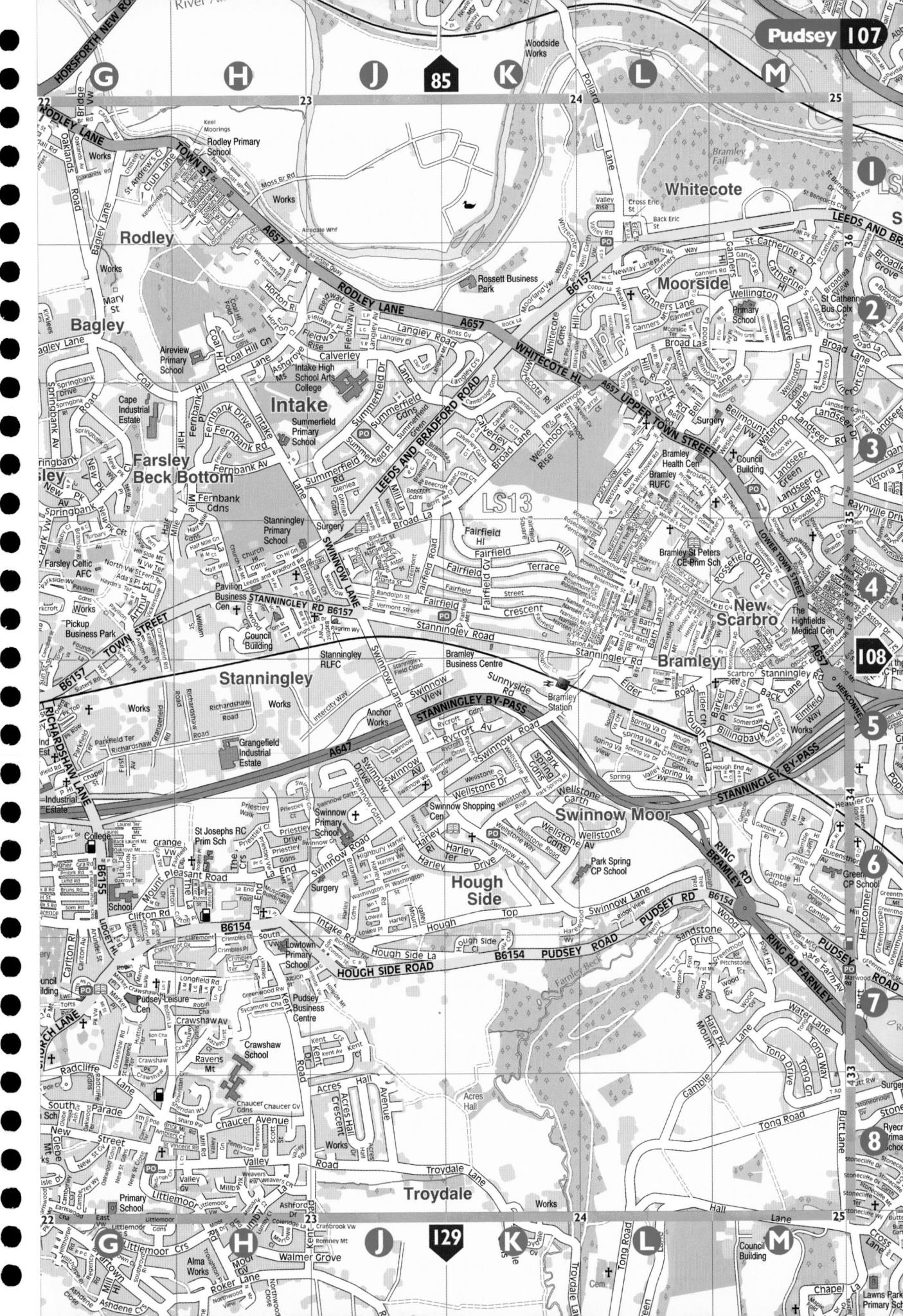

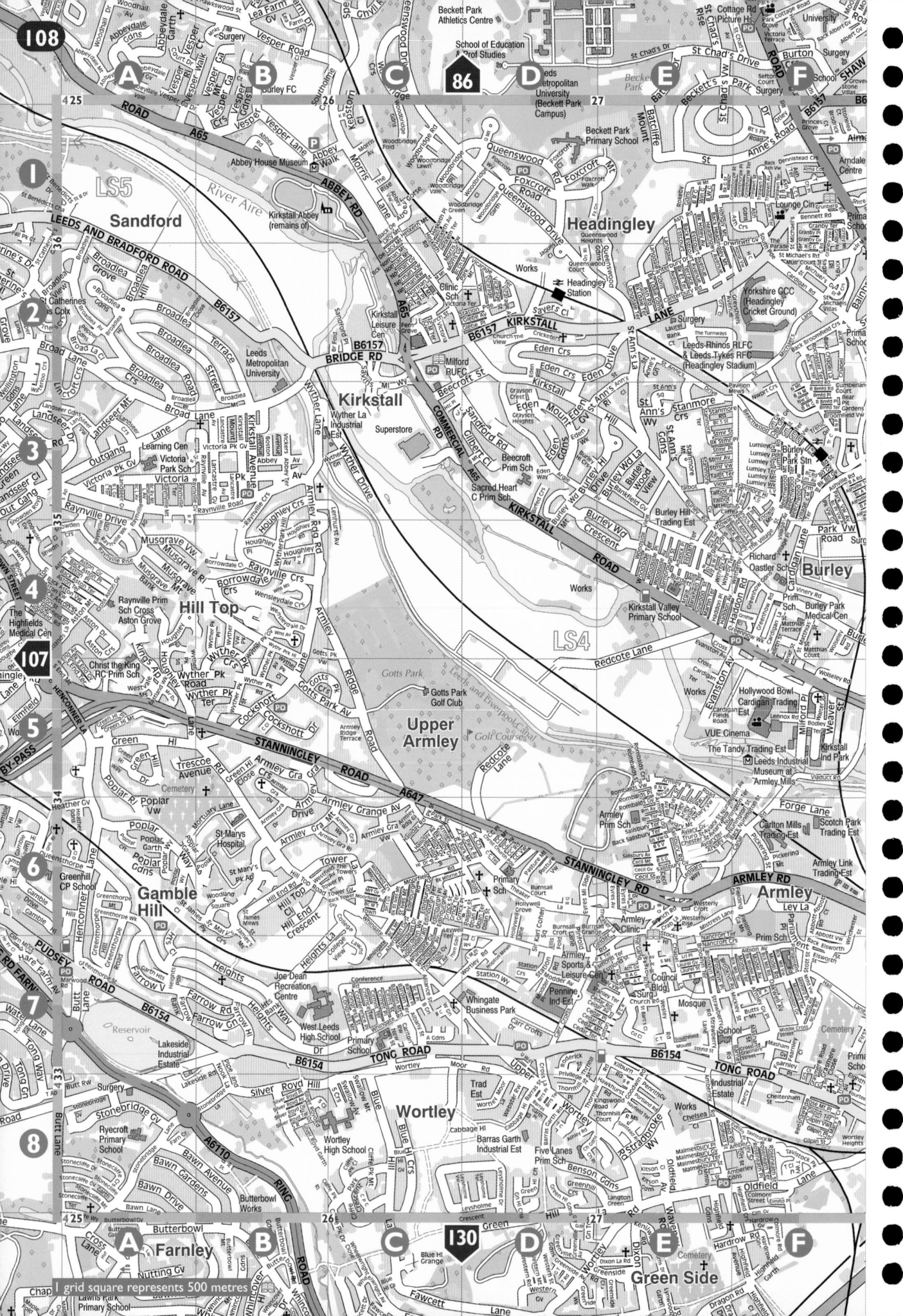

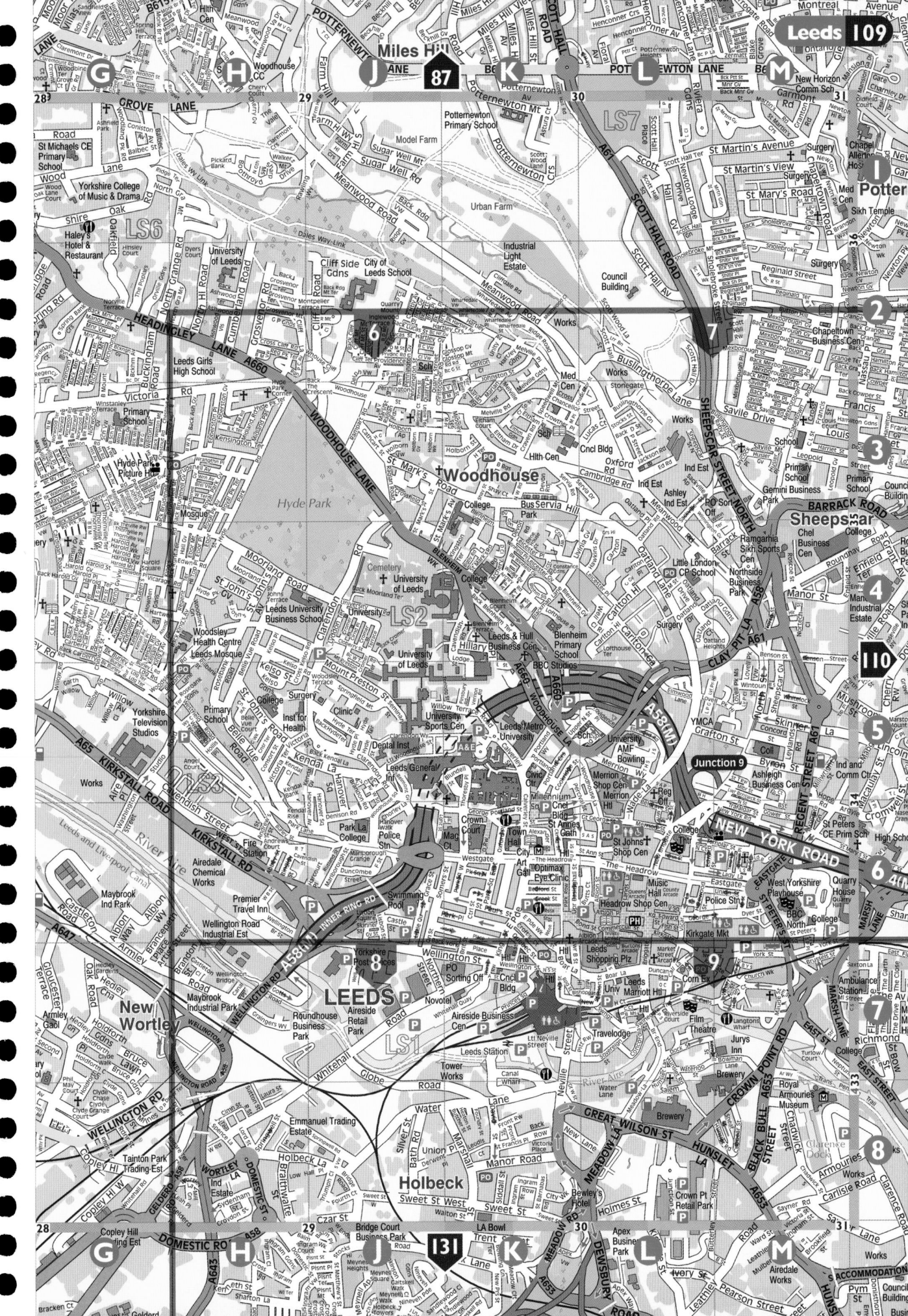

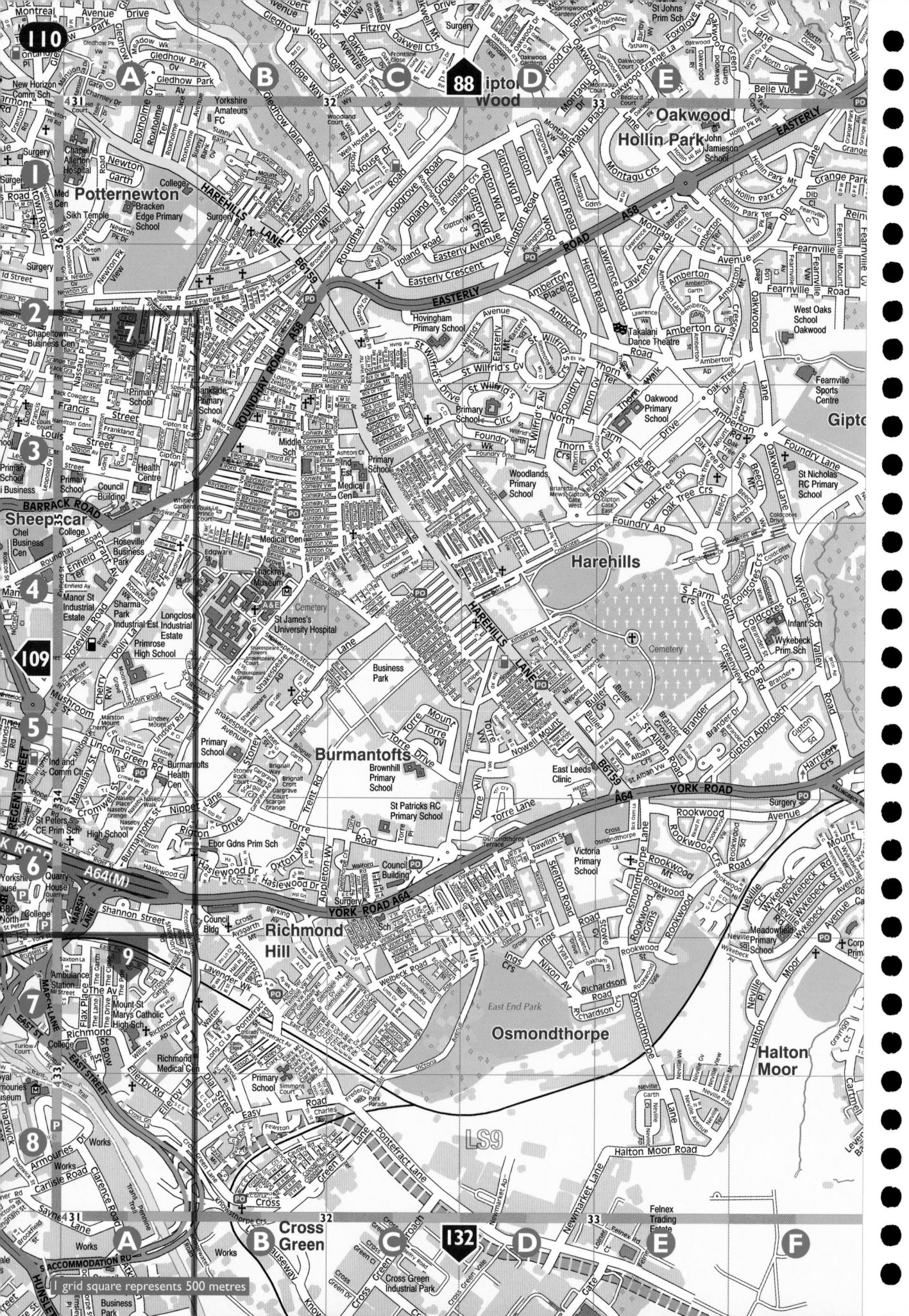

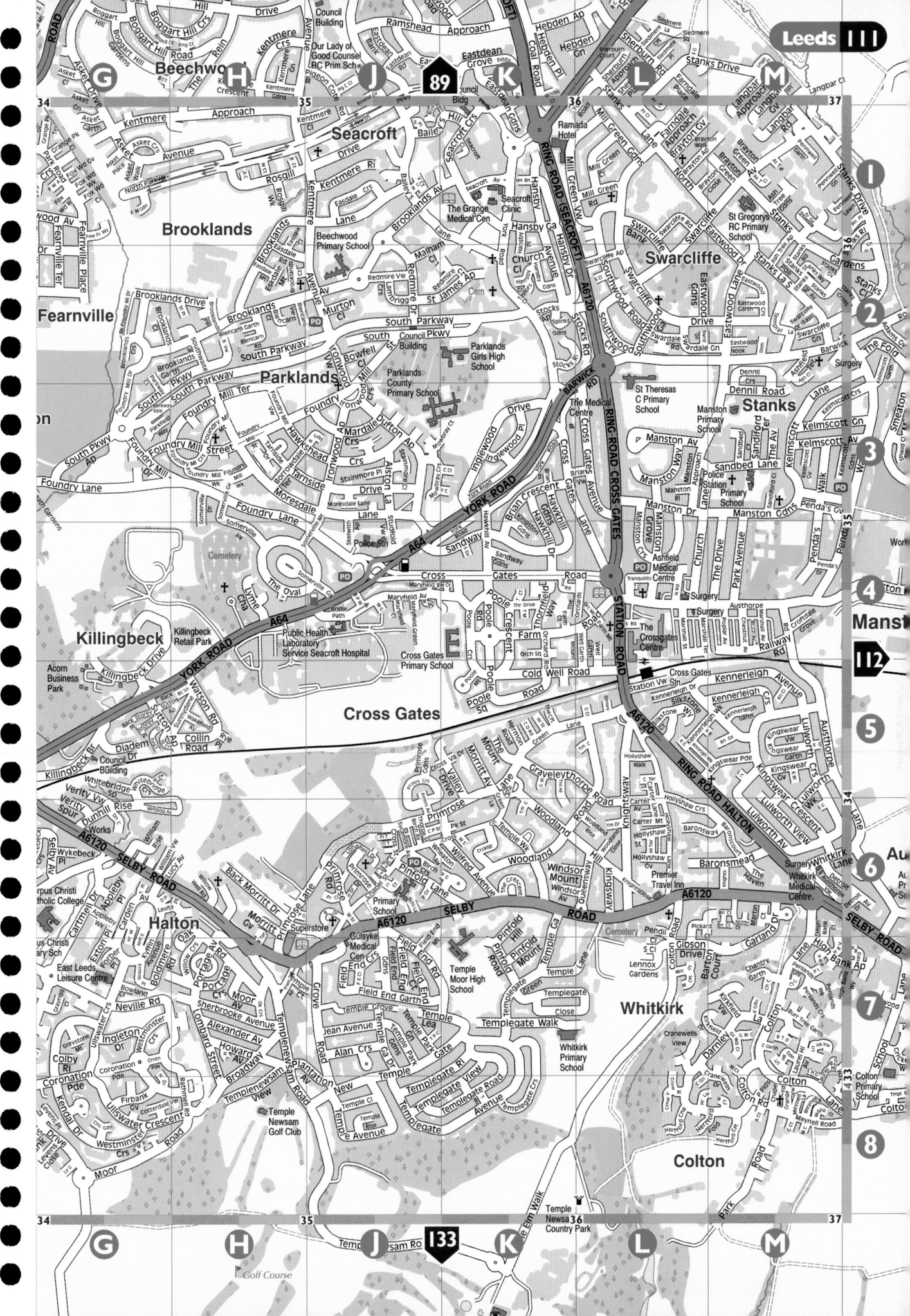

90

Barwick
in Elmet

Barnbow
Carr

Upper
Barnbow Farm

Scholes (Elmete)
Prim School

Scholes Park

Leeds Road

Bog Lane

Barnbow Lane

Carr Beck

Pendas
Fields

John Smeaton
Sports Centre
John Smeaton
Community
High School

Barnbow
Wood

Badgers Mt

Chelsfield Way

Biddenden Road

Sandleas Way

Works

Manston
LS15

Works

Lazencroft
Farm

Manston House

Manston Lane

Barnbow
Common

Barnbow Lane

Leeds Country Way

M1

Austhorpe

Barrowby Lane

Austhorpe
Primary
School

Austhorpe Grove

Barrowby Lane

Barrowby Hall

Barrowby Road

Austhorpe DP

Thorpe Park
Hotel

Century Way

Brown
Moor

Bradbury
Grange

SELBY ROAD

A6120

Colton
Retail
Park

Travelodge

The
Wickets

Colton
Primary
School

Colton Road East

Junction 46

Cross Row

SELBY

ROAD

Swillington
Common

Queensway

Alandale
Road

Alandale
Drive

Kingsway

Westbourne
Terrace

Westbourne

A642

A63

Works

West
Garforth

134

1 grid square represents 500 metres

G   H   J   **91**   K   L   M

I

2

3

ROAD B1217

ABERFORD

Junction

4

Junction 47

114

5

6

7

8

Parlington

Highfield Farm

Home Farm

Highfield Lane

Highfield Lane

Highfield Lane

Long Lane

Cock Beck

Throstle Nest Farm

Parlington Lane

Parlington Hollins

Garforth Golf Club

Golf Course

Ellis Lane

Barwick Road

Park House Farm

Stank House

M1

M1

M1

A642

A656

A656

Silkstone Close

Hawk's Nest Wood

Nanny goat Lane

Barrowby Lane

Lotherton Way

Ash La

Ash Lane

Newhold

Spring Close

New Hold Industrial Est

Elmfield Business Park

East Garforth Prim Sch

East Garforth

Braemar Drive

Gilling Av

Muncaster Rd

Pickering Av

Sturton Grange Lane

ABERFORD   ROAD

Works

St Benedicts RC Primary School

Garforth Station

White Rose Av

Bar Lane

Montague

Sturton Avenue

Firthfields

Caernarvon Avenue

Dunbottle

New

The Chase

Sturton Grange

Surgery

A642

B6137

MAIN ST

Oak Road

Oak Avenue

Oak Drive

Oak Crescent

Oak Royd

Church Ap

Meadow Road

White Rose Cl

Crescent

Garforth Leisure Centre

James Close

Sturton Ave

Ludlow Av

Spofforth Wk

Sturton Grange

FIELD ROAD

Coupland Road

Lyndon Av

Cncl Bldg

Greenway

Medical Cen

Station Fields

Church

Cricketers

Green Lane

Green Lane

East Garforth Station

Woodlands Drive

Green Lane Primary School

GARFORTH

Barleyhill Road

Strawberry Fields Prim Sch

Garforth Clinic

Police Station

LIDGETT LANE

Garforth Community College

Lindsay Road

Lowther Drive

Springmead Drive

Burnham Road

Derwent

Grange Avenue

Oakfield Close

Ninelands Lane Primary School

Ninelands Spur

Glebelands Close

Paddock Close

Works

Hillside

Welland Dr

Witham Way

Thames Way

Airedale Dr

Fosse Way

Ribblesdale Av

Kennet Drive

Kenmere

Trent Avenue

Severn Drive

Highfield

Cotswold

Arran Court

Arran Drive

Long Meadows

Ledston Av

Cliffe House

PO

135

Hazelwood Avenue

Acaster

40   41   42   43

G   H   J   **135**   K   L   M

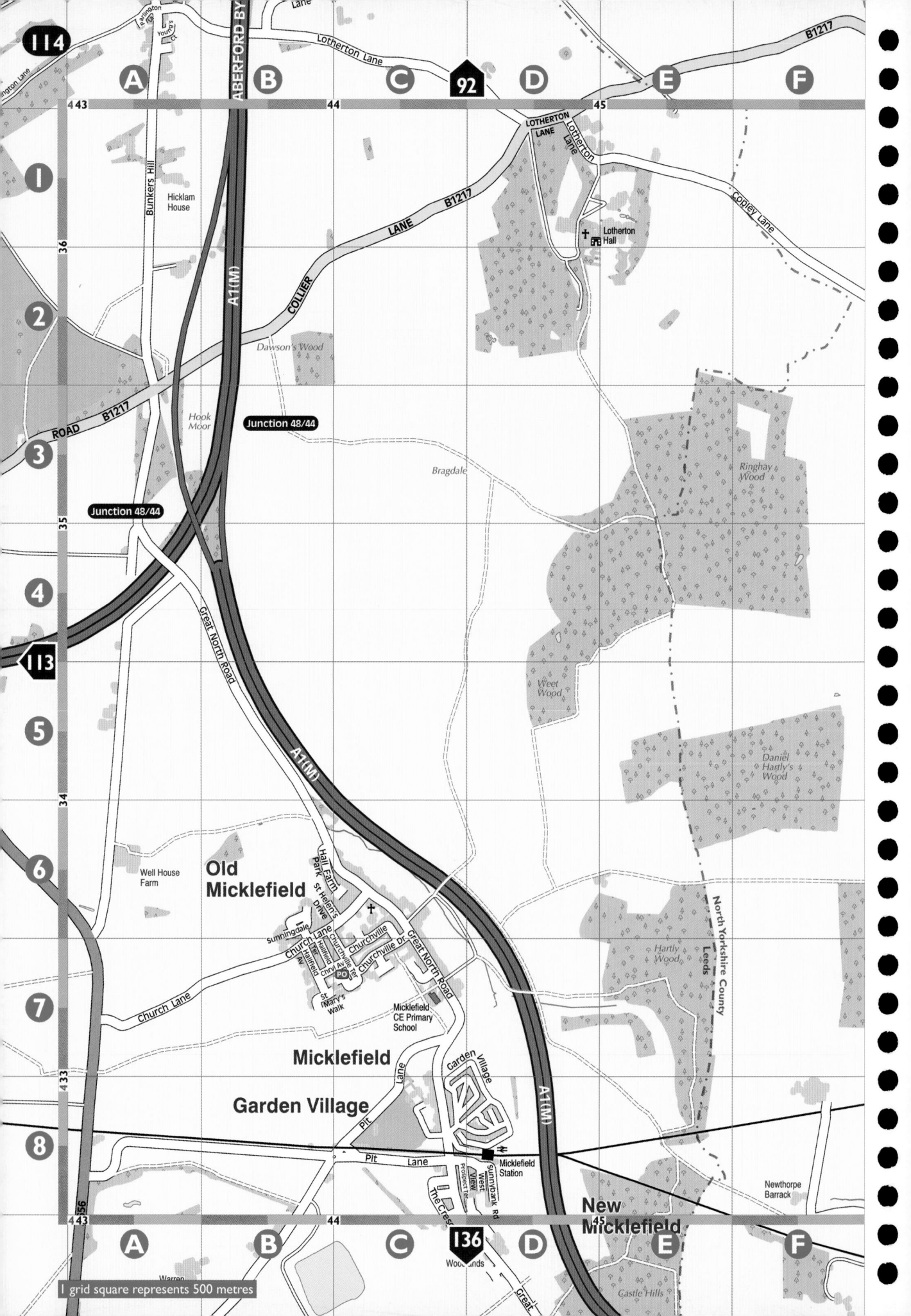

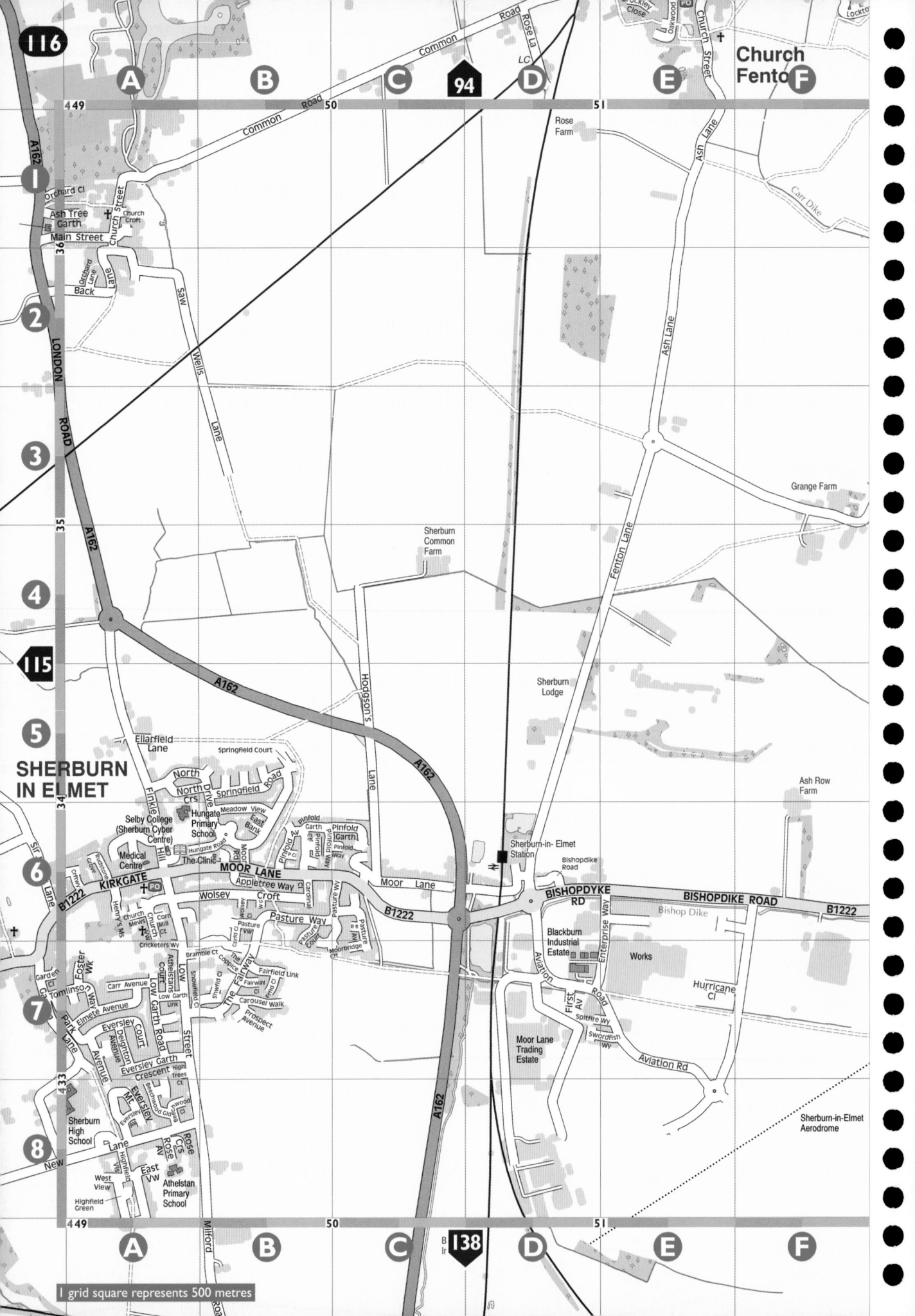

A   B   C   94   D   E   Church
                                    Fento F

449   Common   Road   50   51

Orchard Cl
Ash Tree
Garth
Main Street
Orchard Lane
Back

1
2
3
4

115

5
SHERBURN
IN ELMET

Ellarfield
Lane
Springfield Court
North
North
Drive
Crs
Selby College
(Sherburn Cyber
Centre)
Medical
Centre
The Clinic
KIRKGATE
Wolsey
Pasture Way
Pasture
Cricketers Wy

6

Meadow View
Hungate
Primary
School
Springfield Road
East
Bank
MOOR LANE
Appletree Way
Croft
Pinfold
Pinfold
Garth
Pinfold
Way
B1222

Bramble Ct
Fairfield Link
Athelstan
Court
Low Garth
Carousel Walk
Prospect
Avenue
Eversley
Court
Deighton
Crescent
Eversley Garth
Sherburn
High
School

7
8

West
View
Highfield
Green
Athelstan
Primary
School
East
VW

New   Lane

449   50   138   51

LC
Rose La
Rose
Farm

Ash Lane
Ash Lane

Carr Dike

Grange Farm

Sherburn
Common
Farm

Fenton Lane

Sherburn
Lodge

Ash Row
Farm

Sherburn-in-
Elmet
Station
Bishopdike
Road
BISHOPDYKE
RD
BISHOPDIKE ROAD   B1222

Bishop Dike

Blackburn
Industrial
Estate
Works
Hurricane
Cl
Enterprise Way
Aviation
Road
First
AV
Spitfire Wy
Swordfish
Wy
Moor Lane
Trading
Estate
Aviation Rd

Sherburn-in-Elmet
Aerodrome

A162
LONDON ROAD
A162
A162
Hodgson's Lane
B1222
A162

Saw Wells Lane

Church Street

1 grid square represents 500 metres

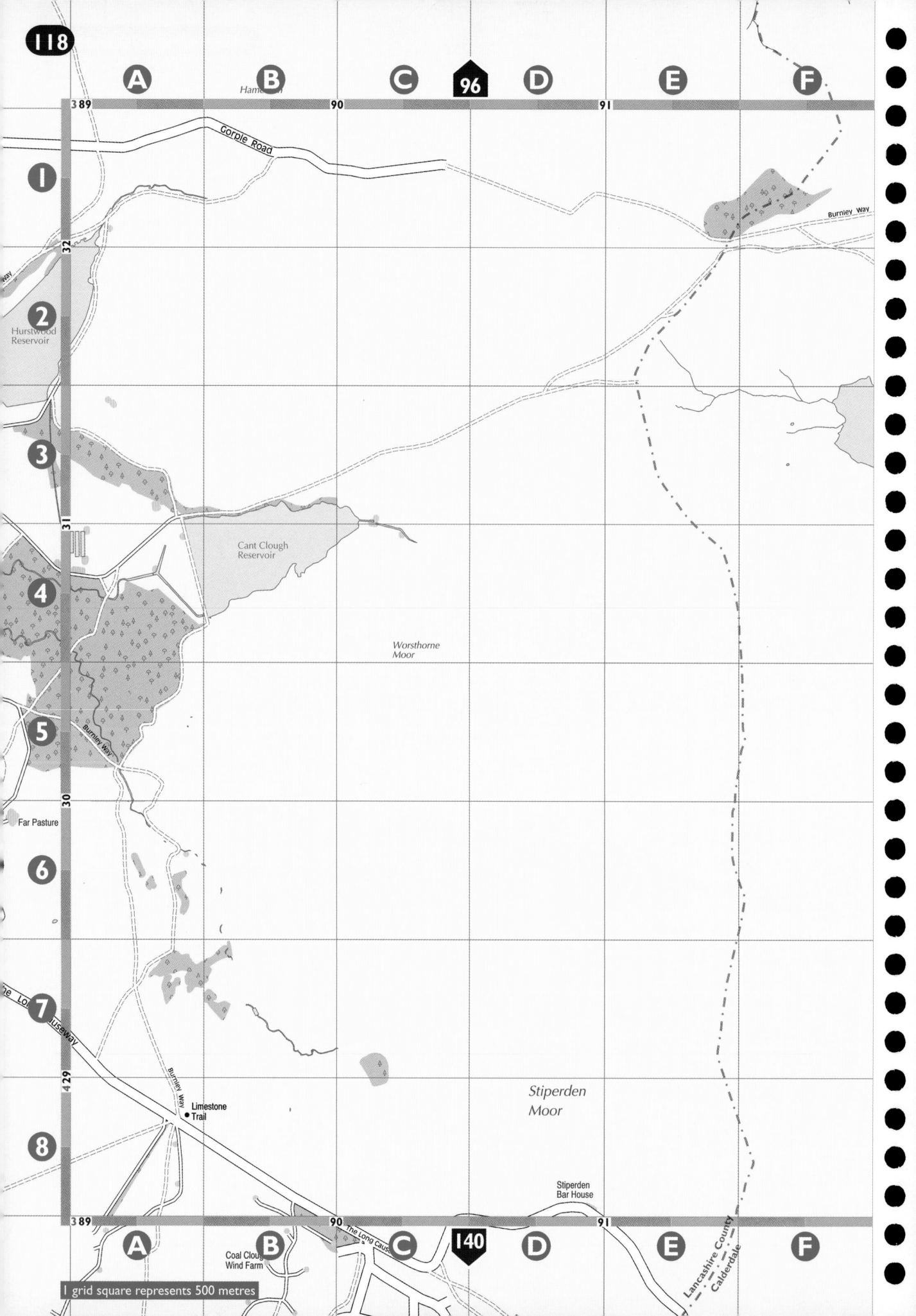

A   B   C   **96**   D   E   F

3 89   90   91

Gorple Road

Hame...n

I

32

2
Hurstwood
Reservoir

3

31

Cant Clough
Reservoir

4

Worsthorne
Moor

5

Burnley Way

30

Far Pasture

6

...Lo... useway

7

4 29

Burnley Way

Limestone
● Trail

Stiperden
Moor

8

Stiperden
Bar House

Coal Clough
Wind Farm

The Long Caus...

Burnley Way

Burnley Way

Lancashire County
Calderdale

3 89   90   91

A   B   **140**   C   D   E   F

1 grid square represents 500 metres

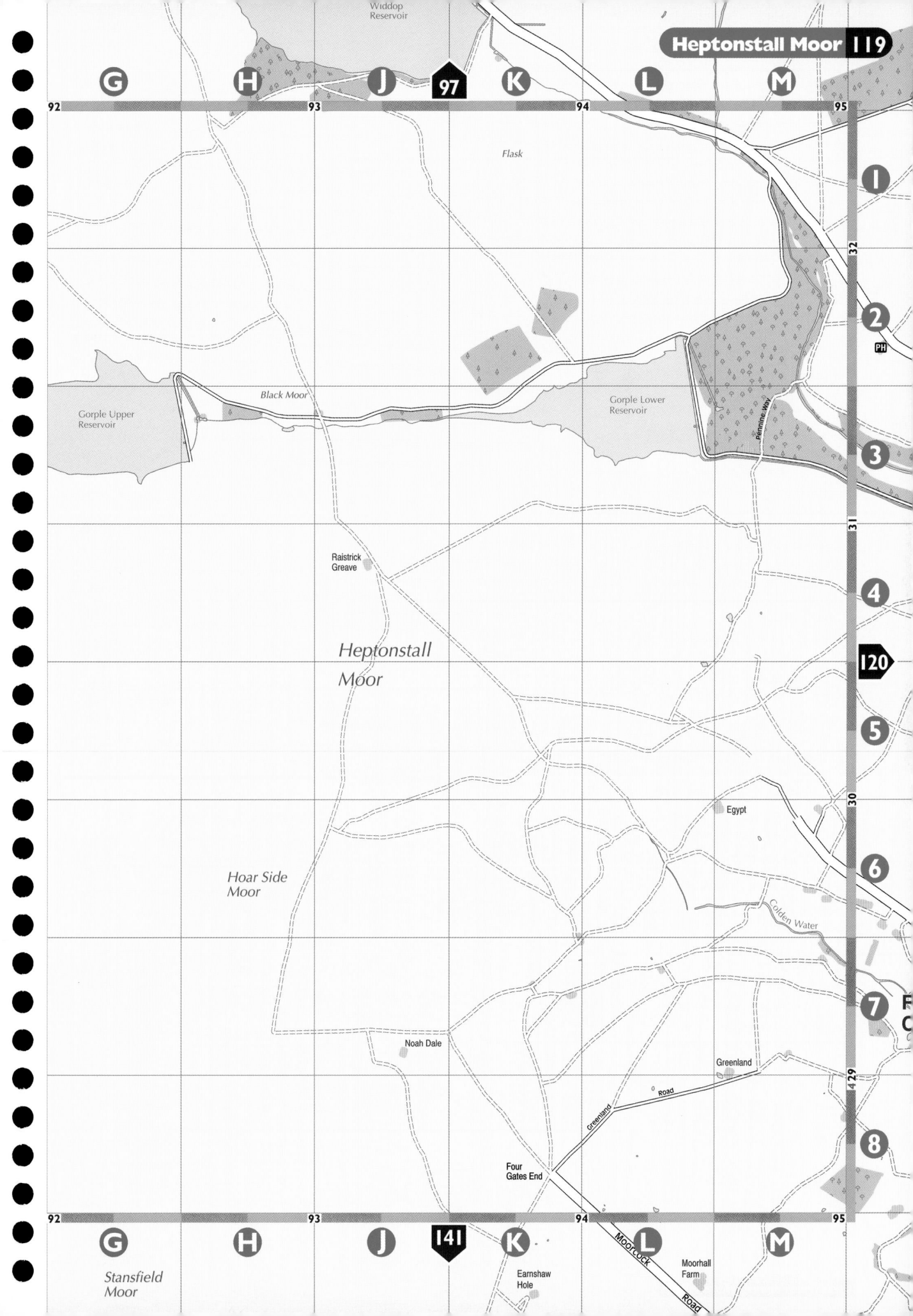

G   H   J   **97**   K   L   M

Widdop
Reservoir

Flask

Gorple Upper
Reservoir

Black Moor

Gorple Lower
Reservoir

Raistrick
Greave

*Heptonstall
Moor*

*Hoar Side
Moor*

Egypt

Colden Water

Noah Dale

Greenland

Greenland   Road

Four
Gates End

I

2
PH

3

4

120

5

6

7   F
C

8

Pennine Way

G   H   J   **141**   K   L   M

*Stansfield
Moor*

Earnshaw
Hole

Moorcock   Road

Moorhall
Farm

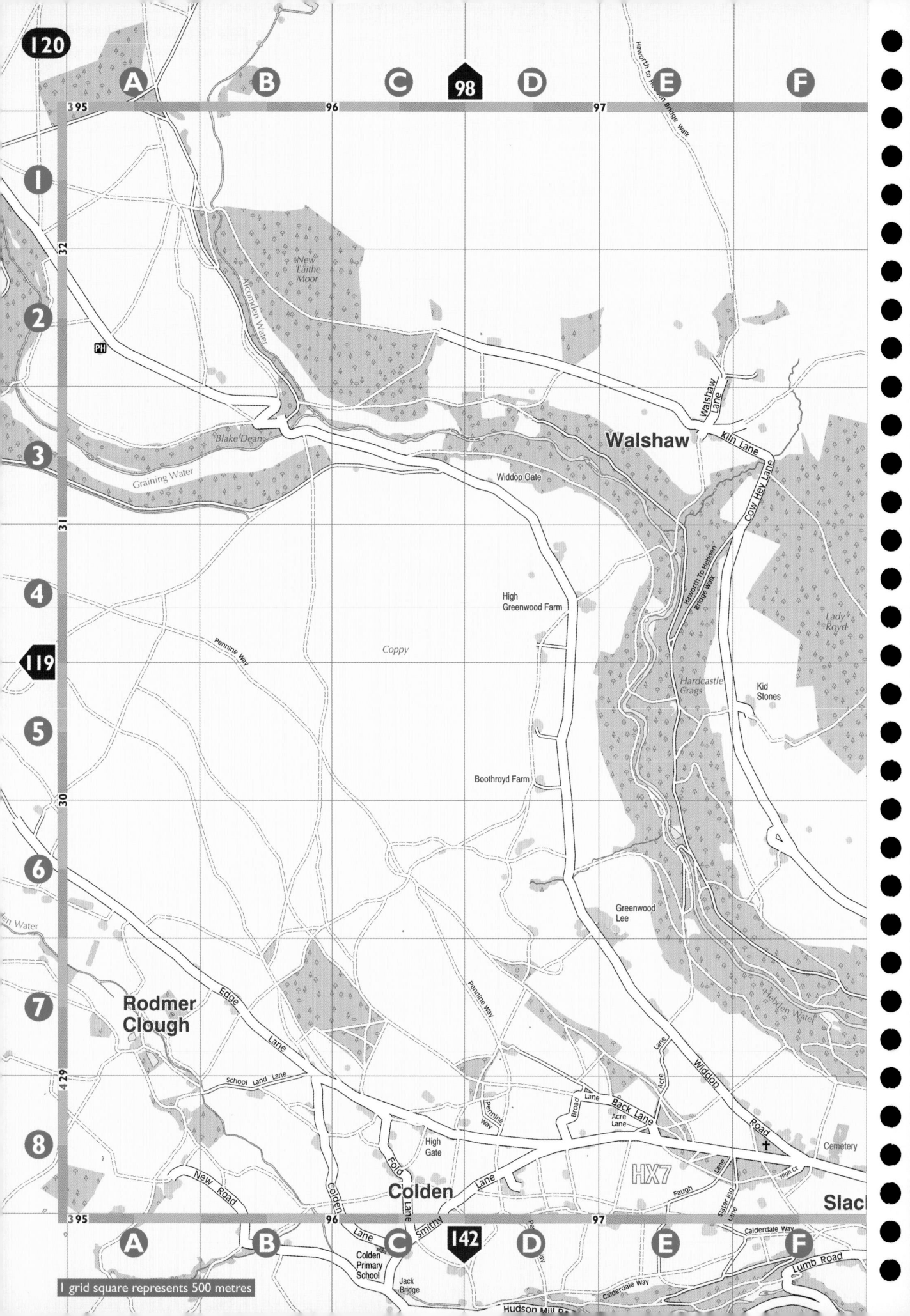

A   B   C   98   D   E   F

3 95   96   98   97

I

32

2

PH

3

Blake Dean

Graining Water

New Laithe Moor

Ashenden Water

Widdop Gate

Walshaw

Walshaw Lane

Kiln Lane

Cow Hey Lane

Haworth to Hebden Bridge Walk

31

4

119

Pennine Way

Coppy

High Greenwood Farm

Hardcastle Crags

Kid Stones

Lady Royd

30

5

Boothroyd Farm

6

Greenwood Lee

Eden Water

7

Rodmer Clough

Edge Lane

Pennine Way

Hebden Water

Widdop Road

School Land Lane

Lane

Acre Lane

Back Lane

4 29

8

New Road

Colden Lane

Fold Lane

High Gate

Pennine Way

Smithy Lane

Broad Lane

Acre Lane

HX7

Faugh Lane

Slater Ing Lane

High Cr

Cemetery

Colden

Slac

3 95   96   97

A   B   C   142   D   E   F

Colden Primary School

Jack Bridge

Calderdale Way

Calderdale Way

Lumb Road

Hudson Mill R

1 grid square represents 500 metres

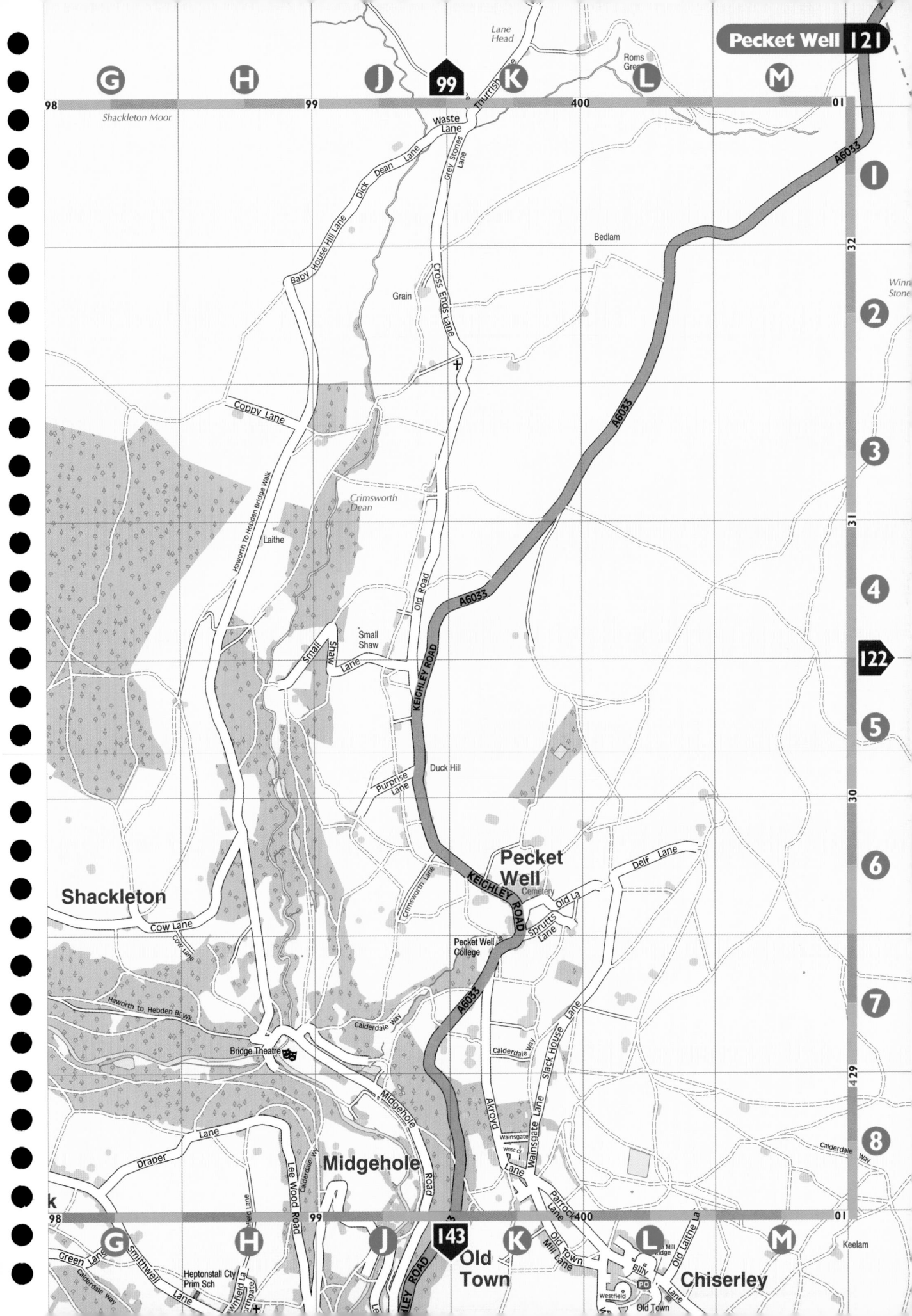

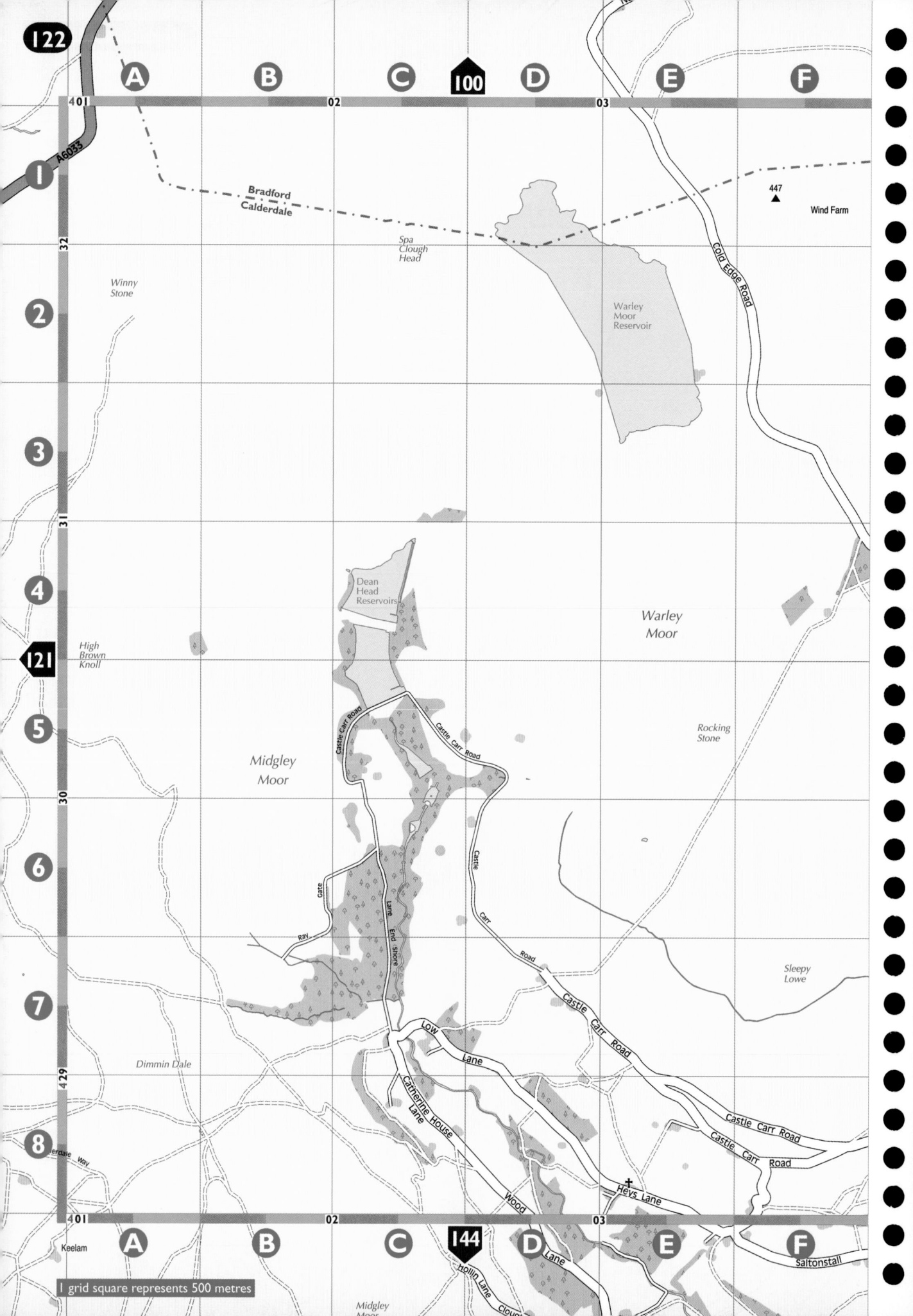

A   B   C   100   D   E   F

401   02   03

A6033

1   Bradford
Calderdale

Spa
Clough
Head

32

Winny
Stone

2   Warley
Moor
Reservoir

447
Wind Farm

3

31

4   Dean
Head
Reservoirs   Warley
Moor

121   High
Brown
Knoll

5   Castle Carr Road   Castle Carr Road

Midgley
Moor   Rocking
Stone

Castle

6   Gate   Carr

Lane   Road

Ray   End Shore   Sleepy
Lowe

7   Castle Carr Road

429   Dimmin Dale   Low
Lane

Catherine House
Lane   Castle Carr Road

Castle Carr
Road

8   erdale Way

Heys Lane

Wood

401   02   03

A   B   C   144   D   E   F

Keelam   Lane   Saltonstall

I grid square represents 500 metres

Midgley
Moor

Hollin Lane   Clough

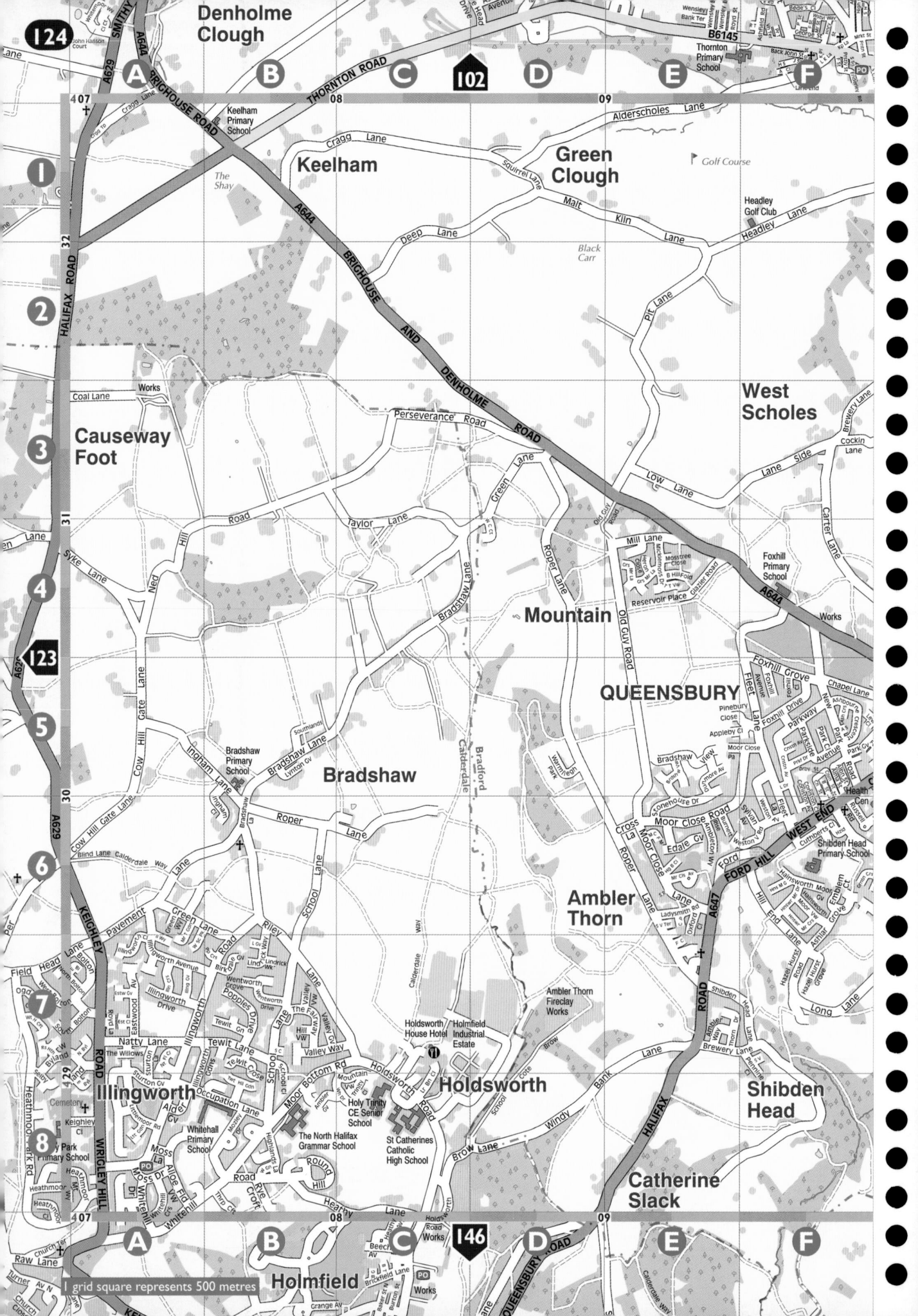

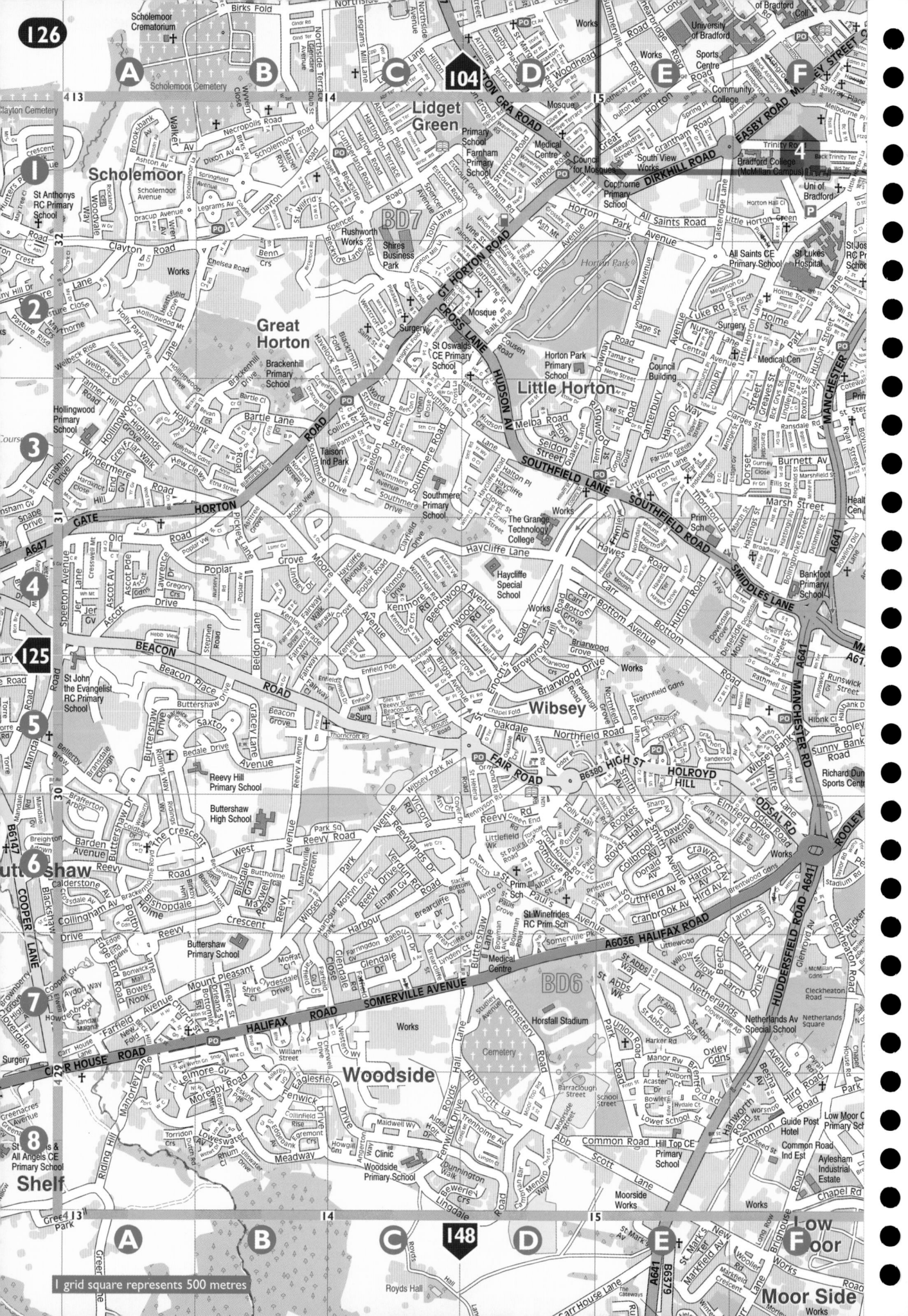

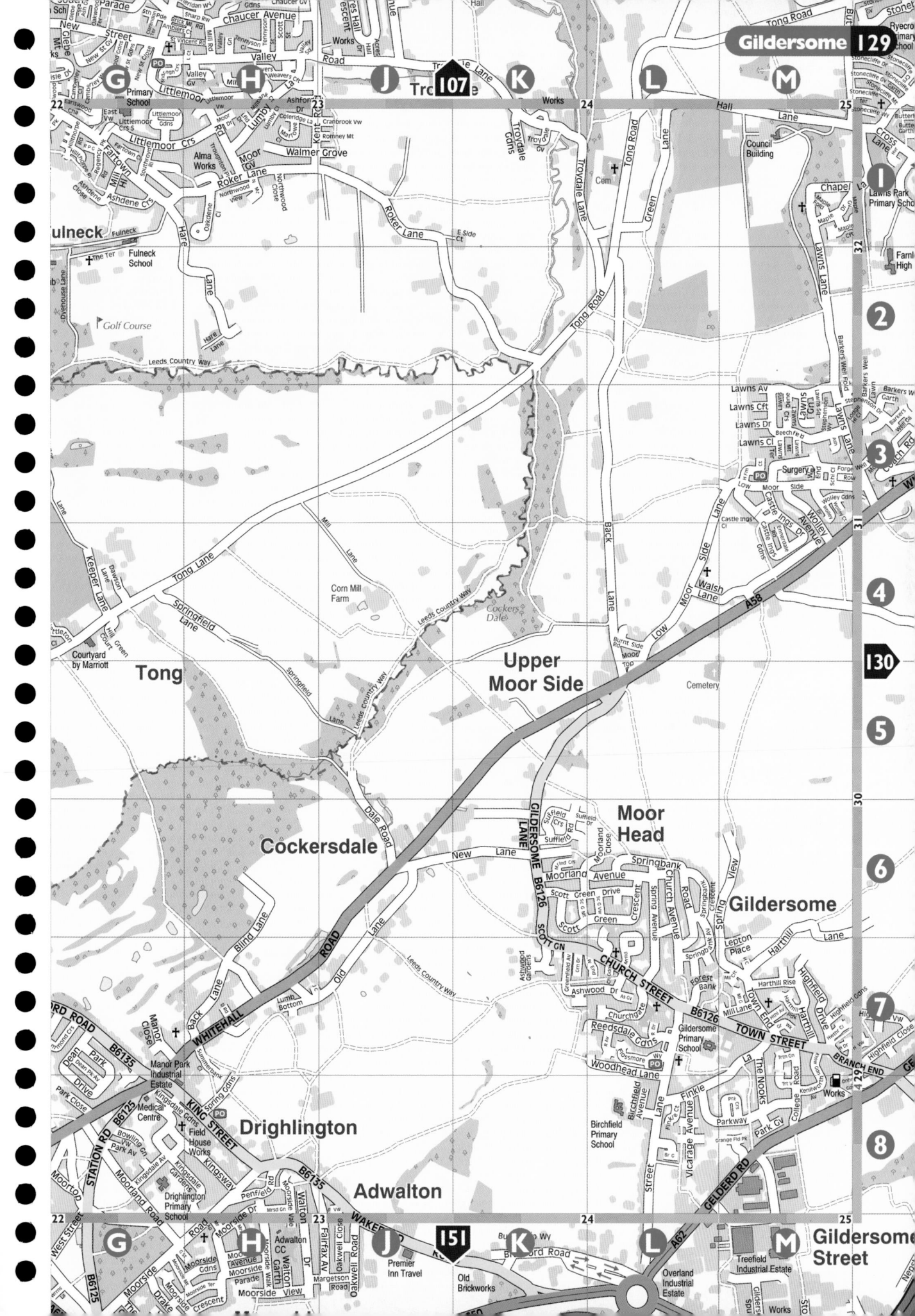

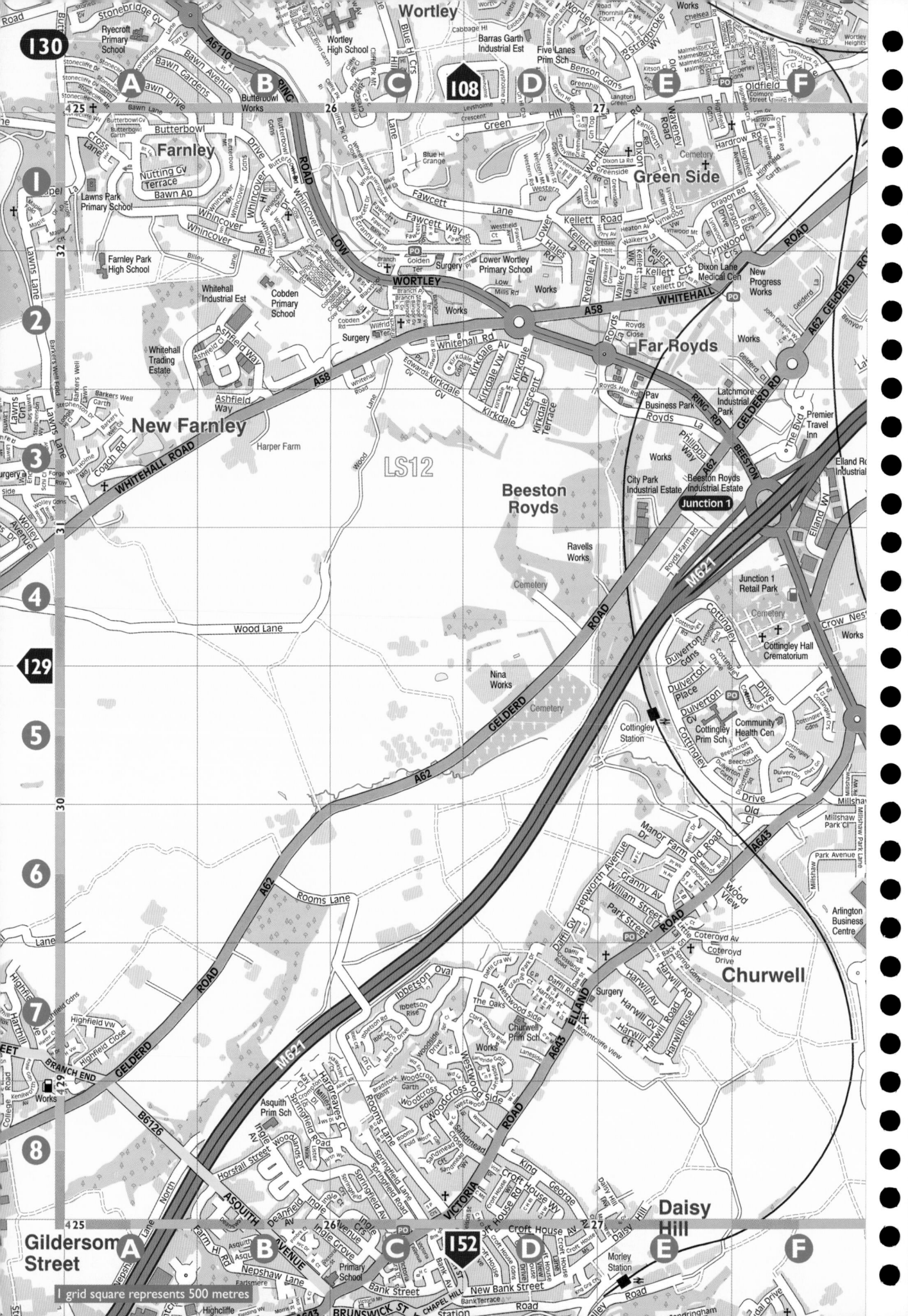

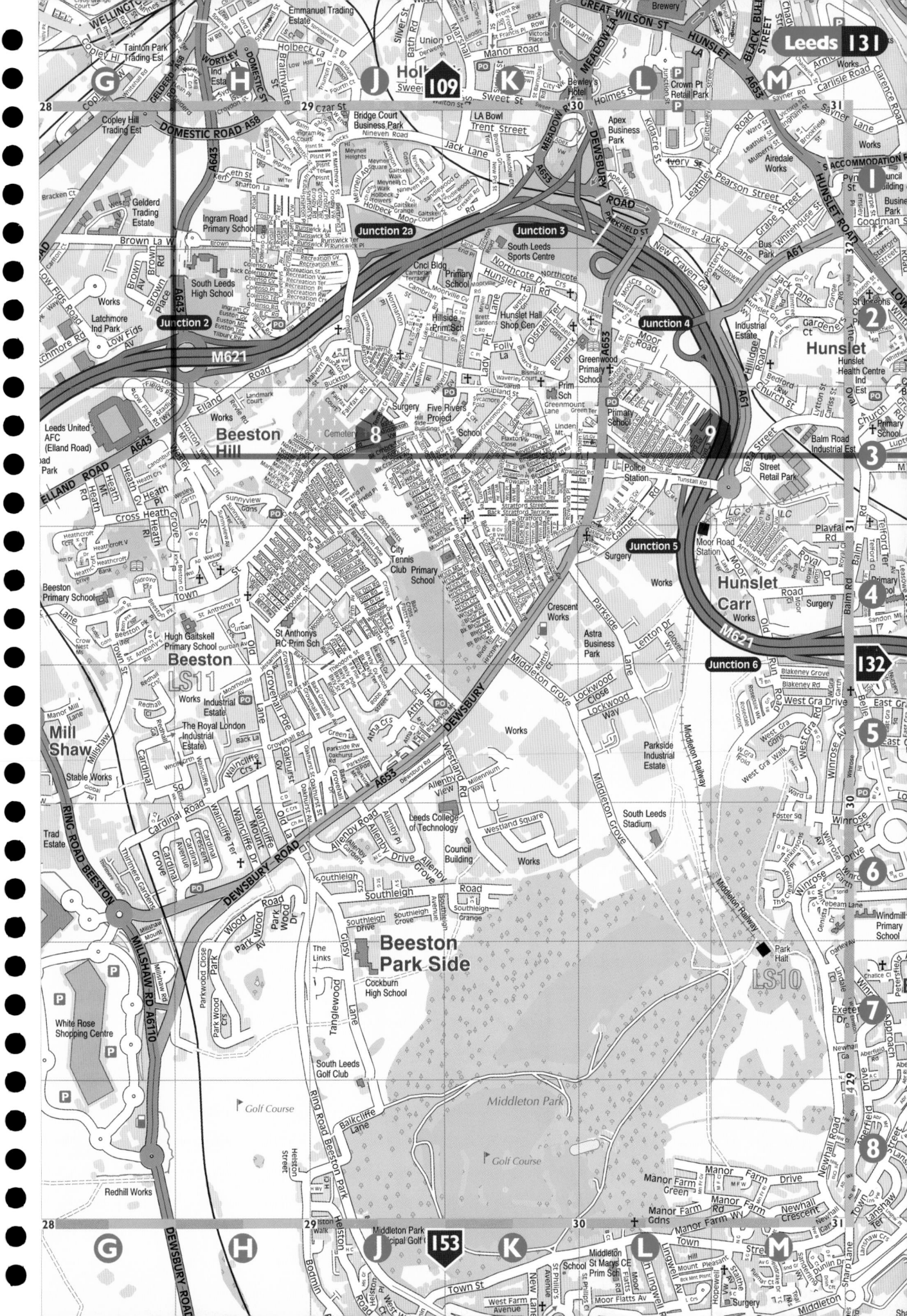

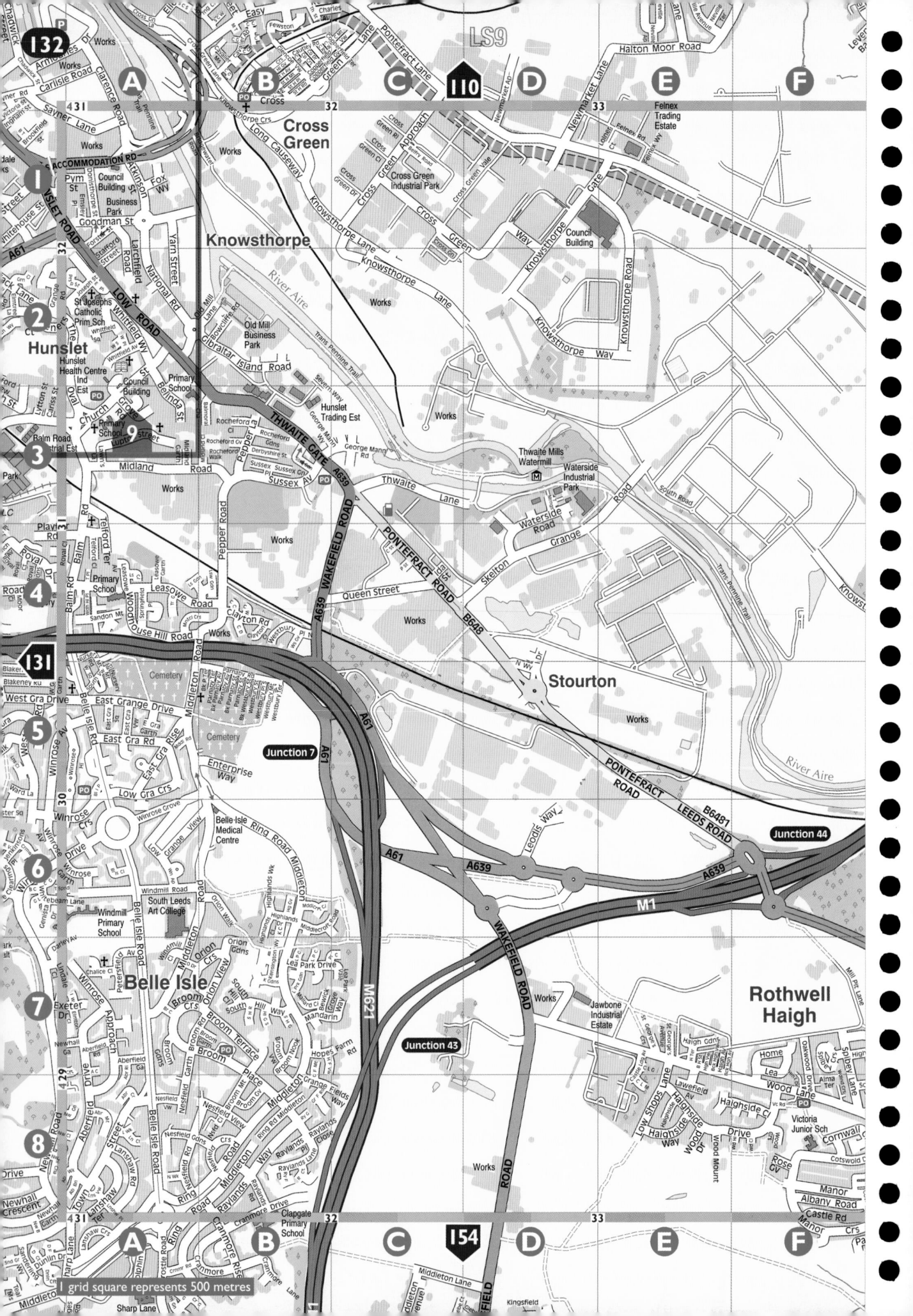

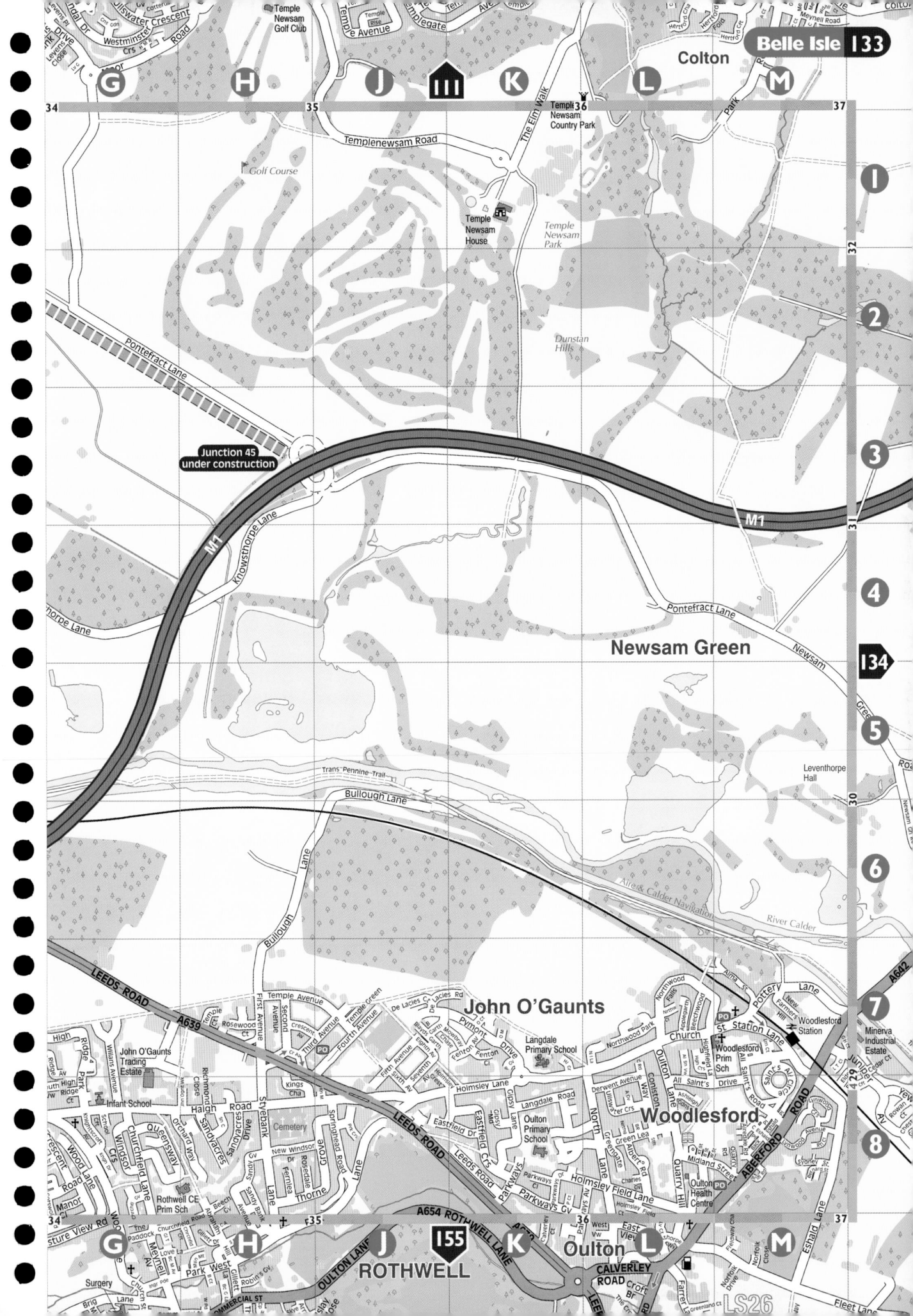

134

437

A   B   Swillington   C   112   D   E   39 A63   F
Common   SELBY ROAD

1

2   Hollinthorpe

3

4

133

5

6

7

8

437   38   C   156   D   E   F
A   B

1 grid square represents 500 metres

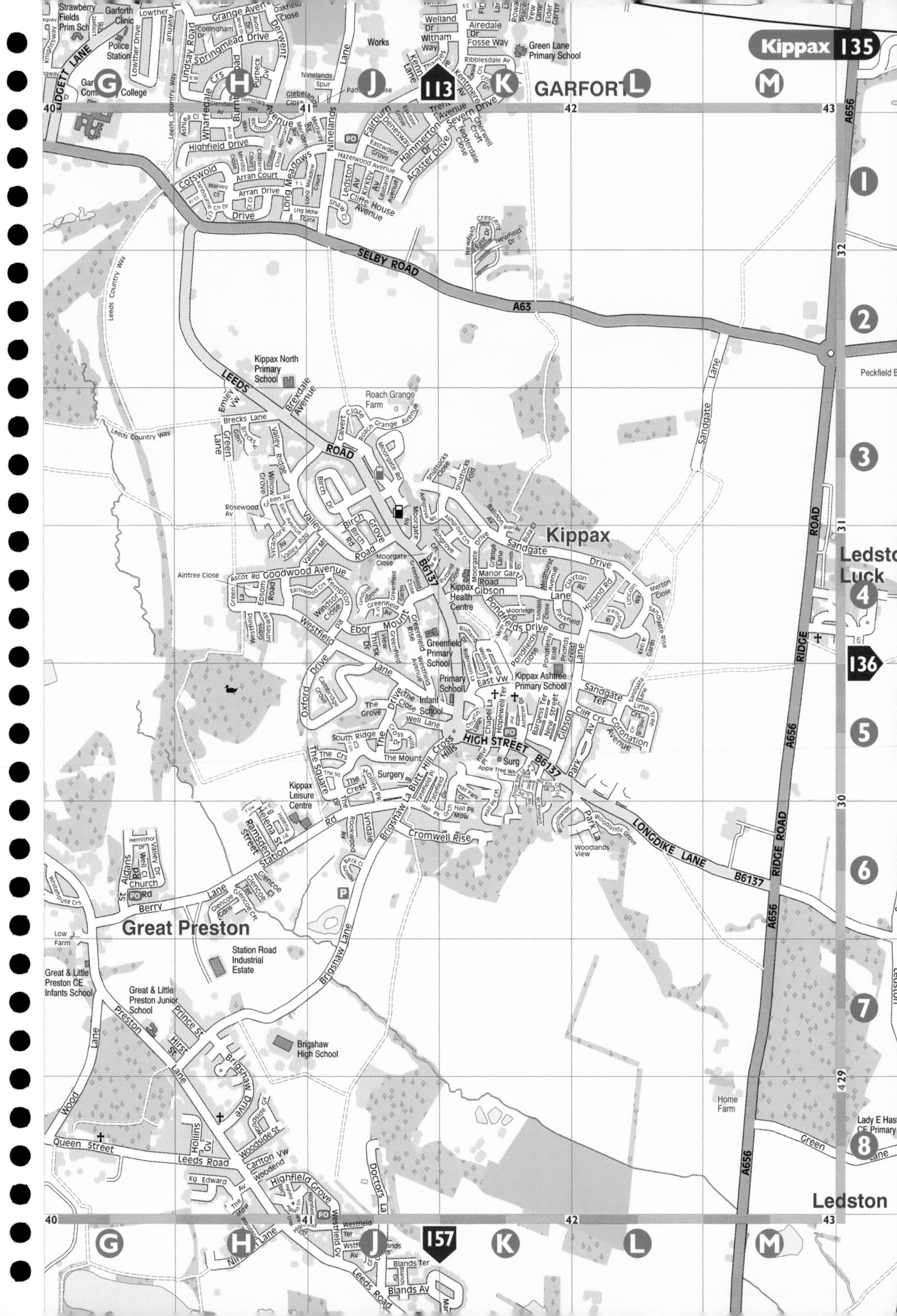

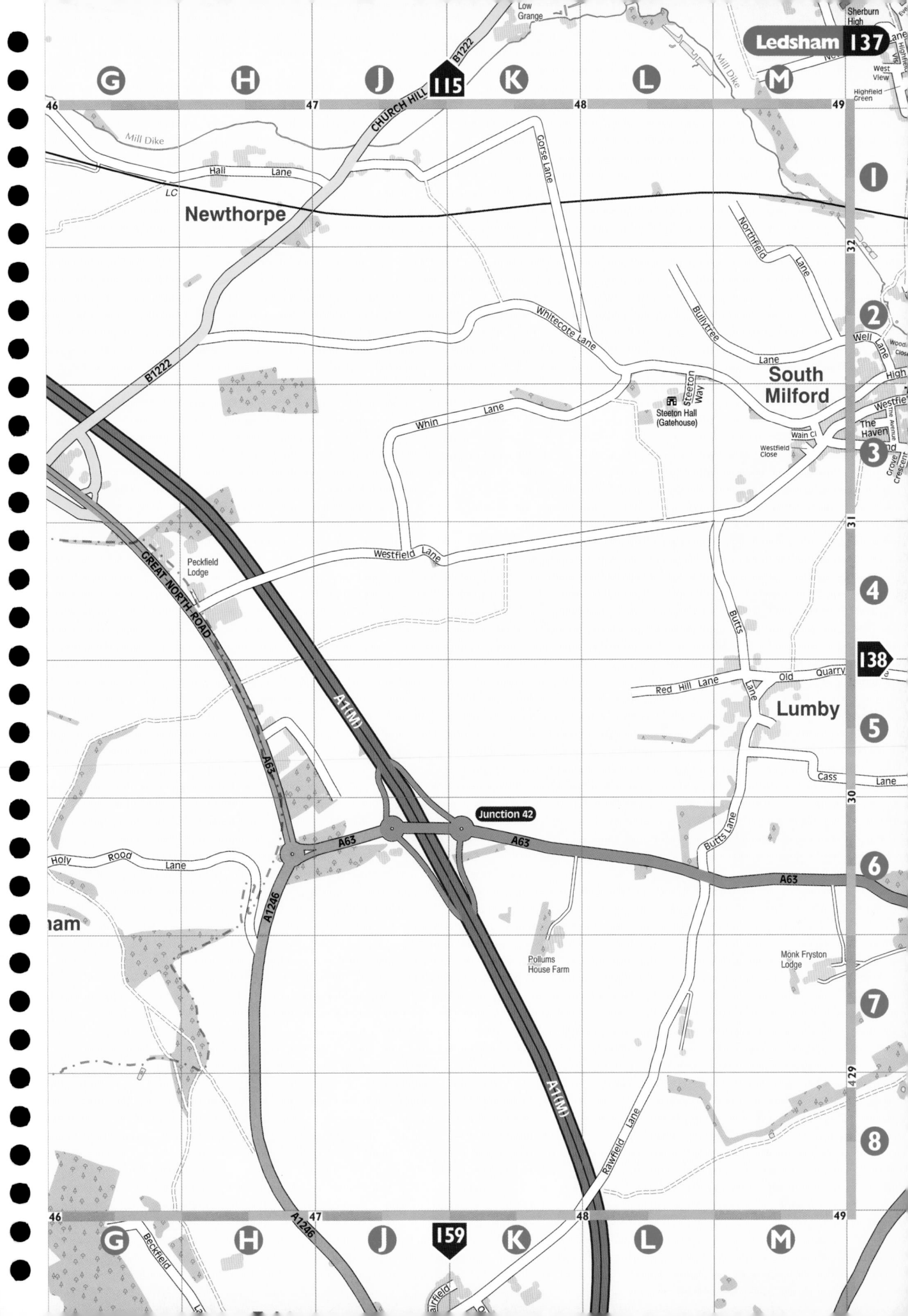

G H J 115 K L M

46 47 CHURCH HILL 48 49

I

Mill Dike

Hall Lane

LC

Newthorpe

B1222

Whitecote Lane

Gorse Lane

Northfield Lane

Bullytree Lane

2

Well Lane

Wood Close

South Milford

High

B1222

Whin Lane

Steeton Way

Steeton Hall (Gatehouse)

Westfie

Westfield Close

Wain Cl

The Haven

The Avenue

Grove Crescent

3

31

Westfield Lane

Peckfield Lodge

GREAT NORTH ROAD

Butts Lane

4

I38

Red Hill Lane

Old Quarry

5

A1(M)

A63

Lumby

Cass Lane

30

Butts Lane

Junction 42

A63

A63

6

Holy Rood Lane

A1246

Pollums House Farm

Monk Fryston Lodge

ham

7

4 29

8

A1(M)

Rawfield Lane

46 47 A1246 48 49

G H J 159 K L M

G H J 117 K L M

52 53 54 55

I
2
3
4
5
6
7
8

32
31
30
29

Lennerton Farm

Milford Hagg Farm

Low Rest Park Farm

Kelton Leys

Habholme Dike

Gascoigne Wood Mine

Hagg Lane

LC

LC

Philip Lane

Painter Lane

Common Lane

Owlet Hall

Common Lane

Fryston Grange

Hagg Bush Farm

Common Lane

Kingston Dr

The Willows

Kingston Drive

Back Lane

Chapel

Siddle House

One Acre Garth

Appletree Drive

Garth Rd

Garth Lane

Bar Lane

Garth Cl

Garth View

Garth Ct

Dunnington

Anson Cl

Garth Drive

Cherwell Ct

Cherwell Croft

A63

Westcroft Lane

Mill La

Hambleton

Fox Lane

Old Lane

Stocking Lane

Fox Lane

Brecks Farm

Lowfield Road

Hagg House

Hillam Road

Pighill Nook Road

Bower's House Farm

Maspin Moor Road

Gateforth Wood

52 53 161 54 55

G H J K L M

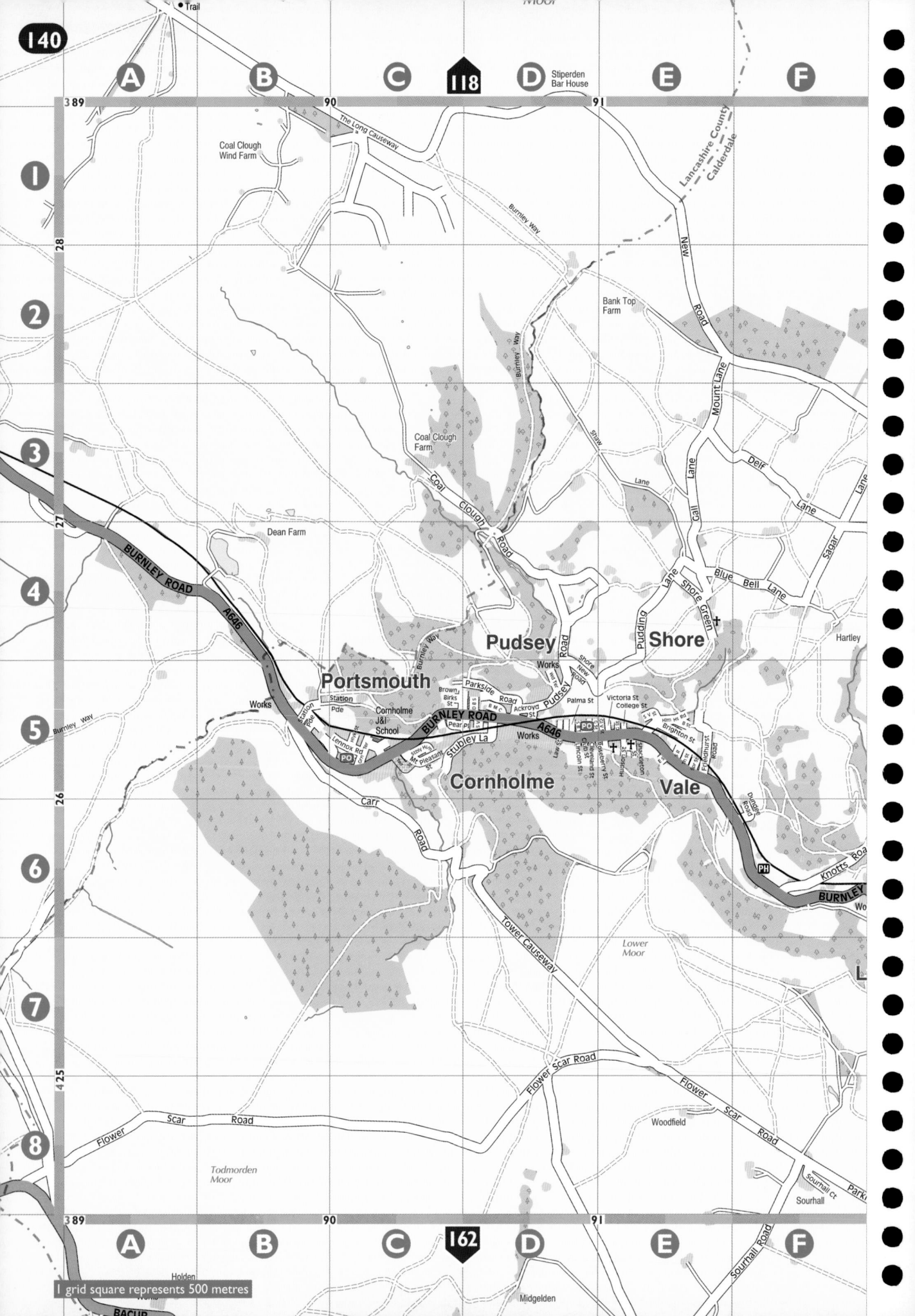

A   B   C   118   D Stiperden Bar House   E   F

389   90   91

The Long Causeway

1

Coal Clough Wind Farm

Burnley Way

28

2

Bank Top Farm

Mount Lane

Coal Clough Farm

Burnley Way

New Road

Lancashire County Calderdale

Call Lane

Lane

Delf Lane

Lane

3

27

BURNLEY ROAD

A646

Dean Farm

Coal Clough Road

Shaw

Sagar Lane

Blue Bell Lane

Shore Green

Hartley

4

Pudsey   Shore

Portsmouth

Burnley Way

Works

Station Rd

Station Pde

Works

Parkside Road

New Road

Pudsey Road

Shore New Road

Palma St

Victoria St College St

Pudding Lane

Shore Lane

Brown Birks St

Ackroyd St

Cornholme J&I School

5

26

Burnley Way

Works

Lennox Rd

PO

BURNLEY ROAD   A646

Mt Pleasant

Pear Pl

Stubley La

Works

Lincoln St

Cleveland St

Gladstone St

Roseberry St

PO

Brighton St

Victoria St

Shackleton

St Joseph's

Brunel St

Fielden St

Fieldhurst Road

Cornholme

Vale

Dundee Road

Carr Road

6

PH

BURNLEY

Knotts Road

Wo

Tower Causeway

Lower Moor

7

425

8

Flower   Scar   Road

Flower Scar Road

Woodfield

Flower Scar Road

Parkin

Todmorden Moor

Souhall Ct

Sourhall

Sourhall Road

389   90   91

A   B   C   162   D   E   F

Holden

Midgelden

BACUP

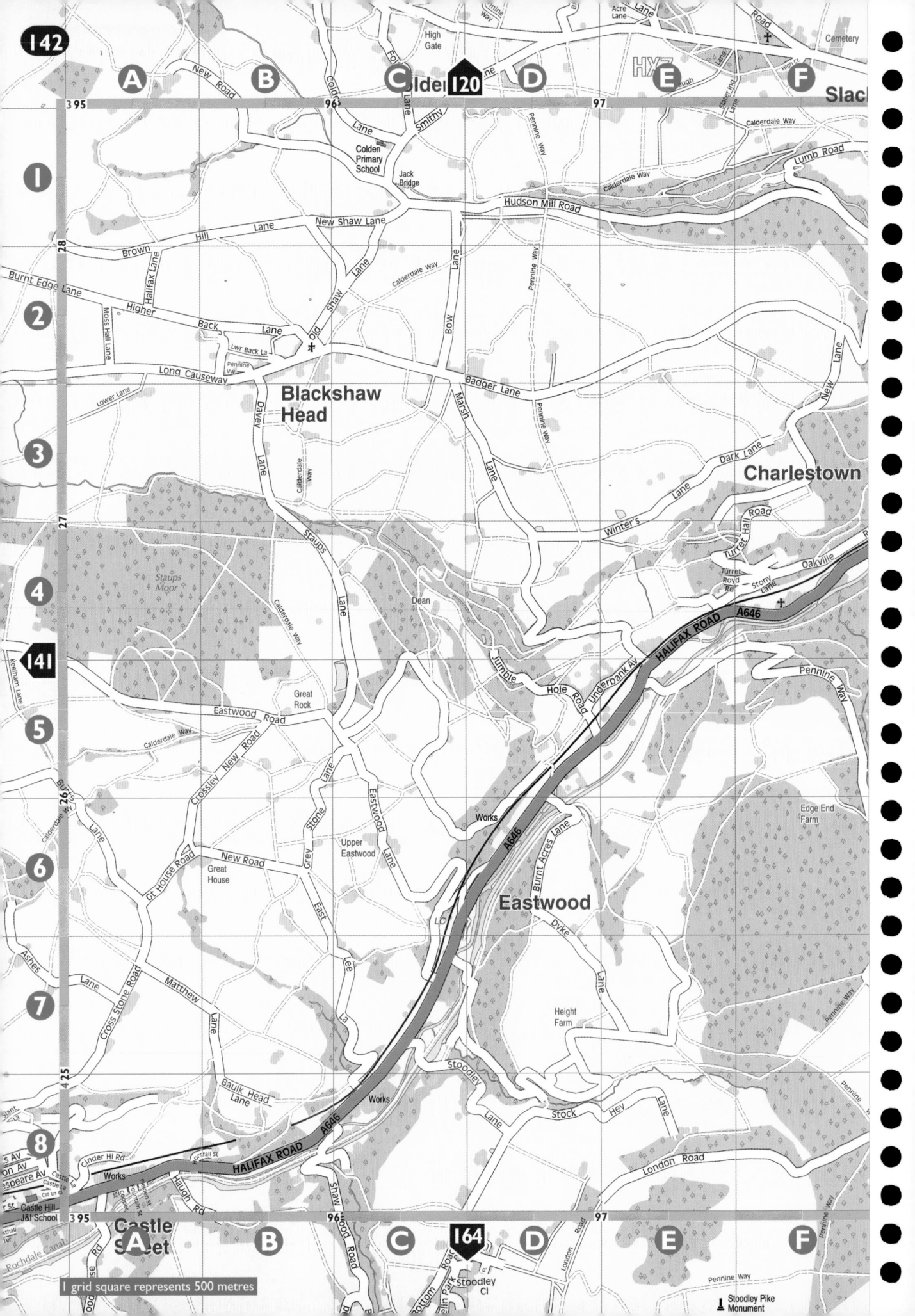

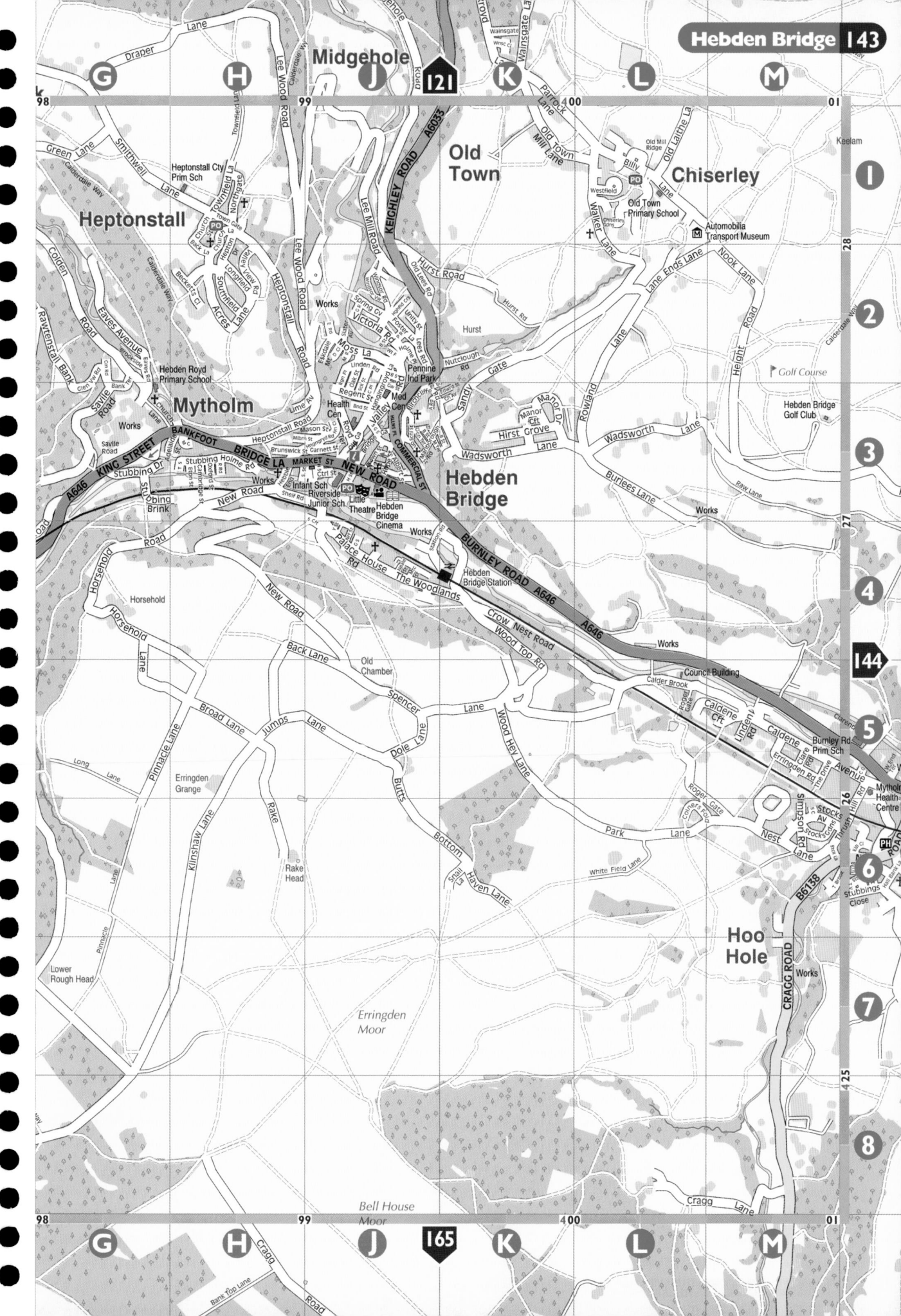

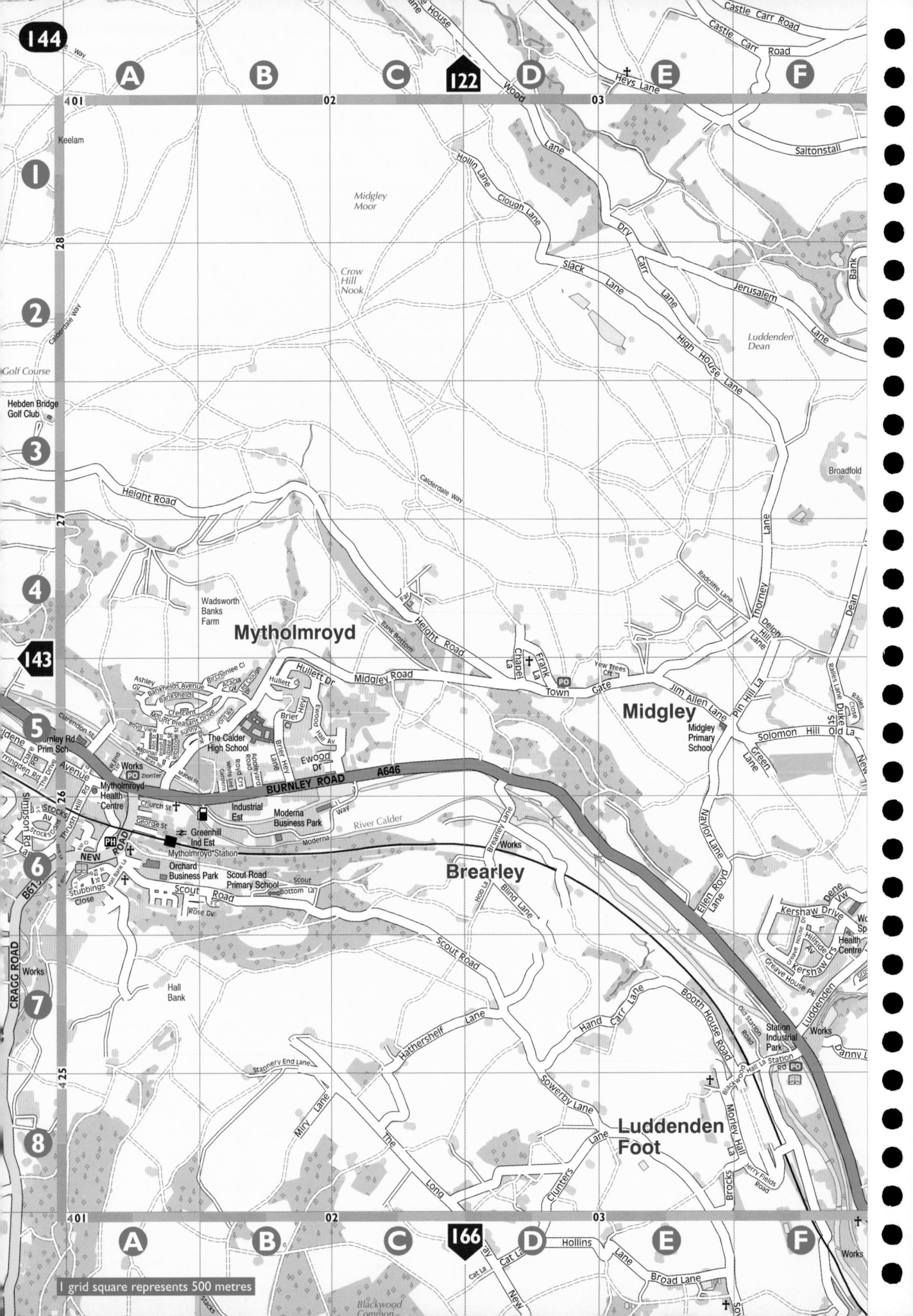

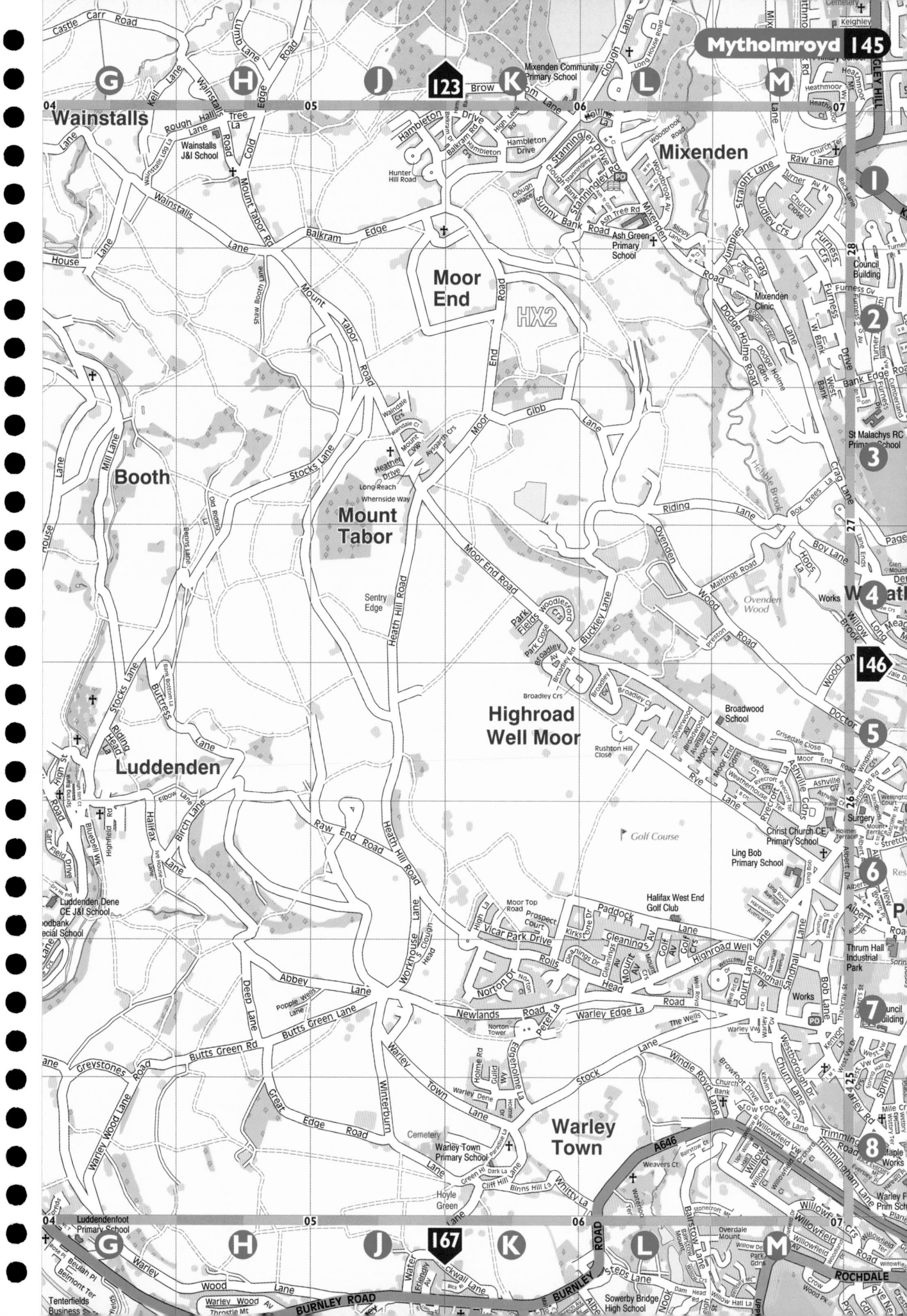

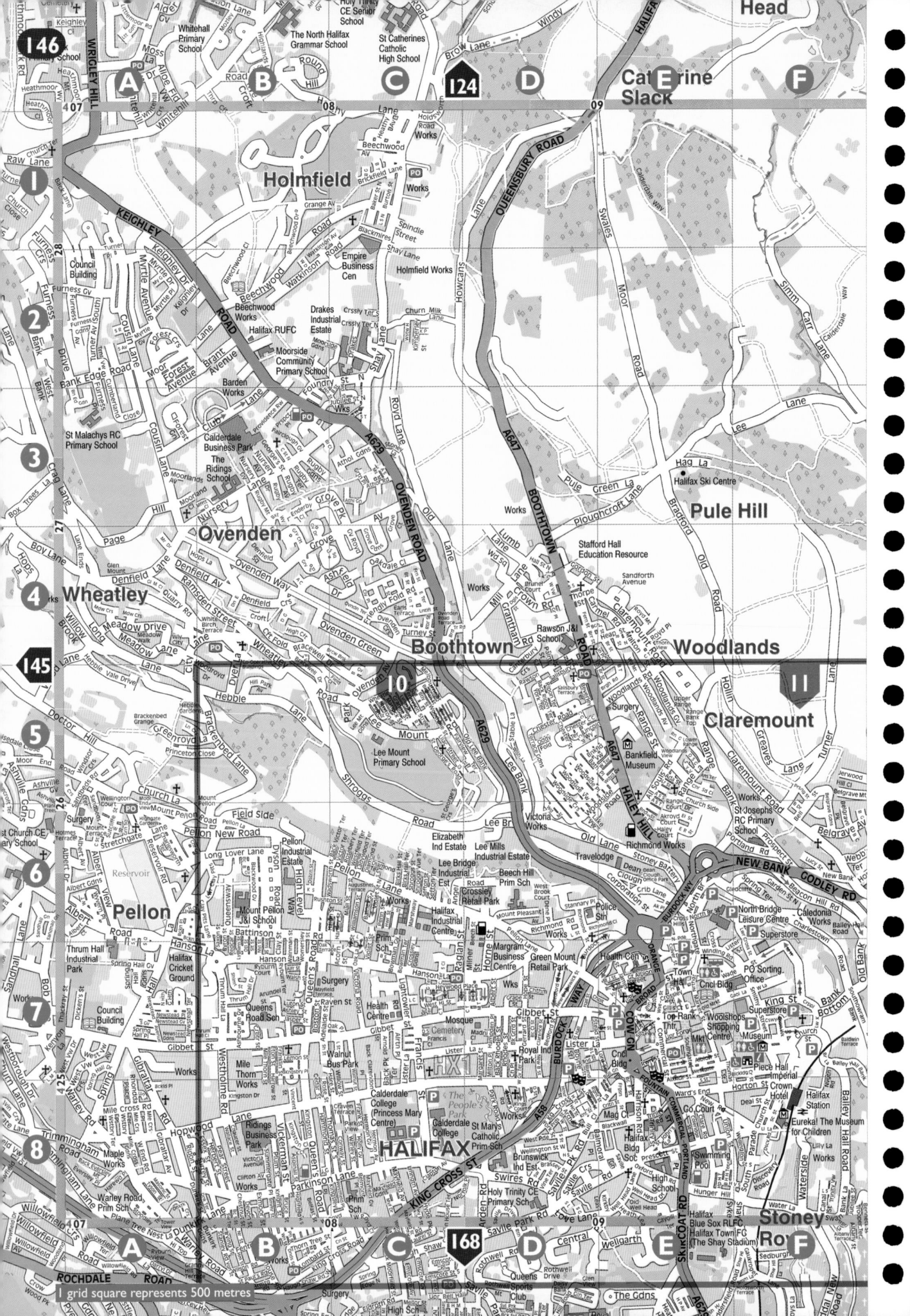

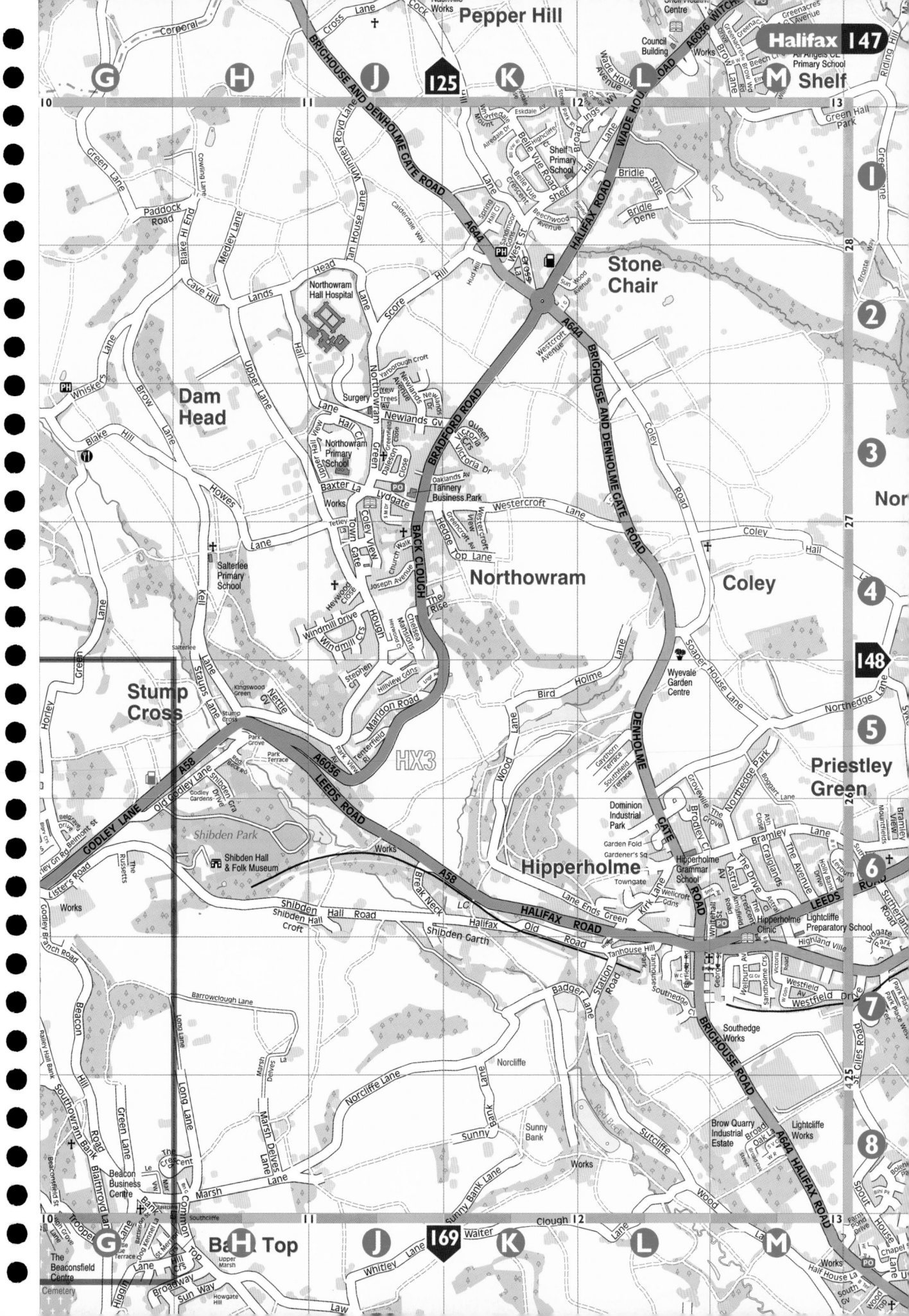

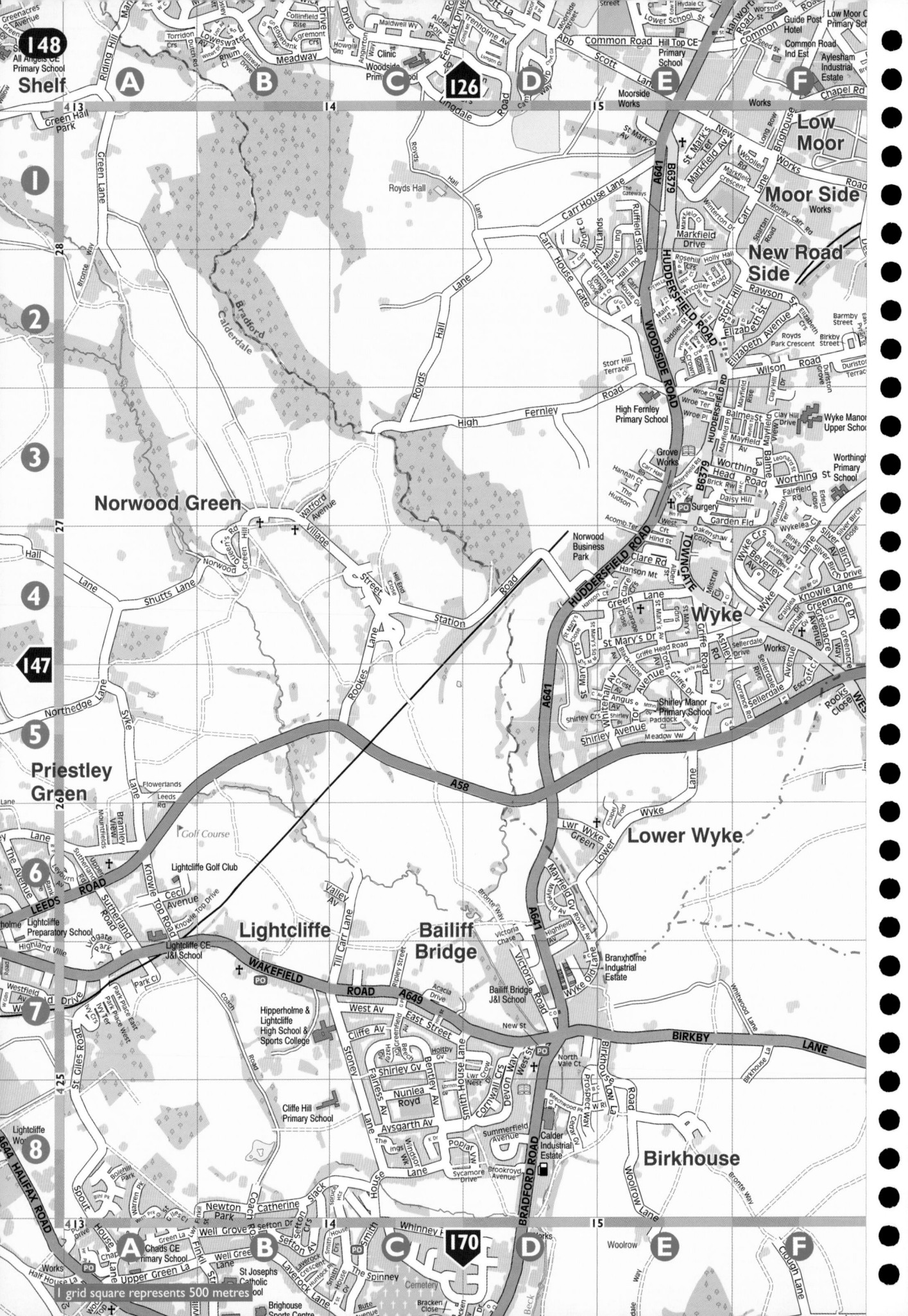

Shelf

A **B** **C** 126 **D** **E** **F**

Low Moor

Moor Side

New Road Side

Norwood Green

Wyke

Priestley Green

147

Lower Wyke

Lightcliffe

Bailiff Bridge

Birkhouse

1 grid square represents 500 metres

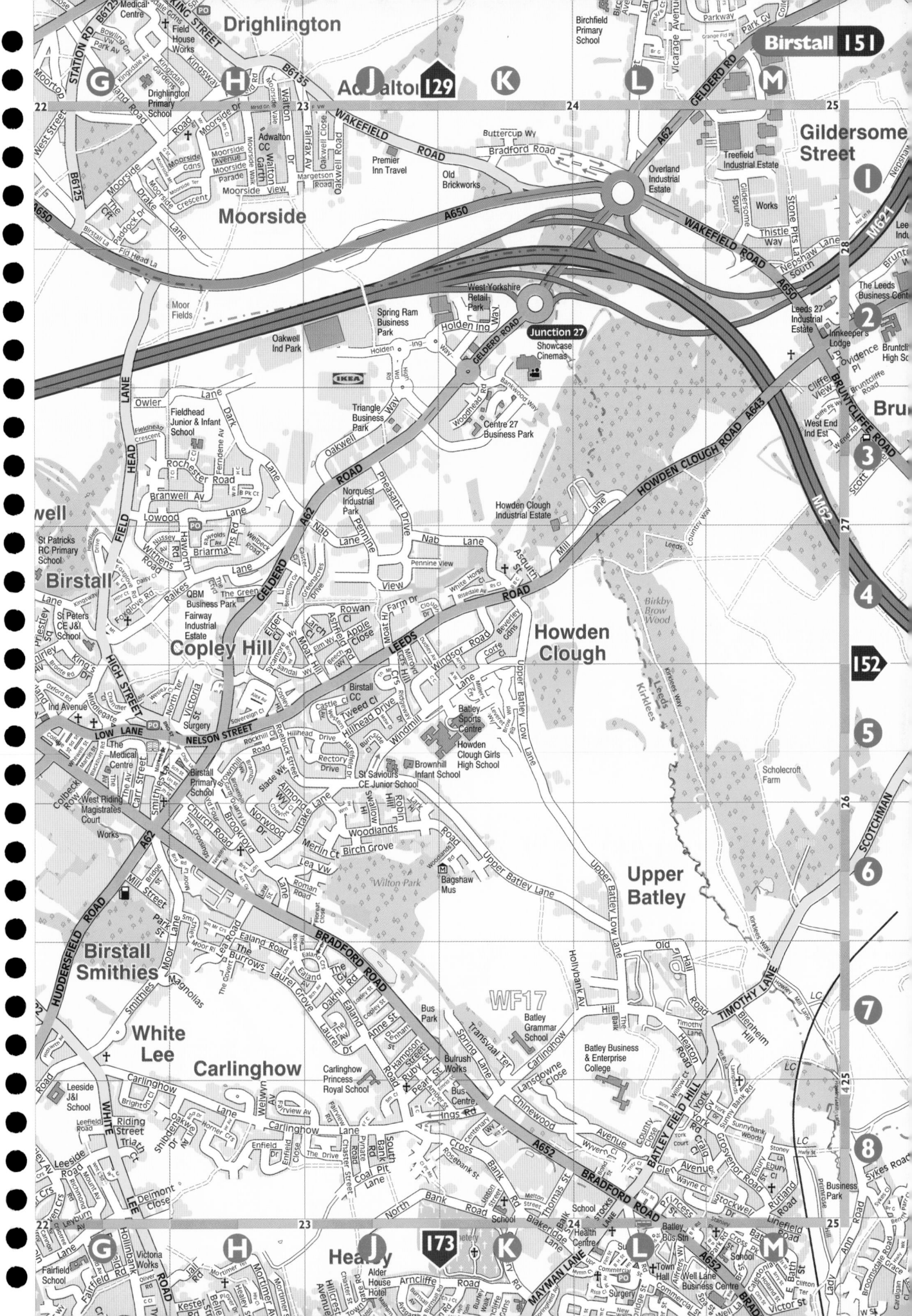

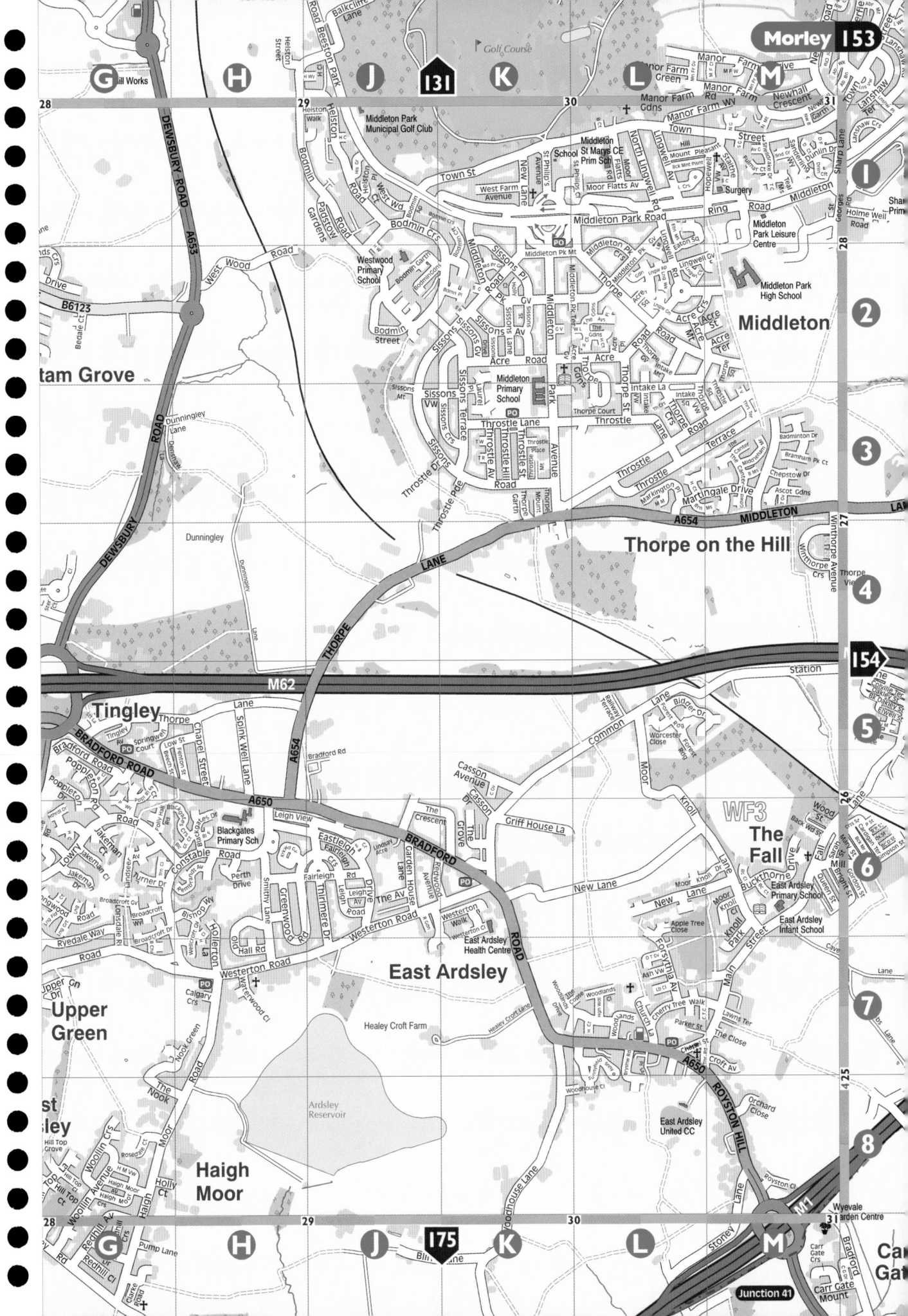

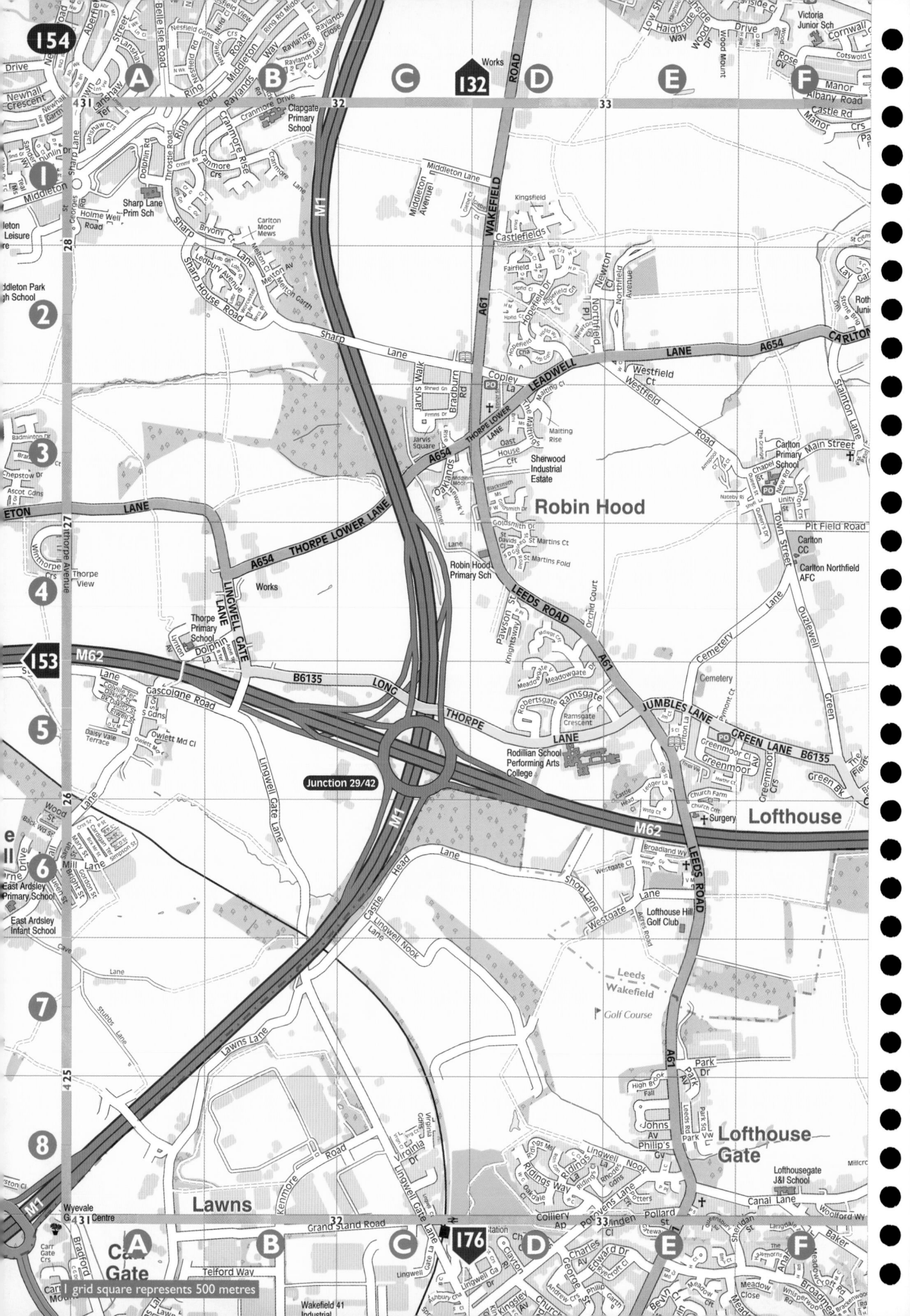

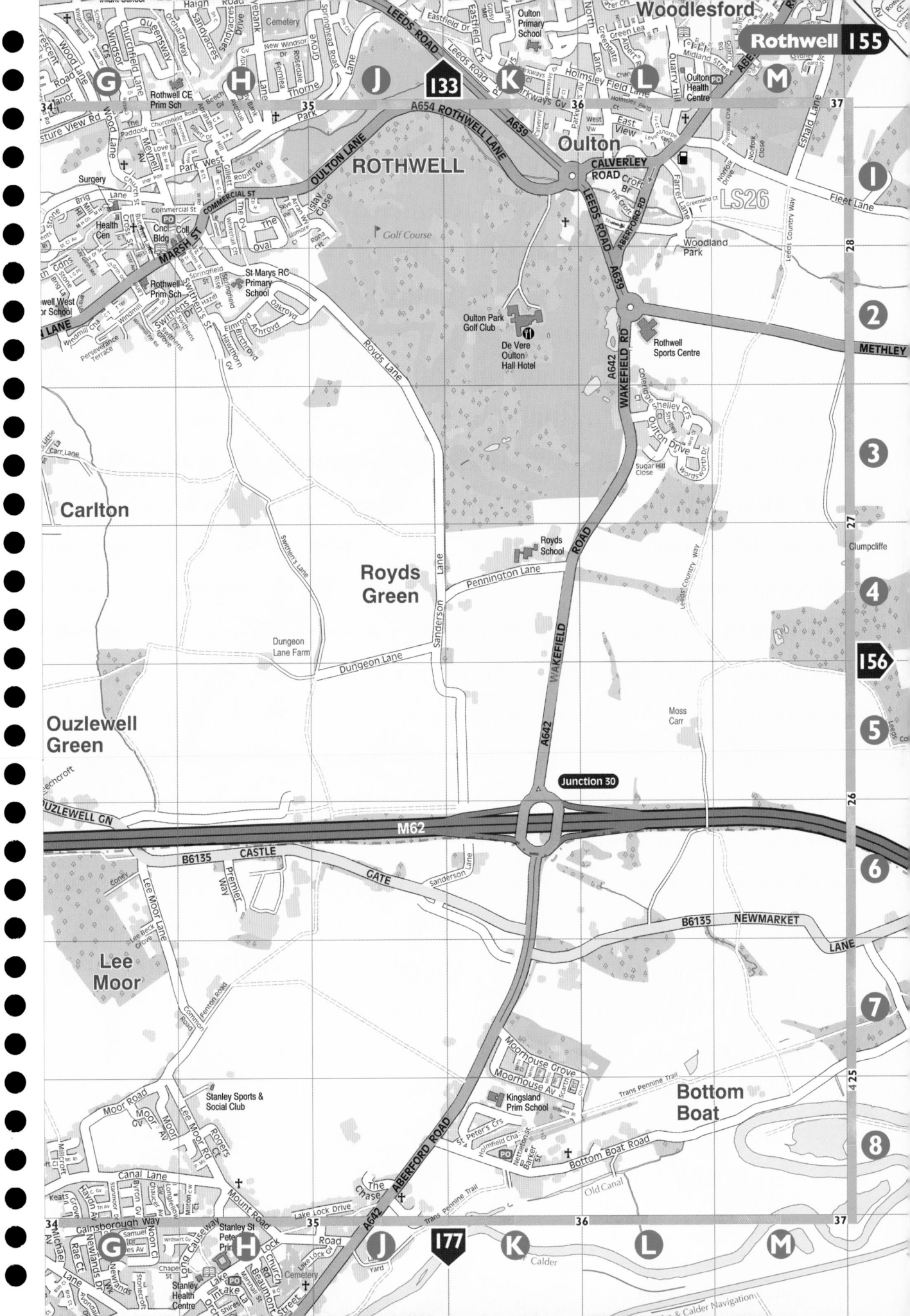

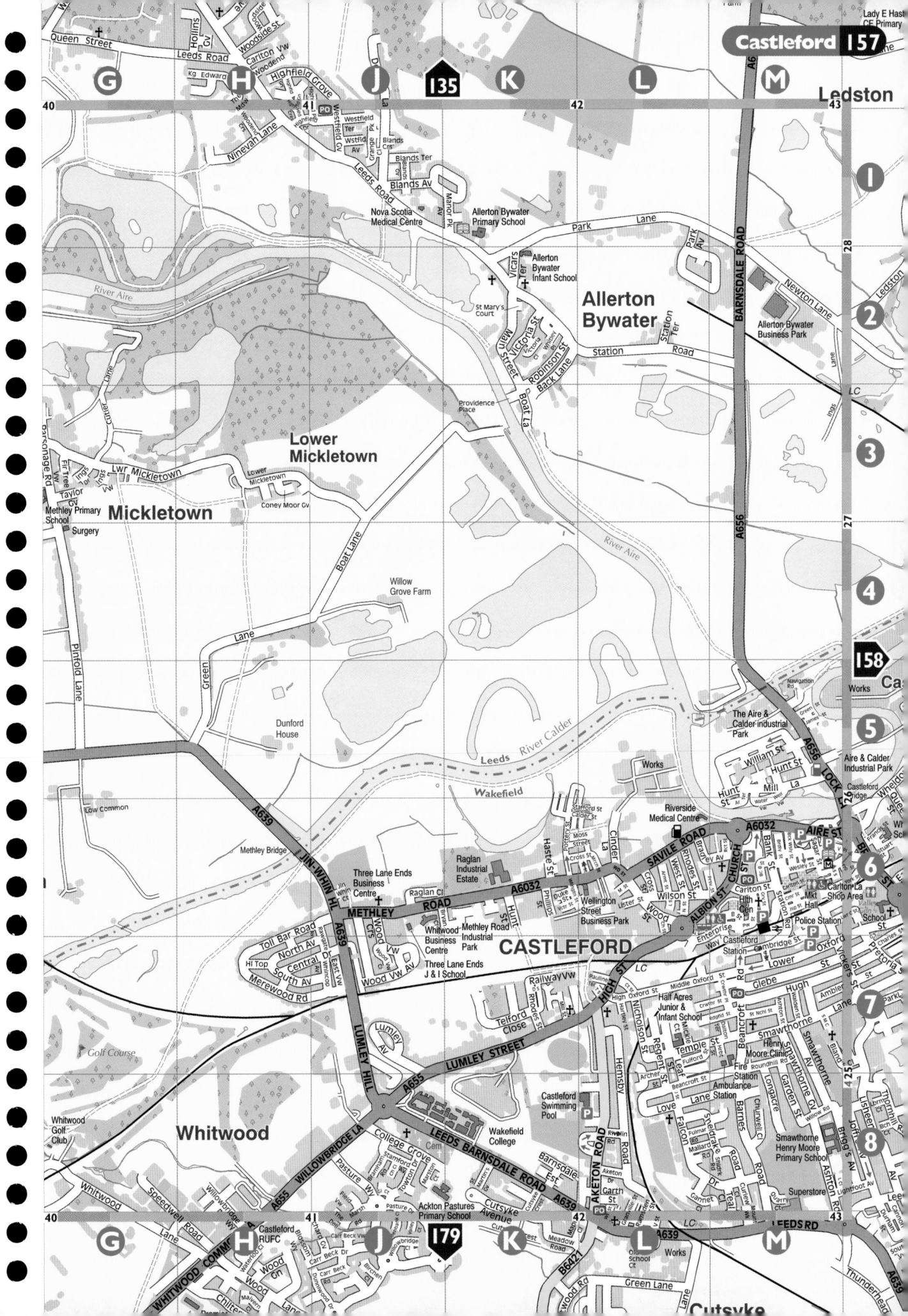

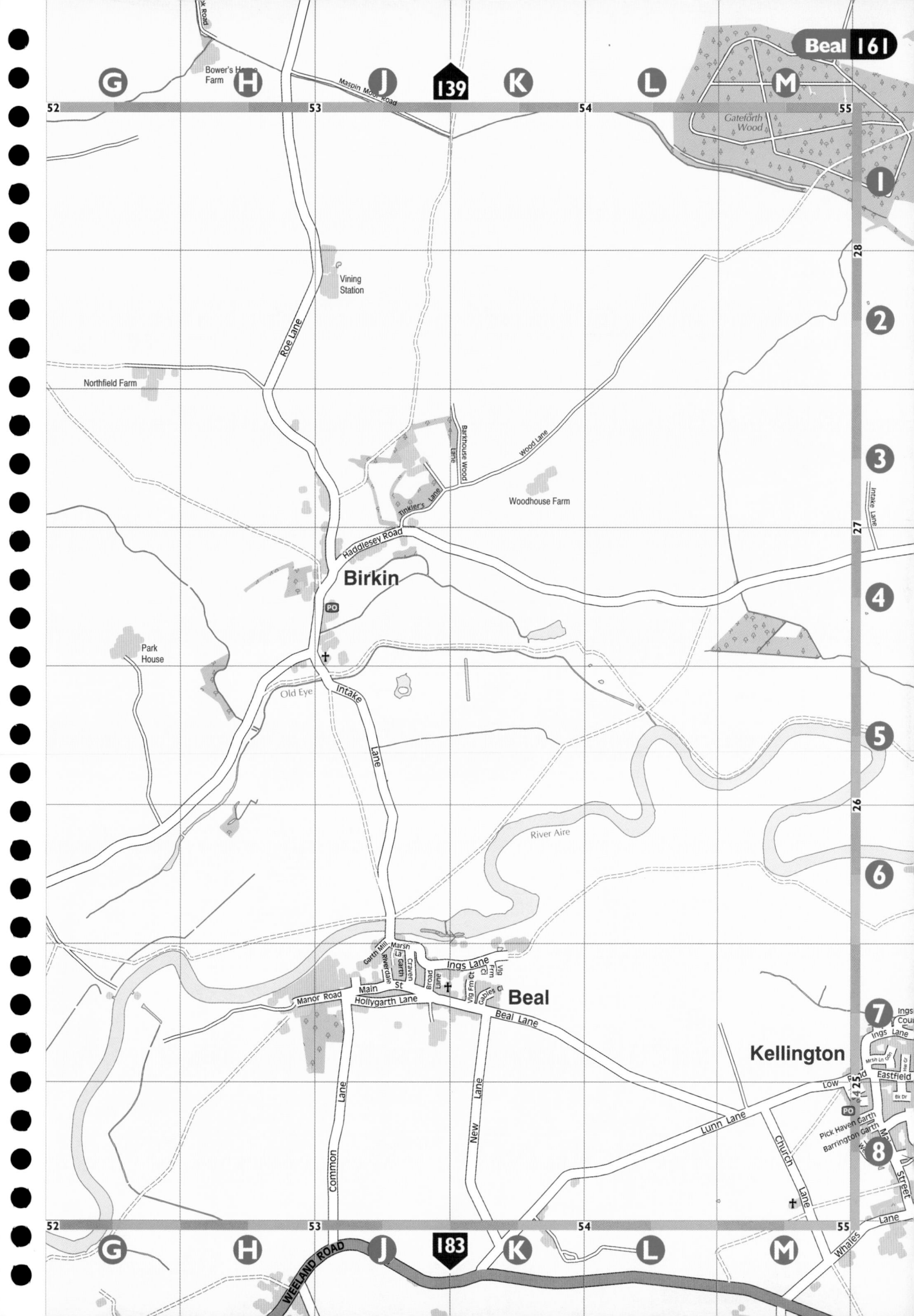

Beal 161

G H J 139 K L M

52 53 54 55

Bower's House Farm

Maspin Moor Road

Gateforth Wood

1

28

Vining Station

2

Roe Lane

3

Intake Lane

27

Northfield Farm

Barkhouse Wood Lane

Wood Lane

Woodhouse Farm

Tinkler's Lane

Haddlesey Road

Birkin

4

PO

Park House

Old Eye

Intake Lane

5

26

River Aire

6

Garth Mill

Marsh La

Riverdale

Craven Garth

Ings Lane

Vtg Frm Ct

Main St

Broad Lane

Coples Cl

Beal

Kellington

Manor Road

Hollygarth Lane

Beal Lane

7

Ings Cou

Ings Lane

Mrsh Ln Cl

Eastfield

Bk Dr

Low Frd

Lane

Common Lane

New Lane

Lunn Lane

Church Lane

PO

Pick Haven Garth

Barrington Garth

8

Whales

52 53 54 55

G H J 183 K L M

WEELAND ROAD

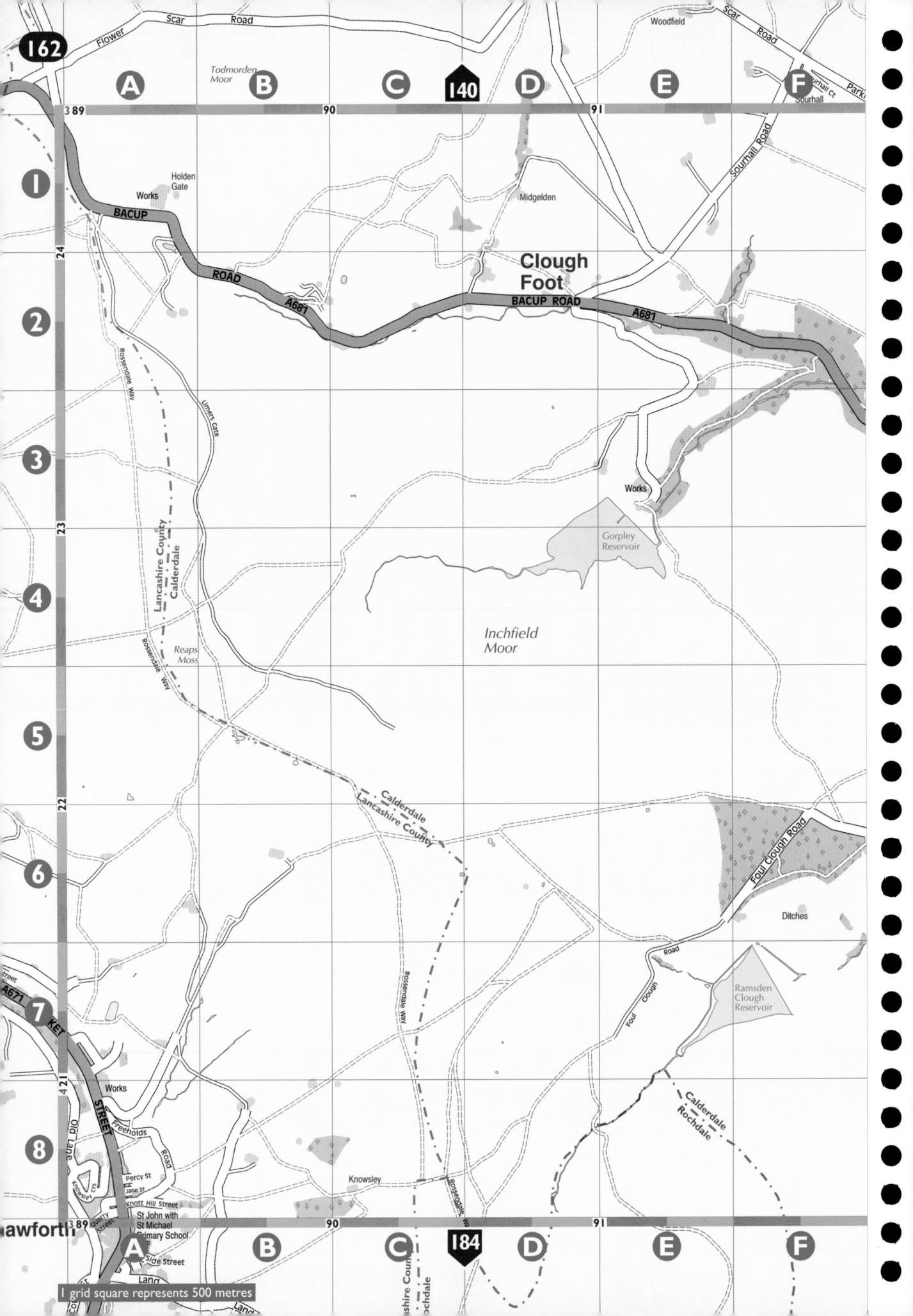

Scar Road

Flower

Woodfield

Scar Road

A B 140 C D E F

Parkwall

Sourhall ct

389 90 91 Sourhall

Todmorden
Moor

1

24

Holden
Gate

Works

BACUP

Midgelden

**Clough
Foot**

2

ROAD

A681

BACUP ROAD A681

Rossendale Way

Ulmers Gate

3

23

Lancashire County

Calderdale

Works

Gorpley
Reservoir

4

Rossendale Way

Reaps
Moss

*Inchfield
Moor*

5

22

Calderdale

Lancashire County

Foul Clough Road

6

Ditches

Road

A671

Rossendale Way

Foul Clough

Ramsden
Clough
Reservoir

KET

7

421

Works

Old Lane

STREET

Freeholds

Road

Calderdale

Rochdale

8

Percy St
Jane st

Knowsley

Rossendale Way

awforth

Knott Hill Street

St John with
St Michael
Primary School

389 90 184 91

A B C D E F

Side Street

Lancashire County

Rochdale

Land

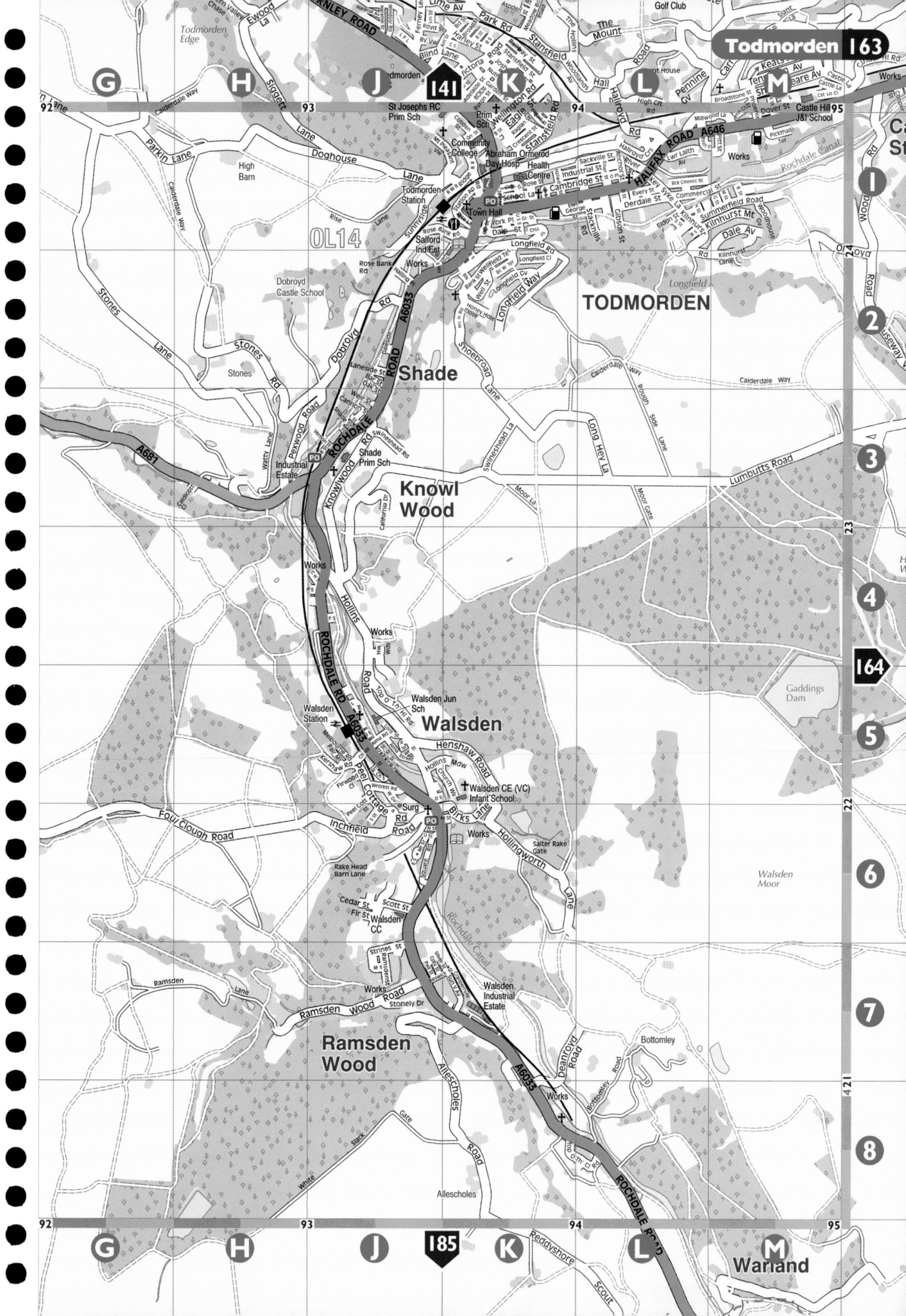

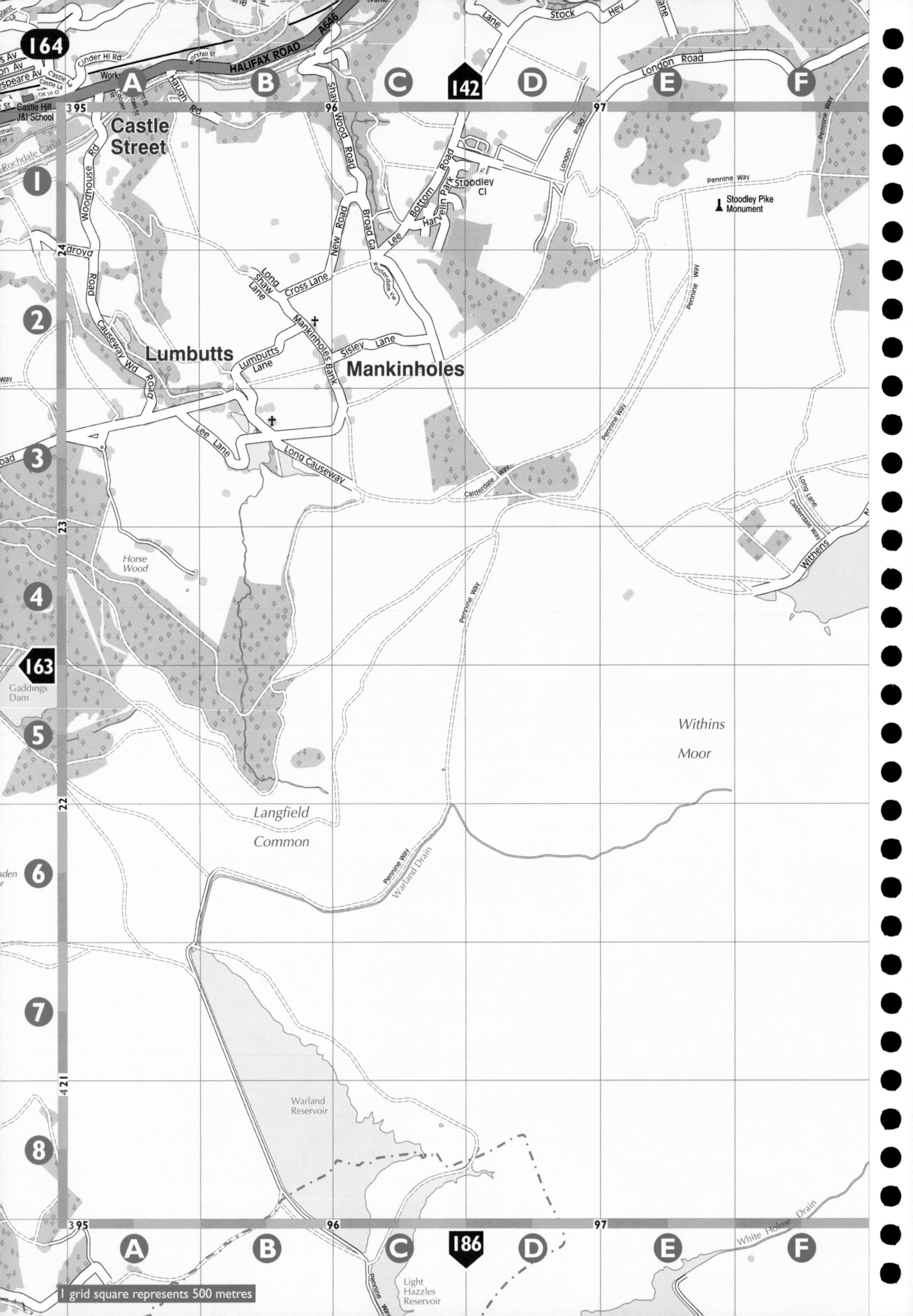

G
H
J
143
K
L
M

Bell House
Moor

I

Cragg
Road

Bank Top Lane

Blaith Royd Lane

Stony Royd Lane

Lane

Upr
Lumb La

Sunny Bank
La

Cragg Brooke

CRAGG ROAD

New La

2

Heseltine

Lane

Castle Gate

B6138

Cragg
Vale

New
Lane

Kirby
Core

Lane

Coppy

Field Head Lane

Hill Top Lane

†

Swine

Lane

Market

Lane

Calderdale Way

Church Way La

†

Works

Cragg Vale
Primary School

High

Lane

Bent Cl La

Folly Hall La

High

24

3

Withens

Lane

Rud Lane

Calderdale Way

Road

New

Withins
Clough
Reservoir

Turley
Holes
Edge

B6138

Clattering

23

4

166

Road

New Road

Stalls Road

5

22

6

Water

Turley Holes
and Higher
House Moor

Blake Moor

Washfold Road

Sykes Gate

EDGE ROAD

Calderdale Way

7

Great
Manshead
Hill

21

8

Turvin
Clough

BLACKSTONE

G
H
J
187
K
L
M

B6138

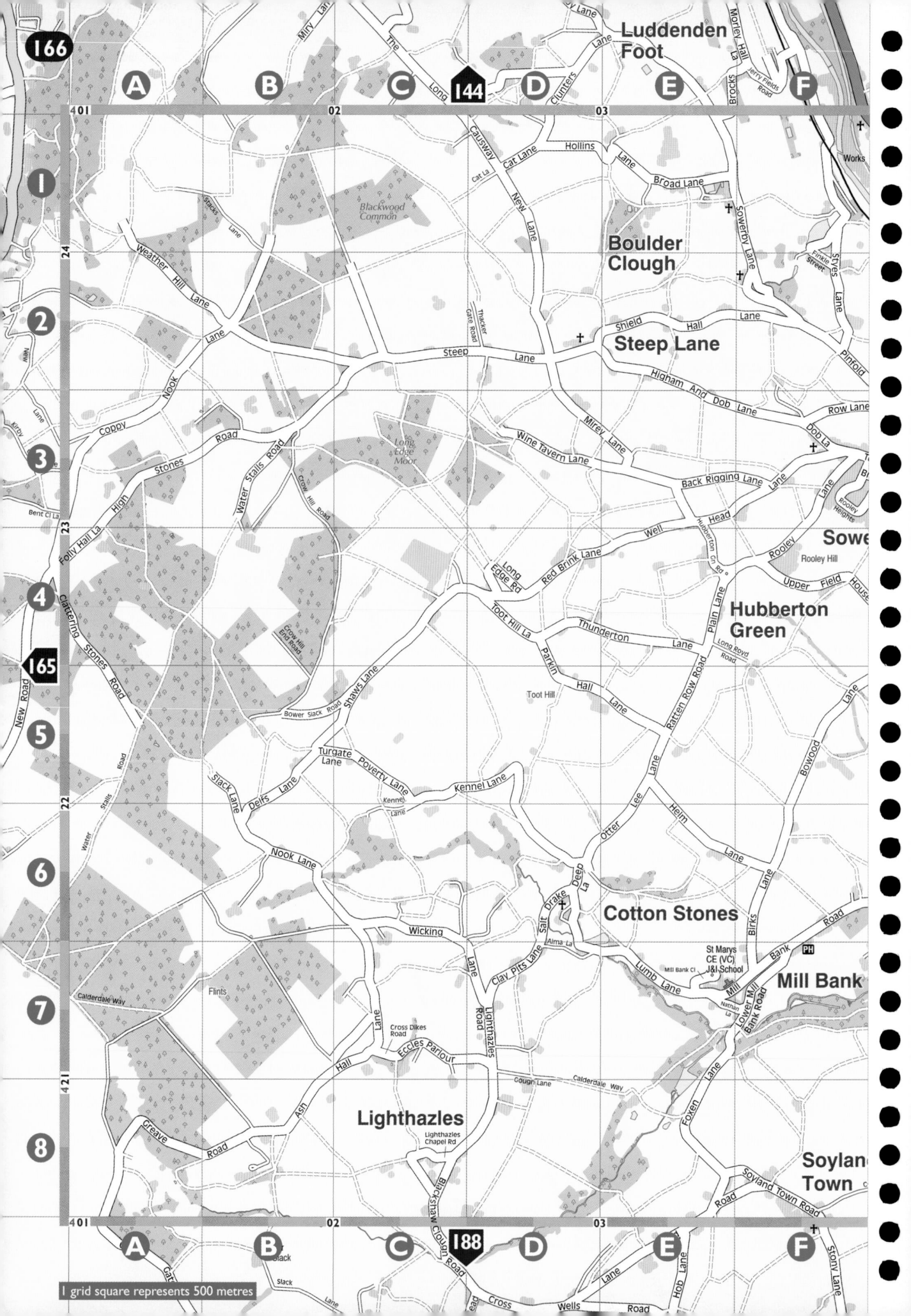

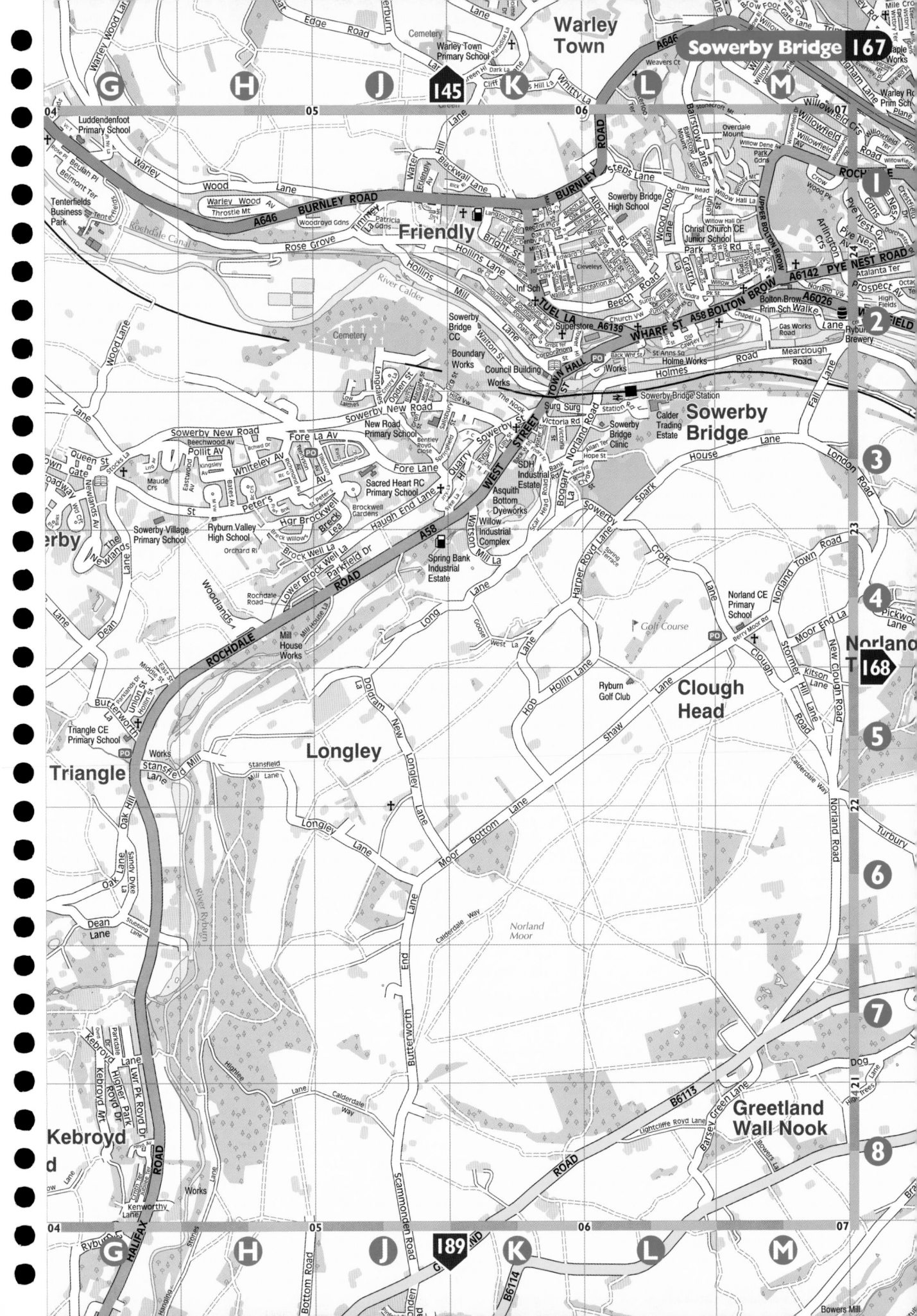

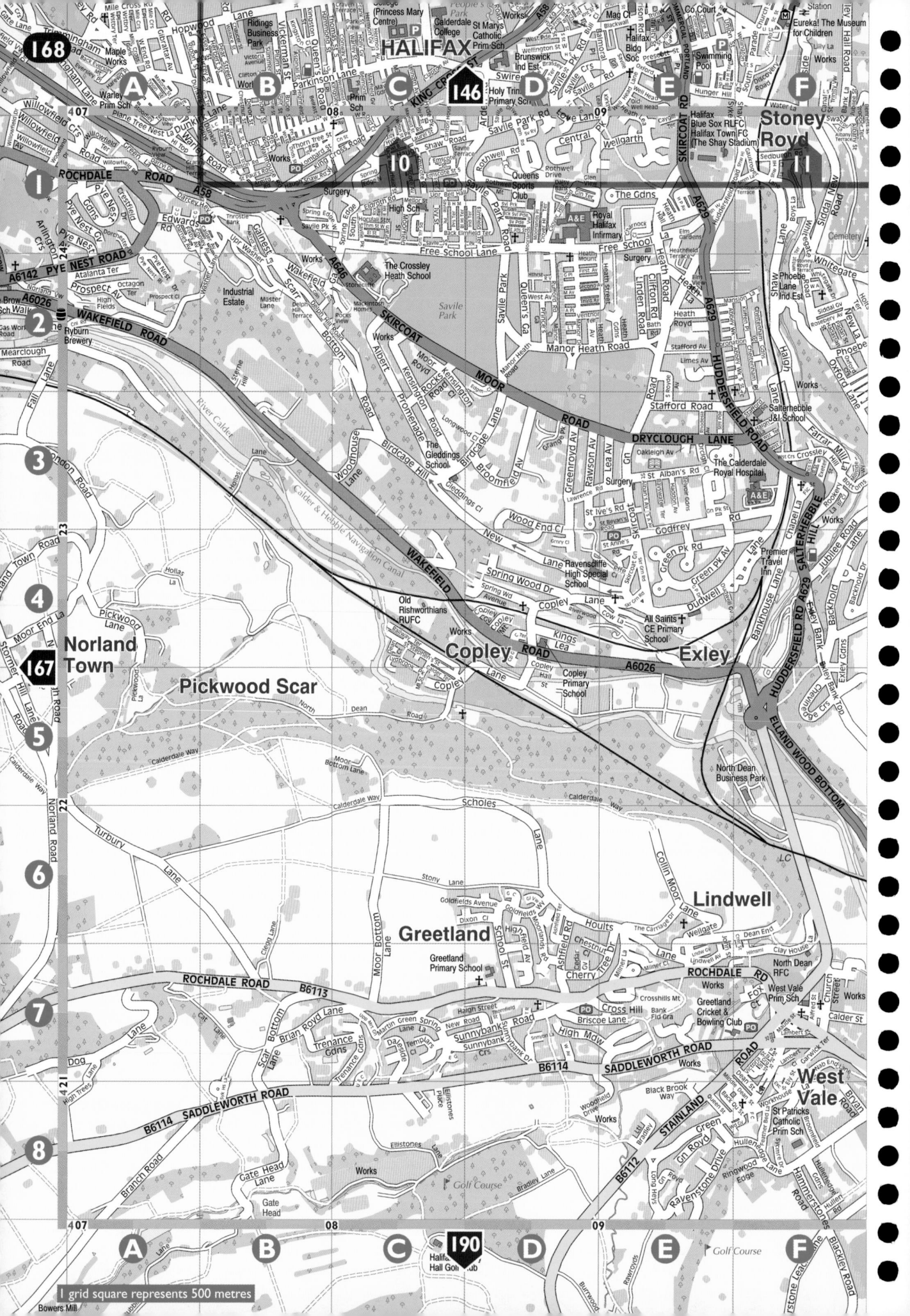

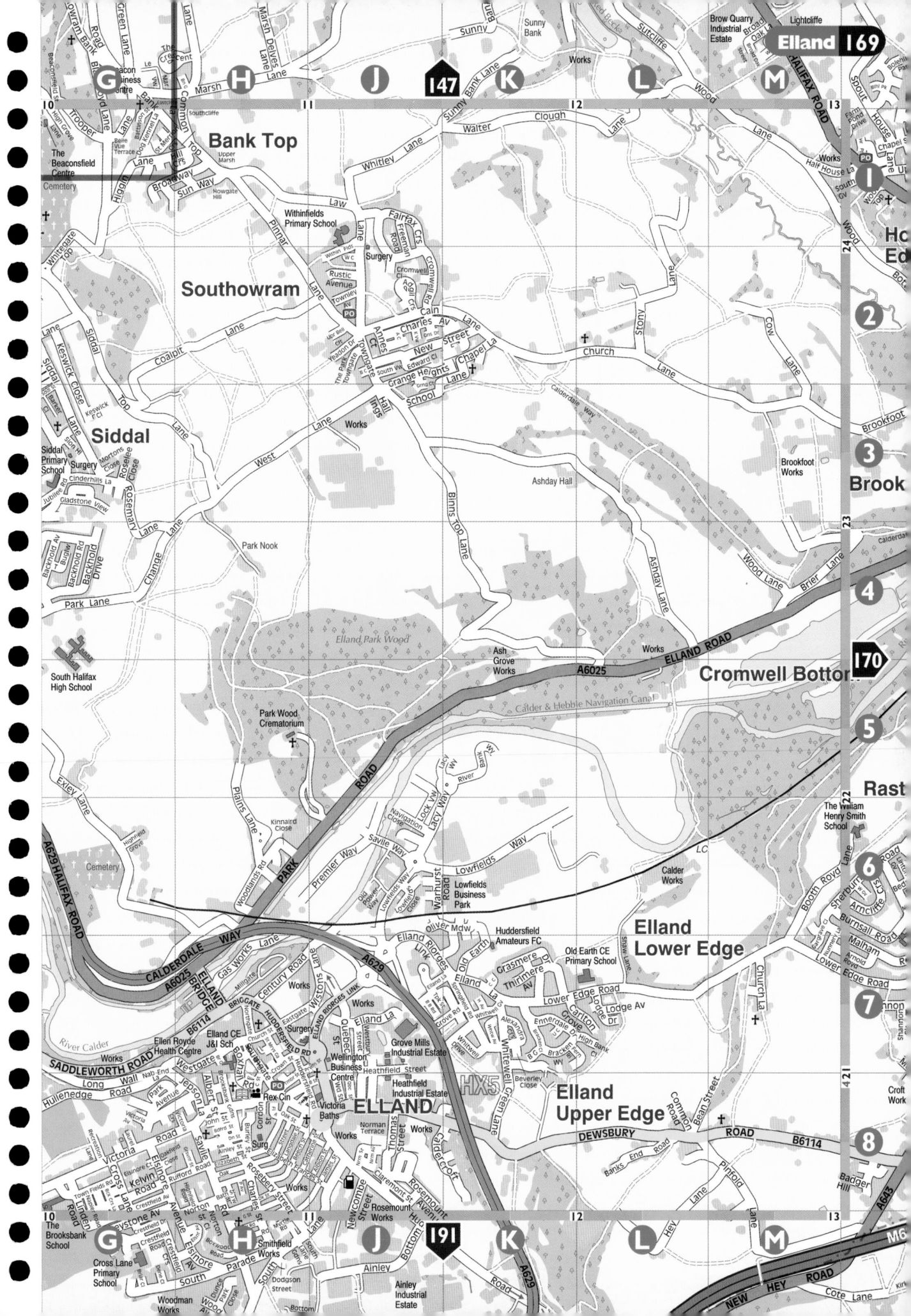

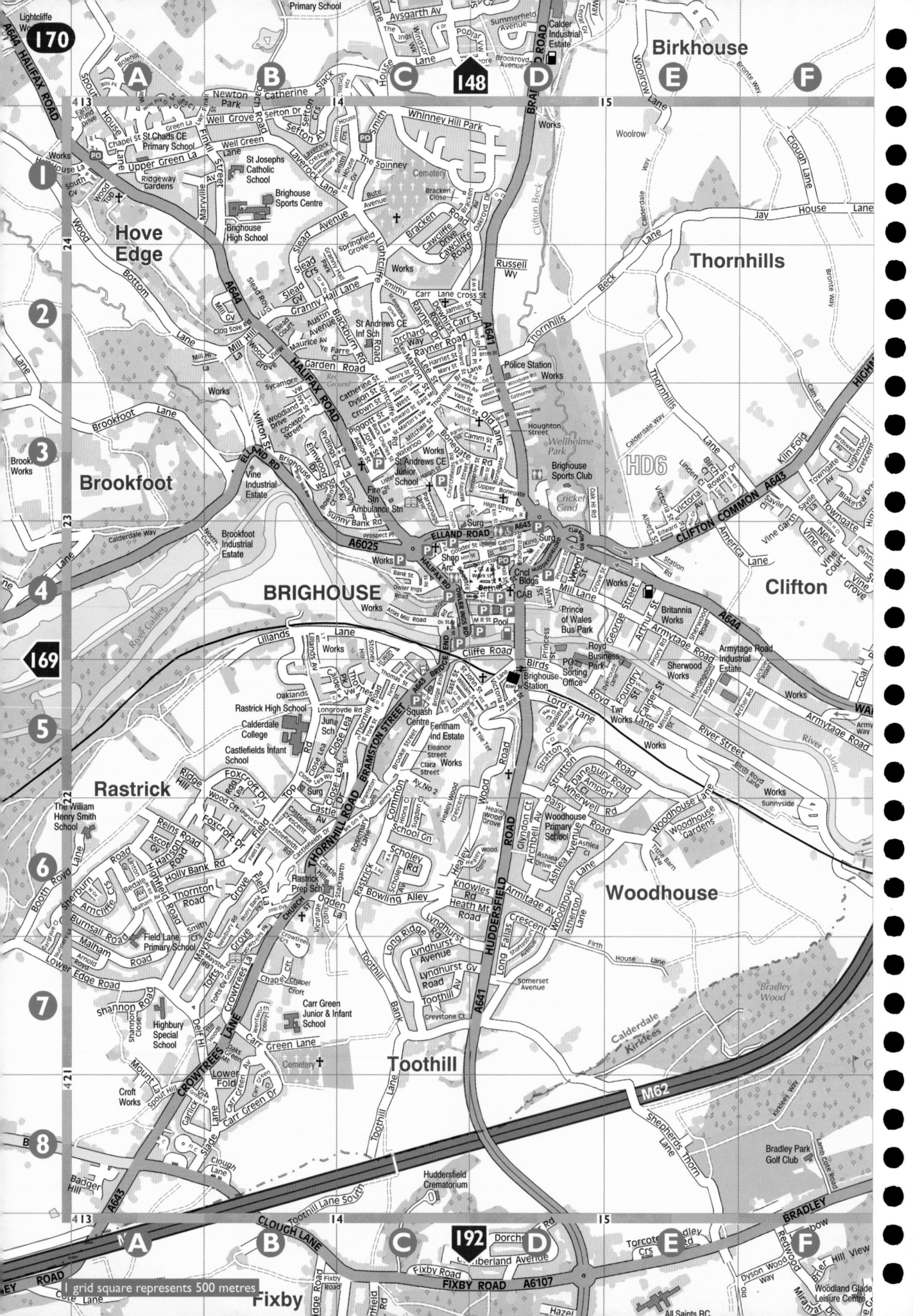

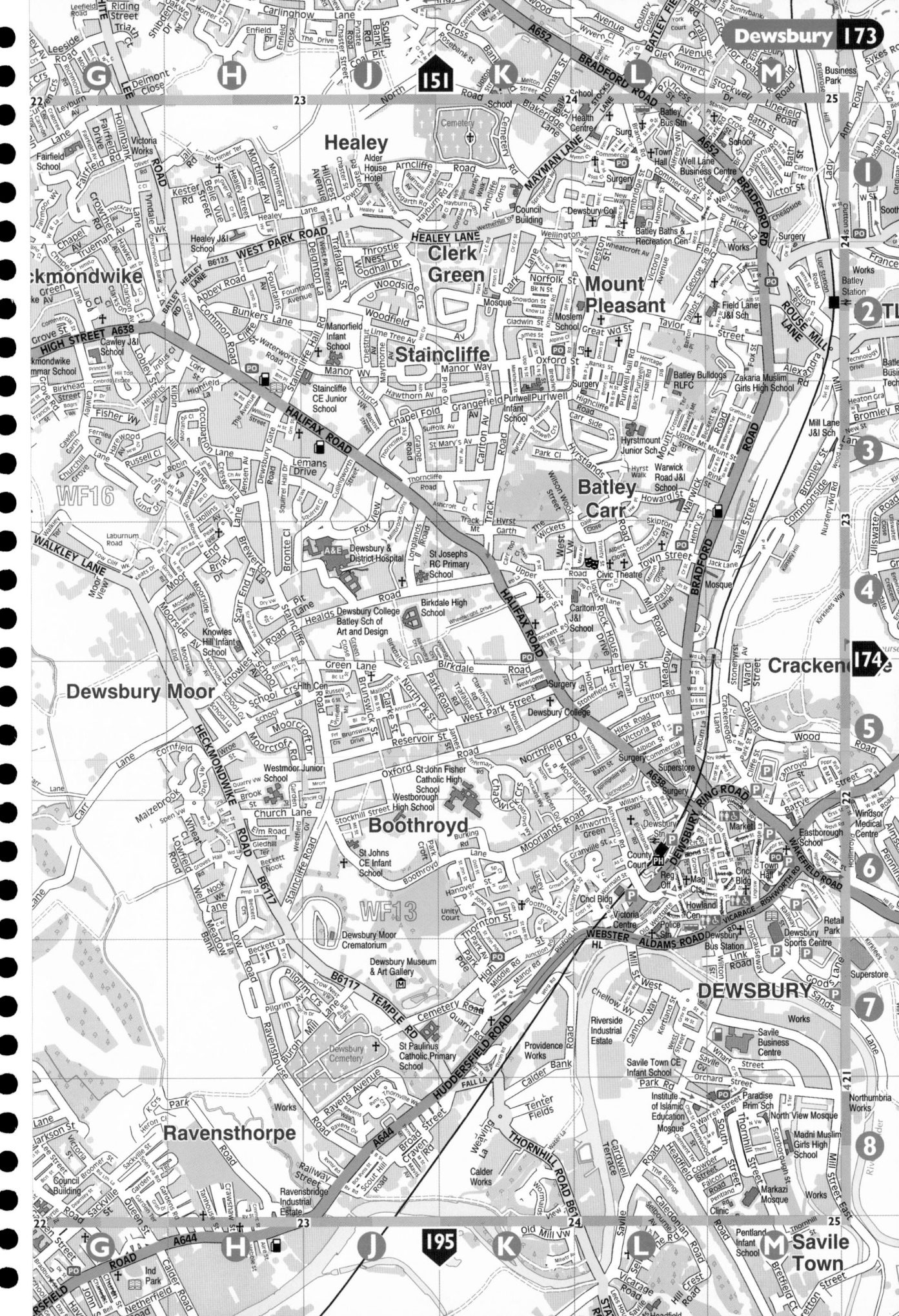

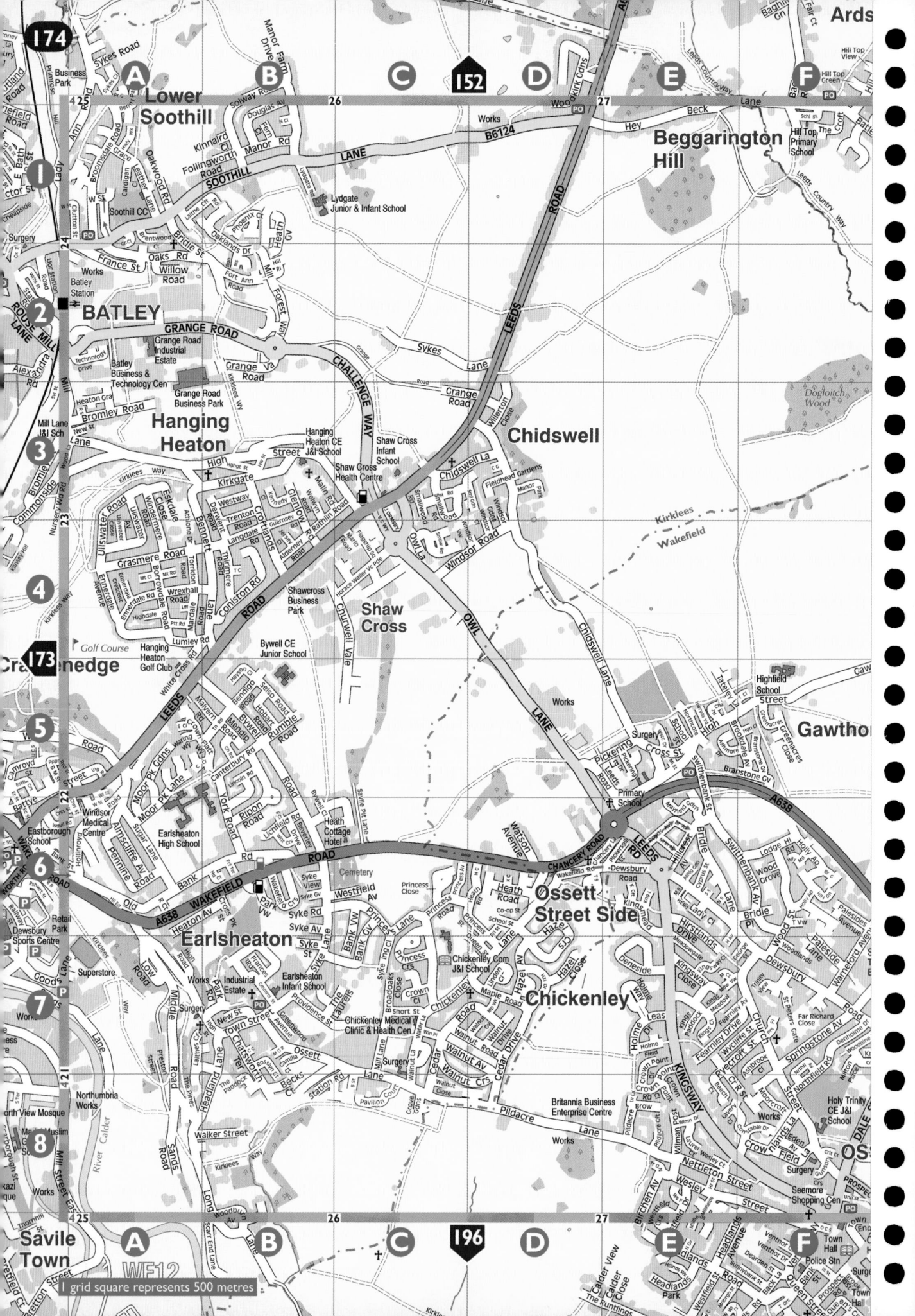

153

176

197

Junction 41

Junction 40

Brandy Carr

Beck Bottom

Kirkhamgate

Jaw Hill

Flushdyke

Shepherd Hill

Reservoir

East Ardsley
United CC

Haigh Moor

Woodhouse
Hall Farm

Red Lodge

Lower
Park Farm

Lodge
Hill

Woodhouse Lane

Blind Lane

Batley Road

Leeds Wakefield

Leeds Country Way

Leeds Country Way

Brandy Carr Road

Jerry Clay Lane

Lindale Lane

Lindale Garth

Sunny Cft

Sunny

Silcoates

Wrenthorpe Lane

Lindale Gv

Lindale Mt

The Mount

Harewood Dr

Childs Rd

Marion Gv

St Paul's Dr

Geary Cres

Geary Av

Billingham Cl

Allan Haigh Cl

St Pauls
J&I CE
School

Gelder
Rd

Jerry
Lane J&I
School

Larkspur

Batley Road

Park Mill Lane

Low Laithes
Golf Club

Golf Course

Laithes
Drive

Laithes Fold

New Park Lane

Flanshaw Way

Willow Road

Willow Fold

Willow
Brick St

Flanshaw Way

Industrial
Estate

Oakes St

Spout Fold

Eagle Gv

Springfield
Gra

Beechwood
Av

Days Inn
Hotel

The Office Village

Carr Gate
Crs

Carr Gate
Mount

yevale
Garden Centre

A650

WF5

Sandbeds
Trading Estate

Ashley
Industrial Estate

Eidon Street

Flushdyke
Primary Sch

A638

B6129

WAKEFIELD ROAD

Cross Keys

Jacksons
Estate

Smith Way

Milner Way

Mortimer Rise

Longlands Trading Estate

Milner

Towngate
Primary School

Works

Spring Mill Lane

A638 WAKEFIELD ROAD

DEWSBURY ROAD

Oakwood Av

Toplar Av

Ashleigh Avenue

Flanshaw Crs

English Martyrs
RC Primary School

Pump Lane

Redhill Av

Redhill Dr

Redhill Cl

Clarke Road

Hill Top Grove

Woollin Crs

Holly Ct

Moor

Rosedale Ct

HM VW

M1

Gawthorpe Lane

Greenlay Drive

New Row

Hawthorn Cl

Westfield

West Crs

West View

Kirkhamgate
Primary School

Caledonia
Court

Piccolins

Green
Avenue

Stoney Lane

WAKEFIELD ROAD

Queen's

Hinchliffe Av

Greatfield Cl

Athold

Indfield Avenue

Towngate

Broadway Drive

The Wheatings

New

Teall St

Sunnydale

Spring Crs

Tumbling Close

Whitley

PO

G H J K L M I 2 3 4 5 6 7 8

28 29 30 31

24 23 22

Boat

G H J 155 K L M

I

2

3

4

178

5

6

7

8

River Calder

Aire & Calder Navigation

Stanley

Hatfield Hall
Golf Club
Golf Course

Stanley Grove
J&I School

Birkwood
Farm

Birkwood Road

Stanley
Ferry

Newland Hall

West Yorkshire
College of
Health Studies
A&E

East
Moor

Wakefield
City High
School

Heath View
Community
School

WF1

Goosehill

Kirkthorpe

Warmf

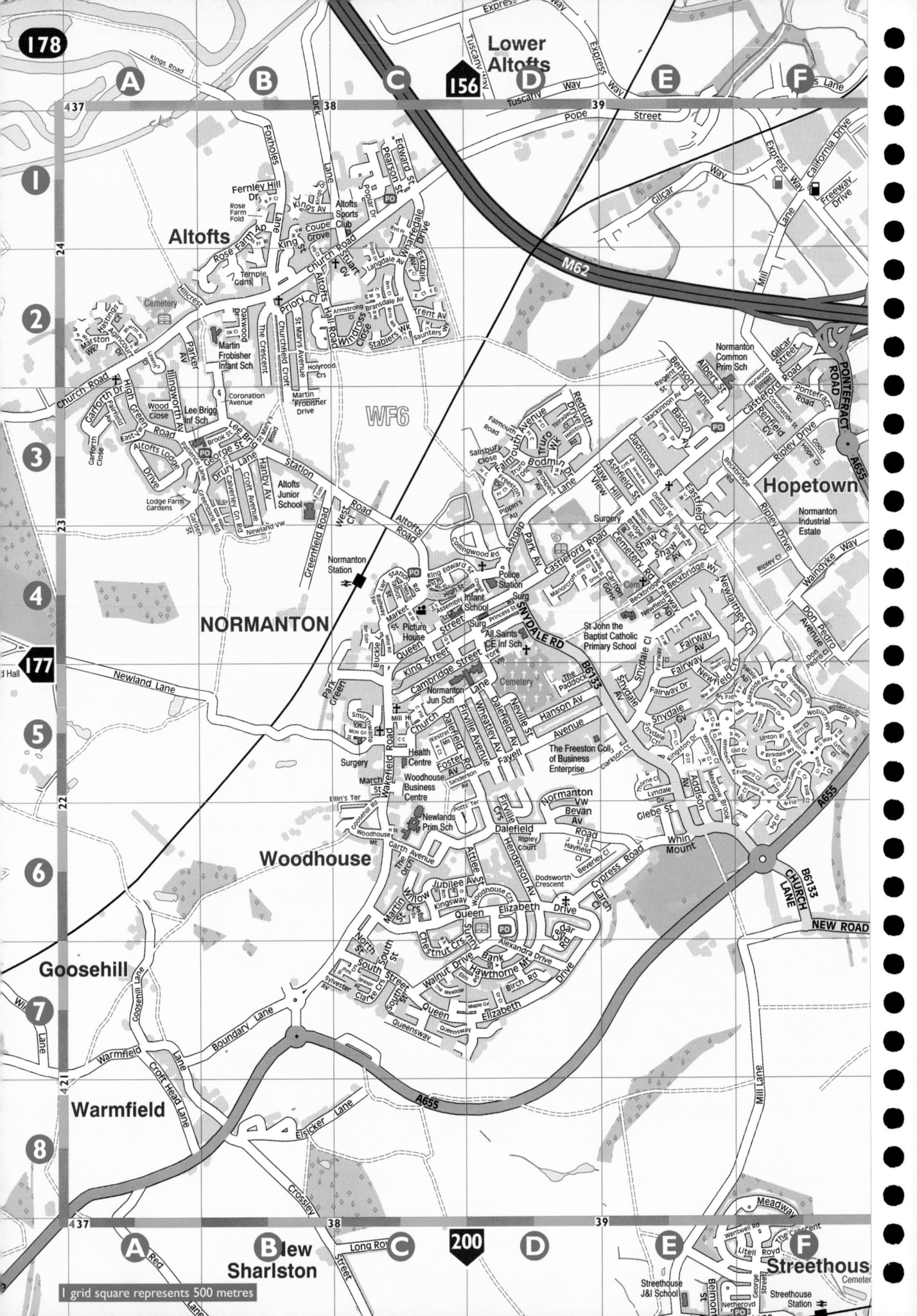

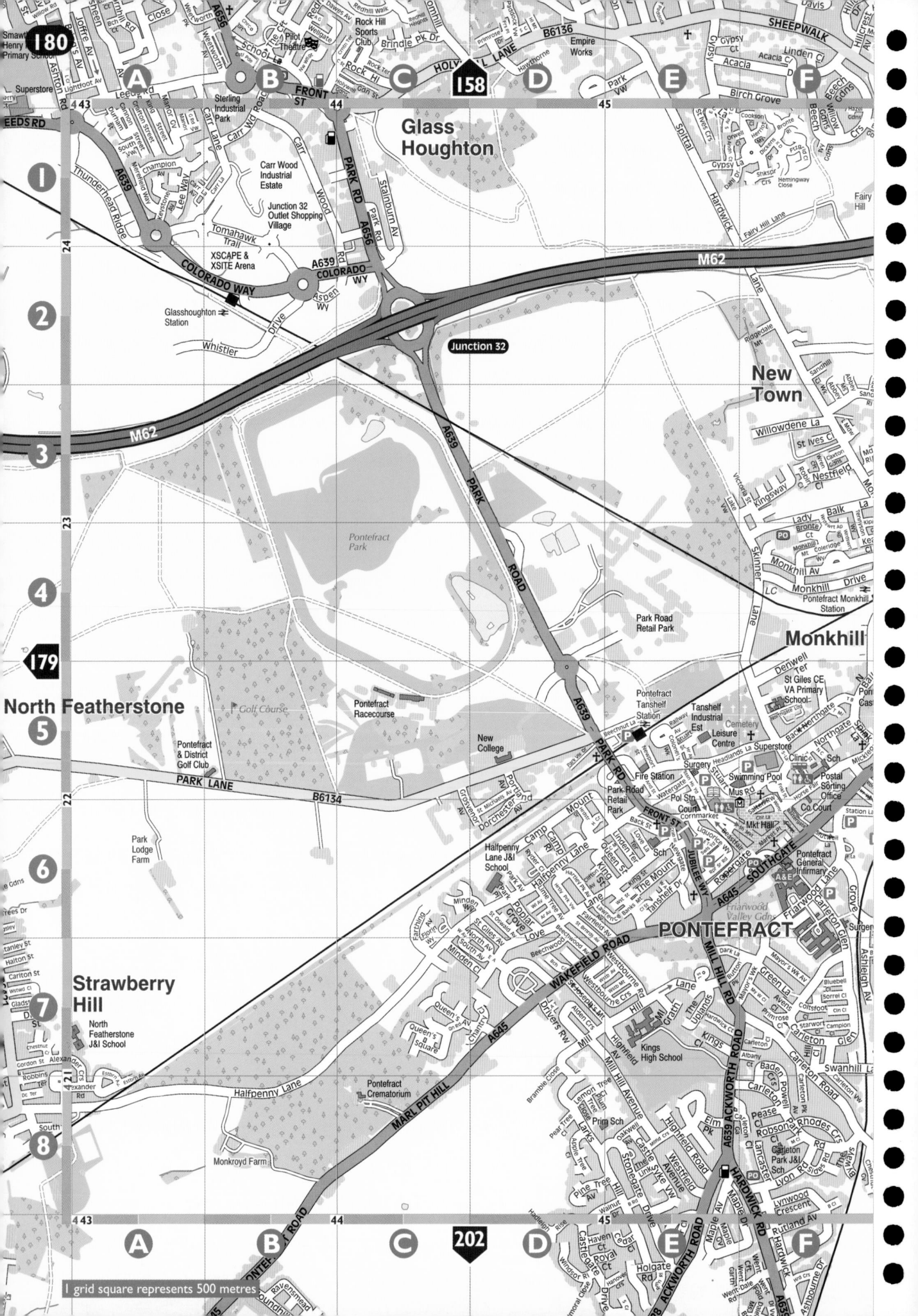

G H B6136 J **159** K A16 L **Ferrybridge** M

Junction 41

STRANGLANDS LANE

46 47 48 B6136 49

LANE Work Hinton

Holmfield Lane Strnglands

New Road

Roundhill Junior School Pollard's Fields King's Castleford Richmond Av Pontefract Road Ferrybridge Infant Sch Med Cen Surgery

Cemetery Houghton Dr Windsor St Andrews FISHERGATE Works

Wordsworth Dr Shelley Dr Crewe Wentcliffe Kingsley Pinders Crs FERRYBRIDGE RD North Vw Clifton F Business PO B6136

Orchard Head Drive Bronte Av Sandringham Av Linden Cl Harewood Elizabeth Vale Knottingley Vale J&I School **2**

Orchard Head Primary School Holmfield Mill Vw Doncaster Road Snowdon Cr Vale **PONTEFRACT RD** Headland

Orchard Head Limetrees Pontefract Road A1 Business Park A162 PONTEFRACT RD Knottingley Station

Queensway Duverton Manor Pk Av Stumpcross La Sowgate La A645 Chevet Business Centre Rossiter Drive Simpsons Mirey Butt La Warren **3** Health Centre

Water La Stumpcross Wy Premier Travel Inn A162 Mirey Butt La Simpsons Lane J&I School Cherry Tree Elm

Works Dandy MI KNOTTINGLEY ROAD Cattlelaith Sycamore Avenue **4**

Black Mill Dam BONDGATE A645 Bexhill Close Longbull Hill Ferrybridge Service Area Travelodge **182**

Baileygate Bondgate Industrial Est Cobblers La A11(M) Junction 33 **5**

Pontefract Castle All Saints Industrial Est Baileygate Industrial Est Northfield Poplar Green Holy Family & St Michaels RC Primary School 22

Baghill Station Eastfield Drive Cobblers Lane Greavefield La Grovehall Lane Grove Hall **6**

Harewood Mt Harefield Road Cobblers Lane Junior School South Vw Gdns Eastbourne

Willow Pk Chequerfield Av Eastbourne Chequerfield View **7**

Grove Town Willow Park Junior School School Road East Drive Rookhill Lane Long A162 Junction 40 421

Friars Nook King's Crescent Rookhill Rd Chequerfield Infant School Spitalgap Lane Marlpit Hodgewood **8**

Chequerfield Long La Street Furlong Lane

Carleton Road The Rookeries Carleton J&I School Havercroft

46 47 48 49

G H Carlton J **203** K L **Darrington** M A1

Carleton High School Darrington CE J&I School Mid Yorkshir Golf Club

G   H   J   **161**   K   L   M

52   53   54   55

1
2
3
4
5
6
7
8

Lunn Lane
Pick Haven Garth
Garth
Street
Whales Lane
24
PO

WEELAND ROAD   A645

The Oval
Shaftesbury Avenue
Sudforth Lane
Weeland Road

ellingley

Turver's Lane
Works

Thornfield House

Southfield Lane

LC
Turver's Lane

LC

Stubbs Bridge

common Lane

Beal Lane

Aire and Calder Navigation

(Knottingley and Goole Canal)

23

Kelli
Com

Wakefield   M62   M62

North Yorkshire County

Cobcroft Lane

Whitefield Lane

22

Cridling Stubbs

croft Lane

Spring Lodge

421

Lane

Grange Farm

Boot

LC

52   53   54   55

G   H   J   **205**   K   L   M

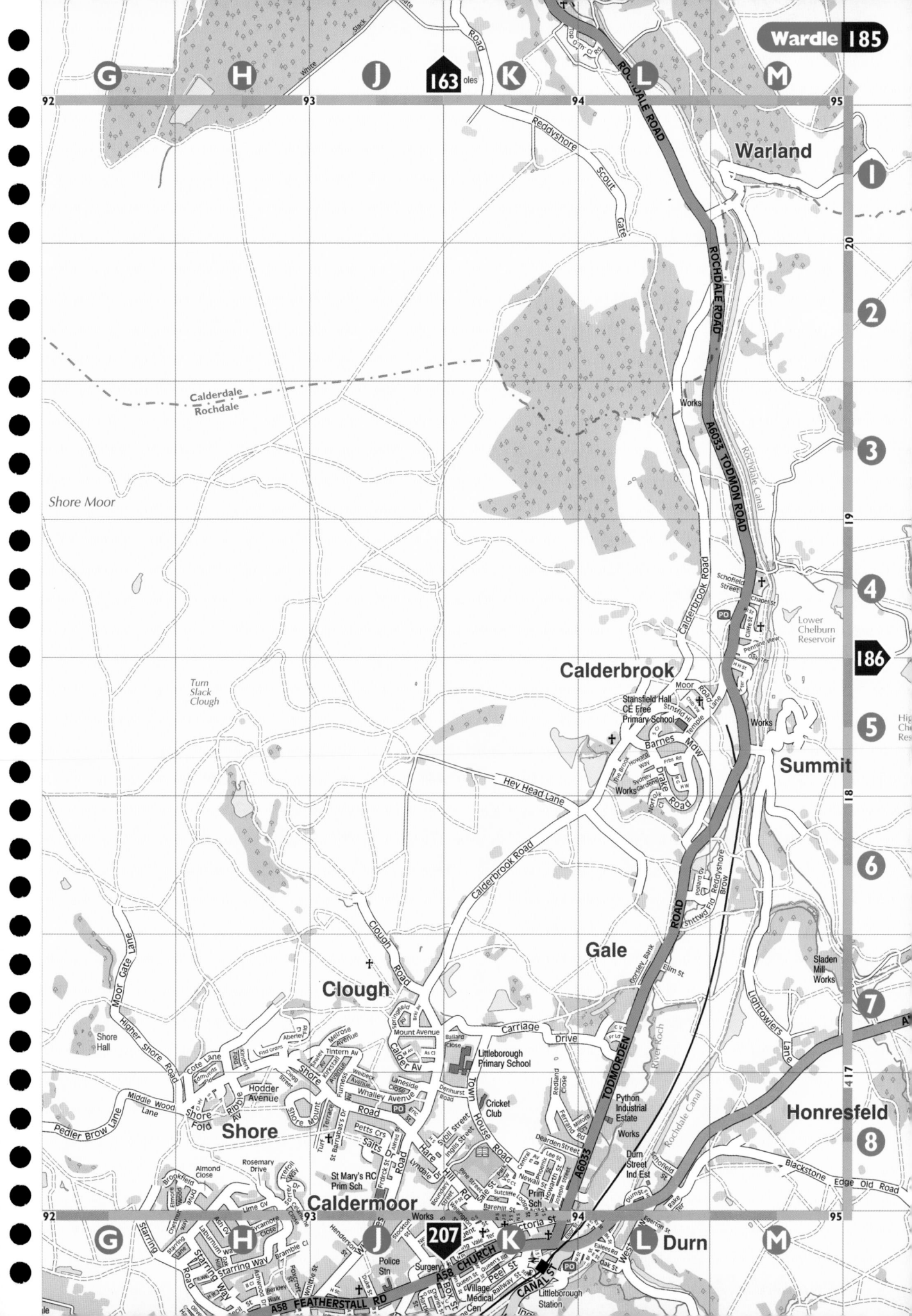

G H J **163** K L M

92 93 94 95

1
2
3
4
186
5
6
7
8

20
19
18
417

Warland

Calderdale
Rochdale

Shore Moor

Works

ROCHDALE ROAD

A6033 TODMON ROAD

Rochdale Canal

Reddyshore

Scout Gate

Schofield
Street

Chapel St

PO

Pennine View

Oak Ter

Lower
Chelburn
Reservoir

Calderbrook Road

Calderbrook

Stansfield Hall
CE Free
Primary School

Stnsfld Hl

Moor
Road Lne

Temple

Works

Summit

Hi
Ch
Res

Barnes Mdw

The Brook

Howard
Way

Sydney
Gardens

Norfolk

Drake Road

Frds Rd

C
HW

Turn
Slack
Clough

Hey Head Lane

Works

Calderbrook Road

Gale

Reddyshore
Brow

Shttwg Fld

Gorsey Bank

Elim St

ROAD

River Roch

Rochdale Canal

Sladen
Mill
Works

Lightowlers Lane

Honresfield

Clough

Clough Road

Springfield

Mount Avenue

Carriage Drive

Littleborough
Primary School

Ballard
Close

Fr Ld

C V

TODMORDEN

A6033

Python
Industrial
Estate

Works

Durn
Street
Ind Est

Blackstone
Edge Old Road

Moor Gate Lane

Higher Shore Road

Shore
Hall

Cote Lane

Shore

Edmunds
Av

Kinders

Aberley

Sawley

Melrose
Avenue

Tintern Av

Whalley Avenue

Furness
Avenue

Weneck
Avenue

Calder Av

Redland
Close

Ferrand Rd

Milnrow

Shore

Middle Wood
Lane

Pedler Brow Lane

Hodder
Avenue

Ripble
AV

Shore
Fold

Shore
Mount

Terrace

St Barnabas's Dr

Turf

Salts
Dr

Petts Crs

Shore
Road

Lyndale

Hare
Hill
Rd

Scoil Street

Ingls Street

PO

Town House Road

Cricket
Club

Dearden Street

Newal

Central

Lee St

Howarth
St

Prim
Sch

Sutcliffe Lodge

Shore

Shore

Almond
Close

Brookfield

Elmore

Rosemary
Drive

Trefoil
Walk

Sorrel Walk

Lime Gv

St Mary's RC
Prim Sch

Caldermoor

Works

Henderson St

Victoria St

Police
Stn

Surgery

207

Bridge St

A58 CHURCH

PO

Village
Medical
Cen

Littleborough
Station

CANAL

Durn

Durn St

Rake

Egerton St

Schofield
St

Eales Rd

Oak St

G H J **207** K L M

92 93 94 95

A58 FEATHERSTALL RD

Starring Road

Starring Way

Berkley
Walk

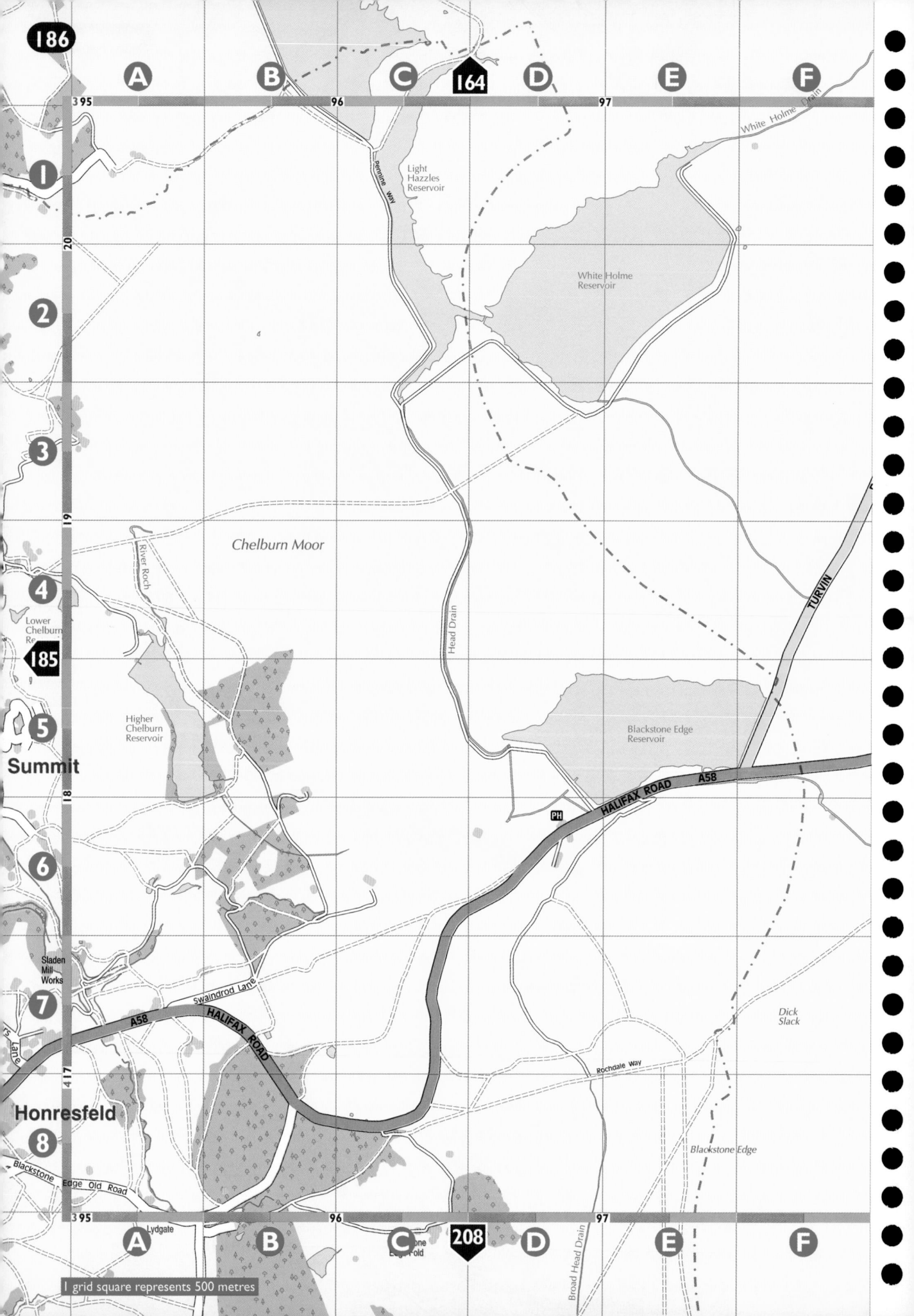

A   B   C   164   D   E   F

3 95   96   97

White Holme Drain

1

Pennine Way

Light
Hazzles
Reservoir

2

White Holme
Reservoir

3

Chelburn Moor

River Roch

4

Lower
Chelburn
Re

185

Head Drain

Higher
Chelburn
Reservoir

5

Summit

Blackstone Edge
Reservoir

TURVIN

HALIFAX ROAD   A58

PH

6

Sladen
Mill
Works

Swaindrod Lane

Dick
Slack

7

A58   HALIFAX ROAD

's Lane

4 17

Rochdale Way

Honresfeld

8

Blackstone
Edge Old Road

Blackstone Edge

Broad Head Drain

A   B   C   208   D   E   F

3 95   96   97

Lydgate   one
Edge Fold

1 grid square represents 500 metres

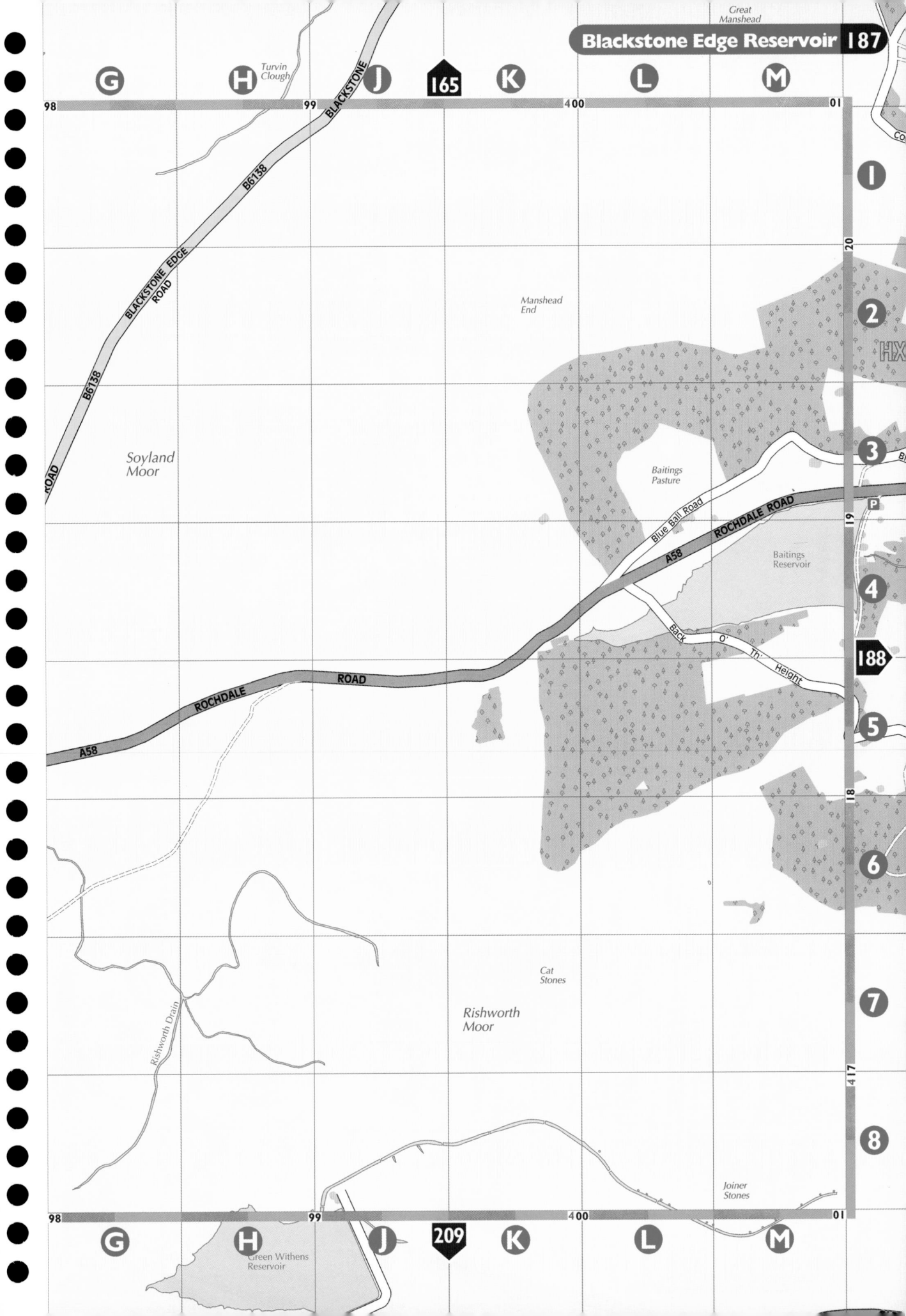

G   H   J   165   K   L   M

Turvin
Clough

BLACKSTONE

98   99   BLACKSTONE   400   01

I

B6138

BLACKSTONE EDGE
ROAD

Great
Manshead

Manshead
End

2

HX

B6138

Baitings
Pasture

3

Br

Soyland
Moor

Blue Ball Road   ROCHDALE ROAD

P

ROAD

A58   19

Baitings
Reservoir

4

Back   O'   Th'   Height

ROCHDALE   ROAD

188

A58   ROCHDALE

5

18

6

Rishworth Drain

Cat
Stones

7

Rishworth
Moor

417

8

Joiner
Stones

98   99   400   01

G   H   J   209   K   L   M

Green Withens
Reservoir

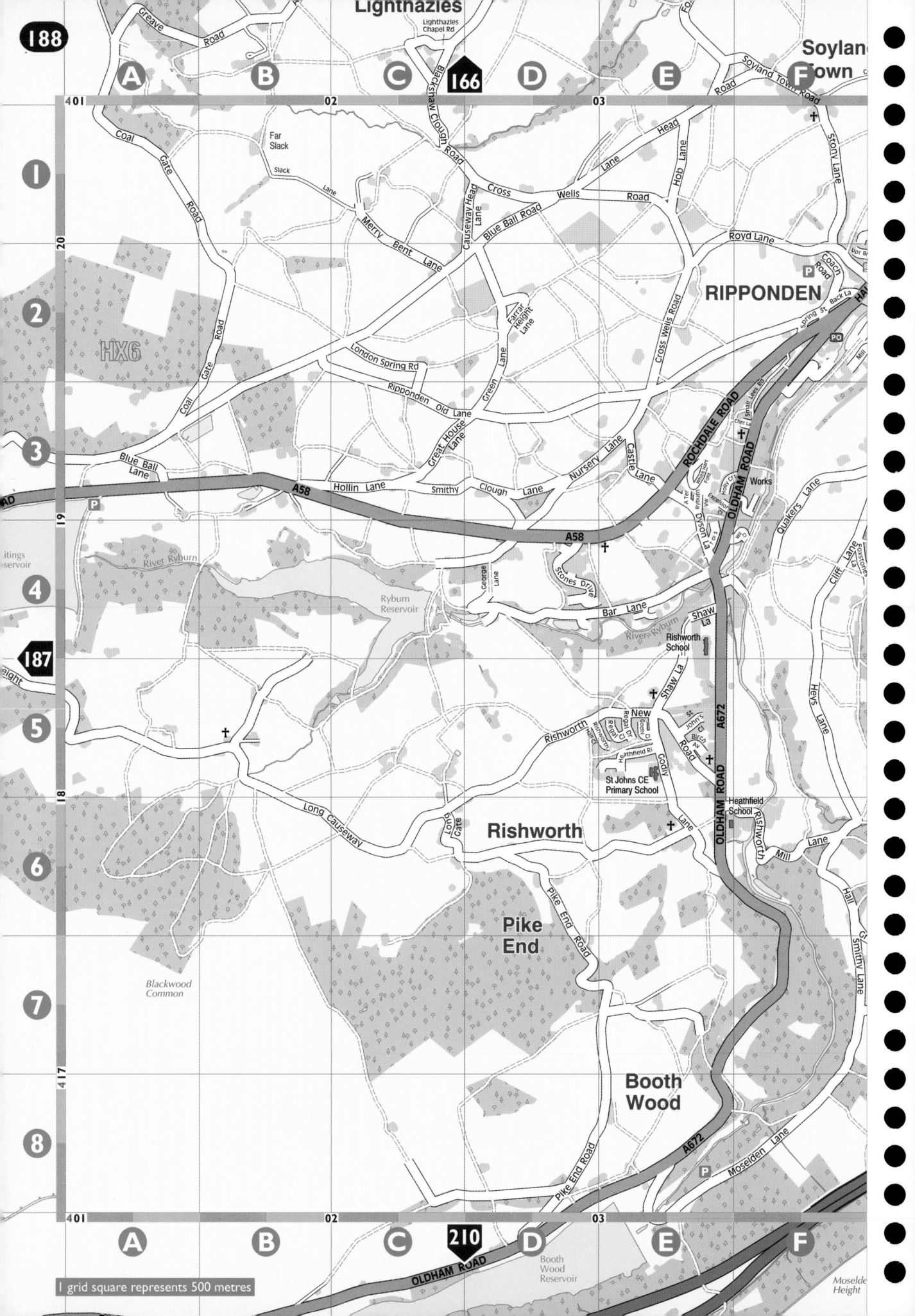

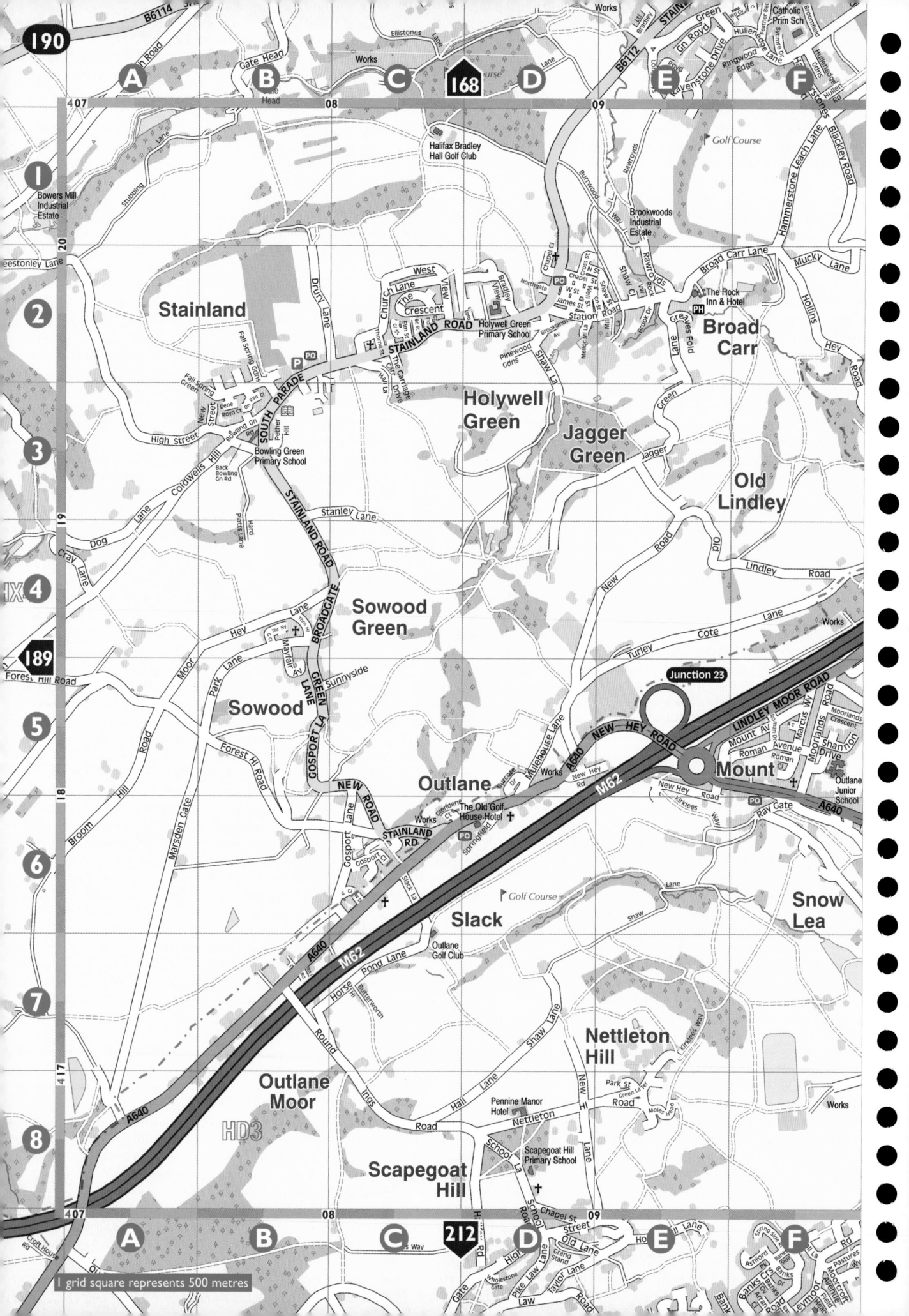

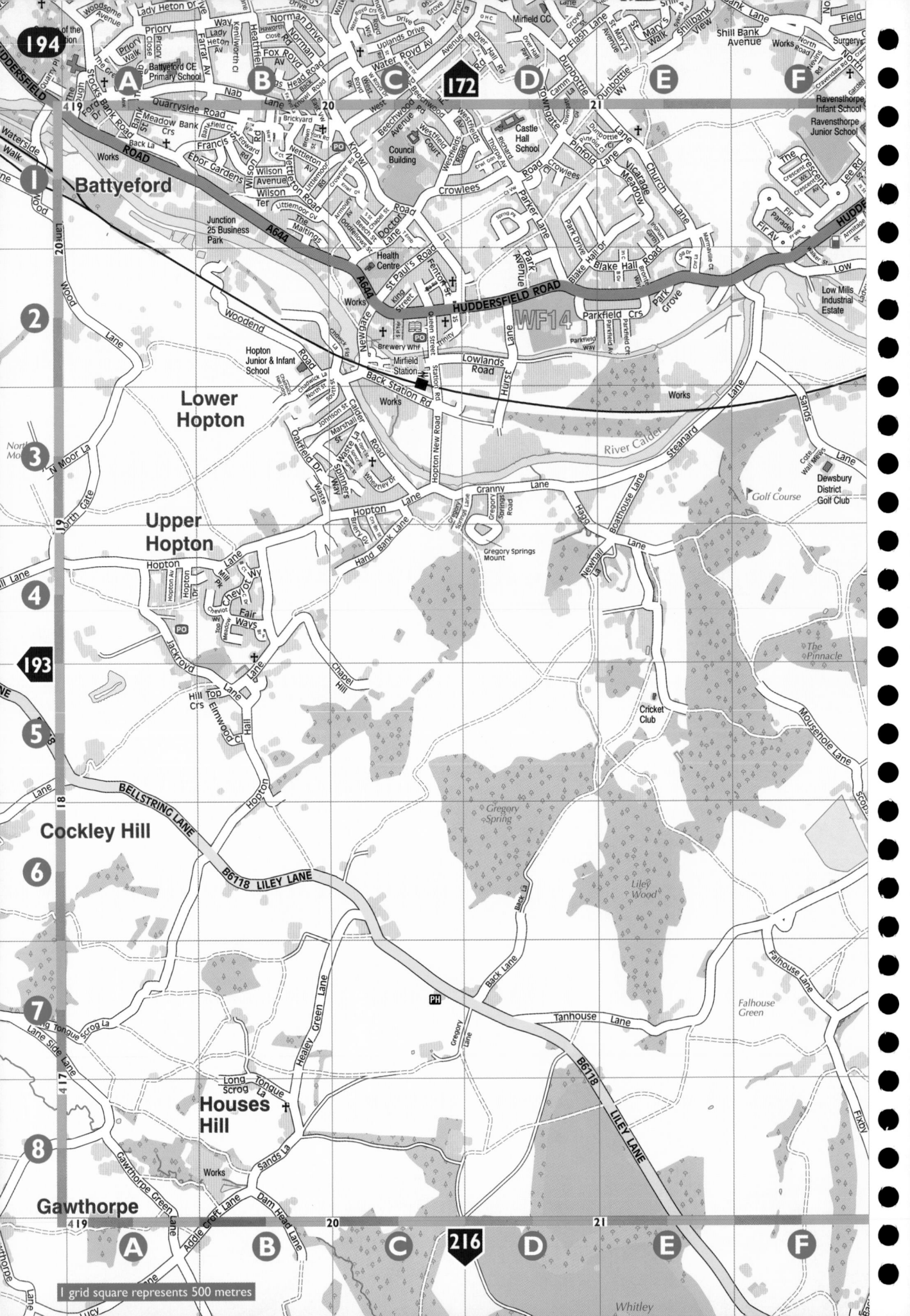

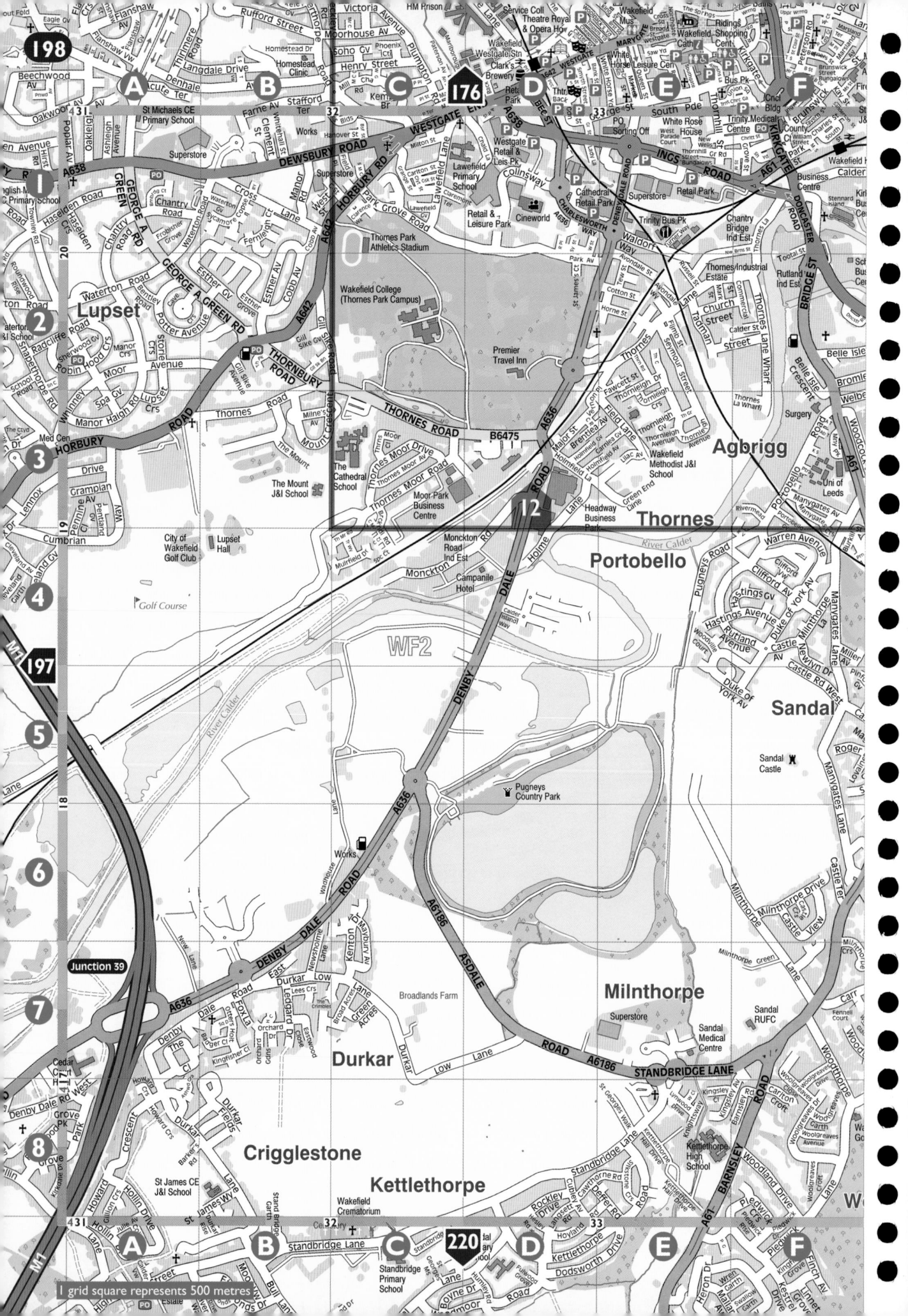

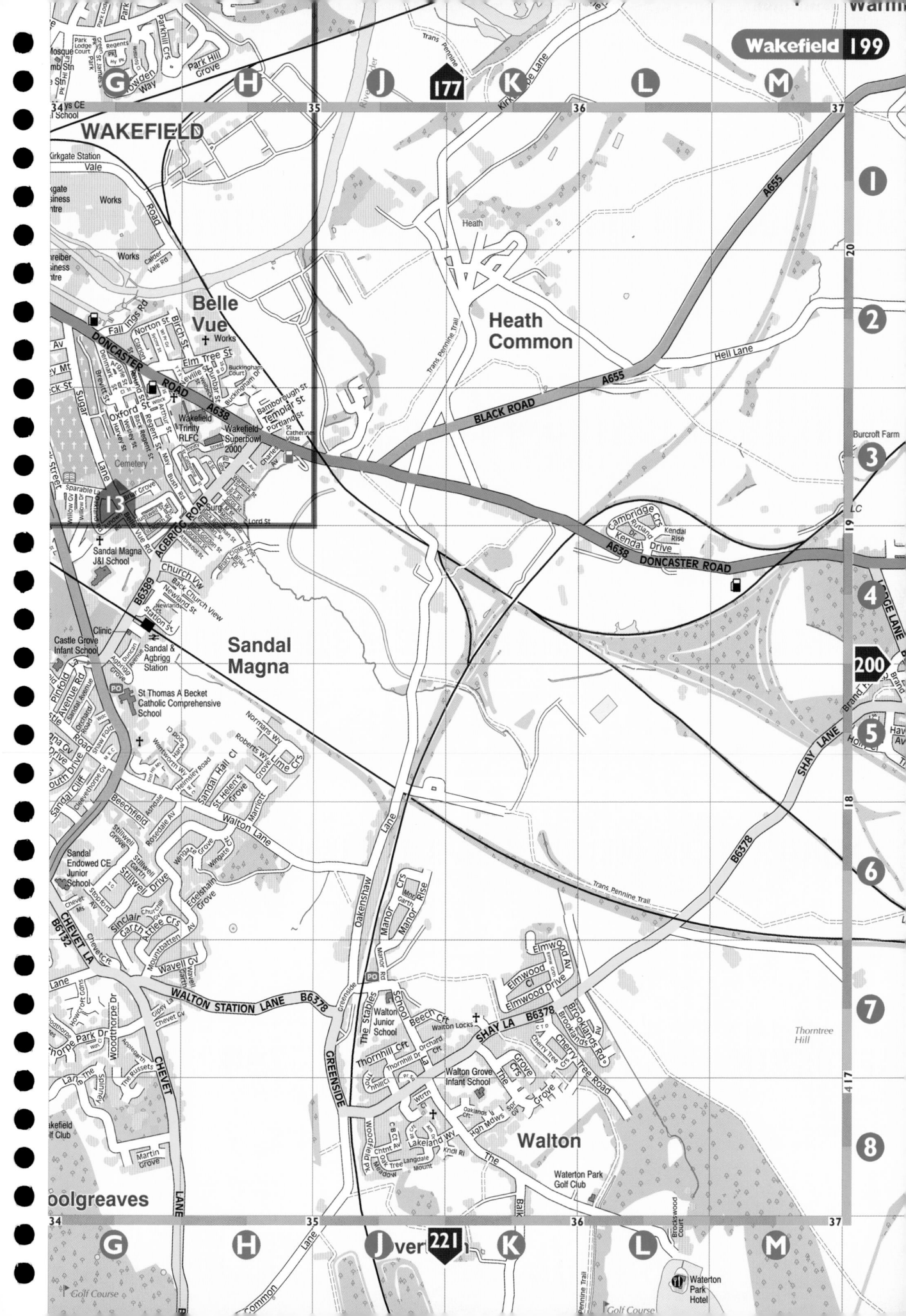

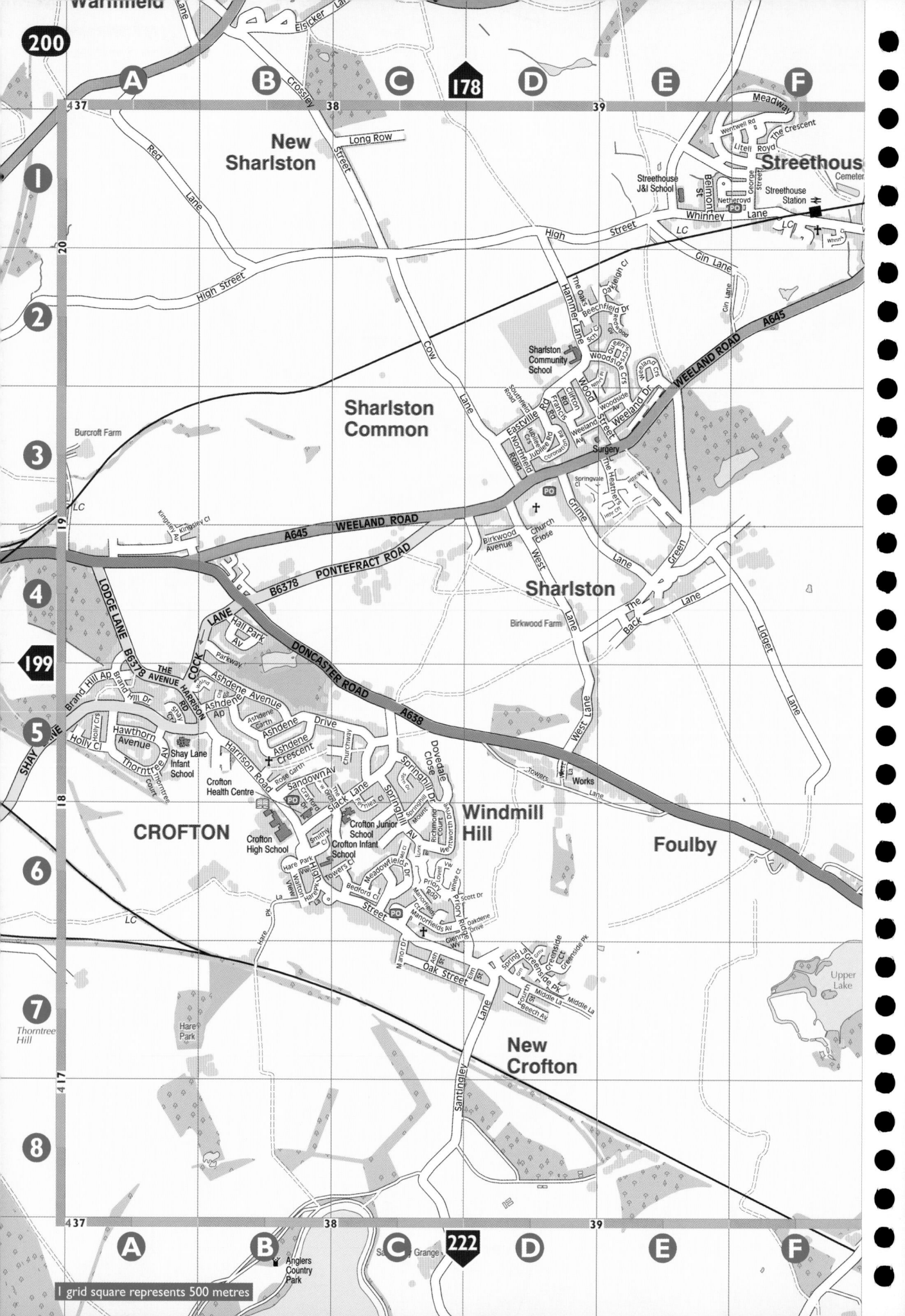

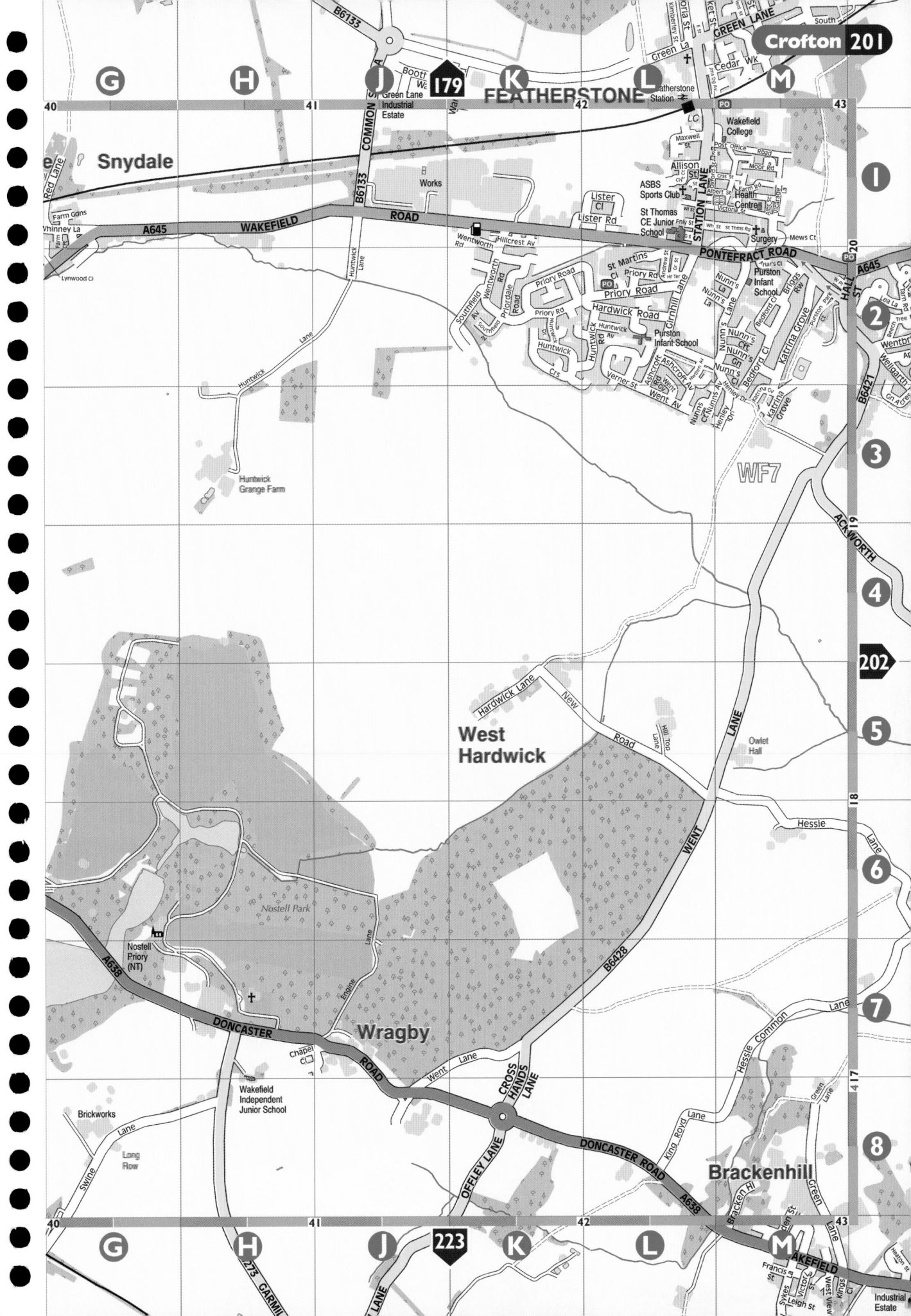

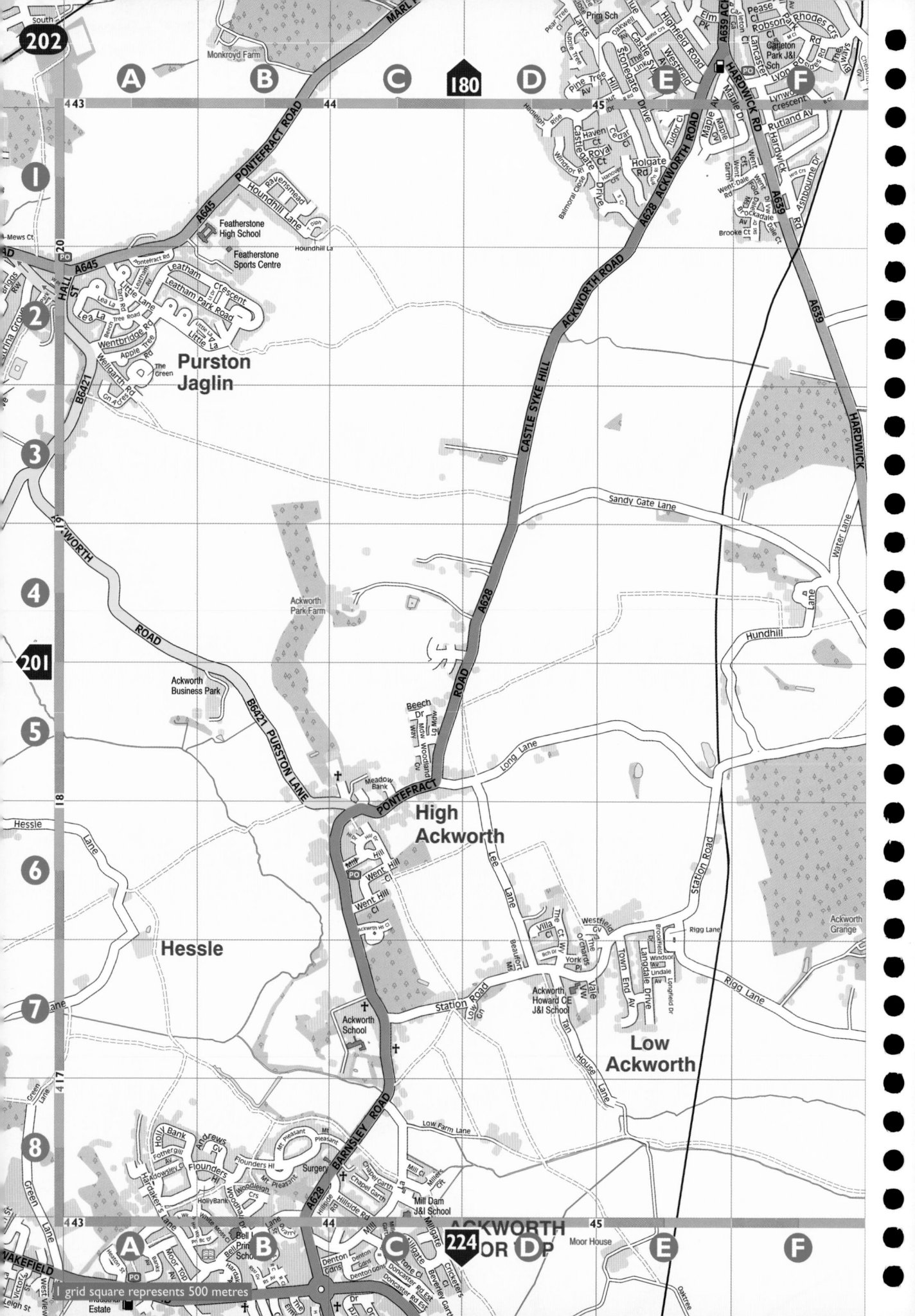

182 Vake Vood

A   B   C   D   E   F

449   50   51

Mid Yorkshire
Golf Club

Havercroft

I
20
2

court
Road
Premier
Travel Inn

Valley
Gdns
Valley   Road

Bank Wood Road

North Lodge Lane

Scrombeck
Farm

Newroad   Works
End

Bank   Wood

Stapleton Park Farm

3
19
4

203

5
18

North Yorkshire County
Wakefield

Stapleton
Park

New Road

Castle Farm

6

Jacksons
Hill

Wentbridge
House Hotel

Jackson's   Lane

Leys   Lane

7

River Went

417

WENT EDGE ROAD B6474

A1

Went Edge Road

8

449   50   51

Kirk Smeaton

A   B   C   226   D   E   F

Main   Street
PO
Kirk Sm
CE Prin
Manor School
Close

Pin   Lane

Norton

I grid square represents 500 metres

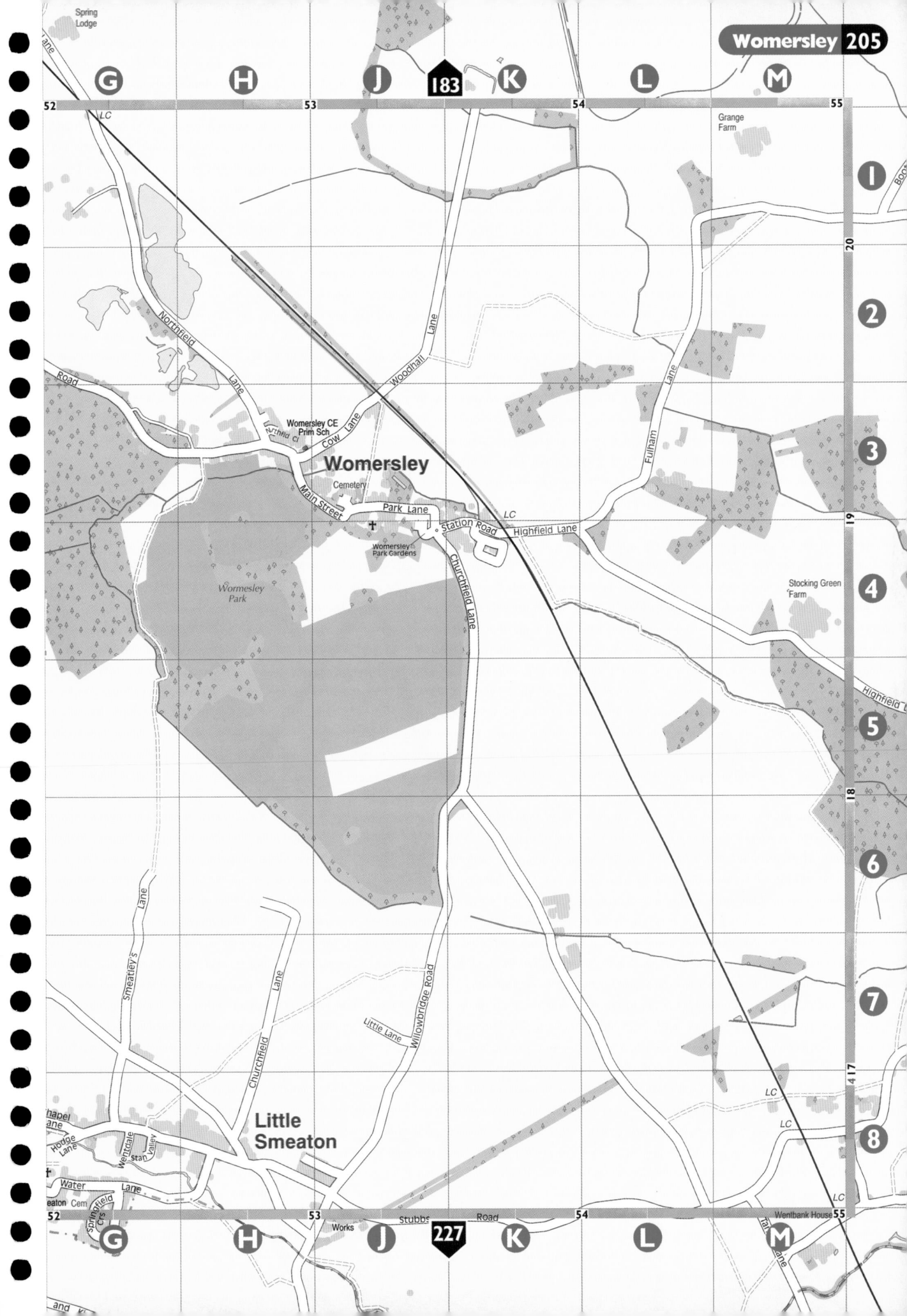

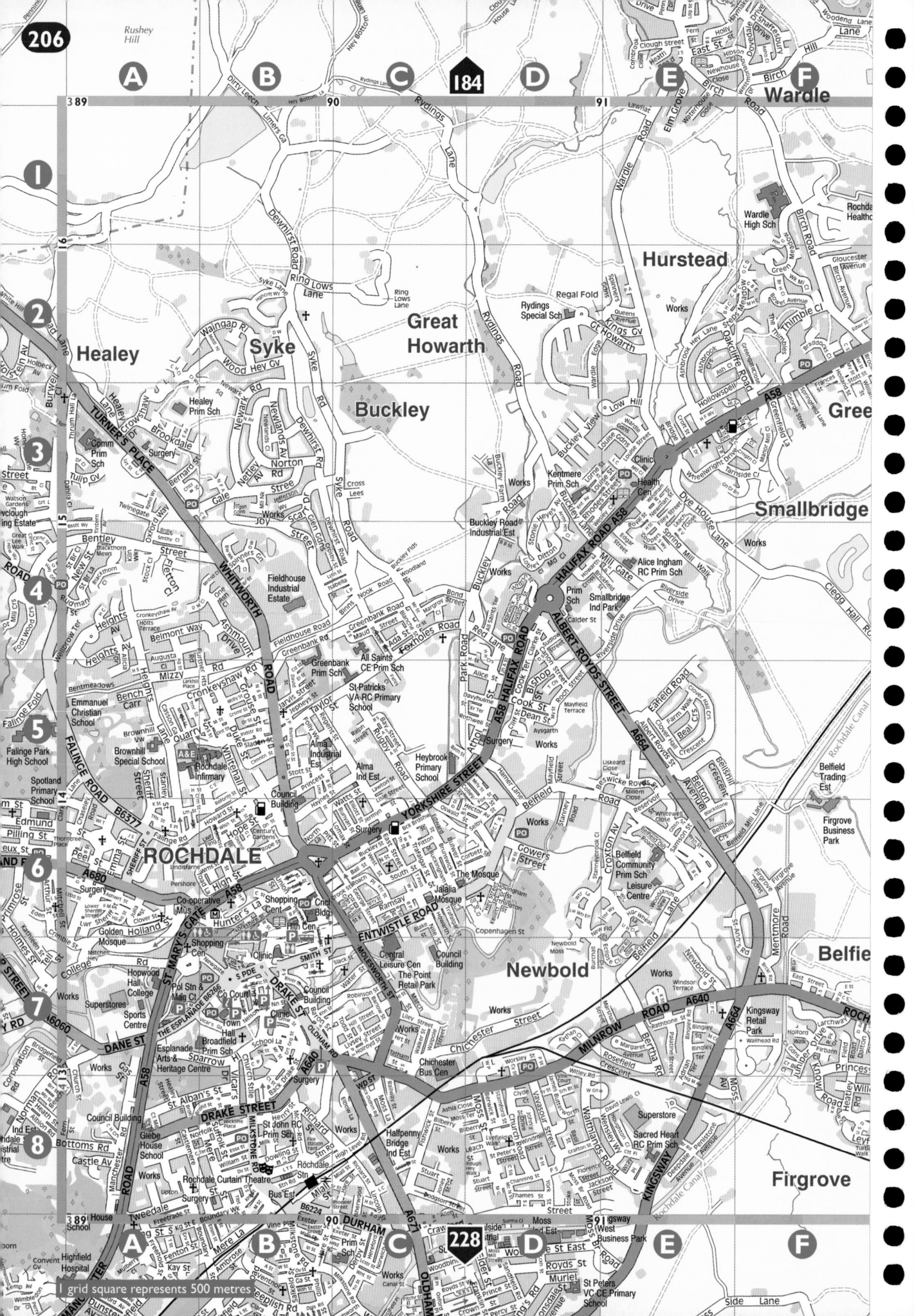

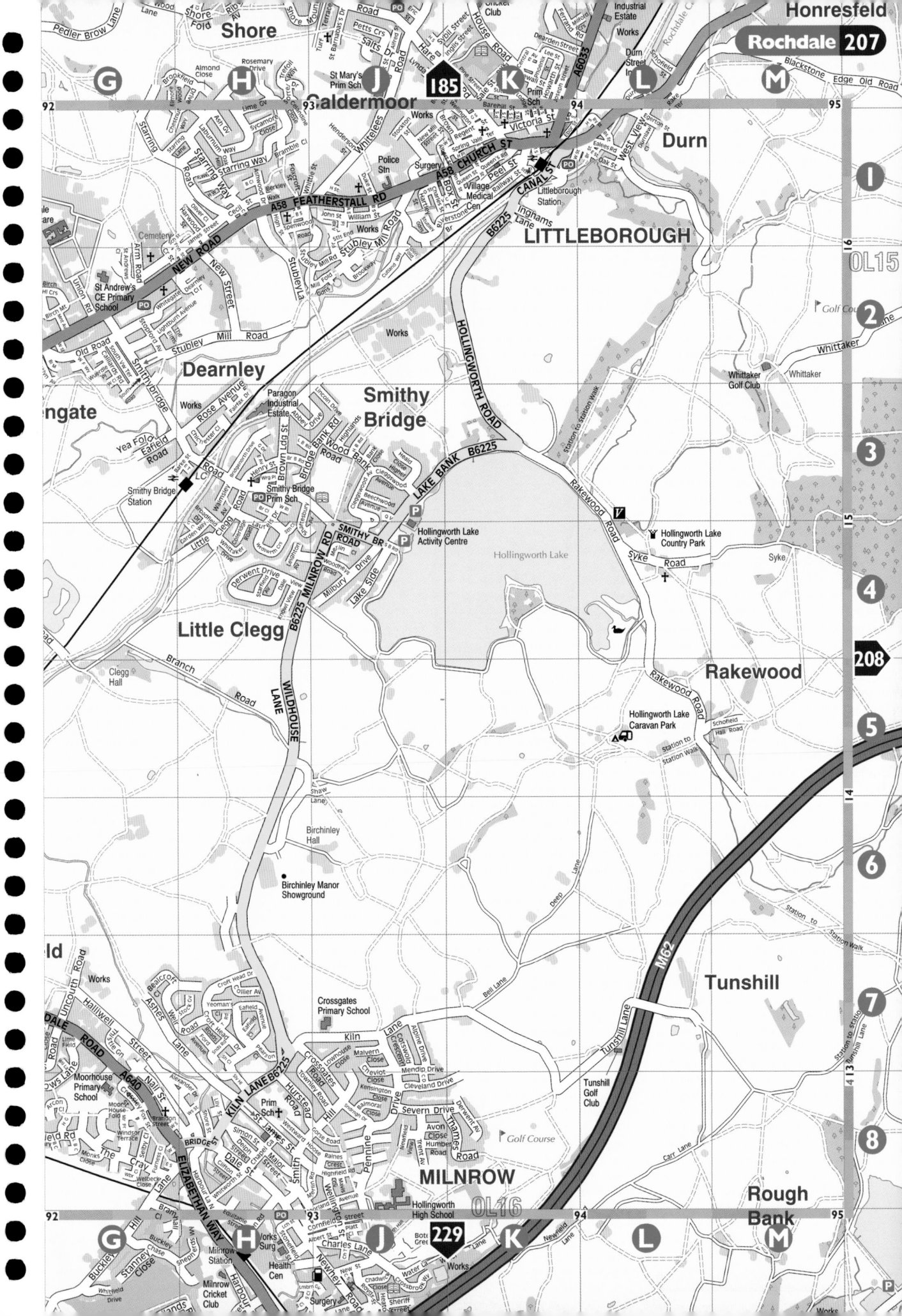

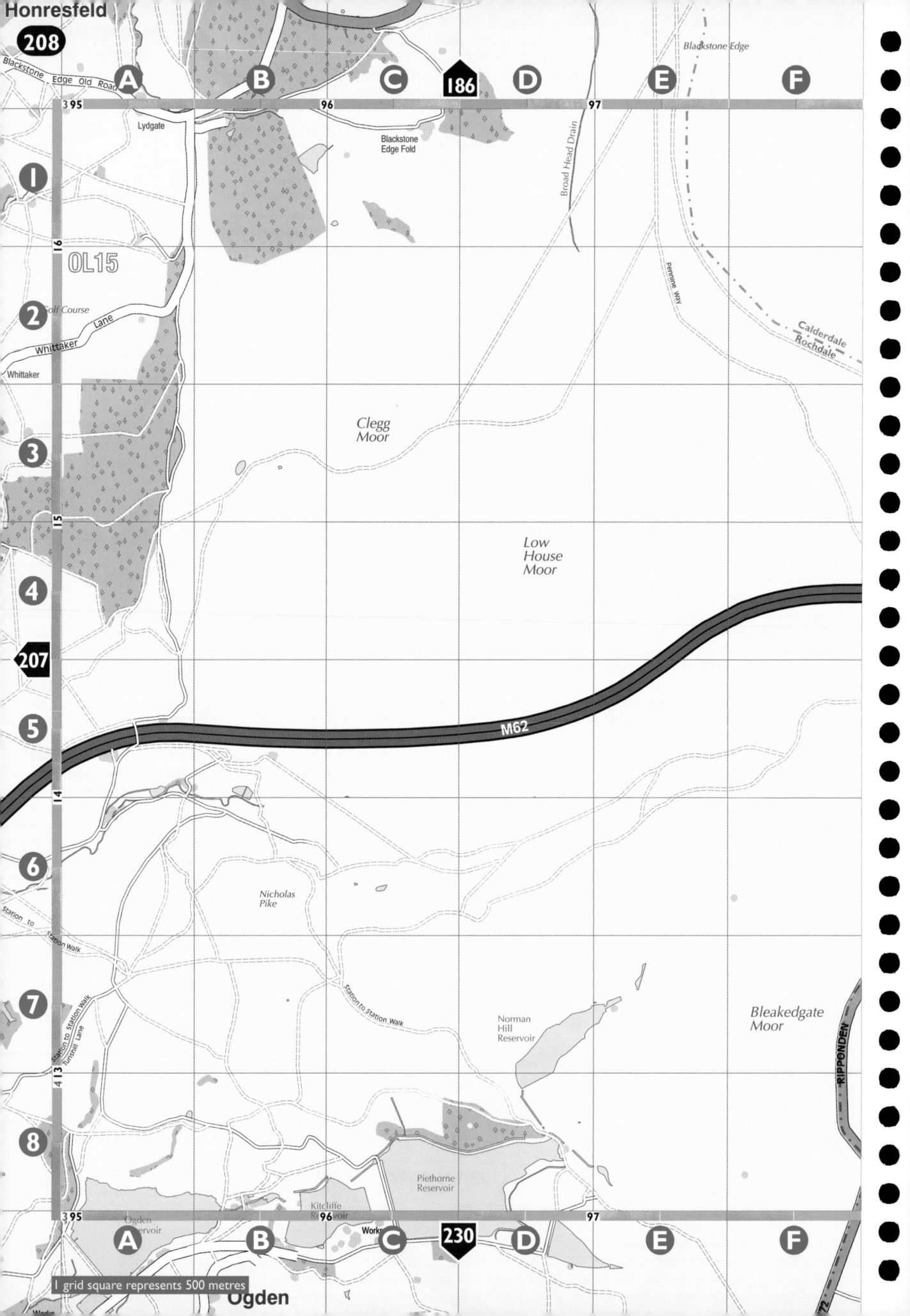

Blackstone Edge Old Road

A   **B**   **C** **186** **D**   **E**   **F**

3 95   96   97

Blackstone Edge

Lydgate

Blackstone Edge Fold

Broad Head Drain

1

16

OL15

Pennine Way

Calderdale
Rochdale

2

Golf Course

Whittaker   Lane

Whittaker

Clegg Moor

3

15

Low House Moor

4

207

M62

5

14

6

Nicholas Pike

Station to Station Walk

7

Station to Station Walk

Turnhill Lane

Station to Station Walk

Norman Hill Reservoir

Bleakedgate Moor

RIPPONDEN

4 13

8

Piethorne Reservoir

Ogden Reservoir

Kitcliffe Reservoir

Works

3 95   96   97

A   **B**   **C** **230** **D**   **E**   **F**

I grid square represents 500 metres

Ogden

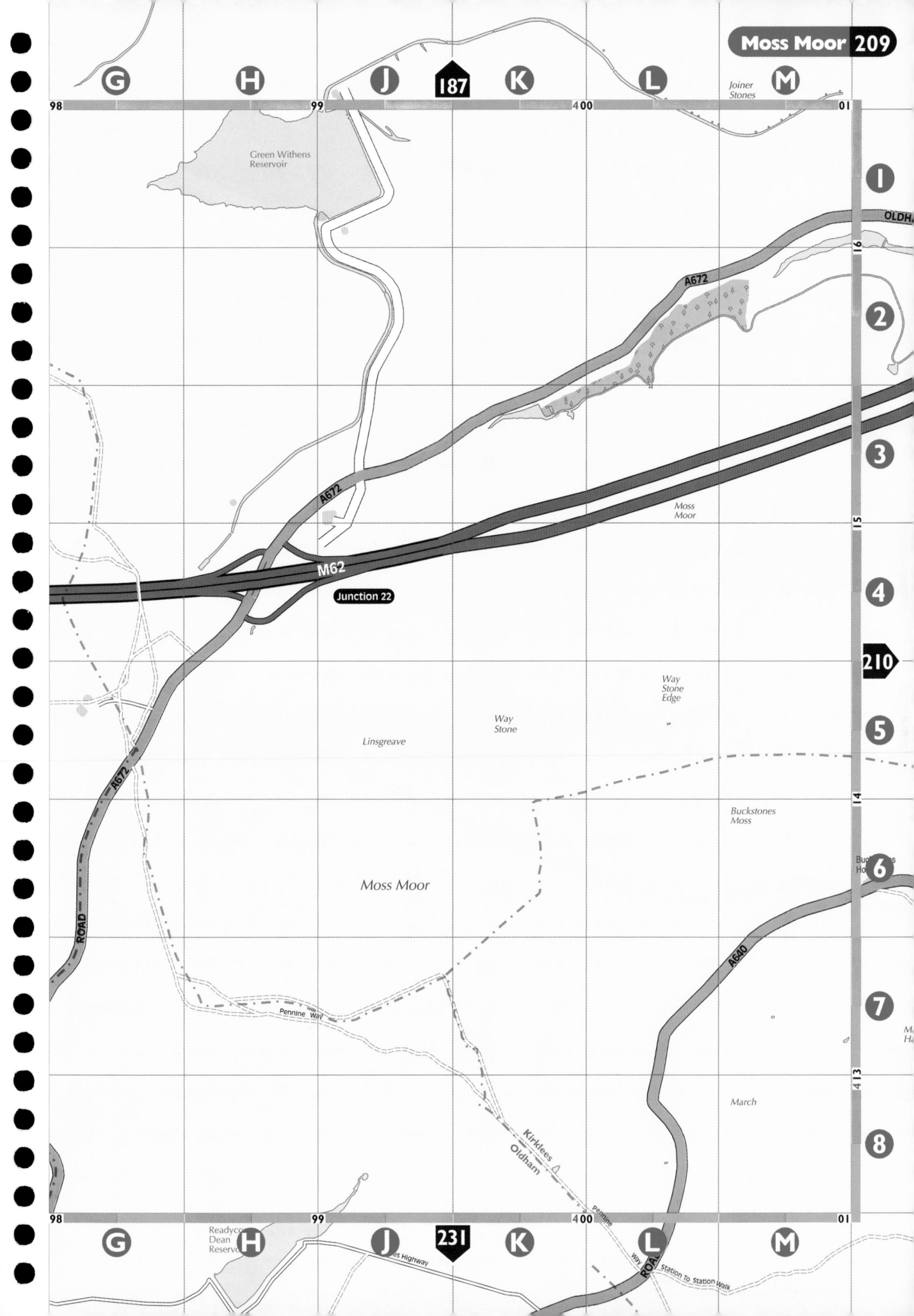

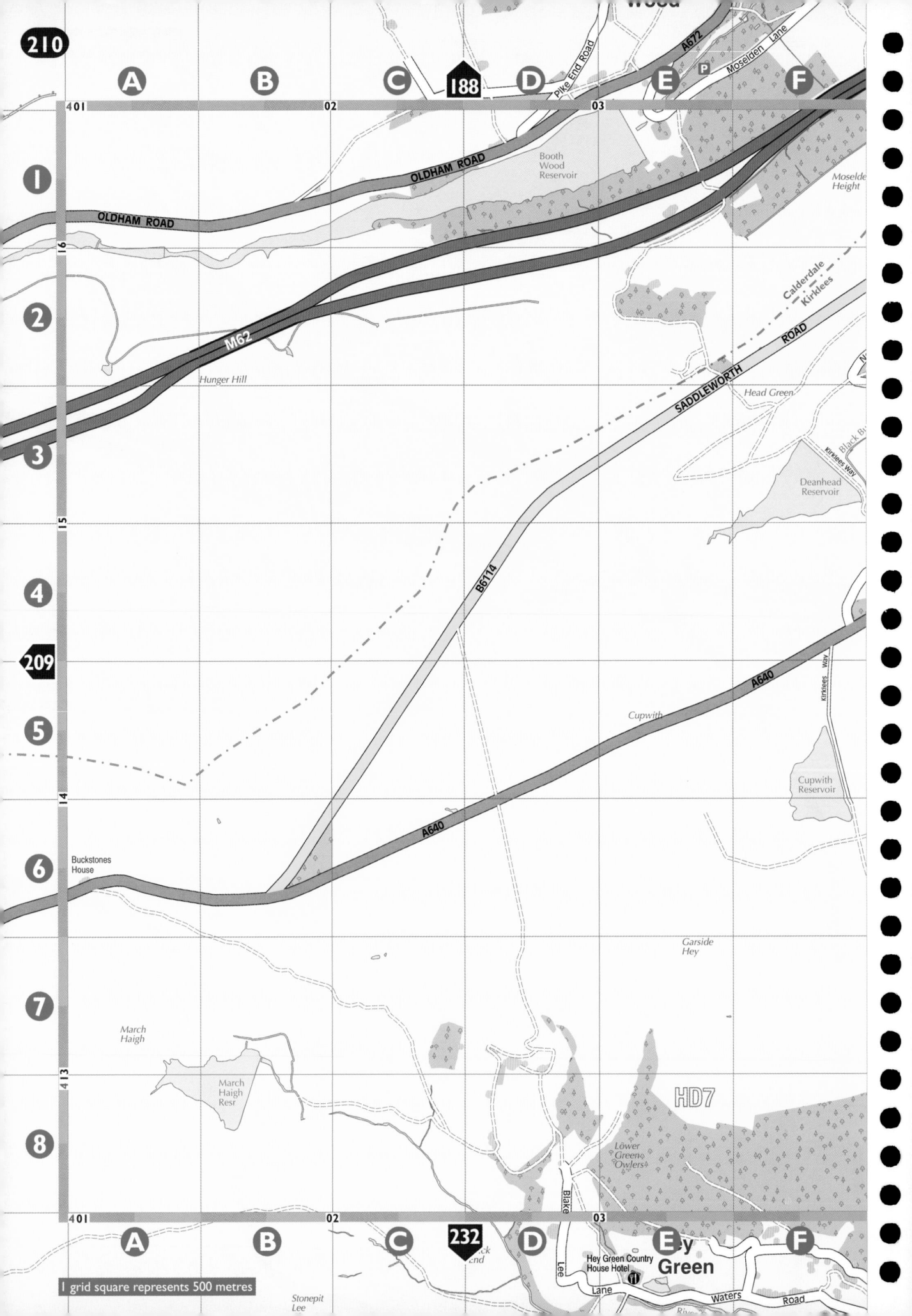

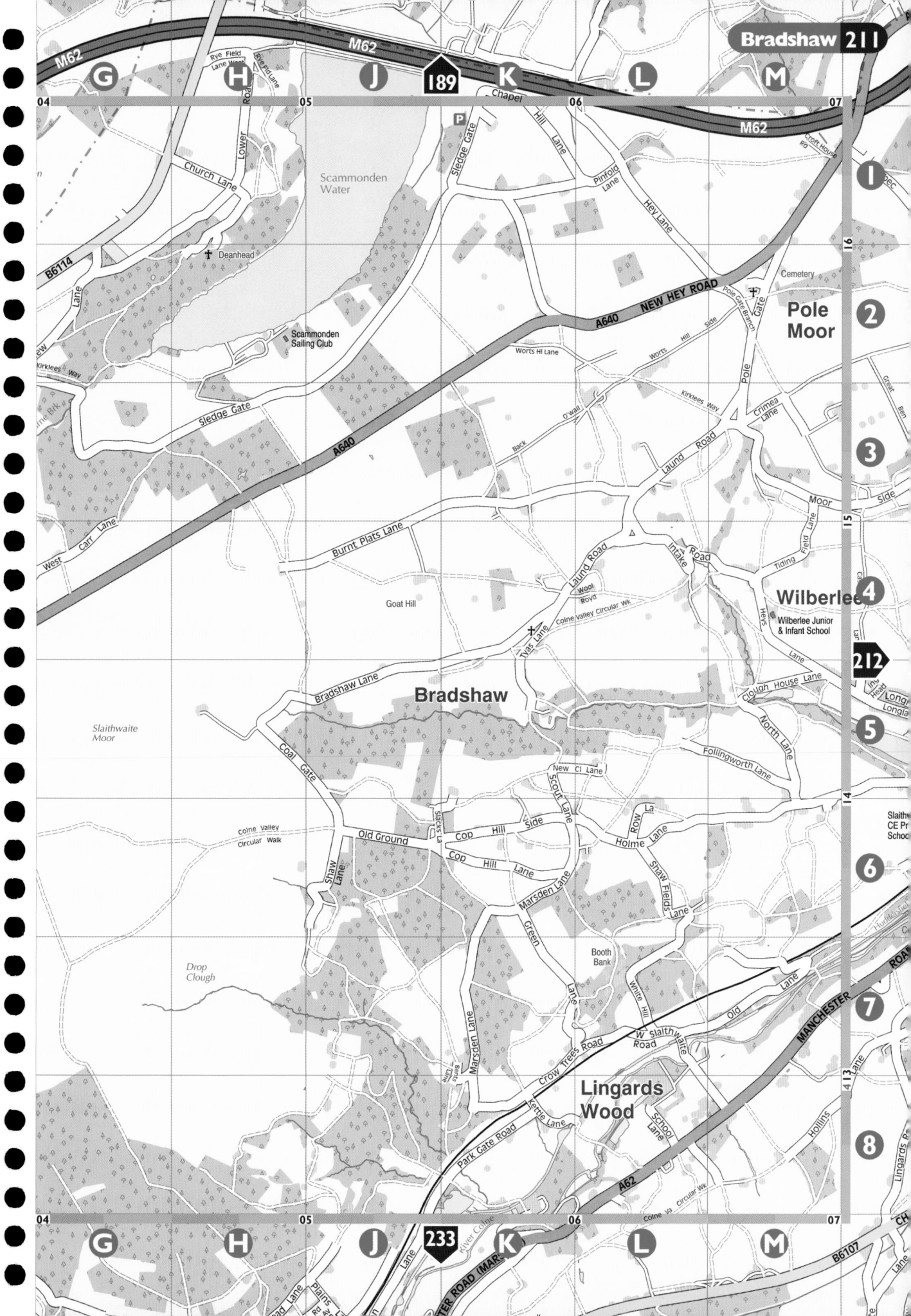

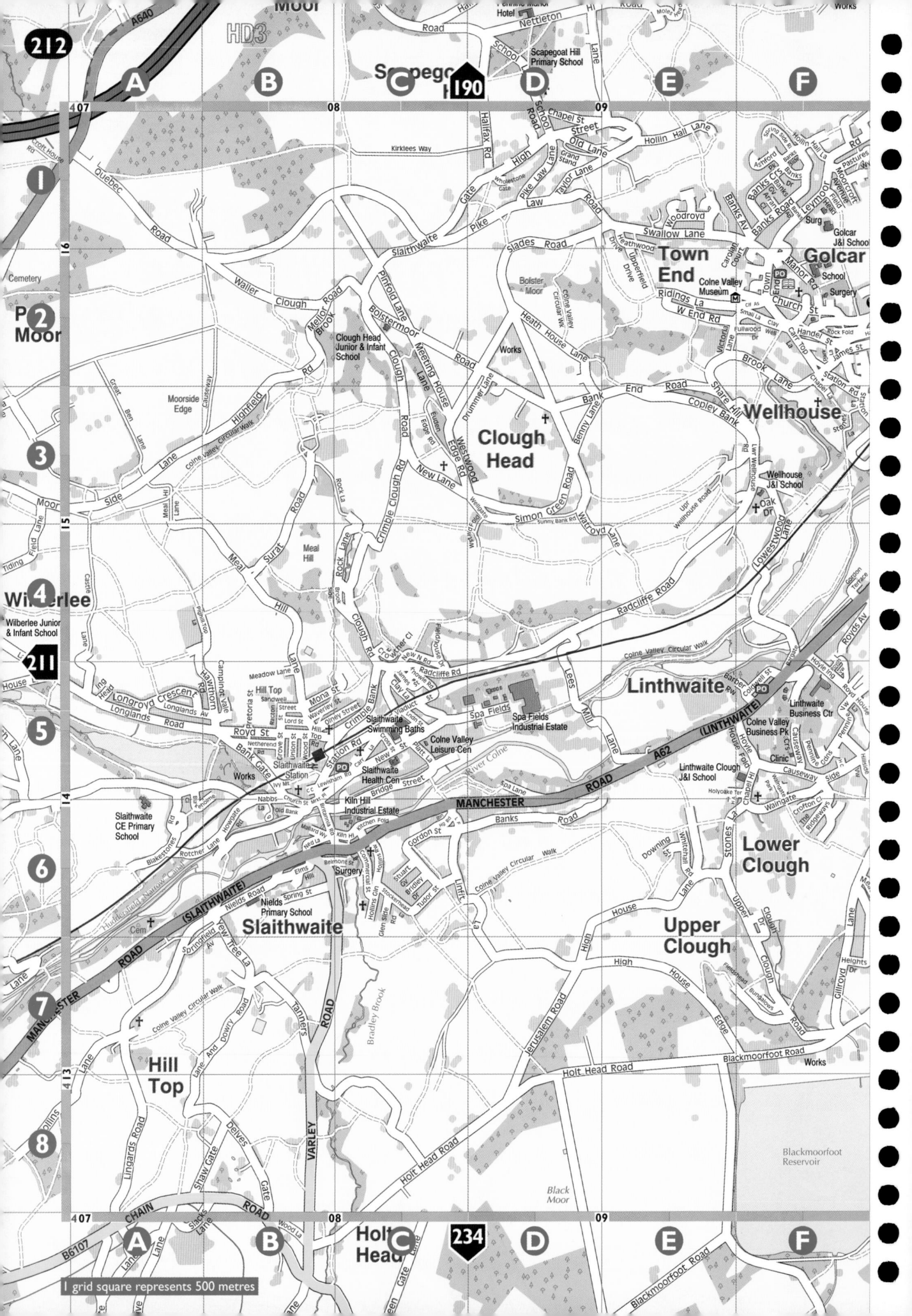

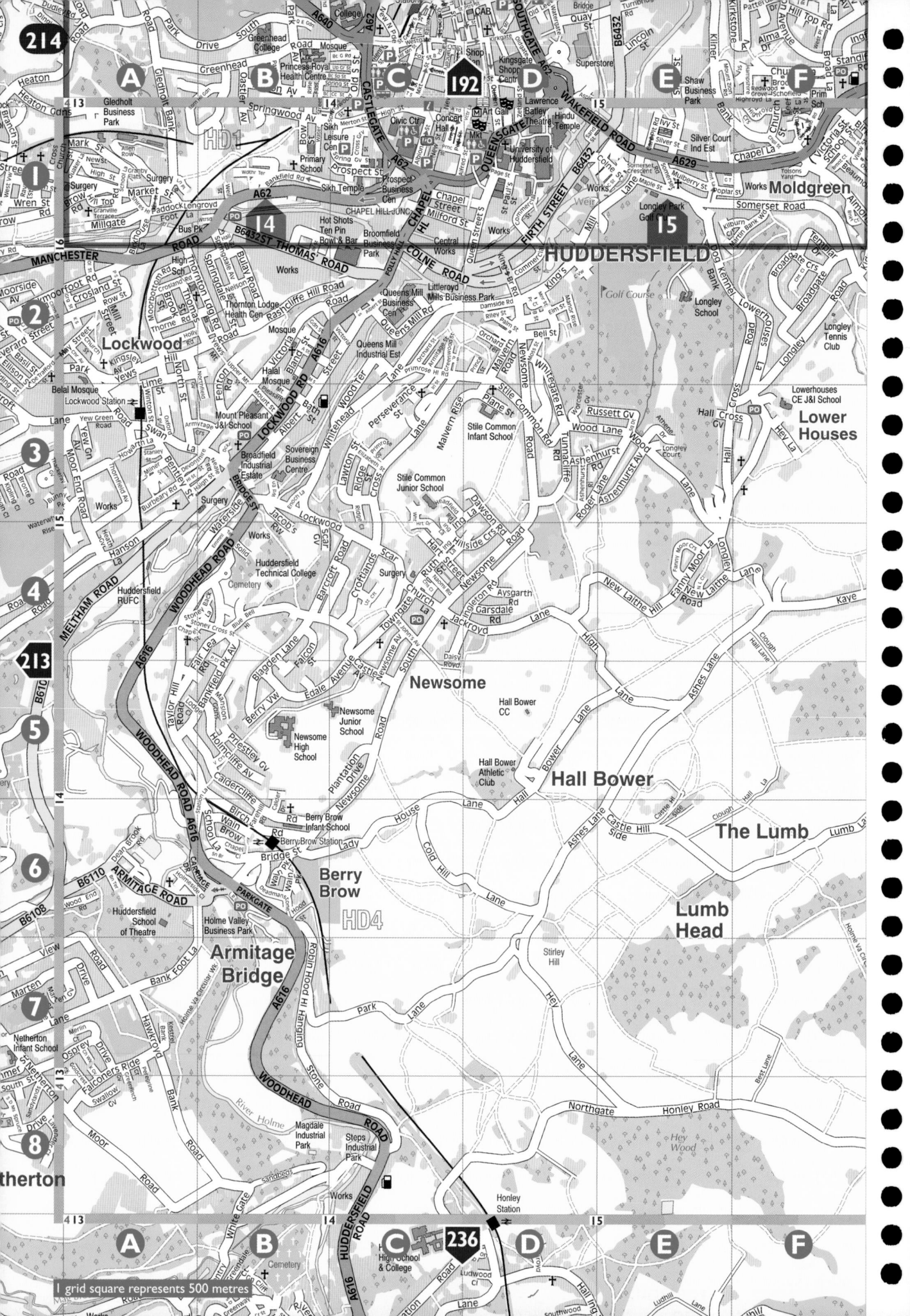

I grid square represents 500 metres

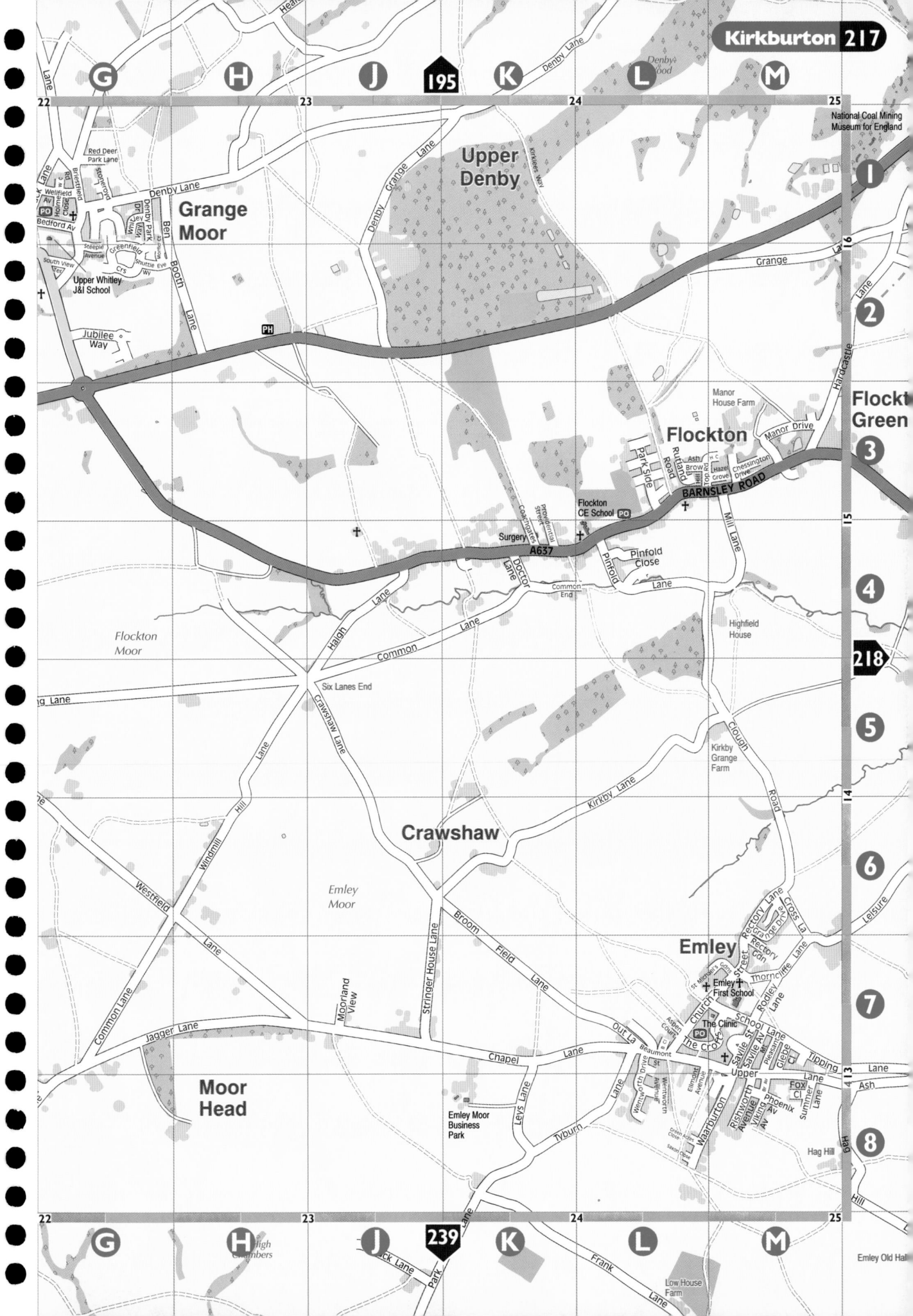

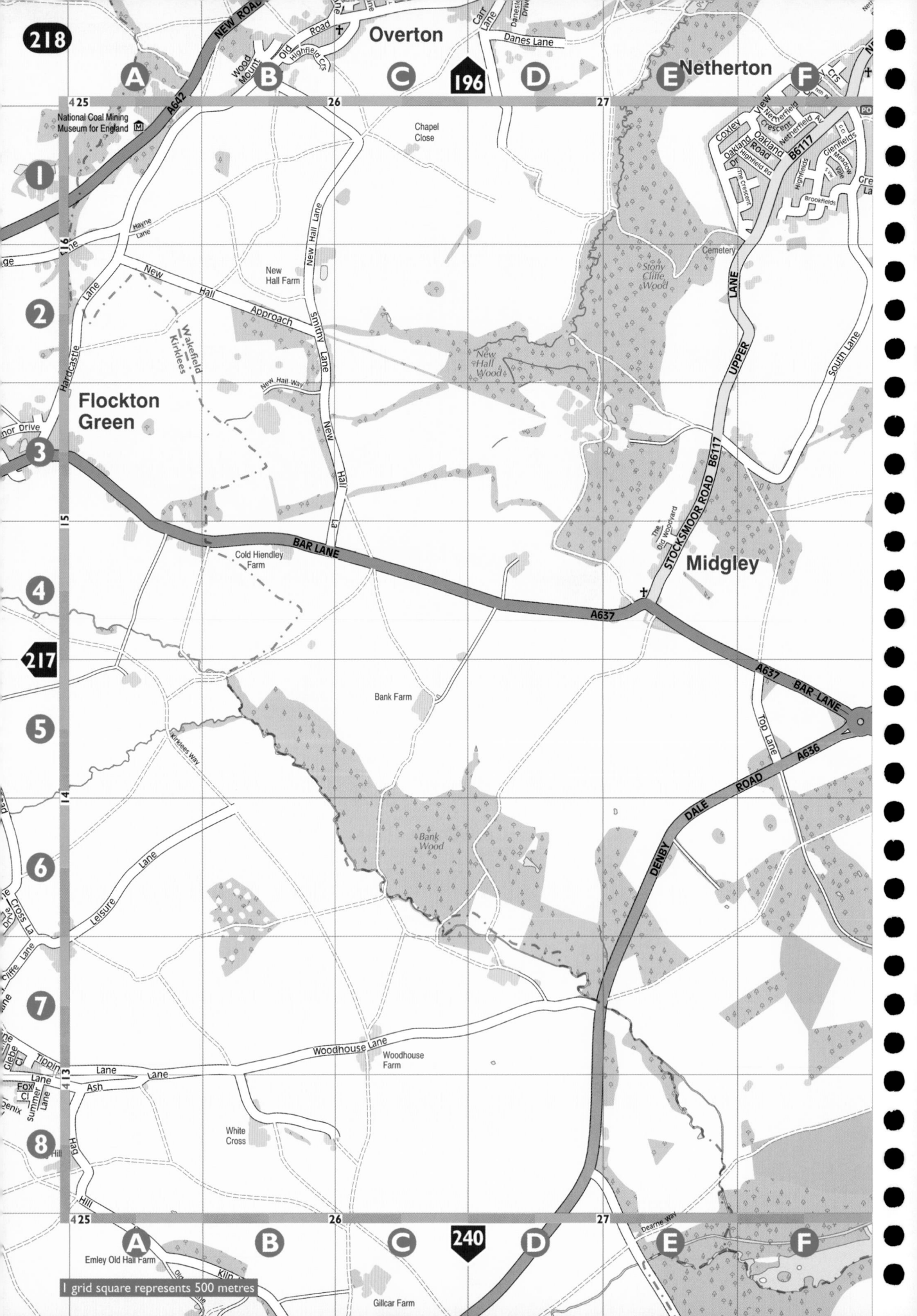

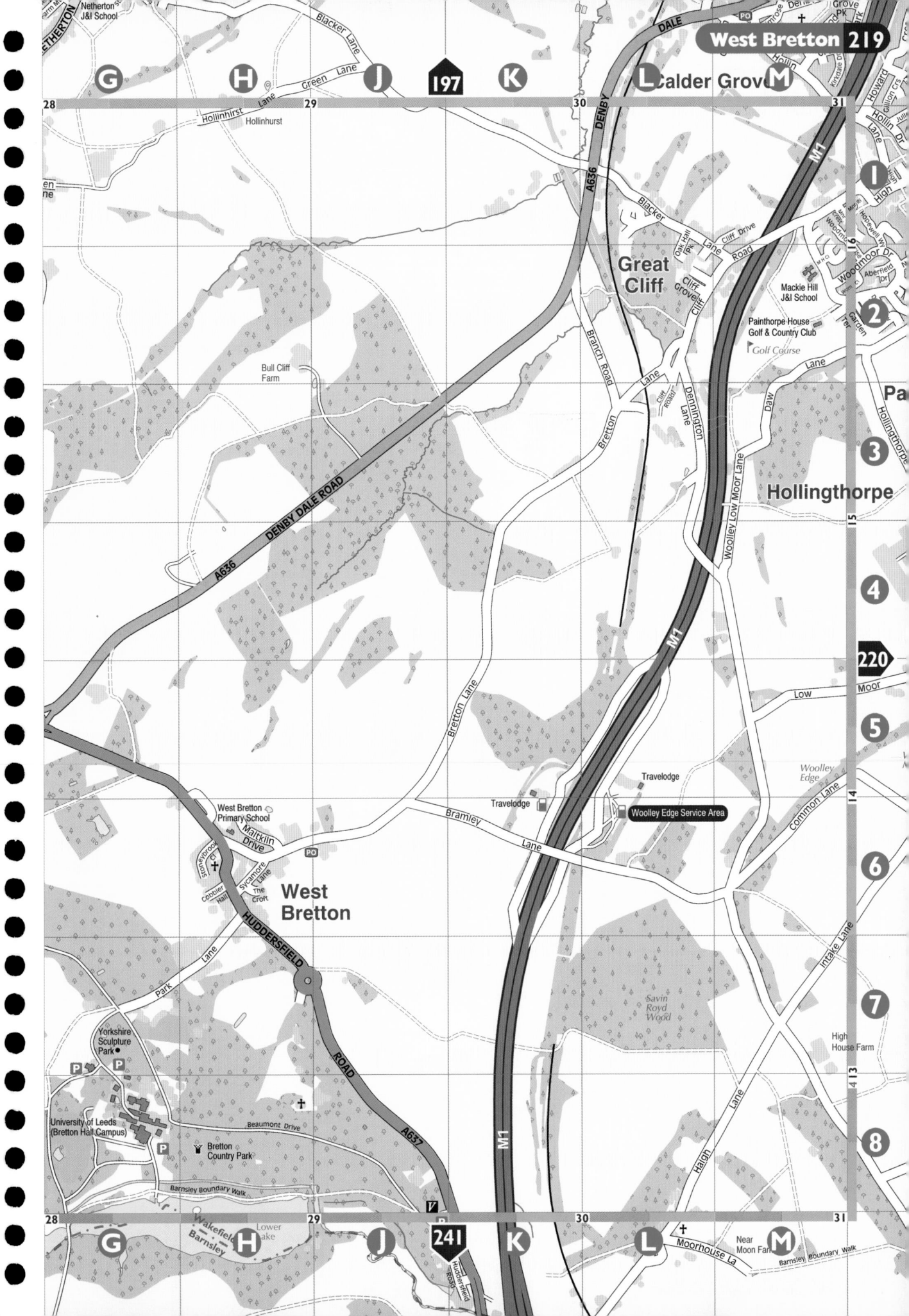

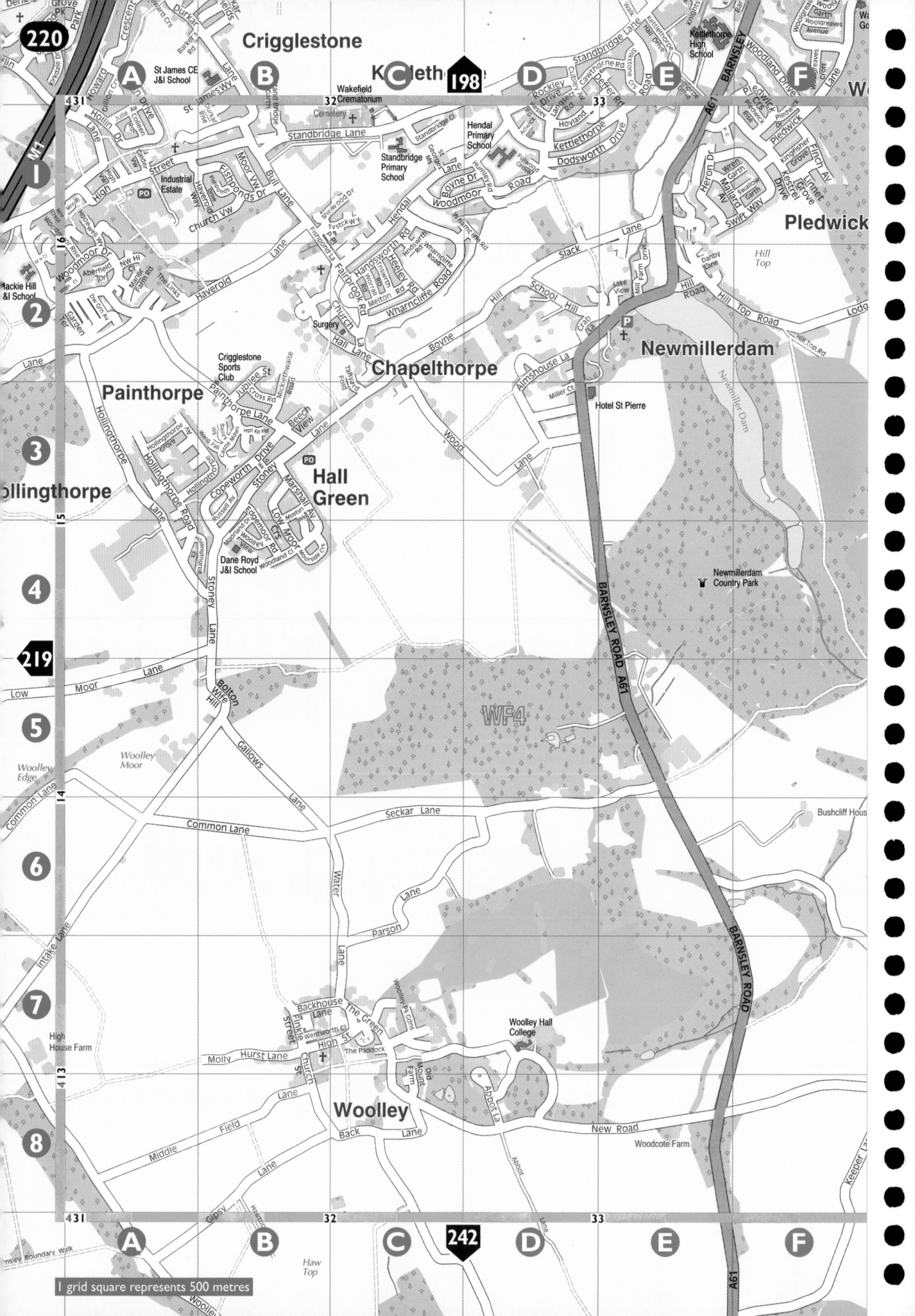

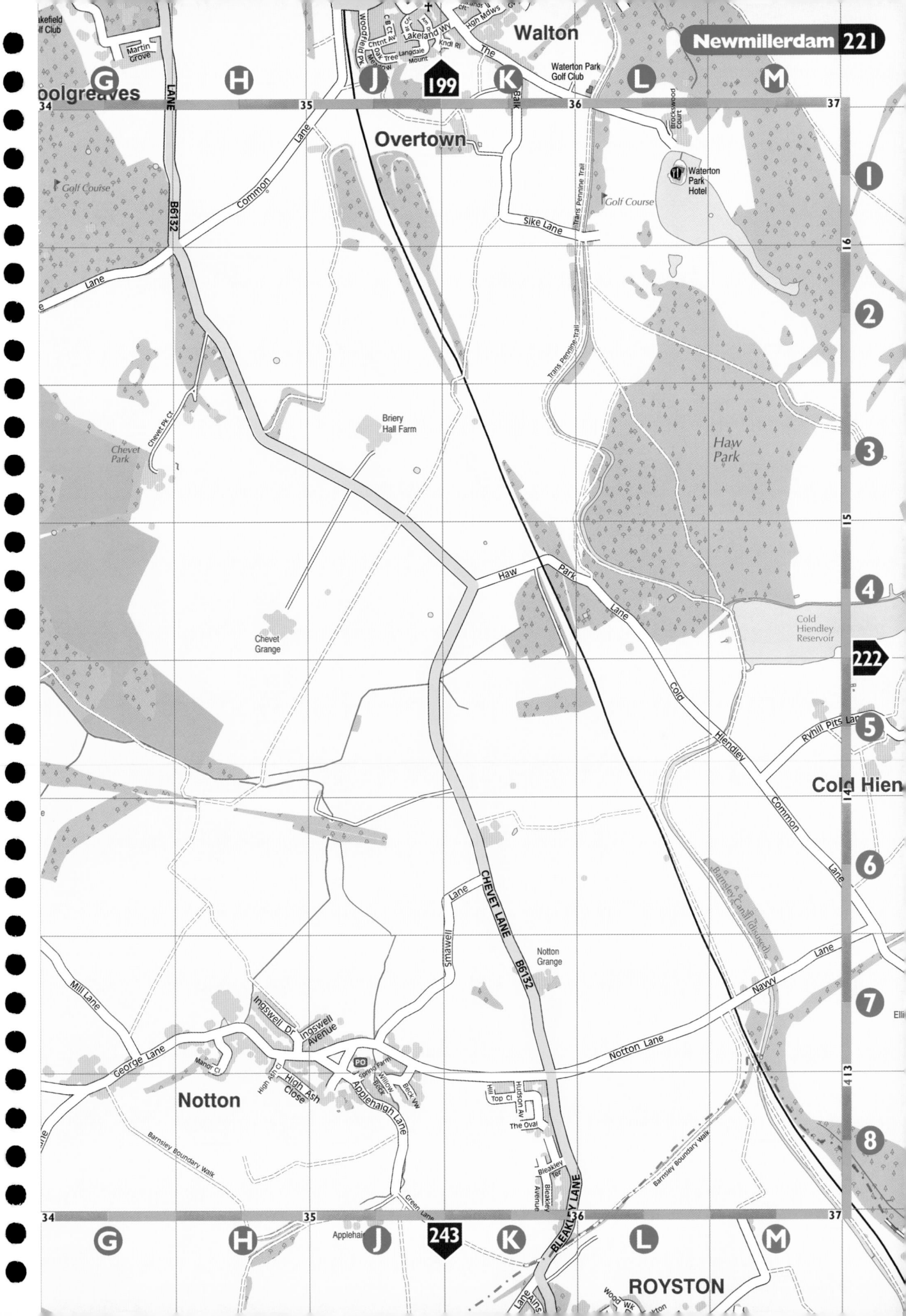

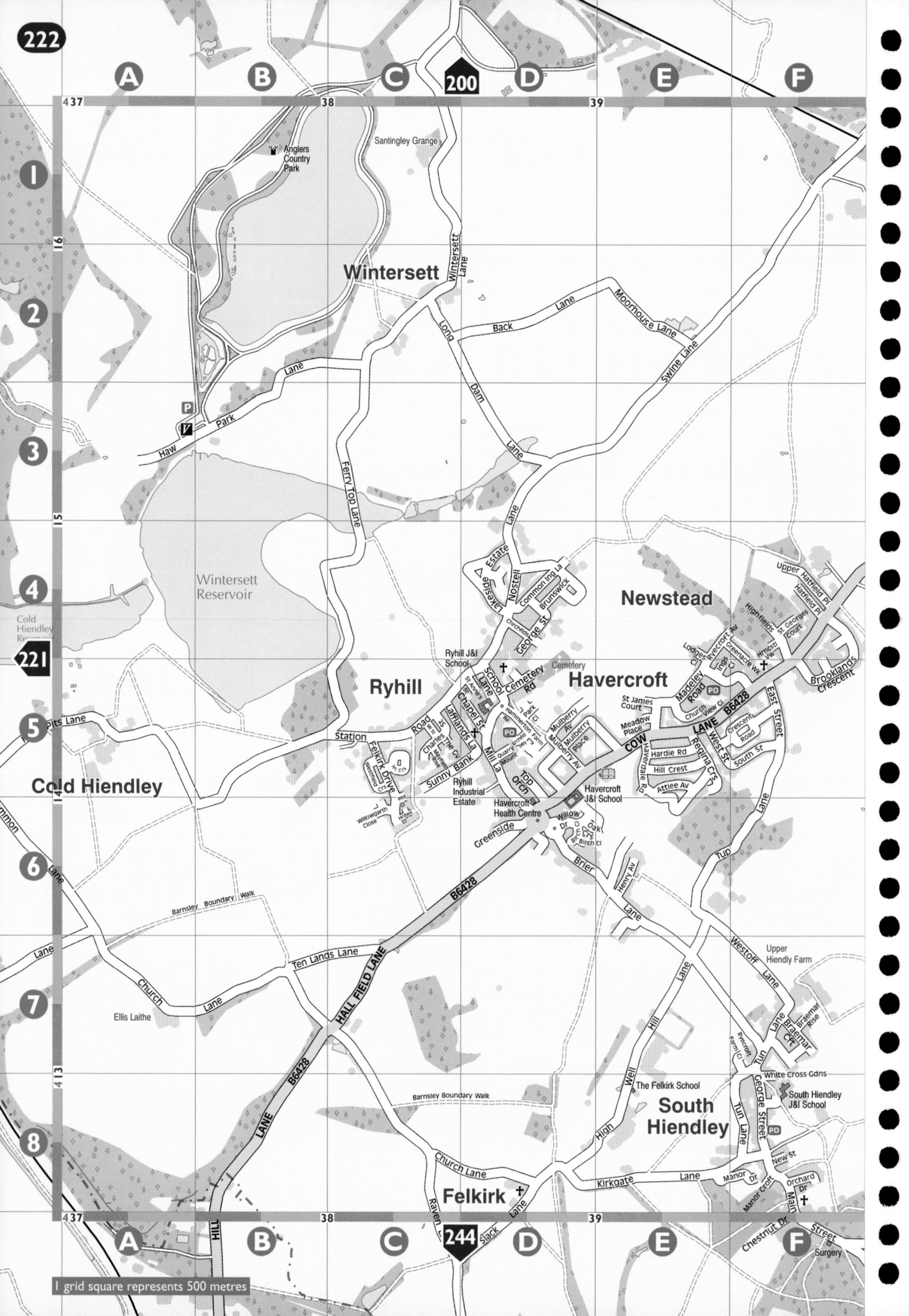

200

A B C D E F

437 38 39

1

16

2

15

3

4

221

Cold Hiendley Reservoir

5

14

6

413

7

8

437 38 39

A B C D E F

244

Anglers Country Park

Santingley Grange

Wintersett

Wintersett Lane

Long Lane

Back Lane

Moorhouse Lane

Swine Lane

Park Lane

Dam Lane

Ferry Top Lane

P
V
Haw Park

Wintersett Reservoir

Lakeside

Nostell

Estate

Common Ing La

Brunswick

Churchridge St

George St

Newstead

Upper Hatfield Pl

Hatfield Pl

St Georges Court

Highfields

Lodges

Ryecroft Av

Greenacre Wk

St Georges Vw

Havercroft

Ryhill

Ryhill J&I School

School Lane

Cemetery Rd

Cemetery

Madeley Road

Church View Cl

Brooklands Crescent

PO

COW LANE

B6428

St James Court

Meadow Place

Crescent Road

West St

East Street

Regina Crs

St Anne's

Chapel St

Croftlands La

The Cl

Park St

Mulberry Av

Mulberry Av

Mulberry Place

Hardie Rd

Hill Crest

Havercroft Rd

Haverdale Rd

South St

Attlee Av

South Hiendley Lane

Tup Lane

Cold Hiendley

Pits Lane

Charles Rd

Sunny Bank

Ryhill Industrial Estate

Mill La

Tod Orch

Quarry

PO

Havercroft Health Centre

Havercroft J&I School

Willow

Dr

Oak

Crs

Birch Cl

Felkirk Drive

Westfield Ct

Willowgarth Close

Greenside

Brier Lane

Henry Av

Station

Barnsley Boundary Walk

Ten Lands Lane

HALL FIELD LANE

B6428

Ellis Laithe

Church Lane

Westoft Lane

Upper Hiendley Farm

Barnsley Boundary Walk

Church Lane

Well Lane

Hill Lane

High Lane

The Felkirk School

South Hiendley

Braemar Rise

Braemar Cl

Tun Lane

White Cross Gdns

South Hiendley J&I School

George Street

PO

New St

Manor Dr

Manor Croft

Orchard Dr

Chestnut Dr

Main Street

Surgery

B6428

HILL LANE

Raven

Slack

Felkirk

Kirkgate

Lane

Lane

Common Lane

Lane

Lane

1 grid square represents 500 metres

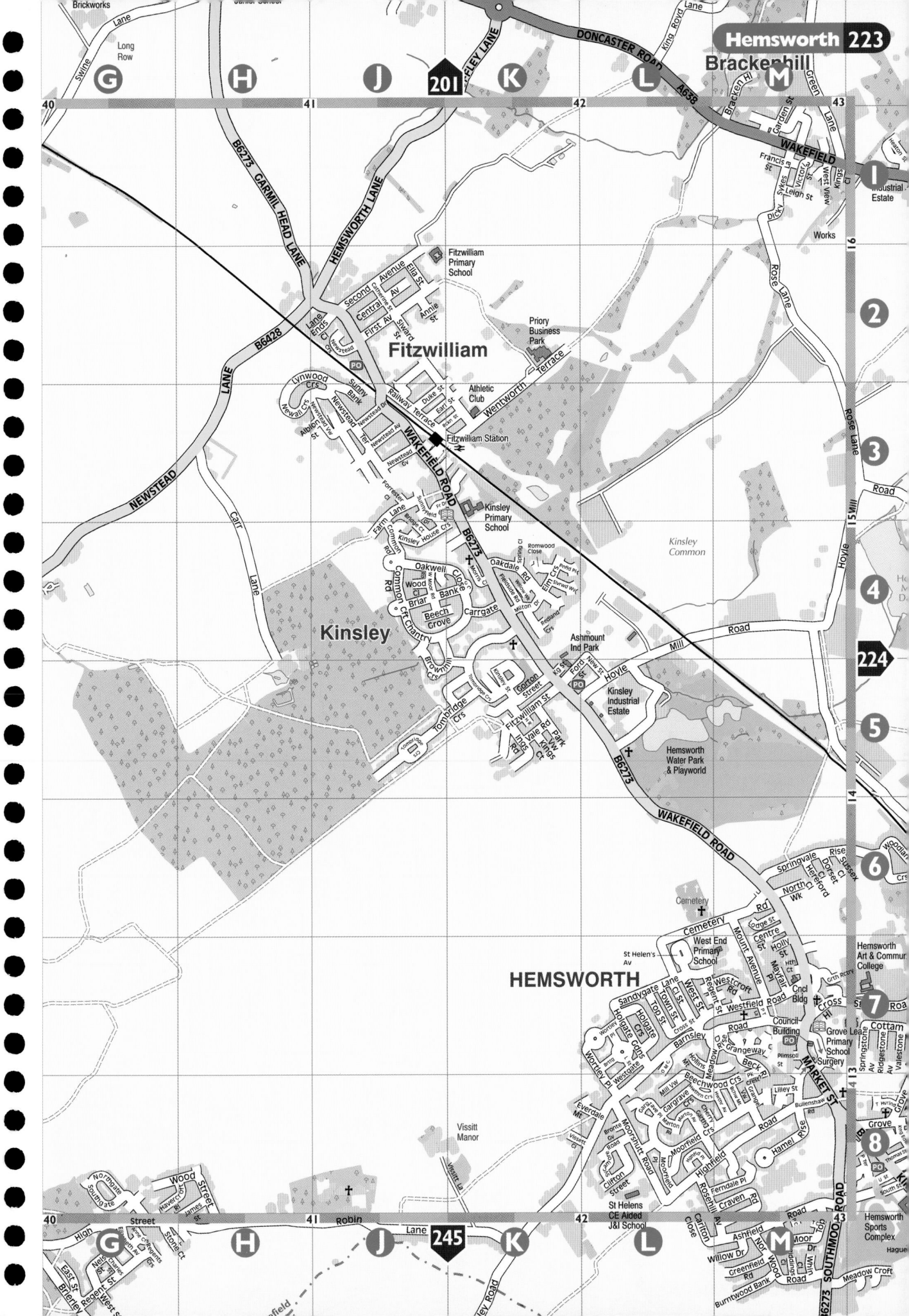

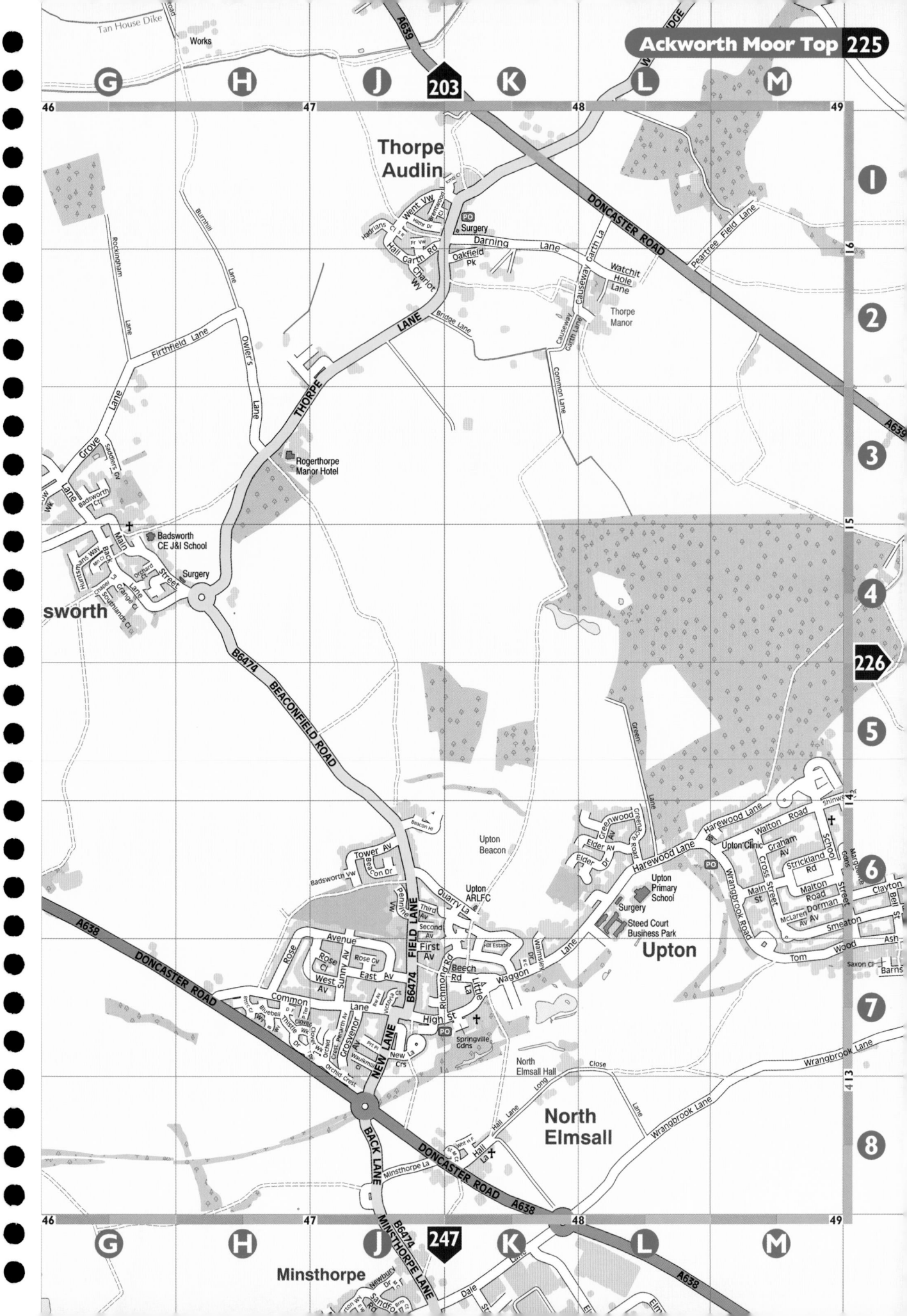

G   H   J   203   K   L   M

46   47   48   49

Thorpe Audlin

I

Went Vw

PO

Surgery

Darning   Lane

Hadrians Ct

Hall Garth Rd

Chariot Wy

Oakfield Pk

Bridge Lane

Carth La

Causeway

Carth Lane

Common Lane

Watchit Hole Lane

Thorpe Manor

Peartree Field Lane

DONCASTER ROAD

A639

16

2

THORPE LANE

Rockingham Lane

Burnhill

Firthfield Lane

Owler's Lane

Rogerthorpe Manor Hotel

15

3

Grove Lane

Sadlers Gv

Badsworth Ct

Main Street

Huntsmans Way

Back Lane

Orchard Ct

Chapel Ln

Grange Ct

Southlands Cl

Badsworth CE J&I School

Surgery

sworth

A639

4

226

B6474 BEACONFIELD ROAD

Beacon Hill

5

14

A638 DONCASTER ROAD

Tower Av

Beacon Dr

Badsworth Vw

Pennine

Quarry La

Third Av

Second Av

First Av

Upton Beacon

Upton ARLFC

Greenwood Av

Elder Av

Elder Dr

Harewood Lane

Green

Shinwell

Harewood Lane

Walton Road

Upton Clinic

Graham Av

Strickland Rd

Cross Street

Malton Road

Dorman Av

McLaren Av

School Street

Clayton

Bell St

Margaret Gdns

6

Rose Ct

Avenue

Sunny Av

Rose Cv

East Av

West Av

Common

Bluebell

Thistle

Clover Wy

Grosvenor Av

Orchid Crest

Pentith Av

Waukmill

New Crs

Pea La

FIELD LANE

B6474

Richmond Rd

Beech Rd

Little

High St

PO

New La

Springville Gdns

Waggon Lane

Walmsley Lane

Upton Primary School

Surgery

Steed Court Business Park

Upton

Main St

Wrangbrook Road

Smeaton

Tom

Wood

Saxon Cl

Ash

Barns

7

13

North Elmsall Hall

Close

Long Lane

Hall Lane

Wrangbrook Lane

Lane

Wrangbrook Lane

NEW LANE

BACK LANE

DONCASTER ROAD   A638

Minsthorpe La

Hall La

North Elmsall

8

46   47   48   49

G   H   J   247   K   L   M

MINSTHORPE LANE

B6474

Minsthorpe

Newbury

Sandford

Dale St

Elm

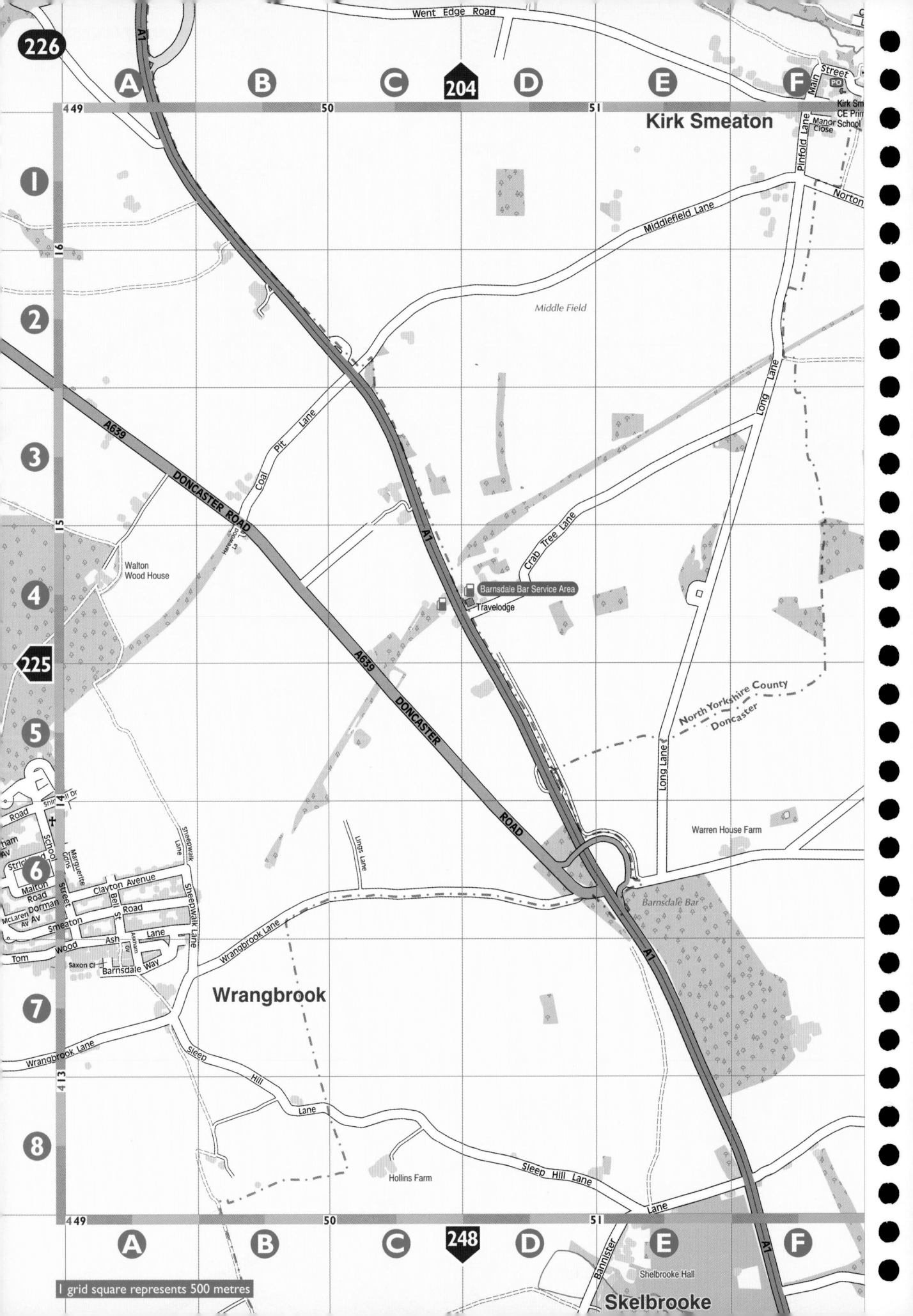

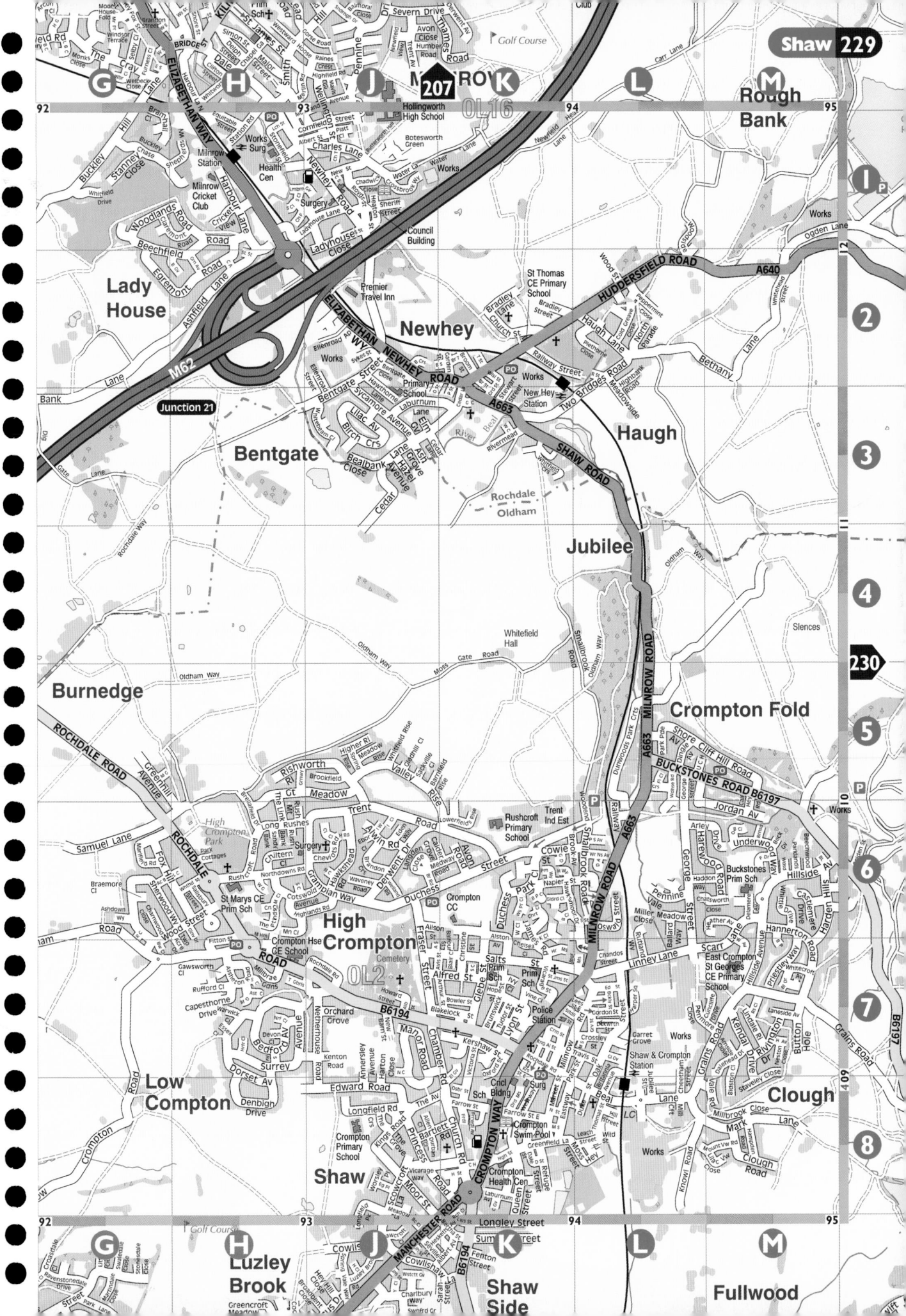

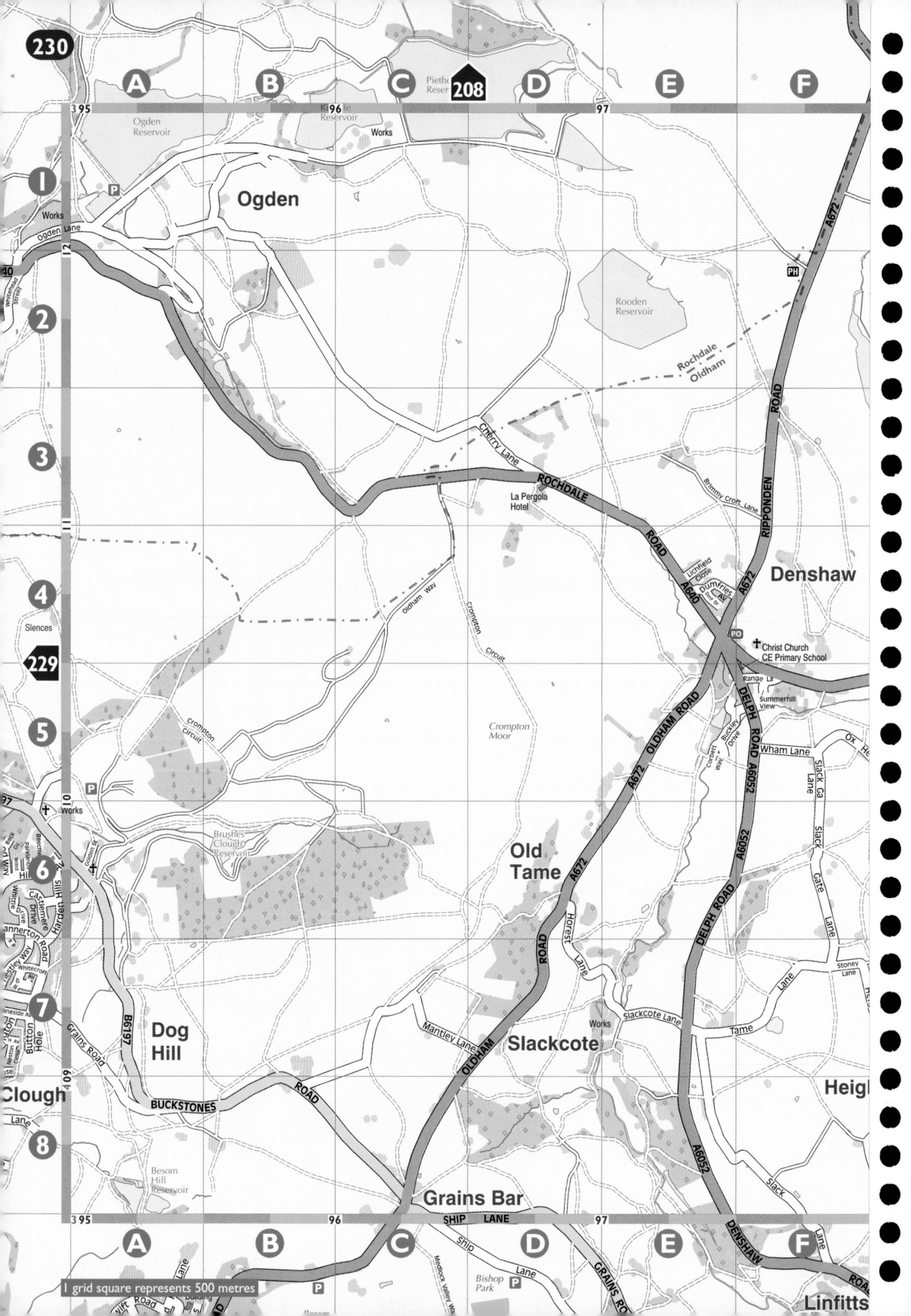

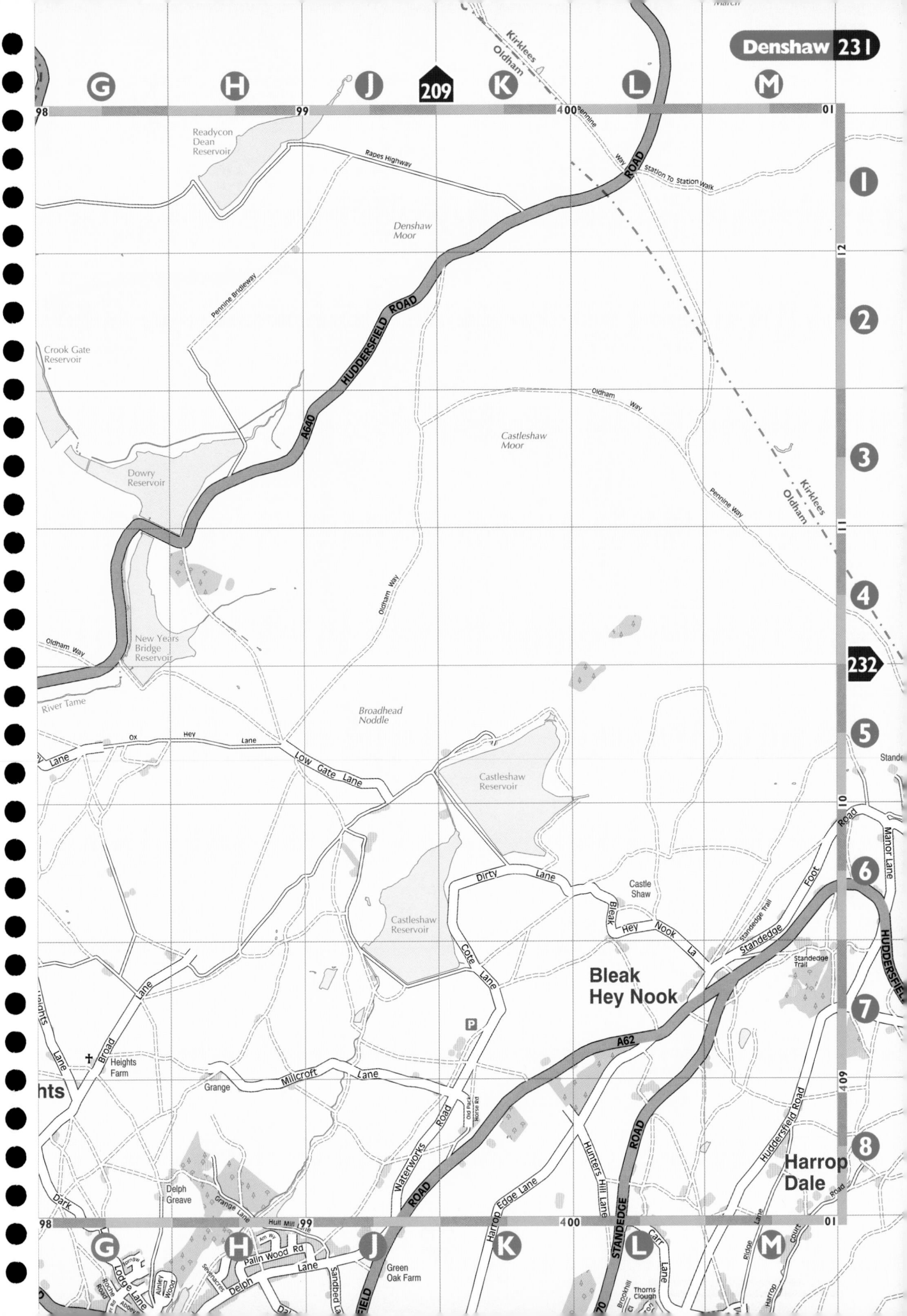

G   H   J   209   K   L   M

98   99   400   01

Readycon Dean Reservoir

Rapes Highway

Kirklees Oldham

Station To Station Walk

Denshaw Moor

Pennine Bridleway

HUDDERSFIELD ROAD

A640

Crook Gate Reservoir

Castleshaw Moor

Oldham Way

Dowry Reservoir

Kirklees Oldham

Pennine Way

232

Oldham Way

New Years Bridge Reservoir

Oldham Way

River Tame

Broadhead Noddle

Ox   Hey   Lane

Lane   Low Gate Lane

Castleshaw Reservoir

Stande

Lane

Castleshaw Reservoir

Dirty   Lane

Castle Shaw

Standedge Trail

Bleak Hey Nook La

Standedge Trail

Standedge Foot

Road

Manor Lane

Core Lane

Standedge Trail

HUDDERSFIELD

P

Bleak Hey Nook

Heights Lane

† Broad

Heights Farm

A62

Grange   Millcroft   Lane

Waterworks   Road

Old Pack Horse Rd

Hunters Hill Lane

STANDEDGE ROAD

Huddersfield Road

409

Harrop Dale

Delph Greave

Grange Lane

Park

Hull Mill Lane

98   99   400   01

G   H   J   K   L   M

Turnpike

Lodge Lane

Ainley Wood

Delph

Palin Wood Rd

Sandbed La

Green Oak Farm

Brookhill

Carr Lane

Ridge La

Thorns Clough

Harrop court

HUDDERSFIELD   70

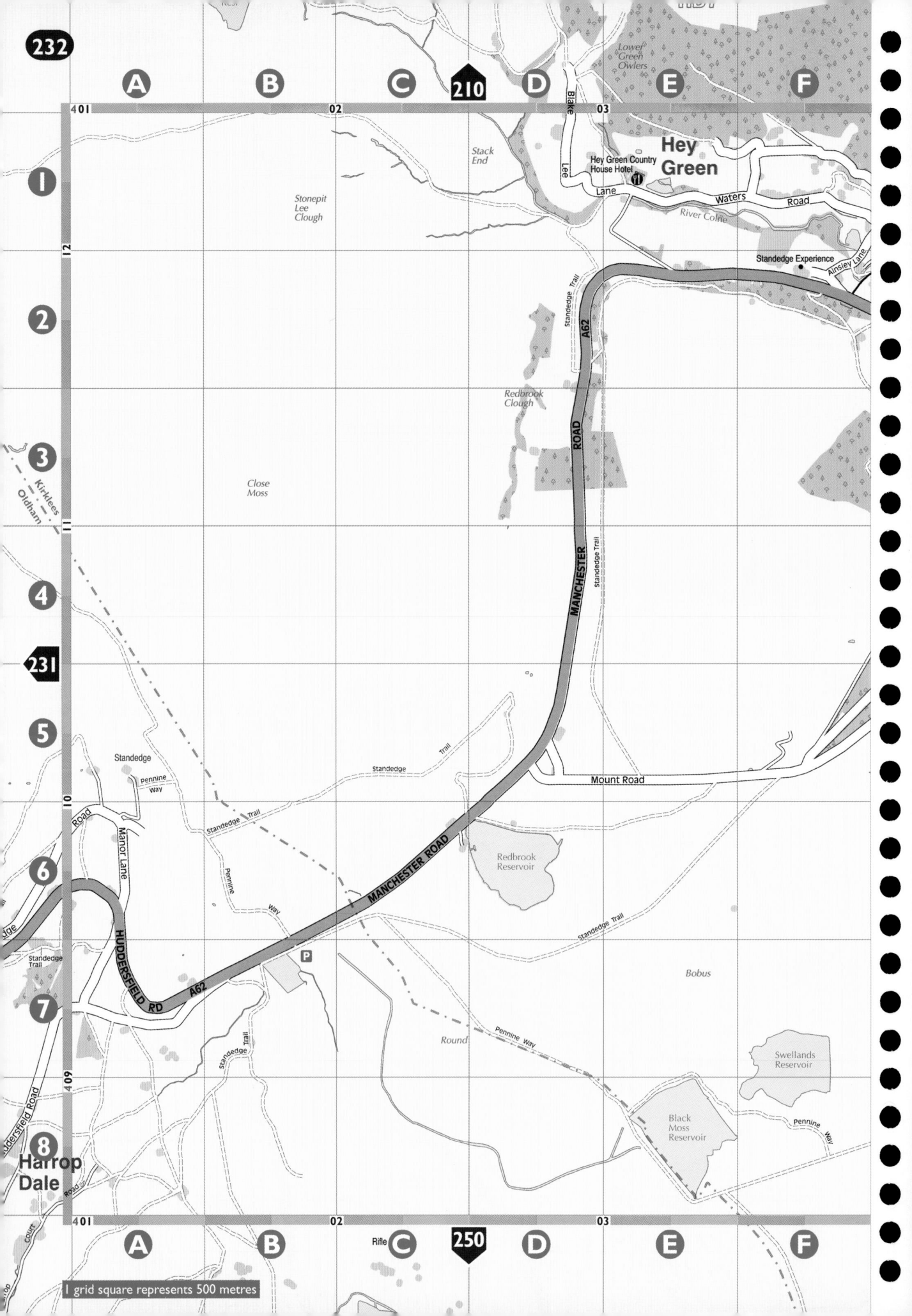

210

A   B   C   D   E   F

401   02   03

1

Stonepit
Lee
Clough

Stack
End

Hey Green Country
House Hotel

Hey
Green

Lower
Green
Owlers

Blake
Lee
Lane

Waters   Road

River Colne

Standedge Experience

Ainsley Lane

12

Standedge Trail

A62

2

Redbrook
Clough

MANCHESTER

ROAD

Kirklees
Oldham

3

Close
Moss

11

Standedge Trail

4

231

5

Standedge

Pennine
Way

Standedge   Trail

Standedge

Trail

Mount Road

Standedge Trail

Road

10

Standedge Trail

Pennine

MANCHESTER ROAD

Redbrook
Reservoir

6

dge

Manor Lane

Way

Standedge Trail

P

Bobus

Swellands
Reservoir

Standedge
Trail

HUDDERSFIELD RD   A62

7

Standedge Trail

Round

Pennine   Way

Pennine   Way

Black
Moss
Reservoir

409

udersfield Road

8

Harrop
Dale

401   02   03

A   B   Rifle C   250   D   E   F

Court

1 grid square represents 500 metres

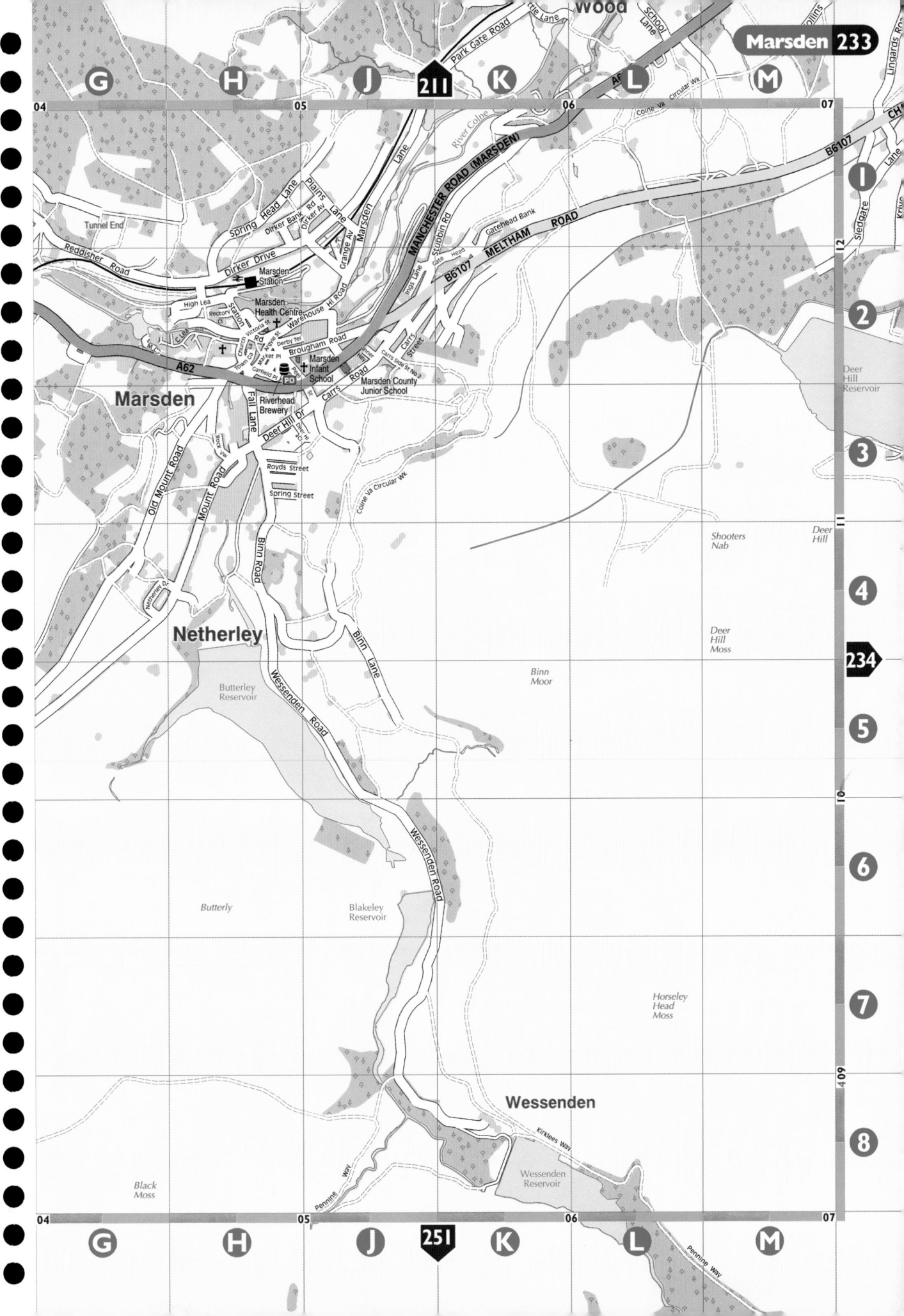

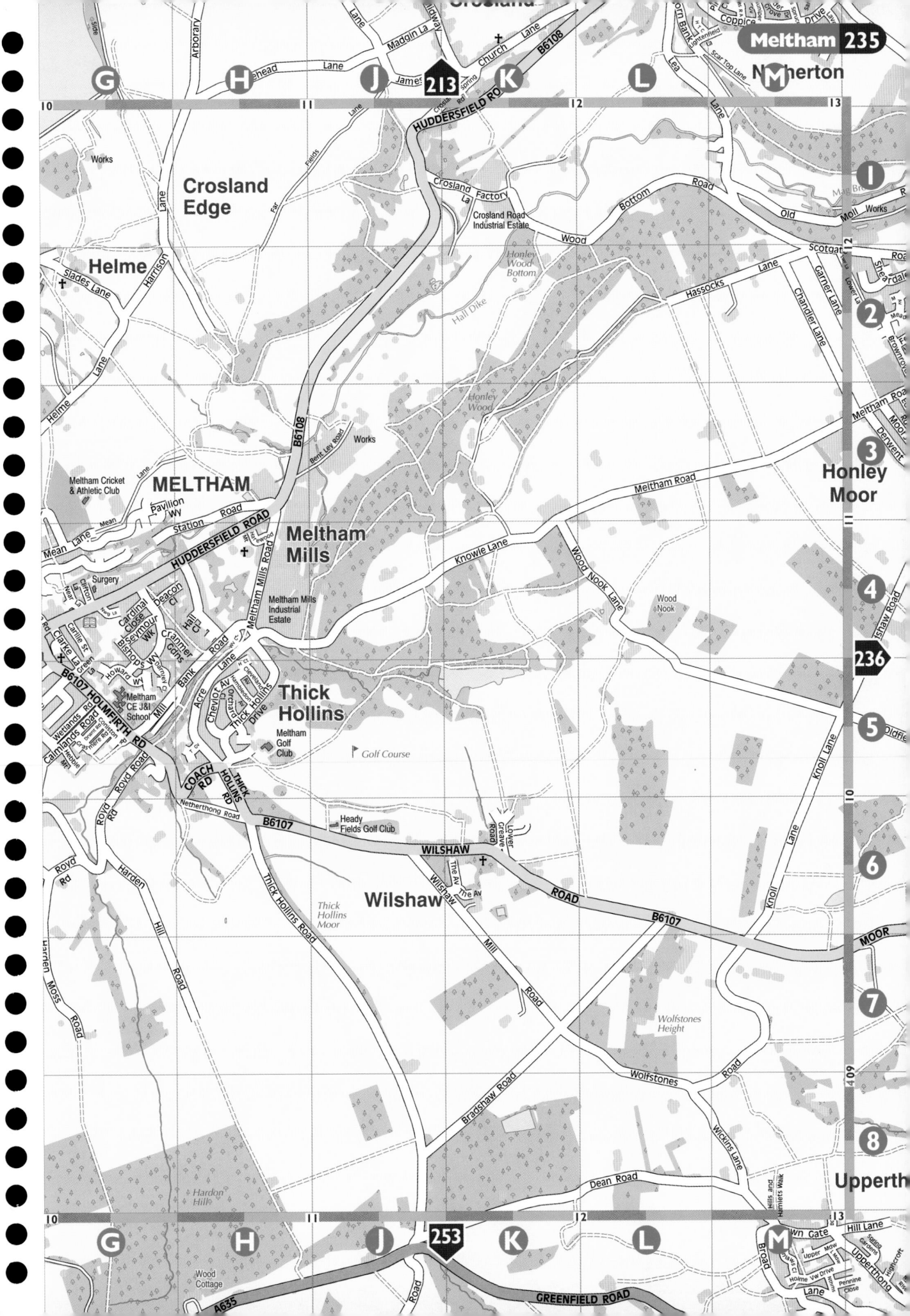

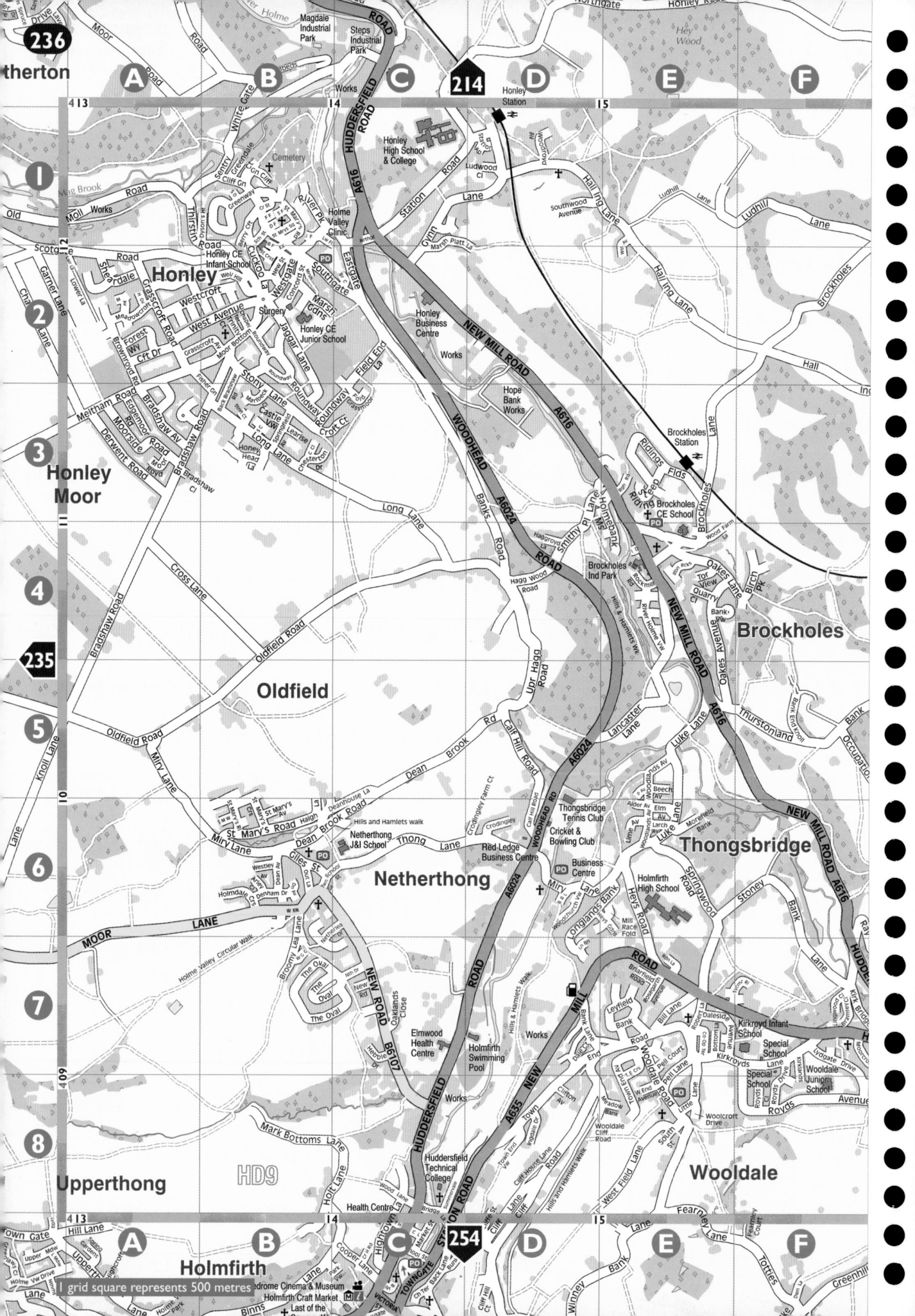

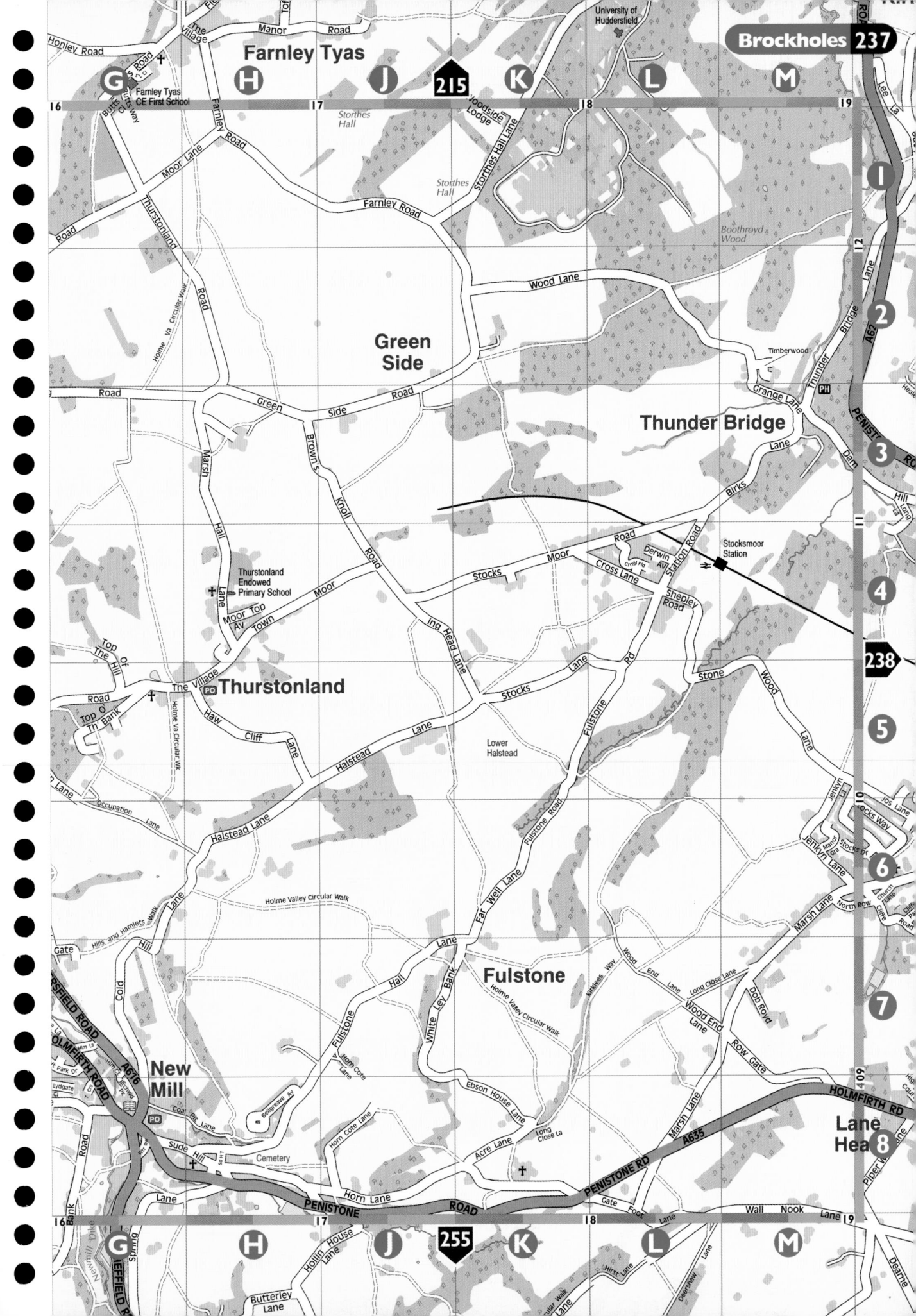

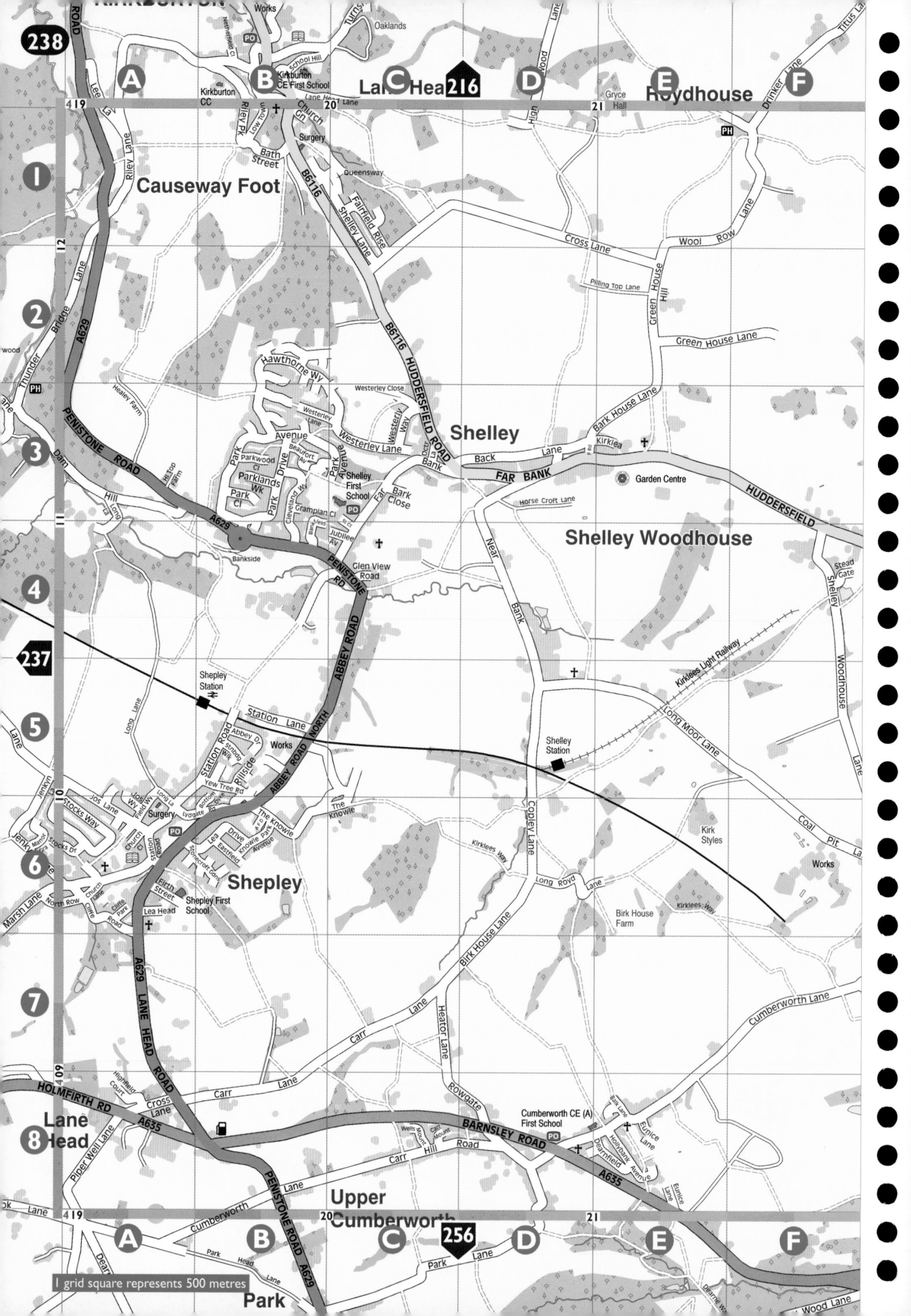

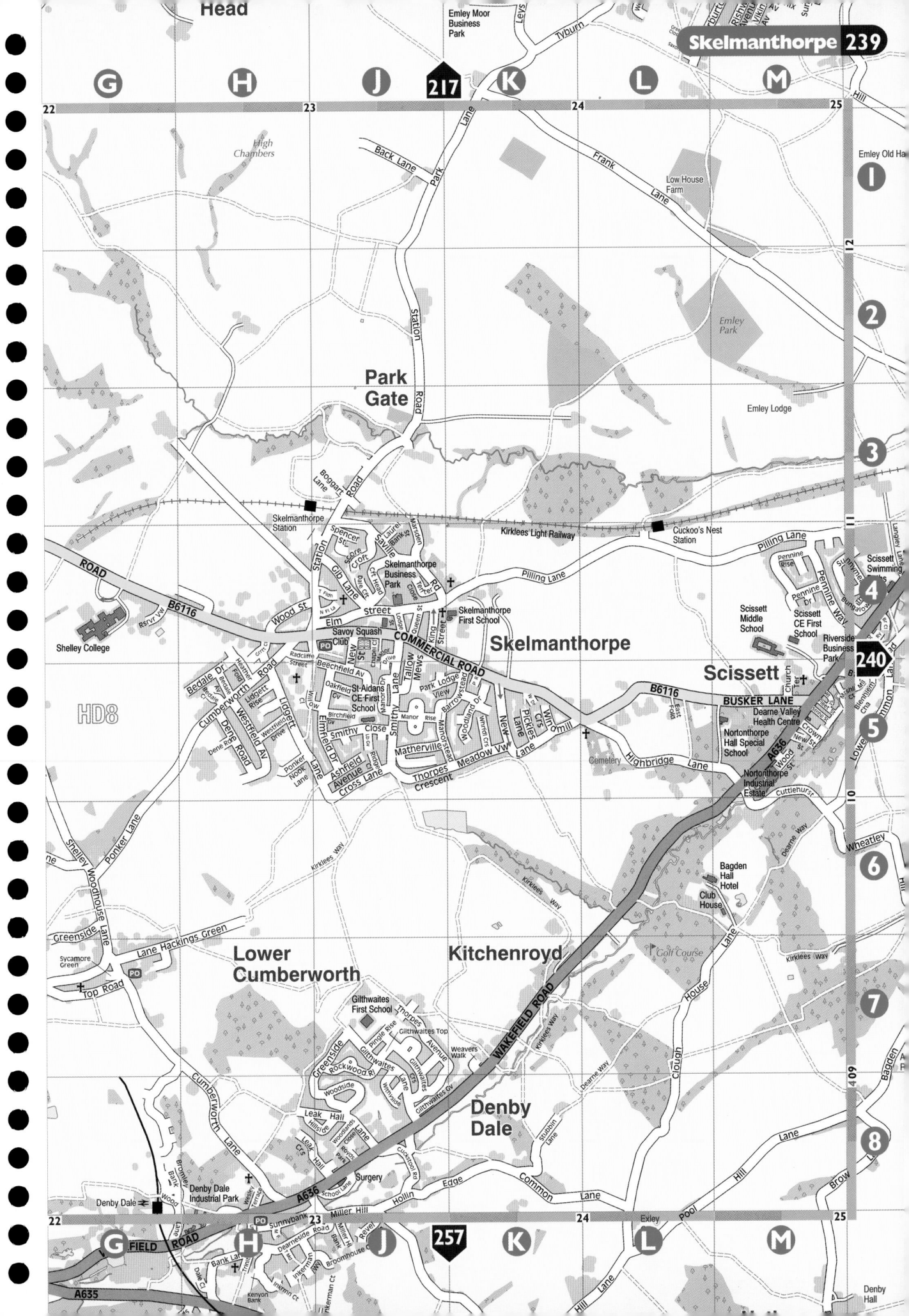

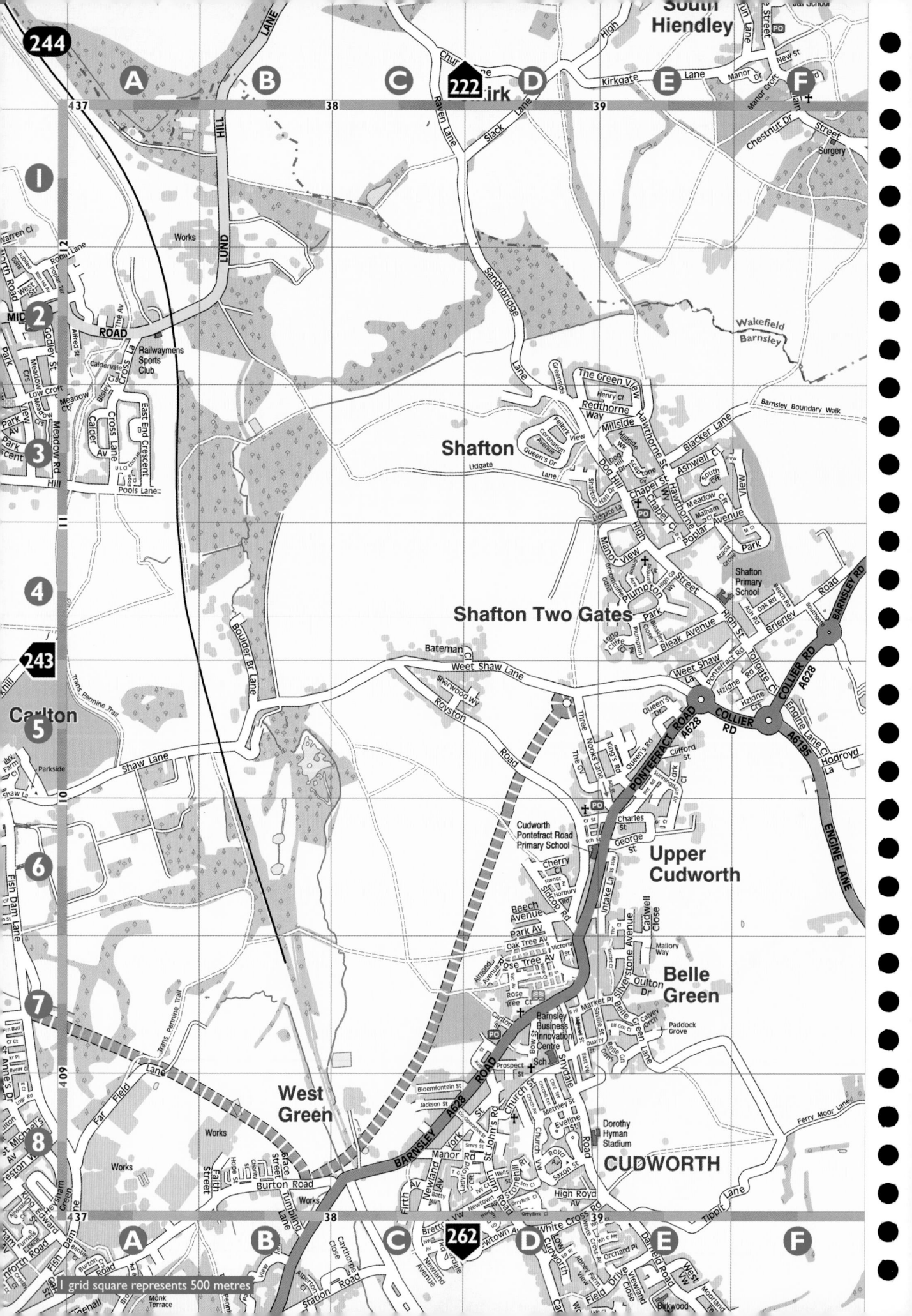

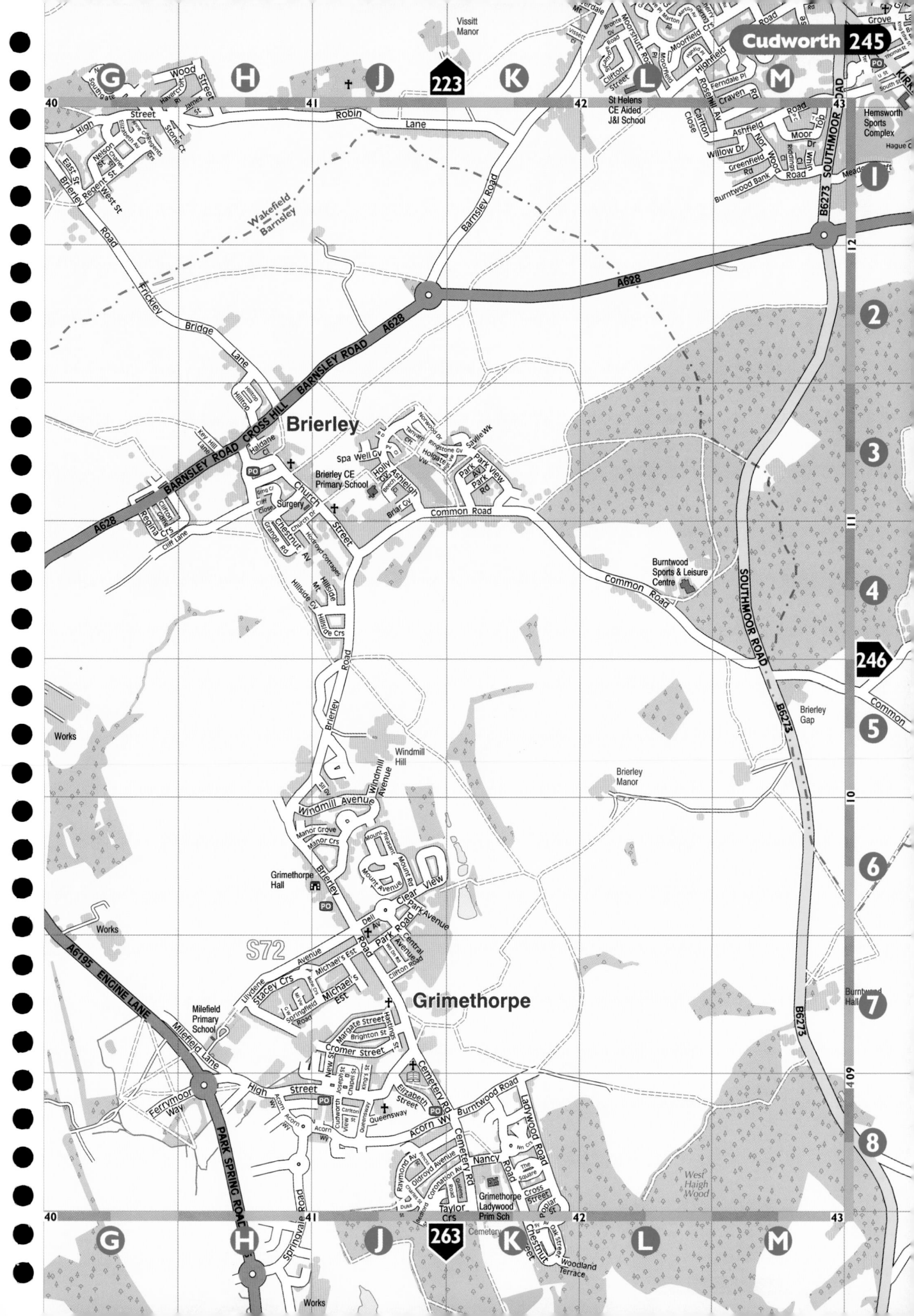

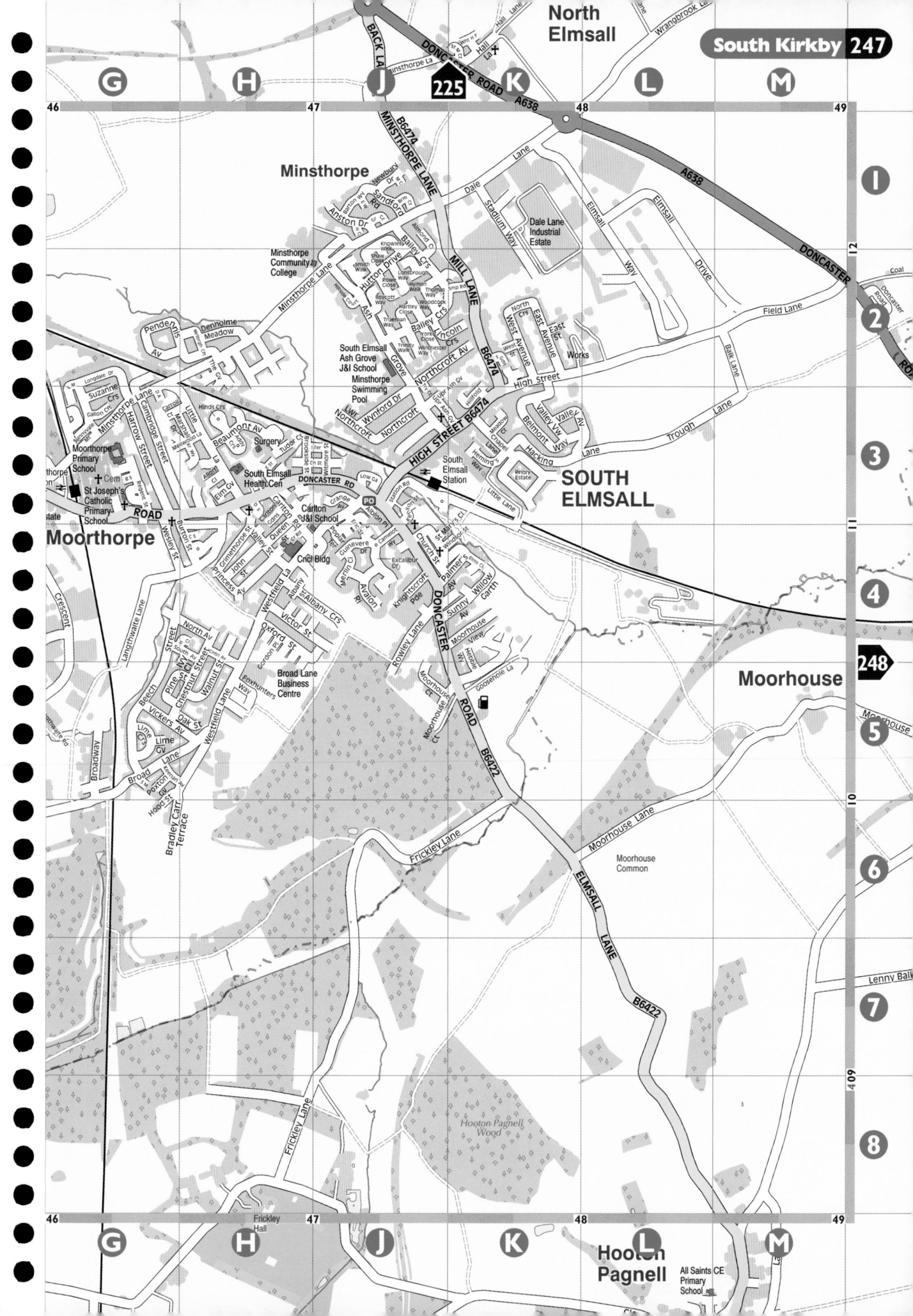

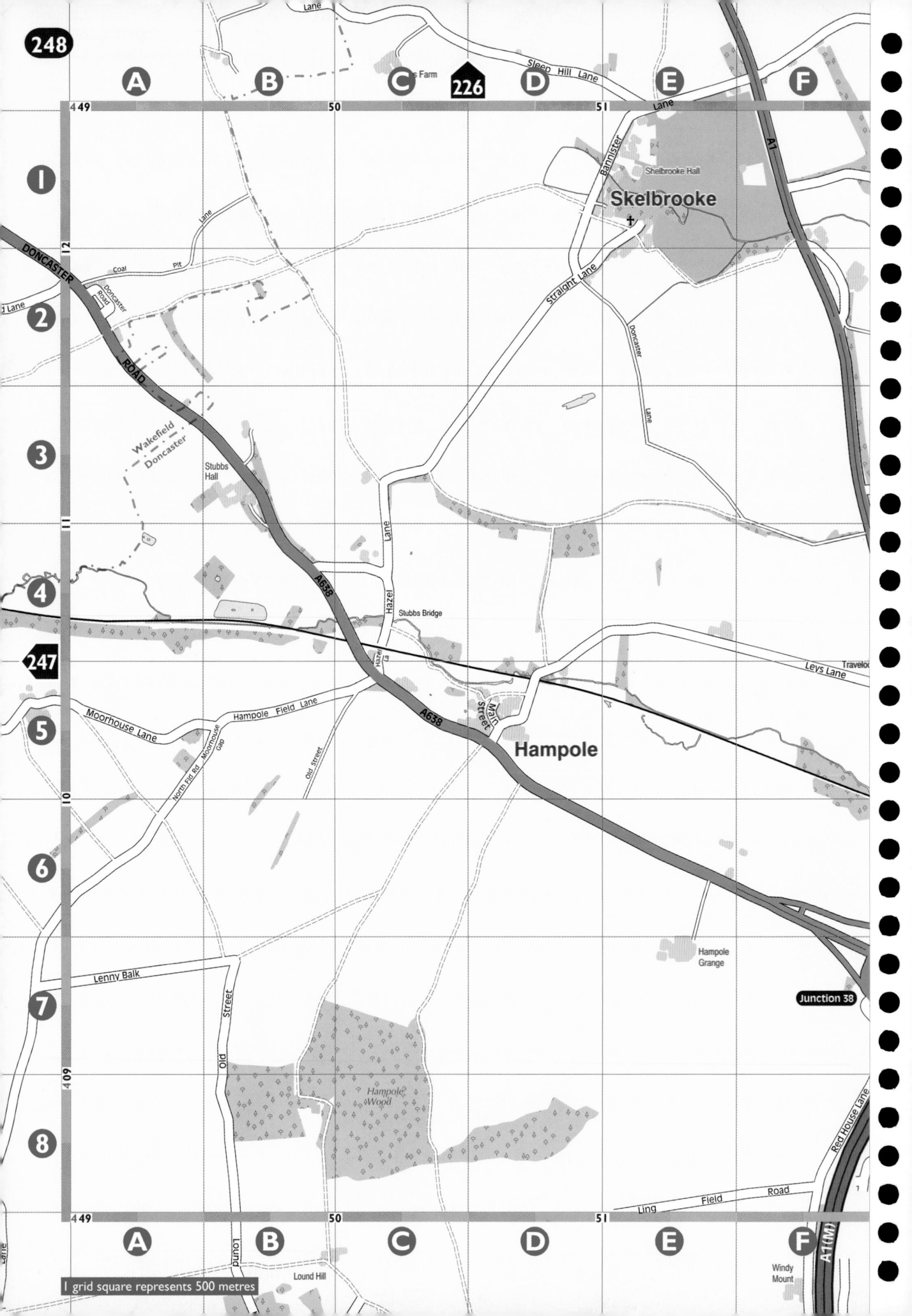

A B C D E F

226

4 49 50 51

I

DONCASTER

Skelbrooke

Bannister

Lane

Shelbrooke Hall

12

2

Coal Pit

Lane

Doncaster Road

Straight Lane

ROAD

Doncaster Lane

3

Wakefield Doncaster

Stubbs Hall

11

Hazel Lane

4

A638

Stubbs Bridge

Hazel La

Leys Lane Travelo

5

Moorhouse Lane

Hampole Field Lane

North Fld Rd Moorhouse Gap

Old Street

A638

Main Street

Hampole

10

6

Hampole Grange

7

Lenny Balk

Old Street

Junction 38

4 09

Red House Lane

8

Hampole Wood

A1(M)

Ling Field Road

4 49 50 51

A B C D E F

Windy Mount

1 grid square represents 500 metres

Lound Hill

Lound Hill

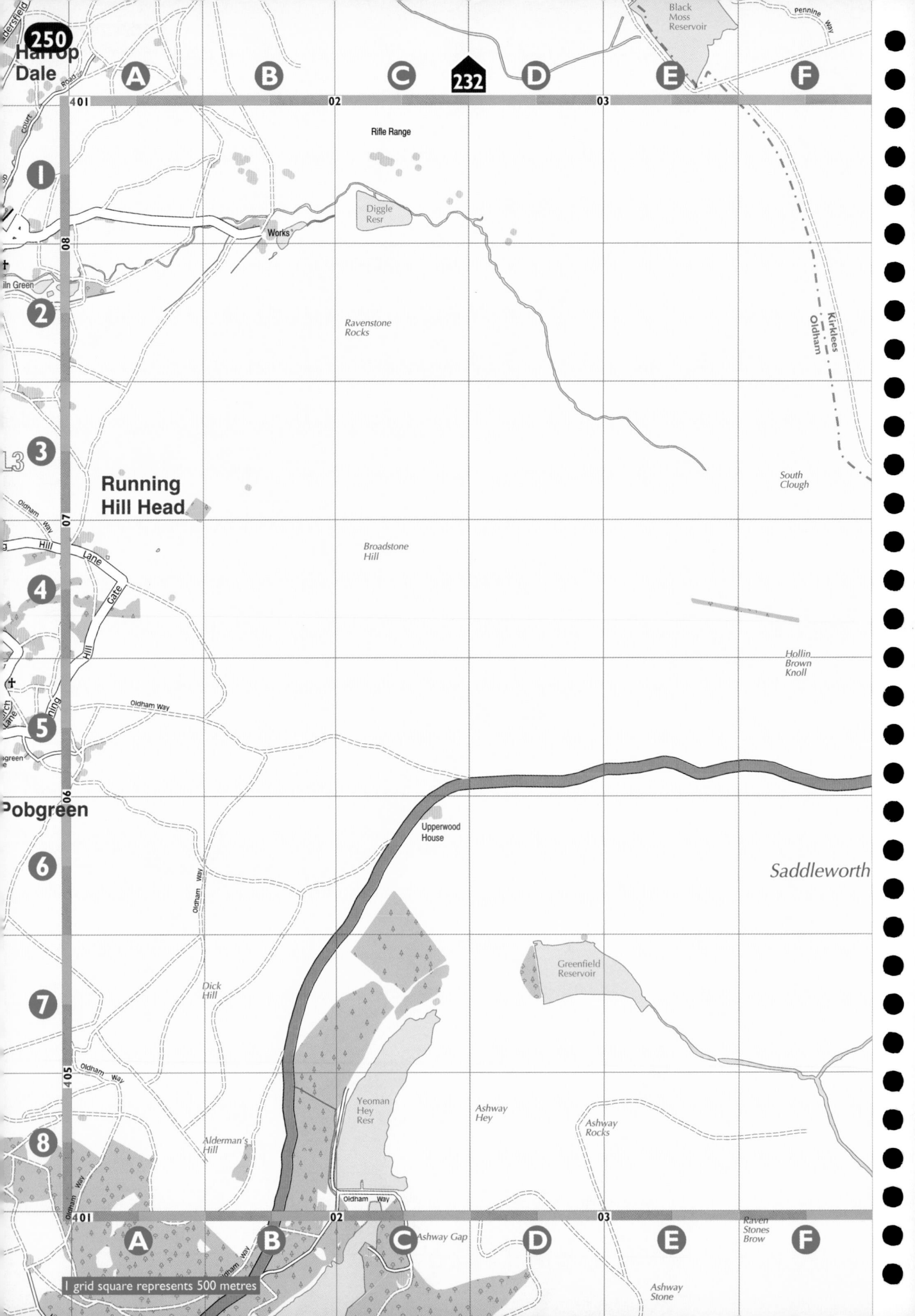

A B C **232** D E F

Rifle Range

Diggle
Resr

Works

Ravenstone
Rocks

South
Clough

**Running
Hill Head**

Broadstone
Hill

Hollin
Brown
Knoll

Oldham Way

Pobgreen

Upperwood
House

Saddleworth

Dick
Hill

Greenfield
Reservoir

Oldham Way

Yeoman
Hey
Resr

Ashway
Hey

Ashway
Rocks

Alderman's
Hill

Oldham Way

A B C Ashway Gap D E Raven
Stones
Brow F

Ashway
Stone

1 grid square represents 500 metres

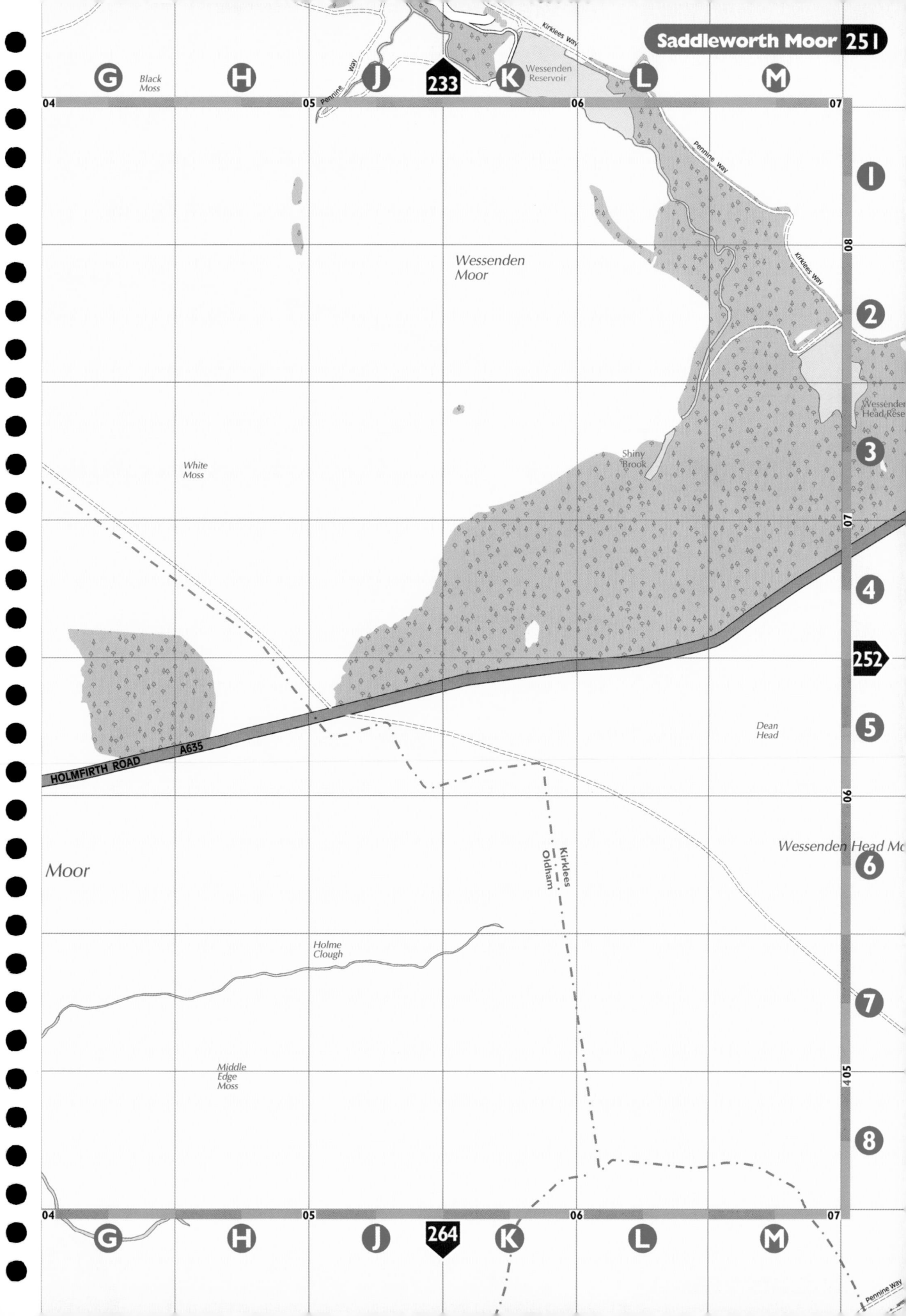

G Black Moss

H

J

233

K Wessenden Reservoir

L

M

Kirklees Way

Pennine Way

1

08

2

Wessenden Moor

Wessenden Head Rese

3

White Moss

Shiny Brook

Kirklees Way

07

4

252

Dean Head

5

06

Holmfirth Road A635

Moor

Wessenden Head Mo

6

Kirklees
Oldham

Holme Clough

7

405

Middle Edge Moss

8

Pennine Way

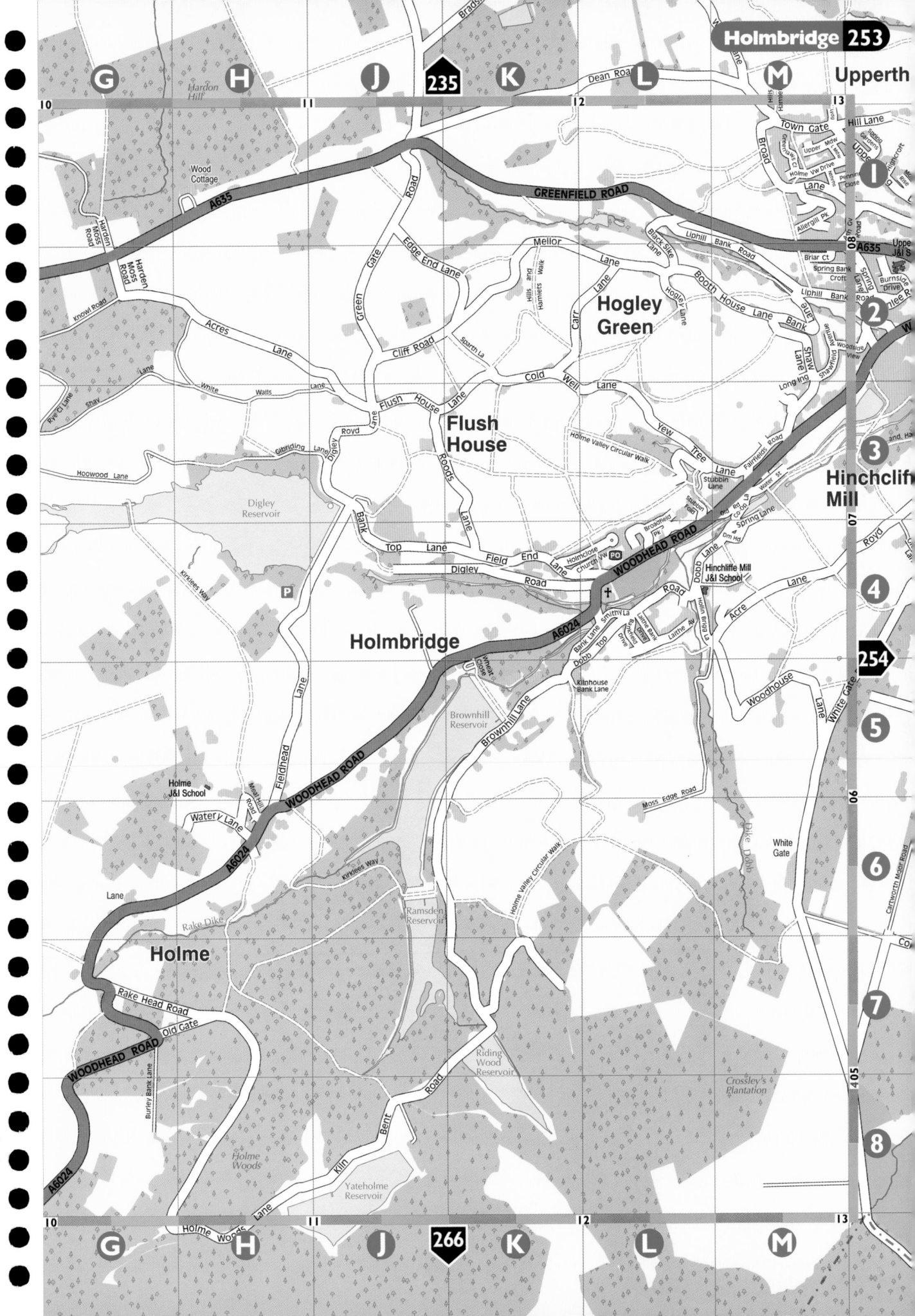

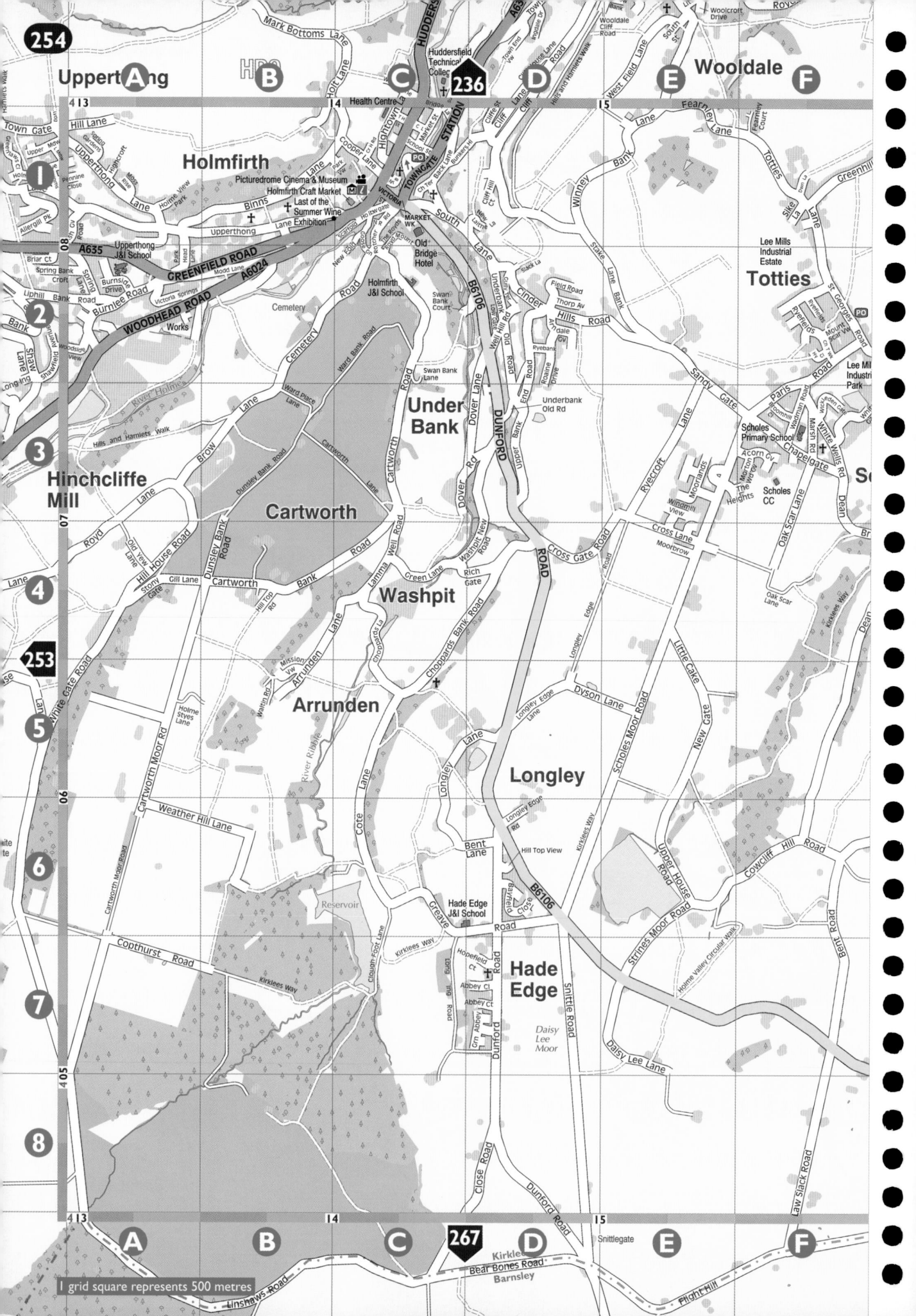

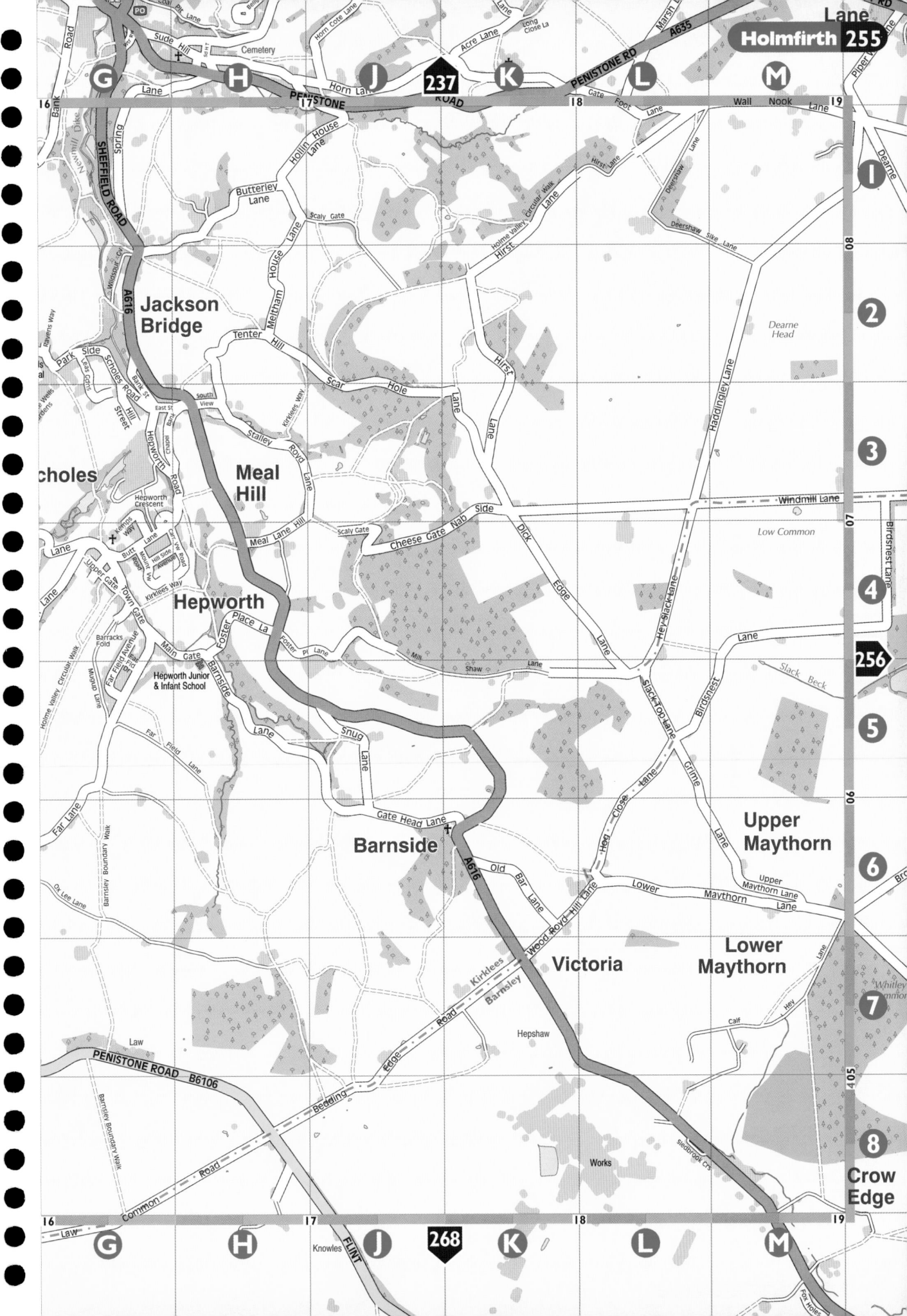

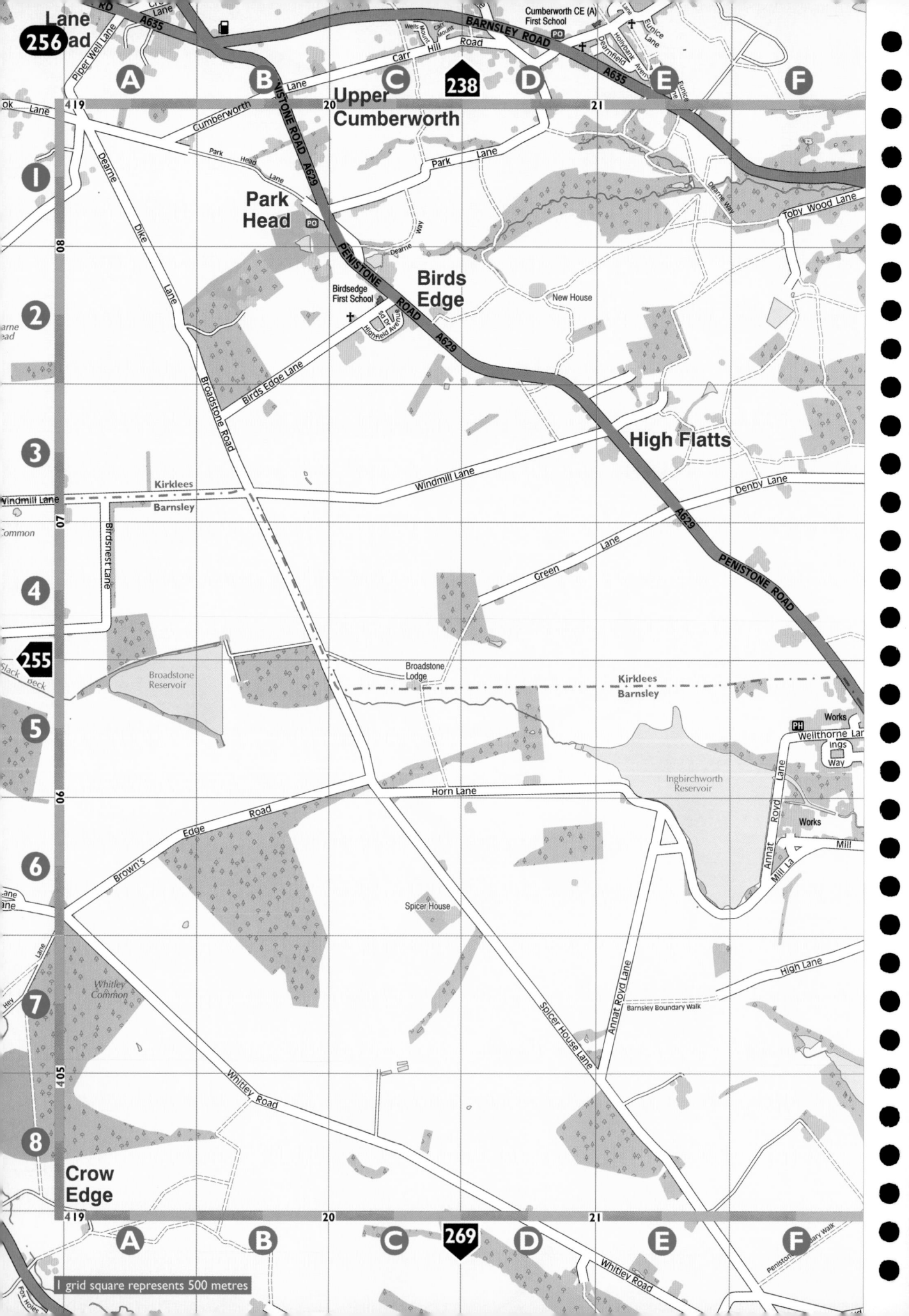

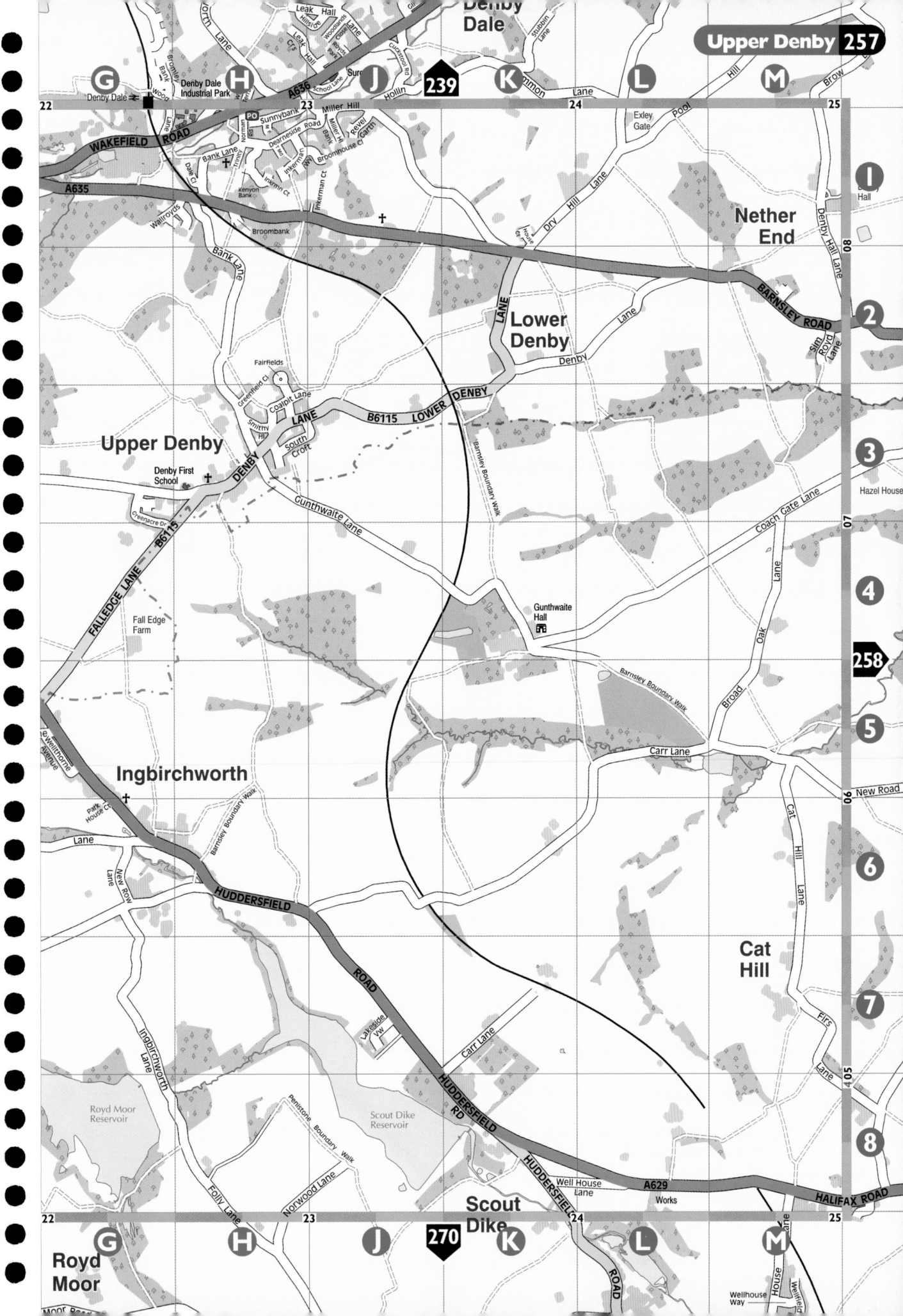

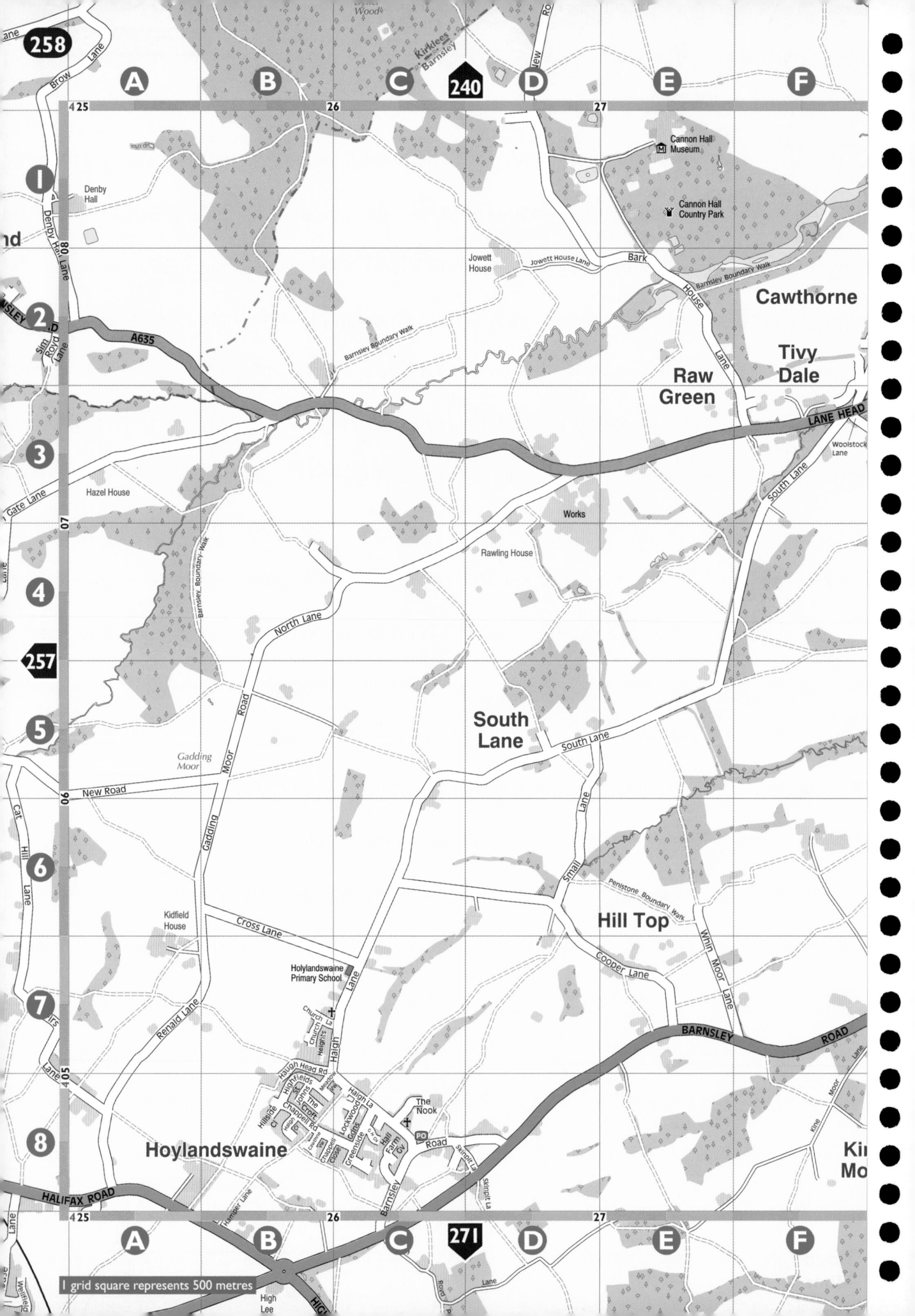

A   B   C   **240**   D   E   F

4 25   26   27

I
Denby Hall

80

2
A635

3
Hazel House

Gate Lane
07

4
North Lane

257

5
Gadding Moor

Road
New Road
90

6
Cat Hill Lane
Gadding

Kidfield House
Cross Lane

Holylandswaine Primary School

7
Renald Lane
405

8
Hoylandswaine

HALIFAX ROAD

4 25   26

A   B   C   **271**   D   E   F

Jowett House
Jowett House Lane
Barnsley Boundary Walk
Bark

Cannon Hall Museum
Cannon Hall Country Park

Cawthorne

Tivy Dale

House Lane

Raw Green

LANE HEAD

Woolstock Lane

South Lane

Works

Rawling House

South Lane
South Lane

Lane

Hill Top
Penistone Boundary Walk

Cooper Lane

Small Lane

Whin Moor Lane

BARNSLEY   ROAD

Church La
Church Heights
Haigh La
Haigh

Haigh Head Rd
Highfields
Hillside Cl
Chappell Rd
Lockwood
The
Greenside
Hall Farm Cv
The Nook
PO
Road
Barnsley
Skimpit La
Skimpit La

Kir Mo

Kine Moor Lane

27

HIGH

High Lee

Halifax Road   Welbeck

1 grid square represents 500 metres

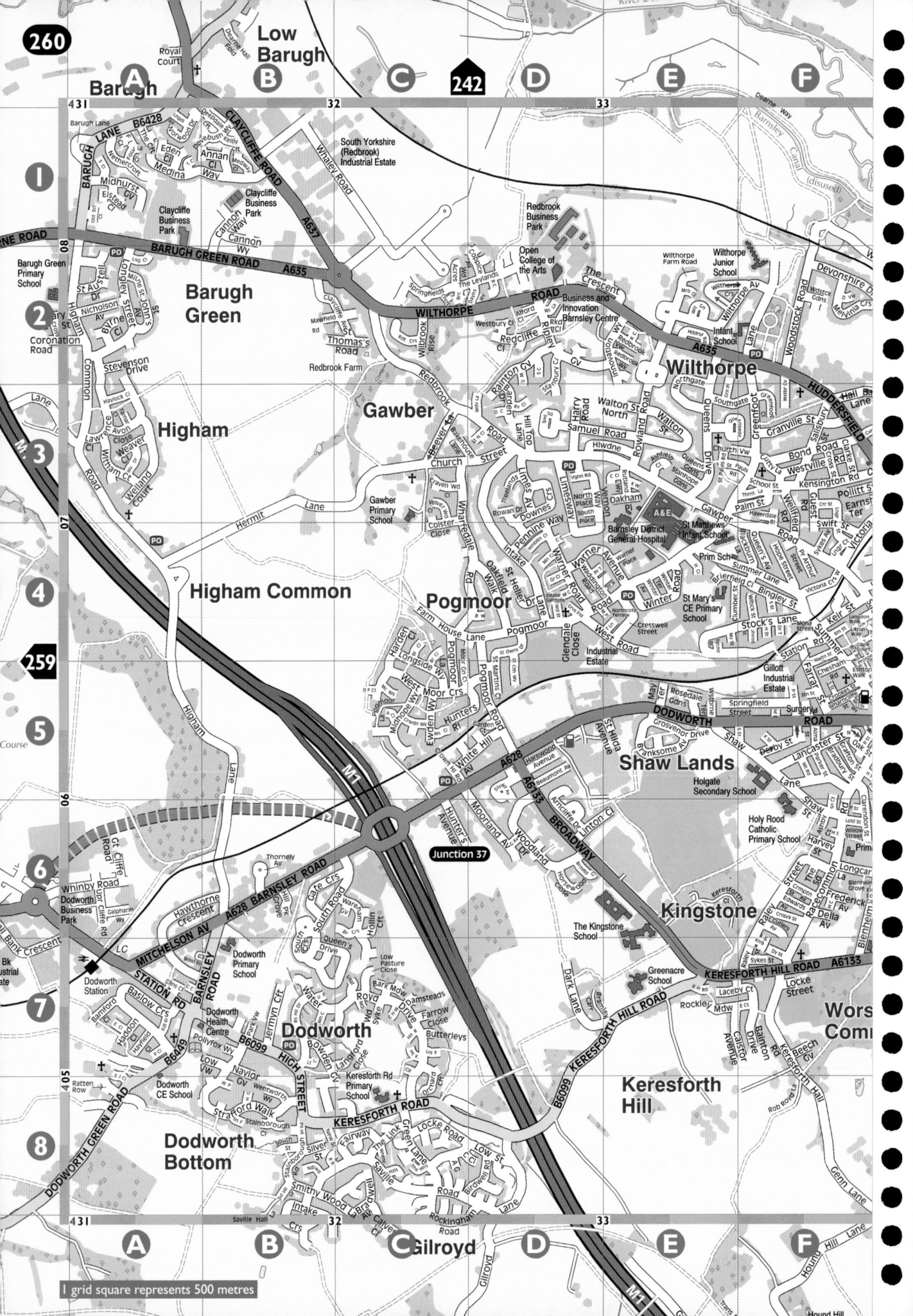

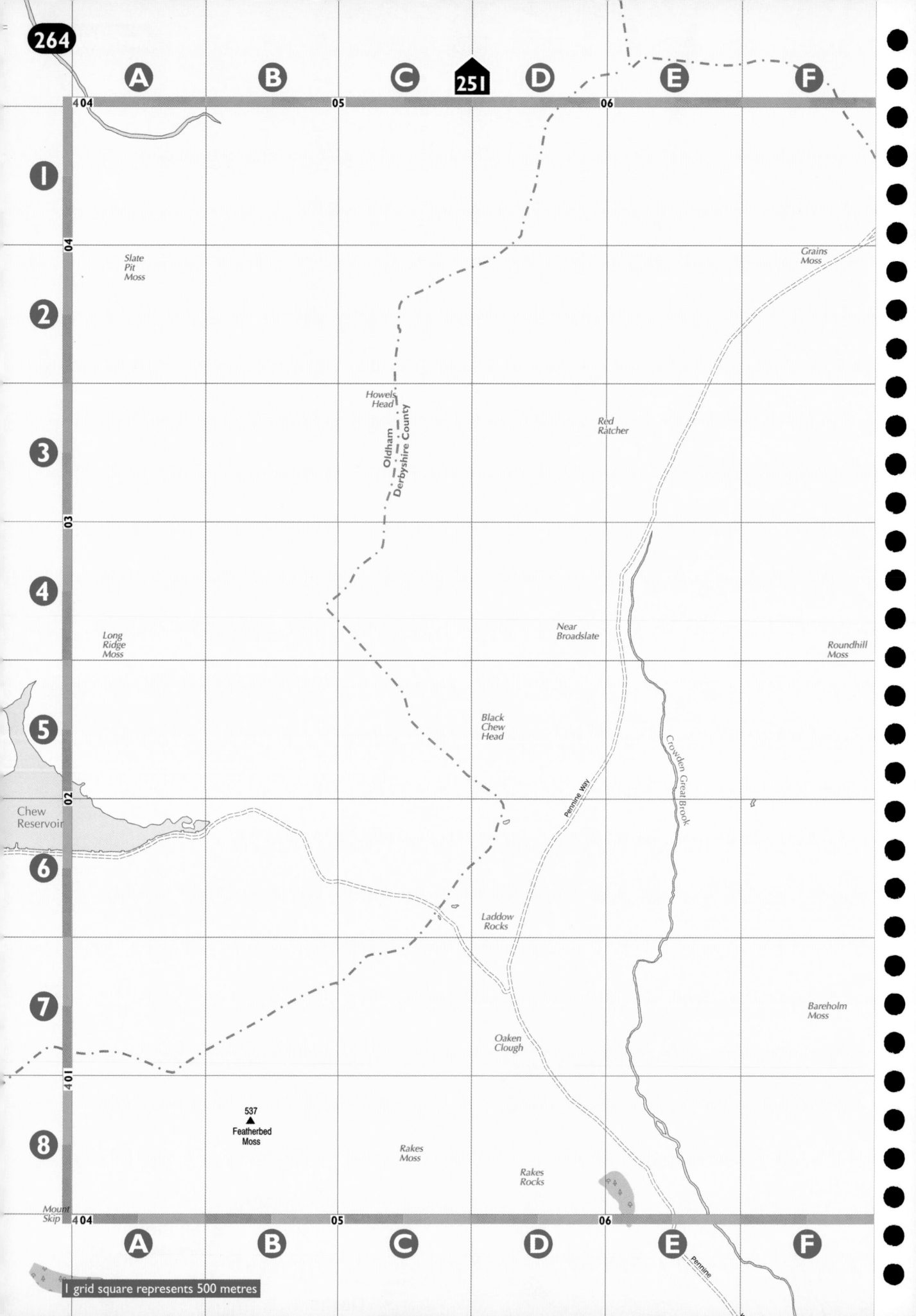

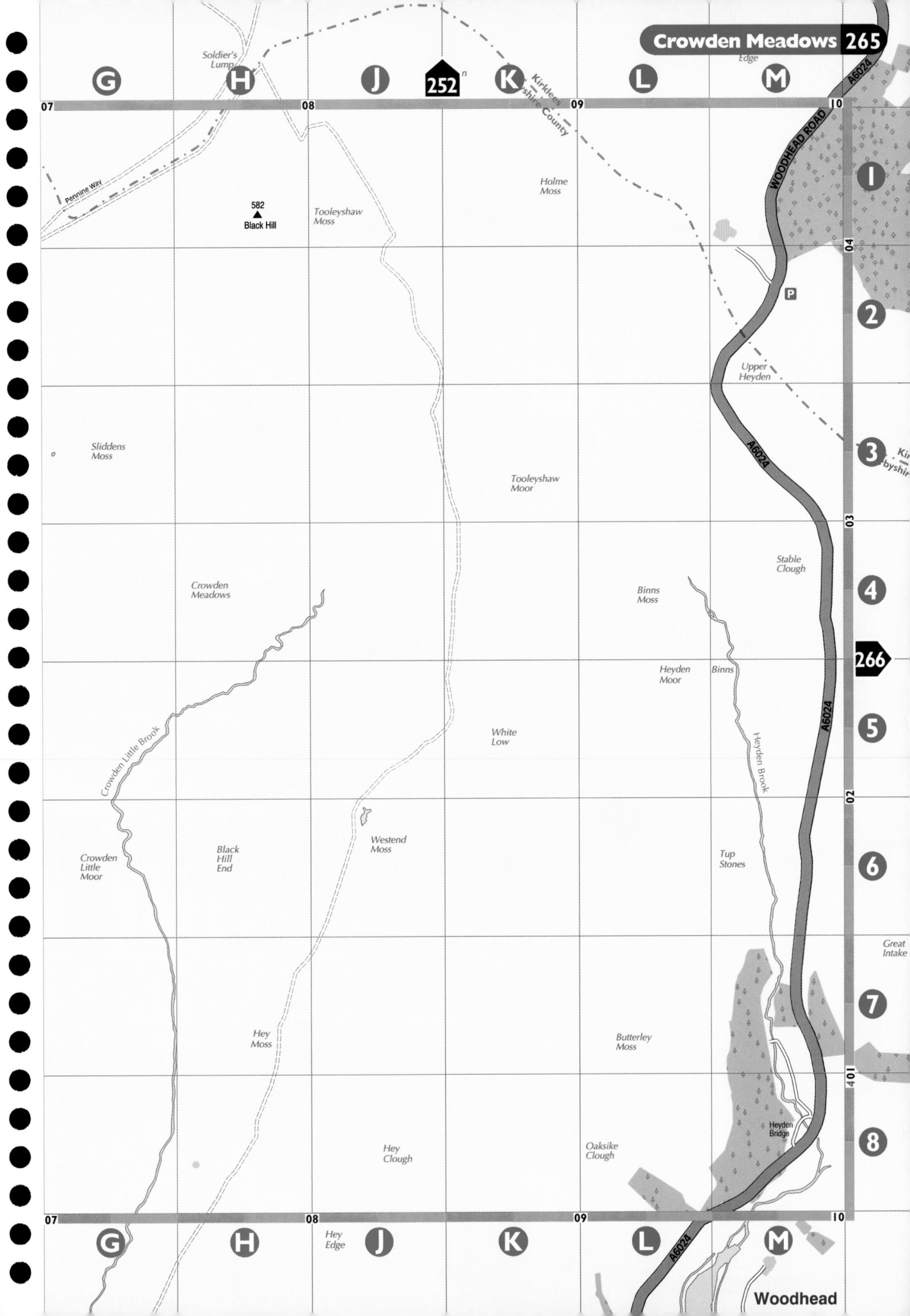

G

H

J

252

K

L

M

I

07

08

Kirklees
shire County

09

WOODHEAD ROAD

10

A6024

Pennine Way

582
▲
Black Hill

Tooleyshaw
Moss

Holme
Moss

Edge

P

Upper
Heyden

A6024

2

Sliddens
Moss

Tooleyshaw
Moor

3

Ki
byshir

03

Stable
Clough

4

Crowden
Meadows

Binns
Moss

266

Heyden
Moor

Binns

5

Crowden Little Brook

White
Low

Heyden Brook

A6024

02

Crowden
Little
Moor

Black
Hill
End

Westend
Moss

Tup
Stones

6

Great
Intake

7

Hey
Moss

Butterley
Moss

01

Heyden
Bridge

8

Hey
Clough

Oaksike
Clough

07

08

09

10

G

H

Hey
Edge

J

K

L

A6024

M

Woodhead

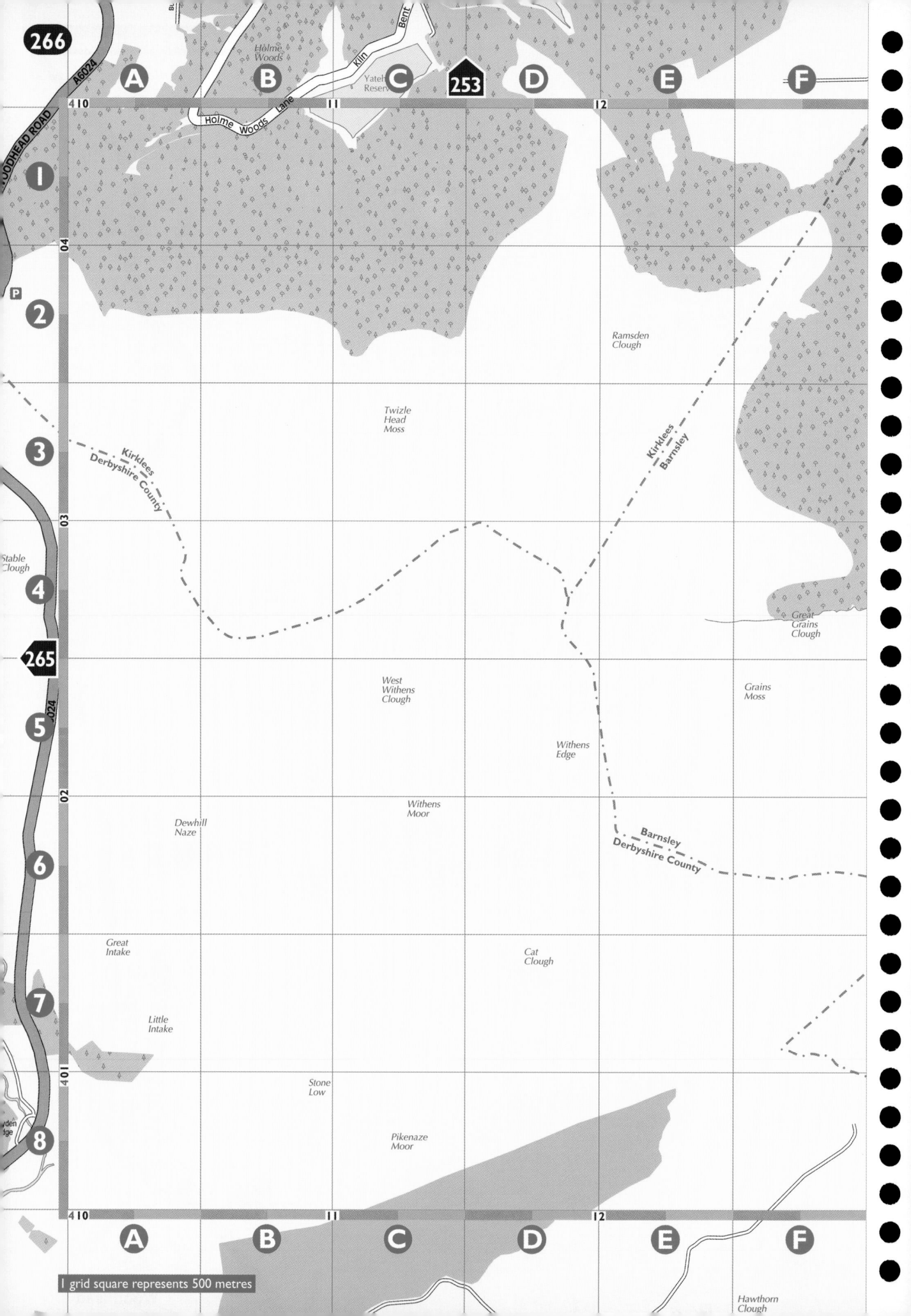

A6024
WOODHEAD ROAD

A   B   C   D   E   F

253

1
2
P
3
4
265
5
6
7
8

Holme Woods Lane
Holme Woods
Kiln
Bent
Yateh
Reserv

Ramsden
Clough

Twizle
Head
Moss

Kirklees
Derbyshire County

Kirklees
Barnsley

Stable
Clough

Great
Grains
Clough

West
Withens
Clough

Grains
Moss

Withens
Edge

Dewhill
Naze

Withens
Moor

Barnsley
Derbyshire County

Great
Intake

Cat
Clough

Little
Intake

Stone
Low

yden
dge

Pikenaze
Moor

Hawthorn
Clough

A   B   C   D   E   F

1 grid square represents 500 metres

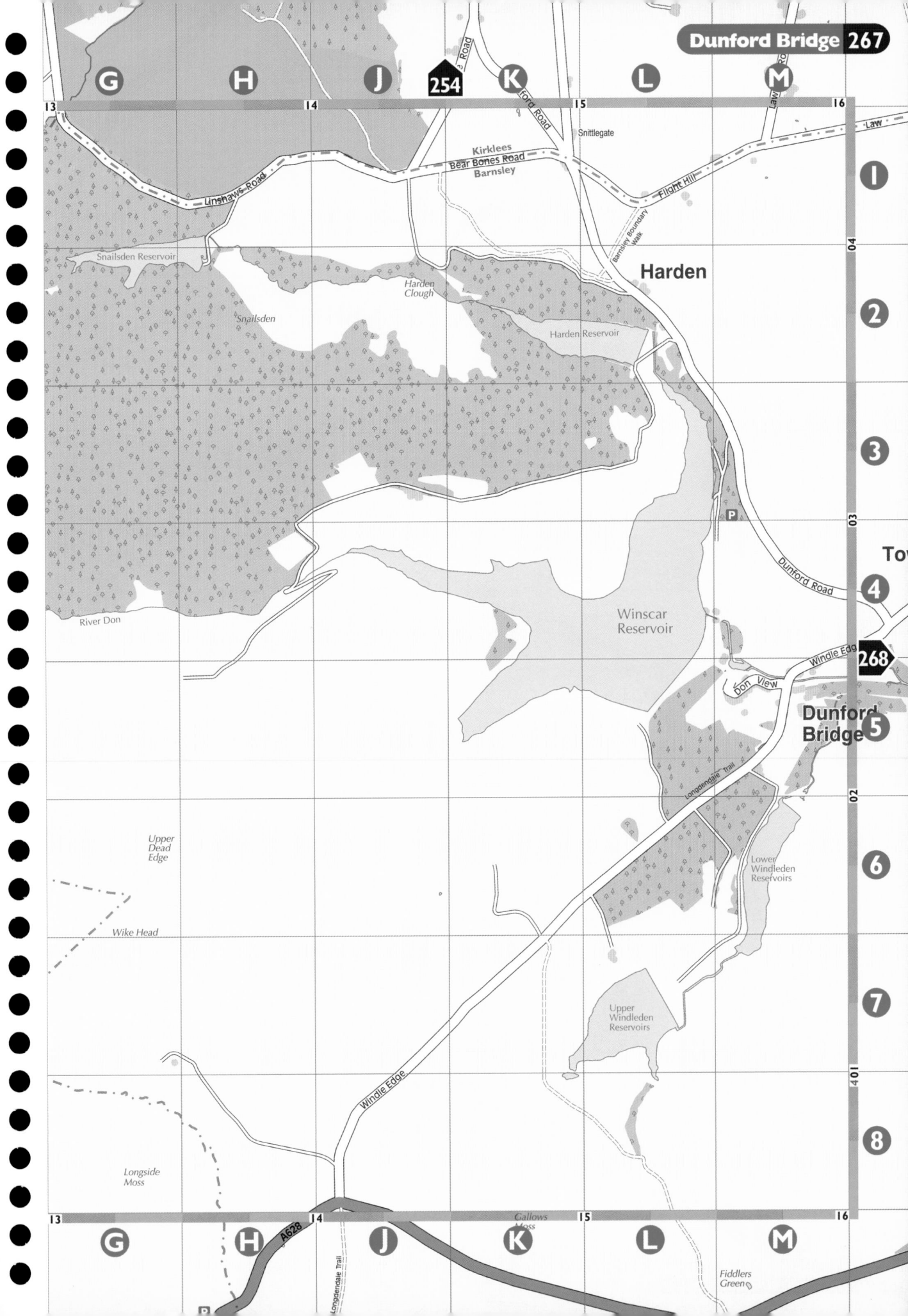

G H J **254** K L M

13 14 15 16

I

Kirklees
Bear Bones Road
Barnsley

Snittlegate

Linshaws Road

Flight Hill

Harden

Barnsley Boundary Walk

Snailsden Reservoir

Harden Clough

Snailsden

Harden Reservoir

2

3

P

Dunford Road

Tov

River Don

Winscar Reservoir

4

Windle Edge **268**

Don View

Dunford Bridge 5

Longdendale Trail

Upper Dead Edge

Lower Windleden Reservoirs

6

Wike Head

7

Upper Windleden Reservoirs

Windle Edge

8

Longside Moss

Gallows Moss

13 14 15 16

G H J K L M

A628

Longdendale Trail

Fiddlers Green

P

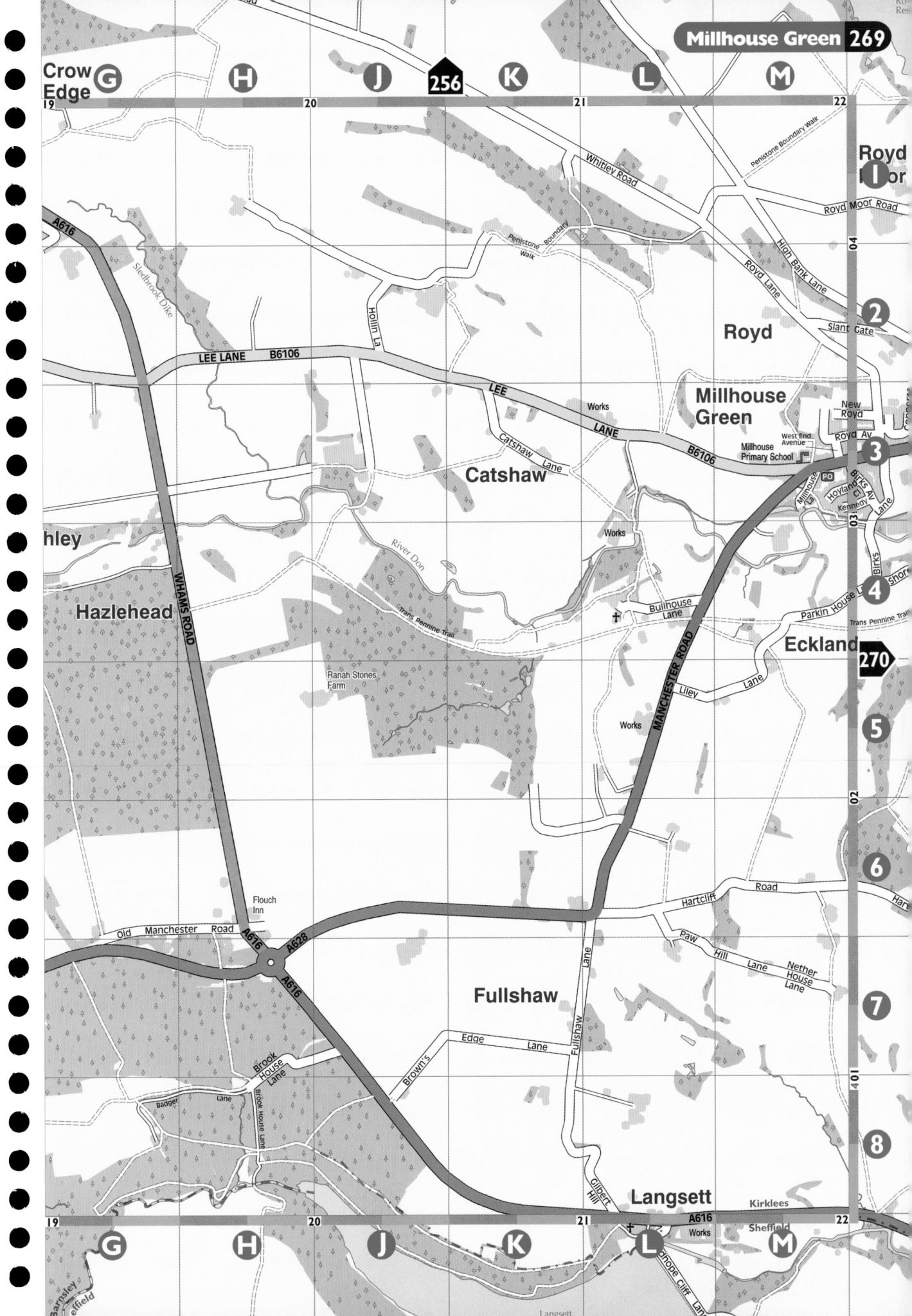

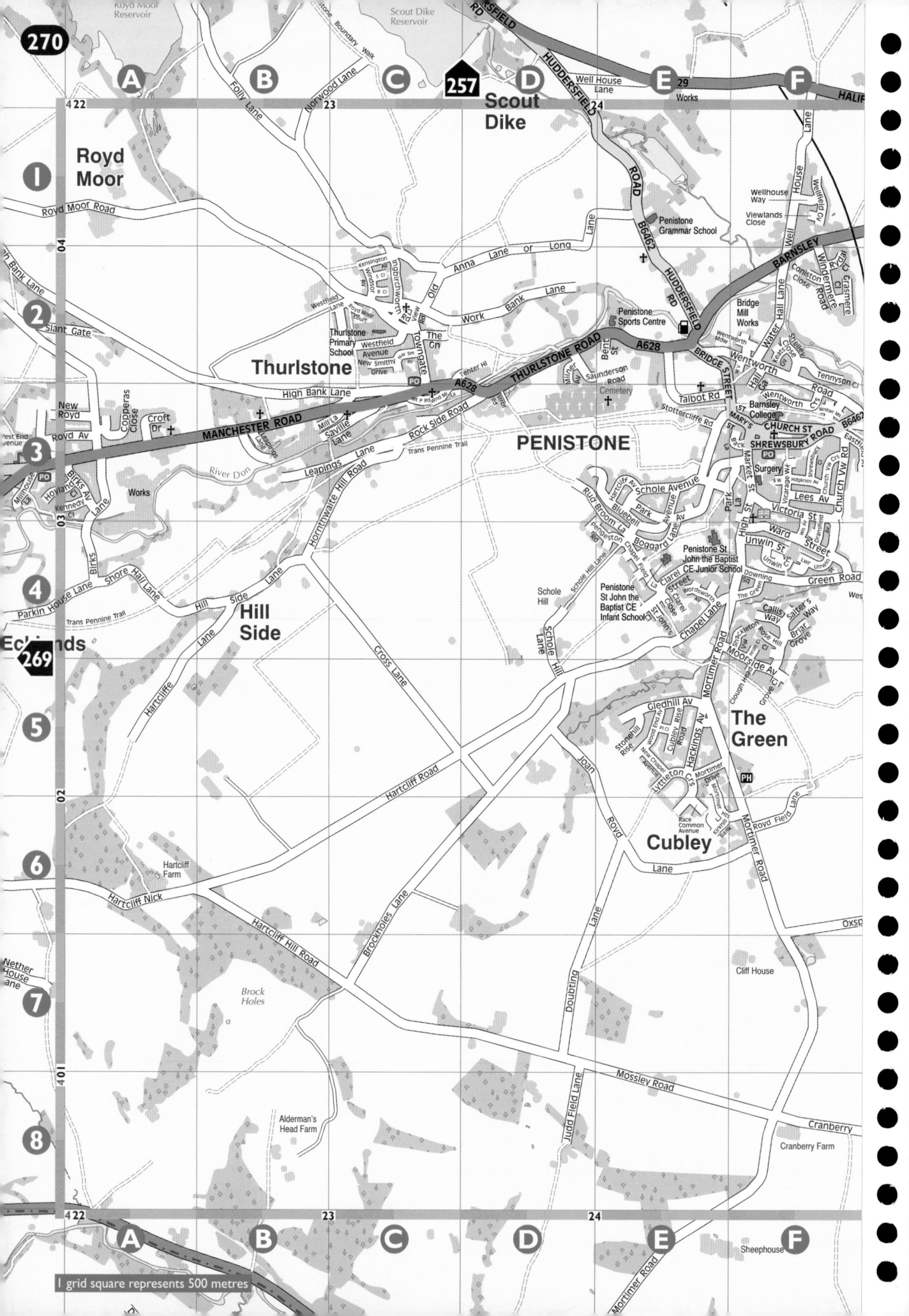

A   B   C   **257** D   E   29   F

Scout Dike

1 Royd Moor

Royd Moor Road

2 Slant Gate

Thurlstone

3 New Royd   Copperas Close   Croft Dr

MANCHESTER ROAD

PENISTONE

4 Parkin House Lane   Hill Side   Shore Hall Lane

Echlands

5

The Green

6 Hartcliff Farm

Hartcliff Nick

Hartcliff Hill Road

Cubley

7 Nether House Lane

Brock Holes

8 Alderman's Head Farm

Cliff House

Cranberry Farm

Sheephouse

A   B   C   D   E   F

I grid square represents 500 metres

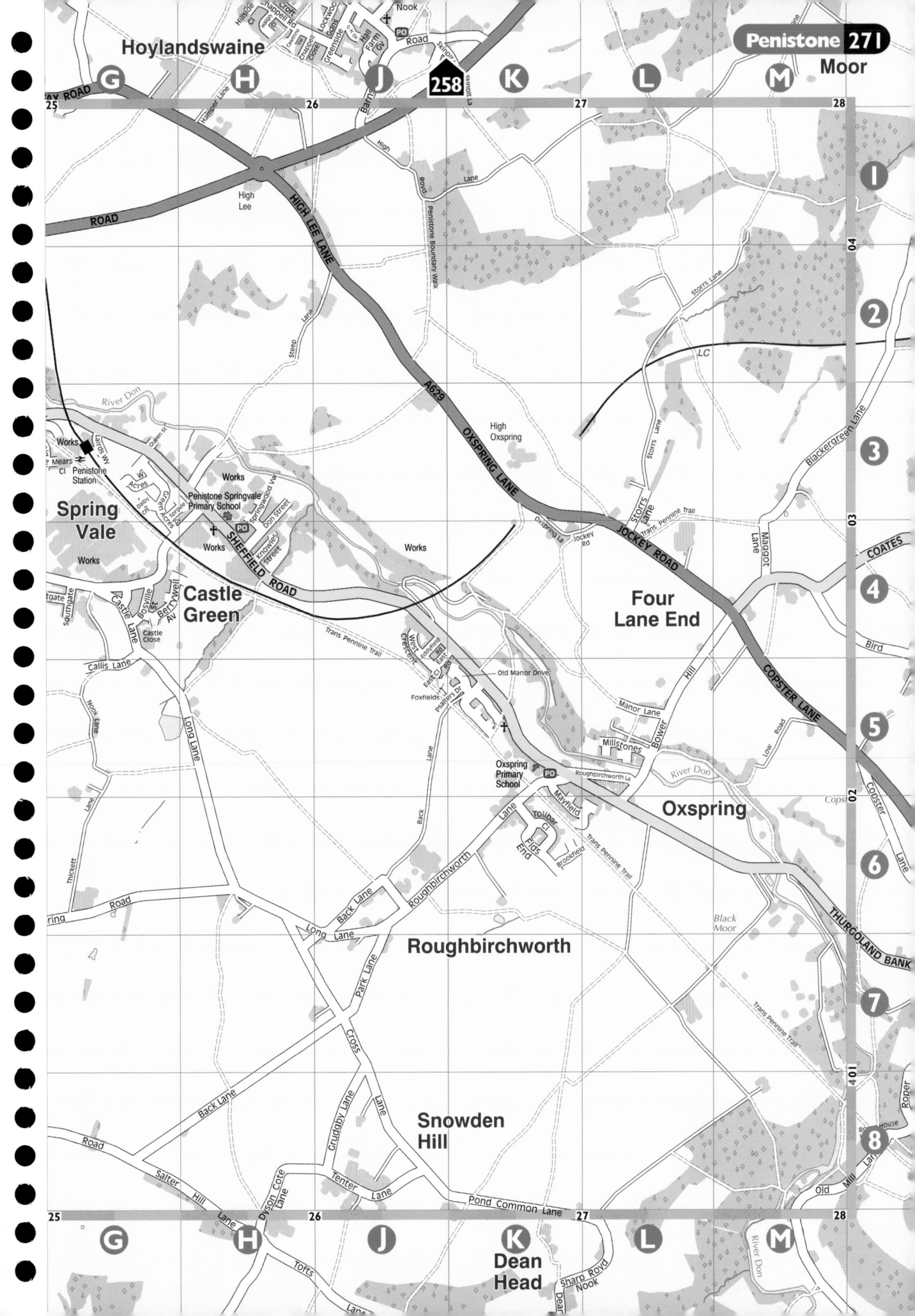

Aberford ...91 M7
Ackton ...179 J6
Ackworth Moor Top ...224 C1
Addingham ...19 G6
Addingham Moorside ...36 F2
Adel ...86 B2
Adwalton ...129 J8
Agbrigg ...13 J9
Ainley Top ...191 K3
Airedale ...158 D7
Aire View ...34 B4
Allerton ...103 L6
Allerton Bywater ...157 L2
Almondbury ...215 H2
Altofts ...178 A1
Alverthorpe ...176 A6
Alwoodley ...87 L1
Alwoodley Gates ...66 A8
Alwoodley Park ...65 H8
Ambler Thorn ...124 D6
Angram ...33 M8
Apperley Bridge ...84 A5
Appleton Roebuck ...75 M4
Ardsley ...262 B7
Armitage Bridge ...214 B7
Armley ...108 F6
Arrunden ...254 B5
Arthington ...43 M8
Arthursdale ...90 B6
Askwith ...40 B1
Athersley North ...243 H6
Athersley South ...243 J7
Austhorpe ...112 A6
Badsworth ...224 F4
Bagley ...107 G2
Baildon ...82 F3
Baildon Green ...82 C4
Bailiff Bridge ...148 C6
Balderstone ...228 B7
Bank End ...18 A5
Bank Top ...105 L1
Bank Top ...169 H1
Bantam Grove ...152 F2
Barcroft ...79 H6
Bardsey ...67 L2
Barkisland ...189 K2
Barkston Ash ...115 L1
Barmbow Carr ...112 E1
Barnside ...255 J6
Barnsley ...261 J7
Barugh ...242 A8
Barugh Green ...260 A2
Barwick in Elmet ...90 E8
Batley ...174 A4
Batley Carr ...173 L3
Battyeford ...194 A1
Beal ...161 K7
Beamsley ...19 G1
Beck Bottom ...175 L3
Beck Foot ...85 G5
Beechcliffe ...57 M5
Beechwood ...89 G8
Beeston ...131 G5
Beeston Hill ...8 D9
Beeston Park Side ...131 J7
Beeston Royds ...130 D3
Beggarington Hill ...174 E1
Belfield ...206 F7
Belle Green ...244 E7
Belle Isle ...132 A7
Belle Vue ...13 K7
Ben Rhydding ...39 G3
Bentgate ...229 J2
Berry Brow ...214 B6
Bickerton ...31 L4
Bierley ...127 K5
Biggin ...117 M4
Bilton in Ainsty ...32 C5
Bingley ...81 G4
Birchencliffe ...191 K4
Birds Edge ...256 C2
Birkby ...14 A1
Birkenshaw ...128 D8
Birkenshaw Bottoms ...150 E2
Birkhouse ...148 E8
Birkin ...161 J4
Birks ...152 C4
Birstall ...151 G4
Birstall Smithies ...151 G7
Blacker ...242 E7
Black Hill ...2 A1
Blackley ...191 G2
Black Moor ...87 J2
Blackmoorfoot ...213 G4
Blackshaw Head ...142 B3
Bleak Hey Nook ...231 L7
Bogthorn ...79 G2
Bolton ...105 H2
Bolton Percy ...73 J7
Bolton Woods ...105 G2
Booth ...145 G3
Boothroyd ...173 J6
Boothtown ...146 C4
Booth Wood ...188 E8
Boston Spa ...48 E7
Bottom Boat ...155 L8
Bottomley ...189 M3
Boulder Clough ...166 E1
Bowling ...127 K2
Bracken Bank ...79 H3
Bracken Hall ...82 A3
Brackenhall ...192 D2
Bracken Hill ...171 L7
Brackenhill ...201 L8
Bracken Park ...67 H7
Brackenthwaite ...26 A3
Bradford ...4 C6
Bradley ...171 H8
Bradley Mills ...15 M1
Bradshaw ...124 B5
Bradshaw ...211 J5
Bradup ...58 D1
Braithwaite ...56 F6
Bramham ...69 M3
Bramhope ...64 B3
Bramley ...107 G4
Brandy Carr ...175 M2
Braythorn ...24 E7
Brearley ...144 C6
Brierley ...245 H5
Briestfield ...195 J7
Brighouse ...170 B4
Briscoerigg ...25 G4
Broad Carr ...190 E2
Brockholes ...236 F4
Brookfoot ...170 A3
Brookhouse ...123 K6
Brooklands ...111 G1
Brotherton ...159 K6
Brown Moor ...112 B7
Bruntcliffe ...152 A3
Brunthwaite ...36 F5
Buckley ...206 C3
Buersil Head ...228 E5
Burghwallis ...249 K2
Burley ...108 F4
Burley in Wharfedale ...39 M5
Burley Woodhead ...39 K8
Burmantofts ...110 B5

Burn Bridge ...26 E2
Burnedge ...229 C5
Burton Salmon ...160 A2
Buttershaw ...125 M6
Byram ...159 M7
Cackleshaw ...78 F4
Calderbrook ...185 M5
Calder Grove ...197 L8
Caldermoor ...185 H8
Calverley ...84 E8
Cambridge ...41 L7
Campsall ...227 M6
Camp Town ...87 K3
Carcroft ...249 L4
Carlecotes ...268 C3
Carleton ...203 H1
Carlinghow ...151 H7
Carlton ...155 C3
Carlton ...243 M5
Carr Gate ...176 A1
Cartworth ...254 B3
Castleford ...157 K7
Castleford Ings ...158 A5
Castle Green ...271 H4
Castle Street ...164 A1
Catherine Slack ...124 E8
Cat Hill ...257 M7
Catshaw ...269 K3
Catterton ...51 L6
Causeway Foot ...124 A3
Causeway Foot ...238 A1
Cawthorne ...258 F2
Chapel Allerton ...87 L7
Chapelthorpe ...220 C2
Chapeltown ...87 L6
Charlestown ...83 C4
Charlestown ...142 F5
Chat Hill ...125 J1
Chequerfield ...181 H8
Chevin End ...61 M1
Chickenley ...174 D7
Chidswell ...174 D3
Chiserley ...143 L1
Church Clough ...74 A3
Church Fenton ...94 F8
Churwell ...130 E7
Claremount ...11 H5
Clayton ...125 L2
Clayton Heights ...125 L4
Clayton West ...240 C4
Cleckheaton ...150 A6
Clerk Green ...173 J2
Cliff End ...191 K8
Clifford ...69 M1
Clifton ...170 F4
Clifton ...41 G1
Clough ...185 J7
Clough ...229 M8
Clough Foot ...162 D2
Clough Head ...167 L5
Clough Head ...212 D3
Cockersdale ...129 H6
Cockley Hill ...193 M6
Colden ...120 C8
Cold Hiendley ...221 M5
Coley ...147 M4
Collingham ...47 H7
Colne Bridge ...193 J1
Colton ...111 L8
Combs ...195 M3
Compton ...47 M8
Cononley ...34 A3
Cookridge ...63 M8
Copley ...168 C4
Copley Hill ...151 H4
Cornholme ...140 C5
Cottingley ...81 J7
Cotton Stones ...166 E6
Cowcliffe ...192 B3
Cowling ...54 E4
Cowmes ...217 H1
Cowthorpe ...30 E1
Coxley ...196 F7
Crackenedge ...173 M5
Cragg Hill ...85 L6
Cragg Vale ...165 M2
Crawshaw ...217 J6
Cridling Stubbs ...183 G7
Crigglestone ...198 B8
Cringles ...18 B8
Crofton ...200 A6
Crompton Fold ...229 L5
Cromwell Bottom ...169 L5
Crosland Edge ...235 H1
Crosland Hill ...213 J4
Crosland Moor ...213 L3
Crossflatts ...59 H8
Cross Gates ...111 J5
Cross Green ...132 B1
Cross Hills ...34 F8
Crossley ...172 D6
Crossley Hall ...104 A7
Cross Roads ...79 G5
Crow Edge ...256 A8
Crow Nest ...81 K3
Cubley ...270 E6
Cudworth ...244 E8
Cudworth Common ...262 F2
Cullingworth ...79 K8
Cundy Cross ...261 M5
Cutsyke ...179 L1
Daisy Hill ...103 M4
Daisy Hill ...130 E8
Dalton ...193 H8
Damems ...79 H4
Dam Head ...172 B6
Darrington ...203 L1
Darton ...242 A6
Daw Cross ...26 C2
Dearnley ...207 H2
Deighton ...193 H2
Denby Dale ...239 K8
Denholme ...101 L6
Denholme Clough ...102 A8
Denholme Edge ...101 L5
Denholme Gate ...123 M1
Denshaw ...230 F4
Denton ...21 J8
Dewsbury ...173 L7
Dewsbury Moor ...173 C5
Dockroyd ...78 E5
Dodworth ...260 B7
Dodworth Bottom ...260 A8
Dodworth Green ...259 M8
Dogley Lane ...215 L5
Draughton ...17 L1
Drighlington ...129 H8
Druid ...150 B4
Dudley Hill ...127 L4
Dunford Bridge ...267 M5
Dunkeswick ...44 H4
Durkar ...198 C7
Durn ...207 L1
Earlsheaton ...174 A7
East Ardsley ...153 J2
East Bierley ...128 B7
Eastburn ...35 J8

East Carlton ...63 G3
East Garforth ...113 L6
East Hardwick ...203 H4
East Keswick ...46 E8
East Moor ...177 H7
East Morton ...59 G5
East Rigton ...68 A1
Eastwood ...142 D6
Eccleshill ...105 K1
Eccup ...65 J5
Ecklands ...269 M4
Edgerton ...191 M6
Egypt ...102 D6
Eldwick ...59 L8
Elland ...169 J8
Elland Lower Edge ...169 L7
Elland Upper Edge ...169 K8
Emley ...217 L7
Esholt ...83 L1
Exley ...168 E4
Facit ...184 A4
Fagley ...105 M3
Fairburn ...159 H1
The Fall ...153 M6
Farnhill ...34 E5
Farnley ...41 M2
Farnley ...130 A1
Farnley ...124 C8
Farnley Bank ...215 G6
Farnley Tyas ...215 H8
Far Royds ...130 E2
Farsley ...106 F3
Farsley Beck Bottom ...107 G3
Fartown ...192 C4
Fearnville ...111 G2
Featherstone ...179 K8
Felkirk ...222 C8
Fell Lane ...2 A6
Fenay Bridge ...215 L2
Ferrybridge ...159 L8
Firgrove ...206 F8
Fishpool ...42 C2
Fitzwilliam ...223 J2
Five Lane Ends ...105 J1
Fixby ...192 B1
Flanshaw ...176 A8
Flockton ...217 L3
Flockton Green ...218 A3
Flushdyke ...175 H7
Flush House ...253 K1
Follifoot ...28 A1
Foulby ...200 E6
Foulridge ...52 A5
Four Lane End ...271 L4
Four Lane Ends ...104 A6
Fox Royd ...195 K4
Friendly ...167 J1
Frizinghall ...104 C1
Fullshaw ...269 K7
Fulneck ...128 F1
Fulstone ...237 J2
Gale ...185 L7
Gamble Hill ...108 A6
Garden Village ...114 B8
Garforth ...135 K1
Gawber ...260 C3
Gawthorpe ...174 F5
Gawthorpe ...193 M8
Gildersome ...129 M6
Gildersome Street ...151 M1
Gill ...54 C5
Gilstead ...59 L8
Gipton ...110 F3
Gipton Wood ...88 D8
Girlington ...104 C5
Glass Houghton ...180 C1
Gledhow ...88 C7
Golcar ...212 F2
Gomersal ...150 E6
Goose Eye ...56 D8
Goosehill ...177 M7
Grains Bar ...230 C8
Grange Moor ...217 H1
Gravel Hole ...228 F7
Great Cliff ...219 L2
Great Horton ...126 B2
Great Howarth ...206 C2
Great Preston ...135 G6
Green Clough ...124 D1
Greengate ...206 F3
Greengates ...83 M7
Green Hill ...92 B6
Green Side ...130 E1
Green Side ...237 J2
Greenside ...215 H1
The Green ...270 F5
Greetland ...168 C6
Greetland Wall Nook ...167 M8
Grimethorpe ...245 J7
Grove Town ...181 G7
Guard House ...57 G7
Guiseley ...61 L6
Hade Edge ...254 D7
Haigh ...241 J2
Haigh Moor ...153 H8
Hainworth ...79 L3
Hainworth Shaw ...79 M3
Halifax ...11 H7
Hall Bower ...214 D5
Hall Green ...220 B3
Halton ...111 G6
Halton Moor ...110 F7
Hambleton ...139 M5
Hampole ...248 D5
Hanging Heaton ...174 A3
Harden ...80 D5
Harden ...267 L2
Hare Croft ...80 B2
Harehills ...110 D4
Harewood ...45 J7
Harewood Hill ...79 G4
Harrop Dale ...231 M8
Hartshead ...171 L5
Hartshead Moor Side ...149 J8
Hartshead Moor Top ...149 G7
Haugh ...229 L3
Havercroft ...222 D5
Hawks Stones ...141 G3
Hawksworth ...61 H6
Hawksworth Wood ...85 M7
Haworth ...78 D7
Hazlehead ...269 G4
Headingley ...108 D1
Healaugh ...51 H2
Healey ...173 J1
Healey ...196 E3
Healey ...206 A2
Heath Common ...199 K2
Heaton ...104 A3
Heaton Royds ...104 B1
Heaton Shay ...104 B1
Hebden Bridge ...143 K3
Heckmondwike ...172 F2
Helme ...235 G2
Hemsworth ...223 K7
Henshaw ...84 C1
Heptonstall ...143 G1
Hepworth ...255 G4
Hessle ...202 A7
Hey Green ...232 E1

High Ackworth ...202 C6
Higham ...260 A3
Higham Common ...260 A4
High Bradley ...16 E6
Highburton ...216 B6
High Crompton ...229 G7
Higher Ogden ...230 B1
High Flatts ...256 E3
High Green ...216 B4
High Hoyland ...240 F5
Highroad Well Moor ...145 K5
Hightown ...171 M1
Hightown Heights ...149 L8
Hilam ...138 E8
Hillfoot ...106 E6
Hill Side ...193 L1
Hill Side ...270 B4
Hill Top ...102 E7
Hill Top ...108 A4
Hill Top ...212 A7
Hill Top ...258 D6
Hinchcliffe Mill ...253 M3
Hipperholme ...147 K6
Hogley Green ...253 L2
Holbeck ...8 D4
Holden Gate ...57 M1
Holdsworth ...124 C8
Hole ...78 D8
Hole Bottom ...141 K7
Hollingthorpe ...219 M3
Hollin Hall ...74 E5
Hollin Park ...110 E1
Hollinthorpe ...134 C2
Holmbridge ...253 J4
Holme ...128 B2
Holme ...253 G7
Holme Wood ...128 B3
Holmfield ...146 B1
Holmfirth ...254 A1
Holt Head ...234 C1
Holt Park ...86 B1
Holywell Green ...190 D3
Honley ...236 A2
Honley Moor ...235 M3
Honresfeld ...185 M8
Hoo Hole ...143 M7
Hopetown ...178 F3
Horbury ...197 J6
Horbury Bridge ...196 F5
Horbury Junction ...197 L6
Horsforth ...85 H4
Horsforth Woodside ...85 L6
Hough Side ...107 K6
Houses Hill ...194 A8
Hove Edge ...170 A1
Howden Clough ...151 K4
Hoylandswaine ...258 A8
Hoyle Mill ...261 L5
Hubberton Green ...166 E4
Huby ...43 L2
Huddersfield ...15 H7
Hungate ...156 B6
Hunslet ...9 K8
Hunslet Carr ...131 M4
Hunsworth ...150 A3
Hurstead ...206 E2
Hutton Wandesley ...33 M4
Ickornshaw ...54 C3
Idle ...83 K6
Idle Moor ...83 H8
Ilkley ...38 C2
Illingworth ...124 A4
Ingbirchworth ...257 C5
Ingmanthorpe ...30 D4
Ingrow ...79 J3
Intake ...107 H3
Ireland Wood ...86 B4
Jackson Bridge ...255 G2
Jagger Green ...190 D3
Jaw Hill ...175 J2
John O'Gaunts ...133 K7
Jubilee ...229 K4
Junction ...217 H1
Kearby Town End ...45 K5
Kebroyd ...166 F8
Keelham ...124 B1
Keighley ...3 H4
Kelbrook ...52 C1
Kelcliffe ...61 M4
Kellingley ...182 F2
Kellington ...161 M7
Kendray ...261 K8
Keresforth Hill ...260 E8
Kettlethorpe ...198 C8
Kexbrough ...241 L5
Kiddal Lane End ...91 G2
Kildwick ...35 G6
Killingbeck ...111 G4
Kine Moor ...258 F8
Kingstone ...223 J4
Kinsley ...223 J4
Kippax ...135 K4
Kirkburton ...216 A8
Kirkby Overblow ...27 K7
Kirkby Wharfe ...72 C8
Kirk Deighton ...29 L5
Kirkhamgate ...175 K4
Kirkheaton ...193 L5
Kirkholt ...228 A3
Kirk Smeaton ...226 E1
Kirkstall ...108 C3
Kirkthorpe ...177 M8
Kitchenroyd ...239 J7
Knottingley ...182 A2
Knowle Park ...2 D8
Knowl Wood ...163 J3
Knowsthorpe ...9 M6
Krumlin ...189 J5
Lady House ...229 G2
Lady Wood ...88 E7
Laisterdyke ...105 M8
Lane Bottom ...101 K4
Lane End ...78 C4
Lane Ends ...55 G2
Lane Ends ...85 H3
Lane Head ...216 C8
Lane Head ...237 M8
Laneshaw Bridge ...53 C7
Langbar ...19 L3
Langsett ...269 L8
Larkfield ...84 F2
Lawns ...154 A8
Lawnswood ...86 C4
Laycock ...56 E7
Leathley ...42 C3
Leaventhorpe ...103 L8
Ledsham ...136 F6
Ledston ...135 M8
Ledston Luck ...136 A4
Leeds ...6 E7
Leeming ...100 F5
Lee Moor ...155 C7
Lees ...79 G6
Lepton ...216 C2
Lepton Edge ...216 E3
Leymoor ...213 G1
Lidget Green ...126 C1
Lidgett Park ...88 C6
Lightcliffe ...148 B6

Lighthazles ...166 C8
Lindley ...24 A7
Lindley ...191 K5
Lindwell ...168 E6
Lingards Wood ...211 L8
Lingbob ...102 F2
Linthwaite ...212 E5
Linton ...47 J4
Littleborough ...207 K1
Little Clegg ...207 G4
Little Fenton ...117 G3
Little Horton ...126 D3
Little Houghton ...263 M6
Little Lepton ...216 C4
Little London ...84 C5
Little Preston ...134 E5
Little Smeaton ...205 H8
Little Thorpe ...171 M6
Littletown ...172 C1
Liversedge ...172 C2
Lockwood ...214 A2
Lofthouse ...154 F6
Lofthouse Gate ...154 E8
Long Lee ...3
Longley ...167 H5
Longley ...254 D5
Long Marston ...33 J3
Longwood ...191 H8
Longwood Edge ...191 G2
Loscoe ...179 H3
Low Ackworth ...202 E7
Low Barugh ...242 B8
Low Bradley ...34 F1
Low Compton ...229 G8
Lower Altofts ...156 D8
Lower Clough ...212 F6
Lower Cumberworth ...239 H7
Lower Denby ...257 K2
Lower Grange ...103 L7
Lower Hopton ...194 A3
Lower Houses ...214 F3
Lower Maythorn ...255 H7
Lower Mickletown ...157 H3
Lower Place ...228 E2
Lower Soothill ...152 A8
Lower Town ...100 F4
Lower Wyke ...148 E6
Low Fold ...85 H6
Low Green ...84 E5
Low Laithes ...262 D7
Low Moor ...148 F1
Low Snaygill ...16 C6
Luddenden ...145 G5
Luddenden Foot ...144 E8
Lumb Foot ...78 B6
Lumb Head ...214 E6
The Lumb ...214 E6
Lumbutts ...164 A2
Lumby ...137 M5
Lundwood ...262 B1
Lupset ...198 A2
Lydgate ...140 F7
Mankinholes ...164 C2
Manningham ...104 E4
Manor Park ...39 M3
Manston ...112 A4
Mapplewell ...242 E5
Marsden ...233 G3
Marsh ...100 D2
Marsh ...191 L8
Meal Hill ...255 H3
Meanwood ...87 G6
Measborough Dike ...261 K6
Meltham ...235 G3
Meltham Mills ...235 H4
Menston ...61 H3
Merchant Fields ...150 A5
Methley ...156 E4
Methley Junction ...156 F6
Methley Lanes ...156 A7
Micklefield ...114 B8
Micklethwaite ...59 G7
Mickletown ...157 G3
Middlecliffe ...263 L7
Middlestown ...196 C7
Middleton ...20 D7
Middleton ...54 C3
Middleton ...153 M2
Midgehole ...121 J8
Midgley ...144 E5
Midgley ...218 E4
Miles Hill ...87 J8
Mill Bank ...166 F7
Millhouse Green ...269 L3
Mill Shaw ...131 C5
Minrow ...207 J8
Milnsbridge ...213 H2
Milnthorpe ...198 E2
Minsthorpe ...247 H1
Mirfield ...172 C7
Mixenden ...145 L1
Moldgreen ...15 K8
Monk Bretton ...261 K2
Monk Fryston ...138 C7
Monkhill ...180 F4
Monkswood ...89 H7
Moor Allerton ...87 M4
Moor End ...48 D6
Moor End ...145 J2
Moorhead ...82 A7
Moor Head ...129 L6
Moor Head ...217 H6
Moorhouse ...247 M5
Moor Side ...100 B2
Moor Side ...148 F1
Moorside ...107 L2
Moorside ...145 J4
Moorside ...216 C4
Moorthorpe ...246 F4
Moor Top ...172 A6
Moortown ...87 L4
Morley ...152 D3
Mount ...190 E5
Mountain ...124 D4
Mount Pleasant ...173 L2
Mount Tabor ...145 J3
Mytholm ...143 H3
Mytholmes ...78 F6
Mytholmroyd ...144 B4
Nab Wood ...81 M6
Netherby ...45 M4
Nether End ...257 M1
Netherthong ...233 H4
Netheroyd Hill ...192 C3
Netherthong ...236 C6
Netherton ...196 F4
Netherton ...213 M8
Nether Yeadon ...84 C1
Nettleton Hill ...190 D7
Newall ...41 J5
Newbold ...206 D7
New Brighton ...81 L8
New Brighton ...152 B2
Newby ...43 K3
New Crofton ...200 D7
New Farnley ...130 A3
New Fryston ...158 F3
Newhey ...229 H3
New Holland ...102 E3
New Lodge ...242 F7

New Micklefield 114 D8
New Mill 237 G7
Newmillerdam 220 E2
New Road Side 54 F3
New Road Side 148 F2
Newsam Green 133 L5
New Scarbro 107 M4
New Sharlston 200 B1
Newsholme 78 C2
Newsome 214 C5
Newstead 222 E4
Newthorpe 137 H1
Newton Hill 176 E3
Newton Kyme 50 A7
New Town 180 F2
New Wortley 109 G7
Noblethorpe 259 G7
Noon Nick 103 K2
Norland Town 167 M4
Normanton 178 B4
Norr 102 F1
Norristhorpe 172 D4
North Deighton 29 L2
North Elmsall 225 K8
North Featherstone 179 M5
Northorpe 172 F7
Northowram 147 K4
North Rigton 26 A7
Norton 227 L3
Norwood Green 148 A3
Notton 221 H8
Oakenshaw 149 G2
Oakes 191 J6
Oakwell 150 F5
Oakwood 110 E1
Oakworth 78 D5
Odsal 127 G6
Ogden 123 M4
Old Bramhope 63 K3
Old Dolphin 125 J4
Oldfield 77 M6
Oldfield 236 B5
Old Lindley 190 F3
Old Micklefield 114 B6
Old Snydale 179 G7
Old Tame 230 D6
Old Town 143 K1
Osmondthorpe 110 D7
Ossett 174 F8
Ossett Spa 197 J3
Ossett Street Side 174 D6
Otley 41 K6
Oulton 155 K1
Ousel Hole 59 G4
Outlane 190 C5
Outlane Moor 190 B8
Outwood 176 C2
Ouzlewell Green 155 C5
Ovenden 146 B4
Overthorpe 195 L4
Overton 196 C8
Overtown 221 J1
Owlet 104 E1
Oxenhope 100 E4
Oxspring 271 L6
Oxton 72 C3
Paddock 213 M1
Painthorpe 220 H3
Pannal 26 E3
Park Gate 239 J2
Park Head 256 B1
Parklands 111 H2
Park Mill 240 C2
Park Villas 88 C5
Parlington 113 L2
Peas Acre 59 G6
Pecket Well 121 K6
Pellon 146 A6
Pendas Fields 112 B3
Penistone 270 D5
Penny Hill 189 L5
Pepper Hill 125 K8
Pickles Hill 78 B5
Pickwood Scar 168 A5
Pike End 188 D6
Pike Law 189 H7
Pledwick 220 F1

Pogmoor 260 C4
Pole Moor 211 M2
Pontefract 180 E6
Pool 42 E7
Poole 160 A3
Portobello 198 D4
Portsmouth 140 B5
Potternewton 110 A1
Potterton 91 G3
Pottery Field 9 J5
Priest Hill 29 L6
Priesthorpe 106 C2
Priestley Green 147 M5
Priestthorpe 81 J2
Prince Royd 191 L4
Pudsey 106 F7
Pudsey 140 D4
Pule Hill 146 E3
Purston Jaglin 202 A2
Quarmby 191 J8
Queensbury 124 D5
Rakewood 207 L5
Ramsden Wood 163 J7
Rastrick 170 A5
Ravenscliffe 106 A2
Ravensthorpe 173 G8
Rawdon 84 E3
Rawdon Carrs 84 F4
Rawfolds 172 A1
Raw Green 258 E2
Rawthorpe 15 M4
Red Hill 158 C7
Richmond Hill 110 B7
Riddlesden 58 C5
Ripponden 188 E2
Rishworth 188 D6
Roberttown 171 M5
Robin Hood 154 D3
Rochdale 206 A6
Rodley 107 G1
Rodmer Clough 120 A7
Rothwell 155 J1
Rothwell Haigh 132 F7
Rough Bank 207 M8
Roughbirchworth 271 J7
Roundhay 88 F6
Rowley Hill 216 A4
Royd 269 M2
Roydhouse 216 E8
Royd Moor 224 D6
Royd Moor 270 A1
Royds Green 155 J4
Royston 243 L1
Running Hill Head 250 A3
Ryecroft 80 A5
Ryhill 222 C5
Ryther 95 M3
St Helen's 261 L1
St John's 92 A5
Salendine Nook 191 G7
Saltaire 82 C5
Sandal 198 F5
Sandal Magna 199 H4
Sandford 108 A1
Sandhill 263 M5
Sandhills 90 A3
Sandy Lane 103 H3
Savile Town 195 M1
Sawood 101 H6
Saxton 93 J8
Scapegoat Hill 190 C8
Scarcroft 67 L5
Scarthingwell 94 A7
Scholemoor 126 A1
Scholes 90 B7
Scholes 149 H6
Scholes 254 F3
Scholey Hill 156 C6
School Green 103 J8
Scissett 239 L5
Scout Dike 257 K8
Seacroft 111 J1
Shackleton 121 G6
Shade 163 J2
Shadwell 89 H2
Shafton 244 C3
Shafton Two Gates 244 C4

Sharlston 200 D4
Sharlston Common 200 C3
Shaw 100 D4
Shaw Cross 229 J6
Shawfield Head 25 J1
Shaw Green 25 J1
Shaw Lands 260 E5
Shay Gate 103 G2
Sheepridge 192 D3
Sheepscar 7 K4
Shelf 125 M8
Shelley 238 C3
Shelley Woodhouse 238 D4
Shepherd Hill 175 H8
Shepley 238 B6
Sherburn in Elmet 115 M5
Shibden Head 124 F8
Shipley 82 C7
Shore 140 E4
Shore 185 H8
Sicklinghall 28 E8
Siddal 169 G3
Silkstone 259 G6
Silsden 36 A5
Skelbrooke 248 E4
Skellow 249 J4
Skelmanthorpe 239 K4
Skipton 16 A4
Slack 120 F8
Slack 190 C6
Slackcote 230 D7
Slaithwaite 212 B6
Slippery Ford 55 L8
Smallbridge 206 F3
Smithies 261 H1
Smithy Bridge 207 J3
Snowden Hill 271 J8
Snow Hill 176 C4
Snow Lea 190 F6
Snydale 201 G1
Soughley 268 F4
South Crosland 213 K8
South Elmsall 247 K5
South Hiendley 222 E3
South Kirkby 246 E5
South Lane 258 D5
South Milford 137 M2
South Ossett 197 G2
Southowram 169 H2
Sowerby 166 F4
Sowerby Bridge 167 L3
Sowood 190 B5
Sowood Green 190 C4
Soyland Town 166 F8
Spacey Houses 28 F3
Spofforth 28 F4
Spring Green 53 J3
Spring Vale 271 G3
Stainburn 25 G8
Staincliffe 173 J2
Staincross 242 D4
Stainland 190 A2
Stairfoot 262 A7
Stanbury 77 L7
Stanks 111 M3
Stanley 177 G2
Stanley Ferry 177 K4
Stanningley 107 H5
Stead 39 J5
Steep Lane 166 E2
Steeton 56 F1
Stockbridge 57 M4
Stone Chair 147 L2
Stone Head 53 M3
Stoneyfield 228 B2
Stoney Royd 11 H8
Stourton 132 D5
Strawberry Hill 180 A7
Streethouse 200 F1
Stutton 71 L7
Summit 185 L5
Summit 228 D7
Sutton 160 B7
Sutton 227 M8
Sutton-in-Craven 56 A1
Sutton Mill 56 A1

Swain House 105 H1
Swallow Hill 242 C7
Swarcliffe 111 L2
Swartha 36 B4
Swillington 134 C4
Swillington Common 112 B8
Swincliffe 150 C2
Swinnow Moor 107 K6
Syke 206 B2
Sympson Green 83 L5
Tadcaster 71 G2
Tandem 215 K1
Tarn 83 G2
Thackley 83 J5
Thackley End 83 H4
Thick Hollins 235 H5
Thongsbridge 236 E6
Thornbury 106 B6
Thorncliff 216 E7
Thorner 90 B1
Thornes 12 E9
Thornham Fold 228 C7
Thornhill 196 B4
Thornhill Edge 195 L6
Thornhill Lees 195 L2
Thornhills 170 E2
Thornton 103 G8
Thorp Arch 49 G6
Thorpe Audlin 225 J1
Thorpe Edge 83 K8
Thorpe on the Hill 153 L4
Thunder Bridge 237 L3
Thurlstone 270 B2
Thurstonland 237 H5
Thwaites 58 B7
Thwaites Brow 58 B8
Tingley 153 G5
Tinshill 86 A3
Tivy Dale 258 F2
Todmorden 163 L2
Toftshaw 127 L6
Tong 129 G5
Tong Park 83 H2
Tong Street 127 M5
Toothill 170 C8
Totties 254 F2
Toulston 70 E1
Town End 212 E2
Town Head 36 B4
Townhead 268 A4
Towton 93 M2
Trawden 74 F4
Triangle 167 G5
Troydale 107 J8
Tunshill 207 L2
Turf Hill 228 F2
Tyersal 128 B1
Ulleskelf 94 E2
Under Bank 254 C3
Undercliffe 105 J4
Upper Armley 108 C5
Upper Batley 151 L6
Upper Brockholes 123 L6
Upper Clough 212 E6
Upper Cudworth 244 E6
Upper Cumberworth 238 C8
Upper Denby 217 K1
Upper Denby 257 G5
Upper Green 153 G7
Upper Heaton 193 J3
Upper Hopton 194 A4
Upper Marsh 100 C2
Upper Maythorn 255 M6
Upper Moor Side 129 K5
Upperthong 235 M8
Upper Town 100 D4
Upton 225 L7
Upwood 58 E2
Utley 57 J5
Vale 140 E5
Victoria 255 K7
Wainstalls 145 G1
Wakefield 12 E2
Walsden 163 J5
Walshaw 120 E3
Walton 49 J2
Walton 199 K8

Wardle 184 F8
Warland 185 M1
Warley Town 145 L2
Warmfield 178 A8
Washpit 254 C4
Water Fryston 159 H4
Wayside Gardens 67 L5
Weardley 44 D8
Weeton 44 B4
Weetwood 86 E6
Well Heads 102 C7
Wellhouse 212 F3
Wellington Hill 89 G5
Wellroyd 84 F5
Wentbridge 203 L7
Wescoe Hill 43 L4
Wessenden 233 K8
West Ardsley 152 F8
West Bowling 127 H3
West Bretton 219 H6
West Carlton 62 D5
West End 85 G4
West End 94 F1
West End 149 K7
Westfield 84 A1
Westfield 172 F1
West Garforth 134 F1
Westgate Hill 128 C6
West Green 244 B8
West Hardwick 201 K5
West Morton 58 C4
Weston 40 D3
West Park 86 D6
West Royd 82 F6
West Scholes 124 F5
West Vale 168 F8
Wetherby 48 B1
Wheatley 145 M4
Wheldale 158 D5
Whinmoor 89 L6
Whins Wood 79 J5
Whitecote 107 L1
White Hill 77 M1
White Lee 151 G7
Whitkirk 111 L7
Whitley Head 56 E2
Whitley Lower 195 G6
Whitwood 157 G8
Wibsey 126 D5
Wighill 50 C4
Wike 66 F5
Wilberlee 211 M4
Wilsden 102 D1
Wilshaw 235 J6
Wilthorpe 260 C2
Windhill 82 F7
Windmill Hill 200 C6
Winewall 74 F2
Wintersett 222 C2
Womersley 205 J3
Woodhall Hills 106 C3
Woodhouse 3 H9
Woodhouse 6 D8
Woodhouse 170 E6
Woodhouse 178 B6
Woodkirk 152 E7
Woodlands 11 H1
Woodlands 146 E4
Woodlesford 133 L8
Wood Row 156 D3
Woodside 126 C8
Wooldale 236 E8
Woolgreaves 198 F8
Woolley 220 C8
Worsbrough Common 260 C7
Wortley 108 C8
Wragby 201 J7
Wrangbrook 226 B7
Wrenthorpe 176 B4
Wrose 83 G8
Wycoller 75 H8
Wyke 148 E4
Yeadon 84 D1

USING THE STREET INDEX

Street names are listed alphabetically. Each street name is followed by its postal town or area locality, the Postcode District, the page number, and the reference to the square in which the name is found.

Standard index entries are shown as follows:

Aachen Wy *HFAX* HX1 ....**10** C9

Street names and selected addresses not shown on the map due to scale restrictions are shown in the index with an asterisk:

Abbeydale *WHIT* OL12 * **206** A6

GENERAL ABBREVIATIONS

ACC...........ACCESS	COTS..........COTTAGES	FLS..........FLATS	IS..........ISLAND	OFF..........OFFICE
ALY..........ALLEY	CP..........CAPE	FM..........FARM	JCT..........JUNCTION	ORCH..........ORCHARD
AP..........APPROACH	CPS..........COPSE	FT..........FORT	JTY..........JETTY	OV..........OVAL
AR..........ARCADE	CR..........CREEK	FWY..........FREEWAY	KG..........KING	PAL..........PALACE
ASS..........ASSOCIATION	CREM..........CREMATORIUM	FY..........FERRY	KNL..........KNOLL	PAS..........PASSAGE
AV..........AVENUE	CRS..........CRESCENT	GA..........GATE	L..........LAKE	PAV..........PAVILION
BCH..........BEACH	CSWY..........CAUSEWAY	GAL..........GALLERY	LA..........LANE	PDE..........PARADE
BLDS..........BUILDINGS	CT..........COURT	GDN..........GARDEN	LDG..........LODGE	PH..........PUBLIC HOUSE
BND..........BEND	CTRL..........CENTRAL	GDNS..........GARDENS	LGT..........LIGHT	PK..........PARK
BNK..........BANK	CTS..........COURTS	GLD..........GLADE	LK..........LOCK	PKWY..........PARKWAY
BR..........BRIDGE	CTYD..........COURTYARD	GLN..........GLEN	LKS..........LAKES	PL..........PLACE
BRK..........BROOK	CUTT..........CUTTINGS	GN..........GREEN	LNDG..........LANDING	PLN..........PLAIN
BTM..........BOTTOM	CV..........COVE	GND..........GROUND	LTL..........LITTLE	PLNS..........PLAINS
BUS..........BUSINESS	CYN..........CANYON	GRA..........GRANGE	LWR..........LOWER	PLZ..........PLAZA
BVD..........BOULEVARD	DEPT..........DEPARTMENT	GRG..........GARAGE	MAG..........MAGISTRATE	POL..........POLICE STATION
BY..........BYPASS	DL..........DALE	GT..........GREAT	MAN..........MANSIONS	PR..........PRINCE
CATH..........CATHEDRAL	DM..........DAM	GTWY..........GATEWAY	MD..........MEAD	PREC..........PRECINCT
CEM..........CEMETERY	DR..........DRIVE	GV..........GROVE	MDW..........MEADOWS	PREP..........PREPARATORY
CEN..........CENTRE	DRO..........DROVE	HGR..........HIGHER	MEM..........MEMORIAL	PRIM..........PRIMARY
CFT..........CROFT	DRY..........DRIVEWAY	HL..........HILL	MKT..........MARKET	PROM..........PROMENADE
CH..........CHURCH	DWGS..........DWELLINGS	HLS..........HILLS	MKTS..........MARKETS	PRS..........PRINCESS
CHA..........CHASE	E..........EAST	HO..........HOUSE	ML..........MALL	PRT..........PORT
CHYD..........CHURCHYARD	EMB..........EMBANKMENT	HOL..........HOLLOW	MNR..........MANOR	PT..........POINT
CIR..........CIRCLE	EMBY..........EMBASSY	HOSP..........HOSPITAL	MS..........MEWS	PTH..........PATH
CIRC..........CIRCUS	ESP..........ESPLANADE	HRB..........HARBOUR	MSN..........MISSION	PZ..........PIAZZA
CL..........CLOSE	EST..........ESTATE	HTH..........HEATH	MT..........MOUNT	QD..........QUADRANT
CLFS..........CLIFFS	EX..........EXCHANGE	HTS..........HEIGHTS	MTN..........MOUNTAIN	QU..........QUEEN
CMP..........CAMP	EXPY..........EXPRESSWAY	HVN..........HAVEN	MTS..........MOUNTAINS	QY..........QUAY
CNR..........CORNER	EXT..........EXTENSION	HWY..........HIGHWAY	MUS..........MUSEUM	R..........RIVER
CO..........COUNTY	F/O..........FLYOVER	IMP..........IMPERIAL	MWY..........MOTORWAY	RBT..........ROUNDABOUT
COLL..........COLLEGE	FC..........FOOTBALL CLUB	IN..........INLET	N..........NORTH	RD..........ROAD
COM..........COMMON	FK..........FORK	IND EST..........INDUSTRIAL ESTATE	NE..........NORTH EAST	RDG..........RIDGE
COMM..........COMMISSION	FLD..........FIELD	INF..........INFIRMARY	NW..........NORTH WEST	REP..........REPUBLIC
CON..........CONVENT	FLDS..........FIELDS	INFO..........INFORMATION	O/P..........OVERPASS	RES..........RESERVOIR
COT..........COTTAGE	FLS..........FALLS	INT..........INTERCHANGE		RFC..........RUGBY FOOTBALL CLUB

274

RI	RISE
RP	RAMP
RW	ROW
S	SOUTH
SCH	SCHOOL
SE	SOUTH EAST
SER	SERVICE AREA
SH	SHORE
SHOP	SHOPPING
SKWY	SKYWAY
SMT	SUMMIT
SOC	SOCIETY
SP	SPUR
SPR	SPRING
SQ	SQUARE
ST	STREET
STN	STATION
STR	STREAM
STRD	STRAND
SW	SOUTH WEST
TDG	TRADING
TER	TERRACE
THWY	THROUGHWAY
TNL	TUNNEL
TOLL	TOLLWAY
TPK	TURNPIKE
TR	TRACK
TRL	TRAIL
TWR	TOWER
U/P	UNDERPASS
UNI	UNIVERSITY
UPR	UPPER
V	VALE
VA	VALLEY
VIAD	VIADUCT
VIL	VILLA
VIS	VISTA
VLG	VILLAGE
VLS	VILLAS
VW	VIEW
W	WEST
WD	WOOD
WHF	WHARF
WK	WALK
WKS	WALKS
WLS	WELLS
WY	WAY
YD	YARD
YHA	YOUTH HOSTEL

POSTCODE TOWNS AND AREA ABBREVIATIONS

AIRE	Airedale
AL/HA/HU	Alwoodley/Harewood/Huby
AWLS/ASK	Adwick le Street/Askern
BAIL	Baildon
BCUP	Bacup
BEE/HOL	Beeston/Holbeck
BFD	Bradford City Centre
BFDE	Bradford east
BGLY	Bingley
BHP/TINH	Bramhope/Tinshill
BIRK/DRI	Birkenshaw/Drighlington
BOW	Bowling
BRAM	Bramley
BRFD/BLYE	Brierfield/Burnley east
BRIG	Brighouse
BSLY	Barnsley
BSLYN/ROY	Barnsley north/Royston
BSPA/BRAM	Boston Spa/Bramham
BTLY	Bentley
BTLY	Batley
BULY	Burley
BVRD	Belle Vue Road
BWCK/EAR	Barnoldswick/Earby
CAS	Castleford
CHAL	Chapel Allerton
CHPT/GREN	Chapeltown/Grenoside
CLAY	Clayton
CLECK	Cleckheaton
COL	Colne
COP/BISH	Copmanthorpe/Bishopthorpe
CUD/GR	Cudworth/Grimethorpe
CUL/QBY	Cullingworth/Queensbury
DEWS	Dewsbury
DOD/DAR	Dodworth/Darton
EARD/LOFT	East Ardsley/Lofthouse
EARL	Earlsheaton
ECHL	Eccleshill
ELL	Elland
FEA/AMT	Featherstone/Ackworth Moor Top
GFTH/SHER	Garforth/Sherburn in Elmet
GIR	Girlington
GLE	Goole
GLSP	Glossop
GSLY	Guiseley
GTHN	Great Horton
GTL/HWG	Greetland/Holywell Green
HARS	Harrogate south
HBR	Hebden Bridge
HDGY	Headingley
HECK	Heckmondwike
HEM/SK/SE	Hemsworth/South Kirby/South Elmsall
HFAX	Halifax
HIPP	Hipperholme
HOLM/MEL	Holmfirth/Meltham
HOR/CROF	Horbury/Crofton
HORS	Horsforth
HTON	Heaton
HUD	Huddersfield
HUDE	Huddersfield east
HUDN	Huddesfield north
HUDS	Huddersfield south
HUDW	Huddersfield west
HWTH	Haworth
IDLE	Idle
ILK	Ilkley
KBTN	Kirkburton
KGHY	Keighley
KNA	Knaresborough
KNOT	Knottingley
KSTL	Kirkstall
LDS	Leeds City Centre
LDSU	Leeds University
LIT	Littleborough
LM/WK	Low Moor/Wyke
LUD/ILL	Luddenden/Illingworth
LVSG	Liversedge
MAR/SLWT	Marsden/Slaithwaite
MDTN	Middleton (Gtr. Man)
MID	Middleton (W.Yorks)
MILN	Milnrow
MIRF	Mirfield
MOR	Morley
MSTN/BAR	Manston/Barwick in Elmet
NORM	Normanton
OLD	Oldham
OLDE	Oldham east
OSM	Osmandthorpe
OSS	Ossett
OT	Otley
PBR	Pateley Bridge
PDSY/CALV	Pudsey/Calverley
PONT	Pontefract
RHAY	Roundhay
ROCH	Rochdale
ROY/SHW	Royton/Shaw
RPDN/SBR	Ripponden/Sowerby Bridge
RTHW	Rothwell
RYKW	Rural York west
SCFT	Seacroft
SEL	Selby
SHPY	Shipley
SKP/WHF	Skipton/Wharfedale
STKB/PEN	Stocksbridge/Penistone
TAD	Tadcaster
TOD	Todmorden
UPML	Uppermill
WBOW	West Bowling
WBSY	Wibsey
WBY	Wetherby
WHIT	Whitworth
WIL/AL	Wilsden/Allerton
WKFDE	Wakefield east
WKFDW/WTN	Wakefield west/Walton
WMB/DAR	Wombwell/Darfield
WOR/ARM	Wortley/Armley
YEA	Yeadon

Index - streets

Aac - Alb

A

Aachen Wy HFAX HX1 10 C9
Aaron Wilkinson Ct
HEM/SK/SE WF9 246 C4
Abaseen Cl BFDE BD3 5 M6
Abber La TAD LS24 51 J3
The Abbe's Cl AWLS/ASK DN6 249 K1
The Abbe's Wk AWLS/ASK DN6 249 M2
Abbey Av KSTL LS5 108 B3
Abbey Cl HOLM/MEL HD9 254 C7
ILK LS29 19 J6
Abbey Ct HOLM/MEL HD9 254 C7
HORS LS18 85 K8
Abbeydale WHIT OL12 * 206 A6
Abbeydale Gdns KSTL LS5 86 A8
Abbeydale Garth KSTL LS5 86 A8
Abbeydale Gv KSTL LS5 86 A8
Abbeydale Mt KSTL LS5 86 A8
Abbeydale V KSTL LS5 86 A8
Abbeydale Wy KSTL LS5 86 A8
Abbey Dr KBTN HD8 238 B5
LIT OL15 207 H3
Abbey Farm Dr KBTN HD8 238 B6
Abbey Farm Vw CUD/GR S72 262 D1
Abbey Gdns PONT WF8 181 G3
Abbey Gorse KSTL LS5 108 C1
Abbey Gn DOD/DAR S75 260 C8
Abbey Gv BSLYN/ROY S71 262 A2
Abbey La BSLYN/ROY S71 262 A5
LUD/ILL HX2 145 H7
Abbey Lea WIL/AL BD15 103 L6
Abbey Ms PONT WF8 180 F2
Abbey Pl HUDN HD2 192 E5
Abbey Rd BTLY WF17 173 H2
HUDN HD2 192 D5
KBTN HD8 238 C5
KSTL LS5 85 M8
Abbey Rd North KBTN HD8 238 B5
Abbey Sq BSLYN/ROY S71 262 A2
Abbey St BVRD LS3 6 B8
Abbey Ter KSTL LS5 108 B3
Abbey Vw KSTL LS5 108 C1
Abbey Wk HIPP HX3 168 E2
KSTL LS5 108 B1
PONT WF8 180 F2
Abbey Wk South HIPP HX3 168 E2
Abbot La HOR/CROF WF4 220 D8
Abbotside Cl IDLE BD10 * 83 L8
Abbots Rd BSLYN/ROY S71 262 B3
Abbot St HUD HD1 14 A4
Abbotsway GFTH/SHER LS25 112 F8
Abbott Ct WOR/ARM LS12 108 F6
Abbott Rd WOR/ARM LS12 108 F6
Abbotts Cl GFTH/SHER LS25 92 A6
Abbotts Ter HFAX HX1 10 C6
Abbott Ter WKFDE WF1 13 H8
Abbott Vw WOR/ARM LS12 108 F6
Abb Scott La LM/WK BD12 126 D8
Abb St HUD HD1 191 M7
Abelia Mt GTHN BD7 104 A8
Abel St LM/WK BD12 148 E2
Aberdeen Dr WOR/ARM LS12 108 C7
Aberdeen Gv WOR/ARM LS12 108 C7
Aberdeen Pl GTHN BD7 126 C1
Aberdeen Rd WOR/ARM LS12 108 C7
Aberdeen Ter CLAY BD14 125 M2
GTHN BD7 104 C8
Aberdeen Wk WOR/ARM LS12 108 C7
Aberfield Bank MID LS10 132 A8
Aberfield Cl MID LS10 132 A7
Aberfield Crest MID LS10 132 A8
Aberfield Dr HOR/CROF WF4 220 A2
MID LS10 132 A8
Aberfield Ga MID LS10 132 A7
Aberfield Mt MID LS10 132 A8
Aberfield Ri MID LS10 132 A8
Aberfield Rd MID LS10 132 A7
Aberfield Wk MID LS10 131 M8
Aberford By-Pass
GFTH/SHER LS25 92 B8
Aberford Rd BSPA/BRAM LS23 69 M5
GFTH/SHER LS25 113 K5
GIR BD8 104 D5
MSTN/BAR LS15 91 G7
RTHW LS26 155 L2
WKFDE WF1 177 G6
Aberley Fold LIT OL15 185 H7
Abingdon Cl ROCH OL11 228 A2
Abingdon St GIR BD8 104 D5
HUDN HD2 192 C5
Abion Ct HOLM/MEL HD9 234 E4
Aboukir St MILN OL16 206 D6
Abraham Hl RTHW LS26 133 H8
Acacia Cl CAS WF10 158 F8
Acacia Dr BRIG HD6 148 C7
CAS WF10 158 E8
WIL/AL BD15 103 J2
Acacia Gv CUD/GR S72 244 E4
HBR HX7 144 B5
Acacia Park Crs IDLE BD10 84 B4
Acacia Park Dr IDLE BD10 84 B4
Acacia Park Ter IDLE BD10 84 B4
Acacia Rd AWLS/ASK DN6 249 J4
Acaster Dr GFTH/SHER LS25 135 J1
LM/WK BD12 126 E8
Accommodation Rd OSM LS9 7 M7
Acer Cl AIRE BD20 56 B1
Acer Wy CLECK BD19 149 H6
Ackroyd Ct CUL/QBY BD13 * 102 F8
Ackroyd St MOR LS27 152 D2
TOD OL14 140 D5
Ackton Cl FEA/AMT WF7 179 J5
Ackton Hall Crs FEA/AMT WF7 179 J6
Ackton La FEA/AMT WF7 179 K6
Ackton Pasture La CAS WF10 179 J2
Ackworth Av YEA LS19 62 E8
Ackworth Bridle Rd PONT WF8 203 G7
Ackworth Crs YEA LS19 62 E8
Ackworth Dr YEA LS19 62 E8
Ackworth House Cl
FEA/AMT WF7 202 C6
Ackworth Rd FEA/AMT WF7 201 M3
PONT WF8 180 E8
Ackworth St WBOW BD5 127 G2
Acme Ter WKFDE WF1 13 H8
Acomb Ter LM/WK BD12 148 E3
Acorn Cl WBSY BD6 126 A8
Acorn Dr SCFT LS14 89 L6
Acorn Gv HOLM/MEL HD9 254 F3
Acorn Pk BAIL BD17 83 G4
Acorn St HFAX HX1 10 C5
Acorn Wy CUD/GR S72 245 J8
OT LS21 42 F8
Acre Av ECHL BD2 105 K1
Acre Barn ROY/SHW OL2 229 G6
Acre Cl ECHL BD2 105 K1
Acre Crs ECHL BD2 105 K1
MID LS10 153 L2
Acre Dr ECHL BD2 105 K1
Acre Fold ILK LS29 18 F6
Acre Gv ECHL BD2 * 105 K1
MID LS10 153 L2
Acre House Av HUDW HD3 191 L6
Acrehowe Ri BAIL BD17 82 F2
Acre La ECHL BD2 105 K2
HBR HX7 120 E8
HOLM/MEL HD9 235 H5
HOLM/MEL HD9 237 K8
HOLM/MEL HD9 253 M4
HWTH BD22 78 E7
WBSY BD6 126 E5
Acre Meadow HWTH BD22 54 E3
Acre Mt MID LS10 153 L2
Acre Pl MID LS10 153 L2
Acre Ri BAIL BD17 82 E2
Acre Rd CUD/GR S72 262 E2
HWTH BD22 54 E3
MID LS10 153 L2
Acresfield COL BB8 * 74 C1
Acres Hall Av PDSY/CALV LS28 107 J8
Acres Hall Crs PDSY/CALV LS28 107 J8
Acres Hall Dr PDSY/CALV LS28 107 J8
Acres La HBR HX7 143 H2
HOLM/MEL HD9 253 H2
Acre Sq MID LS10 153 L2
Acres Rd EARD/LOFT WF3 154 E6
Acres St KGHY BD21 2 E7
The Acres AIRE BD20 55 L2
ILK LS29 19 H5
Acre St HUDW HD3 191 K6
MID LS10 153 L2
Acre Ter MID LS10 153 M2
Acton Flat La HUDW HD3 191 J3
Acton St BFDE BD3 105 L7
WHIT OL12 206 C5
Acute Ter WKFDW/WTN WF2 176 A8
Adam Ct HUDW HD3 191 K5
Adam Cft CUL/QBY BD13 79 M8
Adam La DOD/DAR S75 259 J4
Adams Gv MSTN/BAR LS15 112 A2
Adam St TOD OL14 141 J8
WBSY BD6 126 D5
Ada's Pl PDSY/CALV LS28 107 G4
Ada St BAIL BD17 83 G4
CUL/QBY BD13 124 F5
HIPP HX3 11 H2
KGHY BD21 2 D5
SHPY BD18 82 B6
WHIT OL12 206 C4
Addingford Cl HOR/CROF WF4 197 J6
Addingford Dr HOR/CROF WF4 197 J6
Addingford La HOR/CROF WF4 197 J6
Addingham Gdns
WOR/ARM LS12 108 C7
Addingham Wharfedale Rd
ILK LS29 18 F6
Addison Av BFDE BD3 105 M5
NORM WF6 178 E5
Addison Ct HOR/CROF WF4 197 L4
MSTN/BAR LS15 111 M8
Addison Dr HWTH BD22 78 E8
Addi St BOW BD4 127 L3
Addle Croft La HUDE HD5 216 A1
Addlethorpe La WBY LS22 46 B1
Addy Crs HEM/SK/SE WF9 247 H3
Adelaide Rd AWLS/ASK DN6 227 M3
Adelaide St HBR HX7 143 G3
HFAX HX1 10 B6
TOD OL14 141 K8
WBOW BD5 4 F9
Adel Garth BHP/TINH LS16 86 F1
Adel Grange Cl BHP/TINH LS16 86 E4
Adel Grange Cft
BHP/TINH LS16 * 86 E4
Adel Grange Ms BHP/TINH LS16 86 E4
Adel Gn BHP/TINH LS16 86 F2
Adel La BHP/TINH LS16 86 E2
Adel Md BHP/TINH LS16 86 F2
Adel Ml BHP/TINH LS16 64 F8
Adel Park Cl BHP/TINH LS16 86 E3
Adel Park Ct BHP/TINH LS16 86 E3
Adel Park Cft BHP/TINH LS16 86 E3
Adel Park Dr BHP/TINH LS16 86 E3
Adel Park Gdns BHP/TINH LS16 86 E3
Adel Pasture BHP/TINH LS16 86 E3
Adelphi Rd HUDW HD3 191 L7
Adel Towers Ct BHP/TINH LS16 86 F3
Adel V BHP/TINH LS16 86 F2
Adel Wood Dr BHP/TINH LS16 86 F3
Adel Wood Gv BHP/TINH LS16 86 F3
Adel Wood Pl BHP/TINH LS16 86 F3
Adel Wood Rd BHP/TINH LS16 86 F3
Aden St WHIT OL12 206 C5
Adgil Crs HIPP HX3 169 J2
Adkin Royd DOD/DAR S75 259 H6
Admiral St BEE/HOL LS11 9 G7
Adowsley Cl FEA/AMT WF7 202 A8
Adrian Ter MILN OL16 206 E8
Adwalton Cl BIRK/DRI BD11 150 F1
Adwalton Gn BIRK/DRI BD11 150 F1
Adwalton Gv CUL/QBY BD13 125 H5
Adwick Gv WKFDW/WTN WF2 220 D1
Adwick Pl BULY LS4 108 E4
Agar St GIR BD8 104 B6
Agar Ter GIR BD8 104 B6
Agbrigg Gv WKFDW/WTN WF2 199 G4
Agbrigg Rd WKFDE WF1 13 L9
Agincourt Dr BGLY BD16 81 K3
NORM WF6 178 A2
Agnes Rd BSLY S70 261 G6
DOD/DAR S75 241 M6
Agnes St AIRE BD20 57 L5
Agnes Ter BSLY S70 261 G6
Aimbry Ct HUDE HD5 215 H4
Ainley Bottom ELL HX5 191 J1
Ainley Cl HUDW HD3 191 J4
Ainley Pk MAR/SLWT HD7 213 G2
Ainley Rd HUDW HD3 191 J3
Ainley St ELL HX5 169 H8
Ainsbury Av IDLE BD10 83 K3
Ainsdale Ct BSLYN/ROY S71 261 M1
Ainsdale Gv CUL/QBY BD13 80 A8
Ainsdale Rd BSLYN/ROY S71 243 K1
Ainsley La MAR/SLWT HD7 232 F2
Ainsty Crs WBY LS22 30 A7
Ainsty Dr WBY LS22 30 A7
Ainsty Garth WBY LS22 30 A7
Ainsty Rd WBY LS22 29 M7
WBY LS22 30 A7
Ainsty Vw WBY LS22 30 A7
Ainsworth St MILN OL16 206 C8
Aintree Cl GFTH/SHER LS25 135 H4
Airebank BGLY BD16 81 G3
Aire Cl BAIL BD17 82 D5
Aire Crs AIRE BD20 34 F8
Airedale Av BGLY BD16 81 J8
SKP/WHF BD23 16 D2
Airedale College Mt BFDE BD3 * 5 J1
Airedale College Rd BFDE BD3 5 J1
Airedale College Ter BFDE BD3 5 J2
Airedale Ct SCFT LS14 111 H1
Airedale Crs BFDE BD3 5 J1
Airedale Cft BRAM LS13 107 H1
Airedale Dr CAS WF10 158 E4
GFTH/SHER LS25 113 K8
HIPP HX3 147 K1
HORS LS18 85 H6
Airedale Gdns BRAM LS13 107 H2
Airedale Gv HORS LS18 85 H6
RTHW LS26 * 133 M8
Airedale Hts WKFDW/WTN WF2 197 L2
Airedale Ms AIRE BD20 36 A5
SKP/WHF BD23 16 A3
Airedale Mt AIRE BD20 58 E6
Airedale Pl BAIL BD17 83 G4
Airedale Quay BRAM LS13 107 J2
Airedale Rd BFDE BD3 5 H1
CAS WF10 158 D7
DOD/DAR S75 241 L6
KGHY BD21 58 B6
RTHW LS26 133 M8
Airedale St BGLY BD16 81 H3
ECHL BD2 105 K3
KGHY BD21 3 M3
Airedale Ter MOR LS27 152 D2
RTHW LS26 * 133 M8
Airedale Vw AIRE BD20 34 F7
RTHW LS26 * 133 M8
Airedale Whf BRAM LS13 107 H1
Aire Gv YEA LS19 62 E8
Aire Mt WBY LS22 29 M7
Aire Pl BVRD LS3 109 G5
Aire Rd WBY LS22 29 M7
Aireside Av AIRE BD20 34 D4
Aireside Ter AIRE BD20 34 C3
Aire St AIRE BD20 35 G8
BGLY BD16 81 G1
BRIG HD6 170 D5
CAS WF10 157 M6
DEWS WF13 195 H1
HWTH BD22 78 F7
IDLE BD10 83 J5
KGHY BD21 3 K3
KNOT WF11 182 C1
LDS LS1 8 E1
Aire Ter CAS WF10 157 M6
Aireton Rd BSLY S70 260 F4
Aire Valley Dr AIRE BD20 16 D8
Aire Valley Mt CAS WF10 158 C7
Aire Valley Rd KGHY BD21 3 L2
Airevalley Rd KGHY BD21 3 M3
Aire Vw AIRE BD20 35 M5
AIRE BD20 58 B4
YEA LS19 62 E8
Aire View Av BGLY BD16 81 K6
SHPY BD18 82 C6
Aireview Crs BAIL BD17 82 C5
Aire View Dr AIRE BD20 58 E7
Aire View Ter KGHY BD21 3 M6
Aireview Ter SKP/WHF BD23 * 16 A3
Aireville Av SHPY BD18 104 D1
Aireville Cl AIRE BD20 57 J4
SHPY BD18 104 D1
Aireville Crs AIRE BD20 36 B5
HTON BD9 104 D1
Aireville Dr AIRE BD20 36 B5
HTON BD9 104 D1
Aireville Gra SHPY BD18 104 D1
Aireville Gv HTON BD9 104 D1
Aireville Mt AIRE BD20 58 E7
Aireville Mouny AIRE BD20 36 B5
Aireville Ri HTON BD9 104 D2
Aireville Rd HTON BD9 104 E1
Aireville St AIRE BD20 57 J4
Aireville Ter ILK LS29 40 A5
Aire Wy BAIL BD17 82 C5
Aireworth Cl KGHY BD21 3 M2
Aireworth Gv KGHY BD21 3 M3
Aireworth Rd KGHY BD21 3 M2
Aireworth St KGHY BD21 2 F6
Airey St KGHY BD21 2 D4
Airlie Av RHAY LS8 110 B2
Airlie Pl RHAY LS8 110 B2
Akam Rd BFD BD1 4 C5
Aked's Rd HFAX HX1 10 E7
Aked St BFD BD1 * 5 H6
Aketon Dr CAS WF10 157 L8
Aketon Rd CAS WF10 157 L8
Akroyd Ct HIPP HX3 11 G3
Akroyd La HBR HX7 121 K8
Akroyd Pl HIPP HX3 11 G4
Akroyd Ter LUD/ILL HX2 168 B1
Alabama St HFAX HX1 10 B5
Alanby Dr IDLE BD10 83 L7
Alan Crs MSTN/BAR LS15 111 J7
Alandale Crs GFTH/SHER LS25 112 F8
Alandale Dr GFTH/SHER LS25 112 F8
Alandale Gv GFTH/SHER LS25 112 F8
Alandale Rd GFTH/SHER LS25 112 F7
HUDN HD2 193 G1
Alan Rd DOD/DAR S75 241 M6
Alaska Pl CHAL LS7 88 A8
Alba Cl WMB/DAR S73 263 G8
Albans Cl AL/HA/HU LS17 47 G8
Alban St BOW BD4 127 K2
Albany Cl WMB/DAR S73 262 C8
Albany Ct AIRE BD20 2 D3
PONT WF8 180 F7
Albany Crs HEM/SK/SE WF9 247 H4
Albany Dr HUDE HD5 193 J8
Albany Rd HUDE HD5 193 J8
RTHW LS26 132 F8
Albany Rw ILK LS29 * 61 H2
Albany St HEM/SK/SE WF9 247 H4
HIPP HX3 11 K9
HUD HD1 214 B2
ROCH OL11 228 C1
WBOW BD5 * 127 G2
WBSY BD6 126 E5
WOR/ARM LS12 108 C7
Albany Ter HIPP HX3 11 K9
WOR/ARM LS12 * 108 C7
Albany Wk ILK LS29 38 D3
Alberta Av CHAL LS7 88 A8
Albert Av IDLE BD10 83 L6
LUD/ILL HX2 146 A6
SHPY BD18 82 A5
Albert Cl BTLY WF17 173 L4
Albert Ct LUD/ILL HX2 146 A6
Albert Crs BIRK/DRI BD11 150 D2
CUL/QBY BD13 125 G5
Albert Dr LUD/ILL HX2 145 M6
MOR LS27 152 F1
Albert Gdns LUD/ILL HX2 146 A6
Albert Gv HDGY LS6 86 F8
Albert Pl BFDE BD3 106 A6
HORS LS18 85 L5
Albert Prom HIPP HX3 168 C2
Albert Rd AIRE BD20 34 F8
CUL/QBY BD13 124 F4
KBTN HD8 240 A3
LUD/ILL HX2 146 A6
MOR LS27 152 E1
RPDN/SBR HX6 167 L1
RTHW LS26 133 L8
SHPY BD18 82 B6
Albert Royds St MILN OL16 206 E5
Albert Simmons Way St
ILK LS29 40 A5
Albert Sq AIRE BD20 36 A5
Albert St AIRE BD20 55 M1
BAIL BD17 82 E5
BRIG HD6 170 E3
BSLY S70 261 H5
CAS WF10 157 M6
CLECK BD19 * 149 M6
CUD/GR S72 244 E6
CUL/QBY BD13 102 F8
CUL/QBY BD13 125 H5
ELL HX5 169 H8
FEA/AMT WF7 201 M1
HBR HX7 143 J3
HBR HX7 144 A5
HFAX HX1 10 E5
HUD HD1 214 C2
HWTH BD22 79 H6
KGHY BD21 2 F4
LIT OL15 207 J1
LM/WK BD12 148 E4
LVSG WF15 172 E3
MILN OL16 229 H1
NORM WF6 178 E2
PDSY/CALV LS28 106 F8
ROY/SHW OL2 229 J7
WBSY BD6 126 D6
WIL/AL BD15 102 E2
Albert Ter LM/WK BD12 149 H1
SHPY BD18 82 B5
SKP/WHF BD23 16 B2
Albert Vw LUD/ILL HX2 146 A6
Albert Wk SHPY BD18 82 A6
Albert Wy BIRK/DRI BD11 150 D2
Albert Yd HUD HD1 14 F8
Albion Ar LDS LS1 9 G1
Albion Av WOR/ARM LS12 108 F7
Albion Cl BSPA/BRAM LS23 69 M1
Albion Ct HFAX HX1 11 G5
WKFDE WF1 12 E3
Albion Cft OSS WF5 175 G8
Albion Fold WIL/AL BD15 102 E1
Albion Pl HEM/SK/SE WF9 247 J3
LDS LS1 7 G9
Albion Rd BSLYN/ROY S71 243 L7
EARL WF12 195 M5
IDLE BD10 83 L6
PDSY/CALV LS28 107 G4
Albion St BRIG HD6 170 C3
BSPA/BRAM LS23 69 M1
BTLY WF17 173 M2
CAS WF10 157 L6
CLECK BD19 150 A7
CUL/QBY BD13 101 M6
CUL/QBY BD13 124 F5
DEWS WF13 173 L5
DEWS WF13 * 195 H1
EARD/LOFT WF3 154 F3
ELL HX5 169 J8
HEM/SK/SE WF9 223 H3
HFAX HX1 11 H6
HUD HD1 14 F8
HWTH BD22 79 G6

LDS LS1 .....7 G9
LIT OL15 .....207 J1
LVSG WF15 .....172 C2
MOR LS27 .....152 C2
OT LS21 .....41 K7
PDSY/CALV LS28 .....107 H7
WBSY BD6 .....126 A7
WKFDE WF1 .....176 B7
Albion Ter BSLY S70 .....261 K6
BSPA/BRAM LS23 .....48 F8
Albion Wy WOR/ARM WF12 .....109 G6
Albion Yd SKP/WHF BD23 * 16 C2
Alcester Garth BFDE BD3 * 5 L4
Alcester Pl RHAY LS8 * 110 B2
Alcester Rd RHAY LS8 .....110 B2
Alcester St RHAY LS8 * 110 B2
Alcester Ter RHAY LS8 .....110 B2
Aldams Rd EARL WF12 .....173 L7
Aldbury Cl BSLYN/ROY S71 .....243 K8
Alden Av MOR LS27 .....152 C4
Alden Cl MOR LS27 .....152 C4
Alden Ct MOR LS27 .....152 C4
Alden Crs PONT WF8 .....180 D7
Alden Fold MOR LS27 * 152 C4
Alder Av HOLM/MEL HD9 .....236 E6
KGHY BD21 .....3 K8
WKFDW/WTN WF2 .....176 C6
Alderbank WHIT OL12 .....184 E7
Alder Carr BAIL BD17 .....82 D3
Alder Cl DOD/DAR S75 .....242 C5
Alder Dr PDSY/CALV LS28 .....106 D6
Alder Garth PDSY/CALV LS28 .....106 D6
Alder Gv LUD/ILL HX2 .....124 A8
NORM WF6 .....
Alder Hill Av CHAL LS7 .....87 J7
Alder Hill Gv CHAL LS7 .....87 J7
Alder Holt Dr WBSY BD6 .....126 C8
Aldermanbury BFD BD1 * 4 E7
Alderscholes Cl CUL/QBY BD13 .....102 F8
Alderscholes La CUL/QBY BD13 .....124 E1
Aldersley Av SKP/WHF BD23 .....16 C2
Alderson Dr MILN OL16 .....207 G8
Alderson St AIRE BD20 .....34 F7
Alderstone Ri HUDW HD3 .....191 J4
Alder St HUD HD1 .....15 G4
Aldersyde BTLY WF17 .....151 L7
Aldersyde Rd GSLY LS20 .....61 M6
Alderton Bank AL/HA/HU LS17 .....87 H4
Alderton Crs AL/HA/HU LS17 .....87 H4
Alderton Mt AL/HA/HU LS17 .....87 H4
Alderton Pl AL/HA/HU LS17 .....87 H4
Alderton Ri AL/HA/HU LS17 .....87 H4
Aldham Crs WMB/DAR S73 .....262 C8
Aldonley HUDE HD5 .....215 J2
Aldwych ROCH OL11 .....228 B3
Alegar St BRIG HD6 .....
Alexander Av MSTN/BAR LS15 .....111 H7
Alexander St East HFAX HX1 * .....
Alexander Dr MILN OL16 .....207 G8
Alexander Rd FEA/AMT WF7 .....179 M8
Alexander Sq CLAY BD14 .....125 K2
Alexander St LDS LS1 * 6 F8
WBSY BD6 .....126 C6
Alexandra Av BTLY WF17 .....151 H5
Alexandra Cl RPDN/SBR HX6 .....167 L2
Alexandra Crs SKP/WHF BD23 .....16 B4
Alexandra Crs DEWS WF13 .....173 J4
ELL HX5 .....169 K7
ILK LS29 .....38 C2
Alexandra Dr NORM WF6 .....178 D7
Alexandra Gv HDGY LS6 .....109 G4
PDSY/CALV LS28 .....106 C7
Alexandra Rd AWLS/ASK DN6 .....249 M8
BTLY WF17 .....173 M2
ECHL BD2 .....105 L1
HBR HX7 .....143 J3
HDGY LS6 .....109 G4
HORS LS18 .....85 L5
HUDW HD3 .....191 L6
PDSY/CALV LS28 .....106 E8
SHPY BD18 .....82 D7
Alexandra St CUL/QBY BD13 * 125 G5
GTHN BD7 .....4 A3
HFAX HX1 .....11 G7
LVSG WF15 .....172 C2
Alexandra Ter BSLYN/ROY S71 .....262 B6
ECHL BD2 .....105 L4
YEA LS19 .....62 E7
Alford Cl DOD/DAR S75 .....260 D4
Alford Ter GTHN BD7 .....104 C7
Alfred St East HFAX HX1 * .....
Alfred St BRIG HD6 .....170 D3
BSLYN/ROY S71 .....244 A2
BTLY WF17 .....173 K2
EARL WF12 .....174 A3
GTL/HWG HX4 .....168 F3
HFAX HX1 .....10 B5
HUD HD1 .....14 F7
LIT OL15 .....185 J8
LVSG WF15 .....172 D2
MOR LS27 * 130 E6
ROY/SHW OL2 .....229 J7
Alfreds Wy BTLY WF17 .....173 L1
Alice St CLECK BD19 .....149 M6
GIR BD8 .....4 C3
HWTH BD22 .....78 C8
KGHY BD21 .....3 G4
WHIT OL12 .....206 D5
Alicia Dr WHIT OL12 .....206 A4
Alison Dr ROY/SHW OL2 .....229 J6
Alkincote St KGHY BD21 .....2 F6
All Alone Rd IDLE BD10 .....83 H7
Allanbridge Cl IDLE BD10 .....83 H7
Allandale Av WBSY BD6 .....126 C7
Allandale Rd WBSY BD6 .....126 C7
Allan Haigh Cl
WKFDW/WTN WF2 .....175 M6
Allan St BFDE BD3 .....5 M6
Allan Ter RPDN/SBR HX6 .....167 L3
Allatt Cl BSLY S70 .....261 H6
Allenby Crs BEE/HOL LS11 .....131 J6
Allenby Dr BEE/HOL LS11 .....131 J6
Allenby Gdns BEE/HOL LS11 .....131 J6
Allenby Gv BEE/HOL LS11 .....131 J6
Allenby Pl BEE/HOL LS11 .....131 J6
Allenby Rd BEE/HOL LS11 .....131 J6
Allenby Rd ROY/SHW OL2 .....229 J6
Allenby Vw BEE/HOL LS11 .....131 J6
Allen Cft BIRK/DRI BD11 .....150 C1
Allendale
DOD/DAR S75 .....241 G6
DOD/DAR S75 .....261 G6
Allendale St COL BB8 .....74 B1
Allen Rw HUD HD1 .....14 A8
Allen St MILN OL16 .....228 C1
Allerby Gn WBSY BD6 .....126 B8
Allergill Pk HOLM/MEL HD9 .....253 M1
Allerton Cl WIL/AL BD15 .....103 K5
Allerton Dr AL/HA/HU LS17 .....46 E8
Allerton Grange Av
AL/HA/HU LS17 .....88 A5
Allerton Grange Cl
AL/HA/HU LS17 .....87 L6
Allerton Grange Crs
AL/HA/HU LS17 .....87 M6
Allerton Grange Cft RHAY LS8 .....88 A6

Allerton Grange Dr
AL/HA/HU LS17 .....87 M6
WIL/AL BD15 .....103 K5
Allerton Grange Gdns
AL/HA/HU LS17 .....87 M6
Allerton Grange Ri
AL/HA/HU LS17 .....87 M6
Allerton Grange V AL/HA/HU LS17 .....87 M6
Allerton Grange Wk
AL/HA/HU LS17 .....87 M6
Allerton Grange Wy RHAY LS8 .....87 L7
Allerton Hi CHAL LS7 .....87 L7
Allerton La WIL/AL BD15 .....103 J7
Allerton Ms AL/HA/HU LS17 .....87 L5
Allerton Pk AL/HA/HU LS17 .....87 M7
Allerton Pl AL/HA/HU LS17 .....87 L6
HFAX HX1 .....10 C6
Allerton Rd AL/HA/HU BD15 .....102 F5
Allerton St BULY LS4 .....108 F4
Allescholes Rd TOD OL14 .....163 J7
Alliance St WOR/ARM LS12 .....108 C7
Allington ROCH OL11 * 206 A8
Allinson St WOR/ARM LS12 .....109 G8
Allison Dr HUDN HD2 .....192 C5
Allison Gv COL BB8 .....52 A8
Allison La ECHL BD2 .....104 F2
Allison St FEA/AMT WF7 .....201 L1
Alloe Field Vw LUD/ILL HX2 .....124 A8
Allott Cl HEM/SK/SE WF9 .....247 H3
All Saints Cl DOD/DAR S75 .....259 J6
KBTN HD8 .....240 B4
All Saints Ct KGHY BD21 .....2 E5
All Saints Dr RTHW LS26 .....133 L6
All Saints Rd GTHN BD7 .....126 E1
RTHW LS26 .....133 M7
All Saints Ter WHIT OL12 .....206 D4
All Saints Vw RTHW LS26 .....133 L7
All Souls' Rd HIPP HX3 * 11 G1
All Souls' St HIPP HX3 * 11 G1
All Souls' Ter HIPP HX3 * 11 G1
Allums La OT LS21 .....65 G2
Alma Cl PDSY/CALV LS28 .....106 E3
Alma Cottages HDGY LS6 .....108 F1
Alma Dr HUDE HD5 .....15 L7
Alma La HECK WF16 .....150 F8
RPDN/SBR HX6 .....166 F1
Alma Pl BFDE BD3 .....105 M6
KGHY BD21 .....3 G9
Alma Rd COL BB8 .....52 F8
HDGY LS6 .....108 F1
TOD OL14 .....163 J5
Alma St BOW BD4 .....127 M2
BSLY S70 .....260 E5
CUL/QBY BD13 .....124 F5
HWTH BD22 .....78 E6
KGHY BD21 .....79 L2
LDSU LS9 .....7 M6
RTHW LS26 .....133 M7
SHPY BD18 .....82 F6
TOD OL14 .....163 J5
WHIT OL12 * 206 B5
YEA LS19 .....62 E7
Alma Ter KGHY BD21 .....79 L2
RTHW LS26 .....132 F8
Almond Av CUD/GR S72 .....244 D7
Almondbury Bank HUDE HD5 .....15 M9
Almondbury Cl HEM/SK/SE WF9 .....247 J2
Almondbury Common
HUDS HD4 .....215 H5
Almond Cl HEM/SK/SE WF9 .....247 J2
Almondroyd HECK WF16 .....172 E1
Almond St BFDE BD3 .....105 L8
Almond Wy BTLY WF17 .....151 H5
Almscliffe Av EARL WF12 .....174 A6
Almscliffe Dr AL/HA/HU LS17 .....43 K2
Almscliffe Garth
AL/HA/HU LS17 .....25 M7
Almshouse Hl BSPA/BRAM LS23 .....69 M4
Almshouse La WKFDE WF1 .....17 J5
WKFDW/WTN WF2 .....
Alnwick Vw BHP/TINH LS16 .....86 E7
Alperton Cl BSLYN/ROY S71 .....262 B1
Alpha St KGHY BD21 .....3 J5
Alpine Cl BTLY WF17 .....173 K2
Alpine Dr MILN OL16 .....207 J7
WHIT OL12 .....184 E8
Alpine Ri CUL/QBY BD13 .....102 F7
Alric Dr BSLYN/ROY S71 .....262 A5
Alston Av ROY/SHW OL2 .....229 K6
Alston Cl DOD/DAR S75 .....259 H6
HTON BD9 .....103 M5
Alston La SCFT LS14 .....111 J3
Alston Rd KGHY BD21 .....3 K1
Altar Dr AIRE BD20 .....58 C5
HTON BD9 .....104 D1
Altar La BGLY BD16 .....80 C2
Althorpe Gv IDLE BD10 .....83 J8
Altinkool St WKFDE WF1 .....199 G4
Altofts Hall Rd NORM WF6 .....178 B2
Altofts La CAS WF10 .....156 F8
Altofts Lodge Dr NORM WF6 .....178 C3
Altofts Rd NORM WF6 .....178 C3
Alton Av HUDE HD5 .....193 H7
Alton Gv HTON BD9 .....104 D1
SHPY BD18 .....104 D1
Alton Wy DOD/DAR S75 .....242 C5
Alum Dr HTON BD9 .....104 C3
Alum Ct HTON BD9 .....104 C3
Alvanley Ct GIR BD8 .....103 M6
Alverthorpe Rd
WKFDW/WTN WF2 .....176 B8
Alwen Av HUDN HD2 .....192 B4
Alwin Rd ROY/SHW OL2 .....229 J6
Alwoodley Cha AL/HA/HU LS17 * 88 A1
Alwoodley Court Gdns
AL/HA/HU LS17 .....65 J1
Alwoodley Gdns AL/HA/HU LS17 .....87 J1
Alwoodley Gates
AL/HA/HU LS17 .....66 A8
Alwoodley La AL/HA/HU LS17 .....65 H8
Amberley Crs BSPA/BRAM LS23 .....48 F7
Amberley Gdns WOR/ARM LS12 .....108 E8
Amberley Ri AWLS/ASK DN6 .....249 H4
Amberley St BFDE BD3 .....5 L7
WOR/ARM LS12 .....108 E8
Amber St BTLY WF17 .....151 J1
Amberton Ap RHAY LS8 .....110 E1
Amberton Cl RHAY LS8 .....110 E1
Amberton Crs RHAY LS8 .....110 E2
Amberton Gdns RHAY LS8 .....110 E2
Amberton Garth RHAY LS8 .....110 E2
Amberton Gv RHAY LS8 .....110 E2
Amberton La RHAY LS8 .....110 E2
Amberton Mt RHAY LS8 .....110 E2
Amberton Rd OSM LS9 .....110 E3
Amberton Rd RHAY LS8 .....110 E2
Amberton St RHAY LS8 .....110 E2
Amberton Ter RHAY LS8 .....110 E2
Ambler Gv LUD/ILL HX2 .....124 B8
Amblers Cft IDLE BD10 .....83 K4
Amblers Ter HFAX HX3 .....11 H2
Ambler St CAS WF10 .....157 M7
GIR BD8 .....104 E4
KGHY BD21 .....3 K5
Ambler Wy CUL/QBY BD13 .....124 E7

Ambleside Av HTON BD9 .....104 B4
Ambleside Dr
WKFDW/WTN WF2 .....199 J8
Ambleside Gdns
PDSY/CALV LS28 .....106 E7
Ambleside Gv BSLYN/ROY S71 .....262 C6
RTHW LS26 .....133 C8
Ambleside Rd CAS WF10 .....159 G5
Ambleside Wk WBY LS22 .....29 K8
Ambleton Wy CUL/QBY BD13 .....124 E6
Ambrose St ROCH OL11 .....228 B1
Amelia St SHPY BD18 .....82 B6
America La AIRE BD20 .....56 A6
BRIG HD6 .....170 E4
America Moor La MOR LS27 .....152 C4
Amisfield Rd HIPP HX3 .....147 M6
Amos St HFAX HX1 .....10 B5
Amport Cl BRIG HD6 .....170 D5
Amspool Ct EARD/LOFT WF3 .....154 E3
Amundsen Av ECHL BD2 .....105 J1
Amy Busfield Gn ILK LS29 * 40 A5
Amyroyce Dr SHPY BD18 .....83 G7
Amy St BGLY BD16 .....81 J3
HIPP HX3 .....
Anaheim Dr WKFDE WF1 .....176 F1
Ancaster Crs BHP/TINH LS16 .....86 D7
Ancaster Rd BHP/TINH LS16 .....86 D7
Ancaster Vw BHP/TINH LS16 .....86 D7
The Anchorage BGLY BD16 .....81 H2
Anchor Bridge Wy EARL WF12 .....173 J4
Anchor St HUD HD1 .....15 H6
TOD OL14 .....163 L1
Ancote Cl DOD/DAR S75 .....260 C5
Andersen Ct CAS WF10 .....180 E1
Anderson Av RHAY LS8 .....7 M4
Anderson Mt RHAY LS8 .....7 M4
Anderson St GIR BD8 .....4 A1
PONT WF8 .....180 E5
WKFDW/WTN WF2 .....12 B3
Anderton St AIRE BD20 .....34 F7
WKFDE WF1 .....13 K8
Andover Gn BOW BD4 .....128 A2
Andrew Cl HIPP HX3 .....169 J2
Andrew Crs HUDS HD4 .....213 J5
WKFDE WF1 .....176 D1
Andrew Sq PDSY/CALV LS28 .....106 D7
Andrew St FEA/AMT WF7 .....201 L2
PDSY/CALV LS28 .....106 F4
WKFDE WF1 .....176 D7
Angel Cl BVRD LS3 .....6 A7
Angel Pl BGLY BD16 .....81 J1
Angel Rd HFAX HX1 .....10 D4
Angel St BAIL BD17 .....82 E1
Angel Wy BFD BD1 .....4 C6
Angerton Wy WBSY BD6 .....126 C8
Angram Rd RYKW YO26 .....33 J4
Angus Av LM/WK BD12 .....148 E5
Anlaby St BOW BD4 .....127 M1
Annan Cl DOD/DAR S75 .....260 A1
Annat Royd La STKB/PEN S36 .....256 F5
Anne Crs CUD/GR S72 .....245 G1
Anne Ga BFDE BD3 .....5 H5
Annersley Av ROY/SHW OL2 .....229 J8
Annes Ct HIPP HX3 .....169 J2
Anne St BTLY WF17 .....151 J7
GTHN BD7 .....126 B3
Annie St HEM/SK/SE WF9 .....223 J2
KGHY BD21 * 3 G1
MOR LS27 .....152 D2
RPDN/SBR HX6 .....167 K1
SHPY BD18 .....82 B7
WKFDE WF1 .....176 D2
Anning Fold GFTH/SHER LS25 .....113 K6
Annison St BFDE BD3 .....5 J6
Annottes Cft HUDE HD5 .....193 H7
Ann Pl WBOW BD5 .....
KGHY BD21 .....2 E6
ROCH OL11 .....206 B8
Ann St CUL/QBY BD13 .....101 M5
KGHY BD21 .....2 E6
Anroyd St DEWS WF13 .....173 J5
Ansdell Rd MILN OL16 .....228 D2
Anson Cft SEL YO8 .....139 M5
Anson Gv GTHN BD7 .....126 B4
Anston Dr HEM/SK/SE WF9 .....247 J1
Anthony La BGLY BD16 .....80 D4
Antony Cl HUDW HD3 .....190 F5
Anvil Ct CUL/QBY BD13 .....101 M1
GIR BD8 .....104 C3
Anvil St BRIG HD6 .....170 C3
GIR BD8 .....104 C3
Apex Vw BEE/HOL LS11 .....9 G5
Apex Wy BEE/HOL LS11 .....9 G5
Apperley Gdns IDLE BD10 .....84 A6
Apperley La IDLE BD10 .....84 A6
Apperley Rd IDLE BD10 .....83 M6
Appleby Cl CUL/QBY BD13 .....124 E5
DOD/DAR S75 .....242 B5
Appleby La GFTH/SHER LS25 .....113 K7
MSTN/BAR LS15 .....111 G6
Appleby Pl AWLS/ASK DN6 .....249 H4
Appleby Wk MSTN/BAR LS15 .....111 G6
WBY LS22 .....30 A7
Apple Cl BTLY WF17 .....151 L4
Applegarth RTHW LS26 .....133 L7
WKFDW/WTN WF2 .....199 G5
Applehaigh Cl IDLE BD10 .....83 L7
Applehaigh Gv BSLYN/ROY S71 .....243 J2
Applehaigh La HOR/CROF WF4 .....221 J8
Applehaigh Vw BSLYN/ROY S71 .....243 J2
Applehurst Bank BSLY S70 * 261 K6
Appleshaw Crs
WKFDW/WTN WF2 .....176 B1
Appleton Cl BGLY BD16 .....81 K1
LM/WK BD12 .....149 H1
Appleton Gv OSM LS9 .....110 D6
Appleton Wy OSM LS9 .....110 D6
Appletree Cl EARD/LOFT WF3 .....153 L6
PONT WF8 .....180 D8
Apple Tree Cl EARD/LOFT WF3 .....153 L6
Appletree Dr SEL YO8 .....139 M4
Apple Tree Gdns ILK LS29 .....38 B2
Apple Tree La GFTH/SHER LS25 .....135 K5
Apple Tree Ms GFTH/SHER LS25 .....135 K5
Appletree Wy GFTH/SHER LS25 .....116 B6
Appleyard Rd HBR HX7 .....144 B5
The Approach MSTN/BAR LS15 .....90 B7
April Cl BSLYN/ROY S71 .....261 J2
April Ct LVSG WF15 .....172 C4
April Dr BSLYN/ROY S71 .....261 M2
Apsley Crs GIR BD8 .....4 B1
Apsley St HWTH BD22 .....78 F3
Apsley Vls GIR BD8 .....4 B1
Aquamarine Dr HUDN HD2 .....192 A4
Aqueduct St BSLYN/ROY S71 .....261 H3
Aquila Wy GFTH/SHER LS25 .....171 M1
Arboary La HOLM/MEL HD9 .....213 J8
The Arbour AIRE BD20 .....34 F5
ILK LS29 .....20 C8
The Arcade BSLY S70 * 261 G5
Arcadia St KGHY BD21 .....2 F5
Archbell Av BRIG HD6 .....170 D6

Archer Rd BRIG HD6 .....170 F5
Archer St CAS WF10 .....157 L8
Archery Pl LDSU LS2 .....6 E3
Archery Rd LDSU LS2 .....6 E4
Archery Ter LDSU LS2 .....6 E5
Arches St HFAX HX3 .....10 F7
The Arches HIPP HX3 * 11 H1
Arcon Cl MILN OL16 .....207 G8
Arctic Pde GTHN BD7 .....126 C2
Arctic St AIRE BD20 .....57 K5
HWTH BD22 .....79 G6
Arden Ct HOR/CROF WF4 .....197 J6
HUDE HD5 .....193 L7
Ardennes Cl ECHL BD2 .....105 H2
Arden Rd GIR BD8 .....103 M7
HIPP HX3 .....10 E9
Ardsley Cl BOW BD4 .....128 E3
Argie Av BULY LS4 .....108 D3
Argie Gdns BULY LS4 .....108 D4
Argie Rd BULY LS4 .....108 D4
Argie Ter BULY LS4 .....108 E4
Argyle Av BAIL BD17 .....85 G4
HORS LS18 .....85 K1
Argyle Rd KNOT WF11 .....181 L1
OSM LS9 .....7 K8
Argyle St BOW BD4 .....127 K2
HUDE HD5 .....15 L7
KGHY BD21 .....3 K6
MAR/SLWT HD7 .....213 G2
PDSY/CALV LS28 .....106 C4
ROY/SHW OL2 .....229 J7
Argyll Av PONT WF8 .....180 C6
Argyll Cl BAIL BD17 .....85 G3
HORS LS18 .....85 K1
Arkendale Ms GTHN BD7 * 126 A3
Arkenley La HUDS HD4 .....215 H5
Arkenmore HUDE HD5 .....193 H7
Arksey Mt WOR/ARM LS12 .....108 E6
Arksey Pl WOR/ARM LS12 .....108 E6
Arksey Ter WOR/ARM LS12 .....108 E6
Arkwright Wk MOR LS27 .....130 C3
Arlesford Rd BOW BD4 .....128 A4
Arley Cl HOLM/MEL HD9 .....236 B6
Arley Dr ROY/SHW OL2 .....229 L6
Arley Gv WOR/ARM LS12 .....108 E6
Arley Pl WOR/ARM LS12 .....108 E6
Arley St WOR/ARM LS12 .....108 E6
Arley Ter WOR/ARM LS12 .....108 E6
Arlington Crs LUD/ILL HX2 .....167 M1
Arlington Gv CAS WF10 * 158 B7
RHAY LS8 .....110 D2
Arlington Rd RHAY LS8 .....110 D2
Arlington St BFDE BD3 .....5 L7
HFAX HX1 .....176 D6
Arlington Wy HUDE HD5 .....193 J7
Armadale Av BOW BD4 .....128 B3
Armgill La BGLY BD16 .....104 F2
Armidale Wy ECHL BD2 .....105 H3
Armitage Av BRIG HD6 .....170 D6
Armitage Rd HFAX HX1 .....10 A9
HUDN HD4 .....214 A6
HUDS HD4 .....214 A6
LM/WK BD12 .....149 H2
WKFDW/WTN WF2 .....175 M6
Armitage Sq PDSY/CALV LS28 .....106 C4
Armitage St CAS WF10 .....157 L6
DEWS WF13 .....
Armley Grange Av
WOR/ARM LS12 .....108 B5
Armley Grange Crs
WOR/ARM LS12 .....108 B5
Armley Grange Dr
WOR/ARM LS12 .....108 B6
Armley Grange Mt
WOR/ARM LS12 .....108 B6
Armley Grange Ov
WOR/ARM LS12 .....108 C6
Armley Grange Ri
WOR/ARM LS12 .....108 C6
Armley Grange Vw
WOR/ARM LS12 .....108 C6
Armley Grange Wk
WOR/ARM LS12 .....108 C6
Armley Grove Pl
WOR/ARM LS12 .....108 F7
Armley Lodge Rd
WOR/ARM LS12 .....108 E5
Armley Park Rd WOR/ARM LS12 .....108 E5
Armley Ridge Cl
WOR/ARM LS12 .....108 C6
Armley Ridge Rd
WOR/ARM LS12 .....108 C6
Armley Ridge Ter
WOR/ARM LS12 .....108 D6
Armley Rd WOR/ARM LS12 .....9 K4
Armouries Dr MID LS10 .....9 M9
Armouries Wy MID LS10 .....9 M9
Armoury Av MIRF WF14 .....194 C1
Arm Rd MAR/SLWT HD7 .....207 G1
Armstrong Cl WHIT OL12 .....206 D3
Armstrong Hurst Cl WHIT OL12 .....206 D3
Armstrong St BOW BD4 .....105 M8
PDSY/CALV LS28 .....106 F4
Armstrong Ter PONT WF8 .....180 C7
Armyne Gv BSLYN/ROY S71 .....262 A5
Armytage Crs HUD HD1 .....214 A3
Armytage Rd BRIG HD6 .....170 E6
Armytage Wy BRIG HD6 .....170 F5
Arncliffe Av BSLYN/ROY S71 .....262 A3
Arncliffe Cl HUD HD1 .....14 A4
Arncliffe Crs BRIG HD6 .....170 A6
Arncliffe Dr BSLY S70 .....260 C5
Arncliffe Garth AL/HA/HU LS28 .....106 F4
Arncliffe Gra AL/HA/HU LS17 .....87 M4
Arncliffe Gv HWTH BD22 .....2 C7
Arncliffe Pl HWTH BD22 .....2 C7
Arncliffe Rd BHP/TINH LS16 .....86 C6
BTLY WF17 .....173 J1
HWTH BD22 .....
WKFDE WF1 .....177 H6
Arncliffe St PDSY/CALV LS28 .....106 C4
Arncliffe Ter GTHN BD7 .....104 D8
Arndale Gv HOLM/MEL HD9 .....254 D6
Arnford Cl BFDE BD3 .....5 H3
Arnold Av BSLYN/ROY S71 .....243 J6
Arnold Pl GIR BD8 .....104 C6
Arnold Royd BRIG HD6 .....170 A7
Arnold St GIR BD8 .....4 B1
HFAX HX1 .....10 C6
HUDN HD2 .....192 C1
LVSG WF15 .....172 C2
RPDN/SBR HX6 .....167 K2
Arnside Av AIRE BD20 .....58 D6
Arnside Cl CAS WF10 .....158 F6
ROY/SHW OL2 .....229 M4
Arnside Crs CAS WF10 .....158 F6
Arnside Rd WBOW BD5 .....126 A3
Arran Cl MAR/SLWT HD7 .....212 F1

Arran Ct GFTH/SHER LS25 .....135 H1
Arran Dr GFTH/SHER LS25 .....135 H1
HORS LS18 .....85 K2
Arran Wy RTHW LS26 .....155 H5
Arrunden La HOLM/MEL HD9 .....254 B5
Arthington Av MID LS10 .....131 M4
Arthington Cl EARD/LOFT WF3 .....154 E7
Arthington Garth OT LS21 .....43 H8
Arthington Gv MID LS10 .....131 M4
Arthington La OT LS21 .....43 G7
Arthington Pl MID LS10 .....131 M4
Arthington Rd BHP/TINH LS16 .....64 E5
Arthington St GIR BD8 .....4 A3
MID LS10 .....131 M4
MILN OL16 .....206 D6
Arthington Ter MID LS10 .....131 M4
Arthington Vw MID LS10 .....131 M4
Arthur Av GIR BD8 .....103 M7
Arthur Gv BTLY WF17 .....151 K4
Arthursdale Cl MSTN/BAR LS15 .....90 B7
Arthursdale Dr MSTN/BAR LS15 .....90 B7
Arthursdale Gra MSTN/BAR LS15 .....90 B7
Arthur St BGLY BD16 * 81 H5
BRIG HD6 .....
HWTH BD22 .....78 D4
IDLE BD10 .....83 K8
MAR/SLWT HD7 .....213 G2
PDSY/CALV LS28 .....106 C4
ROY/SHW OL2 .....229 J7
LIT OL15 .....185 K8
Artillery St HECK WF16 .....172 F3
Arum St WBOW BD5 .....126 E3
Arundel Av ROCH OL11 .....228 A2
Arundel Cl BTLY WF17 .....151 K4
Arundel Gdns BSLYN/ROY S71 .....243 J2
Arundell Dr BSLYN/ROY S71 .....262 B2
Arundel Rd AWLS/ASK DN6 .....227 M3
Arundel St GFTH/SHER LS25 .....113 K6
HFAX HX1 .....10 B5
PDSY/CALV LS28 .....106 C4
ROCH OL11 .....228 A2
Arundel Wk BTLY WF17 .....151 K5
Ascot Av GTHN BD7 .....126 A4
Ascot Dr GTHN BD7 .....126 A4
Ascot Gdns GTHN BD7 .....126 A4
MID LS10 .....153 K3
Ascot Gv BRIG HD6 .....170 A6
Ascot Pde GTHN BD7 .....126 A4
Ascot Rd GFTH/SHER LS25 .....135 H4
Ascot Ter OSM LS9 .....14 E1
Asdale Rd HOR/CROF WF4 .....198 C7
Ashbourne Av CLECK BD19 .....149 M8
ECHL BD2 .....105 H3
Ashbourne Bank ECHL BD2 .....105 H3
Ashbourne Cl ECHL BD2 .....105 H3
WHIT OL12 .....184 F8
Ashbourne Crs CUL/QBY BD13 .....124 F5
ECHL BD2 .....105 H3
GFTH/SHER LS25 .....135 H1
Ashbourne Dr CLECK BD19 .....149 M8
ECHL BD2 .....105 H3
PONT WF8 .....202 F1
Ashbourne Gdns CLECK BD19 .....149 M8
ECHL BD2 .....105 H3
Ashbourne Garth ECHL BD2 .....105 H2
Ashbourne Gv ECHL BD2 .....105 H3
HFAX HX1 .....10 A6
Ashbourne Hvn ECHL BD2 .....105 H3
Ashbourne Mt ECHL BD2 .....105 H3
Ashbourne Ri ECHL BD2 .....105 H3
Ashbourne Rd BSLYN/ROY S71 .....243 H7
HWTH BD22 .....79 J2
Ashbourne Vw CLECK BD19 .....149 M8
Ashbourne Wy CLECK BD19 .....149 M8
Ashbrook Cl OSS WF5 .....174 F8
Ashbrook Crs WHIT OL12 .....206 D2
Ashbrooke Pk BEE/HOL LS11 * 131 L4
Ashbrook Hey La WHIT OL12 .....206 E2
Ash Brow HOR/CROF WF4 .....217 L3
Ash Brow Rd HUDN HD2 .....192 D3
Ashburn Cl WBY LS22 .....29 M7
Ashburn Cft WBY LS22 .....29 M7
Ashburn Dr WBY LS22 .....29 M7
Ashburn Gv BAIL BD17 .....82 E2
WBY LS22 .....29 M7
Ashburnham Gv HTON BD9 .....104 D3
Ashburn Pl ILK LS29 .....38 C3
Ashburn Wy WBY LS22 .....29 M7
Ashburton Cl AWLS/ASK DN6 .....249 J4
Ashbury Cha WKFDE WF1 .....176 C1
Ashby Av BRAM LS13 .....107 M4
Ashby Cl BSLY S70 .....260 F6
Ashby Crs BRAM LS13 .....107 M4
Ashby Gdns BRAM LS13 .....107 M4
Ashby Mt BRAM LS13 .....107 M4
Ashby Sq BRAM LS13 .....107 M4
Ashby St BOW BD4 .....127 M4
Ashby Ter BRAM LS13 .....107 M4
Ashby Vw BRAM LS13 .....107 M4
Ash Cl HIPP HX3 .....147 M6
ILK LS29 .....38 A2
WHIT OL12 .....206 E2
Ashcombe Dr KNOT WF11 .....182 B3
Ash Ct CLECK BD19 .....149 H6
Ash Crs EARD/LOFT WF3 .....177 H2
HDGY LS6 .....108 E1
Ash Cft WBSY BD6 .....
Ashcroft Av FEA/AMT WF7 .....201 L2
Ashcroft Rd FEA/AMT WF7 .....201 L3
Ashdale WKFDW/WTN WF2 .....199 G6
Ashday La HIPP HX3 .....169 L4
Ashdene Ap HOR/CROF WF4 .....200 B5
Ashdene Av HOR/CROF WF4 .....200 B5
Ashdene Cl PDSY/CALV LS28 .....129 G1
Ashdene Crs HOR/CROF WF4 .....200 B5
Ashdene Cft PDSY/CALV LS28 .....79 M8
Ashdene Dr HOR/CROF WF4 .....200 B5
Ashdene Garth HOR/CROF WF4 .....200 B5
Ashdene Gv PONT WF8 .....181 H2
Ashdown Rd WKFDE WF1 .....13 J9
Ashdown St BRAM LS13 .....107 L4
Ashdown Wy ROY/SHW OL2 .....229 G6
Ash Dyke Cl DOD/DAR S75 .....241 M7
TOD OL14 .....141 J7
Ashenhurst Av HUDS HD4 .....214 E3
Ashenhurst Ri HUDS HD4 .....214 D3
Ashenhurst Rd HUDS HD4 .....214 D3
TOD OL14 .....141 J7
Ashes La HUDS HD4 .....214 D6
MILN OL16 .....207 L2
TOD OL14 .....141 M7
Ashfield BOW BD4 .....127 M5
EARL WF12 .....195 M2
WBY LS22 .....30 B1
Ashfield Av KBTN HD8 239

MOR LS27 152 B4
ROCH OL11 228 B1
SHPY BD18 104 C1
Ashfield Cl DOD/DAR S75 260 E3
HIPP HX5 146 B4
MSTN/BAR LS15 111 M3
WOR/ARM LS12 130 A2
Ashfield Crs BGLY BD16 81 J4
PDSY/CALV LS28 106 F5
Ashfield Dr BAIL BD17 82 F2
HIPP HX5 146 C4
Ashfield Gv PDSY/CALV LS28 * 107 G5
SHPY BD18 104 C1
Ashfield La MILN OL16 229 H2
Ashfield Pk HDGY LS6 109 G1
Ashfield Pl ECHL BD2 105 M4
OT LS21 * 41 H7
Ashfield Rd BTLY WF17 151 J4
CUL/QBY BD13 102 F8
GTL/HWG HX4 168 D7
HEM/SK/SE WF9 245 M1
HUDN HD2 14 B1
IDLE BD10 84 A5
MOR LS27 152 B4
PDSY/CALV LS28 106 F5
ROCH OL11 228 B1
SHPY BD18 82 A7
Ashfield St HUDN HD2 192 D4
NORM WF6 178 E3
Ashfield Ter EARD/LOFT WF3 154 B4
GTL/HWG HX4 168 D6
HWTH BD22 78 E8
MSTN/BAR LS15 111 M2
Ashfield Wy WOR/ARM LS12 130 B3
Ashford Ct BSLYN/ROY S71 * 243 K1
KBTN HD8 216 B7
Ashford Dr PDSY/CALV LS28 107 H8
Ash Ford Gn WBSY BD6 * 126 B5
Ashford Mnr KBTN HD8 215 M5
Ashford Pk MAR/SLWT HD7 212 F1
Ashgap La NORM WF6 178 D4
Ash Gdns HDGY LS6 * 108 F1
NORM WF6 178 E3
Ash Ghyll Gdns BGLY BD16 * 81 H2
Ash Gn HDGY LS6 108 F3
Ash Gn PONT WF8 181 H5
Ash Gv AIRE BD20 55 L1
AIRE BD20 56 F1
BGLY BD16 81 J5
BIRK/DRI BD11 128 C3
BRIG HD6 170 E4
BSLY S70 261 M7
CLECK BD19 150 C5
COL BB8 * 53 G8
EARD/LOFT WF3 177 H4
HDGY LS6 6 A2
HEM/SK/SE WF9 247 J2
HORS LS18 85 L4
HWTH BD22 78 E8
ILK LS29 38 E1
LIT OL15 207 H1
MILN OL16 229 J3
OT LS21 41 H7
PDSY/CALV LS28 107 G8
PONT WF8 203 L1
ROY/SHW OL2 228 F8
Ashgrove ECHL BD2 105 L3
GTHN BD7 4 C8
IDLE BD10 84 A7
MILN OL16 229 H2
Ashgrove Av HIPP HX3 * 169 G3
Ashgrove Cl GFTH/SHER LS25 135 K3
Ashgrove Cft GFTH/SHER LS25 135 K4
Ashgrove Ms BRAM LS13 107 J2
Ashgrove Mt GFTH/SHER LS25 135 J3
Ash Grove Rd HOLM/MEL HD9 254 A1
Ashgrove Rd AIRE BD20 57 J4
HUDE HD5 193 H4
Ash Hall La RPDN/SBR HX6 166 B8
Ash Hill Dr AL/HA/HU LS17 89 H2
Ash Hill Gdns AL/HA/HU LS17 89 H2
Ash Hill La AL/HA/HU LS17 89 H2
Ashia Cl MILN OL16 206 C8
Ashington Cl ECHL BD2 105 M3
Ashlands Rd ILK LS29 38 E1
Ash La GFTH/SHER LS25 113 J6
GFTH/SHER LS25 117 G1
KBTN HD8 218 A8
TAD LS24 116 F2
Ashlar Cl HWTH BD22 * 78 F7
Ashlar Gv CAS WF10 158 B4
CUL/QBY BD13 124 F7
Ash Lea EARD/LOFT WF3 * 177 H4
KNOT WF11 159 J2
Ashlea Av BRIC HD6 170 D6
GFTH/SHER LS25 135 H1
Ashlea Cl BRIG HD6 170 D6
Ashlea Dr BRIG HD6 170 D6
Ashlea Ga BRAM LS13 107 L2
Ashlea Gn BRAM LS13 107 L3
Ashleigh CUD/QBY S72 245 J3
Ashleigh Av PONT WF8 180 F7
WKFDW/WTN WF2 * 198 A1
Ashleigh Cl KBTN HD8 * 238 D4
Ashleigh Dl HUDN HD2 192 D1
Ashleigh Gdns OSS WF5 174 E6
RTHW LS26 133 L8
Ashleigh Rd BHP/TINH LS16 86 C6
Ashleigh St KGHY BD21 3 G2
Ashleigh St BSLY S70 261 L6
Ashley Av RHAY LS8 110 C4
Ashley Cl CLECK BD19 150 C4
WKFDW/WTN WF2 176 D1
Ashley Ct HEM/SK/SE WF9 246 B5
Ashley Cft BSLYN/ROY S71 243 K1
Ashley Dr BAIL BD17 82 C6
Ashley La BAIL BD17 82 C6
Ashley Park Ms
GFTH/SHER LS25 113 K6
Ashley Rd BGLY BD16 81 J4
LM/WK BD12 148 E4
RHAY LS8 110 C4
WOR/ARM LS12 108 D0
Ashley St HFAX HX1 10 D6
SHPY BD18 82 D6
Ashley Ter OSM LS9 110 C4
Ashmead BSPA/BRAM LS23 * 69 M1
BTLY WF17 173 J3
Ash Meadow Cl HUDN HD2 192 D4
Ashmere Cl HUDN HD2 192 D4
Ashmere Gv BRAM LS13 107 J4
Ashmews IDLE BD10 * 84 A7
Ashmore Dr OSS WF5 174 E5
Ashmore Gdns BOW BD4 * 127 K6
Ashmount CLAY BD14 125 M2
Ash Mt GTHN BD7 126 D1
KGHY BD21 2 C9
Ashmount Dr WHIT OL12 206 A6
Ash Rd AWLS/ASK DN6 249 K4
CUD/QBY S72 245 J3
HDGY LS6 108 E2
Ashroyd RTHW LS26 155 H2
Ash St AIRE BD20 34 F8
CLECK BD19 149 L7
COL BB8 74 E4
EARD/LOFT WF3 177 H4
HOR/CROF WF4 200 C7
HUD HD1 14 B2
HWTH BD22 100 D3
ILK LS29 38 E1

WMB/DAR S73 262 C8
Ash Ter BGLY BD16 81 H4
RPDN/SBR HX6 188 E3
Ashtofts Mt CSLY LS20 62 A5
Ashton Av GTHN BD7 126 A1
RHAY LS8 110 B4
Ashton Clough Rd LVSG WF15 172 C2
Ashton Ct RHAY LS8 110 C3
Ashton Crs EARD/LOFT WF3 154 F3
Ashton Gv RHAY LS8 110 B4
Ashton Mt RHAY LS8 110 B4
Ashton Pl RHAY LS8 110 B4
Ashton Rd CAS WF10 157 M8
RHAY LS8 110 C3
Ashton St BFD BD1 4 C1
CAS WF10 157 M7
RHAY LS8 110 B3
ROCH OL11 228 A1
Ashton Vw RHAY LS8 110 B4
Ashton Wk RHAY LS8 * 110 B4
Ash Tree Ap SCFT LS14 111 M2
Ash Tree Av CUL/QBY BD13 102 D8
Ash Tree Bank SCFT LS14 111 M1
Ash Tree Cl SCFT LS14 111 M1
Ash Tree Gdns LUD/ILL HX2 145 L1
NORM WF6 178 B3
SCFT LS14 111 M1
Ash Tree Garth TAD LS24 115 M1
Ashtree Gv GFTH/SHER LS25 * 135 K5
GTHN BD7 126 B4
Ash Tree Gv SCFT LS14 111 M1
Ash Tree Pk GFTH/SHER LS25 * 135 K5
Ash Tree Rd LUD/ILL HX2 145 L1
Ash Vw EARD/LOFT WF3 153 L7
Ashville Av HDGY LS6 * 108 F3
Ashville Cft LUD/ILL HX2 145 M5
Ashville Gdns LUD/ILL HX2 145 M5
Ashville Gv HDGY LS6 108 F3
LUD/ILL HX2 145 M5
Ashville Rd HDGY LS6 108 F3
Ashville St HIPP HX3 * 10 D1
Ashville Ter HDGY LS6 108 F3
Ashville Vw HDGY LS6 109 G4
Ashwell Cl CUD/QBY S72 244 E5
Ashwell Rd GIR BD8 104 C5
HTON BD9 104 D2
Ashwood St GIR BD8 104 C5
Ashwood Cl HUDN HD2 192 E3
Ashwood Dr AIRE BD20 58 C5
LIT OL15 207 H1
MOR LS27 129 K7
Ashwood Gdns MOR LS27 129 K7
Ashwood Gra HOR/CROF WF4 198 A4
Ashwood Gv CUD/QBY S72 263 M8
HOR/CROF WF4 198 A4
MOR LS27 129 L7
Ashwood Hts HOR/CROF WF4 196 D7
Ashwood St BOW BD4 127 M5
Ashwood Ter HDGY LS6 * 109 H2
Ashwood Vls HDGY LS6 6 A1
LIT OL15 185 J7
Ashworth Gdns DEWS WF13 173 L6
Ashworth Gn DEWS WF13 173 L6
Ashworth Pl WBSY BD6 126 F6
Ashworth Rd DEWS WF13 173 L6
PONT WF8 181 J5
Ashworth St WHIT OL12 206 A6
Askam Av PONT WF8 181 H1
Asket Av SCFT LS14 111 G1
Asket Crs SCFT LS14 111 G1
Asket Dr SCFT LS14 89 G8
Asket Gdns RHAY LS8 * 88 F8
Asket Garth SCFT LS14 111 G1
Asket Gn SCFT LS14 89 G8
Asket Hl SCFT LS14 88 F8
Asket Pl SCFT LS14 111 G1
Asket Wk SCFT LS14 111 G1
Askew Av MOR LS27 152 D4
Askey Crs MOR LS27 152 D4
Askey Av MOR LS27 152 D4
Askham Gv HEM/SK/SE WF9 226 A6
Askham Rd CAS WF10 158 F5
Askwith La OT LS21 22 C8
Askwith Moor Rd OT LS21 22 B1
Aspden St TOD OL14 141 K8
Aspect Gdns PDSY/CALV LS28 106 E6
Aspen Cl KGHY BD21 3 L8
WKFDW/WTN WF2 176 C6
Aspen Ct EARD/LOFT WF3 * 152 E5
KBTN HD8 217 J1
Aspen Gv DEWS WF13 173 K5
Aspen Ri WIL/AL BD15 103 H2
Aspen Wy CAS WF10 180 B2
TAD LS24 71 K3
Aspinall St HBR HX7 144 A5
Aspley Pl HUD HD1 15 H1
Asprey Dr WIL/AL BD15 103 K6
Asquith Av MOR LS27 130 B8
Asquith Cl MOR LS27 152 B1
Asquith Ct LUD/ILL HX2 * 145 M7
Asquith Dr MOR LS27 152 B1
Assembly St LDSU LS2 * 9 H1
NORM WF6 178 A4
Assheton Rd ROY/SHW OL2 229 H7
Astley Av RTHW LS26 134 C5
Astley Cl ROY/SHW OL2 229 H7
Astley La RTHW LS26 134 D6
Astley Wy RTHW LS26 134 D6
Aston Av BRAM LS13 * 107 M4
Aston Cl LVSG WF15 172 B4
Aston Crs BRAM LS13 108 A4
Aston Dr BRAM LS13 108 A4
BSLYN/ROY S71 243 J7
Aston Gv BRAM LS13 108 A4
Aston Mt BRAM LS13 108 A4
Aston Pl BRAM LS13 107 M4
Aston Rd BRAM LS13 107 M4
WBOW BD5 127 G3
Aston St BRAM LS13 107 M4
Aston Ter BRAM LS13 107 M4
Aston Vw BRAM LS13 107 M4
Astor Gv BRAM LS13 107 J4
Astor St BRAM LS13 107 J4
Astra Av HIPP HX3 147 M6
Astral Cl HIPP HX3 147 M6
Astral Vw WBSY BD6 126 C4
Astra Pk BEE/HOL LS11 * 131 L4
Astura Ct CHAL LS7 10 D1
Atalanta Ter LUD/ILL HX2 168 A2
Atha Cl BEE/HOL LS11 131 H5
Atha Crs BEE/HOL LS11 131 J5
Atha St BEE/HOL LS11 131 J5
Athelstans Ct GFTH/SHER LS25 116 A7
Athene Dr HUDS HD4 214 D3
Athersley Crs BSLYN/ROY S71 243 J8
Athersley Rd BSLYN/ROY S71 243 J8
Atherstone WHIT OL12 * 206 B6
Atherton La BRIG HD6 170 D6
Athlone Dr EARL WF12 174 A1

Athlone Gv WOR/ARM LS12 108 E7
Athlone Ri GFTH/SHER LS25 113 K7
Athlone St WOR/ARM LS12 108 E7
Athlone Ter WOR/ARM LS12 108 E7
Athold Dr OSS WF5 197 H1
Athold St OSS WF5 197 H1
Athol Gdns HIPP HX3 146 C3
Athol Gn HIPP HX3 146 C3
Athol Mt HIPP HX3 146 C3
HTON BD9 104 D4
Athol Rd HIPP HX3 146 C3
Athol St HIPP HX3 * 146 D3
KGHY BD21 3 M1
WHIT OL12 206 D5
Atkinson Ct NORM WF6 * 178 C5
Atkinson La PONT WF8 181 H4
Atkinson St MID LS10 9 L5
SHPY BD18 82 D6
Atlanta St BRAM LS13 107 J4
Atlas Mill Rd BRIC HD6 170 C4
Atlas St GIR BD8 104 D5
Atterwith La RYKW YO26 33 H1
Attlee Av HOR/CROF WF4 222 E5
Attlee Crs WKFDW/WTN WF2 199 G7
Attlee Gv WKFDW/WTN WF2 176 E2
Attlee St NORM WF6 178 D6
Aubrey St ROCH OL11 228 B1
Auckland Rd WBSY BD6 126 C5
Audby Ct WBY LS22 30 B8
Audby La WBY LS22 30 B7
Audrey St OSS WF5 197 H3
Audsley's Yd HOR/CROF WF4 197 G5
Augusta Cl WHIT OL12 206 A5
Augusta Dr NORM WF6 178 F6
Augusta St WHIT OL12 206 A6
Auster Bank Av TAD LS24 72 A2
Auster Bank Crs TAD LS24 72 A2
Auster Bank Rd TAD LS24 72 A2
Auster Bank Vw TAD LS24 72 A1
Austfield La GFTH/SHER LS25 138 E7
Austhorpe Av MSTN/BAR LS15 112 A7
Austhorpe Ct MSTN/BAR LS15 112 A7
Austhorpe Dr MSTN/BAR LS15 112 A7
Austhorpe Gdns
MSTN/BAR LS15 112 B6
Austhorpe Gv MSTN/BAR LS15 * 112 A7
Austhorpe La MSTN/BAR LS15 111 M5
Austhorpe Rd MSTN/BAR LS15 112 A6
Austhorpe Vw MSTN/BAR LS15 111 M6
Austin Av BRIG HD6 170 B2
Austin Rd CAS WF10 158 F6
Austin St KGHY BD21 3 J3
Austwick Cl DOD/DAR S75 242 C7
Austwick Wk BSLY S70 * 260 F4
Authorpe Rd CHAL LS7 87 H8
Autumn Av HDGY LS6 109 G4
WBY LS22 30 A6
Autumn Crs HORS LS18 85 M7
Autumn Gv HDGY LS6 109 G4
Autumn Pl HDGY LS6 109 G4
Autumn St HDGY LS6 109 G4
HFAX HX1 * 10 B9
Autumn Ter HDGY LS6 109 G4
Auty Crs EARD/LOFT WF3 177 H1
Auty Sq MOR LS27 152 D3
Avalon Ri HEM/SK/SE WF9 247 J4
Avenel Rd WIL/AL BD15 103 K6
Avenel Ter WIL/AL BD15 103 K6
Avenham Wy BFDE BD3 5 K8
Avens Cl PONT WF8 180 F7
Avenue A BSPA/BRAM LS23 49 K5
Avenue B BSPA/BRAM LS23 49 J5
Avenue C East BSPA/BRAM LS23 49 L4
Avenue C West
BSPA/BRAM LS23 49 K5
Avenue D BSPA/BRAM LS23 49 K6
Avenue Des Hirondelles OT LS21 42 F8
Avenue E East BSPA/BRAM LS23 49 L5
Avenue E West BSPA/BRAM LS23 49 K6
Avenue F BSPA/BRAM LS23 49 J5
Avenue Gdns AL/HA/HU LS17 87 H1
Avenue Hl RHAY LS8 110 B2
Avenue Lawns AL/HA/HU LS17 87 H1
Avenue No 2 BRIC HD6 170 C5
Avenue Rd WBOW BD5 127 H3
WKFDW/WTN WF2 199 G5
Avenue Ter OT LS21 41 H7
The Avenue AL/HA/HU LS17 45 J8
AL/HA/HU LS17 87 J1
AWLS/ASK DN6 227 L5
BGLY BD16 * 81 K6
BSLYN/ROY S71 244 A2
BTLY WF17 151 G5
BTLY WF17 151 J7
CLAY BD14 125 K2
DEWS WF13 173 H3
EARD/LOFT WF3 153 J6
GFTH/SHER LS25 138 A3
HIPP HX3 147 M6
HOLM/MEL HD9 235 K6
HOR/CROF WF4 200 A5
HORS LS18 85 J5
HUDE HD5 15 L8
IDLE BD10 84 A5
MSTN/BAR LS15 90 B6
MSTN/BAR LS15 111 M3
OSM LS9 110 C6
RHAY LS8 88 C6
ROY/SHW OL2 229 J8
TAD LS24 50 C1
WBY LS22 47 J5
WKFDE WF1 * 176 C2
Avenue Victoria RHAY LS8 * 88 C6
Avengcliffe Rd IDLE BD10 88 M8
Aviary Gv WOR/ARM LS12 108 E6
Aviary Mt WOR/ARM LS12 108 E6
Aviary Pl WOR/ARM LS12 108 E6
Aviary Rd WOR/ARM LS12 108 E5
Aviary Rw WOR/ARM LS12 * 108 E6
Aviary St WOR/ARM LS12 108 E6
Aviary Ter WOR/ARM LS12 108 E6
Aviary Vw WOR/ARM LS12 108 E6
Aviation Rd GFTH/SHER LS25 116 E7
Avis St ROY/SHW OL2 229 J7
Avocet Garth MID LS10 153 H1
Avon Cl AL/HA/HU LS17 89 H1
DOD/DAR S75 260 A3
MILN OL16 207 J8
Avon Dr AL/HA/HU LS17 89 G1
Avondale AIRE BD20 2 C3
Avondale Crs SHPY BD18 82 B7
Avondale Gv SHPY BD18 82 B7
Avondale Mt SHPY BD18 82 B7
Avondale Pl HIPP HX3 168 D2
Avondale Rd SHPY BD18 82 B7
Avondale St BRAM LS13 108 A4
COL BB8 74 C4
WKFDW/WTN WF2 12 E6
Avondale Wy
WKFDW/WTN WF2 12 E6
Avon Dr GFTH/SHER LS25 113 H8
Avon Garth WBY LS22 47 L1

Avon Rd ROY/SHW OL2 229 K6
Avon St BSLYN/ROY S71 261 J5
Avon Wk FEA/AMT WF7 179 M7
Axis St MOR LS27 * 152 A1
Aydon Wy BD6 126 A7
Aygill Av HTON BD9 103 M3
Aylesbury St KGHY BD21 79 J2
Aylesford Cl BSLYN/ROY S71 261 J5
Aylesford St MSTN/BAR LS15 112 B3
Aynholme Dr ILK LS29 19 H6
Aynsley Gv WIL/AL BD15 103 K5
Ayres Dr HUDS HD4 213 J5
Ayresome Av RHAY LS8 88 C4
Ayresome Ov WIL/AL BD15 103 J7
Ayreesome Ter RHAY LS8 88 B4
Ayrton St COL BB8 74 A1
Aysgarth MILN OL16 206 D5
Aysgarth Av BRIC HD6 148 C8
BSLYN/ROY S71 262 D6
Aysgarth Cl LM/WK BD12 148 E4
OSM LS9 110 B7
WKFDW/WTN WF2 197 M3
Aysgarth Crs LUD/ILL HX2 145 J5
Aysgarth Dr OSM LS9 110 B7
WKFDW/WTN WF2 197 M3
Aysgarth Fold MID LS10 153 L2
Aysgarth Pl OSM LS9 110 B7
HUDS HD4 214 D4
Aysgarth Rd BTLY WF17 173 J1
Aysgarth Wk OSM LS9 110 B7
Ayton Cl BFDE BD3 5 K4
Ayton Rd HUDW HD3 191 H6
Azealea Ct BFDE BD3 5 L4

B

Baby House Hill La HBR HX7 121 H2
Bachelor La HORS LS18 85 L5
Back Ada St KGHY BD21 2 D5
Back Aireview Ter KGHY BD21 * 3 M6
Back Aireville St AIRE BD20 57 J4
Back Airlie Av RHAY LS8 * 110 B2
Back Airlie Pl RHAY LS8 * 110 B2
Back Albert Gv HDGY LS6 * 86 F8
Back Albert Ter HDGY LS6 * 109 G4
Back Alcester Pl RHAY LS8 * 110 B2
Back Alcester Rd RHAY LS8 * 110 B2
Back Alcester Ter RHAY LS8 * 110 B2
Back Anderton St
WKFDW/WTN WF1 * 13 K8
Back Ann St CUL/QBY BD13 * 101 M5
Back Archery Pl LDSU LS2 6 C4
Back Archery Rd LDSU LS2 6 F5
Back Archery St LDSU LS2 6 F5
Back Archery Ter LDSU LS2 6 F5
Back Ash Gv HDGY LS6 6 A2
Back Ashgrove West GTHN BD7 * 4 C8
Back Ashley Av OSM LS9 * 110 C4
Back Ashley St OSM LS9 110 C4
Back Ash Vw HDGY LS6 * 108 F1
Back Ashville Av HDGY LS6 * 108 F4
Back Ashville Gv HDGY LS6 * 108 F3
Back Ashville Rd HDGY LS6 108 F3
Back Ashville Ter HDGY LS6 * 108 F3
Back Ashwood Ter HDGY LS6 109 H2
Back Aston Pl BRAM LS13 108 A4
Back Aston St BRAM LS13 * 107 M4
Back Aston Vw BRAM LS13 107 M4
Back Athlone Av
WOR/ARM LS12 * 108 E7
Back Athlone Gv
WOR/ARM LS12 108 E7
Back Athlone Ter
WOR/ARM LS12 * 108 E7
Back Atlanta St BRAM LS13 * 107 J4
Back Austhorpe Rd
MSTN/BAR LS15 111 M4
Back Autumn Rd HDGY LS6 * 109 G4
Back Aylesbury Pl HWTH BD22 * 79 J2
Back Baileys Pl BEE/HOL LS11 86 F6
Back Baker St SHPY BD18 * 82 C6
Back Baldovan Ter BFDE BD3 * 110 B2
Back Balfour St BGLY BD16 * 81 H4
KGHY BD21 * 3 H1
Back Bank St PDSY/CALV LS28 107 G4
Back Bank Ter PDSY/CALV LS28 * 107 G4
Back Banstead St RHAY LS8 110 B3
Back Barden Pl WOR/ARM LS12 * 108 C7
Back Barkly Gv BEE/HOL LS11 * 131 K4
Back Barkly Pde BEE/HOL LS11 131 K4
Back Barkly Ter BEE/HOL LS11 * 131 K4
Back Barrowby Vw
MSTN/BAR LS15 * 112 A7
Back Bath Rd BRAM LS13 * 107 L4
Back Beamsley Gv HDGY LS6 * 109 G4
Back Beamsley Mt HDGY LS6 * 109 G4
Back Beamsley Ter HDGY LS6 * 109 G4
Back Beaumont St BTLY WF17 * 173 L5
Back Beck La ILK LS29 19 H5
Back Beech St BGLY BD16 * 81 H4
Back Beech Ter HUD HD1 * 15 G1
Back Beechwood Rd
BULY LS4 * 108 C3
Back Bellbrooke Ter OSM LS9 * 110 D4
Back Belvedere Av
BEE/HOL LS11 131 K4
Back Belvedere Mt
BEE/HOL LS11 131 K4
Back Bentley Av HDGY LS6 * 87 H8
Back Bentley Gv HDGY LS6 87 H8
Back Berkeley Av RHAY LS8 110 C3
Back Berkeley Ter RHAY LS8 * 110 C3
Back Beverley Ter
BEE/HOL LS11 131 K3
Back Blackwood Gv HFAX HX1 * 10 A3
Back Blenheim Av LDSU LS2 6 C2
Back Blenheim Mt GIR BD8 * 104 E4
Back Blenheim Ter LDSU LS2 6 C2
Back Boundary Ter BVRD LS3 * 109 G5
Back Bower Rd ELL HX5 169 J7
Back Bowling Green Rd
HOLM/MEL HD9 236 D3
Back Bradbury St WKFDE WF1 * 13 L9
Back Bradshaw Rd
HOLM/MEL HD9 236 B3
Back Bradshaw St MILN OL16 * 206 D5
Back Breary Av HORS LS18 85 M5
Back Bridge St SKP/WHF BD23 16 B2
Back Briggate BRAM LS13 * 36 M4
Back Brigg Rd PDSY/CALV LS28 * 107 G4
Back Broad La BRAM LS13 * 107 M2
Back Broomfield Crs HDGY LS6 * 108 F3
Back Broomfield Pl HDGY LS6 * 108 F3
Back Broomfield Rd HDGY LS6 * 108 F3
Back Broomfield St KGHY BD21 * 2 F4
Back Brudenell Gv HDGY LS6 * 108 F3
Back Brudenell Mt HDGY LS6 * 109 G4
Back Brudenell Rd HDGY LS6 * 109 G4

Back Brunswick St DEWS WF13 * 173 J5
LDSU LS2 7 H7
Back Burchett Gv HDGY LS6 * 6 D1
Back Burchett Pl HDGY LS6 * 6 D1
Back Burley Hl BULY LS4 108 E4
Back Burley Lodge Rd
HDGY LS6 109 G4
Back Burley Lodge Ter
HDGY LS6 109 G5
Back Burley St BVRD LS3 6 C8
Back Burlington Pl
BEE/HOL LS11 131 K4
Back Burlington Rd
BEE/HOL LS11 131 K4
Back Burton Crs HDGY LS6 * 86 F8
Back Burton Ter
BEE/HOL LS11 131 L3
Back Buxton St KGHY BD21 * 3 J2
Back Byron St LDSU LS2 * 141 K8
Back Camberley St
BEE/HOL LS11 * 131 L3
Back Carberry Pl HDGY LS6 * 109 G4
Back Carberry Rd HDGY LS6 * 109 G4
Back Carberry Ter HDGY LS6 * 109 G4
Back Carter Ter
MSTN/BAR LS15 * 111 L4
Back Cartmel Rd KGHY BD21 * 2 D5
Back Castle Rd KGHY BD21 * 2 F2
Back Cavendish Rd IDLE BD10 83 K7
Back Cavendish St HFAX HX1 * 3 H4
Back Cecil St HUD HD1 14 D7
Back Chapel La HDGY LS6 108 F2
Back Charles St BRIG HD6 170 C3
Back Chatsworth Rd RHAY LS8 * 110 C3
Back Chestnut Av HDGY LS6 * 109 G3
MSTN/BAR LS15 111 M4
Back Chiswick St HDGY LS6 * 109 G4
Back Christ Church Vw
BRAM LS13 * 108 D6
Back Church La BHP/TINH LS16 * 86 E1
KSTL LS5 108 C1
Back Church Vw WKFDE WF1 * 199 G5
Back Claremont Av BVRD LS3 * 6 C7
Back Clarence Rd HORS LS18 85 K7
Back Clarence St HFAX HX1 * 10 E6
Back Clarendon Pl HFAX HX1 * 10 C6
Back Clarkson Vw HDGY LS6 * 6 D1
Back Clayton St RTHW LS26 155 H1
Back Cliff Mt HDGY LS6 * 6 C1
Back Clifton Rd HUD HD1 * 14 A5
Back Clifton Ter OSM LS9 110 D4
Back Clock View St AIRE BD20 * 57 K4
Back Close Lea BRIC HD6 170 C5
Back Close Lea Dr BRIC HD6 * 170 C5
Back Clough HIPP HX3 * 147 J4
Back Coldcotes Av OSM LS9 * 110 D4
Back Colenso Mt BEE/HOL LS11 * 8 B7
Back Colenso Rd BEE/HOL LS11 * 8 B7
KGHY BD21 3 M1
Back Colne Rd AIRE BD20 34 E8
Back Colton Rd
WOR/ARM LS12 * 108 E7
Back Colwyn Pl
BEE/HOL LS11 * 131 K4
Back Colwyn Vw
BEE/HOL LS11 * 131 K4
Back Commerical St TOD OL14 * 163 H1
Back Compton St KGHY BD21 * 3 J3
Back Conway St RHAY LS8 110 B3
Back Cowper Gv RHAY LS8 * 110 C3
Back Cowper St CHAL LS7 110 C4
Back Cranbrook Av
BEE/HOL LS11 * 131 J3
Back Cranbrook Ter
BEE/HOL LS11 * 8 C9
Back Croft House La
AIRE BD20 * 57 J4
Back Cromer Av KGHY BD21 * 79 K2
Back Cromer Ter LDSU LS2 6 E5
Back Cromwell Ter HFAX HX1 * 10 E5
Back Cross Flatts Av
BEE/HOL LS11 * 131 H4
Back Cross Flatts Crs
BEE/HOL LS11 131 H4
Back Cross Flatts Gv
BEE/HOL LS11 * 131 H4
Back Cross Flatts Mt
BEE/HOL LS11 * 131 H4
Back Cross Flatts Pl
BEE/HOL LS11 * 131 H4
Back Cross Flatts Rw
BEE/HOL LS11 * 131 H4
Back Cross Green Crs OSM LS9 * 110 D8
Back Cross Green La OSM LS9 110 D8
Back Crossland St
BEE/HOL LS11 * 8 F9
Back Cross La ELL HX5 169 G5
Back Dalton Av BEE/HOL LS11 * 131 J4
Back Dalton Gv BEE/HOL LS11 131 J4
Back De Lacy Mt KSTL LS5 * 108 C1
Back Delph Mt HDGY LS6 * 6 F3
Back Dent St OSM LS9 * 110 D7
Back Der St TOD OL14 * 163 L1
Back Devonshire La RHAY LS8 * 88 C2
Back Dorset Mt RHAY LS8 * 110 C2
Back Dorset Rd RHAY LS8 110 C2
Back Dorset Ter RHAY LS8 * 110 C2
Back Drake St MILN OL16 206 D8
Back Dudley Hill Rd ECHL BD2 * 5 H1
Back Duke of York St
WKFDE WF1 * 176 F7
Back Duke St FEA/AMT WF7 * 179 L8
Back Dunbar St WKFDE WF1 * 13 L8
Back Durham St ROCH OL11 228 C1
Back East Park Rd OSM LS9 * 110 C7
Back Eaton St KGHY BD21 * 79 J2
Back Ecclesburn Gv OSM LS9 * 110 D7
Back Ecclesburn St OSM LS9 * 110 D7
Back Edensor Rd KGHY BD21 * 2 D5
Back Eldon Rd HUD HD1 * 191 H7
Back Elford Pl RHAY LS8 * 110 B3
Back Elizabeth St WBOW BD5 * 4 E9
Back Ellers Gv RHAY LS8 * 110 B3
Back Ellers Rd RHAY LS8 110 B2
Back Elmfield Ter HFAX HX1 * 168 C1
Back Elsworth St
WOR/ARM LS12 * 108 D7
Back Emily St KGHY BD21 * 3 J3
Back Eric St KGHY BD21 107 L5
3 H2
Back Eshald Pl RTHW LS26 * 133 M8
Back Esmond Ter
WOR/ARM LS12 * 108 D7
Back Estcourt Av HDGY LS6 * 108 E2
Back Estcourt Ter HDGY LS6 * 108 E1
Back Eversley Mt LUD/ILL HX2 * 146 A8
Back Fairford Pl BEE/HOL LS11 * 9 G9
Back Ferguson St HFAX HX1 * 11 G7
Back Field St CUL/QBY BD13 * 102 F8
Back Fitzwilliam St HUD HD1 * 14 D1
Back Florist St KGHY BD21 * 3 M1
Back Fold CLAY BD14 * 125 K1

Back Foster Rd KGHY BD21 ....2 E9
Back Foundry Mill Dr SCFT LS14..111 G2
Back Garden St WKFDE WF1.......12 D3
Back Garton Rd OSM LS9.........110 C7
Back Garton Ter OSM LS9........110 C7
Back Gerrard St HFAX HX1........10 E8
Back Giles St South
  WBOW BD5 *..................126 F1
Back Glenthorpe Mt OSM LS9....110 C6
Back Glossop St HDGY LS6........6 E1
Back Gooder La BRIG HD6.......170 D5
Back Gordon St WKFDE WF1......13 L9
Back Gordon Ter HDGY LS6......87 H8
Back Graham Gv BULY LS4.......108 F3
Back Granby Gv HDGY LS6......108 F2
Back Grange Av CHAL LS7.........7 L1
Back Grange Crs CHAL LS7........7 L1
Back Grange Ter CHAL LS7........7 K1
Back Grange Vw CHAL LS7.........7 K1
Back Grantley St WKFDE WF1.....13 G2
Back Grant St HWTH BD22.........2 C5
Back Granville Ter GSLY LS20....62 B4
Back Great Russell St CTHN BD7...4 A6
Back Greaves St WBOW BD5.....126 F3
Back Gn MOR LS27.............130 C1
Back Greenhead Rd HUD HD1....14 D0
Back Greenmount Ter
  BEE/HOL LS11 *...............8 F9
Back Greenwood St HDGY LS6....87 G7
Back Grimthorpe St HDGY LS6.....6 E1
Back Grosvenor Ter HDGY LS6...109 H2
  HFAX HX1....................10 D6
Back Grouse St KGHY BD21 *......3 J3
Back Grovehall Av
  BEE/HOL LS11................131 J1
Back Grovehall Dr
  BEE/HOL LS11................131 J1
Back Grove Rd ILK LS29.........38 D2
Back Haigh Av RTHW LS26......132 B3
Back Haigh St RTHW LS26......132 E7
Back Haigh Vw RTHW LS26......132 G7
Back Halliday Gv
  WOR/ARM LS12...............108 C6
Back Halliday Pl
  WOR/ARM LS12...............108 C6
Back Hambleton St WKFDE WF1...12 F1
Back Hamilton Av CHAL LS7.......7 L1
Back Hamilton Vw CHAL LS7.......7 L1
Back Harehills Av CHAL LS7....109 M2
Back Harehills Park Vw
  OSM LS9.....................110 D4
Back Harehills Pl RHAY LS8 *...110 B3
Back Harehills Rd RHAY LS8 *...110 B3
Back Hares Av RHAY LS8.......110 B2
Back Hares Mt RHAY LS8.........7 M1
Back Hares Ter RHAY LS8......110 B2
Back Hares Vw RHAY LS8.......110 B2
Back Harold Gv HDGY LS6......109 G4
Back Hartley Av HDGY LS6........6 E1
Back Hartley Gv HDGY LS6........6 D1
Back Hartley St MOR LS27.....152 D3
Back Hatfeild St WKFDE WF1...176 E7
Back Hawksworth Gv KSTL LS5...85 M8
Back Headingley Av HDGY LS6..108 E1
Back Headingley Mt HDGY LS6..108 E1
Back Heddon St HDGY LS6......87 G8
Back Heights Rd
  CUL/OBY BD13................102 D7
Back Henrietta St BTLY WF17...173 L1
Back Hessle Av HDGY LS6......109 G3
Back Hessle Mt HDGY LS6......109 G3
Back Hessle Ter HDGY LS6.....109 G3
Back Hessle Vw HDGY LS6......109 G3
Back Highbury Ter BRAM LS13...87 G8
Back Highfield Rd BRAM LS13..107 M4
Back High St CUL/OBY BD13....102 F8
  YEA LS19....................62 D7
Back Highthorne Gv
  WOR/ARM LS12 *.............108 C6
Back Highthorne St
  WOR/ARM LS12...............108 C6
Back Hillcrest Av CHAL LS7......7 M1
Back Hillcrest Vw CHAL LS7......7 M1
Back Hill Top Av RHAY LS8....110 B2
Back Hill Top Mt RHAY LS8....110 B2
Back Hilton Gv RHAY LS8 *.....110 B2
Back Hilton Pl RHAY LS8......110 B2
Back Hilton Rd RHAY LS8......110 B2
Back Hird St KGHY BD21 *.......2 E7
Backhold Av HIPP HX3.........169 G4
Backhold Dr HIPP HX3.........168 F4
Backhold La HIPP HX3.........168 F4
Backhold Rd HIPP HX3.........169 G4
Back Holywell La
  AL/HA/HU LS17...............88 F1
Back Honoria St HUDN HD2......14 F1
Backhouse La HOR/CROF WF4...220 B7
Back Hovingham Gv RHAY LS8..110 C3
Back Hovingham Mt RHAY LS8..110 C2
Back Hovingham Ter RHAY LS8.110 C3
Back Hyde Ter LDSU LS2.........9 K3
Back Ibbetson Pl LDSU LS2......6 E6
Back Ingledew Crs RHAY LS8....88 D4
Back Irwell St BOW BD4.......127 J1
Back Ivy Av OSM LS9 *........110 D7
Back Ivy Mt OSM LS9 *........110 C6
Back Ivy St OSM LS9..........110 C6
Back John St CUL/OBY BD13...102 F8
Back Karnac Rd RHAY LS8......110 B2
Back Kelso Rd LDSU LS2.........8 B5
Back Kendal La BVRD LS3 *......8 C7
Back Kensington St GIR BD8...104 C6
Back Kensington Ter HDGY LS6...6 A2
Back Kirby St KGHY BD21 *......3 J2
Back Kirkgate SHPY BD18.......82 C7
Back Kitson St OSM LS9.......110 B7
Back Knowl Rd MIRF WF14.....172 B8
Back Laisteridge La CTHN BD7...4 A6
Back Lambton Gv RHAY LS8....110 B2
Back Landseer Av BRAM LS13..108 A3
Back Landseer Gv BRAM LS13..108 A3
Back Landseer Ter BRAM LS13..108 A3
Back La AIRE BD20
  AIRE BD20...................36 A4
  AIRE BD20...................58 F5
  AL/HA/HU LS17...............44 B3
  AWLS/ASK DN6...............227 L2
  AWLS/ASK DN6...............227 L6
  BEE/HOL LS11...............131 H5
  BIRK/DRI BD11...............129 H7
  BRAM LS13..................107 M5
  BRFD/BLYE BD10..............96 C1
  BSLYN/ROY S71..............261 L1
  BSPA/BRAM LS23.............69 M3
  CAS WF10...................157 K3
  COL BB8.....................74 D4
  CUL/OBY BD13...............103 G2
  CUL/OBY BD13...............125 K4
  EARL WF12..................195 G5
  GSLY LS20...................61 M5
  HBR HX7.....................99 J8
  HBR HX7....................120 E8
  HBR HX7....................143 H4
  HECK WF16..................172 F2
  HEM/SK/SE WF9..............225 G4
  HEM/SK/SE WF9..............225 J8
  HOLM/MEL HD9...............254 C1
  HOR/CROF WF4...............200 E4
  HOR/CROF WF4...............216 F1
  HOR/CROF WF4...............220 C8
  HOR/CROF WF4...............222 D8
  HS LS18.....................85 K6
  HTON BD9...................104 C2
  HWTH BD22...................56 D7
  HWTH BD22...................79 J2
  IDLE BD10...................83 J6
  ILK LS29....................40 B5
  KBTN HD8...................238 D2
  KBTN HD8...................239 J1
  KBTN HD8...................240 C3
  LUD/ILL HX2................145 M1
  MIRF WF14..................194 A1
  MIRF WF14..................194 D7
  OSS WF5....................196 F1
  OT LS21.....................40 C2
  PDSY/CALV LS28.............107 G6
  RPDN/SBR HX6...............188 F2
  RYKW YO26...................33 J3
  STKB/PEN S36...............270 F4
  STKB/PEN S36...............271 H8
  TAD LS24...................116 A2
  WBY LS22....................46 D1
  WIL/AL BD15................103 G1
  WKFDW/WTN WF2..............12 D3
  WOR/ARM LS12...............129 L3
  YEA LS19....................84 C1
Back La West BSLYN/ROY S71...243 J2
Back Langdale Gdns HDGY LS6..108 E2
Back Langdale Ter HDGY LS6...108 E2
Back Laurel Mt
  PDSY/CALV LS28.............107 G6
Back Leatham St DEWS WF13...173 J5
Back Leeming St HWTH BD22...100 F5
Back Lime St KGHY BD21 *......79 K3
Back Linden Gv BEE/HOL LS11..131 K4
Back Lindom St CTHN BD7........4 A6
Back Lindom St GIR BD8......104 E4
Back Lodge La BEE/HOL LS11...131 K3
Back Lombard St YEA LS19......84 C2
Back Longroyd Ter
  BEE/HOL LS11 *.............131 L3
Back Lord St HFAX HX1 *.......10 F4
Back Lucas St HDGY LS6.........6 D1
Back Lunan Pl RHAY LS8.......110 B2
Back Lunan Ter RHAY LS8......110 B2
Back Lune St COL BB8 *........74 A2
Back Lyon St CUL/OBY BD13...125 H5
Back Mafeking Av
  BEE/HOL LS11...............131 J5
Back Mafeking Mt
  BEE/HOL LS11 *.............131 J5
Back Malt St HWTH BD22.......79 J1
Back Mannville Rd KGHY BD21....2 D7
Back Manor Dr HDGY LS6......109 G3
Back Manor Gv CHAL LS7.......87 M8
Back Manor St ECHL BD2......105 K3
Back Manor Ter HDGY LS6.....109 G3
Back Market St WBSY BD6 *....126 E5
Back Markham Av RHAY LS8.....88 C4
Back Marriot St DEWS WF13...173 M5
Back Mary St AIRE BD20........34 F6
Back Masham St
  WOR/ARM LS12 *.............108 C5
Back Maud Av BEE/HOL LS11....131 J4
Back Mayville Av HDGY LS6....109 G3
Back Mayville Pl HDGY LS6....109 G3
Back Mayville St HDGY LS6....109 G3
Back Mayville Ter HDGY LS6...109 G3
Back Meadow Vw HDGY LS6....109 G3
Back Melbourne Gv BRAM LS13.107 L4
Back Methley Dr CHAL LS7 *....87 M8
Back Mexborough Av CHAL LS7..7 J1
Back Mexborough Dr CHAL LS7..7 J1
Back Mexborough Gv CHAL LS7..7 J1
Back Mexborough St CHAL LS7..7 J1
Back Meynell Av RTHW LS26...155 G1
Back Middle Cross St
  WOR/ARM LS12 *.............108 C7
Back Middleton Vw
  BEE/HOL LS11................8 D9
Back Midland Rd HDGY LS6......6 A2
Back Milan Av RHAY LS8.......110 B3
Back Milan Rd RHAY LS8.......110 B3
Back Milan St RHAY LS8.......110 C3
Back Minnie St KGHY BD21 *.....2 E7
Back Mitchell Ter BGLY BD16 *..81 H4
Back Mitford Rd
  WOR/ARM LS12...............108 F7
Back Model Av WOR/ARM LS12.108 F7
Back Model Rd WOR/ARM LS12.108 F7
Back Model Ter WOR/ARM LS12.108 F7
Back Model Vw WOR/ARM LS12.108 F7
Back Monk Bridge Dr HDGY LS6.87 H8
Back Monk Bridge Pl HDGY LS6.87 G8
Back Montague St WKFDE WF1..13 L9
Back Moorfield St HFAX HX1...10 C1
Back Moorfield Ter
  WOR/ARM LS12...............108 C6
Back Moorland Ter LDSU LS2....6 C4
Back Moor La HUDS HD4.......213 M7
Back Morning St KGHY BD21 *..79 K2
Back Morritt Dr
  MSTN/BAR LS15..............111 H6
Back Mount Av BTLY WF17.....173 M3
Back Mount Pleasant
  MID LS10...................153 L1
  WKFDE WF1...................13 H2
Back Mount Vw HDGY LS6........6 B1
Back Muff St BOW BD4.........6 B2
Back Myrtle Av BGLY BD16.....81 H4
Back Nansen St BRAM LS13....107 J4
Back Newport Gdns HDGY LS6..108 F3
Back Newport Mt HDGY LS6....108 F3
Back Newport Pl HDGY LS6....108 F3
Back Newton Gv CHAL LS7.....109 M2
Back Newton La CAS WF10.....136 C2
Back Nice Vw RHAY LS8.......110 B2
Back Norfolk St BTLY WF17....173 K2
Back Norman Mt KSTL LS5.....108 E3
Back Norman Pl RHAY LS8......88 C4
Back Norman Ter RHAY LS8.....88 C4
Back Northbrook St CHAL LS7..87 M7
Back Northfield Pl GIR BD8 *....4 B1
Back Northgate PONT WF8.....181 L6
Back North Park Av RHAY LS8..88 B5
Back Norwood St LM/WK BD12 *.149 J2
Back Norwood Gv HDGY LS6...109 G3
Back Norwood Pl HDGY LS6....109 G3
Back Norwood Rd HDGY LS6...109 G3
Back Nowell Crs OSM LS9.....110 D5
Back Nowell Pl OSM LS9......110 D5
Back Nowell Ter OSM LS9.....110 D5
Back Nunington St
  WOR/ARM LS12...............108 F6
Back Nunington Vw
  WOR/ARM LS12...............108 E5
Back Nunroyd Rd
  AL/HA/HU LS17...............87 M5
Back Nursery Mt MID LS10 *...132 A3
Back Oak Av BGLY BD16.......81 H4
Back Oakfield Ter HDGY LS6....87 G8
Back Oakley St
  EARD/LOFT WF3..............154 A5
Back Oakley Ter
  BEE/HOL LS11...............131 L4
Back Oak Rd CHAL LS7 *......109 M1
Back Oakwood Av RHAY LS8....88 B3
Back Oakwood Dr RHAY LS8....88 B3
Back of The Beck
  SKP/WHF BD23 *.............16 B2
Back Oldham Rd MILN OL16...206 C8
Back Osmondthorpe La
  OSM LS9....................110 E6
Back O' The MI BGLY BD16.....80 C5
Back O' Th' Height
  RPDN/SBR HX6...............187 L4
Back Otterburn St KGHY BD21 *..3 G2
Back Outwood La HORS LS18...85 L7
Back Overdale Ter
  MSTN/BAR LS15 *............111 J6
Back O'Wall HUDW HD3........211 K6
Back Oxford St
  EARD/LOFT WF3..............154 A6
Back Paget St KGHY BD21.......2 D5
Back Parish Ghyll Rd ILK LS29..38 D3
Back Parkfield Crs RHAY LS8....88 D4
Back Parkfield Rd
  BEE/HOL LS11...............131 J3
Back Park Ter HFAX HX1......10 C6
Back Park Vw BEE/HOL LS11...131 J3
Back Park View Av BULY LS4..108 F3
Back Parkville Rd BRAM LS13..107 L5
Back Parnaby Av MID LS10....132 B5
Back Parnaby St MID LS10....132 B5
Back Parnaby Ter MID LS10....132 B5
Back Pasture Gv CHAL LS7.....87 M7
Back Pasture Rd RHAY LS8....110 B2
Back Pawson St
  EARD/LOFT WF3..............154 A6
Back Pleasant St
  RPDN/SBR HX6...............167 L1
Back Pollard La BRAM LS13....107 L1
Back Pollard St HUDN HD2....192 D4
Back Potternewton La
  CHAL LS7....................87 L8
Back Potters St CHAL LS7.....87 M8
Back Prospect Pl KGHY BD21....2 F6
Back Prospect Ter CHAL LS9 *.110 B7
Back Providence Av HDGY LS6...6 D1
Back Providence St
  BTLY WF17..................173 L1
Back Purlwell Hall Rd
  BTLY WF17..................173 L3
Back Purlwell La BTLY WF17...173 L2
Back Quarry Mount Ter
  HDGY LS6.....................6 D1
Back Queen St GTL/HWG HX4..168 E8
  HUD HD1.....................15 G7
Back Ravenscar Av RHAY LS8...88 C8
Back Ravens St DEWS WF13...173 J8
Back Raynville Mt BRAM LS13..108 A3
Back Regent Park Ter HDGY LS6..6 B1
Back Regent St WKFDE WF1....13 K8
Back Regent Ter HDGY LS6......6 A4
Back Reginald Mt CHAL LS7 *..109 M2
Back Reginald Pl CHAL LS7....109 M2
Back Reginald St CHAL LS7....109 M2
Back Rhodes St HFAX HX1.....10 E5
Back Ribble St KGHY BD21......58 B6
Back Richardshaw La
  PDSY/CALV LS28.............107 G6
Back Richardson St
  LM/WK BD12.................149 J2
Back Richmond Mt HDGY LS6..109 G3
Back Ridge Mount Ter
  HDGY LS6.....................6 D1
Back Ridge St TOD OL14 *.....163 K1
Back Ridge Vw CHAL LS7.....109 J1
Back Rigging
  RPDN/SBR HX6...............166 E3
Back Ripley St AIRE BD20......58 B5
Back Ripon Ter HIPP HX3......10 F7
Back River St HWTH BD22......78 F7
Back Rd LM/WK BD12.........148 E2
Back Roberts St RTHW LS26 *..133 L8
Back Rochester Ter HDGY LS6..108 F2
Back Rokeby Gdns HDGY LS6..108 E1
Back Roman Gv RHAY LS8......88 C4
Back Roman Pl RHAY LS8......88 C4
Back Roman St RHAY LS8......88 C4
Back Rosebank Crs HDGY LS6...6 A5
Back Rosemont Wk BRAM LS13.107 L4
Back Rossall Rd RHAY LS8.....110 C2
Back Rossington Gv RHAY LS8 *.7 M1
Back Rossington Pl RHAY LS8 *..7 M1
Back Rossington Rd RHAY LS8..110 B2
Back Roundhay Av RHAY LS8...110 B2
Back Roundhay Crs RHAY LS8..110 B2
Back Roundhay Gv RHAY LS8...110 B2
Back Roundhay Pl RHAY LS8 *.110 B2
Back Roundhay Vw RHAY LS8 *.110 B2
Back Rw BEE/HOL LS11.........8 F5
Back Rowland Ter
  BEE/HOL LS11 *.............131 K3
Back Royds St MILN OL16.....228 C1
Back Rupert St KGHY BD21......3 H2
Back Russell St WBOW BD5.....8 D9
Back Ruthven Vw RHAY LS8....110 C3
Back Rydal St HWTH BD22.......2 C5
Back Rylstone St KGHY BD21...3 K2
Back St Alban Crs OSM LS9....110 C6
Back St Elmo Gv OSM LS9 *...110 C6
Back St Ives Mt WOR/ARM LS12.108 C6
Back St Luke's Crs
  BEE/HOL LS11................8 D8
Back St Paul's Rd SHPY BD18 *..82 C7
Back Salisbury Gv
  WOR/ARM LS12...............108 E6
Back Salisbury Ter
  WOR/ARM LS12...............108 E6
Back Salisbury Vw
  WOR/ARM LS12...............108 E6
Back Saltaire Rd North
  SHPY BD18...................82 C6
Back Sandhurst Gv RHAY LS8..110 C3
Back Sandhurst Pl RHAY LS8...110 C3
Back Sandhurst Rd RHAY LS8..110 C3
Back Savile Pde HFAX HX1....168 D1
Back Savile Pl CHAL LS7.......7 J2
Back Savile Rd CHAL LS7.......7 J2
Back School Vw HDGY LS6.....109 G3
Back Seaforth Ter OSM LS9....110 C3
Back Sefton Av BEE/HOL LS11..131 J3
Back Sefton Ter BEE/HOL LS11.131 J3
Back Shaftesbury Av
  RHAY LS8....................88 C5
Back Shaw La KGHY BD21.....79 M3
Back Shepherd's La CHAL LS7..110 A2
Back Shepherd's Pl RHAY LS8..110 B2
Back Sholebroke Av CHAL LS7.109 M1
Back Sholebroke Mt CHAL LS7.109 M1
Back Sholebroke Pl CHAL LS7 *.109 M2
Back Sholebroke Rw CHAL LS7.109 L2
Back Sholebroke Vw CHAL LS7.109 M1
Back Sidlaw Ter CHAL LS7.....110 B2
Back Simpson St KGHY BD21....2 D4
Back Sladen St KGHY BD21.....2 D5
Back Slaithwaite Rd
  EARL WF12..................195 L2
Back Smith Rw WBOW BD5 *..126 E3
Back Somerset Rd
  PDSY/CALV LS28.............106 F6
Back South End Gv
  BRAM LS13..................108 A4
Back South St HUD HD1......213 M1
Back Spencer Mt RHAY LS8 *...7 M2
Back Springfield Mt
  WOR/ARM LS12...............108 C7
Back Springfield Rd ELL HX5 *.169 K7
Back Spring Grove Wk
  HDGY LS6...................109 G4
Back Spring St HUD HD1......14 C7
Back Stanley St OSM LS9 *...110 B4
Back Stanmore Pl BULY LS4...108 E3
Back Stanmore St BULY LS4...108 E3
Back Station Rd
  AIRE BD20...................34 F5
  BTLY WF17..................173 M2
  MIRF WF14..................194 C2
Backstone Gill La
  AL/HA/HU LS17...............66 F5
Back Stone Hall Rd ECHL BD2..105 K2
Backstone La ILK LS29.........38 E3
Backstone Wy ILK LS29........38 E2
Back Storey Pl SCFT LS14.....111 G5
Back Stratford Av
  BEE/HOL LS11...............131 K3
Back Stratford St
  BEE/HOL LS11...............131 K3
Back Stratford Ter
  BEE/HOL LS11...............131 K3
Back St North LUD/ILL HX2...146 C1
Back St CTHN BD7............126 C2
Back Sunnybank Rd HORS LS18..85 K7
Back Sunnydene SCFT LS14....111 G5
Back Sutton Ap SCFT LS14....111 G5
Back Swinton St HFAX HX1....10 A8
Back Sycamore Av BGLY BD16..81 H4
Back Tamworth St BOW BD4...106 B4
Back Tempest Rd
  BEE/HOL LS11...............131 K3
Back Temple Vw BEE/HOL LS11 *..8 D9
Back The Crs HDGY LS6.......6 C5
Back Thornhill St
  PDSY/CALV LS28..............84 D8
Back Thornville Rw HDGY LS6..109 G4
Back Tower Gv WOR/ARM LS12.108 C6
Back Town St HORS LS18......85 K6
Back Trentham Pl
  BEE/HOL LS11...............131 K4
Back Trinity Ter WBOW BD5....4 D9
Back Union St HUD HD1......15 G5
Back Unity St North BGLY BD16..81 H4
Back Unity St South BGLY BD16..81 H4
Back Vicars Rd RHAY LS8 *......7 M2
Back Victoria Gv HDGY LS6...110 D7
Back Victoria Rd HFAX HX1....11 G5
Back Victor Ter HFAX HX1.....10 C3
Back Walmsley Rd HDGY LS6..109 G3
Back Walnut St KGHY BD21 *...79 K3
Back Warwick Ter BTLY WF17..173 M3
Back Waverley Rd ELL HX5....191 H1
Back Webster St DEWS WF13 *..173 L6
Back Wellfield Ter TOD OL14..163 K2
Back Welton Gv HDGY LS6....109 G3
Back Welton Mt HDGY LS6....109 G3
Back Welton Pl HDGY LS6....109 G3
Back Wentworth St HUD HD1..14 D6
Back Wesley St CAS WF10....157 M6
Back Westbourne St LDSU LS2..9 L9
Back Westbury St MID LS10...132 B5
Back Westlock Av OSM LS9...110 C5
Back Weston Rd ILK LS29......38 D2
Back Westover Rd BRAM LS13.107 L4
Back West St RPDN/SBR HX6..167 K3
Back Wetherby Gv BULY LS4..108 E4
Back Wetherby Rd HDGY LS6..88 B8
Back Wharf St RPDN/SBR HX6.167 L2
Back Wickham St
  BEE/HOL LS11...............131 J3
Back William Av
  MSTN/BAR LS15 *............111 L5
Back Wilton Gv HDGY LS6 *....87 G8
Back Winfield Gv LDSU LS2.....6 C4
Back Winston Gdns HDGY LS6..108 E1
Back Winterburn St
  KGHY BD21....................3 G2
Back Woodbine Ter HDGY LS6..87 G8
Back Woodland Park Rd
  HDGY LS6...................109 G1
Back Woodlands Av
  PDSY/CALV LS28.............106 E5
Back Woodlands Ter
  PDSY/CALV LS28.............106 E5
Back Wood St
  EARD/LOFT WF3..............153 M6
  GIR BD8......................4 B3
Back Wright Av HWTH BD22....78 F7
Back York Pl LDS LS1.........9 H9
Back York St LDSU LS2.........9 J1
Bacon St GSLY LS20...........62 B6
Bacup Rd TOD OL14..........162 A1
Baddeley Gdns IDLE BD10.....83 J5
Baden Powell Crs PONT WF8...180 C2
Baden St HWTH BD22..........78 E6
Badger Brow HOLM/MEL HD9..234 B5
Badger Cl HOR/CROF WF4.....198 B7
  ILK LS29....................38 K2
Badger Ga HOLM/MEL HD9....234 F4
Badgergate WIL/AL BD15.....102 C2
Badger Hl BRIG HD6..........169 M8
Badger La HEM/SK/SE WF9....225 J8
  MILN OL16..................228 C3
  STKB/PEN S36...............269 G8
Badgers Ga ILK LS29..........20 C1
Badgers Mt MSTN/BAR LS15...112 A6
Badgerstone Cl AIRE BD20.....58 F5
Badgers Wk HECK WF16.......172 C5
Badgers Wy WBY LS22.........30 A6
Badger Wood Gld WBY LS22...30 A6
Badminton Dr MID LS10......153 M3
Badsworth Ct HEM/SK/SE WF9.225 L5
Badsworth Vw
  HEM/SK/SE WF9.............225 J8
Bagby Rd LDSU LS2............6 E4
Bagden La KBTN HD8.........240 C5
Baghill Ct PONT WF8.........181 H6
Baghill Gn EARD/LOFT WF3...152 B7
Baghill Rd EARD/LOFT WF3...152 F8
Bagley La PDSY/CALV LS28...106 C2
Bagnall Ter WBSY BD6.......126 C5
Baildon Av GFTH/SHER LS25..135 K4
Baildon Cl SCFT LS14.........89 J3
Baildon Dr SCFT LS14.........89 J3
Baildon Gn SCFT LS14.........89 J3
Baildon Holmes BAIL BD17....82 C5
Baildon Pl BAIL BD17.........82 C4
Baildon Rd BAIL BD17.........82 C4
Baildon Wood Ct BAIL BD17...82 B4
Bailey Crs HEM/SK/SE WF9...247 J2
Bailey Hall Bank HIPP HX3....11 K6
Bailey Hall Rd HIPP HX3......11 K4
Bailey Hills Rd BGLY BD16....81 G2
Bailey's Ct SCFT LS14........111 J1
Bailey's Hl SCFT LS14........111 J1
Bailey's La SCFT LS14.......111 J1
Bailey's Lawn SCFT LS14.....111 J1
Bailey St BOW BD4...........127 K1
The Bailey SKP/WHF BD23.....16 C2
Bailey Wells Av WBOW BD5...126 E5
Baillie St MILN OL16 *.......206 B7
Baillie St East MILN OL16....206 C8
Bainbrigge Rd HDGY LS6.....108 F2
Baines St HFAX HX1..........10 C4
  RTHW LS26..................155 G1
Bainton Dr BSLY S70.........260 F7
Baird St WBOW BD5..........127 G2
Bairstow Ct LUD/ILL HX2.....145 L8
Bairstow La LUD/ILL HX2.....145 L8
Bairstow Mt LUD/ILL HX2....167 L1
Bairstow St WIL/AL BD15.....103 J3
Bakehouse La DOD/DAR S75...260 C5
Baker Crs MOR LS27.........152 C3
Baker Fold HFAX HX1.........10 D5
Baker La EARD/LOFT WF3.....176 D1
Baker Rd MOR LS27..........152 C3
Baker's Ct HBR HX7..........143 J2
Baker St ECHL BD2...........105 K4
  HUDW HD3..................191 K6
  MOR LS27...................152 C3
  SHPY BD18...................82 C5
Bakes St BSPA/BRAM LS23....69 L3
Bala St BSLYN/ROY S71......261 K5
Balbec Av HDGY LS6.........109 G1
Balbec St HDGY LS6.........109 G1
Balderstone Hall La MIRF WF14.172 E8
Balderstone Rd ROCH OL11...228 C4
Baldovan Pl RHAY LS8........110 B2
Baldovan Ter RHAY LS8......110 B2
Baldwin La CLAY DD14......125 J3
Baldwin Ter HIPP HX3.......11 K6
Bale Dr IDLE BD10...........83 H6
Balfour St BGLY BD16........81 H4
  BOW BD4....................127 J2
  KGHY BD21....................2 E7
  ROY/SHW OL2...............229 K6
Balk Av EARD/LOFT WF3.....177 M4
Balkcliffe La MID LS10.......131 J8
Balk Crs EARD/LOFT WF3.....177 J4
Balk La CTHN BD7............126 C2
  HEM/SK/SE WF9.............247 M2
  HOR/CROF WF4..............197 H7
  HUDE HD5...................193 K7
  KBTN HD8...................238 E8
Balkram Dr LUD/ILL HX2......145 J1
Balkram Edge LUD/ILL HX2....145 H1
Balkram Rd LUD/ILL HX2......145 J1
Balks LVSG WF15............172 B2
Balk St BTLY WF17...........173 K1
The Balk BTLY WF17.........151 L7
  DOD/DAR S75...............242 E4
Ballantyne Rd IDLE BD10.....83 J4
Ballard Cl LIT OL15.........185 K7
Ballard Wy ROY/SHW OL2....229 L7
Ballater Av HUDS HD4.......213 L4
Ballfield La DOD/DAR S75....241 L6
Ball Grove Dr COL BB8......74 D1
Ballroyd Clough HUDW HD3..191 J8
Ballroyd La HUDW HD3......191 J8
Ball Royd Rd HUDN HD2.....192 D4
Ball St CUL/OBY BD13.......103 G8
Balme La LM/WK BD12.......206 C6
Balme St CLECK BD19.......149 M6
  LM/WK BD12.................148 B5
Balme Ter HWTH BD22 *.....78 E8
Balmfield LVSG WF15........172 C4
Balmfield Crs LVSG WF15....172 C4
Balmoral Av HUDS HD4.......213 L4
Balmoral Cha MID LS10......132 B5
Balmoral Cl MILN OL16......207 J8
  PONT WF8...................181 G5
  STKB/PEN S36...............270 C2
Balmoral Dr KNOT WF11.....181 K7
  RTHW LS26..................156 E3
Balmoral Pl HFAX HX1.......10 A3
Balmoral St HBR HX7........143 J3
Balmoral Wy YEA LS19.......62 C5
Balm Pl BEE/HOL LS11.......8 C5
Balm Rd MID LS10..........132 A4
Balne Av WKFDW/WTN WF2...12 A1
Balne La WKFDW/WTN WF2...12 B1
Bamborough St WKFDE WF1...13 L8
Bamburgh Rd MSTN/BAR LS15.112 A3
Bamford Av BSLYN/ROY S71...243 J8
Bamford Cl DOD/DAR S75....260 A7
Bamford St LIT OL15........207 H1
Bamlett Brow HWTH BD22....78 F7
Banbury Rd PONT WF8.......181 G3
Bancroft Av HUDE HD5......215 G5
Bangor Gv WOR/ARM LS12...130 C2
Bangor Pl WOR/ARM LS12...130 C2
Bangor St MILN OL16 *......206 D8
Bangor Ter WOR/ARM LS12...130 C2
Bangor Vw WOR/ARM LS12...130 C2
Bank IDLE BD10.............83 M8
Bank Av HORS LS18.........85 K6
  MOR LS27...................152 C3
Bank Barn La WHIT OL12....184 F7
Bank Bottom HBR HX7.......144 C4
  HFAX HX1....................11 K6
Bank Bottom La LUD/ILL HX2.145 C5
Bank Cl IDLE BD10..........105 L1
  LIT OL15....................207 J3
Bank Crest BAIL BD17.......81 M7
Bank Crest Ri SHPY BD18....81 M7
Bank Dr WBSY BD6..........126 F6
Bank Edge Gdns LUD/ILL HX2.146 A3
Bank Edge Rd LUD/ILL HX2...145 M3
Bank End Knoll
  HOLM/MEL HD9..............236 F5
Bank End La HUDE HD5......215 G2
  KBTN HD8...................240 C5
Bank End Rd MAR/SLWT HD7..212 D3
Banker St BULY LS4..........108
Bank Fld AL/HA/HU LS17......238 B4
  KBTN HD8...................238 B4
  MAR/SLWT HD7 *............233 J2
Bankfield Av HUDE HD5......193 K6
  SHPY BD18...................81 M7
Bankfield Cl OSS WF5........197 G2
Bankfield Ct HUDE HD5......15 M9
  MIRF WF14..................194 B1
  WKFDW/WTN WF2.............176 B3
Bankfield Dr HOLM/MEL HD9..253 L4
  HWTH BD22...................57 G7
  SHPY BD18...................81 M7
  WKFDW/WTN WF2.............176 B3
Bankfield Gdns BULY LS4.....108

HIPP HX3 147 H8
Bank Field Gra GTL/HWG HX4 168 E7
Bankfield Gv BULY LS4 108 E3
Bankfield La HUDE HD5 193 K6
Bankfield Mt HWTH BD22 57 G7
Bankfield Park Av HUDS HD4 214 B5
Bank Field Rd BTLY WF17 173 L1
Bankfield Rd BULY LS4 * 108 E4
HUD HD1 14 D9
HWTH BD22 57 G6
SHPY BD18 81 M7
Bankfields Av HBR HX7 144 A5
Bankfield St COL BB8 74 D2
HWTH BD22 57 G6
Bankfield Ter BAIL BD17 82 F4
BULY LS4 108 E4
HUDS HD4 214 A6
Bankfield Vw HIPP HX3 10 F2
Bankfield Wk HWTH BD22 57 G7
Bankfield Yd HIPP HX3 * 10 F1
Bankfoot HBR HX7 143 H3
Bank Foot La HUDS HD4 214 A7
Bank Foot Pl BTLY WF17 * 173 L1
Bank Foot Rd HUDS HD4 215 H6
Bank Foot St BTLY WF17 * 173 L1
Bank Gdns HORS LS18 85 K6
Bank Ga MAR/SLWT HD7 212 B5
Bank Gv EARL WF12 174 C7
Bank Hey Bottom La
RPDN/SBR HX6 189 G3
Bankholme Ct BOW BD4 128 B4
Bankhouse PDSY/CALV LS28 128 F1
Bank House Cl MOR LS27 152 C1
Bankhouse Ct PDSY/CALV LS28 128 F1
Bank House La LUD/ILL HX2 144 F2
Bankhouse La HIPP HX3 168 F4
HUDW HD3 213 K1
PDSY/CALV LS28 128 F1
Bankhouse Rd HUDW HD3 213 K1
Banklands AIRE BD20 36 A4
Banklands Av AIRE BD20 36 B4
Banklands La AIRE BD20 36 B4
Bank La AIRE BD20 18 A6
HOLM/MEL HD9 236 D7
HOLM/MEL HD9 253 K4
KBTN HD8 257 H2
WHIT OL12 184 E7
Bank Pde OT LS21 41 H7
Bank Rd AIRE BD20 34 F7
RPDN/SBR HX6 167 K3
Bank Royd La GTL/HWG HX4 189 K5
Banks Ap MAR/SLWT HD7 212 F1
Banks Av FEA/AMT WF7 224 A1
MAR/SLWT HD7 212 E1
PONT WF8 * 180 E6
Banks Crs MAR/SLWT HD7 212 F1
Banks Dr MAR/SLWT HD7 212 F1
Banks End Rd ELL HX5 169 L8
Banksfield Av YEA LS19 62 D6
Banksfield Cl YEA LS19 62 D6
Banksfield Crs YEA LS19 62 D6
Banksfield Gv YEA LS19 62 D6
Banksfield Mt YEA LS19 62 D6
Banksfield Ri YEA LS19 62 D6
Banksfield Rd HBR HX7 144 A5
Banksfields Crs HBR HX7 144 A5
Banksfield Ter HBR HX7 144 A5
Banks Gv MAR/SLWT HD7 212 F1
Bankside KBTN HD8 238 B4
TOD OL14 163 K2
Bank Side St RHAY LS8 110 B3
Banks La AIRE BD20 58 A2
KNOT WF11 182 B2
Banks Mt PONT WF8 180 E6
Bank Sq MOR LS27 152 C1
Banks Rd HOLM/MEL HD9 236 D3
MAR/SLWT HD7 212 D6
MAR/SLWT HD7 212 F1
Banks Side MAR/SLWT HD7 212 F1
Banks St BTLY WF17 173 L2
Bank St BFD BD1 4 F6
BRIG HD6 170 C4
BSLY S70 261 H7
BSLYN/ROY S71 262 A6
CAS WF10 157 M6
CLECK BD19 149 L7
COL BB8 74 E5
CUD/GR S72 244 D7
EARL WF12 173 M6
HOLM/MEL HD9 255 G2
HOR/CROF WF4 197 J5
LDS LS1 7 G9
MIRF WF14 194 A1
MOR LS27 152 C1
OSS WF5 196 F1
ROCH OL11 228 C2
SHPY BD18 82 D6
TOD OL14 163 K2
WBOW BD5 * 126 E5
WBY LS22 48 A1
WKFDE WF1 12 E3
Bank Ter HBR HX7 143 G3
MOR LS27 152 C1
Bank Top HIPP HX3 11 M9
Bank Top Dr AIRE BD20 58 B4
Bank Top La HBR HX7 165 H1
HOLM/MEL HD9 253 J3
OT LS21 64 F3
Bank Top Wy KGHY BD21 58 B8
Bank Vw BAIL BD17 82 D4
EARL WF12 174 C7
HOLM/MEL HD9 236 E4
STKB/PEN S36 * 271 L5
Bank View Ter CHAL LS7 87 K7
Bank Wk BAIL BD17 82 E3
Bankwell Fold WBSY BD6 126 F5
Bankwell Rd HUDW HD3 213 K2
Bankwood BTLY WF17 * 151 K2
Bank Wood Rd PONT WF8 204 B2
Bankwood Wy BTLY WF17 151 K2
Bannerman St LM/WK BD12 149 J1
Banner St BFDE BD3 5 K7
Bannister Cl COL BB8 74 D3
Bannister La AWLS/ASK DN6 248 E1
Bannister Wk HWTH BD22 54 F2
Bannockburn Ct BOW BD4 * 127 J5
Bannockburn Wy NORM WF6 178 A2
Banstead St East RHAY LS8 110 B3
Banstead St West RHAY LS8 110 B3
Banstead Ter East RHAY LS8 110 B3
Banstead Ter West RHAY LS8 * 110 B3
Bantam Cl MOR LS27 152 F2
Bantam Grove La MOR LS27 152 F2
Bantam Grove Vw MOR LS27 152 F2
Bantree Ct IDLE BD10 83 J5
Baptist Fold CUL/QBY BD13 125 G5
Baptist La OSS WF5 197 K2
Baptist Pl BFD BD1 4 D5
Baptist St BTLY WF17 173 J3
Baptist Wy PDSY/CALV LS28 107 J4
Bar Av DOD/DAR S75 242 F6
Barber Rw MAR/SLWT HD7 212 E5
Barberry Av BFDE BD3 106 A6
Barber Sq HECK WF16 172 E2
Barber St BRIG HD6 170 C2
Barclay Cl CUL/QBY BD13 102 A1
Barclay St CHAL LS7 7 J6
Barclyde St ROCH OL11 228 A1
Bar Cft HUDE HD5 193 K5
Barcroft DOD/DAR S75 260 C2
HWTH BD22 79 H6
Barcroft Gv YEA LS19 62 C8
Barcroft Rd HUDS HD4 214 B4
Barden Av WBSY BD6 125 M5
Barden Cl BTLY WF17 173 K1
WOR/ARM LS12 108 C7
Barden Dr BGLY BD16 81 L2
DOD/DAR S75 260 D3
Barden Gn WOR/ARM LS12 108 C7
Barden Gv WOR/ARM LS12 * 108 C7
Barden Mt WOR/ARM LS12 108 C7
Barden Pl WOR/ARM LS12 108 C7
Barden Rd WKFDE WF1 13 M2
Barden St GIR BD8 104 D5
Barden Ter WOR/ARM LS12 108 C7
Bardon Hall Gdns
BHP/TINH LS16 86 E6
Bardon Hall Ms
BHP/TINH LS16 * 86 F7
Bardsey Crs BFDE BD3 5 K6
Bardwell Ct EARD/LOFT WF3 177 G1
Barehill St LIT OL15 185 K8
Barfield Av YEA LS19 62 C8
Barfield Crs AL/HA/HU LS17 88 B1
Barfield Dr YEA LS19 62 C8
Barfield Gv AL/HA/HU LS17 88 C1
Barfield Mt AL/HA/HU LS17 88 C1
Barfield Rd HIPP HX3 147 L7
Bargate MAR/SLWT HD7 212 F5
Bargess Ter GFTH/SHER LS25 135 K5
Barge St HUD HD1 214 B2
Bargrange Av SHPY BD18 82 D8
Bargreen HUDE HD5 193 K5
Barham Ter IDLE BD10 105 M2
Bar House La AIRE BD20 57 H3
Bari Cl WMB/DAR S73 263 G8
Baring Av BFDE BD3 105 M6
Bark Cl KBTN HD8 238 C3
Barker Cl HIPP HX3 169 G3
Barker Ct HUDN HD2 192 A5
Barkerend Rd BFDE BD3 5 J5
Barker Pl BRAM LS13 107 M5
Barker Rd HOR/CROF WF4 197 H4
Barker's Rd HOR/CROF WF4 198 A8
Barker St EARD/LOFT WF3 155 K8
LVSG WF15 172 D2
TOD OL14 141 K8
Barkers Well Fold
WOR/ARM LS12 129 M2
Barkers Well Garth
WOR/ARM LS12 130 A3
Barkers Well Ga
WOR/ARM LS12 130 A3
Barkers Well Lawn
WOR/ARM LS12 130 A3
Barke St MILN OL16 207 G3
Bark House La DOD/DAR S75 258 E2
KBTN HD8 238 D3
Barkhouse Wood La
KNOT WF11 161 K3
Bark La ILK LS29 19 J6
Barkly Av BEE/HOL LS11 131 J5
Barkly Dr BEE/HOL LS11 * 131 J5
Barkly Gv BEE/HOL LS11 131 J4
Barkly Pde BEE/HOL LS11 131 J5
Barkly Pl BEE/HOL LS11 131 J5
Barkly Rd BEE/HOL LS11 131 H4
Barkly St BEE/HOL LS11 131 J5
Barkly Ter BEE/HOL LS11 131 J4
Bark Mdw DOD/DAR S75 260 C7
Barkston Rd BSLYN/ROY S71 243 L8
Bar La AIRE BD20 58 B5
BSPA/BRAM LS23 49 J8
DOD/DAR S75 242 F6
GFTH/SHER LS25 113 J7
HOR/CROF WF4 218 B4
HORS LS18 85 G6
RPDN/SBR HX6 188 E4
SEL YO8 139 M5
WKFDE WF1 176 F5
Barlbro' Pl HUDW HD3 213 J2
Barlby Wy RHAY LS8 88 E8
Barleycorn Cl WKFDE WF1 177 G5
Barley Cote Av AIRE BD20 58 B4
Barley Cote Gv AIRE BD20 58 C4
Barley Cote Rd AIRE BD20 58 B4
Barley Cft DEWS WF13 173 H6
Barleyfield Cl WKFDE WF1 177 G6
Barley Field Ct
MSTN/BAR LS15 * 111 J6
Barleyfields Cl WBY LS22 30 A7
Barleyfields Ct WBY LS22 30 A8
Barleyfields La WBY LS22 30 A8
Barleyfields Ms WBY LS22 * 48 A1
Barleyfields Rd WBY LS22 30 A8
Barleyfields Ter WBY LS22 30 A8
Barleyhill Crs GFTH/SHER LS25 113 G7
Barleyhill La GFTH/SHER LS25 113 G7
Barleyhill Rd GFTH/SHER LS25 113 G7
Barley Horn Rd TAD LS24 94 F2
Barley Ms EARD/LOFT WF3 154 D3
Barley St HWTH BD22 79 J2
Barlow Rd KGHY BD21 2 E3
Barlow St BFDE BD3 5 L5
MILN OL16 206 C7
Barmby Cl OSS WF5 197 H2
Barmby Crs OSS WF5 197 J2
Barmby Fold OSS WF5 197 H2
Barmby Pl ECHL BD2 5 L1
Barmby Rd ECHL BD2 5 L1
Barmby St LM/WK BD12 148 F2
Bar Mt GFTH/SHER LS25 * 113 J7
Barmouth Ter BFDE BD3 5 G1
Barnabas Wk BSLYN/ROY S71 261 H3
Barnaby Rd BGLY BD16 81 L2
Barnard Cl MSTN/BAR LS15 112 A3
Barnard Rd BOW BD4 127 J1
Barnard Wy MSTN/BAR LS15 112 A3
Barnbow La MSTN/BAR LS15 112 D2
Barnbrough St BULY LS4 108 E4
Barnby Av GIR BD8 103 L7
Barnby Royd HUDE HD5 193 G7
Barncroft Cl SCFT LS14 89 H7
Barncroft Dr SCFT LS14 89 G8
Barncroft Gdns SCFT LS14 89 H8
Barncroft Mt SCFT LS14 89 G8
Barncroft Ri SCFT LS14 89 H8
Barncroft Rd SCFT LS14 89 H8
Barnes Av WKFDE WF1 176 C3
Barnes Mdw LIT OL15 185 L5
Barnes Rd CAS WF10 157 M8
GIR BD8 104 B6
Barnes St TOD OL14 163 J5
Barnet Gv MOR LS27 152 C4
Barnet Rd WOR/ARM LS12 108 F7
Barn Field Cl COL BB8 74 C1
Barn Field La WHIT OL12 184 C7
Barnfield Ri ROY/SHW OL2 229 J5
Barnfield St WHIT OL12 206 B4
Barnfold Pl CUD/GR S72 244 E4
Barnsdale Est CAS WF10 157 K8
Barnsdale Ms AWLS/ASK DN6 227 L6
Barnsdale Rd CAS WF10 135 M8
RTHW LS26 156 E5
Barnsdale Vw AWLS/ASK DN6 227 K2
Barnsdale Wy HEM/SK/SE WF9 226 A7
Barnside Cl STKB/PEN S36 * 270 F4
Barnside La HOLM/MEL HD9 255 H5
Barnsley Beck Gv BAIL BD17 82 F3
Barnsley Boundary Wk
DOD/DAR S75 240 F2
DOD/DAR S75 241 M1
HOLM/MEL HD9 267 L2
HOR/CROF WF4 222 A6
KBTN HD8 257 K3
STKB/PEN S36 256 E7
Barnsley Rd CUD/GR S72 244 C8
CUD/GR S72 245 K1
DOD/DAR S75 242 A6
DOD/DAR S75 242 F1
DOD/DAR S75 259 J6
FEA/AMT WF7 224 C2
HEM/SK/SE WF9 246 F3
HOR/CROF WF4 217 L3
KBTN HD8 238 E8
KBTN HD8 240 A5
KBTN HD8 257 M2
STKB/PEN S36 270 F2
WKFDE WF1 13 H7
WKFDW/WTN WF2 220 E4
WMB/DAR S73 263 H7
Barnstone V WKFDE WF1 177 G6
Barn St HWTH BD22 * 100 E4
Barnswick Cl PONT WF8 180 F8
Barnswick Vw BHP/TINH LS16 86 A2
The Barn LM/WK BD12 127 G8
Baron Cl BEE/HOL LS11 8 B8
Baronscourt MSTN/BAR LS15 111 M6
Baronsmead MSTN/BAR LS15 111 L6
Baron St MILN OL16 206 B7
Baronsway MSTN/BAR LS15 111 L6
Barrack Rd CHAL LS7 7 K3
Barracks Fold HOLM/MEL HD9 255 G4
Barracks St HECK WF16 172 E2
Barrack St CHAL LS7 7 J4
Barraclough Sq LM/WK BD12 148 E2
Barraclough St LM/WK BD12 126 D8
Barran St BGLY BD16 81 J3
Barras Garth Pl WOR/ARM LS12 108 D8
Barras Garth Rd
WOR/ARM LS12 108 D8
Barras Pl WOR/ARM LS12 108 D8
Barras St WOR/ARM LS12 108 D8
Barras Ter WOR/ARM LS12 108 D8
Barratt's Rd WKFDE WF1 176 E6
Barrett St AIRE BD20 35 M5
Barrington Cl HIPP HX3 169 J2
Barrington Garth GLE DN14 161 M8
Barrington Pde CLECK BD19 150 C6
Barrowby Av MSTN/BAR LS15 112 A7
Barrowby Crs MSTN/BAR LS15 112 A6
Barrowby La GFTH/SHER LS25 113 G6
MSTN/BAR LS15 112 C6
PBR HG3 27 K8
Barrowby Rd MSTN/BAR LS15 112 B7
Barrowclough La HIPP HX3 147 H7
Barrows La AIRE BD20 56 E2
Barrowstead KBTN HD8 239 J5
Barr St HUD HD1 15 J2
Barr Ter GIR BD8 * 104 B6
Barry St BFD BD1 4 E6
Barsey Green La GTL/HWG HX4 167 L8
Barstow Fall PONT WF8 181 G3
Barstow Sq WKFDE WF1 12 E2
Bar St BTLY WF17 173 M2
TOD OL14 163 J2
Barthorpe Cl BOW BD4 128 B4
Barthorpe Crs CHAL LS7 87 L6
Bartle Cl GTHN BD7 126 B3
Bartle Fold GTHN BD7 126 C2
Bartle Gill Dr BAIL BD17 83 G2
Bartle Gill Ri BAIL BD17 83 G2
Bartle Gill Vw BAIL BD17 * 83 G2
Bartle Gv GTHN BD7 126 B3
Bartle La GTHN BD7 126 B3
Bartle Pl GTHN BD7 126 B3
Bartle Sq GTHN BD7 126 C2
Bartlett Rd ROY/SHW OL2 229 J8
Barton Ct MSTN/BAR LS15 111 L7
Barton Gv BEE/HOL LS11 8 D8
Barton Hl BEE/HOL LS11 * 8 C8
Barton Manor Cl HUDS HD4 213 K4
Barton Mt BEE/HOL LS11 8 D8
Barton Pl BEE/HOL LS11 8 C8
BTLY WF17 173 L2
Barton Rd BEE/HOL LS11 8 C8
Barton St BRIG HD6 * 170 C3
WBOW BD5 126 D3
Barton Ter BEE/HOL LS11 8 D8
Barton Vw BEE/HOL LS11 8 C8
Barton Wy HEM/SK/SE WF9 247 J1
Barugh Green Rd
DOD/DAR S75 260 A2
Barugh La DOD/DAR S75 260 A1
Barwick Gn WBSY BD6 126 A5
Barwick Rd GFTH/SHER LS25 113 G5
SCFT LS14 111 K3
Basford Ct WKFDW/WTN WF2 12 A4
Basford St WKFDW/WTN WF2 12 A4
Basil Ct MILN OL16 * 206 D8
Basil St HUDS HD4 213 M2
MILN OL16 206 D8
WBOW BD5 126 D3
Baslow Crs DOD/DAR S75 260 A7
Baslow Gv HTON BD9 104 B4
Baslow Rd BSLYN/ROY S71 243 K7
Bassett Wy WHIT OL12 206 A4
Batcliffe Dr HDGY LS6 86 E8
Batcliffe Mt HDGY LS6 108 E1
Bateman Cl CUD/GR S72 244 C4
Bateman St GIR BD8 4 D1
Bates Av RPDN/SBR HX6 167 H3
Bates La PONT WF8 203 H1
Bateson St IDLE BD10 84 A7
Bath Cl BRAM LS13 107 L4
Bath Gv BRAM LS13 * 107 L4
Bath La BRAM LS13 107 L4
Bath Pl CLECK BD19 149 M7
HIPP HX3 10 F2
Bath Rd BEE/HOL LS11 8 D4
BRAM LS13 107 L4
CLECK BD19 149 M7
HECK WF16 172 F2
HIPP HX3 168 E2
Bath St BFDE BD3 5 J6
BTLY WF17 173 M1
COL BB8 74 A1
DEWS WF13 173 L5
ELL HX5 169 H8
HFAX HX1 * 11 J7
HUD HD1 14 E5
ILK LS29 38 E1
KBTN HD8 238 B1
KGHY BD21 2 F4
TOD OL14 163 K1
WHIT OL12 206 C5
Batley Av HUD HD1 191 M8
Batley Buildings HUD HD1 14 A5
Batley Ct BAIL BD17 82 F2
Batley Field Hl BTLY WF17 151 L8
Batley Rd EARD/LOFT WF3 174 F1
HECK WF16 173 H2
WKFDW/WTN WF2 175 L5
Batley St HIPP HX3 10 D1
HUDE HD5 15 M7
Batter La YEA LS19 84 E2
Battinson Rd HFAX HX1 10 A4
Battinson St HIPP HX3 11 M9
Battlefield Vw BOW BD4 128 D7
Batty Av CUD/GR S72 244 C8
Battye Av HUDS HD4 213 K3
Battye St BOW BD4 105 L8
EARL WF12 173 M6
Baulk Head La TOD OL14 142 B8
The Baum MILN OL16 * 206 B6
Bavaria Pl GIR BD8 104 D5
Bawn Ap WOR/ARM LS12 130 A1
Bawn Av WOR/ARM LS12 108 A8
Bawn Dr WOR/ARM LS12 108 A8
Bawn Gdns WOR/ARM LS12 108 A8
Bawn La WOR/ARM LS12 108 A8
Bawson Ct CLECK BD19 150 C5
Baxandall St WBOW BD5 126 F3
Baxtergate PONT WF8 180 F6
Baxter La HIPP HX3 147 J3
Baxter Wd AIRE BD20 34 E7
Baycliff Cl BSLYN/ROY S71 243 M7
Bay Cl HUDW HD3 191 L7
Bayfield Cl HOLM/MEL HD9 254 D6
Bay Hall HUD HD1 14 E2
Bay Hall Common Rd HUDN HD2 14 E1
Bay Horse La AL/HA/HU LS17 67 J7
Bay Horse Yd SKP/WHF BD23 16 B2
Bayldons Pl BTLY WF17 * 173 L1
Baylee St HEM/SK/SE WF9 224 A8
Bayne Dr BOW BD4 127 K6
Bay of Biscay WIL/AL BD15 103 K2
Bay St WHIT OL12 206 C5
Bayswater Crs RHAY LS8 110 B3
Bayswater Gv ECHL BD2 105 M4
RHAY LS8 110 B3
Bayswater Mt RHAY LS8 110 B3
Bayswater Pl RHAY LS8 110 B3
Bayswater Rw RHAY LS8 110 B3
Bayswater Ter HIPP HX3 168 E3
RHAY LS8 110 B3
Bayswater Vw RHAY LS8 110 B3
Bayton La HORS LS18 85 H2
YEA LS19 63 G8
Beacon Av MOR LS27 152 D4
Beacon Brow WBSY BD6 125 M4
Beacon Cl BGLY BD16 81 K3
DOD/DAR S75 259 J8
Beacon Ct DOD/DAR S75 259 J8
Beacon Dr HEM/SK/SE WF9 225 J6
Beaconfield Rd
HEM/SK/SE WF9 225 H5
Beacon Gv MOR LS27 152 D4
WBSY BD6 126 B5
Beacon Hl DOD/DAR S75 259 J8
HEM/SK/SE WF9 225 J6
Beacon Hill Rd HIPP HX3 11 J4
Beacon Pl WBSY BD6 126 A5
Beacon Ri ILK LS29 38 A2
Beacon Rd WBSY BD6 126 A4
Beaconsfield Ct
GFTH/SHER LS25 113 H6
Beaconsfield Rd CLAY BD14 125 M2
Beaconsfield St BSLY S70 261 G6
HIPP HX3 11 L8
TOD OL14 163 L1
Beacon St DEWS WF13 173 G8
GTHN BD7 * 126 A4
HUDN HD2 14 E1
ILK LS29 19 J6
Beacon Vw HEM/SK/SE WF9 246 E3
Beaden Dr KBTN HD8 216 A4
Beadon Av HUDE HD5 215 K1
Beagle Av HUDS HD4 213 L5
Bealbank Cl MILN OL16 229 J3
Beal Crs MILN OL16 206 E5
Bealcroft Cl MILN OL16 207 G7
Beal La GLE DN14 161 K7
KNOT WF11 183 H4
ROY/SHW OL2 229 L8
Beamshaw HEM/SK/SE WF9 246 D5
Beamsley Ct SKP/WHF BD23 16 C4
Beamsley Gv BGLY BD16 81 K3
HDGY LS6 109 G4
Beamsley Mt HDGY LS6 * 109 G4
Beamsley Pl HDGY LS6 109 G4
Beamsley Rd HTON BD9 104 D1
Beamsley Ter HDGY LS6 * 109 G4
Beamsley Vw ILK LS29 38 A2
Beamsley Wk HTON BD9 104 C4
Beancroft Rd CAS WF10 157 M7
Beancroft St CAS WF10 157 L8
Beanlands Dr AIRE BD20 34 E8
Beanlands Pde ILK LS29 38 E1
Beanlands Pl AIRE BD20 34 E8
Bean St ELL HX5 169 L8
Bear Bones Rd HOLM/MEL HD9 267 K1
Bear Pit Gdns HDGY LS6 108 F3
Beastfair PONT WF8 180 E6
Beast Market HUD HD1 15 G6
Beatrice St AIRE BD20 57 L5
CLECK BD19 149 M6
HWTH BD22 100 E4
Beaufort Av KBTN HD8 238 B3
Beaufort Gv ECHL BD2 105 J3
Beaufort Ms FEA/AMT WF7 202 D6
Beaulieu Cl DOD/DAR S75 242 E6
Beaulieu Vw DOD/DAR S75 242 E6
Beaumont Av AWLS/ASK DN6 249 H8
BSLY S70 260 D5
HEM/SK/SE WF9 247 H3
HUDE HD5 15 M8
RHAY LS8 88 C4
Beaumont Cl EARD/LOFT WF3 177 H1
LIT OL15 207 H1
Beaumont Dr HOR/CROF WF4 219 H8
Beaumont Park Rd HUDS HD4 213 M5
Beaumont Pl BTLY WF17 173 H2
Beaumont Rd DOD/DAR S75 241 L7
GIR BD8 104 D5
Beaumont St BTLY WF17 173 L3
EARD/LOFT WF3 177 H1
HUD HD1 15 G4
HUDE HD5 15 M8
HUDS HD4 213 L7
HUDW HD3 213 H1
KBTN HD8 217 L7
TOD OL14 141 J8
Beaver Dr DEWS WF13 173 H7
Becca La GFTH/SHER LS25 91 M6
Beck Bottom PDSY/CALV LS28 84 A8
WKFDW/WTN WF2 175 L3
Beckbridge La NORM WF6 178 E4
Beckbridge Rd NORM WF6 178 E3
Beckbridge Wy NORM WF6 178 E4
Beckbury Cl PDSY/CALV LS28 106 F4
Beckbury St PDSY/CALV LS28 106 F4
Beckenham Pl HFAX HX1 146 A6
Beckers Av BTLY WF17 * 151 K4
Beckett Cl HOR/CROF WF4 197 L4
Beckett Crs DEWS WF13 173 H6
Beckett Gv DEWS WF13 173 H7
Beckett Hospital Ter
BSLY S70 * 261 H6
Beckett La DEWS WF13 173 H7
Beckett Nook DEWS WF13 173 H6
Beckett Rd DEWS WF13 173 K4
Becketts Cl HBR HX7 143 H2
Beckett's Park Dr HDGY LS6 108 E1
Beckett's Park Rd HDGY LS6 108 F1
Beckett St BSLYN/ROY S71 261 H4
BTLY WF17 173 L3
OSM LS9 7 M7
Beckett Wk DEWS WF13 173 H7
Beckfield Cl AIRE BD20 35 G8
BRIG HD6 148 D8
Beckfield La KNOT WF11 159 G1
Beckfield Rd BGLY BD16 81 J7
Beckfoot La BGLY BD16 81 H5
Beck Gv ROY/SHW OL2 229 M6
Beck Hl WBSY BD6 126 A7
Beckhill Ap CHAL LS7 87 J8
Beckhill Av CHAL LS7 87 J8
Beckhill Cha CHAL LS7 87 J8
Beckhill Cl CHAL LS7 * 87 J8
Beckhill Dr CHAL LS7 87 J7
Beckhill Fold CHAL LS7 87 J7
Beckhill Gdns CHAL LS7 87 J8
Beckhill Garth CHAL LS7 87 J8
Beckhill Ga CHAL LS7 87 J8
Beckhill Gn CHAL LS7 87 J8
Beckhill Gv CHAL LS7 87 J8
Beckhill Lawn CHAL LS7 * 87 J8
Beckhill Pl CHAL LS7 87 J7
Beckhill Rw CHAL LS7 87 J7
Beckhill V CHAL LS7 87 J7
Beckhill Vw CHAL LS7 87 J8
Beckhill Wk CHAL LS7 87 J7
Beck La BGLY BD16 81 H2
LVSG WF15 172 E3
WBY LS22 47 K5
Beckley Rd WKFDW/WTN WF2 176 B8
Beck Meadow MSTN/BAR LS15 91 G8
Beck Ri HEM/SK/SE WF9 223 M7
Beck Rd BGLY BD16 59 G6
HUD HD1 14 F4
RHAY LS8 110 B2
Becks Ct EARL WF12 174 B8
Beckside COL BB8 74 D3
Beck Side KGHY BD21 3 G6
Beck Side Cl AIRE BD20 34 C4
Beckside Cl ILK LS29 19 G6
ILK LS29 40 A5
Beckside Gdns BHP/TINH LS16 86 F7
HUDE HD5 215 L2
Beckside La GTHN BD7 126 B1
Beckside Rd GTHN BD7 126 C1
Beckside Vw MOR LS27 152 E2
Becks Rd HWTH BD22 2 C6
Beck St KGHY BD21 3 G6
Beck Vw HOR/CROF WF4 221 J8
Beckwith Dr IDLE BD10 105 M1
Bective Rd WKFDW/WTN WF2 176 A7
Bedale EARD/LOFT WF3 152 F6
Bedale Av BRIG HD6 170 A6
KBTN HD8 239 H5
Bedale Cl KBTN HD8 239 H5
Bedale Ct MOR LS27 153 G2
Bedale Dr KBTN HD8 239 H5
WBSY BD6 126 A5
Bedding Edge Rd
HOLM/MEL HD9 255 J8
Bede Ct WKFDE WF1 176 E6
Bede's Cl CUL/QBY BD13 102 F8
Bedford Av HOR/CROF WF4 217 G1
ROY/SHW OL2 229 H7
Bedford Cl BHP/TINH LS16 86 A3
FEA/AMT WF7 201 M3
HOR/CROF WF4 200 C6
KBTN HD8 216 A3
Bedford Ct HORS LS18 85 K5
RHAY LS8 88 E8
Bedford Dr BHP/TINH LS16 86 A3
Bedford Fld HDGY LS6 * 109 J2
Bedford Gdns BHP/TINH LS16 86 A3
Bedford Garth BHP/TINH LS16 86 A3
Bedford Gn BHP/TINH LS16 86 A3
Bedford Gv BHP/TINH LS16 86 A4
Bedford Mt BHP/TINH LS16 86 A4
Bedford Rw MID LS10 9 J8
Bedfords Fold GFTH/SHER LS25 138 D8
Bedford St BOW BD4 5 G8
BSLY S70 261 H7
CUD/GR S72 263 J1
ELL HX5 169 H8
HFAX HX1 10 F6
KGHY BD21 2 E5
LDS LS1 6 F9
TOD OL14 141 G7
Bedford St North HFAX HX1 10 F5
Bedford Ter BSLYN/ROY S71 261 J1
Bedford Vw BHP/TINH LS16 86 A3
Bedivere Rd GIR BD8 103 M7
Bedlam La OT LS21 65 H1
Beech Av CUD/GR S72 244 D6
CUL/QBY BD13 101 L3
EARD/LOFT WF3 177 H2
HOLM/MEL HD9 236 E5
HOR/CROF WF4 200 D7
HORS LS18 85 L7
HUDE HD5 215 H1
MAR/SLWT HD7 213 G1
RPDN/SBR HX6 167 K1
TOD OL14 141 J8
WKFDW/WTN WF2 176 B7
Beech Cl CUD/GR S72 245 J3
GFTH/SHER LS25 138 B2
HEM/SK/SE WF9 246 D4
HIPP HX3 125 M8
IDLE BD10 83 K4
ILK LS29 40 C8
OSM LS9 110 F3
PONT WF8 181 G8
TAD LS24 72 A3
Beech Ct CAS WF10 158 A8
OSS WF5 174 E8
Beech Crs BAIL BD17 82 B5
BFDE BD3 5 M2
CAS WF10 158 F8
PONT WF8 203 L1
Beechcroft EARD/LOFT WF3 154 F5
Beech Cft PONT WF8 181 G3
WKFDW/WTN WF2 199 J7
Beechcroft Cl BEE/HOL LS11 130 E5
Beechcroft Md AL/HA/HU LS17 88 C2
Beechcroft Vw BEE/HOL LS11 130 E5
Beechdale Av BTLY WF17 151 J7
Beech Dr CUL/QBY BD13 101 L3
FEA/AMT WF7 202 C5
GFTH/SHER LS25 138 B2
WOR/ARM LS12 108 E6
Beecher St HIPP HX3 146 D4
KGHY BD21 3 L1
Beeches End BSPA/BRAM LS23 49 G7
Beeches Rd KGHY BD21 3 L2
The Beeches BAIL BD17 82 F2
BIRK/DRI BD11 150 C1
GSLY LS20 62 A4
PDSY/CALV LS28 106 D6
WBY LS22 30 B8
Beechfield WKFDW/WTN WF2 199 G5
WOR/ARM LS12 129 M3
Beechfield Av KBTN HD8 239 J5
Beechfield Dr HOR/CROF WF4 200 D2
Beechfield Rd MILN OL16 229 G1
Beech Gdns CAS WF10 158 F8
Beech Gv AIRE BD20 35 M5
BFDE BD3 5 L2
BGLY BD16 81 L1
BSLY S70 260 F7

CLAY BD14 .... 125 L2
CLECK BD19 .... 150 C5
GFTH/SHER LS25 .... 116 A6
GFTH/SHER LS25 .... 160 A3
HEM/SK/SE WF9 .... 223 J4
HIPP HX3 .... 148 C7
NORM WF6 .... 178 C6
RTHW LS26 .... 133 H8
Beech Grove Av
GFTH/SHER LS25 .... 113 G8
Beech Grove Ter
GFTH/SHER LS25 .... 113 G8
Beech Hl OT LS21 .... 41 J6
PONT WF8 .... 181 D5
Beech La OSM LS9 .... 110 E3
PBR HG3 .... 28 E3
Beech Lees PDSY/CALV LS28 .... 106 E2
Beech Mt OSM LS9 .... 110 F3
Beechmount Cl BAIL BD17 .... 82 F2
Beechnut La PONT WF8 .... 180 E5
Beech Rd AWLS/ASK DN6 .... 227 M5
AWLS/ASK DN6 .... 249 J5
BSPA/BRAM LS23 .... 48 E6
CUD/GR S72 .... 244 F4
ELL HX5 .... 225 K7
RPDN/SBR HX6 .... 167 L2
WBSY BD6 .... 126 E7
Beech Spinney WBY LS22 .... 30 A6
Beech Sq CLAY BD14 .... 125 L2
Beech St AIRE BD20 .... 34 F8
AIRE BD20 .... 56 E1
BGLY BD16 .... 81 H4
BSLY S70 .... 261 H6
EARD/LOFT WF3 .... 153 G5
ELL HX5 .... 169 H8
GTL/HWG HX4 .... 190 C2
HEM/SK/SE WF9 .... 247 G5
HFAX HX1 .... 10 E4
HOLM/MEL HD9 * 254 D4
HUD HD1 .... 213 M1
KGHY BD21 .... 3 L3
MILN OL16 .... 229 J2
MIRF WF14 .... 194 D3
PONT WF8 .... 180 F7
Beech Ter BFDE BD3 .... 5 L3
Beechtree Cl BAIL BD17 .... 82 C4
Beech Tree Ct HUDN HD2 .... 192 A2
Beechtree Rd TAD LS24 .... 71 K4
Beech Vw GFTH/SHER LS25 .... 91 M7
HOR/CROF WF4 .... 220 B3
RPDN/SBR HX6 * 167 K1
Beech Wk BHP/TINH LS16 .... 86 F4
CLECK BD19 .... 150 D2
OSM LS9 .... 110 F3
TAD LS24 .... 71 K3
Beech Wy BTLY WF17 .... 151 K4
Beechwood PONT WF8 .... 180 D7
ROY/SHW OL2 .... 229 M6
RTHW LS26 .... 133 L7
Beechwood Av AIRE BD20 .... 58 B5
BIRK/DRI BD11 .... 128 F7
HIPP HX3 .... 147 K1
LIT OL15 .... 207 J3
LUD/ILL HX2 .... 146 C1
MIRF WF14 .... 194 C1
PONT WF8 .... 180 D6
RPDN/SBR HX6 .... 167 H3
SHPY BD18 .... 82 A7
WBSY BD6 .... 126 C4
WKFDW/WTN WF2 .... 175 M8
Beechwood Cl GFTH/SHER LS25 .... 116 A8
HORS LS18 .... 85 J3
LUD/ILL HX2 .... 146 B2
Beechwood Ct BHP/TINH LS16 * 86 D1
SCFT LS14 .... 89 G8
Beechwood Crs BULY LS4 .... 108 F3
HEM/SK/SE WF9 .... 223 L8
PONT WF8 .... 180 D7
RPDN/SBR HX6 .... 167 H3
Beechwood Cft
GFTH/SHER LS25 * 116 A8
Beechwood Dl FEA/AMT WF7 .... 202 D7
Beechwood Dr LUD/ILL HX2 .... 146 B2
ROY/SHW OL2 .... 228 E8
RPDN/SBR HX6 .... 167 H3
WBSY BD6 .... 126 D4
Beechwood Gld
GFTH/SHER LS25 .... 116 A8
Beechwood Gv BIRK/DRI BD11 .... 128 F7
BULY LS4 .... 108 F3
HOR/CROF WF4 .... 197 L5
HUDN HD2 .... 192 C1
ILK LS29 .... 38 B2
LUD/ILL HX2 * 146 B2
SHPY BD18 .... 82 A7
WBSY BD6 .... 126 D4
Beechwood Mt BULY LS4 .... 108 F3
HEM/SK/SE WF9 .... 223 M8
Beechwood Pk BRIG HD6 .... 148 C8
Beechwood Pl BULY LS4 * 108 F3
KNOT WF11 .... 159 L5
Beechwood Ri WBY LS22 .... 30 A7
Beechwood Rd BULY LS4 .... 108 F3
LUD/ILL HX2 .... 146 B2
MIRF WF14 .... 172 C8
WBSY BD6 .... 126 C4
Beechwood Rw BULY LS4 .... 108 F3
Beechwood St HDGY LS6 .... 108 F3
PDSY/CALV LS28 .... 106 E5
Beechwood Ter BULY LS4 .... 108 F3
Beechwood Vw BULY LS4 .... 108 F3
Beecroft Cl BRAM LS13 .... 107 J3
Beecroft Crs BRAM LS13 .... 107 J3
Beecroft Gdns BRAM LS13 .... 107 J3
Beecroft Mt BRAM LS13 .... 107 J3
Beecroft St KGHY BD21 .... 3 K4
KSTL LS5 .... 108 C3
Beehive St LVSG WF15 .... 172 C4
Beehive St WBSY BD6 .... 126 B7
Beehive Yd WBSY BD6 * 126 B7
Beestonley La GTL/HWG HX4 .... 189 M2
Beeston Park Cft
BEE/HOL LS11 * 131 G4
Beeston Park Garth
BEE/HOL LS11 * 131 G4
Beeston Park Pl BEE/HOL LS11 .... 131 G4
Beeston Park Ter
BEE/HOL LS11 .... 131 G4
Beeston Rd BEE/HOL LS11 .... 131 J3
Beeston's La HLTN/SBR LS17 .... 25 M1
Beeston Sq BSLYN/ROY S71 .... 243 H6
Beever La DOD/DAR S75 .... 260 C3
Beevor Ct BSLYN/ROY S71 .... 261 J5
Beevor St BSLYN/ROY S71 .... 261 K5
Bela Av BOW BD4 .... 127 J4
Belcross Dr HIPP HX3 .... 147 K1
Beldon Brook Gn KBTN HD8 .... 215 M5
Beldon La GTHN BD7 .... 126 B5
Beldon Park Av GTHN BD7 .... 126 B4
Beldon Park Cl GTHN BD7 .... 126 B4
Beldon Pl ECHL BD2 .... 105 K4
Beldon Rd GTHN BD7 .... 126 B4
Belfast St HFAX HX1 .... 10 D4
Belfield Cl MILN OL16 .... 206 E6
Belfield La MILN OL16 .... 206 E6
Belfield Mill La MILN OL16 .... 206 E6
Belfield Old Rd MILN OL16 .... 206 D6
Belford Ct HDGY LS6 .... 87 G5

Belfry Ct WKFDE WF1 .... 176 E1
Belfry Rd OSM LS9 .... 132 C1
The Belfry YEA LS19 .... 62 E8
Belfry Wy NORM WF6 .... 178 D5
Belgrave Av HIPP HX3 .... 11 K3
OSS WF5 .... 197 G3
Belgrave Cl HIPP HX3 .... 11 K3
Belgrave Crs HIPP HX3 .... 11 K3
Belgrave Dr HIPP HX3 .... 11 K3
Belgrave Gdns HIPP HX3 .... 11 K3
Belgrave Gv HIPP HX3 .... 11 K3
Belgrave Ms YEA LS19 * 84 C2
Belgrave Mt HIPP HX3 .... 11 K2
Belgrave Pk HIPP HX3 .... 11 K3
Belgrave Pl AIRE BD20 .... 2 E3
BGLY BD16 .... 81 J3
BSLYN/ROY S71 .... 261 J5
OSS WF5 .... 197 G3
Belgrave Rd LDSU LS2 .... 7 ...
OSS WF5 .... 197 G3
RPDN/SBR HX6 .... 167 K2
SKP/WHF BD23 .... 16 A2
Belgrave Ter HUD HD1 .... 14 D5
WKFDE WF1 .... 176 F6
Belgravia Gdns RHAY LS8 * 110 C1
Belgravia Ms YEA LS19 .... 129 L7
Belgravia Rd WKFDE WF1 .... 176 D6
Belinda St MID LS10 .... 9 M8
Bell Bank Vw BGLY BD16 .... 81 G2
Bellbrooke Av OSM LS9 .... 110 D4
WMB/DAR S73 .... 263 H7
Bellbrooke Gv OSM LS9 .... 110 D4
Bellbrooke Pl OSM LS9 .... 110 D4
Bellbrooke St OSM LS9 .... 110 C4
Bell Dean Rd WIL/AL BD15 .... 103 K6
Belle Green Cl CUD/GR S72 .... 244 E7
Belle Green Gdns CUD/GR S72 .... 244 E7
Belle Green La CUD/GR S72 .... 244 E7
Belle Isle Cl MID LS10 .... 132 A6
Belle Isle Crs WKFDE WF1 .... 13 H7
Belle Isle Pde MID LS10 .... 132 A6
Belle Isle Rd HWTH BD22 .... 78 E8
MID LS10 .... 132 A6
Bellerby Brow WBSY BD6 .... 125 M5
Bellerby Pl AWLS/ASK DN6 .... 249 H4
Bellerby Rd AWLS/ASK DN6 .... 249 H4
Belle View Ri HIPP HX3 .... 147 K1
Belle Vue CUL/QBY BD13 .... 125 C7
GIR BD8 .... 4 C2
ILK LS29 .... 38 D3
RHAY LS8 .... 88 ...
Belle Vue Ct BVRD LS3 * 6 B9
HUDN HD2 .... 192 E3
Belle Vue Dr PDSY/CALV LS28 .... 106 E3
Belle Vue Est HEM/SK/SE WF9 .... 90 B8
Belle Vue Pk HFAX HX1 * 10 B4
Belle Vue Rd HDGY LS6 .... 109 H5
HIPP HX3 .... 147 K1
LDSU LS2 .... 6 ...
MSTN/BAR LS15 .... 90 B3
WKFDE WF1 .... 13 K9
Belle Vue St BTLY WF17 .... 173 H1
Belle Vue Ter HIPP HX3 .... 11 M9
KGHY BD21 .... 3 J6
Bellgreave Av HOLM/MEL HD9 .... 237 H6
Bell Hall Mt HFAX HX1 .... 168 C1
Bell Hall Ter HFAX HX1 .... 168 C1
Bell House Av BOW BD4 .... 127 K5
Bellhouse Crs BOW BD4 .... 127 K6
Bellingham Cl ROY/SHW OL2 .... 229 K6
Bell La BRAM LS13 .... 107 L3
FEA/AMT WF7 .... 224 B1
MILN OL16 .... 207 K7
TAD LS24 .... 95 G2
Bellmount Crs HEM/SK/SE WF9 .... 224 A8
Bellmount Cl BRAM LS13 .... 107 L2
Bellmount Gdns BRAM LS13 .... 107 L2
Bellmount Gn BRAM LS13 .... 107 L2
Bellmount Pl BRAM LS13 .... 107 M3
Bellmount Vw BRAM LS13 .... 107 M3
Belloe St WBOW BD5 .... 126 F2
Bell Rd BRAM LS13 .... 107 L3
Bellshaw St GIR BD8 .... 104 B4
Bellshill Crs MILN OL16 .... 206 E6
Bell Sq AIRE BD20 .... 36 A4
Bell St DEWS WF13 .... 195 C1
HEM/SK/SE WF9 .... 226 A6
HIPP HX3 .... 11 J3
HUDS HD4 .... 214 ...
LM/WK BD12 .... 148 E2
MILN OL16 .... 206 B6
OSM LS9 .... 7 L8
WKFDE WF1 .... 12 D1
Bellstring La HUDE HD5 .... 194 A3
Bellwood Av BSPA/BRAM LS23 .... 48 F8
Belmont CUD/GR S72 * 262 E2
KNOT WF11 .... 159 L5
Belmont Av BAIL BD17 .... 82 D5
BSLYN/ROY S71 .... 261 K1
LM/WK BD12 .... 127 G7
LM/WK BD12 .... 148 B2
MIRF WF14 .... 172 C8
WBSY BD6 .... 126 C4
Belmont Cl BAIL BD17 .... 82 D5
HUD HD1 .... 14 D5
Belmont Crs LM/WK BD12 .... 127 G7
SHPY BD18 .... 82 C6
Belmont Gdns WBSY BD6 .... 126 F7
Belmont Gv LDSU LS2 .... 6 D2
WBSY BD6 .... 126 F7
YEA LS19 .... 84 D1
Belmont Pl HFAX HX1 .... 10 C2
Belmont Ri BAIL BD17 .... 82 D3
Belmont Rd ILK LS29 .... 39 G2
Belmont St ECHL BD2 .... 105 L1
FEA/AMT WF7 .... 200 E1
HIPP HX3 .... 11 J3
HUD HD1 .... 14 D5
MAR/SLWT HD7 .... 212 B6
RPDN/SBR HX6 * 167 G2
SKP/WHF BD23 .... 16 B2
WKFDE WF1 .... 176 D6
Belmont Ter EARD/LOFT WF3 .... 154 B4
LUD/ILL HX2 ....
SHPY BD18 .... 82 C6
Belmont Wy HEM/SK/SE WF9 .... 247 K3
WHIT OL12 .... 206 A4
Belridge Cl DOD/DAR S75 .... 260 D2
Belton Cl MILN OL16 .... 206 D5
Belton Ct HFAX HX1 .... 11 K3
Belton Gv HUDW HD3 .... 191 G4
Belton Rd AIRE BD20 .... 36 A4
Belton St HUDE HD5 .... 215 G1
Belvedere Av CUD/GR S72 .... 244 E4
AL/HA/HU LS17 .... 87 K2
Belvedere Ct AL/HA/HU LS17 .... 88 A2
Belvedere Dr WMB/DAR S73 .... 263 D4
Belvedere Gdns
AL/HA/HU LS17 .... 87 K2
Belvedere Mt BEE/HOL LS11 .... 131 K4
Belvedere Rd AL/HA/HU LS17 .... 87 K2
BTLY WF17 .... 173 K2
Belvedere Ter BEE/HOL LS11 .... 131 K4
GIR BD8 .... 104 D6
Belvedere Vw AL/HA/HU LS17 .... 88 A2

Belvoir Dr KNOT WF11 .... 182 A2
Belvoir Gdns HIPP HX3 .... 168 E3
Belvoir Mdw MILN OL16 .... 207 G2
Bembridge Ct WKFDW/WTN WF2 .... 198 A5
Bempton Ct BTLY WF17 .... 126 D2
Bempton Gv BTLY WF17 .... 151 F4
Bempton Pl BTLY WF17 .... 126 D2
Ben Bank Rd DOD/DAR S75 .... 259 J8
Ben Booth La HOR/CROF WF4 .... 217 G1
Benbow Av IDLE BD10 .... 106 A1
Bence Cl DOD/DAR S75 .... 242 A7
Bence La DOD/DAR S75 .... 241 L7
Bench St COL BB8 .... 74 A1
Bench Carr WHIT OL12 .... 206 A5
Bendigo Rd EARL WF12 .... 174 B5
Benjamin St LVSG WF15 .... 172 D3
WKFDW/WTN WF2 .... 12 A1
Benjamin Sykes Wy
WKFDW/WTN WF2 .... 197 L2
Benn Av GTHN BD7 .... 126 B2
Benn Crs GTHN BD7 .... 126 B2
Bennett Av MSTN/BAR LS15 .... 111 M6
Bennett La EARL WF12 .... 174 A3
Bennett Rd HDGY LS6 .... 108 F1
Bennett St HIPP HX3 .... 11 K8
LVSG WF15 .... 172 D2
SKP/WHF BD23 .... 16 B3
Benn La LUD/ILL HX2 .... 145 K4
Benns La LUD/ILL HX2 .... 145 L4
Benny Parr Cl BTLY WF17 .... 174 A1
Benomley Crs HUDE HD5 .... 215 G3
Benomley Dr HUDE HD5 .... 215 G3
Benomley Fold HUDE HD5 .... 215 G3
Benomley Rd HUDE HD5 .... 215 G3
Ben Rhydding Dr ILK LS29 .... 39 J4
Ben Rhydding Rd ILK LS29 .... 39 J4
Benson Gdns WOR/ARM LS12 .... 108 D8
Benson La NORM WF6 .... 178 E2
Benson St CHAL LS7 .... 7 K5
Bentcliffe Av AL/HA/HU LS17 .... 88 A4
Bentcliffe Cl AL/HA/HU LS17 .... 88 A5
Bentcliffe Ct AL/HA/HU LS17 .... 88 A4
Bentcliffe Dr AL/HA/HU LS17 .... 88 A4
Bentcliffe Gdns AL/HA/HU LS17 .... 88 A4
Bentcliffe Gv AL/HA/HU LS17 .... 88 A4
Bentcliffe La AL/HA/HU LS17 .... 87 M5
Bentcliffe Mt AL/HA/HU LS17 .... 88 A4
Bent Close La HBR HX7 .... 165 M3
Bentfield Cottages CLAY BD14 .... 125 L1
Bentfield Crs MILN OL16 .... 229 J2
Bentgate Cl MILN OL16 .... 229 J3
Bentgate St MILN OL16 .... 229 J3
Bentham Dr BSLYN/ROY S71 .... 261 M2
Bentham Wy DOD/DAR S75 .... 242 C4
Bent La AIRE BD20 .... 55 L1
COL BB8 .... 52 D8
HOLM/MEL HD9 .... 254 C6
Bent Lea HUDN HD2 .... 171 H4
Bentley Av BRIG HD6 .... 148 C7
Bentley Cl BAIL BD17 .... 82 D2
BSLYN/ROY S71 .... 262 A1
Bentley Gdns CHAL LS7 .... 87 H4
Bentley Gv HDGY LS6 .... 87 H4
Bentley La HDGY LS6 .... 87 H4
Bentley Ms WHIT OL12 * 206 A4
Bentley Moor La
AWLS/ASK DN6 .... 249 M7
Bentley Mt HDGY LS6 .... 87 H4
Bentley Pde HDGY LS6 .... 87 H4
Bentley Ri HWTH BD22 ....
Bent Ley Rd HOLM/MEL HD9 .... 235 J3
Bentley Rd WKFDW/WTN WF2 .... 198 A2
Bentley Royd Cl
RPDN/SBR HX6 .... 167 J3
Bentmeadows WHIT OL12 .... 206 A5
Benton Ct HOR/CROF WF4 .... 197 L4
Benton Park Av YEA LS19 .... 84 E1
Benton Park Crs YEA LS19 .... 84 E1
Benton Park Dr YEA LS19 .... 84 E1
Benton Park Rd YEA LS19 .... 84 E1
Bent Rd HOLM/MEL HD9 .... 254 F7
Bents Cl COL BB8 .... 52 D8
Bents Farm Cl LIT OL15 * 207 L1
Bents La MAR/SLWT HD7 .... 211 K7
WIL/AL BD15 .... 80 C3
Bents Rd HUDS HD4 .... 214 D7
Bent St HUDS HD4 .... 214 D1
Benyon Park Wy
WOR/ARM LS12 .... 130 F2
Beresford Rd WBSY BD6 .... 126 D7
Beresford St LM/WK BD12 .... 149 F3
MILN OL16 .... 229 K2
Berkeley Av RHAY LS8 .... 110 C3
Berkeley Crs RHAY LS8 .... 110 C3
Berkeley Cft BSLYN/ROY S71 .... 243 G5
Berkeley Dr MILN OL16 .... 228 D2
Berkeley Gv RHAY LS8 .... 110 C3
Berkeley Mt RHAY LS8 .... 110 C3
Berkeley Rd RHAY LS8 .... 110 C3
Berkeley St RHAY LS8 .... 110 C3
Berkeley Ter RHAY LS8 .... 110 C3
Berkeley Vw RHAY LS8 .... 110 C3
Berking Av OSM LS9 .... 110 B6
Berkley Wk OT LS21 .... 41 H5
Bermondsey Ms OT LS21 .... 41 K7
Bermondsey St OT LS21 .... 41 K7
Bernard St HUDN HD2 .... 193 D3
RTHW LS26 .... 133 M8
WHIT OL12 .... 206 A3
Berne Gv WKFDE WF1 .... 176 E7
Berners St WKFDE WF1 .... 13 H5
Bernesli Cl BSLY S70 .... 261 G4
Bernesli St BSLY S70 ....
Berrington Wy HWTH BD22 .... 78 D3
Berry Bank La HOLM/MEL HD9 .... 236 D6
Berry Cft HOLM/MEL HD9 .... 236 B2
Berryfield Garth OSS WF5 .... 174 F6
Berry La HFAX HX1 .... 11 K6
HOR/CROF WF4 .... 197 K5
KGHY BD21 .... 2 F8
RTHW LS26 .... 135 G6
Berry Moor Rd RPDN/SBR HX6 .... 167 M4
Berry Rd HOLM/MEL HD9 .... 234 E3
Berrys Yd HOR/CROF WF4 .... 197 J4
Berrywell Av STKB/PEN S36 .... 271 G4
Bertha Rd MILN OL16 .... 206 E7
Bertha St PDSY/CALV LS28 .... 106 D4
Bertie St BOW BD4 .... 127 L3
Bertram Dr BAIL BD17 .... 82 B5
Bertram Rd GIR BD8 .... 104 D7
Bertrand St BEE/HOL LS11 .... 8 C7
Berwick Av HECK WF16 .... 150 F9
Berwick St HFAX HX1 .... 11 J6
MILN OL16 .... 206 D8
Bescaby Gv AL/HA/HU LS17 .... 88 A2
Besha Av LM/WK BD12 .... 126 F7
Bessingham Gdns WBSY BD6 .... 126 B6
Best La HUDS HD4 .... 214 F8
HWTH BD22 .... 100 A4
Beswick Cl BFDE BD3 .... 105 M7
Beswick Royds St MILN OL16 .... 206 D5
Beswicke St LIT OL15 .... 207 L1

WHIT OL12 .... 206 A6
Beswick St TOD OL14 .... 163 J7
Bethany La MILN OL16 .... 229 L2
Bethel Gn LIT OL15 * 185 L5
Bethel Rd SHPY BD18 .... 82 F6
BRIG HD6 .... 170 D4
HIPP HX3 .... 146 C4
Betjeman Pl ROY/SHW OL2 .... 229 M7
Betteras Hill Rd
GFTH/SHER LS25 .... 138 A7
Betula Wy KBTN HD8 .... 216 A4
Beulah Gv HDGY LS6 .... 6 E2
Beulah Mt HDGY LS6 * 6 E2
Beulah Pl LUD/ILL HX2 .... 167 G3
Beulah St HIPP HX3 .... 6 E1
Beulah Ter HDGY LS6 * 6 E1
Bevan Av NORM WF6 .... 178 D6
Bevan Dr GTHN BD7 .... 126 B3
Bevan Pl WKFDW/WTN WF2 .... 197 L2
Bevedere Gdns AL/HA/HU LS17 .... 288 A2
Beverley Av BEE/HOL LS11 .... 131 K3
BSLY S70 .... 261 H8
LM/WK BD12 .... 148 B3
NORM WF6 .... 178 D6
Beverley Dr EARL WF12 .... 174 B6
LM/WK BD12 .... 148 B3
Beverley Gdns BTLY WF17 .... 151 K3
Beverley Garth FEA/AMT WF7 .... 224 C1
Beverley Mt BEE/HOL LS11 .... 131 K3
Beverley Pl HIPP HX3 .... 10 E1
MILN OL16 .... 206 C6
Beverley Ri ILK LS29 .... 38 A2
Beverley St BOW BD4 .... 127 H4
Beverley Ter BEE/HOL LS11 .... 131 K3
HIPP HX3 .... 10 E1
Beverley Vw BEE/HOL LS11 .... 8 F9
Beverly Wk GFTH/SHER LS25 .... 113 ...
Beverston ROCH OL11 * 206 A6
Bevin Cl WKFDE WF1 .... 176 E1
Bevin Crs WKFDE WF1 .... 176 E1
Bevor Crs HECK WF16 .... 172 F1
Bewerley Crs LM/WK BD12 .... 126 C8
Bewick Ct WBSY BD6 .... 125 K4
Bewick Gv MID LS10 .... 132 B7
Bexhill Cl PONT WF8 .... 181 H4
Bexley Av RHAY LS8 .... 110 B4
Bexley Gv RHAY LS8 .... 110 B4
Bexley Mt RHAY LS8 .... 110 B4
Bexley Pl RHAY LS8 .... 110 B4
Bexley Rd RHAY LS8 .... 110 B4
Bexley Ter RHAY LS8 .... 110 B4
Bexley Vw RHAY LS8 .... 110 B4
Beza St BEE/HOL LS11 .... 131 M3
Bickerton Wy OT LS21 .... 41 J7
Bidder Dr EARD/LOFT WF3 .... 153 L5
Bideford Av RHAY LS8 .... 88 B3
Bidston Cl ROY/SHW OL2 .... 229 M8
Bierley Hall Gv BOW BD4 .... 127 K6
Bierley House Av BOW BD4 .... 127 K5
Bierley La BOW BD4 .... 127 K5
Bierley Vw BOW BD4 .... 127 L5
Big Meadow Dr ILK LS29 .... 18 F6
Biggin La GFTH/SHER LS25 .... 117 G3
Bilberry Cl CLAY BD14 .... 125 L3
Bilberry Ri HWTH BD22 ....
Bilberry St MILN OL16 .... 206 C8
Bilham Rd KBTN HD8 .... 240 C4
Billams Hl OT LS21 .... 41 J6
Billey La WOR/ARM LS12 .... 130 A2
Billingbauk Dr BRAM LS13 .... 107 M5
Billing Ct YEA LS19 .... 84 F3
Billing Dr YEA LS19 .... 85 G3
Billingham Cl
WKFDW/WTN WF2 .... 175 M6
Billing Vw IDLE BD10 .... 83 L7
Billingwood Dr YEA LS19 .... 84 F3
Bill La HOLM/MEL HD9 .... 236 E7
Billy La HBR HX7 .... 143 L1
Bilsdale Gra WBSY BD6 .... 126 B6
Bilsdale Wy BAIL BD17 .... 82 B4
Bilton Pl GIR BD8 .... 4 B4
Binbrook Vw WIL/AL BD15 * 103 K5
Bingley Bank AL/HA/HU LS17 .... 67 L4
Bingley Ct DOD/DAR S75 * 260 T6
Bingley Lands GSLY LS20 .... 62 A5
Bingley Rd BAIL BD17 .... 60 B8
CUL/QBY BD13 .... 80 B3
HTON BD9 .... 103 M2
ILK LS29 .... 38 A6
KGHY BD21 .... 79 K5
MILN OL16 .... 206 E7
SHPY BD18 .... 81 M6
Bingley Sq MILN OL16 .... 206 E7
Bingley St BVRD LS3 .... 6 B9
DOD/DAR S75 .... 260 F4
GIR BD8 .... 104 C7
Bingley Ter MILN OL16 .... 206 E7
Binham Rd HUDN HD3 .... 191 M6
Binks Fold LM/WK BD12 .... 148 A3
Binks St WBOW BD5 ....
Binks Yd OSS WF5 * 174 F8
Binnie St BFDE BD3 .... 5 L5
Binn La MAR/SLWT HD7 .... 233 J4
Binn Rd MAR/SLWT HD7 .... 233 H4
Binns Hill La LUD/ILL HX2 .... 145 K8
Binns La AIRE BD20 .... 34 C8
GTHN BD7 .... 126 B1
HOLM/MEL HD9 .... 254 F1
Binns Nook Rd WHIT OL12 .... 206 C4
Binns St BGLY BD16 .... 81 J3
Binns Top La HIPP HX3 .... 169 K5
Birch Av AWLS/ASK DN6 .... 249 J5
KBTN HD8 .... 216 A4
MSTN/BAR LS15 .... 111 J6
RPDN/SBR HX6 .... 188 E5
TOD OL14 .... 141 J7
WBOW BD5 .... 127 H4
WHIT OL12 .... 206 F1
Birch Cliff BAIL BD17 .... 82 D4
Birchcliffe Rd HBR HX7 .... 143 J3
Birch Cl BRIG HD6 .... 170 D3
HOR/CROF WF4 .... 222 D6
WBOW BD5 .... 127 H4
Birch Close La BGLY BD16 .... 60 B6
Birch Crs MILN OL16 .... 229 J3
MSTN/BAR LS15 .... 111 J6
Birchdale BGLY BD16 .... 59 H8
Birch Dr GFTH/SHER LS25 .... 135 J3
Birchen Av OSS WF5 .... 196 F5
Birchencliffe Hill Rd HUDW HD3 .... 191 H5
Birchen Cl CAS WF10 ....
The Birches BHP/TINH LS16 .... 64 B3
Birchfield Av MOR LS27 .... 129 G3
Birchfield Garth SCFT LS14 .... 89 L7
Birchfield Gv KBTN HD8 .... 239 J5
Birchfields Av SCFT LS14 .... 89 L7
Birchfields Cl SCFT LS14 .... 89 L7
Birchfields Crs SCFT LS14 .... 89 L7
Birchfields Ri SCFT LS14 .... 89 L7
Birchfield Wk DOD/DAR S75 .... 260 D4

Birch Gn PONT WF8 .... 181 H5
Birch Gv BTLY WF17 .... 151 H5
CAS WF10 .... 158 E8
GFTH/SHER LS25 .... 135 J4
HWTH BD22 .... 79 J2
MAR/SLWT HD7 .... 213 G1
WBOW BD5 .... 127 G5
Birch Hey Cl WHIT OL12 .... 206 E2
Birch Hill Crs WHIT OL12 .... 207 G2
Birch Hill La WHIT OL12 .... 184 F8
Birch Hill Ri HORS LS18 .... 86 A6
Birchington Av HUDW HD3 .... 191 J4
Birchington Cl HUDW HD3 .... 191 K4
Birchington Dr HUDW HD3 .... 191 J4
Birchlands Av WIL/AL BD15 .... 80 D8
Birchlands Gv WIL/AL BD15 .... 80 D8
Birch La LUD/ILL HX2 .... 145 K8
WBOW BD5 .... 127 H3
Birch Ms BHP/TINH LS16 .... 86 F4
Birch Mt WHIT OL12 .... 207 G2
Birch Pk HOLM/MEL HD9 .... 236 F4
Birch Pl HBR HX7 * 143 J3
Birch Rd BSLY S70 .... 261 H8
GFTH/SHER LS25 .... 135 J4
HUDS HD4 .... 214 B6
NORM WF6 .... 178 D7
WHIT OL12 .... 206 F1
Birchroyd RTHW LS26 .... 155 H2
Birchroyd Cl HUDN HD2 .... 191 K4
MOR LS27 .... 152 D4
WHIT OL12 .... 184 E8
WKFDE WF1 .... 13 K4
Birchtree Cl WKFDE WF1 .... 177 H6
Birch Tree Gdns HWTH BD22 .... 79 J2
Birchtree Wy BHP/TINH LS16 * 86 A4
Birch Wk TOD OL14 * 141 K8
Birch Wy WBOW BD5 .... 127 H4
Birchwood Av AIRE BD20 .... 57 K4
AL/HA/HU LS17 .... 88 C3
BTLY WF17 .... 151 H4
Birchwood Cl ILK LS29 .... 38 C2
LVSG WF15 .... 172 D3
Birchwood Dr AIRE BD20 .... 57 K3
Birchwood Hl AL/HA/HU LS17 .... 88 C2
Birchwood Mt AL/HA/HU LS17 .... 88 C2
Birchwood Pk HOLM/MEL HD9 .... 237 G8
Birchwood Rd AIRE BD20 .... 57 J4
Birdale Field La WBY LS22 .... 47 M6
Birdcage Hl HIPP HX3 .... 168 C3
Birdcage La HIPP HX3 .... 168 C3
Birdcage Wk OT LS21 .... 41 J8
Bird Holme La HIPP HX3 .... 147 K5
Birds Edge La KBTN HD8 .... 256 B3
Birdsnest La HOLM/MEL HD9 .... 256 A4
KBTN HD8 .... 256 A4
Birds Royd La BRIG HD6 .... 170 E5
Birdswell Av BRIG HD6 .... 170 F5
The Birdwalk WBSY BD6 .... 125 L4
Birdwell Rd DOD/DAR S75 .... 260 F8
Birfed Crs BULY LS4 .... 108 D3
Birk Av BSLY S70 ....
Birkby Brow Crs BTLY WF17 .... 151 K4
Birkby Fold HUDN HD2 .... 14 B1
Birkby Hall Rd HUDN HD2 .... 14 A1
Birkby Hvn WBSY BD6 .... 126 A6
Birkby La BRIG HD6 .... 148 E7
Birkby Lodge Rd HUDN HD2 .... 14 B1
Birkby Rd HUDW HD3 .... 191 L4
Birk Crs BSLY S70 .... 261 L7
Birkdale Av HUDW HD3 .... 191 J6
CUD/GR S72 .... 244 E6
CUL/QBY BD13 .... 80 A4
Birkdale Cl AIRE BD20 .... 57 J3
Birkdale Dr AL/HA/HU LS17 .... 87 K2
Birkdale Gn AL/HA/HU LS17 .... 87 K2
Birkdale Gv AL/HA/HU LS17 .... 87 K2
DEWS WF13 .... 173 J4
LUD/ILL HX2 .... 124 B7
Birkdale Mt AL/HA/HU LS17 .... 87 K2
Birkdale Pl AL/HA/HU LS17 .... 87 K2
Birkdale Ri AL/HA/HU LS17 .... 87 K2
DEWS WF13 .... 173 J4
MILN OL16 .... 228 D2
Birkdale Rd BSLYN/ROY S71 .... 243 K1
DEWS WF13 .... 173 K5
MILN OL16 .... 228 D2
Birkdale Wk AL/HA/HU LS17 .... 87 K2
Birkenshaw La BIRK/DRI BD11 .... 150 D1
Birkett St CLECK BD19 .... 149 M6
Birk Gn BSLY S70 .... 261 L7
Birkhead St HECK WF16 .... 173 G3
Birkhill CAS WF10 .... 158 E6
Birkhill Crs BIRK/DRI BD11 .... 150 D1
Birkhill Rd BIRK/DRI BD11 .... 150 D1
Birk House La BSLY S70 .... 261 M7
KBTN HD8 .... 238 D7
Birkhouse La BRIG HD6 .... 148 E7
HUDE HD5 .... 15 M8
HUDS HD4 .... 14 B9
Birkhouse Rd BRIG HD6 .... 148 E7
Birkin La KNOT WF11 .... 160 F6
Birklands Moor CLECK BD19 .... 150 T5
Birklands Rd HUDN HD2 .... 192 B4
SHPY BD18 .... 82 C7
Birklands Ter SHPY BD18 .... 82 C7
Birk La MOR LS27 .... 152 A2
Birk Lea St WBOW BD5 .... 127 G2
Birk Rd BSLY S70 .... 261 L7
Birks Av GTHN BD7 .... 126 B1
STKB/PEN S36 .... 270 A3
Birks Fold GTHN BD7 .... 126 B1
Birkshall La BFDE BD3 .... 5 M8
Birks Hall St HFAX HX1 .... 10 D4
Birks Hall Ter HFAX HX1 .... 10 D4
Birksland St BOW BD4 .... 5 L9
Birks La HUDE HD5 .... 215 L8
KBTN HD8 .... 237 M3
RPDN/SBR HX6 .... 166 F6
STKB/PEN S36 .... 270 A4
TOD OL14 .... 163 K6
Birks Rd HUDW HD3 .... 213 J1
Birk St BSLY S70 ....
Birkwith Cl SCFT LS14 .... 89 K6
Birkwood Av CUD/GR S72 .... 262 E2
HOR/CROF WF4 .... 200 D4
Birkwood Rd NORM WF6 .... 206 C5
Birley St HTON BD9 .... 104 D3
Birmingham La
HOLM/MEL HD9 .... 234 E3
Birnam Gv BOW BD4 .... 127 J4
Birr Rd HTON BD9 .... 104 D3
Birstall La BIRK/DRI BD11 .... 151 G1
Birstall Park Ct BTLY WF17 .... 151 K3
Birthwaite Rd DOD/DAR S75 .... 241 K6
Birtwistle Cl COL BB8 .... 74 A1
Bishopdale Dr WBY LS22 .... 47 J3
Bishopdale Holme WBSY BD6 .... 125 K4
Bishopdyke Rd
GFTH/SHER LS25 .... 116 E6
Bishopgate St LDS LS1 .... 13 F1
Bishopgate Wk MILN OL16 .... 228 D2
Bishop St HTON BD9 .... 104 D3
MILN OL16 .... 206 D5
Bishops Wy BSLYN/ROY S71 .... 246 L3
HOLM/MEL HD9 .... 235 G4
MIRF WF14 .... 171 J7

Bishop Wy EARD/LOFT WF3 153 H6
Bisley Cl BSLYN/ROY S71 244 A3
Bismarck Ct BEE/HOL LS11 * 8 F8
Bismarck Dr BEE/HOL LS11 8 F8
Bismarck St BEE/HOL LS11 8 F8
BSLY S70 261 H7
Bitterne Ct WBSY BD6 125 L4
Bittern Ri MOR LS27 152 E3
Black Abbey La AIRE BD20 34 E8
Black Aston Rd BRAM LS13 107 M4
Blackberry Wy CLAY BD14 125 K3
Blackbird Gdns GIR BD8 103 K7
Black Brook Wy GTL/HWG HX4 168 E8
Black Bull St MID LS10 9 J4
Blackburn Cl GIR BD8 103 M7
HIPP HX3 146 B3
Blackburn Ct RTHW LS26 155 H1
Blackburn La DOD/DAR S75 260 F4
KNOT WF11 182 E3
Blackburn Pl BTLY WF17 173 M1
Blackburn Rd BRIG HD6 170 B2
BTLY WF17 151 G5
Blackchapel Dr MILN OL16 228 D3
Black Dyke TOD OL14 * 164 B3
Black Dyke La CUL/QBY BD13 102 D5
Black Edge La CUL/QBY BD13 101 L8
Blacker Crs HOR/CROF WF4 197 G8
Blackergreen La STKB/PEN S36 271 M3
Blacker La CUD/GR S72 244 E3
HOR/CROF WF4 197 J8
Blacker Rd DOD/DAR S75 242 E6
HUDW HD3 14 C3
Blacker Rd North HUDN HD2 * 14 D2
Blackers Ct EARL WF12 195 J2
Blackett St PDSY/CALV LS28 84 D7
Black Gates Ct EARD/LOFT WF3 153 H6
Blackgates Crs EARD/LOFT WF3 153 G6
Blackgates Dr EARD/LOFT WF3 153 H6
Blackgates Fold
EARD/LOFT WF3 153 H6
Black Gates Ri
EARD/LOFT WF3 * 153 H6
Blackheath Cl BSLYN/ROY S71 243 K7
Blackheath Rd BSLYN/ROY S71 243 K7
Blackheath Wk BSLYN/ROY S71 243 K7
Black Hill La AIRE BD20 56 F5
BHP/TINH LS16 64 F5
Black Hill Rd OT LS21 64 E1
Blackhouse Rd HUDN HD2 192 D4
Black La MAR/SLWT HD7 213 G7
Blackledge HFAX HX1 11 J7
Blackley Rd ELL HX5 190 F1
Blackman La LDSU LS2 6 F5
Blackmires LUD/ILL HX2 146 C1
Blackmoorfoot Rd
HOLM/MEL HD9 234 E1
MAR/SLWT HD7 213 G7
Blackmoor La AL/HA/HU LS17 67 K4
Black Moor Rd AL/HA/HU LS17 87 H3
HWTH BD22 78 F8
Blackpool Gv WOR/ARM LS12 130 C2
Blackpool Pl WOR/ARM LS12 130 C2
Blackpool St WOR/ARM LS12 130 C2
Blackpool Ter WOR/ARM LS12 130 C2
Blackpool Vw WOR/ARM LS12 130 B2
Black Rd WKFDE WF1 199 L2
Blackshaw Beck La HIPP HX3 125 J7
Blackshaw Clough Rd
RPDN/SBR HX6 166 C8
Blackshaw Dr WBSY BD6 125 M6
Blackshaw St TOD OL14 163 M1
Black Sike La HOLM/MEL HD9 253 L1
Blacksmith GTHN BD7 126 C2
Blacksmith Fold GTHN BD7 126 C2
Blacksmith La BHP/TINH LS16 65 H5
Blacksmith Ms EARD/LOFT WF3 154 D3
Blacksmiths Fold HUDE HD5 215 H3
Blackstone Av LM/WK BD12 148 E4
MILN OL16 206 E6
Blackstone Edge Old Rd
LIT OL15 185 M8
Blackstone Edge Rd HBR HX7 165 L4
RPDN/SBR HX6 187 G2
Blackthorn Cl WHIT OL12 206 A4
Blackthorn Ct MID LS10 131 M6
Blackthorn La PBR HG3 26 D2
Blackthorn Ms WHIT OL12 206 A4
Blackthorn Wy
WKFDW/WTN WF2 176 C6
Black Wk PONT WF8 181 G4
Blackwall HFAX HX1 10 F7
Blackwall La RPDN/SBR HX6 167 J1
Blackwall Ri RPDN/SBR HX6 167 K1
Blackwood Av BHP/TINH LS16 85 M3
Blackwood Gdns BHP/TINH LS16 85 M3
Black Wood Gv BHP/TINH LS16 85 M3
Blackwood Gv HFAX HX1 10 A4
Blackwood Hall La LUD/ILL HX2 144 E8
Black Wood Mt BHP/TINH LS16 85 M3
Black Wood Ri BHP/TINH LS16 85 M3
Blacup Moor Vw CLECK BD19 149 M7
Blagden La HUDS HD4 214 B5
Blair Cl ROY/SHW OL2 229 K7
Blairsville Gdns BRAM LS13 107 K2
Blairsville Gv BRAM LS13 107 L2
Blaith Royd La HBR HX7 165 H2
Blaithroyd La HIPP HX3 11 L8
Blake Crs GSLY LS20 62 B6
Blake Gv CHAL LS7 87 M8
Blake Hall Dr MIRF WF14 194 D2
Blake Hall Rd MIRF WF14 194 D2
Blake Hl HIPP HX3 147 G3
Blakehill Av ECHL BD2 105 L4
Blake Hill End HIPP HX3 147 H2
Blakehill Ter ECHL BD2 105 L4
Blakeholme Cl MAR/SLWT HD7 212 A5
Blakelaw Dr BRIG HD6 170 F3
Blake Law La BRIG HD6 171 H4
Blake Lee La MAR/SLWT HD7 210 D8
Blakeley Cl BSLYN/ROY S71 243 K7
Blakeley Gv WKFDW/WTN WF2 176 B8
Blakelock St ROY/SHW OL2 229 J7
Blakeney Gv MID LS10 131 M5
Blakeney Rd MID LS10 131 M5
Blakeridge La BTLY WF17 173 K1
Blakestones Rd MAR/SLWT HD7 212 A6
Blake St MILN OL16 206 C6
Blakey Rd WKFDW/WTN WF2 176 B6
Blamires Pl GTHN BD7 126 B3
Blamires St GTHN BD7 126 B3
Blanche St BOW BD4 105 M8
WHIT OL12 206 C4
Blandford Gdns LDSU LS2 6 E5
Blandford Gv LDSU LS2 6 E5
Blands Av CAS WF10 157 J1
Bland's Cl CAS WF10 157 M7
Blands Crs CAS WF10 157 J1
Blands Gv CAS WF10 157 J1
Blands Ter CAS WF10 157 J1
Bland St HFAX HX1 * 10 F6
HUD HD1 214 B2
Blantyre Ct CUL/QBY BD13 79 M8
Blayds Garth RTHW LS26 133 J7
Blayds Ms LDS LS1 9 G2
Blayds St OSM LS9 110 B7
Blayd's Yd LDS LS1 9 G2
Bleachcroft Wy BSLY S70 262 A7
Bleach Mill La ILK LS29 61 G1
Bleak Av CUD/GR S72 244 E4
Bleak Hey Nook La UPML OL3 231 L6
Bleakley Av HOR/CROF WF4 221 K8
Bleakley Cl CUD/GR S72 244 E4
Bleakley La BSLYN/ROY S71 243 K1
Bleakley Ter HOR/CROF WF4 221 K8
Bleak St CLECK BD19 150 E6
Bleak St Lower CLECK BD19 150 E6
Bleasdale Av HUDN HD2 192 B5
KNOT WF11 182 A1
Bleasdale Gv BSLYN/ROY S71 261 J2
Blencarn Cl SCFT LS14 111 H2
Blencarn Garth SCFT LS14 111 H2
Blencarn Rd SCFT LS14 111 H2
Blencarn Vw SCFT LS14 111 H2
Blenheim Av BSLY S70 261 G6
LDSU LS2 6 F4
Blenheim Cl KNOT WF11 181 L2
Blenheim Ct HFAX HX1 * 10 F4
LDSU LS2 * 6 E5
Blenheim Dr BTLY WF17 151 L8
DEWS WF13 173 J5
Blenheim Gv BSLY S70 260 F6
LDSU LS2 6 F5
Blenheim Hl BTLY WF17 151 M7
Blenheim Mt GIR BD8 104 E4
Blenheim Pl IDLE BD10 83 K5
Blenheim Rd BSLY S70 260 F7
GIR BD8 4 B1
WKFDE WF1 176 D6
Blenheim Sq LDSU LS2 6 F4
Blenheim St COL BB8 74 C1
HBR HX7 143 J3
Blenheim Ter LDSU LS2 6 E5
Blenheim Vw LDSU LS2 6 E4
Blenheim Wk LDSU LS2 6 E5
Blenhiem Cha KBTN HD8 240 A5
Blind La AL/HA/HU LS17 89 G2
BGLY BD16 80 F3
BIRK/DRI BD11 129 H7
EARD/LOFT WF3 175 J1
LUD/ILL HX2 124 A6
LUD/ILL HX2 144 D6
TOD OL14 141 J8
Bloemfontein St CUD/GR S72 244 C8
Bloomfield Ri DOD/DAR S75 242 B5
Bloomfield Rd DOD/DAR S75 242 B5
Bloomhouse La DOD/DAR S75 242 A4
Blossom Ct HUDE HD5 193 G8
Blossom Pl MILN OL16 206 B6
Blossom Wy CAS WF10 179 H1
Blucher St BOW BD4 105 M8
BSLY S70 261 G5
COL BB8 74 A2
Blue Ball La RPDN/SBR HX6 188 A3
Blue Ball Rd RPDN/SBR HX6 187 L4
Bluebell Av STKB/PEN S36 270 E3
Bluebell Cl PONT WF8 180 F7
SHPY BD18 104 F1
WIL/AL BD15 * 103 K6
Bluebell Ct BTLY WF17 151 G4
Blue Bell Hl HUDS HD4 214 B4
Blue Bell La TOD OL14 140 E4
Bluebell Rd DOD/DAR S75 242 A3
Bluebell Wk LUD/ILL HX2 145 G6
Bluebell Wy HEM/SK/SE WF9 225 H7
Blueberry Dr ROY/SHW OL2 229 M7
Bluebird Wk BGLY BD16 81 L2
Blue Butts OSS WF5 196 F1
Bluecoat Ct WBY LS22 47 H6
Bluefields ROY/SHW OL2 229 M6
Blue Hill Crs WOR/ARM LS12 108 C8
Blue Hill Gra WOR/ARM LS12 130 C1
Blue Hill Gv WOR/ARM LS12 108 C8
Blue Hill La WOR/ARM LS12 108 C8
Blundell Ct BSLYN/ROY S71 261 M1
Blundell St HEM/SK/SE WF9 247 G3
LDS LS1 6 E7
Bly Rd WMB/DAR S73 263 H8
Blyth Av LIT OL15 * 207 H3
Blythe Av GIR BD8 104 C6
Blythe St GTHN BD7 4 B6
Boardman St TOD OL14 141 K8
Boar La LDS LS1 9 G1
Boathouse La MIRF WF14 194 E4
Boat La CAS WF10 157 K3
Bobbin Mill Cl TOD OL14 140 D5
Bobbin Mill Ct AIRE BD20 56 E1
Bob La LUD/ILL HX2 145 M7
Bodiham Hl GFTH/SHER LS25 113 K6
Bodkin La HWTH BD22 100 A3
Bodley Ter BULY LS4 108 F5
Bodmin Ap MID LS10 153 J1
Bodmin Av SHPY BD18 83 G7
Bodmin Ct BSLYN/ROY S71 261 K3
Bodmin Crs MID LS10 153 J1
Bodmin Cft MID LS10 153 K2
Bodmin Dr NORM WF6 178 D3
Bodmin Gdns MID LS10 153 J2
Bodmin Garth MID LS10 153 J2
Bodmin Pl MID LS10 153 K2
Bodmin Rd MID LS10 153 H1
Bodmin St MID LS10 153 J2
Boggard La STKB/PEN S36 270 E4
Boggart Hl SCFT LS14 89 G8
Boggart Hill Crs SCFT LS14 89 G8
Boggart Hill Dr SCFT LS14 89 G8
Boggart Hill Gdns SCFT LS14 89 G8
Boggart Hill Rd SCFT LS14 89 G8
Boggart La HIPP HX3 147 M5
KBTN HD8 239 J3
RPDN/SBR HX6 167 K3
TAD LS24 95 H2
Bog Green La HUDE HD5 193 K1
Bog La MSTN/BAR LS15 112 C1
Bogthorn HWTH BD22 79 G2
Boland Crs HWTH BD22 79 G3
Boldgrove St EARL WF12 174 C8
Boldmere Rd MSTN/BAR LS15 111 G7
Boldron Holt WBSY BD6 126 B6
Boldshay St BFDE BD3 5 L4
Bold St COL BB8 74 A2
Bold Venture St SKP/WHF BD23 16 B4
Bolehill Pk BRIG HD6 148 A8
Bolingbroke St WBOW BD5 126 F4
Bolland St LM/WK BD12 149 G1
Bolling Rd BOW BD4 5 H8
ILK LS29 38 F2
Bolsover Cl GFTH/SHER LS25 113 K7
Bolstermoor Rd
MAR/SLWT HD7 212 C2
Boltby La WBSY BD6 126 A6
Bolton LUD/ILL HX2 124 A7
Bolton Bridge Rd ILK LS29 38 C2
Bolton Brow RPDN/SBR HX6 167 L2
Bolton Dr ECHL BD2 105 K2
Bolton Gra YEA LS19 62 E8
Bolton Gv ECHL BD2 105 K2
Bolton Hall Rd ECHL BD2 104 F1
SHPY BD18 105 G1
Bolton La ECHL BD2 105 H3
Bolton Rd AIRE BD20 36 A4
BFDE BD3 5 G1
SKP/WHF BD23 19 G1
YEA LS19 62 E8
Bolton St BFDE BD3 5 J5
LM/WK BD12 126 E8
Bolton Ter AIRE BD20 36 A4
Bolton Wy BSPA/BRAM LS23 48 E7
Bolton Wife Hl HOR/CROF WF4 220 B5
Bolus Cl WKFDE WF1 176 E2
Bolus La WKFDE WF1 176 D2
Bond Ct LDS LS1 6 F9
Bondgate AL/HA/HU LS17 45 J7
OT LS21 41 J7
PONT WF8 181 H4
Bondings Ri GFTH/SHER LS25 116 C6
Bond Rd DOD/DAR S75 260 F3
Bond St BRIG HD6 170 C3
BTLY WF17 151 G5
BTLY WF17 151 L8
DEWS WF13 173 L6
HBR HX7 143 J3
HFAX HX1 * 10 F7
LDS LS1 6 F9
PONT WF8 181 G4
TOD OL14 * 163 K1
WHIT OL12 206 C4
WKFDE WF1 12 D1
Bonegate Av BRIG HD6 170 D3
Bonegate Rd BRIG HD6 170 C3
Bone La AWLS/ASK DN6 227 K6
Bonnaccord Ter BTLY WF17 * 173 L2
Bonn Rd HTON BD9 104 C4
Bonwick Ml WBSY BD6 126 A7
Boocock St PDSY/CALV LS28 * 107 G5
Bookers Fld CLECK BD19 150 E7
Bootham Pk HTON BD9 103 M4
Booth House La
HOLM/MEL HD9 253 L2
Booth House Rd LUD/ILL HX2 144 E7
Boothman Wk KGHY BD21 2 D9
Booth Royd IDLE BD10 83 K5
Boothroyd Dr HDGY LS6 109 H1
HUDS HD4 213 K3
Booth Royd Dr IDLE BD10 83 K5
Boothroyd Gn DEWS WF13 173 K6
Booth Royd La BRIG HD6 169 M6
Boothroyd La DEWS WF13 173 K6
Boothroyds Wy FEA/AMT WF7 179 J8
Booth St CAS WF10 157 M6
CLECK BD19 149 M6
CUL/QBY BD13 124 F5
IDLE BD10 83 K7
ILK LS29 40 A4
SHPY BD18 82 F7
Boothtown Rd HIPP HX3 146 D3
Border Cl HUDW HD3 191 H5
Boroughgate OT LS21 41 J6
Borough Rd WKFDE WF1 12 E1
Borrins Wy BAIL BD17 82 F3
Borrough Av RHAY LS8 88 A6
Borrough Vw RHAY LS8 88 A6
Borrowdale Cl AWLS/ASK DN6 249 L5
BSLYN/ROY S71 262 C6
ROY/SHW OL2 228 F8
WOR/ARM LS12 108 B4
Borrowdale Crs
WOR/ARM LS12 108 B4
Borrowdale Cft YEA LS19 62 C7
Borrowdale Dr CAS WF10 158 F5
Borrowdale Rd EARL WF12 174 A4
WKFDW/WTN WF2 176 A7
Borrowdale Ter SCFT LS14 111 H3
Boston Av KSTL LS5 108 B3
Boston Rd WBY LS22 48 A2
Boston St CAS WF10 158 A6
HFAX HX1 10 B6
RPDN/SBR HX6 167 J3
Boston Wk WBSY BD6 126 B6
Bosville St STKB/PEN S36 271 G4
Boswell Cl BSLYN/ROY S71 * 243 K2
Bosworth Av NORM WF6 178 A2
Bosworth Cl WIL/AL BD15 103 K5
Bosworth Rd AWLS/ASK DN6 249 J8
Botany Av ECHL BD2 105 H2
Botany Dr AIRE BD20 59 G4
Botany La KBTN HD8 216 B1
Botesworth Gn MILN OL16 229 J1
Botham Flds HUDW HD3 213 H1
Botham Hall Rd HUDW HD3 213 H1
Botheby Wd SKP/WHF BD23 16 A1
Bottom Boat Rd
EARD/LOFT WF3 155 K8
Bottom Dyke KBTN HD8 238 B6
Bottom La HOLM/MEL HD9 236 E7
Bottomley La GTL/HWG HX4 189 L4
Bottomley Rd TOD OL14 163 L8
Bottomley's Buildings
HDGY LS6 6 E3
Bottomley St BRIG HD6 170 D2
WBOW BD5 126 F2
WBSY BD6 126 B7
Bottoms HIPP HX3 168 F3
Bottoms La BIRK/DRI BD11 150 D2
Boulder Bridge La CUD/GR S72 244 B4
The Boulevard BEE/HOL LS11 130 F3
PDSY/CALV LS28 106 F4
Boulsworth Dr COL BB8 74 E5
Boulsworth Gv COL BB8 74 C1
Boulview Ter COL BB8 74 C1
Boundary Av AIRE BD20 34 E8
Boundary Cl BAIL BD17 82 F2
MSTN/BAR LS15 112 A7
Boundary Dr CUD/GR S72 245 J3
Boundary Farm Rd
AL/HA/HU LS17 87 J3
Boundary La WKFDE WF1 178 B7
Boundary Pl CHAL LS7 7 L4
Boundary Rd DEWS WF13 173 H4
Boundary St BSLY S70 261 K6
CHAL LS7 * 7 L4
LIT OL15 185 J8
LVSG WF15 172 E3
ROCH OL11 228 A1
Boundary Ter DEWS WF13 * 173 K4
The Boundary GIR BD8 104 A5
Boundary Wk ROCH OL11 228 B1
Bourbon Cl WBSY BD6 126 D6
Bourne Ct DOD/DAR S75 242 E4
Bourne Rd ROY/SHW OL2 229 J6
Bourne St IDLE BD10 83 K4
Bourne Wk DOD/DAR S75 242 D4
Bourn View Rd HUDS HD4 213 M7
The Bourse LDS LS1 9 G1
Bowater Ct BOW BD4 128 B4
Bow Beck BOW BD4 5 K9
Bowbridge Rd WBOW BD5 * 127 G3
Bow Bridge Vw TAD LS24 72 B1
Bowcliffe Rd BSPA/BRAM LS23 69 L4
MID LS10 132 B2
Bowden Gv DOD/DAR S75 260 B7
Bower Av WHIT OL12 206 F2
Bower Gn BFDE BD3 * 105 L7
Bower Hl STKB/PEN S36 271 L5
Bower La DEWS WF13 173 H3
Bower Rd MSTN/BAR LS15 112 A3
Bower Slack Rd RPDN/SBR HX6 166 B5
Bowers La GTL/HWG HX4 167 M8
Bower St WBOW BD5 4 E9
The Bower BTLY WF17 151 H6
Bowes Nook WBSY BD6 126 A7
Bowfell Cl SCFT LS14 111 J2
Bowfell Vw BSLYN/ROY S71 261 J2
Bow Gn CLAY BD14 125 M2
Bowland Cl MSTN/BAR LS15 111 G7
ROY/SHW OL2 229 G7
Bowland Gv MILN OL16 229 H2
Bowland St GIR BD8 4 D3
Bow La HBR HX7 142 C2
Bowler Cl LM/WK BD12 126 E8
Bowler St ROY/SHW OL2 229 K7
Bowlers Wk WHIT OL12 206 B4
Bowling Aly BRIG HD6 170 C6
Bowling Av WKFDE WF1 * 176 B4
Bowling Back La BOW BD4 5 K9
Bowling Ct BRIG HD6 170 B3
Bowling Dyke HIPP HX3 11 H4
Bowling Green Ct HUDW HD3 191 G7
Bowling Green Rd
GTL/HWG HX4 190 B3
Bowling Green Ter
BEE/HOL LS11 8 E5
Bowling Green Vw
BIRK/DRI BD11 129 G8
Bowling Hall Rd BOW BD4 127 J3
Bowling Old La WBOW BD5 126 F4
Bowling Park Cl BOW BD4 127 H2
Bowling Park Dr WBOW BD5 127 H3
Bowling St HUDS HD4 213 J2
Bowman Av WBSY BD6 126 D7
Bowman Gv HFAX HX1 10 C5
Bowman La MID LS10 9 J2
Bowman Pl HFAX HX1 * 10 C5
Bowman Rd WBSY BD6 126 D7
Bowman St HFAX HX1 * 10 C5
WKFDE WF1 13 L9
Bowman Ter HFAX HX1 10 D5
Bownas Rd BSPA/BRAM LS23 48 E6
Bowness Av CAS WF10 159 G5
IDLE BD10 105 M2
Bowness Dr HUDE HD5 15 L5
Bowood Av CHAL LS7 87 J7
Bowood Crs CHAL LS7 87 J7
Bowood Gv CHAL LS7 87 J7
Bowood La RPDN/SBR HX6 166 F5
Bow St CUD/GR S72 244 D7
HUD HD1 14 D8
KGHY BD21 3 G5
OSM LS9 9 L2
Bowwood Dr AIRE BD20 58 D6
Boxhall Rd ELL HX5 169 H7
Box La PONT WF8 181 G4
Box St LIT OL15 207 J1
Box Tree Cl GIR BD8 104 A5
Box Trees La LUD/ILL HX2 145 M3
Boxwood Rd ELL HX5 191 H1
Boycott Dr FEA/AMT WF7 224 C1
Boycott Wy HEM/SK/SE WF9 247 J2
Boyd Av BFDE BD3 106 A5
Boy La BOW BD4 127 K7
HIPP HX3 145 M4
The Boyle MSTN/BAR LS15 90 F6
Boyne Dr WKFDW/WTN WF2 220 C1
Boyne Hl HOR/CROF WF4 220 C2
Boyne St HFAX HX1 10 F6
Boynton St WBOW BD5 126 F3
Boynton Ter WBOW BD5 127 G3
Boys La HIPP HX3 168 F1
Bracewell Av WIL/AL BD15 103 J6
Bracewell Bank HIPP HX3 146 B4
Bracewell Dr HIPP HX3 146 B4
Bracewell Gv HIPP HX3 10 C1
Bracewell Rd HOLM/MEL HD9 234 E5
Bracken Av BRIG HD6 170 C1
Bracken Bank Av HWTH BD22 79 H3
Bracken Bank Crs HWTH BD22 79 H3
Bracken Bank Gv HWTH BD22 79 H3
Bracken Bank Wk HWTH BD22 79 H3
Bracken Bank Wy HWTH BD22 79 H3
Brackenbeck Rd GTHN BD7 126 B2
Brackenbed Gra LUD/ILL HX2 146 A5
Brackenbed La HFAX HX1 10 A1
Bracken Cl BRIG HD6 170 C1
ELL HX5 169 K7
MIRF WF14 171 M7
Bracken Ct AL/HA/HU LS17 87 L5
WOR/ARM LS12 131 G1
Brackendale IDLE BD10 83 H4
Brackendale Av IDLE BD10 83 J4
Brackendale Dr IDLE BD10 83 H4
Brackendale Gv IDLE BD10 83 H4
Brackendale Pde IDLE BD10 83 H4
Brackendale Rd
WKFDW/WTN WF2 12 A9
Bracken Edge IDLE BD10 83 L7
RHAY LS8 110 B1
Bracken Ghyll Dr AIRE BD20 35 M4
Bracken Gv HUDN HD2 192 D2
MIRF WF14 171 M7
Bracken Hall Rd HUDN HD2 192 E3
Bracken Hl AL/HA/HU LS17 87 L5
FEA/AMT WF7 223 M1
HEM/SK/SE WF9 246 F2
MIRF WF14 171 M7
Brackenhill Dr GTHN BD7 126 B3
Brackenhill La TAD LS24 95 H7
Brackenholme Royd
WBSY BD6 126 A6
Brackenhurst Pl AL/HA/HU LS17 87 L4
Bracken Mt AIRE BD20 35 M4
Bracken Pk BGLY BD16 81 L3
SCFT LS14 67 J6
Bracken Rd AIRE BD20 56 C1
BRIG HD6 170 C1
HWTH BD22 79 J2
Brackens La HIPP HX3 125 K7
Bracken Sq HUDN HD2 * 192 E2
Bracken St KGHY BD21 79 K2
Brackenthwaite La PBR HG3 25 L3
Bracken Wy ELL HX5 169 K7
Brackenwell La AL/HA/HU LS17 25 M7
Brackenwood Cl ILK LS29 39 G2
RHAY LS8 88 A7
Brackenwood Ct WKFDE WF1 176 F1
Brackenwood Dr RHAY LS8 88 A6
Brackenwood Gn RHAY LS8 88 A6
Brackenwood Rd WKFDE WF1 176 F1
Bradbeck Rd GTHN BD7 104 B7
Bradburn Rd EARD/LOFT WF3 154 C3
Bradbury St BSLY S70 260 F5
DEWS WF13 195 G1
Bradcroft HUDN HD2 15 G1
Bradd Cl LVSG WF15 * 172 D1
Braddocks Cl WHIT OL12 206 F2
Bradfield Cl HUDN HD2 193 G1
Bradford La BFDE BD3 105 M7
Bradford Old Rd BGLY BD16 81 K7
HIPP HX3 146 E3
Bradford Rd AIRE BD20 58 F7
BGLY BD16 81 J5
BIRK/DRI BD11 128 F7
BIRK/DRI BD11 150 C2
BRIG HD6 170 D2
BTLY WF17 150 F5
CLAY BD14 125 M1
CLECK BD19 149 K3
CLECK BD19 150 B8
DEWS WF13 173 L4
EARD/LOFT WF3 153 G5
GSLY LS20 61 L5
HIPP HX3 147 J3
HUD HD1 15 G3
HUDN HD2 192 D2
IDLE BD10 105 J1
ILK LS29 40 B6
KGHY BD21 3 J4
PDSY/CALV LS28 106 B5
SHPY BD18 82 D8
WKFDW/WTN WF2 176 A2
Bradfords Cl BSPA/BRAM LS23 69 L3
Bradford St DEWS WF13 173 M5
KGHY BD21 3 H3
Bradford & Wakefield Rd
BOW BD4 128 E7
Bradlaugh Rd WBSY BD6 126 D5
Bradlaugh Ter WBSY BD6 126 E5
Bradley Av AIRE BD20 35 M4
CAS WF10 157 L6
Bradley Bvd HUDN HD2 192 E3
Bradley Carr Ter
HEM/SK/SE WF9 247 G6
Bradley Grange Gdns
HUDN HD2 171 H8
Bradley Gv AIRE BD20 35 M4
Bradley La GTL/HWG HX4 168 D8
MILN OL16 229 K2
PDSY/CALV LS28 106 D7
Bradley Mills La HUD HD1 15 K2
Bradley Mills Rd HUD HD1 15 K2
Bradley Quarry Cl HUDN HD2 * 171 J8
Bradley Ri AIRE BD20 35 M4
Bradley Rd AIRE BD20 35 M3
HUDN HD2 192 F1
Bradley Smithy Cl WHIT OL12 206 A4
Bradley St BGLY BD16 81 H3
CAS WF10 157 M6
COL BB8 74 B1
HTON BD9 104 E2
MILN OL16 229 K2
Bradley Vw GTL/HWG HX4 190 D2
Bradshaw Av HOLM/MEL HD9 236 A3
Bradshaw Cl DOD/DAR S75 260 C4
HOLM/MEL HD9 236 A3
Bradshaw Crs HOLM/MEL HD9 * 236 A3
Bradshaw La LUD/ILL HX2 124 B6
MAR/SLWT HD7 211 J5
Bradshaw Rd HOLM/MEL HD9 235 K8
Bradshaw St MILN OL16 206 C6
Bradshaw Vw CUL/QBY BD13 124 E5
Bradstock Gdns MOR LS27 130 C8
Brae Av ECHL BD2 105 H3
Braegate La TAD LS24 73 K1
Braemar Cft CUD/GR S72 222 F7
Braemar Dr GFTH/SHER LS25 113 K6
Braemar Ri CUD/GR S72 222 F7
Braemore Cl ROY/SHW OL2 229 G6
Brafferton Arbor WBSY BD6 126 A6
Braine Rd WBY LS22 30 B8
Braithwaite Av HWTH BD22 57 G7
Braithwaite Crs HWTH BD22 2 B4
Braithwaite Dr HWTH BD22 2 A4
Braithwaite Edge Rd HWTH BD22 56 F6
Braithwaite Gv HWTH BD22 2 A4
Braithwaite Rd HWTH BD22 56 F7
Braithwaite Rw MID LS10 * 132 A4
Braithwaite St BEE/HOL LS11 8 B4
Braithwaite Wk HWTH BD22 2 A4
Braithwaite Wy HWTH BD22 2 A4
Brakehouse Cl MILN OL16 207 G8
Bramah St BSLYN/ROY S71 243 L5
Bramble Av BSPA/BRAM LS23 48 D7
Bramble Cl CLAY BD14 125 K3
HWTH BD22 78 F8
LIT OL15 207 H1
PONT WF8 180 D8
Bramble Ct GFTH/SHER LS25 116 A7
OT LS21 42 F8
WKFDE WF1 176 C1
Bramble Gv ELL HX5 169 K7
OT LS21 42 F8
The Brambles ILK LS29 38 B2
Bramble Wk BTLY WF17 151 H5
Brambling Dr WBSY BD6 125 L4
Brambling Ms MOR LS27 152 E2
Bramcote Av BSLYN/ROY S71 243 G6
Bramhall Cl MILN OL16 207 G8
Bramham Dr BAIL BD17 82 F2
Bramham La BSPA/BRAM LS23 68 D3
Bramham Park Ct MID LS10 153 M3
Bramham Rd BGLY BD16 81 J2
BSPA/BRAM LS23 69 M1
CAS WF10 157 J8
SCFT LS14 68 D8
Bramhope Old La OT LS21 63 G2
Bramhope Rd CLECK BD19 149 L6
Bramleigh Dr MOR LS27 130 C8
Bramleigh Gv MOR LS27 130 C8
Bramley Carr BSLY S70 260 D7
Bramley Cl HOLM/MEL HD9 236 F7
HWTH BD22 78 D3
Bramley Crs WKFDE WF1 176 D2
Bramley Fold HIPP HX3 147 M6
Bramley La HIPP HX3 147 M6
HOR/CROF WF4 219 J6
Bramley St BRAM LS13 107 L5
WBOW BD5 127 G2
Bramley Vw HIPP HX3 148 A6
Brampton Ct HEM/SK/SE WF9 247 J1
Bramstan Av BRAM LS13 107 J3
Bramstan Cl BRAM LS13 107 J3
Bramstan Gdns BRAM LS13 107 J3
Bramston Gdns BRIG HD6 170 C6
Bramston St BRIG HD6 170 C5
Brancepeth Pl WOR/ARM LS12 109 G7
Branch Cl WOR/ARM LS12 130 C2
Branch End MOR LS27 129 M7
Branch La HUDW HD3 191 K3
Branch Pl WOR/ARM LS12 130 C2
Branch Rd BTLY WF17 173 L1
CLECK BD19 149 H5
DEWS WF13 173 L6
GTL/HWG HX4 168 A8
HOR/CROF WF4 219 L2
HUDW HD3 191 J2
MILN OL16 207 G5
SKP/WHF BD23 16 B4
WOR/ARM LS12 108 E6
Branch St HUD HD1 213 M1
WOR/ARM LS12 130 C2
Brander Ap OSM LS9 110 E5
Brander Cl IDLE BD10 83 J8
OSM LS9 110 F5
Brander Dr OSM LS9 110 E5
Brander Gv OSM LS9 110 E5
Brander Rd OSM LS9 110 E5
Brander St OSM LS9 110 F4
Brandfort St GTHN BD7 126 C1
Brand Hill Ap HOR/CROF WF4 200 A5
Brand Hill Dr HOR/CROF WF4 200 A5
Brandling Ct MID LS10 153 L1
Brandon Ct AL/HA/HU LS17 88 D1
Brandon Crs AL/HA/HU LS17 67 H8
ROY/SHW OL2 229 J6
Brandon La AL/HA/HU LS17 66 F6
Brandon Rd BVRD LS3 6 C7
Brandon St MILN OL16 207 G8
WOR/ARM LS12 8 A1
Brandon Wy CHAL LS7 109 M1
Brandy Carr Rd
WKFDW/WTN WF2 175 K4
Branksome Av BSLY S70 260 E5
Branksome Ct HTON BD9 * 104 B4
Branksome Crs HTON BD9 104 B4
Branksome Dr SHPY BD18 81 M6
Branksome Gv BGLY BD16 81 L6
Branksome Pl HDGY LS6 109 G4

Branksome St HDGY LS6 * 109 G4
Branksome Ter HDGY LS6 * 109 G4
Bransby Cl PDSY/CALV LS28 ....107 G4
Bransby Ct PDSY/CALV LS28 ....107 G4
Bransby Ri PDSY/CALV LS28 ....107 G4
Bransdale Av GSLY LS20 ....62 A6
    NORM WF6 ....178 C2
Bransdale Cl BAIL BD17 ....82 C2
    GSLY LS20 ....62 A6
    NORM WF6 ....178 C2
Bransdale Clough WBSY BD6 ..126 A5
Bransdale Garth GSLY LS20 ....62 A6
Bransdale Ms NORM WF6 ....178 C2
Bransdale Wk NORM WF6 ....178 C2
Branshaw Dr HWTH BD22 ....79 G1
Branshaw Gv HWTH BD22 ....79 G1
Branshaw Mt HWTH BD22 ....79 G1
Branstone Gv OSS WF5 ....174 F5
Bran St HWTH BD22 ....79 J2
Brant Av LUD/ILL HX2 ....146 B2
Brant Bank La ILK LS29 ....19 L8
Brantcliffe Dr BAIL BD17 ....82 D2
Brantdale Cl HTON BD9 ....103 L2
Brantdale Rd HTON BD9 ....103 L2
Brantford St CHAL LS7 ....87 M8
Brant La TAD LS24 ....71 J7
Brantwood Av HTON BD9 ....103 L2
Brantwood Cl HTON BD9 ....103 L2
Brantwood Crs HTON BD9 ....103 K2
Brantwood Dr HTON BD9 ....103 L2
Brantwood Ov HTON BD9 ....103 K2
Brantwood Rd HTON BD9 ....103 K2
Brantwood Vls HTON BD9 ....103 L2
Branwell Av BTLY WF17 ....151 G3
Branwell Ct HTON BD9 ....104 A4
Branwell Dr HWTH BD22 ....78 E6
Brassey Rd BOW BD4 ....127 J2
Brassey St HFAX HX1 ....10 F8
Brassey Ter BOW BD4 ....127 J2
Brathay Gdns SCFT LS14 ....111 J3
Brat La OT LS21 ....23 J1
Braybrook Ct GIR BD8 ....104 E3
Bray Cl GTHN BD7 * 125 M4
Brayshaw Dr GTHN BD7 ....125 M4
Brayshaw Rd EARD/LOFT WF3 ..153 L7
Brayside Av HUDN HD2 ....192 B4
Braythorne La OT LS21 ....24 F7
Brayton Ap SCFT LS14 ....111 L1
Brayton Cl SCFT LS14 ....111 L1
Brayton Gdns AWLS/ASK DN6 ..227 L5
Brayton Gn SCFT LS14 ....111 M1
Brayton Gv SCFT LS14 ....111 L1
Brayton Wk SCFT LS14 ....111 L1
Brazil St CAS WF10 ....158 A6
Bread St WKFDE WF1 ....12 E2
Breakmoor Av AIRE BD20 ....36 A4
Break Neck HIPP HX3 ....147 J6
Breaks Rd LM/WK BD12 ....126 F8
Brearcliffe Cl WBSY BD6 ....126 C6
Brearcliffe Dr WBSY BD6 ....126 C7
Brearcliffe Rd WBSY BD6 ....126 C7
Brearcliffe St WBSY BD6 ....126 C7
Brearley Gdns LVSG WF15 ....172 C3
Brearley La LUD/ILL HX2 ....144 D6
Brearley St BTLY WF17 ....173 K2
Brearton St BFD BD1 ....4 E3
Breary Av HORS LS18 ....85 M5
Breary Cl BHP/TINH LS16 ....64 A3
Breary La BHP/TINH LS16 ....64 B3
Breary La East BHP/TINH LS16 ....64 B3
Breary Ri BHP/TINH LS16 ....64 B3
Breary Ter HORS LS18 ....85 M5
Breary Wk HORS LS18 ....85 M5
Breck Lea RPDN/SBR HX6 ....167 J4
Brecks Gdns GFTH/SHER LS25 ..135 H3
Brecks La GFTH/SHER LS25 ....135 H3
    RTHW LS26 ....134 E2
Brecks Rd CLAY BD14 ....125 H1
Breck Willows RPDN/SBR HX6 ..167 H4
Brecon Ap OSM LS9 ....110 F4
Brecon Av HUDW HD3 ....191 J5
Brecon Cl IDLE BD10 ....83 K7
    ROY/SHW OL2 ....228 E8
Bredon Av SHPY BD18 ....83 H7
Bredon Cl HEM/SK/SE WF9 ....224 F5
Breeze Cl COL BB8 ....52 A5
Breighton Adown WBSY BD6 ....125 M6
Brellafield Dr ROY/SHW OL2 .....229 H5
Bremner St OT LS21 ....41 K6
Brendon Ct BOW BD4 ....127 M3
    MIRF WF14 ....194 B4
Brendon Dr HUDN HD2 ....191 M5
Brendon Wk BOW BD4 * 127 M4
Brentford Gv WOR/ARM LS12 * ..108 E7
Brentford Rd LM/WK BD12 ....126 E8
Brentlea Av WKFDW/WTN WF2 ...12 D8
Brentwood Cl BTLY WF17 ....174 A1
    LIT OL15 ....207 H3
    PONT WF8 ....225 J1
Brentwood Gdns WBSY BD6 .....126 E6
Brentwood St WOR/ARM LS12 * ..108 E7
Brentwood Ter WOR/ARM LS12 ..108 E7
Bretfield Ct EARL WF12 ....195 M1
Brettas Pk BSLYN/ROY S71 ....261 J1
Brettegate HEM/SK/SE WF9 ......223 L7
Brett Gdns BEE/HOL LS11 ....8 E3
Bretton Cl DOD/DAR S75 ....241 L6
Bretton Ct WBSY BD6 * 126 B6
Bretton La HOR/CROF WF4 ....219 K3
Bretton Rd DOD/DAR S75 ....241 M6
Bretton St EARL WF12 ....195 M1
Bretton Vw CUD/GR S72 ....262 C1
Brevitt St WKFDE WF1 ....12 D4
Brewerton La DEWS WF13 ....173 H4
Brewery Cl HUDW HD3 ....191 H4
Brewery La CUL/OBY BD13 ....124 C7
    CUL/OBY BD13 ....124 C7
    EARL WF12 ....195 L2
    SKP/WHF BD23 ....16 B2
    ILK LS29 ....38 E2
Brewery Rd HWTH BD22 ....79 J3
Brewery St HECK WF16 * 172 C1
    HIPP HX3 ....146 E4
    KGHY BD21 ....3 K4
Brewery Whf MIRF WF14 ....194 C2
Brexdale Av GFTH/SHER LS25 ...135 H3
Brian Crs MSTN/BAR LS15 ....111 K4
Brian Pl MSTN/BAR LS15 ....111 K3
Brian Royd La GTL/HWG HX4 ....168 B7
Brian St HUDW HD3 ....191 H5
Brian Vw MSTN/BAR LS15 ....111 K3
Briar Av HOLM/MEL HD9 ....234 B3
Briar Bank HEM/SK/SE WF9 ......223 J4
Briar Cl ELL HX5 ....191 G1
    HECK WF16 ....172 F1
Briar Ct HOLM/MEL HD9 ....253 K2
Briardale Rd HTON BD9 ....103 K2
Briardene RTHW LS26 * 155 L1
Briar Dr DEWS WF13 ....173 H4
Briarfield Av IDLE BD10 ....83 J7
Briarfield Cl IDLE BD10 ....83 J7
    ILK LS29 ....38 F3
Briarfield Gv SHPY BD18 ....82 D8
Briarfield Gv IDLE BD10 * 83 J7
Briarfield Rd HOLM/MEL HD9 ....236 E7

Briar Ga WBY LS22 ....30 A7
Briar Gv CUD/GR S72 ....245 J3
    STKB/PEN S36 ....270 C4
    WKFDE WF1 ....13 K9
Briarlea Cl YEA LS19 ....62 B1
Briarlyn Av HUDW HD3 ....191 H5
Briarlyn Rd HUDW HD3 ....191 H5
Briarmains Rd BTLY WF17 ....151 H4
Briar Rd AWLS/ASK DN6 ....249 J5
Briarsdale Av WBSY BD6 ....126 C5
Briars Ct COP/BISH YO25 ....73 M5
Briarsdale Cft RHAY LS8 * 110 E3
Briarsdale Cft RHAY LS8 * 110 E3
Briarsdale Garth RHAY LS8 * 110 D3
Briarsdale Hts OSM LS9 * 110 E3
Briars Dr COP/BISH YO23 ....55 M1
Briar Wd SHPY BD18 ....83 G7
Brickbank HUDE HD5 * 215 H3
Brickfield Gv LUD/ILL HX2 ....146 C1
Brickfield La LUD/ILL HX2 ....146 C1
Brickfield St MILN OL16 ....206 D4
Brickfield Ter LUD/ILL HX2 ....146 C1
Brick Mill Rd PDSY/CALV LS28 ...107 G8
Brick Rw LM/WK BD12 ....148 E3
Brick St CLECK BD19 ....149 L7
    OSM LS9 ....9 K1
    WKFDW/WTN WF2 ....12 B5
Brickyard MIRF WF14 ....194 B1
Bride St TOD OL14 ....141 K8
Bridge Bank Rd LIT OL15 ....207 H3
Bridge Cl BSPA/BRAM LS23 ....49 G6
    HOR/CROF WF4 ....196 F5
    KBTN HD8 ....240 A4
Bridge Cl HEM/SK/SE WF9 ....223 J3
    MOR LS27 ....152 D3
Bridge Cft HUDW HD3 ....213 K2
Bridge End BRIG HD6 ....170 C5
    LDS LS1 ....9 H2
Bridge End St TOD OL14 * 140 E5
Bridge Fold KSTL LS5 ....108 C2
Bridge Foot BSPA/BRAM LS23 .....49 G6
Bridge Gdns BSLYN/ROY S71 ...261 J3
Bridge Garth BSPA/BRAM LS23 ...48 F8
    GFTH/SHER LS25 ....138 E2
Bridge Ga HBR HX7 ....143 J3
Bridgegate BSLYN/ROY S71 * ...262 A6
Bridgehouse La HWTH BD22 ......78 E8
Bridge La HIPP HX3 ....125 K7
    HOLM/MEL HD9 ....236 C8
    ILK LS29 ....38 C1
    KNOT WF11 ....182 B1
    PONT WF8 ....225 J2
Bridge Lanes HBR HX7 ....143 H3
Bridgenorth Dr LIT OL15 ....207 H3
Bridge Rd AIRE BD20 ....55 M1
    BEE/HOL LS11 ....8 C4
    BRAM LS13 ....107 G1
    BRIG HD6 ....170 B7
    BSPA/BRAM LS23 ....49 G6
    HOR/CROF WF4 ....197 G5
    HUDN HD2 ....193 K1
    KSTL LS5 ....108 B2
Bridge St AIRE BD20 ....36 A4
    BFD BD1 ....4 F7
    BSLYN/ROY S71 ....261 H4
    BSLYN/ROY S71 * 262 A6
    BTLY WF17 ....151 G6
    BTLY WF17 ....173 M1
    CAS WF10 ....158 A6
    DOD/DAR S75 ....242 A5
    HECK WF16 ....172 E2
    HUD HD1 ....214 B3
    HUD5 HD4 ....214 B6
    HWTH BD22 ....78 D4
    KGHY BD21 ....2 F6
    LDSU LS2 ....7 J8
    MAR/SLWT HD7 ....212 C5
    MILN OL16 ....207 H8
    MOR LS27 ....152 D4
    NORM WF6 ....178 A4
    OT LS21 ....41 J6
    PONT WF8 ....180 F6
    ROY/SHW OL2 * 229 L6
    SKP/WHF BD23 ....16 B2
    STKB/PEN S36 ....270 E2
    TAD LS24 ....71 M3
    TOD OL14 ....163 K1
    WHIT OL12 ....206 E3
    WKFDE WF1 ....13 H6
Bridge Vw BRAM LS13 ....107 G1
Bridgewater HDGY LS6 ....87 G8
Bridgewater Park Dr
    AWLS/ASK DN6 ....249 H4
Bridgewater Rd OSM LS9 ....9 M5
Bridgeway BOW BD4 ....127 L4
Bridge Wood Vw HORS LS18 ......85 M4
Bridgland Av ILK LS29 ....61 J1
Bridgwater Rd HTON BD9 ....104 C4
Bridle Av OSS WF5 ....174 E4
Bridle Cl HOR/CROF WF4 ....197 G7
Bridle Dene HIPP HX3 ....147 L1
Bridle La HOR/CROF WF4 ....147 G7
    OSS WF5 ....174 E4
Bridle Pth MSTN/BAR LS15 ....111 J4
Bridle Path Rd AL/HA/HU LS17 ...88 F1
Bridle Path Wk
    MSTN/BAR LS15 ....111 J4
Bridle Pl OSS WF5 ....174 F6
Bridle Stile HIPP HX3 ....147 L1
Bridle Stile La CUL/OBY BD13 ...125 G4
Bridle St BTLY WF17 ....174 A1
Bridley Dr MAR/SLWT HD7 ....212 B8
Brierdene AIRE BD20 ....36 A4
Brierey Cl DOD/DAR S75 ....242 C6
Brierfield Cl DOD/DAR S75 ....260 H4
Brierfield Gdns MOR LS27 ....129 L8
Brier Hey Cl HBR HX7 ....144 B5
Brier Hey La HBR HX7 ....144 B5
Brier Hill Cl CLECK BD19 ....149 J8
Brier Hill Vw HUDW HD3 ....192 F1
Brierlands Cl GFTH/SHER LS25 ..113 K6
Brierlands Fold
    GFTH/SHER LS25 ....113 K6
Brierlea La GFTH/SHER LS25 .....113 K6
Brier La ELL HX5 ....169 M4
    HOR/CROF WF4 ....218 C1
Brierley Cl SHPY BD18 ....82 B5
Brierley Crs HEM/SK/SE WF9 ....246 E3
Brierley Rd CUD/GR S72 ....245 J6
    CUD/GR S72 ....245 J6
Brier St HIPP HX3 ....146 D4
    KGHY BD21 ....3 K2
Briery Cl ILK LS29 ....38 A2
Briery Fld SHPY BD18 ....104 A3
Briery Gv MIRF WF14 ....194 B1
Briestfield Rd EARL WF12 ....195 H7
    HOR/CROF WF4 ....217 G1
Briggate AIRE BD20 ....36 A4
    BAIL BD17 ....82 D6

    BRIG HD6 ....170 C4
    ELL HX5 ....169 H7
    LDS LS1 ....9 G1
Brigg Gdns HWTH BD22 ....2 B4
Briggland St AL/BD15 ....102 E1
Brigglands WIL/AL BD15 * 102 E1
Brigg's Av CAS WF10 ....157 M8
    WBSY BD6 ....126 C5
Briggs Gv WBSY BD6 ....126 C5
Briggs Pl WBSY BD6 ....126 C5
Briggs Rd BSLYN/ROY S71 ....243 L5
Briggs Rw FEA/AMT WF7 ....201 M2
Briggs St HUDE HD5 ....125 C5
Briggs Ter HUDE HD5 ....115 L7
Briggs Yd OSS WF5 * 196 E1
Brighouse &
Denholme Gate Rd HIPP HX3 ..125 J8
Brighouse & Denholme Rd
    CUL/OBY BD13 ....124 C2
Brighouse Rd CUL/OBY BD13 ...102 A8
    CUL/OBY BD13 ....125 C3
    HIPP HX3 ....147 K3
    HUDW HD3 ....148 F1
    LM/WK BD12 ....148 F1
Brighouse Wood La BRIG HD6 ..170 B3
Brighouse Wood Rw BRIG HD6 ..170 B3
Brighton Av MOR LS27 ....152 B1
Brighton Cliff BRAM LS13 ....107 L4
Brighton Cl BTLY WF17 ....151 G8
Brighton Gv BRAM LS13 ....107 M5
    HFAX HX1 ....10 C4
Brighton Rd ILK LS29 ....39 G3
Brighton St BAIL BD17 ....82 D6
    CUD/GR S72 ....245 J7
    HECK WF16 ....172 F1
    HIPP HX3 ....10 D1
    IDLE BD10 ....83 J5
    TOD OL14 ....140 E5
    WKFDW/WTN WF2 ....12 B5
Brighton Ter CLECK BD19 ....149 H6
Bright St AIRE BD20 ....34 F5
    CLAY BD14 * 125 K2
    COL BB8 ....74 D1
    CUL/OBY BD13 ....125 H5
    DEWS WF13 * 173 L6
    EARD/LOFT WF3 ....153 M6
    MILN OL16 ....207 J8
    MIRF WF14 ....194 B2
    MOR LS27 ....152 C2
    PDSY/CALV LS28 ....107 H4
    RPDN/SBR HX6 ....167 K1
    SKP/WHF BD23 ....16 C3
    TOD OL14 ....163 J3
    WIL/AL BD15 ....103 K5
Bright Ter COL BB8 ....74 D4
Brignall Cft OSM LS9 ....110 B5
Brignall Garth OSM LS9 ....110 B5
Brignall Wy OSM LS9 ....110 B5
Brigshaw Dr CAS WF10 ....135 H7
Brigshaw La CAS WF10 ....135 J7
Brimmy Croft La UPML OL3 ....230 A1
Brinckman St BSLYN/ROY S71 ...261 H6
Brindle Park Dr CAS WF10 ....158 A6
Brindley Cft SKP/WHF BD23 ....16 B3
Brindley Gv GIR BD8 ....103 L7
Brindley Rd AIRE BD20 ....36 B6
Brindley Wy WKFDW/WTN WF2 ..176 B2
Brisbane Av ECHL BD2 ....105 G3
Briscoe La GTL/HWG HX4 ....168 D7
Briscoe Ridge La PBR HG3 ....205 J4
Bristol Av AIRE BD20 ....36 D6
Bristol St CHAL LS7 ....7 K6
    COL BB8 ....74 A1
    HIPP HX3 ....168 F3
Britannia Av ROY/SHW OL2 ......229 L8
Britannia Cl BSLY S70 ....261 H6
    PDSY/CALV LS28 ....107 H4
Britannia Ct BRAM LS13 ....107 J6
Britannia Rd MAR/SLWT HD7 ....212 B6
    MAR/SLWT HD7 ....213 G3
Britannia St BGLY BD16 ....81 J3
    BRAM LS13 ....107 J6
    LDS LS1 ....8 D2
    PDSY/CALV LS28 ....107 H4
    WBOW BD5 ....5 G3
Britannia St CLECK BD19 ....149 M6
Britland Cl DOD/DAR S75 ....260 D6
Briton St BGLY BD16 ....206 C6
Broadacre Rd OSS WF5 ....197 G1
Broad Acres Wy CAS WF10 ....198 C7
Broadacre Wy BAIL BD17 ....83 H7
Broadbent Cft HUDN HD3 ....236 C2
Broad Carr La GTL/HWG HX4 ....190 E2
Broadcroft Cha
    EARD/LOFT WF3 ....153 G7
Broadcroft Dr EARD/LOFT WF3 ..153 G7
Broadcroft Wy EARD/LOFT WF3 ..153 G7
Broad Cut Rd HOR/CROF WF4 ...197 M8
Broadfield Cl BOW BD4 ....128 A3
Broadfield Dr LIT OL15 ....207 H3
Broadfield Pk HOLM/MEL HD9 ..253 L4
Broadfield Stile MILN OL16 ....206 A8
Broadfield St MILN OL16 ....206 A8
Broadfield Wy WIL/AL BD15 ....18 F6
Broadfolds CLAY BD14 ....125 L2
Broadgate GTL/HWG HX4 ....190 B4
    HUDE HD5 ....214 F2
    OSS WF5 ....197 G1
Broad Ga TOD OL14 ....141 L8
Broadgate Av HORS LS18 ....85 M6
Broadgate Ct HORS LS18 ....85 L6
    HUDE HD5 ....214 F2
Broadgate Dr HORS LS18 ....85 L5
Broadgate La HORS LS18 ....85 L5
Broadgate Ms HORS LS18 ....85 M6
Broadgate Ri HORS LS18 ....85 M6
Broad Gates DOD/DAR S75 ....259 H6
Broadgate Wk HORS LS18 ....85 L6
Broad Head La HWTH BD22 ....78 A2
Broad Ings Wy HIPP HX3 ....147 L1
Broadlands AIRE BD20 ....2 A2
Broadlands Rd HOLM/MEL HD9 ..234 F3
Broadlands St BOW BD4 ....127 M2
Broadlands Wy EARD/LOFT WF3 ..154 G6
Broad La BOW BD4 ....107 J4
    BRAM LS13 ....107 J4
    GLE DN14 ....161 J7
    HBR HX7 ....120 D3
    HBR HX7 ....143 H5
    HEM/SK/SE WF9 ....246 A3
    HOLM/MEL HD9 ....253 M1
    HUDE HD5 ....15 M1
    LUD/ILL HX2 ....166 C1
    MILN OL16 ....228 C2
    SCFT LS14 ....111 H2
    TAD LS24 ....53 J4
    TOD OL14 ....141 M4
    UPML OL3 ....231 G7
Broad Lane Cl BRAM LS13 ....108 A2
Broadlea Av BRAM LS13 ....108 A2
Broadlea Cl BRAM LS13 ....108 A2
Broadlea Crs BRAM LS13 ....108 A2
    WBOW BD5 ....127 H4
Broadlea Gdns BRAM LS13 ....108 A2
Broadlea Gv BRAM LS13 ....108 A2
Broadlea Hl BRAM LS13 ....108 A2

Broadlea Mt BRAM LS13 ....108 B3
Broadlea Pl BRAM LS13 ....108 A2
Broadlea Rd BRAM LS13 ....108 A2
Broadlea St BRAM LS13 ....108 A2
Broadlea Ter BRAM LS13 ....108 A2
Broadlea Vw BRAM LS13 ....107 M2
Bradley Cl LUD/ILL HX2 ....145 L5
Bradley Gv LUD/ILL HX2 ....145 L5
Bradley Rd LUD/ILL HX2 ....145 L5
Broadmead CAS WF10 ....158 B6
Broadmeadows WKFDE WF1 ......176 F1
Broad Oak La HIPP HX3 ....147 M8
    STKB/PEN S36 ....268 B3
Broadoaks Cl EARL WF12 ....174 C7
Broad Oak St HIPP HX3 ....147 M8
Broad Shaw La MILN OL16 ....228 A4
Broadstone Rd KBTN HD8 ....256 B2
Broadstones Pk BGLY BD16 * 81 M3
Broadstone Wy BOW BD4 ....128 A2
Broad St BFD BD1 * 4 B2
    DEWS WF13 ....173 J8
    HFAX HX1 ....11 H5
    PDSY/CALV LS28 ....106 C3
    TOD OL14 ....141 K8
Broad Tree Rd HIPP HX3 ....146 C4
Broad Vw OSS WF5 ....197 H1
Broadway BFD BD1 ....4 E1
    BGLY BD16 ....81 J3
    BSLY S70 ....260 D6
    DOD/DAR S75 ....242 D5
    GSLY LS20 ....61 L6
    HIPP HX3 ....169 L1
    HORS LS18 ....85 H7
    HUD HD1 ....15 L5
    KSTL LS5 ....86 A7
    MSTN/BAR LS15 ....111 H8
    PONT WF8 ....181 G7
    RPDN/SBR HX6 ....166 F3
    WKFDW/WTN WF2 ....197 M2
Broadway Av WBOW BD5 ....126 A4
Broadway Cl WBOW BD5 ....126 A4
Broad Way Ct EARL WF12 ....196 A5
Broadway Dr HORS LS18 ....85 K6
Broadway Rd OSS WF5 ....197 H1
Broadwell Rd LUD/ILL HX2 ....145 L5
Brockadale Av PONT WF8 ....202 F1
Brock Bank HUDE HD5 ....148 M6
Brockholes La HOLM/MEL HD9 ..236 E4
    STKB/PEN S36 ....270 C7
Brockholes Rd HOLM/MEL HD9 ..236 F4
Brocklebank Cl BRAM LS13 ....58 D5
Brocklebank Rd MILN OL16 ....206 F7
Brocklehurst Av BOW BD4 ....261 M8
Brocklesby Dr WIL/AL BD15 ....105 K5
Brockley Cl TAD LS24 ....94 E3
Brocks LUD/ILL HX2 ....144 E8
Brockstones GTL/HWG HX4 * 168 B7
Brockwood Ct
    WKFDW/WTN WF2 ....221 L1
Brockwell Gdns RPDN/SBR HX6 ..167 J3
Brock Well La RPDN/SBR HX6 ....167 H4
Brodley Cl HIPP HX3 ....147 L6
Brodrick Ct HDGY LS6 ....108 F1
Broken Banks COL BB8 ....74 A2
Broken Cross HUDE HD5 ....215 G4
Broken Wy WBOW BD5 * 126 A4
Bromcliffe Pk BSLYN/ROY S71 ...262 A1
Bromet Pl ECHL BD2 ....105 K2
Bromfield WHIT OL12 * 206 B6
Bromfield Rd BOW BD4 ....127 J2
Bromley Av HOLM/MEL HD9 * ...236 F7
    ROY/SHW OL2 ....228 D8
Bromley Bank KBTN HD8 ....239 G8
Bromley Gv HWTH BD22 ....79 G1
Bromley Mt WKFDE WF1 ....13 H7
Bromley Rd BGLY BD16 ....81 J3
    BTLY WF17 ....174 A3
    HUDN HD2 ....192 B5
    SHPY BD18 ....82 A6
Bromley St CLECK BD19 ....149 M6
Brompton Av BOW BD4 ....127 J2
Brompton Gv BEE/HOL LS11 ......131 K4
Brompton Mt BEE/HOL LS11 ......131 K4
Brompton Rd BEE/HOL LS11 ......131 K4
Brompton Rw BEE/HOL LS11 * ..131 K4
Brompton Ter BEE/HOL LS11 .....131 K4
Brompton Vw BEE/HOL LS11 .....131 K4
Bronshill Gv WIL/AL BD15 ....103 L5
Bronte Av KNOT WF11 ....181 K2
Bronte Cl BSLYN/ROY S71 ....261 K3
    CLECK BD19 ....150 D5
    DEWS WF13 ....173 H6
    HTON BD9 ....104 A4
    HUDS HD4 ....213 M4
Bronte Ct PONT WF8 ....180 F4
Bronte Dr HWTH BD22 ....79 G6
Bronte Gv EARL WF12 ....223 L8
    MIRF WF14 ....194 B2
Bronte Old Rd CUL/OBY BD13 ...103 G8
Bronte Ri CAS WF10 ....180 F1
Bronte Rd BTLY WF17 ....151 G4
    KGHY BD21 ....3 J3
Bronte St HWTH BD22 * 78 D7
    KGHY BD21 ....3 J3
Bronte Vls HWTH BD22 ....79 H6
Bronte Wy BRFD/BLYE BD10 ....96 D2
    BRIG HD6 ....170 C2
    COL BB8 ....75 H2
    CUL/OBY BD13 ....103 H8
    HWTH BD22 ....125 K6
    MIRF WF14 ....194 B2
Brook Av ROY/SHW OL2 ....229 K6
Brook Cl OSS WF5 ....197 H1
Brookdale WHIT OL12 ....206 A3
Brookdale Av OSS WF5 ....174 E4
Brookdale Bank HUDW HD3 ......213 J1
Brook Dr GTL/HWG HX4 ....190 E2
Brooke Ct PONT WF8 ....202 E1
Brooke Fold HOLM/MEL HD9 .....236 C6
    CLECK BD19 ....150 C5
    HECK WF16 * 172 F1
Brookeville Av HIPP HX3 ....147 L1
Brooke Fld MIRF WF14 ....194 B4
Brookfield ROY/SHW OL2 ....229 J7
Brookfield Av BRAM LS13 ....84 D4
    CAS WF10 ....158 A5
    CLECK BD19 ....149 M5
    HDGY LS6 ....108 F2
    SHPY BD18 ....82 B4
Brookfield Ct NORM WF6 ....178 A4
Brookfield Dr FEA/AMT WF7 ......202 B6
    LIT OL15 ....185 H3
Brookfield Gdns BRAM LS13 ......84 D4
Brookfield Rd BFDE BD3 ....5 M5
    HDGY LS6 ....108 F2
    SHPY BD18 ....82 B4
Brookfield St BRIG HD6 ....170 C5
    HECK WF16 * 172 F1
    OSM LS9 ....10 A9
Brookfields HOR/CROF WF4 ......218 F1
Brookfields Av CLECK BD19 ....149 G6
Brookfields Rd LM/WK BD12 .....148 D5

Brookfield St MID LS10 ....9 K5
    TOD OL14 ....140 E5
Brookfield Ter CLECK BD19 ....149 M5
    MID LS10 * 9 K5
Brookfoot Av BIRK/DRI BD11 .....150 C1
Brookfoot La HIPP HX3 ....169 G3
Brook Gdns HOLM/MEL HD9 .....234 F3
Brook Grain Hl BRIG HD6 ....170 C6
Brook Hey Cl WHIT OL12 ....206 F2
Brookhill Av AL/HA/HU LS17 * 88 A2
Brookhill Cl AL/HA/HU LS17 ....88 A2
Brookhill Crs AL/HA/HU LS17 ....88 A2
Brookhill Dr AL/HA/HU LS17 ....88 A2
Brookhill Gv AL/HA/HU LS17 ....88 A2
Brook Hill La STKB/PEN S36 ....268 B3
Brookhouse Gdns IDLE BD10 ....84 B6
Brook House La STKB/PEN S36 ...269 H8
Brooklands HUDN HD2 ....257 J7
    GTL/HWG HX4 ....190 D2
    SCFT LS14 ....111 J3
Brooklands Cl SCFT LS14 ....111 K7
    WKFDW/WTN WF2 ....199 K7
Brooklands Ct OSS WF5 ....197 H2
    SCFT LS14 ....111 J3
Brooklands Crs HOR/CROF WF4 ..222 F5
    SCFT LS14 ....111 G2
    YEA LS19 ....62 D8
Brooklands Dr SCFT LS14 ....111 G2
    YEA LS19 ....62 D8
Brooklands Garth SCFT LS14 .....111 G3
Brooklands La ILK LS29 ....61 J1
    SCFT LS14 ....111 H2
Brooklands Rd AWLS/ASK DN6 ..249 L7
    WKFDW/WTN WF2 ....199 K7
Brooklands Ter SKP/WHF BD23 ...16 B3
Brookland St MILN OL16 * 228 D3
Brooklands Vw SCFT LS14 ....111 G3
Brooklands Wk ILK LS29 ....61 K1
Brook La AL/HA/HU LS17 ....44 B3
    LVSG WF15 ....171 L2
    MAR/SLWT HD7 ....212 F2
    PDSY/CALV LS28 ....106 D3
Brooklyn Av HUDE HD5 ....193 H8
    LIT OL15 ....185 J7
    MILN OL16 ....206 E7
    WOR/ARM LS12 ....108 E7
Brooklyn Dr CLECK BD19 ....149 M6
Brooklyn Pl WOR/ARM LS12 .....108 E7
Brooklyn Rd CLECK BD19 ....150 A6
Brooklyn St AIRE BD20 ....34 F5
    WOR/ARM LS12 ....108 E7
Brooklyn Ter BRIG HD6 ....170 A1
    WOR/ARM LS12 ....108 E7
Brook Rd DEWS WF13 ....173 K7
Brook Rw GTL/HWG HX4 * 168 B7
Brookroyd Av BRIG HD6 ....148 D8
Brookroyd Gdns BTLY WF17 ......151 H6
Brookroyd La BTLY WF17 ....151 H6
Brooksbank WKFDW/WTN WF2 ..12 C2
Brooksbank Dr MSTN/BAR LS15 ..111 H6
Brooksbank Gdns ELL HX5 ....169 H7
Brooksfield HEM/SK/SE WF9 .....246 F2
Brook Side MAR/SLWT HD7 ....212 C4
Brookside AL/HA/HU LS17 * 88 A1
    HBR HX7 ....143 G2
    HEM/SK/SE WF9 ....224 A7
    WBY LS22 ....30 A4
Brookside Dr BSLY S70 ....261 M8
Brookside Fold HWTH BD22 ....100 E4
Brookside St HEM/SK/SE WF9 ...247 H3
Brook's Pl WHIT OL12 ....206 A6
Brook St CAS WF10 ....158 A3
    DEWS WF13 ....173 H6
    HBR HX7 ....169 J8
    HBR HX7 ....143 J2
    HUD HD1 ....14 E5
    HUD HD1 ....15 H7
    HUDE HD5 ....15 L7
    ILK LS29 ....38 C2
    KGHY BD21 ....2 F8
    LIT OL15 ....207 L1
    LM/WK BD12 ....149 K2
    NORM WF6 ....178 B3
    OSS WF5 ....196 F1
    SKP/WHF BD23 ....184 E8
    WHIT OL12 ....12 E1
    WKFDE WF1 ....12 C1
Brooks Yd DEWS WF13 ....173 K7
    HUD HD1 ....14 F7
    HUDN HD2 ....171 J8
The Brook HBR HX7 ....143 M6
Brookvale BSLYN/ROY S71 ....261 M3
Brookwater Cl HIPP HX3 ....168 F3
Brookway FEA/AMT WF7 * 201 M1
    LIT OL15 ....207 J2
Broombank HUDN HD2 ....257 H1
    KBTN HD8 ....257 H1
Broomcliffe Gdns CUD/GR S72 ..244 F4
Broom Cl BSLY S70 ....261 M8
    DOD/DAR S75 ....242 C5
Broom Crs MID LS10 ....132 A7
Broomcroft CLAY BD14 ....125 K2
Broomcroft Rd OSS WF5 ....196 F2
Broom Cross MID LS10 ....132 A7
Broome Av ECHL BD2 ....105 G3
Broome Cl NORM WF6 ....178 C2
Broomer St DEWS WF13 ....173 K7
Broome Av BHP/TINH LS16 ....86 D2
    CLAY BD14 ....125 J3
    GTL/HWG HX4 ....168 F3
Broomfield Av HIPP HX3 ....168 F3
Broomfield Cl BSLY S70 ....260 D6
    KBTN HD8 ....217 L7
Broomfield Crs HDGY LS6 * 108 F2
Broom Field La KBTN HD8 ....217 K6
Broomfield Pl CLAY BD14 ....125 J3
    HDGY LS6 ....108 F2
Broomfield Rd HDGY LS6 ....108 F2
    HUD HD1 ....191 M8
    HUDN HD2 ....192 C1
    KGHY BD21 ....3 J3
Broomfield Sq ROCH OL11 * 228 B1
Broomfield St CUL/OBY BD13 ....125 G5
    HDGY LS6 * 108 F2
    KGHY BD21 ....3 J3
Broomfield Ter CLECK BD19 ......149 K8
    HDGY LS6 ....108 F2
    HUD HD1 ....191 M8
Broomfield Vw HDGY LS6 ....108 F2
Broom Gdns MID LS10 ....132 A7
Broom Garth MID LS10 ....132 A8
Broom Gv MID LS10 ....132 B8
Broom Hall Av WKFDE WF1 ....176 C4
Broom Hall Crs WKFDE WF1 .....176 C4
Broomhead St CUD/GR S72 ....262 A8
Broomhey Av KBTN HD8 ....217 M8
Broomhill Av AL/HA/HU LS17 ....87 M4
    KGHY BD21 ....2 D1

KNOT WF11 ...182 D3
Broomhill Cl HOLM/MEL HD9 ...254 F3
KNOT WF11 ...182 D3
Broomhill Crs AL/HA/HU LS17 ...87 M4
KNOT WF11 ...182 D3
Broomhill Dr AL/HA/HU LS17 ...87 M5
KGHY BD21 ...2 D9
KNOT WF11 ...182 D3
Broomhill Gv KGHY BD21 ...2 D9
KNOT WF11 ...182 D3
Broomhill Mt KGHY BD21 ...2 D9
KNOT WF11 ...182 D3
Broom Hill Rd GTL/HWG HX4 ...190 A6
Broomhill Sq KNOT WF11 ...182 D3
Broomhill Wk KGHY BD21 ...79 J2
KNOT WF11 ...182 D3
Broomhouse Cl KBTN HD8 ...257 J1
Broom Mt MID LS10 ...132 B8
Broom Nook MID LS10 ...132 A7
Broom Pl MID LS10 ...132 A7
Broom Rd MID LS10 ...132 A7
TAD LS24 ...71 K4
Broomsdale Rd BTLY WF17 ...174 A1
Broom St BOW BD4 ...5 C8
CLECK BD19 ...149 K8
KGHY BD21 ...3 H7
MILN OL16 ...229 G5
Broom Ter MID LS10 ...132 B7
Broom Vw MID LS10 ...132 B7
Broomy Lea La HOLM/MEL HD9 ...236 B7
Broster Av HWTH BD22 ...2 B4
Brotherton Av WKFDE WF1 ...13 H3
Brougham Rd HIPP HX3 ...10 F1
MAR/SLWT HD7 ...233 H2
Brougham St HIPP HX3 ...11 G1
SKP/WHF HX5 ...16 C3
Broughton Av BOW BD4 ...127 K5
OSM LS9 ...110 C4
Broughton Rd HUDS HD4 ...213 K3
SKP/WHF BD23 ...16 A5
Broughton Ter PDSY/CALV LS28 ...107 F6
Brow Bottom La LUD/ILL HX2 ...123 K8
Browcliff AIRE BD20 ...36 C2
Brow Cl BSLY S70 ...261 H8
Browfield Vw HWTH BD22 ...79 G1
Browfoot SHPY BD18 ...82 F7
Browfoot Dr LUD/ILL HX2 ...145 M7
Brow Foot Gate La LUD/ILL HX2 ...145 M8
Browgate BAIL BD17 ...82 F2
Brow Grains Rd HOLM/MEL HD9 ...234 C5
Brow La CLAY BD14 ...125 J5
HIPP HX3 ...124 C8
HIPP HX3 ...125 M8
HIPP HX3 ...147 J3
HOLM/MEL HD9 ...254 A3
KBTN HD8 ...239 M8
Brow Rd HDU HD1 ...14 A9
Brown Av BEE/HOL LS11 ...131 G2
Brown Bank La AIRE BD20 ...36 B3
Brown Bank Rd LIT OL15 ...207 H3
Brownberrie Av HORS LS18 ...85 L5
Brownberrie Crs HORS LS18 ...85 K3
Brownberrie Dr HORS LS18 ...85 L5
Brownberrie Gdns HORS LS18 ...85 K3
Brownberrie La HORS LS18 ...85 J3
Brownberrie Wk HORS LS18 ...85 L3
Brownberry Gv HWTH BD22 ...125 M7
Brown Birks St TOD OL14 ...140 F5
Brown Hill Av OSM LS9 ...110 C4
Brownhill Cl BTLY WF17 * ...151 H5
Brown Hill Crs OSM LS9 ...110 C4
Brownhill Crs HEM/SK/SE WF9 ...223 H4
Brown Hill Dr BIRK/DRI BD11 ...128 C8
Brownhill Dr BIRK/DRI BD11 ...128 C8
Brownhill La COL BB8 ...52 B7
HBR HX7 ...142 A2
Brownhill La HOLM/MEL HD9 ...253 H5
Brownhill Rd BTLY WF17 ...151 H5
Brown Hill Ter OSM LS9 ...110 C4
Brownhill Vw WHIT OL12 ...206 H5
Browning Av HIPP HX3 * ...168 F3
Browning Rd HUDN HD2 ...192 F3
Browning St BFDE BD3 ...5 L6
Brown La East BEE/HOL LS11 ...8 A6
Brown La West WOR/ARM LS12 ...131 G1
Brown Lee La WIL/AL BD15 ...102 C2
Brown Lodge St LIT OL15 ...207 H3
Brown Pl BEE/HOL LS11 ...131 G2
Brown Rd BEE/HOL LS11 ...131 G2
Brownroyd Av BSLYN/ROY S71 ...243 L4
Brown Royd Av HUDE HD5 ...15 M3
Brownroyd Hill Rd WBSY BD6 ...126 D5
Brownroyd St HOLM/MEL HD9 ...236 A2
Brownroyd St GIR BD8 ...104 D7
Brownroyd Wk WBOW BD5 ...126 D4
Browns Cl AIRE BD20 ...34 E1
Brown's Edge La STKB/PEN S36 ...269 J8
Brown's Edge Rd STKB/PEN S36 ...256 A6
Brownside Rd MILN OL16 ...206 D3
Brown's Knoll Rd HUDS HD4 ...237 H3
Brown Springs La HWTH BD22 ...79 K2
Brown's St BTLY WF17 * ...173 K2
Brown St KGHY BD21 ...3 J3
LIT OL15 ...207 J1
MIRF WF14 ...194 B3
Brow Rd HWTH BD22 ...78 F8
Browsfield Rd ILK LS29 ...18 F6
Browsholme St KGHY BD21 * ...2 F7
ROCH OL11 ...228 C2
Brow Top Rd HWTH BD22 ...79 G7
Brow Wood Crs ECHL BD2 ...105 C3
Brow Wood Ri HIPP HX3 ...125 M8
Brow Wood Rd BTLY WF17 ...151 K5
HIPP HX3 ...125 M8
Browwood Ter WBSY BD6 ...126 B7
Bruce Av BSLY S70 ...261 H6
Bruce Gdns WOR/ARM LS12 ...109 G3
Bruce Lawn WOR/ARM LS12 ...109 G3
Bruce St HFAX HX1 ...10 A3
Brudenell Av HDGY LS6 ...6 A1
Brudenell Gv HDGY LS6 ...6 A3
Brudenell Mt HDGY LS6 ...6 A1
Brudenell Rd HDGY LS6 ...109 G3
Brudenell St HDGY LS6 ...6 A1
Brudenell Vw HDGY LS6 ...6 A3
Brunel Cl HTON BD9 ...104 C4
Brunel Ct HIPP HX3 ...146 D4
Brunel Rd WKFDW/WTN WF2 ...176 B2
Brunswick CROF/CROF WF4 ...222 C4
Brunswick Cl BSLYN/ROY S71 ...243 G1
Brunswick Ct LDSU LS2 ...7 J1
Brunswick Dr DEWS WF13 ...173 J1
Brunswick Gdns GFTH/SHER LS25 ...113 H7
HFAX HX1 ...10 F7
Brunswick Pl IDLE BD10 ...83 M7
PDSY/CALV LS28 ...107 G6
Brunswick Rw LDSU LS2 ...7 J8

Brunswick St BGLY BD16 ...81 K3
BTLY WF17 * ...173 L1
CUL/QBY BD13 ...80 A8
CUL/QBY BD13 ...125 H5
DEWS WF13 ...173 J5
HBR HX7 ...143 H3
HECK WF16 * ...172 F7
HUD HD1 ...14 E6
MILN OL16 ...206 C6
MOR LS27 ...152 C1
ROY/SHW OL2 ...229 K7
WKFDE WF1 ...13 G4
Brunswick St Bungalows WKFDE WF1 ...13 H5
Brunswick Ter LDSU LS2 ...7 G7
Bruntcliffe Av MOR LS27 ...152 A1
Bruntcliffe Cl MOR LS27 ...152 B2
Bruntcliffe Dr MOR LS27 ...152 B2
Bruntcliffe La MOR LS27 ...152 B2
Bruntcliffe Rd MOR LS27 ...151 M2
Bruntcliffe Wy MOR LS27 ...152 A1
Brunthwaite Br AIRE BD20 ...36 C7
Brunthwaite Bridge La AIRE BD20 ...36 B7
Brunthwaite La AIRE BD20 ...36 C5
Brussels St OSM LS9 ...9 K1
Bryan Cl CAS WF10 ...157 J6
Bryan Rd GTL/HWG HX4 ...168 F8
HUDW HD3 ...191 M6
Bryanstone Rd BOW BD4 ...127 K4
Bryan St BRIG HD6 ...170 C5
PDSY/CALV LS28 ...106 D7
Bryan St North PDSY/CALV LS28 ...106 F7
Bryan Ter HUDW HD3 ...191 G8
Bryer St DEWS WF13 ...173 L5
Bryngate RTHW LS26 ...133 L8
Bryony Ct MID LS10 ...154 A1
Bubwith Gv LUD/ILL HX2 * ...146 A8
Buckden Ct AIRE BD20 ...36 A4
Buckden Rd BSLY S70 ...260 F4
HUDW HD3 ...191 M6
Buckfast Ct IDLE BD10 ...61 H7
Buckingham Av HDCY LS6 * ...109 G2
Buckingham Ct BSLYN/ROY S71 ...243 K2
WKFDE WF1 * ...13 L7
Buckingham Crs CLAY BD14 ...125 M1
Buckingham Dr HDGY LS6 ...109 G3
WKFDE WF1 ...13 L8
Buckingham Gv HDGY LS6 ...109 G2
Buckingham Mt HDGY LS6 ...109 G3
Buckingham Park Cl ROY/SHW OL2 ...229 K6
Buckingham Rd HDGY LS6 ...109 G3
Buckingham St MILN OL16 ...206 C6
Buckingham Vw BSLYN/ROY S71 ...243 K2
KNOT WF11 ...159 M7
Buckland Pl HFAX HX1 ...146 A8
Buck La BAIL BD17 ...83 H3
Buckle La ILK LS29 ...61 L2
NORM WF6 ...178 C5
Buckley Brook St WHIT OL12 ...206 D4
Buckley Cha MILN OL16 ...229 G1
Buckley Cl BSLY S70 ...261 H6
Buckley Dr UPML OL3 ...230 E5
Buckley Farm La WHIT OL12 ...206 D3
Buckley Flds WHIT OL12 ...206 C4
Buckley Hill La MILN OL16 ...229 G1
Buckley La LUD/ILL HX2 ...145 L4
WHIT OL12 ...206 D3
Buckley Rd WHIT OL12 ...206 D4
Buckley St MILN OL16 ...206 C6
ROY/SHW OL2 ...229 L7
Buckley Vw TOD OL14 ...141 J8
WHIT OL12 ...206 D3
Buckley Wood Bottom TOD OL14 ...163 K1
Buck Mill La IDLE BD10 ...83 J3
Buck Pk CUL/QBY BD13 * ...102 A4
Buckrose St HUD HD1 ...14 F1
Buckrose Ter HUDN HD2 ...14 E1
Buck Stone Av AL/HA/HU LS17 ...87 J2
Buck Stone Cl AL/HA/HU LS17 ...87 J2
Buck Stone Crs AL/HA/HU LS17 ...87 J2
Buck Stone Dr YEA LS19 ...84 C3
Buck Stone Gdns AL/HA/HU LS17 ...87 J2
Buck Stone Garth AIRE BD20 ...58 F5
Buck Stone Gn AL/HA/HU LS17 ...87 H2
Buck Stone Gv AL/HA/HU LS17 ...87 H2
Buck Stone La HWTH BD22 ...55 G4
Buck Stone Mt AL/HA/HU LS17 ...87 H2
Buck Stone Ov AL/HA/HU LS17 ...87 H2
Buck Stone Ri AL/HA/HU LS17 ...87 H2
Buck Stone Rd AL/HA/HU LS17 ...87 H2
Buckstones Rd OLD OL3 ...230 H1
ROY/SHW OL2 ...229 L5
Buck Stone Vw AL/HA/HU LS17 * ...87 H2
Buck Stone Wy AL/HA/HU LS17 ...87 H2
Buck St BFDE BD3 ...5 K8
COL BB8 ...74 A1
CUL/QBY BD13 ...102 A6
Buckthorne Cl EARD/LOFT WF3 ...153 M6
Buckthorne Ct EARD/LOFT WF3 ...153 M6
Buckthorne Dr EARD/LOFT WF3 ...153 M6
Buckthorne Fold EARD/LOFT WF3 * ...153 M6
Buckton Cl BEE/HOL LS11 * ...8 C8
Buckton Mt BEE/HOL LS11 ...8 C8
Buckton Vw BEE/HOL LS11 ...8 C8
Bude Ct BSLYN/ROY S71 ...261 L3
Bude Rd BEE/HOL LS11 ...131 K4
WBOW BD5 ...127 H5
Buersil Av WIL/AL BD15 ...228 D2
Buersil St MILN OL16 ...228 D3
Bula Cl GFTH/SHER LS25 ...135 K4
Bulay Rd HUD HD1 ...214 D2
Bullace Trees La LVSG WF15 ...171 M3
Bull Close La HFAX HX1 ...10 F7
Bullcroft Cl AWLS/ASK DN6 ...249 L5
Bullenshaw Rd HEM/SK/SE WF9 ...223 M8
Bullenshaw Vis HEM/SK/SE WF9 * ...224 C8
Buller Cl OSM LS9 ...110 D5
Buller Ct OSM LS9 ...110 D5
Buller Gv OSM LS9 ...110 D5
Buller St BOW BD4 ...127 L1
RTHW LS26 ...133 L8
Bullerthorpe La RTHW LS26 ...134 A6
Bullfields Cl EARL WF12 ...196 A4
The Bullfield BGLY BD16 ...80 D5
Bull Gn HFAX HX1 ...11 G7
Bull Green Rd HUDW HD3 ...191 H8
Bull Haw La DOD/DAR S75 ...258 B5
Bullhouse La STKB/PEN S36 ...269 L4
Bull La HEM/SK/SE WF9 ...246 D4
HOR/CROF WF4 ...220 B1
Bullough La RTHW LS26 ...133 H7
Bull Ring HOFT WF1 * ...12 E7
Bull Royd Av GIR BD8 ...104 A6
Bull Royd Crs GIR BD8 ...104 A6
Bull Royd Dr GIR BD8 ...104 A6
Bull Royd La GIR BD8 ...104 A6
Bullstyle Rd PONT WF8 ...170 H7
Bullytree La GFTH/SHER LS25 ...137 L2
Bulwer St MILN OL16 ...206 C6
Bundria Ct GIR BD8 ...104 E4

Bungalow Rd AIRE BD20 ...34 D8
The Bungalows HIPP HX3 ...169 G4
KBTN HD8 ...240 A4
Bunkers HI GFTH/SHER LS25 ...114 A1
HOLM/MEL HD9 ...254 C1
SKP/WHF BD23 ...16 C2
Bunker's Hill La HWTH BD22 ...78 F1
Bunny Pk HUDS HD4 ...213 M3
Bunting Dr WBSY BD6 ...125 K5
Bunyan St WHIT OL12 ...206 C6
Burbeary Rd HUDS HD4 ...214 A3
Burberry Cl BOW BD4 ...127 L6
Burchall Fld MILN OL16 ...206 D7
Burchett Gv HDGY LS6 ...6 D1
Burchett Pl HDGY LS6 ...6 D1
Burchett Ter HDGY LS6 ...6 D1
Burcote Pl CTHN BD7 ...104 D8
Burdett Ter BULY LS4 ...108 E4
Burdock Wy HFAX HX1 ...10 F6
Burfitts Rd HUDW HD3 ...191 K7
Burghley Ms MID LS10 ...153 M3
Burgh Mill Gdns DEWS WF13 ...173 J7
Burgh Mill La DEWS WF13 ...173 J7
Burghwallis La AWLS/ASK DN6 ...249 L1
Burghwallis Rd AWLS/ASK DN6 ...227 J1
Burkill St DEWS WF13 ...173 K6
Burking Rd DEWS WF13 ...173 K6
Burleigh St HFAX HX1 * ...198 F4
Burley Bank La HOLM/MEL HD9 ...253 G8
Burley Cl GFTH/SHER LS25 ...138 B2
Burley Ct AIRE BD20 ...56 E1
Burley Hill Crs BULY LS4 ...108 C3
Burley Hill Dr BULY LS4 ...108 D3
Burley La HORS LS18 ...85 K7
ILK LS29 ...40 C8
Burley Lodge Pl HDGY LS6 * ...109 G5
Burley Lodge Rd HDGY LS6 ...109 G5
Burley Lodge St HDGY LS6 ...109 G5
Burley Lodge Ter HDGY LS6 ...109 G4
Burley Ms AIRE BD20 ...56 E1
Burley Rd BULY LS4 ...108 E3
Burley St BVRD LS3 ...8 B8
ECHL BD2 ...104 F2
ELL HX5 ...169 H8
Burley Wk BTLY WF17 ...173 K1
Burley Wood Crs BULY LS4 ...108 C3
Burley Wood La BULY LS4 ...108 C3
Burley Wood Mt BULY LS4 ...108 C3
Burley Wood Vw BULY LS4 ...108 C3
Burlington Ar BSLY S70 ...261 H5
Burlington Pl BEE/HOL LS11 ...131 K4
Burlington Rd BEE/HOL LS11 ...131 K4
Burlington St GIR BD8 ...4 D2
HFAX HX1 ...10 B5
ROCH OL11 ...228 C2
Burmantofts St OSM LS9 ...9 L8
Burn Bridge La PBR HG3 ...26 E4
Burn Bridge Ov PBR HG3 ...26 D2
Burn Bridge Rd PBR HG3 ...26 D2
Burned Gv HIPP HX3 ...125 L7
Burneston Gdns WBSY BD6 ...126 A6
Burnett Av WBOW BD5 ...126 F3
Burnett Pl WBOW BD5 ...126 F3
Burnett Ri CUL/QBY BD13 ...124 E6
Burnett St BFD BD1 ...5 H5
Burnham Av BOW BD4 ...127 K5
DOD/DAR S75 ...242 D5
Burnham Rd GFTH/SHER LS25 ...135 H1
Burniston Cl WIL/AL BD15 ...102 C3
Burnlee Rd HOLM/MEL HD9 ...254 A2
Burnley Rd COL BB8 ...74 D5
HBR HX7 ...143 K4
RPDN/SBR HX6 ...167 K1
TOD OL14 ...140 D4
TOD OL14 ...141 M8
Burnleys Ct RTHW LS26 ...156 F5
Burnleys Dr RTHW LS26 ...156 F5
Burnleys Ms RTHW LS26 ...156 F6
Burnleys Vw RTHW LS26 ...156 F5
Burnleyville CLECK BD19 ...150 F3
Burnley Rd BRFD/BLYE BB10 ...118 A7
TOD OL14 ...118 F1
Burnsall Rd HUDW HD3 ...191 L4
BRIG HD6 ...169 M6
BTLY WF17 ...173 J1
Burns Av HEM/SK/SE WF9 ...246 B5
Burnsall Ct BTLY WF17 ...150 F4
Burnsdale AL/HA/HU LS17 ...103 J3
Burns Hi ILK LS29 ...19 G6
Burnside Av SKP/WHF BD23 ...16 B4
Burnside Cl BTLY WF17 ...151 H5
Burnside Ct HOLM/MEL HD9 ...254 A2
Burnside Dr HOLM/MEL HD9 ...254 A2
Burnside Rd HUD HD1 ...14 D6
Burns Wy BSPA/BRAM LS23 ...48 F8
Burnt Acres La TOD OL14 ...142 D6
Burnt Edge La HBR HX7 ...141 M2
Burnt House Cl TOD OL14 ...141 J8
Burnt Plats La MAR/SLWT HD7 ...211 J4
Burnt Side Rd WOR/ARM LS12 ...129 L4
Burntwood Av HEM/SK/SE WF9 ...246 A4
Burntwood Bank HEM/SK/SE WF9 ...245 M1
Burnt Wood Crs HEM/SK/SE WF9 ...246 B5
Burntwood Dr HEM/SK/SE WF9 ...246 A5
Burntwood Gv HEM/SK/SE WF9 ...246 E5
Burnt Wood La CUD/GR S72 ...246 A5
Burntwood Rd CUD/GR S72 ...245 K8
Burnup Gv CLECK BD19 ...149 L2
Burnwells Av IDLE BD10 ...83 J4
Burrage St IDLE BD10 ...81 H7
Burras Av OT LS21 ...41 H7
Burras Dr OT LS21 ...41 H7
Burras La OT LS21 ...41 H7
Burras Rd BOW BD4 ...127 K4

Burrel Cl WBY LS22 ...48 C1
Burrell St WKFDE WF1 ...13 H3
The Burrows BTLY WF17 ...151 H7
Burrow St WBOW BD5 ...4 E8
Burr Tree Dr MSTN/BAR LS15 ...111 M7
Burr Tree Garth MSTN/BAR LS15 * ...111 M7
Burr Tree V MSTN/BAR LS15 * ...111 M7
Burrwood Wy GTL/HWG HX4 ...190 D1
Burton Acres La KBTN HD8 ...216 A7
Burton Acres Ms KBTN HD8 ...216 A6
Burton Acres Wy KBTN HD8 ...216 A7
Burton Av BEE/HOL LS11 ...9 C9
BSLYN/ROY S71 ...261 M2
Burton Bank Rd BSLYN/ROY S71 ...261 G2
Burton Crs BSLYN/ROY S71 ...262 A1
HDGY LS6 ...86 F8
Burton Ms AL/HA/HU LS17 ...87 M1
Burton Rd BEE/HOL LS11 ...9 G9
BSLYN/ROY S71 ...261 J3
Burton Rw BEE/HOL LS11 ...9 H8
Burton Royd La KBTN HD8 ...216 D7
Burtons Ar LDS LS9 ...9 G1
Burton St AIRE BD20 ...57 K5
BEE/HOL LS11 ...9 G8
BOW BD4 ...127 J2
BSLYN/ROY S71 ...261 J3
CAS WF10 ...160 C2
Burton Ter BEE/HOL LS11 ...131 L3
BSLYN/ROY S71 ...261 K6
Burwood Rd HUDW HD3 ...191 K6
Busely Ct MOR LS27 ...152 B1
Busfield St BGLY BD16 ...81 H3
BOW BD4 ...127 K3
Bush Hill Fold CUL/QBY BD13 ...124 E4
Bush St SE HEM/SK/SE WF9 ...224 A8
Busker La KBTN HD8 ...239 M5
Busk La TAD LS24 ...95 G7
Buslingthorpe Gn CHAL LS7 ...7 G2
Buslingthorpe La CHAL LS7 ...7 J2
Bussey Ct HDGY LS6 ...6 E1
Busy La SHPY BD18 ...83 G5
Butcher Hill Station Rd HEM/SK/SE WF9 ...224 A6
Butcher La RTHW LS26 ...155 G1
Butcher St BEE/HOL LS11 ...8 E3
BFD BD1 ...4 C7
Bute Av BRIG HD6 ...170 C1
Bute St ECHL BD2 ...104 F2
Butler La BAIL BD17 ...82 F2
Butler St East BFDE BD3 ...5 K4
Butler St West BFDE BD3 ...5 K4
Butterbowl Dr WOR/ARM LS12 ...130 A1
Butterbowl Gdns WOR/ARM LS12 ...130 B1
Butterbowl Garth WOR/ARM LS12 ...130 A1
Butterbowl Gv WOR/ARM LS12 ...130 A1
Butterbowl Lawn WOR/ARM LS12 ...130 A1
Butterbowl Mt WOR/ARM LS12 ...130 B1
Butterbowl Rd WOR/ARM LS12 ...130 B1
Buttercross AWLS/ASK DN6 ...249 J4
Buttercross Cl AWLS/ASK DN6 ...249 J3
Buttercross Dr CUD/GR S72 ...263 G6
Buttercup Wy HEM/SK/SE WF9 ...225 H7
Butterfield St OSM LS9 ...9 M8
Butterley La BSLY S70 ...261 M8
Butterley Rd HEM/SK/SE WF9 ...255 H1
Butterleys DOD/DAR S75 ...260 C7
Butterley St MID LS10 ...9 H5
Buttermeade Cl WBSY BD6 ...126 A6
Buttermere Av COL BB8 ...52 B8
WBY LS22 ...29 L8
Buttermere Cft WKFDW/WTN WF2 ...199 J8
Buttermere Dr HUDE HD5 ...15 L6
Buttermere Rd ROY/SHW OL2 ...228 F7
Buttermere Wy BSLYN/ROY S71 * ...262 D6
Butternab Rdg HUDS HD4 ...213 M6
Butternab Rd HUDS HD4 ...213 L6
Buttershaw Dr WBSY BD6 ...126 A6
Buttershaw La LVSG WF15 ...171 K1
WBSY BD6 ...126 D7
Butterton Cl DOD/DAR S75 ...242 E5
Butterwick Gdns WBY LS22 ...47 L1
Butterwood Cl HUDS HD4 ...213 M6
Butterworth End La RPDN/SBR HX6 ...167 J7
Butterworth Hall MILN OL16 ...229 J1
Butterworth La RPDN/SBR HX6 ...167 C7
Butterworth St LIT OL15 ...207 J1
Butt Hedge RYKW YO26 ...33 J4
Butt Hill GFTH/SHER LS25 ...135 J5
Buttholme Ga WBSY BD6 ...126 B6
Butt La HOLM/MEL HD9 ...255 C4
HWTH BD22 ...78 E7
IDLE BD10 ...83 K6
WOR/ARM LS12 ...130 D7
Button Hole ROY/SHW OL2 ...229 M7
Button Pk PONT WF8 ...180 E7
Buttress La LUD/ILL HX2 ...145 L2
The Butts Av MILN OL16 ...206 B7
Butts Bottom HBR HX7 ...143 J5
Butts Cl HUDS HD4 ...237 J5
Butts Ct LDS LS1 ...9 G7
Butts Garth SCFT LS14 ...90 B1
Butts Green La LUD/ILL HX2 ...145 H7
Butts Green Rd LUD/ILL HX2 ...145 H7
Butts HI CLECK BD19 ...150 C6
Butts La GFTH/SHER LS25 ...137 L6
HOR/CROF WF4 ...196 E1
TOD OL14 ...141 M5
Butts Mt WOR/ARM LS12 ...108 D8
Butts Rd HUDS HD4 ...215 G8
The Butts MILN OL16 ...206 B7
Butts Wy HUDS HD4 ...215 G8
Butts Yd CLECK BD19 ...149 M7
Buxton Av HTON BD9 ...104 E2
Buxton Crs MILN OL16 ...228 D2
Buxton La MILN OL16 ...228 D2
Buxton Pl WKFDE WF1 ...176 D6
Buxton Rd BSLYN/ROY S71 ...243 J7
Buxton St HIPP HX3 ...10 C1
HTON BD9 ...104 D4
KGHY BD21 ...3 H7
Buxton Wy HIPP HX3 ...10 C1
HUD HD1 ...14 F8
Byland LUD/ILL HX2 ...123 H4
Byland Cl BSPA/BRAM LS23 ...48 E7
Byland Gv WIL/AL BD15 ...103 H4
Byland Wy BSLYN/ROY S71 ...261 L4
Byram Ar HUD HD1 * ...14 F6
Byram Park Av KNOT WF11 ...160 A6

Byram Park Rd KNOT WF11 ...159 M6
Byram St HUD HD1 ...14 F6
Byre Wy HWTH BD22 * ...79 G1
Byrl St KGHY BD21 ...3 H2
Byron Av AWLS/ASK DN6 ...227 L5
Byron Dr BSLYN/ROY S71 ...167 J7
Byron Gv DEWS WF13 ...173 G4
EARD/LOFT WF3 ...155 G8
Byron Ms BGLY BD16 ...81 J1
Byron Rd COL BB8 ...74 C1
Byron St BFDE BD3 ...5 L4
HFAX HX1 ...10 A5
LDSU LS2 ...7 J7
RPDN/SBR HX6 ...167 K1
SKP/WHF BD23 ...16 C3
TOD OL14 ...141 F8
The Byways PONT WF8 ...180 F8
Bywell Cl EARL WF12 ...174 B5
Bywell Rd EARL WF12 ...174 B5

C

Cabbage HI WOR/ARM LS12 ...108 D8
Cabin Rd OT LS21 ...63 K1
Cad Beeston Ms BEE/HOL LS11 * ...8 C9
Cadney Cft HFAX HX1 ...11 G7
Cadogan Av HUDW HD3 ...191 K6
Cadwell Cl CUD/GR S72 ...244 E6
Caenarvon Cl BTLY WF17 ...151 H4
Caernarvon Av GFTH/SHER LS25 ...113 K7
Caesar St ROCH OL11 ...228 C2
Cain Cl OSM LS9 ...110 B7
Cain La HIPP HX3 ...169 G2
Caina Cl Av CSLY LS20 ...61 L5
Cairn Cl AIRE BD20 ...57 J4
Cairns Cl ECHL BD2 ...105 H3
Caister Cl BTLY WF17 ...151 H4
Caister Gv KGHY BD21 * ...79 K2
Caister St KGHY BD21 ...79 K2
Caister Wy KGHY BD21 ...79 K2
Caistor Gv BSLY S70 ...260 F2
Calcaria Crs TAD LS24 ...71 K4
Calcaria Rd TAD LS24 ...71 K4
Calde Ct LM/WK BD12 ...127 L6
Caidene Av HBR HX7 ...143 M5
LM/WK BD12 ...127 G8
Caldene Cft HBR HX7 ...143 L5
Calder Av BSLYN/ROY S71 ...244 D3
LIT OL15 ...185 J2
LUD/ILL HX2 ...168 B1
Calder Bank Rd EARL WF12 ...173 K8
Calder Banks CUL/QBY BD13 ...125 J5
Calder Brook HBR HX7 ...143 L5
Calderbrook Rd LIT OL15 ...185 K6
Caldercliffe Rd HUDS HD4 ...214 B5
Calder Cl OSS WF5 ...196 E1
CAS WF10 ...29 M6
Calder Crs BSLY S70 ...261 H5
Caldercroft ELL HX5 ...169 J8
Calderdale Wy BRIG HD6 ...170 E1
ELL HX5 ...169 C7
GTL/HWG HX4 ...168 C6
HBR HX7 ...164 F3
HIPP HX3 ...147 J1
Calder Dr HUDS HD4 ...214 B6
Calder Edge TOD OL14 * ...142 C7
Calder Gv HBR HX7 ...144 A5
ROY/SHW OL2 ...229 J6
Calder Island Wy WKFDW/WTN WF2 ...198 D4
Calder Rd DEWS WF13 ...195 G1
MIRF WF14 ...194 C3
Calderstone Av WBSY BD6 ...125 M6
Calderstone Ct HOR/CROF WF4 ...196 C2
Calder St BRIG HD6 ...170 E5
CAS WF10 ...157 K6
GTL/HWG HX4 ...168 C6
MILN OL16 ...206 D4
TOD OL14 ...163 K1
WKFDE WF1 ...12 F7
Calder Ter HBR HX7 * ...143 H3
HIPP HX3 ...168 A3
Caldervale Rd BSLYN/ROY S71 ...244 A2
Calder Vale Rd HOR/CROF WF4 ...197 L6
WKFDE WF1 ...13 H4
Calder Vw BRIG HD6 ...170 B5
HOR/CROF WF4 ...220 A1
OSS WF5 ...196 C5
Calder Wy AIRE BD20 ...36 A6
Caldicott Cl WKFDW/WTN WF2 ...175 K4
Caledonian Rd EARL WF12 ...173 L8
Caledonia Rd BTLY WF17 ...173 M1
KGHY BD21 ...3 H7
Caledonia St BOW BD4 ...5 H9
WBOW BD5 ...4 F7
Calf Hey LIT OL15 ...185 L6
Calf Hey La STKB/PEN S36 ...255 M7
Calf Hey North ROCH OL11 ...228 C2
Calf Hey Rd ROY/SHW OL2 ...229 M6
Calf Hey South ROCH OL11 ...228 C2
Calf Hill Rd HOLM/MEL HD9 ...236 D6
Calgary Crs EARD/LOFT WF3 ...153 H7
Calgary Pl CHAL LS7 * ...87 M8
California Crs BSLY S70 ...261 G2
California Dr CAS WF10 ...178 A1
HOR/CROF WF4 ...197 L5
TOD OL14 ...163 J4
California Gdns BSLY S70 ...261 H6
California La CLECK BD19 ...150 D5
California Ms MOR LS27 ...130 D8
MOR LS27 * ...152 C2
California Ter BSLY S70 ...261 G2
Callards Rd MILN OL16 ...207 G2
Callis La STKB/PEN S36 ...271 G5
Callis Wy STKB/PEN S36 ...270 F4
Call La LDS LS1 ...9 H1
The Calls LDSU LS2 ...9 J1
Calmlands Rd HOLM/MEL HD9 ...234 D5
Calpin Cl IDLE BD10 * ...83 K6
Calton Gv KGHY BD21 ...58 B8
Calton St HUD HD1 ...15 G3
KGHY BD21 ...2 E8
Calver Av HWTH BD22 ...2 B3
Calver Gv KGHY BD21 ...2 E5
Calverley Av BFDE BD3 ...105 M6
BRAM LS13 ...107 K3
Calverley Ct BRAM LS13 * ...107 K3
RTHW LS26 ...155 K1
Calverley Cutting IDLE BD10 ...84 B6
Calverley Dr BRAM LS13 ...107 K3
Calverley Gdns BRAM LS13 ...107 J2
Calverley Garth BRAM LS13 ...107 K3
Calverley Gn NORM WF6 ...178 B3
Calverley Green Rd NORM WF6 ...178 B3
Calverley Gv BRAM LS13 ...107 K3
HORS LS18 ...85 H6
PDSY/CALV LS28 ...84 E8
Calverley Moor Av PDSY/CALV LS28 ...106 C5

Cemetery La AIRE BD20 ....57 K4
  EARD/LOFT WF3 ....154 E5
  RPDN/SBR HX6 ....167 J3
Cemetery Rd BEE/HOL LS11 ....8 C8
  BGLY BD16 ....81 G2
  BSLY S70 ....261 H6
  BTLY WF17 ....173 K1
  CUD/GR S72 ....245 K8
  DEWS WF13 ....173 J7
  GIR BD8 ....104 B7
  HECK WF16 ....172 F2
  HEM/SK/SE WF9 ....223 L7
  HOLM/MEL HD9 ....2 B2
  HOR/CROF WF4 ....222 D5
  HUD HD1 ....14 C4
  HWTH BD22 ....78 C7
  NORM WF6 ....178 E4
  PDSY/CALV LS28 ....106 F6
  WBSY BD6 ....126 D7
  YEA LS19 ....62 E7
Centenary Rd BAIL BD17 ....83 H2
Centenary Sq EARL WF12 ....195 K2
Centenary Wy BTLY WF17 ....151 K8
Central Av BAIL BD17 ....82 D4
  CUD/GR S72 ....245 J7
  HEM/SK/SE WF9 ....223 J2
  HEM/SK/SE WF9 ....247 H4
  HUDN HD2 ....192 D4
  HWTH BD22 ....79 H3
  LIT OL15 ....185 K8
  LVSG WF15 ....171 K1
  SHPY BD18 ....82 D7
  WBOW BD5 ....126 E3
Central Av East LVSG WF15 ....171 K1
Central CI HUDN HD2 ....192 D4
Central Dr BSLYN/ROY S71 ....243 L3
  CAS WF10 ....157 H7
  HUDN HD2 ....192 D3
  HWTH BD22 ....79 H3
Central Pk HFAX HX1 ....10 F4
Central Rd HUDN HD2 ....192 D4
Central St DEWS WF13 ....173 L6
  HBR HX7 ....143 J3
  HFAX HX1 ....11 G6
  LDS LS1 ....6 E3
Centre La TAD LS24 ....71 M5
Centre St HECK WF16 * 172 E2
  HEM/SK/SE WF9 ....223 M7
  HEM/SK/SE WF9 ....247 H5
  WBOW BD5 * 126 E3
Centre Vale CI LIT OL15 ....185 L7
Centuria Wk HUDW HD3 ....191 G6
Centurion Wy CLECK BD19 ....149 L4
Century Gdns WHIT OL12 ....206 B2
Century PI GIR BD8 ....4 A1
Century Rd ELL HX5 ....169 H7
Century St KGHY BD21 ....79 K2
Century Wy MSTN/BAR LS15 ....112 B7
Ceres Rd WBY LS22 ....48 B1
Chaddlewood Cl HORS LS18 ....85 L5
Chadwell Springs BGLY BD16 ....81 J7
Chadwick CI WBOW BD5 ....229 J1
Chadwick Crs DEWS WF13 ....173 K5
Chadwick Fold La MIRF WF14 ....194 C2
Chadwick Hall Gdns
  MIRF WF14 ....194 B3
  MIRF WF14 ....194 B3
Chadwick St MID LS10 ....9 K3
  MILN OL16 ....20 C7
Chadwick St South MID LS10 ....9 K4
Chaffinch Rd GIR BD8 ....103 L7
Chaffinch Wk HUDS HD4 ....214 A4
Chain Bar Rd CLECK BD19 ....149 L5
Chain St MAR/SLWT HD7 ....234 A1
Chain St BFD BD1 ....4 D5
  CAS WF10 ....157 L6
Chalcroft CI HECK WF16 ....173 G1
Chald La WKFDW/WTN WF2 ....12 A4
Chalfont Rd BHP/TINH S16 * 86 D7
Chalice CI MID LS10 ....123 A7
Challenge Wy BOW BD4 ....127 M2
  BTLY WF17 ....174 B2
Challis Gv WBOW BD5 ....127 G3
Chalner Av MOR LS27 ....152 B4
Chalner St MOR LS27 ....152 B4
Chaloner Gn WKFDE WF1 ....176 F6
Chaloner Rd WKFDE WF1 ....176 F6
Chalwood HUDN HD2 ....193 G2
Chamber Rd RPDN/SHW OL2 ....229 J7
Champion Av CAS WF10 ....180 A1
Champness Hall MILN OL16 * 206 B7
Chancellor St HDGY LS6 ....6 F2
Chancel PI MILN OL16 ....206 B7
Chancel Wy BSLYN/ROY S71 ....261 L4
Chancery La HUD HD1 * 14 F7
  OSS WF5 ....174 D6
  ROY/SHW OL2 ....229 L7
  WKFDE WF1 ....12 E4
Chancery Rd EARL WF12 ....174 D6
Chandler CI BTLY WF17 ....151 K8
Chandler La HOLM/MEL HD9 ....235 M2
Chandlers CI WKFDE WF1 ....12 F5
The Chandlers MID LS10 ....9 J2
Chandos Av RHAY LS8 ....88 A7
Chandos Fold RHAY LS8 ....88 A7
Chandos Gdns RHAY LS8 ....88 A6
Chandos Garth RHAY LS8 ....88 A6
Chandos Gn RHAY LS8 ....88 A6
Chandos PI RHAY LS8 ....88 B7
Chandos St BOW BD4 ....5 G8
  KGHY BD21 ....2 F8
Chandos Ter RHAY LS8 ....88 A7
Chandos Wk RHAY LS8 ....88 A7
Changegate HWTH BD22 ....78 D6
Changegate Ct HWTH BD22 ....78 D7
Change La HIPP HX3 ....169 G4
Channing Sq MILN OL16 * 206 D8
Channing Sq MILN OL16 ....206 D8
Channing Wy BFD BD1 ....4 D7
Chantrell Ct LDSU LS2 ....9 J1
Chantry CI PONT WF8 ....180 D7
Chantry Ct MSTN/BAR LS15 ....111 M7
Chantry Garth MSTN/BAR LS15 ....111 M7
Chantry Gv BSLYN/ROY S71 ....243 L5
Chantry La TAD LS24 ....92 E2
Chantry Rd WKFDW/WTN WF2 ....198 A2
Chapel Av BSLYN/ROY S71 ....243 L5
  HBR HX7 ....143 K3
  HECK WF16 ....173 G1
Chapel Bank HOLM/MEL HD9 ....255 G8
Chapel Cft CUD/GR S72 ....244 B6
  EARL WF12 ....195 M4
  GFTH/SHER LS25 ....113 G7
  GTL/HWG HX4 ....190 D7
  HOR/CROF WF4 ....201 H7
  HUDS HD4 ....214 B6
  KBTN HD8 ....239 G7
  TAD LS24 ....94 F7
  WBY LS22 ....31 L5
Chapel Ct MSTN/BAR LS15 ....111 J6
Chapel Cft HDGY LS6 ....170 D7
Chapel Field La STKB/PEN S36 ....270 E4
Chapelfields HEM/SK/SE WF9 ....246 D4
Chapel Fold BTLY WF17 ....173 L6
  LM/WK BD12 ....148 E6

MSTN/BAR LS15 ....111 J6
PDSY/CALV LS28 * 107 G8
WBSY BD6 ....126 D5
Chapel Garth FEA/AMT WF7 ....202 C8
Chapelgate HOLM/MEL HD9 ....254 F3
Chapel Ga MILN OL16 ....207 H8
Chapel Gv BGLY BD16 ....81 G1
Chapel HI HUD HD1 ....14 C4
  HUD8 ....240 A4
  LIT OL15 ....185 K8
  MIRF WF14 ....194 C5
  MOR LS27 ....152 C1
  SKP/WHF BD23 ....16 B1
  WBY LS22 ....45 M4
  YEA LS19 ....62 D7
Chapel Hill Jct HUD HD1 ....14 C4
Chapel Hill La HUD3 ....189 K8
  OT LS21 ....43 K6
Chapel Hill Rd OT LS21 ....42 F8
Charlestown Est FEA/AMT WF7 ....224 C2
Charlestown Rd HIPP HX3 ....11 J4
Charlesworth Ct EARL WF12 ....195 M4
Charlesworth Dr CUD/GR S72 ....245 J8
Charlesworth Gv LUD/ILL HX2 ....146 A6
Charlesworth PI
  EARD/LOFT WF3 ....153 K6
Charlesworth Sq CLECK BD19 ....150 C8
Charlesworth Ter LUD/ILL HX2 ....146 A6
Charlesworth Wy
  WKFDW/WTN WF2 ....12 D5
Charlotte CI BTLY WF17 ....151 H3
Charlotte Ct HWTH BD22 ....78 F6
Charlotte Gv OSS WF5 ....197 H2
Charlotte St ROCH OL11 ....207 L8
  WKFDE WF1 ....12 F4
Charlotte Wd WKFDE WF1 * 13 C4
  OSM LS9 ....110 C7
Charlton Gv AIRE BD20 ....36 B6
Charlton Mt OSM LS9 ....110 C7
Charlton PI OSM LS9 ....110 C7
Charlton Rd OSM LS9 ....110 C7
Charlton St OSM LS9 ....110 C7
Charnley Dr CHAL LS7 ....88 A8
Charnock Gv HFAX HX1 ....168 E1
Charnwood Bank HECK WF16 ....173 G1
Charnwood CI ECHL BD2 ....105 L4
  ROY/SHW OL2 ....229 G6
Charnwood Gv ECHL BD2 ....105 L4
Charnwood Rd ECHL BD2 ....105 L4
Charterhouse Rd IDLE BD10 ....83 K5
Charteris Rd GIR BD8 ....103 M7
Charter St MILN OL16 ....228 D7
Chartists Wy MOR LS27 ....152 C3
Chartwell Ct AL/HA/HU LS17 ....88 D1
Charville Gdns AL/HA/HU LS17 ....89 H1
Chaseley Rd WHIT OL12 ....206 A6
The Chase AIRE BD20 ....33 J5
  EARD/LOFT WF3 ....155 J8
  GFTH/SHER LS25 ....113 K7
  WBY LS22 ....30 B8
  YEA LS19 ....84 D2
Chassum Gv HTON BD9 ....104 C4
Chaster St BTLY WF17 ....151 J8
Chatham Crs COL BB8 ....52 A8
  COL BB8 ....52 A8
Chatham St BFDE BD3 ....5 H1
  HFAX HX1 ....10 E5
  RPDN/SBR HX6 ....167 K1
Chat Hill Rd CUL/QBY BD13 ....125 K1
Chatswood Av BEE/HOL LS11 ....131 H6
Chatswood Crs BEE/HOL LS11 ....131 H6
Chatswood Dr BEE/HOL LS11 ....131 H6
Chatsworth Av PDSY/CALV LS28 ....106 C6
  PONT WF8 ....181 G3
Chatsworth CI HUDE HD5 ....214 D3
  RHAY LS8 ....110 C3
  ROY/SHW OL2 ....229 L6
Chatsworth Crs
  PDSY/CALV LS28 ....106 C6
Chatsworth Dr
  PDSY/CALV LS28 ....106 C6
  WBY LS22 ....29 J3
Chatsworth Fall
  PDSY/CALV LS28 ....106 C6
Chatsworth Ms MOR LS27 * 152 E3
Chatsworth Ri DOD/DAR S75 * 260 B8
Chatsworth PI
  PDSY/CALV LS28 ....106 C6
Chatsworth Rd
  BSLYN/ROY S71 ....243 J8
  PDSY/CALV LS28 ....106 C6
  RHAY LS8 ....110 C3
Chatsworth St KGHY BD21 ....3 K4
  WHIT OL12 ....206 A3
Chatsworth Ter EARL WF12 ....174 B7
Chatts Wood Fold LM/WK BD12 ....149 K1
Chaucer Av EARD/LOFT WF3 ....155 G8
  PDSY/CALV LS28 ....107 H8
Chaucer CI HOLM/MEL HD9 ....236 B5
Chaucer Gdns PDSY/CALV LS28 ....107 H8
Chaucer Gv PDSY/CALV LS28 ....107 H8
Chaucer St HFAX HX1 ....10 A7
Cheapside BFD BD1 ....4 F5
  BSLY S70 ....261 H5
  BTLY WF17 ....173 M1
  CLECK BD19 ....150 A7
  HFAX HX1 ....11 H6
  HIPP HX3 ....125 L8
  NORM WF6 ....178 D4
Cheddington Gv WIL/AL BD15 ....103 K6
Cheese Gate Nab Side
  HOLM/MEL HD9 ....255 J4
Cheetham HI MIRF WF14 ....172 B7
Cheetham St HBR HX7 ....143 J3
  MILN OL16 ....206 B6
  ROY/SHW OL2 ....229 K8
Chelburn Vw LIT OL15 ....185 L5
Chellow Gdns WIL/AL BD15 * 103 J4
Chellow Grange Rd HTON BD9 ....103 L4
Chellow La HTON BD9 ....103 L4
Chellow St WBOW BD5 ....126 F4
Chellow Wy EARL WF12 ....195 K6
Chelmsford Rd BFDE BD3 * 105 L6
Chelmsford Ter BFDE BD3 ....105 L6
Chelsea CI ROY/SHW OL2 ....229 K7
Chelsea Man HIPP HX3 ....147 J4
Chelsea St KGHY BD21 ....2 E8
Chelston Wy GFTH/SHER LS15 ....112 B3
Cheltenham Av ILK LS29 ....39 G5
Cheltenham Ct HFAX HX1 ....168 F2
Cheltenham Gdns HFAX HX1 ....168 F2
Cheltenham PI HIPP HX3 ....168 F2
Cheltenham Rd LUD/ILL HX2 ....146 A6
Cheltenham St WOR/ARM LS12 ....108 F1
Chelwood Av RHAY LS8 ....88 B3
  BAIL BD17 ....82 D6
  BFD BD1 ....4 D6
  BGLY BD16 ....81 H3
  BSLY S70 ....261 G6
  BTLY WF17 ....173 L2
  CAS WF10 ....158 A7
  CLECK BD19 ....150 C6
  COL BB8 ....74 A1
  CUD/GR S72 ....244 D6
Chelwood Crs RHAY LS8 ....88 B4
Chelwood Dr RHAY LS8 ....88 B3
  WIL/AL BD15 ....103 K7
Chelwood Gv RHAY LS8 ....88 B3
Chelwood Mt RHAY LS8 ....88 B3
Chelwood PI RHAY LS8 ....88 B3
Chenies CI SCFT LS14 ....111 G5
Chepstow CI GFTH/SHER LS25 ....113 K7

Chepstow Dr MID LS10 ....153 M3
Chequerfield Av PONT WF8 ....181 H6
Chequerfield CI CAS WF10 ....157 J8
Chequerfield Dr PONT WF8 ....181 H6
Chequerfield La PONT WF8 ....181 H7
Chequerfield Mt PONT WF8 ....181 H7
Chequerfield Rd PONT WF8 ....181 H6
Chequers CI PONT WF8 ....181 H7
Chequers Ct MILN OL16 ....206 C7
Cheriton Av AWLS/ASK DN6 ....249 J8
Cheriton Dr CUL/QBY BD13 ....125 H5
Cherry CI BSLYN/ROY S71 ....243 J2
  CUD/GR S72 ....244 D6
Cherry Ct HDGY LS6 ....87 K8
  HFAX HX1 ....10 D4
  OSM LS9 ....10 E4
Cherry Flds ECHL BD2 ....105 G2
Cherry Garth AWLS/ASK DN6 ....227 G6
Cherry Gv HDGY LS6 ....87 K8
  ILK LS29 ....38 D3
  ROY/SHW OL2 ....229 G7
Cherry Hall Dr ROY/SHW OL2 * 229 G7
Cherry Hills DOD/DAR S75 ....242 C5
Cherry La KBTN HD8 ....240 B4
  LIT OL15 ....230 D3
Cherry Lea Ct YEA LS19 ....84 D2
Cherry Nook Rd HUDN HD2 ....193 G2
Cherry PI OSM LS9 ....7 L7
Cherry Ri SCFT LS14 ....89 L6
Cherry Rw OSM LS9 ....7 L7
Cherrys Rd BSLYN/ROY S71 ....261 M4
Cherry St HWTH BD22 ....79 G6
Cherry Tree Av IDLE BD10 * 83 M8
  KNOT WF11 ....182 A3
Cherry Tree CI DOD/DAR S75 * 242 E5
  MAR/SLWT HD7 ....213 G1
Cherry Tree Ct EARD/LOFT WF3 ....153 L7
Cherry Tree Crs
  PDSY/CALV LS28 ....106 F3
  WKFDW/WTN WF2 ....199 K7
Cherry Tree Dr GTL/HWG HX4 ....168 D7
  PDSY/CALV LS28 ....106 F3
  WKFDW/WTN WF2 ....199 K7
Cherry Tree Gdns SHPY BD18 ....83 H5
Cherry Tree Ri KGHY BD21 ....3 K8
Cherry Tree Rd
  WKFDW/WTN WF2 ....199 K7
Cherry Tree Rw BGLY BD16 ....80 D7
Cherry Tree Wk
  EARD/LOFT WF3 ....153 L7
  HOLM/MEL HD9 ....254 F2
  LDS LS1 * 9 K1
Cherrywood CI SCFT LS14 ....89 K5
Cherrywood Gdns SCFT LS14 ....89 K5
Chertsey CI ROY/SHW OL2 ....229 K6
Chervana Ct BOW BD4 ....128 A2
Cherwell Cft GFTH/SHER LS25 ....135 K1
  SEL YO8 ....139 M5
Cherwell Dr WBSY BD6 ....126 D7
Chesham Rd BSLY S70 ....260 F5
Chesham St GTHN BD7 ....4 B7
  KGHY BD21 ....3 K4
Chesil Bank HUDW HD3 ....191 H6
Chesilton Av HUD HD1 ....191 K7
Chesney Av MID LS10 ....9 J7
Chesnut End BSPA/BRAM LS23 ....49 H5
Chessington Dr
  HOR/CROF WF4 ....217 M3
Chester Ct HIPP HX3 ....10 F1
Chester Gv HIPP HX3 ....10 F1
Chester PI HIPP HX3 ....10 F1
Chester Rd HIPP HX3 ....10 F1
Chester St GTHN BD7 ....4 D8
  HIPP HX3 ....10 F1
  RPDN/SBR HX6 ....167 K1
  WOR/ARM LS12 ....108 E6
Chesterton Ct HOR/CROF WF4 ....197 L4
  MSTN/BAR LS15 ....111 M8
Chesterton Dr HOLM/MEL HD9 ....236 B5
Chestnut Av AWLS/ASK DN6 ....249 K5
  BSPA/BRAM LS23 ....48 E6
  BTLY WF17 ....173 L2
  CUD/GR S72 ....245 H3
  HDGY LS6 ....109 H3
  MSTN/BAR LS15 ....111 M4
  TOD OL14 ....141 J7
  WBY LS22 ....29 M8
  WKFDW/WTN WF2 ....199 J8
Chestnut CI FEA/AMT WF7 ....179 M7
  GTL/HWG HX4 ....168 D6
  HUDS HD4 ....214 C4
  HWTH BD22 * 2 B1
  ILK LS29 ....39 G3
Chestnut Crs BSLY S70 ....261 H7
  SHPY BD18 ....82 A7
Chestnut Ct NORM WF6 ....178 C6
  CUD/GR S72 ....244 F1
Chestnut Dr BHP/TINH S16 ....86 D1
  CUD/GR S72 ....244 F1
Chestnut Gdns WOR/ARM LS12 ....108 D8
Chestnut Garth HUDW HD3 * 191 K7
Chestnut Gn GFTH/SHER LS25 ....138 D2
Chestnut Gv BSPA/BRAM LS23 ....48 E6
  ECHL BD2 ....104 F2
  HDGY LS6 ....109 G3
  HEM/SK/SE WF9 ....247 H5
  HOR/CROF WF4 ....200 B5
  PDSY/CALV LS28 ....84 D8
  PONT WF8 ....180 F8
Chestnut Mdw MIRF WF14 ....172 B7
Chestnut PI HDGY LS6 ....109 G3
Chestnut Ri WOR/ARM LS12 ....108 D7
Chestnut Rd HDGY LS6 ....109 G3
The Chestnuts PONT WF8 ....181 H2
Chestnut St CUD/GR S72 ....263 K1
  HDGY LS6 ....109 G3
  HEM/SK/SE WF9 ....247 H5
  HFAX HX1 ....10 A8
  HUDN HD2 ....192 D3
Chestnut Ter EARL WF12 ....195 L3
  WKFDW/WTN WF2 ....176 D3
Chestnut Wy BHP/TINH S16 ....86 D1
  LIT OL15 ....207 G1
Chevet Cft WKFDW/WTN WF2 ....199 G6
Chevet La HOR/CROF WF4 ....221 K6
  WKFDW/WTN WF2 ....221 G1
Chevet Ms WKFDW/WTN WF2 ....199 G7
Chevet Mt WIL/AL BD15 ....103 J7
Chevet Park Ct
  WKFDW/WTN WF2 ....221 G1
Chevet Ri BSLYN/ROY S71 ....243 J2
Chevet Vw BSLYN/ROY S71 ....243 J2
Chevin Av ILK LS29 ....61 K1
  OT LS21 ....41 K8
Chevinedge Crs HIPP HX3 ....168 F5
Chevin End Rd ILK LS29 ....61 L2
Chevington Ct YEA LS19 * 84 C3
Chevins CI BTLY WF17 ....151 H3
Chevin Side OT LS21 ....41 J8
Cheviot Av HOLM/MEL HD9 ....235 L5
  OT LS21 ....41 K8
Cheviot CI HEM/SK/SE WF9 ....224 B7

MILN OL16 ....207 J7
Cheviot Ct GFTH/SHER LS25 ....135 H1
Cheviot La LM/WK BD12 ....126 E8
Cheviot PI KNOT WF11 ....182 A2
Cheviots Rd ROY/SHW OL2 ....229 J6
Cheviot Wy MIRF WF14 ....194 B4
Cheyne Wk KGHY BD21 * 2 B1
Chichester CI LIT OL15 ....207 H3
Chichester St MILN OL16 ....206 C7
  WOR/ARM LS12 * 108 E6
Chickenley La EARL WF12 ....174 C7
Chidswell Gdns EARL WF12 ....174 C3
Chidswell La EARL WF12 ....174 C3
Child La LVSG WF15 ....172 B4
Childs La SHPY BD18 ....83 G8
Childs Rd WKFDW/WTN WF2 ....175 M6
Chiltern Av CAS WF10 ....179 H1
  HUDW HD3 ....191 J5
  KNOT WF11 ....182 A2
Chiltern CI GFTH/SHER LS25 ....135 H1
  ROY/SHW OL2 ....229 H6
Chiltern Ct BRAM LS13 ....107 G3
  GFTH/SHER LS25 ....135 H1
  HEM/SK/SE WF9 ....224 B7
Chiltern Dr FEA/AMT WF7 ....224 B1
  MIRF WF14 ....194 B4
Chiltern Rd EARL WF12 ....174 B5
Chiltern Wy LVSG WF15 ....171 M1
Chilton St BSLY S70 ....261 G6
Chilver Dr BOW BD4 ....128 C4
Chilwell CI BSLYN/ROY S71 ....243 H5
Chilwell Gdns BSLYN/ROY S71 ....243 H5
Chimney La KBTN HD8 ....215 M2
Chinewood Av BTLY WF17 ....151 K8
Chippendale Ri IDLE BD10 ....103 M6
  OT LS21 ....41 J7
Chipping Fold MILN OL16 ....229 H1
Chirton Gv RHAY LS8 ....110 C1
Chiserley Gdns HBR HX7 ....143 L1
Chislehurst PI WBOW BD5 ....126 C3
Chiswick St HDGY LS6 ....109 G5
Chiswick Ter HDGY LS6 ....109 G5
Choppards Bank Rd
  HOLM/MEL HD9 ....254 C5
Choppards La HOLM/MEL HD9 ....254 C5
Chorley La BVRD LS3 ....6 C8
Chrisharben Pk CLAY BD14 ....125 L3
Chrismoor IDLE BD10 ....83 J7
Christ Church Av
  WOR/ARM LS12 ....108 D6
Christ Church Mt
  WOR/ARM LS12 ....108 D6
Christ Church Pde
  WOR/ARM LS12 ....108 D6
Christ Church PI
  WOR/ARM LS12 ....108 D6
Christ Church Rd
  WOR/ARM LS12 ....108 D6
Christ Church Ter
  WOR/ARM LS12 ....108 D6
Christ Church Vw
  WOR/ARM LS12 ....108 D6
Christine St ROY/SHW OL2 ....229 K7
Christopher Rd HDGY LS6 ....6 D1
Christopher St WBOW BD5 ....126 E3
Christopher Ter WBOW BD5 ....126 E3
Churchbalk Dr PONT WF8 ....181 G8
Churchbalk La PONT WF8 ....181 G7
Church Bank BFD BD1 ....5 G6
  RPDN/SBR HX6 ....167 L2
Church Bank La HBR HX7 ....143 L5
Churchbank Wy EARL WF12 ....195 L2
Church Cswy BSPA/BRAM LS23 ....49 H5
Church CI DOD/DAR S75 ....242 A6
  HECK WF16 ....172 F2
  HOR/CROF WF4 ....200 D4
  KBTN HD8 ....238 A6
  LUD/ILL HX2 ....145 M1
  RTHW LS26 ....134 C4
  SCFT LS14 ....111 K2
Churchcourt AIRE BD20 ....58 B4
Church Ct GTHN BD7 * 179 G5
  NORM WF6 ....178 C6
  YEA LS19 ....62 D8
Church Crs HOR/CROF WF4 ....197 G8
  RTHW LS26 ....134 D5
  TAD LS24 ....71 K7
  YEA LS19 ....62 D8
Church Cft EARD/LOFT WF3 ....154 E6
  TAD LS24 ....116 A1
Church Dr AL/HA/HU LS17 ....67 K1
  CUD/GR S72 ....245 H4
Church Farm SCFT LS14 ....68 B8
Church Farm CI
  EARD/LOFT WF3 ....154 E6
  NORM WF6 ....178 B2
Churchfarm Garth
  AL/HA/HU LS17 ....89 H2
Church Farm Vw
  MSTN/BAR LS15 ....91 G7
Church Fenton La TAD LS24 ....94 F2
Churchfield BSLY S70 ....261 G4
Churchfield Av CUD/GR S72 ....244 D8
  DOD/DAR S75 ....241 K6
Churchfield CI DOD/DAR S75 ....241 K6
  LVSG WF15 ....172 C2
Churchfield Crs CUD/GR S72 ....244 D8
Churchfield Cft NORM WF6 ....178 B2
  RTHW LS26 ....155 H1
Chinewood Gv RTHW LS26 ....155 G1
Churchfield La AWLS/ASK DN6 ....205 K4
  CAS WF10 ....158 B8
  DOD/DAR S75 ....133 G8
  RTHW LS26 ....133 G8
Church Field Rd AWLS/ASK DN6 ....227 M5
Churchfield Rd RTHW LS26 ....155 G1
  NORM WF6 ....178 B2
Churchfields ECHL BD2 ....105 M4
  HOR/CROF WF4 ....222 D4
  HUDN HD2 ....193 H3
Churchfields Rd BRIG HD6 ....170 C3
  BTLY WF17 ....173 L1
Church Flds CUD/GR S72 ....244 D8
Church Gdns AL/HA/HU LS17 * 67 M3
  GFTH/SHER LS25 ....113 H8
  MOR LS27 ....129 L7
  OT LS21 ....42 E7
Church Garth CAS WF10 ....158 B8
Church Gn GIR BD8 ....104 D5
  KBTN HD8 ....216 D8
  LUD/ILL HX2 ....146 A5
Church Gv BSLYN/ROY S71 ....261 L2

HDGY LS6 .....87 G7
HEM/SK/SE WF9 .....246 E4
HORS LS18 .....85 K5
Church Hts *STKB/PEN* S36 .....258 B7
Church Hl *AL/HA/HU* LS17 .....25 M8
   BAIL BD17 .....82 F2
   BHP/TINH LS16 .....63 M3
   BSLYN/ROY S71 .....243 M3
   BSPA/BRAM LS23 .....69 M3
   GFTH/SHER LS25 .....137 J1
   PBR HG3 .....28 E3
   SCFT LS14 .....68 C8
Church Hill Gdns
   PDSY/CALV LS28 .....107 H4
Church Hill Gn
   PDSY/CALV LS28 .....107 H4
Church Hill Mt
   PDSY/CALV LS28 .....107 H4
Churchill Gdns *LDSU* LS2 .....6 E5
Churchill Gv *HECK* WF16 .....173 C3
   WKFDW/WTN WF2 .....199 G6
Churchill Rd *CUL/OBY* BD13 .....105 H8
Churchill St *TOD* OL14 .....141 G6
Churchill Wy *AIRE* BD20 .....35 G7
Church La *AL/HA/HU* LS17 .....45 H7
   AWLS/ASK DN6 .....249 L8
   BAIL BD17 .....83 L1
   BHP/TINH LS16 .....86 E2
   BRIG HD6 .....170 C4
   BSLY LS70 .....261 G4
   CHAL LS7 .....87 M8
   CLECK BD19 .....150 E6
   COP/BISH VO23 .....73 K6
   CUD/GR S72 .....222 C8
   DEWS WF13 .....173 H6
   DOD/DAR S75 .....240 F3
   DOD/DAR S75 .....259 H2
   EARD/LOFT WF3 .....152 F7
   EARD/LOFT WF3 .....153 L7
   EARL WF12 .....196 A4
   ELL HX5 .....169 M7
   FEA/AMT WF7 .....178 F6
   FEA/AMT WF7 .....179 L5
   GFTH/SHER LS25 .....113 M7
   GFTH/SHER LS25 .....114 A7
   GFTH/SHER LS25 .....135 K5
   GFTH/SHER LS25 .....138 D6
   GLE DN14 .....161 M8
   GTL/HWG HX4 .....190 C2
   HBR HX7 .....143 H1
   HDGY LS6 .....87 H7
   HECK WF16 .....172 F2
   HIPP HX3 .....169 L2
   HOR/CROF WF4 .....197 G7
   HOR/CROF WF4 .....220 C2
   HEM/SK/SE WF9 .....246 K6
   HORS LS18 .....85 K5
   HUDE HD5 .....15 K7
   HUDE HD5 .....193 K7
   HUDS HD4 .....214 C4
   HUDW HD3 .....211 H1
   KBTN HD8 .....238 A6
   KBTN HD8 .....240 B4
   LUD/ILL HX2 .....146 A5
   LVSG WF15 .....171 K3
   LVSG WF15 .....172 A4
   MAR/SLWT HD7 .....213 G5
   MAR/SLWT HD7 .....233 H2
   MILN OL16 * 206 B7
   MIRF WF14 .....194 E2
   MSTN/BAR LS15 .....111 L4
   NORM WF6 .....178 C5
   OT LS21 .....24 F8
   OT LS21 .....40 D4
   OT LS21 .....42 E7
   PBR HG3 .....28 E3
   PDSY/CALV LS28 .....107 G7
   PONT WF8 .....180 F6
   PONT WF8 .....203 M1
   RPDN/SBR HX6 .....188 F3
   RTHW LS26 .....134 C5
   RTHW LS26 .....156 E4
   STKB/PEN S36 .....258 B7
   TAD LS24 .....50 C4
   TAD LS24 .....71 K6
   WBSY BD6 .....126 D6
   WBY LS22 .....47 K5
   WKFDE WF1 .....176 D1
Church Lane Av *WKFDE* WF1 .....176 D1
Church Mdw *BSPA/BRAM* LS23 .....69 M3
   BTLY WF17 .....150 F5
Church Ms *BSPA/BRAM* LS23 .....48 F6
   GFTH/SHER LS25 .....116 A6
Church Mt *HEM/SK/SE* WF9 .....246 K4
   HORS LS18 .....85 K5
Church Pk *LVSG* WF15 .....172 A4
Church Pl *GFTH/SHER* LS25 .....113 H7
   HFAX HX1 .....10 E7
Church Rd *AIRE* BD20 .....55 M1
   BTLY WF17 .....151 H6
   DOD/DAR S75 .....242 A6
   EARD/LOFT WF3 .....177 H1
   HORS LS18 .....85 K6
   LVSG WF15 .....172 A4
   MILN OL16 .....206 D8
   NORM WF6 .....177 M3
   OSM LS9 .....9 L2
   ROY/SHW OL2 .....229 K8
   RTHW LS26 .....135 G6
   TOD OL14 .....141 G6
   WBSY BD6 .....126 D6
   WOR/ARM LS12 .....9 J1
Church Rw *LDSU* LS2 .....9 J1
Church Side *RTHW* LS26 .....156 E4
Church Side Cl *HIPP* HX3 .....11 H2
Church Side Dr *HIPP* HX3 .....11 H2
Churchside Vls *RTHW* LS26 .....156 E4
Church Sq *GFTH/SHER* LS25 .....113 H7
Church Stile *MILN* OL16 .....206 B7
Church St *AIRE* BD20 .....34 F7
   BGLY BD16 .....81 J4
   BRIG HD6 .....170 B6
   BSLY S70 .....261 G4
   BSLYN/ROY S71 .....243 L5
   BSLYN/ROY S71 .....243 M5
   BSPA/BRAM LS23 .....48 F7
   CAS WF10 .....157 M6
   CLECK BD19 .....150 A7
   COL BB8 .....74 E4
   CUD/GR S72 .....244 D8
   CUD/GR S72 .....245 H3
   CUL/OBY BD13 * 79 M8
   DEWS WF13 .....195 G1
   DOD/DAR S75 .....242 A6
   DOD/DAR S75 .....242 E5
   DOD/DAR S75 .....259 G1
   DOD/DAR S75 .....260 C3
   EARL WF12 .....173 M6
   ELL HX5 .....169 M7
   GIR BD8 .....104 D5
   GSLY LS20 .....62 A5
   GTL/HWG HX4 .....168 F7
   HBR HX7 .....143 H1
   HECK WF16 .....172 F3
   HEM/SK/SE WF9 .....247 J4
   HFAX HX1 .....11 J7
   HOLM/MEL HD9 * 237 H8

HOR/CROF WF4 .....220 B7
HUD HD1 .....14 F6
HUD HD1 .....213 L1
HUDE HD5 .....15 L8
HUDS HD4 .....214 A2
HWTH BD22 .....78 D7
HWTH BD22 .....100 E4
ILK LS29 .....19 J6
ILK LS29 .....38 C2
ILK LS29 .....217 L7
KCHY BD21 .....2 F6
KCHY BD21 .....3 J4
KNOT WF11 .....159 L6
KSTL LS5 .....108 C2
LIT OL15 .....207 K1
LVSG WF15 .....171 L1
LVSG WF15 .....171 L1
MAR/SLWT HD7 .....212 B5
MAR/SLWT HD7 .....212 F2
MID LS10 .....9 J3
MILN OL16 .....206 F5
MILN OL16 .....229 K2
MOR LS27 .....129 C7
MOR LS27 .....152 C1
OSS WF5 .....174 F7
ROCH OL11 .....206 A7
RTHW LS26 .....133 L7
RTHW LS26 .....155 G1
RYKW YO26 .....32 D5
SHPY BD18 .....82 F6
SKP/WHF BD23 .....16 B3
STKB/PEN S36 .....270 F3
TAD LS24 .....94 E8
TAD LS24 .....95 G1
TAD LS24 .....116 A1
TOD OL14 .....141 H6
WBSY BD6 .....126 A8
WBY LS22 .....48 A1
WKFDE WF1 .....12 F6
YEA LS19 .....62 C8
Church Ter *HOLM/MEL* HD9 .....254 C7
   LUD/ILL HX2 .....123 J7
   MILN OL16 .....229 J1
Church Top *HEM/SK/SE* WF9 .....246 E4
Church Vw *AWLS/ASK* DN6 .....249 L8
   CLECK BD19 .....149 K6
   CUD/GR S72 .....244 D8
   DOD/DAR S75 .....260 E3
   GFTH/SHER LS25 .....136 A4
   GFTH/SHER LS25 .....138 A3
   HEM/SK/SE WF9 .....246 E4
   HOLM/MEL HD9 .....253 M4
   HOR/CROF WF4 .....220 A1
   KSTL LS5 .....108 C2
   RPDN/SBR HX6 .....167 L2
   WKFDE WF1 .....199 D8
Church View *HOR/CROF* WF4 .....222 B5
Church View Crs *STKB/PEN* S36 .....270 F3
Church View Ms
   BSPA/BRAM LS23 .....69 M1
Church View Rd *STKB/PEN* S36 * 270 F3
Church Vls *HEM/SK/SE* WF9 .....246 E4
Churchville *GFTH/SHER* LS25 .....114 C7
Churchville Av *GFTH/SHER* LS25 .....114 B7
Churchville Dr *GFTH/SHER* LS25 .....114 B7
Churchville Ter *GFTH/SHER* LS25 .....114 B6
Church Wk *BTLY* WF17 .....173 J3
   EARL WF12 .....147 J4
   HIPP HX3 .....147 A4
   LDSU LS2 .....9 J5
   TOD OL14 .....163 H7
Churchway *HOR/CROF* WF4 .....200 C5
Church Wy *KCHY* BD21 .....3 D8
   MOR LS27 * 152 C1
Church Wood Av
   BHP/TINH LS16 .....86 E8
Churchwood Cl
   MAR/SLWT HD7 .....212 B5
Church Wood Mt *HDGY* LS6 .....86 E8
Church Wood Rd
   BHP/TINH LS16 .....86 E8
Churcroft *DOD/DAR* S75 .....260 C4
Churn La *LUD/ILL* HX2 .....145 M7
Churn Milk La *HIPP* HX3 .....146 C2
Churwell Av *DEWS* WF13 .....173 H3
Churwell Cl *CAS* WF10 .....157 M8
Churwell V *EARL* WF12 .....174 C4
Cinder Hl Rd *TOD* OL14 .....142 A8
Cinderhills La *HIPP* HX3 .....169 G3
Cinder Hills Rd *HOLM/MEL* HD9 .....254 D2
Cinder Hills Wy *DOD/DAR* S75 .....260 C5
Cinder La *BSPA/BRAM* LS23 .....48 F6
   CAS WF10 .....157 L6
   OT LS21 .....42 B1
The Circle *PONT* WF8 .....181 G7
The Circuit *AWLS/ASK* DN6 .....249 H8
Cirrus Vw *FEA/AMT* WF7 .....224 B1
City La *HIPP* HX3 .....146 A5
City Link *BEE/HOL* LS11 .....8 F1
City Sq *LDS* LS1 .....8 F1
City Wk *BEE/HOL* LS11 .....8 F1
Clanricarde St *BSLYN/ROY* S71 .....261 G3
Clapgate *OT* LS21 .....41 J4
Clapham Dene Rd
   MSTN/BAR LS15 .....111 K5
Clapham St *CUL/OBY* BD13 .....102 A4
Clapton Av *HFAX* HX1 .....10 D8
Clara Dr *PDSY/CALV* LS28 .....84 C7
Clara Rd *ECHL* BD2 .....105 H1
Clara St *BRIG* HD6 .....170 C5
   HUD HD1 .....14 F2
   HUDS HD4 .....213 J3
   PDSY/CALV LS28 .....106 F4
   ROCH OL11 .....228 B3
Clarebont Av *BVRD* LS3 * 6 C7
   ECHL BD2 .....83 D8
Claremont Ct *HDGY* LS6 .....87 G8
Claremont Crs *ECHL* BD2 .....83 G8
   HDGY LS6 .....109 H1
Claremont Dr *HDGY* LS6 .....87 G8
Claremont Gdns *BGLY* BD16 .....81 J3
Claremont Gv *BVRD* LS3 * 6 C7
   ECHL BD2 .....83 G8
   PDSY/CALV LS28 .....107 G7
Claremont Pl *WOR/ARM* LS12 .....108 C7
Claremont Rd *DEWS* WF13 .....173 H5
   MILN OL16 .....229 J1
   SHPY BD18 .....83 G8
Claremont St *CLECK* BD19 * 149 M6
   ELL HX5 .....169 J3
   HUD HD1 .....14 E4
   RPDN/SBR HX6 * 167 L2
   RTHW LS26 * 133 L7
   WKFDE WF1 .....13 K7
   WOR/ARM LS12 .....108 C7
Claremont Ter *GTHN* BD7 .....4 C8
   WKFDW/WTN WF2 .....12 B5

WOR/ARM LS12 .....108 C7
Claremont Vw *BVRD* LS3 * 6 C7
Claremont Vls *BVRD* LS3 * 6 C7
Claremount *HDGY* LS6 .....87 G8
Claremount Rd *HDGY* LS6 .....87 G8
   HIPP HX3 .....146 C2
Claremount Ter *HIPP* HX3 .....146 K4
Clarence Dr *HORS* LS18 .....85 K7
   ILK LS29 .....40 B8
Clarence Gdns *HORS* LS18 .....85 K7
Clarence Rd *BSLYN/ROY* S71 .....243 K2
   HORS LS18 .....85 K7
   MID LS10 .....9 L4
   SHPY BD18 .....82 B6
   WKFDW/WTN WF2 .....12 D8
Clarence St *BRAM* LS13 .....107 L5
   BTLY WF17 .....173 M1
   CLECK BD19 .....149 M7
   COL BB8 .....74 C1
   COL BB8 .....74 E4
   HFAX HX1 .....10 C3
Clarence Ter *PDSY/CALV* LS28 .....106 F6
Clarence Wk *WKFDW/WTN* WF2 .....12 A5
Clarendon Ct *WKFDE* WF1 .....176 B7
Clarendon Pl *CUL/OBY* BD13 .....124 E6
   HFAX HX1 .....10 C5
   LDSU LS2 .....6 C5
Clarendon Rd *BGLY* BD16 .....81 K2
   BSPA/BRAM LS23 .....48 C5
   LDSU LS2 .....6 C5
Clarendon Ter *PDSY/CALV* LS28 .....107 G8
Clarendon Wy *LDSU* LS2 .....6 C5
Clare Rd *CLECK* BD19 .....149 L7
   HBR HX7 .....143 M5
   HFAX HX1 .....11 H7
   LM/WK BD12 .....148 E4
Clare St *HFAX* HX1 .....11 H7
Clarges St *WBOW* BD5 .....126 C3
Clarion St *WKFDE* WF1 .....13 K7
Clark Av *OSM* LS9 .....110 B5
Clark Ct *FEA/AMT* WF7 .....179 K5
Clark Crs *NORM* WF6 .....178 C2
Clarke Crs *NORM* WF6 .....178 C2
Clarke Gv *WKFDE* WF1 .....177 G5
Clarke Hall Rd *EARD/LOFT* WF3 .....177 G4
Clarke La *HOLM/MEL* HD9 .....235 G4
Clarke St *DEWS* WF13 .....172 F8
   DOD/DAR S75 .....260 A7
   MILN OL16 .....206 D4
   PDSY/CALV LS28 .....84 D8
Clark Gv *OSM* LS9 .....110 B5
Clark La *OSM* LS9 .....110 B5
Clark Mt *OSM* LS9 .....110 B5
Clark Rd *OSM* LS9 .....110 B5
Clark Rw *OSM* LS9 .....110 B8
Clarks Ct *AWLS/ASK* DN6 .....249 K6
Clarkson Av *HECK* WF16 .....173 G2
Clarkson Ct *NORM* WF6 .....178 C4
Clarkson Dr *GFTH/SHER* LS25 .....160 A3
Clarkson St *DEWS* WF13 .....172 F8
Clarkson Vw *HDGY* LS6 .....6 D1
Clark Spring Ri *MOR* LS27 .....130 D7
Clark Ter *OSM* LS9 .....110 B7
Clark Vw *OSM* LS9 * 110 B7
Clarney Av *WMB/DAR* S73 .....263 H8
Clarney Pl *WMB/DAR* S73 .....263 H8
Clattering Stones Rd *HBR* HX7 .....165 M4
Clay Butts *HUDN* HD2 .....192 A4
Claycliffe Av *DOD/DAR* S75 .....260 B2
Claycliffe Rd *DOD/DAR* S75 .....260 B1
Claycliffe Ter *BSLY* S70 * 260 F6
Clayfield *GTHN* BD7 .....126 B1
Clay Hill Dr *MAR/SLWT* HD7 .....212 C5
Clay House La *GTL/HWG* HX4 .....168 F7
Clay La *MAR/SLWT* HD7 .....212 C5
Claymore Ri *AIRE* BD20 .....36 B6
Clay Pit La *CHAL* LS7 .....7 H6
Claypit La *GFTH/SHER* LS25 .....136 D7
   SCFT LS14 .....90 B1
Clay Pits La *HFAX* HX1 .....10 A4
   RPDN/SBR HX6 .....166 C1
Clay St *HFAX* HX1 .....10 B5
   RPDN/SBR HX6 .....167 L2
Clayton Av *GFTH/SHER* LS25 .....135 K4
   HEM/SK/SE WF9 .....226 A6
Clayton Cl *MID* LS10 .....132 B4
Clayton Ct *FEA/AMT* WF7 .....201 L1
   MID LS10 .....132 B4
Clayton Dr *MID* LS10 .....132 B4
Clayton Flds *HUDN* HD2 .....192 A1
Clayton Fold *AIRE* BD20 .....35 G4
Clayton Gv *YEA* LS19 .....62 D7
Clayton Hall Rd *AIRE* BD20 .....35 G4
Clayton Holt *HEM/SK/SE* WF9 .....246 D5
Clayton La *CLAY* BD14 * 125 K3
   WBOW BD5 .....127 G2
Clayton Ms *NORM* WF6 .....178 C2
Clayton Pl *NORM* WF6 .....178 C2
Clayton Ri *AIRE* BD20 .....2 D2
Clayton Rd *GTHN* BD7 .....126 B1
   MID LS10 .....132 B4
Claytons Buildings
   FEA/AMT WF7 .....179 M6
Clayton St *COL* BB8 .....74 A2
   RTHW LS26 * 155 H1
   WHIT OL12 .....206 D4
   WKFDW/WTN WF2 .....12 B4
Clayton Vw *HEM/SK/SE* WF9 .....246 D5
Clayton Wy *MID* LS10 .....132 B4
Clayton Wood Bank
   BHP/TINH LS16 .....86 B5
Clayton Wood Cl
   BHP/TINH LS16 .....86 B5
Clayton Wood Ct
   BHP/TINH LS16 .....86 B5
Clayton Wood Ri
   BHP/TINH LS16 .....86 B5
Clayton Wood Rd
   BHP/TINH LS16 .....86 B5
Clay Well *MAR/SLWT* HD7 .....212 F2
The Clearings *MID* LS10 .....131 M6
Clear Vw *CUD/GR* S72 .....222 C7
Cleasby Rd *ILK* LS29 .....61 J3
Cleavesty La *AL/HA/HU* LS17 .....46 D7
Cleckheaton Rd *WBSY* BD6 .....126 D7
Cleeve Hl *YEA* LS19 .....84 D2
Cleevethorpe Gv
   WKFDW/WTN WF2 .....199 G6
Clegg Hall Rd *MILN* OL16 .....206 H7
Clegg La *GTL/HWG* HX4 .....168 B7
Clegg St *LIT* OL15 .....185 H7
Cleggswood Av *LIT* OL15 .....207 J1
Clement St *NORM* WF6 .....178 F5
Clement Ct *MILN* OL16 * 206 H7
Clementina St *WHIT* OL12 .....206 B5

Clement Royds St *WHIT* OL12 * 206 A6
Clement St *GIR* BD8 .....104 B6
   HUD HD1 .....14 D3
   HUDS HD4 .....213 M2
   RPDN/SBR HX6 * 167 K2
   WKFDW/WTN WF2 .....198 B1
Clement Ter *EARL* WF12 .....173 L8
   RTHW LS26 .....155 C2
Cleopatra Pl *BRAM* LS13 .....107 C5
Clerk Green St *BTLY* WF17 .....173 K2
Clevedon Pl *HIPP* HX3 .....146 K2
Cleveland Av *HIPP* HX3 * 168 F2
Cleveland Dr *MILN* OL16 .....207 J8
Cleveland Garth
   WKFDW/WTN WF2 .....197 M4
Cleveland Gv
Cleveland Pl *HBR* HX7 .....143 J3
Cleveland Rd *HTON* BD9 .....104 D3
   HUD HD1 .....191 M7
Cleveland St *COL* BB8 .....52 B8
   TOD OL14 .....140 D5
Cleveland Wy *KBTN* HD8 .....238 B4
Cleveleys Av *BEE/HOL* LS11 .....8 B7
Cleveleys Mt *BEE/HOL* LS11 * 8 B7
Cleveleys St *BEE/HOL* LS11 * 8 B7
Cleveleys Ter *BEE/HOL* LS11 * 8 B7
Clevlands Cl *ROY/SHW* OL2 .....229 J6
   HUDW HD3 .....191 K8
Cliff Ct *HOR/CROF* WF4 * 219 M2
Cliff Crs *GFTH/SHER* LS25 .....135 L5
Cliffdale Rd *CHAL* LS7 .....109 K2
Cliffe Ash *MAR/SLWT* HD7 .....212 F2
Cliffe Av *BAIL* BD17 .....82 E3
   BGLY BD16 .....80 C5
   HIPP HX3 .....148 D3
Cliffe Ct *BSLYN/ROY* S71 .....261 L3
   DOD/DAR S75 .....260 A7
Cliffe Crest *HOR/CROF* WF4 .....197 K4
Cliffedale Crs *BSLY* S70 .....261 K8
Cliffe Dr *YEA* LS19 .....84 D4
Cliffe End Rd *HUDW* HD3 .....191 K8
Cliffe Gdns *SHPY* BD18 .....82 D6
Cliffe House Av
   GFTH/SHER LS25 .....135 J1
Cliffe La *BAIL* BD17 .....82 E3
   BSLYN/ROY S71 .....261 L3
   CLECK BD19 .....150 A5
   CUL/OBY BD13 .....103 G7
   YEA LS19 .....84 D3
Cliffe La South *BAIL* BD17 .....82 E5
Cliffe La West *BAIL* BD17 .....82 E4
Cliffe Mill Fold *AIRE* BD20 .....58 G6
Cliffe Mt *CLECK* BD19 .....150 C5
   MOR LS27 * 151 J4
Cliffe Park Cha *WOR/ARM* LS12 .....108 C1
Cliffe Park Cl *WOR/ARM* LS12 .....108 C1
Cliffe Park Crs *WOR/ARM* LS12 .....130 C1
Cliffe Park Dr *WOR/ARM* LS12 .....108 C1
Cliffe Park Mt *WOR/ARM* LS12 .....108 B8
Cliffe Park Wy *MOR* LS27 .....151 M3
Cliffe Rd *BFDE* BD3 .....105 H4
   BRIG HD6 .....170 C4
   KBTN HD8 .....238 B4
   KCHY BD21 .....79 K2
Cliffestone Dr *AIRE* BD20 .....58 F4
Cliffe St *BTLY* WF17 .....173 K2
   CUL/OBY BD13 .....102 F7
   DEWS WF13 .....173 M5
   HBR HX7 .....143 J3
   HOLM/MEL HD9 .....254 D1
   KBTN HD8 .....240 B4
Cliffe Ter *BAIL* BD17 .....82 E3
   GIR BD8 .....4 C1
   KCHY BD21 .....79 L2
   RPDN/SBR HX6 .....166 F7
   WIL/AL BD15 .....103 H4
Cliffe Vw *KBTN* HD8 .....240 B4
Cliffewood Ri *KBTN* HD8 .....240 B4
Cliff Gdns *LUD/ILL* HX2 .....168 A1
Cliff Gv *HOR/CROF* WF4 * 219 L2
Cliff Hill Ct *HOLM/MEL* HD9 .....254 D1
Cliff Hill La *LUD/ILL* HX2 .....145 K8
Cliff Hollins La *LM/WK* BD12 .....127 M8
Cliff House La *HOLM/MEL* HD9 .....254 C1
Cliff La *CUD/GR* S72 .....245 G4
   HDGY LS6 .....6 B1
   HOLM/MEL HD9 .....254 D1
   RPDN/SBR HX6 .....188 F4
   YEA LS19 .....12 D1
Cliff Mt *HDGY* LS6 .....6 C1
Cliff Mount St *HDGY* LS6 .....6 C1
Cliff Mount Ter *HDGY* LS6 .....6 C1
Clifford Av *ILK* LS29 .....38 C1
   WKFDW/WTN WF2 .....198 F4
Clifford Ct *BSPA/BRAM* LS23 * 70 A1
Clifford Hodgson Pl
   MOR LS27 * 130 D7
Clifford Moor Rd
   BSPA/BRAM LS23 .....48 D7
Clifford Pl *MOR* LS27 .....130 D7
Clifford Rd *BAIL* BD17 .....82 E4
   BSPA/BRAM LS23 .....49 G7
   BSPA/BRAM LS23 .....69 M3
   HEM/SK/SE WF9 .....246 B4
   ILK LS29 .....20 C8
Clifford St *AIRE* BD20 .....35 M4
   COL BB8 .....74 A1
   CUD/GR S72 .....244 E5
   HEM/SK/SE WF9 .....247 H4
   ROCH OL11 .....228 B5
   SKP/WHF BD23 .....16 B3
   WBOW BD5 .....6 A9
Clifford Vw *WKFDW/WTN* WF2 .....198 F4
Cliff Pde *WKFDE* WF1 .....12 D1
Cliff Park Av *WKFDE* WF1 .....12 D1
Cliff Rd *HDGY* LS6 .....6 C1
   HOLM/MEL HD9 .....253 M1
   HOLM/MEL HD9 .....254 C1
   HOR/CROF WF4 .....219 L2
Cliff Side Gdns *HDGY* LS6 .....109 J1
Cliff St *HWTH* BD22 .....78 F7
   MILN OL16 .....206 E6
   PONT WF8 .....180 E6
   WKFDW/WTN WF2 .....176 B7
Cliff Ter *BSLYN/ROY* S71 .....261 J7
   HDGY LS6 .....6 C1
Cliff Vale Rd *SHPY* BD18 .....104 D1

Cliff Villa Ct *WKFDE* WF1 .....12 C1
Cliff Wood Av *SHPY* BD18 .....82 D8
Clifton Av *BSLYN/ROY* S71 .....243 G6
   EARD/LOFT WF3 .....177 G1
   HFAX HX1 .....10 A1
   HOLM/MEL HD9 .....236 D8
   HOR/CROF WF4 .....197 J4
   OSM LS9 .....110 C5
   PONT WF8 .....180 D5
Clifton Cl *BSLYN/ROY* S71 .....243 G6
   HOR/CROF WF4 .....197 H4
Clifton Common *HOLM/MEL* HD6 .....170 F6
Clifton Ct *DEWS* WF13 .....173 H5
Clifton Crs *BSLYN/ROY* S71 .....243 H5
   HOR/CROF WF4 .....197 J4
Clifton Dr *HOR/CROF* WF4 .....197 J4
   PDSY/CALV LS28 .....107 G6
Clifton Gdns *CUD/GR* S72 .....245 G3
   ROY/SHW OL2 * 110 C5
Clifton Hl *PDSY/CALV* LS28 .....107 G6
Clifton La *HOLM/MEL* HD9 .....235 G4
   OT LS21 .....41 G3
Clifton Pl *PDSY/CALV* LS28 .....107 G6
   SHPY BD18 .....176 D6
   WKFDE WF1 .....176 D6
Clifton Rd *BRIG* HD6 .....170 D4
   HIPP HX3 .....168 E2
   HOR/CROF WF4 .....200 D3
   HUD HD1 .....14 A5
   PDSY/CALV LS28 .....107 G6
Clifton Side *HUDN* HD2 .....171 H8
Clifton St *BSLY* S70 .....261 J4
   COL BB8 .....74 D4
   GIR BD8 .....4 C1
   HEM/SK/SE WF9 .....223 L8
   HIPP HX3 .....10 C1
   HWTH BD22 .....2 C7
   MILN OL16 .....228 C1
   RPDN/SBR HX6 .....167 L2
Clifton Ter *BTLY* WF17 .....173 M1
   OSM LS9 .....110 C5
Clifton Vw *KBTN* HD8 .....240 B4
   OSM LS9 .....110 C5
Clifton Vls *GIR* BD8 .....4 C1
Cliftonville Rd *MILN* OL16 .....228 C6
Clipston Av *HDGY* LS6 .....87 H8
Clipstone Av *BSLYN/ROY* S71 .....243 H6
Clipstone St *WBOW* BD5 .....6 A9
Clipston St *HDGY* LS6 .....87 H8
Clipston Ter *HDGY* LS6 * 87 H8
Clive Pl *GTHN* BD7 .....126 D1
Clive Rd *PBR* HG3 .....28 C7
Clive Ter *GTHN* BD7 .....126 D1
Cloberry St *LDSU* LS2 .....6 D1
Clock La *CUL/OBY* BD13 .....101 M5
Clock Row Av *HEM/SK/SE* WF9 .....246 F3
Clock Row Gv *HEM/SK/SE* WF9 .....246 F3
Clock View St *AIRE* BD20 .....57 K5
Clog Br *BRIG* HD6 .....38 A5
Clog Sole Rd *BRIG* HD6 .....170 B2
The Cloisters *HFAX* HX1 .....10 C9
   MILN OL16 .....206 B7
Cloisters Wy *BSLYN/ROY* S71 * 261 M4
Close Head Dr *CUL/OBY* BD13 .....102 C8
Close Head La *CUL/OBY* BD13 .....102 C8
Close Lea *HWTH* BD22 .....54 E5
Close Lea Av *BRIG* HD6 .....170 B5
Close Lea Dr *BRIG* HD6 .....170 B6
Close Lea Wy *BRIG* HD6 .....170 B5
Close Rd *CAS* WF10 .....158 B7
Closes Rd *BRIG* HD6 .....170 B5
Close St *HEM/SK/SE* WF9 .....246 F3
The Close *AL/HA/HU* LS17 .....67 L1
   AL/HA/HU LS17 .....67 L1
   AWLS/ASK DN6 .....227 M3
   BSLYN/ROY S71 .....243 L5
   BSLYN/ROY S71 .....262 A3
   BSPA/BRAM LS23 .....69 M3
   EARD/LOFT WF3 .....153 M7
   GFTH/SHER LS25 .....135 J5
   GSLY LS20 .....61 L6
   HOR/CROF WF4 .....198 A7
   KBTN HD8 .....240 A4
   MSTN/BAR LS15 .....90 F8
   OSM LS9 .....9 H3
   PONT WF8 .....181 H7
   SCFT LS14 .....90 E3
   SKP/WHF BD23 .....16 B3
   TAD LS24 .....93 M3
   WBY LS22 .....47 K6
Cloth Hall St *DEWS* WF13 .....173 H6
   HUD HD1 .....14 F7
   LDSU LS2 .....9 H1
Cloudberry Wy *DOD/DAR* S75 .....242 H5
Cloudsdale Av *WBOW* BD5 .....127 G2
Clough Av *AIRE* BD20 .....56 K1
Clough Bank *LUD/ILL* HX2 .....145 K1
Clough Bank La *HWTH* BD22 .....56 A8
Clough Ct *CUL/OBY* BD13 .....102 A8
Clough Dr *BTLY* WF17 .....151 J4
   KBTN HD8 .....215 M4
   MAR/SLWT HD7 .....212 F6
Clough Foot La
   HOLM/MEL HD9 .....254 C7
Clough Ga *HOR/CROF* WF4 .....216 F1
   HWTH BD22 .....78 F4
Clough Gate Dr
   HOR/CROF WF4 .....216 F1
Clough Gn *DOD/DAR* S75 .....258 D3
Clough Hall La *HUDS* HD4 .....214 E6
Clough Head *STKB/PEN* S36 .....258 F7
Clough Hey *MAR/SLWT* HD7 .....233 H2
Clough House La *HUDN* HD2 .....192 B4
Clough House La *GTL/HWG* HX4 .....189 H3
   KBTN HD8 .....239 L8
   MAR/SLWT HD7 .....212 F6
   WHIT OL12 .....184 D8
Clough La *BRIG* HD6 .....170 B8
   BRIG HD6 .....170 F1
   HBR HX7 .....143 L2
   HUD HD1 .....213 L1
   HUDN HD2 .....192 B1
   HWTH BD22 .....78 E3
   LUD/ILL HX2 .....145 K1
   LVSG WF15 .....171 M2
Clough Lea *MAR/SLWT* HD7 .....233 H2
Clough Ml *TOD* OL14 .....141 H5
Clough Pk *KBTN* HD8 .....215 M4
Clough Pl *LUD/ILL* HX2 .....145 K1
Clough Rd *HOR/CROF* WF4 .....217 M5
   HUDN HD2 .....192 C4
   MAR/SLWT HD7 .....212 C2
   ROY/SHW OL2 .....229 M8
   RPDN/SBR HX6 .....167 M4
   TOD OL14 .....163 H5
Clough St *MOR* LS27 .....152 D2
   WBOW BD5 .....117 G3
   WHIT OL12 .....184 E8
Clough Ter *LIT* OL15 .....185 J7
The Clough *KBTN* HD8 .....215 M3
   MIRF WF14 .....172 A8
Clough Wy *KBTN* HD8 .....215 M4

Clovelly Av BEE/HOL LS11 .....131 K3
Clovelly Gv BEE/HOL LS11 .....131 K3
Clovelly Pl BEE/HOL LS11 .....131 K3
Clovelly Rw BEE/HOL LS11 .....131 K3
Clovelly St BEE/HOL LS11 .....131 K3
Clover Ct PDSY/CALV LS28 .....84 C8
Clover Crs PDSY/CALV LS28 .....84 C7
Cloverdale HIPP HX3 .....125 M7
Clover Hall Crs MILN OL16 .....206 E5
Clover Hl LVSG WF15 .....171 M1
SKP/WHF BD23 .....16 D1
Clover Hill Rd HFAX HX1 .....10 F8
Clover Hill Rd HFAX HX1 .....168 D1
Clover Hill Ter HFAX HX1 .....168 D1
Clover Hill Vw HFAX HX1 * 168 D1
Cloverlands Dr DOD/DAR S75 .....242 E6
Clover Ri KGHY LS20 .....3 M5
Clover St WBOW BD5 .....126 D3
WHIT OL12 .....206 A6
Clover Vw MILN OL16 * 206 E7
Cloverville Bd WBSY BD6 .....126 E7
Clover Wk HEM/SK/SE WF9 .....225 J7
Clubhouses Cft HOR/CROF WF4 .....197 L3
Club La LS13 .....107 G1
LUD/ILL HX2 .....146 B3
Club Rw CHAL LS7 .....87 L2
YEA LS19 .....62 E7
Club St BSLYN/ROY S71 .....261 L2
GTHN BD7 .....104 B8
TOD OL14 .....140 D5
Clumber Dr CLECK BD19 .....150 D7
Clumber St DOD/DAR S75 .....260 E4
Cluntergate HOR/CROF WF4 .....197 K5
Clunters La LUD/ILL HX2 .....144 D8
Clutton St BTLY WF17 .....174 A1
Clyde Ap WOR/ARM LS12 * 109 G8
Clyde Cha WOR/ARM LS12 .....109 G8
Clyde Ct MILN OL16 .....206 D8
WOR/ARM LS12 .....109 G8
Clyde Gra WOR/ARM LS12 .....109 G8
Clydesdale Dr WBSY BD6 .....126 B7
Clyde St BSLYN/ROY S71 .....261 H3
RPDN/SBR HX6 .....167 K3
WKFDW WF1 .....13 K1
Clyde Vw WOR/ARM LS12 * 109 G8
Clyde Wk WOR/ARM LS12 .....109 G8
Coach Gate La STKB/PEN S36 .....257 M4
Coachgates HOR/CROF WF4 .....217 K4
Coach House Dr HUDE HD5 .....215 H1
Coach House La BSLY S70 .....261 H8
Coach La CLECK BD19 * 150 A6
OT LS21 .....24 D8
Coach Rd BAIL BD17 .....63 J7
GSLY LS20 .....61 M7
HIPP HX3 .....148 B7
HOLM/MEL HD9 .....235 H5
HUDN HD2 .....192 B4
RPDN/SBR HX6 .....188 F2
WKFDE WF1 .....176 E1
WOR/ARM LS12 .....130 A3
Coach St SKP/WHF BD23 .....16 B2
Coach Street Yd
SKP/WHF BD23 * 16 B2
Coalby Wk BSLY S70 * 261 G4
Coal Clough La TOD OL14 .....140 C4
Coal Ga MAR/SLWT HD7 .....211 H5
Coal Gate Rd RPDN/SBR HX6 .....188 A4
Coal Hill Dr BRAM LS13 .....107 H2
Coal Hill Fold BRAM LS13 .....107 H1
Coal Hill Gdns BRAM LS13 .....107 H2
Coal Hill Gn BRAM LS13 .....107 H2
Coal Hill La PDSY/CALV LS28 .....107 G2
Coal La LUD/ILL HX2 .....124 A3
Coal Pit La BRIG HD6 .....170 F5
BTLY WF17 .....151 J8
COL BB8 .....74 B7
CUD/GR S72 .....262 E1
HEM/SK/SE WF9 .....248 A2
HOLM/MEL HD9 .....237 G8
KBTN HD8 .....238 F6
PONT WF8 .....226 B3
Coalpit La HIPP HX3 .....169 C2
KBTN HD8 .....257 H3
Coal Pit Ms BTLY WF17 .....151 J8
Coal Rd AL/HA/HU LS17 .....67 G6
AL/HA/HU LS17 .....89 K8
SCFT LS14 .....89 K8
Coates Cl EARL WF12 .....174 A5
Coate's La AIRE BD20 .....35 H1
Coates St WBOW BD5 .....126 F2
Coates Ter WBOW BD5 .....126 F2
Cobb Av WKFDW/WTN WF2 .....198 B2
Cobbler Hall HOR/CROF WF4 .....219 H4
Cobbler's La PONT WF8 .....181 H5
Cobcroft La WEN WF11 .....182 F7
KNOT WF11 .....183 K5
Cobcroft Rd HUDN HD2 .....14 F1
Cobden Av WOR/ARM LS12 .....130 F1
Cobden Ct HFAX HX1 .....10 F4
Cobden Gv WOR/ARM LS12 .....130 B2
Cobden Ms MOR LS27 .....152 C1
Cobden Pl WOR/ARM LS12 .....130 C2
Cobden Rd WOR/ARM LS12 .....130 C2
Cobden St CLAY BD14 .....125 K2
CUL/QBY BD13 .....125 H5
IDLE BD10 .....83 K7
TOD OL14 .....163 K1
WIL/AL BD15 .....103 J5
WOR/ARM LS12 .....130 B2
Cobden Ter ELL HX5 * 191 H1
WOR/ARM LS12 .....130 B2
Cobham Pde WKFDE WF1 * 176 D2
Cobham Wk MSTN/BAR LS15 .....112 B4
Cob La BWCK/EAR BB18 .....52 D2
Cockburn Cl BEE/HOL LS11 .....9 C9
Cockburn Wy BEE/HOL LS11 .....9 C9
Cockerham Av DOD/DAR S75 .....261 G3
Cockerham St DOD/DAR S75 .....261 G3
Cockermouth La
HOR/CROF WF4 .....216 E4
Cockhill La COL BB8 .....52 D6
Cock Hill La HIPP HX3 .....147 J8
Cocking La ILK LS29 .....36 E1
Cockin La CLAY BD14 .....125 C3
CUL/QBY BD13 .....124 F3
Cock La HOR/CROF WF4 .....200 A5
Cockley Hill La HUDE HD5 .....193 J6
Cockley Mdw HUDE HD5 .....193 J6
Cock Pit La GTL/HWC HX4 .....189 C6
Cockroft Gv WBO BD3 .....5 J5
Cockshott Dr WOR/ARM LS12 .....108 B5
Cockshott La IDLE BD10 .....83 J6
WOR/ARM LS12 .....108 B5
Cockshott Pl ILK LS29 .....19 G6
Coggil St MID LS10 .....132 C4
Coiners Fold HBR HX7 .....143 H5
Colbeck Rw BTLY WF17 .....151 G6
Colbert Av ILK LS29 .....39 G5
Colby Ri MSTN/BAR LS15 .....111 C7
Coldbeck Dr WBSY BD6 .....126 A6
Coldcotes Av OSM LS9 .....110 D4
Coldcotes Crs OSM LS9 .....110 D4
Coldcotes Dr OSM LS9 .....110 E4
Coldcotes Garth OSM LS9 .....110 F4
Coldcotes Gv OSM LS9 .....110 F4

Coldcotes Vw OSM LS9 .....110 E4
Coldcotes Wk OSM LS9 .....110 F4
Cold Edge Rd LUD/ILL HX2 .....122 C1
LUD/ILL HX2 .....145 H1
Colden St HWTH BD22 * 143 H3
Colden La HBR HX7 .....120 B8
Colders Dr HOLM/MEL HD9 .....234 F5
Colders Gn HOLM/MEL HD9 .....234 F4
Cold Greave Cl MILN OL16 .....229 L2
Cold Hiendley Common La
HOR/CROF WF4 .....221 L5
Coldhill La GFTH/SHER LS25 .....115 H1
Cold Hill La HOLM/MEL HD9 .....237 G2
HUDS HD4 .....214 C6
Cold Royd La HUDE HD5 .....193 J7
Coldshaw Top HWTH BD22 .....78 E8
Coldstream St HWTH BD22 .....78 E8
Cold Well La HOLM/MEL HD9 .....253 K2
Cold Well La HOLM/MEL HD9 .....253 K2
Coldwells Hi GTL/HWC HX4 .....190 A3
Cold Well La MSTN/BAR LS15 * 111 K5
Coldwell St MAR/SLWT HD7 .....212 F5
Colehill Wy BOW BD4 .....127 L6
Coleman St BFDE BD3 .....5 G2
WOR/ARM LS12 .....8 A3
Colenso Gdns BEE/HOL LS11 .....8 B7
Colenso Gv BEE/HOL LS11 .....8 B7
BD21 * 3 M1
Colenso Mt BEE/HOL LS11 .....8 B7
Colenso Pl BEE/HOL LS11 .....8 B7
Colenso Rd BEE/HOL LS11 .....8 B7
Colenso Ter BEE/HOL LS11 .....8 B7
Colenso Wk KGHY BD21 .....3 M1
Colenso Wy KGHY BD21 .....3 M1
Coleridge Av BSLYN/ROY S71 .....261 K2
Coleridge Cl RTHW LS26 .....155 L1
Coleridge Crs
WKFDW/WTN WF2 .....176 B3
Coleridge Gdns IDLE BD10 .....83 L6
Coleridge La PDSY/CALV LS28 .....129 H1
Coleridge Rd LIT OL15 .....207 H4
Coleridge St HFAX HX1 .....11 H1
Coleridge Wy PONT WF8 .....180 F4
Coles Wy AIRE BD20 .....57 M4
Coley Hall La HIPP HX3 .....147 M4
Coley Rd HIPP HX3 .....147 L3
Coley Vw HIPP HX3 .....147 J3
Colinsway WKFDW/WTN WF2 .....12 C4
Collbrook Av WBSY BD6 .....126 E6
Colleen Rd HOR/CROF WF4 .....220 A1
College Ct AIRE BD20 .....34 E1
College Dr LIT OL15 * 38 D3
College Farm La WBY LS22 .....47 K3
College Gv CAS WF10 .....157 J8
WKFDE WF1 * 176 D7
College Grove Cl WKFDE WF1 .....176 D6
College Grove Rd WKFDE WF1 .....176 E6
College Grove Vw WKFDE WF1 * 176 E6
College La AIRE BD20 .....16 F8
College Lawns WOR/ARM LS12 .....108 C6
College Rd AIRE BD20 .....34 F1
BGLY BD16 .....59 J8
CAS WF10 .....158 D7
MOR LS27 .....129 M8
College St BTLY WF17 .....151 G5
HUDS HD4 .....213 M2
TOD OL14 .....140 E5
College Ter HFAX HX1 * 168 B1
College Vw WOR/ARM LS12 .....108 C7
Collier Av MILN OL16 .....207 H7
Collier Hag La COP/BISH YO23 .....33 M8
Collier La BAIL BD17 .....82 D2
GFTH/SHER LS25 .....114 B2
Collier Rd CUD/GR S72 .....244 F5
Colliers Cl SHPY BD18 .....82 A7
Colliers La AL/HA/HU LS17 .....89 G2
Colliers Wy KBTN HD8 .....240 B2
Colliery Ap WKFDE WF1 .....176 D1
Collindale Cl IDLE BD10 .....84 A8
Collinfield Ri WBSY BD6 .....126 B8
Collinge St HWTH BD22 .....54 F3
Collinge St ROY/SHW OL2 * 229 K7
Collingham Av WBSY BD6 .....125 M6
Collingham Dr GFTH/SHER LS25 .....113 H8
Collingwood Rd NORM WF6 .....178 C4
Collin Moor La GTL/HWC HX4 .....168 E6
Collin Rd SCFT LS14 .....111 H5
Collins Cl DOD/DAR S75 .....260 F4
HWTH BD22 .....79 G6
Collinson St CLECK BD19 .....149 M6
Collins St BOW BD4 .....127 K1
GTHN BD7 .....126 C3
Collyer Vw ILK LS29 .....39 G1
Colmore Gv WOR/ARM LS12 .....130 F1
Colmore Rd WOR/ARM LS12 .....108 C7
Colmore St WOR/ARM LS12 .....130 E1
Colne Hurst HUDN HD2 .....193 G2
Colne La COL BB8 .....74 A2
Colne Rd AIRE BD20 .....55 H1
BWCK/EAR BB18 .....52 B2
COL BB8 .....74 A2
HUD HD1 .....214 C2
HWTH BD22 .....54 C4
Colne Rd (Goodley) HWTH BD22 .....78 E4
Colne St HUD HD1 .....14 B9
Colne Vale Rd HUDW HD3 .....213 J2
Colne Valley Circular Wk
MAR/SLWT HD7 .....211 H6
MAR/SLWT HD7 .....212 D2
ELL HX5 .....169 K7
STKB/PEN S36 .....270 F2
Coniston Cl CUL/QBY BD13 .....124 F5
DOD/DAR S75 .....242 C4
HDGY LS6 .....130 C1
HUDE HD5 .....215 L6
Coniston Ct EARD/LOFT WF3 .....154 E7
Coniston Dr CAS WF10 .....159 G7
Coniston Crs WKFDE WF1 .....177 G6
Coniston Gdns CAS WF10 .....159 G7
MSTN/BAR LS15 .....111 G7
Coniston Gv COL BB8 .....52 B8
HTON BD9 .....104 B3
ROY/SHW OL2 .....228 F8
Coniston Rd BSLYN/ROY S71 .....261 J5
EARL WF12 .....174 B4
GTHN BD7 .....126 A3
HOLM/MEL HD9 .....235 G6
NORM WF6 .....133 L2
Coniston Wy RTHW LS26 .....133 L7
WBY LS22 .....29 K8
Connaught Av ROCH OL11 .....228 D4
Connaught Fold HUDN HD2 .....193 G1
Connaught Rd ILK LS29 .....37 G6
Cononley La AIRE BD20 .....34 C4
Cononley Rd AIRE BD20 .....34 D6
Consort Av ROY/SHW OL2 .....228 F8
Consort St BVRD LS3 .....8 D1
SKP/WHF BD23 .....16 C2
Consort Vw BVRD LS3 .....8 D1
Consort Wk BVRD LS3 .....8 D1
Constable Dr OSS WF5 .....174 E8
Constable Rd EARD/LOFT WF3 .....153 H6
ILK LS29 .....38 F3
The Combs EARL WF12 .....196 A5
Commerce Ct BOW BD4 .....127 M2

Commercial Buildings
LM/WK BD12 .....149 K2
Commercial Ct LDS LS1 .....9 G2
Commercial Rd DEWS WF13 .....173 L5
KBTN HD8 .....239 J4
KSTL LS5 .....108 C3
Commercial St BFD BD1 * 5 G5
BRIC HD6 .....170 C4
BSLY S70 .....261 J6
BTLY WF17 .....174 B1
CAS WF10 .....157 M6
CLECK BD19 .....150 A7
CUL/QBY BD13 .....101 M6
CUL/QBY BD13 .....103 G8
CUL/QBY BD13 .....124 F5
DEWS WF13 .....173 H8
EARL WF12 .....174 B7
HBR HX7 .....143 J3
HECK WF16 .....173 G2
HFAX HX1 .....11 H7
HUD HD1 .....14 C4
LDS LS1 .....9 G9
LDS LS1 .....7 G9
MAR/SLWT HD7 .....212 C6
MOR LS27 .....152 C2
RTHW LS26 .....155 H1
SHPY BD18 .....82 D6
TAD LS24 .....71 M3
TOD OL14 .....163 L1
WKFDE WF1 .....12 F6
Commercial Vls
PDSY/CALV LS28 .....106 F8
Commondale Wy BOW BD4 .....127 J8
Common End HOR/CROF WF4 .....217 K4
Common End La KBTN HD8 .....215 M4
Common Holme La ILK LS29 .....20 A8
Common Ing La
HOR/CROF WF4 .....222 D4
Common La AWLS/ASK DN6 .....227 M3
BSLYN/ROY S71 .....243 L2
BTLY DN5 .....246 B8
EARD/LOFT WF3 .....153 L5
GFTH/SHER LS25 .....138 B2
GLE DN14 .....161 J8
HEM/SK/SE WF9 .....225 H7
HIPP HX3 .....147 H8
HOR/CROF WF4 .....219 M6
KBTN HD8 .....217 C7
KNOT WF11 .....182 F3
KNOT WF11 .....183 G4
PONT WF8 .....225 K2
SEL YO8 .....139 K4
TAD LS24 .....95 C3
WKFDW/WTN WF2 .....221 H1
Common Rd BTLY WF17 .....173 H2
CUD/GR S72 .....245 A5
CUD/GR S72 .....246 A5
EARD/LOFT WF3 .....155 H7
ELL HX5 .....169 L8
HEM/SK/SE WF9 .....223 J4
HUD HD1 .....14 E2
LM/WK BD12 .....126 D8
TAD LS24 .....116 B1
Common Road Av
HEM/SK/SE WF9 .....246 C5
Commonside BTLY WF17 .....173 M4
LVSG WF15 .....172 A4
Common Side La FEA/AMT WF7 .....179 J8
The Common EARL WF12 .....195 M3
Como Av GIR BD8 .....104 B3
Como Gdns GIR BD8 .....104 B3
Como Gv GIR BD8 .....104 B3
Compeigne Av AIRE BD20 .....58 B5
Compton Av OSM LS9 .....110 C4
Compton Crs OSM LS9 .....110 C4
Compton Pl OSM LS9 .....110 C4
Compton La AL/HA/HU LS17 .....68 B1
WBY LS22 .....47 L8
Compton Mt OSM LS9 .....110 C4
Compton Rd OSM LS9 .....110 C4
Compton Rw OSM LS9 .....110 C4
Compton St BOW BD4 .....127 L4
KGHY BD21 .....3 J3
OSM LS9 .....110 C4
Compton Ter OSM LS9 .....110 C4
Compton Vw OSM LS9 .....110 C4
Concordia St LDS LS1 .....9 G5
Concord St HARM/MEL HD9 .....236 B2
LDSU LS2 .....7 J7
Concrete St HIPP HX3 .....10 D1
Condor Cl WBSY BD6 .....125 L5
Conduit St GIR BD8 .....4 A1
Cone La DOD/DAR S75 .....259 J7
Coney La KGHY BD21 .....3 H6
Coney Moor Gv RTHW LS26 .....157 H3
Coney Wk DEWS WF13 .....173 H4
Coney Warren La
EARD/LOFT WF3 .....155 G6
Conference Pl WOR/ARM LS12 .....108 C7
Conference Rd WOR/ARM LS12 .....108 C7
Conference Ter WOR/ARM LS12 .....108 C7
Congress Mt WOR/ARM LS12 .....108 C7
Congress St WOR/ARM LS12 .....108 C7
Congreve Ap AL/HA/HU LS17 .....47 G8
Congreve Wy AL/HA/HU LS17 .....47 G8
Conisborough La
GFTH/SHER LS25 .....113 K7
Coniston Av CUL/QBY BD13 .....124 F5

Constance Wy CHAL LS7 .....6 F4
Constantine Rd MILN OL16 .....206 B7
Constitutional St HFAX HX1 .....10 C9
Conway Av RHAY LS8 .....110 B3
Conway Crs BTLY WF17 .....173 L4
FEA/AMT WF7 .....179 L5
HOLM/MEL HD9 .....234 F1
Conway Dr RHAY LS8 .....110 B3
Conway Gv RHAY LS8 .....110 B3
Conway Mt RHAY LS8 .....110 B3
Conway Pl RHAY LS8 .....110 B3
Conway Rd RHAY LS8 .....110 B3
WKFDW/WTN WF2 .....176 A7
Conway St BSLY S70 .....261 M6
HFAX HX1 .....10 C7
PDSY/CALV LS28 .....106 C3
RHAY LS8 .....110 B3
Conway Ter RHAY LS8 .....110 B3
Conway Vw RHAY LS8 .....110 B3
Conyers Yd OSS WF5 * 175 G7
Cooke Crs CLECK BD19 .....150 C6
Cookson St BRIG HD6 .....170 B3
Cook La CL MILN OL16 .....206 D5
Cook Ter MILN OL16 .....206 D6
Cook House Rd COL BB8 .....52 A6
Cook La HECK WF16 .....172 E2
Cookridge Av BHP/TINH LS16 .....64 A8
Cookridge Dr BHP/TINH LS16 .....63 M8
Cookridge Gv BHP/TINH LS16 .....64 A8
Cookridge La BHP/TINH LS16 .....64 A7
Cookridge St LDSU LS2 .....6 F8
Cooksland La FEA/AMT WF7 .....179 G5
Cookson Cl CAS WF10 .....180 F1
Cookson St BRIG HD6 .....170 B3
Cook Cl MILN OL16 .....206 D5
Cook Ter MILN OL16 .....206 D6
Coombe HI CUL/QBY BD13 .....125 K4
Coombe Rd HUDW HD3 .....213 H1
Co-operative Buildings
BRIC HD6 .....148 D7
HIPP HX3 .....146 B4
Co-operative St CUD/GR S72 .....244 D5
EARD/LOFT WF3 .....154 C5
EARL WF12 .....174 D6
HOR/CROF WF4 .....197 J5
MIRF WF14 .....194 C3
MOR LS27 .....152 C1
ROY/SHW OL2 * 229 K7
TOD OL14 .....163 J7
WKFDW/WTN WF2 .....12 A4
Co-operative Ter
HOLM/MEL HD9 .....236 E7
Cooper Bridge Rd HUDN HD2 .....171 M3
Cooper Cl BGLY BD16 .....81 J1
Cooperfields LUD/ILL HX2 .....167 G1
Cooper Gv WBSY BD6 .....125 M7
Cooper La HOLM/MEL HD9 .....254 C1
STKB/PEN S36 .....258 D7
WBSY BD6 .....125 M5
Cooper Rd DOD/DAR S75 .....241 L6
WBY LS22 .....48 A1
Cooper St TOD OL14 .....142 A8
WHIT OL12 .....206 F2
Cooper Ter MILN OL16 .....206 E4
Co-op La HOLM/MEL HD9 .....253 M3
Copeland St BOW BD4 .....127 M1
Copenhagen Sq MILN OL16 .....206 C6
Copenhagen St MILN OL16 .....206 C6
Cope St BSLY S70 .....261 H7
Copeworth Dr HOR/CROF WF4 .....220 B3
Copgrove Cl BOW BD4 .....128 A3
Copgrove Ct BOW BD4 .....128 A3
Copgrove Rd BOW BD4 .....128 A3
RHAY LS8 .....110 C1
Copley Av AL/HA/HU LS17 .....168 A4
Copley Bank Rd MAR/SLWT HD7 .....211 K6
Copley Gth HIPP HX3 .....168 A4
Copley Gv HIPP HX3 .....168 A4
Copley Hall St WOR/ARM LS12 .....109 G8
Copley HI BTLY WF17 .....151 H5
WOR/ARM LS12 .....109 G8
Copley Hill Wy WOR/ARM LS12 .....131 G5
Copley La EARD/LOFT WF3 .....154 D2
GFTH/SHER LS25 .....114 E1
HIPP HX3 .....168 A4
KBTN HD8 .....238 D6
Copley Mt HIPP HX3 .....168 A4
Copley St BTLY WF17 .....151 J7
ROY/SHW OL2 * 229 K6
WBOW BD5 .....126 D3
WOR/ARM LS12 * 109 G8
Copley Ter HIPP HX3 .....168 A4
Copley Yd WOR/ARM LS12 .....109 G8
Copperas House Ter TOD OL14 .....163 A4
Copperas Rw GTL/HWC HX4 * 168 A7
Copper Beech Ct
WKFDW/WTN WF2 .....199 H8
Copper Cl BSLY S70 .....261 H6
Copperfield Av OSM LS9 * 110 D7
Copperfield Cl GFTH/SHER LS25 .....116 B7
Copperfield Crs OSM LS9 .....110 C7
Copperfield Dr OSM LS9 .....110 C8
Copperfield Gv OSM LS9 .....110 D8
Copperfield Mt OSM LS9 .....110 D8
Copperfield Pl OSM LS9 .....110 C8
Copperfield Rw OSM LS9 .....110 D8
Copperfield Ter OSM LS9 .....110 D8
Copperfield Vw OSM LS9 .....110 D8
Copperfield Wk OSM LS9 .....110 D8
Coppertop Ms PONT WF8 .....181 G3
Coppice Cl WKFDE WF1 .....177 G6
Coppice Cft HUDS HD4 .....213 M8
Coppice Gra YEA LS19 .....62 M8
Coppice Head RTHW LS26 .....155 H1
The Coppice AIRE BD20 .....34 E8
GFTH/SHER LS25 .....116 B7
HFAX HX1 .....10 B7
HUDN HD2 .....192 D4
ILK LS29 .....20 C8
MIRF WF14 * 172 B6
MSTN/BAR LS15 .....90 F8
YEA LS19 .....84 B1
Coppice Vw IDLE BD10 .....83 G8
Coppice Wy RHAY LS8 .....88 C8
Coppice Wood Av GSLY LS20 .....62 C5
GTHN BD7 .....104 C8
Coppice Wood Crs YEA LS19 .....62 C5
Coppice Wood Gv GSLY LS20 .....62 C5
GTHN BD7 .....104 C8
Coppice Wood Ri YEA LS19 .....62 C5
The Coppies LM/WK BD12 .....148 C2
Coppin Hall Gv MIRF WF14 .....171 M8
Coppin Hall La MIRF WF14 .....171 M8
Coppy Cl BGLY BD16 .....81 J8
Coppy La AIRE BD20 .....34 B2
BRAM LS13 .....107 L2
HBR HX7 .....121 H3
HWTH BD22 .....55 L7
Coppy Nook La HBR HX7 .....166 A3
Coppy Rd AIRE BD20 .....56 D1
ILK LS29 .....19 G6

Coppy Wood Dr ILK LS29 .....20 D7
The Copse BGLY BD16 .....81 M3
CLECK BD19 .....149 H7
EARD/LOFT WF3 .....153 K7
FEA/AMT WF7 .....179 L5
ILK LS29 .....40 A6
Copster La STKB/PEN S36 .....271 M5
Copthorne Gdns HUDN HD2 .....193 H1
Copthurst Rd HOLM/MEL HD9 .....254 A7
Coptrod Head Cl WHIT OL12 .....206 A2
Copt Royd Gv YEA LS19 .....62 C7
Corban St BOW BD4 .....128 A1
Corbett St MILN OL16 .....206 C6
Corbett Wy UPML OL3 .....230 E5
Corby St HUDN HD2 .....192 C5
Cordingley Cl BOW BD4 .....128 A5
Cordingley St BOW BD4 .....128 A5
Corfe Cl BTLY WF17 .....151 K4
Corn Bank HUDS HD4 .....213 L8
Cornbrook Cl WHIT OL12 .....184 E8
Cornerstones Cl ILK LS29 .....19 J6
Cornfield DEWS WF13 .....173 G5
Cornfield Av HUD HD3 .....213 H1
Cornfield St MILN OL16 .....229 H1
TOD OL14 * 141 M8
Corn Market HFAX HX1 .....11 H6
Cornmarket PONT WF8 .....180 E6
Corn MI ILK LS29 .....61 K2
Cornmill Cl AL/HA/HU LS17 .....67 M3
Corn Mill Ct GFTH/SHER LS25 .....116 A6
WOR/ARM LS12 .....107 M7
Cornmill Crs LVSG WF15 .....172 C3
Cornmill Dr LVSG WF15 .....172 D3
Corn Mill La CLAY BD14 .....125 H1
ILK LS29 .....23 H1
Cornmill La AL/HA/HU LS17 .....67 M3
LVSG WF15 .....172 D3
Cornrace Vw HUD HD1 .....214 D2
Cornstone Fold
WOR/ARM LS12 .....107 L7
Corn St HWTH BD22 .....79 J2
Cornus Gdns MID LS10 .....131 M6
Cornwall Av AIRE BD20 .....35 L5
Cornwall Cl BSLYN/ROY S71 .....261 K2
RTHW LS26 * 132 F2
Cornwall Crs BAIL BD17 .....63 L8
BRIC HD6 .....148 D8
RTHW LS26 .....132 F8
Cornwall Pl GIR BD8 .....4 D2
Cornwall Rd BGLY BD16 .....81 K4
GIR BD8 .....4 D2
KGHY BD21 .....3 M1
Cornwall Ter GIR BD8 .....4 D2
Coronation Av CUD/GR S72 .....244 D3
CUD/GR S72 .....245 J4
GFTH/SHER LS25 .....135 L5
IDLE BD10 .....83 M2
NORM WF6 .....178 B3
Coronation Bungalows
GFTH/SHER LS25 .....135 L5
Coronation Mt HWTH BD22 .....2 B4
Coronation Pde
MSTN/BAR LS15 .....111 G8
Coronation Rd DOD/DAR S75 .....259 M2
HIPP HX3 .....168 C2
HOR/CROF WF4 .....200 D3
Coronation St BSLYN/ROY S71 .....261 L2
CAS WF10 .....158 B5
EARD/LOFT WF3 * 154 F3
ELL HX5 .....169 H8
GTL/HWC HX4 .....168 F6
LM/WK BD12 .....149 J1
NORM WF6 .....178 B3
WKFDW/WTN WF2 .....176 B4
WMB/DAR S73 .....263 K8
Coronation Ter BSLYN/ROY S71 .....262 B6
CAS WF10 .....158 C4
RPDN/SBR HX6 .....167 C8
Coronation Wk HWTH BD22 .....2 B4
Coronation Wy HWTH BD22 .....57 G6
Corporal La CUL/QBY BD13 .....125 G8
Corporation St BSLY S70 .....261 J7
DEWS WF13 .....173 M6
ECHL BD2 .....105 L3
HIPP HX3 .....11 G4
HUD HD1 .....14 F8
MOR LS27 .....152 C2
RPDN/SBR HX6 .....167 K2
Corporation Yd BTLY WF17 * 173 K1
Corrance Rd LM/WK BD12 .....148 F5
Corrie St BSLY S70 .....261 J8
Cortina Ri WMB/DAR S73 * 263 G8
Cotchers La TAD LS24 .....93 K6
Cote Farm La IDLE BD10 .....83 H6
Cotefields Av PDSY/CALV LS28 .....106 C4
Cote Gap CUL/QBY BD13 * 102 F7
Cote La HOLM/MEL HD9 .....254 C6
HUDN HD2 .....191 M1
LIT OL15 .....185 H4
PDSY/CALV LS28 .....106 C4
UPML OL3 .....231 K7
WIL/AL BD15 .....103 J3
Coteroyd Av MOR LS27 .....130 E6
Coteroyd Dr MOR LS27 .....130 E7
The Cote PDSY/CALV LS28 .....106 E4
Cote Wall Ms MIRF WF14 .....194 F3
Cotewall Rd WBOW BD5 .....126 F3
Cotswold Av ROY/SHW OL2 .....229 H6
SHPY BD18 .....83 G7
Cotswold Cl DOD/DAR S75 .....260 D4
HEM/SK/SE WF9 .....224 B7
Cotswold Crs MILN OL16 .....207 J7
Cotswold Dr GFTH/SHER LS25 .....135 H1
KNOT WF11 * 182 K2
LVSG WF15 .....171 M1
RTHW LS26 .....132 F3
Cotswold Ms KBTN HD8 .....216 B7
Cotswold Rd RTHW LS26 .....132 F8
WKFDW/WTN WF8 .....197 M1
Cottage Gn GIR BD8 .....104 B6
Cottage Ms HWTH BD22 * 78 D7
Cottage Rd HDGY LS6 .....86 F8
IDLE BD10 .....83 J7
HUDN HD2 .....192 D4
Cottam Av CTHN BD7 .....104 D8
Cottam Cft HEM/SK/SE WF9 .....224 A7
Cottam Ter GTHN BD7 .....104 D8
Cotterdale WIL/AL BD15 .....103 J3
Cotterdale Holt WBY LS22 .....47 J3
Cotterdale Vw MSTN/BAR LS15 .....111 G8
Cotterill Rd KNOT WF11 .....181 M3
Cottesmore Cl DOD/DAR S75 .....260 E3
Cottingley Cha BEE/HOL LS11 .....130 E4
Cottingley Cliffe Rd BGLY BD16 .....81 L8
Cottingley Crs BEE/HOL LS11 .....130 F5
Cottingley Dr BEE/HOL LS11 .....130 E4
BGLY BD16 .....81 J6
Cottingley Fold BEE/HOL LS11 .....130 F5
Cottingley Gdns BEE/HOL LS11 .....130 F5
Cottingley Gn BEE/HOL LS11 .....130 F5
Cottingley Gv BEE/HOL LS11 .....130 F5
Cottingley Manor Pk
BGLY BD16 .....81 K7
Cottingley Moor Rd BGLY BD16 .....103 J1
Cottingley New Rd BGLY BD16 .....81 K7
Cottingley Rd BEE/HOL LS11 .....130 E4
WIL/AL BD15 .....103 J3
Cottingley Ter GIR BD8 * 4 D2
Cottingley V BEE/HOL LS11 .....130 F5

Cotton Fold *MILN* OL16 ....206 E8
Cotton St *OSM* LS9 ....9 K2
WKFDW/WTN WF2 ....12 E6
Cotton Tree La *COL* BB8 ....74 C1
Couford Gv *HUDN* HD2 ....193 J2
Coule Royd *HUDE* HD5 ....193 G7
Coultas Cl *ILK* LS29 ....61 K2
Counting House Ms
  SKP/WHF BD23 ....16 B2
Count St *MILN* OL16 ....228 C2
County Ar *LDS* LS1 ....
County Cl *BTLY* WF17 ....151 L8
County Wy *BSLY* S70 ....69 H4
Coupe Gv *NORM* WF6 ....178 B1
Coupland Pl *BEE/HOL* LS11 ....8 E8
Coupland Rd *BEE/HOL* LS11 ....8 E8
  GFTH/SHER LS25 ....113 G8
Coupland St *BEE/HOL* LS11 ....8 E9
Court Dr *KSTL* LS5 ....86 A8
Courtenay Cl *BFDE* BD3 ....106 A7
Courtenays *SCFT* LS14 * 111 K2
Courthouse St *OT* LS21 ....41 J6
Court La *LUD/ILL* HX2 ....145 M7
  SKP/WHF BD23 ....
Courts Leet *LM/WK* BD12 ....148 E2
The Court *AL/HA/HU* LS17 ....87 H1
  LVSG WF15 ....172 A2
  SHPY BD18 ....82 A7
The Courtyards *SCFT* LS14 * 89 K7
The Court Yd *HOR/CROF* WF4 ....220 C7
The Courtyard *BTLY* WF17 ....151 H4
  HUDS HD4 ....213 M2
  PONT WF8 ....181 G3
  WKFDW/WTN WF2 ....197 M5
Cousen Av *BIRK/DRI* BD11 ....126 B1
Cousen Rd *GTHN* BD7 ....126 D2
Cousin La *AL/HA/HU* LS17 ....146 A2
Coutances Wy *ILK* LS29 ....39 J2
Coventry St *BOW* BD4 ....127 K2
  LUD/ILL HX2 ....146 A7
  ROCH OL11 ....206 B8
Coverdale Garth *WBY* LS22 ....47 J6
Coverdale Wy *BAIL* BD17 ....83 C2
Cover Dr *WBSY* BD6 ....126 C6
  WMB/DAR S73 ....263 K8
Coverley Ri *YEA* LS19 ....62 B7
The Covert *BTLY* WF17 ....151 H7
The Covert *IDLE* BD10 ....83 M6
Covey Clough Ct *MIRF* WF14 * 194 B5
Cowcliffe Hill Rd *HUDN* HD2 ....192 B4
Cowcliff Hill Rd
  HOLM/MEL HD9 ....254 F6
Cow Close Gv *WOR/ARM* LS12 ....130 B1
Cow Close La *LM/WK* BD12 ....149 G4
Cow Close Rd *WOR/ARM* LS12 ....130 B1
Cowdray Dr *CLECK* BD19 ....149 H6
Cowdry Cl *EARL* WF12 ....196 A4
Cowfold St *TOD* OL14 ....141 K8
Cow Ga *HUDW* HD3 ....191 H8
Cowgill St *GIR* BD8 ....4 A1
Cow Gn *HFAX* HX1 ....11 G6
Cow Hey La *HBR* HX7 ....120 F3
Cow Heys *HUDE* HD5 ....193 G7
Cow Hill Gate La *LUD/ILL* HX2 ....124 A6
Cowhurst Av *TOD* OL14 ....141 H7
Cowie St *ROY/SHW* OL2 ....229 K6
Cow La *AWLS/ASK* DN6 ....205 J3
  HBR HX7 ....121 G7
  HIPP HX3 ....169 M2
  HIPP HX3 ....
  HOR/CROF WF4 ....200 C7
  HOR/CROF WF4 ....222 E1
  HWTH BD22 ....54 D1
  RPDN/SBR HX6 ....166 F8
Cowlersley La *MAR/SLWT* HD7 ....213 J4
Cowley Crs *HTON* BD9 ....103 J2
Cowley Rd *BRAM* LS13 ....107 H1
Cowling Br *AIRE* BD20 ....35 L6
Cowling Hill La *HWTH* BD22 ....54 A3
Cowling La *HIPP* HX3 ....147 H1
Cowm St *WHIT* OL12 ....184 A1
Cowm Top La *ROCH* OL11 ....228 A4
Cowpasture Rd *ILK* LS29 ....38 E3
Cowper Av *OSM* LS9 ....110 C4
Cowper Crs *OSM* LS9 ....110 C4
Cowper Gv *RHAY* LS8 ....110 C3
Cowper Mt *OSM* LS9 ....110 C3
Cowper Rd *OSM* LS9 ....110 C4
Cowper St *CHAL* LS7 ....7 L2
  EARL WF12 ....173 L8
  SKP/WHF BD23 ....16 C3
Cowper Ter *OSM* LS9 ....110 C4
Cowrakes Cl *HUDW* HD3 ....191 J5
Cowrakes Rd *HUDW* HD3 ....191 H5
Cowroyd Pl *HIPP* HX3 ....11 J3
Cowslip St *HUD* HD1 * 213 M1
Coxley Crs *HOR/CROF* WF4 ....196 F8
Coxley La *HOR/CROF* WF4 ....196 F7
Coxley Vw *HOR/CROF* WF4 ....218 E1
Coxwold Hil *WBY* LS22 ....30 A7
Coxwold Vw *WBY* LS22 ....30 A8
Crabgate Dr *AWLS/ASK* DN6 ....249 G4
Crabgate La *AWLS/ASK* DN6 ....249 G4
Crab Hi *PONT* WF8 ....180 E6
Crab La *WKFDW/WTN* WF2 ....220 D2
  WOR/ARM LS12 ....108 D2
Crabtree Av *HECK* WF16 ....173 C1
Crabtree Dr *CUD/GR* S72 ....263 M3
Crabtree Gn *WBY* LS22 ....47 K6
Crabtree Hi *WBY* LS22 ....47 K6
Crabtree La *AL/HA/HU* LS17 ....46 E7
Crab Tree La *PONT* WF8 ....226 D4
Crabtree Pl *GTHN* BD7 ....126 C2
Crabtree St *GTHN* BD7 ....126 C2
  HFAX HX1 ....10 A6
Crabtree Wy *EARD/LOFT* WF3 * 153 H7
Crackenedge La *DEWS* WF13 ....173 M6
Crackenedge Ter *DEWS* WF13 ....173 L6
Crack La *WIL/AL* BD15 ....102 F1
Cracoe Rd *BFDE* BD3 ....5 M7
Craddock Rd *COL* BB8 ....74 A1
Crag Cl *AIRE* BD20 ....55 L2
  LUD/ILL HX2 ....145 M2
Crag Gdns *BSPA/BRAM* LS23 ....69 M4
Cragg Av *HORS* LS18 ....85 K6
Cragg Bottom Rd *HWTH* BD22 ....76 F6
Cragg Dr *ILK* LS29 ....39 H3
Cragg La *CUL/QBY* BD13 ....124 B1
  GTHN BD7 ....126 C3
  HBR HX7 ....143 L8
Cragg Rd *HBR* HX7 ....165 H1
  HBR HX7 ....165 M2
  HORS LS18 ....85 L6
Cragg Ter *GTHN* BD7 ....126 C3
  HORS LS18 ....85 L6
Cragg Top *CUL/QBY* BD13 ....124 A1
Cragg Vw *AIRE* BD20 ....36 A4
Cragg Wood Dr *YEA* LS19 ....84 C3
Craggwood Rd *HORS* LS18 ....85 L7
Crag Hill Av *BHP/TINH* LS16 ....64 C3
Crag Hill Rd *IDLE* BD10 ....83 J4
Crag Hill Vw *BHP/TINH* LS16 ....64 C3
Crag La *AIRE* BD20 ....34 E2
  AIRE BD20 ....55 L2
  AL/HA/HU LS17 ....25 L8
  AL/HA/HU LS17 ....43 L2
  AL/HA/HU LS17 ....87 H1
  LUD/ILL HX2 ....145 M2

Crag Mt *PONT* WF8 ....180 E6
Crag Pl *KGHY* BD21 ....79 L2
Crag Rd *SHPY* BD18 ....82 E8
Cragside Cl *KSTL* LS5 ....86 A7
Cragside Crs *KSTL* LS5 ....86 A7
Cragside Gdns *KSTL* LS5 ....86 A7
Cragside Gv *KSTL* LS5 ....85 M7
Cragside Mt *KSTL* LS5 ....86 A7
Cragside Pl *KSTL* LS5 ....86 A7
Cragside Wk *KSTL* LS5 ....86 A7
The Crag *BSPA/BRAM* LS23 ....69 M4
Crag Vw *AIRE* BD20 ....34 C5
  AL/HA/HU LS17 ....43 K2
  IDLE BD10 ....83 L7
Crag View Rd *SKP/WHF* BD23 ....16 D3
Craig Cl *BTLY* WF17 ....151 L8
Craiglands *HIPP* HX3 ....147 M6
  MILN OL16 ....228 D4
Craiglands Pk *ILK* LS29 ....38 E3
Craiglea Dr *ILK* LS29 ....38 E3
Craiglea Dr *LM/WK* BD12 ....148 F4
Craigmore Ct *BOW* BD4 ....128 B4
Craigmore Dr *ILK* LS29 ....39 G2
Crake Dr *WBSY* BD6 ....125 L5
Cramlands *DOD/DAR* S75 ....260 C7
Cranberry Av *TOD* OL14 ....163 K7
Cranberry Rd *STKB/PEN* S36 ....270 F8
Cranborne Dr *DOD/DAR* S75 ....242 B5
Cranbourne Rd *HTON* BD9 ....103 M4
Cranbourne St *COL* BB8 ....52 A8
  WBSY BD6 ....126 E6
Cranbrook Pl *WBOW* BD5 ....127 G3
Cranbrook St *BSLY* S70 ....262 F6
  CLAY BD14 ....125 K2
  WBOW BD5 ....127 G3
Cranbrook Vw *PDSY/CALV* LS28 ....129 J1
Cranewells Dr *MSTN/BAR* LS15 ....111 L7
Cranewells Gn *MSTN/BAR* LS15 ....111 L7
Cranewells Ri *MSTN/BAR* LS15 ....111 L8
Cranewells V *MSTN/BAR* LS15 ....111 L8
Cranewells Vw *MSTN/BAR* LS15 ....111 L7
Cranfield Dr *AWLS/ASK* DN6 ....249 H4
Cranford Gdns *BSLYN/ROY* S71 ....243 K2
  ILK LS29 ....38 E3
Cranford Pl *WIL/AL* BD15 ....102 E1
Crangle Flds *HUDS* HD4 ....237 L4
Cranleigh Mt *KGHY* BD21 ....2 C9
Cranmer Bank *AL/HA/HU* LS17 ....87 J3
Cranmer Cl *AL/HA/HU* LS17 ....87 J3
Cranmer Gdns *AL/HA/HU* LS17 ....87 J3
  HOLM/MEL HD9 ....235 G4
Cranmer Ri *AL/HA/HU* LS17 ....87 J2
Cranmer Rd *AL/HA/HU* LS17 ....87 J3
  BFDE BD3 ....5 G1
Cranmore Crs *MID* LS10 ....154 A1
Cranmore Dr *MID* LS10 ....154 A1
Cranmore Gdns *MID* LS10 ....154 A1
Cranmore Garth *MID* LS10 ....154 A1
Cranmore Gn *MID* LS10 ....154 A1
Cranmore Gv *MID* LS10 ....154 A1
Cranmore La *MID* LS10 ....154 A1
Cranmore Ri *MID* LS10 ....154 A1
Cranmore Rd *MID* LS10 ....154 B1
Cranston Cl *BSLYN/ROY* S71 ....261 M2
Cranwood Dr *HUDE* HD5 ....193 J8
Craven Av *AIRE* BD20 ....36 A5
  CUL/QBY BD13 ....103 C8
Craven Cl *BSLYN/ROY* S71 ....243 J4
  CLECK BD19 ....150 E6
Craven Ct *AIRE* BD20 ....36 A5
  GIR BD8 ....104 B6
  HFAX HX1 ....10 C7
  HWTH BD22 ....54 F2
  SKP/WHF BD23 ....16 C2
Craven Crs *ILK* LS29 ....19 G6
Cravendale Rd *DEWS* WF13 ....172 F8
Craven Dr *AIRE* BD20 ....36 A5
  CLECK BD19 ....150 E6
Craven Edge *HFAX* HX1 ....10 C7
Craven Gdns *ROCH* OL11 * 228 A1
Craven Garth *GLE* DN14 ....161 J7
Craven Gv *AIRE* BD20 ....36 B5
Craven La *CLECK* BD19 ....150 E6
Craven Pk *ILK* LS29 ....61 H1
Craven Rd *DEWS* WF13 ....173 J8
  HDGY LS6 ....6 F3
  HEM/SK/SE WF9 ....246 F3
  KGHY BD21 ....3 L2
Craven St *BFDE* BD3 ....5 H4
  COL BB8 ....
  DEWS WF13 ....172 F8
  HUDS HD4 ....213 J2
  OT LS21 ....41 K7
  SKP/WHF BD23 ....16 B3
  WKFDE WF1 ....12 F1
Craven Ter *HFAX* HX1 ....10 C7
Craven Wood Cl *DOD/DAR* S75 ....260 C3
Crawford Av *WBSY* BD6 ....126 E6
Crawford Dr *WKFDW/WTN* WF2 ....176 B7
Crawford St *BOW* BD4 ....127 J2
  MILN OL16 ....228 C1
Crawshaw Av *HEM/SK/SE* WF9 ....246 F3
Crawshaw Av *PDSY/CALV* LS28 ....107 H7
Crawshaw Gdns
  PDSY/CALV LS28 ....107 G7
Crawshaw Hl *PDSY/CALV* LS28 ....107 G7
Crawshaw La *HOR/CROF* WF4 ....217 J5
Crawshaw Pk *PDSY/CALV* LS28 ....107 G7
Crawshaw Ri *PDSY/CALV* LS28 ....107 G8
Crawshaw Rd *PDSY/CALV* LS28 ....107 G7
Crawshaw St *DEWS* WF13 ....173 H8
Crawthorne Crs *HUDN* HD2 ....193 G2
Crayford Dr *HOR/CROF* WF4 ....200 B5
Cray La *GTL/HWG* HX4 ....189 M4
The Cray *MILN* OL16 ....207 G8
Crediton Av *WIL/AL* BD15 ....103 K6
Crediton Ct *WIL/AL* BD15 ....103 K6
Crescent Av *AL/HA/HU* LS17 ....87 M2
  RTHW LS26 ....133 H7
Crescent Gra *BEE/HOL* LS11 ....9 H7
Crescent Rd *HOR/CROF* WF4 ....222 C5
  HUDN HD2 ....14 D7
  HUDS HD4 ....213 M7
Crescent Rdyd *HUDE* HD5 ....215 J1
Crescent St *TOD* OL14 ....163 K1
Crescent Ter *ILK* LS29 ....38 D2
The Crescent *AL/HA/HU* LS17 ....25 M8
  AL/HA/HU LS17 ....65 M8
  BAIL BD17 ....82 E4
  BGLY BD16 ....59 G8
  BHP/TINH LS16 ....86 C2
  BIRK/DRI BD11 ....128 C7
  CAS WF10 ....158 B8
  CUD/GR S72 ....244 D7
  DEWS WF13 ....173 J6
  DOD/DAR S75 ....260 D2
  EARD/LOFT WF3 ....153 J6
  FEA/AMT WF7 ....200 F1
  GFTH/SHER LS25 ....113 J6
  GFTH/SHER LS25 ....114 C8
  GFTH/SHER LS25 ....135 J5
  GSLY LS20 ....61 L6
  GTL/HWG HX4 ....190 C2
  HIPP HX3 ....147 M6
  HOLM/MEL HD9 ....237 G8
  HOR/CROF WF4 ....218 E1
  ILK LS29 ....39 G1

  IDLE BD10 ....83 J6
  KBTN HD8 ....216 C7
  LVSG WF15 ....171 K6
  MSTN/BAR LS15 ....111 K6
  NORM WF6 ....178 B2
  OT LS21 ....41 J4
  PDSY/CALV LS28 ....107 H6
  ROY/SHW OL2 ....229 K8
  WBSY BD6 ....125 M5
  WBY LS22 ....46 E1
Crescent Towers *BEE/HOL* LS11 * 9 G7
Crescent Vw *AL/HA/HU* LS17 ....65 M8
  HWTH BD22 ....79 J3
Creskeld Crs *BHP/TINH* LS16 ....64 B5
Creskeld Dr *BHP/TINH* LS16 ....64 A3
Creskeld Gdns *BHP/TINH* LS16 ....64 A3
Creskeld Garth *BHP/TINH* LS16 ....64 B3
Creskeld La *BHP/TINH* LS16 ....64 B3
Creskeld Pk *BHP/TINH* LS16 ....64 A3
Creskeld Wy *WIL/AL* BD15 ....103 H4
Creskell Rd *BEE/HOL* LS11 ....8 E8
Cresswell Mt *GTHN* BD7 ....126 A4
Cresswell Pl *GTHN* BD7 ....126 A4
Cresswell St *DOD/DAR* S75 ....260 A4
Cresswell Ter *GTHN* BD7 ....126 A4
Crest Av *HUDE* HD5 * 215 G5
  LM/WK BD12 ....148 E5
Crest Dr *PONT* WF8 ....181 G8
Crestfield Av *ELL* HX5 ....169 G8
Crestfield Crs *ELL* HX5 ....191 G1
Crestfield Dr *ELL* HX5 ....191 G1
  LUD/ILL HX2 ....168 A1
Crestfield Rd *ELL* HX5 ....191 G1
Crest Hl *RTHW* LS26 ....134 C5
Crest Hill Rd *HUDN* HD2 ....192 B4
Crest Mt *PONT* WF8 ....181 G8
Crest Rd *HUDW* HD3 ....191 J7
The Crest *GFTH/SHER* LS25 ....115 J7
  HUDN HD2 ....171 G8
  RTHW LS26 ....134 C5
Crestville Cl *CLAY* BD14 ....125 M1
Crestville Rd *CLAY* BD14 ....125 M1
Crestville Ter *CLAY* BD14 ....125 M1
Crestwood Cl *BOW* BD4 ....127 K5
Creswell La *DEWS* WF13 ....173 H3
Crewe Av *KNOT* WF11 ....181 K2
Crewe La *CAS* WF10 ....158 F7
Crib La *HIPP* HX3 ....11 G4
Crich Av *BSLYN/ROY* S71 ....243 J7
Cricketers Ap
  WKFDW/WTN WF2 ....176 A3
Cricketers Cl *FEA/AMT* WF7 ....224 C1
  GFTH/SHER LS25 ....113 J8
Cricketers Fold *AL/HA/HU* LS17 ....89 G2
Cricketers Gn *YEA* LS19 ....62 B3
Cricketers Ter *WOR/ARM* LS12 ....108 E7
The Cricketers *BULY* LS4 ....108 C4
Cricketers Vw *AL/HA/HU* LS17 ....89 G2
Cricketers Wk *GFTH/SHER* LS25 ....116 A7
Cricket Vw *MILN* OL16 ....229 H1
Cricklegate *MSTN/BAR* LS15 ....111 K6
Cricklegate *MSTN/BAR* LS15 ....111 K6
Crimble Bank *MAR/SLWT* HD7 ....212 C5
Crimble Clough Rd
  MAR/SLWT HD7 ....212 C4
Crimbles Ct *PDSY/CALV* LS28 ....107 H7
Crimbles Pl *PDSY/CALV* LS28 ....107 H7
Crimbles Rd *PDSY/CALV* LS28 ....107 H7
Crimbles Ter *PDSY/CALV* LS28 ....107 H7
The Crimbles *HOR/CROF* WF4 ....198 B2
Crimea La *HUDW* HD3 ....211 M3
Crimple Gn *GFTH/SHER* LS25 ....113 K8
Crimple Mdw *PBR* HD3 ....26 E2
Crimshaw La *HBR* HX7 ....121 J6
Crimsworth La *HBR* HX7 ....121 M1
Crinan Ct *NORM* WF6 ....178 C2
Cringles La *ROCH* OL11 ....228 A5
Cripplegate *HFAX* HX1 ....11 K5
Cripple Gate La *ROCH* OL11 ....228 A5
Croasdale Gdns
  AWLS/ASK DN6 ....249 L6
Crodingley Farm Ct
  HOLM/MEL HD9 ....236 D6
Crodingley *HOLM/MEL* HD9 ....236 D6
Croft Av *BGLY* BD16 ....58 F8
  BSLYN/ROY S71 ....243 K3
  EARD/LOFT WF3 ....153 M7
  KNOT WF11 ....182 C1
  NORM WF6 ....178 B3
  NORM WF6 ....178 A3
  OT LS21 ....41 G7
  PDSY/CALV LS28 ....106 F3
Croft Bank *BIRK/DRI* BD11 ....150 C1
Croft Br *RTHW* LS26 ....155 L1
Croft Chantry *HEM/SK/SE* WF9 ....223 J4
Croft Cl *DOD/DAR* S75 ....242 C5
Croft Ct *HOLM/MEL* HD9 ....236 B3
  HORS LS18 ....85 K5
  ILK LS29 * 61 H1
Croftdale Gv *MSTN/BAR* LS15 ....111 M4
Croft Dr *BSLYN/ROY* S71 ....243 H7
  BSPA/BRAM LS23 ....69 M3
  DOD/DAR S75 ....242 C5
  HOLM/MEL HD9 ....236 A2
  ILK LS29 ....61 J2
  STKB/PEN S36 ....270 A3
Croft End *WBY* LS22 ....47 L1
Crofters Cl *IDLE* BD10 ....83 G6
Crofters Lea *YEA* LS19 ....62 B8
Crofters Ml *AIRE* BD20 ....55 H1
Croft Fld *AIRE* BD20 ....36 A6
Croft Fold *HIPP* HX3 ....146 B4
Croft Foulds Ct
  GFTH/SHER LS25 ....113 H7
Croft Gdns *MOR* LS27 ....152 A5
Croft Head *KBTN* HD8 ....239 H1
Croft Head Dr *MILN* OL16 ....207 H7
Croft Head La *WKFDE* WF1 ....178 A7
Croft Hi *AIRE* BD20 ....54 E8
Croft House Av *MOR* LS27 ....152 A5
Croft House Cl *MOR* LS27 ....130 D8
  WBSY BD6 ....126 D6
Croft House Ct
  PDSY/CALV LS28 * 107 G6
Croft House Dr *MOR* LS27 ....152 A5
Croft House Gdns *MOR* LS27 ....152 A5
Croft House Gv *MOR* LS27 ....152 A5
Croft House La *AIRE* BD20 ....54 D8
  MOR LS27 ....152 A5
Croft House Mt *MOR* LS27 * 152 A5
Croft House Ri *MOR* LS27 ....130 D8
Croft House Rd *HUDW* HD3 ....211 M1
  MOR LS27 ....152 A5
  WBSY BD6 ....126 D6
Croft House Vw *MOR* LS27 ....152 A5
Croft House Wk *MOR* LS27 ....130 D8
Croft House Wy *MOR* LS27 ....130 D8
Croftlands *BTLY* WF17 ....174 B3

  IDLE BD10 ....83 J6
  KNOT WF11 ....182 C1
Croft La *BSPA/BRAM* LS23 ....49 J2
  TAD LS24 ....49 M8
Crofton Cl *MAR/SLWT* HD7 ....212 F6
Crofton Ri *AL/HA/HU* LS17 ....89 J2
Crofton Rd *HTON* BD9 ....104 C3
Crofton Ter *AL/HA/HU* LS17 ....89 J2
Croft Pk *ILK* LS29 ....61 H2
Croft Pl *BRIC* HD6 ....169 K5
Croft Ri *RHPP* HX3 ....146 B4
  ILK LS29 ....61 J2
Croft Rd *BGLY* BD16 ....58 F8
  BSLY S70 ....261 L7
  BSPA/BRAM LS23 ....69 J3
Croft's Ct *LDS* LS1 6
Croftside Cl *SCFT* LS14 ....111 K3
The Crofts *AIRE* BD20 ....35 G5
  AIRE BD20 ....55 G2
  BTLY WF17 ....173 H2
  KBTN HD8 ....217 C7
Croft St *AIRE* BD20 ....34 E8
  BFD BD1 ....6 G8
  BIRK/DRI BD11 ....150 C1
  BRIC HD6 ....170 C4
  DEWS WF13 ....173 L6
  HBR HX7 ....143 J3
  HECK WF16 ....172 F3
  HUD HD1 ....213 L1
  IDLE BD10 ....83 L6
  KGHY BD21 ....2 E6
  OT LS21 ....41 K7
  PDSY/CALV LS28 ....106 F3
  RPDN/SBR HX6 * 167 G3
  SHPY BD18 ....82 D7
  WBSY BD6 ....126 E5
  WHIT OL12 ....206 E3
The Croft *BIRK/DRI* BD11 ....151 L1
  CAS WF10 ....158 B8
  COL BB8 ....52 A7
  DOD/DAR S75 ....260 A1
  EARD/LOFT WF3 ....174 F1
  HEM/SK/SE WF9 ....219 H6
  HOR/CROF WF4 ....219 H6
  KNOT WF11 ....182 C1
  MSTN/BAR LS15 ....111 K5
  RTHW LS26 ....155 L1
  SCFT LS14 ....67 M6
  SKP/WHF BD23 ....17 M1
  STKB/PEN S36 ....258 B8
  WBY LS22 ....47 J6
Croftway *ILK* LS29 ....61 J2
Croftway *MSTN/BAR* LS15 ....111 J2
Croisdale Cl *LVSG* WF15 ....172 A2
Cromack Vw *PDSY/CALV* LS28 ....106 C7
Cromarty Av *HUDS* HD4 ....213 L4
Cromarty Dr *HUDS* HD4 ....213 L4
Cromer Av *KGHY* BD21 * 2 E9
Cromer Gv *KGHY* BD21 * 2 E9
Cromer Pl *LDSU* LS2 ....6 C5
Cromer Rd *KGHY* BD21 ....2 E9
  LDSU LS2 ....6 C5
Cromer St *CUD/GR* S72 ....245 J7
  HFAX HX1 ....10 A9
  KGHY BD21 ....2 E9
  LDSU LS2 ....6 C5
  ROY/SHW OL2 * 229 K7
  WHIT OL12 ....206 A3
Cromer Ter *LDSU* LS2 ....6 C5
Cromford Av *BSLYN/ROY* S71 ....243 K8
Crompton Av *BSLY* S70 ....260 F6
  ROCH OL11 ....228 D3
Crompton Circuit
  ROY/SHW OL2 ....230 C4
Crompton Dr *MOR* LS27 ....130 B8
Crompton St *ROY/SHW* OL2 ....229 K7
Crompton Wy *ROY/SHW* OL2 ....229 K8
Cromwell Bottom Dr
  BRIC HD6 ....170 C2
  KNOT WF11 ....159 M6
Cromwell Ct *AWLS/ASK* DN6 * 249 J4
  BGLY BD16 ....103 K2
  BIRK/DRI BD11 ....150 F1
  HUDE HD5 ....215 H3
Cromwell Gv *AWLS/ASK* DN6 ....249 J4
  MID LS10 ....131 M6
  OSM LS9 ....7 L7
Cromwell Mt *BSLY* S70 ....261 G8
  MID LS10 ....131 M6
  OSM LS9 ....7 L7
Cromwell Pl *OSS* WF5 ....174 F7
Cromwell Ri *GFTH/SHER* LS25 ....135 J6
Cromwell Rd *CAS* WF10 ....158 E7
  HIPP HX3 ....169 J2
  ROY/SHW OL2 ....228 B3
Cromwell St *OSM* LS9 ....7 L8
  SKP/WHF BD23 ....16 C3
Cronkeyshaw Av *WHIT* OL12 ....206 A4
Cronkeyshaw Rd *WHIT* OL12 ....206 A5
Cronkhill La *BSLYN/ROY* S71 ....243 M5
Crooked La *IDLE* BD10 ....83 J6
Crooke House La
  BSLYN/ROY S71 ....263 H5
Crooke La *WIL/AL* BD15 ....102 E2
Crookes La *BSLYN/ROY* S71 ....243 J3
Crookes St *BSLY* S70 ....260 F5
Crook St *MILN* OL16 ....206 C6
Cropper Ga *LDS* LS1 6
Croppers Ct *CUL/QBY* BD13 ....125 H5
Cropstones *BSPA/BRAM* LS23 ....69 M4
Cropton Rd *BSLYN/ROY* S71 ....243 K3
Crosby Av *BEE/HOL* LS11 ....8 B7
Crosby Pl *BEE/HOL* LS11 ....8 B6
Crosby Rd *BEE/HOL* LS11 ....8 B6
  CUD/GR S72 ....244 D6
  KGHY BD21 ....
  WHIT OL12 ....206 B4
Crosby St *BEE/HOL* LS11 ....8 B6
  CUD/GR S72 ....244 D6
  KGHY BD21 ....
Crosby Ter *BEE/HOL* LS11 ....8 B6
Crosby Vw *BEE/HOL* LS11 ....8 B6
Croscombe Wk *WBOW* BD5 ....
Croset Av *HUDE* HD5 ....15 G8
Crosland Ct *HUDW* HD3 ....191 H6
Crosland Factory La
  HUDS HD4 ....235 J1
Crosland Hill Rd *HUDS* HD4 ....213 K3
Crosland Rd *HUD* HD1 ....214 A2
  HUDW HD3 ....191 H2
Crosland Spring Rd *HUDS* HD4 ....235 J1
Crosland St *HUDS* HD4 ....214 C2
Crosley Vw *BGLY* BD16 ....81 K4
Crosley Wood Rd *BGLY* BD16 ....81 K4
Cross Albert Pl *WOR/ARM* LS12 ....108 F7
Cross Alcester Rd *RHAY* LS8 ....110 B2
Cross Alma St *OSM* LS9 ....110 B5
Cross Ar *RTHW* LS26 ....133 H7
Cross Aysgarth Mt *OSM* LS9 ....110 B6
Cross Bank Rd *BTLY* WF17 ....151 K8
Cross Banks *SHPY* BD18 ....82 D7
Cross Bank St *MIRF* WF14 ....194 C3
Cross Banstead St *RHAY* LS8 * 110 B3
Cross Barstow St *BEE/HOL* LS11 ....9 G4

Cross Bath Rd *BRAM* LS13 ....107 L4
Crossbeck Cl *ILK* LS29 ....38 D3
Crossbeck Rd *ILK* LS29 ....38 D3
Cross Beck Rd *RHAY* LS8 * 110 B2
Cross Belgrave St *LDSU* LS2 ....7 K8
Cross Bellbrooke Av *OSM* LS9 ....110 D4
Cross Bell St *OSM* LS9 * 7 K8
Cross Bentley La *HDGY* LS6 ....87 H4
Cross Birch St *MOR* LS27 ....152 D4
Crossbrook Wy *MILN* OL16 ....229 J1
Cross Burley Lodge Rd
  HDGY LS6 ....109 G4
Cross Cardigan Ter *BULY* LS4 ....108 C3
Cross Catherine St *OSM* LS9 ....9 M1
Cross Chancellor St *HDCY* LS6 ....6 F1
Cross Chapel St *HDGY* LS6 ....108 F1
Cross Church St *HUD* HD1 ....15 G3
Cross Cliff Rd *HDGY* LS6 ....6 D1
Cross Cottages *HUD* HD1 ....191 M7
Cross Cowper St *CHAL* LS7 ....7 K2
Cross Crown St *CLECK* BD19 ....149 M7
Crossdale Av *WBSY* BD6 ....125 M6
Cross Dawlish Gv *OSM* LS9 ....110 D6
Cross Dikes Rd *RPDN/SBR* HX6 ....166 C7
Cross Easy Rd *OSM* LS9 * 110 B8
Cross Elford St *RHAY* LS8 * 110 B3
Cross Emily St *KGHY* BD21 * 3 H3
Cross Ends La *HBR* HX7 ....121 J2
Cross Eric St *KGHY* BD21 ....3 H2
Cross Eshald Pl *RTHW* LS26 ....133 M8
Cross Evanston Av *BULY* LS4 ....108 B4
Cross Farm Ct *HWTH* BD22 ....100 C3
Cross Fld *GTL/HWG* HX4 ....190 C2
Cross Field Ct *ROY/SHW* OL2 ....229 L5
Crossfield Cl *HWTH* BD22 ....100 D3
  WHIT OL12 ....184 E7
Crossfield Ct *HOR/CROF* WF4 ....196 B8
Crossfield La
  AWLS/ASK DN6 ....249 J4
Crossfield Pl *ROCH* OL11 ....228 C2
Crossfield Rd *HWTH* BD22 ....100 D3
  WHIT OL12 ....184 E8
Crossfields *HOR/CROF* WF4 ....196 C8
Cross Flds *HUDE* HD5 ....193 G7
Crossfield St *LDSU* LS2 6
Cross Firs St *HUDW* HD3 ....213 K1
Cross Flatts Av *BEE/HOL* LS11 ....131 J4
Cross Flatts Crs *BEE/HOL* LS11 ....131 H4
Cross Flatts Dr *BEE/HOL* LS11 ....131 H4
Cross Flatts Gv *BEE/HOL* LS11 ....131 J4
Cross Flatts Mt *BEE/HOL* LS11 ....131 J4
Cross Flatts Pde *BEE/HOL* LS11 ....131 H4
Cross Flatts Pl *BEE/HOL* LS11 ....131 H4
Cross Flatts Rd *BEE/HOL* LS11 ....131 H4
Cross Flatts Rw *BEE/HOL* LS11 ....131 H4
Cross Flatts St *BEE/HOL* LS11 ....131 H4
Cross Flatts Ter *BEE/HOL* LS11 ....131 H4
Cross Foundry St *DEWS* WF13 * 195 G1
Cross Fountaine St *LDS* LS1 * 7 J8
Cross Francis St *CHAL* LS7 ....7 K2
Crossgate *DOD/DAR* S75 ....242 D5
  OT LS21 ....41 J7
Cross Gate Rd *HOLM/MEL* HD9 ....254 D4
Cross Gates Av *MSTN/BAR* LS15 ....111 L3
Cross Gates La *BGLY* BD16 ....80 E3
  MSTN/BAR LS15 ....111 K3
Crossgates Rd *MILN* OL16 ....207 F8
Cross Gates Rd *MSTN/BAR* LS15 ....111 K3
Cross Glen Rd *BHP/TINH* LS16 ....86 E7
Cross Granby Ter *HDGY* LS6 * 108 F1
Cross Grange Av *RHAY* LS8 ....7 M2
Cross Grasmere St
  WOR/ARM LS12 ....108 F7
Cross Gn *OT* LS21 ....41 K6
Cross Green Ap *OSM* LS9 ....132 C1
Cross Green Av *OSM* LS9 ....110 B8
Cross Green Cl *OSM* LS9 ....132 C1
Cross Green Crs *OSM* LS9 ....110 B8
Cross Green Dr *OSM* LS9 ....132 C1
Cross Green Gv *OSM* LS9 ....110 B8
Cross Green La *MSTN/BAR* LS15 ....111 H8
  OSM LS9 ....9 M3
Cross Green Ri *OSM* LS9 ....132 C1
Cross Green Rd *HUDE* HD5 ....193 J8
  OSM LS9 ....110 B8
Cross Green Rw *HDGY* LS6 ....87 G7
Cross Green V *OSM* LS9 ....132 C1
Cross Green Wy *OSM* LS9 ....132 C1
Cross Grove St *HUD* HD1 ....14 E8
Cross Hands La *HOR/CROF* WF4 ....201 M8
Cross Hartley Av *HDGY* LS6 ....6 D1
Cross Heath Gv *BEE/HOL* LS11 ....131 J3
Cross Henley Rd *BRAM* LS13 ....107 L4
Cross Hi *CUD/GR* S72 ....245 H3
  GTL/HWG HX4 ....168 C2
  HEM/SK/SE WF9 ....223 M4
  HIPP HX3 ....11 H4
  KNOT WF11 ....159 J2
Cross Hill *AWLS/ASK* DN6 ....249 H4
Cross Hill La *LVSG* WF15 ....171 K3
Cross Hills Dr *GFTH/SHER* LS25 ....135 J5
Cross Hills *HIPP* HX3 ....11 J5
Crosshills Mt *GTL/HWG* HX4 ....168 C2
Crosshills Rd *AIRE* BD20 ....34 C4
Cross Hilton Gv *RHAY* LS8 ....110 B2
Cross House Ct *LM/WK* BD12 * 149 G2
Cross Ingledew Crs *RHAY* LS8 ....88 D4
Cross Ingram Rd *BEE/HOL* LS11 ....8 B5
The Crossings *BTLY* WF17 ....151 H6
Cross Ivy Mt *OSM* LS9 ....110 C6
Cross Kelso Rd *LDSU* LS2 ....6 B6
Cross Keys *OSS* WF5 ....175 J7
Cross Keys Ct *HOR/CROF* WF4 ....197 K5
Crossland Rd *MOR* LS27 ....130 D7
Crossland St *BEE/HOL* LS11 * 8 F9
Crossland Ter *BEE/HOL* LS11 ....8 B5
Cross La *BGLY* BD16 ....81 H3
  BIRK/DRI BD11 ....151 H1
  BRIC HD6 ....171 G5
  BSLYN/ROY S71 ....244 A3
  CUL/QBY BD13 ....124 E6
  ELL HX5 ....169 G8
  GSLY LS20 ....62 D3
  GTHN BD7 ....125 J8
  HIPP HX3 ....125 J8
  HOLM/MEL HD9 ....236 A4
  HUDS HD4 ....214 C3
  HUDS HD4 ....237 L4
  HWTH BD22 ....100 F2
  KBTN HD8 ....238 A8
  KBTN HD8 ....239 J7
  STKB/PEN S36 ....258 B6
  STKB/PEN S36 ....270 C4
  STKB/PEN S36 ....271 J7
  TOD OL14 ....164 B2
  WIL/AL BD15 ....80 F7
  WKFDW/WTN WF2 ....198 A1
Cross Lea Farm Rd *KSTL* LS5 ....86 A1
Cross Lee *TOD* OL14 ....141 H7
Cross Leeds St *KCHY* BD21 ....2 F5
Cross Lee Ga *TOD* OL14 ....141 H7

Cross Lee Rd TOD OL14 141 H7
Cross Lees WHIT OL12 206 C3
Crossley Cl MIRF WF14 172 C6
Crossley Gdns HFAX HX1 10 D5
Crossley Gv MIRF WF14 172 C6
Crossley Hall Ms GIR BD8 104 A7
Crossley Hall St GIR BD8 103 M7
Crossley Hl HIPP HX3 168 F3
Crossley La HUDE HD5 193 J7
MIRF WF14 172 C6
Crossley New Rd TOD OL14 142 A6
Crossley Pl SKP/WHF BD23 16 B2
Crossley St BRIG HD6 170 D5
CUL/QBY BD13 125 H5
FEA/AMT WF7 201 M1
GTHN BD7 126 D1
HFAX HX1 11 G5
HOR/CROF WF4 200 C1
MILN OL16 207 G8
ROY/SHW OL2 229 L7
TOD OL14 163 K1
WBY LS22 48 A1
WKFDE WF1 178 B8
Crossley Ter BTLY WF17 173 L3
Crossley Ter North LUD/ILL HX2 146 C2
Crossley Ter South LUD/ILL HX2 146 C2
Crossley Vw MIRF WF14 172 D6
Cross Lidgett Pl RHAY LS8 88 B6
Cross Louis St CHAL LS7 7 K3
Crossman Dr NORM WF6 178 E3
Cross Maude St LDSU LS2 * 9 J1
Cross Milan Rd RHAY LS8 110 C3
Crossmoor Cl AIRE BD20 35 L5
Crossmount St BTLY WF17 173 L3
Cross Osmondthorpe La
OSM LS9 110 E6
Cross Park Av CAS WF10 158 B7
Cross Park St BTLY WF17 173 M1
EARL WF12 174 B6
HOR/CROF WF4 197 J5
MSTN/BAR LS15 111 J6
Cross Peel St MOR LS27 152 D2
Cross Pipes Rd
WKFDW/WTN WF2 176 A6
Cross Quarry St HDGY LS6 6 D1
Cross Queen St NORM WF6 178 C4
Cross Reginald Mt CHAL LS7 * 7 J1
Cross Reginald Pl CHAL LS7 * 7 K1
Cross Rink St BTLY WF17 173 M3
Cross River St KGHY BD21 * 3 L1
Cross Rd EARL WF12 195 L4
GIR BD8 104 D5
HOR/CROF WF4 196 D8
HOR/CROF WF4 220 B3
HORS LS18 85 J6
IDLE BD10 83 L6
LM/WK BD12 149 H1
Cross Roseville Rd RHAY LS8 7 M3
Cross Rosse St SHPY BD18 * 82 D6
Cross Roundhay Av RHAY LS8 110 B1
Cross Rw MSTN/BAR LS15 112 C8
Cross Ryecroft St OSS WF5 174 E8
Cross St Michael's La
HDGY LS6 * 108 F2
Cross Skelton St COL BB8 74 A1
Cross Speedwell St HDGY LS6 6 F2
Cross Sq WKFDE WF1 12 E2
Cross Stamford St CHAL LS7 7 K6
Cross Stone Rd TOD OL14 142 A7
Cross St BRIG HD6 170 C2
BSLYN/ROY S71 261 L2
BTLY WF17 173 L1
CAS WF10 157 L6
CLAY BD14 125 L2
CUD/GR S72 245 K8
DOD/DAR S75 259 M2
DOD/DAR S75 260 F3
EARD/LOFT WF3 154 A6
EARL WF12 173 M7
GTL/HWG HX4 * 168 F7
GTL/HWG HX4 190 D2
HEM/SK/SE WF9 223 L7
HEM/SK/SE WF9 225 M6
HFAX HX1 11 H4
HOLM/MEL HD9 236 B2
HOR/CROF WF4 197 K5
HWTH BD22 54 E3
LM/WK BD12 149 J2
LVSG WF15 172 C4
MAR/SLWT HD7 212 C5
MILN OL16 206 F7
MSTN/BAR LS15 111 J6
OSS WF5 174 E5
PONT WF8 * 180 F6
RTHW LS26 155 G1
SKP/WHF BD23 16 B3
WBSY BD6 * 126 B7
WBY LS22 48 A1
WKFDE WF1 12 E2
Cross St West LUD/ILL HX2 * 146 A6
Cross Sun St BFD BD1 5 G4
Cross Ter RTHW LS26 155 G1
The Cross MSTN/BAR LS15 91 G7
Cross Valley Dr MSTN/BAR LS15 111 J5
Crossway BGLY BD16 81 H7
The Crossways OT LS21 41 J4
Cross Wells Rd RPDN/SBR HX6 188 E2
Cross Westfield Rd BVRD LS3 * 6 B7
Cross Wingham St CHAL LS7 * 7 K4
Cross Woodstock St LDSU LS2 * 6 E4
Cross York St LDSU LS2 9 J1
Crowden Wk DOD/DAR S75 260 C5
Crowgill Rd SHPY BD18 82 D6
Crow Hill End Rd
RPDN/SBR HX6 166 B4
Crow Hill Rd HBR HX7 166 B3
Crow La HUDW HD3 213 J2
OT LS21 41 J7
Crowlees Cl MIRF WF14 194 D1
Crowlees Gdns MIRF WF14 194 D1
Crowlees Rd MIRF WF14 194 C1
Crown & Anchor Yd
PONT WF8 * 180 E6
Crown Av BSLY S70 261 J7
CUD/GR S72 262 E2
Crown Cl BSLY S70 261 H7
EARL WF12 174 C7
Crown Dr LM/WK BD12 148 E2
Crow Nest La BEE/HOL LS11 130 F4
Crownest La BGLY BD16 81 J2
Crow Nest Ms BEE/HOL LS11 131 G4
Crow Nest Pk DEWS WF13 * 173 J7
Crownest Rd BGLY BD16 81 J3
Crow Nest Rd HBR HX7 143 K4
Crow Nest Vw DEWS WF13 173 J7
Crown Flatt Wy EARL WF12 174 A5
Crown Gdns MILN OL16 228 C1
Crown Gn HUDW HD3 213 J2
Crown Hill Rd DOD/DAR S75 260 C5
Crownlands La OSS WF5 174 F8
Crown La HOLM/MEL HD9 254 C1
Crown Point Cl OSS WF5 174 E8
Crown Point Dr OSS WF5 174 E8
Crown Point Rd MID LS10 9 J3
OSS WF5 174 E8
Crown Rd HIPP HX3 146 D4
Crown St BFD BD1 4 B5
BRIG HD6 170 C3
BSLY S70 261 J7
CLECK BD19 149 M7
ELL HX5 169 H8
HBR HX7 143 J3
HFAX HX1 11 G6
HOLM/MEL HD9 236 B1
ILK LS29 40 B5
KBTN HD8 239 M5
LDSU LS2 9 H1
LM/WK BD12 148 E2
LVSG WF15 172 D2
MILN OL16 228 D1
OSS WF5 197 G3
ROY/SHW OL2 * 229 K7
Crown Well Hl BSLYN/ROY S71 262 B6
Crown Yd HEM/SK/SE WF9 246 F3
Crowshaw Dr WHIT OL12 206 A3
Crowther Av PDSY/CALV LS28 84 B8
Crowther Cl MAR/SLWT HD7 212 C4
Crowther Fold BGLY BD16 80 D5
Crowther Pl CAS WF10 157 M7
HDGY LS6 6 F2
Crowther Rd HECK WF16 173 G1
MIRF WF14 194 C1
Crowther St BTLY WF17 173 H1
CAS WF10 157 L7
CLECK BD19 149 M6
HUD HD1 * 15 H8
IDLE BD10 83 M7
LIT OL15 207 G2
LM/WK BD12 148 E2
MILN OL16 228 C2
Crowther Wk WBOW BD5 4 E9
Crow Tree Cl BAIL BD17 82 F3
Crow Tree La GIR BD8 104 A5
Crowtrees Ct YEA LS19 84 D3
Crowtrees Crs BRIG HD6 170 B6
Crowtrees La BRIG HD6 170 B7
Crowtrees Pk BRIG HD6 170 B7
Crow Trees Pk YEA LS19 84 D2
Crow Trees Rd MAR/SLWT HD7 211 K8
Crow Wood La GTL/HWG HX4 189 L4
Crow Wood Pk LUD/ILL HX2 167 M1
Croxall Dr EARD/LOFT WF3 177 G1
Croxton Av MILN OL16 206 E6
Croydon Av ROY/SHW OL2 228 E8
Croydon Rd GTHN BD7 126 B2
Croydon St BEE/HOL LS11 8 A5
Crumack La HWTH BD22 101 G3
Crummock Wy BSLYN/ROY S71 262 D6
Crystal Ct HFAX HX1 10 D5
Crystal Pl WKFDE WF1 * 13 H3
Crystal Ter BOW BD4 127 L3
Cubley Av WKFDW/WTN WF2 198 D8
Cubley Rise Rd STKB/PEN S36 270 E5
Cuckoo La HOLM/MEL HD9 236 B2
Cuckstool Rd KBTN HD8 239 J8
Cudbear St MID LS10 9 J3
Cudworth Vw CUD/GR S72 245 J8
Cullingworth Rd
CUL/QBY BD13 101 M1
Cullingworth St DEWS WF13 173 J3
Culver St HFAX HX1 11 G5
Culvert St MILN OL16 228 D4
Cumberland Av HUDN HD2 192 C1
Cumberland Cl LUD/ILL HX2 146 A2
Cumberland Ct HDGY LS6 108 F3
Cumberland Dr BSLYN/ROY S71 262 C6
Cumberland Rd CAS WF10 159 G4
GTHN BD7 126 C1
HDGY LS6 6 A1
ROCH OL11 228 B4
Cumberland St SKP/WHF BD23 16 B3
Cumberworth La KBTN HD8 238 F7
KBTN HD8 256 A1
Cumberworth Rd KBTN HD8 239 H5
Cumbrian Cl ROY/SHW OL2 229 H6
Cumbrian Wy
WKFDW/WTN WF2 197 M4
Cuncliffe Dr ROY/SHW OL2 229 M7
Cunliffe La BAIL BD17 83 K1
Cunliffe Rd GIR BD8 104 E4
ILK LS29 38 D2
Cunliffe Ter GIR BD8 104 F3
Cunliffe Vls HTON BD9 104 F3
Cupstone Cl AIRE BD20 58 F5
Cure Hl HWTH BD22 78 D3
Curlew Cl CAS WF10 157 M8
ILK LS29 38 A2
Curlew Ct AIRE BD20 35 K8
Curlew Ri MOR LS27 152 F3
Curlew St WBOW BD5 126 E3
Curly Hl ILK LS29 20 D8
Currer Av BOW BD4 127 K5
Currerbell Ms CUL/QBY BD13 103 H8
Currer La ILK LS29 19 L2
Currer St BFD BD1 5 G6
Currer Wk AIRE BD20 35 K8
Curtis Ct CUL/QBY BD13 * 79 M8
Curwen Crs HECK WF16 172 F1
Curzon Rd BFDE BD3 5 M6
ROCH OL11 228 B4
Curzon St HUDN HD2 193 J1
Cuthbert Mayne Ct MILN OL16 206 A8
Cuthberts Cl CUL/QBY BD13 124 F6
Cutland Wy LIT OL15 207 J2
Cutler Heights La BOW BD4 127 L3
Cutler La RTHW LS26 157 G3
Cutler Pl BOW BD4 127 M2
Cutlers Av BSLY S70 260 F6
Cut Rd KNOT WF11 159 J2
Cutsyke Av CAS WF10 157 K8
Cutsyke Crest CAS WF10 179 K1
Cutsyke Rd CAS WF10 179 K2
Cuttlehurst KBTN HD8 239 M5
Cutts Field Vw
BSLYN/ROY S71 * 243 K1
Cutty La DOD/DAR S75 260 F3
Cyndor Ct CAS WF10 159 G8
Cypress Ct WKFDW/WTN WF2 198 C4
Cypress Fold KBTN HD8 216 A3
Cypress Gdns MILN OL16 206 F7
Cypress Rd BSLY S70 261 K7
NORM WF6 178 D6
Cyprus Av IDLE BD10 83 H5
WKFDE WF1 176 C6
Cyprus Crs MIRF WF14 172 F7
Cyprus Dr IDLE BD10 83 H5
Cyprus Gv GFTH/SHER LS25 113 G7
WKFDE WF1 176 C6
Cyprus Mt WKFDE WF1 176 C6
Cyprus Rd GFTH/SHER LS25 113 G7
Cyprus St OSS WF5 174 E6
WKFDE WF1 176 D6
Cyprus Ter GFTH/SHER LS25 113 G7
Cyril St ROY/SHW OL2 229 L7
Czar St BEE/HOL LS11 8 C5

D

Dacre Av WKFDW/WTN WF2 197 L2
Dacre Cl LVSG WF15 172 B2
Dacre Ct TAD LS24 93 J8
Dacre Rd ROCH OL11 228 B2
Daffels Wood Cl BOW BD4 127 K6
Daffil Av MOR LS27 130 D7
Daffil Grange Ms MOR LS27 * 130 D7
Daffil Grange Wy MOR LS27 130 D7
Daffil Gv MOR LS27 130 D7
Daffil Rd MOR LS27 130 D7
Daffodil Cl WHIT OL12 206 A3
Daffodil Ct WIL/AL BD15 103 K6
Dagenham Rd BOW BD4 127 L3
Dahl Dr CAS WF10 180 E1
The Dairies NORM WF6 * 178 E3
Daisy Bank HFAX HX1 10 F9
Daisy Bank St TOD OL14 140 D5
Daisy Cl BTLY WF17 151 G4
Daisy Cft AIRE BD20 36 B5
Daisyfield Rd BRAM LS13 * 107 M5
Daisy Fold HEM/SK/SE WF9 225 H7
Daisy Hl AIRE BD20 36 B5
EARL WF12 173 L6
LM/WK BD12 148 E3
MOR LS27 152 E1
Daisy Hill Av MOR LS27 130 E8
Daisy Hill Back La HTON BD9 104 A4
Daisy Hill Cl MOR LS27 * 130 E8
Daisy Hill Gv HTON BD9 104 A4
Daisy Hill La HTON BD9 104 A4
Daisy Lea La HUDW HD3 191 L5
Daisy Lee La HOLM/MEL HD9 254 E7
Daisy Mt RPDN/SBR HX6 167 J1
Daisy Rd BRIG HD6 170 D6
Daisy Royd HUDS HD4 214 C4
Daisy St BRIG HD6 170 C4
GTHN BD7 126 C3
HFAX HX1 10 E7
HWTH BD22 79 G6
WHIT OL12 206 A6
Daisy Vale Ms EARD/LOFT WF3 154 A5
Daisy Vale Ter EARD/LOFT WF3 154 A5
Dalby Av BFDE BD3 105 M5
Dalby Cft STKB/PEN S36 271 G3
Dalby St BFDE BD3 * 105 L6
Dalcross Gv WBOW BD5 127 H2
Dalcross St WBOW BD5 127 G2
Dale Av TOD OL14 163 M1
Dale Cl BSLYN/ROY S71 243 J7
BTLY WF17 173 L4
GSLY LS20 61 K6
KBTN HD8 257 H1
OSS WF5 175 G8
Dale Ct HOLM/MEL HD9 236 D7
OSS WF5 * 174 F8
PONT WF8 202 F1
Dalecourt ILK LS29 * 39 G1
Dale Crs AIRE BD20 56 E1
Dale Cft GFTH/SHER LS25 113 G6
ILK LS29 38 A2
KBTN HD8 239 J4
Dale Croft Ri WIL/AL BD15 103 J4
Dalecroft Rd AWLS/ASK DN6 249 K6
Dalefield Av NORM WF6 178 D5
Dalefield Rd NORM WF6 178 D6
Dalefield Wy NORM WF6 178 D6
Dale Garth BAIL BD17 82 D3
Dale Gv SHPY BD18 83 G5
Dalehead Dr ROY/SHW OL2 229 M7
Dale La HECK WF16 172 F1
HEM/SK/SE WF9 247 K1
Dale Ms PONT WF8 202 F1
Dale Park Av BHP/TINH LS16 85 M2
Dale Park Cl BHP/TINH LS16 85 M2
Dale Park Gdns BHP/TINH LS16 85 M2
Dale Park Ri BHP/TINH LS16 85 M2
Dale Park Wk BHP/TINH LS16 85 M2
Dale Rd BIRK/DRI BD11 129 J6
Dales Dr GSLY LS20 61 K6
Daleside EARL WF12 195 L5
GTL/HWG HX4 168 C7
TOD OL14 163 J2
Daleside Av HOLM/MEL HD9 236 E7
PDSY/CALV LS28 106 C6
Daleside Cl PDSY/CALV LS28 106 B5
Daleside Gv LM/WK BD12 149 H2
PDSY/CALV LS28 106 C6
Daleside Rd AIRE BD20 58 C5
BFDE BD3 106 B5
SHPY BD18 83 G5
Daleside Wk WBOW BD5 127 H4
Daleson Cl HIPP HX3 147 J3
Dale Stone Cl KNOT WF11 * 159 L5
Dale St BFD BD1 4 F5
HUDW HD3 191 J8
KGHY BD21 3 L1
MILN OL16 206 E7
OSS WF5 174 F8
ROY/SHW OL2 229 K8
RPDN/SBR HX6 167 K2
SHPY BD18 82 D7
TOD OL14 163 K1
Dalesway BGLY BD16 81 K1
Dales Wy BHP/TINH LS16 65 G8
BHP/TINH LS16 86 F6
GSLY LS20 61 K6
ILK LS29 37 M1
Dales Way Link BAIL BD17 82 A1
BHP/TINH LS16 64 C3
HDGY LS6 87 G7
OT LS21 63 H2
Daleswood Av BSLY S70 260 D5
The Dale GFTH/SHER LS25 92 A6
Dale Vw AIRE BD20 36 A4
AIRE BD20 56 E1
HEM/SK/SE WF9 224 B8
ILK LS29 38 A2
LIT OL15 207 H4
PONT WF8 202 F1
Dale View Cl KGHY BD21 3 M7
Daleview Ct BAIL BD17 82 C4
Dale View Gv KGHY BD21 3 M6
Dale View Rd KGHY BD21 3 L8
Dallam Av SHPY BD18 82 A6
Dallam Rd SHPY BD18 82 A6
Dallam Wk SHPY BD18 82 B6
Dalmeny Av HUDS HD4 213 L4
Dalmeny Cl HUDS HD4 213 L3
Dalmeny Ter BRAM LS13 * 107 G1
ROCH OL11 228 B2
Dalton Av BEE/HOL LS11 131 J4
MILN OL16 206 F7
Dalton Bank Rd HUDE HD5 193 J5
Dalton Cl MILN OL16 206 F7
Dalton Clowes HUDE HD5 193 G7
Dalton Fold Rd HUDE HD5 15 L5
Dalton Green La HUDE HD5 193 J7
Dalton Gv BEE/HOL LS11 131 J4
HUDE HD5 193 G7
Dalton La BSPA/BRAM LS23 69 G4
KGHY BD21 3 K4
Dalton Rd BEE/HOL LS11 131 J4
KGHY BD21 3 L4
Dalton St RPDN/SBR HX6 167 K1
Dalton Ter BSLY S70 261 J6
CAS WF10 157 M7
GIR BD8 104 D6
KGHY BD21 3 L2
Dalton Wk AWLS/ASK DN6 249 K2
Damask St HFAX HX1 * 10 F4
Dam Br COP/BISH YO23 33 L7
Damems La HWTH BD22 79 H4
Dam Head HOLM/MEL HD9 253 M4
Dam Head La HUDE HD5 194 B8
Dam Head Rd RPDN/SBR HX6 167 L1
Dam Hl COP/BISH YO23 33 M7
KBTN HD8 237 M3
Dam La TAD LS24 93 J8
YEA LS19 62 E7
Damon Av IDLE BD10 106 A2
Dampier St TOD OL14 163 J5
Damside KGHY BD21 2 F6
Damside Rd HUDS HD4 214 D2
Damson Ct CLAY BD14 125 L3
Damsteads DOD/DAR S75 260 C7
Danby Av BOW BD4 127 K6
Danby La WKFDW/WTN WF2 220 E2
Danby Wk OSM LS9 110 B7
Dandy Mill Av PONT WF8 181 H4
Dandy Mill Cft PONT WF8 181 H4
Dandy Mill Vw PONT WF8 181 H4
Danebury Rd BRIG HD6 170 D5
Danecourt Rd BOW BD4 128 A3
Danefield Ter OT LS21 41 K6
Dane Hill Dr BOW BD4 128 A2
Danella Crs WKFDW/WTN WF2 176 B4
Danella Gv WKFDW/WTN WF2 176 B4
Danes La HOR/CROF WF4 196 D8
Danesleigh Dr HOR/CROF WF4 196 D8
Dane St ROCH OL11 206 A7
Daniel Ct BOW BD4 128 B4
Dan La WBSY BD6 125 L5
Danny La LUD/ILL HX2 144 F7
Dansk Wy ILK LS29 38 F1
Danum Dr BAIL BD17 82 E4
Darcey Hey La LUD/ILL HX2 168 A1
Darfield Av RHAY LS8 110 C3
Darfield Crs RHAY LS8 110 C3
Darfield Gv RHAY LS8 110 B3
Darfield Pl RHAY LS8 110 C3
Darfield Rd CUD/GR S72 262 F2
RHAY LS8 110 C3
Darfield St GIR BD8 4 D4
RHAY LS8 110 C3
Darkfield La PONT WF8 181 H2
Dark La BSLY S70 260 D7
BTLY WF17 151 H3
BTLY WF17 173 K2
HBR HX7 142 E3
HUDE HD5 215 J3
HWTH BD22 78 B5
HWTH BD22 100 E3
LUD/ILL HX2 145 K8
OT LS21 42 F1
PBR HG3 29 G1
PONT WF8 180 E7
UPML OL3 231 G8
Darkwood Cl AL/HA/HU LS17 88 C2
Darkwood Wy AL/HA/HU LS17 88 C2
Darley Av BSLY S70 261 H8
BSLYN/ROY S71 243 J8
MID LS10 131 M7
Darley Cl BSLYN/ROY S71 243 J8
Darley Rd LVSG WF15 172 B1
ROCH OL11 228 B2
Darley St AIRE BD20 57 K5
BFD BD1 4 F5
HECK WF16 172 F2
Darley Ter DOD/DAR S75 260 F4
Darlington Rd ROCH OL11 228 B3
Darnell Ter BEE/HOL LS11 9 G3
Darnes Av LUD/ILL HX2 168 A1
Darning La PONT WF8 225 K1
Darnley Av WKFDW/WTN WF2 12 A1
Darnley Cl HOLM/MEL HD9 235 G5
Darnley La MSTN/BAR LS15 111 L8
Darren St BOW BD4 106 A8
Darrington Pl BSLYN/ROY S71 262 A3
Darrington Rd PONT WF8 203 G4
Darryl Dr LUD/ILL HX2 168 A1
Dartmouth Av HUDE HD5 215 J3
MOR LS27 152 C4
Dartmouth Ms MOR LS27 152 B3
Dartmouth Ter GIR BD8 104 E4
Darton Hall Cl DOD/DAR S75 242 B5
Darton La DOD/DAR S75 242 C6
Darton Rd DOD/DAR S75 259 H1
Darton St BSLY S70 261 M6
Dartree Cl WMB/DAR S73 263 H8
Dartree Wk WMB/DAR S73 263 H8
Darwin St WBOW BD5 126 E3
Datchett Ter ROCH OL11 228 B2
Daventry Rd ROCH OL11 228 B3
Davey La HBR HX7 142 B3
David La DEWS WF13 173 L4
David Lewis Cl MILN OL16 206 E8
David St BEE/HOL LS11 8 E3
CAS WF10 157 K7
WHIT OL12 206 B5
WKFDE WF1 * 13 J7
David St North WHIT OL12 * 206 B5
Davies Av RHAY LS8 88 C6
Davis Av CAS WF10 158 F8
Davyhulme St WHIT OL12 206 C5
Dawcross Ri PBR HG3 26 C2
Dawes Av CAS WF10 158 B8
Daw Green Av HOR/CROF WF4 220 A2
Daw La HOR/CROF WF4 197 L6
Dawlish Av OSM LS9 110 D6
Dawlish Crs OSM LS9 110 C6
Dawlish Gv OSM LS9 110 D7
Dawlish Mt OSM LS9 110 D6
Dawlish Pl OSM LS9 110 D6
Dawlish Rd OSM LS9 110 D6
Dawlish Rw OSM LS9 110 D6
Dawlish St OSM LS9 110 D6
Dawlish Ter OSM LS9 110 D6
Dawnay Rd WBOW BD5 126 E2
Dawn St ROY/SHW OL2 * 229 K8
Daw Royds HUDE HD5 215 J1
Dawson Av WBSY BD6 126 E6
Dawson Hl MOR LS27 152 C1
Dawson La BOW BD4 127 L5
BOW BD4 129 G4
Dawson Mt BOW BD4 127 L5
Dawson Pl BOW BD4 127 L5
KGHY BD21 3 H8
Dawson Rd BEE/HOL LS11 131 J3
HUDS HD4 214 D3
KGHY BD21 3 H8
Dawsons Meadow
PDSY/CALV LS28 106 E4
Dawson St BOW BD4 127 L4
EARD/LOFT WF3 152 F5
IDLE BD10 83 K4
PDSY/CALV LS28 * 106 F5
SKP/WHF BD23 16 C3
Dawson Ter BOW BD4 127 L5
Dawson Wy KGHY BD21 3 H9
Dawtrie Cl CAS WF10 158 F7
Dawtrie St CAS WF10 158 F6
Dayhouse Wy DOD/DAR S75 260 D2
Daykin Cl DOD/DAR S75 241 M6
Day St BSLY S70 261 G6
DEWS WF13 195 G1
HUD HD1 15 J9
Deacon Cl BFDE BD3 * 105 M4
HOLM/MEL HD9 235 G4
Deacon St MILN OL16 206 D5
Deacons Wy BSLYN/ROY S71 261 L3
Deadmanstone HUDS HD4 214 B6
Dealburn Rd LM/WK BD12 148 F1
Deal St HFAX HX1 11 J7
KGHY BD21 3 L3
Dean Av HOLM/MEL HD9 236 B6
RHAY LS8 88 C8
Dean Bank Dr MILN OL16 228 D5
Dean Beck Av WBSY BD6 127 G6
Dean Beck Ct WBSY BD6 * 127 H6
Dean Bridge La
HOLM/MEL HD9 254 F3
Dean Brook Rd
HOLM/MEL HD9 236 C5
HUDS HD4 214 A6
Dean Cl GIR BD8 103 M5
WKFDW/WTN WF2 176 B4
Dean Clough HIPP HX3 11 G4
Dean Clough Office Pk
HIPP HX3 11 G3
Dean Ct HIPP HX3 168 C4
RHAY LS8 88 C8
Deancourt ROCH OL11 228 A2
Dean Edge Rd HWTH BD22 77 J6
Dean End GTL/HWG HX4 168 F6
Deanery Gdns IDLE BD10 105 L1
Deanfield Av MOR LS27 152 B1
Dean Fold KBTN HD8 215 M6
Dean Hall Cl MOR LS27 * 152 B2
Dean Head HORS LS18 63 J6
LIT OL15 * 185 L3
Dean House La GTL/HWG HX4 189 M6
LUD/ILL HX2 144 F4
Deanhouse La HOLM/MEL HD9 236 B6
Deanhurst Gdns MOR LS27 129 M8
Dean La CUL/QBY BD13 102 E5
GSLY LS20 61 H6
HOLM/MEL HD9 254 F4
HORS LS18 63 J6
HWTH BD22 56 B8
RPDN/SBR HX6 167 G4
Dean La Head CUL/QBY BD13 * 102 F5
Dean Park Av BIRK/DRI BD11 129 G7
Dean Park Dr BIRK/DRI BD11 129 G8
Dean Rd HOLM/MEL HD9 235 L8
WBSY BD6 126 F6
Deanroyd Rd TOD OL14 163 K7
Dean's Laithe KGHY BD21 3 J5
Deanstones Crs CUL/QBY BD13 125 G6
Deanstones La CUL/QBY BD13 125 G6
Dean St BSLY S70 260 F5
COL BB8 74 D4
ELL HX5 169 H8
GTL/HWG HX4 168 F7
HUDW HD3 191 K7
HWTH BD22 78 F7
ILK LS29 38 E1
MILN OL16 206 D5
Deans Wy BSLYN/ROY S71 261 L2
Deansway MOR LS27 130 B8
Deanswood Cl AL/HA/HU LS17 87 J3
Deanswood Dr AL/HA/HU LS17 87 H3
Deanswood Gn AL/HA/HU LS17 87 H3
Deanswood Hl AL/HA/HU LS17 87 H3
Deanswood Pl AL/HA/HU LS17 87 J3
Deanswood Ri AL/HA/HU LS17 87 H3
Deanswood Vw AL/HA/HU LS17 87 J3
Deanwood Av WIL/AL BD15 103 J4
Deanwood Crs WIL/AL BD15 103 J4
Deanwood Wk WIL/AL BD15 103 J4
Dearden St LIT OL15 185 K8
OSS WF5 196 F1
RPDN/SBR HX6 167 K1
Dearne Cft WBY LS22 30 A6
Dearne Dike La KBTN HD8 256 A1
Dearne Fold HUDW HD3 191 K5
Dearne Hall Fold DOD/DAR S75 242 B8
Dearne Hall Rd DOD/DAR S75 242 B8
Dearne Pk KBTN HD8 240 A4
Dearne Royd KBTN HD8 240 A4
Dearneside Rd KBTN HD8 257 H1
Dearne St DOD/DAR S75 242 A5
HEM/SK/SE WF9 247 H3
Dearne Wy DOD/DAR S75 241 L3
DOD/DAR S75 242 D7
KBTN HD8 239 L8
KBTN HD8 256 C2
Dearnfield KBTN HD8 238 E8
Dearnley Cl LIT OL15 207 H2
Dearnley St DEWS WF13 173 G8
Dearnley Vw DOD/DAR S75 260 F2
Dee Ct HWTH BD22 78 E4
Deepcar La CUD/GR S72 263 G3
Deep Dl BSPA/BRAM LS23 48 E5
Deepdale Av MILN OL16 206 E8
ROY/SHW OL2 228 E6
Deepdale Cl BAIL BD17 82 C4
Deepdale Cft DOD/DAR S75 260 B1
Deepdale La BSPA/BRAM LS23 48 D5
Deep La BRIG HD6 171 G4
CLAY BD14 125 L1
CUL/QBY BD13 124 C2
HUDS HD4 213 K3
LIT OL15 207 K6
LUD/ILL HX2 145 H7
RPDN/SBR HX6 166 D6
Deeplish Rd ROCH OL11 228 B1
Deeplish St ROCH OL11 228 B1
Deer Croft Av HUDW HD3 191 H6
Deer Croft Crs HUDW HD3 191 H6
Deer Croft Rd HUDW HD3 191 H5
Deer Hill Cl MAR/SLWT HD7 233 H3
Deer Hill Ct HOLM/MEL HD9 234 E4
Deer Hill Cft MAR/SLWT HD7 233 H3
Deer Hill Dr MAR/SLWT HD7 233 H3
Deer Hill End Rd
HOLM/MEL HD9 234 B3
Deer Park Ct GFTH/SHER LS25 138 C6
Deershaw La KBTN HD8 255 L1
Deershaw Sike La KBTN HD8 255 L1
Deerstone Rdg WBY LS22 30 A6
Defarge Ct WBOW BD5 127 G3
Deffer Rd WKFDW/WTN WF2 198 D8
Deganwy Dr HUDE HD5 193 L4
Deighton Av GFTH/SHER LS25 116 A7
Deighton Cl WBY LS22 30 B8
Deighton La BTLY WF17 173 J1
Deighton Rd HUDN HD2 192 F3
PBR HG3 29 G3
WBY LS22 30 A6
Deighton Vw HDGY LS6 87 G5
De Lacey Ms BOW BD4 127 L4
De Lacies Ct RTHW LS26 133 J7
De Lacies Rd RTHW LS26 133 J7
De Lacy Av BOW BD4 * 127 K6
FEA/AMT WF7 179 L5
HUDE HD5 215 H2
Delacy Crs CAS WF10 158 F5
De Lacy Mt KSTL LS5 108 C2
De Lacy Ter PONT WF8 181 G6
Delamere Av ROY/SHW OL2 229 M6
Delamere Rd MILN OL16 228 E2
Delamere St WBOW BD5 126 F4
Delaware Ct BOW BD4 127 K6
Delf Hl BRIG HD6 170 A7
Delf La HBR HX7 121 L6
TOD OL14 140 F3
Delfs La RPDN/SBR HX6 166 B6
Delius Av IDLE BD10 105 M1
Della Av BSLY S70 260 F6
Dell Av CUD/GR S72 245 J6
Dell Cft AIRE BD20 35 L5
Dellside Fold CUL/QBY BD13 79 M8

The Dell *AL/HA/HU* LS17 ....67 M3
CAS WF10 ....179 J1
Delph Dr BD13 ....80 A8
HUDN HD2 ....192 D2
Delmont CI *BTLY* WF17 ....151 L4
Delph CI *DOD/DAR* S75 ....259 J5
Delph Croft Vw *KGHY* BD21* 3 G4
Delph Crs *CLAY* BD14 ....125 K2
Delph Ct *CLAY* BD14 ....125 K2
Delph Dr *CLAY* BD14 ....125 K2
Delph Gv *CLAY* BD14 ....125 K2
Delph HI *BAIL* BD17 ....82 E2
PDSY/CALV LS28 ....107 G6
Delph Hill Castle *LUD/ILL* HX2 *...145 M8
Delph Hill La *LUD/ILL* HX2 ....144 F4
Delph Hill Rd *LUD/ILL* HX2 ....168 B2
Delph Hill Ter *LUD/ILL* HX2 ....168 B3
Delph La *HDGY* LS6 ....6 D1
HUDS HD4 ....213 M7
Delph Mt *UPML* OL3 ....230 F6
Delph St *HFAX* HX1 ....10 F7
MILN OL16 ....207 H4
Delph Ter *CLAY* BD14 ....125 K2
The Delph *FEA/AMT* WF7 ....202 B1
Delph Vw *HDGY* LS6 ....6 C1
Delph Wood CI *BGLY* BD16 ....81 L5
Delverne Gv *ECHL* BD2 ....105 L3
Delves Ga *MAR/SLWT* HD7 ....212 B8
Delves Wood Rd *HUDS* HD4 ....213 H6
Denbigh Dr *ROY/SHW* OL2 ....229 H8
Denbrook Av *BOW* BD4 ....128 B5
Denbrook CI *BOW* BD4 ....128 B5
Denbrook Crs *BOW* BD4 ....128 B5
Denbrook Wk *BOW* BD4 ....128 B5
Denbrook Wy *BOW* BD4 ....128 B5
Denbury Mt *BOW* BD4 ....128 A4
Denby CI *BTLY* WF17 ....150 F5
LVSG WF15 ....172 E3
Denby Ct *HWTH* BD22 ....78 D5
Denby Crest *PONT* WF8 ....203 L1
Denby Dale Rd *HOR/CROF* WF4 ....218 C6
WKFDW/WTN WF2 ....12 D7
Denby Dale Rd East
HOR/CROF WF4 ....198 A7
Denby Dale Rd West
HOR/CROF WF4 ....197 M8
Denby Dr *BAIL* BD17 ....82 D5
Denby Grange La
HOR/CROF WF4 ....217 J1
Denby Hall La *KBTN* HD8 ....257 M1
Denby Hill Rd *HWTH* BD22 ....78 D4
Denby La *HOR/CROF* WF4 ....217 G1
KBTN HD8 ....256 F3
WIL/AL BD15 ....103 K5
Denby Mt *HWTH* BD22 ....100 E4
Denby Park Dr
HOR/CROF WF4 ....217 G1
Denby PI *RPDN/SBR* HX6 ....167 K1
Denby Rd *BSLYN/ROY* S71 ....243 H7
KGHY BD21 ....3 G9
PONT WF8 ....203 L1
Denby St *GIR* BD8 ....4 B3
Denby Vw *EARL* WF12 ....195 M5
Dence Gn *BOW* BD4 * 128 A1
Dence PI *MSTN/BAR* LS15 ....111 G6
Dendrum CI *HWTH* BD22 ....78 C5
Dene Bank *BGLY* BD16 ....59 J3
Dene CI *ELL* HX5 ....191 G5
Dene Crs *GTHN* BD7 ....126 A2
Dene Gv *AIRE* BD20 ....36 A4
Dene HI *BAIL* BD17 ....82 B3
Denehill *HTON* BD9 ....103 M4
Dene House La *LDSU* LS2 ....6 F4
Dene Mt *WIL/AL* BD15 ....103 L5
Dene Pk *KBTN* HD8 ....216 E2
Dene PI *HFAX* HX1 ....10 F4
Dene Rd *KBTN* HD8 ....239 K5
WBSY BD6 ....125 M5
Dene Royd CI *GTL/HWG* HX4 ....190 F5
Dene Royd Ct *GTL/HWG* HX4 ....190 B3
Deneside OSS WF5 ....174 A4
Deneside Mt *WBOW* BD5 ....126 E5
Deneside Ter *WBOW* BD5 ....126 F4
Deneswav *GFTH/SHER* LS25 ....135 J1
Dene Vw *LUD/ILL* HX2 ....144 F6
Deneway *PDSY/CALV* LS28 ....106 A2
Denfield Av *HIPP* HX3 ....146 A4
Denfield Crs *HIPP* HX3 ....146 B4
Denfield Edge *HIPP* HX3 ....146 B4
Denfield Gdns *HIPP* HX3 ....146 B4
Denfield La *HIPP* HX3 ....146 A4
Denfield Sq *HIPP* HX3 ....146 B4
Denham Av *WKFDW/WTN* WF2 ....176 A8
Denham Av *MOR* LS27 ....152 C4
Denham Dr *HOLM/MEL* HD9 ....236 B6
Denham St *BRIG* HD6 ....170 C4
BTLY WF17 ....151 J7
Denholme Av *MOR* LS27 ....152 C3
Denholme Gate Rd *HIPP* HX3 ....147 L5
Denholme Meadow
HEM/SK/SE WF9 ....247 H2
ROCH OL11 ....228 B1
Denhurst Rd *LIT* OL15 ....185 J8
Denison St *BSLY* S70 ....261 H6
YEA LS19 ....62 D1
Denmark St *MILN* OL16 ....206 C6
WKFDE WF1 ....13 J7
Dennil La *MSTN/BAR* LS15 ....111 M2
Dennil Rd *MSTN/BAR* LS15 ....111 M3
Dennington La *HOR/CROF* WF4 ....219 L3
Dennis La *AIRE* BD20 ....35 J3
Dennison Fold *BOW* BD4 ....128 A1
Dennison HI *OT* LS21 ....41 K6
Dennistead Crs *HDGY* LS6 ....108 F1
Denshaw Dr *MOR* LS27 ....152 E2
Denshaw Gv *MOR* LS27 ....152 E2
Denshaw La *EARD/LOFT* WF3 ....153 L2
Denshaw Rd *UPML* OL3 ....230 A1
Denstone St *WKFDE* WF1 ....13 L5
Dent Dr *WKFDE* WF1 ....177 H6
Denton Av *RHAY* LS8 ....88 C4
Denton Dr *BGLY* BD16 ....81 L2
Denton Gdns *FEA/AMT* WF7 ....224 C1
Denton Gv *RHAY* LS8 * 88 B4
Denton Rd *ILK* LS29 ....38 C1
ILK LS29 ....38 D4
Denton St *BSLYN/ROY* S71 ....261 H4
WHIT OL12 ....206 B5
Denton Ter *CAS* WF10 ....158 A6
Dent St *OSM* LS9 ....110 B7
Denver Rd *ROCH* OL11 ....228 D4
Denwell Ter *PONT* WF8 ....180 F5
Derby PI *BFDE* BD3 * 105 M7
Derby Rd *BFDE* BD3 ....106 A7
YEA LS19 ....84 D2
Derbyshire St *MID* LS10 ....132 B5
Derby St *BSLY* S70 ....260 F5
CLAY BD14 * 125 K2
CUL/OBY BD13 ....124 F5
GTHN BD7 ....126 D2
ROCH OL11 ....228 C1
Derby Ter *MAR/SLWT* HD7 ....233 H2
Derdale St *TOD* OL14 ....163 H7
Derry HI *ILK* LS29 ....61 H3

Derry Hill Gdns *ILK* LS29 ....61 H2
Derry La *ILK* LS29 ....61 H2
Der St *TOD* OL14 ....163 L1
Derwent Av *GFTH/SHER* LS25 ....113 H8
MILN OL16 ....207 K8
RTHW LS26 ....133 L8
WIL/AL BD15 ....102 E2
Derwent CI *BSLYN/ROY* S71 ....243 K7
COL BD13 ....52 C8
HBR HX7 ....143 J7
Derwent Crs *BSLYN/ROY* S71 ....243 K7
Derwent Dr *BHP/TINH* LS16 ....86 F2
CAS WF10 ....159 G5
ROY/SHW OL2 ....229 H7
Derwent Gv *WKFDW/WTN* WF2 ....176 B8
KNOT WF11 ....182 A4
Derwent Ri *WBY* LS22 ....29 M6
Derwent Rd *BSLYN/ROY* S71 ....243 J7
EARL WF12 ....174 B3
ECHL BD2 ....105 J3
HOLM/MEL HD9 ....235 G5
HOLM/MEL HD9 ....236 A3
Derwent St *KGHY* BD21 ....176 B8
WHIT OL12 ....206 B5
Derwentwater Gv *HDGY* LS6 ....108 G2
Derwentwater Ter *HDGY* LS6 ....108 F1
Derwin Av *HUDS* HD4 ....237 L4
De Trafford St *HUDS* HD4 ....213 M3
Detroit Av *MSTN/BAR* LS15 ....111 M6
Detroit Dr *MSTN/BAR* LS15 ....112 A6
Deveron Gv *HUD* HD3 ....14 B3
Devine CI *ROY/SHW* OL2 ....228 F8
Devon CI *LDSU* LS2 ....6 E4
ROY/SHW OL2 ....229 H7
Devon Rd *CHAL* LS7 ....6 E4
Devonshire Av *RHAY* LS8 ....88 C4
Devonshire CI *RHAY* LS8 ....88 C5
Devonshire Crs *RHAY* LS8 ....88 B5
Devonshire Dr *DOD/DAR* S75 ....260 F2
Devonshire Gdns *CHAL* LS7 ....6 F3
Devonshire La *RHAY* LS8 ....88 C4
Devonshire PI *SKP/WHF* BD23 * 16 E3
Devonshire Rd *ROCH* OL11 ....228 B4
Devonshire St *HUDS* HD4 ....214 A3
KGHY BD21 ....2 E4
SKP/WHF BD23 ....16 E3
Devonshire St West *KGHY* BD21 ....2 D5
Devonshire Ter *GIR* BD8 ....104 C4
Devon St *HFAX* HX1 ....10 A8
ROCH OL11 ....206 A8
Devon Wy *BRIG* HD6 ....148 D8
Dewar CI *WBY* LS22 ....47 J3
Dewhirst PI *BOW* BD4 * 105 M8
Dewhirst Rd *BAIL* BD17 ....82 F4
BRIG HD6 ....170 C2
WHIT OL12 ....206 B1
Dewhirst Wy *WHIT* OL12 ....206 B1
Dewhurst Rd *HUDN* HD2 ....192 D4
Dew Meadow CI *WHIT* OL12 ....206 A4
Dewsbury Gate Rd
DEWS WF13 ....173 H3
Dewsbury Ring Rd
DEWS WF13 ....173 L6
Dewsbury Rd *BEE/HOL* LS11 ....9 G5
CLECK BD19 ....150 A7
EARL WF12 ....174 B4
ELL HX5 ....169 L8
OSS WF5 ....174 F7
WKFDW/WTN WF2 ....197 M1
Deyne Rd *HUDS* HD4 ....213 L7
Diadem Dr *SCFT* LS14 ....111 G5
Dial St *OSM* LS9 ....110 B7
Diamond Av *HEM/SK/SE* WF9 ....247 G3
Diamond St *BFD* BD1 ....5 G7
BTLY WF17 * 151 K8
HFAX HX1 ....10 C4
HUD HD1 ....15 H5
HUDE HD5 ....15 M8
HWTH BD22 ....79 J2
Diamond Ter *HFAX* HX1 ....10 C3
Dibb La *YEA* LS19 ....62 E3
Dib CI *RHAY* LS8 ....110 F1
Dib La *RHAY* LS8 ....110 F1
Dick Dean La *HBR* HX7 ....121 J1
Dick Edge La *HOLM/MEL* HD9 ....255 K4
Dicken Gn *ROCH* OL11 ....228 B2
Dicken Green La *ROCH* OL11 ....228 B2
Dickens Dr *CAS* WF10 ....180 F1
Dicken's St *LUD/ILL* HX2 ....146 A7
WBOW BD5 ....127 G5
Dickin Ct *RPDN/SBR* HX6 * 189 G2
Dickinson St *WKFDE* WF1 ....176 E6
Dickinson PI *BSLY* S70 ....261 H7
Dickinson St *HORS* LS18 ....85 L4
WKFDE WF1 ....176 E7
Dickinson Ter *FEA/AMT* WF7 ....179 M8
Dick La *BFDE* BD3 ....106 B6
BOW BD4 ....128 A1
HWTH BD22 ....54 F2
Dickson St *COL* BD8 ....74 A1
Dick's Garth Rd *ILK* LS29 ....61 J2
Dickson St *COL* BD8 ....74 A1
Dicky Sykes La *FEA/AMT* WF7 ....223 M1
Digby Rd *ILK* LS29 ....61 J2
ROCH OL11 ....228 B2
Dig Gate La *MILN* OL16 ....229 G1
Diggle St *ROY/SHW* OL2 ....229 K8
Digle Rd *HOLM/MEL* HD9 ....253 K4
Digley Royd La *HOLM/MEL* HD9 ....253 L8
Dillington Rd *BSLY* S70 ....261 H7
Dillington Sq *BSLY* S70 ....261 H7
Dillington Ter *BSLY* S70 ....261 H7
Dimple Gdns *OSS* WF5 ....196 F2
Dimples La *AIRE* BD20 ....58 F6
HWTH BD22 ....78 C7
Dimple Wells CI *OSS* WF5 ....196 F2
Dimple Wells La *OSS* WF5 ....196 F2
Dimple Wells Rd *OSS* WF5 ....196 F2
Dineley Av *TOD* OL14 ....141 M7
Dingle Av *ROY/SHW* OL2 ....229 L5
Dingle Rd *HUD* HD1 ....191 M8
Dingley Rd *HUDW* HD3 ....191 M8
Dirker Av *MAR/SLWT* HD7 ....233 J1
Dirker Bank Rd *MAR/SLWT* HD7 ....233 H1
Dirker Dr *MAR/SLWT* HD7 ....233 H1
Dirkhill Rd *GTHN* BD7 ....126 D1
Dirkhill St *GTHN* BD7 ....126 D1
Dirty La *UPML* OL3 ....231 K6
Dirty Leech *WHIT* OL12 ....184 D4
Discovery Wk *HFAX* HX1 ....11 H4
Disney CI *HUDS* HD4 ....213 M3
Dispensary Wk *HFAX* HX1 ....11 J5
Disraeli Gdns *BEE/HOL* LS11 ....8 F8
Disraeli Ter *BEE/HOL* LS11 ....8 F8
Ditton Mead CI *WHIT* OL12 ....206 D4
Division La *WHIT* OL12 ....206 D4
Dixon Av *GTHN* BD7 ....126 C1
Dixon CI *AIRE* BD20 ....56 B1
GTL/HWG HX4 ....168 C6
Dixon La *WOR/ARM* LS12 ....130 C1
Dixon Lane Rd *WOR/ARM* LS12 ....130 C1
Dixon St *AIRE* BD20 ....56 A1
FEA/AMT WF7 ....179 M7

Dixon's Yd *WKFDE* WF1 * 13 G3
Dobbin Dr *ROCH* OL11 ....228 B3
Dobb La *HOLM/MEL* HD9 ....253 L4
Dobb Top Rd *HOLM/MEL* HD9 ....253 H5
Dob St *BSLY* S70 ....261 H6
Dob La *RPDN/SBR* HX6 ....166 F3
Dob Royd *KBTN* HD8 ....237 M7
Dobroyd Rd *TOD* OL14 ....163 J2
Dobson Av *BEE/HOL* LS11 ....9 G9
Dobson Gv *BEE/HOL* LS11 ....9 G9
Dobson PI *BEE/HOL* LS11 ....9 G9
Dobson Ter *BEE/HOL* LS11 ....9 G9
Dobson Vw *BEE/HOL* LS11 ....9 G9
Dockery *HUD* HD1 ....214 D3
Dockfield PI *BAIL* BD17 ....82 E5
Dockfield Rd *BAIL* BD17 ....82 E6
Dockfield Ter *BAIL* BD17 ....82 E6
Dock La *SHPY* BD18 ....82 E6
Dockray St *COL* BD8 ....74 A1
Dockroyd La *HWTH* BD22 ....78 A1
Dock St *MID* LS10 ....9 H2
Doctor Fold *HOLM/MEL* HD9 ....236 B1
Doctor HI *IDLE* BD10 ....83 K7
LUD/ILL HX2 ....145 M5
Doctor La *HOR/CROF* WF4 ....217 K4
IDLE BD10 ....83 K5
KBTN HD8 ....238 C1
MIRF WF14 ....194 C1
Doctors La *CAS* WF10 ....135 J8
Dodd CI *MILN* OL16 ....228 D4
Dodgeholme CI *LUD/ILL* HX2 ....145 M2
Dodge Holme Gdns
LUD/ILL HX2 ....145 M2
Dodge Holme Rd *LUD/ILL* HX2 ....145 M2
Dodgson Av *CHAL* LS7 ....7 L2
Doddie La *HUDW* HD3 ....191 H4
Dodsworth Crs *NORM* WF6 ....178 D6
Dodsworth Dr
WKFDW/WTN WF2 ....220 D1
Dodworth Green Rd
DOD/DAR S75 ....259 M8
Dodworth Rd *BSLY* S70 ....260 E5
Dog HI *CUD/GR* S72 ....244 D3
Dog Hill La *CUD/GR* S72 ....244 D3
Doghouse La *TOD* OL14 ....163 J1
Dog Kennel Bank *HUDE* HD5 ....15 K9
Dog Kennel HI *DOD/DAR* S75 ....259 G3
Dog Kennel La *HIPP* HX3 ....11 M9
Dog La *GTL/HWG* HX4 ....168 A7
Dogley Villa Ct *KBTN* HD8 ....215 M5
Doldram La *RPDN/SBR* HX6 ....167 J5
Dole La *HBR* HX7 ....143 J5
Doles Av *BSLYN/ROY* S71 ....243 K3
Doles Crs *BSLYN/ROY* S71 ....243 K3
Dole St *CUL/OBY* BD13 ....103 G8
Dolfin PI *HUDN* HD2 ....193 H1
Doll La *CUL/OBY* BD13 ....102 A1
Dolly La *OSM* LS9 ....7 L6
Dolphin Ct *OSM* LS9 ....9 M1
Dolphin La *EARD/LOFT* WF3 ....154 A4
Dolphin Rd *MID* LS10 ....154 A1
Dolphin St *OSM* LS9 ....9 M1
Dolphin Ct *BRAM* LS13 ....107 K4
Dombey St *HFAX* HX1 ....10 D6
Domestic Rd *BEE/HOL* LS11 ....131 C1
Domestic St *BEE/HOL* LS11 ....8 B5
Dominion Av *CHAL* LS7 ....87 M8
Dominion CI *CHAL* LS7 ....87 M8
Donald Aldred Dr *ILK* LS29 ....40 A6
Donald Av *WBSY* BD6 ....126 E6
Donald St *PDSY/CALV* LS28 ....106 F4
Don Av *WBY* LS22 ....29 M6
Doncaster La *AWLS/ASK* DN6 ....248 C1
Doncaster Rd *BSLY* S70 ....261 H5
BSLYN/ROY S71 ....262 B4
FEA/AMT WF7 ....224 C1
HEM/SK/SE WF9 ....225 J8
HEM/SK/SE WF9 ....247 J4
HOR/CROF WF4 ....199 L4
KNOT WF11 ....181 L2
PONT WF8 ....203 J8
PONT WF8 ....181 J6
WMB/DAR S73 ....263 K8
Doncaster Road Est
FEA/AMT WF7 ....224 C1
Doncaster St *HIPP* HX3 ....168 F3
Don Ct *AIRE* BD20 ....36 A5
Don Dr *BSLY* S70 ....261 M7
Donisthorpe St *MID* LS10 ....9 L5
WBOW BD5 * 7 K8
Donnington *ROCH* OL11 * 206 A8
Don Pedro Av *NORM* WF6 ....178 A4
Don Pedro CI *NORM* WF6 ....178 A4
Don St *KGHY* BD21 ....2 E3
STKB/PEN S36 ....271 H4
Don Vw *STKB/PEN* S36 ....267 M5
Dorchester Ct *BOW* BD4 * 128 A3
Dorchester Crs *BAIL* BD17 ....83 H2
BOW BD4 ....128 A3
Dorchester Dr *LUD/ILL* HX2 ....168 A1
YEA LS19 ....62 E3
Dorchester Rd *HUDN* HD2 ....192 D1
TAD LS24 ....51 G2
Dorian CI *IDLE* BD10 ....83 M8
Dorman Av *HEM/SK/SE* WF9 ....225 M6
Dorothy St *KGHY* BD21 ....79 J3
ROY/SHW OL2 ....229 H7
Dorset Av *RHAY* LS8 ....110 C2
ROY/SHW OL2 ....229 H7
Dorset CI *HEM/SK/SE* WF9 ....223 M6
WBOW BD5 ....126 E5
Dorset Gv *PDSY/CALV* LS28 * 107 G6
Dorset Mt *RHAY* LS8 ....110 C2
Dorset Rd *RHAY* LS8 ....110 C2
Dorset St *HUD* HD1 ....14 D2
RHAY LS8 * 110 C2
ROCH OL11 ....206 B8
SKP/WHF BD23 ....16 C3
WBOW BD5 ....126 E5
Dorset Ter *RHAY* LS8 ....110 C3
Dorts Crs *TAD* LS24 ....95 G5
Dotterel Gln *MOR* LS27 ....152 E3
Doubting La *EARL* WF12 ....195 M5
STKB/PEN S36 ....270 D7
Doubting Rd *EARL* WF12 ....195 M5
Douglas Av *BTLY* WF17 ....174 B1
HUDE HD5 ....215 G1
Douglas Dr *BOW* BD4 * 127 L2
Douglas Rd *BOW* BD4 ....127 L2
COL BD8 ....52 A8
EARL WF12 ....195 L3
HIPP HX3 ....146 D4
Dovebush Wy *DOD/DAR* S75 ....260 A1
Dovecote CI *HOR/CROF* WF4 ....199 J4
Dovecote Dr *CAS* WF10 ....136 A3
Dovecot Ms *BSLYN/ROY* S71 ....261 J2
Dovedale CI *HIPP* HX3 ....125 K8
HOR/CROF WF4 ....200 A1
Dovedale Dr *WHIT* OL12 ....184 F8
Dovedale Gdns
MSTN/BAR LS15 ....112 B3

Dovedale Garth
MSTN/BAR LS15 ....112 B3
Dovelands *BFDE* BD3 ....55 M2
Dover La *HOLM/MEL* HD9 ....254 D5
Dover Rd *HOLM/MEL* HD9 ....254 D5
Dover St *BFDE* BD3 ....5 K7
GFTH/SHER LS25 ....113 K7
MILN OL16 * 206 F7
TOD OL14 ....163 M1
Dovesdale Gv *WBOW* BD5 ....126 E4
Dovesdale Rd *WBOW* BD5 ....126 E4
Dove St *SHPY* BD18 ....82 B6
Dowkell La *BSPA/BRAM* LS23 ....49 G5
Dowker St *HFAX* HX1 ....10 B9
Dowley Gap La *BGLY* BD16 ....81 K5
Dowling St *ROCH* OL11 ....206 B8
Downes Crs *DOD/DAR* S75 ....260 D3
Downham St *BFDE* BD3 ....5 K7
Downing CI *BFDE* BD3 ....5 K5
Downing Sq *STKB/PEN* S36 ....270 G4
Downing St *MAR/SLWT* HD7 ....212 G6
Downland Crs *KNOT* WF11 ....182 D1
Downshutts La
HOLM/MEL HD9 ....254 F1
Downside Crs *WIL/AL* BD15 ....103 J3
Dracup Av *GTHN* BD7 ....126 A1
Dracup Rd *GTHN* BD7 ....126 B3
Dradishaw Rd *AIRE* BD20 ....35 M5
Dragon Ct *WOR/ARM* LS12 * 8 F7
Dragon Crs *WOR/ARM* LS12 ....130 F1
Dragon Dr *WOR/ARM* LS12 ....130 E1
Dragon Rd *WOR/ARM* LS12 ....130 E1
Drake La *BIRK/DRI* BD11 ....151 L1
Drake Rd *LIT* OL15 ....185 L5
Drakes Rd *HIPP* HX3 ....146 C2
Drake St *BFD* BD1 ....5 G3
MILN OL16 ....206 B7
Dransfield Av *STKB/PEN* S36 ....270 F4
Draper La *HBR* HX7 ....121 G6
Draughton Gv *WBOW* BD5 ....126 D5
Draughton St *WBOW* BD5 ....126 D5
Drayton Manor Yd
BEE/HOL LS11 * 9 G7
Dray Vw *DEWS* WF13 ....173 H4
Drewry Rd *KGHY* BD21 ....2 C5
Drewton Rd *BFD* BD1 ....4 D5
Drift La *HOR/CROF* WF4 ....199 K8
Drill Pole *GIR* BD8 ....4 C2
Drill St *HWTH* BD22 ....78 E8
KGHY BD21 ....3 C4
Drinker La *KBTN* HD8 ....216 E5
Driver PI *WOR/ARM* LS12 ....109 G6
Drivers Rw *PONT* WF8 ....180 F2
Driver Ter *AIRE* BD20 ....36 A4
WOR/ARM LS12 ....109 G6
The Drive *BSLYN/ROY* S71 ....261 J1
AL/HA/HU LS17 ....65 J8
BGLY BD16 ....59 G8
BHP/TINH LS16 ....86 A1
BTLY WF17 ....151 J8
GFTH/SHER LS25 ....135 J5
HBR HX7 ....143 K5
HIPP HX3 ....147 M6
IDLE BD10 ....83 M8
ILK LS29 ....38 D4
MSTN/BAR LS15 ....111 M4
OSM LS9 ....9 L2
RHAY LS8 ....88 C4
RTHW LS26 ....134 C5
SKP/WHF BD23 ....16 D1
Drovers Wy *ECHL* BD2 ....105 G3
Drub La *CLECK* BD19 ....150 A4
Druggist La *ILK* LS29 ....19 K6
Druids St *CLAY* BD14 ....125 K2
Drummer La *MAR/SLWT* HD7 ....212 G4
Drummond Av *BHP/TINH* LS16 ....86 F3
Drummond Ct *BHP/TINH* LS16 ....86 F3
Drummond Rd *BHP/TINH* LS16 ....86 E3
GIR BD8 ....4 A2
Drury Av *HORS* LS18 ....85 L6
Drury CI *HORS* LS18 ....85 K6
Drury Farm Ct *DOD/DAR* S75 ....260 C5
Drury La *GTL/HWG* HX4 ....190 B2
HORS LS18 ....85 K6
NORM WF6 ....26 F3
PBR HG3 ....26 F3
WKFDE WF1 ....12 D7
Dry Carr La *LUD/ILL* HX2 ....144 E1
Dryclough Av *HUDS* HD4 ....213 H6
Dryclough CI *HIPP* HX3 ....168 E3
Dryclough La *HIPP* HX3 ....168 E3
Dryclough Rd *HUDS* HD4 ....213 H3
Dryden St *BSLYN/ROY* S71 ....261 J4
Dryden St *BFD* BD1 * 5 H7
BGLY BD16 ....81 H3
Dry Hill La *KBTN* HD8 ....257 H3
Dubb La *BGLY* BD16 ....81 J3
Duchess Park CI *ROY/SHW* OL2 ....229 K6
Duchess St *ROY/SHW* OL2 ....229 K6
Duchy Av *HTON* BD9 ....104 A3
Duchy Crs *HTON* BD9 ....104 A3
Duchy Dr *HTON* BD9 ....104 A3
Duchy Gv *HTON* BD9 ....104 A3
Duchy Vs *HTON* BD9 ....104 A3
Duchywood *HTON* BD9 ....104 A3
Ducie St *IDLE* BD10 ....83 K5
Duckett CI *PDSY/CALV* LS28 ....106 A2
Duckett St *SKP/WHF* BD23 ....16 C3
Ducking Pond CI *HWTH* BD22 ....78 B4
Duckworth Gv *HTON* BD9 ....104 A4
Duckworth La *HTON* BD9 ....104 A5
Duckworth Ter *HTON* BD9 ....104 A4
Dudley Av *BTLY* WF17 ....191 L4
HUD HD1 ....191 M8
Dudley Crs *LUD/ILL* HX2 ....145 M1
Dudley Gv *BOW* BD4 ....127 L4
Dudley Hill Rd *ECHL* BD2 ....105 M8
Dudley St *BOW* BD4 ....127 L4
COL BD8 ....74 A1
Dudwell Gv *HIPP* HX3 * 168 F4
Dudwell La *HIPP* HX3 ....168 F4
Duffield CI *GFTH/SHER* LS25 * 116 B6
Dufton Ap *SCFT* LS14 ....111 J3
Duich Rd *WBSY* BD6 ....126 A8
Duinen St *WBOW* BD5 ....5 M9
Duke Crs *BSLY* S70 ....261 H6
Duke of York Av
WKFDW/WTN WF2 ....198 A4
Duke of York St *WKFDE* WF1 ....176 B4
Dukes HI *ILK* LS29 ....20 C5
Duke St *AIRE* BD20 ....57 K5
BFD BD1 ....5 L4
BSLY S70 ....261 H6
CAS WF10 ....157 K6
CUD/GR S72 ....245 J3
DEWS WF13 ....195 G1
ELL HX5 ....169 L5
HEM/SK/SE WF9 ....223 J4
HWTH BD22 ....78 F7
LIT OL15 ....207 J1
LUD/ILL HX2 ....144 F5
ROY/SHW OL2 ....229 L8

SKP/WHF BD23 ....16 C2
WHIT OL12 ....206 B5
Duke Wood Rd *KBTN* HD8 ....240 A4
PONT WF8 ....181 H3
Dulverton CI *BEE/HOL* LS11 ....130 E4
Dulverton Gdns *BEE/HOL* LS11 ....130 E4
Dulverton Garth *BEE/HOL* LS11 ....130 E4
Dulverton Gn *BEE/HOL* LS11 ....130 E5
Dulverton Gv *BEE/HOL* LS11 ....130 E5
BOW BD4 ....127 M3
Dulverton PI *BEE/HOL* LS11 ....130 E5
Dulverton Ri *PONT* WF8 ....181 H3
Dulverton Sq *BEE/HOL* LS11 ....130 F5
Dulverton Wy *PONT* WF8 ....181 H3
Dumfries Av *UPML* OL3 ....230 E4
Dumfries Dr *UPML* OL3 ....230 E4
Dunbar Cft *CUL/OBY* BD13 ....125 H5
Dunbar St *WKFDE* WF1 ....13 L7
Dunbottle CI *MIRF* WF14 ....194 D1
Dunbottle La *MIRF* WF14 ....172 D8
Dunbottle Wy *MIRF* WF14 ....172 E8
Duncan Av *OT* LS21 ....40 F8
WKFDW/WTN WF2 ....199 G4
Duncan St *LDS* LS1 ....9 G1
...............4 F9
Dunce Mire Rd
GFTH/SHER LS25 ....138 C7
Dunce Park CI *ELL* HX5 ....191 H4
Duncombe Rd *GIR* BD8 ....104 B7
Duncombe St *GIR* BD8 ....104 C7
LDS LS1 ....8 C1
Duncombe Wy *GTHN* BD7 ....104 C7
Dundas St *HFAX* HX1 ....10 E9
HUD HD1 ....14 E7
KGHY BD21 ....2 D7
Dundee Rd *TOD* OL14 ....140 F6
Dunderdale Crs *CAS* WF10 ....158 F5
Dunford Rd *HOLM/MEL* HD9 ....254 D5
Dungeon La *RTHW* LS26 ....155 J5
Dunhill Crs *OSM* LS9 ....111 G6
Dunhill Ri *OSM* LS9 ....111 G6
Dunkeswick La *AL/HA/HU* LS17 ....26 C7
Dunkirk Crs *HFAX* HX1 ....146 A8
Dunkirk Hill *HFAX* HX1 ....168 A1
Dunkirk Ri *AIRE* BD20 ....58 A4
WHIT OL12 * 206 A7
Dunkirk St *HFAX* HX1 ....146 A8
Dunkirk Ter *HFAX* HX1 ....146 A8
Dunlin CI *MOR* LS27 ....152 F3
Dunlin Ct *MID* LS10 ....153 M1
Dunlin Cft *MID* LS10 ....153 M1
Dunlin Dr *MID* LS10 ....153 M1
Dunlin Fold *MID* LS10 ....153 M1
Dunlin Wy *GIR* BD8 ....103 L7
Dunlop Av *ROCH* OL11 ....228 A3
Dunmere CI *BSLYN/ROY* S71 ....261 J1
Dunmore Av *CUL/OBY* BD13 ....124 E5
Dunnington Dr *WKFDW/WTN* WF2 ....199 G4
Dunningley La *EARD/LOFT* WF3 ....153 H4
Dunnington Dr *SEL* YO8 ....139 M5
Dunnington Wk *LM/WK* BD12 ....126 C8
Dunniwood Dr *CAS* WF10 ....179 J1
Dunnock Av *WBSY* BD6 ....125 K5
Dunnock Cft *MOR* LS27 ....152 E5
Dunrobin Av *GFTH/SHER* LS25 ....113 K7
Dunsford Av *BOW* BD4 ....127 K6
Dunsley Bank Rd
HOLM/MEL HD9 ....254 B4
Dunsley Ter *HEM/SK/SE* WF9 ....246 C4
Dunsmore Dr *HUDW* HD3 ....191 H4
Dunstable *WHIT* OL12 * 206 B6
Dunstan CI *OSS* WF5 ....197 G2
Dunstan Gv *CLECK* BD19 ....150 B2
Dunstarn Dr *BHP/TINH* LS16 ....86 F1
Dunstarn Gdns *BHP/TINH* LS16 ....87 G1
Dunstarn La *BHP/TINH* LS16 ....86 F1
Dunster Av *ROCH* OL11 ....228 A1
Dunwood Av *ROY/SHW* OL2 ....229 L6
Dunwood Park Cts
ROY/SHW OL2 ....229 L6
Dunwoods Park Cts
ROY/SHW OL2 ....229 L5
Durban Av *BEE/HOL* LS11 ....131 H4
Durban CI *ROY/SHW* OL2 ....229 L1
Durban Crs *BEE/HOL* LS11 ....131 H4
Durden Ms *ROY/SHW* OL2 ....229 K8
Durham Rd *GIR* BD8 ....104 C5
Durham St *CAS* WF10 ....180 A1
LUD/ILL HX2 ....146 A6
ROCH OL11 ....228 C1
Durham Ter *GIR* BD8 ....104 C5
Durkar Fids *HOR/CROF* WF4 ....198 A8
Durkar La *HOR/CROF* WF4 ....198 C7
Durkar Low La *HOR/CROF* WF4 ....198 C7
Durkar Ri *HOR/CROF* WF4 ....198 B8
Durkheim Ct *BFDE* BD3 * 105 L7
Durley Av *HTON* BD9 ....104 B3
Durling Dr *SHPY* BD18 ....83 G7
Durlston Gv *LM/WK* BD12 ....148 E2
Durlston Ter *LM/WK* BD12 ....148 F2
Durnlaw CI *LIT* OL15 ....207 L1
Durn St *LIT* OL15 ....185 L8
Durrance St *HWTH* BD22 ....2 A7
Durrant CI *WBY* LS22 ....29 J5
Dutton Gn *SCFT* LS14 ....89 J6
Dutton Wy *SCFT* LS14 ....89 J7
Duxbury Ri *CHAL* LS7 ....6 F4
Dyehouse Dr *CLECK* BD19 ....149 L4
Dye House La *MILN* OL16 ....206 D1
WIL/AL BD15 ....102 D1
Dyehouse La *BRIG* HD6 ....170 E5
PDSY/CALV LS28 ....129 G2
Dyehouse Rd *LM/WK* BD12 ....149 H1
Dyer La *HIPP* HX3 ....10 D1
Dyers Ct *HDGY* LS6 ....109 H2
LIT OL15 ....185 L8
Dyer St *LDSU* LS2 ....7 J9
Dyke CI *MIRF* WF14 ....172 C5
Dyke La *TOD* OL14 ....142 D6
Dymond Gv *LVSG* WF15 ....172 C3
Dymond Rd *LVSG* WF15 ....172 C3
Dymond Vw *LVSG* WF15 ....172 C3
Dyson La *HOLM/MEL* HD9 ....254 D5
RPDN/SBR HX6 ....188 D3
Dyson PI *HIPP* HX3 * 168 F3
Dyson Rd *HFAX* HX1 ....10 B4
Dyson's HI *HOLM/MEL* HD9 ....236 D1
Dyson St *BFD* BD1 ....5 H2
BRIG HD6 ....170 C3
BSLY S70 ....260 F7
HTON BD9 ....104 C2
HUDE HD5 ....193 G8
Dyson Wood Wy *HUDN* HD2 ....192 F1

Eafield Av *MILN* OL16 ....207 H7
Eafield CI *MILN* OL16 ....207 H7
Eafield Rd *MILN* OL16 ....206 G5
Eagle Gv *WKFDW/WTN* WF2 ....175 M8
Eaglesfield Dr *WBSY* BD6 ....126 B8
Eagle St *HWTH* BD22 ....79 G7
KGHY BD21 ....2 F1

TOD OL14 ....163 K1
Ealand Av *BTLY* WF17 ....151 H7
Ealand Cl *BTLY* WF17 ....151 H7
Ealand Rd *BTLY* WF17 ....151 J7
Ealees Rd *LIT* OL15 ....207 L1
Ealing Ct *BTLY* WF17 ....151 J8
Eaming Vw *BSLYN/ROY* S71 ....261 J3
Earl Crag Vw *HWTH* BD22 ....55 G2
Earles Av *HUDE* HD5 ....215 G5
Earle St *FEA/AMT* WF7 ....179 L8
MOR LS27 ....152 B1
Earls Ter *HIPP* HX3 ....146 C4
Earl St *EARL* WF12 ....174 D7
HEM/SK/SE WF9 ....223 J7
HWTH BD22 ....78 E8
KGHY BD21 ....2 F2
WBOW BD5 ....4 E9
WKFDE WF1 ....13 G1
Earls Wd *AIRE* BD20 ....55 L2
Earlswood *LM/WK* BD12 * 148 F3
Earlswood Av *RHAY* LS8 ....88 B4
Earlswood Cha
PDSY/CALV LS28 ....107 J7
Earlswood Crs
GFTH/SHER LS25 ....135 H4
Earlswood Md
PDSY/CALV LS28 ....129 G1
Earl Ter *HIPP* HX3 ....146 C4
Earnshaw Av *WHIT* OL12 ....206 A3
Earnshaw Ter *DOD/DAR* S75 ....260 F3
Easby Av *BTLY* WF17 ....173 H2
Easby Cl *ILK* LS29 ....38 B2
Easby Dr *ILK* LS29 ....38 B2
Easby Rd *WBOW* BD5 ....4 C9
Easdale Cl *SCFT* LS14 ....111 H1
Easdale Crs *SCFT* LS14 ....111 J1
Easdale Mt *SCFT* LS14 ....111 J1
Easdale Rd *SCFT* LS14 ....111 H1
Easingwood Dr *HUDE* HD5 ......193 K5
East Acres *KNOT* WF11 ....160 C4
East Av *AIRE* BD20 ....34 F8
HEM/SK/SE WF9 ....225 J7
HOR/CROF WF4 ....197 L5
HUDW HD3 ....191 L5
KGHY BD21 ....3 H7
PONT WF8 ....180 D7
East Bank *GFTH/SHER* LS25 ....116 B6
East Bath St *BTLY* WF17 ....173 M1
East Beck Ct *OT* LS21 ....40 D1
East Bolton *LUD/ILL* HX2 ....8 A1
Eastborough Crs *DEWS* WF13 ...173 M5
Eastbourne Av *FEA/AMT* WF7 ...180 A7
Eastbourne Cl *PONT* WF8 ....181 J6
Eastbourne Crs *PONT* WF8 ....181 J6
Eastbourne Dr *PONT* WF8 ....181 J6
Eastbourne Rd *HTON* BD9 ....104 D1
Eastbourne St *ROCH* OL11 ....228 B1
Eastbourne Ter *PONT* WF8 ......181 H6
Eastbourne Vw *PONT* WF8 ......181 H6
Eastbrook Ct
BSPA/BRAM LS23 * 69 M4
Eastburn Br *AIRE* BD20 ....35 H8
Eastbury Av *WBSY* BD6 ....125 M5
East Busk La *OT* LS21 ....41 L6
East Byland *LUD/ILL* HX2 ....124 A8
East Cswy *BHP/TINH* LS16 ....86 F1
East Causeway Cl
BHP/TINH LS16 ....86 F1
East Causeway Crs
BHP/TINH LS16 ....86 F2
East Causeway V
BHP/TINH LS16 ....87 G2
East Chevin Rd *OT* LS21 ....62 F1
Eastcliffe *HIPP* HX3 ....11 M8
East Cl *PONT* WF8 ....203 G1
STKB/PEN S36 ....271 J5
East Dale Cl *HEM/SK/SE* WF9 ..224 B7
Eastdean Bank *SCFT* LS14 ....89 K8
Eastdean Dr *SCFT* LS14 ....89 K8
Eastdean Gdns *SCFT* LS14 ....89 K8
Eastdean Ga *SCFT* LS14 ....89 K8
Eastdean Gv *SCFT* LS14 ....89 K8
Eastdean Ri *SCFT* LS14 ....89 K8
Eastdean Rd *SCFT* LS14 ....89 J8
East Dene *AIRE* BD20 ....36 A4
East Down *CAS* WF10 ....158 C6
East Dr *GFTH/SHER* LS25 ....135 K1
PONT WF8 ....181 H7
Easterly Av *RHAY* LS8 ....110 C3
Easterly Crs *RHAY* LS8 ....110 C2
Easterly Cross *RHAY* LS8 ....110 D2
Easterly Garth *RHAY* LS8 ....110 D2
Easterly Gv *RHAY* LS8 ....110 C2
Easterly Mt *RHAY* LS8 ....110 D2
Easterly Rd *RHAY* LS8 ....110 C2
Easterly Sq *RHAY* LS8 ....110 D2
Easterly Vw *RHAY* LS8 ....110 D2
Eastfield *KBTN* HD8 ....238 B6
Eastfield Av *KNOT* WF11 ....182 B3
STKB/PEN S36 ....270 F3
TAD LS24 ....72 B1
Eastfield Crs *DOD/DAR* S75 ....242 F6
RTHW LS26 ....133 K8
Eastfield Dr *KBTN* HD8 ....216 A7
PONT WF8 ....181 H6
RTHW LS26 ....133 J8
Eastfield Gdns *BOW* BD4 ....128 A3
Eastfield Gv *NORM* WF6 ....178 E3
Eastfield La *CAS* WF10 ....158 A6
Eastfield Pl *AIRE* BD20 ....55 M1
Eastfield Rd *KNOT* WF11 ....182 B3
MIRF WF14 ....172 F8
East Field St *OSM* LS9 ....9 M1
East Fold *KBTN* HD8 ....239 L5
Eastgate *BHP/TINH* LS16 ....63 M3
BSLY S70 ....261 G4
ELL HX5 ....169 H7
HEM/SK/SE WF9 ....224 A4
HOLM/MEL HD9 ....236 C2
OSM LS9 ....7 J9
Eastgate Cl *BHP/TINH* LS16 .....63 M3
East Gate St *MILN* OL16 ....206 B6
East Grange Cl *MID* LS10 * 132 A5
East Grange Dr *MID* LS10 ....132 A5
East Grange Garth *MID* LS10 ...132 A5
East Grange Rd *MID* LS10 ....132 A5
East Grange Sq *MID* LS10 ....132 A5
East Grange Vw *MID* LS10 ......132 A5
Easthorpe Ct *ECHL* BD2 ....105 M2
East King St *OSM* LS9 ....9 L2
Eastlands *HUDE* HD5 ....215 H3
Eastland Wk *BRAM* LS13 ....108 A5
East Lee La *TOD* OL14 ....142 B6
Eastleigh *WBSY* BD6 ....88 B4
East Leigh Ct *LVSG* WF15 ....172 N4
Eastleigh Dr *RHAY* LS8 ....88 B4
East Moor Cl *RHAY* LS8 ....88 B4
East Moor Dr *RHAY* LS8 ....88 C5
Eastmoor Gv *BSLY* S70 ....243 L4
East Moor La *BHP/TINH* LS16 ...86 F2
East Moor Rd *RHAY* LS8 ....88 B4
Eastmoor Rd *WKFDE* WF1 ......176 E6
East Mt *BRIC* HD6 ....170 C3

East Neville St *SKP/WHF* BD23 ..16 C3
Easton Pl *HUDW* HD3 ....191 K7
East Pde *AIRE* BD20 ....56 F1
BAIL BD17 ....82 C2
BFD BD1 ....5 J5
ILK LS29 ....38 E2
ILK LS29 ....61 J2
KGHY BD21 ....3 H5
LDS LS1 ....9 J5
RPDN/SBR HX6 ....167 M1
East Parade Wk *LDS* LS1 ....9 J5
East Park Dr *OSM* LS9 ....110 C7
East Park Gv *OSM* LS9 ....110 C7
East Park Mt *OSM* LS9 ....110 C8
East Park Pde *OSM* LS9 ....110 C8
East Park Pl *OSM* LS9 ....110 C8
East Park Rd *HIPP* HX3 ....10 C1
OSM LS9 ....110 B7
PBR HC3 ....28 F4
East Park St *MOR* LS27 ....152 B3
OSM LS9 ....110 C7
East Park Ter *OSM* LS9 ....110 C8
East Park Vw *OSM* LS9 ....110 C7
East Pinfold *BSLYN/ROY* S71 ...243 L3
East Ridge Vw
GFTH/SHER LS25 ....113 L6
East Rd *LM/WK* BD12 ....126 F8
STKB/PEN S36 ....271 J5
East Royd *HWTH* BD22 ....78 F4
East Side Ct *PDSY/CALV* LS28 ..129 K1
East Squire La *GIR* BD8 ....104 E4
East St *BRIC* HD6 ....170 C5
BTLY WF17 ....173 L1
CUD/GR S72 ....245 G1
HEM/SK/SE WF9 ....247 K2
HIPP HX3 ....148 C7
HUD LS29 ....255 G3
HOR/CROF WF4 ....197 L5
HUDW HD3 ....191 K5
LIT OL15 ....207 L1
MAR/SLWT HD7 ....213 C3
MILN OL16 ....206 C6
MILN OL16 ....206 F7
OSM LS9 ....9 L2
RPDN/SBR HX6 ....167 G4
WHIT OL12 ....184 E8
WKFDE WF1 ....176 E4
WMB/DAR S73 ....263 J8
YEA LS19 ....62 E8
East Vw *AIRE* BD20 ....36 A4
AWLS/ASK DN6 ....227 M5
CAS WF10 ....157 J7
CLECK BD19 ....149 J8
COL BB8 ....74 E4
CUD/GR S72 ....244 D7
GFTH/SHER LS25 ....116 A8
GFTH/SHER LS25 ....135 K5
HUD HD1 ....14 A4
KNOT WF11 ....182 C2
LUD/ILL HX2 * 145 G5
MIRF WF14 ....172 E8
MSTN/BAR LS15 * 111 L4
NORM WF6 ....178 A3
OSS WF5 ....197 G3
PDSY/CALV LS28 ....129 G1
RTHW LS26 ....155 L1
WBSY BD6 ....125 L4
YEA LS19 ....62 E8
East View Rd *YEA* LS19 ....62 E8
East View Ter *LM/WK* BD12 ....148 F2
Eastville Rd *HOR/CROF* WF4 ...200 D5
Eastway *MIRF* WF14 ....172 B7
ROY/SHW OL2 ....229 K8
Eastway Pk *MIRF* WF14 ....172 B7
Eastwick Vw *WIL/AL* BD15 * ...103 K5
Eastwood Av *LUD/ILL* HX2 ......124 A7
RPDN/SBR HX6 ....167 H3
WKFDW/WTN WF2 ....176 A7
Eastwood Cl *HOR/CROF* WF4 ..198 B7
LUD/ILL HX2 ....124 A7
Eastwood Dr *SCFT* LS14 ....111 M2
Eastwood Gdns *SCFT* LS14 ......111 L2
Eastwood Garth *SCFT* LS14 .....111 L2
Eastwood Gv *GFTH/SHER* LS25 ..135 J1
LUD/ILL HX2 ....124 A7
Eastwood La *SCFT* LS14 ....111 M2
TOD OL14 ....142 C5
Eastwood Nook *SCFT* LS14 .....111 M2
Eastwood Rd *TOD* OL14 ....141 J3
Eastwood St *BOW* BD4 ....127 H1
BRIC HD6 ....170 D3
HIPP HX3 ....146 C4
LIT OL15 ....207 K1
Easy Rd *OSM* LS9 ....110 B8
Eaton Ms *MID* LS10 ....153 L1
Eaton Pl *HEM/SK/SE* WF9 ......224 A7
Eaton Rd *ILK* LS29 ....38 C3
Eaton Sq *MID* LS10 ....153 L2
Eaton Wk *HEM/SK/SE* WF9 ....247 J1
Eaves Av *HBR* HX7 ....143 C2
Eaves Rd *HBR* HX7 ....143 C2
Eaves Ms *SKP/WHF* BD23 ....16 A3
Ebberston Gv *HDGY* LS6 ....6 A2
Ebberston Pl *HDGY* LS6 ....6 A2
Ebenezer Pl *BFD* BD1 ....5 G7
Ebenezer St *BFD* BD1 ....5 G7
PDSY/CALV LS28 ....106 F3
Ebor Cl *ROY/SHW* OL2 ....229 J6
Ebor Gdns *MIRF* WF14 ....194 A1
Ebor Mt *GFTH/SHER* LS25 ......135 J4
HDGY LS6 ....6 A4
Ebor Pl *HDGY* LS6 ....6 A4
Ebor St *HDGY* LS6 ....6 A4
LIT OL15 ....207 L1
Ebor Vw *AL/HA/HU* LS17 * 44 F8
AL/HA/HU LS17 ....46 E6
AL/HA/HU LS17 ....65 L2
ILK LS29 ....39 M8
OSM LS9 ....62 C1
Ebson House La
HOLM/MEL HD9 ....237 K8
Ebury Cl *BTLY* WF17 ....151 M8
Ebury St *BTLY* WF17 ....151 M8
Ecclesburn Av *OSM* LS9 ....110 C7
Ecclesburn Rd *OSM* LS9 ....110 C7
Ecclesburn St *OSM* LS9 ....110 C7
Ecclesburn Ter *OSM* LS9 ....110 C7
Eccles Cl *ECHL* BD2 ....105 K2
Eccles Parlour *RPDN/SBR* HX6 ..166 C7
Eccup La *BHP/TINH* LS16 ....65 H6
Eccup Moor Rd *BHP/TINH* LS16 ..65 J2
Echo St *LVSG* WF15 ....172 N4
Eclipse Cl *MILN* OL16 ....206 F7
Edale Av *HUDS* HD4 ....214 B5
Edale Cl *HUDE* HD5 ....193 N6
Edale Gv *WBSY* BD6 ....125 L6
Edale Ri *DOD/DAR* S75 ....260 A7
Edale Wy *BHP/TINH* LS16 ....64 B1
Eddercliff Crs *CLECK* BD19 ......150 C8
Edderthorpe La *RTHW* LS26 ....133 K8
Edderthorpe St *BFDE* BD3 ....5 K7
Eddison Cl *BHP/TINH* LS16 ....86 F1

Eddison St *PDSY/CALV* LS28 ...106 F4
Eddystone Ri *KNOT* WF11 ....181 M2
Edelshain Gv *WKFDW/WTN* WF2 ..199 H6
Eden Av *OSS* WF5 ....174 F8
WKFDW/WTN WF2 ....197 M1
Eden Crs *BULY* LS4 ....108 D2
Eden Ct *BULY* LS4 ....108 D2
Edendale *CAS* WF10 ....158 B6
Eden Dr *BULY* LS4 ....108 D2
Edenfield Cl *BSLYN/ROY* S71 ..243 M8
Eden Gdns *BULY* LS4 ....108 D3
Eden La *HUDN* HD2 ....192 C1
Eden Mt *BULY* LS4 ....108 D3
Eden Rd *BULY* LS4 ....108 D2
Edensor Rd *KGHY* BD21 ....2 E1
Eden Wk *BULY* LS4 ....108 D3
ROY/SHW OL2 ....229 J6
Ederoyd Av *PDSY/CALV* LS28 ..106 D5
Ederoyd Crs *PDSY/CALV* LS28 ..106 D5
Ederoyd Dr *PDSY/CALV* LS28 ..106 D5
Ederoyd Gv *PDSY/CALV* LS28 ..106 C5
Ederoyd Mt *PDSY/CALV* LS28 ..106 C5
Ederoyd Ri *PDSY/CALV* LS28 ...106 C5
Edgar St *CLAY* BD14 ....125 M2
MILN OL16 ....206 F4
Edgbaston Cl *AL/HA/HU* LS17 ..65 J8
Edgbaston Wk *AL/HA/HU* LS17 ..65 J8
Edge Av *OSS* WF5 ....195 M5
Edgebank Av *WBSY* BD6 ....126 B8
Edgecliffe Pl *BSLYN/ROY* S71 ..261 J1
Edge Cl *EARL* WF12 ....196 A5
MAR/SLWT HD7 ....213 C2
Edge End Gdns *WBSY* BD6 ......126 A7
Edge End La *HOLM/MEL* HD9 ..235 J3
Edge End Rd *WBSY* BD6 ....126 A7
Edgehill Cl *CUL/QBY* BD13 ......125 H5
Edge Hill Cl *HUDE* HD5 ....15 L4
Edgeholme La *LUD/ILL* HX2 ....145 K7
Edge Jct *EARL* WF12 ....195 M5
Edgelands Ri *CUD/GR* S72 ......262 D1
Edge La *EARL* WF12 ....196 A5
HBR HX7 ....143 E8
Edge Rd *EARL* WF12 ....196 A5
HBR HX7 ....143 E8
Edge Terr *HUDW* HD3 ....191 H1
Edgemoor Cl *BOW* BD4 ....128 A6
HIPP HX3 ....148 C8
Edgemoor Rd *HOLM/MEL* HD9 ..236 A5
HOR/CROF WF4 ....220 B3
Edge Rd *EARL* WF12 ....196 A6
Edgerton Cl *TAD* LS24 ....71 K3
Edgerton Ct *TAD* LS24 ....71 L3
Edgerton Dr *TAD* LS24 ....71 K3
Edgerton Garth *TAD* LS24 ....71 K3
Edgerton Gn *HUD* HD1 ....14 B4
Edgerton Grove Rd *HUD* HD1 ...14 B4
Edgerton La *HUD* HD1 ....14 A4
Edgerton Rd *BHP/TINH* LS16 ....87 H2
HUDW HD3 ....191 H1
Edge Ter *HUDW* HD3 ....191 H7
Edge Top Rd *EARL* WF12 ....195 L5
Edge Vw *EARL* WF12 ....196 A5
MAR/SLWT HD7 ....213 C2
Edgeware Rd *HUDE* HD5 ....193 J8
Edgware Av *RHAY* LS8 ....110 B4
Edgware Gv *RHAY* LS8 ....110 B4
Edgware Mt *RHAY* LS8 ....110 B4
Edgware Pl *RHAY* LS8 ....110 B4
Edgware Rw *RHAY* LS8 * 110 B4
Edgware St *RHAY* LS8 ....110 B4
Edgware Ter *RHAY* LS8 ....110 B4
Edgware Vw *RHAY* LS8 ....110 B4
Edinburgh Av *WOR/ARM* LS12 ..108 C6
Edinburgh Cl *BSLYN/ROY* S71 ..261 K2
Edinburgh Gv *WOR/ARM* LS12 ..108 C6
Edinburgh Pl *GFTH/SHER* LS25 ..113 K7
WOR/ARM LS12 ....108 C6
Edinburgh Rd *WOR/ARM* LS12 ..108 C6
Edinburgh Ter *WOR/ARM* LS12 ..108 C6
Edington Whit OL12 * 206 B6
Edlington Cl *BOW* BD4 ....128 A5
Edmonton Cl *DOD/DAR* S75 * ..260 D4
Edmonton Pl *CHAL* LS7 ....87 M4
Edmunds Fold *LIT* OL15 ....185 H8
Edmund St *GTHN* BD7 ....4 E8
ROY/SHW OL2 ....229 L7
TOD OL14 ....163 K6
Edrich Cl *LM/WK* BD12 ....127 G8
Edroyd Pl *PDSY/CALV* LS28 ....106 F3
Edroyd St *PDSY/CALV* LS28 ....106 F3
Education Rd *CHAL* LS7 ....7 H1
Edward Av *LIT* OL15 ....207 H3
Edward Cl *BSLY* S70 ....261 L7
Edward Dr *WKFDW/WTN* WF2 ..176 A1
Edward Pl *HEM/SK/SE* WF9 ....224 B7
Edward Rd *AWLS/ASK* DN6 .....249 K6
AWLS/ASK DN6 ....249 M8
MIRF WF14 ....194 B1
ROY/SHW OL2 ....229 J8
Edwards Rd *LUD/ILL* HX2 ....168 A1
Edward St *BOW* BD4 ....5 G8
BRIG HD6 ....170 D3
CLECK BD19 ....172 C1
DOD/DAR S75 ....242 E6
HBR HX7 ....143 K3
LDSU LS2 ....10 D3
MILN OL16 ....206 C6
NORM WF6 ....178 C1
RPDN/SBR HX6 ....167 K2
SHPY BD18 ....82 B6
WHIT OL12 ....206 F2
WKFDE WF1 * 176 F7
Edward Turner Cl
LM/WK BD12 ....126 E8
Edwin Av *OSL* LS20 ....61 M5
Edwin Rd *HDGY* LS6 ....6 A4
Edwins Cl *BSLYN/ROY* S71 .....243 J7
Eel Holme View St *AIRE* BD20 ..57 K4
Eel Mires Garth *WBY* LS22 ....30 B8
Effingham Rd *BGLY* BD16 ....80 C5
Egerton Gv *WIL/AL* BD15 ....103 H5
Egerton Pl *ROY/SHW* OL2 ......229 J6
Egerton St *LIT* OL15 ....207 L1
RPDN/SBR HX6 ....167 K2
Eggleston Dr *BOW* BD4 ....128 B4
Egglestone Sq
BSPA/BRAM LS23 ....48 E7
Eggleston St *BRAM* LS13 ....107 H1
Egmanton Rd *BSLYN/ROY* S71 ..243 M5
Egremont Crs *WBSY* BD6 ....126 B8
Egremont St *MILN* OL16 ....229 G2
Egremont Ter *RPDN/SBR* HX6 ..167 J1
Egypt Rd *CUL/QBY* BD13 ....102 E6
Eider Cl *WBSY* BD6 ....126 B8
Eiffel Buildings *HBR* HX7 ....143 J5
Eighth Av *LVSG* WF15 ....172 N4
WOR/ARM LS12 ....108 F8
Eightlands Av *BRAM* LS13 ......107 M4
Eightlands La *BRAM* LS13 ....107 M4
Eightlands Rd *DEWS* WF13 .....173 L6
Ekota Pl *RHAY* LS8 ....110 B2
Elam Wood Rd *AIRE* BD20 ....57 L3
Elbow La *ROCH* OL11 ....206 C8
ECHL BD2 ....105 K4

LUD/ILL HX2 ....145 G6
Elder Av *HEM/SK/SE* WF9 ......225 L6
Elderberry Cl *AIRE* BD20 ....12 A1
Elder Cl *BTLY* WF17 ....151 H4
Elder Cft *BRAM* LS13 ....107 L5
Elder Garth *GFTH/SHER* LS25 ..113 K8
HEM/SK/SE WF9 ....225 K6
Elder Gn *WKFDW/WTN* WF2 ....12 A1
Elder Gv *HUDN* HD4 ....213 M8
WKFDW/WTN WF2 ....12 A1
Elder Grove Ms *HUDS* HD4 * ...213 M8
Elder La *HUDN* HD2 ....193 L1
Elder Lea *OSS* WF5 * 197 J1
Elder Mt *BRAM* LS13 * 107 L5
Elder Pl *BRAM* LS13 ....107 L5
Elder Ri *RTHW* LS26 ....133 M8
Elder Rd *BRAM* LS13 ....107 L5
HUDN HD2 ....193 H1
Elder St *AIRE* BD20 ....57 H1
BRAM LS13 ....107 L5
IDLE BD10 ....84 A7
MILN OL16 ....228 D1
Elderwood Gdns *IDLE* BD10 ...106 A1
Eldon Ar *BSLY* S70 * 261 H4
Eldon Dr *BFD* BD1 ....4 D4
CLECK BD19 ....150 A7
Eldon Rd *HUD* HD1 ....191 M7
HECK WF16 ....172 E2
HIPP HX3 ....11 H3
OSS WF5 ....175 H7
TOD OL14 ....163 L1
Eldon St North *BSLYN/ROY* S71 ..261 H4
Eldroth Mt *HFAX* HX1 ....168 C1
Eldroth Rd *HFAX* HX1 ....168 C1
Eldwick Cft *BGLY* BD16 ....81 L1
Eleanor Dr *PDSY/CALV* LS28 ....84 B7
Eleanor St *BRIC* HD6 ....170 C5
HUD HD1 ....14 F2
Eleventh Av *LVSG* WF15 ....171 L1
Elford Gv *RHAY* LS8 ....110 B3
Elford Pl East *RHAY* LS8 ....110 B3
Elford Pl West *RHAY* LS8 ....110 B3
Elford Rd *RHAY* LS8 * 110 B3
Elgin Cl *HUDS* HD4 ....213 L4
Elia St *RHAY* LS8 * 110 B3
Eliot Cr *BSLY* LS20 ....62 B6
Eliots Cl *OSM* LS9 ....180 E1
Eli St *WBOW* BD5 ....127 K5
Elizabeth Ct *PONT* WF8 ....181 G4
Elizabethan Wy *MILN* OL16 ....207 G8
Elizabeth Av *CUD/GR* S72 ......245 G1
LM/WK BD12 ....148 F2
Elizabeth Cl *LM/WK* BD12 ......148 F2
Elizabeth Crs *LM/WK* BD12 ....148 F2
Elizabeth Dr *RPDN/SBR* HX6 ..167 K1
KNOT WF11 ....181 L2
LM/WK BD12 ....148 F2
Elizabeth Frances St *ELL* HX5 ..169 H8
Elizabeth Gdns *WKFDE* WF1 ...176 E6
Elizabeth Gv *MOR* LS27 ....152 E1
ROY/SHW OL2 ....229 K8
Elizabeth Pl *SCFT* LS14 ....111 J1
Elizabeth St *BGLY* BD16 * 81 J3
CUD/GR S72 ....245 J8
ELL HX5 ....169 H8
GTL/HWG HX4 ....168 F7
HDCY LS6 ....6 A2
HUDS HD4 ....214 C3
KGHY BD21 ....58 B7
LM/WK BD12 ....148 E2
LVSG WF15 ....172 A2
WBOW BD5 ....4 E9
WKFDE WF1 ....199 G5
Elland Br *ELL* HX5 ....169 H7
Elland Cl *BSLYN/ROY* S71 ....243 G7
Elland La *ELL* HX5 ....169 K7
Elland Riorges Link *ELL* HX5 ...169 J7
Elland Rd *BEE/HOL* LS11 ....131 G3
BEE/HOL LS11 ....130 F4
BRIG HD6 ....170 C4
ELL HX5 ....169 L5
MOR LS27 ....130 C2
RPDN/SBR HX6 ....189 G2
Elland St *CAS* WF10 ....158 A6
Elland Wy *BEE/HOL* LS11 ....130 F4
Elland Wood Bottom *ELL* HX5 ..168 A4
Ellar Carr Rd *CUL/QBY* BD13 ....79 L7
IDLE BD10 ....83 L4
Ellarfield La *GFTH/SHER* LS25 ..116 A5
Ellar Gdns *ILK* LS29 ....61 K1
Ella St *HEM/SK/SE* WF9 ....223 J7
Ellenroad Ap *MILN* OL16 ....229 J2
Ellen Royd La *LUD/ILL* HX2 ....144 E6
Ellen Royd St *HIPP* HX3 ....11 H3
Ellen St *BGLY* BD16 ....81 J3
Ellenthorpe Rd *BAIL* BD17 ....82 A4
Ellerby La *OSM* LS9 ....9 L3
Ellerby Rd *OSM* LS9 ....9 L2
Ellercroft Av *GTHN* BD7 ....104 C8
Ellercroft Rd *GTHN* BD7 ....104 C8
Ellercroft Ter *GTHN* BD7 ....104 C8
Ellerker La *SCFT* LS14 ....90 D1
Ellerker Rd *SCFT* LS14 ....68 C5
Eller Ms *SKP/WHF* BD23 ....16 A3
Ellers Gv *RHAY* LS8 ....110 B3
Ellerslie Ct *HUDW* HD3 ....214 D1
Ellers Rd *AIRE* BD20 ....55 M2
RHAY LS8 ....110 B2
Ellerton St *BFDE* BD3 ....105 L7
Ellesmere Av *COL* BB8 ....74 B1
Ellesmere St *ROCH* OL11 ....206 E7
Ellington St *BSLY* S70 ....260 F7
Ellin's Ter *NORM* WF6 ....178 B5
Ellinthorpe St *BOW* BD4 ....127 K1
Elliot St *SKP/WHF* BD23 ....16 B2
Elliott St *AIRE* BD20 ....35 M5
SHPY BD18 ....82 C6
WHIT OL12 ....206 A1
Elliston Av *DOD/DAR* S75 ....242 F6
Ellistones Gdns *GTL/HWG* HX4 ..168 E7
Ellistones La *GTL/HWG* HX4 ....168 E7
Ellis Yd *DEWS* WF13 * 173 L4
Ellmont Av *KBTN* HD8 ....217 L8
Elm Av *KBTN* HD8 ....239 J4
Elton Gv *WBSY* BD6 ....126 C5
Ellwood Cl *CHAL* LS7 ....87 H7
Elm Av *EARD/LOFT* WF3 ....177 H2
GFTH/SHER LS25 ....135 H4
HOLM/MEL HD9 ....236 C2
RPDN/SBR HX6 ....167 K1
TOD OL14 ....141 K7
Elmbridge Cl *BSLYN/ROY* S71 ..244 A3
Elm Ct *OSS* WF5 ....197 G3
PONT WF8 ....181 G4
PONT WF8 ....203 L1

Elm Crs *AIRE* BD20 ....58 F6
HEM/SK/SE WF9 ....223 K4
Elmet Dr *MSTN/BAR* LS15 ....91 G7
Elmete Av *GFTH/SHER* LS25 ...116 A7
MSTN/BAR LS15 ....90 B8
Elmete Cl *RHAY* LS8 ....88 B8
Elmete Ct *RHAY* LS8 ....88 B8
Elmete Cft *MSTN/BAR* LS15 .....90 B8
Elmete Dr *RHAY* LS8 ....88 E7
Elmete Gra *RHAY* LS8 ....88 B8
Elmete Hl *RHAY* LS8 ....88 E7
Elmete La *AL/HA/HU* LS17 ....89 G4
RHAY LS8 ....88 F6
Elmete Mt *RHAY* LS8 ....88 E7
Elmete Rd *CAS* WF10 ....158 F5
Elmete Wk *RHAY* LS8 ....88 E7
Elmete Wy *RHAY* LS8 ....89 G8
Elmet Rd *MSTN/BAR* LS15 ....91 G8
Elmfield *BAIL* BD17 ....82 F2
Elmfield Av *HUDW* HD3 ....213 H1
Elmfield Ct *BIRK/DRI* BD11 ....150 C2
MOR LS27 ....152 C3
Elmfield Dr *KBTN* HD8 ....233 J5
WBSY BD6 ....126 E6
Elmfield Gv *WOR/ARM* LS12 * ..108 F8
Elmfield Pl *WOR/ARM* LS12 ....108 F8
Elmfield Rd *AIRE* BD20 ....57 K1
HUDN HD2 ....192 A5
MOR LS27 ....152 D4
Elmfield Ter *HFAX* HX1 ....168 D1
HUDE HD5 ....15 L8
Elmfield Wy *BRAM* LS13 ....107 M5
Elm Gdns *CAS* WF10 ....158 F5
HFAX HX1 ....168 E1
AIRE BD20 ....35 M5
CLECK BD19 ....150 C6
HECK WF16 ....172 E1
HEM/SK/SE WF9 ....247 H3
HIPP HX3 ....125 M8
HOR/CROF WF4 ....197 K5
HWTH BD22 ....79 J7
ILK LS29 ....40 B6
MILN OL16 ....3 J3
ROCH OL11 ....228 A1
SHPY BD18 ....87 F5
WHIT OL12 ....206 E1
Elmhurst Cl *AL/HA/HU* LS17 ....88 C2
Elmhurst Gdns *AL/HA/HU* LS17 ..88 C2
Elmhurst Gv *KNOT* WF11 ....182 A3
Elmore Wd *LIT* OL15 ....185 G8
Elm Pk *PONT* WF8 ....180 E8
Elm Pl *BSLYN/ROY* S71 ....261 M1
KNOT WF11 ....182 A3
RPDN/SBR HX6 ....167 K1
Elm Rd *AIRE* BD20 ....55 L1
AWLS/ASK DN6 ....249 K8
DEWS WF13 ....173 H6
HEM/SK/SE WF9 ....224 A7
NORM WF6 ....178 C7
SHPY BD18 ....82 F7
Elm Rw *BSLYN/ROY* S71 ....261 L5
Elmroyd *RTHW* LS26 ....155 H2
Elmsall Dr *HEM/SK/SE* WF9 ....247 L1
Elmsall La *AWLS/ASK* DN6 .....247 L1
Elmsall St *GIR* BD8 ....4 D3
Elmsall Wy *HEM/SK/SE* WF9 ...247 L1
Elmsdale Cl *HEM/SK/SE* WF9 ..247 K4
Elms Hl *MAR/SLWT* HD7 ....212 B6
Elmsley St *AIRE* BD20 ....56 E1
The Elms *FEA/AMT* WF7 ....224 B1
CSLY LS20 ....62 A5
LIT OL15 ....207 G2
Elm St *COL* BB8 ....4 A1
GTL/HWG HX4 ....190 C2
HDGY LS6 ....5 M4
HOR/CROF WF4 ....200 D7
HUDS HD4 ....214 D2
HWTH BD22 ....79 J3
KBTN HD8 ....239 J4
WHIT OL12 ....8 B1
Elm Ter *PONT* WF8 ....180 E8
Elmton Cl *MID* LS10 ....132 A7
Elm Tree Av *WBSY* BD6 ....126 E6
Elm Tree Cl *KGHY* BD21 ....3 K8
LVSG WF15 ....172 K4
MSTN/BAR LS15 ....91 H5
WBSY BD6 ....126 F6
Elm Tree Gdns *WBSY* BD6 ......126 E6
Elmtree La *MID* LS10 ....9 K7
Elm Tree St *WKFDE* WF1 ....19 K3
Elm Vw *AIRE* BD20 ....35 K8
HIPP HX3 ....168 E2
The Elm Wk *MSTN/BAR* LS15 ..133 K1
Elm Wy *BTLY* WF17 ....151 J4
Elmwood Av *AWLS/ASK* DN6 ..249 H8
HUD HD1 ....14 E5
MSTN/BAR LS15 ....91 F7
WKFDW/WTN WF2 ....199 K7
Elmwood Cha *MSTN/BAR* LS15 ..90 F7
Elmwood Cl *HUD* HD1 ....14 E5
MIRF WF14 ....194 B5
WKFDW/WTN WF2 ....199 K7
Elmwood Dr *BRIC* HD6 ....170 B3
HWTH BD22 ....79 H1
WKFDW/WTN WF2 ....199 K7
Elmwood Garth
WKFDW/WTN WF2 ....199 K7
Elmwood La *LDSU* LS2 ....7 H6
MSTN/BAR LS15 ....90 F7
Elmwood Pl *BFDE* BD3 ....105 L5
Elmwood Rd *HWTH* BD22 ....79 H1
LDSU LS2 ....7 G6
Elm Wood St *BRIC* HD6 ....170 D2
Elmwood St *HFAX* HX1 ....146 B8
Elmwood Ter *HWTH* BD22 ....79 H2
Flghaborough Cl *HBR* HX7 ......144 A6
Elsdon Gv *WBOW* BD5 ....127 G5
Elsham Ter *BULY* LS4 ....108 C1
Elsie St *AIRE* BD20 ....55 L1
HWTH BD22 ....79 H6
Elsinore Av *ELL* HX5 ....169 G8
Elsinore Ct *ELL* HX5 * 169 G8
Elstead Cl *DOD/DAR* S75 ....260 A1
Elsworth St *WOR/ARM* LS12 ..108 F7
Eltham Cl *HDGY* LS6 ....6 E2
Eltham Dr *HDGY* LS6 ....6 E2
Eltham Gdns *HDGY* LS6 ....6 E2
Eltham Gv *WBSY* BD6 ....126 C6
Eltham Ri *HDGY* LS6 ....6 E2
Elvaston Rd *MOR* LS27 ....152 C4
Elvey Cl *ECHL* BD2 ....105 M2
Elvey St *WKFDE* WF1 ....176 E7
Elwell Cl *BRIG* HD6 ....157 M7
Elwell St *EARD/LOFT* WF3 ......154 A5
Elwyn Gv *WBOW* BD5 ....127 G3
Elwyn Rd *WBOW* BD5 ....127 H3
Ely St *GTL/HWG* HX4 ....168 F7
The Embankment *MIRF* WF14 ..124 F6
Emblem Ct *CUL/QBY* BD13 .....124 F6
Emblem Ter *WKFDE* WF1 ....13 G9
Embleton Rd *RTHW* LS26 ....156 E5
Emerald St *BTLY* WF17 ....151 J8

HUD HD1.....15 G3
HWTH BD22.....79 J2
Emerson Av HTON BD9.....103 M3
Emily Cl BSLYN/ROY S71.....261 K6
Emily Hall WIL/AL BD15.....102 F1
Emily St KGHY BD21.....3 H3
Emley Vw GFTH/SHER LS25.....135 K3
Emma St WHIT OL12.....206 A4
Emmanuel Ter HUDS HD4.....214 B4
Emmeline Cl IDLE BD10 *.....83 K6
Emmet Cl BIRK/DRI BD11.....150 D1
Emmfield Dr HTON BD9.....104 C3
Emm La HTON BD9.....104 C3
Emmott Ct COL BB8.....53 G8
Emmott Dr YEA LS19.....84 F5
Emmott Farm Fold HWTH BD22.....78 E8
Emmott Ct COL BB8.....52 F7
Empress St COL BB8.....74 A1
Emscote Av HFAX HX1.....10 D3
Emscote Gdns HFAX HX1.....10 D3
Emscote Gv HFAX HX1.....10 D3
Emscote Pl HFAX HX1.....10 D3
Emscote St South HFAX HX1.....10 D3
Emsley Av OSS S72.....262 E2
Emsley Cl BOW BD4.....127 K6
Emsley Pl MID LS10.....9 L6
Emville Av AL/HA/HU LS17.....88 F1
Enderby Cl HIPP HX3.....146 B3
Enderley Rd CUL/QBY BD13.....102 F3
Endor Gv ILK LS29.....40 B7
Endor Crs ILK LS29.....40 B7
Endsleigh Pl CLAY BD14 *.....125 J2
Enfield YEA LS19.....62 D8
Enfield Av CHAL LS7.....7 L4
Enfield Cl BTLY WF17.....151 L8
Enfield Dr BTLY WF17.....151 K8
Enfield Pde WBSY BD6.....126 C5
Enfield Rd BAIL BD17.....82 E4
Enfield Side Rd HWTH BD22.....99 M1
Enfield St CHAL LS7.....7 L4
  KGHY BD21.....2 E4
Enfield Ter CHAL LS7.....7 L4
Enfield Wk WBSY BD6.....126 C5
Engine La CUD/GR S72.....244 F6
  HOR/CROF WF4.....197 J6
  HOR/CROF WF4.....201 J7
Engine Lane Cl CUD/GR S72.....244 F5
England La KNOT WF11.....182 C2
Englefield Cl BOW BD4.....128 A4
Englefield Crs BOW BD4.....128 A4
Ennerdale Av EARL WF12.....174
  ROY/SHW OL2.....228 C7
Ennerdale Cl WBY LS22.....29 L8
Ennerdale Crs EARL WF12.....174 A4
Ennerdale Dr ECHL BD2.....105 K3
  ELL HX5.....169 K7
Ennerdale Rd BSLYN/ROY S71.....262 D6
  EARL WF12.....174 A4
  ECHL BD2.....105 J3
  WKFDW/WTN WF2 *.....176 B8
  WOR/ARM LS12.....129 M4
Ennerdale Wy WOR/ARM LS12 *.....129 M4
Enoch La HUDS HD4.....214 B3
Enterprise Wy AIRE BD20.....16 C7
  CAS WF10.....157 L7
  GFTH/SHER LS25.....116 E7
  IDLE BD10.....83 K8
  MID LS10.....132 B5
Entwistle St MILN OL16.....207 H8
Entwistle Rd MILN OL16.....206 D7
Envoy St BEE/HOL LS11.....9 G8
Epsom Rd GFTH/SHER LS25.....135 H4
Epsom Wy HUDE HD5.....193 L5
Epworth Pl HWTH BD22.....78 D3
  MID LS10.....9 L7
Equitable St MILN OL16.....229 H1
Eric St BRAM LS13.....107 L1
  HEM/SK/SE WF9.....247 J3
  KGHY BD21.....3 H2
  LIT OL15.....185 J8
Ermysted St SKP/WHF BD23.....16 C2
Ernest St DEWS WF13.....173 M5
  TOD OL14.....163 L1
Ernest Ter WHIT OL12.....206 D5
Erringden Rd HBR HX7.....143 H5
Erringden St TOD OL14.....163 L1
Escroft Cl WK/WK BD12.....148 F5
Eshald La RTHW LS26.....155 M1
Eshald Pl RTHW LS26.....133 M8
Esholt Av BAIL BD17.....83 K1
Eshton Av LM/WK BD12.....149 H1
Eshton Ct DOD/DAR S75.....242 C4
Eshton Vw BSLY S70.....260 F5
Eskdale Av HIPP HX3.....147 K1
  NORM WF6.....178 C2
  ROY/SHW OL2.....228 F7
Eskdale Cl EARL WF12.....174 A4
  NORM WF6.....178 C2
Eskdale Ct NORM WF6.....178 C2
Eskdale Gv GFTH/SHER LS25.....113 J8
Eskdale Mt HBR HX7.....143 J2
  SCFT LS14.....111 H2
Eskdale Ri WIL/AL BD15.....103 K6
Eskdale Rd BSLYN/ROY S71.....262 C6
  WKFDW/WTN WF2.....176 A7
Esk Gdns WBY LS22.....30 A6
Eskine Pde WBSY BD6.....126 B5
  WOR/ARM LS12.....108 C7
Esmond Ter WOR/ARM LS12.....108 C7
The Esplanade MILN OL16.....206 A7
Essex Cl ROY/SHW OL2.....229 H7
Essex Rd BSLY S70.....261 H7
Essex St BFDE BD3.....5 K8
  COL BB8.....74 A2
  HFAX HX1.....10 A7
  ROCH OL11.....206 B8
Estcourt Av HDGY LS6.....108 C1
Estcourt Dr PONT WF8.....203 M2
Estcourt Gv GTHN BD7.....126 C1
Estcourt Rd GTHN BD7.....126 C1
  PONT WF8.....203 M2
Estcourt Ter HDGY LS6.....108 C1
Esther Av WKFDW/WTN WF2.....198 A3
Esther Gv WKFDW/WTN WF2.....198 A3
Esthwaite Gdns
  MSTN/BAR LS15 *.....111 J2
Ethel Ct MILN OL16 *.....206 D8
Ethel St AIRE BD20.....57 K5
Etna St GTHN BD7.....126 B3
Eton Av HUDE HD5.....193 L6
Eton St HBR HX7.....143 H3
  HFAX HX1.....10 B6
Euden Edge Rd
  MAR/SLWT HD7.....212 A2
Eunice La KBTN HD8.....238 E8
Euston Gv BEE/HOL LS11.....8 A8
Euston Mt BEE/HOL LS11.....8 A8
Euston Ter BEE/HOL LS11.....8 A8
Evanston Av BULY LS4.....108 C5
Eva St WHIT OL12.....206 C4
Eveline St CUD/GR S72.....244 G4
Evelyn Av BFDE BD3.....106 A6
Evelyn Pl WOR/ARM LS12.....108 C8
Evelyn Ter BSLY S70 *.....261 J6
Evens Ter WBOW BD5.....127 G4

Everard St HUDS HD4.....213 M2
Everdale Mt HEM/SK/SE WF9.....223 K8
  HEM/SK/SE WF9.....247 G3
Everest Av SHPY BD18.....83 G7
Everest St ROCH OL11.....228 C4
Evereigh St OSM LS9.....110 C6
Eversham Gv IDLE BD10.....83 K7
Eversley Dr BOW BD4.....127 J7
Eversley Garth Crs
  GFTH/SHER LS25.....116 A7
Eversley Ldg GFTH/SHER LS25.....116 A8
  LUD/ILL HX2 *.....146 A8
Eversley Mt GFTH/SHER LS25.....116 A8
  LUD/ILL HX2 *.....146 A8
Eversley Pl LUD/ILL HX2.....146 A8
Eversley Rd HBR HX7.....143 J2
Every St TOD OL14.....163 L1
Evesham Gv IDLE BD10.....83 K7
Ewart Pl GTHN BD7.....126 C3
Ewart St BOW BD13 *.....125 C3
  GTHN BD7.....126 C3
Ewden Wy DOD/DAR S75.....260 C5
Ewood Dr HBR HX7.....144 B5
Ewood Hall Av HBR HX7.....144 B5
Ewood La TOD OL14.....161 J5
Exbury WHIT OL12.....206 A6
Excalibur Dr HEM/SK/SE WF9.....247 J4
Excelsior Cl RPDN/SBR HX6.....188 E3
Excelsior Ter MILN OL16.....207 H3
Exchange HOLM/MEL HD9.....236 B2
Exchange Sq BFD BD1 *.....5 G2
Exchange St CLECK BD19.....149 M5
  GTL/HWG HX4.....168 F8
  HEM/SK/SE WF9.....247 H3
  NORM WF6.....178 C4
Exe St WBOW BD5.....126 E5
Exeter Dr MID LS10.....131 M7
Exeter St ROCH OL11.....228 B1
Exeter St HIPP HX3.....168 F3
  ROCH OL11.....228 B1
  RPDN/SBR HX6.....167 L2
Exhibition Rd SHPY BD18.....82 B6
Exley Av KGHY BD21.....2 C9
Exley Bank HIPP HX3.....168 F4
Exley Bank Top HIPP HX3.....168 F4
Exley Crs KGHY BD21.....2 C9
Exley Dr KGHY BD21.....2 D9
Exley Gdns HIPP HX3.....168 F5
Exley Gv KGHY BD21.....2 C9
Exley Head HWTH BD22.....2 B9
Exley Head Vw HWTH BD22.....57 G6
Exley La ELL HX5.....169 G5
Exley Mt GTHN BD7.....104 B8
  KGHY BD21.....2 C9
Exley Rd KGHY BD21.....2 D7
Exley St KGHY BD21.....2 D9
Exley Wy KGHY BD21 *.....79 J2
Exmoor St HFAX HX1.....10 A8
Exmouth Pl BFDE BD3.....5 L3
Exmouth Sq ROCH OL11 *.....228 C3
Exmouth St ROCH OL11.....228 C3
Express Wy NORM WF6.....156 D8
Exton Pl MSTN/BAR LS15.....111 J2
Eyam Cl DOD/DAR S75.....260 A7
Eyres Av WOR/ARM LS12.....108 E6
Eyres Gv WOR/ARM LS12.....108 E6
Eyres Mill Side WOR/ARM LS12.....108 D6
Eyres St WOR/ARM LS12.....108 E6
Eyres Ter WOR/ARM LS12.....108 E6
Eyre St BTLY WF17.....173 M2
  HUDE HD5.....195 K2
Eyrie Ap MOR LS27.....152 E3

F

Factory La BOW BD4.....127 K4
  HUDW HD3.....213 K2
Factory St BOW BD4.....127 L4
Fagley Crs ECHL BD2.....105 L4
Fagley Cft ECHL BD2.....105 M4
Fagley Dr ECHL BD2.....105 L4
Fagley La ECHL BD2.....105 M3
Fagley Pl ECHL BD2.....105 L4
Fagley Rd ECHL BD2.....105 L4
Fagley Ter ECHL BD2.....105 L4
Fair Bank SHPY BD18.....82 E8
Fairbank Rd GIR BD8.....104 C5
Fairbanks RPDN/SBR HX6.....167 L2
Fairbank Ter GIR BD8.....104 C5
Fairbrook Rd HOR/CROF WF4.....220 C2
Fairburn Ct HIPP HX3 *.....169 J2
Fairburn Dr GFTH/SHER LS25.....135 J1
Fairburn Gdns ECHL BD2.....106 A2
Fairclough Gv LUD/ILL HX2.....146 B3
Fairfax Av BIRK/DRI BD11.....151 J1
  BOW BD4.....127 L5
  FEA/AMT WF7.....179 L5
  KNOT WF11.....181 M3
Fairfax Cl COP/BISH YO23 *.....73 J7
  SCFT LS14.....111 K3
Fairfax Crs BOW BD4.....127 L5
  HIPP HX3.....169 J1
Fairfax Dr LIT OL15.....207 H3
Fairfax Gdns ILK LS29.....61 H1
Fairfax Gv YEA LS19.....62 B7
Fairfax Rd BEE/HOL LS11.....8 C9
  BGLY BD16.....81 J3
  CUL/QBY BD13.....79 M7
  ILK LS29.....61 H1
  PONT WF8.....181 G6
Fairfax St AIRE BD20.....5 M5
  BOW BD4.....127 L5
  HWTH BD22.....78 F9
  OT LS21.....41 J7
  SKP/WHF BD23.....16 C3
Fairfax Vw BOW BD4 *.....128 B7
  HORS LS18.....85 K2
Fairfield CUL/QBY BD13.....101 M6
  KNOT WF11.....159 L6
Fairfield Av BRAM LS13.....107 J4
  HECK WF16.....173 H1
  NORM WF6.....178 A3
  OSS WF5.....197 H2
  PDSY/CALV LS28.....107 H6
  PONT WF8.....180 C6
Fairfield Cl CAS WF10.....158 C7
  GFTH/SHER LS25.....116 B7
  OSS WF5.....197 H2
  RTHW LS26.....154 D2
Fairfield Crs BRAM LS13.....107 J4
  DEWS WF13.....173 J5
Fairfield Dr BAIL BD17.....83 G2
  HECK WF16.....173 H1
  OSS WF5.....197 H2
Fairfield Gdns OSS WF5.....197 H2
  RTHW LS26.....154 D2
Fairfield Gv BRAM LS13.....107 K4
  RTHW LS26 *.....154 D2

Fairfield Hl BRAM LS13.....107 K4
Fairfield La BRAM LS13.....160 D2
  RTHW LS26.....154 D2
Fairfield Link GFTH/SHER LS25.....116 B7
Fairfield Ms DEWS WF13.....173 J5
Fairfield Mt BRAM LS13.....107 K4
  OSS WF5.....197 H2
Fairfield Ri KBTN HD8.....238 C1
Fairfield Rd BRAM LS13.....107 J4
  GIR BD8.....104 D5
  HECK WF16.....173 G1
  LM/WK BD12.....148 F3
  OSS WF5.....197 G2
Fairfields CAS WF10.....159 G7
  KBTN HD8.....257 H2
Fairfield Sq BRAM LS13.....107 K3
Fairfields Rd HOLM/MEL HD9.....253 M5
Fairfield Ter BRAM LS13.....107 K4
  EARL WF12.....174 B6
  OSS WF5.....197 H2
Fairfield Wy TAD LS24.....71 L3
Fairford Av BEE/HOL LS11.....9 G9
Fairford Mt HDGY LS6.....87 G5
Fairford Ter BEE/HOL LS11.....9 G9
Fairhaven Gn IDLE BD10.....83 L7
Fair Isle Ct KGHY BD21.....3 G4
Fairlands Rd HUDS HD4.....214 D4
Fairlands Ri MILN OL16.....228 D4
Fair Lea Rd HUDS HD4.....214 A5
Fairleigh Crs EARD/LOFT WF3.....153 J6
Fairleigh Rd EARD/LOFT WF3.....153 H6
Fairless Av HIPP HX3.....148 C7
Fairmoor Wy HECK WF16.....173 C1
Fairmount Pk SHPY BD18.....82 A7
Fairmount Ter KGHY BD21.....58 B8
Fair Rd WBSY BD6.....126 D5
Fair Vw LVSG WF15.....172 B1
  PONT WF8.....203 L5
Fairview Av BTLY WF17.....151 H8
Fairview Ct BAIL BD17.....82 D5
Fairview Crs BTLY WF17.....151 J8
Fairview Rd BTLY WF17.....151 J8
Fair Vw Rd HWYS HX3.....10 D1
Fairway DOD/DAR S75.....260 C8
  GSLY LS20.....61 L5
  GTHN BD7.....126 B5
  IDLE BD10.....84 B5
  NORM WF6.....178 E5
  SHPY BD18.....82 B7
Fairway Av NORM WF6.....178 E5
  GTHN BD7.....126 B5
Fairway Cl GFTH/SHER LS25.....116 B7
  GSLY LS20.....61 L6
  GTHN BD7.....126 B5
  NORM WF6.....178 E5
Fairway Crs HWTH BD22.....78 F8
  ROY/SHW OL2.....228 F8
Fairway Dr GTHN BD7.....126 B4
  NORM WF6.....178 E5
Fairway Gdns NORM WF6.....178 E5
Fairway Gv GTHN BD7.....126 B4
Fairway Mdw NORM WF6.....178 E5
The Fairways MIRF WF14.....194 B4
  AIRE BD20.....57 J3
  HTON BD9.....104 A1
  TAD LS24.....71 L5
The Fairway AL/HA/HU LS17.....65 L8
  FEA/AMT WF7.....179 M5
  GFTH/SHER LS25.....116 B7
  HUDN HD2.....192 C2
  LUD/ILL HX2.....124 B7
  PDSY/CALV LS28.....106 C5
Fairway Wk GTHN BD7.....126 B4
Fairweather Ms GIR BD8 *.....104 A3
Fairy Dell BGLY BD16.....81 J7
Fairy Hill La CAS WF10.....180 F1
Faith St BSLYN/ROY S71.....244 B8
  HEM/SK/SE WF9.....246 F2
Falcon Cliffe AIRE BD20.....56 E1
Falcon Cl AWLS/ASK DN6.....249 K8
  OT LS21.....41 J7
Falcon Dr CAS WF10.....157 L8
Falconers Rd HUDS HD4.....214 A8
Falcon Ms GIR BD8 *.....104 A3
  MOR LS27.....152 E3
Falcon Rd BGLY BD16.....81 H1
Falcon St GTHN BD7.....126 C1
  HIPP HX3.....168 F3
  HUDS HD4.....214 A5
Falhouse La EARL WF12.....194 F7
Falinge Ms WHIT OL12.....206 A6
Falinge Rd WHIT OL12.....206 A6
Falkland Ct AL/HA/HU LS17.....87 L5
Falkland Crs AL/HA/HU LS17.....87 L5
Falkland Gv AL/HA/HU LS17.....87 L5
Falkland Mt AL/HA/HU LS17.....87 L5
Falkland Ri AL/HA/HU LS17.....87 L5
Falkland Rd AL/HA/HU LS17.....87 L5
  IDLE BD10.....106 A2
Fall Bank Crs DOD/DAR S75.....259 M6
Fall Brow Cl LUD/ILL HX2.....125 J3
Falledge La STKB/PEN S36.....257 J8
Fall Head La DOD/DAR S75.....259 K5
Fall Ings Rd WKFDE WF1.....13 L1
Fall La DEWS WF13.....173 K8
  EARD/LOFT WF3.....153 M6
  LVSG WF15.....171 G1
  MAR/SLWT HD7.....233 H3
  PBR HX3.....85 B3
  RPDN/SBR HX6.....167 M5
Fallow Cft HUDN HD2.....193 H1
Fallow Fld SKP/WHF BD23.....16 D1
Fallowfield Cl BOW BD4.....127 L6
Fallowfield Dr BOW BD4.....127 L6
Fallowfield Gdns BOW BD4.....127 L6
Fallow La HWTH BD22.....56 C8
Fall Park Ct BRAM LS13.....107 M1
Fall Rd LVSG WF15.....172 A5
Fall Spring Gdns GTL/HWG HX4.....190 B2
Fall Spring Gn GTL/HWG HX4.....190 A2
Fallswood Gv BRAM LS13.....107 M2
Fall Vw DOD/DAR S75.....259 J4
Fall Wood St HWTH BD22.....78 F8
Falmouth Av BFDE BD3.....5 L1
  NORM WF6.....178 C4
Falmouth Cl BSLYN/ROY S71.....261 L4
Falmouth Crs NORM WF6.....178 C4
Falmouth Rd NORM WF6.....178 C4
Falmouth St ROCH OL11.....228 C1
Falsgrave Av ECHL BD2.....105 M4
Fanny La TAD LS24.....71 K7
Fanny Moor Crs HUDE HD5.....214 E6
Fanny Moor La HUDE HD5.....214 E6
Fanny St KGHY BD21.....2 E6
  SHPY BD18.....82 B6
Far Bank KBTN HD8.....238 D5
Farcliffe Pl GIR BD8.....104 D5
Farcliffe Rd GIR BD8.....104 D5
Farcliffe Ter GIR BD8.....104 D5

Far Common Rd MIRF WF14.....172 A6
Far Cft KBTN HD8.....216 C4
Far Crook IDLE BD10.....89 H5
Fardale ROY/SHW OL2.....229 K8
Far Dene KBTN HD8.....215 M6
Farehill Rd HUDS HD4.....214 B6
Far Field Av HOLM/MEL HD9.....255 G4
Farfield Av BTLY WF17 *.....151 H1
  GFTH/SHER LS25.....106 E3
  PDSY/CALV LS28.....106 E3
  WBSY BD6.....126 A7
Farfield Ct AL/HA/HU LS17.....88 A1
  GFTH/SHER LS25.....112 F7
Farfield Crs WBSY BD6.....126 A7
Far Field Dr HOLM/MEL HD9.....255 G4
Farfield Dr PDSY/CALV LS28.....106 E4
Farfield Gv PDSY/CALV LS28.....106 E3
Far Field La BSLYN/ROY S71.....244 A8
  HOLM/MEL HD9.....255 G5
Farfield Ri PDSY/CALV LS28.....106 E3
Farfield Rd BAIL BD17.....82 E2
  HUDE HD5.....215 H3
  SHPY BD18.....82 C7
Far Fields La HOLM/MEL HD9.....255 H1
  HTON BD9.....104 C4
Farfield Ter HTON BD9.....104 C4
Far Field Ter CLECK BD19.....149 M5
Faringdon ROCH OL11 *.....206 A8
Farlands Ri MILN OL16.....228 E3
Far La HBR HX7.....144 C4
  HOLM/MEL HD9.....255 G6
Far Lawns BSLYN/ROY S71.....243 M5
Farlea Dr ECHL BD2.....105 L3
Farleton Dr ECHL BD2.....105 M4
Farley Crs HWTH BD22.....78 F8
Farm Cl BSLY S70.....260 E3
  FEA/AMT WF7.....201 L2
  MSTN/BAR LS15.....111 K4
Farm Cft FEA/AMT WF7.....201 L1
Farm Gdns FEA/AMT WF7.....201 L2
Farm Hill Crs CHAL LS7.....109 J1
Farm Hl North CHAL LS7.....87 J8
Farm Hill Rd CHAL LS7.....109 J1
  MOR LS27.....152 A1
Farm Hill South CHAL LS7.....109 J1
Farm Hill Wy CHAL LS7.....109 J1
Farm House La HEM/SK/SE WF9.....223 J4
Far Moss AL/HA/HU LS17.....87 J1
Farm Pond Dr BRIG HD6.....170 A1
Far Reef Cl HORS LS18.....85 L4
Farrar La BHP/TINH LS16.....86 A7
Farm Rd BSLY S70.....261 L2
  FEA/AMT WF7.....201 L1
  MSTN/BAR LS15.....111 K4
Farmstead Rd IDLE BD10.....83 L8
Farm Wk LIT OL15.....207 H1
  MILN OL16.....206 E5
Farm Wy WMB/DAR S73.....263 J8
Farnboro St TOD OL14.....163 J4
Farndale Ap SCFT LS14.....111 L1
Farndale Cl GFTH/SHER LS25.....135 H1
  WBY LS22.....29 L8
Farndale Garth SCFT LS14.....89 L8
Farndale Pl SCFT LS14.....89 L8
Farndale Rd BAIL BD17.....82 C4
  WIL/AL BD15.....102 E2
Farne Av WKFDW/WTN WF2.....198 B1
Farnham Cl BAIL BD17.....82 F2
  BHP/TINH LS16.....86 A7
  SCFT LS14.....89 K5
Farnham Cft SCFT LS14.....89 K5
Farnley Cl GTHN BD7.....126 D1
Farnham Rd GTHN BD7.....126 D1
Farnham Wy MIRF WF14.....172 A6
Farnlee HUDW HD3.....191 K5
Farnley Cl ILK LS29.....23 J1
Farnley Crs WOR/ARM LS12.....108 A8
Farnley La OT LS21.....42 A3
Farnley Pk OT LS21.....41 K2
Farnley Vw BIRK/DRI BD11.....129 J3
Farrar Av MIRF WF14.....172 A6
Farrar Ct BRAM LS13.....107 J3
Farrar Cft BHP/TINH LS16.....86 C2
Farrar Dr MIRF WF14.....172 A7
Farrar Gv BHP/TINH LS16.....86 C2
Farrar Height La
  RPDN/SBR HX6.....188 D2
Farrar Mill La HIPP HX3.....168 F4
Farrar St BSLY S70.....260 F5
Farriers Ct DOD/DAR S75 *.....260 C7
Farriers Pl CAS WF10.....158 D7
Farrier Wy EARD/LOFT WF3.....154 D3
Farringdon Cl BOW BD4.....128 A3
Farringdon Dr BOW BD4.....128 A3
Farringdon Gv WBSY BD6.....126 C7
Farringdon Sq BOW BD4.....128 A3
Farrow Bank WOR/ARM LS12.....108 A7
Farrow Cl DOD/DAR S75.....260 C7
Farrowdale Av ROY/SHW OL2.....229 K8
Farrow Gn WOR/ARM LS12.....108 A7
Farrow Hl WOR/ARM LS12.....108 A7
Farrow Rd WOR/ARM LS12.....108 A7
Farrow St ROY/SHW OL2.....229 K8
Farrow St East ROY/SHW OL2.....229 K8
Farrow V WOR/ARM LS12.....108 A7
Farside Gn WBOW BD5.....126 E5
Farthing Av PONT WF8.....180 C7
Fartown PDSY/CALV LS28.....129 G1
Fartown Cl PDSY/CALV LS28.....129 G1
Fartown Green Rd HUDN HD2.....192 D5
Far View Bank HUDE HD5.....215 H1
Farway BOW BD4.....128 A2
Far Well Fold YEA LS19.....84 F5
Far Well La HOLM/MEL HD9.....237 K6
Faugh La HBR HX7.....120 E8
Favell Av NORM WF6.....178 D5
Faversham Wk BOW BD4 *.....128 A2
Favordale Rd COL BB8.....52 C8
Fawcett Av WOR/ARM LS12.....130 C1
Fawcett Bank WOR/ARM LS12.....130 C1
Fawcett Cl WOR/ARM LS12.....130 C1
Fawcett Dr WOR/ARM LS12.....130 C1
Fawcett Gdns WOR/ARM LS12.....130 C1
Fawcett La WOR/ARM LS12.....130 C1
Fawcett Pl BOW BD4.....127 L6
Fawcett V WOR/ARM LS12.....130 C1
Fawcett Vw WOR/ARM LS12.....130 C1
Fawkes Dr OT LS21.....40 D4
Faxfleet St WBOW BD5.....126 F5
Faye Gdns BOW BD4.....127 M5
Fearnley Av OSS WF5.....174 E7
Fearnley Cl WKFDW/WTN WF2.....12 E7
Fearnley La HUDS HD4.....215 H8

Fearnley Cft CLECK BD19.....150 D6
Fearnley Dr OSS WF5.....174 E7
Fearnley La HOLM/MEL HD9.....254 E1
Fearnley Pl WOR/ARM LS12.....108 F7
  FEA/AMT WF7.....201 L1
Fearnside Fold
  HOR/CROF WF4 *.....197 K4
Fearnsides's Cl GIR BD8.....104 D6
Fearnsides Ter GIR BD8.....104 D6
Fearnville Av RHAY LS8.....110 F2
Fearnville Cl RHAY LS8.....110 F2
Fearnville Dr BOW BD4.....127 M1
  RHAY LS8.....110 F2
Fearnville Gv BSLYN/ROY S71.....243 L3
  RHAY LS8.....110 F3
Fearnville Mt RHAY LS8.....110 F1
Fearnville Pl RHAY LS8.....111 G1
Fearnville Rd RHAY LS8.....111 G1
Fearnville Ter RHAY LS8.....111 G1
Fearnville Vw RHAY LS8.....110 F2
Feast Fld HORS LS18.....85 K5
Featherbank Av HORS LS18.....85 K6
Featherbank Gv HORS LS18.....85 K6
Featherbank Ter HORS LS18.....85 K6
Featherbank Wk HORS LS18.....85 K6
Featherbed Cl GTL/HWG HX4.....168 F8
Feather Bed La ELL HX5.....168 F8
Featherstall Brook Vie
  LIT OL15.....207 J1
Featherstall Rd LIT OL15.....207 H1
Featherstone La FEA/AMT WF7.....179 M6
Federation St WBOW BD5.....127 H4
Felbrigg Av HWTH BD22.....2 C7
Felcote Av HUDE HD5.....215 L1
Felcourt Dr BOW BD4.....128 A4
Felcourt Fold BOW BD4.....128 A4
Felkirk Dr HOR/CROF WF4.....222 C5
Felkirk Vw CUD/GR S72.....244 C3
Felks Stile Rd HUDS HD4.....213 H4
Fell Crs HWTH BD22.....2 A8
Fell Greave Crs HUDN HD2.....192 E2
Fell Greave Rd HUDN HD2.....192 D1
Fell Gv HUDN HD2.....192 D2
Fell La HWTH BD22.....2 B7
Fellowsides La OSS WF5.....197 G1
The Fellows HUDS HD4.....213 L7
Fellside TOD OL14.....164 F1
Fellside Cl WBOW BD5.....127 H4
Fellside Gdns LIT OL15.....185 H7
Fellwood Av HWTH BD22.....79 G6
Fellwood Cl HWTH BD22.....79 G6
Felnex Cl OSM LS9.....132 E1
Felnex Crs OSM LS9.....132 E1
Felnex Rd OSM LS9.....132 E1
Felnex Sq OSM LS9.....132 E1
Felnex Wy OSM LS9.....132 E1
Fenay Bankside KBTN HD8.....215 M3
Fenay Bridge Rd HUDE HD5.....215 L3
Fenay La HUDE HD5.....215 J3
  KBTN HD8.....215 J3
Fenay Lea Dr HUDE HD5.....215 J3
Fenby Av BOW BD4.....127 K2
Fenby Cl BOW BD4.....127 L3
Fenby Gdns BOW BD4.....127 L3
Fenby Gv BOW BD4.....127 L3
Fencote Crs ECHL BD2.....105 M3
Fender Rd WBSY BD6.....126 B5
Fennec Rd BAIL BD17.....83 C2
Fennel Cl RTHW LS26.....133 L6
Fennell Ct WKFDW/WTN WF2.....198 F7
Fensome Wy WMB/DAR S73.....263 H8
Fenton Av RTHW LS26.....133 L6
Fenton Cl HEM/SK/SE WF9.....246 D5
  RTHW LS26.....133 L5
Fenton La GFTH/SHER LS25.....116 E4
Fenton Ms ROCH OL11 *.....228 A1
Fenton Rd EARD/LOFT WF3.....155 H7
  HFAX HX1.....10 A9
  HUD HD1.....214 B3
Fentongate EARD/LOFT WF3.....154 E5
Fenton Sq HUD HD1.....14 C9
Fenton St BSLY S70 *.....260 F5
  EARD/LOFT WF3.....153 H5
  ILK LS29.....40 B5
  LDSU LS2.....6 F6
  MIRF WF14.....194 C2
  ROCH OL11.....228 A1
Fenwick Dr WBSY BD6.....126 B8
Fenwick St ROCH OL11.....206 B8
Ferguson Gdns WHIT OL12.....206 B3
Ferguson St HFAX HX1.....11 G7
Fern Av HOLM/MEL HD9.....234 E3
Fern Bank AWLS/ASK DN6.....249 K8
Fernbank Av BRAM LS13.....107 H3
  HWTH BD22.....79 H2
Fernbank Cl BRAM LS13.....107 H3
Fernbank Dr BAIL BD17.....82 C5
  BGLY BD16.....81 J3
  BRAM LS13.....107 H3
Fernbank Gdns BRAM LS13 *.....107 H3
Fernbank Pl BRAM LS13.....107 H3
Fernbank Rd BFDE BD3.....5 L2
  BRAM LS13.....107 H3
Fern Cha SCFT LS14.....67 J7
Ferncliffe Dr AIRE BD20.....57 H4
  BAIL BD17.....82 D3
Ferncliffe Rd BGLY BD16.....81 J3
  SHPY BD18.....82 B6
Ferncliffe Ter BRAM LS13.....107 K4
Fern Cl BTLY WF17.....174 B1
Fern Ct AIRE BD20.....57 J4
Fern Cft LVSG WF15.....171 L2
  SCFT LS14.....67 J7
  WKFDW/WTN WF2.....176 A3
Ferndale Av CLAY BD14.....125 J5
  MILN OL16.....228 E5
Ferndale Gv HTON BD9.....104 A2
  HUDN HD2.....192 D2
Ferndale Pl HEM/SK/SE WF9.....223 L8
Ferndene BGLY BD16.....81 K3
Ferndene Av BTLY WF17.....151 H8
Ferndown Gn WBOW BD5.....126 F3
Ferney Lee Rd TOD OL14.....141 J8
Fernfield Ter HIPP HX3 *.....146 D2
Fern Gdns ILK LS29.....38 C3
Fern Gv KSTL LS5.....108 E1
Fern Hill Av SHPY BD18.....82 B7
Fern Hill Gv SHPY BD18.....82 B7
Fern Hill Mt SHPY BD18.....82 B7
Fern Hill Rd SHPY BD18.....82 B7
Fernhurst Cl MIRF WF14.....172 C8
Fernhurst Crs MIRF WF14.....172 C8
Fernhurst Lea MIRF WF14.....172 C8
Fernhurst Rd MIRF WF14.....172 C8
Fernhurst Wy MIRF WF14.....172 C8
Fernlea RTHW LS26.....133 H8
Fernlea Cl HWTH BD22.....79 G3
  HOR/CROF WF4.....200 C5
Fernlea Gv MAR/SLWT HD7.....213 G3
Fern Lea Rd HUDW HD3.....191 J5
Fern Lea St RPDN/SBR HX6.....167 K3
Fern Lea Vw PDSY/CALV LS28.....107 G4
Fernleigh Ct WKFDW/WTN WF2.....198 B1
Fernley Gdns LM/WK BD12.....148 B1
Fernley Green Cl KNOT WF11.....182 C2

Fernley Green Rd KNOT WF11 ....182 D2
Fernley Hill Dr NORM WF6.........178 D1
Fern Ri ELL HX5......................169 K7
Fernside Av HUDE HD5..............215 H2
Fernside Cl HUDE HD5...............215 J1
Fernside Crs HUDE..................215 H1
Fern St BOW BD4.....................127 M3
  COL BB8..............................52 B8
  HIPP HX3............................146 D4
  HUDN HD2............................14 E2
  KGHY BD21.............................3 G3
  WHIT OL12...........................184 E8
Fern Ter AIRE BD20..................58 B5
  GIR BD8..............................104 E4
  PDSY/CALV LS28....................107 C4
Fern Valley Cha TOD OL14.........141 H8
Fern Wy SCFT LS14....................67 J7
Fernwood RHAY LS8...................88 C5
Ferrand Av BGLY BD16................81 H3
Ferrand La BGLY BD16................81 H3
  CLECK BD19.........................150 D5
Ferrand Ldg LIT OL15................185 L7
Ferrand Rd LIT OL15.................185 K8
Ferrands Cl BGLY BD16...............80 D5
Ferrands Park Wy BGLY BD16.......80 D5
Ferrara Cl WMB/BAR DARS73......263 G8
Ferriby Cl ECHL BD2.................105 M3
Ferrybridge By-Pass
  KNOT WF11..........................159 L8
Ferrybridge Rd CAS WF10..........158 A6
  KNOT WF11..........................181 M2
  PONT WF8............................181 G4
Ferry La EARD/LOFT WF3...........177 H4
Ferry Moor La CUD/GR S72.........244 D4
Ferrymoor Wy CUD/GR S72.........245 G8
Ferry Top La HOR/CROF WF4.......222 D4
Festival Av SHPY BD18................82 F6
Feversham St BFDE BD3................5 J7
Fewston Av OSM LS9.................110 B8
  WKFDE WF1..........................177 H6
Fewston Ct OSM LS9.................110 B8
Fiddle La GTL/HWG HX4.............189 J3
Fidler La GFTH/SHER LS25.........113 J3
Field Cl HECK WF16.................150 F8
  HIPP HX3.............................10 E1
  WMB/BAR DARS73...................263 J8
Fieldcroft Ct MIRF WF14............194 B1
Field Dr CUD/GR S72.................262 D1
  TAD LS24.............................72 D1
Fieldedge La AIRE BD20.............58 C4
Field End MSTN/BAR LS15..........111 J7
Field End Av MSTN/BAR LS15 *....111 J7
Field End Cl MSTN/BAR LS15.......111 J7
Field End Crs MSTN/BAR LS15.....111 J7
Field End Gdns
  MSTN/BAR LS15.....................111 J7
Field End Garth
  MSTN/BAR LS15.....................111 J7
Field End Gn MSTN/BAR LS15 *....111 J7
Field End Gv MSTN/BAR LS15 *....111 J7
Field End La HOLM/MEL HD9.......236 C2
  HOLM/MEL HD9......................253 K4
Field End Mt MSTN/BAR LS15......111 J7
Field End Rd MSTN/BAR LS15......111 J7
Fieldens Pl BTLY WF17...............151 J8
Fielden Sq TOD OL14................163 K2
Fielden St TOD OL14................142 A8
Fieldfare Dr WBSY BD6..............125 K5
Fieldgate Rd IDLE BD10.............83 M7
Field Head MAR/SLWT HD7.........212 F1
Fieldhead Cl PONT WF8.............181 H5
Fieldhead Ct BSPA/BRAM LS23....48 E7
Fieldhead Crs BTLY WF17...........151 G3
Fieldhead Dr AIRE BD20..............34 F3
  GSLY LS20............................61 L6
  MSTN/BAR LS15.....................91 H7
Fieldhead Gdns EARL WF12.........174 D3
Field Head La BTLY WF17............151 G4
  HBR HX7.............................165 K2
  HWTH BD22..........................100 C1
  LUD/ILL HX2.........................123 M7
Fieldhead La HOLM/MEL HD9......253 H5
Fieldhead Paddock
  BSPA/BRAM LS23....................48 E6
Fieldhead Rd GSLY LS20.............61 L6
Fieldhead St GTHN BD7.............104 D8
Fieldhead Wy LVSG WF15...........172 E1
Fieldholme Cl AL/HA/HU LS17.......87 L4
Field House Cl WBY LS22..............47 L1
Fieldhouse Dr AL/HA/HU LS17......87 L4
  MAR/SLWT HD7.....................212 C4
Fieldhouse Lawn
  AL/HA/HU LS17......................87 L4
Fieldhouse Rd HUD HD1..............15 J2
  WHIT OL12...........................206 B4
Fieldhouse Wk WKFDE WF1..........12 F1
Field Hurst CLECK BD19.............149 H7
  GTL/HWG HX4......................189 K1
Fieldhurst Ct BOW BD4..............127 K6
Fielding Ct MOR LS27................152 B1
Fielding Ga WOR/ARM LS12.........108 F6
Fielding Gate Ms
  WOR/ARM LS12.....................108 F6
Fielding Wy MOR LS27................152 B1
Field La BRIC HD6....................170 B6
  BSLY S70............................262 A7
  BTLY WF17...........................173 L2
  DEWS WF13..........................172 F8
  GFTH/SHER LS25....................92 B6
  HEM/SK/SE WF9.....................225 J7
  HEM/SK/SE WF9.....................247 M2
  HUDS HD4...........................215 H8
  OSS WF5.............................174 F4
Field Pl WKFDW/WTN WF2..........12 A4
Field Rd HOLM/MEL HD9.............254 D2
  MILN OL16...........................206 F7
Fields Ri HUDE HD5..................193 K6
Fields Rd HUDN HD8.................215 M3
  LM/WK BD12.........................149 G1
The Fields EARD/LOFT WF3.........154 F5
Field St BFD BD1.......................6 D7
  DEWS WF13 *........................173 G8
  ROCH OL11..........................228 C2
Fields Wy HUDE HD5.................193 K6
Field Ter MSTN/BAR LS15...........111 J6
Field Top Rd BRIG HD6..............170 B6
Field Vw CAS WF10..................157 J8
  HIPP HX3............................146 B4
  WMB/BAR DARS73..................238 A6
Fieldway CLAY BD14.................125 K2
  ILK LS29..............................39 L6
  MILN OL16...........................228 D3
Fieldway Av BRAM LS13.............107 G3
Fieldway Cha DEWS WF13..........155 M1
Fieldway Cl BRAM LS13..............107 G3
Fieldway Ri BRAM LS13..............107 H2
Fife St BSLY S70......................260 F5
Fifth Av BFDE BD3...................105 L5
  RTHW LS26..........................133 J7
Fifth Av West LVSG WF15...........171 K2

Filbert St HUDN HD2..................14 E1
Filey Av BSLYN/ROY S71............243 M2
Filey St BFDE BD3.......................5 H7
  MILN OL16...........................206 F4
Filley Royd CLECK BD19.............149 M8
Fillingfir Dr BHP/TINH LS16.........86 B6
Fillingfir Rd BHP/TINH LS16.........86 B6
Fillingfir Wk BHP/TINH LS16.........86 B6
Finance St LIT OL15.................207 G1
Finch Av WKFDW/WTN WF2........220 F1
Finch Cl BGLY BD16...................81 L2
Finching Gv MIRF WF14.............172 C6
Finchley St WBOW BD5.............126 F3
Finchley Wy MOR LS27.............152 C3
Finch St WBOW BD5.................126 F2
Findon Ter IDLE BD10................106 A3
Fine Garth Cl BSPA/BRAM LS23....69 M3
Finghall Rd AWLS/ASK DN6.........249 H4
Fink Hl HORS LS18....................85 J6
Finkil St BRIC HD6...................170 A1
Finkin Av EARD/LOFT WF3..........177 G4
Finkin Cft EARD/LOFT WF3.........177 G4
Finkin La EARD/LOFT WF3..........177 G4
Finkle Cl MOR LS27.................129 L8
Finkle Hl GFTH/SHER LS25.........116 A5
Finkle La MOR LS27.................129 L8
  HOR/CROF WF4.....................220 B7
  LUD/ILL HX2........................166 F2
Finsbury Dr ECHL BD2.................83 H8
Finsbury Rd LDS LS1....................6 F5
Finthorpe La HUDE HD5.............215 J3
Fir Av WHIT OL12....................194 F1
Firbank Gn ECHL BD2 *.............105 M4
Firbank Gv MSTN/BAR LS15........111 G8
Fir Bank Rd ROY/SHW OL2.........228 F8
Firbeck BGLY BD16....................80 D6
Firbeck Rd BSPA/BRAM LS23.......69 M3
Fire Station Yd ROCH OL11..........206 B8
Firethorn Cl GIR BD8 *..............104 C6
Firgrove Av MILN OL16..............206 F6
Firgrove Gdns MILN OL16...........206 F6
Firham Cl BSLYN/ROY S71...........243 J2
Fir La ROY/SHW OL2.................228 F8
Fir Pde DEWS WF13..................194 F1
Fir Rd HUD HD1......................191 M8
Firs La STKB/PEN S36................257 M7
First Av AL/HA/HU LS17...............68 A1
  BFDE BD3...........................105 L5
  GFTH/SHER LS25....................116 D7
  HEM/SK/SE WF9.....................223 J2
  HEM/SK/SE WF9.....................225 J7
  HEM/SK/SE WF9.....................246 B5
  HIPP HX3............................168 D2
  HOR/CROF WF4.....................197 H5
  HUDE HD5...........................193 H7
  LUD/ILL HX2.........................166 F2
  OSM LS9.............................110 F3
  PDSY/CALV LS28....................107 G5
  RTHW LS26..........................133 H7
  WBY LS22.............................29 K8
  WKFDE WF1..........................176 D4
  WOR/ARM LS12......................108 F7
  YEA LS19.............................84 E1
First St LM/WK BD12..................127 G8
Firth Av BEE/HOL LS11..............131 J4
  BRIC HD6............................170 C3
  CUD/GR S72.........................262 C1
Firthcliffe Dr LVSG WF15............172 D1
Firthcliffe Gv LVSG WF15............172 D1
Firthcliffe La LVSG WF15............172 D1
Firthcliffe Mt LVSG WF15............150 D8
Firthcliffe Pde LVSG WF15..........172 D1
Firthcliffe Pl LVSG WF15............172 D1
Firthcliffe Rd LVSG WF15............172 D1
Firthcliffe Ter LVSG WF15...........172 D1
Firthcliffe Vw LVSG WF15............172 D1
Firthcliffe Wk LVSG WF15...........172 D1
Firth Cl EARD/LOFT WF3.............177 K8
Firthfield La HEM/SK/SE WF9.......225 J4
Firth Gv BEE/HOL LS11..............131 J4
Firth House La BRIG HD6............170 D7
  GTL/HWG HX4......................189 L6
Firth La WIL/AL BD15................102 L1
Firth Mt BEE/HOL LS11..............131 J4
Firth Rd BEE/HOL LS11..............131 J4
  HTON BD9...........................104 C3
Firth St BRIC HD6....................170 C5
  BSLYN/ROY S71.....................261 J4
  CHAL LS7.............................7 K6
  KBTN HD8...........................238 D7
  SKP/WHF BD23.......................16 C4
Firths Yd DEWS WF13 *.............173 L4
Firth Vw BEE/HOL LS11..............131 J4
Firtree Ap AL/HA/HU LS17...........87 K3
Firtree Av GFTH/SHER LS25........113 K8
Fir Tree Cl AL/HA/HU LS17...........87 L2
Firtree Crs TAD LS24..................71 K4
Fir Tree Gdns AL/HA/HU LS17.......87 L2
  IDLE BD10............................83 M8
Fir Tree Gn AL/HA/HU LS17.........87 L2
Fir Tree La AL/HA/HU LS17..........87 L3
Fir Tree Ri AL/HA/HU LS17..........87 L3
Fir Tree Vw AL/HA/HU LS17.........87 L3
Firville Av NORM WF6................157 G3
Firville Crs NORM WF6...............178 D5
Fir Wk DEWS WF13..................194 F1
Firwood Cl TOD OL14................163 J5
Fishbeck La AIRE BD20................36 C2
Fish Dam La BSLYN/ROY S71.......243 M6
Fishergate KNOT WF11...............181 M1
Fisher Gn HOLM/MEL HD9...........236 A2
Fisher Gv OSS WF5...................197 H2
Fisher St KNOT WF11................182 A2
Fisher Wy HECK WF16................173 L3
Fishponds Dr HOR/CROF WF4......220 B1
Fishponds La HOR/CROF WF4......220 B1
Fish St LDS LS1.........................7 H9
Fishwick St MILN OL16..............206 C6
Fitton St MILN OL16.................206 C6
Fitts La AL/HA/HU LS17...............45 J1
Fitzgerald Cl CAS WF10.............180 F1
Fitzgerald St WBOW BD5..............4 D9
Fitzroy Dr RHAY LS8...................88 C8
Fitzroy St BFDE BD3....................5 M6
Fitzwilliam St BOW BD4.............128 A4
  BSLY S70............................260 F5
  HEM/SK/SE WF9.....................225 K3
  HUD HD1.............................14 D6
Five Acres DOD/DAR S75.............259 H4
Five Lane Ends BHP/TINH LS16.....64 F6
  HOLM/MEL HD9 *...................254 A1
Five Oaks BAIL BD17...................82 C4
Fixby Av LUD/ILL HX2................168 A1

Fixby La EARL WF12..................194 F8
Fixby Park Dr HUDN HD2............192 A4
Fixby St HUDN HD2..................192 C3
Flagship Sq EARL WF12.............174 C4
Flannel St WHIT OL12 *.............206 C6
Flanshaw Av
  WKFDW/WTN WF2.................176 A8
Flanshaw Crs
  WKFDW/WTN WF2.................176 A8
Flanshaw Gv
  WKFDW/WTN WF2.................176 A8
Flanshaw La
  WKFDW/WTN WF2.................175 M8
Flanshaw Rd
  WKFDW/WTN WF2.................176 A8
Flanshaw St
  WKFDW/WTN WF2.................176 A8
Flanshaw Vw
  WKFDW/WTN WF2.................176 A8
Flanshaw Wy
  WKFDW/WTN WF2.................175 L7
Flasby St KGHY BD21...................3 G2
Flash La MIRF WF14..................172 D8
Flass La CAS WF10...................179 L2
Flat Nook BGLY BD16 *...............81 K3
Flatts La MSTN/BAR LS15............90 F8
Flavell Cl HEM/SK/SE WF9.........246 D5
Flawith Dr SCFT LS14...............105 M4
Flaxen Ct WBSY BD6.................126 F5
Flax Meadow HUDW HD3...........191 H8
Flax Pl OSM LS9.........................9 L2
Flaxton Cl BEE/HOL LS11..............8 E9
Flaxton Gdns BEE/HOL LS11.........8 E9
Flaxton Gn ECHL BD2................105 M4
Flaxton Pl GTHN BD7................104 D8
Flaxton Vw BEE/HOL LS11............8 E9
Fledborough Rd WBY LS22...........47 L1
Fleece St KGHY BD21...................3 H5
  MILN OL16...........................206 B7
  WBSY BD6............................126 B7
Fleet Hill Crs BSLYN/ROY S71......261 J4
Fleet Cl CUL/QBY BD13...............124 F5
  RTHW LS26..........................155 M1
Fleet La KBTN HD8...................239 M5
Fleet Thro Rd HORS LS18.............85 K8
Fleetwood Av BSLYN/ROY S71......261 L1
Fleminghouse La HUDE HD5........215 K2
Fleming Pl BSLY S70.................261 G6
Fleming St BTLY WF17................173 L1
Fletcher Av AIRE BD20................36 A4
Fletcher Crs BRIG HD6...............170 A8
Fletcher La ECHL BD2................104 F1
Fletcher Rd WBSY BD6..............126 D5
Fletcher St ROCH OL11..............228 C1
Fletton Cl WHIT OL12................206 A4
Fletton Ter ECHL BD2................105 K4
Flexbury Av MOR LS27...............152 C3
Flight Hl HOLM/MEL HD9............267 L1
Flint La HOLM/MEL HD9.............268 C1
Flintmill La BSPA/BRAM LS23......48 F3
Flinton Gv ECHL BD2................105 M4
Flint St HUDN HD2....................15 G1
Flockton Av BOW BD4...............127 J2
Flockton Cl BOW BD4...............127 J2
Flockton Crs BOW BD4..............127 J2
Flockton Dr BOW BD4...............127 J2
Flockton Gv BOW BD4...............127 J2
Flockton Rd BOW BD4...............127 J2
  KBTN HD8...........................238 D3
Floral Av CHAL LS7....................87 L8
Floreat Cl BTLY WF17................151 J6
Florence Av OSM LS9................110 C4
  WIL/AL BD15.........................80 D8
Florence Mt OSM LS9 *..............110 C4
Florence Pl OSM LS9................110 C4
Florence St BFDE BD3...............105 L8
  CAS WF10...........................157 M6
  MILN OL16...........................206 D8
  OSM LS9.............................110 C4
Florida Rd WIL/AL BD15.............103 G1
Florin Wy PONT WF8.................180 C7
Florist St KGHY BD21...................3 M1
Flossmore Wy MOR LS27............129 J3
Flounders Hl FEA/AMT WF7.........202 B8
Flower Acre ELL HX5.................169 H8
Flower Bank AIRE BD20.............105 H2
  RPDN/SBR HX6.....................167 H3
Flower Cl YEA LS19....................62 C7
Flower Ct ECHL BD2 *...............105 L3
Flower Cft HWTH BD22...............2 B9
Flower Garth IDLE BD10............105 M1
Flower Hvn HTON BD9...............103 M2
Flower Hl HTON BD9.................104 B2
Flowerlands HIPP HX3...............148 A5
Flower Scar Rd TOD OL14..........140 A8
Floyd St WBOW BD5.................126 D3
Flush LVSG WF15....................172 D2
Flush House La
  HOLM/MEL HD9....................253 J3
Fold Grassmoor
  HOLM/MEL HD9....................236 C6
Foldings Av CLECK BD19............149 H6
Foldings Cl CLECK BD19.............149 G6
Foldings Ct CLECK BD19.............149 G6
Foldings Gv CLECK BD19.............149 G6
Foldings Pde CLECK BD19...........149 G6
The Foldings KBTN HD8.............239 J4
Fold La HBR HX7.....................120 C8
  HWTH BD22..........................54 E3
The Fold MSTN/BAR LS15...........112 A2
Foljambe St WKFDW/WTN WF2...12 F6
Folkestone St BFDE BD3...............5 M5
Folkton Holme ECHL BD2...........105 M4
Follett Av HUDS HD4.................213 L4
Follifoot La PBR HG3...................27 H5
Follifoot Rd PBR HG3..................27 G2
Follingworth La
  MAR/SLWT HD7.....................211 L5
Follingworth Rd BTLY WF17.........174 A1
Folly Hall HUD HD1...................214 C2
The Folly Hall Gdns WBSY BD6....126 D6
Folly Hall La HBR HX7...............166 M4
Folly Hall Rd EARD/LOFT WF3.....153 G6
Folly Hall Wk WBSY BD6............126 C6
Folly La BEE/HOL LS11...............130 B7
  BSPA/BRAM LS23....................69 M4
  STKB/PEN S36.......................257 M8
Folly Rd HUDN HD2..................192 C3
Folly Vw BSPA/BRAM LS23...........69 M4
Folly View Rd HWTH BD22 *.........78 F8
Fontmell Cl BOW BD4...............128 A4
Football YEA LS19.....................62 E8
Forber Gv BOW BD4..................127 K1
Forber Pl MSTN/BAR LS15...........111 G7
Ford CUL/QBY BD13...................80 D6
Ford Dr MIRF WF14..................194 A1
Ford Hl HEM/SK/SE WF9.............223 K5
Ford St HEM/SK/SE WF9.............223 K5
  KGHY BD21.............................3 L1
Fordyce Ct BOW BD4.................128 A4
Fore La RPDN/SBR HX6..............167 J3
Fore Lane Av RPDN/SBR HX6......167 H3

Foreside Bottom La
  CUL/QBY BD13.......................123 M2
Foreside La CUL/QBY BD13..........123 K1
Forest Av LUD/ILL HX2..............146 A3
Forest Bank MOR LS27..............129 L7
Forest Cl WKFDE WF1...............177 C5
Forest Crs LUD/ILL HX2..............146 A2
Forest Ga OT LS21.....................41 J7
Forest Gn LUD/ILL HX2..............146 A3
Forest Hill Gdns HUDW HD3 *......190 C6
Forest Hill Rd GTL/HWG HX4.......189 M5
Forest Rdg EARD/LOFT WF3........153 C5
Forest Rd BSLYN/ROY S71...........243 H6
  HUDE HD5...........................215 G1
Forest Wy HOLM/MEL HD9.........236 A2
Forge Gn PBR HG3....................28 A1
Forge Hill La KNOT WF11...........182 A1
Forge La AL/HA/HU LS17..............66 F5
  EARL WF12...........................195 K2
  HOR/CROF WF4.....................197 L6
  LVSG WF15...........................172 A4
  WOR/ARM LS12.....................108 F6
Forge Rw WOR/ARM LS12...........129 M3
Forge Vw BFD BD1....................56 E1
Forman's Dr EARD/LOFT WF3......154 C1
Formby Av HUDN HD2..............192 B3
Formby Ct BSLYN/ROY S71.........243 M8
Forrest Av HUD HD1.................191 M7
Forrester Cl HEM/SK/SE WF9......223 J3
Forrester Dr ROY/SHW OL2.........229 M6
Forrester's Cl AWLS/ASK DN6......227 L3
Forster Dr HECK WF16...............173 L3
Forster Pl WOR/ARM LS12...........130 C2
Forster Sq BFD BD1.....................5 G6
Forster St MID LS10....................9 L6
Forsythia Av EARD/LOFT WF3......153 L7
Fort Ann Rd BTLY WF17.............174 B2
Fortis Wy HUDW HD3................191 J7
Fortshot La AL/HA/HU LS17.........66 D5
Forum Vw PONT WF8.................225 J1
Foss Av WBY LS22.....................29 M7
Fosse Wy GFTH/SHER LS25.........113 K8
Foster Av AIRE BD20...................35 K4
  CUL/QBY BD13......................103 H8
  HUDS HD4...........................213 L4
  NORM WF6...........................178 C5
Foster Cl ILK LS29.....................40 B6
  MOR LS27............................152 C1
Foster Gdns HWTH BD22..............2 B5
Foster La HBR HX7...................143 J2
Foster Park Gv CUL/QBY BD13....102 A5
Foster Park Rd CUL/QBY BD13....102 A5
Foster Park Vw CUL/QBY BD13....102 A5
Foster Place La HOLM/MEL HD9...255 H4
Foster Sq KGHY BD21...................2 E9
Foster Sq BSLY S70...................261 H6
  CUL/QBY BD13......................124 F5
  MOR LS27 *..........................152 C2
Foster Wk GFTH/SHER LS25........113 J4
Foston Cl ECHL BD2..................106 A4
Foston La ECHL BD2.................105 M4
Fothergill Av FEA/AMT WF7.........202 A8
Foulcauseway La OT LS21.............41 M7
Foul Clough Rd TOD OL14..........162 F6
Foulds St COL BB8.....................74 D3
Foulds' Ter BGLY BD16................81 J2
Foundry Ap OSM LS9.................110 D3
Foundry Av OSM LS9.................110 D3
  RHAY LS8............................110 D3
Foundry Dr RHAY LS8................110 D3
Foundry La BOW BD4................128 A4
  KNOT WF11..........................182 C2
  OSM LS9.............................110 F3
  PDSY/CALV LS28....................107 G4
Foundry Mill Crs SCFT LS14........111 J3
Foundry Mill Dr SCFT LS14.........111 J3
Foundry Mill Gdns SCFT LS14......111 J3
Foundry Mill Mt SCFT LS14.........111 J3
Foundry Mill St SCFT LS14.........111 J3
Foundry Mill Ter SCFT LS14........111 J3
Foundry Pl OSM LS9.................110 D3
Foundry St BEE/HOL LS11.............8 E7
  BRIG HD6............................170 C5
  BSLY S70............................261 G6
  CLECK BD19.........................149 M6
  DEWS WF13.........................173 M6
  DEWS WF13.........................195 G1
  HFAX HX1.............................11 H4
  OSM LS9...............................9 L6
  RPDN/SBR HX6.....................167 K3
Foundry St North LUD/ILL HX2....146 B3
Foundry Wk RHAY LS8...............110 D3
Fountain Cl DOD/DAR S75...........242 A5
  LVSG WF15...........................172 B5
Fountain Dr LVSG WF15.............172 B5
Fountain Gv HUDW HD3.............213 H3
Fountains Av BSPA/BRAM LS23.....48 F7
  BTLY WF17...........................173 J2
Fountain St CUL/QBY BD13.........125 C5
  HECK WF16..........................172 E1
  HFAX HX1............................11 C6
  LDS LS1................................6 D5
  LM/WK BD12.........................126 E8
  LVSG WF15...........................172 B5
  MOR LS27............................152 B4
  RPDN/SBR HX6.....................188 F2
Fountain Ter LM/WK BD12..........148 E4
Fountain Wy BSLYN/ROY S71......261 M3
  WKFDE WF1..........................177 H5
Fountain Ter LM/WK BD12 *........148 E4
Four Lanes Cl EARL WF12..........196 A4
Four Lanes Cl DOD/DAR S75.......260 A1
Four Stalls End LIT OL15.............207 J2
Fourteenth Av WOR/ARM LS12....109 G8
Fourth Av BFDE BD3...................5 J7
  KGHY BD21............................3 D7
  LVSG WF15...........................171 K1
  RTHW LS26..........................133 J7
  WBY LS22.............................48 E7
  WKFDE WF1..........................176 D4
Fourth Ct BEE/HOL LS11...............8 C8
Fourth St HOR/CROF WF4............200 D7
  LM/WK BD12.........................127 G8
Fowlers Garth HWTH BD22 *........78 F5
Fowler St BOW BD4..................127 K1
Foxbridge Wy NORM WF6...........179 M5
Foxcliff KNOT WF11...................159 M5
Fox Cl KBTN HD8.....................217 M8
Fox Ct GTL/HWG HX4................168 F7
Fox Covert Rd or
  Whin Covert La
  PONT WF8............................227 G4
Foxcroft Cl CUL/QBY BD13..........124 E1
  HDGY LS6............................108 D1

Foxcroft Dr BRIG HD6................170 B5
Foxcroft Gn HDGY LS6...............108 D1
Foxcroft Mt HDGY LS6...............108 D1
Foxcroft Rd HDGY LS6...............108 D1
Foxcroft St LIT OL15.................207 H1
Foxcroft Wk HDGY LS6...............108 D1
Foxcroft Wy HDGY LS6...............108 D1
Foxen La RPDN/SBR HX6............166 E8
Foxfields STKB/PEN S36.............271 J5
Foxfield Wk BSLY S70................261 M8
Foxglove Av RHAY LS8.................88 E8
Foxglove Folly
  WKFDW/WTN WF2.................176 A6
Foxglove Rd BTLY WF17.............151 G4
  HUDE HD5...........................215 C2
Fox Heads La PBR HG3................28 C6
Fox Hl ROY/SHW OL2...............229 G6
Foxhill BAIL BD17......................82 C3
  WBY LS22.............................30 A8
Foxhill Av BHP/TINH LS16...........86 F5
  CUL/QBY BD13......................124 F5
Foxhill Cl CUL/QBY BD13............124 F5
Foxhill Crs BHP/TINH LS16...........86 F5
Foxhill Dr BHP/TINH LS16............86 F5
  CUL/QBY BD13......................124 F5
Foxhill Gv BHP/TINH LS16............86 F5
  CUL/QBY BD13......................124 F5
The Foxhills BHP/TINH LS16.........85 M2
Foxhole La PDSY/CALV LS28.........84 D8
Foxholes Cl WHIT OL12.............206 D8
Foxholes Crs PDSY/CALV LS28.....84 M8
Foxholes La NORM WF6.............178 B1
Foxholes Rd WHIT OL12.............206 C4
Foxhunters Wy
  HEM/SK/SE WF9.....................247 H5
Fox La CFTH/SHER LS25.............139 K4
  HOR/CROF WF4.....................198 B2
  WKFDW/WTN WF2.................176 C5
Foxlow Av HUDE HD5................193 G6
Foxroyd Cl BSLYN/ROY S71.........262 B6
Fox Royd Dr MIRF WF14............172 B6
Foxroyd La EARL WF12..............195 J3
Fox Royd La MIRF WF14.............172 B6
Foxstone Ri BAIL BD17................83 G3
Foxstones La RPDN/SBR HX6......188 E4
Fox St BGLY BD16......................81 H3
  BTLY WF17...........................173 K2
  CLECK BD19.........................149 K7
  HUD HD1.............................14 F7
  MILN OL16...........................206 D6
  NORM WF6...........................178 D3
  WBOW BD5 *........................126 E3
Fox Ter PONT WF8....................181 G4
Foxton Gdns MOR LS27..............152 B3
Fox Vw DEWS WF13.................173 J4
Fox Wy MID LS10........................9 M6
Fox Wood Av RHAY LS8..............111 G1
Fox Wood Gv RHAY LS8..............111 G1
Foxwood Farm Wy RHAY LS8.......111 G1
Fox Wood Ri RHAY LS8...............111 G1
Fox Wood Wk WBY LS22..............30 A7
Foxwood Wk WBY LS22................30 A7
Frain Cl PONT WF8...................181 G7
Fraisthorpe Md ECHL BD2..........105 M4
France Fold HOLM/MEL HD9.......236 D1
Frances Rd EARL WF12..............174 D7
Frances St AIRE BD20.................35 K4
  BRIG HD6............................170 C3
  MILN OL16...........................206 F3
  PDSY/CALV LS28....................106 F4
France St BTLY WF17.................174 A2
Francis Av HUDW HD3 *.............213 L1
Francis Cl HFAX HX1...................10 D1
Francis Gv BEE/HOL LS11...........131 K3
Francis Rd HOR/CROF WF4.........200 D3
Francis St BOW BD4....................5 J9
  CAS WF10...........................158 A6
  CHAL LS7 *............................7 L1
  FEA/AMT WF7.......................223 M1
  HECK WF16..........................173 G3
  HFAX HX1.............................10 D7
  HUDS HD4...........................213 J2
  MIRF WF14..........................194 B1
Francis Vw MIRF WF14..............194 B1
Francus Rd BSLYN/ROY S71........243 L5
Frank Cl EARL WF12.................196 A4
Frank La EARL WF12.................196 A4
  KBTN HD8...........................239 L1
  LUD/ILL HX2........................144 D4
Franklin St HFAX HX1................10 B6
  MILN OL16...........................228 D1
Frank Peel Cl HECK WF16...........172 F2
Frank Pl GTHN BD7..................126 D2
Frank St GTHN BD7..................126 D2
  HFAX HX1.............................10 C7
Fraser Av HORS LS18..................85 J3
Fraser Rd PDSY/CALV LS28..........84 B8
Fraser St GIR BD8.......................4 B3
  MILN OL16...........................228 D2
  OSM LS9.............................110 D5
  ROY/SHW OL2.......................229 H7
Freakfield La LVSG WF15............171 K4
Frederick Av BSLY S70...............260 D6
  OSM LS9.............................110 C8
  WKFDE WF1...........................13 L9
Frederick Cl IDLE BD10...............83 H5
Frederick St HUDS HD4.............213 L2
  KGHY BD21.............................3 K4
  LIT OL15.............................185 L3
  LVSG WF15...........................172 B5
  PDSY/CALV LS28....................106 F3
  WKFDE WF1..........................12 F2
Frederic Pl BSLY S70..................261 H7
Fred's Pl BOW BD4...................127 L3
Fred St KGHY BD21.....................2 A8
Freeholds St ROCH OL11............228 A1
Freehold St ROCH OL11.............228 A1
Freely Flds BSPA/BRAM LS23.......69 M4
Freely La BSPA/BRAM LS23..........69 M4
Freeman Rd HIPP HX3...............169 H1
Freeman St BSLY S70.................261 H6
Freemans Wy WBY LS22..............30 B8
Freemans St BRAM LS13............107 J4
Freemans Wy BSLY S70..............261 H5
Free School La HFAX HX1............168 D1
Freeston Dr NORM WF6.............178 D3
Freeston Dr NORM WF6 *...........178 D3
Freestone Ms WOR/ARM LS12......107 L7
Freetown St WOR/ARM LS12 *......178 A2
Freetrade St ROCH OL11............228 A1
Freeway Dr CAS WF10...............178 F1
Fremantle Gv BOW BD4.............128 A4
Fremantle Pl MSTN/BAR LS15......111 G7
French St MSTN/BAR LS15...........111 G7
  AWLS/ASK DN6.....................249 J5
Frensham Av MOR LS27.............152 B3
Frensham Dr CAS WF10..............158 F8
  GTHN BD7...........................125 M3
Frensham Gv GTHN BD7.............125 M4
Frensham Wy GTHN BD7............125 M3
Freshfield Gdns WIL/AL BD15......103 K5

Fresh Mdw NORM WF6 ...178 E5
Freston Av WKFDE WF1 ...177 M8
Friar Ct IDLE BD10 ...83 L8
Friar Pl HUDN HD2 ...193 H1
Friar's Cl FEA/AMT WF7 ...201 L2
Friars Crs ROCH OL11 ...228 B4
Friars Nook PONT ...181 G7
Friar's Rd BSLYN/ROY S71 ...262 A3
Friarwood La PONT WF8 ...180 F6
Frickley Bridge La CUD/GR S72 ...245 G2
Frickley La BTLY OL15 ...247 H8
Friedhurst Rd TOD OL14 ...140 E5
Friendly Av RPDN/SBR HX6 ...167 J1
Friendly Fold Rd HIPP HX3 ...146 C4
Friendly St CUL/QBY BD13 ...102 F8
  HIPP HX3 ...146 C4
  HUD HD1 ...15 G5
Frieston WHIT OL12 * ...206 B6
Frimley Dr WBOW BD5 ...126 E4
Frith St HWTH BD22 ...79 G6
Frizinghall Rd HTON BD9 ...104 E3
Frizley Gdns HTON BD9 ...104 E3
Frobisher Gv WKFDW/WTN WF2 * ...198 A1
Frobisher Rd LIT OL15 ...185 L5
Frodingham Vis ECHL BD2 ...105 M4
Frogmoor Av LM/WK BD12 * ...149 H1
Frontline Cl RHAY LS8 ...88 C3
Front Rw BEE/HOL LS11 ...8 E3
Front St BEE/HOL LS11 ...8 E3
  BSPA/BRAM LS23 ...69 L3
  CAS WF10 ...158 B8
  PONT ...180 E6
Frost Hl LVSG WF15 ...172 D2
Fruit St KGHY BD21 ...3 L3
Fryergate WKFDW/WTN WF2 ...176 B7
Fryston Common La
  GFTH/SHER LS25 ...138 C5
Fryston La KNOT WF11 ...159 J7
Fryston Rd CAS WF10 ...158 D8
Fuchsia Cft RTHW LS26 ...134 A8
Fulford Av HUDN HD2 ...192 C4
Fulford Cl NORM WF6 ...178 C4
Fulford St CAS WF10 ...157 L7
Fulford Wk ECHL BD2 ...105 M4
Fulham St AWLS/ASK DN6 ...205 L3
Fulham Pl BEE/HOL LS11 ...8 E9
Fulham St BEE/HOL LS11 ...8 E9
Fullerton Cl AWLS/ASK DN6 ...249 H4
Fullerton St BFDE BD3 ...5 J7
Fullshaw Wk STKB/PEN S36 ...269 K7
Fulmar Ct MID LS10 ...153 M1
Fulmar Ms GIR BD8 * ...103 L7
Fulmar Rd CAS WF10 ...157 L8
Fulmer Cl BSLYN/ROY S71 ...243 K8
Fulneck PDSY/CALV LS28 ...129 G1
Fulneck Cl HUDN HD2 ...192 B3
Fulstone Hall La
  HOLM/MEL HD9 ...237 J2
Fulstone Rd KBTN HD8 ...237 L5
Fulton Pl BHP/TINH LS16 ...86 E7
Fulton St BFD BD1 ...4 D6
Fulwood Gv WKFDW/WTN WF2 ...220 D1
Furnace Gv LM/WK BD12 ...149 H1
Furnace Inn St BOW BD4 ...127 M1
Furnace Rd BIRK/DRI BD11 ...128 C8
Furnace Rd BOW BD4 ...127 J8
  LM/WK BD12 ...149 H1
Furnbrook Gdns HUDE HD5 ...193 L7
Furness Av LIT OL15 ...185 J8
  LUD/ILL HX2 ...146 A2
  WKFDW/WTN WF2 ...176 A4
Furness Cl MILN OL16 ...207 G8
Furness Crs LUD/ILL HX2 ...146 A2
Furness Dene BSLYN/ROY S71 ...261 M1
Furness Dr LUD/ILL HX2 ...145 M2
  WKFDW/WTN WF2 ...176 A4
Furness Gdns LUD/ILL HX2 ...146 A2
Furness Gv LUD/ILL HX2 ...145 M2
Further Heights Rd WHIT OL12 ...206 A4
Furzegate WHIT OL12 ...228 C5
Fusden La CLECK BD19 ...150 C5
Fyfe Crs BAIL BD17 ...82 F4
Fyfe Gv BAIL BD17 ...83 G4
Fyfe La BAIL BD17 ...83 G4
Fylde Cl BSLYN/ROY S71 ...243 M8

G

Gables Cl GLE DN14 ...161 K7
The Gables BAIL BD17 ...83 G3
  HORS LS18 ...85 L4
  HWTH BD22 ...2 D5
The Gabriels ROY/SHW OL2 ...229 H7
Gadding Moor Rd
  STKB/PEN S36 ...258 B6
Gagewell Dr HOR/CROF WF4 ...197 K4
Gagewell La HOR/CROF WF4 ...197 K4
Gagewell Vw HOR/CROF WF4 ...197 K4
Gainest LUD/ILL HX2 ...168 D1
Gainford Dr GFTH/SHER LS25 ...113 H8
Gain La BFDE BD3 ...105 M5
Gainsborough Av
  BHP/TINH LS16 ...86 D1
Gainsborough Cl BFDE BD3 ...105 J4
Gainsborough Ct
  SKP/WHF BD23 ...16 A2
Gainsborough Dr
  BHP/TINH LS16 ...86 D1
  ROCH OL11 ...228 A3
Gainsborough Wy
  BSLYN/ROY S71 ...261 K3
  EARD/LOFT WF3 ...177 L7
Gaisby La ECHL BD2 ...104 E2
Gaisby Mt SHPY BD18 ...104 F1
Gaisby Pl SHPY BD18 ...82 F8
Gaisby Ri SHPY BD18 ...82 F8
Gaitskell Ct BEE/HOL LS11 ...8 D6
Gaitskell Gra BEE/HOL LS11 ...8 D6
Gaitskell Wk BEE/HOL LS11 ...8 D6
Gatefield Gn WBSY BD6 ...126 B8
Gale Ct OT LS21 ...24 E7
Gales Ter ROCH OL11 ...228 A1
Gale St KGHY BD21 ...3 G1
  WHIT OL12 ...206 B3
Gall La TOD OL14 ...140 C4
Gallogate La AL/HA/HU LS17 ...44 B4
Gallon Cft HEM/SK/SE WF9 ...247 G3
Galloway Ct PDSY/CALV LS28 ...106 C5
Galloway La PDSY/CALV LS28 ...106 C5
Galloway Rd IDLE BD10 ...83 M7
Galloway St HUD HD1 ...15 H3
Gallows Hl CAS WF10 ...158 C7
  OT LS21 ...41 L6
Gallows La HOR/CROF WF4 ...220 D4
Galpharm Wy DOD/DAR S75 ...260 A6
Galsworthy Av HTON BD9 ...103 M3
Galway St BSLYN/ROY S71 ...243 L2
Gamble Hl BRAM LS13 ...107 M6
Gamble Hill Cl BRAM LS13 ...107 M6
Gamble Hill Dr BRAM LS13 ...107 M6
Gamble Hill Gn BRAM LS13 ...107 M6

Gamble Hill Lawn BRAM LS13 ...107 M6
Gamble Hill Pl BRAM LS13 ...107 M6
Gamble Hill Ri BRAM LS13 ...107 M6
Gamble Hill Vw BRAM LS13 ...107 M6
Gamel Vw SEL YO8 ...139 M4
The Gang WOR/ARM LS12 ...108 E6
Ganners Cl BRAM LS13 ...107 L2
Ganners Gn BRAM LS13 ...107 L2
Ganners Gv BRAM LS13 * ...107 L2
Ganners Hl BRAM LS13 ...107 M2
Ganners La BRAM LS13 ...107 L2
Ganners Mt BRAM LS13 ...107 L2
Ganners Ri BRAM LS13 ...107 M2
Ganners Rd BRAM LS13 ...107 L2
Ganners Wk BRAM LS13 ...107 L2
Ganners Wy BRAM LS13 ...107 L2
Gannerthorpe Cl LM/WK BD12 ...148 E3
Gannet Cl CAS WF10 ...157 L8
Ganny Rd BRIG HD6 ...170 D4
Ganton Cl HDGY LS6 ...6 F1
Ganton Pl BSLYN/ROY S71 ...243 G7
Ganton Wy HUDN HD2 ...192 B3
Gaol La HFAX HX1 ...11 H5
Garden Av CLECK BD19 ...150 C8
Garden Cl AIRE BD20 ...34 D8
  CLECK BD19 ...172 C1
  GFTH/SHER LS25 ...115 M7
  LIT OL15 ...207 H4
  LM/WK BD12 ...148 E2
  OSS WF5 ...197 G5
Garden Ct BSLY S70 ...260 D5
Garden Dr DEWS WF13 ...173 G8
Gardeners Ct MID LS10 ...9 K8
Gardener's Sq HIPP HX3 ...147 L6
Garden Fld LM/WK BD12 ...148 E3
Garden Fold HX3 ...147 L6
Garden House Cl
  BSLYN/ROY S71 ...261 L1
  RTHW LS26 ...156 F3
Garden House La
  EARD/LOFT WF3 ...153 J6
Garden La GFTH/SHER LS25 ...115 M7
  HTON BD9 ...104 B3
  KNOT WF11 ...182 C1
  MILN OL16 ...206 C6
Garden Pde CLECK BD19 ...150 C8
Garden Pl DEWS WF13 ...173 H5
Garden Rd BRIG HD6 ...170 C8
Gardens Rd DEWS WF13 ...173 G8
Gardens St HTON BD9 ...104 C2
The Gardens BGLY BD16 ...81 M3
  HFAX HX1 ...168 E1
  MID LS10 ...153 L2
  MOR LS27 ...152 B4
  PDSY/CALV LS28 ...106 C3
Garden St BSLY S70 ...261 H6
  CAS WF10 ...157 M8
  DEWS WF13 ...172 C1
  FEA/AMT WF7 ...223 M1
  HECK WF16 * ...172 F3
  HUD HD1 ...214 B2
  HWTH BD22 ...229 H6
  MILN OL16 ...229 H6
  NORM WF6 ...178 A3
  TOD OL14 ...141 H7
Garden St North HIPP HX3 * ...12 D4
Garden Ter DEWS WF13 ...173 J4
  HBR HX7 ...143 J3
  HOR/CROF WF4 ...220 A7
  HTON BD9 ...104 C3
  ROY/SHW OL2 ...228 E7
Garden Vw BGLY BD16 ...81 J3
  CLECK BD19 ...150 C8
Garden Village
  GFTH/SHER LS25 ...114 C7
Garden Wk CLECK BD19 ...172 C1
Garden Wy LIT OL15 ...207 H4
Gardiner Rw BOW BD4 ...127 K4
Gare Forth Av BSPA/BRAM LS23 ...35 L8
Garfield Av GIR BD8 ...104 D4
Garfield Pl MAR/SLWT HD7 ...212 F1
Garfield St HIPP HX3 * ...10 D1
  TOD OL14 ...140 E5
  WIL/AL BD15 ...103 J5
Garfit Hl BTLY WF17 ...150 F6
Garforth Cl NORM WF6 ...178 A7
Garforth Ct MIRF WF14 ...172 C7
Garforth Dr WKFDE WF1 ...178 A3
Garforth Rd KGHY BD21 ...3 M2
Garforth St HUDS HD4 ...213 L7
  WIL/AL BD15 ...103 K5
Garnet Av BEE/HOL LS11 ...131 L3
Garnet Crs BEE/HOL LS11 ...131 L3
Garnet Gv BEE/HOL LS11 ...131 L3
Garnet La TAD LS24 ...71 H6
Garnet Pde BEE/HOL LS11 * ...131 L3
Garnet Pl BEE/HOL LS11 ...131 L3
Garnet Rd BEE/HOL LS11 ...131 L4
Garnet Ter BEE/HOL LS11 ...131 L4
Garnett St BFDE BD3 ...5 H7
  DEWS WF13 ...173 H3
  HBR HX7 ...143 J3
  OT LS21 ...41 J6
Garnet Vw BEE/HOL LS11 ...131 L3
Garret Gv ROY/SHW OL2 ...229 H4
Garret Ct KBTN HD8 ...239 H4
Garsdale Av IDLE BD10 ...83 L7
Garsdale Crs BAIL BD17 ...83 G2
Garsdale Fold WBY LS22 ...47 J5
Garsdale Wk KNOT WF11 ...182 A4
Garth AL/HA/HU LS17 ...87 K5
  NORM WF6 ...178 C6
  WBY LS22 ...47 K6
Garth Barn Cl HTON BD9 ...104 C5
Garth Cl SEL YO8 ...139 M4
Garth Dr AL/HA/HU LS17 ...87 K5
  SEL YO8 ...139 M4
Garth End WBY LS22 ...47 K6
Garth Gv AIRE BD20 ...34 D4
Garth Land Wy BOW BD4 ...127 L2
Garth La SEL YO8 ...139 M4
Garth Mt GLE DN14 ...161 J7
Garth Rd AL/HA/HU LS17 ...87 K5
  SEL YO8 ...139 M4

Garth St CAS WF10 ...157 L8
  KGHY BD21 ...2 D5
The Garth GFTH/SHER LS25 ...113 J7
  OSM LS9 ...9 J1
  WBY LS22 ...47 K6
Garth Vw SEL YO8 ...139 M4
Garthwaite Mt WIL/AL BD15 ...103 K4
Garth Wk AL/HA/HU LS17 ...87 K5
Garth Willow BULY LS4 ...109 G5
Garth Willow Av SCFT LS14 ...89 K6
Garton Av OSM LS9 ...110 C7
Garton Gv OSM LS9 ...110 C7
Garton Rd OSM LS9 ...110 C7
Garton Ter OSM LS9 ...110 C7
Garton Vw OSM LS9 ...110 C7
Garvey Vw WBOW BD5 ...127 G2
Garwick Ter GTL/HWG HX4 ...168 F7
Gascoigne Av MSTN/BAR LS15 ...90 F8
Gascoigne Ct MSTN/BAR LS15 ...90 F8
Gascoigne Rd EARD/LOFT WF3 ...154 A5
  MSTN/BAR LS15 ...90 F8
Gascoigne Vw MSTN/BAR LS15 ...90 F8
Gashouse La WBY LS22 ...48 A1
Gaskell Cl LIT OL15 * ...185 J8
Gaskell Dr HOR/CROF WF4 ...197 J4
Gaskell St WKFDW/WTN WF2 ...12 A1
Gasson St HUDS HD4 ...213 J2
Gas St HWTH BD22 * ...78 F7
  ROCH OL11 ...206 A7
  SKP/WHF BD23 ...16 B3
Gas Works La BSPA/BRAM LS23 ...49 H7
  ELL HX5 ...169 H7
Gas Works Rd KGHY BD21 ...3 K6
  RPDN/SBR HX6 ...167 M2
Gasworks St HUD HD1 ...15 H5
  LVSG WF15 ...172 D2
Gate Crs DOD/DAR S75 ...260 D6
Gatefield Mt LM/WK BD12 ...126 D8
Gate Foot La KBTN HD8 ...237 L5
Gate Head MAR/SLWT HD7 ...233 J2
Gatehead Bank MAR/SLWT HD7 ...233 K1
Gate Head La GTL/HWG HX4 ...168 B8
  HOLM/MEL HD9 ...255 J6
Gatehouse LIT OL15 * ...185 M8
Gate House Cft RTHW LS26 ...133 M7
Gateland Dr AL/HA/HU LS17 ...89 G3
Gateland La AL/HA/HU LS17 ...89 G3
Gateon House La
  AL/HA/HU LS17 ...67 J2
Gatesgarth Crs HUDN HD3 ...191 J5
Gate St ROCH OL11 ...228 B1
Gateway WKFDE WF1 ...176 E1
The Gateways LM/WK BD12 ...148 E1
Gathorne Cl RHAY LS8 ...7 M1
Gathorne St BRIG HD6 ...170 D3
  GTHN BD7 ...126 D2
  RHAY LS8 ...7 M1
Gathorne Ter RHAY LS8 ...7 M1
Gaukroger La HFAX HX1 ...11 J9
Gauk St KNOT WF11 ...159 J2
  KNOT WF11 ...159 L6
Gavin Cl BFDE BD3 ...106 A7
Gawber Rd DOD/DAR S75 ...260 D6
Gawsworth Cl ROY/SHW OL2 ...229 H7
Gawthorpe Dr BGLY BD16 ...81 H1
Gawthorpe Green La
  HUDE HD5 ...194 A8
Gawthorpe La KBTN HD8 ...215 M1
  OSS WF5 ...174 F5
  WKFDW/WTN WF2 ...175 J4
Gawthorpe St WIL/AL BD15 ...80 D8
Gay La OT LS21 ...41 J7
  TAD LS24 ...95 H8
Gayle Cl LM/WK BD12 ...148 E4
Gayle Ct BSLY S70 ...260 F4
Gaynor St BFD BD1 ...4 A4
Gaythorne Rd ECHL BD2 ...105 L4
  WBOW BD5 ...127 G3
Gaythorne Ter CLAY BD14 ...125 J2
Gaython Ter HIPP HX3 ...147 L5
Geary Cl WKFDW/WTN WF2 ...175 M4
Geary Dr WKFDW/WTN WF2 ...175 M6
Geecroft La WBY LS22 ...46 E1
Geelong Cl ECHL BD2 ...105 H3
Gelder Cl WKFDW/WTN WF2 ...175 M6
Gelder Cft WKFDW/WTN WF2 * ...175 M6
Gelderd La WOR/ARM LS12 ...130 F2
Gelderd Pl WOR/ARM LS12 ...130 F2
Gelderd Pl BEE/HOL LS11 ...8 A4
Gelderd Rd BEE/HOL LS11 ...130 F3
  BTLY WF17 ...151 H4
  MOR LS27 ...130 A7
  MOR LS27 ...130 D5
Gelder Rd WOR/ARM LS12 ...108 D7
Gelder Ter HUDE HD5 ...15 K9
Geneva Gv WKFDE WF1 ...176 E1
Genista Dr MID LS10 ...131 M6
Genn La BSLY S70 ...260 F8
Genoa St DOD/DAR S73 ...263 G7
Gentian Cl WKFDW/WTN WF2 ...176 A7
George A Green Rd
  WKFDW/WTN WF2 ...198 A2
George Av HUDN HD2 ...14 B2
George Buckley Ct
  HEM/SK/SE WF9 ...246 C4
George & Crown Yd
  WKFDE WF1 ...12 E2
George La HOR/CROF WF4 ...221 G8
  RPDN/SBR HX6 ...188 D4
George Mann Rd MID LS10 ...132 C3
George Mann Wy MID LS10 ...132 B3
George Sq BSLY S70 ...261 G5
  HFAX HX1 ...11 G6
George's Sq CUL/QBY BD13 ...79 M8
  KGHY BD21 ...2 F1
George's St LUD/ILL HX2 ...146 B3
George St AWLS/ASK DN6 ...249 K4
  BAIL BD17 * ...82 E5
  BFD BD1 ...5 H7
  BRIG HD6 ...170 C5
  BSLY S70 ...261 J5
  BTLY WF17 ...173 L2
  CLECK BD19 ...149 M6
  CUD/GR S72 ...222 F8
  CUD/GR S72 ...244 E6
  CUL/QBY BD13 * ...102 A5
  CUL/QBY BD13 ...102 F8
  DEWS WF13 ...173 G4
  DEWS WF13 ...195 G5
  DOD/DAR S75 ...260 D5

  ILK LS29 ...19 H6
  LDS LS1 ...7 H9
  LIT OL15 * ...207 K1
  LVSG WF15 ...172 C2
  MILN OL16 ...206 C6
  MILN OL16 ...206 C6
  NORM WF6 ...178 B3
  OSS WF5 ...174 C7
  ROY/SHW OL2 ...229 L6
  RPDN/SBR HX6 ...167 K2
  SHPY BD18 ...82 B6
  SKP/WHF BD23 ...16 C5
  TOD OL14 ...163 K1
  WKFDE WF1 ...12 E3
  WKFDE WF1 ...176 D1
  YEA LS19 ...84 D2
George Yd BSLY S70 ...261 G5
Georgia Ms OSS WF5 ...197 G2
Gerald Cl BSLY S70 ...261 H6
Gerald Crs BSLY S70 ...261 M6
Gerald Pl BSLY S70 ...261 H6
Gerald Rd BSLY S70 ...261 L7
Geraldton Av ECHL BD2 ...105 G3
Gerald Wk BSLY S70 ...261 M6
Gervase Rd HOR/CROF WF4 ...197 J5
Gernhill Av HUDN HD2 ...192 B1
Gerrard St HFAX HX1 ...10 E6
  ROCH OL11 ...228 C5
Ghyllbank AIRE BD20 ...36 A4
Ghyll Beck Dr OT LS21 ...40 F8
  YEA LS19 ...85 G3
Ghyll Cl AIRE BD20 ...56 E1
Ghyll Dr HWTH BD22 ...78 E8
Ghyll Mt YEA LS19 ...85 G3
Ghyll Rd HDGY LS6 ...86 C8
Ghyll Royd GSLY LS20 ...62 A7
  ILK LS29 ...38 B2
Ghyllroyd Av BIRK/DRI BD11 ...150 A1
Ghyllroyd Dr BIRK/DRI BD11 ...150 A1
The Ghyll BGLY BD16 ...81 J6
  MID LS10 ...192 C2
Ghyll Wd ILK LS29 ...38 A3
Ghyll Wood Dr BGLY BD16 ...81 J6
Gib St HFAX HX1 ...146 A8
Gibb La LUD/ILL HX2 ...145 K3
Gibb St HWTH BD22 ...54 E8
Gib La BFDE BD3 ...239 J4
Gibraltar Av HFAX HX1 ...146 A8
Gibraltar Island Rd MID LS10 ...132 B2
Gibraltar Rd HFAX HX1 ...146 A7
  PDSY/CALV LS28 ...106 C7
Gibriding La HOLM/MEL HD9 ...253 H1
Gibside La AIRE BD20 ...34 B4
Gibson Av WKFDW/WTN WF2 ...176 B1
Gibson Dr MSTN/BAR LS15 ...111 J7
Gibson La GFTH/SHER LS25 ...135 K5
Gibson St BFDE BD3 ...5 M7
  HUDW HD3 ...191 H1
  MILN OL16 ...206 C6
  TOD OL14 ...163 K1
Gilbert Cha KSTL LS5 ...108 C3
Gilbert Cl KSTL LS5 ...108 C3
Gilbert Gv BSLY S70 ...261 M6
  HUDS HD4 ...213 M3
Gilbert Mt KSTL LS5 ...108 C3
Gilbert St BULY LS4 ...108 C3
Gilbert St PDSY/CALV LS28 * ...106 F4
Gilbrook Wy MILN OL16 ...228 D4
Gilcar St NORM WF6 ...178 F2
Gilcar Wy NORM WF6 ...178 E1
Gilderdale Cl ROY/SHW OL2 ...229 K6
Gildersome Cross MOR LS27 * ...129 L8
Gildersome La MOR LS27 ...129 K8
Gildersome Sp MOR LS27 ...151 M1
Gilead Rd HUDW HD3 ...191 G1
Giles Hill La HIPP HX3 ...125 K7
Giles St HOLM/MEL HD9 ...236 D5
  WBSY BD6 ...126 C5
Gillann St KNOT WF11 ...182 C2
Gill Bank Rd ILK LS29 ...20 C3
Gill Beck Cl BAIL BD17 ...83 G2
Gill Cl ILK LS29 ...18 F6
Gillemere Gv ROY/SHW OL2 ...229 L7
Gillett Dr RTHW LS26 ...155 H1
Gillett La RTHW LS26 ...155 H1
Gilling Av GFTH/SHER LS25 ...113 K6
Gillingham Gn BOW BD4 ...128 A3
Gillion Crs HOR/CROF WF4 ...220 A1
Gill La BAIL BD17 ...84 A2
  HOLM/MEL HD9 ...254 A4
  HWTH BD22 ...54 D1
  ILK LS29 ...19 L7
  WBY LS22 ...46 B3
Gillroyd La MAR/SLWT HD7 ...212 C2
Gillroyd Pl MOR LS27 ...152 B3
Gillroyd Ri GTHN BD7 ...104 D7
Gill's Buildings
  WKFDW/WTN WF2 ...176 B8
Gill St HFAX HX1 ...11 G6
Gill Sike Av WKFDW/WTN WF2 ...198 B2
Gill Sike Bungalows
  WKFDW/WTN WF2 ...198 B2
Gill Sike Gv WKFDW/WTN WF2 ...198 B2
Gill Sike Rd WKFDW/WTN WF2 ...198 B2
The Gills OT LS21 ...41 J4
Gillstone Dr HWTH BD22 ...78 F8
Gill St WKFDE WF1 ...12 E1
Gill's Yd WKFDE WF1 ...12 E1
Gillygate PONT WF8 ...180 F6
Gilmour St BFDE BD3 ...5 M5
Gilpin Pl WOR/ARM LS12 ...108 F8
Gilpin St BFDE BD3 ...5 M5
  WOR/ARM LS12 ...108 F8
Gilpin Ter WOR/ARM LS12 ...108 F8
Gilstead Ct BGLY BD16 ...81 L3
Gilstead Dr BGLY BD16 ...81 L3
Gilstead La BGLY BD16 ...81 L3
Gilstead Wy ILK LS29 ...38 D1
Gilthwaites Crs KBTN HD8 ...239 J8
Gilthwaites Gv KBTN HD8 ...239 J8
Gilthwaites La KBTN HD8 ...239 J7
Gilthwaites Top KBTN HD8 ...239 J7
Glynda Cl 104 A7
Gin La FEA/AMT WF7 ...200 F2
Gindhill La OT LS21 ...25 J1
The Ginnel AL/HA/HU LS17 ...67 L4
Gipsy La BEE/HOL LS11 ...131 J6
  DOD/DAR S75 ...242 B1
  RTHW LS26 ...133 K8
  WKFDW/WTN WF2 ...199 G3
Gipsy Md RTHW LS26 ...133 K8
Gipton Ap OSM LS9 ...110 C6
Gipton Av RHAY LS8 ...110 A3
Gipton Ga East OSM LS9 ...110 C5
Gipton Ga West RHAY LS8 ...110 C5
Gipton Sq OSM LS9 ...110 C5
Gipton St RHAY LS8 ...110 A5
Gipton Wood Av RHAY LS8 ...110 C3
Gipton Wood Crs RHAY LS8 ...110 C3
Gipton Wood Gv RHAY LS8 ...110 C3
Gipton Wood Pl RHAY LS8 ...110 C3
Gipton Wood Rd RHAY LS8 ...110 C3
Girlington Rd GIR BD8 ...104 C6

Girnhill La FEA/AMT WF7 ...201 L2
Gisbourne Rd HUDN HD2 ...193 G1
Gisburn Rd ROCH OL11 ...228 C3
  WKFDE WF1 ...177 H6
Gisburn St KGHY BD21 ...3 H5
Gissing Rd WKFDW/WTN WF2 ...197 M2
The Glade PDSY/CALV LS28 ...106 C4
  SCFT LS14 ...67 K7
Gladstone Av WKFDE WF1 ...177 H5
Gladstone Crs ROCH OL11 ...228 C3
Gladstone Rd HFAX HX1 * ...10 D5
  YEA LS19 ...84 D2
Gladstone St BFDE BD3 ...105 L8
  BGLY BD16 * ...81 H4
  CLECK BD19 ...149 M7
  CUL/QBY BD13 ...125 J5
  FEA/AMT WF7 ...179 M7
  GTL/HWG HX4 ...190 C2
  KGHY BD21 ...2 E6
  NORM WF6 ...178 B3
  PDSY/CALV LS28 ...106 E3
  SKP/WHF BD23 ...16 B2
  TOD OL14 ...140 D5
  WIL/AL BD15 ...103 K5
Gladstone Ter CAS WF10 ...158 A6
  MOR LS27 * ...152 C2
Gladstone Vw HIPP HX3 ...169 G3
Gladwin St BTLY WF17 ...173 K2
Glaisdale Cl AIRE BD20 ...36 A6
Glaisdale Ct WIL/AL BD15 ...103 J3
Glaisdale Gv HIPP HX3 ...147 M7
Glamis Cl GFTH/SHER LS25 ...113 K6
Glanville Ter WMB/B S73 ...155 G5
Glasshouse St MID LS10 ...9 K6
Glasshouse Vw MID LS10 ...153 K2
Glastonbury WHIT OL12 * ...206 A6
Glastonbury Dr HUDN HD3 ...213 H1
Glazier Rd CUL/QBY BD13 ...124 E4
Gleanings Av LUD/ILL HX2 ...145 L7
Gleanings Dr LUD/ILL HX2 ...145 K7
Glebe Av KSTL LS5 ...108 D2
Glebe Cl COP/BISH YO23 ...73 J7
  KBTN HD8 ...217 M7
Glebe Ct RTHW LS26 ...154 D1
Glebe Field Cha WBY LS22 ...29 M8
Glebe Field Cl WBY LS22 ...29 L8
Glebe Field Cft WBY LS22 ...29 M8
Glebe Field Dr WBY LS22 ...29 L8
Glebe Field Garth WBY LS22 ...29 L8
Glebe Field Holt WBY LS22 ...29 L8
Glebe Ga EARL WF12 ...196 A5
Glebelands Cl GFTH/SHER LS25 ...113 K8
Glebelands Dr HDGY LS6 ...86 F8
Glebe La KNOT WF11 ...182 B2
Glebe Mt PDSY/CALV LS28 ...107 G8
Glebe Pl KSTL LS5 ...108 D2
Glebe Rd AWLS/ASK DN6 ...227 M5
Glebe St CAS WF10 ...157 M7
  HUD HD1 ...14 A4
  NORM WF6 ...178 E4
  PDSY/CALV LS28 ...107 G8
  ROY/SHW OL2 ...229 M7
Glebe Ter HDGY LS6 ...86 F7
Gledcliffe HIPP HX3 ...11 H4
Gleddings Cl HIPP HX3 ...168 C3
Gledhill Av STKB/PEN S36 ...270 E6
Gledhill Cl ROY/SHW OL2 ...229 J5
Gledhill Rd BFDE BD3 ...5 M7
Gledhill St TOD OL14 ...141 H7
Gledhill Ter DEWS WF13 ...172 F1
Gledholt Bank HUD HD1 ...14 B7
Gledholt Rd HUD HD1 ...14 A5
Gledhow Av RHAY LS8 ...88 B6
Gledhow Dr HWTH BD22 ...100 A2
Gledhow Grange Vw RHAY LS8 ...88 B7
Gledhow Grange Wk RHAY LS8 ...88 B7
Gledhow La HDGY LS6 ...87 M7
  RHAY LS8 ...88 B7
Gledhow Mt RHAY LS8 ...7 M4
Gledhow Park Av RHAY LS8 ...88 A8
Gledhow Park Crs CHAL LS7 * ...88 A8
Gledhow Park Dr CHAL LS7 ...87 M8
Gledhow Park Gv CHAL LS7 ...88 A8
Gledhow Park Rd CHAL LS7 ...88 A8
Gledhow Park Vw CHAL LS7 ...88 A8
Gledhow Pl RHAY LS8 ...7 M4
Gledhow Ri RHAY LS8 ...88 B8
Gledhow Ter RHAY LS8 ...7 M4
Gledhow Towers RHAY LS8 * ...88 A7
Gledhow Vale Rd CHAL LS7 ...87 L6
  RHAY LS8 ...88 B8
Gledhow Valley Rd CHAL LS7 ...87 M6
Gledhow Wood Av RHAY LS8 ...88 B7
Gledhow Wood Cl RHAY LS8 ...88 B8
Gledhow Wood Ct RHAY LS8 ...110 C1
Gledhow Wood Gv RHAY LS8 ...88 B8
Gledhow Wood Rd RHAY LS8 ...88 B7
Glenaire SHPY BD18 ...83 G5
Glenaire Dr BAIL BD17 ...82 C5
Glen Av BTLY WF17 ...151 M8
Glenavon Dr ROY/SHW OL2 ...229 H6
Glenbrook Dr GTHN BD7 ...104 D7
Glencoe Cl GFTH/SHER LS25 ...135 H6
Glencoe Cft GFTH/SHER LS25 ...135 H6
Glencoe Gdns GFTH/SHER LS25 ...135 H6
Glencoe Ter GFTH/SHER LS25 ...135 H6
  LVSG WF15 ...172 D3
Glencoe Vw OSM LS9 ...10 B8
Glen Ct OT LS21 ...157 J8
Glen Dr BGLY BD16 ...81 H7
Glendale HOR/CROF WF4 ...197 H5
Glendale Cl DOD/DAR S75 ...260 D5
  WBSY BD6 ...126 C7
Glendale Dr WBSY BD6 ...126 C7
Glendare Av GTHN BD7 ...104 B8
Glendare Rd GTHN BD7 ...104 B8
Glendare Ter GTHN BD7 ...104 B8
Glen Dene BGLY BD16 ...81 H7
  EARL WF12 * ...174 B6
  ILK LS29 ...19 K2
Glendene Ct HUDW HD3 ...190 C5
Glendower Pk BHP/TINH LS16 ...86 D1
Gleneagles Cl NORM WF6 ...178 C5
Gleneagles Ct NORM WF6 ...178 C5
Gleneagles Dr NORM WF6 ...178 C5
Gleneagles Rd AL/HA/HU LS17 ...87 K2
  FEA/AMT WF7 ...179 M5
Gleneagles Wy HUDN HD2 ...192 B3
Glenfield WBY LS22 ...29 M8
Glenfield Av WBSY BD6 ...126 F6
Glen Gdns WHIT OL12 ...206 B3
Glen Garth KGHY BD21 ...3 K9
Glen Gv MOR LS27 ...152 C3
Glenholme SHPY BD18 ...83 C5
Glenholme Heath HFAX HX1 ...146 A4
Glenholme Pk CLAY BD14 ...125 J3
Glenholme Rd GIR BD8 ...104 D5
  PDSY/CALV LS28 ...106 C4

Glenholm Rd BAIL BD17 .....82 E3
Glenhurst BOW BD4 .....127 M5
Glenhurst Av KGHY BD21 .....3 J9
Glenhurst Dr KGHY BD21 .....3 J8
Glenhurst Gv KGHY BD21 .....3 J8
Glenhurst Rd SHPY BD18 .....82 A6
Glenlea Cl BRAM LS13 .....107 J3
Glenlea Gdns BRAM LS13 .....107 J3
Glen Lee La KGHY BD21 .....79 M2
Glenlee Rd GTHN BD7 .....104 B8
Glenlow Rd BTLY WF17 .....174 B3
Glenlyon Av AIRE BD20 .....57 J5
Glenlyon Dr AIRE BD20 .....57 J5
Glenmere Mt YEA LS19 .....62 F7
Glenmoor Av BSLY S70 .....260 D6
Glenmore Ct ECHL BD2 .....105 L5
Glenmore Ct BHP/TINH LS16 .....64 A3
Glen Mt BGLY BD16 .....81 H7
  HIPP HX3 .....146 A3
  ILK LS29 .....61 K3
  MOR LS27 .....152 D3
Glen Mount Cl HIPP HX3 .....146 A4
Glenn Wy HOR/CROF WF4 .....200 C7
Glen Ri BAIL BD17 .....82 C4
Glen Rd BAIL BD17 .....81 M2
  BHP/TINH LS16 .....86 F7
  MOR LS27 .....152 D3
Glenrose Dr GTHN BD7 .....104 A8
Glenroyd SHPY BD18 .....83 C5
Glenroyd Av WBSY BD6 .....126 F5
Glenroyd Cl PDSY/CALV LS28 .....106 E7
Glensdale Est MOR LS27 .....152 E4
Glensdale Gv OSM LS9 .....110 C6
Glensdale Mt OSM LS9 .....110 B7
Glensdale Rd OSM LS9 .....110 B7
Glensdale St OSM LS9 .....110 B7
Glensdale Ter OSM LS9 .....110 B7
Glenside Av SHPY BD18 .....83 C5
Glenside Cl HUDW HD3 .....191 M6
Glen Side Rd MAR/SLWT HD7 .....212 C6
Glenside Rd SHPY BD18 .....83 H5
Glenstone Gv GTHN BD7 .....104 B7
Glen Ter HFAX HX1 .....168 D1
The Glen TOD OL14 .....141 J7
Glenthorpe Av OSM LS9 .....110 C6
Glenthorpe Crs OSM LS9 .....110 C6
Glenthorpe Ter OSM LS9 .....110 C6
Glenton Sq HTON BD9 .....104 C4
Glen Vw BGLY BD16 .....80 D5
  HFAX HX1 .....10 F9
Glenview Av HTON BD9 .....104 A3
Glenview Cl SHPY BD18 .....81 L7
Glenview Dr SHPY BD18 .....81 L8
Glenview Gv SHPY BD18 .....81 M7
Glen View Rd BGLY BD16 .....81 L1
  HBR HX7 .....143 G3
  KGHY HD8 .....238 C4
Glenview Rd SHPY BD18 .....81 M7
Glen Vw St TOD OL14 .....140 E5
Glenview Ter SHPY BD18 .....81 L8
Glen Wy BGLY BD16 .....59 L8
Glenwood Av BAIL BD17 .....82 A5
Global Av BEE/HOL LS11 .....131 G5
Globe Ct LVSG WF15 .....172 C4
Globe Fold GIR BD8 * 4 A3
Globe Rd WOR/ARM LS12 * 8 C2
Glossop Gv HDGY LS6 .....6 C1
Glossop Mt HDGY LS6 .....6 C1
Glossop St HDGY LS6 .....6 C1
Glossop Vw HDGY LS6 .....6 E1
Gloucester Av AIRE BD20 .....35 L5
  BFDE BD3 .....105 M5
  WHIT OL12 .....206 F2
Gloucester Ct
  WKFDW/WTN WF2 .....176 B3
  WOR/ARM LS12 * 109 G6
Gloucester Gv
  WKFDW/WTN WF2 .....197 M1
Gloucester Pl
  WKFDW/WTN WF2 .....197 M1
Gloucester Rd BGLY BD16 .....81 K4
  WKFDW/WTN WF2 .....197 L1
Gloucester Ter WOR/ARM LS12 .....109 G7
Glover Ct WBOW BD5 .....127 G2
Glovershaw La BAIL BD17 .....60 A8
Glover Wy BEE/HOL LS11 .....131 L4
Glydegate WBOW BD5 .....4 E7
Glyndon Ct BRIG HD6 .....170 D4
Glynn Ter GIR BD8 .....104 D6
Glynwed Ct BSLY/WHF BD23 .....16 A3
Gobind Marg BFDE BD3 .....5 J6
Godfrey Rd HIPP HX3 .....168 E4
Godfrey St GIR BD8 .....103 M7
Godley Branch Rd HIPP HX3 .....11 L4
Godley Gdns HIPP HX3 .....147 H5
Godley La HIPP HX3 .....11 K3
Godley Rd HIPP HX3 .....11 K4
Godley St BSLY/ROY S71 .....243 M2
Godly Cl RPDN/SBR HX6 .....188 E5
Godly La RPDN/SBR HX6 .....188 E5
Godwin St BFD BD1 .....4 E6
Goff Well La KGHY BD21 .....79 L4
Goit Side BFD BD1 .....4 C6
Goit Stock La BGLY BD16 .....80 D6
Goit Stock Ter BGLY BD16 .....80 D6
Goker Brow Rd
  HOLM/MEL HD9 .....234 D4
Goldbourne Dr ROY/SHW OL2 .....229 K6
Goldcrest Av GIR BD8 .....103 G7
Goldcrest Ct HUDS HD4 .....214 A7
Gold Cft BSLY S70 .....261 J6
Golden Butts Rd ILK LS29 .....38 E2
Golden Sq HOR/CROF WF4 .....197 K5
Golden St ROY/SHW OL2 .....230 A6
Golden Ter WOR/ARM LS12 .....130 C2
Golden View Dr KGHY BD21 .....58 B8
Goldfields Av GTL/HWG HX4 .....168 C6
Goldfields Cl GTL/HWG HX4 .....168 B6
Goldfields Dr GTL/HWG HX4 .....168 C6
Goldfields Wy GTL/HWG HX4 .....168 B6
Goldington Av HUDW HD3 .....191 H6
Goldington Dr HUDW HD3 .....191 H6
Goldsmith Dr EARD/LOFT WF3 .....154 D4
Gold St BSLY S70 .....261 J6
Goldthorpe Vls
  AWLS/ASK DN6 * 227 M3
Golf Av LUD/ILL HX2 .....145 L7
Golf Crs LUD/ILL HX2 .....145 L7
Golf La LUD/ILL HX2 .....152 A6
Golf Links Av TAD LS24 .....71 L4
Golf Links Rd TAD LS24 .....71 L4
Golf Links Crs TAD LS24 .....71 K4
Gomersal La CLECK BD19 .....150 C7
Gomersal Rd CLECK BD19 .....150 E8
Gondal Ct WBOW BD5 .....126 E3
Gooder Av BSLY/ROY S71 .....243 J3
Gooder La BRIG HD6 .....170 C6
Gooder St BRIG HD6 .....170 C4
Goodfellow Cl BGLY BD16 .....81 K8
Good Hope Cl NORM WF6 .....178 F3
Goodman St MID LS10 .....9 M6
Goodrich ROCH OL11 * 206 A8
Goodrick La AL/HA/HU LS17 .....65 K7
Good Shepherd La MILN OL16 .....206 K7
Goods La EARL WF12 .....173 M7
Goodwin Pl HUDN HD2 .....193 H1
Goodwin Rd WOR/ARM LS12 .....108 D8
Goodwood ILK LS29 .....20 D1
  MID LS10 .....153 M3

Goodwood Av GFTH/SHER LS25 .....135 H4
Goody Cross La RTHW LS26 .....134 D4
Goose Cote La KGHY BD21 .....3 G4
Goose Cote Wy HWTH BD22 .....79 G3
Goosedale Ct BOW BD4 .....128 C3
Goose Eye HWTH BD22 .....56 D8
Goosegate Ri GFTH/SHER LS25 .....134 F1
Goosegate LUD/ILL HX2 * 124 B8
Goose Gn HOLM/MEL HD9 .....254 C1
Goose Hi HECK WF16 .....172 F2
Goosehill La WKFDE WF1 .....178 A7
Goosehill Rd NORM WF6 .....178 C6
Goosehole La HEM/SK/SE WF9 .....247 K5
Goose La CSLY LS20 .....60 F5
  WHIT OL12 .....206 B8
Goose West La RPDN/SBR HX6 .....167 K4
Gordale Cl BTLY WF17 .....173 K1
Gordon Av OSS WF5 .....174 F1
Gordon Ct LIT OL15 .....185 K8
  MIRF WF14 .....172 E8
Gordon Dr HDGY LS6 .....87 G8
Gordon Pl HEM/SK/SE WF9 .....247 H5
Gordon St AIRE BD20 .....55 M1
  BSLY S70 .....262 A6
  CLAY BD14 * 125 K1
  COL BB8 .....74 A1
  EARD/LOFT WF3 .....154 A6
  ELL HX5 .....169 H8
  FEA/AMT WF7 .....179 M7
  HIPP HX3 .....146 D4
  HWTH BD22 * 79 G6
  ILK LS29 .....38 E2
  KGHY BD21 .....2 E4
  MAR/SLWT HD7 .....212 C6
  MILN OL16 .....229 K3
  ROCH OL11 .....228 C1
  ROY/SHW OL2 .....229 L7
  RPDN/SBR HX6 .....167 J3
  TOD OL14 * 163 L1
  WBOW BD5 .....5 G9
  WKFDE WF1 .....199 H4
Gordon Ter AIRE BD20 .....34 B3
  IDLE BD10 .....83 K5
  MAR/SLWT HD7 .....212 F4
Goring Park Av OSS WF5 .....197 J2
Gorrel St ROCH OL11 .....228 C1
Gorse La GFTH/SHER LS25 .....137 J1
Gorse Lea MID LS10 .....131 M6
Gorse Rd HUDW HD3 .....191 L8
  MILN OL16 .....207 H8
Gorsley Bank LIT OL15 .....185 L7
Gorston St HEM/SK/SE WF9 .....223 K5
Goschen St SKP/WHF BD23 * 16 D1
Gosport Cl HUDW HD3 .....190 C6
Gosport La GTL/HWG HX4 .....190 B5
Gosside Gv NORM WF6 .....178 E5
Gothic Mt FEA/AMT WF7 .....179 M6
Gothic St CUL/QBY BD13 .....125 G5
Gotts Park Av WOR/ARM LS12 .....108 B5
Gotts Park Crs WOR/ARM LS12 .....108 B5
Gotts Park Vw WOR/ARM LS12 .....108 B4
Gotts Rd WOR/ARM LS12 .....8 B1
Gott's Ter EARL WF12 .....57 J4
Gott St HWTH BD22 .....79 H6
Gough La RPDN/SBR HX6 .....166 D8
Goulbourne St KGHY BD21 .....2 E7
Governor's Yd WKFDE WF1 .....176 F7
Gowers St MILN OL16 .....206 D6
Gower St LDSU LS2 .....7 J8
  WBOW BD5 .....127 G2
Gracechurch St GIR BD8 * 4 A4
Grace Leather La BTLY WF17 .....174 A1
Grace St BSLY/ROY S71 .....244 B3
  KGHY BD21 .....3 K5
  LDS LS1 .....6 D9
  WHIT OL12 .....206 C4
Gracey La WBSY BD6 .....126 B5
Grafton Cl BAIL BD17 .....82 F2
  KNOT WF11 .....182 B1
Grafton Ct MILN OL16 * 206 D8
Grafton Pl HIPP HX3 .....146 C3
Grafton Rd KGHY BD21 .....2 C8
Grafton St BSLY S70 .....260 F5
  BTLY WF17 .....173 M3
  CAS WF10 .....158 A8
  CHAL LS7 .....7 H7
  KGHY BD21 .....2 E9
  MILN OL16 .....206 D8
  WBOW BD5 .....4 E9
Gragwood Cl HORS LS18 .....85 L7
Graham Av BULY LS4 .....108 F3
  HEM/SK/SE WF9 .....225 M6
Graham Dr CAS WF10 .....158 F3
Graham Gv BULY LS4 .....108 F3
Graham Mt BULY LS4 .....108 F3
Graham's Orch BSLY S70 .....261 G5
Graham St BULY LS4 .....108 F3
  HTON BD9 .....104 C4
Graham Ter BULY LS4 .....108 F3
Graham Wk MOR LS27 .....129 M7
Graingers Wy WOR/ARM LS12 .....8 C6
Grains Bd ROY/SHW OL2 .....229 J7
Grain St WBOW BD5 .....126 D3
Gramfield Rd HUDS HD4 .....213 K3
Grammar School St BFD BD1 .....4 E4
Grampian Av WKFDW/WTN WF2 .....198 A3
Grampian Cl DOD/DAR S75 .....260 D4
Grampian Wy ROY/SHW OL2 .....229 J6
  KBTN HD8 .....238 B3
Granary Ct ECHL BD2 .....105 L1
Granary Whf LDS LS1 * 8 F2
Granby Av HDGY LS6 .....108 F1
Granby Ct HEM/SK/SE WF9 .....247 J1
Granby Dr AIRE BD20 .....58 B5
Granby Flats HUD HD1 .....14 A8
Granby Gv HDGY LS6 .....108 F1
Granby La AIRE BD20 .....58 B5
Granby Mt HDGY LS6 .....108 F1
Granby Pl HDGY LS6 .....108 F1
Granby Rd HDGY LS6 .....108 F2
  HEM/SK/SE WF9 .....247 J1
Granby St BOW BD4 .....5 H9
  CUL/QBY BD13 .....125 G5
Granby Ter HDGY LS6 .....108 F1
Granby Vw HDGY LS6 .....108 F2
Grand Ar LDS LS1 * 7 H8
Grand Cross Rd HUDE HD5 .....193 G8
Grandidge St ROCH OL11 .....228 A1
Grandsmere Pl HIPP HX3 .....168 B1
Grand Stand MAR/SLWT HD7 .....212 D1
Grand Stand Rd
  EARD/LOFT WF3 .....176 D1
Grange Av BFDE BD3 .....106 B6
  BOW BD4 .....128 C6
  BSPA/BRAM LS23 .....49 J3
  CHAL LS7 * 7 L1
  GFTH/SHER LS25 .....113 H6
  HEM/SK/SE WF9 .....247 J3
  HUDN HD2 .....192 B5
  ILK LS29 .....38 F2
  ILK LS29 .....61 H1
  LUD/ILL HX2 .....146 B1
  MAR/SLWT HD7 .....233 J2
  MILN OL16 .....229 H2

  PBR HG3 .....28 E3
  SHPY BD18 .....82 A6
  TAD LS24 .....72 A2
  WIL/AL BD15 .....103 L6
  YEA LS19 .....62 E8
Grange Bank HIPP HX3 .....125 E3
Grange Bank La HUDE HD5 .....15 L4
Grange Br AIRE BD20 .....35 J6
Grange Cl AL/HA/HU LS17 .....67 M3
  CUD/GR S72 .....245 K1
  HEM/SK/SE WF9 .....225 C4
  HORS LS18 .....85 H6
  HUDW HD3 .....190 C6
  YEA LS19 .....62 F7
Grange Crs AIRE BD20 .....58 A5
  BSLY/ROY S71 .....262 A4
  CHAL LS7 .....7 L1
  TAD LS24 .....71 M2
  YEA LS19 .....62 E8
Grange Ct AL/HA/HU LS17 .....87 L1
  BGLY BD16 .....81 J7
  HIPP HX3 .....169 J3
  MSTN/BAR LS15 .....90 B8
Grange Dr AIRE BD20 .....58 A5
  BFDE BD3 .....106 B6
Grange Est ILK LS29 .....38 F2
Grange Farm Cl ILK LS29 .....61 H1
Grangefield Av BTLY WF17 .....173 J3
  ILK LS29 .....40 B5
Grange Field Pk MOR LS27 .....129 L8
Grangefield Rd
  PDSY/CALV LS28 .....107 G5
Grange Fields Mt MID LS10 .....132 B8
Grange Fields Rd MID LS10 .....132 B8
Grange Fields Wy MID LS10 .....132 B8
Grange Gv AIRE BD20 .....58 A5
  BFDE BD3 .....106 B6
Grange Hts HIPP HX3 .....169 J3
Grange Holt AL/HA/HU LS17 .....87 L1
Grange La AWLS/ASK DN6 .....249 J4
  BRIG HD6 .....171 G4
  BSLY/ROY S71 .....262 A5
  GFTH/SHER LS25 .....135 K4
  HOR/CROF WF4 .....217 M2
  HWTH BD22 .....78 B3
  KBTN HD8 .....237 M3
  UPML OL3 .....231 H8
Grange Mt YEA LS19 .....62 E8
Grange Pk BAIL BD17 .....82 D3
  HIPP HX3 .....168 D3
Grange Park Cl CAS WF10 .....157 J1
  MOR LS27 * 130 D7
  RHAY LS8 .....111 G1
Grange Park Ct MOR LS27 .....130 D7
Grange Park Crs RHAY LS8 .....110 F1
Grange Park Dr BGLY BD16 .....81 J6
  MOR LS27 .....130 D7
Grange Park Gv RHAY LS8 .....110 F1
Grange Park Ms MOR LS27 .....130 D7
Grange Park Pl RHAY LS8 .....111 G1
Grange Park Rd BGLY BD16 .....81 J6
  RHAY LS8 .....110 F1
Grange Park Ter RHAY LS8 .....111 G1
Grange Park Wy MOR LS27 * 130 D7
Grange Rd AIRE BD20 .....34 F5
  AIRE BD20 .....56 C1
  AIRE BD20 .....58 A5
  AWLS/ASK DN6 .....227 M5
  BGLY BD16 .....81 K2
  BSLY/ROY S71 .....243 J3
  BTLY WF17 .....173 J3
  BTLY WF17 .....174 A2
  CAS WF10 .....158 F5
  CLECK BD19 .....149 L6
  CUD/GR S72 .....245 H4
  HUDN HD3 .....191 G8
  ILK LS29 .....40 A5
  MID LS10 .....9 K7
  TAD LS24 .....72 A2
  WIL/AL BD15 .....103 L6
  YEA LS19 .....62 E8
The Grange Rd BHP/TINH LS16 .....86 D5
Grange St HIPP HX3 .....10 C1
  KGHY BD21 .....3 H3
  WKFDW/WTN WF2 .....12 A4
Grange Ter CHAL LS7 * 7 K1
  MAR/SLWT HD7 .....233 J2
  MOR LS27 .....130 D7
  PDSY/CALV LS28 .....107 G6
  SHPY BD18 .....82 D8
  WIL/AL BD15 .....103 L6
The Grange AWLS/ASK DN6 .....249 J4
  EARD/LOFT WF3 .....154 F3
  GFTH/SHER LS25 .....113 K7
Grange Valley Rd BTLY WF17 .....174 B2
Grange Vw BFDE BD3 * 106 B6
  CHAL LS7 .....7 K1
  EARL WF12 .....195 M5
  HEM/SK/SE WF9 .....223 M8
  MSTN/BAR LS15 .....111 M8
  OT LS21 .....39 J6
  PDSY/CALV LS28 .....107 G6
  TAD LS24 .....93 M2
Grange View Gdns
  AL/HA/HU LS17 .....89 H5
Grangeway GIR BD8 .....103 L6
  HEM/SK/SE WF9 .....223 M8
Grangewood Ct WKFDE WF1 .....176 F1
Grangewood Gdns
  BHP/TINH LS16 .....86 D5
Granham Acre CUD/GR S72 .....244 E4
Granhamthorpe BRAM LS13 .....107 L4
Granny Av MOR LS27 .....130 E6
Granny Hall Gv BRIG HD6 .....170 B2
Granny Hall La BRIG HD6 .....170 B2
Granny Hall Pk BRIG HD6 .....170 B2
Granny Hill Ter HFAX HX1 .....168 A1
Granny La MIRF WF14 .....194 D3
  WOR/ARM LS12 .....130 C1
Grant Av RHAY LS8 .....7 L4
Grantham Pl GTHN BD7 .....4 B9
  HIPP HX3 .....146 D4
Grantham Rd GTHN BD7 .....4 A9
  HIPP HX3 .....146 D4
Grantham Ter GTHN BD7 .....4 B9
Grantley Pl HUDN HD2 .....192 F1
Grantley St WKFDE WF1 .....13 G1
Grantley Wy WKFDE WF1 .....13 H1
Granton Rd CHAL LS7 .....87 G5
Granton St BFDE BD3 .....105 L7
Grant St BSLY S70 .....5 J5
  HWTH BD22 .....2 C5
Granville Av PONT WF8 * 180 C6
Granville Ct MILN OL16 .....229 K3
  OT LS21 .....41 H7
Granville Pl WIL/AL BD15 .....103 K5
Granville Rd HTON BD9 .....7 M6
  OSM LS9 .....10 D3
Granville St CAS WF10 .....179 L1
  CLAY BD14 .....125 L2
  COL BB8 .....74 A1

  DEWS WF13 .....173 K6
  DOD/DAR S75 .....260 F3
  ELL HX5 .....169 H8
  FEA/AMT WF7 .....201 L2
  KGHY BD21 .....3 J9
  LVSG WF15 .....172 D3
  NORM WF6 .....178 D4
  PDSY/CALV LS28 .....106 E6
  PDSY/CALV LS28 .....107 H4
  SKP/WHF BD23 .....16 A2
  TOD OL14 * 163 J3
Granville Ter BGLY BD16 .....81 J3
  HUD HD1 .....14 A9
  SHPY BD18 .....104 D1
  YEA LS19 .....62 F7
Grape St HFAX HX1 .....10 E6
  KGHY BD21 .....3 L5
  MID LS10 .....9 C1
  WIL/AL BD15 .....103 K5
Grasleigh Av WIL/AL BD15 .....103 J4
Grasleigh Wy WIL/AL BD15 .....103 J4
Grasmere Av WBY LS22 .....47 L1
Grasmere Cl CAS WF10 .....159 K3
  STKB/PEN S36 .....270 F2
  WOR/ARM LS12 .....108 F8
Grasmere Crs DOD/DAR S75 .....242 F3
Grasmere Dr ELL HX5 .....169 K7
  WBY LS22 .....47 L1
Grasmere Rd AWLS/ASK DN6 .....249 L5
  BSLY/ROY S71 .....261 J3
  EARL WF12 .....174 A4
  ECHL BD2 .....105 J3
  HOLM/MEL HD9 .....235 M3
  HUD HD1 .....14 A5
  LM/WK BD12 .....149 G3
  ROY/SHW OL2 .....228 F8
  WKFDW/WTN WF2 .....176 A7
  WOR/ARM LS12 .....108 F8
Grasmere St WHIT OL12 .....206 B5
Grasscroft HUDE HD5 .....215 H4
Grasscroft Ct HEM/SK/SE WF9 .....236 A2
Grasscroft Rd HOLM/MEL HD9 .....236 A2
  HUD HD1 .....191 M7
Grassington Rd
  SKP/WHF BD23 .....16 B3
Gratrix La RPDN/SBR HX6 .....167 L2
Grattan Rd BFD BD1 .....4 D6
Gravelleythorpe Ri
  MSTN/BAR LS15 .....111 K5
Gravelleythorpe Rd
  MSTN/BAR LS15 .....111 K5
Gravelly Hill La AL/HA/HU LS17 .....43 J1
Gray Av SHPY BD18 .....104 F1
Gray Ct MSTN/BAR LS15 * 111 M6
Gray Hall Cl GTL/HWG HX4 * 190 B3
Grayrigg Cl MSTN/BAR LS15 .....111 G7
Grayrigg Dr MSTN/BAR LS15 .....110 F7
Grayshon Dr WBSY BD6 .....126 E5
Grayshon St BIRK/DRI BD11 .....151 G1
Grayson Crest BULY LS4 .....108 D3
Grayson Hts BULY LS4 .....108 D3
Gray's Rd BSLY/ROY S71 .....243 L5
Gray St LVSG WF15 .....172 A2
Graywood Crs BOW BD4 .....127 M3
Graywood Dr BOW BD4 .....127 M2
Great Albion St HFAX HX1 .....11 H5
Great Ben La MAR/SLWT HD7 .....212 A4
Great Bent Cl WHIT OL12 .....206 V4
Great Cliffe Rd DOD/DAR S75 .....260 A6
Great Cross St BFD BD1 .....5 G7
Great Edge Rd LUD/ILL HX2 .....145 H8
Greatfield Cl OSS WF5 .....175 G1
Greatfield Dr OSS WF5 .....175 G8
Greatfield Gdns OSS WF5 .....175 G8
Great Gates Cl ROCH OL11 .....228 C2
Great Gates Rd ROCH OL11 .....228 C4
Great George St LDS LS1 .....6 D8
  MILN OL16 .....206 B7
Great Horton Rd GTHN BD7 .....4 A6
Great House La TOD OL14 .....142 A6
Great Howarth WHIT OL12 .....206 D2
Great Meadow ROY/SHW OL2 .....229 H5
Great Northern St HUD HD1 .....15 G3
  MOR LS27 .....152 C3
Great North Rd AWLS/ASK DN6 .....249 H8
  GFTH/SHER LS25 .....114 A4
Great Pasture ILK LS29 .....40 B4
Great Pond St DEWS WF13 * 195 H1
Great Russell Ct GTHN BD7 .....4 A6
Great Russell St GTHN BD7 .....104 D7
Great Wilson St BEE/HOL LS11 .....8 E5
Greatwood Av SKP/WHF BD23 .....16 C5
Great Wood St BTLY WF17 .....173 L2
Greave Cl HUDN HD2 .....192 D1
Greavefield La PONT WF8 .....181 K6
Greave House Dr LUD/ILL HX2 .....144 F3
Greave House Flds LUD/ILL HX2 .....145 G4
Greave House La KBTN HD8 .....215 M3
Greave House Pk LUD/ILL HX2 .....144 F7
Greave House Ter KBTN HD8 .....215 M3
Greave Rd HOLM/MEL HD9 .....254 C6
  RPDN/SBR HX6 .....166 A8
Greaves Av WKFDW/WTN WF2 .....197 L3
Greaves Cft HEM/SK/SE WF9 .....215 M3
Greaves Fold DOD/DAR S75 .....260 D4
  GTL/HWG HX4 .....190 E2
Greaves Smithy ILK LS29 .....19 L7
Greaves St CAS WF10 .....157 M6
  ROY/SHW OL2 * 229 L7
  WBOW BD5 .....126 F3
Greave St ROY/SHW OL2 .....229 L7
Greave Vw BFDE BD3 * 106 B6
  TOD OL14 .....163 M1
Grebe Cl ROY/SHW OL2 .....229 G5
Green Abbey HOLM/MEL HD9 .....254 D7
Green Acre La LM/WK BD12 .....148 F4
Green Acre Cl KBTN HD8 .....257 H6
Greenacre Cl LM/WK BD12 .....148 F4
Greenacre Dr KBTN HD8 .....257 J6
Greenacre Pk YEA LS19 .....84 D1
Greenacre Park Av YEA LS19 .....84 D1
Greenacre Park Ms YEA LS19 .....84 D1
Greenacre Park Ri YEA LS19 .....84 D1
Green Acres FEA/AMT WF7 .....202 A3
  HOR/CROF WF4 .....198 C7
  ILK LS29 .....39 M6
  STKB/PEN S36 .....271 J3
Greenacres HIPP HX3 .....125 M8
  OSS WF5 .....174 F5
  SKP/WHF BD23 .....16 D1
Greenacres Cl OSS WF5 .....174 F5
Greenacres Ct CAS WF10 .....158 C6
Greenacres Dr AIRE BD20 .....57 J4
  BTLY WF17 .....151 J4
  HIPP HX3 .....125 M8
Greenacres Gv HIPP HX3 .....125 M8
Greenacre Wk HOR/CROF WF4 .....222 K4
Greenacre Wy LM/WK BD12 .....148 F4

Green Av AIRE BD20 .....35 M4
  GFTH/SHER LS25 .....135 H3
  HECK WF16 .....173 G2
Green Balk La KBTN HD8 .....257 G8
Greenbank BSLY/ROY S71 .....243 H5
Green Bank CLECK BD19 .....150 B8
  EARD/LOFT WF3 .....154 F5
Greenbank Cl CAS WF10 .....179 J1
Greenbank Dr LIT OL15 .....207 H3
Greenbank Rd NORM WF6 .....178 B3
  NORM WF6 .....178 A3
  WHIT OL12 .....206 C4
  WHIT OL12 .....103 L6
Greenbanks Av HORS LS18 .....85 K4
Greenbanks Cl HORS LS18 .....85 L4
Greenbanks Dr HORS LS18 .....85 K4
Green Bridge Cl ROCH OL11 * 228 C7
Green Cha HDGY LS6 * 87 G7
Green Cliff HOLM/MEL HD9 .....236 B1
Greencliffe Av BAIL BD17 .....82 D3
  AIRE BD20 .....35 H8
  BTLY WF17 .....174 A2
  DEWS WF13 .....173 J4
  HDGY LS6 * 87 G7
Green Ct CLECK BD19 .....149 H6
  GTHN BD7 .....104 D7
  MSTN/BAR LS15 .....90 A7
Green Crs HDGY LS6 * 87 G7
  MAR/SLWT HD7 .....213 G1
Green Cft HEM/SK/SE WF9 .....223 K4
Greencroft Av HIPP HX3 .....147 K3
Greencroft Cl IDLE BD10 .....83 J7
Greendale Ct HOLM/MEL HD9 .....236 B1
Greendown Cl ILK LS29 .....38 F7
Green End BRIG HD6 .....170 C2
  CLAY BD14 .....125 K2
Green End Rd AIRE BD20 .....59 G5
  WBSY BD6 .....126 D6
Greenfell Cl HWTH BD22 .....2 C7
Greenfield Av GFTH/SHER LS25 .....135 J4
  CSLY LS20 .....61 K7
  HIPP HX3 .....148 C7
  HUDW HD3 .....191 J7
  MOR LS27 .....129 K7
  SHPY BD18 .....82 E8
Greenfield Cl GFTH/SHER LS25 .....135 J4
  GTL/HWG HX4 .....190 B4
  HDGY LS6 * 147 J3
  ILK LS29 .....40 B7
  KBTN HD8 .....257 H3
  OSS WF5 .....197 J2
Greenfield Ct BHP/TINH LS16 .....86 D2
  HWTH BD22 .....2 C7
Greenfield Crs CUL/QBY BD13 .....80 A3
  HOR/CROF WF4 .....217 G2
Greenfield Dr CLECK BD19 .....149 H6
  MOR LS27 .....129 K7
Greenfield Gdns AIRE BD20 .....35 H8
Greenfield Garth
  GFTH/SHER LS25 .....135 J4
Greenfield La BOW BD4 .....127 K8
  CSLY LS20 .....61 J7
  GTHN BD7 .....126 B2
  IDLE BD10 .....83 K5
  MILN OL16 .....206 F3
  ROCH OL11 .....228 C2
  ROY/SHW OL2 .....229 K8
Greenfield Mt
  WKFDW/WTN WF2 .....176 B4
Greenfield Pl GIR BD8 * 4 B1
  HIPP HX3 .....148 C7
Greenfield Ri GFTH/SHER LS25 .....135 J4
  HEM/SK/SE WF9 .....245 M1
  HOLM/MEL HD9 .....235 K1
  NORM WF6 .....178 B4
  OSM LS9 .....9 M1
  OSS WF5 .....197 J2
Greenfields HECK WF16 .....172 E1
Greenfield St ROCH OL11 .....228 C2
Greenfields Wy ILK LS29 .....40 B7
  TOD OL14 .....140 C5
Greenfield V GFTH/SHER LS25 .....135 J4
Greenfield Vw GFTH/SHER LS25 .....135 J4
Greenfield Wy
  WKFDW/WTN WF2 .....176 B4
Greenfinch Gv HUDS HD4 .....214 A7
Greenfinch Wy WIL/AL BD15 .....103 K7
Greenfold La WBY LS22 .....48 B1
Greenfoot Cl DOD/DAR S75 .....260 F3
Greenfoot La DOD/DAR S75 .....260 F3
Green Gdns MAR/SLWT HD7 .....213 G1
Greengate AIRE BD20 .....35 M4
  RTHW LS26 .....133 L8
Greengate Cl WHIT OL12 .....206 F2
Green Gate La MAR/SLWT HD7 .....234 C1
Green Gate Rd HOLM/MEL HD9 .....253 J2
  KGHY BD21 .....3 G7
Greengate Rd KGHY BD21 .....3 G7
  PONT WF8 .....227 H4
Greengates Av LM/WK BD12 .....148 E5
Green Grove Bank MILN OL16 .....206 E3
Green Haggs La PBR HG3 .....28 A8
Green Hall Pk HIPP HX3 .....147 M1
Greenhead Av HUDE HD5 .....215 H1
Greenhead Ct HUD HD1 .....57 J4
Greenhead Dr AIRE BD20 .....57 J4
Greenhead La BRIG HD6 .....170 A8
  HUDE HD5 .....215 H1
Green Head Rd AIRE BD20 .....57 K4
  BHP/TINH LS16 .....86 D8
  KGHY BD21 .....14 C7
Green Hi HUDN HD2 .....192 D2
  LUD/ILL HX2 .....145 K8
Greenhill Av BSLY/ROY S71 .....261 J3
  PONT WF8 .....227 H4
  ROY/SHW OL2 .....229 G5
Green Hill Bank Rd
  HOLM/MEL HD9 .....254 F1
Green Hill Cha WOR/ARM LS12 .....108 D5
Green Hill Cl WOR/ARM LS12 .....108 D5
Greenhill Crs WOR/ARM LS12 .....108 D8
Green Hill Cft WOR/ARM LS12 .....108 D8
Greenhill Dr BGLY BD16 .....80 G7
Greenhill Dr BRAM LS13 .....108 A5
Green Hill Gdns WOR/ARM LS12 .....108 D8
Greenhill Holt
  WOR/ARM LS12 * 108 D8
Green Hill La BFDE BD3 .....105 L7
  BGLY BD16 .....54 D5
  WOR/ARM LS12 .....130 D1
Green Hill Mt WOR/ARM LS12 .....108 D5
Green Hill Mt PONT WF8 .....181 A5
Green Hill Rd BRAM LS13 .....108 A5
  HUDW HD3 .....191 C0
  WKFDE WF1 .....13 H1
Greenhills YEA LS19 .....84 E3
Greenhill St BFDE BD3 .....105 L8
Green Hill Wy BRAM LS13 .....108 A5

Greenholme Cl ILK LS29 40 B4
Greenholme Ct BOW BD4 128 B4
Green House Hl KBTN HD8 238 E2
Green House La KBTN HD8 238 E2
Greenhouse Rd HUDN HD2 192 C4
Greenhow Cl BULY LS4 108 F4
Greenhow Gdns BULY LS4 108 F4
Greenhow Pk ILK LS29 39 M5
Greenhow Rd BULY LS4 108 F4
Greenhow Wk BULY LS4 108 E4
Greenland CUL/QBY BD13 * 125 H4
Greenland Av CUL/QBY BD13 * 124 F6
Greenland Ct RTHW LS26 155 L1
Greenland Rd HBR HX7 119 L8
Greenland Vls CUL/QBY BD13 125 G6
Green La AIRE BD20 17 J8
AIRE BD20 34 D8
AIRE BD20 35 J8
AL/HA/HU LS17 44 E2
AWLS/ASK DN6 249 G3
BAIL BD17 82 C2
BAIL BD17 82 D5
BEE/HOL LS11 131 J5
BHP/TINH LS16 85 M2
BRIG HD6 170 A1
BRIG HD6 171 H4
BSPA/BRAM LS23 49 G7
CAS WF10 135 M8
CAS WF10 158 B4
CAS WF10 179 L1
CLECK BD19 149 M4
CUL/QBY BD13 103 G8
CUL/QBY BD13 124 D3
CUL/QBY BD13 125 G1
CUL/QBY BD13 125 G7
DEWS WF13 173 J5
DOD/DAR S75 260 C8
EARD/LOFT WF3 154 E5
ECHL BD2 105 M3
FEA/AMT WF7 179 M8
FEA/AMT WF7 201 M8
GFTH/SHER LS25 113 J7
GFTH/SHER LS25 135 H4
GIR BD8 4 B2
GTHN BD7 * 126 C1
GTL/HWG HX4 168 E8
GTL/HWG HX4 189 H6
GTL/HWG HX4 190 B5
HBR HX7 143 G1
HEM/SK/SE WF9 225 L5
HEM/SK/SE WF9 246 D4
HIPP HX3 11 M7
HIPP HX3 147 G1
HIPP HX3 148 A1
HOLM/MEL HD9 235 G5
HOLM/MEL HD9 254 C4
HOR/CROF WF4 196 B8
HOR/CROF WF4 197 H8
HOR/CROF WF4 197 M6
HOR/CROF WF4 218 F1
HOR/CROF WF4 221 J8
HORS LS18 85 K7
HWTH BD22 52 B2
HWTH BD22 78 F4
IDLE BD10 83 J6
ILK LS29 19 G5
ILK LS29 39 L8
ILK LS29 40 A3
KBTN HD8 256 D4
LM/WK BD12 148 E4
LM/WK BD12 149 H2
LUD/ILL HX2 124 A6
LUD/ILL HX2 144 F5
LUD/ILL HX2 168 A1
LVSG WF15 171 M3
MAR/SLWT HD7 211 K6
MSTN/BAR LS15 111 K5
OT LS21 41 H5
PDSY/CALV LS28 106 F8
PONT WF8 180 F7
RPDN/SBR HX6 188 D3
RTHW LS26 157 H5
TAD LS24 71 K7
WBY LS22 47 H6
WHIT OL12 * 206 A6
WKFDW/WTN WF2 176 A6
WOR/ARM LS12 129 L1
YEA LS19 84 E1
Green Lane Cl HOR/CROF WF4 196 B7
Green Lane Ter MAR/SLWT HD7 190 E8
Greenlaws Cl HOLM/MEL HD9 253 M1
Greenlay Dr WKFDW/WTN WF2 175 K4
Green Lea RTHW LS26 133 L8
Greenlea Av YEA LS19 62 B8
Green Lea Cl BSPA/BRAM LS23 49 G7
Greenlea Cl YEA LS19 84 B1
Greenlea Mt YEA LS19 62 B8
Greenlea Rd YEA LS19 62 B8
Greenlees St WHIT OL12 206 B6
Green Meadow COL BB8 74 D4
WHIT OL12 206 F2
WIL/AL BD15 102 F2
Greenmires La OT LS21 25 H6
Greenmoor Av EARD/LOFT WF3 154 E5
WOR/ARM LS12 107 M7
Greenmoor Cl EARD/LOFT WF3 154 E5
Greenmoor Crs
EARD/LOFT WF3 154 F6
Green Mt BOW BD4 * 127 M3
HUDE HD5 15 M7
OSS WF5 * 196 F2
Greenmount Ct
BEE/HOL LS11 * 131 K3
Greenmount La BEE/HOL LS11 8 F9
Greenmount Pl BEE/HOL LS11 8 E9
Green Mount Rd
CUL/QBY BD13 103 G8
Greenmount St BEE/HOL LS11 8 E9
Greenmount Ter BEE/HOL LS11 8 F9
Greenock Pl WOR/ARM LS12 108 C6
Greenock Rd WOR/ARM LS12 * 108 C6
Greenock St WOR/ARM LS12 108 C6
Greenock Ter WOR/ARM LS12 108 C6
Green Pk WKFDE WF1 13 J2
Green Park Av HIPP HX3 168 E4
OSS WF5 197 G2
Green Park Dr HIPP HX3 168 E4
Green Park Rd HIPP HX3 168 E4
Green Park St HIPP HX3 168 E3
Green Pasture Cl OSM LS9 110 E6
Green Pl ECHL BD2 * 105 K4
Green Rd BAIL BD17 82 D4
HDGY LS6 87 H7
LVSG WF15 172 C1
STKB/PEN S36 270 F4
Green Rw RTHW LS26 156 F5
Green Royd GTL/HWG HX4 168 E8
Greenroyd Av CLECK BD19 149 M4
HIPP HX3 168 D3
Greenroyd Cl HIPP HX3 168 D4
Greenroyd Ct PONT WF8 203 L1
Greenroyd Crs HFAX HX1 * 10 A2
Greenroyd Cft HUDN HD2 14 A1
Greenroyd Dr AIRE BD20 55 M2
Greenroyde ROCH OL11 * 228 A1
Greenroyd Gv AIRE BD20 55 M2
Greenroyd La LUD/ILL HX2 146 A5
Greens End Rd HOLM/MEL HD9 234 F4
Greenset Vw BSLYN/ROY S71 243 G5
Greenshank Ms MOR LS27 152 F2
Greenside CLECK BD19 150 A7
CUD/GR S72 244 D2
DOD/DAR S75 242 E5
HECK WF16 172 E2
HOR/CROF WF4 222 D6
KBTN HD8 239 G7
LM/WK BD12 149 J2
PDSY/CALV LS28 106 F8
STKB/PEN S36 258 C8
WKFDW/WTN WF2 199 J7
Greenside Av DOD/DAR S75 242 E5
HUDE HD5 215 J1
WOR/ARM LS12 130 D1
Greenside Cl WOR/ARM LS12 130 E1
Greenside Ct HOR/CROF WF4 200 D7
MOR LS27 * 129 M7
Greenside Crs HUDE HD5 215 J1
Greenside Dr HUDE HD5 215 J1
WOR/ARM LS12 130 E1
Greenside Gv PDSY/CALV LS28 106 F8
Greenside La CUL/QBY BD13 79 M8
GIR BD8 104 B7
Greenside Mt MIRF WF14 172 D7
Greenside Pk HOR/CROF WF4 200 D7
Greenside Pl DOD/DAR S75 242 D5
Green Side Rd HUDS HD4 237 H3
Greenside Rd MIRF WF14 172 D7
WOR/ARM LS12 130 D1
Greenside Ter WOR/ARM LS12 130 D1
Greenside Wk WOR/ARM LS12 130 D1
Green Sq GFTH/SHER LS25 * 135 K5
Green's Sq LUD/ILL HX2 146 A6
Green St BFD BD1 5 H6
CAS WF10 157 M5
GTL/HWG HX4 190 D2
HUD HD1 14 F5
HWTH BD22 54 E3
HWTH BD22 78 E8
HWTH BD22 100 E4
Greensway GFTH/SHER LS25 113 G7
Green Sykes Rd AIRE BD20 56 B6
Green Ter BEE/HOL LS11 9 G9
ECHL BD2 105 K4
Green Terrace Sq HFAX HX1 168 C1
The Green AL/HA/HU LS17 87 M4
BGLY BD16 59 G7
BGLY BD16 59 J8
BGLY BD16 * 81 M3
BOW BD4 128 B7
BTLY WF17 151 H4
CAS WF10 158 F6
COL BB8 52 B8
FEA/AMT WF7 202 A2
GFTH/SHER LS25 113 J8
GFTH/SHER LS25 135 J5
GSLY LS20 62 A6
HOR/CROF WF4 200 E4
HOR/CROF WF4 220 C7
HORS LS18 85 K6
HUDN HD2 192 F1
MAR/SLWT HD7 * 233 H2
MIRF WF14 172 A8
OSS WF5 196 F2
OT LS21 41 H5
PDSY/CALV LS28 106 F2
STKB/PEN S36 270 C2
STKB/PEN S36 270 F4
WKFDW/WTN WF2 176 A3
Greenthorpe Hl BRAM LS13 108 A7
Greenthorpe Mt BRAM LS13 108 A6
Greenthorpe Rd
WOR/ARM LS12 108 A7
Greenthorpe St BRAM LS13 108 A7
Greenthorpe Wk BRAM LS13 108 A6
Greenthwaite Cl AIRE BD20 2 D1
Greenton Av CLECK BD19 149 G5
Greenton Crs CUL/QBY BD13 124 F6
Greentop HOR/CROF WF4 200 D7
PDSY/CALV LS28 106 F8
Green Top WOR/ARM LS12 130 D1
Green Top Gdns
WOR/ARM LS12 130 D1
Green Top St GIR BD8 104 A7
Greenups Ter RPDN/SBR HX6 167 K2
Green Vw HDGY LS6 87 G7
SCFT LS14 67 L6
Greenview HOR/CROF WF4 200 D7
Greenview Cl OSM LS9 110 A4
Green View Ct RHAY LS8 88 C6
Greenview Mt OSM LS9 110 A4
The Green Vw CUD/GR S72 244 D2
Greenville Av WOR/ARM LS12 130 D1
Greenville Dr LM/WK BD12 127 G7
Greenville Gdns
WOR/ARM LS12 130 D1
Green Wy AIRE BD20 34 E7
LUD/ILL HX2 124 A6
SCFT LS14 67 L6
Greenway GSLY LS20 61 L7
HOLM/MEL HD9 236 B1
HUDW HD3 213 H1
MSTN/BAR LS15 111 L5
ROY/SHW OL2 229 H5
Greenway Cl MSTN/BAR LS15 111 L5
Greenway Dr WIL/AL BD15 103 K7
Greenway Rd WBOW BD5 127 G4
The Greenway BFDE BD3 5 L3
Greenwell Ct OSM LS9 110 E6
Greenwell Rw CLAY BD14 125 K2
Greenwood Av EARL WF12 174 B7
ECHL BD2 105 J1
HEM/SK/SE WF9 225 L6
Greenwood Cl NORM WF6 178 D7
Greenwood Ct HDGY LS6 * 87 G7
Greenwood Dr ECHL BD2 105 J2
Greenwood Mt ECHL BD2 105 J2
HDGY LS6 87 G7
Green Wood Pk HDGY LS6 87 G7
Greenwood Rd BAIL BD17 82 D5
EARD/LOFT WF3 153 H6
WKFDE WF1 13 H1
Greenwood Rw
PDSY/CALV LS28 107 H7
Greenwood St DEWS WF13 173 K6
HBR HX7 143 J3
HUDS HD4 214 C2
LIT OL15 207 K1
MILN OL16 206 B7
Greenwood Ter BSLY S70 261 G4
Greetland Rd GTL/HWG HX4 189 J1
Greggs Ct BSLY S70 261 M6
Gregory Ct CLAY BD14 125 L2
Gregory Crs GTHN BD7 126 A4
Gregory Dr KBTN HD8 216 B8
Gregory La HUDE HD5 194 C7
Gregory Rd CAS WF10 180 A1
Gregory Springs La MIRF WF14 194 C3
Gregory Springs Mt
MIRF WF14 194 D4
Gregory Springs Rd MIRF WF14 194 D3
Gregory St BTLY WF17 * 174 A1
Grenfell Dr BFDE BD3 105 M6
Grenfell Rd BFDE BD3 105 M6
Grenfell Ter BFDE BD3 105 M6
Grenley St KNOT WF11 182 C2
Grenville Pl DOD/DAR S75 260 E3
Grenville Wk HOR/CROF WF4 220 B3
Gresham Av ECHL BD2 105 H2
Gresley Rd KGHY BD21 3 H5
Grey Cl WKFDE WF1 176 D3
Grey Ct WKFDE WF1 176 D3
Greycourt Cl ECHL BD2 83 J8
HFAX HX1 10 C8
Greyfriars Av HUDN HD2 193 G2
Greyfriar Wk GTHN BD7 126 A3
Grey Gables HOR/CROF WF4 197 G8
Greyshiels Av HDGY LS6 108 E2
Greyshiels Cl HDGY LS6 108 E2
Greystone Av ELL HX5 190 G1
Greystone Cl BSPA/BRAM LS23 49 G7
ILK LS29 40 A4
Greystone Ct BRIG HD6 170 C7
Greystone Crs IDLE BD10 83 L8
Grey Stone La TOD OL14 142 B6
Greystone Mt MSTN/BAR LS15 111 G7
Greystone Pk GFTH/SHER LS25 92 A5
Greystones Cl GFTH/SHER LS25 92 A5
Greystones Ct RHAY LS8 88 D7
Greystones Dr HWTH BD22 79 H3
OSS WF5 197 G2
Grey Stones La HBR HX7 121 K1
Greystones La HWTH BD22 55 M8
Greystones Mt HWTH BD22 79 H4
Greystones Ri HWTH BD22 79 H3
Greystones Rd LUD/ILL HX2 145 G7
Grey St WKFDE WF1 176 D3
Griffe Dr LM/WK BD12 148 E5
Griffe Gdns HWTH BD22 78 D4
Griffe Head Crs LM/WK BD12 * 148 E4
Griffe Head Rd LM/WK BD12 148 E4
Griffe Rd HWTH BD22 77 M6
LM/WK BD12 148 E4
Griff House La EARD/LOFT WF3 153 K6
Grime La HOLM/MEL HD9 255 L5
HOR/CROF WF4 200 D3
Grimescar Mdw HUDN HD2 191 M4
Grimescar Rd HUDW HD3 191 L3
Grimethorpe St
HEM/SK/SE WF9 247 H4
Grimpit Hl HOR/CROF WF4 * 221 J8
Grimscar Av HUDN HD2 192 B5
Grimthorpe Av HDGY LS6 * 108 E1
Grimthorpe Pl HDGY LS6 108 F1
Grimthorpe St HDGY LS6 108 F1
Grimthorpe Ter HDGY LS6 108 F1
Grisedale Av HUDN HD2 192 B5
ROY/SHW OL2 228 E6
Grisedale Cl GTHN BD7 126 B3
LUD/ILL HX2 145 M5
Gritstone Cl ILK LS29 40 A4
Grizedale Cl WBY LS22 29 K8
Grosmont Rd BRAM LS13 107 L4
Grosmont Ter BRAM LS13 107 L4
Grosvenor Av HEM/SK/SE WF9 225 J7
KBTN HD8 216 A3
PONT WF8 180 C5
SHPY BD18 82 B6
Grosvenor Dr BSLY S70 260 E5
Grosvenor Gdns AL/HA/HU LS17 43 L3
Grosvenor Hl CHAL LS7 7 G4
Grosvenor Mt HDGY LS6 109 H2
Grosvenor Pk CHAL LS7 87 L7
Grosvenor Park Gdns HDGY LS6 6 B1
Grosvenor Rd BTLY WF17 151 M8
GIR BD8 4 C2
HDGY LS6 6 B1
HUDE HD5 193 G8
SHPY BD18 82 B7
Grosvenor St COL BB8 74 B1
EARL WF12 173 L7
ELL HX5 169 H8
HECK WF16 172 F1
WKFDE WF1 13 L9
Grosvenor Ter GIR BD8 4 C2
HDGY LS6 109 H2
HECK WF16 * 172 F2
HFAX HX1 10 D6
WBY LS22 30 A8
Grosvenor Wy KBTN HD8 216 A3
Grouse Moor La CUL/QBY BD13 124 E4
Grouse St KGHY BD21 3 H3
WHIT OL12 206 B5
Grove Av HDGY LS6 87 G8
HEM/SK/SE WF9 224 A8
HEM/SK/SE WF9 226 A6
HIPP HX3 146 B4
ILK LS29 38 B3
PDSY/CALV LS28 106 F7
PONT WF8 * 181 G6
SHPY BD18 104 D1
Grove Cl CLECK BD19 150 A6
ECHL BD2 105 J2
STKB/PEN S36 270 B2
Grove Ct HDGY LS6 87 G8
HIPP HX3 146 C4
PDSY/CALV LS28 106 F7
Grove Crs BSPA/BRAM LS23 49 G7
GFTH/SHER LS25 138 A3
LUD/ILL HX2 144 F7
WKFDW/WTN WF2 199 K7
Grove Crs South
BSPA/BRAM LS23 49 G8
Grove Cft HIPP HX3 146 B4
Grove Dr HEM/SK/SE WF9 246 D4
HIPP HX3 146 B3
Grove Edge HIPP HX3 146 B4
Grove Farm Cl BHP/TINH LS16 86 B2
Grove Farm Crs BHP/TINH LS16 86 A3
Grove Farm Cft BHP/TINH LS16 86 A2
Grove Farm Dr BHP/TINH LS16 86 A2
Grove Gdns BSPA/BRAM LS23 49 H7
EARL WF12 174 C8
HDGY LS6 87 G8
HIPP HX3 146 C4
Grovehall Av BEE/HOL LS11 131 H5
Grovehall Dr BEE/HOL LS11 131 H4
Grovehall La PONT WF8 181 K6
Grovehall Pde BEE/HOL LS11 131 H5
Grovehall Rd BEE/HOL LS11 131 H5
Grove Head HEM/SK/SE WF9 246 D4
Grove House Crs ECHL BD2 105 J2
Grove House Dr ECHL BD2 105 J2
Grove House Rd ECHL BD2 105 J2
Grovelands ECHL BD2 105 J3
Grove La CLECK BD19 150 D5
HDGY LS6 109 G1
HEM/SK/SE WF9 224 A8
HEM/SK/SE WF9 225 G3
HEM/SK/SE WF9 246 D4
KNOT WF11 182 A2
Grove Lea Cl HEM/SK/SE WF9 224 A8
Grove Lea Crs PONT WF8 181 G7
Grove Lea Wk PONT WF8 181 G7
Grove Marsh Lea
HEM/SK/SE WF9 * 224 B7
Grove Mill Ct OT LS21 41 G7
Grove Mt HEM/SK/SE WF9 246 D4
PONT WF8 * 181 G6
Grove Nook HUDW HD3 191 H8
Grove Pk HIPP HX3 146 B3
HOR/CROF WF4 197 M8
Grove Pl BSPA/BRAM LS23 49 G7
HEM/SK/SE WF9 224 A8
The Grove Prom ILK LS29 38 D2
Grove Ri AL/HA/HU LS17 87 H1
PONT WF8 * 181 G6
Grove Rd BSPA/BRAM LS23 49 G7
DOD/DAR S75 * 242 C5
ELL HX5 169 J7
HBR HX7 143 J2
HDGY LS6 87 G8
HECK WF16 173 G2
HOR/CROF WF4 197 J5
HORS LS18 85 K6
HUD HD1 15 H4
ILK LS29 38 A2
ILK LS29 61 J2
MID LS10 9 L9
MSTN/BAR LS15 111 J7
PDSY/CALV LS28 106 F7
PONT WF8 180 F6
SHPY BD18 104 D1
WKFDE WF1 12 F4
Grove Royd HIPP HX3 146 C4
Groves Hall Rd DEWS WF13 173 H6
Grove Sq CLECK BD19 * 150 D5
HIPP HX3 146 B4
Grove St BRIG HD6 170 D4
BSLYN/ROY S71 261 J5
DEWS WF13 173 L6
HECK WF16 173 G2
HEM/SK/SE WF9 246 D4
HUDW HD3 191 G8
LDS LS1 6 C9
LVSG WF15 172 D4
MAR/SLWT HD7 212 B5
MIRF WF14 172 D8
OSS WF5 196 F2
PDSY/CALV LS28 * 107 G4
ROCH OL11 228 A1
RPDN/SBR HX6 167 M2
WKFDE WF1 13 G4
Grove St South HFAX HX1 * 10 B6
Grove Ter GTHN BD7 * 4 D7
HEM/SK/SE WF9 224 A8
PDSY/CALV LS28 106 F7
The Grove AL/HA/HU LS17 46 D8
AL/HA/HU LS17 87 H1
BAIL BD17 82 E2
BGLY BD16 59 G8
BTLY WF17 151 J7
CUD/GR S72 244 D5
EARD/LOFT WF3 153 K6
GFTH/SHER LS25 135 J5
HECK WF16 150 E8
HEM/SK/SE WF9 247 H2
HIPP HX3 147 L6
HOLM/MEL HD9 235 H5
HOR/CROF WF4 222 C5
HORS LS18 85 K6
HUDN HD2 192 D4
IDLE BD10 83 K7
IDLE BD10 83 M7
ILK LS29 38 C2
NORM WF6 * 178 D4
PDSY/CALV LS28 106 F7
ROY/SHW OL2 229 J8
RTHW LS26 134 D4
SHPY BD18 82 A7
SKP/WHF BD23 16 E3
WKFDW/WTN WF2 199 K7
YEA LS19 84 C2
Groveville HIPP HX3 147 L5
Groveway ECHL BD2 105 J2
Grove Wy HEM/SK/SE WF9 246 D4
Grovewood HDGY LS6 86 F8
Grudgby La STKB/PEN S36 271 J8
Grunberg Rd HDGY LS6 108 F1
Grunberg St HDGY LS6 * 108 F1
Guard House Av HWTH BD22 2 C5
Guard House Dr HWTH BD22 2 C4
Guard House Gv HWTH BD22 2 B5
Guard House Rd HWTH BD22 2 B5
Guernsey Rd EARL WF12 174 B4
Guest La DOD/DAR S75 259 J6
Guest Rd DOD/DAR S75 260 F3
Guildford Rd BSLYN/ROY S71 243 K2
Guildford St HBR HX7 143 J4
MILN OL16 206 C7
OSS WF5 196 F2
Guild Wy LUD/ILL HX2 145 K8
Guillemot Ap MOR LS27 152 F3
Guinevere Dr HEM/SK/SE WF9 247 J4
Guiseley Dr ILK LS29 61 K4
Gully Ter HOLM/MEL HD9 254 D2
Gunson Crs OSS WF5 174 F8
Gunter Rd WBY LS22 30 C8
Gunthwaite La KBTN HD8 257 H3
Gunthwaite Top KBTN HD8 * 257 H3
Gurbax Ct BFDE BD3 106 A7
Gurney Cl WBOW BD5 126 F3
Guygroft OT LS21 41 H6
Guys Cft WKFDW/WTN WF2 197 L2
Guy St BOW BD4 5 G8
Gwyn Holme DEWS WF13 * 173 H4
Gwynne Av BFDE BD3 106 A5
Gynn La HOLM/MEL HD9 236 C2
Gypsy Ct CAS WF10 158 E8
Gypsy La CAS WF10 158 E8
Gypsy Wood Cl
MSTN/BAR LS15 111 M7
Gypsy Wood Crest
MSTN/BAR LS15 111 M7

H

Hacking La HEM/SK/SE WF9 247 K3
Hackings Av STKB/PEN S36 270 E5
Hadassah St HIPP HX3 168 F2
Haddingley La KBTN HD8 255 M3
Haddlesey Rd KNOT WF11 161 J4
Haddon Av BULY LS4 108 E4
HIPP HX3 168 E3
Haddon Cl CLECK BD19 150 D6
DOD/DAR S75 260 A7
HEM/SK/SE WF9 247 J1
Haddon Pl BULY LS4 108 E4
Haddon Rd BSLYN/ROY S71 243 K8
BULY LS4 108 F4
Haddon St ROCH OL11 228 A1
Haddon Wy ROY/SHW OL2 229 L6
Hadfield Rd HECK WF16 172 F1
Hadleigh Ct AL/HA/HU LS17 87 M4
Hadleigh Ri PONT WF8 180 D8
Hadrian Cl CAS WF10 158 E5
Hadrian's Cl HUDW HD3 191 G6
PONT WF8 225 J1
Hag Farm Rd ILK LS29 40 A7
Hagg La GFTH/SHER LS25 139 H2
MIRF WF14 194 D3
Haggroyd La HOLM/MEL HD9 236 D4
Haggs Hill Rd OSS WF5 197 J1
Haggs La WKFDW/WTN WF2 197 L1
Haggs Rd PBR HG3 27 K1
Hagg Wood Rd
HOLM/MEL HD9 236 D4
Hag Hill La KBTN HD8 217 M8
Hag La HIPP HX3 146 E3
Hague Crs HEM/SK/SE WF9 246 A1
Hague Park Cl
HEM/SK/SE WF9 * 246 D3
Hague Park Dr
HEM/SK/SE WF9 246 D3
Hague Park Gdns
HEM/SK/SE WF9 246 D3
Hague Park La
HEM/SK/SE WF9 246 D3
Hague Park Wk
HEM/SK/SE WF9 246 D3
Hague Ter HEM/SK/SE WF9 224 A8
Haigh Av RTHW LS26 132 E7
Haigh Beck Vw IDLE BD10 83 L7
Haigh Cl STKB/PEN S36 258 B8
Haigh Cnr IDLE BD10 83 M7
Haigh Cft BSLYN/ROY S71 243 K2
Haigh Cross HUDW HD3 * 191 H4
Haigh Fold ECHL BD2 105 L3
Haigh Gdns RTHW LS26 132 E7
Haigh Hall IDLE BD10 83 M7
Haigh La DOD/DAR S75 241 K2
HIPP HX3 168 F3
HOLM/MEL HD9 236 B6
HOR/CROF WF4 217 J4
STKB/PEN S36 258 C8
Haigh Ms DOD/DAR S75 * 241 L1
Haigh Moor Av
EARD/LOFT WF3 153 G8
Haigh Moor Crs
EARD/LOFT WF3 153 G8
Haigh Moor Rd
EARD/LOFT WF3 175 G1
Haigh Moor St WKFDE WF1 176 F6
Haigh Moor Vw
EARD/LOFT WF3 153 G8
Haigh Moor Wy
BSLYN/ROY S71 243 K2
Haigh Rd RTHW LS26 133 H8
Haighside RTHW LS26 132 E8
Haighside Cl RTHW LS26 132 E8
Haighside Dr RTHW LS26 132 E8
Haighside Wy RTHW LS26 132 E8
Haighs Sq HUDE HD5 15 M5
Haigh St BOW BD4 127 K3
BRIG HD6 170 C3
GTL/HWG HX4 168 C7
HFAX HX1 10 B4
HUDS HD4 214 A3
ROCH OL11 206 C8
Haigh Ter RTHW LS26 132 E7
Haigh Vw RTHW LS26 132 E7
Haigh Wood Crs BHP/TINH LS16 85 M3
Haigh Wood Gn
BHP/TINH LS16 * 85 M4
Haigh Wood Rd BHP/TINH LS16 85 L3
Hailhead Dr PONT WF8 181 H5
Haincliffe Rd KGHY BD21 79 K2
Haines Pk RHAY LS8 * 7 L4
Hainsworth Moor Crs
CUL/QBY BD13 124 F6
Hainsworth Moor Dr
CUL/QBY BD13 124 F6
Hainsworth Moor Garth
CUL/QBY BD13 124 F6
Hainsworth Moor Gv
CUL/QBY BD13 124 F6
Hainsworth Moor Vw
CUL/QBY BD13 124 F6
Hainsworth Rd AIRE BD20 36 B6
Hainsworth Sq PDSY/CALV LS28 106 F3
Hainsworth St RTHW LS26 155 G2
WOR/ARM LS12 * 109 G8
Hainworth Crag Rd KGHY BD21 79 J4
Hainworth La KGHY BD21 79 K3
Hainworth Rd KGHY BD21 79 L2
Hainworth Wood Rd KGHY BD21 79 K2
Hainworth Wood Rd North
KGHY BD21 3 G9
Haise Mt DOD/DAR S75 242 C5
Halcyon Hl CHAL LS7 87 L6
Halcyon Wy WBOW BD5 126 E3
Haldane Cl CUD/GR S72 245 H3
Haldane Crs WKFDE WF1 177 G6
Hales Rd WOR/ARM LS12 130 D1
Halesworth Crs BOW BD4 128 A3
Haley Ct HIPP HX3 11 G3
Haley Hl HIPP HX3 11 G3
Half Acre Rd CUL/QBY BD13 102 D7
Half House La BRIG HD6 169 M1
Half Mile BRAM LS13 107 G4
Half Mile Cl PDSY/CALV LS28 107 H4
Half Mile Ct PDSY/CALV LS28 107 H4
Half Mile Gdns BRAM LS13 107 H4
Half Mile Gn PDSY/CALV LS28 107 H4
Half Mile La BRAM LS13 107 H3
Half Moon La WKFDE WF1 177 K7
Half Moon St HUD HD1 14 F7
Halfpenny La FEA/AMT WF7 180 B8
Half St KGHY BD21 2 F3
Halifax La HBR HX7 142 A2
LUD/ILL HX2 145 G6
Halifax Old Rd HIPP HX3 147 K6
HUDN HD2 192 B4
Halifax Rd BRFD/BLYE BB10 96 D5
BRIG HD6 170 C4
CLECK BD19 149 G7
CUL/QBY BD13 79 M8
CUL/QBY BD13 101 M7
CUL/QBY BD13 124 E8
DEWS WF13 173 H3
ELL HX5 169 G7
HIPP HX3 147 K2
HUDW HD3 191 L5
HWTH BD22 79 H7
LIT OL15 186 B7
LUD/ILL HX2 123 M2
LVSG WF15 171 L1
MAR/SLWT HD7 212 D1
MILN OL16 206 D5
RPDN/SBR HX6 188 F2
STKB/PEN S36 257 L8
TOD OL14 142 D6
TOD OL14 163 L1
WBSY BD6 126 B7
Halifax Ter BSLYN/ROY S71 261 G2
Haliwell St LIT OL15 207 L1
Hallam La OT LS21 40 C1
Hallamshire Ms
WKFDW/WTN WF2 197 L2
Hallam's Yd SKP/WHF BD23 16 B2
Hallas Gv HUDE HD5 215 G1
Hallas La CUL/QBY BD13 102 A1
KBTN HD8 216 C8
Hallas Rd KBTN HD8 216 B8
Hall Av AIRE BD20 55 M2
HUD HD1 14 C9
IDLE BD10 105 M1
Hall Balk La DOD/DAR S75 260 F3
Hallbank Cl WBOW BD5 126 F5
Hall Bank Dr BGLY BD16 81 H2
Hallbank Dr WBOW BD5 126 F5
Hall Bank La HBR HX7 144 A6
Hall Bower La HUDS HD4 214 D6
Hallcliffe BAIL BD17 82 F2
Hall Cliffe Ct HOR/CROF WF4 197 J4
Hall Cliffe Crs HOR/CROF WF4 197 J4
Hall Cliffe Gv HOR/CROF WF4 197 K4
Hall Cliffe Ri HOR/CROF WF4 197 K4
Hall Cliffe Rd HOR/CROF WF4 197 K4
Hall Cl AIRE BD20 55 L2
BHP/TINH LS16 64 A2

BSPA/BRAM LS23 ....49 G7
HIPP HX3 ....147 J3
HOLM/MEL HD9 ....235 M4
ILK LS29 ....39 M5
LVSG WF15 ....172 C5
Hall Ct KNOT WF11 ....159 L6
Hall Cft HOR/CROF WF4 ....197 G8
SKP/WHF BD23 ....16 A2
ILK LS29 ....19 K7
Hallcroft Dr HOR/CROF WF4 ....197 K6
ILK LS29 ....19 K7
Hallcroft Gdns MILN OL16 ....207 D8
Hallcroft Ri BSLYN/ROY S71 ....243 K3
Hall Cross Gv HUDS HD4 ....214 E6
Hall Cross Rd HUDS HD5 ....214 E3
Hall Dr AIRE BD20 ....55 M2
BHP/TINH LS16 ....86 A2
ILK LS29 ....39 M5
LVSG WF15 ....172 D4
Hall Farm Gv STKB/PEN S36 ....258 C8
Hall Farm Pk GFTH/SHER LS25 ....114 B6
Hallfield Av GFTH/SHER LS25 ....114 B7
Hallfield Crs WBY LS22 ....48 B1
Hallfield Dr BAIL BD17 ....82 E3
Hall Field La HOR/CROF WF4 ....222 C7
Hallfield La WBY LS22 ....30 B8
Hall Fld Pl BD1 ....4 C1
Hallfield Rd GIR BD8 ....4 C1
Hallfield St BFD BD1 ....4 E4
Hallfield Ter GFTH/SHER LS25 ....114 B7
Hall Gdns AIRE BD20 ....35 C5
Hall Garth Cl TAD LS24 ....95 C1
Hall Garth Rd PONT WF8 ....225 J1
Hall Ga STKB/PEN S36 ....270 C8
Hall Green La AL/HA/HU LS17 ....26 A1
GTL/HWG HX4 ....188 F6
Hall Gv DOD/DAR S75 ....242 E5
HDGY LS6 ....6 A4
Halliday Av WOR/ARM LS12 ....108 C6
Halliday Dr WOR/ARM LS12 ....108 C6
Halliday Gv WOR/ARM LS12 ....108 C6
Halliday Mt WOR/ARM LS12 * 108 C6
Halliday Pl WOR/ARM LS12 ....108 C6
Halliday Rd GFTH/SHER LS25 ....113 G7
WOR/ARM LS12 ....108 C6
Halliday St PDSY/CALV LS28 ....107 G6
Halliley St DEWS WF13 ....173 K6
Hall Ing La HOLM/MEL HD9 ....236 D1
Halling Pl TOD OL14 ....163 J2
Hall Ing Rd HOLM/MEL HD9 ....236 F2
Hall Ings BFD BD1 ....4 F7
HIPP HX3 ....169 J3
Halliwell St MILN OL16 ....207 C7
WHIT OL12 ....206 A6
Hall La BHP/TINH LS16 ....64 B8
BOW BD4 ....5 H9
CAS WF10 ....136 B8
CHAL LS7 ....109 M1
EARL WF12 ....196 A4
GFTH/SHER LS25 ....137 H1
HEM/SK/SE WF9 ....225 K8
HIPP HX3 ....147 H2
HOR/CROF WF4 ....220 C2
HORS LS18 ....85 J5
KBTN HD8 ....216 A7
MAR/SLWT HD7 ....190 C8
OT LS21 ....22 B8
OT LS21 ....42 C4
SHPY BD18 ....82 F6
TAD LS24 ....117 C1
WOR/ARM LS12 ....107 L8
WOR/ARM LS12 ....108 F7
Hall Lee Rd HUDW HD3 ....191 L5
Hall Mdw COL BB8 ....74 D5
Hall Ms BSPA/BRAM LS23 ....49 G7
Hall Orchards Av WBY LS22 ....30 E4
Hallowes Gv CUL/QBY BD13 ....101 M1
Hallowes Park Rd
CUL/QBY BD13 ....101 M1
Hallows Ct HUDE HD5 * 215 H3
Hallows Rd KCHY BD21 ....3 M1
The Hallows AIRE BD20 ....2 C2
Hall Park Av HOR/CROF WF4 ....200 B4
HORS LS18 ....85 K5
LVSG WF15 ....171 K4
Hall Park Cl HORS LS18 ....85 J5
Hall Park Ct GFTH/SHER LS25 ....135 K5
Hall Park Cft GFTH/SHER LS25 ....135 K6
Hall Park Garth HORS LS18 ....85 J5
Hall Park Mdw GFTH/SHER LS25....135 K6
Hall Park Mt HORS LS18 * 85 J5
Hall Park Orch GFTH/SHER LS25 ....135 J6
Hall Park Ri GFTH/SHER LS25 * 135 K5
HORS LS18 ....85 J5
Hall Park Rd BSPA/BRAM LS23 ....49 G7
Hall Pl BSLYN/ROY S71 ....261 L2
OSM LS9 ....110 B7
Hall Ri BHP/TINH LS16 ....64 A8
ILK LS29 ....39 M5
Hall Rise Cl BHP/TINH LS16 ....64 A8
Hall Rise Cft BHP/TINH LS16 ....64 A8
Hall Rd COL BB8 ....74 D5
IDLE BD10 ....105 M1
RTHW LS26 ....134 D5
WKFDW/WTN WF2 ....197 M2
WOR/ARM LS12 ....108 E7
Hall Royd SHPY BD18 ....82 D7
Hallroyd Crs TOD OL14 ....163 L1
Hall Royd La DOD/DAR S75 ....259 J4
Hallroyd Pl TOD OL14 * 163 L1
Hall Royd Rd DOD/DAR S75 ....259 J4
Hall Royd Wk DOD/DAR S75 ....259 J4
Hallside Cl BAIL BD17 ....83 H1
Hall Stone Ct HIPP HX3 * 147 L1
Hall St AIRE BD20 ....34 F7
BRIG HD6 ....170 D4
FEA/AMT WF7 ....202 A2
HWTH BD22 ....191 H7
HWTH BD22 ....78 F3
WBSY BD6 ....126 E5
Hall St North HIPP HX3 ....146 D4
Hall Ter AIRE BD20 * 58 B5
Hall Wy AIRE BD20 ....55 L2
Hallwood Gn IDLE BD10 ....106 A1
Halstead Dr ILK LS29 ....40 C8
Halstead Gv DOD/DAR S75 ....242 G4
Halstead La HUDS HD4 ....237 J3
Halstead Pl BFDE BD3 ....126 C3
Halsteads Wy AIRE BD20 ....55 M3
Halton Cl HUDE HD5 ....215 H2
Halton Dr MSTN/BAR LS15 ....111 J6
Halton Moor Av OSM LS9 ....110 F7
Halton Moor Rd
MSTN/BAR LS15 ....111 J4
OSM LS9 ....110 F7
Halton Pl WBOW BD5 ....126 D3
Halton St FEA/AMT WF7 ....179 M7
Hamber Cote La AIRE BD20 ....36 B4
Hamble Ct DOD/DAR S75 * 242 E6
Hambledon Av BOW BD4 ....127 K5
HOLM/MEL HD9 ....235 H5
Hambleton Bank LUD/ILL HX2 ....145 L1
Hambleton Cl LUD/ILL HX2 ....145 L1
Hambleton Crs LUD/ILL HX2 ....145 L1
Hambleton Dr LUD/ILL HX2 ....145 L1
Hambleton St WKFDE WF1 ....176 F7
Hamel Ri HEM/SK/SE WF9 ....223 M8

Hamer Hall Crs WHIT OL12 ....206 D4
Hamer La MILN OL16 ....206 D5
The Hame GTL/HWG HX4 * 190 B3
Hamilton Av CHAL LS7 ....7 L1
Hamilton Ct NORM WF6 ....178 D5
Hamilton Gdns CHAL LS7 ....7 K2
Hamilton Pl CHAL LS7 ....7 L1
Hamilton Ter CHAL LS7 * 7 M2
Hamilton Vw CHAL LS7 ....7 L1
Hammer La HOR/CROF WF4 ....200 D2
Hammerstone Leach La
ELL HX5 ....190 F1
Hammerstones Rd ELL HX5 * 168 F8
Hammerton Dr
GFTH/SHER LS25 ....135 J1
Hammerton Farm Av
HOR/CROF WF4 ....222 D5
Hammerton Gv
PDSY/CALV LS28 ....107 H7
Hammerton Rd HUDN HD2 ....192 C4
Hammerton St BFDE BD3 ....5 J7
CLAY BD14 ....107 G2
Hammond Crs BIRK/DRI BD11 ....128 F7
Hammond Pl HTON BD9 ....104 C3
Hammond Rd KNOT WF11 ....181 M3
Hammond St HFAX HX1 ....10 B7
HUDN HD2 ....192 D5
OSM LS9 * 9 M4
Hammonds Yd HUD HD1 * 14 F7
Hamm Strasse BFD BD1 ....4 F4
Hampden Cl KNOT WF11 ....181 K1
Hampden Pl HFAX HX1 ....10 E6
WBOW BD5 ....126 F2
Hampden Rd ROY/SHW OL2 ....229 M8
Hampden St WBOW BD5 ....126 F2
Hamper La STKB/PEN S36 ....271 H1
Hampole Balk AWLS/ASK DN6 ....249 H5
Hampole Field La
AWLS/ASK DN6 ....248 B5
Hampshire Cl ILK LS29 ....38 F2
PONT WF8 ....181 G3
Hampshire St HUDE HD5 ....15 L1
Hampson Pl IDLE BD10 ....83 K6
OSM LS9 ....110 B7
Hampton St HFAX HX1 ....10 A9
Hampton Ter OSM LS9 ....110 B7
Hamworth Dr HWTH BD22 ....78 F4
Hamza St BTLY WF17 ....173 K2
Hanbury Cl BSLYN/ROY S71 ....261 M2
Hanbury Gdns GFTH/SHER LS25 ....113 H6
Hanby Av NORM WF6 ....178 B3
Hand Bank La MIRF WF14 ....194 C4
Hand Carr La LUD/ILL HX2 ....144 D7
Handel St GTHN BD7 ....4 B5
MAR/SLWT HD7 ....212 F2
Handel Ter HUDE HD5 * 15 L8
Handsworth Rd
WKFDW/WTN WF2 ....220 C2
Hanging Chadder La
ROY/SHW OL2 ....228 E7
Hanging Gate La HWTH BD22 ....100 C1
Hangingroyd Cl HBR HX7 ....143 J3
Hangingroyd La HBR HX7 ....143 J3
Hanging Stone Rd HUDS HD4 ....214 B7
Hangingstone Rd ILK LS29 ....38 C1
Hanging Stones La
RPDN/SBR HX6 ....189 G1
Hanging Wood Wy CLECK BD19....149 L4
Hangthwaite Rd
AWLS/ASK DN6 ....249 M7
Hanley Rd MOR LS27 ....152 C3
Hannah Ct LM/WK BD12 ....148 E5
Hannas Royd DOD/DAR S75 ....260 C7
Hannerton Rd ROY/SHW OL2 ....229 M6
Hanover Av BVRD LS3 ....6 C7
Hanover Cl GIR BD8 ....104 C5
Hanover Crs PONT WF8 ....202 E1
Hanover Gdns DEWS WF13 ....173 K6
WBOW BD5 * 126 F1
Hanover La BVRD LS3 ....6 D8
Hanover Mt BVRD LS3 ....6 B7
Hanover Pl BTLY WF17 ....173 M1
GFTH/SHER LS25 ....135 K5
KNOT WF11 ....159 L5
Hanover Sq BFD BD1 ....4 D5
BVRD LS3 ....6 C8
Hanover St AIRE BD20 ....34 F5
BTLY WF17 ....173 L1
DEWS WF13 ....173 K6
HFAX HX1 ....10 F7
KGHY BD21 ....3 C5
LIT OL15 ....207 J1
RPDN/SBR HX6 ....167 M1
WKFDW/WTN WF2 ....12 A4
Hanover Wk LDS LS1 ....6 C8
Hanover Wy BVRD LS3 ....6 C8
ILK LS29 ....40 A5
Hansby Av NORM WF6 ....178 D5
Hansby Bank SCFT LS14 ....111 K1
Hansby Cl SCFT LS14 ....111 K1
Hansby Dr SCFT LS14 ....111 K1
Hansby Gdns SCFT LS14 ....111 K1
Hansby Ga SCFT LS14 ....111 K1
Hansby Pl SCFT LS14 ....111 K1
Hanson Av NORM WF6 ....178 D5
Hanson Ct LM/WK BD12 ....148 D4
Hanson Fold LM/WK BD12 ....148 E5
Hanson La HFAX HX1 ....10 A5
HUDS HD4 ....214 A4
Hanson Mt LM/WK BD12 ....148 E4
Hanson Rd BRIG HD6 ....170 A4
HOLM/MEL HD9 ....234 E5
Hanson St BSLY S70 ....261 H5
Hanworth Rd LM/WK BD12 ....126 F8
Harbeck Dr BGLY BD16 ....80 D6
Harborough Hill Rd
BSLYN/ROY S71 ....261 H5
Harbour Crs WBSY BD6 ....126 A6
Harbour La MILN OL16 ....229 H1
Harbour La North MILN OL16 ....207 H1
Harbour Pk WBSY BD6 ....126 B7
Harclo Rd KGHY BD21 ....3 L2
Harcourt Av CUL/QBY BD13 ....102 F7
Harcourt Dr ILK LS29 ....19 H5
MOR LS27 ....152 B1
Harcourt Pl LDS LS1 ....9 J8
Harcourt St BOW BD4 ....127 K3
WKFDW/WTN WF2 ....198 B1
Hardaker La BAIL BD17 ....82 C4
Hardaker's Ap FEA/AMT WF7 ....224 B1
Hardaker's La FEA/AMT WF7 ....202 B1
Hardaker St GIR BD8 ....4 C1
Hardcastle Av PONT WF8 ....180 C5
Hardcastle La HOR/CROF WF4 ....217 M3
Harden Brow La BGLY BD16 ....80 C5
Harden Dr DOD/DAR S75 ....260 C4
Harden Gv IDLE BD10 ....106 A3
KCHY BD21 ....3 M9
Harden Hill Rd HOLM/MEL HD9 ....235 G6
Harden Hills Rd ROY/SHW OL2 ....229 M6
Harden Moss Rd
HOLM/MEL HD9 ....234 F7
Harden Rd BGLY BD16 ....80 E5
KCHY BD21 ....3 M9

Hardgate La HWTH BD22 ....79 H8
Hardie Av HOR/CROF WF4 ....222 E5
Hardings La AIRE BD20 ....35 C2
ILK LS29 ....19 M3
Hardings La AIRE BD20 ....20 C6
Hard Ings Rd KGHY BD21 ....3 H1
Hardistry Dr PONT WF8 ....180 D6
Hardknot Cl GTHN BD7 ....126 A3
Hardknott Cl GTHN BD7 ....126 A3
Hard Nese La HWTH BD22 ....100 B5
Hard Platts La GTL/HWG HX4 ....190 B6
Hardrow Gn WOR/ARM LS12 ....130 E3
Hardrow Gv WOR/ARM LS12 ....130 F1
Hardrow Rd WOR/ARM LS12 ....130 E1
Hardrow Ter WOR/ARM LS12 * 130 F1
Hardwick Cl HOR/CROF WF4 ....222 C6
PONT WF8 ....202 F1
Hardwick Cft CHAL LS7 ....87 M8
Hardwicke St ROCH OL11 ....228 C3
Hardwick Gv DOD/DAR S75 ....260 B8
Hardwick Rd FEA/AMT WF7 ....201 L2
PONT WF8 ....180 C5
Hardwick St KGHY BD21 ....2 F1
Hardy Av MOR LS27 ....130 E6
Hardy Cl ROCH OL11 ....228 B3
Hardy Ct MOR LS27 ....152 D2
Hardy Cft WKFDE WF1 ....13 C3
Hardy Gv BEE/HOL LS11 ....131 J3
Hardy Pl BRIG HD6 ....170 A1
Hardy St BEE/HOL LS11 ....131 J3
BOW BD4 ....5 G8
BRIG HD6 ....170 A1
MOR LS27 ....152 D2
Hardy Ter BEE/HOL LS11 ....131 J3
Hardy Vw BEE/HOL LS11 ....131 J3
Hareball Av WKFDW/WTN WF2 ....176 A7
Harecroft Rd OT LS21 ....41 J5
Hare Farm Av WOR/ARM LS12 ....107 M7
Hare Farm Cl WOR/ARM LS12 ....107 M7
Harefield Cl AIRE BD20 ....56 C1
Harefield Dr BTLY WF17 ....153 J5
Harefield East MSTN/BAR LS15....111 J6
Harefield Rd PONT WF8 ....181 H6
Harefield West MSTN/BAR LS15....111 J6
Harefield Pk RHAY LS8 ....191 L4
Harehill Av RHAY LS8 ....
Harehill Cl IDLE BD10 ....83 K5
Hare Hill Rd LIT OL15 ....185 J8
Harehills La HWTH BD22 ....77 L5
OSM LS9 ....110 D4
Harehills Park Av OSM LS9 * 110 D3
Harehills Park Ter OSM LS9 ....110 D4
Harehills Park Vw OSM LS9 ....110 D3
Harehills Pl RHAY LS8 ....110 B3
Harehills Rd RHAY LS8 ....110 B3
Harehill St TOD OL14 ....141 J8
Hare La PDSY/CALV LS28 ....129 H2
Hare Park Av LVSG WF15 ....171 L2
Hare Park Cl LVSG WF15 ....171 L2
Harepark Dr LVSG WF15 ....171 L2
Hare Park La HOR/CROF WF4 ....200 B7
LVSG WF15 ....171 L2
Hare Park Vw HOR/CROF WF4 ....200 B6
Hares Av RHAY LS8 ....110 B2
Hares Mt RHAY LS8 ....7 M1
Hares Rd RHAY LS8 ....110 B2
Hares Ter RHAY LS8 ....110 B2
Hare St HFAX HX1 ....10 B6
ROCH OL11 ....228 B1
Hares Vw RHAY LS8 ....110 B2
Harewood Av AIRE BD20 ....56 C1
AL/HA/HU LS17 ....45 K8
BSLY S70 ....260 D5
HECK WF16 ....173 H4
LUD/ILL HX2 ....145 M6
NORM WF6 ....178 E3
Harewood Dr
WKFDW/WTN WF2 ....175 M5
Harewood Ga AL/HA/HU LS17....45 J7
Harewood Gv HECK WF16 ....173 G3
Harewood La HEM/SK/SE WF9....225 L6
PONT WF8 ....226 B4
Harewood Ms HOLM/MEL HD9 ....235 H4
Harewood Mt HOLM/MEL HD9 ....235 H4
Harewood Pl LUD/ILL HX2 ....146 A4
Harewood Ri HWTH BD22 ....79 H3
Harewood Rd AL/HA/HU LS17....46 D7
HWTH BD22 ....79 G4
ROY/SHW OL2 ....229 L6
SKP/WHF BD23 ....16 A2
WBY LS22 ....47 H6
WKFDE WF1 ....177 H6
Harewood St BFDE BD3 ....5 M6
LDSU LS2 ....14 B1
Harewood Vw PONT WF8 ....181 G6
Harewood Wy BRAM LS13 ....107 K6
Hargrave Crs ILK LS29 ....21 H2
Hargreaves Av MOR LS27 ....130 B7
Hargreaves Cl MOR LS27 ....130 B7
Harker Rd WBSY BD6 ....126 E7
Harker Ter PDSY/CALV LS28 ....106 F5
Harland Cl ECHL BD2 ....105 G4
Harland Sq LDSU LS2 ....6 D3
Harlech Av BEE/HOL LS11 ....131 K4
Harlech Crs BEE/HOL LS11 ....131 K4
Harlech Gv BEE/HOL LS11 ....131 K4
Harlech Mt BEE/HOL LS11 ....131 K4
Harlech Park Ct BEE/HOL LS11 ....131 K4
Harlech Rd BEE/HOL LS11 ....131 K4
Harlech St BEE/HOL LS11 ....131 K4
Harlech Ter BEE/HOL LS11 ....131 K4
Harlech Wy GFTH/SHER LS25 ....113 G6
Harley Cl BRAM LS13 ....107 J5
Harley Dr BRAM LS13 ....107 J5
Harley Gdns PDSY/CALV LS28 ....107 J5
Harley Gn BRAM LS13 ....107 J5
Harley Ri BRAM LS13 ....107 J5
Harley Rd BRAM LS13 ....107 J5
Harley St BRIC HD6 ....170 C5
TOD OL14 ....141 J8
Harley Ter BRAM LS13 ....107 J5
Harley Vw BRAM LS13 ....107 J5
Harley Wk BRAM LS13 ....107 J5
Harley Wd TOD OL14 ....141 J8
Harlington Ct MOR LS27 ....152 C4
Harlington Rd MOR LS27 ....152 C4
Harlow Ct RHAY LS8 ....88 E7
Harlow Rd GTHN BD7 ....127 G2
Harmby Cl AWLS/ASK DN6 ....249 H4
Harmon Cl BOW BD4 ....127 L6
Harold Av BSLYN/ROY S71 ....262 A4
Harold Gdns MOR LS27 ....152 C4
Harold Gv HDGY LS6 ....109 G4

Harold Mt HDGY LS6 ....109 G4
Harold Pl HDGY LS6 ....109 G4
Harold Rd HDGY LS6 ....109 G4
Harold Sq HDGY LS6 ....109 G4
Harold St BGLY BD16 ....81 G2
HDGY LS6 ....109 G4
MILN OL16 ....206 D4
Harold Ter HDGY LS6 ....109 G4
Harold Vw HDGY LS6 ....109 G4
Harold Wk HDGY LS6 ....109 G4
Harpe Inge HUDE HD5 ....193 G7
Harper Av IDLE BD10 ....83 K5
Harper Crs IDLE BD10 ....83 L5
Harper Ga BOW BD4 ....128 B2
Harper Gv AIRE BD20 ....55 M2
IDLE BD10 ....83 K5
Harper La YEA LS19 ....62 D9
Harper Royd La
RPDN/SBR HX6 ....167 K4
Harpers La ROY/SHW OL2 ....229 L7
Harpers Sq AIRE BD20 ....55 M2
Harper St LDSU LS2 ....9 J1
ROCH OL11 ....228 A3
Harp Rd HUDW HD3 ....
Harrap St WKFDW/WTN WF2....175 M8
Harrier Cl GIR BD8 ....103 K7
Harrier Wy MOR LS27 ....152 F2
Harriet Cl BSLY S70 * 261 J7
Harriet St BRIC HD6 ....170 C2
CHAL LS7 * 7 K2
GIR BD8 ....104 D6
Harriett St MILN OL16 ....206 C7
Harrington Ct BSLYN/ROY S71 ....262 A2
HOLM/MEL HD9 ....235 H5
Harris Ct GTHN BD7 ....5 J5
BGLY BD16 ....81 J4
Harrison Crs OSM LS9 ....110 C5
Harrison La HOLM/MEL HD9 ....235 G2
Harrison Rd HFAX HX1 ....11 G7
HOR/CROF WF4 ....200 B5
Harrisons Av PDSY/CALV LS28 ....107 J4
Harrison St BGLY BD16 ....81 J4
LDS LS1 ....9 L8
TOD OL14 * 140 D5
Harris St BFD BD1 ....5 J5
BGLY BD16 ....81 J4
Harrogate Pl BFDE BD3 ....105 J4
Harrogate Ringway PBR HG3 ....26 C4
Harrogate Rd AL/HA/HU LS17 ....43 L3
AL/HA/HU LS17 ....43 M1
AL/HA/HU LS17 ....44 F7
AL/HA/HU LS17 ....66 B5
AL/HA/HU LS17 * 87 M4
CHAL LS7 ....87 L8
ECHL BD2 ....83 M8
IDLE BD10 ....83 M8
PBR HG3 ....26 D5
PBR HG3 ....28 F5
WBY LS22 ....29 H6
YEA LS19 ....84 E1
Harrogate Ter BFDE BD3 ....105 J4
Harrogate Vw AL/HA/HU LS17 ....88 E1
Harrop Av MOR LS27 ....152 C3
Harrop Gv MOR LS27 ....152 D4
Harrop La WIL/AL BD15 ....102 D3
Harrop Ter MOR LS27 ....152 C3
Harrop Well La PONT WF8 ....180 D7
Harrowby Crs BHP/TINH LS16 ....86 D7
Harrowby Rd BHP/TINH LS16 ....86 D7
Harrow Ms ROY/SHW OL2 ....229 K7
Harrow St HEM/SK/SE WF9 ....247 G3
HFAX HX1 ....10 B7
ROCH OL11 * 228 D4
Harry La CLAY BD14 ....125 K2
HWTH BD22 ....100 D3
Harry Rd DOD/DAR S75 ....260 D3
Harry St BOW BD4 ....127 L3
Hartcliff Av STKB/PEN S36 ....270 E3
Hartcliffe La STKB/PEN S36 ....270 A5
Hartcliff Hill Rd
STKB/PEN S36 ....270 B6
Hartcliff Nick STKB/PEN S36 ....270 A4
Hartcliff Rd STKB/PEN S36 ....269 L6
Harthill MOR LS27 ....129 M7
Harthill Av MOR LS27 ....129 M7
Harthill Cl MOR LS27 ....129 M7
Harthill La MOR LS27 ....129 M7
Harthill Paddock MOR LS27 ....129 M7
Harthill Ri MOR LS27 ....129 M7
Hartington Dr BSLYN/ROY S71 ....261 H2
Hartington St BTLY WF17 ....173 L3
KGHY BD21 ....3 G3
Hartington Ter GTHN BD7 ....126 C1
Hartland Rd BOW BD4 ....128 A2
Hartlebury ROCH OL11 * 206 A8
Hartley Av HDGY LS6 ....6 D1
Hartley Cl HEM/SK/SE WF9 ....247 J2
Hartley Ct LVSG WF15 ....172 C3
Hartley Crs HDGY LS6 ....6 E1
Hartley Gdns HDGY LS6 ....6 D1
Hartley Gv HDGY LS6 ....6 D1
Hartley Hl LDSU LS2 ....7 H7
Hartley La ROCH OL11 ....228 A3
Hartley Park Av PONT WF8 ....180 D6
Hartley Park Vw PONT WF8 ....180 D6
Hartley Pl HWTH BD22 ....54 F3
MOR LS27 * 152 D3
Hartley's Buildings MOR LS27 ....152 D3
Hartley's Sq AIRE BD20 ....58 F5
Hartley St BOW BD4 ....127 J1
CAS WF10 ....157 L7
DEWS WF13 ....173 L5
HFAX HX1 ....10 C4
LIT OL15 ....207 J1
MILN OL16 * 206 F7
MOR LS27 ....152 D3
WHIT OL12 ....184 E8
Hartley Ter FEA/AMT WF7 ....201 G6
Hartlington Ct BAIL BD17 * 83 G3
Hartman Pl HTON BD9 ....104 B4
Harton Cl ROY/SHW OL2 ....164 C1
Hartwell Rd HDGY LS6 ....109 G4
Harvard Av ROCH OL11 ....228 C2
Harvelin Pk TOD OL14 ....164 C1
Harvest Ct PONT WF8 ....181 G3
Harvest Cft HFAX HX1 * 10 E6
Harvest Ms OSS WF5 ....197 G5
Harvest Mt IDLE BD10 ....83 H6
Harvey Rd HUDE HD5 ....215 G4
Harvey St BSLY S70 ....260 F6
WHIT OL12 ....184 E8
WKFDE WF1 ....13 K8
Harwill Ap MOR LS27 ....130 E7
Harwill Cft MOR LS27 ....130 E7
Harwill Gv MOR LS27 ....130 E7
Harwill Ri MOR LS27 ....130 E7
Harwill Rd MOR LS27 ....130 E7
Harwood Cl HUDE HD5 ....215 H1
WKFDW/WTN WF2 ....199 G5
Harwood St LIT OL15 ....207 H1
Harwood Ter BSLYN/ROY S71 ....262 A4

Haselden Crs
WKFDW/WTN WF2 ....197 M1
Haselden Rd
WKFDW/WTN WF2 ....197 M1
Haslam Cl BFDE BD3 ....5 K4
Haslam Gv SHPY BD18 ....83 G8
Haslemere Cl BOW BD4 ....127 M3
Haslewood Cl OSM LS9 ....7 M9
Haslewood Ct OSM LS9 ....110 B6
Haslewood Dene OSM LS9 ....110 B6
Haslewood Dr OSM LS9 ....110 B6
Haslewood Gdns OSM LS9 ....110 B6
Haslewood Ms OSM LS9 ....110 B6
Haslewood Cft OSM LS9 ....110 B6
Haslewood Sq OSM LS9 ....110 B6
Haslewood Vw OSM LS9 ....110 B6
Hasley Rd ILK LS29 ....40 B6
Haslingden Dr HTON BD9 ....104 B4
Hassocks La HOLM/MEL HD9 ....235 L2
Hassocks Rd HOLM/MEL HD9 ....234 E3
Haste St CAS WF10 ....157 K6
Hastings Av WBOW BD5 ....126 F4
WKFDW/WTN WF2 ....198 E4
Hastings Ct AL/HA/HU LS17 ....89 G2
NORM WF6 ....178 A2
Hastings Crs CAS WF10 ....158 D7
Hastings Gv WKFDW/WTN WF2 ....198 F4
Hastings Pl WBOW BD5 ....126 F4
Hastings St CUD/CR S72 ....245 L7
ROCH OL11 ....228 B1
WBOW BD5 ....126 F4
Hastings Ter WBOW BD5 ....126 F4
Hastings Wk CAS WF10 ....158 D7
Hastings Wy WBY LS22 ....47 H6
Hatchet La LM/WK BD12 ....149 J2
Hatfield Cl BSLYN/ROY S71 ....243 G7
Hatfield Gdns BSLYN/ROY S71 ....243 G7
Hatfield Pl HOR/CROF WF4 ....222 F4
Hatfield Rd ECHL BD2 ....105 K4
Hatfield St WKFDE WF1 ....176 E7
Hatfield Vw WKFDE WF1 ....176 E6
Hathaway Av HTON BD9 ....103 M3
Hathaway Dr SCFT LS14 ....89 K6
Hathaway La SCFT LS14 ....89 K5
Hathaway Ms SCFT LS14 ....89 K5
Hathershelf La LUD/ILL HX2 ....144 C7
Hatton Cl WBSY BD6 ....126 F6
Haugh End La RPDN/SBR HX6 ....167 J4
Haugh Head Rd STKB/PEN S36 ....258 B8
Haugh La MILN OL16 ....229 L2
Haugh Rd TOD OL14 ....142 A8
Haugh Shaw Cft HFAX HX1 ....10 D9
Haugh Shaw Rd HFAX HX1 ....10 C9
Haugh Shaw Rd West
HFAX HX1 ....168 B1
Haughs La HUDW HD3 ....191 H7
Haughs Rd HUDW HD3 ....191 J7
Hauxley Ct ILK LS29 ....38 F1
Hauxwell Cl AWLS/ASK DN6 ....249 H4
Hauxwell Dr YEA LS19 ....62 D8
Havelock Sq BSLY S70 ....260 F6
CUL/QBY BD13 ....103 G1
DEWS WF13 ....195 G1
GTHN BD7 ....126 B2
Haven Cha BHP/TINH LS16 ....86 A3
Haven Ct BHP/TINH LS16 ....86 A3
PONT WF8 ....202 D1
Haven Cft BHP/TINH LS16 ....86 A3
Haven Gdns BHP/TINH LS16 ....86 A3
Haven Garth BHP/TINH LS16 ....86 A3
Haven Gn BHP/TINH LS16 ....86 A3
Haven La HBR HX7 ....143 K6
Haven Mt BHP/TINH LS16 ....86 A3
Haven Ri BHP/TINH LS16 ....86 A3
Haven St TOD OL14 * 165 L1
The Haven GFTH/SHER LS25 ....138 A3
IDLE BD10 ....83 L8
MSTN/BAR LS15 ....111 M6
Haven Vw BHP/TINH LS16 ....86 A3
Havercroft OSS WF5 ....197 G1
WOR/ARM LS12 ....130 A1
Havercroft La PONT WF8 ....204 A1
Havercroft Ri CUD/CR S72 ....223 G8
Havercroft Wy BTLY WF17 ....173 H1
Haverdale Ri DOD/DAR S75 ....260 F3
Haverdale Rd HOR/CROF WF4 ....222 E5
The Haverlands
HEM/SK/SE WF9 ....224 A8
Haveroid La HOR/CROF WF4 ....220 B1
Haveroid Wy HOR/CROF WF4 ....220 A1
Haverthwaites Dr
GFTH/SHER LS25 ....92 A3
Havertop La NORM WF6 ....179 H4
Haw Av YEA LS19 ....62 E6
Hawber Cote Dr AIRE BD20 * 36 B4
Hawber La AIRE BD20 ....36 A4
Haw Cliff La HUDS HD4 ....237 H5
Haw Ct DOD/DAR S75 ....259 H6
Hawes Av WBOW BD5 ....126 E4
WBOW BD5 ....126 E4
Hawes Cl CAS WF10 ....158 D6
Hawes Crs WBOW BD5 ....52 B8
Hawes Dr COL BB8 ....126 E4
WBOW BD5 ....126 E4
Hawes Gv WBOW BD5 ....126 E4
Hawes Mt WBOW BD5 ....126 E4
Hawes Rd WBOW BD5 ....126 E4
Hawes Ter WBOW BD5 ....126 E4
Haweswater Cl WBY LS22 ....47 K1
Haw Hill Vw NORM WF6 ....178 D3
Hawkcliffe Vw AIRE BD20 ....35 L3
Hawke Av HECK WF16 ....173 G1
Hawke Wy LM/WK BD12 ....127 M6
Hawkhill Av GSLY LS20 ....61 M6
MSTN/BAR LS15 ....111 K3
Hawkhill Dr MSTN/BAR LS15 ....111 K3
Hawkhill Gdns MSTN/BAR LS15 ....111 K3
Hawkhills CHAL LS7 ....88 A7
Hawkhurst Rd WOR/ARM LS12 ....108 E8
Hawkingcroft Rd
HOR/CROF WF4 ....197 H5
Hawkins Dr CHAL LS7 ....7 L2
Hawkins Wy LIT OL15 ....185 L5
Hawkroyd Bank Rd HUDS HD4 ....214 F8
Hawksbridge La HWTH BD22 ....100 B3
Hawkshead Cl WBOW BD5 ....127 L5
Hawkshead Crs SCFT LS14 ....111 H3
Hawkshead Dr ROY/SHW OL2 ....228 G3
WBOW BD5 ....127 L5
Hawkshead Rd ROY/SHW OL2 ....229 G5
Hawkshead Wk WBOW BD5 * 127 G1
Hawksley Ct MOR LS27 ....130 B7
Hawksmoor Dr ROY/SHW OL2 ....229 K6
Hawk's Nest Gdns East
AL/HA/HU LS17 ....87 M2
Hawk's Nest Gdns South
AL/HA/HU LS17 ....87 M2
Hawk's Nest Gdns West
AL/HA/HU LS17 ....87 M2
Hawk's Nest Ri AL/HA/HU LS17....87 M2
Hawkstone Av GSLY LS20 ....61 L2
Hawkstone Vw GSLY LS20 ....61 L2
Hawk St KGHY BD21 * 3 J3
Hawksworth Av HTON BD9 ....104 B3
KSTL LS5 ....86 A7
Hawkswood Crs KSTL LS5 ....86 A7

Hawkswood Gv KSTL LS5....86 A7
Hawkswood Mt KSTL LS5....86 A7
Hawkswood Pl KSTL LS5....86 A8
Hawkswood St KSTL LS5....86 B8
Hawkswood Ter KSTL LS5....86 B8
Hawksworth Av GSLY LS20....61 M7
Hawksworth Cl ILK LS29....61 J3
Hawksworth Dr ILK LS29....61 J3
Hawksworth La ILK LS29....61 H6
Hawksworth Rd BAIL BD17....61 L9
 HORS LS18....85 M7
Hawksworth St ILK LS29....38 D2
Hawkwell Bank
 BSLYN/ROY S71....262 C6
Haw La YEA LS19....62 E6
Hawley Cl MOR LS27....152 B4
Hawley St COL BB8....74 E1
Hawley Ter IDLE BD10....106 A2
Hawley Wy MOR LS27....152 B4
Haworth Cl BSLYN/ROY S71....261 K3
 MIRF WF14....172 B8
Haworth La YEA LS19....62 E6
Haworth Rd BTLY WF17....151 H4
 HTON BD9....104 A3
 HWTH BD22....79 G6
 WIL/AL BD15....102 C2
Haworth to Hebden
 Bridge Wk HBR HX7....99 G3
 HBR HX7....120 E4
 HWTH BD22....99 M4
Haw Park La HOR/CROF WF4....222 A3
 WKFDW/WTN WF2....221 K4
Hawshaw Rd WBSY BD6....53 J2
Hawsworth Rd DOD/DAR S75....260 C8
Hawthorn Av BFDE BD3....106 A6
 BTLY WF17....173 J3
 HOR/CROF WF4....200 A5
 KNOT WF11....181 M3
 TAD LS24....71 K5
 YEA LS19....62 D7
Hawthorn Cl BRIG HD6....170 E8
 ILK LS29....18 F6
 TAD LS24....71 L5
 WKFDW/WTN WF2....175 K4
Hawthorn Cs EARD/LOFT WF3....154 E5
Hawthorn Crs CHAL LS7 *....87 M7
 ROY/SHW OL2....229 K8
 YEA LS19....62 D7
Hawthorn Cft TAD LS24....71 K5
Hawthorn Dr BRAM LS13....106 F1
 IDLE BD10....83 L7
 YEA LS19....62 E6
Hawthorne Av CAS WF10....158 D8
 FEA/AMT WF7....201 L2
 HEM/SK/SE WF9....223 M8
 SHPY BD18....104 F1
 WBY LS22....47 B7
Hawthorne Cl HOR/CROF WF4....217 M3
 KBTN HD8....215 M3
 MOR LS27....129 M7
Hawthorne Ct DOD/DAR S75....241 K6
Hawthorne Crs AWLS/ASK DN6....249 J5
 DOD/DAR S75....260 A6
 HEM/SK/SE WF9....223 L8
Hawthorne Dr MOR LS27....129 M7
Hawthorne Gdns
 BHP/TINH LS16....86 D1
Hawthorne La MILN OL16....229 J2
Hawthorne Mt NORM WF6....178 D7
Hawthorne Ri SCFT LS14....89 L1
Hawthorne St AIRE BD20....35 M5
 BSLY S70....261 G6
 CUD/GR S72....244 E3
Hawthorne Vw MOR LS27....130 A7
Hawthorne Wy CUD/GR S72....244 E3
Hawthorn Gv BRAM LS13....106 F1
 DOD/DAR S75....259 J5
 ILK LS29....40 B7
 RTHW LS26....155 H2
Hawthorn La CHAL LS7 *....87 M7
Hawthorn Mt CHAL LS7 *....87 M7
Hawthorn Pl TOD OL14 *....141 K8
Hawthorn Rd EARD/LOFT WF3....87 M7
 MAR/SLWT HD7....212 A5
 YEA LS19....62 D7
The Hawthorns AIRE BD20....34 E8
 OSS WF5....197 G3
 WKFDE WF1....176 F1
Hawthorn St BFDE BD3....106 A6
 HFAX HX1 *....10 C1
 HIPP HX3 *....147 M6
Hawthorn Ter HFAX HX1 *....10 C1
 HUDS HD3....213 L2
 OSS WF5....197 G3
Hawthorn V CHAL LS7 *....87 M7
Hawthorn Vw BAIL BD17....82 F5
 CHAL LS7 *....87 M7
Hawthorn Wk LIT OL15....207 H1
Hawtop La DOD/DAR S75....220 B8
Hayburn Gdns BTLY WF17....173 K1
Hayburn Rd BTLY WF17....173 J1
Haycliffe Av CTHN BD7....126 C4
Haycliffe Dr CTHN BD7....126 B4
Haycliffe Gv CTHN BD7....126 C4
Haycliffe Hill Rd WBOW BD5....126 D4
Haycliffe La WBOW BD5....126 D4
Haycliffe Rd WBOW BD5....126 D3
Haycliffe Ter WBOW BD5....126 D4
Hay Cft IDLE BD10....83 H6
Hayden St BFDE BD3....5 J5
Haydn Av EARD/LOFT WF3....155 G8
Haydn's Ter PDSY/CALV LS28....107 J7
Hayes Cft BSLY S70....261 H5
Hayfield Av BSPA/BRAM LS23....48 E6
 HUDW HD3....191 J7
Hayfield Cl DOD/DAR S75....260 A7
 HOLM/MEL HD9....254 F2
 NORM WF6....178 D6
The Hayfields HWTH BD22....79 G1
Hayfield Ter WOR/ARM LS12....108 E8
Hayhills La AIRE BD20....35 M2
Hayhills Rd AIRE BD20....36 A4
Hayleigh Av BRAM LS13....107 L3
Hayleigh Mt BRAM LS13....107 L4
Haylock Cl DOD/DAR S75....260 A3
Haymaker Cl WHIT OL12....184 E8
Hayne La HOR/CROF WF4....218 A1
Haynes St KGHY BD21....3 J5
Hays La LUD/ILL HX2....206 B6
Hayson Cl EARL WF12....174 B5
Haythorns Av AIRE BD20....35 M5
Haythorns Mt AIRE BD20....35 M5
Hayton Dr WBY LS22....48 B2
Hayton Wood Vw
 GFTH/SHER LS25....92 A3
The Haywain ILK LS29....38 F3
Haywood Av HUDW HD3....191 L8
Haywood Gv ILK LS29....39 H2
Hazel Av MILN OL16 *....174 D7
 MILN OL16....229 J3
 SCFT LS14....89 J6
Hazel Bank WKFDW/WTN WF2....176 A6
Hazel Beck BGLY BD16....81 J6

Hazel Cl BIRK/DRI BD11....128 C8
 EARL WF12....174 D7
 PBR HG3....26 D2
Hazel Ct RTHW LS26....155 H2
 WKFDW/WTN WF2....176 C6
Hazel Cft SHPY BD18....82 A7
Hazelcroft IDLE BD10....105 M2
Hazel Gdns CAS WF10....180 F1
Hazel Gv AIRE BD20....55 L1
 BTLY WF17....173 J2
 HIPP HX3....148 C7
 HOR/CROF WF4....217 M3
 HUDN HD2....192 D1
 PONT WF8....181 G4
Hazel Grove Rd AIRE BD20....55 L1
Hazelheads BAIL BD17....82 C2
Hazelhurst Av BCLY BD16....81 H6
Hazelhurst Brow HTON BD9....103 M4
Hazelhurst Ct BFDE BD3....105 L3
 PDSY/CALV LS28....107 H7
Hazel Hurst Gv CUL/QBY BD13....124 F7
Hazel Hurst Rd CUL/QBY BD13....124 F7
Hazelhurst Rd HTON BD9....103 M4
Hazelhurst Ter HTON BD9....103 M4
Hazel La AWLS/ASK DN6....248 C5
Hazelmere Av BGLY BD16....81 J6
Hazel Mt SHPY BD18....82 C7
Hazel Ri RTHW LS26....155 E5
Hazel Rd KNOT WF11....182 A3
Hazelshaw DOD/DAR S75....260 C8
Hazel Wk HTON BD9....103 M4
Hazelwood BSLYN/ROY S71....261 J1
Hazelwood Av AIRE BD20....58 B5
 GFTH/SHER LS25....135 J1
Hazelwood Ct WKFDE WF1....176 B6
Hazelwood Rd HEM/SK/SE WF9....223 K6
 WKFDE WF1....176 B6
Hazelwood St TOD OL14....163 K1
Hazledene Cs CUD/GR S72....244 B3
Hazledene Rd CUD/GR S72....244 B3
Headfield Rd EARL WF12....173 L8
 HUDS HD4....214 C3
Headfield Vw EARL WF12....195 M2
Headingley Crs HDGY LS6....108 F2
Headingley La HDGY LS6....109 G2
Headingley Mt HDGY LS6....108 E1
Headingley Rd AWLS/ASK DN6....227 M3
Headingley Vw HDGY LS6....108 F2
Headland Gv WBSY BD6....126 B5
Headland La EARL WF12....174 B8
Headlands Cl OSS WF5....196 E1
Headlands Cl LVSG WF15....172 D3
Headlands La KNOT WF11....181 L4
 PONT WF8....180 E5
Headlands Pk OSS WF5....196 E1
Headlands Rd HUD HD1....14 E4
 LVSG WF15....172 C2
 OSS WF5....196 E1
Headlands St LVSG WF15....172 C3
 WHIT OL12....206 A5
Headlands Wk OSS WF5....196 E1
Headley La BSPA/BRAM LS23....70 A4
 CUL/QBY BD13....124 F1
The Headrow LDS LS1....6 F8
Headwell La TAD LS24....115 L1
Healaugh La RYKW YO26....33 G5
Heald Cl LIT OL15....207 H1
Healdfield Rd CAS WF10....158 B6
Heald Rd DEWS WF13....173 J4
Heald St CAS WF10....158 B6
Healdwood Cl CAS WF10....158 C6
Healdwood Rd CAS WF10....158 C6
Healey Av BGLY BD16....81 J4
Healey Cl BTLY WF17....173 J2
Healey Crs OSS WF5....196 F3
Healey Croft La
 EARD/LOFT WF3....153 K7
Healey Dr OSS WF5....196 F3
Healey Farm KBTN HD8....238 A3
Healey Green La HUDE HD5....193 L8
Healey La BGLY BD16....81 K5
 BTLY WF17....173 J1
 EARL WF12....195 M8
 WHIT OL12....206 A3
Healey Rd BGLY BD16....81 K5
Healey St BTLY WF17....173 H1
 MILN OL16....206 A8
Healey Wood Crs BRIG HD6....170 C6
Healey Wood Gdns BRIG HD6....170 C6
Healey Wood Gv BRIG HD6....170 C6
Healey Wood Rd BRIG HD6....170 C6
Healing St ROCH OL11....228 C1
Heap La BFDE BD3....5 J3
Heap St BFDE BD3....5 J5
 HIPP HX3....146 E4
Heath Av HIPP HX3....168 D2
Heathcliff HWTH BD22....78 D7
Heathcliffe Cl BTLY WF17....151 H4
Heath Cl EARL WF12....174 D6
 MAR/SLWT HD7....213 G2
Heathcote Ri HWTH BD22....78 F6
Heath Crs AIRE BD20....16 E8
 BEE/HOL LS11....131 G3
Heathcroft Bank BEE/HOL LS11....131 G4
Heathcroft Crs BEE/HOL LS11....131 G4
Heathcroft Dr BEE/HOL LS11....131 G4
Heathcroft Ri BEE/HOL LS11....131 G4
Heathcroft V BEE/HOL LS11....131 G4
Heath Dr AIRE BD20....16 E8
 BSPA/BRAM LS23....48 D7
Heather Av ROY/SHW OL2....229 M6
Heather Bank LIT OL15 *....185 M8
Heatherbank Av HWTH BD22....79 H2
Heather Bank Cl CUL/QBY BD13....101 M1
Heather Cl EARD/LOFT WF3....176 F1
 HEM/SK/SE WF9....246 F7
 OSS WF5....197 H3
Heather Ct BTLY WF17....151 G4
 EARD/LOFT WF3....191 H1
 ILK LS29....38 D3
Heather Dr LUD/ILL HX2....145 J3
Heatherfield Crs HUD HD1....191 M8
Heatherfield Rd HUD HD1....191 M8
Heather Fold KBTN HD8....239 H4
Heather Gdns BRAM LS13....108 A6
Heather Gv HUD HD1....67 L7
 MILN OL16....229 J3
 SCFT LS14....89 J6
Heather Gv BRAM LS13....107 M6
 HTON BD9....103 K3
 KGHY BD21....2 B3
Heathergrove Fold HUDE HD5....15 L4

Heather Knowle DOD/DAR S75....260 C7
Heatherlands Av
 CUL/QBY BD13....101 M4
Heather Ri ILK LS29....40 A6
Heather Rd BDT BD17 *....82 F2
 HOLM/MEL HD9....234 F5
Heather Side BAIL BD17....82 D2
The Heathers HOR/CROF WF4....200 E5
Heatherstones HIPP HX3....168 E2
Heather V SCFT LS14....89 K8
Heelis St BSLY S70....261 H6
Heather Vw BGLY BD16....81 M1
 HOR/CROF WF4....200 E5
 SKP/WHF BD23....16 D3
Heathfield BHP/TINH LS16....86 D1
 MIRF WF14....172 B8
Heathfield Cl BGLY BD16....81 J2
 EARD/LOFT WF3....153 H7
Heathfield Gv GTHN BD7....126 C6
 HIPP HX3 *....168 F3
Heathfield La BSPA/BRAM LS23....48 D6
Heathfield Ms MAR/SLWT HD7....213 G2
Heathfield Pl HIPP HX3 *....168 E2
Heathfield Ri RPDN/SBR HX6....188 E5
Heathfield Rd MAR/SLWT HD7....213 G2
 OSS WF5....174 E6
Heathfield St ELL HX5....169 J8
Heathfield Ter HDGY LS6....86 F8
 HFAX HX1....168 E1
Heath Gdns HIPP HX3....168 E2
Heath Gv AIRE BD20....38 D7
 BEE/HOL LS11....131 G3
 BTLY WF17....174 B2
 HUDS HD4....214 A4
 PDSY/CALV LS28....106 C7
Heath Hall HFAX HX1....168 E1
Heath Hall Av WBOW BD4....127 K5
Heath Hill Rd LUD/ILL HX2....145 J4
Heath House La
 MAR/SLWT HD7....212 D7
Heath House Ml
 MAR/SLWT HD7 *....212 D7
Heati la HIPP HX3 *....168 E2
Heath Lea HFAX HX1....11 G8
Heathmoor Cl IDLE BD10....83 J7
 LUD/ILL HX2....123 M8
Heathmoor Mt LUD/ILL HX2....123 M8
Heathmoor Park Rd
 LUD/ILL HX2....123 M8
Heathmoor Wy LUD/ILL HX2....123 M8
Heath Mt BEE/HOL LS11....131 G3
Heathness Rd AIRE BD20....18 F5
Heath Pk ILK LS29....38 B3
Heath Park Av HFAX HX1....168 E1
Heath Pl BEE/HOL LS11....131 G3
Heath Ri BEE/HOL LS11....131 G3
Heath Rd BEE/HOL LS11....131 G3
 BFDE BD3....5 L2
 EARL WF12....174 D6
 HFAX HX1....168 E1
 MAR/SLWT HD7....213 G6
 WHIT OL12....206 A5
Heath Royd HIPP HX3....168 E2
Heath St BFDE BD3....105 L7
 BGLY BD16....81 J3
 HIPP HX3....168 E2
 LVSG WF15....172 C4
Heath Ter BFDE BD3....5 M6
Heath Vw HFAX HX1....11 H8
Heath View St EARL WF12....174 D6
Heath Wk EARL WF12 *....174 D6
Heathwood Dr MAR/SLWT HD7....212 E1
Heathy Av LUD/ILL HX2....146 C1
Heathy La LUD/ILL HX2....124 A4
Heatley Rd MILN OL16....206 F8
Heaton Av AIRE BD20....58 E7
 CLECK BD19....149 L7
 EARL WF12....174 A6
 HUDE HD5....193 L6
 WOR/ARM LS12....130 E1
Heaton Cl BGLY BD16....81 K2
Heaton Crs BGLY BD16 *....81 K2
Heaton Dr BAIL BD17....82 D2
 BGLY BD16....81 K2
Heaton Fold La HUD HD1....191 M8
Heaton Gdns HUD HD1....191 M8
Heaton Gra BTLY WF17....174 A3
Heaton Gv CLECK BD19 *....149 L7
 HTON BD9....104 D2
 SHPY BD18....82 E7
Heaton Hl WBSY BD6....126 A7
Heaton Moor Rd HUDE HD5....193 L5
Heaton Park Dr HTON BD9....104 B3
Heaton Park Rd HTON BD9....104 B3
Heaton Rd BTLY WF17....151 L7
 HTON BD9....104 C3
 HUD HD1....191 M8
Heaton Royds SHPY BD18 *....104 B1
Heaton Royds La SHPY BD18....104 B1
Heaton St BEE/HOL LS11....8 E7
 BOW BD4....5 J9
 BRIG HD6....170 C4
 CLECK BD19....149 M6
 FEA/AMT WF7....224 A1
 MILN OL16....229 J1
Heator La KBTN HD8....238 C7
Hebble Brook Cl LUD/ILL HX2....145 L2
Hebble Butt Cl MILN OL16 *....207 G8
Hebble Dr HOLM/MEL HD9....236 C7
Hebble End HBR HX7....143 H3
Hebble Gdns LUD/ILL HX2....146 A3
Hebble La HFAX HX1....10 A1
 HOLM/MEL HD9....234 F6
Hebble Mt HOLM/MEL HD9....235 G5
Hebble St DEWS WF13....195 H1
 HUD HD1....15 G3
Hebble Vale Dr LUD/ILL HX2....146 A4
Hebble Wy HEM/SK/SE WF9....247 K4
Hebb Vw GTHN BD7....126 A4
Hebden Ap SCFT LS14....89 K8
Hebden Bridge Rd HWTH HX7....100 A7
Hebden Cl SCFT LS14 *....89 K8
Hebden Gn SCFT LS14....89 K8
Hebden Pl SCFT LS14....89 K8
Hebden Rd HWTH BD22....78 D7
 WKFDE WF1....177 G6
Heber Cl AIRE BD20....36 B6
Heber Pl LIT OL15....207 K1
Heber's Ghyll Dr ILK LS29....38 A3
Heber's La GFTH/SHER LS25....116 A6
Heber St KGHY BD21....2 F6
Heckmondwike Rd
 DEWS WF13....173 H6
Hector Av MILN OL16....206 C6
Hector Cl WBSY BD6....126 E5
Heddle Ri WKFDW/WTN WF2....175 M7
Heddon Cl WBOW BD5....127 G1
Heddon Gv WBOW BD5....4 F9
Heddon St HDGY LS6....87 G8
Heddon Wk WBOW BD5 *....127 G1
Hedge Cl WBOW BD5....127 G1
Hedge Hill Rd STBR/PEN S36 *....270 C3
Hedge Side GIR BD8....104 A4
Hedge Top La HIPP HX3....147 J3

Hedge Wy GIR BD8....104 A5
Hedley Cha WOR/ARM LS12....109 G7
Hedley Cl WKFDE WF1....176 D3
Hedley Gdns WOR/ARM LS12....109 G7
Hedley Gn WOR/ARM LS12....109 G7
Heeley Rd WKFDW/WTN WF2....220 C2
Heidelberg Rd HTON BD9....104 C4
Height Av RPDN/SBR HX6....166 F5
Height La KWTH BD22....100 F4
 SKP/WHF BD23....17 M3
Heights Av HBR HX7....143 H7
Heights Bank WOR/ARM LS12....108 B7
Heights Cl WHIT OL12....206 A4
 WOR/ARM LS12....108 A6
Heights Ct LVSG WF15....171 K1
Heights Dr MAR/SLWT HD7....212 F7
 WOR/ARM LS12....108 A7
Heights La AIRE BD20....35 K2
 BGLY BD16....59 J7
 HECK WF16....173 G3
 HTON BD9....103 M3
 UPML OL3....230 F7
 WHIT OL12....206 A5
 WOR/ARM LS12....108 A7
Heights Pde WOR/ARM LS12....108 A6
The Heights HOLM/MEL HD9....254 E5
Heights Vw MAR/SLWT HD7 *....212 D1
 WOR/ARM LS12....108 A7
Helena Cl BSLY S70....261 J6
Helena Pl GFTH/SHER LS25....135 H6
Helena St GFTH/SHER LS25....135 H6
Helena Wy BOW BD4....127 L6
Helene Ct HUDW HD3....191 K6
Helen Rose Ct SHPY BD18 *....104 A1
Helensburgh Cl DOD/DAR S75....260 C8
Helen St HUDS HD4....214 A3
 SHPY BD18....82 B6
Hellewell St WBSY BD6....126 D1
Hell La WKFDE WF1 *....199 M2
Hellwood La SCFT LS14....67 J2
Helme La HOLM/MEL HD9....235 G3
Helme Pk HOLM/MEL HD9....234 F5
Helm La HUDE HD5....193 L7
 RPDN/SBR HX6....166 E5
Helmshore Wy ROY/SHW OL2....229 K6
Helmsley Ct MID LS10....153 L2
Helmsley Dr BHP/TINH LS16....86 D7
Helmsley Rd BHP/TINH LS16....86 D7
 BSPA/BRAM LS23....48 D6
 WKFDW/WTN WF2....199 G5
Helmsley St BOW BD4....127 J2
Helston Cl MID LS10....131 H8
Helston Crs BSLYN/ROY S71....261 L3
Helston Cft MID LS10....153 L1
Helston Garth MID LS10....153 J1
Helston Gv HOLM/MEL HD9....236 F5
Helston Pl MID LS10....153 H1
Helston Rd MID LS10....131 H8
Helston Sq MID LS10....131 H8
Helston Wk MID LS10....131 H8
Helston Wy MID LS10....131 J8
Helted Wy HUDE HD5....215 G3
Heming's Wy HEM/SK/SE WF9....247 K3
Hemingway Cl CAS WF10....180 F1
 MID LS10....9 M9
Hemingway Garth MID LS10....9 M9
Hemingway Gn MID LS10....9 M9
Hemingway Rd IDLE BD10....83 M6
Hemishor Dr RTHW LS26....135 G6
Hemsby Dr KGHY BD21....79 J3
Hemsby Rd KGHY BD21....79 J3
Hemsby St KGHY BD21....79 J3
Hemsworth La
 HEM/SK/SE WF9....223 J2
Hemsworth Rd
 HEM/SK/SE WF9....246 A1
Henacrewood Ct
 CUL/QBY BD13....125 G3
Henbury St CHAL LS7....7 K6
Henconner Av CHAL LS7....87 L8
Henconner Crs CHAL LS7....87 L8
Henconner Dr CHAL LS7....87 L8
Henconner Gdns CHAL LS7....87 L8
Henconner La BRAM LS13....107 M5
 CHAL LS7....87 L8
Hendal La WKFDW/WTN WF2....220 C1
Hendford Dr BFDE BD3....5 K5
Hendriff Pl WHIT OL12 *....206 B5
Hen Holme La AIRE BD20....36 A7
Henley Av BRAM LS13....107 L4
 EARL WF12....196 A4
 WBOW BD5....127 G4
 YEA LS19....84 F3
Henley Cl WBOW BD5....127 H4
 YEA LS19....84 F3
Henley Cft HUDE HD5....193 G8
Henley Dr FEA/AMT WF7....201 M3
 YEA LS19....84 F3
Henley Gv BRAM LS13....107 L4
 WBOW BD5....127 G4
Henley Hl YEA LS19....84 F3
Henley Mt YEA LS19....84 F3
Henley Pl BRAM LS13....107 L4
Henley Rd BRAM LS13....107 L4
 EARL WF12....196 A4
 WBOW BD5....127 H4
Henley St BRAM LS13....107 L4
 WHIT OL12....206 A5
Henley Ter BRAM LS13....107 L4
 ROCH OL11....228 A1
Henley Vw BRAM LS13....107 L4
Henrietta St BTLY WF17....173 L1
Henry Av HOR/CROF WF4....222 A2
 WOR/ARM LS12....130 D1
Henry Cl CUD/GR S72....244 D3
Henry Frederik Av HUDS HD4....213 L7
Henry Moore Ct CAS WF10....158 D7
Henry Ralph Av HUDS HD4....213 L5
Henry Ms GFTH/SHER LS25....116 A6
Henry St BRIG HD6....170 C2
 BTLY WF17....173 K1
 CLAY BD14....125 L2
 CUL/QBY BD13....102 F8
 HFAX HX1....10 C1
 HUD HD1....14 A1
 KGHY BD21....3 G4
 LIT OL15....207 H3
 ROCH OL11....228 A1
 WBSY BD6 *....126 D1
 WKFDW/WTN WF2....12 A3
Henry Ter YEA LS19....62 B7
Henshall St BSLY S70....261 G6
Henshaw Av YEA LS19....62 D8

Henshaw Crs YEA LS19....62 D8
Henshaw La YEA LS19....62 D8
Henshaw Ov YEA LS19....62 D8
Henshaw Rd TOD OL14....163 J5
Henshaw Woods TOD OL14....163 J5
Henson Gv CAS WF10....158 D8
Henthorn St ROY/SHW OL2....229 K8
Henton Ct OSM LS9....15 M5
Hepton Dr HBR HX7....143 H3
Hepworth Av MOR LS27....130 A8
Hepworth Crs HOLM/MEL HD9....255 G3
 MOR LS27....130 E8
Hepworth Dr MIRF WF14....172 E4
Hepworth Rd HOLM/MEL HD9....255 G3
Herbalist St WOR/ARM LS12....108 B5
Herbert Pl BFDE BD3....106 A6
Herbert St BGLY BD16....81 G1
 CAS WF10....157 M7
 CLAY BD14....125 L2
 HFAX HX1....10 A7
 SHPY BD18....82 B6
 WBOW BD5....126 F2
Hereford Cl HEM/SK/SE WF9....223 H1
 ROY/SHW OL2....229 H7
Hereford St ROCH OL11....228 C1
Hereford Wy WBOW BD4 *....127 J2
Heritage Ms HFAX HX1 *....11 J7
Heritage Pk BGLY BD16....59 J8
Heritage Rd BTLY WF17....173 L2
Heritage Wy HWTH BD22....78 E4
Hermit La DOD/DAR S75....260 B4
Hermit St HWTH BD22....79 J4
Hermon Av HFAX HX1....10 C7
Hermon Gv HFAX HX1....10 C7
Hermon Rd MSTN/BAR LS15....111 K5
Hermon St MSTN/BAR LS15....111 K5
Heron Cl AIRE BD20....35 K8
 AL/HA/HU LS17....88 B2
 BGLY BD16....80 C5
 CUL/QBY BD13....124 E4
 DEWS WF13....173 J3
Heron Ct MOR LS27....152 F2
Heron Dr WKFDW/WTN WF2....220 E1
Heron Gv AL/HA/HU LS17....88 C2
Herriot Ms CAS WF10....180 F1
Herschel Rd GIR BD8....103 L7
Hertford Cha MSTN/BAR LS15....111 L8
Hertford Cl MSTN/BAR LS15....111 M8
Hertford Cft MSTN/BAR LS15....111 M8
Hertford Fold MSTN/BAR LS15....111 L8
Hertford Lawn
 MSTN/BAR LS15....111 L8
Hertfordshire Park Cl
 ROY/SHW OL2 *....229 K6
Heseltine La HBR HX7....165 J2
Hesheth St BOW BD4....127 L3
Hesketh La EARD/LOFT WF3....152 F6
 KSTL LS5....108 C1
Hesketh Mt KSTL LS5....108 C1
Hesketh Pl KSTL LS5....108 C1
Hesketh Rd KSTL LS5....108 C1
 MILN OL16....206 E7
Hesketh Ter KSTL LS5....108 C1
Hesley Rd WKFDW/WTN WF2....198 D8
Hessle Av HDGY LS6....109 G3
Hessle Common La
 HOR/CROF WF4....201 M7
Hessle La HOR/CROF WF4....201 M6
Hessle Mt HDGY LS6....109 G3
Hessle Pl HDGY LS6....109 G3
Hessle Rd HDGY LS6....109 G3
Hessle Ter HDGY LS6....109 G3
Hessle Vw HDGY LS6....109 G3
Hessle Wk HDGY LS6....109 G3
Hetchell Vw AL/HA/HU LS17....67 L4
Hetton Dr BFDE BD3....105 M8
Hetton Rd RHAY LS8....110 D2
Heuthwaite Av WBY LS22....48 B2
Hever Gv HUDE HD5 *....215 G3
Heversham Av ROY/SHW OL2....229 M7
Hew Clews GTHN BD7....126 A3
Hew Royd IDLE BD10....83 M5
Hey Beck La EARL WF12....174 E1
Heybeck Wk BOW BD4....128 B4
Hey Bottom La WHIT OL12....184 C8
Heybrook St MILN OL16....206 E7
Hey Crs HOLM/MEL HD9....234 F6
Heyden Br GLSP SK13....265 M8
Heyford Ct ECHL BD2....104 F3
Heygate Cl BAIL BD17....82 F2
Heygate La BAIL BD17....82 F2
 BSPA/BRAM LS23....70 B2
Hey Head La LIT OL15....185 K5
 TOD OL14....141 M7
Hey La HUDE HD5....214 F3
 HUDS HD3....214 D7
 HUDW HD3....189 L7
Heys Av CUL/QBY BD13....103 H8
Heys Cl KNOT WF11....182 C2
Heys Crs CUL/QBY BD13....103 J8
Heys Gdns HOLM/MEL HD9....236 G6
Heysham Dr BOW BD4....128 B3
Heysham Gn BSLYN/ROY S71....261 M1
Hey Slack La KBTN HD8....235 L4
Heys La LUD/ILL HX2....122 E8
 MAR/SLWT HD7....211 M4
 RPDN/SBR HX6....188 C3
Hey St BRIG HD6....170 D2
 GTHN BD7....126 D6
 MILN OL16....206 D6
The Hey ROY/SHW OL2 *....230 A3
Heywood Cl HIPP HX3....147 J4
Heywood Ct HIPP HX3....147 J4
Heywood Pl HFAX HX1....10 D5
Heywood St HFAX HX1....10 D5
Hibbert Ter BSLY S70 *....261 H7
Hibson Cl WHIT OL12....184 E8
Hick La BTLY WF17....173 M1
Hickleton Ct ROY/SHW OL2....230 A3
Hickson Dr BSLYN/ROY S71....262 A2
Hick St BFD BD1 *....5 H6
Higgin Farm LUD/ILL HX2 *....146 C1
Higgin La HIPP HX3....169 G1
Higham Common Rd
 DOD/DAR S75....260 A2
Higham & Dob La
 RPDN/SBR HX6....166 E2
Higham La DOD/DAR S75....260 A5
Higham Vw DOD/DAR S75....241 M7
Higham Wy GFTH/SHER LS25....113 H6
High Ash SHPY BD18....83 G1
High Ash Av AL/HA/HU LS17....88 B1
High Ash Crs AL/HA/HU LS17....88 A1
High Ash Dr AL/HA/HU LS17....88 A1
High Ash Mt AL/HA/HU LS17....88 A1
High Ash Pk WIL/AL BD15....103 H5
High Bank AIRE BD20....16 E8
High Bank Ap MSTN/BAR LS15....111 M7
High Bank Cl ELL HX5....169 L7

ILK LS29 * ... 19 H6
MSTN/BAR LS15 ... 111 M6
High Bank Gdns
MSTN/BAR LS15 ... 112 A7
High Bank Ga
MSTN/BAR LS15 * ... 111 M7
High Bank La SHPY BD18 ... 81 M8
STKB/PEN S36 ... 269 M1
High Bank PI MSTN/BAR LS15 ... 111 M7
High Banks CI AIRE BD20 ... 58 B4
High Bank Vw MSTN/BAR LS15 ... 111 M7
High Bank Wy MSTN/BAR LS15 ... 111 M7
High Barn CI ROCH OL11 ... 228 A1
High Bradley La AIRE BD20 ... 16 B1
Highbridge La KBTN HD8 ... 239 L5
Highbridge Ter WBOW BD5 ... 127 H5
High Brook Fall
EARD/LOFT WF3 ... 154 E8
High Brooms Rd HUDN HD2 ... 192 A5
High Bury CI CUL/QBY BD13 ... 124 E6
Highbury CI HDGY LS6 ... 87 G8
Highbury La HDGY LS6 ... 87 G8
Highbury PI BRAM LS13 ... 107 J6
HDGY LS6 ... 87 G8
Highbury Rd HDGY LS6 ... 87 G8
Highbury St HDGY LS6 ... 87 G8
Highbury Ter HDGY LS6 ... 87 G8
Highbury Wy ROY/SHW OL2 ... 228 F8
High Busy La IDLE BD10 ... 83 H6
High Cliffe BULY LS4 ... 108 E3
Highcliffe Av HUDN HD2 ... 192 B4
Highcliffe Ct HWTH BD22 ... 147 K1
Highcliffe Dr LUD/ILL HX2 ... 145 M7
Highcliffe Rd BTLY WF17 ... 173 L3
MOR LS27 ... 152 B2
High Cliffe Ter WBY LS22 ... 48 A4
High CI DOD/DAR S75 ... 241 M5
GSLY LS20 ... 61 K6
HUDE HD5 ... 215 G3
MAR/SLWT HD7 ... 213 G6
OSS WF5 ... 174 F5
YEA LS19 ... 84 D3
High Ct HBR HX7 ... 120 F8
LDSU LS2 ... 9 J1
High Court La LDSU LS2 ... 9 J1
High Crest MAR/SLWT HD7 ... 213 G4
High Cft CUL/QBY BD13 ... 125 G5
HIPP HX3 ... 146 B4
Highcroft HOLM/MEL HD9 ... 254 A1
WBY LS22 ... 47 J6
Highcroft CI PDSY/CALV LS28 ... 106 C1
High Croft Crs HUDE HD5 ... 215 H3
High Croft Dr BSLYN/ROY S71 ... 243 H7
Highcroft Gdns EARD/LOFT WF3 ... 58 B8
High Croft Rd TOD OL14 ... 141 L8
High Croft Wy AIRE BD20 ... 58 F5
Highcroft Wy WIL/AL BD15 ... 206 B2
High Cross La HIPP HX3 ... 125 J7
Highdale EARL WF12 ... 174 A4
Highdale Cft IDLE BD10 ... 83 K6
Higher Ashenhurst TOD OL14 ... 141 J7
Higher Back La HBR HX7 ... 142 A2
Higher Bank Rd LIT OL15 ... 207 J3
Higher Brockwell
RPDN/SBR HX6 ... 167 H3
Higher Cleggswood Av
LIT OL15 ... 207 J3
Higher Coach Rd BAIL BD17 ... 81 M4
Higher Downs GIR BD8 ... 103 M6
Higher Grange Rd
PDSY/CALV LS28 ... 107 C6
Higher Intake Rd ECHL BD2 ... 105 L3
Higher Lodge St AIRE BD20 ... 34 D8
Higher Park Royd Dr
RPDN/SBR HX6 ... 167 C7
Higher Ri ROY/SHW OL2 ... 229 J5
Higher School St SHPY BD18 * ... 82 B6
Higher Shore Rd WHIT OL12 ... 185 G7
Higher Wheat La MILN OL16 ... 206 B6
Higherwood CI KGHY BD21 ... 3 M5
Highfell Ri HWTH BD22 ... 79 G1
High Fernley Ct LM/WK BD12 * ... 148 C3
High Fernley Rd LM/WK BD12 ... 148 C3
Highfield BOW BD4 ... 127 M4
EARD/LOFT WF3 ... 152 F5
HIPP HX3 ... 147 K1
Highfield Av BRIG HD6 ... 148 D6
BSLY S70 ... 261 H8
BSLYN/ROY S71 ... 243 J8
COL BB8 ... 52 A5
GTL/HWG HX4 ... 168 D6
HIPP HX3 ... 125 M7
HOLM/MEL HD9 ... 234 F3
IDLE BD10 ... 83 J7
KBTN HD8 ... 256 C2
PONT WF8 ... 180 E7
PONT WF8 ... 181 J2
WOR/ARM LS12 ... 130 F1
Highfield CI AIRE BD20 ... 58 B4
FEA/AMT WF7 ... 179 M6
MOR LS27 ... 130 A7
WOR/ARM LS12 ... 130 F1
Highfield Ct HWTH BD22 ... 78 E4
KBTN HD8 ... 238 A8
LVSG WF15 ... 172 B4
Highfield Crs BAIL BD17 ... 82 E1
CAS WF10 ... 157 H1
HBR HX7 ... 143 J2
HOLM/MEL HD9 ... 234 F3
HOR/CROF WF4 ... 196 B8
HTON BD9 ... 103 M2
PDSY/CALV LS28 ... 106 F6
RTHW LS26 ... 133 L7
WOR/ARM LS12 ... 108 F8
Highfield Dr BTLY WF17 ... 151 G4
CAS WF10 ... 157 H1
GFTH/SHER LS25 ... 135 H1
HTON BD9 ... 103 M2
LVSG WF15 ... 172 A2
MOR LS27 ... 129 M7
WKFDW/WTN WF2 ... 176 A6
YEA LS19 ... 84 C1
Highfield Gdns EARL WF12 ... 195 M3
HTON BD9 ... 103 M3
MOR LS27 ... 129 M7
WOR/ARM LS12 ... 108 E8
Highfield Garth WOR/ARM LS12 ... 130 F1
Highfield Gra HOR/CROF WF4 ... 197 J5
Highfield Gn CAS WF10 ... 135 H8
GFTH/SHER LS25 ... 116 A8
PDSY/CALV LS28 ... 106 F6
Highfield Gv CAS WF10 ... 135 H8
ELL HX5 ... 169 G6
IDLE BD10 ... 83 J7
High Field La HWTH BD22 ... 78 E3
Highfield La AIRE BD20 ... 36 A4
AWLS/ASK DN6 ... 227 L5
DEWS WF13 ... 173 H3
GFTH/SHER LS25 ... 136 F2
HOLM/MEL HD9 ... 234 E3
HUDE HD5 ... 215 L1
KGHY BD21 ... 2 D3
MSTN/BAR LS15 ... 112 F1
RTHW LS26 ... 133 L7
Highfield Ms AIRE BD20 ... 58 E5
Highfield Mt EARL WF12 ... 196 A5
RTHW LS26 * ... 133 L8

Highfield PI CAS WF10 ... 135 J8
GIR BD8 ... 4 B1
HEM/SK/SE WF9 ... 223 L8
HFAX HX1 ... 10 B8
MOR LS27 ... 152 D3
Highfield Range WMB/DAR S73 ... 263 J7
Highfield Ri BRAM LS13 ... 107 M4
BRIG HD6 ... 170 A6
CLECK BD19 ... 149 L7
ELL HX5 ... 169 H8
GFTH/SHER LS25 ... 92 A6
HEM/SK/SE WF9 ... 223 L8
HOLM/MEL HD9 * ... 234 F3
HOR/CROF WF4 ... 197 J5
HOR/CROF WF4 ... 218 F1
HTON BD9 ... 104 E1
IDLE BD10 ... 83 J8
KBTN HD8 ... 216 A7
KGHY BD21 ... 2 C3
LUD/ILL HX2 ... 145 G6
MILN OL16 ... 206 E6
PDSY/CALV LS28 ... 106 E6
PONT WF8 ... 180 E8
WMB/DAR S73 ... 263 J8
Highfields Rd DOD/DAR S75 ... 241 K6
Highfield St BRAM LS13 * ... 107 M4
KGHY BD21 ... 2 F4
PDSY/CALV LS28 ... 106 E6
Highfield Ter EARL WF12 ... 195 M3
HFAX HX1 ... 10 B8
PDSY/CALV LS28 ... 106 E6
SHPY BD18 ... 82 A6
Highfield Vw MOR LS27 ... 130 A7
Highfield Vls GFTH/SHER LS25 ... 116 A8
Highfold YEA LS19 ... 84 C1
High Fold La AIRE BD20 ... 57 J4
Highgate AIRE BD20 ... 34 E7
HTON BD9 ... 104 B2
Highgate Av KBTN HD8 ... 216 B3
Highgate CI CUL/QBY BD13 ... 125 L4
Highgate Crs KBTN HD8 ... 216 A3
Highgate Dr KBTN HD8 ... 216 B3
ROY/SHW OL2 ... 228 E7
Highgate Gdns LUD/ILL HX2 ... 146 A6
Highgate Gv CLAY BD14 ... 125 L4
Highgate La HUDE HD5 ... 193 M4
KBTN HD8 ... 215 M3
Highgate Rd CUL/QBY BD13 ... 125 L4
EARL WF12 ... 173 M6
HTON BD9 ... 104 C2
Highgate St BTLY WF17 ... 174 B3
High Gate Wk KBTN HD8 * ... 216 B3
High Gn KBTN HD8 ... 216 B4
High Green Dr AIRE BD20 ... 35 M4
High Green Rd NORM WF6 ... 178 A2
Highgrove Ct NORM WF6 ... 178 B1
High Grove La HIPP HX3 ... 11 L9
High Holly Garth KGHY BD21 * ... 3 K7
High House Av ECHL BD2 ... 105 J2
High House Edge
MAR/SLWT HD7 ... 212 E7
High House La LUD/ILL HX2 ... 144 E2
MAR/SLWT HD7 ... 212 D7
High House Rd ECHL BD2 ... 105 J2
High Hoyland La DOD/DAR S75 ... 240 D7
High Keep Fold
HOR/CROF WF4 ... 220 B3
Highland CI PONT WF8 ... 181 H3
Highlands ILK LS29 ... 40 A6
Highlands CI GTHN BD7 ... 126 A3
MID LS10 ... 132 B7
Highlands Dr GTHN BD7 ... 126 A3
MID LS10 ... 132 B6
Highlands La LUD/ILL HX2 ... 124 B8
Highlands Rd ROY/SHW OL2 ... 229 H6
The Highlands LVSG WF15 ... 171 M1
Highlands Wk MID LS10 ... 132 B6
Highland Ville HIPP HX3 ... 147 M7
High La HBR HX7 ... 165 L3
HUDS HD4 ... 214 D4
HWTH BD22 ... 54 D5
LUD/ILL HX2 ... 145 K6
PBR HG3 ... 28 B4
STKB/PEN S36 ... 256 F7
High Lea MAR/SLWT HD7 ... 233 H2
Highlea CI YEA LS19 ... 84 B1
Highlee La RPDN/SBR HX6 ... 167 H4
High Lee La STKB/PEN S36 ... 271 H1
High Lees Rd LUD/ILL HX2 ... 145 K1
High Level Rd ROCH OL11 ... 206 C8
High Level Wy HFAX HX1 ... 10 B3
Highley Hall Cft BRIG HD6 ... 171 G4
Highley Pk BRIG HD6 ... 171 G4
High Meadow AIRE BD20 ... 57 J5
High Mdw EARL WF12 ... 195 L5
GTL/HWG HX4 ... 168 D2
WIL/AL BD15 ... 102 D1
WKFDW/WTN WF2 ... 199 K8
High Mil ILK LS29 * ... 19 J5
High Mill La ILK LS29 ... 19 J5
Highmoor BAIL BD17 ... 82 C3
High Moor Av AL/HA/HU LS17 ... 88 A4
High Moor CI AL/HA/HU LS17 ... 88 A4
High Moor Crs AL/HA/HU LS17 ... 88 A4
Highmoor Crs BRIG HD6 ... 170 F3
High Moor Dr AL/HA/HU LS17 ... 88 A3
Highmoor La BRIG HD6 ... 170 F3
Highmoor Rd PBR HG3 ... 25 L4
Highmoor Wk BAIL BD17 ... 82 C4
Highoak Garth HWTH BD22 ... 78 E4
High Oxford St CAS WF10 ... 157 L7
High Park Crs HTON BD9 ... 104 A3
High Park Dr HTON BD9 ... 103 M3
High Park Gv HTON BD9 ... 104 A3
High Pastures HWTH BD22 ... 79 G1
High Poplars ECHL BD2 ... 105 H2
High Rdg HOR/CROF WF4 ... 197 G8
High Ridge Av RTHW LS26 ... 132 F7
High Ridge Pk RTHW LS26 ... 133 G7
High Ridge Wy BHP/TINH LS16 ... 64 B7
High Rd EARL WF12 ... 174 A7
Highroad Well La LUD/ILL HX2 ... 145 L2
Highroyd KBTN HD8 ... 216 B3
High Royd Av CUD/GR S72 ... 244 D8
Highroyd Crs HUDE HD5 ... 215 L7
Highroyd La HUDE HD5 ... 15 L7
High Royd La STKB/PEN S36 ... 271 J1
High Royds Dr ILK LS29 ... 61 J3
High Spring Gardens La
... 2 D1
High Spring Rd KGHY BD21 ... 58 B8
Highstone Av BSLY S70 ... 261 G7
Highstone Crs BSLY S70 ... 261 G7
Highstone La BSLY S70 ... 261 H8
Highstone Rd BSLY S70 ... 261 H7
High Stones Rd HBR HX7 ... 166 A3

Highstone V BSLY S70 ... 261 G7
High St AIRE BD20 ... 55 M1
AIRE BD20 ... 56 E1
AWLS/ASK DN6 ... 227 L6
AWLS/ASK DN6 ... 227 M3
AWLS/ASK DN6 ... 249 L6
BRIG HD6 ... 170 D3
BSLYN/ROY S71 ... 243 K3
BSLYN/ROY S71 ... 261 L2
BSPA/BRAM LS23 ... 48 D6
BSPA/BRAM LS23 ... 69 M4
BSPA/BRAM LS23 ... 70 A4
BTLY WF17 ... 151 G4
BTLY WF17 ... 174 B3
CAS WF10 ... 157 L7
CLECK BD19 ... 149 M6
COL BB8 ... 74 A1
CUD/GR S72 ... 244 E4
CUD/GR S72 ... 245 G1
CUD/GR S72 ... 245 H8
CUL/QBY BD13 ... 102 F8
CUL/QBY BD13 ... 125 K5
DEWS WF13 ... 173 K7
DOD/DAR S75 ... 242 C4
DOD/DAR S75 ... 259 H7
DOD/DAR S75 ... 260 B7
EARL WF12 ... 174 B7
EARL WF12 ... 195 L5
GFTH/SHER LS25 ... 135 K5
GTL/HWG HX4 ... 168 F7
GTL/HWG HX4 ... 190 A3
HECK WF16 ... 173 J5
HEM/SK/SE WF9 ... 225 J7
HEM/SK/SE WF9 ... 247 K3
HFAX HX1 ... 10 F7
HOLM/MEL HD9 * ... 236 B2
HOR/CROF WF4 ... 197 J5
HOR/CROF WF4 ... 200 A2
HOR/CROF WF4 ... 200 B6
HOR/CROF WF4 ... 200 D1
HOR/CROF WF4 ... 220 A1
HOR/CROF WF4 ... 220 B7
HUD HD1 ... 14 F2
IDLE BD10 ... 83 K6
KBTN HD8 ... 240 D4
KGHY BD21 ... 2 F5
KNOT WF11 ... 159 L5
KNOT WF11 * ... 181 L1
LIT OL15 ... 207 H1
LUD/ILL HX2 ... 145 G5
MAR/SLWT HD7 ... 212 D1
MOR LS27 ... 152 D3
NORM WF6 ... 178 C4
PBR HG3 ... 28 E4
PDSY/CALV LS28 ... 106 F5
ROY/SHW OL2 ... 229 K8
SKP/WHF BD23 ... 16 C2
STKB/PEN S36 ... 270 F4
TAD LS24 ... 71 L3
WBSY BD6 ... 126 E5
WBY LS22 ... 48 A1
WHIT OL12 ... 206 A6
WKFDW/WTN WF2 ... 199 J6
High St * ... 62 E7
High Street Ct LUD/ILL HX2 ... 145 G5
Highthorne CI BFDE BD3 ... 105 M8
Highthorne Ct AL/HA/HU LS17 * ... 88 B2
Highthorne Dr AL/HA/HU LS17 ... 88 B2
Highthorne Gn ROY/SHW OL2 ... 228 E6
Highthorne Mt AL/HA/HU LS17 ... 88 B2
Highthorne St WOR/ARM LS12 * ... 108 C6
Highthorne Vw
WOR/ARM LS12 ... 108 C6
High Thorns DOD/DAR S75 ... 259 H6
Hightown La HOLM/MEL HD9 ... 254 C1
Hightown Rd CLECK BD19 ... 149 M7
Hightown Vw LVSG WF15 ... 171 M3
High Trees Ct GFTH/SHER LS25 ... 116 A7
High Trees La GTL/HWG HX4 ... 167 M8
High Vw BSLYN/ROY S71 ... 243 K3
HOR/CROF WF4 ... 220 A1
High View Ct WMB/DAR S73 ... 263 J7
Highway GSLY LS20 ... 61 L7
High Weardley La CUD/GR S72 ... 222 E8
High Well Hill La CUD/GR S72 ... 222 E8
High Wheatley ILK LS29 ... 39 G3
High Wicken CI CUL/QBY BD13 ... 124 B5
High Wd ILK LS29 ... 39 H3
Highwood Av AL/HA/HU LS17 ... 87 L4
Highwood CI DOD/DAR S75 ... 241 L6
Highwood Crs AL/HA/HU LS17 ... 87 L4
High Woodlands
EARD/LOFT WF3 ... 153 L7
High Wood Rd BTLY WF17 ... 151 J5
Higson Ct HUDE HD5 ... 193 J7
Hildbrord Rd BTLY WF17 ... 173 M2
Hilda St HTON BD9 ... 104 C2
OSS WF5 ... 174 E4
Hild Av CUD/GR S72 ... 262 F2
Hilam Common La
GFTH/SHER LS25 ... 138 F8
Hillam Hall La GFTH/SHER LS25 ... 138 D8
Hillam Hall Vw GFTH/SHER LS25 ... 138 D8
Hillam La GFTH/SHER LS25 ... 160 A1
Hillam Rd ECHL BD2 ... 104 F3
SEL YO8 ... 139 L7
Hillam St WBOW BD5 ... 126 D3
Hillary PI LDSU LS2 ... 8 E5
Hillary St DEWS WF13 ... 173 H3
Hillbro Ct BAIL BD17 * ... 82 F2
Hill Brow CI WIL/AL BD15 ... 103 J5
Hill CI BAIL BD17 ... 82 D4
HUDW HD3 ... 191 H5
PONT WF8 ... 180 F7
Hillcote Dr WBOW BD5 ... 127 G2
Hill Court Av BRAM LS13 ... 107 L2
Hillcourt Crs BRAM LS13 ... 107 L2
Hill Court Dr BRAM LS13 ... 107 L2
Hillcourt Gv BRAM LS13 ... 107 L2
Hill Crs BTLY WF17 ... 151 J5
ILK LS29 ... 40 B7
YEA LS19 ... 84 E1
Hillcrest HOR/CROF WF4 ... 222 E6
WBY LS22 ... 47 G6
Hillcrest BHP/TINH LS16 * ... 63 J2
GFTH/SHER LS25 ... 138 D7
HEM/SK/SE WF9 * ... 223 M8
Hillcrest Av AIRE BD20 ... 36 A4
BTLY WF17 ... 173 J4
CAS WF10 ... 158 F8
HEM/SK/SE WF9 ... 223 M8
HOR/CROF WF4 ... 7 M2
TAD LS24 ... 71 K4
Hillcrest Ct TAD LS24 ... 71 K4

Hill Crest Dr CUL/QBY BD13 ... 101 M5
CUL/QBY BD13 ... 125 H6
Hillcrest Dr CAS WF10 ... 158 F8
CUL/QBY BD13 ... 125 H6
Hillcrest Mt BHP/TINH LS16 ... 86 A2
CAS WF10 ... 158 F8
CLECK BD19 ... 149 M7
Hill Crest PI CHAL LS7 ... 7 M1
Hillcrest PI CUL/QBY BD13 ... 101 M5
Hillcrest Ri BHP/TINH LS16 ... 86 A7
Hill Crest Rd CUL/QBY BD13 ... 101 M5
CUL/QBY BD13 ... 102 F7
GFTH/SHER LS25 ... 135 L1
Hillcrest Rd CAS WF10 ... 159 G8
CUL/QBY BD13 ... 125 H6
Hillcrest Vw CHAL LS7 ... 7 M1
Hill Cft CUL/QBY BD13 ... 103 G7
Hill Croft CI PONT WF8 ... 203 M1
Hill Dr FEA/AMT WF7 ... 202 C6
Hill End EARL WF12 ... 174 A6
Hill End CI HIPP HX3 ... 148 C4
Hill End Crs WOR/ARM LS12 ... 108 B6
Hill End Gv CUL/QBY BD13 ... 126 A3
Hill End La HOLM/MEL HD9 ... 80 A6
CUL/QBY BD13 ... 124 F6
HWTH BD22 ... 54 A4
Hill End Rd DOD/DAR S75 ... 242 E7
WOR/ARM LS12 ... 108 B6
Hillesley Rd EARL WF12 ... 174 C3
Hillfold HEM/SK/SE WF9 ... 223 K3
Hill Foot SHPY BD18 ... 81 M7
Hillfoot Av PDSY/CALV LS28 ... 106 D6
Hillfoot Crs PDSY/CALV LS28 ... 106 D6
Hill Foot La PBR HG3 ... 26 C2
Hillfoot Ri PDSY/CALV LS28 ... 106 D6
Hillgarth EARL WF12 ... 195 M5
KNOT WF11 ... 182 A3
Hill Green Ct BOW BD4 ... 129 G4
Hill Gv HUDW HD3 ... 191 H5
Hill Grove Lea HUDW HD3 ... 191 H5
Hill Gv South MID LS10 ... 132 B7
Hillhead Dr BTLY WF17 ... 151 J5
Hill House Edge La HWTH BD22 ... 77 G4
Hillhouse La HUD HD1 ... 14 F2
Hill House La HWTH BD22 ... 100 E5
Hill House Rd HOLM/MEL HD9 ... 254 A4
Hillam Hall CI GFTH/SHER LS25 ... 138 D8
Hillidge Rd MID LS10 ... 9 J8
Hillidge Sq MID LS10 ... 9 J7
Hillingdon Wy AL/HA/HU LS17 ... 87 J1
Hillings La ILK LS29 ... 60 F2
Hill Lands LM/WK BD12 ... 148 D2
Hill La COL BB8 ... 52 D8
HOLM/MEL HD9 ... 253 J3
Hill Mount Pleasant MID LS10 ... 153 L1
Hill Park Av HIPP HX3 ... 10 A1
Hill Park Gv DOD/DAR S75 ... 260 B6
Hill Ri BTLY WF17 ... 174 B2
SKP/WHF BD23 ... 16 E4
Hill Rise Av BRAM LS13 ... 107 L2
Hill Rise Gv BRAM LS13 ... 107 L2
Hill Rd CAS WF10 ... 158 B7
Hills & Hamlets Wk
HOLM/MEL HD9 ... 235 M8
Hillside BSLYN/ROY S71 ... 262 C6
GFTH/SHER LS25 ... 113 J8
KBTN HD8 ... 239 H8
KNOT WF11 ... 159 M7
PBR HG3 ... 28 A1
Hill Side Av HOLM/MEL HD9 ... 255 G6
HUDN HD2 ... 192 D4
HWTH BD22 ... 78 D4
LUD/ILL HX2 ... 144 F7
ROY/SHW OL2 ... 229 M7
RPDN/SBR HX6 ... 167 G8
Hillside Ct GFTH/SHER LS25 ... 138 D7
HEM/SK/SE WF9 ... 247 J2
ILK LS29 ... 61 H2
Hillside Crs CUD/GR S72 ... 245 J4
HUDS HD4 ... 214 C4
SKP/WHF BD23 ... 16 E3
Hillside Gv CUD/GR S72 ... 245 H4
HWTH BD22 ... 78 D4
PDSY/CALV LS28 ... 107 J7
Hill Side La STKB/PEN S36 ... 270 A4
Hill Side Mt PDSY/CALV LS28 ... 107 G4
Hillside Mt CUD/GR S72 ... 245 J4
PDSY/CALV LS28 ... 107 G4
PONT WF8 ... 181 G6
Hillside Rd GSLY LS20 ... 61 M4
HUDS HD4 ... 214 C4
SKP/WHF BD23 ... 16 E3
BGLY BD16 ... 81 H3
Hill Side Rd BFDE BD3 ... 5 J5
BGLY BD16 ... 81 H3
Hillside Rd CHAL LS7 ... 87 M7
FEA/AMT WF7 ... 202 C8
PBR HG3 ... 26 E2
PONT WF8 ... 181 G6
SHPY BD18 ... 82 E8
Hillside Ter BAIL BD17 * ... 82 E2
Hillside Vw MAR/SLWT HD7 ... 212 E5
PDSY/CALV LS28 ... 107 H7
RPDN/SBR HX6 ... 167 K3
Hill St BEE/HOL LS11 ... 8 D9
ILK LS29 ... 19 G6
STKB/PEN S36 ... 258 D8
WKFDW/WTN WF2 ... 197 M3
Hill Top CAS WF10 ... 157 H7
DOD/DAR S75 ... 259 G2
HEM/SK/SE WF9 * ... 225 K3
HFAX HX1 ... 168 A1
ILK LS29 ... 38 C4
ILK LS29 ... 40 A5
WOR/ARM LS12 ... 71 K7
Hill Top Av BSLYN/ROY S71 ... 261 G5
RHAY LS8 ... 88 B6
Hilltop CI CUD/GR S72 ... 245 H3
Hill Top Av EARD/LOFT WF3 ... 153 G8
WKFDW/WTN WF2 * ... 220 E2
Hilltop CI CAS WF10 ... 158 C5
HEM/SK/SE WF9 * ... 223 K3
HOR/CROF WF4 ... 7 M2
TAD LS24 ... 71 K7
Hill Top Cottages HTON BD9 ... 104 A4
Hill Top Crs MIRF WF14 ... 194 A5

Hill Top Cft HUDS HD4 ... 213 L8
Hill Top Dr HUDW HD3 ... 191 J6
ROCH OL11 ... 228 C4
Hill Top Est HECK WF16 ... 173 G2
Hill Top Farm KBTN HD8 ... 257 H1
Hill Top Gdns EARD/LOFT WF3 * ... 153 G8
Hill Top Gn EARD/LOFT WF3 ... 152 F8
Hill Top Gv EARD/LOFT WF3 ... 153 G8
WIL/AL BD15 ... 103 J5
Hill Top La BGLY BD16 ... 59 J6
EARD/LOFT WF3 ... 152 F8
HBR HX7 ... 153 K5
HOR/CROF WF4 ... 201 L5
PBR HG3 ... 26 B1
WIL/AL BD15 ... 103 J5
Hill Top Ms KNOT WF11 ... 182 B2
Hill Top Mt RHAY LS8 ... 110 B2
Hill Top PI HDGY LS6 ... 6 A4
RHAY LS8 ... 110 B2
Hill Top Rd CUL/QBY BD13 ... 102 D7
HOLM/MEL HD9 ... 254 B6
HOR/CROF WF4 ... 217 M3
HUD HD1 ... 14 A9
HUDE HD5 ... 215 L4
HUDW HD3 ... 191 H5
HWTH BD22 ... 78 D4
KGHY BD21 ... 79 J3
MAR/SLWT HD7 ... 212 B5
WKFDW/WTN WF2 ... 220 F2
WOR/ARM LS12 ... 108 B6
Hill Top Vw EARD/LOFT WF3 ... 152 F8
HOLM/MEL HD9 ... 254 D6
Hill Top Wk HWTH BD22 ... 2 A4
Hill Top Wy HWTH BD22 ... 2 A4
Hill Vw LUD/ILL HX2 ... 124 B7
Hillview Gdns HIPP HX3 ... 147 J5
Hill View Mt CHAL LS7 ... 87 M7
Hill View PI CHAL LS7 ... 87 M7
Hill View Ter CHAL LS7 * ... 87 M7
Hillway GSLY LS20 ... 61 L7
Hilmian Wy HEM/SK/SE WF9 ... 246 B1
Hilton Av SHPY BD18 ... 104 D1
Hilton Ct BHP/TINH LS16 ... 63 J2
Hilton Crs BAIL BD17 ... 82 F2
Hilton Dr SHPY BD18 ... 104 D1
Hilton Gra BHP/TINH LS16 ... 63 K3
Hilton Gv GTHN BD7 ... 104 C8
RHAY LS8 ... 110 B2
SHPY BD18 ... 104 D1
Hilton Ms BHP/TINH LS16 ... 63 J3
Hilton PI RHAY LS8 ... 110 B2
Hilton Rd GTHN BD7 ... 104 C8
RHAY LS8 ... 110 B2
SHPY BD18 ... 104 D1
Hilton St DOD/DAR S75 ... 260 F4
HBR HX7 ... 143 J6
RHAY LS8 * ... 110 B2
Hilton Ter RHAY LS8 ... 110 B2
Hinchcliffe Av OSS WF5 ... 197 H1
Hinchcliffe St BFDE BD3 ... 5 L3
Hinchliffe Av BAIL BD17 ... 82 F4
Hind Ct HOLM/MEL HD9 ... 234 C1
Hindle PI MOR LS27 ... 130 A7
Hindle St BSLY S70 ... 260 F5
Hindley Rd LVSG WF15 ... 172 C3
Hindley Wk GTHN BD7 ... 125 M4
Hinds Crs HEM/SK/SE WF9 ... 247 K5
Hind St LM/WK BD12 ... 148 E4
Hinsley Ct HDGY LS6 ... 109 G2
Hinton WHIT OL12 * ... 206 A6
Hinton Ct PONT WF8 ... 181 G3
Hinton La KNOT WF11 ... 159 J8
Hions CI BRIG HD6 ... 170 C6
Hipswell St BFDE BD3 ... 105 L6
Hird Av WBSY BD6 ... 126 E6
Hird Rd LM/WK BD12 ... 126 F8
Hird St BAIL BD17 ... 82 D6
BEE/HOL LS11 ... 8 D9
KGHY BD21 ... 2 F1
Hirds Yd SKP/WHF BD23 ... 16 E3
Hirst Av HECK WF16 ... 172 F1
Hirst Gv HBR HX7 ... 143 K3
Hirstlands Av OSS WF5 ... 174 E6
Hirstlands Dr OSS WF5 ... 174 E6
Hirst La HOLM/MEL HD9 ... 255 K2
SHPY BD18 ... 82 B6
Hirst Lodge Ct ECHL BD2 ... 105 H2
Hirst Mill Crs SHPY BD18 ... 82 A5
Hirst Rd DEWS WF13 ... 173 L5
WKFDW/WTN WF2 ... 135 G7
Hirst St CAS WF10 ... 157 J3
TOD OL14 * ... 140 D7
Hirst Wood Crs SHPY BD18 ... 82 A6
Hirst Wood Rd SHPY BD18 ... 81 M6
Hive St HWTH BD22 ... 2 D7
Hobart Rd CAS WF10 ... 158 F6
EARL WF12 ... 174 E5
Hobberley La AL/HA/HU LS17 ... 89 H3
Hobb Nook La OT LS21 ... 22 C7
Hob Cote La HWTH BD22 ... 78 B5
Hobcroft Ter AWLS/ASK DN6 ... 228 E6
Hob La HUDS HD4 ... 213 K4
HWTH BD22 ... 77 L7
LUD/ILL HX2 ... 144 D2
RPDN/SBR HX6 ... 167 K5
RPDN/SBR HX6 ... 188 L1
Hockney Rd GIR BD8 ... 104 D6
Hodder Av LIT OL15 ... 185 H8
Hodge La PONT WF8 ... 205 G8
Hodgewood La PONT WF8 ... 181 M8
Hodgkinson Av STKB/PEN S36 ... 270 F2
Hodgson Av AL/HA/HU LS17 ... 88 C3
BIRK/DRI BD11 ... 105 M6
Hodgson Crs AL/HA/HU LS17 ... 88 C3
Hodgson Fold AL/HA/HU LS17 ... 18 F5
Hodgson La BIRK/DRI BD11 ... 128 D2
Hodgson PI MOR LS27 ... 130 D7
Hodgson's La GFTH/SHER LS25 ... 116 C5
Hodgson St MOR LS27 ... 152 E5
WKFDE WF1 ... 176 D2
Hodroyd Cottages CUD/GR S72 ... 245 H4
Hodroyd La CUD/GR S72 ... 244 F5
Hodster La CUD/GR S72 ... 263 M2
Hofmann St HUDW HD3 ... 213 J2
Hogarth Rd ROCH OL11 ... 228 B4
Hog Close La HOLM/MEL HD9 ... 255 L6
Hogley La HOLM/MEL HD9 ... 253 G7
Holays HUDE HD5 ... 193 G7
Holbeck La BEE/HOL LS11 ... 8 B4
Holbeck Moor Rd BEE/HOL LS11 ... 8 C6
Holbeck Towers BEE/HOL LS11 ... 8 C6
Holborn Ap HDGY LS6 ... 6 D2
Holborn Ct HDGY LS6 ... 6 D2
WBSY BD6 ... 147 G2
Holborn Gdns HDGY LS6 ... 6 D2
Holborn Gn HDGY LS6 ... 6 D2
Holborn Gv HDGY LS6 ... 6 D2
Holborn St HDGY LS6 ... 6 D2
Holborn Ter HDGY LS6 ... 6 E2
Holborn Vw HDGY LS6 ... 6 D2
Holborn Wk HDGY LS6 ... 6 D2
Holby Sq WKFDW/WTN WF2 * ... 197 L2
Holden Ct BSLY S70 ... 261 G5
Holden Ing Wy BTLY WF17 ... 151 K2
Holden La AIRE BD20 ... 36 C7
BAIL BD17 ... 82 C7
Holden St WHIT OL12 * ... 206 C4

Holderness Rd KNOT WF11 .....182 A1
Holderness St TOD OL14 .....163 L1
Holdforth Cl WOR/ARM LS12 .....109 G7
Holdforth Gdns WOR/ARM LS12 .....109 G7
Holdforth Gn WOR/ARM LS12 .....109 G8
Holdforth Pl WOR/ARM LS12 .....109 G7
Holdsworth Av HECK WF16 .....151 C7
Holdsworth Ct CLECK BD19 .....149 M7
Holdsworth Rd LUD/ILL HX2 .....124 C7
Holdsworth St BFD BD1 .....5 G4
  CLECK BD19 .....149 M6
  SHPY BD18 .....78 E1
Holdsworth Ter HFAX HX1 .....168 F1
Hole Bottom Rd TOD OL14 .....141 M8
Hole La AIRE BD20 .....35 K2
Holes La KNOT WF11 .....182 A2
Holford Wk MILN OL16 .....206 F7
Holgate Crs HEM/SK/SE WF9 .....223 L7
Holgate Gdns HEM/SK/SE WF9 .....223 L7
Holgate Mt BSLY S70 .....261 H8
Holgate Pl PONT WF8 .....202 E1
Holgate Vw CUD/GR S72 .....245 J3
Holker St GTHN BD8 .....104 D6
  KGHY BD21 .....3 G5
Holland Ri WHIT OL12 * 206 A4
Holland Rd GFTH/SHER LS25 .....135 L4
Holland St BTLY WF17 .....173 M1
  MILN OL16 .....206 F2
  WHIT OL12 .....206 A4
Hollas La RPDN/SBR HX6 .....168 A4
Hollerton La EARD/LOFT WF3 .....153 H6
The Hollies WOR/ARM LS12 * 108 E7
Hollin Av HUDW HD3 .....191 M7
Hollinbank La HECK WF16 .....173 G1
Hollin Brigg La HOLM/MEL HD9 .....253 L6
Hollin Close La ECHL BD2 .....105 G3
Hollin Ct BHP/TINH LS16 * 86 F7
Hollin Crs BHP/TINH LS16 .....86 F7
Hollin Cft DOD/DAR S75 .....260 C6
Hollin Dr BHP/TINH LS16 .....86 F7
  HOR/CROF WF4 .....220 A1
Hollin Edge KBTN HD8 .....239 J8
Hollin End BHP/TINH LS16 .....86 F7
Hollin Ga OT LS21 .....40 F4
Hollingbourne Rd
  MSTN/BAR LS15 .....112 B4
Hollin Greaves La HIPP HX3 * 11 H1
Hollings Rd GIR BD8 .....104 D6
Hollings Sq GIR BD8 .....104 D6
  PDSY/CALV LS28 .....84 D7
Hollings St BGLY BD16 .....81 K7
  GIR BD8 .....104 D6
Hollings Ter GIR BD8 .....104 D6
The Hollings WHIT LS26 .....156 D3
Hollingthorpe Av
  HOR/CROF WF4 .....220 A3
Hollingthorpe Ct
  HOR/CROF WF4 .....220 A4
Hollingthorpe Gv
  HOR/CROF WF4 .....220 A3
Hollingthorpe La
  HOR/CROF WF4 .....220 A3
Hollingthorpe Rd
  HOR/CROF WF4 .....220 A3
Hollington St COL BB8 .....74 D7
Hollingwood Av GTHN BD7 .....126 B2
Hollingwood Ct GTHN BD7 .....126 A2
Hollingwood Dr GTHN BD7 .....126 A2
Hollingwood Ga ILK LS29 .....38 A3
Hollingwood La GTHN BD7 .....126 A3
Hollingwood Mt GTHN BD7 .....126 A2
Hollingworth Fold LIT OL15 * 207 L4
Hollingworth Rd KNOT WF11 .....182 A3
  TOD OL14 .....163 K6
Hollingworth Rd LIT OL15 .....207 K6
Hollin Hall Dr ILK LS29 .....38 A3
Hollin Hall La HUDE HD5 .....193 M4
  MAR/SLWT HD7 .....212 F1
Hollin Head Rd SHPY BD18 .....82 E8
Hollin Hill BAIL BD17 .....83 H2
Hollin Hill Av RPDN/SBR HX6 .....110 E3
Hollinhirst La HOR/CROF WF4 .....219 H1
Hollin House La
  HOLM/MEL HD9 .....255 H1
  KBTN HD8 .....240 B7
Hollin La BHP/TINH LS16 .....86 F7
  HBR HX7 .....144 C1
  HOR/CROF WF4 .....197 M8
  RPDN/SBR HX6 .....167 K5
  SHPY BD18 .....82 F8
  STKB/PEN S36 .....269 J2
Hollin Mt BHP/TINH LS16 .....86 F7
Hollin Park Av RHAY LS8 .....110 E1
Hollin Park Ct PDSY/CALV LS28 .....84 C8
Hollin Park Crs RHAY LS8 .....110 F1
Hollin Park Dr PDSY/CALV LS28 .....84 C8
Hollin Park Mt RHAY LS8 .....110 F1
Hollin Park Pl RHAY LS8 .....110 E1
Hollin Park Rd PDSY/CALV LS28 .....84 C8
  RHAY LS8 .....110 E1
Hollin Park Ter RHAY LS8 .....110 E1
Hollin Ri SHPY BD18 * 82 E8
Hollin Rd BHP/TINH LS16 .....86 F7
  SHPY BD18 .....82 E8
Hollinroyd Rd EARL WF12 .....174 A6
Hollins Av DEWS WF13 .....173 H4
Hollins Bank RPDN/SBR HX6 .....167 K5
Hollins Bank La AIRE BD20 .....56 F2
Hollins Beck Cl GFTH/SHER LS25 .....135 J6
Hollins Cl AIRE BD20 .....57 H4
Hollins Gln MAR/SLWT HD7 .....211 M8
Hollins Gv CAS WF10 .....135 H8
Hollins Hey Rd GTL/HWG HX4 .....190 F2
Hollins Hl BAIL BD17 .....61 K8
Hollins La AIRE BD20 .....57 H3
  LUD/ILL HX2 .....145 L1
  LUD/ILL HX2 .....166 D1
  MAR/SLWT HD7 .....211 M8
  RPDN/SBR HX6 .....167 K1
Hollins Meadow TOD OL14 .....163 J5
Hollins Mill La RPDN/SBR HX6 .....167 J2
Hollins Mt HEM/SK/SE WF9 .....223 M7
Hollins Pl HBR HX7 .....143 J5
Hollin Ter HUDW HD3 .....191 L7
  TOD OL14 .....163 J5
Hollins Rd DEWS WF13 .....173 H4
  TOD OL14 .....163 J4
Hollins Rw MAR/SLWT HD7 .....212 C1
Hollins St TOD OL14 .....163 J6
The Hollins DOD/DAR S75 .....260 C6
  TOD OL14 .....141 K8
Hollin St RPDN/SBR HX6 .....167 G5
Hollins Wood Gv CUD/GR S72 .....262 E2
Hollin Ter HUDW HD3 .....191 E8
Hollins Vw BHP/TINH LS16 * 86 F7
Hollin Wood Cl SHPY BD18 .....82 A7
Hollinwood Vw AIRE BD20 .....58 A7
Hollis Pl BVRD LS3 6
Hollowdene DOD/DAR S75 .....260 D3
Hollowfield Cft LM/WK BD12 .....149 K1
Hollowgate HOLM/MEL HD9 .....254 C1
Hollowspell WHIT OL12 .....206 A3
The Hollow HOLM/MEL HD9 .....234 E4
Holly Ap OSS WF5 .....174 F6
Holly Av BHP/TINH LS16 * 85 M3
Holly Bank FEA/AMT WF7 .....202 B8

  GFTH/SHER LS25 .....113 K8
  HDGY LS6 .....86 F8
  HEM/SK/SE WF9 * 223 M7
Hollybank Av BTLY WF17 .....151 K7
Hollybank Dr HIPP HX3 .....147 M6
Hollybank Gdns GTHN BD7 .....126 A3
Holly Bank Gv GTHN BD7 .....126 A3
Holly Bank Pk BRIG HD6 .....170 B6
Holly Bank Rd BRIG HD6 .....170 B6
  HUDW HD3 .....191 K5
Hollybank Rd GTHN BD7 .....126 A3
Holly Bush Ct BSPA/BRAM LS23 .....49 G7
Hollybush Gn WBY LS22 .....47 L6
Holly Cl HEM/SK/SE WF9 .....247 H4
  HOR/CROF WF4 .....200 A5
  MID LS10 .....153 K2
Holly Crs HOR/CROF WF4 .....200 A5
  RPDN/SBR HX6 .....188 E3
Hollycroft Ct BHP/TINH LS16 .....86 C1
Holly Dene OSS WF5 .....174 F6
Holly Dr BHP/TINH LS16 .....85 M3
Hollyfield Av HUDW HD3 .....191 J7
Hollygarth La GLE DN14 .....161 J7
Holly Gv BTLY WF17 .....173 K2
  CUD/GR S72 .....245 J3
  HFAX HX1 .....10 C7
  HUDW HD3 .....191 J5
Holly Hall La LM/WK BD12 .....148 E2
Holly Mede OSS WF5 .....174 F6
Hollynsmill GTL/HWG HX4 .....168 F7
Hollyoake Av MAR/SLWT HD7 .....212 C6
Holly Pk AL/HA/HU LS17 .....43 L1
  Crs LS18 .....85 H5
Holly Park Dr GTHN BD7 .....126 A2
Holly Park Gv GTHN BD7 .....126 A2
Holly Park Mills
  PDSY/CALV LS28 * 84 C8
  PDSY/CALV LS28 * 107 G2
Holly Rd BSPA/BRAM LS23 .....48 E6
  HUD HD1 .....14 A6
Hollyshaw Crs MSTN/BAR LS15 .....111 L6
Hollyshaw Gv MSTN/BAR LS15 .....111 L6
Hollyshaw La MSTN/BAR LS15 .....111 L6
Hollyshaw Ter MSTN/BAR LS15 .....111 L6
Hollyshaw Wk MSTN/BAR LS15 .....111 L6
Holly St HEM/SK/SE WF9 .....223 M7
  WBSY BD6 .....125 M4
  WHIT OL12 .....184 E8
  WKFDW/WTN WF2 .....176 C6
Holly Tree La MSTN/BAR LS15 .....112 A8
Hollywell Gv WOR/ARM LS12 .....108 D7
Hollywell La WOR/ARM LS12 .....108 D7
Holman Av GFTH/SHER LS25 .....135 H5
Holmcliffe Av HUDS HD4 .....214 B5
Holmclose HOLM/MEL HD9 .....253 K4
Holmdale Crs HOLM/MEL HD9 .....236 B6
Holmdene Dr MIRF WF14 .....172 C8
Holme Av HUDE HD5 .....215 G1
Holmebank Ms
  HOLM/MEL HD9 .....236 D3
Holme Cl AIRE BD20 .....34 F8
  HOR/CROF WF4 .....217 G1
Holme Ct HOLM/MEL HD9 .....237 G7
Holme Crs COL BB8 .....74 D3
Holme Cft HOR/CROF WF4 .....198 B7
Holme Dr LUD/ILL HX2 .....145 K8
Holme Farm Cl WBSY BD6 .....125 M5
Holme Farm Ct WOR/ARM LS12 .....139 H1
Holme Farm La
  BSPA/BRAM LS23 .....68 C4
Holme Fld OSS WF5 .....174 E7
Holmefield Rd AIRE BD20 .....55 M1
  HUDW HD3 .....191 G8
Holme Gv ILK LS29 .....40 A8
Holme House La HWTH BD22 .....78 E1
Holme House Rd TOD OL14 .....140 E5
Holme House St LIT OL15 .....185 M5
Holme Ings ILK LS29 .....19 L7
Holme La AIRE BD20 .....55 M1
  BOW BD4 .....128 A5
  HOLM/MEL HD9 .....237 G7
  MAR/SLWT HD7 .....211 L6
  WKFDW/WTN WF2 .....198 D4
Holme Leas Dr OSS WF5 .....174 E7
Holme Mill La HWTH BD22 .....2 F
Holme Pk ILK LS29 .....40 B7
Holme Park Ct HUDS HD4 * 214 A6
Holme Pl HBR HX7 .....143 J7
Holme Rd LUD/ILL HX2 .....145 K8
Holmeside Cl HUDS HD4 .....214 A6
Holme South LUD/ILL HX2 .....145 K8
Holme St BEE/HOL LS11 .....9 G4
  GIR BD8 .....104 C4
  WHIT OL12 .....206 B3
Holmes Ter LUD/ILL HX2 * 145 M6
Holmes St BRIG HD6 .....148 C7
  COL BB8 .....74 D1
  HBR HX7 .....143 J3
  HWTH BD22 .....78 C7
  LVSG WF15 .....172 D2
  TOD OL14 .....141 G7
  WBOW BD5 .....126 F2
Holme Styes La
  HOLM/MEL HD9 .....254 A5
Holme Ter LIT OL15 .....185 M5
Holme Top La WBOW BD5 .....126 F2
Holme Top St WBOW BD5 .....126 F2
Holme Valley Circular Wk
  HOLM/MEL HD9 .....253 K3
  HUDS HD4 .....214 A7
Holme View Dr
  HOLM/MEL HD9 .....254 A1
Holme View Pk
  HOLM/MEL HD9 .....254 A1
Holme Wy OSS WF5 .....174 E7
Holme Well Rd MID LS10 .....153 L6
Holme Wood Rd BOW BD4 .....127 M3
  HWTH BD22 .....2 B7
Holme Woods La
  HWTH BD22 .....78 B1
Holmfield KBTN HD8 * 240 B4
Holmfield Av WKFDW/WTN WF2 .....12 D9
Holmfield Cha EARD/LOFT WF3 * 155 K8
Holmfield Cl KBTN HD8 .....240 B4
  PONT WF8 .....181 H5
Holmfield Dr MAR/SLWT HD7 .....213 H2
  RHAY LS8 88
Holmfield Gv WKFDW/WTN WF2 .....12 D9
Holmfield La PONT WF8 .....181 H5
  WKFDW/WTN WF2 .....12 D9
Holmfirth Rd HOLM/MEL HD9 .....235 G5
  HOLM/MEL HD9 .....236 C1
  KBTN HD8 .....237 M8
Holmsley Av HEM/SK/SE WF9 .....246 C4
Holmsley Crest RTHW LS26 .....133 J7
Holmsley Field Ct RTHW LS26 .....133 L8
Holmsley Field La RTHW LS26 .....133 K8
Holmsley Garth RTHW LS26 .....133 K7

Holmsley Gv HEM/SK/SE WF9 .....246 C4
Holmsley La CUD/GR S72 .....246 A4
  RTHW LS26 .....133 K8
Holmsley Mt HEM/SK/SE WF9 .....246 C4
Holmwood Cl HDGY LS6 .....87 H6
Holmwood Crs HDGY LS6 .....87 H6
Holmwood Dr HDGY LS6 .....87 G6
Holmwood Gv HDGY LS6 .....87 G6
Holmwood Ms HDGY LS6 .....87 H6
Holmwood Vw HDGY LS6 .....87 H6
Holroyd Hl WBSY BD6 .....126 C6
Holroyd Mill La AIRE BD20 .....59 G6
Holroyd St CHAL LS7 7
  MILN OL16 .....206 C7
Holsworthy Rd BOW BD4 .....128 A3
Holt Av BHP/TINH LS16 .....86 C1
  HUDN 192 B5
Holtby Gv BRIG HD6 .....148 C7
Holt Cl BHP/TINH LS16 .....86 B1
Holt Crs BHP/TINH LS16 .....86 B1
Holtdale Av BHP/TINH LS16 .....86 B1
Holtdale Cl BHP/TINH LS16 .....86 B1
Holtdale Cft BHP/TINH LS16 .....86 B1
Holtdale Dr BHP/TINH LS16 .....86 B1
Holtdale Fold BHP/TINH LS16 .....86 B1
Holtdale Gdns BHP/TINH LS16 .....86 B1
Holtdale Garth BHP/TINH LS16 .....86 B1
Holtdale Gn BHP/TINH LS16 .....86 B1
Holtdale Gv BHP/TINH LS16 .....86 B1
Holtdale Lawn BHP/TINH LS16 .....86 B1
Holtdale Pl BHP/TINH LS16 .....86 B1
Holtdale Rd BHP/TINH LS16 .....86 B1
Holtdale Vw BHP/TINH LS16 .....86 B1
Holtdale Wy BHP/TINH LS16 .....86 B1
Holt Dr BHP/TINH LS16 .....86 C1
Holt Farm Cl BHP/TINH LS16 .....86 C1
Holt Farm Ri BHP/TINH LS16 .....86 C1
Holt Gdns BHP/TINH LS16 .....86 B1
  IDLE BD10 .....83 H6
Holt Garth BHP/TINH LS16 .....86 C1
Holt Ga BHP/TINH LS16 .....86 B1
Holt Head Rd MAR/SLWT HD7 .....212 D8
Holt Park Ap BHP/TINH LS16 .....86 C1
Holt Park Av BHP/TINH LS16 .....86 C1
Holt Park Cl BHP/TINH LS16 .....86 C1
Holt Park Crs BHP/TINH LS16 .....86 C1
Holt Park Dr BHP/TINH LS16 .....86 C1
Holt Park Gdns BHP/TINH LS16 .....86 C1
Holt Park Gra BHP/TINH LS16 .....86 C1
Holt Park Gn BHP/TINH LS16 .....86 C1
Holt Park Gv BHP/TINH LS16 .....86 C1
Holt Park La BHP/TINH LS16 .....86 C1
Holt Park Ri BHP/TINH LS16 .....86 C1
Holt Park Rd BHP/TINH LS16 .....86 C1
Holt Park V BHP/TINH LS16 .....86 C1
Holt Park Vw BHP/TINH LS16 .....86 C1
Holt Ri BHP/TINH LS16 .....86 C1
Holt Rd BHP/TINH LS16 .....86 C1
Holts La CLAY BD14 .....125 H4
Holts Ter HIPP HX3 * 168 F2
  WHIT OL12 .....206 A4
The Holt SHPY BD18 .....82 E7
Holt Vw BHP/TINH LS16 .....86 B1
Holt Vw BHP/TINH LS16 .....86 C1
Holwick Cl DOD/DAR S75 * 259 H6
Holwick Ct BSLY S70 * 261 H8
Holybrook Av IDLE BD10 .....83 M8
Holycroft St KGHY BD21 .....2 B
Holyoake Av BGLY BD16 .....81 H5
  BTLY WF17 .....173 J1
Holyoake St TOD OL14 .....140 C5
Holyoake Ter HOR/CROF WF4 .....197 C5
  MAR/SLWT HD7 212
Holyrood Crs NORM WF6 .....178 B2
Holy Rood La GFTH/SHER LS25 .....137 G6
Holy St ROCH OL11 .....228 D4
Holywell Ash La GIR BD8 4
Holywell Gdns CAS WF10 .....158 B8
Holywell La AL/HA/HU LS17 .....88 C1
  CAS WF10 .....158 C8
Holywell Mt CAS WF10 .....158 C8
Homefield Av MOR LS27 .....152 C4
Home Lea RTHW LS26 .....132 F7
Home Lea Dr RTHW LS26 .....132 F7
Homestead Dr
  WKFDW/WTN WF2 .....176 A6
Homestead Gdns WHIT OL12 .....206 F1
The Homestead HECK WF16 173
Home View Ter GIR BD8 .....104 D5
Honey Head La
  HOLM/MEL HD9 .....236 B3
Honey Hole Cl TOD OL14 .....163 K2
Honey Hole Rd TOD OL14 .....163 K2
Honey Pot La BAIL BD17 * 82 D3
Honeysuckle Cl
  WKFDW/WTN WF2 .....176 A7
Honeysuckle Dr EARL WF12 .....195 M3
Honeywell Cl BSLYN/ROY S71 .....261 H3
Honeywell Gv BSLYN/ROY S71 .....261 G3
Honeywell La BSLYN/ROY S71 .....261 G3
Honeywell Pl BSLYN/ROY S71 .....261 G3
Honeywell St BSLYN/ROY S71 .....261 H3
Honley Rd HUDS HD4 .....214 E8
Honley Sq HOR/CROF WF4 .....197 J5
Honoria St HUD HD1 .....14 F1
The Hoods BRIG HD6 .....170 D7
Hood St HEM/SK/SE WF9 .....247 G6
  HUDS HD4 .....214 B6
Hoopoe Ms WIL/AL BD15 .....103 K7
Hooton Crs HOR/CROF WF4 .....222 A7
Hoowood La HOLM/MEL HD9 .....253 G3
Hopbine Av WBOW BD5 .....127 G4
Hopbine Rd WBOW BD5 .....127 G4
Hope Av SHPY BD18 .....82 F6
  WBOW BD5 .....126 E4
Hopefield Cha EARD/LOFT WF3 .....154 D2
Hopefield Cl RTHW LS26 .....154 D2
Hopefield Ct EARD/LOFT WF3 .....153 L7
  EARD/LOFT WF3 .....154 D2
Hopefield Crs RTHW LS26 .....154 D2
Hopefield Dr EARD/LOFT WF3 .....154 D2
Hopefield Gdns
  EARD/LOFT WF3 .....154 D2
Hopefield Gn RTHW LS26 .....154 D2
Hopefield Gv RTHW LS26 * 154 D2
Hopefield Ms EARD/LOFT WF3 .....154 D2
Hopefield Pl RTHW LS26 .....154 D2
Hopefield Vw RTHW LS26 .....154 D2
Hopefield Wy BOW BD4 .....127 K5
  RTHW LS26 .....154 D2
Hope Hall St HFAX HX1 .....11 H4
Hope Hall Ter HFAX HX1 .....11 H5
Hope Hill Vw BGLY BD16 .....81 J7
Hope La BAIL BD17 .....82 D3
Hope Pl BVRD LS3 8
Hope Rd LDSU LS2 .....7 K8
Hopes Farm Mt MID LS10 .....132 B7
Hopes Farm Rd MID LS10 .....132 B7
Hopes Farm Vw MID LS10 .....132 B7
Hope St BSLYN/ROY S71 .....244 B8
  CAS WF10 .....158 A3

  DEWS WF13 .....173 L5
  DOD/DAR S75 .....242 E6
  DOD/DAR S75 .....260 F4
  HBR HX7 .....143 J3
  HFAX HX1 .....10 C5
  HUDW HD3 * 213 K1
  MOR LS27 .....152 C2
  NORM WF6 .....178 C6
  OSS WF5 .....197 H3
  ROY/SHW OL2 .....229 K7
  RPDN/SBR HX6 .....167 J3
  WBOW BD5 .....206 B6
  WKFDE WF1 .....176 E7
Hope St East CAS WF10 .....157 M6
Hope St West CAS WF10 .....157 L7
Hope Vw SHPY BD18 .....82 E7
Hopewell Pl BSLY S70 .....261 M6
Hopewell St GFTH/SHER LS25 .....135 K5
  MID LS10 .....153 M1
Hopewell Wy HOR/CROF WF4 .....220 A1
Hopkinson Dr BOW BD4 .....127 L5
Hopkinson Rd HUDN 192 D2
Hopkinson St COL BB8 * 74 D3
  LUD/ILL HX2 .....146 B3
Hopkin St BOW BD4 .....128 A5
Hopps's Rd AIRE BD20 .....34 C5
Hopton Av BOW BD4 .....127 M5
  MIRF WF14 .....194 A4
Hopton Dr MIRF WF14 .....194 A4
Hopton Hall La HUDE HD5 .....194 B6
Hopton La MIRF WF14 .....194 A4
Hopton Ms WOR/ARM LS12 .....108 D7
Hopton New Rd MIRF WF14 .....194 C3
Hopwood Bank HORS LS18 .....85 L4
Hopwood Cl HORS LS18 .....85 L4
Hopwood Gv CAS WF10 .....158 D7
Hopwood La HFAX HX1 .....10 A7
Hopwood Rd HORS LS18 .....85 L4
Horace Waller VC Pde
  EARL WF12 .....174 C4
Horbury Ms HOR/CROF WF4 .....197 H4
Horbury Rd CUD/GR S72 .....244 D6
  OSS WF5 .....197 G3
Horest La HUDW HD3 .....230 D6
Horley Green Rd HIPP HX3 .....11 L2
Hornbeam Av
  WKFDW/WTN WF2 .....176 C6
Hornbeam Cl WIL/AL BD15 .....103 H2
Hornbeam Gn PONT WF8 .....181 H5
Hornbeam Wy SCFT LS14 .....89 L6
Hornby St BSLY S70 .....261 H7
  HFAX HX1 * 10 B8
Hornby Ter HFAX HX1 * 10 B8
Horncastle St CLECK BD19 .....150 A7
Horncastle Vw HOR/CROF WF4 .....222 F4
Horn Cote La HOLM/MEL HD9 .....237 J8
Horn Cft DOD/DAR S75 .....259 G1
Horner Av BTLY WF17 .....151 H8
Horner Crs BTLY WF17 .....151 H8
Hornes La DOD/DAR S75 .....242 E5
Horne St HFAX HX1 .....10 E5
  WKFDW/WTN WF2 .....12 D6
Hornington Br COP/BISH YO23 .....73 L1
Horn La AIRE BD20 .....37 G6
  HOLM/MEL HD9 .....237 J8
  STKB/PEN S36 .....256 C5
Hornsea Dr WIL/AL BD15 .....102 E3
Hornthwaite Hill Rd
  STKB/PEN S36 .....270 D4
Horse Bank Dr HUDS HD4 * 214 A8
  HUDW HD3 .....191 G5
  LUD/ILL HX2 * 145 M7
Horse Carr Vw BSLYN/ROY S71 .....262 C4
Horse Cl La KBTN HD8 .....238 D3
Horse Fair PONT WF8 .....180 F6
Horsefair WBY LS22 .....48 A1
Horsehold La HBR HX7 .....143 G4
Horsehold Rd HBR HX7 .....143 G4
Horse Pond La HUDW HD3 .....190 C7
Horseshoe Ct WIL/AL BD15 .....102 B8
Horsewood Cl BSLY S70 .....260 D6
Horsfall St HFAX HX1 .....168 C1
  MOR LS27 .....130 B8
  TOD OL14 .....142 A8
Horsfall Vls TOD OL14 * 142 A8
Horsforth New Rd BRAM LS13 .....85 G8
Horsham Ct HWTH BD22 .....79 G1
Horsman Rd BOW BD4 * 128 A4
Horsley St WBSY BD6 .....126 E5
Horsman St BOW BD4 .....128 A5
Horton Cl BRAM LS13 .....107 H2
Horton Garth BRAM LS13 .....107 H2
Horton Grange Rd GTHN BD7 .....104 D8
Horton Hall Cl WBOW BD5 .....126 F1
Horton Park Av GTHN BD7 .....126 D1
Horton Ri BRAM LS13 .....107 H2
Horton St HECK WF16 .....172 F3
  HFAX HX1 .....11 H7
  OSS WF5 .....174 E8
Hospital La BHP/TINH LS16 .....86 B4
Hospital Rd AIRE BD20 .....58 C5
Hostingley La EARL WF12 .....196 B5
Hothfield St AIRE BD20 .....35 M5
Hough HIPP HX3 .....147 J4
Hough End Av BRAM LS13 .....107 L5
Hough End Cl BRAM LS13 .....107 L5
Hough End Crs BRAM LS13 * 107 L5
Hough End Ct BRAM LS13 .....107 L5
Hough End Garth BRAM LS13 .....107 L5
Hough End Gdns BRAM LS13 .....107 L5
Hough End La BRAM LS13 .....107 L5
Hough Gv BRAM LS13 .....107 L5
Houghley Av WOR/ARM LS12 .....108 A3
Houghley Cl WOR/ARM LS12 .....108 B3
Houghley Crs WOR/ARM LS12 .....108 B3
Houghley La WOR/ARM LS12 .....108 A3
Houghley Pl WOR/ARM LS12 .....108 A3
Houghley Sq WOR/ARM LS12 .....108 A3
Hough Side Cl PDSY/CALV LS28 .....107 J7
Hough Side La PDSY/CALV LS28 .....107 J7
Hough Side Rd PDSY/CALV LS28 .....107 J7
Hough Ter BRAM LS13 .....107 L5
Hough Top BRAM LS13 .....107 J5
Hough Tree Rd BRAM LS13 .....107 L5
Hoults La GTL/HWG HX4 .....168 F5
House Ct KBTN HD8 * 240 B4
House Grove Dr KBTN HD8 .....240 A4
Hovingham Av RHAY LS8 .....110 C5
Hovingham Gv RHAY LS8 .....110 C5
Hovingham Mt RHAY LS8 .....110 C5
Hovingham Ter RHAY LS8 .....110 C5
Howard Av HUDW HD3 .....191 H4
  MSTN/BAR LS15 .....111 H7
Howard Ct MSTN/BAR LS15 .....111 H7
Howard Crs HOR/CROF WF4 .....198 A8
Howard Dr FEA/AMT WF7 .....224 D2
Howard Pl BTLY WF17 .....173 L1
  MILN OL16 .....206 B0
Howard Rd HUDW HD3 .....191 H4

Howards Dean HWTH BD22 .....78 F5
Howard St BSLY S70 .....261 H7
  BTLY WF17 .....173 L3
  HFAX HX1 .....10 C4
  OSS WF5 * 174 F7
  ROY/SHW OL2 .....229 J7
  WBOW BD5 .....206 B6
  WKFDE WF1 .....176 E7
Howard Wv HOLM/MEL HD9 .....235 G5
  LIT OL15 .....185 L5
Howarth Av AIRE BD20 .....105 J1
Howarth Crs ECHL BD2 * 105 J1
Howarth Cross St MILN OL16 .....206 E3
Howarth Farm Wy WHIT OL12 .....206 E3
Howarth La HUDS HD4 .....214 A3
Howarth Pl CHAL LS7 .....7 H6
  LIT OL15 .....185 K8
Howbeck Av AIRE BD20 .....58 C5
Howbeck Dr AIRE BD20 .....58 C5
Howcans La HIPP HX3 .....146 C2
Howcroft Gdns
  WKFDW/WTN WF2 .....199 G7
Howden Av AIRE BD20 .....57 J4
  AWLS/ASK DN6 .....249 G5
Howdenbrook HIPP HX3 .....125 M7
Howden Cl BOW BD4 .....128 B7
  DOD/DAR S75 .....242 B5
  HUDS HD4 .....213 H4
Howden Clough Rd MOR LS27 .....151 L3
Howden Gdns HDGY LS6 .....109 G4
Howden Pl HDGY LS6 .....109 G4
Howden Rd AIRE BD20 .....36 B5
Howden Wy WKFDE WF1 .....13 L5
Howell La CUD/GR S72 .....246 A8
Howes La HIPP HX3 .....147 H3
Howgate IDLE BD10 .....83 L6
Howgate Hl HIPP HX3 .....169 H1
Howgate Rd MAR/SLWT HD7 .....212 B6
Howgill Gn WBSY BD6 .....126 C8
Howhill Quarry Rd PBR HG3 .....25 M1
Howley Mill La MOR LS27 .....151 M7
Howley Park Cl MOR LS27 .....152 B4
Howley Park Rd MOR LS27 .....152 B4
Howley Park Rd East
  MOR LS27 .....152 C5
Howley Wk BTLY WF17 .....151 M8
  BTLY WF17 .....174 A1
Howroyd La EARL WF12 .....195 G3
  GTL/HWG HX4 .....189 K2
Howroyd's Yd OSS WF5 .....174 E8
Howson Cl GSLY LS20 .....62 B6
Hoxton St BEE/HOL LS11 .....9 A9
Hoxton St GIR BD8 .....104 C6
Hoylake Av HUDN 192 B3
Hoyland Rd WKFDW/WTN WF2 .....220 D1
Hoyle Court Av BAIL BD17 .....83 G3
Hoyle Court Dr BAIL BD17 .....83 G3
Hoyle Court Rd BAIL BD17 .....83 G3
Hoyle Fold HWTH BD22 .....2 A4
Hoyle House Fold
  MAR/SLWT HD7 .....212 F5
Hoyle Ing MAR/SLWT HD7 .....212 F4
Hoyle Ing Rd CUL/QBY BD13 .....103 H8
Hoyle Mill Rd BSLY S70 .....261 M6
  HEM/SK/SE WF9 .....223 M4
Hoyle's Ter MILN OL16 * 207 G8
Hubberton Green Rd
  RPDN/SBR HX6 .....166 E3
Hubert St BFDE BD3 .....5 M8
  HUDW HD3 .....191 G5
  LUD/ILL HX2 * 145 M7
Huddersfield Rd BRIG HD6 .....170 D4
  DEWS WF13 .....194 F1
  DOD/DAR S75 .....241 K1
  DOD/DAR S75 .....260 F3
  ELL HX5 .....191 J1
  HFAX HX1 .....168 E1
  HOLM/MEL HD9 .....235 G4
  HOLM/MEL HD9 .....236 C1
  HOR/CROF WF4 .....219 H6
  HUDW HD3 .....191 J2
  KBTN HD8 .....238 F3
  LM/WK BD12 .....148 E3
  MILN OL16 .....229 L2
  MIRF WF14 .....171 M8
  MIRF WF14 .....194 C2
  STKB/PEN S36 .....257 H6
  STKB/PEN S36 .....270 E2
  UPML OL3 .....231 L1
  WBSY BD6 .....126 D3
Huddleston Ct EARL WF12 .....174 B6
Hud Hl HIPP HX3 .....147 K2
Hudroyd HUDE HD5 .....215 H3
Hudson Av GTHN BD7 .....126 B2
  HOR/CROF WF4 .....221 K8
Hudson Cl GTHN BD7 .....126 D3
  TAD LS24 .....71 M1
  WBY LS22 29
Hudson Crs GTHN BD7 .....126 D3
Hudson Gdns GTHN BD7 .....126 D3
Hudson Gv OSM LS9 .....110 C5
Hudson Ms BSPA/BRAM LS23 .....49 G7
Hudson Mill Rd HBR HX7 .....142 D3
Hudson Pl OSM LS9 * 110 C5
Hudson Rd OSM LS9 .....110 C5
Hudson St BFDE BD3 .....105 M7
  OSM LS9 .....110 C5
  PDSY/CALV LS28 * 106 F5
  TOD OL14 .....163 J5
The Hudson LM/WK BD12 .....148 E3
Hudson Vw TAD LS24 .....71 M1
Hudson Wy TAD LS24 .....71 M1
Hudswell Rd MID LS10 10
Hudswell St WKFDE WF1 .....13 K9
Hughenden Dr CUL/QBY BD13 .....103 J8
Hughenden Vw CUL/QBY BD13 .....103 J8
Hughenden Wk CUL/QBY BD13 .....103 J8
Hugh St CAS WF10 .....158 M7
  MILN OL16 .....206 D1
Hughtrede St MILN OL16 * 228 D3
Hugill St CUL/QBY BD13 .....102 F8
Hulbert Cft HUDE HD5 .....215 H2
Hulbert St BGLY BD16 .....81 J4
Hullenedge Gdns ELL HX5 .....168 F8
Hullenedge La GTL/HWG HX4 .....168 F8
Hullenedge Rd ELL HX5 .....168 F8
Hullen Rd ELL HX5 .....168 F8
Hullett Cl HBR HX7 .....144 B5
Hullett Dr HBR HX7 .....144 B5
Hull St MOR LS27 .....152 C2
Hulme Sq CAS WF10 .....158 D3
Humber Cl AWLS/ASK DN6 .....249 J5
  MAR/SLWT HD7 .....212 B6
Humber Ct AWLS/ASK DN6 .....249 J5
Humberside Wy
  BSLYN/ROY S71 .....243 M8
Humboldt St BFD BD1 .....5 J6
Hulme Crest BTLY WF17 .....173 L1
Hume St MILN OL16 .....206 D1
Humley Rd WKFDW/WTN WF2 .....220 D1
Hundhill La PONT WF8 .....202 F4
Hungate Cl TAD LS24 .....93 J7

Hungate La RTHW LS26 156 B5
Hungate Rd GFTH/SHER LS25 116 A6
Hungerford Rd HUDW HD3 191 M6
Hunger Hl HFAX HX1 11 H8
ILK LS29 20 E7
MOR LS27 152 C3
Hunger Hills Av HORS LS18 85 J5
Hunger Hills Dr HORS LS18 85 J5
Hunningley La BSLY S70 261 M6
Hunslet Green Wy MID LS10 9 J7
Hunslet Hall Rd BEE/HOL LS11 8 E7
Hunslet La MID LS10 9 H3
Hunslet Rd MID LS10 9 H3
Hunston Av HUDW HD3 191 K7
Hunsworth La BIRK/DRI BD11 128 A8
CLECK BD19 149 M5
Hunt Cl BSLYN/ROY S71 * 261 L2
Hunter Hill Rd LUD/ILL HX2 145 J1
Hunter's Av BSLY S70 260 C6
Hunterscombe Ct BGLY BD16 81 M1
Hunters Ct HTON BD9 103 L2
Hunters Gn CUL/QBY BD13 79 M7
Hunters Hill La UPML OL3 231 L8
Hunter's La MILN OL16 206 B6
TOD OL14 141 J8
Hunters Meadow AIRE BD20 36 A4
Hunters Park Av CLAY BD14 125 M1
Hunters Ri DOD/DAR S75 260 C5
Hunters Wk WBY LS22 30 A6
Huntingdon Av HUDN HD2 193 H1
Huntingdon Rd BRIG HD6 170 E5
Huntock Pl BRIG HD6 170 B1
Huntsman Fold
WKFDW/WTN WF2 175 M8
Huntsmans Cl AIRE BD20 2 D2
BGLY BD16 81 L1
HUDS HD4 213 M6
Huntsmans Wy
HEM/SK/SE WF9 225 G4
Hunt St CAS WF10 157 K6
Huntwick Av FEA/AMT WF7 201 L2
Huntwick Crs FEA/AMT WF7 201 K2
Huntwick Dr FEA/AMT WF7 201 K2
Huntwick La FEA/AMT WF7 201 J2
Huntwick Rd FEA/AMT WF7 201 L2
Hurricane Cl GFTH/SHER LS25 116 E7
Hurrs Rd SKP/WHF BD23 16 D2
Hurstead Gn WHIT OL12 * 206 F2
Hurstead Rd MILN OL16 207 H8
Hurst Knowle HUDE HD5 215 J2
Hurst La MIRF WF14 194 D3
Hurst Meadow MILN OL16 228 D4
Hurst Rd HBR HX7 143 K2
Hurst St ROCH OL11 228 C1
Hurstville Av BIRK/DRI BD11 128 B8
Hurstwood HUDN HD2 193 G2
Huskar Cl DOD/DAR S75 259 H6
Husler Gv CHAL LS7 7 J3
Husler Pl CHAL LS7 7 J3
The Hustings LVSG WF15 * 172 C2
Hustlergate BFD BD1 4 F6
Hustlers Rw HDGY LS6 86 F6
Hustler St BFDE BD3 5 L2
Hutchinson's Pl KSTL LS5 108 C3
Hutson St WBOW BD5 126 F2
Hutton Dr HECK WF16 173 G2
HEM/SK/SE WF9 247 J2
Hutton Rd WBOW BD5 126 E4
Hutton St RYKW YO26 33 K4
Hutton Ter IDLE BD10 105 M1
PDSY/CALV LS28 107 G7
Hydale Cl KGHY BD21 3 L8
Hydale Ct LM/WK BD12 126 E8
Hyde Gv KGHY BD21 3 J2
Hyde Pk HFAX HX1 10 D8
WKFDE WF1 13 K3
Hyde Park Cl HDGY LS6 6 A4
Hyde Park Cnr HDGY LS6 6 B2
Hyde Park Pl HDGY LS6 6 B2
Hyde Park Rd HDGY LS6 6 A4
HFAX HX1 10 C9
Hyde Park St HFAX HX1 10 D8
Hyde Park Ter HDGY LS6 6 B2
Hyde Pl LDSU LS2 6 C7
Hyde St IDLE BD10 83 K5
LDSU LS2 6 C7
Hyde Ter LDSU LS2 6 C7
Hydro Cl ILK LS29 39 H3
Hyman Wk HEM/SK/SE WF9 247 J2
Hyne Av BOW BD4 127 L5
Hyrst Garth BTLY WF17 173 K4
Hyrstlands Rd BTLY WF17 173 K3
Hyrst Wk BTLY WF17 173 L3

I

Ibberson Av DOD/DAR S75 242 C6
Ibbetson Cl MOR LS27 130 C7
Ibbetson Ct MOR LS27 130 C7
Ibbetson Cft MOR LS27 130 C7
Ibbetson Dr MOR LS27 130 C7
Ibbetson Ov MOR LS27 130 C7
Ibbetson Ri MOR LS27 130 C7
Ibbetson Rd MOR LS27 130 C7
Ibbotroyd Av TOD OL14 141 J7
Ibbotson Flats HUD HD1 15 G6
Ibbottson St WKFDE WF1 13 L9
Ibsley WHIT OL12 * 206 A6
Ida St MID LS10 132 C4
WBOW BD5 126 E3
Iddesleigh St BOW BD4 105 L8
Idlecroft Rd IDLE BD10 83 K6
Idle Rd ECHL BD2 105 K2
Idlethorp Wy IDLE BD10 83 L7
Ilbert Av BOW BD4 127 L5
Ilford St MOR LS27 152 D2
Ilkley Hall Ms ILK LS29 38 D3
Ilkley Hall Pk ILK LS29 38 D3
Ilkley Rd AIRE BD20 58 B4
ILK LS29 19 L8
ILK LS29 39 M3
OT LS21 41 G7
Illingworth Av LUD/ILL HX2 124 A7
NORM WF6 178 A2
Illingworth Cl LUD/ILL HX2 124 A7
YEA LS19 84 E1
Illingworth Crs LUD/ILL HX2 124 A7
Illingworth Dr LUD/ILL HX2 124 A7
Illingworth Gdns LUD/ILL HX2 124 A8
Illingworth Gv LUD/ILL HX2 124 A7
Illingworth Rd LM/WK BD12 149 H2
LUD/ILL HX2 124 A7
Illingworth St OSS WF5 196 F1
Illingworth Wy LUD/ILL HX2 124 A7
Illsley Rd WMB/DAR S73 263 J8
Ilminster ROCH OL11 * 206 A8
Imperial Ar HUD HD1 14 F7
Imperial Av WKFDW/WTN WF2 176 B4
Imperial Rd HDU HD1 14 A4
Inchfield Rd TOD OL14 163 J6
The Incline HIPP HX3 11 K4
Independent St WBOW BD5 126 E3
Indus Cl HECK WF16 173 G2
Industrial Av BTLY WF17 * 150 F5
Industrial Rd RPDN/SBR HX6 167 K2
Industrial St BGLY BD16 81 H3
BRIG HD6 170 D3
CLECK BD19 149 H6
HOR/CROF WF4 197 L6
HUDS HD4 214 C3
HWTH BD22 2 C7
LVSG WF15 172 A2
OSM LS9 110 B5
TOD OL14 163 K1
WKFDE WF1 * 12 F1
Industrial Ter HFAX HX1 168 D1
HUDE HD5 215 J1
Industry Rd BSLYN/ROY S71 243 L7
WHIT OL12 206 B5
Industry St LIT OL15 207 K1
TOD OL14 163 J5
Infirmary Rd DEWS WF13 173 K5
Infirmary St BFD BD1 4 D5
LDS LS1 6 F9
Ingbirchworth La
STKB/PEN S36 257 G7
Ingbirchworth Rd
STKB/PEN S36 270 C2
Ingdale Dr HOLM/MEL HD9 236 D8
Ing Fld LM/WK BD12 149 J2
Ingfield Av HUDE HD5 15 M7
OSS WF5 175 G8
Ingham Cl LUD/ILL HX2 124 B6
Ingham Cft MIRF WF14 194 E2
Ingham Garth MIRF WF14 194 E1
Ingham La LUD/ILL HX2 124 B5
Ingham Rd EARL WF12 195 M3
Ingham's Av PDSY/CALV LS28 106 D6
Inghams Ct HIPP HX3 * 10 D1
Inghams La LIT OL15 207 K1
Inghams Ter PDSY/CALV LS28 106 D6
Ingham St MID LS10 9 K5
Ingham's Vw PDSY/CALV LS28 106 D6
Ing Head MAR/SLWT HD7 212 A5
Inghead Gdns HIPP HX3 147 K2
Ing Head La HUDS HD4 237 J4
Ing La HUDS HD4 214 C4
Ingle Av MOR LS27 130 B8
Ingleborough Cl BOW BD4 128 A3
Ingleborough Dr MOR LS27 152 E4
Ingleby Cl ROY/SHW OL2 229 J6
Ingleby Dr TAD LS24 71 M2
Ingleby Pl GTHN BD7 104 C8
Ingleby Rd GIR BD8 104 C7
Ingleby St GIR BD8 104 C7
Ingleby Wy MID LS10 132 A7
ROY/SHW OL2 229 J6
Ingle Ct KBTN HD8 215 M2
MOR LS27 130 B8
Ingle Crs MOR LS27 152 C1
Ingledew Crs RHAY LS8 88 D4
Ingledew Dr RHAY LS8 88 D5
Ingle Gv MOR LS27 152 B1
Ingle Rw CHAL LS7 87 L8
Ingleton Cl BEE/HOL LS11 131 K3
Ingleton Dr MSTN/BAR LS15 111 G7
Ingleton Gv BEE/HOL LS11 131 K3
Ingleton Pl BEE/HOL LS11 131 K3
Ingleton Rd HUDS HD4 214 D4
Ingleton St BEE/HOL LS11 131 K3
Ingleton Wk BSLY S70 * 260 F4
Inglewood DOD/DAR S75 242 B5
Inglewood Av HUDW HD3 191 L5
Inglewood Dr OT LS21 41 H7
SCFT LS14 111 K3
Inglewood Pl SCFT LS14 111 K3
Inglewood Ter HDGY LS6 * 6 D1
Inglis St LIT OL15 185 K8
Ingram Cl BEE/HOL LS11 8 B5
Ingram Ct BEE/HOL LS11 8 B5
Ingram Crs BEE/HOL LS11 8 A7
KNOT WF11 181 M3
Ingram Gdns BEE/HOL LS11 8 B5
Ingram Pde RTHW LS26 155 G1
Ingram Rd BEE/HOL LS11 8 B7
Ingram Rw BEE/HOL LS11 8 F4
Ingram Sq HFAX HX1 * 168 C1
Ingram St BEE/HOL LS11 8 F4
HFAX HX1 168 C1
KGHY BD21 79 K3
Ingram Vw BEE/HOL LS11 8 B6
Ingrow Br KGHY BD21 * 79 K2
Ingrow La HWTH BD22 79 H2
Ingrow St HWTH BD22 79 J2
Ings Av GSLY LS20 61 M4
Ings Cl HEM/SK/SE WF9 246 F3
HOR/CROF WF4 222 E5
Ings Ct GSLY LS20 61 L4
Ings Crs EARL WF12 195 L4
GSLY LS20 61 L5
LVSG WF15 172 D2
OSM LS9 110 D7
Ings Dr AIRE BD20 16 E8
RTHW LS26 157 G3
Ings Holt HEM/SK/SE WF9 246 F3
Ings La AIRE BD20 34 D1
AWLS/ASK DN6 249 J5
BSPA/BRAM LS23 49 J6
CAS WF10 157 M3
CUD/GR S72 263 L6
EARL WF12 195 L4
GLE DN14 161 J7
GSLY LS20 61 L4
MAR/SLWT HD7 233 J2
TAD LS24 50 C6
Ings Mere Ct KNOT WF11 159 J2
Ings Mill Av KBTN HD8 240 B3
Ings Mill Dr KBTN HD8 240 B4
Ings Rd AIRE BD20 35 K7
BTLY WF17 151 K8
EARL WF12 174 A5
HEM/SK/SE WF9 223 K5
HUDE HD5 215 J2
LVSG WF15 172 D1
OSM LS9 110 D7
TAD LS24 95 G1
WKFDE WF1 12 D4
The Ings BRIG HD6 148 C8
KBTN HD8 240 B4
Ing St BFDE BD3 105 M7
Ings Vw CAS WF10 158 D6
RTHW LS26 157 G3
Ings Vil LVSG WF15 172 E4
Ings Wk HEM/SK/SE WF9 246 F3
Ings Wy AIRE BD20 36 B6
GIR BD8 104 A6
KBTN HD8 216 B3
STKB/PEN S36 256 F5
Ingswell Av HOR/CROF WF4 221 H7
Ingswell Dr HOR/CROF WF4 221 H7
Ingthorns La GFTH/SHER LS25 138 B5
Ingthorpe La GFTH/SHER LS25 138 C6
Ingthorpe Wy GFTH/SHER LS25 138 C5
Ingwell Ct WKFDE WF1 13 G3
Ingwell St WKFDE WF1 13 G3
Ingwell Ter CLECK BD19 150 A7
Inholmes La TAD LS24 49 L2
TAD LS24 71 K3
Inkerman Ct KBTN HD8 257 J1
Inkerman St BOW BD4 127 M2
ECHL BD2 105 M2
WHIT OL12 * 206 B5
Inkerman Wy KBTN HD8 257 H1
Inkersley Rd BFD BD1 4 E2
Ink St MILN OL16 206 B7
Inmoor Rd BOW BD4 128 D7
Inner Hey MAR/SLWT HD7 233 J2
Inner Ring Rd LDS LS1 6 C9
The Innings IDLE BD10 83 J6
Innovation Wy DOD/DAR S75 260 E2
Institute Rd ECHL BD2 105 L1
Institute St AIRE BD20 34 E8
Intake MAR/SLWT HD7 213 G1
Intake Cl EARD/LOFT WF3 177 H1
Intake Crs COL BB8 52 B8
DOD/DAR S75 260 B8
Intake Gdns DOD/DAR S75 260 D4
Intake Gv ECHL BD2 105 L4
Intake La AIRE BD20 56 C2
BRAM LS13 107 H3
BTLY WF17 151 H6
CUD/GR S72 244 E6
DOD/DAR S75 260 D4
EARD/LOFT WF3 177 H1
HOLM/MEL HD9 234 B2
HOR/CROF WF4 219 M7
HUDS HD4 213 H7
KNOT WF11 161 J5
MID LS10 153 L3
OSS WF5 197 G1
YEA LS19 84 F3
Intake Mt MID LS10 153 L2
Intake Rd ECHL BD2 105 L4
MAR/SLWT HD7 211 L4
PDSY/CALV LS28 107 J6
Intake Sq MID LS10 153 L3
Intake Ter ECHL BD2 105 L4
The Intake GFTH/SHER LS25 135 K5
Intake Vw MID LS10 153 L3
Interchange Wy
BSLYN/ROY S71 261 H4
Intercity Wy PDSY/CALV LS28 107 J5
Intermezzo Dr MID LS10 132 D5
Invargarry Cl GFTH/SHER LS25 113 K6
Inverness Rd GFTH/SHER LS25 113 K7
Invertrees Av YEA LS19 84 E2
Iona Pl HIPP HX3 146 D4
Iona St HIPP HX3 10 F1
Ipswich St ROCH OL11 228 B1
Iqbal Ct BFDE BD3 * 105 M8
Ireland Crs BHP/TINH LS16 86 B3
Ireland St BGLY BD16 81 G3
Ireland Ter BGLY BD16 81 G3
Ireton St GTHN BD7 104 D8
Iron Rw ILK LS29 40 B5
Iron St CLECK BD19 149 L7
Ironwood Ap SCFT LS14 111 J3
Ironwood Crs SCFT LS14 111 J3
Ironwood Vw SCFT LS14 111 J2
Irving St HFAX HX1 10 A9
Irving Ter CLAY BD14 125 L3
Irwell St BOW BD4 127 J1
Irwin Ap MSTN/BAR LS15 111 H7
Irwin Av WKFDE WF1 177 G7
Irwin Crs WKFDE WF1 177 G7
Irwin St PDSY/CALV LS28 106 F4
Isaac St GIR BD8 104 D6
Isabella St WHIT OL12 206 B4
Isherwood St ROCH OL11 228 C1
Island Dr HOLM/MEL HD9 236 E4
The Island HOR/CROF WF4 * 197 G6
Islay Cl RTHW LS26 155 J1
Isles St GIR BD8 104 B6
Issott St BSLYN/ROY S71 261 H3
Ivanhoe Rd GTHN BD7 126 D1
Iveagh Ct MILN OL16 * 206 D8
Ivegate BFD BD1 4 E6
COL BB8 52 A5
YEA LS19 62 D8
Ive House La LUD/ILL HX2 145 G6
Iver Wy SHPY BD18 82 C7
Ivesen Garth BHP/TINH LS16 86 C4
Iveson Ap BHP/TINH LS16 86 C4
Iveson Cl BHP/TINH LS16 86 B4
Iveson Ct BHP/TINH LS16 86 B4
Iveson Crs BHP/TINH LS16 86 B4
Iveson Dr BHP/TINH LS16 86 B4
Iveson Gdns BHP/TINH LS16 86 B4
Iveson Garth BHP/TINH LS16 86 C4
Iveson Gn BHP/TINH LS16 86 B4
Iveson Gv BHP/TINH LS16 86 B4
Iveson Lawn BHP/TINH LS16 86 C4
Iveson Ri BHP/TINH LS16 86 C4
Iveson Rd BHP/TINH LS16 86 B4
Ives St BAIL BD17 82 D6
Ivory St BEE/HOL LS11 9 H5
Ivy Av OSM LS9 110 D6
Ivy Bank La HWTH BD22 78 E8
Ivy Cha BRAM LS13 107 K7
Ivy Cl HEM/SK/SE WF9 247 H5
PBR HG3 28 A1
ROY/SHW OL2 229 K7
WKFDE WF1 177 G6
Ivy Ct CUD/GR S72 244 D8
ILK LS29 38 D3
Ivy Crs HIPP HX3 148 A7
OSM LS9 110 C7
Ivy Farm Cl BSLYN/ROY S71 243 M5
Ivy Gdns BRAM LS13 107 M2
CAS WF10 180 F1
Ivy Garth CHAL LS7 87 M8
Ivy Gv OSM LS9 110 D6
SHPY BD18 82 A7
WKFDE WF1 177 G6
Ivy House Rd WBOW BD5 127 G5
Ivy La BSPA/BRAM LS23 48 E6
LUD/ILL HX2 123 M8
WIL/AL BD15 103 J5
WKFDE WF1 177 G6
Ivy Mt MAR/SLWT HD7 212 B5
OSM LS9 110 C6
Ivy Pl AIRE BD20 34 F7
BRAM LS13 107 M2
Ivy Rd KGHY BD21 3 M6
OSM LS9 110 C7
SHPY BD18 82 A7
Ivy St BRIG HD6 170 B3
FEA/AMT WF7 179 M8
HFAX HX1 168 C1
HUD HD1 15 J8
HUDS HD4 213 L2
KGHY BD21 2 F3
OSM LS9 110 C6
Ivy Ter BRIG HD6 170 B3
BSLY S70 * 261 J6
HEM/SK/SE WF9 247 H3
HIPP HX3 148 A7
KGHY BD21 58 B8
Ivy Vw OSM LS9 110 C6

J

Jacana Wy WBSY BD6 125 L5
Jacinth Ct HUDN HD2 192 E4
Jack Br HBR HX7 142 C1
Jack Close Orch
BSLYN/ROY S71 243 L2
Jackdaw Cl WIL/AL BD15 103 K7
Jackdaw La BSPA/BRAM LS23 48 E6
Jack Field La AIRE BD20 55 J2
Jack Hl HUDN HD2 14 E1
Jack Hill La OT LS21 23 H2
Jackie Smart Ct CHAL LS7 7 L2
Jackie Smart Rd WBOW BD5 127 G2
Jack La BEE/HOL LS11 8 E5
DEWS WF13 173 M4
MID LS10 9 K7
Jackman Dr HORS LS18 85 M7
Jackroyd La HUDS HD4 214 C4
MIRF WF14 194 A4
Jackson Av RHAY LS8 88 B7
Jackson Hill La CUL/QBY BD13 125 H7
Jackson La GTL/HWG HX4 189 J1
Jackson Mdw GTL/HWG HX4 189 J1
Jackson Rd CHAL LS7 7 G3
Jackson's La AIRE BD20 35 G1
EARL WF12 195 J4
PONT WF8 204 A7
Jackson St AIRE BD20 55 M1
BFDE BD3 5 K8
CUD/GR S72 244 C8
MILN OL16 206 D8
WHIT OL12 184 E8
Jacksons Yd BSLY S70 * 260 F5
Jack Taylor Ct WHIT OL12 * 206 D5
Jacky La HWTH BD22 78 E8
Jacobs Cft CLAY BD14 125 K2
Jacobs Hall Ct DOD/DAR S75 * 241 L6
Jacobs La HWTH BD22 78 F6
Jacob's Rw HUDS HD4 214 B3
Jacob St LDSU LS2 7 H7
WBOW BD5 126 F2
Jacob's Well La WKFDE WF1 12 F1
Jacques Gv AIRE BD20 36 B5
Jacques Pl BSLYN/ROY S71 261 M4
Jaggar La HOLM/MEL HD9 236 B2
Jagger Green La GTL/HWG HX4 190 E3
Jagger La HUDE HD5 193 J6
KBTN HD8 217 G7
Jail Rd BTLY WF17 173 H1
Jakeman Cl EARD/LOFT WF3 153 G6
Jakeman Ct EARD/LOFT WF3 153 G6
Jakeman Dr EARD/LOFT WF3 153 G6
James Av AIRE BD20 56 C1
RHAY LS8 88 B6
James Butterworth Ct
MILN OL16 * 206 D8
James Butterworth St
MILN OL16 206 D7
James Cl GFTH/SHER LS25 113 J7
James Ct WBY LS22 47 K6
James Duggan Av
FEA/AMT WF7 179 L8
James Ga BFD BD1 4 E6
James Gibbs Cl FEA/AMT WF7 * 179 M8
James Hill St LIT OL15 * 207 K1
James La HUDS HD4 213 J8
James Mason Ct HUD HD1 191 M7
James Rd AWLS/ASK DN6 249 M7
ROY/SHW OL2 229 K6
James St AIRE BD20 * 34 F7
BFD BD1 4 E5
BIRK/DRI BD11 * 128 C8
BRIG HD6 170 C2
BSLYN/ROY S71 261 H4
BTLY WF17 173 K2
CAS WF10 157 M5
COL BB8 * 74 A1
CUD/GR S72 245 H1
CUL/QBY BD13 102 F7
DEWS WF13 173 K5
ELL HX5 169 J8
GTL/HWG HX4 190 D2
HWTH BD22 78 D4
LIT OL15 207 H1
LVSG WF15 172 D3
MAR/SLWT HD7 212 C5
MAR/SLWT HD7 212 F2
MIRF WF14 172 C7
WHIT OL12 206 C6
WIL/AL BD15 103 L5
YEA LS19 84 D2
Jamie Ct IDLE BD10 83 M8
Jane St CUL/QBY BD13 101 M5
SHPY BD18 82 B6
WHIT OL12 162 A8
WHIT OL12 206 A6
Janesway GFTH/SHER LS25 135 H4
Janet St HWTH BD22 79 G6
Japonica Wy BFDE BD3 105 L5
Jaques Cl HDGY LS6 108 D2
Jardine Av FEA/AMT WF7 179 M8
Jardine Rd BGLY BD16 81 J3
Jarratt St GIR BD8 104 D5
Jarratt St East GIR BD8 104 D5
Jarrom Cl BOW BD4 127 M2
Jarvis Sq EARD/LOFT WF3 154 C3
Jarvis St WHIT OL12 206 B5
Jarvis Wk EARD/LOFT WF3 154 C3
Jasmine Gdns HFAX HX1 10 B8
Jason Ter BTLY WF17 * 151 J4
Jasper La PBR HG3 27 K8
Jasper St HFAX HX1 10 B6
IDLE BD10 83 K6
Javelin Cl IDLE BD10 83 K8
Jay House La BRIG HD6 170 F1
Jay St HWTH BD22 78 F8
Jean Av MSTN/BAR LS15 111 J7
Jebb La DOD/DAR S75 241 H2
Jefferson Wy WHIT OL12 206 B3
Jenkin Dr HOR/CROF WF4 197 H5
Jenkin La HOR/CROF WF4 197 H5
Jenkin Rd HOR/CROF WF4 197 H5
Jenkinson Cl BEE/HOL LS11 8 D5
Jenkinson Lawn BEE/HOL LS11 8 D6
Jenkinsons Pl MID LS10 131 M6
Jenkinson St BTLY WF17 173 L4
Jenkyn La KBTN HD8 237 M6
Jennetts Crs OT LS21 41 H7
Jennings Cl AIRE BD20 36 B6
Jennings Pl GTHN BD7 126 C2
Jennings St GTHN BD7 126 C2
Jenny Gill Crs SKP/WHF BD23 16 D3
Jenny La BAIL BD17 82 F2
MIRF WF14 172 D7
Jensen Av DEWS WF13 173 H3
Jepheys Pl WHIT OL12 206 B5
Jepheys St WHIT OL12 206 B5
Jepson La ELL HX5 169 H8
Jeremy La HECK WF16 172 F2
Jer Gv GTHN BD7 126 A4
Jer La GTHN BD7 126 A4
Jermyn Cft DOD/DAR S75 260 B7
Jermyn St BFDE BD3 5 G5
WHIT OL12 206 C6
Jerrold St LIT OL15 207 K1
Jerry Clay Dr
WKFDW/WTN WF2 176 A4
Jerry Clay La
WKFDW/WTN WF2 175 M3
Jerry Cft SKP/WHF BD23 16 C2
Jerry Fields Rd LUD/ILL HX2 144 F8
Jerry La AIRE BD20 37 H5
RPDN/SBR HX6 167 J3
Jersey Cl EARL WF12 174 B4
Jerusalem La LUD/ILL HX2 144 F2
Jerusalem Rd MAR/SLWT HD7 212 D7
Jervaulx Cl BSPA/BRAM LS23 48 E7
Jervaulx Crs GIR BD8 4 B3
Jerwood Hill Cl HIPP HX3 11 K2
Jesmond Av BSLYN/ROY S71 243 K3
HTON BD9 104 B4
Jesmond Gv DEWS WF13 173 K5
HTON BD9 104 B4
Jessamine Av BEE/HOL LS11 131 H5
Jessamine St DEWS WF13 194 F1
Jesse St GIR BD8 103 M7
WBOW BD5 127 G1
Jessop Av HUDE HD5 215 J3
Jessop Fold HOLM/MEL HD9 236 B1
Jessop St CAS WF10 157 M6
WKFDW/WTN WF2 12 E7
Jewitt La WBY LS22 47 L7
Jew La HWTH BD22 100 E4
Jew Leys La COP/BISH YO23 73 M8
Jilley Royd La HUDN HD2 192 C2
Jill Kilner Dr ILK LS29 39 M6
Jill La MIRF WF14 172 E7
Jim Allen La LUD/ILL HX2 144 E5
Jim Laker Pl SHPY BD18 82 B7
Jim La HUD HD1 191 M8
Jinnah Ct GIR BD8 4 C3
Jinny Moor La RTHW LS26 134 A6
Jin Whin Ct CAS WF10 157 J6
Jin-Whin Hl CAS WF10 157 H6
Joan Royd HECK WF16 150 F8
Joan Royd La STKB/PEN S36 270 D5
Joba Av BFDE BD3 5 M6
Jockey Rd STKB/PEN S36 271 L4
Joffre Av CAS WF10 158 A8
John Ashworth St WHIT OL12 206 D5
John Booth Cl LVSG WF15 172 B4
John Carr Av HOR/CROF WF4 197 J4
John Charles Wy WOR/ARM LS12 130 F2
John Escritt Rd BGLY BD16 81 J4
John Gilmour Wy ILK LS29 39 M6
John Haigh Rd MAR/SLWT HD7 212 C6
John Hanson Ct CUL/QBY BD13 102 A8
John Naylor La LUD/ILL HX2 167 G1
John Nelson Cl BTLY WF17 * 151 H5
Johnny La OT LS21 41 J8
John O'Gaunts Wk RTHW LS26 133 H8
John Ormsby VC Wy
EARL WF12 174 C3
John Roberts Cl ROCH OL11 * 228 A1
Johns Av EARD/LOFT WF3 154 E8
John's Crs WKFDW/WTN WF2 176 A4
Johns La ELL HX5 191 H2
Johnson St BFDE BD3 105 M7
BGLY BD16 81 H3
DOD/DAR S75 260 F4
MIRF WF14 194 B3
Johnson Ter MOR LS27 152 D2
Johnston WHIT OL12 * 206 A6
Johnston Av LIT OL15 * 207 H3
Johnston St HDGY LS6 6 E2
WKFDE WF1 13 H3
John St AWLS/ASK DN6 249 L8
BAIL BD17 82 E5
BFD BD1 4 E5
BOW BD4 128 A5
BRIG HD6 170 C3
BSLY S70 261 H5
BTLY WF17 151 G5
CAS WF10 157 L8
CLAY BD14 125 L2
CUD/GR S72 263 M7
CUL/QBY BD13 79 M8
CUL/QBY BD13 101 M6
CUL/QBY BD13 102 F8
DEWS WF13 173 L4
DEWS WF13 195 G1
EARL WF12 * 174 A5
ELL HX5 169 H8
GTL/HWG HX4 168 E6
HDGY LS6 109 G3
HECK WF16 * 172 F3
HEM/SK/SE WF9 247 H4
HFAX HX1 11 G6
HUDW HD3 213 K2
HWTH BD22 78 F4
LIT OL15 207 J1
MILN OL16 206 E3
SHPY BD18 82 C6
WKFDE WF1 13 H3
YEA LS19 84 D2
John St West RPDN/SBR HX6 167 K2
John William St CLECK BD19 149 M6
ELL HX5 169 H8
HUD HD1 14 F5
LVSG WF15 172 E2
Jonathan Garth ILK LS29 * 19 G6
Jones St MILN OL16 206 C8
Jons Av HEM/SK/SE WF9 246 C4
Jordan Av ROY/SHW OL2 229 M6
Jordan Wy ECHL BD2 105 L5
Joseph Av HIPP HX3 147 J4
Josephine Rd HUDS HD4 213 J3
Joseph St BFD BD1 5 J6
BOW BD4 128 A5
BSLY S70 261 G6
CUD/GR S72 245 J8
LIT OL15 185 K8
MID LS10 9 L7
Josephs Well LDS LS1 * 6 D8
Joshua St TOD OL14 141 K8
Jos La KBTN HD8 238 A6
Jos Wy KBTN HD8 238 A5
Jowett House La
DOD/DAR S75 258 D2
Jowett Park Crs IDLE BD10 83 J4
Jowett's La AIRE BD20 17 M6
Jowett St BFD BD1 4 B5
Joy St WHIT OL12 206 B4
Jubilee Av KBTN HD8 238 C4
NORM WF6 178 C6
WKFDE WF1 176 E2
Jubilee Ct SHPY BD18 * 82 E6
Jubilee Crs HOR/CROF WF4 200 D3
WKFDE WF1 176 E2
Jubilee Cft BIRK/DRI BD11 129 H7
Jubilee Dr KGHY BD21 2 C9
Jubilee Gdns BSLYN/ROY S71 243 M2
Jubilee La HUDS HD4 213 H3
Jubilee Pl MOR LS27 152 D2
Jubilee Rd HIPP HX3 168 F4
HOR/CROF WF4 200 D3
Jubilee St GIR BD8 4 D2
HBR HX7 144 A5
HIPP HX3 11 K8
HOR/CROF WF4 220 B3
MOR LS27 152 D2
ROY/SHW OL2 229 L7
Jubilee St North LUD/ILL HX2 146 C3
Jubilee Ter HIPP HX3 * 11 K8
MOR LS27 152 D2
RPDN/SBR HX6 167 G8
Jubilee Trees ILK LS29 39 L7
Jubilee Wy HOR/CROF WF4 217 G2
PONT WF8 180 E6
SHPY BD18 82 F6
Judd Field La STKB/PEN S36 270 D8
Judy Haigh La EARL WF12 195 M6
Judy La HUDN HD2 192 D3
Judy Rw BSLYN/ROY S71 261 L2

Julian Dr CUL/QBY BD13 125 L4
Julian St HUDE HD5 * 215 G1
Julia St WHIT OL12 206 A6
Julie Av HOR/CROF WF4 220 A1
Jumb Beck Cl ILK LS29 40 B6
Jumble Dyke BRIG HD6 170 B6
Jumble Hole Rd TOD OL14 142 D4
Jumbles Ct EARD/LOFT WF3 154 E5
Jumbles La EARD/LOFT WF3 154 E5
Jumble Wd KBTN HD8 215 M3
Jumples LUD/ILL HX2 145 M2
Jumples Cl LUD/ILL HX2 145 M2
Jumps La HBR HX7 143 H5
TOD OL14 141 G5
Junction Aly MILN OL16 206 B7
Junction La OSS WF5 197 J2
Junction Rd BAIL BD17 82 E6
DEWS WF13 173 K7
Junction St BSLY S70 261 K6
MID LS10 9 H4
June St KGHY BD21 3 H2
Juniper Av RTHW LS26 133 M7
Juniper Cl WKFDW/WTN WF2 176 A6
Juniper Dr MILN OL16 206 F8
Juniper Gv HUDS HD4 213 M8
Juniper Pl OSM LS9 110 D5
Jureshi Vw GIR BD8 4 B1
Justin Wy HUDS HD4 213 J5

K

Kaffir Rd HUDW HD3 191 M6
Karnac Rd RHAY LS8 110 B2
Karon Dr HOR/CROF WF4 197 K5
Kathan Cl MILN OL16 206 D7
Katherine St SHPY BD18 82 B6
Katrina Gv FEA/AMT WF7 201 M3
Kaycell St BOW BD4 127 K4
Kay Cl MOR LS27 130 B7
Kaye Hl CUL/QBY BD13 79 M8
Kaye La HUDE HD5 214 F4
Kaye St BSLYN/ROY S71 261 H4
EARL WF12 173 M8
HECK WF16 172 F3
Kay's Ter BSLY S70 262 A7
Kay St HTON BD9 104 E1
ROCH OL11 228 A1
WKFDE WF1 13 H3
Kearby Cliff WBY LS22 45 M4
Keats Av TOD OL14 141 M8
Keats Cl PONT WF8 180 F4
Keats Dr HECK WF16 173 G4
Keats Gv EARD/LOFT WF3 155 G8
STKB/PEN S36 270 F2
Keat St HUDS HD4 214 A2
Kebble Ct CLECK BD19 150 D7
Keble Garth GFTH/SHER LS25 135 L4
Kebroyd La RPDN/SBR HX6 167 G7
Kebroyd Mt RPDN/SBR HX6 167 G7
Kebs Rd HBR HX7 141 K3
Kedleston Rd RHAY LS8 88 B3
Keeldar Cl GTHN BD7 126 D3
Keelham Dr YEA LS19 84 E2
Keelham La AIRE BD20 57 J4
TOD OL14 141 M4
Keel Moorings BRAM LS13 107 H1
Keenan Av HEM/SK/SE WF9 247 G5
Keeper La BOW BD4 128 F3
HOR/CROF WF4 220 F8
Keeton St OSM LS9 7 M9
Keighley Cl LUD/ILL HX2 123 M8
Keighley Dr LUD/ILL HX2 146 A2
Keighley Pl PDSY/CALV LS28 107 G4
Keighley Rd AIRE BD20 16 C8
AIRE BD20 34 F7
AIRE BD20 35 M7
BGLY BD16 59 G8
BGLY BD16 80 C3
COL BB8 53 K7
COL BB8 74 B1
COL BB8 74 E3
CUL/QBY BD13 79 M6
HBR HX7 121 J5
HTON BD9 104 E3
HWTH BD22 54 E3
HWTH BD22 79 G3
HWTH BD22 100 E3
ILK LS29 38 A6
LUD/ILL HX2 123 M5
LUD/ILL HX2 124 A6
SKP/WHF BD23 16 B4
Keir Hardie Cl LVSG WF15 172 D2
Keir Hardy Cl LVSG WF15 * 172 D2
Keir St BSLY S70 260 F4
Keir Ter BSLY S70 * 260 F4
Kelburn Gv HWTH BD22 78 D3
Kelby Cft DOD/DAR S75 260 B1
Kelcbar Cl TAD LS24 71 K2
Kelcbar Hl TAD LS24 71 J2
Kelcbar Wy TAD LS24 71 K2
Kelcliffe Av GSLY LS20 62 A5
Kelcliffe La GSLY LS20 61 M4
Keldholme Cl BRAM LS13 107 G1
Keldholme Rd BRAM LS13 * 107 H1
Keldregate HUDN HD2 193 H1
Kell Beck OT LS21 41 H4
Kellett Av WOR/ARM LS12 130 E2
Kellett Crs WOR/ARM LS12 130 E2
Kellett Dr WOR/ARM LS12 130 E2
Kellett Gv WOR/ARM LS12 130 E1
Kellett La WOR/ARM LS12 130 D1
Kellett Mt WOR/ARM LS12 * 130 E2
Kellett Pl WOR/ARM LS12 130 E2
Kellett Rd WOR/ARM LS12 130 D1
Kellett St MILN OL16 206 D6
Kellett Ter WOR/ARM LS12 * 130 E2
Kellett Wk WOR/ARM LS12 130 E1
Kell La HIPP HX3 147 H4
LUD/ILL HX2 123 G8
Kelloe St CLECK BD19 149 L5
Kell St BGLY BD16 81 J3
Kelmore Gv WBSY BD6 126 A8
Kelmscott Av MSTN/BAR LS15 111 M3
Kelmscott Crs MSTN/BAR LS15 111 M3
Kelmscott Gdns
MSTN/BAR LS15 112 A3
Kelmscott Garth
MSTN/BAR LS15 112 A3
Kelmscott Gn MSTN/BAR LS15 111 M3
Kelmscott Gv MSTN/BAR LS15 111 M3
Kelmscott La MSTN/BAR LS15 111 M3
Kelsall Av HDGY LS6 109 G4
Kelsall Gv HDGY LS6 109 G5
Kelsall Pl HDGY LS6 109 G4
Kelsall Rd HDGY LS6 109 G4
Kelsall St MILN OL16 * 206 B6
Kelsall Ter HDGY LS6 109 G4
Kelsey St HFAX HX1 10 B4
Kelsey Ter BSLY S70 * 261 H7
Kelso Gdns LDSU LS2 6 B6
Kelso Gv HUDE HD5 193 J8
Kelso Pl LDSU LS2 6 B5
Kelso Rd LDSU LS2 6 B5
Kelso St LDSU LS2 6 B6
Kelvin Av HUDE HD5 193 G8
LUD/ILL HX2 145 M7
Kelvin Crs LUD/ILL HX2 145 M8
Kelvin Rd ELL HX5 169 G8
Kelvin Wy ECHL BD2 105 L4
Kemp's Br WKFDW/WTN WF2 12 A4
Kemps Wy HOLM/MEL HD9 255 G4
Kempton Rd GFTH/SHER LS25 135 J4
Kemsing Wk MSTN/BAR LS15 112 B3
Ken Churchill Dr
HOR/CROF WF4 197 J4
Kendal Bank BVRD LS3 6 B7
Kendal Cl BVRD LS3 6 B7
CAS WF10 159 G7
Kendal Cft CAS WF10 159 G7
Kendal Dr CAS WF10 158 F6
HOR/CROF WF4 199 L4
MSTN/BAR LS15 111 G8
ROY/SHW OL2 229 M7
Kendal Gdns CAS WF10 158 F7
RYKW YO26 32 C1
Kendal Garth CAS WF10 159 G7
Kendal Gv BSLYN/ROY S71 262 G6
BVRD LS3 6 C7
Kendal La BVRD LS3 6 B7
Kendall Av SHPY BD18 82 A6
Kendall Mellor Ct KGHY BD21 2 F4
Kendal Ri BVRD LS3 6 B8
HOR/CROF WF4 199 L4
WKFDW/WTN WF2 199 J8
Kendal Rd BVRD LS3 6 C7
Kendal St KGHY BD21 3 J6
Kendal Wk BVRD LS3 * 6 B7
Kendell St MID LS10 9 H2
Kendray St BSLY S70 261 H5
Kenilworth ROCH OL11 * 206 A8
Kenilworth Av MOR LS27 129 M8
Kenilworth Cl MIRF WF14 172 B8
Kenilworth Dr BRIG HD6 148 C8
Kenilworth Gdns MOR LS27 129 M7
Kenilworth Rd MILN OL16 228 E1
WOR/ARM LS12 130 E1
Kenilworth St BOW BD4 127 J2
Kenion St MILN OL16 206 B7
Kenley Av WBSY BD6 126 C5
Kenley Mt WBSY BD6 126 C4
Kenley Pde GTHN BD7 126 B4
Kenmore Av CLECK BD19 149 L6
Kenmore Cl CLECK BD19 149 L6
Kenmore Crs CLECK BD19 149 L6
WBSY BD6 126 C4
Kenmore Dr CLECK BD19 149 L6
WBSY BD6 126 C4
Kenmore Gv CLECK BD19 149 L6
WBSY BD6 126 C4
Kenmore Rd CLECK BD19 149 L6
EARD/LOFT WF3 176 B1
WBSY BD6 126 C4
Kenmore Vw CLECK BD19 149 L6
Kenmore Wk WBSY BD6 126 C4
Kenmore Wy CLECK BD19 149 L6
Kennedy Av HUDN HD2 192 C1
Kennedy Cl BTLY WF17 174 B3
STKB/PEN S36 269 M3
Kennel La HWTH BD22 100 A4
RPDN/SBR HX6 166 C5
Kennels La SCFT LS14 68 B6
Kennerleigh Av
MSTN/BAR LS15 111 M5
Kennerleigh Crs
MSTN/BAR LS15 111 M5
Kennerleigh Dr
MSTN/BAR LS15 111 L5
Kennerleigh Garth
MSTN/BAR LS15 111 M5
Kennerleigh Gln
MSTN/BAR LS15 111 L5
Kennerleigh Gv
MSTN/BAR LS15 111 M5
Kennerleigh Ri
MSTN/BAR LS15 111 L5
Kennerleigh Wk
MSTN/BAR LS15 111 L5
Kenneth St BEE/HOL LS11 8 A6
Kennet La GFTH/SHER LS25 113 J8
Kenny St WBOW BD5 126 F1
Kensington Av ROY/SHW OL2 228 E8
SCFT LS14 68 C8
STKB/PEN S36 270 C2
Kensington Cl BTLY WF17 173 K2
HIPP HX3 168 C2
MILN OL16 207 J8
Kensington Ct MID LS10 132 B6
Kensington Gdns MID LS10 132 B7
Kensington Rd DOD/DAR S75 260 F3
HIPP HX3 168 C2
WKFDE WF1 176 D6
Kensington St GIR BD8 104 C5
KGHY BD21 2 E7
ROCH OL11 228 A2
Kensington Ter HDGY LS6 6 A2
Kensington Wy MID LS10 132 B7
Kenstone Crs IDLE BD10 83 J7
Kent Av AIRE BD20 35 M5
PDSY/CALV LS28 107 J7
Kent Cl BSLYN/ROY S71 243 L2
PDSY/CALV LS28 107 J7
Kent Crs PDSY/CALV LS28 107 J7
Kent Dr PDSY/CALV LS28 107 J7
Kentmere IDLE BD10 83 H8
Kentmere Ap SCFT LS14 111 G1
Kentmere Av GFTH/SHER LS25 113 K8
LM/WK BD12 149 G5
SCFT LS14 89 H7
WHIT OL12 206 D3
Kentmere Cl SCFT LS14 111 H1
Kentmere Crs SCFT LS14 89 H8
Kentmere Gdns SCFT LS14 89 H8
Kentmere Ga SCFT LS14 89 H7
Kentmere Gn SCFT LS14 89 H8
Kentmere Ri SCFT LS14 111 J1
Kent Ms BGLY BD16 81 K4
Kenton Dr HOR/CROF WF4 198 C7
Kenton Rd ROY/SHW OL2 229 J7
Kenton Wy BOW BD4 * 128 A3
Kent Rd BGLY BD16 81 K3
PDSY/CALV LS28 107 H7
Kent St HFAX HX1 10 F7
ROCH OL11 206 B8
Kenwood Cl BSLY S70 261 M6
Kenworthy Cl BHP/TINH LS16 86 C1
Kenworthy Gdns BHP/TINH LS16 86 C1
Kenworthy Garth
BHP/TINH LS16 86 C1
Kenworthy Ga BHP/TINH LS16 86 C1
Kenworthy La RPDN/SBR HX6 167 G8
Kenworthy Ri BHP/TINH LS16 86 C1
Kenworthy Rd BSLY S70 261 G7
Kenworthy St MILN OL16 206 E7
Kenworthy Ter MILN OL16 206 E7
Kenworthy V BHP/TINH LS16 86 C1
Kenya Mt HWTH BD22 2 A3
Kenyon Bank KBTN HD8 257 H1
Kenyon La LUD/ILL HX2 145 M7
Kenyon St HEM/SK/SE WF9 247 J3
Kepler Gv RHAY LS8 7 M4
Kepler Mt RHAY LS8 7 M4
Kepler Ter RHAY LS8 7 M4
Kepstorn Cl KSTL LS5 108 C1
Kepstorn Ri KSTL LS5 108 C1
Kepstorn Rd BHP/TINH LS16 86 D7
Keren Gv WKFDW/WTN WF2 176 A4
Keresforth Cl BSLY S70 260 E6
Keresforth Hall Rd BSLY S70 260 F7
Keresforth Hill Rd BSLY S70 260 E7
Keresforth Rd DOD/DAR S75 260 B8
Kerry Garth HORS LS18 85 K5
Kerry Hl HORS LS18 85 L5
Kerry St HORS LS18 85 K5
Kershaw Av CAS WF10 158 D7
Kershaw Ct LUD/ILL HX2 * 144 F6
Kershaw Crs LUD/ILL HX2 144 F7
Kershaw Dr LUD/ILL HX2 144 F6
Kershaw La KNOT WF11 181 M3
Kershaw Rd TOD OL14 163 J5
Kershaw St BFDE BD3 105 M7
ROY/SHW OL2 229 K7
WHIT OL12 * 206 B6
Kershaw St East ROY/SHW OL2 229 K7
Kertland St EARL WF12 173 L7
Kester Rd BTLY WF17 173 H1
Kesteven Cl BOW BD4 128 B4
Kesteven Ct BOW BD4 128 B4
Kesteven Rd BOW BD4 128 A4
Kestrel Bank HUDS HD4 214 A7
Kestrel Cl AL/HA/HU LS17 88 B2
Kestrel Dr AWLS/ASK DN6 249 K8
ECHL BD2 105 J2
WKFDW/WTN WF2 220 F1
Kestrel Garth MOR LS27 152 F2
Kestrel Gv AL/HA/HU LS17 88 B2
Kestrel Ms NORM WF6 178 C5
Kestrel Mt ECHL BD2 105 J2
Kestrel Vw CLECK BD19 149 M5
Keswick Av HUDW HD3 191 J5
Keswick Cl HIPP HX3 169 G3
TOD OL14 141 H7
Keswick Dr CAS WF10 159 G6
WKFDW/WTN WF2 176 A7
Keswick Gra AL/HA/HU LS17 67 L1
Keswick La AL/HA/HU LS17 67 L2
Keswick Rd DOD/DAR S75 242 C4
Keswick St BOW BD4 127 M1
Keswick Vw AL/HA/HU LS17 68 A1
Keswick Wk BSLYN/ROY S71 262 D6
Kettle La MAR/SLWT HD7 211 K8
Kettleman Br TAD LS24 72 A5
Kettlethorpe Hall Dr
WKFDW/WTN WF2 198 E8
Kettlethorpe Rd
WKFDW/WTN WF2 220 D1
Kettlewell Dr WBOW BD5 126 D3
Ketton Wk DOD/DAR S75 260 E3
Kew Hl HUDW HD3 191 H3
Kew Rd ROCH OL11 228 C3
Kexbrough Dr DOD/DAR S75 241 L6
Key Hill La CUD/GR S72 245 H3
Keystone Av CAS WF10 180 A1
Key Syke La TOD OL14 163 L1
Khalaq Ct BFDE BD3 5 M4
Khus Wk KGHY BD21 79 L2
Kibroyd Dr DOD/DAR S75 241 L7
Kidacre St BEE/HOL LS11 9 H5
Kiddal La MSTN/BAR LS15 91 G3
Kidroyd La HUDE HD5 214 F2
Kilburn Cl HUDE HD5 15 K9
Kilburn La DEWS WF13 173 L5
Kilburn Rd WOR/ARM LS12 108 E7
Kilby St WKFDE WF1 176 D7
Kildare Crs ROCH OL11 228 C4
WIL/AL BD15 103 J5
Kildare Ter WOR/ARM LS12 109 G8
Killingbeck Br OSM LS9 110 F5
SCFT LS14 111 G5
Killingbeck Dr SCFT LS14 111 G5
Killinghall Av ECHL BD2 5 M1
Killinghall Dr ECHL BD2 5 M1
Killinghall Gv ECHL BD2 5 L1
Killinghall Rd BFDE BD3 105 L5
Kiln Bent Rd HOLM/MEL HD9 253 J8
Kiln Ct HUDW HD3 191 G5
Kilner Bank HUDE HD5 15 K4
Kilnerdeyne Ter MILN OL16 * 206 A8
Kilner Rd WBSY BD6 * 126 C5
Kilners Cft ILK LS29 19 H6
Kiln Fold BRIG HD6 170 F3
Kiln Hl MAR/SLWT HD7 212 C6
Kiln Hill La AIRE BD20 37 J8
Kilnhouse Bank La
HOLM/MEL HD9 253 K5
Kilnhurst La TOD OL14 163 M2
Kilnhurst Mt TOD OL14 163 L1
Kilnhurst Rd TOD OL14 163 L1
Kiln La HBR HX7 120 E3
KBTN HD8 240 B1
MILN OL16 207 J7
Kilnsea Mt BOW BD4 128 A3
Kilnsey Fold AIRE BD20 35 M4
Kilnsey Gv WKFDE WF1 177 G7
Kilnsey Hl BTLY WF17 173 M4
Kilnsey Ms BAIL BD17 82 D3
Kilnsey Rd BFDE BD3 5 M7
WKFDE WF1 177 G6
Kilnshaw La HBR HX7 143 H6
Kiln Wk WHIT OL12 206 A4
Kilpin Hill La DEWS WF13 173 H3
Kilroyd Av CLECK BD19 149 M4
Kilroyd Dr CLECK BD19 150 A4
Kimberley Pl HIPP HX3 146 C2
OSM LS9 110 D4
Kimberley Rd OSM LS9 110 D4
Kimberley St BFDE BD3 105 L8
BRIG HD6 170 D3
FEA/AMT WF7 179 L8
HIPP HX3 146 C2
ILK LS29 38 E1
WKFDE WF1 13 H8
Kimberley Vw OSM LS9 110 D5
Kimberly Cl PONT WF8 225 K1
Kinara Cl KGHY BD21 3 M2
Kinder Av HUDS HD4 213 H4
Kinders Fold LIT OL15 185 H7
Kineholme Dr OT LS21 40 F8
Kine Moor La STKB/PEN S36 258 F8
King Albert St ROY/SHW OL2 229 K7
King Alfred's Dr HDGY LS6 87 J5
King Alfred's Wy HDGY LS6 87 J5
King Charles St LDS LS1 * 7 G9
King Cliffe Rd HUDN HD2 14 E1
King Cl AL/HA/HU LS17 87 H2
King Cross Rd HFAX HX1 10 B9
King Cross St HFAX HX1 10 C9
King Dr AL/HA/HU LS17 87 H2
King Edward Av CAS WF10 135 H8
HORS LS18 85 L5
King Edward Crs HORS LS18 85 L5
King Edward Rd
CUL/QBY BD13 102 F8
COL BB8 52 F8
King Edwards Gdns BSLY S70 260 F6
King Edward St AIRE BD20 55 M1
BSLYN/ROY S71 243 M8
EARL WF12 195 K3
HEM/SK/SE WF9 224 A8
HFAX HX1 * 11 H6
LDS LS1 7 H9
NORM WF6 178 C4
King Edwin's Ct RHAY LS8 110 C1
Kingfield GSLY LS20 62 B4
Kingfisher Cl AL/HA/HU LS17 88 B2
HOR/CROF WF4 198 B7
Kingfisher Ct KGHY BD21 3 H5
NORM WF6 178 C5
Kingfisher Crs DEWS WF13 173 G8
Kingfisher Gv GIR BD8 103 L7
HUDS HD4 214 A7
WKFDW/WTN WF2 220 F1
Kingfisher Ms MOR LS27 152 E3
Kingfisher Reach WBY LS22 47 J5
Kingfisher Rd AWLS/ASK DN6 249 K8
The Kingfishers AIRE BD20 36 A6
Kingfisher Wy AL/HA/HU LS17 88 B2
King George Av CHAL LS7 87 M7
HORS LS18 85 L5
MOR LS27 130 D8
King George Cft MOR LS27 152 D1
King George Gdns CHAL LS7 * 87 M7
King George Rd HORS LS18 85 L5
King George St WKFDE WF1 176 C3
King George Ter BSLY S70 * 261 K6
King La AL/HA/HU LS17 65 G7
AL/HA/HU LS17 87 K3
King Royd La HOR/CROF WF4 201 L8
Kings Ap BRAM LS13 108 A4
Kings Av CAS WF10 158 C7
HDGY LS6 109 G5
ILK LS29 38 C2
NORM WF6 178 B1
King's Bridge Rd HUD HD1 214 D2
Kingsbury Pl HFAX HX1 10 B6
Kings Cha RTHW LS26 133 H8
Kings Cl FEA/AMT WF7 223 M1
ILK LS29 38 A2
OSS WF5 174 E7
OT LS21 41 L7
PONT WF8 180 E7
Kings Ct HEM/SK/SE WF9 223 K5
HFAX HX1 10 E7
King's Crs PONT WF8 181 G7
Kings Cft GFTH/SHER LS25 112 F8
HEM/SK/SE WF9 246 D4
OSS WF5 174 E6
King's Croft Gdns
AL/HA/HU LS17 87 M5
Kingsdale Av BIRK/DRI BD11 129 G8
ECHL BD2 105 J3
Kingsdale Ct SCFT LS14 89 H8
Kingsdale Crs ECHL BD2 105 J3
Kingsdale Dr ECHL BD2 105 J3
Kingsdale Gdns BIRK/DRI BD11 129 G8
Kingsdale Gv ECHL BD2 105 H3
King's Dr BTLY WF17 151 G4
ECHL BD2 83 H8
NORM WF6 178 B1
Kingsfield RTHW LS26 154 D1
Kings Ga BFDE BD3 4 F1
Kings Gv BGLY BD16 81 J2
WHIT OL12 206 E2
Kings Head Dr MIRF WF14 * 172 B8
Kings Head Rd MIRF WF14 172 B8
Kings Lea HIPP HX3 168 D4
LVSG WF15 172 E4
OSS WF5 174 E6
Kingsley Av BHP/TINH LS16 86 D1
BIRK/DRI BD11 150 D2
ECHL BD2 105 G3
FEA/AMT WF7 179 M6
HOR/CROF WF4 200 A3
HUDS HD4 214 A2
KNOT WF11 181 L1
RPDN/SBR HX6 167 H3
WKFDE WF1 176 D1
WKFDW/WTN WF2 198 E8
Kingsley Cl BIRK/DRI BD11 150 D2
BSLYN/ROY S71 243 J8
HOR/CROF WF4 200 A4
WKFDE WF1 176 D1
WKFDW/WTN WF2 198 E8
Kingsley Crs BAIL BD17 82 E4
BIRK/DRI BD11 150 D2
Kingsley Dr BHP/TINH LS16 86 D1
BIRK/DRI BD11 150 D2
CAS WF10 180 F1
Kingsley Garth WKFDE WF1 176 D1
Kingsley Pl HFAX HX1 10 B8
Kingsley Rd BHP/TINH LS16 86 D1
COL BB8 52 F8
Kingsmark Fwy LM/WK BD12 127 H8
Kings Md RTHW LS26 133 J8
Kingsmead OSS WF5 174 E6
SCFT LS14 89 J6
Kingsmead Dr SCFT LS14 89 H5
Kings Meadow OSS WF5 174 E7
Kings Meadow Cl WBY LS22 29 M7
Kings Meadow Dr WBY LS22 29 M7
Kings Meadow Gv WBY LS22 29 M7
Kings Meadow Ms WBY LS22 29 M7
Kings Meadow Vw WBY LS22 29 M7
Kingsmill Cl MOR LS27 152 B1
King's Mill La HUDS HD4 214 D2
King's Mt CHAL LS7 87 L6
KNOT WF11 181 K1
Kings Paddock OSS WF5 174 E7
King's Pl HDGY LS6 108 F2
King's Rd BGLY BD16 81 G1
BHP/TINH LS16 64 D5
CUD/GR S72 244 E5
ECHL BD2 105 G4
HDGY LS6 109 G4
ILK LS29 38 B2
MILN OL16 228 D1
NORM WF6 156 A8
ROY/SHW OL2 229 J8
SKP/WHF BD23 16 D2
King's St CUD/GR S72 245 J8
Kingston Av HUDE HD5 193 G8
Kingston Cl HFAX HX1 10 B7
ROY/SHW OL2 229 K7
WIL/AL BD15 102 E2
Kingston Ct HFAX HX1 10 B8
Kingston Crs SEL YO8 139 M4
Kingston Dr HFAX HX1 10 A7
NORM WF6 178 F5
ROY/SHW OL2 228 E8
SEL YO8 139 M4
Kingstone Pl BSLY S70 260 F7
Kingston Gdns MSTN/BAR LS15 111 K3
Kingston Gv IDLE BD10 83 K5
Kingston Rd IDLE BD10 83 K5
Kingston St HFAX HX1 10 B7
Kingston Ter LDSU LS2 6 E4
King St AIRE BD20 * 36 A5
BIRK/DRI BD11 129 H8
BRIG HD6 170 D4
BSLY S70 261 H6
CAS WF10 158 A8
CLECK BD19 150 A6
COL BB8 74 A1
HBR HX7 143 G3
HBR HX7 144 A6
HECK WF16 172 F2
HEM/SK/SE WF9 223 K5
HFAX HX1 11 J5
HOR/CROF WF4 196 F5
HUD HD1 15 G7
HUDW HD3 191 K6
IDLE BD10 105 L1
KBTN HD8 239 J4
KGHY BD21 2 F7
LDS LS1 8 E1
MILN OL16 206 B7
MIRF WF14 194 C2
MOR LS27 152 C3
NORM WF6 178 B2
NORM WF6 178 C5
OSS WF5 197 G2
PDSY/CALV LS28 106 F5
PONT WF8 180 E6
RPDN/SBR HX6 * 167 G3
TOD OL14 141 M8
WKFDE WF1 12 E2
YEA LS19 62 E7
YEA LS19 84 C2
King St East ROCH OL11 228 A1
King St South ROCH OL11 228 A1
Kings Vw HIPP HX3 169 J2
Kingsway AIRE BD20 58 C5
AL/HA/HU LS17 43 M2
BGLY BD16 81 J4
BIRK/DRI BD11 129 H8
BTLY WF17 151 G4
DOD/DAR S75 242 C5
EARD/LOFT WF3 177 H4
ECHL BD2 83 H8
GFTH/SHER LS25 112 F8
MILN OL16 206 E8
MSTN/BAR LS15 111 L6
NORM WF6 178 C6
OSS WF5 174 E7
PONT WF8 180 F3
SKP/WHF BD23 16 D1
Kingsway Cl OSS WF5 174 E7
Kingsway Ct AL/HA/HU LS17 87 M5
OSS WF5 174 E7
Kingsway Dr ILK LS29 38 C2
Kingsway Garth
GFTH/SHER LS25 112 E8
Kingswear Cl MSTN/BAR LS15 111 M5
Kingswear Crs MSTN/BAR LS15 111 M5
Kingswear Garth
MSTN/BAR LS15 111 M5
Kingswear Gln MSTN/BAR LS15 111 M5
Kingswear Gv MSTN/BAR LS15 111 M5
Kingswear Pde MSTN/BAR LS15 111 M5
Kingswear Ri MSTN/BAR LS15 111 M5
Kingswear Vw MSTN/BAR LS15 111 M5
Kingswell Av WKFDE WF1 176 E2
Kingswood Av RHAY LS8 88 C3
Kingswood Crs RHAY LS8 88 B3
Kingswood Dr RHAY LS8 88 B3
Kingswood Gdns RHAY LS8 88 B3
Kingswood Gn HIPP HX3 147 H5
Kingswood Gv RHAY LS8 88 C3
Kingswood Pl GTHN BD7 126 C2
Kingswood Rd WOR/ARM LS12 108 D8
Kingswood St GTHN BD7 126 C2
Kingswood Ter GTHN BD7 * 126 C2
Kingwell Crs BSLY S70 261 H8
Kinnaird Cl BTLY WF17 174 A1
ELL HX5 169 H6
Kinsley House Crs
HEM/SK/SE WF9 223 J4
Kinsley St HEM/SK/SE WF9 223 K5
Kiplin Dr AWLS/ASK DN6 227 L3
Kipling Cl HUDS HD4 213 M3
Kipling Ct IDLE BD10 83 M7
Kipling Gv PONT WF8 180 F4
Kippax Mt OSM LS9 110 B7
Kippax Pl OSM LS9 110 B7
Kipping La CUL/QBY BD13 102 F8
Kipping Pl CUL/QBY BD13 102 F8
Kirby Cote La HBR HX7 165 M3
Kirby St KGHY BD21 3 J2
Kirk Beston Cl BEE/HOL LS11 131 G4
Kirkbourne Gv BAIL BD17 83 G4
Kirk Bridge La HOLM/MEL HD9 236 F7
Kirkbridge Wy
HEM/SK/SE WF9 247 H3
Kirkburn Pl GTHN BD7 104 D8
Kirkby Av BSLYN/ROY S71 243 J6
GFTH/SHER LS25 135 J1
Kirkby Cl HEM/SK/SE WF9 246 E3
Kirkbygate HEM/SK/SE WF9 246 A1
Kirkby La HOR/CROF WF4 217 L6
PBR HG3 45 M2
Kirkby Leas HFAX HX1 11 G8
Kirkby Rd HEM/SK/SE WF9 224 A8
Kirkcaldy Fold NORM WF6 178 F5
Kirk Cl EARL WF12 174 D6
Kirk Cross Crs BSLYN/ROY S71 243 L4
Kirkdale CAS WF10 158 E7
Kirkdale Av WOR/ARM LS12 130 D2
Kirkdale Crs WOR/ARM LS12 130 D3
Kirkdale Dr HOR/CROF WF4 197 M8
WOR/ARM LS12 130 D2
Kirkdale Gdns WOR/ARM LS12 130 C2
Kirkdale Gv WOR/ARM LS12 130 C2
Kirkdale Mt WOR/ARM LS12 130 D3
Kirkdale Ter WOR/ARM LS12 130 D3
Kirkdale Vw WOR/ARM LS12 130 D3
Kirkdale Wy BOW BD4 128 B5
Kirk Dr BAIL BD17 82 C2
Kirkfield Av SCFT LS14 68 C8
Kirkfield Cl DOD/DAR S75 259 H2
Kirkfield Crs SCFT LS14 68 C8
Kirkfield Dr MSTN/BAR LS15 111 L7
Kirkfield Gdns MSTN/BAR LS15 111 M7
Kirkfield La SCFT LS14 68 C8
Kirkfields BAIL BD17 83 G2
Kirkfield Vw MSTN/BAR LS15 111 M7
Kirkfield Wy BSLYN/ROY S71 243 L4
Kirkgate AIRE BD20 35 G6
AIRE BD20 36 A5
BFD BD1 4 E6
BTLY WF17 150 F5
BTLY WF17 174 B3
GFTH/SHER LS25 116 A6
HUD HD1 15 G7
LDS LS1 7 H9
LDSU LS2 9 J1
OT LS21 41 J6
SHPY BD18 82 C7
TAD LS24 71 M3
WKFDE WF1 12 F2
Kirkgate La CUD/GR S72 222 E8
Kirkham Av WKFDW/WTN WF2 175 K3
Kirkham Cl BSLYN/ROY S71 261 L3
Kirkham Pl BSLYN/ROY S71 243 M7
Kirkham Rd GTHN BD7 * 104 D8
Kirkham St BRAM LS13 107 H1
Kirkham La KNOT WF11 159 K8
Kirkhill Bank STKB/PEN S36 270 E6
Kirk Ings Yd LDSU LS2 * 9 J1
Kirklands HOLM/MEL HD9 236 F7
LVSG WF15 172 C2
Kirklands Av BAIL BD17 83 G3
Kirklands Cl BAIL BD17 83 G4
YEA LS19 62 C7
Kirklands Gdns BAIL BD17 83 G3
Kirklands La BAIL BD17 83 G3
Kirklands Rd BAIL BD17 82 F3
Kirklands Vls BAIL BD17 * 83 G3
Kirk La HIPP HX3 147 L6
RYKW YO26 32 B1
YEA LS19 62 C7
Kirklea KBTN HD8 238 E3
Kirk Lea Crs HUDW HD3 191 L6

Kirklees Cl PDSY/CALV LS28 107 G2
Kirklees Cft PDSY/CALV LS28 106 F2
Kirklees Dr PDSY/CALV LS28 106 F2
Kirklees Garth PDSY/CALV LS28 106 F2
Kirklees Ri PDSY/CALV LS28 106 F2
Kirklees Rd WIL/AL BD15 103 K7
Kirklees Wy BIRK/DRI BD11 150 B1
BTLY WF17 151 L5
CLECK BD19 149 J3
EARL WF12 174 A7
HOLM/MEL HD9 255 H3
HUDN HD2 192 B3
KBTN HD8 237 L7
KBTN HD8 238 D6
KBTN HD8 239 J5
KBTN HD8 239 K7
MAR/SLWT HD7 210 F5
MAR/SLWT HD7 212 C1
MAR/SLWT HD7 233 K8
OSS WF5 196 D2
Kirkley Av LM/WK BD12 148 E5
Kirkroyds La HOLM/MEL HD9 236 E7
Kirkstall WHIT OL12 * 206 A6
Kirkstall Av KSTL LS5 108 B3
LIT OL15 185 J8
Kirkstall Gv GIR BD8 103 M7
Kirkstall Hl BULY LS4 108 D3
Kirkstall La KSTL LS5 108 D2
Kirkstall Mt KSTL LS5 108 B3
Kirkstall Rd BSLYN/ROY S71 243 G7
BULY LS4 108 D3
BVRD LS3 6 A8
Kirkstone Av HUDE HD5 15 K6
Kirkstone Dr CLECK BD19 150 D6
LUD/ILL HX2 145 K6
ROY/SHW OL2 228 E8
Kirkthorpe La WKFDE WF1 177 K8
Kirkwall Av OSM LS9 110 D7
Kirkwall Dr BOW BD4 128 A3
Kirk Wy BSLYN/ROY S71 261 M3
Kirkway ROCH OL11 228 B4
Kirkwood Av BHP/TINH LS16 85 M2
Kirkwood Cl BHP/TINH LS16 85 M1
Kirkwood Crs BHP/TINH LS16 85 M1
Kirkwood Dr BHP/TINH LS16 85 M1
HUDW HD3 191 J6
Kirkwood Gdns BHP/TINH LS16 86 A1
Kirkwood Gn HUDW HD3 191 K6
Kirkwood Gv BHP/TINH LS16 85 M2
EARD/LOFT WF3 153 H6
Kirkwood La BHP/TINH LS16 85 M1
Kirkwood Ri BHP/TINH LS16 86 A1
Kirkwood Vw BHP/TINH LS16 86 A1
Kirkwood Wy BHP/TINH LS16 86 A1
Kismet Gdns BFDE BD3 105 L6
Kistyaen Gdns HOLM/MEL HD9 234 E3
Kitchener Av OSM LS9 110 D5
Kitchener Gv OSM LS9 110 D4
Kitchener Mt OSM LS9 110 D5
Kitchener Pl OSM LS9 110 D5
Kitchener St LM/WK BD12 149 J1
OSM LS9 110 D5
RTHW LS26 133 L8
Kitchen Fold MAR/SLWT HD7 212 C6
Kitchen St MILN OL16 206 C6
Kite Ms GIR BD8 103 L7
Kit La AIRE BD20 17 L8
Kitson Cl WOR/ARM LS12 108 E8
Kitson Dr BSLYN/ROY S71 261 M3
Kitson Gdns WOR/ARM LS12 108 E8
Kitson Hill Crs MIRF WF14 172 B8
Kitson Hill Rd MIRF WF14 172 A8
Kitson La RPDN/SBR HX6 167 M5
Kitson Rd MID LS10 9 J6
Kitson St EARD/LOFT WF3 152 F5
OSM LS9 110 B7
SHPY BD18 82 E7
Kitson Wood Rd TOD OL14 141 G6
Kitter St WHIT OL12 206 D3
Kliffen Pl HIPP HX3 168 F2
Knaresborough Dr HUDN HD2 192 C4
Knave Cl HOR/CROF WF4 197 L4
Knavesmire RTHW LS26 154 D1
Knightsbridge Wk BOW BD4 127 K6
Knightsclose MSTN/BAR LS15 111 L6
Knights Cft WBY LS22 30 B7
Knightscroft Av RTHW LS26 133 G8
Knightscroft Dr RTHW LS26 133 G8
Knightscroft Pde
HEM/SK/SE WF9 247 J4
Knight's Fold GTHN BD7 126 C2
Knightshill MSTN/BAR LS15 111 M6
Knight St HFAX HX1 10 B9
HUD HD1 15 G5
Knightsway EARD/LOFT WF3 154 D5
GFTH/SHER LS25 134 F1
MSTN/BAR LS15 111 L6
WKFDW/WTN WF2 198 E8
Knoll Cl OSS WF5 174 F7
Knoll La HOLM/MEL HD9 235 M6
Knoll Pk EARD/LOFT WF3 153 M7
Knoll Park Dr BAIL BD17 82 D5
The Knoll BSPA/BRAM LS23 69 L3
PDSY/CALV LS28 106 C3
ROY/SHW OL2 * 229 L8
Knoll Wood Pk HORS LS18 85 M6
Knott Hill St WHIT OL12 162 A8
Knottingley Rd PONT WF8 181 J4
Knott La AIRE BD20 56 B1
YEA LS19 85 G5
Knotts Rd TOD OL14 140 F6
Knotty La KBTN HD8 216 C3
Knowle Av BULY LS4 108 F3
HUDE HD5 215 G1
Knowle Gv BULY LS4 108 F3
Knowle La HOLM/MEL HD9 235 K4
LM/WK BD12 148 F4
Knowle Mt BULY LS4 108 F4
Knowle Park Av KBTN HD8 238 B6
Knowle Pl BULY LS4 108 F3
Knowler Cl LVSG WF15 172 C1
Knowler Hl LVSG WF15 172 C2
Knowle Rd BSLY S70 261 K8
BULY LS4 * 108 F3
MAR/SLWT HD7 212 C5
Knowler Wy LVSG WF15 172 C1
Knowles Av BOW BD4 127 M4
Knowles Hl DEWS WF13 173 H5
Knowles Hill Rd DEWS WF13 173 H5
Knowles La BOW BD4 127 M4
BTLY WF17 173 K2
CLECK BD19 150 D3
Knowle Spring Rd
KGHY BD21 * 2 E8
Knowles Rd BRIG HD6 170 C6
BTLY WF17 173 K2
Knowles St BOW BD4 127 L5
CUL/QBY BD13 101 M6
STKB/PEN S36 271 H4
Knowles Vw BOW BD4 127 M4
Knowles Wk HEM/SK/SE WF9 247 J1
Knowle Ter BULY LS4 108 E4
The Knowle KBTN HD8 238 C6
Knowle Top Dr HIPP HX3 148 A6
Knowle Top Rd HIPP HX3 148 A6
Knowl Gv MIRF WF14 194 C1
Knowl Rd HOLM/MEL HD9 252 F2
MAR/SLWT HD7 213 G2
MILN OL16 206 F8
MIRF WF14 194 C1
ROY/SHW OL2 229 L8
Knowl Syke St WHIT OL12 184 E7
Knowl Vw LIT OL15 207 H4
Knowlwood Rd TOD OL14 163 J3
Knowsley Av TOD OL14 * 163 J5
Knowsley Crs WHIT OL12 162 A8
Knowsley St BFDE BD3 5 K7
BSLY S70 260 F5
WHIT OL12 206 A6
Knowsthorpe Crs OSM LS9 110 B8
Knowsthorpe Ga OSM LS9 132 D2
Knowsthorpe La OSM LS9 132 C2
Knowsthorpe Rd OSM LS9 132 E2
Knowsthorpe Wy OSM LS9 132 D2
Knox St BRAM LS13 106 F1
Knutsford Gv BOW BD4 128 A4
Knutsford Ms BOW BD4 * 128 A4
Komla Cl BFD BD1 5 H5
Krive La MAR/SLWT HD7 234 A1
Kyffin Av MSTN/BAR LS15 111 G7
Kyffin Pl BOW BD4 128 A1

L

Laburnum Av ROY/SHW OL2 229 K8
Laburnum Cl EARD/LOFT WF3 153 L7
Laburnum Ct CAS WF10 158 A8
HOR/CROF WF4 197 H5
Laburnum Dr BAIL BD17 82 F2
Laburnum Gv BRIG HD6 148 C8
CLECK BD19 150 C5
HOR/CROF WF4 197 H5
HUDW HD3 213 H1
HWTH BD22 79 G6
KBTN HD8 239 J5
Laburnum La MILN OL16 229 J3
Laburnum Pl GIR BD8 4 B2
IDLE BD10 84 A6
Laburnum Rd DEWS WF13 173 G4
SHPY BD18 104 F1
WKFDE WF1 12 D1
Laburnum St GIR BD8 4 B2
PDSY/CALV LS28 106 F5
Laburnum Ter HUD HD1 * 15 G3
ROCH OL11 228 A2
Laburnum Wy LIT OL15 207 H1
Laceby Cl IDLE BD10 83 L6
Lacey Ct BSLY S70 260 E7
Lacey St DEWS WF13 173 K6
Lachman Rd COL BB8 74 D3
Lacy Av TOD OL14 163 J5
Lacy Gv WBY LS22 48 B2
Lacy St HEM/SK/SE WF9 223 L7
Lacy Wy ELL HX5 169 K5
Ladbroke Gv BOW BD4 * 128 A5
Ladderbanks La BAIL BD17 82 F2
Ladock Cl BSLYN/ROY S71 261 K3
Lady Ann Rd BTLY WF17 173 M1
Lady Balk La PONT WF8 180 F4
Lady Beck Cl LDSU LS2 7 J8
Ladybower Av MAR/SLWT HD7 213 G4
Lady Cl OSS WF5 174 E6
Lady Gap La AWLS/ASK DN6 249 L1
Lady Hartley Ct COL BB8 52 F8
Lady Heton Av MIRF WF14 172 B8
Lady Heton Cl MIRF WF14 * 172 A8
Lady Heton Dr MIRF WF14 172 B8
Lady Heton Gv MIRF WF14 172 A8
Ladyhouse Cl MILN OL16 229 J2
Lady House La HUDS HD4 214 C6
Ladyhouse La MILN OL16 229 H1
Lady La BGLY BD16 59 J8
LDSU LS2 7 H9
WKFDE WF1 12 D4
Ladymead BSLYN/ROY S71 261 K2
Lady Park Av BGLY BD16 59 J8
Lady Park Ct AL/HA/HU LS17 88 A2
Lady Pit La BEE/HOL LS11 8 F9
Ladyroyd Cft CUD/GR S72 244 D8
Ladyroyd Dr BIRK/DRI BD11 128 A8
Ladysmith Rd CUL/QBY BD13 124 E6
Ladywell Cl WBOW BD5 127 G3
Ladywell La LVSG WF15 171 K3
Ladywood Gra RHAY LS8 * 88 F8
Ladywood Md RHAY LS8 88 F8
Ladywood Rd CUD/GR S72 245 K8
Lady Wood Rd RHAY LS8 88 D7
Ladywood Ter HFAX HX1 10 C3
Ladywood Wy DEWS WF13 194 F2
Lafflands La HOR/CROF WF4 222 C5
Lairds Wy STKB/PEN S36 271 G3
Lairum Ri BSPA/BRAM LS23 69 M1
Laisterdyke BFDE BD3 105 M8
Laisteridge La GTHN BD7 4 B8
WBOW BD5 126 E1
Laith Cl BHP/TINH LS16 86 B3
Laithe Av HOLM/MEL HD9 253 L4
Laithe Bank Dr HOLM/MEL HD9 253 L4
Laithe Cl AIRE BD20 35 M4
Laithe Cft DOD/DAR S75 260 B7
Laithe Croft Rd BTLY WF17 174 A1
Laithe Gv WBSY BD6 126 C4
Laithe Rd WBSY BD6 126 D5
Laithes Cha WKFDW/WTN WF2 175 M7
Laithes Cl BSLYN/ROY S71 243 K7
WKFDW/WTN WF2 175 M7
Laithes Ct WKFDW/WTN WF2 175 M7
Laithes Crs BSLYN/ROY S71 243 H7
WKFDW/WTN WF2 175 M7
Laithes Cft EARL WF12 174 A7
Laithes Dr WKFDW/WTN WF2 175 M7
Laithes Fold WKFDW/WTN WF2 175 M7
Laithes La BSLYN/ROY S71 243 J7
Laithes Vw WKFDW/WTN WF2 175 M7
Laith Gdns BHP/TINH LS16 86 B3
Laith Garth BHP/TINH LS16 86 B3
Laith Gn BHP/TINH LS16 86 B3
Laith Rd BHP/TINH LS16 86 B3
Laith Staid La GFTH/SHER LS25 115 K6
Lake Bank LIT OL15 207 J3
Lakeland Cl CUD/GR S72 262 D1
Lakeland Crs AL/HA/HU LS17 65 J8
Lakeland Dr AL/HA/HU LS17 65 K8
ROY/SHW OL2 * 228 E6
Lakeland Wy WKFDW/WTN WF2 199 J8
Lake Lock Dr EARD/LOFT WF3 177 H1
Lake Lock Gv EARD/LOFT WF3 177 H1
Lake Lock Rd EARD/LOFT WF3 177 H1
Lake Rw BOW BD4 5 M9
Lakeside AIRE BD20 59 G4
KGHY BD21 * 54 B8
Lake Side LIT OL15 207 J4
Lakeside Cha YEA LS19 84 E2
Lakeside Cl ILK LS29 38 C1
Lakeside Ct HUDW HD3 191 K6
Lakeside Est HOR/CROF WF4 222 D4
Lakeside Gdns YEA LS19 84 E2
Lakeside Mdw PONT WF8 180 F3
Lakeside Pk NORM WF6 178 F5
Lakeside Rd WOR/ARM LS12 108 A8
Lakeside Ter YEA LS19 84 E2
Lakeside Vw STKB/PEN S36 257 J7
YEA LS19 84 E2
Lake St BOW BD4 5 M9
KGHY BD21 3 L1
Lake Ter MID LS10 131 M4
Lake Vw HIPP HX3 10 F3
PONT WF8 180 E3
WKFDW/WTN WF2 220 E2
Lake View Ct RHAY LS8 88 E6
Lake Yd EARD/LOFT WF3 177 J1
Lamb Cote Rd HUDN HD2 170 F8
Lambecroft BSLYN/ROY S71 243 L5
Lambe Flatt DOD/DAR S75 241 L6
Lambert Av RHAY LS8 88 B8
Lambert Cl GTL/HWG HX4 168 F7
Lambert Dr RHAY LS8 88 B8
Lambert Fold DOD/DAR S75 260 C7
Lambert Pl ECHL BD2 105 K4
Lambert Rd BSLY S70 261 L7
Lambert St COL BB8 74 E4
GTL/HWG HX4 168 F7
SKP/WHF BD23 16 C3
Lambert Wk BSLY S70 261 L6
Lambeth St COL BB8 74 D1
Lamb Hall Rd HUDW HD3 191 G6
Lamb Hey MAR/SLWT HD7 * 212 D5
Lamb Inn Rd KNOT WF11 182 C2
Lamb La BSLYN/ROY S71 261 L1
Lambourne Av IDLE BD10 105 M1
Lambourne Gv MILN OL16 229 H1
Lambra Rd BSLY S70 261 H5
Lambrigg Crs SCFT LS14 111 J2
Lamb Springs La BAIL BD17 83 J1
Lambton Gv RHAY LS8 110 B2
Lambton Pl RHAY LS8 110 B2
Lambton St RHAY LS8 * 110 B2
Lambton Ter RHAY LS8 110 B2
Lambton Vw RHAY LS8 * 110 B2
Lamma Well Rd
HOLM/MEL HD9 254 C4
Lampards Cl WIL/AL BD15 103 J4
Lamplands BTLY WF17 151 M7
Lanark Dr HORS LS18 85 J2
Lanark Ri HOR/CROF WF4 200 C6
Lancar Ct BSLYN/ROY S71 261 J2
Lancaster Cl PONT WF8 180 F8
Lancaster Ct KGHY BD21 2 D8
Lancaster Crs HUDE HD5 215 H2
Lancaster Ga BSLY S70 261 G5
Lancaster La HOLM/MEL HD9 236 E5
Lancaster St BSLY S70 260 F5
CAS WF10 158 F5
Lancastre Av KSTL LS5 108 B3
Lancastre Gv KSTL LS5 108 B3
Lancet Ri EARD/LOFT WF3 154 C3
Land Ga WHIT OL12 184 A1
Landmark Ct BEE/HOL LS11 8 A9
Landor St KGHY BD21 * 3 K3
Lands Beck Wy LVSG WF15 172 B2
Landscove Av BOW BD4 128 A4
Lansdown Av
HEM/SK/SE WF9 246 C5
Landseer Av BRAM LS13 108 A3
EARD/LOFT WF3 153 G6
Landseer Cl BRAM LS13 107 M3
Landseer Crs BRAM LS13 107 M3
Landseer Dr BRAM LS13 107 M3
Landseer Gdns BRAM LS13 107 M3
Landseer Gn BRAM LS13 107 M3
Landseer Gv BRAM LS13 108 A3
Landseer Mt BRAM LS13 108 A3
Landseer Ri BRAM LS13 107 M3
Landseer Rd BRAM LS13 107 M3
Landseer Ter BRAM LS13 108 A3
Landseer Vw BRAM LS13 108 A3
Landseer Wk BRAM LS13 108 A3
Lands Head La HIPP HX3 147 H2
Lands La GSLY LS20 62 A5
IDLE BD10 105 L1
LDS LS1 7 G9
Landsmoor Gv BGLY BD16 81 K1
Land St PDSY/CALV LS28 106 F3
Lane & Dowry Rd
MAR/SLWT HD7 212 A8
Lane End CUL/QBY BD13 102 F8
PDSY/CALV LS28 107 H6
Lane End Ct AL/HA/HU LS17 87 H1
Lane End Cft AL/HA/HU LS17 87 H1
Lane End Fold PDSY/CALV LS28 107 H6
Lane End Mt PDSY/CALV LS28 107 H6
Lane End Pl BEE/HOL LS11 8 E6
Lane Ends LUD/ILL HX2 146 A4
Lane Ends Cl GIR BD8 104 A6
HEM/SK/SE WF9 223 H2
Lane Ends Gn HIPP HX3 147 K6
Lane Ends La HBR HX7 143 L2
HWTH BD22 54 F2
Lane Hackings Gn KBTN HD8 239 G7
Lane Head La KBTN HD8 216 B8
LUD/ILL HX2 123 L6
Lane Head Ri DOD/DAR S75 242 C4
Lane Head Rd DOD/DAR S75 258 F3
KBTN HD8 238 A7
RPDN/SBR HX6 188 E1
Lane House La COL BB8 74 E4
Lane House Rd HWTH BD22 54 B2
Lane Side CUL/QBY BD13 124 F3
WIL/AL BD15 102 D2
Laneside KBTN HD8 216 C7
MOR LS27 130 D7
Laneside Av ROY/SHW OL2 229 M7
Lane Side Cl LM/WK BD12 148 E2
Laneside Cl LIT OL15 185 J8
MOR LS27 130 D7
Laneside Fold MOR LS27 130 D7
Laneside Gdns MOR LS27 130 D8
Lane Side La HUDE HD5 193 L7
Laneside St TOD OL14 163 J2
The Lanes PDSY/CALV LS28 107 H6
The Lane AL/HA/HU LS17 87 H1
OSM LS9 9 L2
Lane Top BRIG HD6 * 148 F7
Lang Av BSLYN/ROY S71 262 A4
Langbar Ap SCFT LS14 111 M1
Langbar Av HTON BD9 103 M3
Langbar Cl SCFT LS14 89 M8
Langbar Garth SCFT LS14 89 M8
Langbar Gn SCFT LS14 89 M8
Langbar Gv SCFT LS14 111 M1
Langbar Rd ILK LS29 20 C8
SCFT LS14 111 M1
Langcliffe Cl DOD/DAR S75 242 C4
Lang Crs BSLYN/ROY S71 262 A4
Langdale Av EARD/LOFT WF3 176 F1
GIR BD8 104 A6
HDGY LS6 108 E1
LM/WK BD12 149 G5
MILN OL16 228 E6
NORM WF6 178 C2
Langdale Cl CAS WF10 159 G4
WBY LS22 29 M8
Langdale Ct BGLY BD16 81 J2
Langdale Crs LUD/ILL HX2 146 A5
Langdale Dr CUL/QBY BD13 124 F5
FEA/AMT WF7 202 E7
HUDE HD5 15 K5
NORM WF6 178 C2
WKFDW/WTN WF2 176 A8
Langdale Gdns HDGY LS6 108 E2
Langdale Ms NORM WF6 * 178 C2
Langdale Mt WKFDW/WTN WF2 199 J8
Langdale Ri COL BB8 52 B8
Langdale Rd AWLS/ASK DN6 249 K5
BSLYN/ROY S71 261 H5
DOD/DAR S75 260 A1
EARL WF12 174 B4
IDLE BD10 106 A2
RTHW LS26 133 K8
Langdales RPDN/SBR HX6 167 J2
Langdale Sq WKFDW/WTN WF2 176 B8
Langdale St ELL HX5 169 H8
Langdale Ter HDGY LS6 108 E2
Langden Cl ROY/SHW OL2 229 J6
Langdon Wk BSLY S70 260 F4
Langford Cl DOD/DAR S75 260 C7
Langford La ILK LS29 40 B5
Langford Ride ILK LS29 40 B5
Langford Rd ILK LS29 40 A5
Lang Kirk Cl AIRE BD20 35 G6
Langlands Rd BGLY BD16 81 J7
Lang La ECHL BD2 * 104 F2
Langley Av BGLY BD16 81 J2
BOW BD4 127 K5
BRAM LS13 107 J2
Langley Cl BRAM LS13 107 J2
Langley Crs BAIL BD17 83 G3
BRAM LS13 107 K3
Langley Garth BRAM LS13 107 J2
Langley Gv BGLY BD16 81 J2
Langley La BAIL BD17 83 G2
KBTN HD8 240 A2
Langley Mt BRAM LS13 107 J2
Langley Pl BRAM LS13 107 J2
Langley Rd BGLY BD16 81 J2
BRAM LS13 107 J2
Langold Dr AWLS/ASK DN6 227 M3
Langport Cl CUL/QBY BD13 125 H5
Langroyd Rd COL BB8 52 A8
Langsett Cft HUDN HD2 193 G1
Langsett Rd BSLYN/ROY S71 243 G7
WKFDW/WTN WF2 220 D1
Langthorne Ct MOR LS27 152 E4
Langthwaite La
HEM/SK/SE WF9 247 G4
Langthwaite Rd
HEM/SK/SE WF9 246 F5
Langton Av BOW BD4 127 K5
Langton Cl CLECK BD19 150 C4
Langton Gn WOR/ARM LS12 108 E8
Langton St RPDN/SBR HX6 167 K1
Langtons Whf LDSU LS2 9 J2
Langton Ter ROCH OL11 228 A2
Langwith Av WBY LS22 47 J6
Langwith Dr WBY LS22 47 G6
Langwith Valley Rd WBY LS22 47 G6
Lansdale Ct BOW BD4 128 B4
Lansdowne Av CAS WF10 158 B7
Lansdowne Cl BAIL BD17 83 H3
BTLY WF17 151 K8
Lansdowne Crs DOD/DAR S75 241 M7
Lansdowne Pl WBOW BD5 4 D8
Lansdowne St WOR/ARM LS12 108 E8
Lanshaw Bank SKP/WHF BD23 19 K1
Lanshaw Cl MID LS10 132 A8
Lanshaw Crs MID LS10 154 A1
Lanshaw Pl MID LS10 132 A8
Lanshaw Rd MID LS10 132 A8
Lanshaw Ter MID LS10 154 A1
Lanshaw Vw MID LS10 132 A8
Lanshaw Wk MID LS10 132 A8
Lanyon Wy BSLYN/ROY S71 261 K3
Lapage St BFDE BD3 105 L7
Lapage Ter BFDE BD3 * 105 L7
Lapwing Cl GIR BD8 103 K6
Larch Av HOLM/MEL HD9 236 E6
Larch Cl BTLY WF17 151 J4
HUDE HD5 * 193 K5
HWTH BD22 78 F4
LVSG WF15 172 E3
NORM WF6 178 D6
Larch Dl HUDN HD2 192 C2
Larch Dr WBSY BD6 126 E7
Larchfield Pl BSLYN/ROY S71 261 M1
Larchfield Rd MID LS10 9 L7
Larchfield Wy HOR/CROF WF4 222 D5
Larch Gv BGLY BD16 81 H1
Larch Hl WBSY BD6 126 F7
Larch Hill Crs WBSY BD6 126 F6
Larch La GFTH/SHER LS25 113 K8
Larchmont CLAY BD14 125 L2
Larch Pl BSLY S70 261 L8
Larch Rd HUD HD1 213 L1
Larch St KGHY BD21 79 K2
Larchway MILN OL16 206 F7
Larch Wd SCFT LS14 67 L7
Larkfield Av YEA LS19 84 E2
Larkfield Crs YEA LS19 84 E2
Larkfield Dr YEA LS19 84 E2
Larkfield Mt YEA LS19 84 E2
Larkfield Rd PDSY/CALV LS28 107 G6
YEA LS19 84 E2
Larkfield Ter KGHY BD21 3 M7
Lark Hl BTLY WF17 151 J5
Lark Hill Av CLECK BD19 149 K8
Larkhill Cl RHAY LS8 88 A6
Lark Hill Dr CLECK BD19 149 K7
Larkhill Gn AL/HA/HU LS17 88 A5
Larkhill Pl WHIT OL12 206 A5
Larkhill Rd AL/HA/HU LS17 88 A5
Larkhill Vw RHAY LS8 88 A6
Larkhill Wk RHAY LS8 88 A5
Larkhill Wy AL/HA/HU LS17 88 A5
Larks Hl PONT WF8 180 D8
Larkspur Wy WKFDW/WTN WF2 176 A7
Lark St BGLY BD16 81 H3
COL BB8 52 A8
HWTH BD22 78 F4
KGHY BD21 2 E4
Lark V BGLY BD16 81 L2
Larwood Av IDLE BD10 106 A2
Lascelles Hall Rd HUDE HD5 193 K7
Lascelles Mt RHAY LS8 * 110 B3
Lascelles Pl RHAY LS8 110 B3
Lascelles Rd HECK WF16 173 G3
Lascelles Rd East RHAY LS8 110 B3
Lascelles Rd West RHAY LS8 * 110 B3
Lascelles St RHAY LS8 110 B3
Lascelles Ter RHAY LS8 110 B3
Lascelles Vw RHAY LS8 110 B3
Lastingham Gn WBSY BD6 * 126 A5
Lastingham Rd BRAM LS13 107 H1
Latchmere Av BHP/TINH LS16 86 B6
Latchmere Cl BHP/TINH LS16 86 C6
Latchmere Crest
BHP/TINH LS16 86 B6
Latchmere Cross
BHP/TINH LS16 86 B6
Latchmere Dr BHP/TINH LS16 86 B6
Latchmere Rd BHP/TINH LS16 86 B6
Latchmere Vw BHP/TINH LS16 86 B6
Latchmere Wk BHP/TINH LS16 86 C5
Latchmore Rd WOR/ARM LS12 130 F2
Latham Ct CLECK BD19 150 D4
Latham La CLECK BD19 150 C3
Latham Lea CLECK BD19 150 C5
Latimer St BFDE BD3 105 M8
Latin St MILN OL16 * 206 A8
Launceston Dr BOW BD4 128 A4
Laund Rd HUDW HD3 191 H6
MAR/SLWT HD7 211 L3
Launton Wy WBOW BD5 126 F2
Laura St BRIG HD6 170 C5
HIPP HX3 11 G2
WOR/ARM LS12 8 B3
Laurel Av BSLY S70 261 M7
Laurel Bank BGLY BD16 * 81 M2
KBTN HD8 239 J4
Laurel Bank Cl LUD/ILL HX2 124 C8
Laurel Bank Ct BULY LS4 108 E2
Laurel Cl AL/HA/HU LS17 67 L1
ELL HX5 169 G8
HIPP HX3 125 L7
Laurel Ct MILN OL16 * 206 D8
OSS WF5 174 E8
Laurel Crs KGHY BD21 2 E3
Laurel Dr BTLY WF17 151 J7
Laurel Fold WOR/ARM LS12 * 108 E7
Laurel Gv AIRE BD20 35 M5
BGLY BD16 81 G1
BTLY WF17 151 H7
KGHY BD21 2 E3
WOR/ARM LS12 108 E7
Laurel Hill Av MSTN/BAR LS15 111 M7
Laurel Hill Cft
MSTN/BAR LS15 * 111 M7
Laurel Hill Gdns
MSTN/BAR LS15 111 M7
Laurel Hill Gv MSTN/BAR LS15 111 M7
Laurel Hill Vw MSTN/BAR LS15 111 M7
Laurel Hill Wy MSTN/BAR LS15 111 M8
Laurel Mt CHAL LS7 * 109 M1
HFAX HX1 * 10 D9
PDSY/CALV LS28 107 G6
Laurel Pk WIL/AL BD15 102 E2
Laurel Pl MID LS10 153 K3
WOR/ARM LS12 108 E7
Laurels Dr LIT OL15 207 H4
The Laurels BGLY BD16 * 81 K3
EARL WF12 174 C7
RHAY LS8 88 B8
Laurel St BFDE BD3 105 L8
HFAX HX1 10 D9
WOR/ARM LS12 108 E7
Laurel Ter AWLS/ASK DN6 249 J4
PDSY/CALV LS28 107 G6
Laurence Av RTHW LS26 133 M7
Laurie Pl WHIT OL12 * 206 B5
Lavender Ct HUDS HD4 213 M8
SHPY BD18 104 F1
Lavender Cft HECK WF16 173 G2
Lavender Hl IDLE BD10 105 L1
Lavender Wk OSM LS9 110 B7
Lavenham Pl AWLS/ASK DN6 249 G4
Laverhills LVSG WF15 171 M1
Laverock Crs BRIG HD6 170 B1
Laverock La BRIG HD6 170 B1
Laverton Rd BOW BD4 127 K2
Lavery Cl OSS WF5 174 E8
Lavinia Ter CLAY BD14 125 M2
Lawcliffe Crs HWTH BD22 78 F6
Law Cl WBY LS22 30 B7
Law Common Rd
HOLM/MEL HD9 268 A1
Lawefield Av RTHW LS26 132 E8
Lawefield Gv
WKFDW/WTN WF2 12 B5
Lawefield La
WKFDW/WTN WF2 12 B5
Lawflat WHIT OL12 206 E1
Lawkholme Crs KGHY BD21 3 G4
Lawkholme La KGHY BD21 3 H2
Law La HIPP HX3 169 J1
Lawn Av AWLS/ASK DN6 249 H8
ILK LS29 40 B5
Lawndale AWLS/ASK DN6 249 H4
Lawndale Fold DOD/DAR S75 * 242 B5
Lawn Rd ILK LS29 40 B5
Lawns Av WOR/ARM LS12 129 M3
Lawns Cl NORM WF6 178 A2
WOR/ARM LS12 129 M3
Lawns Ct WKFDW/WTN WF2 176 A1
Lawns Crs WOR/ARM LS12 129 M3
Lawns Cft WOR/ARM LS12 129 M3
Lawns Dene WOR/ARM LS12 129 M3
Lawns Dr WOR/ARM LS12 129 M3
Lawns Gn WOR/ARM LS12 129 M3
Lawns Hall Cl BHP/TINH LS16 86 D3
Lawn's La MID LS10 9 L9
WKFDW/WTN WF2 176 A1
WOR/ARM LS12 129 M1
Lawns Mt WOR/ARM LS12 129 M3
Lawns Sq WOR/ARM LS12 129 M3
Lawns Ter EARD/LOFT WF3 153 M7
WOR/ARM LS12 129 M3
The Lawns HOR/CROF WF4 196 C8
Lawnswood Gdns
BHP/TINH LS16 86 D4
Lawnswood Rd KGHY BD21 2 C8
Lawrence Av PONT WF8 180 D6
RHAY LS8 110 E2
Lawrence Cl DOD/DAR S75 260 A5
Lawrence Crs HECK WF16 150 F8
RHAY LS8 110 E2
Lawrence Dr GTHN BD7 126 A4
Lawrence Gdns RHAY LS8 110 E1
Lawrence Rd HIPP HX3 168 D3
HUD HD1 14 A5
RHAY LS8 110 E2
Lawrence St HIPP HX3 * 10 D1
Lawrence Wk RHAY LS8 110 E2
Law Slack Rd HOLM/MEL HD9 267 M1
Lawson Rd BRIG HD6 170 D4
Lawson St BFDE BD3 5 G3
WOR/ARM LS12 * 108 D7
Lawson Wood Dr HDGY LS6 87 H5
Law St BOW BD4 127 L4
BTLY WF17 151 H6
CLECK BD19 149 M5
TOD OL14 140 D5
Lawton St HUDS HD4 214 C3
WHIT OL12 206 C5
Laxton Rd BSLYN/ROY S71 243 H6
Laycock Flds HWTH BD22 54 E3
Laycock La HWTH BD22 56 E8
Laycock Pl CHAL LS7 7 J3
Laycock St MILN OL16 206 F3
Lay Garth Cl RTHW LS26 * 155 G1
Laygarth Dr HUDE HD5 193 L8
Lay Garth Gdns RTHW LS26 154 F2
Lay Garth Gn RTHW LS26 155 G2
Lay Garth Md RTHW LS26 155 G2
Lay Garth Pl RTHW LS26 155 G2
Lay Garth Sq RTHW LS26 155 G2
Laythe Barn Cl MILN OL16 207 G8
Layton Av YEA LS19 85 G3
Layton Cl YEA LS19 85 G4
Layton Crs YEA LS19 84 F3
Layton Dr YEA LS19 85 G3
Layton La YEA LS19 85 G3
Layton Mt YEA LS19 84 F3
Layton Park Av YEA LS19 85 G4
Layton Park Cl YEA LS19 84 F3
Layton Park Cft YEA LS19 85 G4
Layton Park Dr YEA LS19 85 G4
Layton Ri HORS LS18 85 H3
Layton Rd YEA LS19 85 G3
Lazenby Dr WBY LS22 29 M8
Lazenby Fold WBY LS22 29 M8
Lea Av HIPP HX3 168 E3
Leabank Av GFTH/SHER LS25 135 J1
Leach Cl MILN OL16 206 E4

Leach Crs AIRE BD20....58 A4
Leache's Br AIRE BD20....57 M4
Leach Ri AIRE BD20....58 M4
Leach Rd AIRE BD20....57 M4
Leach St MILN OL16....206 D8
  MILN OL16....229 H1
  ROY/SHW OL2....229 L8
Lea Cl BRIG HD6....170 C2
Lea Ct GTHN BD7....126 A4
Lea Cft BSPA/BRAM LS23....69 M1
  MIRF WF14....172 C8
  OT LS21....41 J7
Leadenhall St HFAX HX1....10 B9
Lea Dr KBTN HD8....238 D6
Leadwell La EARD/LOFT WF3....154 D3
Lea Farm Crs KSTL LS5....86 B8
Lea Farm Dr KSTL LS5....86 B8
Lea Farm Gv KSTL LS5....86 B8
Lea Farm Mt KSTL LS5....86 A7
Lea Farm Pl KSTL LS5....86 B8
Lea Farm Rd KSTL LS5....86 B7
Lea Farm Rw KSTL LS5....86 B7
Lea Farm Wk KSTL LS5....86 B7
Leafield Av ECHL BD2....105 L3
  HUDW HD3....191 G8
Leafield Bank HUDW HD3....191 G8
Leafield Cl AL/HA/HU LS17....87 K4
  HUDN HD2....192 F2
Leafield Crs ECHL BD2....105 K3
Leafield Dr AL/HA/HU LS17....87 K4
  ECHL BD2....105 L2
  PDSY/CALV LS28....129 H1
Leafield Gra AL/HA/HU LS17....87 K4
Leafield Gv ECHL BD2....105 L3
Leafield Ter ECHL BD2....105 L3
Leafield Wy HFAX HX1....10 L6
Leaf St CAS WF10....157 L7
  HWTH BD22 *....79 C6
Leafsway WBSY BD6 *....126 B8
Lea Head KBTN HD8....238 A6
Leah Pl WOR/ARM LS12....8 A4
Leah St LIT OL15 *....207 K1
Leake St CAS WF10....158 A6
Leak Hall Crs KBTN HD8....239 H8
Leak Hall La KBTN HD8....239 H8
Lea La FEA/AMT WF7....202 A2
  HUDS HD4....202 A2
Lea Mill Park Cl YEA LS19....62 C7
Lea Mill Park Rd YEA LS19....62 C7
Leamington Dr IDLE BD10....83 L6
Leamington Rd ILK LS29....38 E1
Leamington St HTON BD9....104 D4
  WHIT OL12....206 A6
Leamington Ter ILK LS29....38 E1
Leamside Av BOW BD4....128 A4
Lea Park Cl MID LS10....132 B7
Lea Park Cft MID LS10....132 B7
Lea Park Dr MID LS10....132 B7
Lea Park Gdns MID LS10....132 B7
Lea Park Garth MID LS10 *....132 B7
Lea Park Vw MID LS10....132 B7
Lea Park Wy MID LS10....132 C7
Leapings La STKB/PEN S36....270 B3
Learlse HOLM/MEL HD9....236 D5
Lea Rd BSLYN/ROY S71....243 K7
  BTLY WF17....151 H7
Learoyd St HUD HD1....15 H4
Leas Gdns HOLM/MEL HD9....255 C2
Leaside Dr CUL/QBY BD13....109 F7
Lea Side Gdns HUDW HD3....191 G8
Leasowe Av MID LS10....132 A4
Leasowe Cl MID LS10....132 A4
Leasowe Gdns MID LS10....132 A4
Leasowe Garth MID LS10....132 A4
Leasowe Rd MID LS10....132 A4
Lea St HUD HD1....14 F2
  HUDW HD3....191 L5
Leatham Av FEA/AMT WF7....202 A2
Leatham Crs FEA/AMT WF7....202 A2
Leatham Dr FEA/AMT WF7....202 B2
Leatham Park Rd
  FEA/AMT WF7....202 A2
Leatham Royd
  MAR/SLWT HD7 *....233 J7
The Lea GFTH/SHER LS25....135 H1
Leather Bank ILK LS29....40 A3
Leathley Av ILK LS29....61 K3
Leathley Br OT LS21....42 C5
Leathley Crs ILK LS29....61 K3
Leathley La ILK LS29....61 K2
  OT LS21....42 C3
Leathley Rd ILK LS29....61 K2
  MID LS10....9 H5
Leathley St MID LS10....9 J5
The Leavens IDLE BD10....83 M6
Leaventhorpe Av GIR BD8....103 L7
Leaventhorpe Cl GIR BD8....103 M7
Leaventhorpe Gv
  CUL/QBY BD13....103 L8
Leaventhorpe La
  CUL/QBY BD13....103 L8
Leaventhorpe Wy GIR BD8....103 M7
Lea Vw BTLY WF17....151 H7
Leavington Cl LM/WK BD12....126 D8
Leaway WHIT OL12....184 D1
Ledbury Av MID LS10....154 A2
Ledbury Cl MID LS10....154 A2
Ledbury Dr MID LS10....154 A2
Ledbury Gn MID LS10....154 A2
Ledbury Gv MID LS10 *....154 A2
Ledbury Pl BOW BD4....127 J2
Ledgard Dr BSLYN/ROY S71....243 H8
Ledgard Dr HOR/CROF WF4....198 D7
Ledgard Wy WOR/ARM LS12....108 C6
Ledgate La GFTH/SHER LS25....159 M2
Ledger La EARD/LOFT WF3....154 C5
  WKFDE WF1....176 D1
Ledger Pl WKFDE WF1....176 D2
Ledston Av GFTH/SHER LS25....135 J1
Ledston Mill La CAS WF10....136 A4
Lee Bank HIPP HX3....10 E2
Lee Beck Gv EARD/LOFT WF3....155 G2
Lee Bottom Rd TOD OL14....164 C1
Lee Br HFAX HX1....10 D8
Lee La BGLY BD16....80 B8
Lee Cl WIL/AL BD15....80 E8
Lee Clough Dr HBR HX7....144 B5
Lee Cft KGHY BD21....58 C8
  OSS WF5....197 G2
Leeds Barnsdale Rd CAS WF10....157 J8
Leeds & Bradford Rd
  BRAM LS13....107 J3
Leeds Country Wy
  AL/HA/HU LS17....65 M2
  HORS LS18....85 J1
  MOR LS27....129 J7
  OSS WF5....175 J7
  PDSY/CALV LS28....106 B3
  RTHW LS26....134 C6
  SCFT LS14....68 A4
  WKFDE WF1....176 H4
Leeds La RTHW LS26....134 D1
Leeds Old Rd BFDE BD3....105 M6
  HECK WF16....150 H4
Leeds Rd AL/HA/HU LS17....67 M3

BFD BD1....5 H6
BHP/TINH LS16....63 M3
BTLY WF17....151 L4
CAS WF10....135 H8
CAS WF10....179 M1
EARD/LOFT WF3....154 D4
EARL WF12....174 A5
GSLY LS20....62 A6
HIPP HX3....147 J5
HIPP HX3....147 M6
HUD HD1....193 G4
ILK LS29....38 E1
LVSG WF15....172 E1
MIRF WF14....172 A6
MSTN/BAR LS15....112 A2
OSS WF5....174 E6
OT LS21....41 K7
PBR HG3....27 C2
RTHW LS26....132 E6
RTHW LS26....133 K8
RTHW LS26....155 L1
RTHW LS26....156 D3
SHPY BD18....82 F6
TAD LS24....71 H4
WBY LS22....47 H7
WKFDE WF1....176 D6
YEA LS19....84 E3
Leeds St KGHY BD21....2
Lee Fair Ct EARD/LOFT WF3....152 H2
Leefield Rd HECK WF16....151 G8
Leef St HUDE HD5....15 L1
Lee Gn MIRF WF14....172 C8
Lee Head HUDN HD2....14 C2
Leeke Av HOR/CROF WF4....197 J4
Lee La BGLY BD17....80 E7
  DOD/DAR S75....242 F4
  FEA/AMT WF7....202 D6
  HIPP HX3....146 F3
  HORS LS18....85 K4
  HWTH BD22....100 B3
  KBTN HD8....216 A8
  STKB/PEN S36....269 H2
  TOD OL14....164 A3
Lee La East HORS LS18....85 K4
Lee La West HORS LS18....85 K4
Lee Mill Rd HBR HX7....143 J1
Leeming St BFD BD1....5 H6
Lee Moor La EARD/LOFT WF3....155 C6
Lee Moor Rd EARD/LOFT WF3....155 H8
Lee Mount Gdns HIPP HX3....10 C1
Lee Mount Rd HIPP HX3....10 C1
Lee Orchards BSPA/BRAM LS23....48 F6
Lee Rd DEWS WF13....194 F1
Lees Av EARL WF12....195 L2
  STKB/PEN S36....270 F3
Lees Bank Av HWTH BD22....79 C6
Lees Bank Dr HWTH BD22 *....79 C6
Lees Bank Hl HWTH BD22....79 C6
Lees Bank Rd HWTH BD22....79 C6
Lees Cl CUL/QBY BD13....79 L8
  HUDE HD5....193 H7
Lees Crs HOR/CROF WF4....198 B7
Lees Dr EARL WF12 *....195 K2
Lees Hall Rd EARL WF12....195 K2
Lees Holm EARL WF12....195 L1
Lees House Rd EARL WF12....195 L1
Leeside Av HUDN HD2....192 D2
Leeside Rd HECK WF16....151 G8
Lees Mill La MAR/SLWT HD7....212 D5
Lees Moor Rd CUL/QBY BD13....79 L8
Lees Rd HBR HX7....143 J2
Lee St BFD BD1....4
  BRIG HD6....170 C2
  CUL/QBY BD13....124 D1
  DEWS WF13....173 G8
  LIT OL15....185 K8
  LVSG WF15....172 C1
  WKFDE WF1....12 E2
Leesworth Ct HWTH BD22 *....79 C6
Lee Wy WIL/AL BD15 *....180 A1
  KBTN HD8....216 A7
Lee Wood Rd HBR HX7....121 H8
Legion St GFTH/SHER LS25....138 A4
Legrams Av GTHN BD7....126 C8
Legrams La GTHN BD7....104 C8
Legrams Mill La GTHN BD7....104 D7
Legrams St GTHN BD7....104 C8
Legrams Ter GTHN BD7....4
Leicester Cl LDSU LS2....6 F4
Leicester Gv LDSU LS2....6 F4
Leicester Pl LDSU LS2....6 F4
Leicester St BOW BD4....127 J2
  ROCH OL11....228 C1
Leicester Ter HIPP HX3....168 D1
Leigh Av EARD/LOFT WF3....153 J6
Leigh Rd EARD/LOFT WF3....153 H6
Leigh St FEA/AMT WF7....223 M1
  MILN OL16....206 F7
  RPDN/SBR HX6....167 L1
Leighton Av LIT OL15....207 H4
Leighton Cl BSLYN/ROY S71....261 L1
Leighton Pl LDS LS1....6 B6
Leighton St LDS LS1....6 B6
Leigh Vw EARD/LOFT WF3....153 H6
Leisure La KBTN HD8....218 A6
Leith Ct EARL WF12....196 A5
Leith St KCHY BD21....2
Lemans Dr DEWS WF13....173 M6
Le Marchant Av HUDW HD3....191 L6
Le Mar Vw HIPP HX3....11 M8
Lemon St HFAX HX1....10 D8
  MOR LS27....129 K6
Lemon Tree Cl PONT WF8....180 D6
Lenacre La KBTN HD8....216 F5
Lenham Cl MOR LS27....152 C1
Lenhurst Av WOR/ARM LS12....108 A6
Lennerton La GFTH/SHER LS25....117 G8
Lennie St KGHY BD21....2
Lennon Dr GIR BD8....104 D1
Lennox Dr WKFDW/WTN WF2....174 A8
Lennox Gdns MSTN/BAR LS15....111 L7
Lennox Rd BULY LS4....108 F5
  TOD OL14....140 C5
Lennox Wy RTHW LS26....134 D6
Lenton Av BEE/HOL LS11....131 H3
Lenton Dr BEE/HOL LS11....131 J3
Lenton Vls IDLE BD10....83 K5
Leodis Ct BEE/HOL LS11....8 E5
Leodis Wy RTHW LS26....134 D6
Leonardin Cl ROY/SHW OL2....229 H4
Leonard's Pl BGLY BD16....81 J4
Leonard St BGLY BD16....81 J4
  HUDN HD2....192 D5
  LM/WK BD12....148 F3
Leopold Gdns CHAL LS7....7 L3
Leopold Gv BSLY S70....260 D7
  CHAL LS7....7 K3
  OSS WF5....197 J2
Lepton Gdns BSLY S70....261 M8
Lepton La KBTN HD8....216 C6
Lepton Pl MOR LS27....129 M7

Lesley Wy HUDS HD4....213 J5
Leslie Av YEA LS19....62 D6
Leslie Rd BSLY S70....261 M7
Leslie St HUDN HD2....14 D1
Leslie Ter HDGY LS6....6 D2
Lesmere Gv GTHN BD7....126 B4
Lessarna Ct BOW BD4 *....127 L1
Letchworth Av ROCH OL11....228 C1
Leven Gdns WBY LS22....29 M7
Levens Bank MSTN/BAR LS15....110 F8
Levens Cl MSTN/BAR LS15....111 G8
Levens Garth MSTN/BAR LS15....111 G8
Levens Pl MSTN/BAR LS15....111 G8
Leventhorpe Ct RTHW LS26....155 L1
Leventhorpe Wy RTHW LS26....155 L1
Leveret Wy BTLY WF17....151 K5
Lever Av WBSY BD6....126 C5
Levita Gv BOW BD4....127 M2
Levita Pl BOW BD4....127 M2
  MSTN/BAR LS15....111 G6
Lewin Gv CAS WF10....158 F6
Lewis Cl CUL/QBY BD13....124 F5
Lewisham Ct ROY/SHW OL2 *....228 C1
Lewisham Gv MOR LS27....152 D2
Lewisham Rd MAR/SLWT HD7....212 B5
Lewisham St MOR LS27....152 A5
Lewis Rd BSLYN/ROY S71....262 A2
Lewis St HFAX HX1....10 F4
Lexington Cl BOW BD4....127 K6
Leyburn Av HECK WF16....173 L1
  HIPP HX3....147 M6
Leyburn Gv BGLY BD16....81 J2
  SHPY BD18....82 C7
Leyburn Rd AWLS/ASK DN6....249 H4
Leyden Ri WIL/AL BD15....103 K6
Leyfield BAIL BD17....82 C3
Leyfield Bank HOLM/MEL HD9....236 D7
Leyfield Rd MILN OL16....206 H8
Ley Fleaks Rd IDLE BD10....83 K7
Leygards La HOLM/MEL HD9....234 D5
Leyland Cl COL BB8....74 D7
Leyland Cft HUDN HD2....171 G8
Leyland Rd BTLY WF17....150 F5
  CAS WF10....158 F6
Leylands Av HTON BD9....104 B3
Leylands Gv HTON BD9....104 B3
Leylands La HTON BD9....104 B3
  KGHY BD21....2 K7
Leylands Rd LDSU LS2....7
Leylands Ter HTON BD9....104 B3
The Leylands DOD/DAR S75....260 C2
Ley La WOR/ARM LS12....108 A7
Leymoor Rd MAR/SLWT HD7....212 F1
Leys Cl IDLE BD10....83 J5
Leysholme Crs WOR/ARM LS12....108 C6
Leysholme Dr WOR/ARM LS12....108 C6
Leysholme Ter WOR/ARM LS12....108 C8
Leysholme Vw WOR/ARM LS12....108 C6
Leyside Gv WIL/AL BD15....103 K4
Ley La AWLS/ASK DN6....248 F5
  BSPA/BRAM LS23....49 C7
  KBTN HD8....217 K8
  KNOT WF11....182 B4
  PONT WF8....204 E7
Leys Rd PONT WF8....182 B8
The Leys HEM/SK/SE WF9....246 C5
Leyton Crs IDLE BD10 *....83 K7
Leyton Dr IDLE BD10....83 K7
Leyton Gv IDLE BD10....83 K7
Leyton St WHIT OL12....206 B4
Ley Top La WIL/AL BD15....103 L6
Leywell Ter WOR/ARM LS12....108 C6
Libbey St GIR BD8....104 D5
Lichen Cl BOW BD4....127 C6
Lichfield Cl UPML OL3....230 E4
Lichfield Mt ECHL BD2....105 G2
Lichfield Rd EARL WF12....174 B6
Lichfield Ter MILN OL16....228 E2
Lickless Av HORS LS18....85 M5
Lickless Dr HORS LS18....85 M5
Lickless Gdns HORS LS18....85 M5
Lickless Ter HORS LS18....85 M5
Lidgate Cl DEWS WF13....173 L4
Lidgate Crs HEM/SK/SE WF9....246 C5
Lidgate La CUD/GR S72....244 D3
  DEWS WF13....173 L4
Lidget Av GTHN BD7....126 B1
Lidget Cft AIRE BD20....34 E1
Lidget Hl PDSY/CALV LS28....107 G6
Lidget La HOR/CROF WF4....200 F4
Lidget Pl GTHN BD7....126 B1
Lidget Rd AIRE BD20....34 E1
Lidgett Av RHAY LS8....88 B7
Lidgett Cl GFTH/SHER LS25....113 G8
  RHAY LS8....88 B6
Lidgett Crs RHAY LS8....88 B7
Lidget Ter CLAY BD14....125 M2
  GTHN BD7....126 B1
Lidgett Gv RHAY LS8....88 B7
Lidgett Hl RHAY LS8....88 B7
Lidgett La AL/HA/HU LS17....88 A5
  GFTH/SHER LS25....113 C8
  RHAY LS8....88 B5
Lidget Mt RHAY LS8....88 B5
Lidgett Park Av RHAY LS8....88 B6
Lidgett Park Gdns RHAY LS8....88 B6
Lidgett Park Gv RHAY LS8....88 C5
Lidgett Park Ms RHAY LS8....88 B5
Lidgett Park Rd RHAY LS8....88 B5
Lidgett Park Vw RHAY LS8....88 B5
Lidgett Pl RHAY LS8....88 C7
Lidgett Rl RHAY LS8....239 H5
Lidgett Wk RHAY LS8....88 B7
Lifton Pl LDSU LS2....6 D1
Light Bank La AIRE BD20....36 E2
Lightburn Av LIT OL15....207 G2
Lightcliffe Rd BRIG HD6....170 C2
Lightcliffe Royd La
  GTL/HWG HX4....167 L8
Lightenfield La HUDS HD4....213 L8
Lightfoot Av CAS WF10....157 M8
Lightfoot Cl CAS WF10....157 M8
Lighthazles Chapel Rd
  RPDN/SBR HX6....166 C8
Lighthazles Rd RPDN/SBR HX6....166 D7
Light La WKFDW/WTN WF2....176 A4
Lightowler Cl HFAX HX1....10 D5
Lightowler Rd HFAX HX1....10 D5
Lightowlers La LIT OL15....185 M7
Light St WBSY BD6....126 A5
Lightridge Cl HUDN HD2....192 B2
Lightridge Rd HUDN HD2....192 B2
Lilac Cl BRIG HD6....170 E3
  ILK LS29....19 J6
Lilac Gv BOW BD4....105 M4
  CLECK BD19....150 C5
  SHPY BD18....104 F1
Lilac Rd ROCH OL11....228 A5
Lilac View Cl ROY/SHW OL2....229 M8

STKB/PEN S36....269 L5
Liley St MILN OL16....206 C7
Lilian St BOW BD4....127 L3
Lillands Av BRIG HD6....170 B4
Lillands La BRIG HD6....170 B4
Lillands Ter BRIG HD6....170 B4
Lilley La HEM/SK/SE WF9....223 M8
Lilley Ter HEM/SK/SE WF9....246 C5
Lilly La HIPP HX3....11 J7
Lilly St RPDN/SBR HX6....167 K3
Lily Cft GIR BD8....104 D4
Lily St GIR BD8....104 C5
  MILN OL16....207 H8
  TOD OL14....141 J8
Lilythorne Av WBY LS22....83 L6
Lime Av HBR HX7....143 H5
  ILK LS29....18 F6
Lime Crs HEM/SK/SE WF9....247 G5
Lime Rd MILN OL16....207 G7
Limers Ga TOD OL14....162 B3
  WHIT OL12....206 B1
Limes Av DOD/DAR S75....242 C6
  DOD/DAR S75....260 D3
  HIPP HX3....168 A2
Limes Cl DOD/DAR S75....242 E4
Lime St BGLY BD16....81 H3
  COL BB8....52 A8
  GTHN BD7....126 C2
  HUDS HD4....214 A3
  HWTH BD22....78 A8
  KGHY BD21....2 F5
  OSS WF5....197 G2
Limes Tree La HOLM/MEL HD9....253 J8
Lime Tree Av BSPA/BRAM LS23....48 F6
  BTLY WF17....173 J2
  PONT WF8....180 D6
Lime Tree Ct RTHW LS26....133 M2
Lime Tree Gdns
  HEM/SK/SE WF9 *....223 M8
Lime Tree Gv BIRK/DRI BD11 *....128 C7
Limetrees PONT WF8....181 J2
Lime Trees Sq SHPY BD18....81 M6
Limewood Ap SCFT LS14....89 J7
Limewood Rd SCFT LS14....89 J7
Linburn Cl BSLYN/ROY S71....243 J2
Linby Rd BSLYN/ROY S71....243 H6
Lincoln Av HECK WF16....172 F1
  LVSG WF15....172 C4
Lincoln Ct ROCH OL11....206 C8
Lincoln Crs HEM/SK/SE WF9....247 J2
Lincoln Dr LIT OL15....207 J3
  LVSG WF15....172 C4
Lincoln Green Ct OSM LS9....7 L7
Lincoln Green Rd OSM LS9....7 L7
Lincoln Gv HUDE HD5....215 J2
  LVSG WF15....172 B4
Lincoln Leach Ct ROCH OL11 *....228 B1
Lincoln Rd EARL WF12....174 B6
  OSM LS9....7 L6
  RTHW LS26....134 B5
Lincoln St CAS WF10....158 A6
  HUD HD1....15 J7
  ROCH OL11....206 C8
  TOD OL14....140 D5
Lincoln Wk GFTH/SHER LS25....135 L4
Lincoln Wy HIPP HX3....10 F2
Lincombe Bank RHAY LS8....88 A7
Lincombe Dr RHAY LS8....88 A7
Lincombe Mt RHAY LS8....88 A7
Lincombe Ri RHAY LS8....88 A7
Lincroft Av HUDE HD5....215 C5
Lincroft Crs BRAM LS13....107 M3
Lincs Wold LVSG WF15....171 K2
Lindale Cl MID LS10....131 M7
Lindale Garth
  WKFDW/WTN WF2....175 L4
Lindale Cl AL/HA/HU LS17....67 M2
  BRIG HD6....170 E8
  CAS WF10....158 E8
  EARL WF12....174 D7
  KNOT WF11....181 J7
Linden Gdns BEE/HOL LS11....131 L3
Linden Gv BEE/HOL LS11....9 G8
  HIPP HX3....106 A6
  TOD OL14....140 D5
Linden Mt BEE/HOL LS11....131 L3
Linden Pl BEE/HOL LS11....131 L3
  HIPP HX3....143 J2
Linden Ri KGHY BD21....3 L8
Linden Rd BEE/HOL LS11 *....131 L3
  BEE/HOL LS11 *....131 L3
  HFAX HX5....169 G8
  HBR HX7....143 J2
  HIPP HX3....168 E2
  HUDN HD2....192 B5
Linden Ter PONT WF8....180 E6
Linden Wy WBY LS22....29 H7
Lindhurst Rd BSLYN/ROY S71....243 H6
Lindisfarne WHIT OL12....206 A6
Lindisfarne Rd SHPY BD18....82 C3
Lindley Br OT LS21....42 A1
Lindley Dr GTHN BD7....126 A4
Lindley Moor Rd HUDW HD3....190 F5
Lindley Rd ELL HX5....191 H2
  WBOW BD5....126 E5
Lindon Wk HUDN HD2....213 L8
  SKP/WHF BD23....16 B3
Lindrick Cl CUD/GR S72....244 E5
  NORM WF6....186 E8
Lindrick Gv HUD OL14....124 D7
Lindrick Wy LUD/ILL HX2....124 D7
Lindsay Acre EARD/LOFT WF3....153 J6
Lindsay Av WKFDW/WTN WF2....197 L4
Lindsay Rd GFTH/SHER LS25....113 H8
Lindsey Ct OSM LS9....7 M7
Lindsey Gdns OSM LS9....7 L7
Lindsey Mt OSM LS9....7 M7
Lindsey Rd OSM LS9....7 M7

Lindwell Av GTL/HWG HX4....168 E7
Lindwell Gv GTL/HWG HX4....168 E7
Linefield Rd BTLY WF17....151 M1
Lineham Ct LVSG WF15....172 C4
Lineholme Av TOD OL14....141 G7
Linfit Fold MAR/SLWT HD7....212 C6
Linfit La KBTN HD8....216 D6
  MAR/SLWT HD7....212 C6
Lingards Rd MAR/SLWT HD7....260 F4
Lingards Rd MAR/SLWT HD7....212 A8
Lingards Ter MAR/SLWT HD7 *....211 L8
Lingard St BFD BD1....5 G4
  DOD/DAR S75....260 F3
Ling Bob WBY LS22 *....31 J3
Ling Bob Cft LUD/ILL HX2....145 L1
Lingcrag Gdns HWTH BD22....54 F2
Ling Cft BSPA/BRAM LS23....48 D5
Lingcroft La WBY LS22....31 J3
Lingdale Rd LM/WK BD12....126 C8
Lingfield Ap AL/HA/HU LS17....87 K3
Lingfield Bank AL/HA/HU LS17....87 K3
Lingfield Cl AL/HA/HU LS17....87 K3
Lingfield Crs AL/HA/HU LS17....87 K3
  WBSY BD6....125 L4
Lingfield Dr AL/HA/HU LS17....87 K3
  HWTH BD22....79 J5
Lingfield Gdns AL/HA/HU LS17....87 K3
Lingfield Ga AL/HA/HU LS17....87 K3
Lingfield Gn AL/HA/HU LS17....87 K3
Lingfield Gv AL/HA/HU LS17....87 K3
  WIL/AL BD15....103 K3
Lingfield Mt AL/HA/HU LS17....87 L3
  WIL/AL BD15....102 E2
Lingfield Rd WBSY BD6....125 L4
Lingfield Vw AL/HA/HU LS17....87 K3
Lingfield Wk AL/HA/HU LS17....87 K3
  WIL/AL BD15....102 E2
Ling Park Ap WIL/AL BD15....102 E2
Ling Park Av WIL/AL BD15....102 E2
Ling Royd Av LUD/ILL HX2....145 M6
Lings La DOD/DAR S75....260 C7
Lingthwaite DOD/DAR S75....260 C7
Lingwell Ap MID LS10....153 L2
Lingwell Av MID LS10....153 L1
Lingwell Cha EARD/LOFT WF3....154 C8
Lingwell Ct EARD/LOFT WF3....154 C8
Lingwell Crs MID LS10....153 L1
Lingwell Gdns MID LS10....153 L2
Lingwell Gate Crs WKFDE WF1....176 C1
Lingwell Gate Dr WKFDE WF1....176 C1
Lingwell Gate La
  EARD/LOFT WF3....154 B5
Lingwell Gn MID LS10....153 L2
Lingwell Gv MID LS10 *....153 L2
Lingwell Ms MID LS10....153 L2
Lingwell Nook La
  EARD/LOFT WF3....154 C6
Lingwell Rd MID LS10....153 L1
Lingwell Vw MID LS10 *....153 L2
Lingwell Wk MID LS10....153 L2
Lingwood Av GIR BD8....104 B5
Lingwood Cl HOLM/MEL HD9....236 F7
Lingwood Rd GIR BD8....104 B6
Lingwood Ter GIR BD8....104 B6
Link Rd EARL WF12....173 M7
  HUD HD1....191 H8
  WKFDE WF1....176 D6
Links Av CLECK BD19....150 C1
The Links BEE/HOL LS11....131 J5
  FEA/AMT WF7....179 M5
  HOR/CROF WF4....200 E7
  TAD LS24....71 L4
Links Vw DOD/DAR S75....242 D4
The Link DOD/DAR S75....260 C8
  PONT WF8....180 E8
  ROY/SHW OL2....229 H5
  RTHW LS26....134 B5
Linkway AWLS/ASK DN6 *....227 M3
  BCLY BD16....81 J7
Linnet Cl GIR BD8 *....103 L6
  MIRF WF14....172 C6
Linnet Ct MOR LS27....129 L1
Linnet Gv WKFDW/WTN WF2....220 F1
Linnet St KGHY BD21....3 H3
Linney La ROY/SHW OL2....229 L7
Linnhe Av WBSY BD6....126 C8
Linshaws Rd HOLM/MEL HD9....267 H1
Linton Av AIRE BD20....36 A4
  AL/HA/HU LS17....88 B2
  BTLY WF17....173 J1
  WBY LS22....88 A2
Linton Cl AL/HA/HU LS17....88 A2
  BSLY S70....260 D6
  LVSG WF15....172 B1
Linton Common WBY LS22....47 L5
Linton Ct SKP/WHF BD23....16 A3
Linton Crs AL/HA/HU LS17....88 A2
Linton Dr AL/HA/HU LS17....88 A2
Linton Gv AL/HA/HU LS17....88 A2
  BRIG HD6....170 A6
Linton Hills Rd WBY LS22....47 L3
Linton La WBY LS22....29 H7
Linton Mdw WBY LS22....47 L4
Linton Ri AL/HA/HU LS17....88 A1
  NORM WF6....178 F5
Linton Rd AL/HA/HU LS17....88 A1
  WBY LS22....47 K5
  WKFDE WF1....13 M2
Linton St BOW BD4....127 H2
  HWTH BD22....2 A1
Linton Vw AL/HA/HU LS17....88 A1
Lion Chambers HUD HD1 *....14 F4
Lionel St OSS WF5....197 G2
Liphill Bank Rd
  HOLM/MEL HD9....253 M2
Lippersley La AIRE BD20....18 C3
Lipscomb St HUDW HD3....213 K1
Liquorice Wy PONT WF8....180 E6
Lisbon Sq LDS LS1....6 C9
Lisbon St LDS LS1....6 D9
Lisheen Av CAS WF10....158 A7
Lisheen Gv CAS WF10....158 A7
Liskeard Cl MILN OL16....206 E5
Lisker Av OT LS21....41 K7
Lisker Ct OT LS21....41 K7
Lisker Dr OT LS21....41 K7
Lisle St WHIT OL12....206 C6
Lismore Cl RTHW LS26....155 H1
Lismore Rd AIRE BD20....2 E2
Lister Av BOW BD4....127 L4
Lister Cl FEA/AMT WF7....201 K1
Lister Ct HFAX HX1....10 D6
Lister's Rd HIPP HX3....11 L4
Lister St BOW BD4....127 L4
  BRIG HD6....170 C3
  CAS WF10....157 G6
  HFAX HX1....11 H5
  HUDE HD5....193 G4
Listerdale LVSG WF15....172 C1
Lister Gdns GIR BD8....104 E4
  HORS LS18....85 L1
Listerhills Rd GTHN BD7....4 D4
Listerhills Science Pk GTHN BD7....4 B6
Lister La ECHL BD2....105 J3
  HFAX HX1....10 D6

ILK LS29 .....38 C2
KGHY BD21 .....2 E7
Lister Vw GIR BD8 .....4 A2
Lister Wk MOR LS27 .....130 B8
Listing Av LVSG WF15 .....172 C1
Listing Ct LVSG WF15 .....172 D1
Listing Dr LVSG WF15 .....172 C1
Listing La LVSG WF15 .....172 D1
Litell Royd FEA/AMT WF7 .....200 F1
Little Baines St HFAX HX1 .....10 C5
Little Bradley GTL/HWG HX4 .....168 C8
Little Brunswick St HUD HD1 .....14 C4
Little Cake HOLM/MEL HD9 .....254 E4
Little Catterton La TAD LS24 .....72 C1
Little Church La RTHW LS26 .....156 C4
Little Clegg Rd LIT OL15 .....207 H4
Little Cote IDLE BD10 .....83 J5
Little Cross St LDS LS1 .....7 G9
WBOW BD5 .....127 G4
Littlefield Gv OSS WF5 .....175 G8
Littlefield St OSS WF5 .....197 G1
Littlefield Wk WBSY BD6 .....126 D6
Little Fold HUDS HD4 * 214 A6
Little Fountain St MOR LS27 .....152 C2
Little Green La HECK WF16 .....172 E1
Little Hemsworth
HEM/SK/SE WF9 .....224 A8
Little Hew Royd IDLE BD10 .....83 H6
Littleholme St TOD OL14 .....163 J3
Little Horton Gn WBOW BD5 .....126 E1
Little Horton La WBOW BD5 .....4 E8
WBOW BD5 .....126 E3
Little Howarth Wy WHIT OL12 * 206 C2
Little Ings Cl TAD LS24 .....95 G5
Little King St LDS LS1 .....8 F1
Littlelands BGLY BD16 .....81 J7
Littlelands Ct BGLY BD16 * 81 J7
Little La AIRE BD20 .....59 G6
AWLS/ASK DN6 .....205 J7
EARD/LOFT WF3 .....155 C3
FEA/AMT WF7 .....202 A2
HBR HX7 .....25 K7
HEM/SK/SE WF9 .....225 K7
HEM/SK/SE WF9 .....247 H3
HOLM/MEL HD9 .....236 D6
HOLM/MEL HD9 * 254 E4
HTON BD9 .....104 B4
ILK LS29 .....38 E2
MOR LS27 .....130 E6
Little Lane Ct MOR LS27 .....130 E6
Littlemoor Cl CUL/QBY BD13 .....125 J5
Littlemoor Ct PDSY/CALV LS28 .....107 H6
Littlemoor Crs PDSY/CALV LS28 .....129 G1
Littlemoor Crs South
PDSY/CALV LS28 .....129 G1
Littlemoor Gdns LUD/ILL HX2 .....124 A8
PDSY/CALV LS28 .....129 G1
Littlemoor Gv MIRF WF14 .....194 B1
Littlemoor La LUD/ILL HX2 .....90 B1
Little Moor Pl WOR/ARM LS12 .....108 D7
Littlemoor Rd LUD/ILL HX2 .....124 A8
MIRF WF14 .....194 B1
PDSY/CALV LS28 .....107 G8
Little Moor Vw PDSY/CALV LS28 * 107 H6
Little Neville St LDS LS1 * 8 F2
Little New Cl DOD/DAR S75 .....260 D3
Little Pk IDLE BD10 .....84 A5
Little Queen St LDS LS1 .....8 D1
Littlethorpe Hl LVSG WF15 .....171 M4
Littlethorpe La LVSG WF15 .....171 M4
Little Westfields
BSLY/ROY S71 * 243 L3
Littlewood Cl WBSY BD6 .....126 E7
Littlewood Ct HUDS HD4 .....214 C4
Little Wood Dr CLECK BD19 .....149 M4
Little Woodhouse BRIG HD6 .....170 C5
Little Woodhouse St LDSU LS2 .....6 D7
Littleworth La BSLYN/ROY S71 .....261 M5
Litton Cft WKFDE WF1 * 13 H1
Littondale Dr BAIL BD17 .....83 G2
Litton Rd HWTH BD22 .....2 C7
Litton Wk BSLY S70 .....260 F4
Litton Wy SCFT LS14 .....89 K6
Liversedge Hall La LVSG WF15 .....172 C3
Livingstone Cl ECHL BD2 .....83 H8
Livingstone Crs
BSLYN/ROY S71 .....261 K1
Livingstone Rd ECHL BD2 .....104 C2
Livingstone St HIPP HX3 .....10 C1
Livingstone St North
LUD/ILL HX2 .....146 C1
Livingstone Ter BSLY S70 * 261 G6
Livinia Gv CHAL LS7 .....6 C2
Livsey St MILN OL16 .....206 C7
Lloyds Dr LM/WK BD12 .....127 G8
Lloyd St TOD OL14 .....141 K8
Lobley Cl WHIT OL12 .....206 D4
Lobley St HECK WF16 .....173 G2
Locarno Av HTON BD9 .....103 J5
Locherbie Gn WIL/AL BD15 * 103 J5
Lochy Rd WBSY BD6 .....126 B8
Lockbridge Wy HUDW HD3 .....213 K2
Lockeaflash Crs BSLY S70 .....261 M8
Locke Av BSLY S70 .....261 H8
Locke Ct DOD/DAR S75 .....260 C6
Locke St BSLY S70 .....260 F7
Lockhart St MILN OL16 .....228 C1
NORM WF6 .....156 B8
Locksley Rd BRIG HD6 .....170 F5
The Locks BGLY BD16 .....81 H2
Lock St EARL WF12 .....195 M2
HIPP HX3 * 11 K8
TOD OL14 .....163 J3
Lockton Ct TAD LS24 .....94 F8
Lock Vw ELL HX5 .....169 K6
Lock Wy DEWS WF13 .....195 G2
Lockwood Av MIRF WF14 .....172 D7
Lockwood Cl BEE/HOL LS11 .....131 K5
HUDW HD3 .....191 L1
Lockwood Gdns
STKB/PEN S36 .....258 C8
Lockwood La BSLY S70 .....261 H1
Lockwood Rd HUD HD1 .....214 B3
Lockwood Scar HUDS HD4 .....214 B3
Lockwood St LM/WK BD12 .....149 G1
SHPY BD18 * 82 B6
WBSY BD6 .....126 E5
Lockwood's Yd HUD HD1 * 14 F7
Lockwood Wy BEE/HOL LS11 .....131 L5
Locomotion Br HUD HD1 .....15 H6
Lode Pit La BGLY BD16 .....81 M2
Lodge Av WOR/ARM LS12 .....108 D7
Lodge Bank Rd LIT OL15 .....207 H5
Lodge Cl HUDS HD4 .....214 A5
Lodge Dr ELL HX5 .....169 L7
MIRF WF14 .....194 C2
Lodge Farm Cl EARL WF12 .....195 M2
Lodge Farm Gdns NORM WF6 .....178 A3
Lodge Gate Cl CUL/QBY BD13 .....102 A5
Lodge Hl BAIL BD17 .....82 B3
Lodge Hill Rd WOR/ARM LS12 .....129 M5
Lodge Hill Rd OSS WF5 * 174 F6
Lodge La CROF WF4 .....200 A4
HOR/CROF WF4 .....200 A4
LUD/ILL HX2 * 145 G1
LVSG WF15 .....172 F4

WKFDW/WTN WF2 .....220 F2
Lodge Pl ELL HX5 * 169 L7
Lodge Rd AWLS/ASK DN6 .....249 K6
PDSY/CALV LS28 .....106 F6
Lodges Cl HOR/CROF WF4 .....222 E4
Lodge St CUL/QBY BD13 .....79 M8
HEM/SK/SE WF9 .....223 M8
KBTN HD8 .....239 J4
LDS LS1 .....6 C5
LIT OL15 .....185 K8
WHIT OL12 .....184 E8
Lodge Ter BEE/HOL LS11 * 131 K4
The Lodge MAR/SLWT HD7 .....213 K4
Lodore Pl ECHL BD2 .....105 K3
Lodore Rd ECHL BD2 .....105 J3
Loft St GIR BD8 .....104 B6
Logwood St HUD HD1 .....214 C2
Loiner Ct OSM LS9 .....132 E1
Lomax St WHIT OL12 .....206 B6
Lombard La DOD/DAR S75 .....260 C3
Lombardi Ct OSS WF5 .....197 H2
Lombard St HFAX HX1 .....10 B9
MSTN/BAR LS15 .....111 H7
YEA LS19 .....84 C1
Lombardy Garth
WKFDW/WTN WF2 .....176 B6
Lomond Av HORS LS18 .....85 K2
Lomond Ter MILN OL16 .....228 C2
Londesboro Gv OSM LS9 .....110 C7
Londesboro Ter OSM LS9 .....110 C7
London La YEA LS19 .....84 C2
London Rd MAR/SLWT HD7 .....212 C5
RPDN/SBR HX6 .....167 M3
TAD LS24 .....115 M2
TOD OL14 .....164 D1
London Spring Rd
RPDN/SBR HX6 .....188 C2
London St YEA LS19 .....84 C2
Long Acre BSLYN/ROY S71 .....243 K5
Longacre CAS WF10 .....157 M8
Long Acre La HWTH BD22 .....78 F6
Longacres HWTH BD22 .....26 F5
Long Acre Wk PBR HX3 .....26 F5
Longbottom Av AIRE BD20 .....36 B5
Longbottom Ter HIPP HX3 * 168 F2
Longbow Cl HUDN HD2 .....192 F1
Longbow Cl HUDN HD2 .....192 F1
Longbow Rd HUDN HD2 .....192 F1
Longbrook La BSLY S70 .....260 F6
Longcar La BSLY S70 .....260 F6
EARD/LOFT WF3 .....177 H1
FEA/AMT WF7 .....195 M3
HBR HX7 .....142 A2
HWTH BD22 .....101 J5
OSM LS9 .....132 B1
RPDN/SBR HX6 .....188 B3
TOD OL14 .....164 B3
WKFDE WF1 .....176 F6
Longcauseway EARL WF12 .....173 M6
The Long Cswy
BRFD/BLYE BB10 .....140 C1
LUD/ILL HX2 .....144 C8
Long Cliffe Cl CUD/GR S72 .....244 E4
Long Cl LM/WK BD12 .....148 D2
Long Close La HEM/SK/SE WF9 .....225 K8
HOLM/MEL HD9 .....237 K8
OSM LS9 .....110 B7
Long Crest PONT WF8 .....181 G8
Long Cft DOD/DAR S75 .....242 D5
KGHY BD21 .....3 H6
Longcroft Cft BFD BD1 .....4 D6
Longcroft Rd ILK LS29 .....39 G3
Long Croft St MAR/SLWT HD7 .....213 G2
Longdale Cft BSLYN/ROY S71 .....261 K2
Longdale Dr HEM/SK/SE WF9 .....247 G2
Long Dam La HOR/CROF WF4 .....222 C2
Longden Av HUDS HD4 .....213 L4
Longdike Cl GFTH/SHER LS25 .....135 K5
Longdike La GFTH/SHER LS25 .....135 L6
Longden Av KBTN HD8 .....216 A3
Longdon Wk KBTN HD8 .....216 A3
Long Edge Rd RPDN/SBR HX6 .....166 D4
Long Fallas Crs BRIG HD6 .....170 D7
Longfellow Gv EARD/LOFT WF3 .....152 F5
Longfield GTL/HWG HX4 .....190 D2
HBR HX7 .....143 H2
Longfield Av HIPP HX3 .....147 J5
HUDE HD5 .....15 M5
MAR/SLWT HD7 .....213 G1
PDSY/CALV LS28 .....107 H7
TOD OL14 .....163 K2
Longfield Ct HECK WF16 .....172 F2
PDSY/CALV LS28 .....107 H7
Longfield Dr BRAM LS13 * 107 H1
BRAM LS13 .....107 H2
DOD/DAR S75 .....242 D5
FEA/AMT WF7 .....201 G4
MSTN/BAR LS15 .....111 J6
Longfield Garth BRAM LS13 .....107 H1
Longfield Gv PDSY/CALV LS28 .....107 H7
TOD OL14 .....163 K2
Longfield Mt PDSY/CALV LS28 .....107 H7
Longfield Rd HECK WF16 .....172 F2
PDSY/CALV LS28 .....107 H7
ROY/SHW OL2 .....229 J8
TOD OL14 .....163 K1
Longfield Ter PDSY/CALV LS28 * 107 G7
WKFDW/WTN WF2 .....12 B7
Longfield Wy TOD OL14 .....163 K2
Longford Ter GTHN BD7 .....126 B1
Long Ga HWTH BD22 .....55 L7
RPDN/SBR HX6 .....188 C6
Long Grove Av HUDE HD5 .....193 G8
Long Heads La
GFTH/SHER LS25 .....138 C8
Long Hey La TOD OL14 .....163 L3
Long Heys HWTH BD22 * 101 J4
Long Hill End HWTH BD22 .....54 E5
Long Hill Rd HUDN HD2 .....192 D2
Longhouse Dr CUL/QBY BD13 .....101 M6
Longhouse La CUL/QBY BD13 .....101 M6
Long House Rd LUD/ILL HX2 .....123 L8
Long Ing HOLM/MEL HD9 .....253 M3
Long Ing La HOLM/MEL HD9 .....254 D3
Longlands HOLM/MEL HD9 .....212 A5
Longlands Bank
HOLM/MEL HD9 .....236 D7
Longlands Cl DOD/DAR S75 .....242 D6
Longlands Dr DOD/DAR S75 .....242 D6
HWTH BD22 .....78 F6
Longlands Rd DEWS WF13 .....173 J4
HWTH BD22 .....46 E1
KGHY BD21 .....3 L3
WHIT OL12 .....206 D3
Longlands St BFD BD1 * 4 D6
Long La BGLY BD16 .....80 C3
COL BB8 .....52 F6
CUL/QBY BD13 .....124 F7
DEWS WF13 .....173 L3
EARL WF12 .....174 B8
FEA/AMT WF7 .....202 D5
HBR HX7 .....143 G5
HBR HX7 .....164 E3
HIPP HX3 .....146 A4

HIPP HX3 .....147 H8
HOLM/MEL HD9 .....236 B3
HOR/CROF WF4 .....216 F5
HTON BD9 .....103 M1
HUDE HD5 .....193 G8
HWTH BD22 .....54 D1
KBTN HD8 .....238 A3
KBTN HD8 .....240 B3
MSTN/BAR LS15 .....90 F7
PONT WF8 .....181 J7
PONT WF8 .....226 E5
RPDN/SBR HX6 .....167 J4
STKB/PEN S36 .....271 H5
WIL/AL BD15 .....102 F5
Long Lee La KGHY BD21 .....3 K8
Long Lee Ter KGHY BD21 .....3 M8
Longley Cl HOLM/MEL HD9 .....254 C5
Longley Ct HUDS HD4 .....214 E3
Longley Edge La
HOLM/MEL HD9 .....254 D5
Longley Edge Rd
HOLM/MEL HD9 .....254 C5
Longley La HOLM/MEL HD9 .....214 E4
HUDE HD5 .....214 E4
RPDN/SBR HX6 .....167 H6
Longley Rd HUDE HD5 .....214 F2
Longman Rd BSLY S70 .....261 G3
Long Meadow COL BB8 * 74 C1
FEA/AMT WF7 .....202 C5
SKP/WHF BD23 .....16 D1
Long Meadow Ct
GFTH/SHER LS25 .....135 J1
Long Meadow Ga
GFTH/SHER LS25 .....135 H1
Long Mdw BHP/TINH LS16 .....64 A4
ECHL BD2 .....105 G2
GFTH/SHER LS25 .....135 H1
ILK LS29 .....40 A4
Long Moor La KBTN HD8 .....238 E5
Long Preston Cha IDLE BD10 * 84 A7
Long Reach LUD/ILL HX2 .....145 J3
Long Riddings ILK LS29 .....19 G5
Long Rdg BRIG HD6 .....170 B8
Longridge Rd BSLYN/ROY S71 .....243 M8
Long Rw HOR/CROF WF4 .....200 C6
HORS LS18 .....85 L5
LM/WK BD12 .....148 F1
Longroyd IDLE BD10 .....83 H6
Longroyd Av BEE/HOL LS11 .....131 H6
Longroyd Crs BEE/HOL LS11 .....131 L1
MAR/SLWT HD7 .....212 A5
Longroyd Crs North
BEE/HOL LS11 .....9 H9
Long Royd Rd RPDN/SBR HX6 .....166 E4
Longroyd Cl BRIG HD6 .....170 B6
Longroyde Gv BRIG HD6 .....170 B6
Longroyde Rd BRIG HD6 .....170 B5
Longroyd Farm
HOR/CROF WF4 .....196 D7
Longroyd Gv BEE/HOL LS11 .....131 H6
Longroyd La KBTN HD8 .....14 B9
Longroyd La KBTN HD8 .....238 D6
Longroyd Pl BEE/HOL LS11 .....131 L3
HUD HD1 .....14 B9
Longroyd St North
BEE/HOL LS11 .....9 H9
Longroyd Ter MID LS10 .....131 L3
Longroyd Vw BEE/HOL LS11 .....131 L3
Long Rushes ROY/SHW OL2 .....229 H6
Long Shaw La TOD OL14 .....164 B2
Longside La GTHN BD7 .....4 B7
Longside Wy DOD/DAR S75 .....260 C4
Longsight Rd DOD/DAR S75 .....242 C5
Long St BOW BD4 .....5 L9
Long Thorpe La
EARD/LOFT WF3 .....154 C5
Long Tongue Scrog La
HUDE HD5 .....193 M7
Long Wall ELL HX5 .....169 G8
Longwood Av BGLY BD16 .....81 G1
Longwood Cl AL/HA/HU LS17 .....88 D1
Longwood Ct EARD/LOFT WF3 .....155 G6
Longwood Crs AL/HA/HU LS17 .....88 D1
Longwood Edge Rd
HUDW HD3 .....191 G6
Longwood Fold
EARD/LOFT WF3 .....153 G6
Longwood Garth
EARD/LOFT WF3 .....153 G6
Longwood Ga HUDW HD3 .....191 H8
Longwood House Rd
HUDN HD2 * 192 C3
Longwood Rd
EARD/LOFT WF3 .....152 F6
HUDW HD3 .....213 K4
Longwood Wk KNOT WF11 .....182 C1
Longwood V EARD/LOFT WF3 .....153 G6
Longwood Vw BGLY BD16 .....81 G1
Longwood Wy AL/HA/HU LS17 .....88 D1
Lonsbrough Av HECK WF16 .....172 F1
Lonsbrough Flats HUD HD1 .....15 G6
Lonsbrough Wy
HEM/SK/SE WF9 .....247 J2
Lonsdale Av BSLYN/ROY S71 .....262 D6
BTLY WF17 .....151 H7
MILN OL16 .....228 D1
Lonsdale Cl MID LS10 .....131 M5
Lonsdale Mdw
BSPA/BRAM LS23 .....48 F7
Lonsdale Ri EARD/LOFT WF3 .....153 G6
Lonsdale Rd WKFDE WF1 .....176 D6
Lonsdale St BFDE BD3 .....5 L4
Lonsdale Ter LVSG WF15 * 172 C2
Lord La HWTH BD22 .....78 D6
Lordsfield Pl BOW BD4 .....127 M5
Lord's La BRIG HD6 .....170 D5
Lord Sq MILN OL16 * 206 B7
Lord St BSLYN/ROY S71 .....261 L4
DEWS WF13 .....173 H3
EARL WF12 .....174 D7
HFAX HX1 .....10 F6
HUD HD1 .....15 G6
KGHY BD21 .....3 G3
MAR/SLWT HD7 .....212 B5
RPDN/SBR HX6 .....167 L1
TOD OL14 .....163 J5
WKFDE WF1 .....13 G6
WOR/ARM LS12 .....8 B3
Lord Ter WOR/ARM LS12 .....8 B3
Loris St BOW BD4 .....127 M3
Lorne St BOW BD4 .....127 K5
HWTH BD22 .....79 H6
KGHY BD21 .....3 L3
WHIT OL12 .....206 D3
Lorry Bank CHAL LS7 .....7 G1
Loscoe Cl NORM WF6 .....179 G4
Loscoe La NORM WF6 .....179 G4
Loshpot La WBY LS22 .....30 C4
Lothersdale Rd AIRE BD20 .....34 C7
Lotherton La GFTH/SHER LS25 .....112 B8
Lotherton Wy GFTH/SHER LS25 .....113 H6
Loughrigg St WBOW BD5 .....127 G5
Loughrigg Wk FEA/AMT WF7 .....224 A1

Louisa St CAS WF10 .....157 L6
IDLE BD10 * 83 K6
Louis Av WBOW BD5 .....126 E2
Louise Cl WHIT OL12 .....206 D3
Louise Gdns WHIT OL12 .....206 D3
Louise St WHIT OL12 .....206 D3
Louis Gv CHAL LS7 .....7 L3
Louis Le Prince Ct RHAY LS8 .....110 B3
Louis St CHAL LS7 .....7 L3
Lovaine Gv WKFDW/WTN WF2 .....198 C5
Love La CAS WF10 .....157 L8
HFAX HX1 .....10 F8
OSS WF5 .....174 B8
PONT WF8 .....180 D7
RTHW LS26 .....155 C1
WKFDW/WTN WF2 .....12 C1
Love Lane Ter PONT WF8 .....180 E6
Lovell Park Cl CHAL LS7 .....7 J6
Lovell Park Ga CHAL LS7 .....7 H6
Lovell Park Ga CHAL LS7 * 7 J6
Lovell Park Hts CHAL LS7 .....7 J6
Lovell Park Hl CHAL LS7 .....7 J5
Lovell Park Ms CHAL LS7 * 7 H6
Lovell Park Rd CHAL LS7 .....7 H5
Lovell Park Vw CHAL LS7 * 7 J6
Lovell Vw HOR/CROF WF4 .....200 C6
Low Ash Av SHPY BD18 .....82 A7
Low Ash Crs SHPY BD18 .....83 G7
Low Ash Dr SHPY BD18 .....82 F7
Low Ash Gv SHPY BD18 .....83 G7
Low Ash Rd SHPY BD18 .....83 G7
Low Bank Dr HWTH BD22 .....78 D5
Low Bank La HWTH BD22 .....78 D3
Low Banks AIRE BD20 .....58 B4
Low Beck ILK LS29 .....38 F1
Low Cl BGLY BD16 .....81 K4
ILK LS29 .....38 C1
Low Cliff Wk HECK WF16 .....173 G4
Low Close St LDSU LS2 .....6 D3
Low Common RTHW LS26 .....157 G6
Low Cft BSLYN/ROY S71 .....243 M5
Lowcroft WBY LS22 .....47 J5
Low Crompton Rd
ROY/SHW OL2 .....228 F8
Low Cudworth La CUD/GR S72 .....262 D1
Lowdale EARL WF12 .....174 A4
Lowell Av GTHN BD7 .....126 B1
Lowell Pl BRAM LS13 .....107 J6
Lower Ashgrove WBOW BD5 .....4 D8
Lower Back La HBR HX7 .....142 B2
Lower Bankhouse
PDSY/CALV LS28 * 128 C2
Lower Basinghall St LDS LS1 * 6 E4
Lower Bower La DEWS WF13 .....173 H3
Lower Brock Well La
RPDN/SBR HX6 .....167 H4
Lower Brunswick St LDSU LS2 * 7 J7
Lower Cambridge St
CAS WF10 .....157 M6
Lower Castlereagh St
BSLY S70 * 261 C5
Lower Clifton St
RPDN/SBR HX6 .....167 L2
Lower Clyde St RPDN/SBR HX6 .....167 K3
Lower Common La AWLS/ASK DN6 .....240 A5
Lower Constable Rd ILK LS29 .....38 F3
Low Cow Cl LM/WK BD12 * 149 H4
Lower Cross St HFAX HX1 .....11 J4
Lower Crow Nest Dr BRIG HD6 .....148 D7
Lower Denby La KBTN HD8 .....257 J7
Lower Edge Rd ELL HX5 .....169 K7
Lower Ellistones
GTL/HWG HX4 * 168 C7
Lower Falinge WHIT OL12 .....206 C1
Lower Ferney Lee TOD OL14 .....141 J8
Lowerfields Ri ROY/SHW OL2 .....229 K6
Lower Finkil St BRIG HD6 .....170 A1
Lower Fitzwilliam St HUD HD1 .....15 C5
Lower Fold BRIG HD6 .....170 D8
HOLM/MEL HD9 .....236 B1
Lower Ga HUDW HD3 .....213 K4
Lower George St TOD OL14 .....163 K1
WBSY BD6 * 126 D5
Lower Globe St GIR BD8 .....4 A4
Lower Gra HUDN HD2 * 171 G8
Lower Grattan Rd BFD BD1 * 4 D5
Lower Greave Rd
HOLM/MEL HD9 .....235 K6
Lower Green Av CLECK BD19 .....149 H6
Lower Hall Cl LVSG WF15 .....172 C3
Lower Hall Crs HUDS HD4 .....193 L8
Lower Hall Dr LVSG WF15 .....172 C3
Lower Hall La LVSG WF15 .....172 C3
Lower Hall Mt LVSG WF15 .....172 B2
Lower Hall Rd HUDS HD5 .....193 L8
Lower Heights Rd
CUL/QBY BD13 .....102 C6
Lower Hey HOLM/MEL HD9 .....234 F4
Lower High Royds
DOD/DAR S75 .....242 C6
Lower Holme BAIL BD17 .....82 E5
Lower House La HUD HD1 .....83 H5
Lower House La KBTN HD8 .....216 C4
Lower Houses La HUDE HD5 .....214 F2
Lowerhouses La HUDE HD5 .....214 F2
Lowerhouses Rd HUDW HD3 * 191 K8
Lower Kipping La
CUL/QBY BD13 .....102 F8
Lower Kirkgate BFD BD1 .....4 F6
HFAX HX1 * 11 K6
Lower Laith Av TOD OL14 .....163 L1
Lower La BIRK/DRI BD11 .....149 M1
BOW BD4 .....127 L2
CLECK BD19 .....150 D7
HBR HX7 .....142 A3
HOLM/MEL HD9 .....235 M2
MILN OL16 .....228 F2
Lower Langwith WBY LS22 .....47 L3
Lower Lark La CLECK BD19 .....149 K7
Lower Maythorn La
HOLM/MEL HD9 .....255 L6
Lower Mdw HOLM/MEL HD9 .....253 M1
Lower Mickletown RTHW LS26 .....157 H3
Lower Mill Bank Rd
RPDN/SBR HX6 .....166 F7
Lower Newlands BRIG HD6 .....170 D5
Lower Northcroft
HEM/SK/SE WF9 .....247 J1
Lower Northfield La
HEM/SK/SE WF9 .....246 E3
Lower North St BTLY WF17 .....151 J5
Lower Oxford St CAS WF10 .....157 M7
Lower Park Grn AIRE BD20 .....35 L5
Lower Park Royd Dr
RPDN/SBR HX6 .....167 G2
Lower Peel St DEWS WF13 .....173 L5
Lower Quarry Rd HUDN HD2 .....171 J7
Lower Range HIPP HX3 * 11 H7
Lower Rd HUDW HD3 .....189 M8
Lower Rushton Rd BFDE BD3 .....106 A2
Lower Sandhills SCFT LS14 .....90 A3
Lower School St LM/WK BD12 .....126 E8
SHPY BD18 .....82 B6
Lower Sheriff St WHIT OL12 .....206 A6
Lower Sheriff St WHIT OL12 .....206 A6

Lower Station Rd NORM WF6 .....178 C4
Lower St ROCH OL11 .....228 C2
Lower Thomas St BSLY S70 .....261 G5
Lower Tofts Rd PDSY/CALV LS28 .....107 G7
Lower Town BRAM LS13 .....107 M4
Lower Tweedale St ROCH OL11 .....228 B8
Lower Union St SKP/WHF BD23 .....16 B3
Lower Unwin St STKB/PEN S36 .....270 F4
Lower Viaduct St HUD HD1 .....15 G4
Lower Warrengate WKFDE WF1 .....12 F2
Lower Wellhouse Rd
MAR/SLWT HD7 .....212 F3
Lower Wellington Rd ILK LS29 .....38 E2
Lower Westfield Rd GIR BD8 * 104 C5
Lower Wheat End MILN OL16 .....206 D6
Lower Wortley Rd
WOR/ARM LS12 .....130 D1
Lower Wyke Gn LM/WK BD12 .....148 B6
Lower Wyke La LM/WK BD12 .....148 C7
Lower York Ct WKFDE WF1 .....176 E7
Lower York St WKFDE WF1 .....12 E1
Lowestwood La
MAR/SLWT HD7 .....212 F4
Loweswater Av WBSY BD6 .....126 B8
Low Farm RTHW LS26 .....135 G6
Low Farm La FEA/AMT WF7 .....202 C5
Low Farm La COP/BISH YO23 .....73 J7
Lowfield Crs AIRE BD20 .....36 B5
HEM/SK/SE WF9 .....224 A7
Lowfields Av AIRE BD20 .....131 G2
Lowfield Cl ELL HX5 .....169 J6
Lowfields Rd BEE/HOL LS11 .....131 G3
WOR/ARM LS12 .....130 C3
Lowfields Wy ELL HX5 .....169 K6
Low Fold AIRE BD20 .....35 L8
CLECK BD19 .....149 H6
ECHL BD2 .....105 H4
Low Garth Link
GFTH/SHER LS25 .....116 A7
Low Garth Rd GFTH/SHER LS25 .....116 A7
Low Ga HEM/SK/SE WF9 .....247 J3
HOLM/MEL HD9 .....254 D3
Low Gate La UPML OL3 .....231 H5
Low Gipton Crs OSM LS9 .....110 C3
Low Grange Crs MID LS10 .....132 A5
Low Grange Vw MID LS10 .....132 A6
Low Gn FEA/AMT WF7 .....202 D7
GTHN BD7 .....126 C3
KNOT WF11 .....182 D2
YEA LS19 .....84 D3
Low Green Ter GTHN BD7 .....126 C3
Low Hall Pl BEE/HOL LS11 .....9 K2
Low Hall Rd ILK LS29 .....61 L2
YEA LS19 .....84 F6
Low Hl WHIT OL12 .....206 E3
Low Hills La HUDW HD3 .....191 J5
Low Holland KNOT WF11 .....159 J2
Lowhouse Cl MILN OL16 .....207 J7
Low House Dr AIRE BD20 .....36 A6
Low House Fold LVSG WF15 .....172 B2
Low Laithes RPDN/SBR HX6 .....167 J3
Lowlands Cl BSLYN/ROY S71 .....261 K6
Lowlands Rd MIRF WF14 .....194 D2
Low La AIRE BD20 .....34 A3
AIRE BD20 .....35 L1
AIRE BD20 .....36 B3
BRIG HD6 .....148 E8
BTLY WF17 .....151 G5
CLAY BD14 .....125 J1
CUL/QBY BD13 .....124 E3
HBR HX7 .....122 C7
HOR/CROF WF4 .....196 D6
HORS LS18 .....85 M5
ILK LS29 .....25 H8
PBR HX3 .....28 C5
Low Mdw ROY/SHW OL2 .....228 F8
Low Ml ILK LS29 .....19 L7
Low Mill La DEWS WF13 .....194 F2
ILK LS29 .....19 K6
KGHY BD21 .....3 J4
Low Mill Rd OSS WF5 .....196 E5
Low Mills GSLY LS20 .....62 A6
Low Mills Rd WOR/ARM LS12 .....130 D2
Low Moor Crs HOR/CROF WF4 .....220 B3
Low Moor La HOR/CROF WF4 .....219 M5
Low Moor Side MID LS10 .....129 M3
Low Moorside Cl
WOR/ARM LS12 * 130 A3
Low Moor Side La
WOR/ARM LS12 .....129 L4
Low Moor St LM/WK BD12 .....126 F8
Low Moor Ter LUD/ILL HX2 .....145 M8
Lowood La BTLY WF17 .....151 G3
Low Park Rd ILK LS29 .....39 K1
Low Pasture Cl DOD/DAR S75 .....260 C7
Low Rd DEWS WF13 .....173 H6
EARL WF12 .....174 A7
EARL WF12 .....195 L5
CLE DN14 .....161 M8
HUDS HD4 .....214 B6
MID LS10 .....9 M8
STKB/PEN S36 .....271 M5
Lowry Rd EARD/LOFT WF3 .....153 G4
Lowry Vw KGHY BD21 .....3 H8
Low Shops La RTHW LS26 .....132 E8
Low's Pl WHIT OL12 .....206 C4
Low Spring Rd KGHY BD21 .....3 M6
Low St DOD/DAR S75 * 3 H5
DOD/DAR S75 .....260 D8
EARD/LOFT WF3 .....153 G5
GFTH/SHER LS25 .....116 A7
KGHY BD21 .....3 G5
KNOT WF11 .....159 L7
Lowswater Rd KNOT WF11 .....182 A4
Lowther Av GFTH/SHER LS25 .....113 C8
ROY/SHW OL2 .....228 E6
Lowther Crs RTHW LS26 .....134 B4
Lowther Dr GFTH/SHER LS25 .....113 G8
RTHW LS26 .....134 B4
Lowther St BFDE BD3 .....5 M1
RHAY LS8 .....110 B2
Low Town KBTN HD8 .....238 B1
Lowtown PDSY/CALV LS28 .....107 H6
Low Vw DOD/DAR S75 .....260 A2
Low Wy BSPA/BRAM LS23 .....48 F8
Low Wd WIL/AL BD15 .....102 F2
Low Wood Dr AIRE BD20 .....57 K3
Low Wood Rd ILK LS29 .....39 H4
Loxley Gv WBY LS22 .....29 M6
Loxley Mt AWLS/ASK DN6 .....227 L6
Loxley Rd BSLYN/ROY S71 .....262 B3
Loxley St BTLY WF17 .....151 J7
Lucas Ct CHAL LS7 .....7 J2
Lucas Gv North RYKW YO26 .....32 A1
Lucas Gv South RYKW YO26 .....32 A1
Lucas Pl HDGY LS6 .....9 G1
Lucas Rd RYKW YO26 .....32 A1
Lucas St HDGY LS6 .....9 G1
Luck La HUD HD1 .....191 M7
Lucknow St ROCH OL11 .....228 B1

Lucy Av MSTN/BAR LS15 ....111 G6
Lucy Hall Dr BAIL BD17 ....82 A4
Lucy La KBTN HD8 ....216 A1
Lucy St HIPP HX3 ....11 K3
Luddenden La LUD/ILL HX2 ....144 F7
Ludgate Rd ROCH OL11 ....228 C4
Ludhill La HOLM/MEL HD9 ....236 F1
Ludlam St WBOW BD5 ....127 G1
Ludlow Av GFTH/SHER LS25 ....113 K7
Ludolf Dr AL/HA/HU LS17 ....89 G2
Ludwell Cl EARL WF12 ....196 B5
Ludwood Cl HOLM/MEL HD9 ....236 C1
Lugano Gv WMB/DAR S73 ....263 G8
Luke La HOLM/MEL HD9 ....236 E6
Luke Rd WBOW BD5 ....126 E2
Lulworth Av MSTN/BAR LS15 ....111 M6
Lulworth Cl BSLY S70 ....261 K6
MSTN/BAR LS15 ....111 M5
Lulworth Crs MSTN/BAR LS15 ....111 M5
Lulworth Garth
MSTN/BAR LS15 ....111 M6
Lulworth Gv BOW BD4 ....127 M4
Lulworth Vw MSTN/BAR LS15 ....111 M6
Lulworth Wk MSTN/BAR LS15 ....111 M6
Lumb Bottom BIRK/DRI BD11 ....129 H7
Lumbfoot Rd HWTH BD22 ....78 A7
Lumb Gill La ILK LS29 ....19 K8
Lumb La GIR BD8 ....4 B1
HIPP HX3 ....146 D4
HUDS HD4 ....214 F6
HWTH BD22 ....54 C5
LUD/ILL HX2 ....123 H8
LVSG WF15 ....172 B4
RPDN/SBR HX6 ....166 E7
Lumb Rd HBR HX7 ....142 F1
Lumbrook Cl HIPP HX3 ....147 L3
Lumbutts La TOD OL14 ....164 B2
Lumbutts Rd TOD OL14 ....163 M3
Lumby Cl PDSY/CALV LS28 ....129 H1
Lumby Hl GFTH/SHER LS25 ....138 D7
Lumby La AL/HA/HU LS17 ....46 C8
GFTH/SHER LS25 ....138 B4
PDSY/CALV LS28 ....129 H1
Lumby St IDLE BD10 * 83 K6
Lumley Av BULY LS4 ....108 F3
CAS WF10 ....157 J7
Lumley Gv BULY LS4 ....108 F3
Lumley Hl CAS WF10 ....157 J7
Lumley Mt BULY LS4 ....108 F3
Lumley Pl BULY LS4 ....108 F3
Lumley Rd BULY LS4 ....108 F3
EARL WF12 ....174 A4
Lumley St BULY LS4 ....108 F3
CAS WF10 ....157 K7
Lumley Ter BULY LS4 ....108 F3
Lumley Vw BULY LS4 ....108 F3
Lumley Wk BULY LS4 ....108 F3
Lunan Pl RHAY LS8 ....110 B2
Lunan Ter RHAY LS8 ....110 B2
Lund Av BSLYN/ROY S71 ....262 B3
Lund Cl BSLYN/ROY S71 ....262 B3
Lund Crs BSLYN/ROY S71 ....262 B3
Lund Dr HECK WF16 ....173 G3
Lund Head La PBR HG3 ....45 L1
Lund Hill La BSLYN/ROY S71 ....222 B8
Lund La BSLYN/ROY S71 ....262 B3
HWTH BD22 ....56 D8
Lund Sike La GFTH/SHER LS25 ....138 C3
Lund St BGLY BD16 ....81 J3
GIR BD8 ....104 A7
KGHY BD21 ....3 G3
Lune St COL BB8 ....74 A2
Lunnfields La KNOT WF11 ....159 K2
Lunn La GLE DN14 ....161 L8
Lunn Rd CUD/GR S72 ....244 D8
Lupset Crs WKFDW/WTN WF2 ....198 A3
Lupton Av OSM LS9 ....110 C6
Lupton St GIR BD8 ....4 D2
MID LS10 ....9 L9
Lustre St KGHY BD21 ....2 D5
Luther Pl HUDW HD3 ....14 A3
Luther Wy ECHL BD2 ....105 H3
Luton St HFAX HX1 ....10 B5
HUDS HD4 ....213 H3
KGHY BD21 ....2 F5
Lutterworth Dr AWLS/ASK DN6 ....249 J8
Luttrell Cl BHP/TINH LS16 ....86 C4
Luttrell Crs BHP/TINH LS16 ....86 C4
Luttrell Gdns BHP/TINH LS16 ....86 C4
Luttrell Pl BHP/TINH LS16 ....86 C4
Luttrell Rd BHP/TINH LS16 ....86 C4
The Lutyens ILK LS29 ....38 B4
Luxor Av RHAY LS8 ....110 B2
Luxor Rd RHAY LS8 ....110 B2
Luxor St RHAY LS8 ....110 C2
Luxor Vw RHAY LS8 ....110 B2
Lyceum Pas MILN OL16 * 206 B7
Lydbrook Pk HIPP HX3 ....168 C4
Lyddon Ter LDSU LS2 ....6 C5
Lydford ROCH OL11 * 206 A8
Lydgate HIPP HX3 ....147 J3
KBTN HD8 ....216 C3
OSM LS9 ....110 B5
Lydgate Cl HOLM/MEL HD9 ....237 G8
Lydgate Dr HOLM/MEL HD9 ....236 F7
KBTN HD8 ....216 C3
Lydgate Pk HIPP HX3 ....148 A7
Lydgate Pl PDSY/CALV LS28 ....84 C7
Lydgate Ri HEM/SK/SE WF9 * 246 F3
Lydgate Rd BTLY WF17 ....174 B1
KBTN HD8 ....238 A6
Lydgate St PDSY/CALV LS28 ....84 C7
Lydget Ct AIRE BD20 ....57 J5
Lydgetts HOLM/MEL HD9 ....253 M1
Lydia St LDSU LS2 ....7 J8
Lyefield Wk MILN OL16 ....206 D8
Lyme Cha SCFT LS14 ....111 H4
Lymington Dr BOW BD4 ....128 A2
Lynch Av GTHN BD7 ....126 B3
Lyncroft ECHL BD2 ....105 H2
Lynda Gv OSS WF5 ....197 J2
Lyndale GFTH/SHER LS25 ....135 J6
Lyndale Crs HECK WF16 ....173 G2
Lyndale Dr LIT OL15 ....185 J8
SHPY BD18 ....83 H7
WKFDW/WTN WF2 ....176 A4
Lyndale Gv NORM WF6 ....178 E5
Lyndale Ms DEWS WF13 ....173 H8
Lyndale Rd BGLY BD16 ....81 L1
Lyndean Gdns IDLE BD10 ....83 J7
Lynden Av SHPY BD18 ....83 G6
Lynden Ct WBSY BD6 ....126 C7
Lyndhurst BGLY BD16 * 81 H2
Lyndhurst Av BRIG HD6 ....170 C7
Lyndhurst Cl MSTN/BAR LS15 ....90 B7
Lyndhurst Crs MSTN/BAR LS15 ....90 B7
Lyndhurst Dr AWLS/ASK DN6 ....227 M3
Lyndhurst Gv WIL/AL BD15 ....103 L5
Lyndhurst Grove Rd BRIG HD6 ....170 C7
Lyndhurst Rd BRIG HD6 ....170 C6
HUDW HD3 ....191 K6
MSTN/BAR LS15 ....90 B8
Lyndhurst Vw MSTN/BAR LS15 ....90 B8
Lyndon Av BSPA/BRAM LS23 ....69 L3
GFTH/SHER LS25 ....113 G7
Lyndon Cl BSPA/BRAM LS23 ....69 L3
Lyndon Crs BSPA/BRAM LS23 ....69 L3
Lyndon Rd BSPA/BRAM LS23 ....69 L3
Lyndon Sq BSPA/BRAM LS23 ....69 L3
Lyndon Ter BGLY BD16 ....81 J3
Lyndon Wy BSPA/BRAM LS23 ....69 L3
Lyndum Gv GFTH/SHER LS25 ....135 J4
Lyndum Vls AWLS/ASK DN6 * 227 L3
Lynfield Dr HTON BD9 ....103 M3
LVSG WF15 ....171 K1
Lynfield Mt SHPY BD18 ....83 G6
Lynmoor Ct IDLE BD10 ....83 J7
Lynndale Av AIRE BD20 ....34 F7
HUDN HD2 ....192 B5
Lynnfield Gdns
MSTN/BAR LS15 ....90 B8
Lynnwood Gdns
PDSY/CALV LS28 ....106 E8
Lynsey Gdns BOW BD4 ....127 K7
Lynthorne Rd HTON BD9 ....104 E2
Lynton Av BSPA/BRAM LS23 ....48 F6
EARD/LOFT WF3 ....154 A4
HTON BD9 ....104 B3
HUD HD1 ....14 C7
Lynton Dr AIRE BD20 ....58 B5
HTON BD9 ....104 A4
SHPY BD18 ....82 C7
Lynton Gv LUD/ILL HX2 ....124 B5
Lynton Pl DOD/DAR S75 ....241 M6
Lynton Ter CLECK BD19 * 149 M6
Lynton Vls HTON BD9 ....104 B4
Lynwood Av RTHW LS26 ....133 M8
SHPY BD18 ....83 G6
WOR/ARM LS12 ....130 E2
Lynwood Cl BIRK/DRI BD11 ....150 D1
FEA/AMT WF7 ....201 G2
Lynwood Ct HWTH BD22 ....79 G1
Lynwood Crs HEM/SK/SE WF9 ....223 H3
HFAX HX1 ....10 A9
PONT WF8 ....180 F8
RTHW LS26 ....133 M8
WOR/ARM LS12 ....130 E2
Lynwood Dr BSLYN/ROY S71 ....243 L5
WKFDW/WTN WF2 ....198 E8
Lynwood Garth WOR/ARM LS12 ....130 E1
Lynwood Gv WOR/ARM LS12 ....130 E1
Lynwood Ms BOW BD4 ....128 B4
Lynwood Mt WOR/ARM LS12 ....130 E1
Lynwood Ri WOR/ARM LS12 ....130 E1
Lynwood Vw WOR/ARM LS12 ....130 E1
Lyon Rd AIRE BD20 ....35 H8
PONT WF8 ....180 F8
Lyon St CUL/QBY BD13 ....102 F7
CUL/QBY BD13 ....125 H5
ROY/SHW OL2 ....229 K7
Lysander Wy BGLY BD16 ....81 K8
Lytham Av BSLYN/ROY S71 ....261 M1
Lytham Cl NORM WF6 ....178 F5
SKP/WHF BD23 ....16 E3
Lytham Dr CUL/QBY BD13 ....125 K4
Lytham Gdns SKP/WHF BD23 ....16 E3
Lytham Gv WOR/ARM LS12 ....130 C2
Lytham Pl WOR/ARM LS12 ....130 C2
Lytham St WHIT OL12 ....206 A3
Lytham Wy HUDW HD3 ....191 K6
Lyttleton Crs STKB/PEN S36 ....270 E5
Lytton Rd GIR BD8 ....104 B6
Lytton St HIPP HX3 ....11 H2
MID LS10 ....9 K9

M

Mabel Royd GTHN BD7 ....126 B1
Mabel St COL BB8 ....74 B1
HBR HX7 ....144 A5
Mabgate OSM LS9 ....7 K7
Mabgate Gn OSM LS9 ....7 K8
Macaulay Rd HUDN HD2 ....14 C1
Macaulay St OSM LS9 ....7 L8
Macham St HUD HD1 ....214 B2
Mackie Hill Cl HOR/CROF WF4 ....219 M2
Mackingstone Dr HWTH BD22 ....78 D3
Mackingstone La HWTH BD22 ....78 D3
Mackinnon Av NORM WF6 ....178 E3
Mackintosh Homes
LUD/ILL HX2 ....168 C2
Maclure Rd ROCH OL11 ....206 B8
Macturk Gv GIR BD8 * 104 C5
Maddocks St SHPY BD18 ....82 C6
Madeley Rd HOR/CROF WF4 ....222 E5
Madeley Sq CAS WF10 ....158 E5
Maden's Sq LIT OL15 ....207 K1
Madgin La HUDS HD4 ....213 J8
Madison Av BOW BD4 ....128 A5
Madni Cl HFAX HX1 ....10 E6
Mafeking Av BEE/HOL LS11 ....131 J5
Mafeking Gv BEE/HOL LS11 ....131 J5
Mafeking Mt BEE/HOL LS11 ....131 J5
Magdalene Cl BHP/TINH LS16 ....86 C3
Magdalene Flds NORM WF6 ....178 F6
Magdalene Rd
WKFDW/WTN WF2 ....197 L1
Magdalen Rd HOLM/MEL HD9 ....252 E1
Magdalin Dr PDSY/CALV LS28 ....107 J4
Maggot La STKB/PEN S36 ....271 M4
Magna Gv WKFDW/WTN WF2 ....198 F5
Magnolia Cl CUD/GR S72 ....244 F4
Magnolia Dr WIL/AL BD15 ....103 H2
Magnolias BTLY WF17 ....151 G7
Magpie Cl WBSY BD6 ....125 L5
Magpie La MOR LS27 ....152 D3
Maidstone St BFDE BD3 ....105 L7
Maidwell Wy WBSY BD6 ....126 C8
Mail Cl MSTN/BAR LS15 ....112 A3
Main Av HUDS HD4 ....213 H4
Main Ga HOLM/MEL HD9 ....255 G4
Main Rd AIRE BD20 ....35 G6
AIRE BD20 ....58 F6
CUL/QBY BD13 ....101 M6
Mainspring Rd WIL/AL BD15 ....102 E1
Main St AIRE BD20 ....34 B4
AIRE BD20 ....34 E1
AIRE BD20 ....34 E4
AIRE BD20 ....34 E8
AIRE BD20 ....55 M1
AL/HA/HU LS17 ....44 B4
AL/HA/HU LS17 ....67 L1
AL/HA/HU LS17 ....88 F1
AL/HA/HU LS17 ....89 G2
AWLS/ASK DN6 ....205 H3
AWLS/ASK DN6 ....248 D5
BAIL BD17 ....83 L1
BGLY BD16 ....81 H3
BGLY BD16 ....81 K8
BSPA/BRAM LS23 ....49 J2
CAS WF10 ....157 K2
CAS WF10 ....158 A1
COP/BISH YO23 ....73 M5
CUD/GR S72 ....222 F8
EARD/LOFT WF3 ....153 M7
EARD/LOFT WF3 ....154 F3
GFTH/SHER LS25 ....92 A3
GFTH/SHER LS25 ....92 A7
GFTH/SHER LS25 ....113 G7
GFTH/SHER LS25 ....138 B6
GFTH/SHER LS25 ....138 D6
GFTH/SHER LS25 ....160 A3
GLE DN14 ....161 J7
GSLY LS20 ....61 G6
HEM/SK/SE WF9 ....225 G4
HEM/SK/SE WF9 ....225 M6
HWTH BD22 ....77 M8
HWTH BD22 ....78 E7
ILK LS29 ....19 G6
ILK LS29 ....40 A4
ILK LS29 ....61 H2
LM/WK BD12 ....148 E2
MSTN/BAR LS15 ....90 B8
MSTN/BAR LS15 ....90 F7
OT LS21 ....42 E7
PBR HG3 ....26 E2
PONT WF8 ....204 F8
RTHW LS26 ....156 F3
SCFT LS14 ....90 B2
TAD LS24 ....50 A7
TAD LS24 ....93 K8
TAD LS24 ....94 E8
TAD LS24 ....94 F1
TAD LS24 ....94 F7
WBY LS22 ....29 M5
WBY LS22 ....31 K4
WBY LS22 ....46 D1
WBY LS22 ....47 K4
WIL/AL BD15 ....102 E2
Maister Pl HWTH BD22 ....78 D3
Maitland Cl WHIT OL12 ....206 E3
WIL/AL BD15 ....103 K7
Maitland Pl BEE/HOL LS11 ....8 D7
Maitland St TOD OL14 ....163 J6
Maizebrook DEWS WF13 ....173 G6
Maize St HWTH BD22 * 79 J2
Major St MILN OL16 ....207 H8
WKFDW/WTN WF2 ....12 D8
Malais La AIRE BD20 ....55 J1
Malcolm Cl BSLY S70 ....261 M6
Malden Rd HDGY LS6 ....87 G5
Maldon St ROCH OL11 ....228 B1
Malham Av BRIG HD6 ....170 A6
HTON BD9 ....103 L3
Malham Cl CUD/GR S72 ....244 E3
SCFT LS14 ....111 J2
Malham Ct BSLY S70 * 260 F4
Malham Dr BTLY WF17 ....173 J1
LVSG WF15 ....172 B5
Malham Rd BRIG HD6 ....170 A7
WKFDE WF1 ....13 L1
Malham Sq WKFDE WF1 ....13 M1
Malincroft DOD/DAR S75 ....242 D6
Malin Rd EARL WF12 ....174 B3
Mallard Av WKFDW/WTN WF2 ....220 E1
Mallard Cl IDLE BD10 ....105 L1
MID LS10 ....132 B7
Mallard Ct GIR BD8 ....103 L7
Mallard Rd CAS WF10 ....157 L8
The Mallards AIRE BD20 ....36 A5
Mallard Vw HWTH BD22 ....100 E4
Mallard Wy MAR/SLWT HD7 ....212 B6
MOR LS27 ....152 F2
Mallinson St DEWS WF13 ....173 J5
Mallory Cl GTHN BD7 ....104 B7
Mallory Wy CUD/GR S72 ....244 E7
Mallow Cft MILN OL16 ....228 E2
Malmesbury Cl BOW BD4 ....128 A4
WOR/ARM LS12 ....108 E8
Malmesbury Gv WOR/ARM LS12 ....108 E8
Malmesbury Pl WOR/ARM LS12 ....108 E8
Malmesbury St WOR/ARM LS12 ....108 E8
Malmesbury Ter
WOR/ARM LS12 ....108 E8
Malsis Rd KGHY BD21 ....2 D7
Maltby Ct MSTN/BAR LS15 * 111 M7
Malthouse Cl SCFT LS14 ....67 L6
Malthouse La PBR HG3 ....26 E5
Malthouse Rd BSLYN/ROY S71 ....261 H5
Malting Cl EARD/LOFT WF3 ....154 D3
Malting Ri EARD/LOFT WF3 ....154 D3
Maltings Ct BEE/HOL LS11 ....9 G8
Maltings Rd BEE/HOL LS11 ....9 H8
LUD/ILL HX2 ....145 M4
The Maltings EARD/LOFT WF3 ....154 D3
HDGY LS6 * 109 G4
MIRF WF14 ....194 B1
PONT WF8 ....180 F5
Malt Kiln Cft WKFDW/WTN WF2 ....199 G5
Maltkiln Dr HOR/CROF WF4 ....219 H6
Maltkiln La CAS WF10 ....158 A6
Malt Kiln La CUL/QBY BD13 ....124 D1
GFTH/SHER LS25 ....135 K5
Malt Kiln Ter TAD LS24 ....71 K7
Malton Pl BSLYN/ROY S71 ....243 G7
Malton Rd HEM/SK/SE WF9 ....225 M6
Malton St HIPP HX3 ....146 E4
RPDN/SBR HX6 ....167 K1
Malt St HWTH BD22 * 79 J2
Malvern Brow HTON BD9 ....103 M4
Malvern Cl CAS WF10 ....179 H1
DOD/DAR S75 ....260 D4
MILN OL16 ....207 J7
ROY/SHW OL2 ....229 H6
Malvern Crs AIRE BD20 ....57 M3
Malvern Gv BEE/HOL LS11 ....8 D8
HTON BD9 ....103 M5
Malvern Ri BEE/HOL LS11 ....8 D8
HUDS HD4 ....214 C3
Malvern Rd BEE/HOL LS11 ....8 D8
EARL WF12 ....174 A5
HTON BD9 ....103 M5
HUDS HD4 ....214 D2
KNOT WF11 ....182 A2
Malvern St BEE/HOL LS11 ....8 C8
Malvern Vw BEE/HOL LS11 ....8 C8
Manchester Rd HUD HD1 ....14 C9
HUDW HD3 ....213 M2
MAR/SLWT HD7 ....212 D6
MAR/SLWT HD7 ....232 C6
ROCH OL11 ....206 A8
STKB/PEN S36 ....269 L5
WBOW BD5 ....126 F3
Manchester Rd (Linthwaite)
MAR/SLWT HD7 ....211 L8
Manchester Rd (Marsden)
MAR/SLWT HD7 ....233 J2
Manchester Rd (Slaithwaite)
MAR/SLWT HD7 ....211 M7
Mandale Gv WBSY BD6 ....125 M6
Mandale Rd WBSY BD6 ....125 M6
Mandarin Wy MID LS10 ....132 B7
Mandeville Crs WBSY BD6 ....126 B6
Mangrill La BSPA/BRAM LS23 ....68 F8
SCFT LS14 ....69 G8
Manitoba Pl CHAL LS7 ....88 A8
Mankinholes Bank TOD OL14 ....164 B2
Manley Ct GFTH/SHER LS25 ....135 H1
Manley Dr WBY LS22 ....29 K8
Manley Gv ILK LS29 ....38 F2
Manley Ri ILK LS29 ....38 F3
Manley Rd ILK LS29 ....38 F3
Manley St BRIG HD6 ....170 C3
Mannerley Gv CLECK BD19 ....150 D8
Mannheim Rd HTON BD9 ....104 C4
Manningham La GIR BD8 ....4 C1
Mannville Gv HWTH BD22 ....2 C7
Mannville Pl HWTH BD22 ....2 C7
Mannville Rd KGHY BD21 ....2 D8
Mannville St HWTH BD22 ....2 C7
Mannville Ter GTHN BD7 ....4 D8
Mannville Wk HWTH BD22 * 2 C7
Mannville Wy HWTH BD22 ....2 C7
Manor Av HDGY LS6 ....109 G2
OSS WF5 ....197 H3
Manor Cha RYKW YO26 ....33 H2
Manor Cl AWLS/ASK DN6 ....227 L3
BHP/TINH LS16 ....63 M3
BIRK/DRI BD11 ....129 G7
GIR BD8 ....103 M6
HEM/SK/SE WF9 ....225 G4
HIPP HX3 ....168 D2
HOR/CROF WF4 ....221 H7
OSS WF5 ....197 H3
PONT WF8 ....226 F1
RTHW LS26 ....133 G8
YEA LS19 ....62 D7
Manor Cottage Ms SCFT LS14 ....67 L8
Manor Ct AL/HA/HU LS17 ....89 H2
BGLY BD16 * 81 J7
KNOT WF11 ....159 J1
OSS WF5 ....197 H3
Manor Crs CUD/GR S72 ....245 H6
OT LS21 ....42 E7
RTHW LS26 ....154 F1
WKFDW/WTN WF2 ....198 A2
WKFDW/WTN WF2 ....199 J6
Manor Crest HOR/CROF WF4 ....219 M1
Manor Cft CUD/GR S72 ....244 F1
HBR HX7 ....143 K3
MSTN/BAR LS15 ....111 L7
Manorcroft NORM WF6 ....178 D4
Manor Dr BGLY BD16 ....81 J7
CUD/GR S72 ....222 E8
FEA/AMT WF7 ....179 L5
HBR HX7 ....143 K3
HDGY LS6 ....109 G3
HIPP HX3 ....168 D2
HOR/CROF WF4 ....200 C7
HOR/CROF WF4 ....217 M3
KBTN HD8 ....239 J5
MIRF WF14 ....171 M7
OSS WF5 ....197 H3
Manor Farm HEM/SK/SE WF9 * 225 G4
Manor Farm Cl AWLS/ASK DN6 ....249 K8
BGLY BD16 ....81 K8
BSLYN/ROY S71 ....243 M6
MID LS10 ....131 M8
Manor Farm Crs MOR LS27 ....130 E6
Manor Farm Dr BTLY WF17 ....152 B8
MID LS10 ....131 L8
MOR LS27 ....130 E6
Manor Farm Gdns MID LS10 ....131 L8
Manor Farm Gn MID LS10 ....131 L8
Manor Farm Gv MID LS10 ....131 L8
Manor Farm Ri MID LS10 ....131 M8
Manor Farm Rd
HOR/CROF WF4 ....220 A2
MID LS10 ....131 L8
Manor Farm Wk MID LS10 ....131 M8
Manor Farm Wy MID LS10 ....153 L1
Manorfield Dr HOR/CROF WF4 ....197 J4
Manorfields Av
HOR/CROF WF4 ....200 C6
Manorfields Ct
HOR/CROF WF4 ....200 C6
Manor Fold BGLY BD16 ....81 K8
Manor Gdns BSLYN/ROY S71 ....262 C6
CUL/QBY BD13 ....101 M1
EARL WF12 * 174 C4
OT LS21 ....42 E7
SCFT LS14 ....68 C8
Manor Garth GFTH/SHER LS25 ....136 F6
MSTN/BAR LS15 ....111 L7
PBR HG3 ....28 E3
WKFDW/WTN WF2 ....199 J6
Manor Garth Rd EARL WF12 ....174 B7
GFTH/SHER LS25 ....135 K4
Manor Gra KBTN HD8 ....237 M6
Manor Gv AIRE BD20 ....58 C6
BSLYN/ROY S71 ....243 K5
CAS WF10 ....158 A8
CHAL LS7 ....87 M8
CUD/GR S72 ....245 H6
HEM/SK/SE WF9 ....246 C5
OSS WF5 ....197 H3
Manor Haigh Rd
WKFDW/WTN WF2 ....198 A3
Manor Heath Rd HIPP HX3 ....168 D2
Manor House Cft
BHP/TINH LS16 ....86 F3
Manor House La
AL/HA/HU LS17 ....88 B1
Manor House Rd WIL/AL BD15 ....80 E8
Manor La OSS WF5 ....197 H3
SHPY BD18 ....83 G5
STKB/PEN S36 ....271 L5
TAD LS24 ....50 F4
UPML OL3 ....232 A6
Manorley La HIPP HX3 ....126 A8
Manor Mill Cl MILN OL16 ....206 F3
Manor Mill La BEE/HOL LS11 ....131 G5
Manor Occupation Rd
BSLYN/ROY S71 ....243 K2
Manor Pk CAS WF10 ....136 A8
DOD/DAR S75 ....259 H7
EARL WF12 ....174 D3
GIR BD8 ....103 M6
HWTH BD22 ....54 E3
HWTH BD22 ....78 E4
MIRF WF14 ....171 L7
PONT WF8 ....203 M1
SCFT LS14 ....67 L7
Manor Park Av CAS WF10 ....157 K1
PONT WF8 ....181 H3
Manor Park Gdns CLECK BD19 ....150 C3
Manor Park Wy KBTN HD8 ....215 M4
Manor Ri HOR/CROF WF4 ....220 A1
HUDS HD4 ....214 D2
ILK LS29 ....38 F2
KBTN HD8 ....239 J5
WKFDW/WTN WF2 ....199 J6
Manor Rd AIRE BD20 ....57 J4
BEE/HOL LS11 ....8 E4
BGLY BD16 ....81 K7
BTLY WF17 ....174 B1
COL BB8 ....52 A7
CUD/GR S72 ....244 C8
DEWS WF13 ....173 K7
GLE DN14 ....161 H7
HORS LS18 ....85 J6
HUDS HD4 ....215 H8
KBTN HD8 ....240 C2
MAR/SLWT HD7 ....212 F2
MOR LS27 ....130 E6
OSS WF5 ....197 J2
ROY/SHW OL2 ....229 J7
RTHW LS26 ....132 F8
TAD LS24 ....71 L6
TAD LS24 ....71 M2
WKFDW/WTN WF2 ....198 B1
WKFDW/WTN WF2 ....199 J7
Manor Rw BFD BD1 ....4 E4
WBSY BD6 ....126 E7
Manor Sq YEA LS19 ....62 D7
Manorstead KBTN HD8 ....239 J5
Manor St BSLYN/ROY S71 ....243 M6
CHAL LS7 ....7 K5
CLECK BD19 ....149 H8
EARL WF12 ....173 M6
ECHL BD2 ....105 K3
HUDS HD4 ....214 D2
OT LS21 ....41 J6
Manor Ter ECHL BD2 ....105 K3
HDGY LS6 ....109 G2
Manor Vw CAS WF10 ....180 A1
CUD/GR S72 ....244 E4
HDGY LS6 ....109 G2
PDSY/CALV LS28 ....107 G7
Manor Wy AIRE BD20 ....55 L2
BTLY WF17 ....173 K2
Manscombe Rd WIL/AL BD15 ....103 L5
Manse Crs ILK LS29 ....40 A5
Manse Dr HUDS HD4 ....213 J3
Mansel Ms BOW BD4 ....128 A5
Manse Rd ILK LS29 ....40 A5
Manse St BFDE BD3 ....105 L7
Manse Wy AIRE BD20 ....34 E8
Mansfield Av BGLY BD16 ....81 L1
Mansfield Crs AWLS/ASK DN6 ....249 K4
Mansfield Rd BSLYN/ROY S71 ....243 H6
GIR BD8 ....104 E4
ILK LS29 ....40 A5
Mansion Gdns HUDS HD4 ....214 B5
Mansion Ga CHAL LS7 ....87 M8
Mansion Gate Dr CHAL LS7 ....88 A8
Mansion Gate Sq CHAL LS7 ....88 A8
Mansion La HIPP HX3 ....168 E2
RHAY LS8 ....88 D5
Manston Ap MSTN/BAR LS15 ....111 L3
Manston Av MSTN/BAR LS15 ....111 L3
Manston Crs MSTN/BAR LS15 ....111 L3
Manston Dr MSTN/BAR LS15 ....111 L3
Manston Gdns MSTN/BAR LS15 ....111 M3
Manston Gv MSTN/BAR LS15 ....111 L3
Manston La MSTN/BAR LS15 ....112 A4
Manston Ri MSTN/BAR LS15 ....111 L3
Manston Wy MSTN/BAR LS15 ....111 L3
Mantley La ROY/SHW OL2 ....230 C7
Manygates Av WKFDE WF1 ....13 H9
Manygates Ct WKFDE WF1 ....13 H8
Manygates Crs WKFDE WF1 ....13 H9
Manygates La
WKFDW/WTN WF2 ....198 F4
Manygates Pk WKFDE WF1 ....13 H8
Manywells Brow
CUL/QBY BD13 ....101 L3
Manywells Crs CUL/QBY BD13 ....101 M1
Manywells La CUL/QBY BD13 ....101 K1
Maple Av BFDE BD3 ....106 A6
HUDW HD3 ....213 H1
HWTH BD22 ....78 F4
PONT WF8 ....202 E1
Maple Beven Gv WKFDE WF1 ....176 F6
Maple Cl BSLY S70 ....261 K7
CAS WF10 ....179 K1
GFTH/SHER LS25 ....138 A3
HUDE HD5 ....193 L5
ROY/SHW OL2 * 229 H6
Maple Ct OSS WF5 ....197 G3
Maple Cft AL/HA/HU LS17 ....88 A3
WOR/ARM LS12 ....129 M1
Maple Dr PONT WF8 ....180 E8
WBY LS22 ....30 A7
WOR/ARM LS12 ....129 M1
Maple Fold WOR/ARM LS12 ....129 M1
Maple Gdns AL/HA/HU LS17 ....68 A1
Maple Gv AIRE BD20 ....2 C1
CLECK BD19 ....150 C5
HUDN HD2 ....192 C2
NORM WF6 ....178 D7
PONT WF8 ....202 E1
WOR/ARM LS12 ....129 M1
Maple Ri RTHW LS26 * 155 G2
Maple Rd DOD/DAR S75 ....242 C5
EARL WF12 ....174 D7
Maple St HFAX HX1 ....10 B9
HUD HD1 ....15 J9
TOD OL14 ....163 J7
WKFDW/WTN WF2 ....176 B6
Maple Wk EARL WF12 ....174 D7
Maple Wy SCFT LS14 ....89 L6
Maplin Av HUDW HD3 ....191 H5
Maplin Dr HUDW HD3 ....191 H5
Mapplewell Crs OSS WF5 ....197 G1
Mapplewell Dr DOD/DAR S75 ....242 E6
OSS WF5 ....197 G1
Marbridge Ct WBSY BD6 ....126 D4
Marchant St CAS WF10 ....157 L6
Marchbank Rd BFDE BD3 ....105 L6
March Cote La BGLY BD16 ....81 J8
March St MILN OL16 ....206 C7
NORM WF6 ....178 C5
Marchwood Gv CLAY BD14 ....125 M1
Marcia Cl IDLE BD10 ....83 L8
Marcroft Pl ROCH OL11 ....228 C2
Marcus Wy HUDW HD3 ....190 F5
Mardale Av ROY/SHW OL2 ....228 E6
Mardale Crs SCFT LS14 ....111 J3
Mardale Rd EARL WF12 ....174 A4
Mardyke WHIT OL12 * 206 A6
Margaret Av AL/HA/HU LS17 ....67 M2
MILN OL16 ....206 E7
Margaret Cl MOR LS27 ....130 E8
Margaret St AIRE BD20 ....2 D3
HFAX HX1 ....10 E6
ROY/SHW OL2 * 229 K8
WKFDE WF1 ....176 C2
WKFDE WF1 ....176 D7
Margate RTHW LS26 * 133 L8
Margate Rd BOW BD4 ....127 J2
Margate St CUD/GR S72 ....245 J7
RPDN/SBR HX6 ....167 J3
Margerison Crs ILK LS29 ....39 G3
Margerison Rd ILK LS29 ....39 G3
Margetson Rd BIRK/DRI BD11 ....151 H1
Margroy Cl WHIT OL12 ....206 C4
Marguerite Gdns
HEM/SK/SE WF9 ....226 A6
Marian Gv BEE/HOL LS11 * 131 K3
Marian Rd HDGY LS6 ....6 E2
Marian Ter HDGY LS6 ....6 E2
Maria St ILK LS29 ....40 A4
Marie Cl HUDE HD5 ....193 L8
Marigold St ROCH OL11 ....228 B1
Marina Crs MOR LS27 ....152 B3
Marina Ter MAR/SLWT HD7 ....213 G1
Marine Villa Rd KNOT WF11 ....182 B2
Marion Av WKFDW/WTN WF2 ....175 M6
Marion Cl HEM/SK/SE WF9 ....246 C4
Marion Dr SHPY BD18 ....82 E7
Marion Gv WKFDW/WTN WF2 ....175 M6
Marion St BGLY BD16 * 81 J3
BRIG HD6 ....170 C2
GTHN BD7 ....4 A5
Marizon Gv WKFDE WF1 * 176 E7
Mark Bottoms La
HOLM/MEL HD9 ....236 B8
Mark Cl IDLE BD10 ....83 L6
Markenfield Dr ROY/SHW OL2 ....229 H7
Market Ar CLECK BD19 * 150 A7
Market Av HUD HD1 ....14 F7
Market Balcony HFAX HX1 * 11 H6
Market Cl BSLYN/ROY S71 ....261 J5
Market Ct CUL/QBY BD13 ....103 G8
Market Hl BSLY S70 ....261 G5
Market Pde BSLY S70 * 261 H5
Market Pl CLECK BD19 ....150 A7
COL BB8 ....74 A1
CUD/GR S72 ....244 D7

DEWS WF13 ...173 M6
HECK WF16 ...172 F5
HUD HD1 ...14 F7
KGHY BD21 ...3 G5
MAR/SLWT HD7 ...212 B6
MAR/SLWT HD7 ...233 H2
NORM WF6 ...178 C4
OT LS21 ...41 J6
PDSY/CALV LS28 ...107 G7
PONT WF8 ...180 F6
WBY LS22 ...48 A1
Market Sq SHPY BD18 ...82 D6
Market St AIRE BD20 ...56 E1
  BFD BD1 ...4 F6
  BGLY BD16 ...81 H5
  BRIG HD6 ...170 D4
  BSLY S70 ...261 G5
  BTLY WF17 ...151 G5
  CLECK BD19 ...150 A7
  COL BB8 ...74 A1
  CUD/GR S72 ...244 D7
  CUL/QBY BD13 ...102 F8
  DEWS WF13 ...173 M5
  FEA/AMT WF7 ...179 L8
  HBR HX7 ...143 H3
  HECK WF16 ...172 F3
  HEM/SK/SE WF9 ...225 M7
  HFAX HX1 ...11 H6
  HOLM/MEL HD9 ...254 C1
  HUD HD1 ...14 A9
  HUD HD1 ...14 F7
  HUDW HD3 ...213 K1
  KGHY BD21 ...3 C6
  NORM WF6 ...178 C4
  OT LS21 ...41 J7
  ROY/SHW OL2 ...229 K8
  SHPY BD18 ...82 D7
  STKB/PEN S36 ...270 F5
  WKFDE WF1 ...12 E3
Market Street Ar LDS LS1 ...9 H1
Market Wk HOLM/MEL HD9 ...254 C1
  HUD HD1 * ...14 F7
  MAR/SLWT HD7 * ...233 H2
Market Wy WKFDE WF1 ...12 F2
Markfield Av LM/WK BD12 ...148 E1
Markfield Cl LM/WK BD12 ...148 E1
Markfield Crs LM/WK BD12 ...148 E1
Markfield Dr LM/WK BD12 ...148 E1
Markham Av AWLS/ASK DN6 ...249 L5
  RHAY LS8 ...110 B2
  YEA LS19 ...84 E1
Markham Crs YEA LS19 ...84 E1
Markham Cft YEA LS19 ...84 E1
Markham St BTLY WF17 ...173 K2
  WKFDW/WTN WF2 ...12 B3
Markington Ms MID LS10 ...153 L3
Markington Pl MID LS10 ...153 L3
Mark La ROY/SHW OL2 ...229 M8
  TOD OL14 ...141 H7
  WBY LS22 ...30 D4
Mark St BSLY S70 ...261 G5
  HUD HD1 ...14 A8
  LVSG WF15 ...172 D1
  WBOW BD5 ...127 G3
  WHIT OL12 * ...206 B9
  WKFDE WF1 ...12 F6
Marland Rd KGHY BD21 ...3 M3
Marlbeck Cl HOLM/MEL HD9 ...236 B3
Marlborough Av HIPP HX3 ...168 D2
  KNOT WF11 ...159 M7
  TAD LS24 ...71 K4
Marlborough Cft
  HEM/SK/SE WF9 * ...247 K2
Marlborough Dr TAD LS24 ...71 K4
Marlborough Gdns
  DEWS WF13 ...173 K4
  LDSU LS2 ...6 C8
Marlborough Gra LDS LS1 ...6 C8
Marlborough Gv ILK LS29 ...38 F3
Marlborough Rd GIR BD8 ...4 B1
  HBR HX7 ...143 J3
  HUDN HD2 * ...192 D1
  SHPY BD18 ...82 C7
Marlborough Sq ILK LS29 ...38 F3
Marlborough St KGHY BD21 ...3 J3
  LDS LS1 ...6 C9
  OSS WF5 ...196 E4
  WKFDW/WTN WF2 ...12 B3
Marlborough Ter BSLY S70 ...261 G6
  DEWS WF13 * ...173 K4
  HBR HX7 ...143 J3
Marldon Rd HIPP HX3 ...147 J5
Marled Cl HECK WF16 ...172 F1
Marley Cl GIR BD8 ...104 A6
Marley Ct BGLY BD16 ...58 F7
Marley Gv BEE/HOL LS11 ...131 H5
Marley La CUL/QBY BD13 ...125 G3
Marley Pl BEE/HOL LS11 ...131 H5
Marley St BEE/HOL LS11 ...131 H5
  BFDE BD3 ...5 J6
  KGHY BD21 ...2 F1
Marley Ter BEE/HOL LS11 ...131 H5
Marley Vw BEE/HOL LS11 ...131 H5
  BGLY BD16 ...58 F7
Marlfield Rd ROY/SHW OL2 ...229 M6
Marling Rd HUDW HD3 ...191 K5
Marlo Rd EARL WF12 ...174 C4
Marlott Rd SHPY BD18 ...82 F6
Marlow Cl HUDE HD5 ...193 H8
Marlowe Cl PDSY/CALV LS28 ...129 H1
Marlowe Ct GFTH/SHER LS25 ...113 H7
Marlow St KGHY BD21 ...3 M3
Marl Pit Hl PONT WF8 ...180 C8
Marmaville Ct MIRF WF14 ...194 E1
Marmion Av GIR BD8 ...103 L7
Marne Av CLAY BD14 ...126 A2
Marne Crs IDLE BD10 ...88 K7
Marquis Av LM/WK BD12 ...149 K1
Marriner Rd KGHY BD21 ...3 G7
Marriner's Dr HTON BD9 ...104 D2
Marriner Wk KGHY BD21 ...3 G7
Marriott Gv WKFDW/WTN WF2 ...199 H6
Marsala Wk WMB/DAR S73 ...263 H8
Marsden Av BEE/HOL LS11 ...131 J4
Marsden Ca MILN OL16 ...228 E6
Marsden Ga GTL/HWG HX4 ...190 A6
Marsden Gv BEE/HOL LS11 ...131 J4
Marsden La MAR/SLWT HD7 ...233 J1
Marsden Mt BEE/HOL LS11 ...131 J4
Marsden Pl BEE/HOL LS11 ...131 J4
Marsden St KBTN HD8 ...239 J1
Marsden Vw BEE/HOL LS11 ...131 J4
Marsett Wy SCFT LS14 ...89 K6
Marsh HOLM/MEL HD9 ...236 B2
  PDSY/CALV LS28 ...106 E7
  MSTN/BAR LS15 ...111 M4
Marshall Av HEM/SK/SE WF9 ...247 G3
Marshall Mill Ct KBTN HD8 ...239 M5
Marshall St AIRE BD20 ...57 K5
  BEE/HOL LS11 ...8 E4
  EARD/LOFT WF3 ...177 H4
  MILN OL16 ...206 F4
  MIRF WF14 ...194 C3
  MOR LS27 ...152 C2
  MSTN/BAR LS15 ...111 L4

YEA LS19 ...62 D7
Marshall Ter MSTN/BAR LS15 ...111 L4
Marsham Gv HUDW HD3 * ...191 L7
Marsh Cr PDSY/CALV LS28 ...106 E7
Marsh Cft KNOT WF11 ...159 L1
Marsh Delves La HIPP HX3 ...147 H8
Marsh End KNOT WF11 ...182 C1
Marshfield Pl WBOW BD5 ...126 F3
Marshfield St WBOW BD5 ...126 F3
Marsh Gdns HOLM/MEL HD9 ...236 B2
Marsh Grove Rd HUDW HD3 ...191 M6
Marsh Hall La HUDS HD4 ...237 H3
Marsh La BIRK/DRI BD11 ...150 C1
  COP/BISH YO23 ...73 J8
  GLE DN14 ...161 J7
  HBR HX7 ...142 C3
  HIPP HX3 ...11 M8
  HWTH BD22 ...100 E2
  KNOT WF11 ...237 L8
  KNOT WF11 ...160 B8
  MSTN/BAR LS15 ...9 K1
Marsh Platt La
  HOLM/MEL HD9 ...236 C2
Marsh Rd CAS WF10 ...179 J1
Marsh St HOLM/MEL HD9 ...254 F3
Marsh St CLECK BD19 ...150 A8
  HDGY LS6 ...6 D2
  RTHW LS26 ...155 G2
  WBOW BD5 ...126 F4
Marsh Ter PDSY/CALV LS28 ...106 E7
Marsh V HDGY LS6 ...6 D3
Marshway HFAX HX1 ...10 D4
Marsh Wy WKFDE WF1 ...12 F1
Marsland Av WKFDE WF1 ...13 H3
Marsland Ct CLECK BD19 ...149 M4
Marsland Pl BFDE BD3 ...105 M7
  WKFDE WF1 ...13 H2
Marsland St WKFDE WF1 ...13 H3
Marsland St WKFDE WF1 ...13 H3
Marston Av MOR LS27 ...152 C3
Marston Cl CUL/QBY BD13 ...125 H5
Marston Ct CAS WF10 ...157 J8
Marston Crs BSLYN/ROY S71 ...243 H8
Marston Rd RYKW YO26 ...32 F1
Marston Wk NORM WF6 ...178 A2
Marston Wy WBY LS22 ...29 L8
Marten Dr HUDS HD4 ...213 M7
Marten Gv HUDS HD4 ...213 M7
Marten Rd BEE/HOL LS11 ...8 E3
Martha's Ter MILN OL16 ...206 E3
Martin Bank Wd HUDE HD5 ...15 L9
Martin Cl BFDE BD3 ...105 M8
Martin Ct MSTN/BAR LS15 ...111 M6
  WBSY BD6 ...125 L5
Martin Cft DOD/DAR S75 ...259 H6
Martindale Dr BRAM LS13 ...108 A5
Martindale Wk AWLS/ASK DN6 ...249 L6
Martin Frobisher Dr
  NORM WF6 ...178 B3
Martingale Dr MID LS10 * ...153 H7
Martin Green La GTL/HWG HX4 ...168 C7
Martin Gv WKFDW/WTN WF2 ...199 C8
Martin's Rd BSLYN/ROY S71 ...262 A3
Martin St BRIG HD6 * ...170 D3
  BTLY WF17 ...151 G5
  NORM WF6 ...178 C4
Martin Ter BULY LS4 ...108 E4
Marton Av HEM/SK/SE WF9 ...223 M6
Marton Dr BFDE BD3 ...105 M7
Marwood Rd WOR/ARM LS12 ...107 M7
Mary Ann Ct BSLYN/ROY S71 ...261 M4
Maryfield Av MSTN/BAR LS15 ...111 J4
Maryfield Cl MSTN/BAR LS15 ...111 J4
Maryfield Gdns
  MSTN/BAR LS15 ...111 J4
  OSS WF5 ...197 G3
Maryfield Ms MSTN/BAR LS15 ...111 J4
Maryfield V MSTN/BAR LS15 ...111 J4
Margate WKFDE WF1 ...12 E3
Mary's Pl DOD/DAR S75 ...260 D4
Mary St AIRE BD20 ...34 F5
  BOW BD4 ...127 L1
  BRIG HD6 ...170 C2
  CUL/QBY BD13 ...102 A5
  CUL/QBY BD13 ...102 F8
  DOD/DAR S75 ...259 M2
  EARD/LOFT WF3 ...154 A6
  HWTH BD22 ...100 A4
  LM/WK BD12 ...148 E2
  PDSY/CALV LS28 ...107 G2
  SHPY BD18 ...82 C7
Mary St Caravan Site BOW BD4 ...127 L1
Maryville Av BRIG HD6 ...170 B1
Masefield Av HTON BD9 ...103 J3
Masefield St GSLY LS20 ...62 B6
Masham Gv WOR/ARM LS12 ...108 F7
Masham Pl HTON BD9 ...104 B4
Masham St WOR/ARM LS12 ...108 F7
Masonic St HFAX HX1 ...146 A8
Mason St HBR HX7 ...143 H3
  MILN OL16 ...206 B7
Masons Wy BSLY S70 ...261 L8
Maspin Moor Rd
  GFTH/SHER LS25 ...139 J8
Massey Flds HWTH BD22 ...78 F5
Massey Fold PBR HX3 ...28 E4
Master La LUD/ILL HX2 ...168 B2
Matherville KBTN HD8 ...239 J5
Matlock Rd BSLYN/ROY S71 ...243 K8
Matlock St HIPP HX3 ...10 C1
  HUDS HD4 ...213 M2
Matrix Ct BEE/HOL LS11 ...131 K5
Matterdale Cl EARL WF12 ...174 A4
Matterdale Rd EARL WF12 ...174 A4
Matthew Cl AIRE BD20 ...58 A5
  COL BB8 ...74 A2
Matthew La HOLM/MEL HD9 ...234 D8
Matthew St AIRE BD20 ...34 E1
  HOLM/MEL HD9 ...234 E4
  TOD OL14 ...142 A7
Matty Marsden La OSS WF5 ...197 G4
Maud Av BEE/HOL LS11 ...131 J4
Maude Av BAIL BD17 ...82 E4
Maude Crs RPDN/SBR HX6 ...167 G3
Maude St GTL/HWG HX4 ...168 F7
  HIPP HX3 ...146 C2
  LDSU LS2 ...9 J2
Maud La OT LS21 ...23 J2
Maud Pl BEE/HOL LS11 ...131 K3
Maudsley St BFDE BD3 ...5 L7
  WKFDE WF1 ...206 C4
Maufe Wy ILK LS29 ...38 D3
Maureen St WHIT OL12 ...206 C4
Maurice Av BRIG HD6 ...170 C1
Mavis Av BHP/TINH LS16 ...64 A8
Mavis Gv BHP/TINH LS16 ...86 A1
Mavis La BHP/TINH LS16 ...64 A8
Mavis Rd DEWS WF13 ...173 H3
Mavis St BFDE BD3 ...5 L5
  DEWS WF13 ...173 J8

Mawcroft Cl YEA LS19 ...84 C1
Mawcroft Grange Dr YEA LS19 ...84 C1
Mawfield Rd DOD/DAR S75 ...260 B2
Mawfield MILN OL16 ...228 D3
Mawson St SHPY BD18 ...82 B6
Maw St BOW BD4 ...127 H1
Maxwell Av DEWS WF13 ...173 J4
Maxwell Rd ILK LS29 ...126 B6
  WBSY BD6 ...126 B6
Maxwell St FEA/AMT WF7 ...201 L1
  MOR LS27 ...152 B3
May Av CUL/QBY BD13 ...103 G8
Mayberry Dr DOD/DAR S75 ...259 H5
Maybury Av HOR/CROF WF4 ...198 C6
May Bush Rd WKFDE WF1 ...13 K9
May Day Gn BSLY S70 ...261 H5
May Day Green Ar BSLY S70 * ...261 H5
Mayfair WBOW BD5 ...126 F2
Mayfair Av GTL/HWG HX4 ...190 B4
Mayfair Pl HEM/SK/SE WF9 ...223 M7
Mayfair Wy BOW BD4 ...127 M1
Mayfield BSLYN/ROY S71 ...261 K2
  STKB/PEN S36 ...271 K5
Mayfield Av BRIG HD6 ...148 D6
  HFAX HX1 ...10 C8
  HUDE HD5 ...193 H8
  ILK LS29 ...38 F2
  LM/WK BD12 ...148 E3
Mayfield Cl AIRE BD20 ...34 E8
  ILK LS29 ...38 F2
Mayfield Ct OSS WF5 ...197 G3
Mayfield Dr AIRE BD20 ...58 E6
  DOD/DAR S75 ...242 A7
  HIPP HX3 ...146 A4
Mayfield Gdns HFAX HX1 ...10 C8
  ILK LS29 ...38 F1
  OSS WF5 ...174 E6
Mayfield Gv BAIL BD17 ...82 F3
  BRIG HD6 ...148 D6
  HFAX HX1 ...10 C8
  HUDE HD5 ...193 H8
  WIL/AL BD15 ...80 D8
Mayfield Pl HFAX HX1 ...10 C8
  LM/WK BD12 ...148 E3
Mayfield Ri HOR/CROF WF4 ...222 C5
  LM/WK BD12 ...148 F3
Mayfield Rd HBR HX7 ...143 J2
  ILK LS29 ...38 E2
  KGHY BD21 ...2 E2
Mayfield St HFAX HX1 ...10 D8
  MILN OL16 ...206 D5
Mayfields Wy HEM/SK/SE WF9 ...246 D5
Mayfield Ter CLAY BD14 ...125 L2
  HFAX HX1 ...10 B5
  LM/WK BD12 ...148 E3
  MILN OL16 ...206 D5
Mayfield Ter South HFAX HX1 * ...10 D8
Mayfield Vw LM/WK BD12 ...148 F3
Mayflower St BSLYN/ROY S71 ...261 M4
Maylea Dr OT LS21 ...40 F8
Mayman La BTLY WF17 ...173 K1
Maynes Cl EARL WF12 ...195 M4
Mayo Av WBOW BD5 ...126 F5
Mayo Cl RHAY LS8 ...88 F8
Mayo Crs WBOW BD5 ...127 G5
Mayo Dr WBOW BD5 ...127 G5
Mayo Gv WBOW BD5 ...127 G5
Mayo Rd WBOW BD5 ...127 G5
Mayors Wk CAS WF10 ...159 G7
Mayor's Walk Av PONT WF8 ...180 F7
Mayor's Walk Cl PONT WF8 ...180 F7
Maypole Rd HUDN HD2 ...192 E3
Mayster Gv BRIG HD6 ...170 A7
Mayster Rd BRIG HD6 ...170 A7
May St CLECK BD19 ...149 M6
  HUDS HD4 ...213 M2
  HWTH BD22 ...78 F8
  KGHY BD21 ...3 H2
May Ter BSLY S70 ...260 E5
  OSM LS9 ...110 B8
Maythorne Cl BTLY WF17 ...173 J3
Maythorne Crs CLAY BD14 ...125 M2
Maythorne Dr CLAY BD14 ...125 M1
May Tree Cl CLAY BD14 ...125 M1
Mayville Av AIRE BD20 ...58 D6
  HDGY LS6 ...109 G3
Mayville Pl HDGY LS6 ...109 G3
Mayville Rd HDGY LS6 ...109 G3
Mayville St HDGY LS6 ...108 F3
Mayville Ter HDGY LS6 ...109 G3
Mazebrook Av CLECK BD19 ...150 A4
Mazebrook Crs CLECK BD19 ...150 A4
McBride Wy WBY LS22 ...48 B1
McLaren Av HEM/SK/SE WF9 ...225 M6
McLaren Flds BRAM LS13 ...107 M4
McLintock Wy BSLY S70 ...260 F5
McMahon Dr CUL/QBY BD13 ...125 L4
McMillan Gdns WBSY BD6 ...126 F7
McNaught St MILN OL16 ...206 D8
Mead Cl MSTN/BAR LS15 ...112 A4
The Meade GFTH/SHER LS25 ...113 H7
Mead Gv MSTN/BAR LS15 ...112 A4
Meadow Bank DEWS WF13 ...173 H6
  FEA/AMT WF7 ...202 C5
  HOR/CROF WF4 ...222 E5
Meadowbank Av WIL/AL BD15 ...103 K5
Meadow Bank Crs MIRF WF14 ...194 A1
Meadow Bottom Rd TOD OL14 ...141 M4
Meadow Brook Cl NORM WF6 ...178 F1
Meadow Cl AIRE BD20 ...34 B3
  AL/HA/HU LS17 ...67 M1
  BGLY BD16 ...80 D5
  BSPA/BRAM LS23 ...48 E6
  BTLY WF17 ...151 J5
  HIPP HX3 ...125 M8
  LVSG WF15 ...172 D3
  WKFDE WF1 ...176 F1
Meadow Crs BSLYN/ROY S71 ...243 M3
  CUD/GR S72 ...245 H7
  HIPP HX3 ...146 A4
Meadow Cft AIRE BD20 ...34 B3
  BGLY BD16 * ...80 D5
  BEE/HOL LS11 ...131 H5
  CUD/GR S72 ...244 E5
  GTL/HWG HX4 ...189 K2
  HEM/SK/SE WF9 ...245 M1
  HUDN HD2 ...193 H1
  HWTH BD22 ...57 G8
  WKFDE WF1 ...176 F1
Meadow Croft Cl IDLE BD10 ...83 H5
Meadowcroft Cl WKFDE WF1 * ...176 F1
Meadowcroft Crs CAS WF10 ...158 C6
Meadowcroft Ms CAS WF10 ...158 C6
  OSM LS9 * ...9 M2
Meadowcroft Ri WBOW BD5 ...127 J4
Meadowcroft Rd WKFDE WF1 ...176 F1
Meadow Dr BSLYN/ROY S71 ...261 M2

HIPP HX3 ...146 A4
LVSG WF15 ...172 B5
Meadow End BHP/TINH LS16 ...64 A4
Meadowfield MILN OL16 ...228 D3
Meadowfield Cl
  HEM/SK/SE WF9 * ...223 J4
Meadowfield Ri
  EARD/LOFT WF3 ...155 K8
Meadowfields Cl
  HOR/CROF WF4 ...200 C6
Meadowfields Dr
  HOR/CROF WF4 ...200 C6
Meadow Garth BHP/TINH LS16 ...64 B4
  TAD LS24 ...72 A1
  WKFDE WF1 ...176 E1
Meadowgate OSS WF5 ...174 E7
Meadowgate Cft
  EARD/LOFT WF3 ...154 D4
Meadowgate Dr
  EARD/LOFT WF3 ...154 D5
Meadowgate V
  EARD/LOFT WF3 ...154 D5
Meadow Gn MAR/SLWT HD7 ...212 F6
Meadowhurst Gdns
  PDSY/CALV LS28 ...106 F7
Meadowland Ri CUD/GR S72 ...262 E1
Meadowlands CLECK BD19 ...149 G5
Meadow La AIRE BD20 ...34 B3
  BEE/HOL LS11 ...14 E7
  DEWS WF13 ...173 L5
  DOD/DAR S75 ...242 A7
  HIPP HX3 ...146 A4
  LVSG WF15 ...172 B5
  MAR/SLWT HD7 ...212 B5
  ROY/SHW OL2 ...229 J3
  WKFDW/WTN WF2 ...176 B7
Meadow Lea AIRE BD20 ...34 E8
Meadow Pk HUDE HD5 ...193 K4
Meadow Park Crs
  PDSY/CALV LS28 ...106 D4
Meadow Park Dr
  PDSY/CALV LS28 ...106 D4
Meadow Ri HEM/SK/SE WF9 ...223 J4
  ROY/SHW OL2 ...229 J5
  SKP/WHF BD23 ...16 D7
Meadow Rd BEE/HOL LS11 ...8 F5
  BSLYN/ROY S71 ...243 M3
  CAS WF10 ...179 K1
  GFTH/SHER LS25 ...113 J7
  IDLE BD10 ...84 A6
Meadowside MILN OL16 ...229 L2
Meadows Morvern
  HEM/SK/SE WF9 ...224 B7
The Meadows BHP/TINH LS16 ...86 B5
  CAS WF10 ...135 H8
  GFTH/SHER LS25 ...138 A3
  GFTH/SHER LS25 ...138 D6
  KBTN HD8 ...257 H1
  WBOW BD5 ...126 E5
Meadow St BSLYN/ROY S71 ...261 M4
  HUDS HD4 ...191 M7
The Meadow SCFT LS14 ...67 M6
Meadow V HOR/CROF WF4 ...218 F1
  WKFDE WF1 ...176 E1
Meadow Va AL/HA/HU LS17 ...87 J1
Meadow Vw GFTH/SHER LS25 ...116 B6
  HDGY LS6 ...109 G3
  HWTH BD22 ...78 B8
  KBTN HD8 ...239 K5
  LM/WK BD12 ...148 E5
  MSTN/BAR LS15 ...91 C6
  OSS WF5 ...197 G3
  STKB/PEN S36 ...258 D8
  WBOW BD5 ...126 E5
Meadow Wk CHAL LS7 ...88 A8
  HEM/SK/SE WF9 ...224 F3
  HIPP HX3 ...146 A4
  LIT OL15 ...207 H1
Meadow Wy AL/HA/HU LS17 ...87 J1
  CAS WF10 ...158 C6
  EARD/LOFT WF3 ...152 F7
  FEA/AMT WF7 ...202 C5
  TAD LS24 ...72 A2
Mead Rd MSTN/BAR LS15 ...112 A4
Meadstead Dr BSLYN/ROY S71 ...243 K3
Mead St HUDN HD2 ...14 F1
Mead Vw BOW BD4 * ...128 A3
Mead Wy KBTN HD8 ...216 A7
  MSTN/BAR LS15 ...112 A4
Meadway FEA/AMT WF7 ...178 F6
  WBSY BD6 ...126 B8
Meagill Ri OT LS21 ...40 F4
Meal Hill La HOLM/MEL HD9 ...255 H4
  MAR/SLWT HD7 ...212 B4
Meal Hill Rd HOLM/MEL HD9 ...253 H5
Mean La HOLM/MEL HD9 ...235 C4
  MAR/SLWT HD7 ...233 H5
Meanwood Cl CHAL LS7 ...6 F1
Meanwood Gv HDGY LS6 ...87 G5
Meanwood Rd CHAL LS7 ...7 J5
  HDGY LS6 ...87 H4
Meanwood Valley Cl CHAL LS7 ...87 H8
Meanwood Valley Dr CHAL LS7 ...87 H8
Meanwood Valley Gn CHAL LS7 ...87 H8
Meanwood Valley Gv CHAL LS7 ...87 H8
Meanwood Valley Mt CHAL LS7 ...87 H8
Mearclough Rd RPDN/SBR HX6 ...167 M2
Mears Cl STKB/PEN S36 ...271 C3
Medway PDSY/CALV LS28 ...106 E4
Medhurst Av GFTH/SHER LS25 ...135 K4
Medina Wy DOD/DAR S75 ...260 A1
Medley La HIPP HX3 ...147 H2
Medley St CAS WF10 ...158 A7
  WHIT OL12 ...206 B5
Medlock Rd HOR/CROF WF4 ...197 J5
Medway CUL/QBY BD13 ...125 K2
  HUDE HD5 * ...193 K4
Medway Av GFTH/SHER LS25 ...135 J1
Medway Cl DOD/DAR S75 ...260 B1
Medway Rd ROY/SHW OL2 ...229 J6
Meeting House La
  MAR/SLWT HD7 ...212 C2
Megasson Gv WBOW BD5 ...126 E2
Meg La HUDW HD3 ...213 K1
Megnaway WBOW BD5 ...127 G2
Melba Rd WBOW BD5 ...126 D3
Melbourne Av
  WKFDW/WTN WF2 ...176 B3
Melbourne Cl ROCH OL11 ...228 A6
Melbourne Gv BFDE BD3 ...106 A6
  BRAM LS13 ...107 L4
Melbourne Ms
  WKFDW/WTN WF2 ...176 A2
Melbourne Pl WBOW BD5 ...4 D3
Melbourne Rd ROCH OL11 ...228 C4
  TOD OL14 ...163 J5
  WKFDE WF1 ...176 F1
Melbourne St HBR HX7 ...143 H3
  HIPP HX3 ...10 D1
  LDSU LS2 ...10 A1
  LVSG WF15 ...172 D3
  MOR LS27 ...152 B3
  PDSY/CALV LS28 ...106 F4
Melcombe Wk BOW BD4 ...128 A2
Meldon Wy WBOW BD5 ...125 L5
Melford Cl DOD/DAR S75 ...242 D5
Melford Ri DOD/DAR S75 ...260 C5
Mellor Brook MAR/SLWT HD7 ...212 B2
Mellor La HOLM/MEL HD9 ...253 K2

Mellor Mill La GTL/HWG HX4 ...190 D2
Mellor St BRIG HD6 * ...170 C4
  HFAX HX1 ...168 C1
Mellwood La HEM/SK/SE WF9 ...247 G3
Melrose Av WLIT OL15 ...185 J7
Melrose Cl HUDE HD5 ...193 H8
Melrose Dr ILK LS29 ...40 A4
Melrose Gv HORS LS18 ...86 A6
Melrose Pl HORS LS18 ...85 M6
  PDSY/CALV LS28 ...106 F8
Melrose St GTHN BD7 ...126 C2
  HIPP HX3 ...10 D1
Melrose Ter ELL HX5 * ...169 H8
Melrose Wk HORS LS18 ...85 M6
Melrose Wy BSLYN/ROY S71 ...261 M4
Meltham House La
  HOLM/MEL HD9 ...255 H2
Meltham Mills Rd
  HOLM/MEL HD9 ...235 H4
Meltham Rd HOLM/MEL HD9 ...235 L3
  HUDS HD4 ...213 L7
  MAR/SLWT HD7 ...233 K7
Melton Av MID LS10 ...154 B2
Melton Cl HEM/SK/SE WF9 ...247 J1
  MID LS10 ...154 B1
Melton Garth MID LS10 ...154 B2
Melton Ms HWTH BD22 ...78 F7
Melton Rd HOR/CROF WF4 ...220 C2
Melton St BTLY WF17 ...151 K8
Melton Ter IDLE BD10 ...106 A1
Melton Wy BSLYN/ROY S71 ...243 L1
  LVSG WF15 ...172 B5
Melville Cl HDGY LS6 ...6 E5
Melville Gdns HDGY LS6 ...6 E5
Melville Gv ILK LS29 ...39 G2
Melville Pl HDGY LS6 ...6 E5
Melville Rd HDGY LS6 ...6 E6
Melville St GTHN BD7 ...126 C2
Melvinia Crs CUD/GR S72 ...260 F2
Memorial Dr HDGY LS6 ...87 H7
Mendip Av HUDW HD3 ...191 J5
Mendip Rd DOD/DAR S75 ...260 C1
  GFTH/SHER LS25 ...135 H1
Mendip Dr MILN OL16 ...207 H8
Mendip Rd EARL WF12 ...174 B5
Mendips Cl ROY/SHW OL2 ...229 H6
Mendip Wy LM/WK BD12 ...126 D8
Menin Dr BAIL BD17 ...82 F1
Menston Dr ILK LS29 ...61 J3
Menston Old La ILK LS29 ...40 B8
Mentmore Rd MILN OL16 ...206 F7
Mercer Cl HUDS HD4 ...213 L7
Merchants Quay OSM LS9 * ...9 K2
Merchants Wy MSTN/BAR LS15 ...112 A3
Mercia Wy MSTN/BAR LS15 ...112 A3
Mercury Rw OT LS21 ...41 J7
Merefield Av ROCH OL11 ...228 A1
Merefield Rd ROCH OL11 ...228 A1
Merefield St ROCH OL11 ...228 A1
Merefield Ter ROCH OL11 * ...228 A1
Mere La ROCH OL11 ...228 B1
Mere St ROCH OL11 ...206 B9
Merewood Rd CAS WF10 ...180 A1
Meriden Av GFTH/SHER LS25 ...135 H1
Merinall Cl MILN OL16 ...206 F7
Merlin Cl AWLS/ASK DN6 ...249 K8
  HEM/SK/SE WF9 ...247 J4
  LIT OL15 ...207 J4
  MOR LS27 ...152 D3
Merlin Ct BTLY WF17 ...151 H6
  HUDS HD4 ...214 A7
  KGHY BD21 * ...2 F5
Merlin Gv CIR BD8 ...103 L7
Merlin Rd MILN OL16 ...207 J4
Merlinwood Dr BAIL BD17 ...82 F2
Merlyn-Rees Av MOR LS27 ...152 C2
Merrion HIPP HX3 ...11 M9
Merrion Pl LDS LS1 ...7 H8
Merrion St LDSU LS2 ...7 G8
Merrion Wy LDSU LS2 ...7 G7
Merrivale Rd WIL/AL BD15 ...103 J6
Merrybank La AL/HA/HU LS17 ...43 K1
Merry Bent La RPDN/SBR HX6 ...188 D3
Merrybents St TOD OL14 ...163 M1
Merrydale Rd BOW BD4 ...127 J8
Merryman Hall MILN OL16 * ...206 D4
Merton Av PDSY/CALV LS28 ...106 F4
Merton Cl GFTH/SHER LS25 ...135 L4
Merton Dr PDSY/CALV LS28 ...106 E4
Merton Fold WBOW BD5 ...127 G6
Merton Gdns PDSY/CALV LS28 ...106 E4
Merton Rd GTHN BD7 ...4 D8
Merton St HUD HD1 ...14 D8
Merville Av BAIL BD17 ...82 E1
Metcalfe St BOW BD4 ...127 K2
Methley Dr CHAL LS7 ...87 M8
Methley Gv CHAL LS7 ...87 L8
Methley La CHAL LS7 ...87 M8
  RTHW LS26 ...156 A2
Methley Mt CHAL LS7 ...87 M8
Methley Pl CHAL LS7 ...87 L8
Methley Rd CAS WF10 ...157 J6
Methley St CUD/GR S72 ...244 D8
Methley Ter CHAL LS7 ...87 L8
Methley Vw CHAL LS7 ...87 M8
Metro Gv LM/WK BD12 ...148 E5
Mews Ct FEA/AMT WF7 ...201 M1
The Mews NORM WF6 ...178 D3
Mexborough Av CHAL LS7 ...90 B1
Mexborough Dr CHAL LS7 ...7 J1
Mexborough Gv CHAL LS7 ...7 J1
Mexborough Pl CHAL LS7 ...7 J1
Mexborough Rd CHAL LS7 ...7 K2
Mexborough St CHAL LS7 ...7 J1
Meynell Ap BEE/HOL LS11 ...155 G1
Meynell Ct MSTN/BAR LS15 ...111 M7
Meynell Hts BEE/HOL LS11 ...8 D6
Meynell La MSTN/BAR LS15 ...111 M8
Meynell Mt RTHW LS26 ...155 H1
Meynell Rd MSTN/BAR LS15 ...111 M8
Meynell Sq BEE/HOL LS11 ...8 D6
Meynell Wk BEE/HOL LS11 ...8 D6
Meyrick Av WBY LS22 ...30 C8
Meyrick Dr DOD/DAR S75 ...241 M7
Miall St HFAX HX1 ...10 C4
  ROCH OL11 ...206 C9
Michael Av EARD/LOFT WF3 ...155 J7
Michael Rd BSLYN/ROY S71 ...262 A4
Michael's Est CUD/GR S72 ...245 J7
Mickelden Wy DOD/DAR S75 ...260 C5
Mickle Ct CAS WF10 ...157 L7
Mickledore Cl GTHN BD7 * ...126 A8
Mickledore Ct GTHN BD7 ...126 A3
Mickledore Rdg GTHN BD7 ...126 A3
Micklefield Ct YEA LS19 ...84 D2
Micklefield La YEA LS19 ...84 D2
Micklefield Ms YEA LS19 * ...84 D2
Micklefield Rd YEA LS19 ...84 D2
Micklegate PONT WF8 ...180 F5
Micklemoss Dr CUL/QBY BD13 ...124 E4
Micklethwaite Dr
  CUL/QBY BD13 ...125 G6
Micklethwaite La BGLY BD16 ...59 G8
Micklethwaite Rd
  HOR/CROF WF4 ...220 B3
Micklethwaite Vw WBY LS22 ...48 A2

Mickletown Rd *RTHW* LS26 ......156 E3
Mickley St *CAS* WF10 ......108 E7
Middlebrook Cl *GIR* BD8 ......104 A7
Middlebrook Crs *GIR* BD8 ......103 M8
Middlebrook Dr *GIR* BD8 ......103 M7
Middlebrook Hl *GIR* BD8 ......103 M7
Middlebrook Ri *GIR* BD8 ......103 M7
Middlebrook Vw *GIR* BD8 ......104 A7
Middlebrook Wk *GIR* BD8 ......104 A7
Middlebrook Wy *GIR* BD8 ......103 M8
Middleburn St *BSLY* S70 ......261 J7
Middlecliffe Dr *STKB/PEN* S36 ......268 F1
Middlecliff La *CUD/GR* S72 ......263 L6
Middlecroft Cl *MID* LS10 ......132 B6
Middlecroft Rd *MID* LS10 ......132 B6
Middle Cross St *WOR/ARM* LS12 ......108 F7
Middle Dean St *GTL/HWG* HX4 ......168 C7
Middlefield La *HOR/CROF* WF4 ......220 B8
Middle Field La *PONT* WF8 ......226 E1
Middle Field Rd *DEWS* WF13 ......173 J5
Middlegate *BTLY* WF17 ......151 G6
Middlegate Ct *BOW* BD4 ......127 K6
Middle Hall Cl *LVSG* WF15 ......172 B3
Middleham Ct *BOW* BD4 * 128 A3
Middleham Moor
  EARD/LOFT WF3 ......154 C3
  MID LS10 ......153 M3
Middle Hl *WHIT* OL12 ......206 A5
Middle La *BDAN* BD14 ......125 L1
  HOR/CROF WF4 ......200 A1
  KNOT WF11 ......182 C3
  WBY LS22 ......47 L4
Middlemoor *SCFT* LS14 ......89 K6
Middle Oxford St *CAS* WF10 ......157 L7
Middle Rd *DEWS* WF13 ......173 K7
  EARL WF12 ......174 A7
Middlesex St *BSLY* S70 ......261 H1
Middle St *RPDN/SBR* HX6 ......167 G4
Middlethorne Cl *AL/HA/HU* LS17 ......88 D2
Middlethorne Ct
  AL/HA/HU LS17 ......88 C1
Middlethorne Ms
  AL/HA/HU LS17 ......88 D1
Middlethorne Ri
  AL/HA/HU LS17 ......88 C2
Middleton Av *ILK* LS29 ......38 D1
  OSM LS9 ......110 B5
  RTHW LS26 ......154 C1
Middleton Cl *MOR* LS27 ......152 D2
Middleton Ct *LVSG* WF15 ......172 A2
Middleton Gv *BEE/HOL* LS11 ......131 L5
  MOR LS27 * 152 D2
Middleton La *MID* LS10 ......153 M4
  RTHW LS26 ......154 C1
Middleton Park Av *MID* LS10 ......153 L2
Middleton Park Crs *MID* LS10 ......153 L2
Middleton Park Gn *MID* LS10 ......153 L2
Middleton Park Gv *MID* LS10 ......153 L2
Middleton Park Mt *MID* LS10 ......153 L2
Middleton Park Pl *MID* LS10 ......153 L2
Middleton Park Rd *MID* LS10 ......153 L1
Middleton Park Ter *MID* LS10 ......153 L2
Middleton Rd *ILK* LS29 ......38 C2
  MID LS10 ......132 A5
  MOR LS27 ......152 A5
Middleton St *GIR* BD8 ......104 D5
Middleton Ter *MOR* LS27 ......152 D2
Middleton Wy *KNOT* WF11 ......182 B2
Middleway *AIRE* BD20 ......36 B5
Middle Wy *KGHY* BD21 ......3 L4
Middle Wood La *WHIT* OL12 ......185 G8
Middlewoods *DOD/DAR* S75 ......260 C7
Midge Hall Cl *ILK* LS29 ......40 A5
Midgeham Gv *BGLY* BD16 ......80 C5
Midgehole Rd *HBR* HX7 ......121 J8
Midgley Gdns *HDGY* LS6 ......6 D2
Midgley Pl *HDGY* LS6 ......6 E2
Midgley Ri *PONT* WF8 ......180 F3
  ILK LS29 ......40 A5
Midgley St *COL* BB8 ......74 E2
Midgley Ter *HDGY* LS6 ......6 E2
Midge Wy *DOD/DAR* S75 ......260 C5
Midhurst Dr *DOD/DAR* S75 ......260 A1
Midhurst St *ROCH* OL11 ......228 B1
Midland Cl *MID* LS10 ......132 B3
Midland Garth *MID* LS10 ......9 M9
Midland Hl *BGLY* BD16 ......81 H3
Midland Pas *HDGY* LS6 ......6 D2
Midland Rd *BAIL* BD17 ......82 F4
  BSLYN/ROY S71 ......243 M2
  GIR BD8 ......104 F4
  HDGY LS6 ......6 B2
  HTON BD9 ......104 E1
  MID LS10 ......132 A3
  PONT WF8 ......181 G5
Midland St *BSLY* S70 ......261 H4
  HUD HD1 ......15 G2
  RTHW LS26 ......133 L8
  SKP/WHF BD23 ......16 A3
Midland Ter *ECHL* BD2 ......104 F4
  HTON BD9 ......104 E1
  KGHY BD21 * 3 G2
Mid Point *BFDE* BD3 ......106 B6
Midway *HUDS* HD4 ......213 J8
Midway Av *BGLY* BD16 ......81 J7
Milan Rd *RHAY* LS8 ......110 D3
Milan St *RHAY* LS8 ......110 C3
Milbury Dr *LIT* OL15 ......207 J4
Milden Pl *BSLY* S70 ......261 J7
Mildred Sylvester Wy
  NORM WF6 ......179 G4
Mile Cross Gdns *HFAX* HX1 ......146 A8
Mile Cross Pl *HFAX* HX1 ......146 A8
Mile Cross Rd *HFAX* HX1 ......146 A8
Mile Cross Ter *HFAX* HX1 ......146 A8
Mile End *HOLM/MEL* HD9 ......234 F5
Milefield La *CUD/GR* S72 ......245 G7
Milefield Vw *CUD/GR* S72 ......245 H7
Miles Garth *AL/HA/HU* LS17 ......47 H8
Miles Hill Av *CHAL* LS7 ......87 K5
Miles Hill Crs *BOW* BD4 ......127 L5
  CHAL LS7 ......87 K5
Miles Hill Gv *CHAL* LS7 ......87 K5
Miles Hill Mt *CHAL* LS7 ......87 K8
Miles Hill Pl *CHAL* LS7 ......87 K8
Miles Hill Rd *CHAL* LS7 ......87 K8
Miles Hill Sq *CHAL* LS7 ......87 K8
Miles Hill St *CHAL* LS7 ......87 K8
Miles Hill Ter *CHAL* LS7 ......87 K8
Miles Hill Vw *CHAL* LS7 ......87 K8
Mileswood *CUD/GR* S72 ......263 M3
Mile Thorn St *HFAX* HX1 ......10 B6
Milford Crs *LIT* OL15 ......185 L4
Milford Gv *BRIG* BD19 ......150 C3
Milford Pl *BULY* LS4 ......108 F5
  HTON BD9 ......104 C3
Milford Rd *GFTH/SHER* LS25 ......138 A2
Milford St *HUD* HD1 ......14 F9
  WHIT OL12 ......206 B5
Milgate St *BSLYN/ROY* S71 ......243 J5
Milkstone Pl *ROCH* OL11 * 206 B8
Milkstone Rd *ROCH* OL11 ......206 B8
Milk St *WBOW* BD5 206
Millars Wk *HEM/SK/SE* WF9 ......246 C5
Mill Av *HUDE* HD5 ......193 J7
Millbank *PDSY/CALV* LS28 ......107 H8
Mill Bank Cl *RPDN/SBR* HX6 ......166 E7

Millbank Ct *PDSY/CALV* LS28 ......129 H1
Mill Bank Rd *HOLM/MEL* HD9 ......235 G5
  RPDN/SBR HX6 ......
Mill Banks *AIRE* BD20 ......36 A6
Millbeck Ap *MOR* LS27 ......152 E2
Millbeck Cl *GIR* BD8 ......103 L8
Millbeck Dr *BGLY* BD16 ......80 C5
Millbrae Gdns *ROY/SHW* OL2 ......229 H1
Mill Br *SKP/WHF* BD23 ......16 B2
Millbrook Gdns *DEWS* WF13 ......173 J4
Mill Carr Hill Rd *BOW* BD4 ......127 K8
Mill Chase Cft
  WKFDW/WTN WF2 ......12 A3
Mill Chase Rd
  WKFDW/WTN WF2 ......12 A3
Mill Ct *FEA/AMT* WF7 ......202 C8
Millcroft *EARD/LOFT* WF3 ......154 F8
  OT LS21 ......42 F7
Millcroft La *UPML* OL3 ......231 H8
Mill Croft Ri *EARD/LOFT* WF3 ......155 G8
Mill Dam *BSPA/BRAM* LS23 ......70 A1
Milldale Cl *BOW* BD4 ......127 J7
Mill Dam *PONT* WF8 ......181 G7
Millenium Ct *PDSY/CALV* LS28 * 107 H6
Millennium Rd *AIRE* BD20 ......
Millennium Sq *LDS* LS1 ......9 J2
Millennium Wy *BEE/HOL* LS11 ......131 K5
Miller Av *WKFDW/WTN* WF2 ......198 F4
Miller Ct *WKFDW/WTN* WF2 ......220 D3
Miller Garth *FEA/AMT* WF7 ......224 C1
Millergate *BFD* BD1 ......4 E6
Millers Ct *LVSG* WF15 ......172 D4
Millers Cft *BTLY* WF17 ......151 K5
Millers Dale *AMT* WF7 ......202 C8
Millers Dl *MOR* LS27 ......130 D8
Millersdale Cl *BOW* BD4 ......127 J7
Mill Farm Dr *WKFDW/WTN* WF2 ......220 E2
Millfield Cl *HUDW* HD3 ......191 H7
Millfield Crs *PONT* WF8 ......180 E8
Mill Field Rd *BGLY* BD16 ......81 K7
Millfield Gv *MILN* OL16 ......206 D8
Millfield Rd *HOR/CROF* WF4 ......197 L8
Millfields *AIRE* BD20 ......35 M5
  OSS WF5 ......196 E1
Mill Fold Gdns *LIT* OL15 ......207 G7
Mill Fold Wy *RPDN/SBR* HX6 ......188 F2
Mill Forest Wy *BTLY* WF17 ......174 B2
Mill Garth *MOR* LS27 ......129 M7
Mill Garth St *WBY* LS22 ......47 K6
Millgarth St *LDSU* LS2 ......7 J9
Millgate *ELL* HX5 ......169 F7
  FEA/AMT WF7 ......224 C1
  HUD HD1 ......14 A9
  HUDS HD4 ......215 K4
Mill Ga *MILN* OL16 ......206 D4
Mill Grath *PONT* WF8 ......180 E7
Mill Gn *BEE/HOL* LS11 ......8 A4
Mill Green Cl *SCFT* LS14 ......111 K1
Mill Green Gdns *SCFT* LS14 ......111 K1
Mill Green Garth *SCFT* LS14 * 111 K1
Mill Green Rd *SCFT* LS14 ......111 K1
Mill Green Vw *SCFT* LS14 ......111 K1
Mill Gv *BRIG* HD6 ......170 B2
Millhaven Ms *GIR* BD8 ......104 E4
Mill Hey *WHIT* BD22 ......78 F7
Mill Hl *FEA/AMT* WF7 ......202 C6
  HWTH BD22 ......78 E7
  LDS LS1 ......9 G1
Mill Hill Av *PONT* WF8 ......180 D7
Mill Hill La *PONT* WF8 ......203 M1
Mill Hill Sq *RTHW* LS26 ......155 G1
Mill Hill Top *BGLY* BD16 ......80 D6
Mill House Cl *WHIT* OL12 ......206 F2
Mill House La *RPDN/SBR* HX6 ......167 H4
Millhouse La *STKB/PEN* S36 ......269 M3
Mill House Ri *BOW* BD4 * 127 K5
Milligan Av *ECHL* BD2 * 105 H1
Milligan Ct *BGLY* BD16 ......80 C5
Milligans Pl *AIRE* BD20 * 34 F7
Mill La *AIRE* BD20 ......16 B8
  AIRE BD20 ......56 E1
  AL/HA/HU LS17 ......68 A2
  AWLS/ASK DN6 ......249 H4
  AWLS/ASK DN6 ......249 K8
  BIRK/DRI BD11 ......128 C8
  BOW BD4 ......129 J3
  BRAM LS13 ......107 J3
  BRIG HD6 ......170 D4
  BSPA/BRAM LS23 ......49 G6
  BTLY WF17 ......151 G6
  BTLY WF17 ......173 M2
  CAS WF10 ......157 M5
  CAS WF10 ......178 F2
  CLECK BD19 ......149 M3
  COP/BISH YO23 ......33 M1
  CUL/OBY BD13 ......124 E4
  DOD/DAR S75 ......242 A5
  EARD/LOFT WF3 ......153 M6
  EARL WF12 ......174 C7
  FEA/AMT WF7 ......178 F8
  FEA/AMT WF7 ......178 F8
  GFTH/SHER LS25 ......138 A2
  GSLY LS20 ......60 F6
  GTL/HWG HX4 ......190 E2
  HEM/SK/SE WF9 ......246 C5
  HEM/SK/SE WF9 ......247 K2
  HIPP HX3 ......146 D4
  HOR/CROF WF4 ......217 M3
  HOR/CROF WF4 ......221 K1
  HOR/CROF WF4 ......221 K7
  HUDE HD5 ......193 K1
  HWTH BD22 ......78 C3
  HWTH BD22 ......100 E3
  LUD/ILL HX2 ......123 G3
  LUD/ILL HX2 ......145 G3
  MOR LS27 ......152 A3
  OT LS21 ......41 J6
  OT LS21 ......41 M6
  PBR HG3 ......26 F2
  PBR HG3 ......28 E3
  PONT WF8 ......181 H3
  RTHW LS26 ......156 F3
  SKP/WHF BD23 ......16 E2
  STKB/PEN S36 ......256 F6
  STKB/PEN S36 ......270 B3
  TAD LS24 ......71 L6
  TAD LS24 ......71 M2

  TAD LS24 ......95 M4
  WBOW BD5 ......127 G1
  WBY LS22 ......46 A3
  WBY LS22 ......47 M3
Millmoor Cl *HTON* BD9 ......103 M4
Mill Nook OL12 ......206 B3
Millom Cl *MILN* OL16 ......206 E5
Mill Pk *MIRF* WF14 ......194 B4
Mill Pit La *RTHW* LS26 ......132 F3
Mill Pond Cl *HDGY* LS6 ......87 G8
Mill Pond Gv *HDGY* LS6 ......87 G8
Mill Pond La *HDGY* LS6 ......87 G8
Mill Pond Sq *HDGY* LS6 ......87 G8
Mill Race Fold *HOLM/MEL* HD9 ......236 E6
Mill Rd *DEWS* WF13 ......173 L4
Mill Rw *AIRE* BD20 ......35 H8
Mill Royd St *BRIG* HD6 ......170 D4
Millshaw *BEE/HOL* LS11 ......130 F5
Millshaw Mt *BEE/HOL* LS11 ......131 G6
Millshaw Park Av *MOR* LS27 ......130 F6
Millshaw Park Ln *BEE/HOL* LS11 ......130 F6
Millshaw Park La
  BEE/HOL LS11 ......130 F5
Millshaw Park Wy
  BEE/HOL LS11 ......130 F5
Millside *CUD/GR* S72 ......244 D3
Millside Wk *CUD/GR* S72 ......244 E3
Millside Wy *HIPP* HX3 ......168 F3
Millstone Cl *FEA/AMT* WF7 ......224 C1
Millstone Ri *LVSG* WF15 ......172 D4
Millstones *STKB/PEN* S36 ......271 L5
Millstream Cl *AIRE* BD20 ......58 C5
Mill St *AIRE* BD20 ......56 A1
  BFD BD1 ......5 G4
  BTLY WF17 ......151 G6
  CAS WF10 ......157 K7
  CUL/OBY BD13 ......79 M8
  HEM/SK/SE WF9 ......246 C4
  HIPP HX3 ......168 C5
  HUDS HD4 ......214 A2
  MOR LS27 ......152 C3
  OSM LS9 ......11 G3
  WBSY BD6 ......126 C5
Mill St East *EARL* WF12 ......173 M8
Mill St West *EARL* WF12 ......173 M8
Mill Vw *HEM/SK/SE* WF9 ......223 L8
  ILK LS29 ......40 A4
  KNOT WF11 ......181 K2
  WKFDW/WTN WF2 ......175 M3
Millward St *HOR/CROF* WF4 ......222 C5
Millwater Av *EARL* WF12 ......195 K4
Millwood La *TOD* OL14 ......163 L1
Millwright Cl *MAR/SLWT* HD7 ......2 K7
Milne Ct *MSTN/BAR* LS15 ......111 M8
Milner Av *STKB/PEN* S36 ......270 D3
Milner Bank *OT* LS21 ......40 F8
Milner La *EARD/LOFT* WF3 ......154 C3
  GTL/HWG HX4 ......168 E7
  SCFT LS14 ......68 B6
  TAD LS24 ......93 J7
Milner Rd *BAIL* BD17 ......82 D5
Milner's La *PONT* WF8 ......205 M2
Milner's Rd *YEA* LS19 ......62 B8
Milner St *HFAX* HX1 ......10 E5
  HUDS HD4 ......214 A3
  OSS WF5 ......174 E5
Milner Wy *OSS* WF5 ......175 G5
Milne's Gv *CAS* WF10 ......158 D7
Milnes St *BSLY* S70 * 261 J6
  WOR/ARM LS12 ......109 G8
Milne St *DOD/DAR* S75 ......260 A2
  ROY/SHW OL2 ......229 K8
Milngate OL16 ......228 E3
Miln Rd *HUD* HD1 ......14 C2
Milnrow Rd *LIT* OL15 ......207 H4
  MILN OL16 ......206 D7
  ROY/SHW OL2 ......229 J6
Milnthorpe Cl *BSPA/BRAM* LS23 ......69 L3
Milnthorpe Crs
  WKFDW/WTN WF2 ......198 F7
Milnthorpe Dr
  WKFDW/WTN WF2 ......198 F6
Milnthorpe Gdns
  BSPA/BRAM LS23 ......69 L3
Milnthorpe Garth
  BSPA/BRAM LS23 ......69 L4
Milnthorpe Gn
  WKFDW/WTN WF2 ......198 E7
Milnthorpe La
  BSPA/BRAM LS23 ......69 L3
  WKFDW/WTN WF2 ......198 F7
Milnthorpe Wy
  BSPA/BRAM LS23 ......69 L3
Milroyd Crs *BTLY* WF17 ......151 J4
Milton Av *LVSG* WF15 ......172 E3
  RPDN/SBR HX6 ......167 L1
Milton Cl *HOR/CROF* WF4 ......197 M8
  LVSG WF15 ......172 E3
Milton Ct *EARD/LOFT* WF3 ......155 H8
Milton Crs *WKFDW/WTN* WF2 ......197 M3
Milton Dr *HEM/SK/SE* WF9 ......223 K4
  LVSG WF15 ......172 E4
  MSTN/BAR LS15 ......90 B7
Milton Gdns *LVSG* WF15 ......172 E3
Milton Gv *DEWS* WF13 ......173 L4
Milton Pl *HFAX* HX1 ......10 E4
  OSS WF5 ......174 F1
Milton Rd *AWLS/ASK* DN6 ......249 L5
  LVSG WF15 ......172 E3
  PBR HG3 ......26 F2
  WKFDW/WTN WF2 ......197 L2
Milton Sq *HECK* WF16 * 172 F2
Milton St *CAS* WF10 ......157 K7
  CUD/GR S72 ......263 M4
  CUL/OBY BD13 ......102 A6
  GTHN BD7 ......4 A7
  HECK WF16 ......172 F2
  MILN OL16 ......206 B6
  RPDN/SBR HX6 ......167 K1
  SKP/WHF BD23 ......16 C3
  WKFDW/WTN WF2 ......12 B4
Milton Ter *CLECK* BD19 ......149 G6
  HFAX HX1 ......10 E4
  KSTL LS5 ......108 C2
Minden Cl *PONT* WF8 ......180 D7
Minden Wy *PONT* WF8 ......180 D7
Minerva St *HUDS* HD4 ......213 H3
Minnie St *HWTH* BD22 ......78 B8
  KGHY BD21 ......2 E7
Minorca Mt *CUL/OBY* BD13 ......101 M5
Minster Dr *BOW* BD4 ......127 M1
Minster St *BSLYN/ROY* S71 ......261 M3
Minsthorpe La *HEM/SK/SE* WF9 ......225 J8
  HEM/SK/SE WF9 ......247 J1
Mint St *ECHL* BD2 ......105 K4
  HUD HD1 ......191 M7
Miramar *HUDN* HD2 ......192 F1
Mire Rdg *COL* BB8 ......74 C3

Mires La *TAD* LS24 ......94 F4
Mirey Butt La *KNOT* WF11 ......181 M3
Mirey La *RPDN/SBR* HX6 ......166 D3
Mirfield Av *ECHL* BD2 ......105 J1
Mirry La *WOR/ARM* LS12 ......108 A5
Miry La *HBR* HX7 ......144 B8
  HOLM/MEL HD9 ......236 B6
  MSTN/BAR LS15 ......91 H4
  YEA LS19 ......62 D7
Mission St *BRIG* HD6 ......170 E5
Mission Vw *HOLM/MEL* HD9 ......254 B5
The Mistal *IDLE* BD10 ......83 H6
Mistral Gv *LM/WK* BD12 ......148 C4
Mistral Gv *LVSG* WF15 ......171 K1
Mistress Ln *WOR/ARM* LS12 ......108 C5
Mitcham Dr *HTON* BD9 ......104 C4
Mitchell Av *HUDE* HD5 ......215 J1
Mitchell Cl *IDLE* BD10 ......83 L5
Mitchell Hey *WHIT* OL12 ......206 A7
Mitchell La *IDLE* BD10 ......83 L5
  IDLE BD10 ......83 L5
Mitchell Sq *WBOW* BD5 ......127 G2
Mitchell St *BRIG* HD6 ......170 C3
Mitchelson Av *DOD/DAR* S75 ......260 A7
Mitchel Sq *AIRE* BD20 ......36 A5
Mitford Pl *WOR/ARM* LS12 ......108 F7
Mitford Rd *WOR/ARM* LS12 ......108 F7
Mitford Ter *WOR/ARM* LS12 ......108 F7
Mitre Ct *BOW* BD4 ......127 M3
Mitre St *DEWS* WF13 ......173 J6
  HUD HD1 ......14 A4
Mixenden Cl *LUD/ILL* HX2 ......145 L1
Mixenden La *LUD/ILL* HX2 ......123 M8
Mixenden Rd *LUD/ILL* HX2 ......145 L1
Mizzy Rd *WHIT* OL12 ......206 A5
Moat Crs *IDLE* BD10 ......83 L6
Moat Hl *BTLY* WF17 ......151 J4
Moat Hill Farm Dr *BTLY* WF17 ......151 J4
Modder Av *WOR/ARM* LS12 ......108 D7
Modder Pl *WOR/ARM* LS12 ......108 D7
Model Av *WOR/ARM* LS12 ......108 F7
Model Rd *WOR/ARM* LS12 ......108 F7
Model Ter *WOR/ARM* LS12 ......108 F7
Modena Ct *WMB/DAR* S73 ......263 G8
Moderna Wy *HBR* HX7 ......144 B6
Moffat Cl *WBSY* BD6 ......126 B7
Moffatt Cl *LUD/ILL* HX2 ......146 B3
Moles Head *MAR/SLWT* HD7 ......190 B6
Molesworth St *MILN* OL16 ......206 C7
Molly Hurst La *HOR/CROF* WF4 ......220 D7
Mona St *DOD/DAR* S75 ......260 A4
  MAR/SLWT HD7 ......212 B5
  WKFDW/WTN WF2 ......176 A3
Monckton Dr *CAS* WF10 ......158 A8
Monckton Rd
  WKFDW/WTN WF2 ......198 C4
Mond Av *BFDE* BD3 ......105 M3
Monk Barn Cl *BGLY* BD16 * 81 J2
Monk Bridge Av *HDGY* LS6 ......87 G8
Monk Bridge Dr *HDGY* LS6 ......87 H8
Monk Bridge Gv *HDGY* LS6 ......87 H8
Monk Bridge Mt *HDGY* LS6 ......87 H8
Monk Bridge Pl *HDGY* LS6 ......87 H8
Monk Bridge Rd *HDGY* LS6 ......87 G8
Monk Bridge St *HDGY* LS6 ......87 H8
Monk Bridge Ter *HDGY* LS6 ......87 H8
Monkfield *MIRF* WF14 ......172 A8
Monkhill Av *PONT* WF8 ......180 E8
Monkhill Dr *PONT* WF8 ......180 E8
Monkhill La *PONT* WF8 ......180 E8
Monkhill Mt *PONT* WF8 ......180 D7
Monk Ings *BTLY* WF17 ......150 F5
Monk Ings Av *BTLY* WF17 ......150 E5
Monkmans Wharfe *AIRE* BD20 ......35 M5
Monks Cl *MILN* OL16 ......207 G8
Monk St *GTHN* BD7 ......4 C4
Monks Wy *BSLYN/ROY* S71 ......261 M3
Monkswood *KSTL* LS5 ......86 B5
Monkswood Av *SCFT* LS14 ......89 H6
Monkswood Bank *SCFT* LS14 ......89 H6
Monkswood Cl *SCFT* LS14 ......89 H6
Monkswood Dr *SCFT* LS14 ......89 H6
Monkswood Ga *SCFT* LS14 * 89 J6
Monkswood Gn *SCFT* LS14 ......89 H6
Monkswood Hl *SCFT* LS14 ......89 H6
Monkswood Ri *SCFT* LS14 ......89 H6
Monkswood Wk *SCFT* LS14 ......89 J6
Monk Ter *BSLYN/ROY* S71 ......262 A1
Monkton Wy *BSLYN/ROY* S71 ......243 A1
Monkwood Rd *WKFDE* WF1 ......176 D7
Monmouth St *COL* BB8 ......74 C1
  ROCH OL11 ......206 B8
Monsal Crs *BSLYN/ROY* S71 ......243 J7
Monson Av *PDSY/CALV* LS28 ......84 D3
Mons Rd *TOD* OL14 ......141 G7
Montague Av *RHAY* LS8 ......110 E1
Montague Crs *GFTH/SHER* LS25 ......113 J3
Montague Pl *GFTH/SHER* LS25 ......113 J3
Montague St *COL* BB8 ......52 A3
  CUD/GR S72 ......244 E6
  RPDN/SBR HX6 ......167 K1
  WBOW BD5 ......126 E3
Montagu Gdns *RHAY* LS8 ......110 E1
Montagu Gv *RHAY* LS8 ......110 E1
Montagu Pl *RHAY* LS8 ......110 D1
Montagu Rd *WBY* LS22 ......30 C8
Montagu St *RHAY* LS8 ......110 D2
Montagu Vw *RHAY* LS8 ......110 D1
Montcalm Crs *EARD/LOFT* WF3 ......177 H3
  MID LS10 ......132 A4
Monterey Dr *WIL/AL* BD15 ......103 H3
Montfort Cl *HORS* LS18 ......85 J3
Montgomery Av
  BHP/TINH LS16 ......86 E7
Montgomery St *SKP/WHF* BD23 ......16 C3
Montpelier Ter *HDGY* LS6 ......109 H2
Montreal Av *CHAL* LS7 ......87 M8
Montreal St *TOD* OL14 ......163 J6
Montrose Av *DOD/DAR* S75 ......242 C6
Montrose St *ECHL* BD2 ......104 F2
Montserrat Rd *BOW* BD4 ......128 C4
Monument La *PONT* WF8 ......181 G7
Monument Ms *PONT* WF8 ......181 G7
Moody St *WBOW* BD5 ......5 G9
Moor Allerton Av
  AL/HA/HU LS17 ......88 A4
Moor Allerton Crs
  AL/HA/HU LS17 ......88 A4
Moor Allerton Dr
  AL/HA/HU LS17 ......88 B4
Moor Allerton Gdns
  AL/HA/HU LS17 ......87 M4
  EARD/LOFT WF3 ......155 J1
  MSTN/BAR LS15 ......111 H7

Moorbottom *CLECK* BD19 ......149 K8
Moor Bottom *HOLM/MEL* HD9 ......236 B2
Moor Bottom La *BGLY* BD16 ......81 J3
  GTL/HWG HX4 ......168 C5
  KGHY BD21 ......79 K4
  RPDN/SBR HX6 ......167 J6
Moor Bottom Rd
  GTL/HWG HX4 ......189 H1
  LUD/ILL HX2 ......124 B8
Moorbottom Rd *HUD* HD1 ......214 A2
Moorbridge Cft
  GFTH/SHER LS25 ......116 B7
Moorbrow *HOLM/MEL* HD9 ......254 D4
Moor Cl *HUDS* HD4 ......213 L5
  MID LS10 ......131 M4
Moor Close Av *CUL/OBY* BD13 ......124 E6
Moor Close Farm Ms
  CUL/OBY BD13 ......124 E6
Moor Close La *CUL/OBY* BD13 ......124 E6
Moor Close Pde *CUL/OBY* BD13 ......124 E6
Moor Close Rd *CUL/OBY* BD13 ......124 E6
Moorcock Rd *HBR* HX7 ......141 L1
Moor Cottage Cl *HUDS* HD4 ......213 M7
Moor Crs *BEE/HOL* LS11 ......9 G8
Moor Crescent Cha
  BEE/HOL LS11 ......9 G7
Moorcrest Ri *DOD/DAR* S75 ......242 C6
Moor Cft *HUDS* HD4 ......213 L3
  BGLY BD16 ......81 K1
  BHP/TINH LS16 ......86 F2
Moorcroft *DEWS* WF13 ......173 J5
  OSS WF5 ......173 J5
  ROCH OL11 ......228 B8
Moorcroft Av *BFDE* BD3 ......105 M5
  HWTH BD22 ......78 F3
  MAR/SLWT HD7 ......212 F1
Moorcroft Dr *BOW* BD4 ......128 A3
  DEWS WF13 ......173 H5
Moorcroft Park Dr
  HOLM/MEL HD9 ......236 F7
Moorcroft Rd *BOW* BD4 ......128 B5
  DEWS WF13 ......173 H5
Moorcroft Ter *BOW* BD4 ......128 B6
Moor Dr *HDGY* LS6 ......86 B3
  HWTH BD22 ......78 E3
  OT LS21 ......41 M6
  PDSY/CALV LS28 ......129 H1
Moore Av *GTHN* BD7 ......126 B4
Moor Edge High Side
  BGLY BD16 ......80 C3
Moor End Av *LUD/ILL* HX2 ......145 L5
Moor End Gdns *LUD/ILL* HX2 ......145 M5
Moor End La *DEWS* WF13 ......173 H4
  RPDN/SBR HX6 ......
Moor End Rd *HUDS* HD4 ......214 A3
  LUD/ILL HX2 ......145 K4
Moor End Vw *LUD/ILL* HX2 ......146 A5
Moore Vw *GTHN* BD7 ......126 B4
Moor Farm Gdns *CHAL* LS7 * 87 L7
Moorfield *MOR* LS27 ......129 L7
Moorfield Av *BFDE* BD3 ......105 M5
  CLECK BD19 ......149 G7
  ILK LS29 ......61 H2
  LIT OL15 ......185 J7
  WOR/ARM LS12 ......108 D6
Moorfield Cl *YEA* LS19 ......62 F8
Moorfield Ct *HOR/CROF* WF4 ......217 G2
  YEA LS19 ......62 F8
Moorfield Crs *HEM/SK/SE* WF9 ......223 K7
  PDSY/CALV LS28 ......108 C6
  WOR/ARM LS12 ......108 C6
  YEA LS19 ......62 F8
Moorfield Cft *YEA* LS19 ......62 F8
Moorfield Dr *BAIL* BD17 ......82 E1
  HWTH BD22 ......78 F3
  YEA LS19 ......62 F8
Moorfield Gdns
  PDSY/CALV LS28 ......106 E8
Moorfield Gv *PDSY/CALV* LS28 ......106 E8
  WOR/ARM LS12 ......108 C6
Moorfield Hamlet
  ROY/SHW OL2 ......229 H7
Moorfield Ms *ROY/SHW* OL2 ......229 K7
Moorfield Pl *HEM/SK/SE* WF9 ......223 K7
  IDLE BD10 ......83 K6
  WHIT OL12 * 206 A5
Moor Field Rd *GTL/HWG* HX4 ......189 G6
Moorfield Rd *BGLY* BD16 ......81 J7
  HUDN HD2 ......192 D5
  ILK LS29 ......39 G2
  WOR/ARM LS12 ......108 C6
Moorfield Vw *LVSG* WF15 ......172 A5
Moorfield Wy *CLECK* BD19 ......149 G7
  ILK LS29 ......39 H3
Moor Flatts Av *MID* LS10 ......153 L1
Moor Flatts Rd *MID* LS10 ......153 L1
Moorfoot La *AIRE* BD20 ......34 C5
Moorgarth Av *BFDE* BD3 ......105 L5
Moorgate *BAIL* BD17 ......82 A7
Moorgate Av *BFDE* BD3 ......105 L5
  GFTH/SHER LS25 ......135 J3
Moorgate Cl *GFTH/SHER* LS25 ......135 J3
Moorgate Dr *GFTH/SHER* LS25 ......135 J3
Moorgate Ri *GFTH/SHER* LS25 ......135 J4
Moorgate Rd *GFTH/SHER* LS25 ......135 J3
Moor Gate St *HFAX* HX1 * 10 B9
Moor Grange Ri *BHP/TINH* LS16 ......86 C6
Moor Grange Vw
  BHP/TINH LS16 ......86 C6
Moor Green Cl *DOD/DAR* S75 ......260 C4
Moor Gv *EARD/LOFT* WF3 ......155 G8
  HIPP HX3 ......
  PDSY/CALV LS28 ......129 H1
Moorhead Av *SHPY* BD18 ......82 A7
Moorhead Crs *SHPY* BD18 ......82 A7
Moorhead La *SHPY* BD18 ......82 A7
Moorhead Ter *SHPY* BD18 ......82 A7
Moor Hey La *ELL* HX5 ......191 L1
Moor Hill Ct *HUDW* HD3 * 191 G6
Moor Hill Rd *HUDW* HD3 ......191 G6
Moorhouse Av *BEE/HOL* LS11 ......131 H5
  EARD/LOFT WF3 ......155 K7
  ECHL BD2 ......105 J1
  WKFDW/WTN WF2 ......
Moorhouse Cl *EARD/LOFT* WF3 ......155 K7
  NORM WF6 ......
Moorhouse Ct *BOW* BD4 ......128 B7
  HEM/SK/SE WF9 ......247 J6
  HWTH BD22 ......100 E3
Moorhouse Crs
  WKFDW/WTN WF2 ......12 A2
Moorhouse Farm *MILN* OL16 ......207 G8
Moor House Fold *MILN* OL16 ......207 G8
Moorhouse Gap
  AWLS/ASK DN6 ......248 B5
Moorhouse Gv *EARD/LOFT* WF3 ......155 K7

Moorhouse La *AWLS/ASK* DN6 247 L6
BIRK/DRI BD11 128 C7
DOD/DAR S75 241 L1
HOR/CROF WF4 222 E2
HWTH BD22 100 D2
Moorhouse Ter
EARD/LOFT WF3 155 K8
Moorhouse Vw
EARD/LOFT WF3 155 K8
HEM/SK/SE WF9 247 K4
The Moorings *AL/HA/HU* LS17 88 A1
IDLE BD10 83 M6
MID LS10 132 D3
Moor Knoll Cl *EARD/LOFT* WF3 153 M6
Moor Knoll Dr *EARD/LOFT* WF3 153 L6
Moor Knoll La *EARD/LOFT* WF3 153 L5
Moorland Av *BAIL* BD17 82 F2
BGLY BD16 59 L8
BSLY S70 260 D6
DOD/DAR S75 242 D4
GSLY LS20 62 A5
HDGY LS6 6 A4
MILN OL16 229 H1
MOR LS27 129 K6
Moorland Cl *LUD/ILL* HX2 146 A3
MAR/SLWT HD7 213 G7
MOR LS27 129 L6
Moorland Crs *BAIL* BD17 82 F2
DOD/DAR S75 242 D4
GSLY LS20 62 A4
ILK LS29 61 J1
ILK LS29 61 K4
MOR LS27 129 K6
Moorland Dr *AL/HA/HU* LS17 87 L5
BIRK/DRI BD11 128 D7
GSLY LS20 62 A4
HOR/CROF WF4 220 B4
PDSY/CALV LS28 106 C6
Moorland Gdns *AL/HA/HU* LS17 87 M4
Moorland Garth *AL/HA/HU* LS17 87 L5
Moorland Gv *PDSY/CALV* LS28 106 C6
Moorland Ings *AL/HA/HU* LS17 87 L5
Moorland Pl *LM/WK* BD12 149 G1
Moorland Ri *HOLM/MEL* HD9 234 E5
Moorland Rd *BHP/TINH* LS16 63 L4
BIRK/DRI BD11 129 G8
HDGY LS6 6 B4
PDSY/CALV LS28 106 C5
Moorlands *HOLM/MEL* HD9 254 E3
ILK LS29 38 C4
Moorlands Av *BFDE* BD3 105 M5
BIRK/DRI BD11 128 C7
DEWS WF13 173 K5
HWTH BD22 79 H2
LUD/ILL HX2 146 A3
MIRF WF14 * 172 B8
OSS WF5 174 E6
YEA LS19 62 F8
Moorlands Av North
DEWS WF13 173 K5
Moorlands Ct *GTL/HWG* HX4 * 168 D6
WBY LS22 48 B1
Moorlands Crs *HUDW* HD3 190 F5
Moorlands Dr *LUD/ILL* HX2 146 A4
YEA LS19 62 F8
Moorlands Pl *HFAX* HX1 168 D1
Moorlands Rd *BIRK/DRI* BD11 128 C7
DEWS WF13 173 K6
GTL/HWG HX4 168 D6
HUDW HD3 190 F5
Moorlands St *ROY/SHW* OL2 229 L7
The Moorlands *AL/HA/HU* LS17 88 A2
WBY LS22 48 B1
Moorland St *WHIT* OL12 206 A5
Moorlands Vw *HFAX* HX1 168 D1
WBY LS22 48 B1
Moorland Ter *CUD/GR* S72 262 E1
GFTH/SHER LS25 113 G8
KGHY BD21 58 B8
Moorland Vw *AL/HA/HU* LS17 87 L4
BRAM LS13 107 K2
KBTN HD8 217 J7
KBTN HD8 240 C4
LM/WK BD12 149 G1
RPDN/SBR HX6 167 H3
Moorland Wk *AL/HA/HU* LS17 87 L4
Moor La *AIRE* BD20 56 B1
AL/HA/HU LS17 67 J1
BSPA/BRAM LS23 48 F1
BTLY WF17 151 H6
CLECK BD19 150 D4
GFTH/SHER LS25 116 C6
GSLY LS20 62 A4
HOLM/MEL HD9 236 A7
HUDS HD4 213 M7
HUDS HD4 237 G1
ILK LS29 18 C4
ILK LS29 18 F6
ILK LS29 39 M6
ILK LS29 61 G2
KBTN HD8 216 C7
LUD/ILL HX2 146 A2
OT LS21 22 D6
OT LS21 40 D3
PBR HG3 45 L3
PONT WF8 203 G2
RYKW YO26 32 D4
TAD LS24 51 L5
TAD LS24 71 H6
TAD LS24 95 M4
TOD OL14 163 K3
WBY LS22 48 B6
Moorlea Dr *BAIL* BD17 82 F3
Moorleigh Cl *GFTH/SHER* LS25 135 K4
Moorleigh Dr *GFTH/SHER* LS25 135 K4
Moor Park Av *HDGY* LS6 86 F8
HUDS HD4 213 L5
Moor Park Cl *ILK* LS29 18 F6
Moor Park Ct *EARL* WF12 * 174 A5
Moor Park Crs *ILK* LS29 18 F6
Moor Park Dr *BFDE* BD3 105 M6
HDGY LS6 86 F8
ILK LS29 18 F6
Moor Park Gdns *EARL* WF12 174 A6
Moor Park Gv *ILK* LS29 19 G6
Moor Park La *EARL* WF12 174 A6
Moor Park Mt *HDGY* LS6 86 F7
Moor Park Rd *BFDE* BD3 * 105 L6
Moor Park Vls *HDGY* LS6 87 G8
Moor Park Wy *ILK* LS29 19 G6
Moor Rd *BEE/HOL* LS11 9 G8
BHP/TINH LS16 63 M4
EARD/LOFT WF3 155 G8
FEA/AMT WF7 201 M1
GFTH/SHER LS25 116 B6
HDGY LS6 86 F8
ILK LS29 39 H5
LIT OL15 185 L5
MID LS10 131 M4
Moor Royd *HIPP* HX3 168 C2
HOLM/MEL HD9 236 A3
Moorroyd St *OSS* WF5 174 E6
Moorshutt Rd
HEM/SK/SE WF9 223 L8
Moor Side *BSPA/BRAM* LS23 48 D6
Moorside *BAIL* BD17 82 F1
CLECK BD19 149 J8
HTON BD9 104 A4
ROCH OL11 228 B3
Moorside Ap *BIRK/DRI* BD11 151 H1
Moorside Av *AIRE* BD20 56 C1
BIRK/DRI BD11 128 C7
BIRK/DRI BD11 151 H1
DEWS WF13 173 H4
ECHL BD2 105 M4
HUDS HD4 213 M2
STKB/PEN S36 270 E4
Moorside Cl *BIRK/DRI* BD11 151 H1
DOD/DAR S75 242 D6
ECHL BD2 105 L3
Moorside Ct *ILK* LS29 38 C3
Moorside Crs *BIRK/DRI* BD11 151 G1
DEWS WF13 173 H4
HOR/CROF WF4 220 B4
Moorside Cft *ECHL* BD2 105 L4
Moorside Dr *BIRK/DRI* BD11 151 H1
BRAM LS13 107 L2
Moorside End *DEWS* WF13 173 H4
Moorside Gdns *BIRK/DRI* BD11 151 H1
ECHL BD2 105 L3
LUD/ILL HX2 146 B2
Moorside Gn *BIRK/DRI* BD11 129 H8
Moor Side La *HWTH* BD22 100 B1
MAR/SLWT HD7 211 M3
Moorside La *BFDE* BD3 105 M7
ILK LS29 37 G2
OT LS21 22 B7
Moorside Maltings
BEE/HOL LS11 9 G8
Moorside Mt *BIRK/DRI* BD11 151 G1
Moorside Pde *BIRK/DRI* BD11 151 H1
Moorside Pl *BFDE* BD3 105 M7
DEWS WF13 173 H4
Moorside Ri *CLECK* BD19 149 K7
Moorside Rd *BFDE* BD3 105 M7
BIRK/DRI BD11 151 G1
DEWS WF13 173 H4
ECHL BD2 105 L3
HOLM/MEL HD9 236 A3
HUDE HD5 193 L4
WIL/AL BD15 102 E2
Moorside St *BRAM* LS13 107 L2
LM/WK BD12 126 D8
Moorside Ter *BIRK/DRI* BD11 151 H1
BRAM LS13 107 L2
ECHL BD2 105 M4
Moorside V *BIRK/DRI* BD11 129 H8
Moorside Vw *BIRK/DRI* BD11 151 H1
Moorside Wk *BIRK/DRI* BD11 151 H1
Moor Stone Pl *HIPP* HX3 * 147 L1
Moor St *CUL/QBY* BD13 * 125 G5
HWTH BD22 78 F3
ROY/SHW OL2 229 J8
Moor Ter *ECHL* BD2 105 L5
Moorthorpe Av *BFDE* BD3 105 M5
Moortop *BIRK/DRI* BD11 128 F8
Moor Top *BIRK/DRI* BD11 150 F1
MIRF WF14 172 A8
OT LS21 61 M1
WOR/ARM LS12 129 L4
Moor Top Av *FEA/AMT* WF7 224 A1
HUDS HD4 237 H4
Moor Top Dr *HEM/SK/SE* WF9 245 M1
Moor Top Gdns *LUD/ILL* HX2 124 A7
Moor Top La *HOR/CROF* WF4 216 F5
Moor Top Rd *HUDE* HD5 193 L4
LM/WK BD12 126 D8
LUD/ILL HX2 145 K6
Moor Vw *BEE/HOL* LS11 8 D6
BOW BD4 * 128 C6
HECK WF16 173 G4
HOLM/MEL HD9 234 E3
HOR/CROF WF4 220 B1
MIRF WF14 172 C5
Moor View Av *SHPY* BD18 82 C6
Moor View Cl *CAS* WF10 158 B7
Moor View Ct *AIRE* BD20 58 E7
IDLE BD10 * 83 J5
Moorview Cft *ILK* LS29 61 H1
Moorview Dr *SHPY* BD18 83 H7
Moorview Gv *KGHY* BD21 3 K8
Moorview Rd *SKP/WHF* BD23 16 D3
Moorview Wy *SKP/WHF* BD23 16 E2
Moorville Av *BFDE* BD3 105 M5
Moorville Cl *BEE/HOL* LS11 8 E8
Moorville Ct *BEE/HOL* LS11 8 D7
Moorville Dr *BIRK/DRI* BD11 128 C7
Moorville Gv *BEE/HOL* LS11 8 D7
Moorville Rd *BEE/HOL* LS11 8 E7
Moorway *GSLY* LS20 61 K5
Moor Wy *HWTH* BD22 78 E3
Moorwell Pl *ECHL* BD2 105 K2
Moravian Pl *WBOW* BD5 * 126 F2
Morefield Bank
HOLM/MEL HD9 236 E6
Moresby Rd *WBSY* BD6 126 A8
Moresdale La *SCFT* LS14 111 J3
Morgan St *LIT* OL15 207 K1
Morlands Cl *DEWS* WF13 173 H3
Morley Av *BFDE* BD3 105 M5
KNOT WF11 182 C2
Morley Carr Rd *LM/WK* BD12 148 F1
Morley Fold *KBTN* HD8 257 H1
Morley Hall La *LUD/ILL* HX2 144 E8
Morley La *HUDW* HD3 213 J2
Morley St *GTHN* BD7 4 E7
MILN OL16 206 D5
Morningside *GIR* BD8 104 D5
Morningside Cl *MILN* OL16 * 206 D8
Morning St *KGHY* BD21 79 K2
Mornington Rd *BGLY* BD16 81 J3
ILK LS29 38 E2
ROCH OL11 228 C3
Mornington St *KGHY* BD21 2 F3
Mornington Vls *GIR* BD8 4 C1
Morpeth Pl *OSM* LS9 9 L3
Morpeth St *CUL/QBY* BD13 125 G5
GTHN BD7 4 B6
Morphet Ter *CHAL* LS7 * 7 H6
Morrell Crs *WKFDW/WTN* WF2 176 B3
Morris Av *KSTL* LS5 108 C1
Morris Cl *HEM/SK/SE* WF9 223 K4
Morris Flds *NORM* WF6 178 E5
Morris Gv *KSTL* LS5 108 C2
Morris La *KSTL* LS5 108 C1
Morris Mt *KSTL* LS5 108 C2
Morrison Pl *WMB/DAR* S73 263 J8
Morrison Rd *WMB/DAR* S73 263 H8
Morrison St *CAS* WF10 158 A7
Morris Pl *MOR* LS27 152 B1
Morris Vw *KSTL* LS5 108 C2
Morritt Av *MSTN/BAR* LS15 111 K5
Morritt Gv *MSTN/BAR* LS15 111 H6
Mortech Pk *MSTN/BAR* LS15 * 90 F7
Mortimer Av *BFDE* BD3 105 M5
BTLY WF17 173 H1
Mortimer Dr *STKB/PEN* S36 270 E5
Mortimer Hts *STKB/PEN* S36 270 E5
Mortimer Ri *OSS* WF5 175 G8
Mortimer Rw *BFDE* BD3 105 M8
HOR/CROF WF4 197 H5
Mortimer St *BTLY* WF17 173 H1
CLECK BD19 * 149 M7
GIR BD8 104 B6
Mortimer Ter *BTLY* WF17 173 H1
Morton Cl *BSLYN/ROY* S71 261 M1
Morton Crs *CAS* WF10 158 B7
Morton Gn *HUDE* HD5 215 J2
Morton Gv *AIRE* BD20 58 F6
EARL WF12 195 K3
Morton La *AIRE* BD20 58 F7
Morton Pde *WKFDW/WTN* WF2 12 B3
Morton Rd *BOW* BD4 127 M1
Mortons Cl *HIPP* HX3 169 G3
The Mortons *HUDW* HD3 * 191 H6
Morton Wy *HUDW* HD3 191 G5
Morton Wood Gv
HOLM/MEL HD9 254 F3
Mortuary La *WOR/ARM* LS12 108 A6
Morwick Gv *MSTN/BAR* LS15 90 A8
Moselden La *RPDN/SBR* HX6 188 E8
Moseley Pl *HDGY* LS6 6 F2
Moseley Wood Ap
BHP/TINH LS16 85 M2
Moseley Wood Av
BHP/TINH LS16 63 M8
Moseley Wood Bank
BHP/TINH LS16 85 M1
Moseley Wood Cl
BHP/TINH LS16 85 M2
Moseley Wood Crs
BHP/TINH LS16 85 M1
Moseley Wood Cft *HORS* LS18 85 L2
Moseley Wood Dr
BHP/TINH LS16 85 M1
Moseley Wood Gdns
BHP/TINH LS16 85 M2
Moseley Wood Gn
BHP/TINH LS16 85 M1
Moseley Wood Gv
BHP/TINH LS16 85 M1
Moseley Wood La
BHP/TINH LS16 64 A8
Moseley Wood Ri
BHP/TINH LS16 85 L1
Moseley Wood Vw
BHP/TINH LS16 64 A8
Moseley Wood Wk
BHP/TINH LS16 85 M1
Moseley Wood Wy
BHP/TINH LS16 63 M8
Moser Av *ECHL* BD2 105 J1
Moser Crs *ECHL* BD2 105 J1
Moss Av *MILN* OL16 206 E8
Moss Bridge Rd *BRAM* LS13 107 H1
MILN OL16 206 D8
Moss Carr Av *KGHY* BD21 80 B1
Moss Carr Gv *KGHY* BD21 * 80 B1
Moss Carr Rd *KGHY* BD21 80 B1
Mossdale Av *HTON* BD9 103 L3
Moss Dr *LUD/ILL* HX2 124 A8
Moss Edge Rd *HOLM/MEL* HD9 253 L6
Moss End La *HWTH* BD22 54 A4
Moss Gdns *AL/HA/HU* LS17 87 J1
Moss Gate Rd *ROY/SHW* OL2 229 J5
Moss Gv *ROY/SHW* OL2 229 G5
Moss Hall La *HBR* HX7 142 A2
Moss Hey St *ROY/SHW* OL2 229 K8
Moss La *HBR* HX7 143 J2
LUD/ILL HX2 124 A8
MILN OL16 206 C8
Mossley Rd *STKB/PEN* S36 270 E8
Moss Mill St *MILN* OL16 228 D1
Moss Ri *AL/HA/HU* LS17 87 J1
HOLM/MEL HD9 254 A1
Moss Rw *WIL/AL* BD15 80 E8
Moss Side *HTON* BD9 104 A4
Moss Side La *MILN* OL16 228 E1
Moss Side St *WHIT* OL12 184 A1
Moss St *CAS* WF10 157 K6
CUL/QBY BD13 102 E7
HUDS HD4 214 D2
HWTH BD22 79 G6
MILN OL16 206 D8
Moss Syke *SCFT* LS14 67 L6
Moss Ter *MILN* OL16 206 C8
Mosstree Cl *CUL/QBY* BD13 124 E4
Moss Va *AL/HA/HU* LS17 87 J1
Mossy Bank Cl *CUL/QBY* BD13 125 G4
Mostyn Gv *WBSY* BD6 126 C6
Mostyn Mt *HIPP* HX3 146 C3
Mostyn Wk *HOR/CROF* WF4 220 B3
Motley La *GSLY* LS20 62 A4
Mottram St *BSLYN/ROY* S71 261 H4
Moule Ri *GFTH/SHER* LS25 113 K5
Moulson Ct *WBOW* BD5 127 G3
Mountain Crs *EARL* WF12 195 M4
Mountain Rd *EARL* WF12 195 M4
Mountain Vw *LUD/ILL* HX2 124 C8
SHPY BD18 82 F8
Mountain Wy *HUDE* HD5 193 L7
Mount Av *CUD/GR* S72 245 J6
ECHL BD2 105 K1
HECK WF16 151 G8
HEM/SK/SE WF9 223 M6
HUDW HD3 190 E5
LIT OL15 185 J7
LUD/ILL HX2 145 L7
WHIT OL12 207 G2
WKFDW/WTN WF2 176 B2
Mountbatten Av *WKFDE* WF1 176 E1
WKFDW/WTN WF2 199 G7
Mountbatten Crs *WKFDE* WF1 176 E1
Mountbatten Gdns *HUDW* HD3 191 K7
Mountbatten Gv *WKFDE* WF1 176 F2
Mountcliffe Vw *MOR* LS27 130 D7
Mount Cl *BSLY* S70 261 H7
Mount Ct *PDSY/CALV* LS28 107 G6
Mount Crs *CLECK* BD19 149 M6
LUD/ILL HX2 145 L7
WKFDW/WTN WF2 198 B3
Mount Dr *AL/HA/HU* LS17 65 K8
Mountfield Av *HUDE* HD5 215 K2
Mountfield Rd *HUDE* HD5 215 K1
Mountfields *HIPP* HX3 148 A6
Mountfields Wk
HEM/SK/SE WF9 246 D5
Mount Gdns *AL/HA/HU* LS17 65 K8
CLECK BD19 149 M6
Mount Gv *ECHL* BD2 105 K1
Mountjoy Rd *HUD* HD1 14 C5
Mount La *BRIG* HD6 170 A7
TOD OL14 140 E3
Mountleigh Cl *BOW* BD4 127 J8
Mount Pellon *LUD/ILL* HX2 10 A3
Mount Pellon Rd *LUD/ILL* HX2 146 A6
Mount Pl *SHPY* BD18 82 D6
Mount Pleasant *AIRE* BD20 58 E7
BRAM LS13 107 K2
CAS WF10 158 B8
CUD/GR S72 245 J6
CUL/QBY BD13 101 M6
EARL WF12 * 174 A7
FEA/AMT WF7 202 B8
GFTH/SHER LS25 135 K6
GIR BD8 * 104 E4
GSLY LS20 62 A4
HUD HD1 214 B3
ILK LS29 19 H6
ILK LS29 38 E3
KBTN HD8 217 M7
LIT OL15 * 185 L6
WBSY BD6 126 A7
Mount Pleasant Av *HFAX* HX1 10 E4
RHAY LS8 110 B1
Mount Pleasant Ct
PDSY/CALV LS28 107 G6
Mount Pleasant Dr *HBR* HX7 144 A5
Mount Pleasant Gdns
RHAY LS8 * 110 B1
Mount Pleasant La *HUDE* HD5 215 L2
Mount Pleasant Rd
PDSY/CALV LS28 107 G6
Mount Pleasant St
FEA/AMT WF7 179 M8
HUDE HD5 15 L6
TOD OL14 140 C5
Mount Pleasant Vw *TOD* OL14 163 J1
Mount Preston *LDSU* LS2 6 C6
Mount Preston St *LDSU* LS2 6 C6
Mount Ri *AL/HA/HU* LS17 65 K8
Mount Rd *CUD/GR* S72 245 J6
EARD/LOFT WF3 155 H8
ECHL BD2 105 K1
HUD HD1 191 M8
MAR/SLWT HD7 232 D5
WBSY BD6 126 C5
Mount Royd *AWLS/ASK* DN6 * 227 K3
GIR BD8 104 E4
Mount Scar Vw
HOLM/MEL HD9 254 F2
Mountside Cl *WHIT* OL12 206 B4
Mount St *BFDE* BD3 5 K7
BSLY S70 261 G6
BSLYN/ROY S71 262 B6
BTLY WF17 173 M3
CLECK BD19 149 M6
ECHL BD2 105 K1
HFAX HX1 10 F6
HUD HD1 214 B3
HUDS HD4 * 213 J2
HWTH BD22 2 D5
RPDN/SBR HX6 167 K2
WHIT OL12 * 206 A6
Mount St West *LUD/ILL* HX2 * 146 A6
Mount Tabor Rd *LUD/ILL* HX2 145 H2
Mount Tabor St
PDSY/CALV LS28 * 106 E7
Mount Ter *BTLY* WF17 173 L3
ECHL BD2 105 K1
LUD/ILL HX2 146 A6
The Mount *AL/HA/HU* LS17 65 K8
BTLY WF17 151 G4
CAS WF10 158 E7
GFTH/SHER LS25 135 J5
MSTN/BAR LS15 90 F8
MSTN/BAR LS15 111 K5
PONT WF8 180 E6
TOD OL14 141 L8
WKFDW/WTN WF2 175 M5
WKFDW/WTN WF2 198 B3
YEA LS19 * 84 F3
Mount Vernon Av *BSLY* S70 261 H7
Mount Vernon Crs *BSLY* S70 261 J8
Mount Vernon Rd *BSLY* S70 261 H8
YEA LS19 84 E2
Mount Vw *HWTH* BD22 78 D4
LUD/ILL HX2 145 J3
Mount View Ct *CLECK* BD19 149 L6
Mount View Rd
HOLM/MEL HD9 255 G4
ROY/SHW OL2 229 L8
Mount Wk *CAS* WF10 157 M8
Mount Zion Rd *HUDE* HD5 15 K7
Mousehole La *MIRF* WF14 194 F5
Moverley Flatts *PONT* WF8 181 G7
Mowat Ct *LVSG* WF15 171 K1
Mowbray Cha *RTHW* LS26 133 J7
Mowbray Cl *CUL/QBY* BD13 101 L1
Mowbray Ct *SCFT* LS14 111 J3
Mowbray Crs *SCFT* LS14 111 J3
Moxon Cl *PONT* WF8 180 F8
Moxon Gv *WKFDE* WF1 176 D3
Moxon Pl *WKFDW/WTN* WF2 197 L1
Moxon Sq *WKFDE* WF1 176 F7
Moxon St *WKFDE* WF1 176 E2
Moxon Wy *WKFDE* WF1 176 E2
Moynihan Cl *RHAY* LS8 110 D2
Mozley Dr *LUD/ILL* HX2 124 B8
Mucky La *GTL/HWG* HX4 190 F2
Muddy La *WBY* LS22 47 K3
Muffit La *CLECK* BD19 150 F6
Muff St *BOW* BD4 5 L9
Mug Mill La *EARL* WF12 196 A6
Mugup La *HOLM/MEL* HD9 255 G5
Muir Ct *HDGY* LS6 108 F2
Muirfield Av *FEA/AMT* WF7 179 L5
Muirfield Dr *WKFDW/WTN* WF2 198 C4
Muirhead Ct *BOW* BD4 128 A4
Muirhead Dr *BOW* BD4 128 A4
Muirhead Fold *BOW* BD4 128 A4
The Muirlands *HUDN* HD2 193 G1
Mulberry Av *BHP/TINH* LS16 86 F2
HOR/CROF WF4 222 D5
Mulberry Cha *OT* LS21 42 F8
Mulberry Cl *ROCH* OL11 228 A1
Mulberry Ct *GFTH/SHER* LS25 138 B2
MAR/SLWT HD7 213 G1
Mulberry Gdns *RTHW* LS26 156 D4
Mulberry Garth *BHP/TINH* LS16 86 F3
BSPA/BRAM LS23 49 G6
Mulberry Pl *HOR/CROF* WF4 222 E5
Mulberry Ri *BHP/TINH* LS16 86 F2
Mulberry St *HUD* HD1 15 K8
KGHY BD21 3 J3
MID LS10 9 J5
PDSY/CALV LS28 107 G7
Mulberry Ter *HUD* HD1 * 14 F3
Mulberry Vw *BHP/TINH* LS16 86 F3
Mulcture Hall Rd *HFAX* HX1 11 J5
Mulehouse La *HUDW* HD3 190 D5
Mulgrave St *BFDE* BD3 5 L8
Mullins Ct *OSM* LS9 110 B8
Mullion Av *HOLM/MEL* HD9 236 A2
Mumford St *WBOW* BD5 127 G3
Munby St *GIR* BD8 104 A7
Muncaster Rd *GFTH/SHER* LS25 113 K6
Munster St *BOW* BD4 127 K3
Munton Cl *WBSY* BD6 * 126 A8
Murdoch Pl *BSLYN/ROY* S71 243 G7
Murdoch St *KGHY* BD21 58 B6
Murgatroyd St *SHPY* BD18 82 D6
WBOW BD5 127 G4
Muriel St *MILN* OL16 228 D1
Murray Rd *HUDN* HD2 14 C3
Murray St *WBOW* BD5 * 126 E3
Murton Cl *SCFT* LS14 111 J2
Musabbir Sq *WHIT* OL12 * 206 C6
Museum Ct *ECHL* BD2 105 L4
Museum St *OSM* LS9 110 B5
Musgrave Bank *BRAM* LS13 108 A4
Musgrave Buildings
PDSY/CALV LS28 107 H6
Musgrave Dr *ECHL* BD2 105 L4
Musgrave Gv *ECHL* BD2 105 L4
Musgrave Mt *BRAM* LS13 108 A4
ECHL BD2 105 L4
Musgrave Ri *BRAM* LS13 108 A4
Musgrave Rd *ECHL* BD2 105 L4
Musgrave St *BTLY* WF17 * 151 G5
Musgrave Vw *BRAM* LS13 108 A4
Mushroom St *CHAL* LS7 7 K6
Musselburgh St *GTHN* BD7 4 A5
Mutton La *WIL/AL* BD15 102 F4
Myers Av *ECHL* BD2 105 J2
Myers Cft *HUDE* HD5 193 H8
OT LS21 41 J7
Myers La *ECHL* BD2 105 J2
Mylor Ct *BSLYN/ROY* S71 261 L3
Myrtle Av *BGLY* BD16 * 81 H4
DEWS WF13 195 G1
LUD/ILL HX2 146 A2
Myrtle Ct *BGLY* BD16 81 H4
Myrtle Dr *HWTH* BD22 79 H5
LUD/ILL HX2 146 A2
Myrtle Gdns *LUD/ILL* HX2 146 A2
Myrtle Gv *BGLY* BD16 81 H4
HUDW HD3 191 K8
LUD/ILL HX2 146 A2
Myrtle Pl *BGLY* BD16 81 H3
LUD/ILL HX2 146 A2
Myrtle Rd *DEWS* WF13 * 195 G1
ELL HX5 191 H1
Myrtle St *BFDE* BD3 105 L8
BGLY BD16 81 J3
DOD/DAR S75 260 E4
HUD HD1 15 G4
Myson Av *PONT* WF8 181 H2
Mytholm Bank *HBR* HX7 * 143 G3
Mytholm Cl *HBR* HX7 143 H3
Mytholmes La *HWTH* BD22 78 E7

N

Nabbs La *MAR/SLWT* HD7 212 B6
Nabb Vw *HOLM/MEL* HD9 * 254 D2
Nab Crs *HOLM/MEL* HD9 234 E4
Nabcroft La *HUDS* HD4 213 M3
Nabcroft Ri *HUDS* HD4 * 213 M2
Nab End La *ELL* HX5 169 G8
GTL/HWG HX4 168 F7
Nab La *BTLY* WF17 151 J4
MIRF WF14 172 B8
SHPY BD18 81 M7
The Nab *MIRF* WF14 172 A8
Naburn Ap *SCFT* LS14 89 K5
Naburn Cha *SCFT* LS14 89 L7
Naburn Cl *SCFT* LS14 89 K7
Naburn Dr *SCFT* LS14 89 K7
Naburn Gdns *SCFT* LS14 89 K6
Naburn Gn *SCFT* LS14 89 K7
Naburn Pl *SCFT* LS14 89 K6
Naburn Rd *SCFT* LS14 89 K7
Naburn Vw *SCFT* LS14 89 L7
Naburn Wk *SCFT* LS14 89 L7
Nab Vw *AIRE* BD20 36 B3
Nab Water La *HWTH* BD22 100 E8
Nab Wood Bank *SHPY* BD18 81 M7
Nab Wood Cl *SHPY* BD18 * 82 A7
Nab Wood Crs *SHPY* BD18 81 M7
Nab Wood Dr *BGLY* BD16 81 M8
Nab Wood Gdns *SHPY* BD18 82 A7
Nab Wood Gv *SHPY* BD18 81 M7
Nab Wood Mt *SHPY* BD18 81 M7
Nab Wood Pl *SHPY* BD18 81 M7
Nab Wood Ri *SHPY* BD18 81 M7
Nab Wood Rd *SHPY* BD18 81 M8
Nab Wood Ter *SHPY* BD18 81 M7
Nairn Cl *HUDS* HD4 213 L4
Nall St *MILN* OL16 207 G8
Nancroft Crs *WOR/ARM* LS12 108 E7
Nancroft Ter *WOR/ARM* LS12 108 E7
Nancy Crs *CUD/GR* S72 245 K8
Nancy Rd *CUD/GR* S72 245 K8
Nanny Goat La
GFTH/SHER LS25 113 G6
Nanny La *TAD* LS24 95 G8
Nanny Marr Rd *WMB/DAR* S73 263 K8
Nansen Av *BRAM* LS13 107 K4
Nansen Gv *BRAM* LS13 107 K4
Nansen Mt *BRAM* LS13 107 K4
Nansen Pl *BRAM* LS13 107 K4
Nansen St *BRAM* LS13 107 J4
Nansen Ter *BRAM* LS13 107 K4
Nansen Vw *BRAM* LS13 107 K4
Nantwich Av *WHIT* OL12 206 B3
Naomi Rd *HUDS* HD4 214 C4
Napier Mt *BSLY* S70 261 H8
Napier Rd *BFDE* BD3 105 M7
ELL HX5 169 G8
Napier St *BFDE* BD3 105 M7
CUL/QBY BD13 125 H5
KGHY BD21 3 J6
ROY/SHW OL2 229 K6
Napier Ter *BFDE* BD3 105 M7
Naples St *GIR* BD8 104 D5
Nares St *HWTH* BD22 79 G6
KGHY BD21 2 E4
Narrowboat Whf *BRAM* LS13 107 H1
Narrow La *BGLY* BD16 80 D5
The Narrows *BGLY* BD16 80 D5
Naseby Gdns *OSM* LS9 * 7 L7
Naseby Garth *OSM* LS9 7 L7
Naseby Gra *OSM* LS9 7 L8
Naseby Pl *OSM* LS9 7 L8
Naseby Ri *CUL/QBY* BD13 125 H5
Naseby Ter *OSM* LS9 7 M8
Naseby Vw *OSM* LS9 * 7 L8
Naseby Wk *OSM* LS9 7 M8
Nashville Rd *HWTH* BD22 2 D7
Nashville St *HWTH* BD22 2 D7
Nashville Ter *HWTH* BD22 2 D7
Nassau Pl *CHAL* LS7 7 L1
Nateby Ri *EARD/LOFT* WF3 154 E3
Nathan La *RPDN/SBR* HX6 166 E7
National Rd *MID* LS10 9 M7
Nat La *AL/HA/HU* LS17 43 J1
Natty Fields Cl *LUD/ILL* HX2 124 A7
Natty La *LUD/ILL* HX2 124 A7
Nature Wy *WBSY* BD6 126 A7
Navigation Cl *ELL* HX5 169 J6
Navigation Ri *HUDW* HD3 213 K2
Navigation Rd *CAS* WF10 157 M5
EARL WF12 195 K2
HIPP HX3 11 K7
Navigation Wk *MID* LS10 9 H2
Navvy La *BSLYN/ROY* S71 221 M7
Naylor Ct *DEWS* WF13 173 M5
Naylor Gv *DOD/DAR* S75 260 B7
Naylor La *LUD/ILL* HX2 144 E6
Naylors Garth *HDGY* LS6 109 H1
Naylor St *DEWS* WF13 173 K4
HFAX HX1 10 A5
OSS WF5 174 E6
Neale Rd *HUD* HD1 214 B3
Neale St *HBR* HX7 143 J4
Neal St *WBOW* BD5 4 E8
Near Bank *KBTN* HD8 238 D4
Nearcliffe Rd *HTON* BD9 104 C4
Near Crook *IDLE* BD10 83 H5
Near La *HOLM/MEL* HD9 235 G4
Neath Gdns *OSM* LS9 110 F3
Necropolis Rd *GTHN* BD7 126 B1
Ned Hill Rd *LUD/ILL* HX2 124 A4
Ned La *BOW* BD4 128 B2
MAR/SLWT HD7 212 B6
Needles Inn La *RTHW* LS26 133 L7
Needlewood *DOD/DAR* S75 260 B8
Nell Gap Av *HOR/CROF* WF4 196 C7
Nell Gap Crs *HOR/CROF* WF4 196 C7

Nell Gap La HOR/CROF WF4 196 C7
Nelson Av BSLYN/ROY S71 261 J2
Nelson Ct MOR LS27 152 B4
RTHW LS26 156 F3
Nelson Cft GFTH/SHER LS25 112 F8
Nelson Pl CUL/QBY BD13 125 G5
MOR LS27 152 C1
Nelson Rd ILK LS29 38 D2
Nelson St BFD BD1 4 F7
BSLY S70 261 G5
BTLY WF17 151 H5
BTLY WF17 * 173 J1
CUD/GR S72 245 G1
CUL/QBY BD13 125 G5
DEWS WF13 * 173 L6
HUD HD1 214 B2
HWTH BD22 79 G6
LIT OL15 207 K1
LVSG WF15 172 D3
MILN OL16 206 B7
NORM WF6 178 E3
OT LS21 41 J7
RPDN/SBR HX6 167 M2
SKP/WHF BD23 16 C3
WIL/AL BD15 103 L5
Nene St WBOW BD5 126 E2
Nepshaw La MOR LS27 152 B1
Nepshaw La North MOR LS27 152 A1
Nepshaw La South MOR LS27 151 M2
Neptune St OSM LS9 9 K2
Nesfield Cl MID LS10 132 B8
Nesfield Crs MID LS10 132 B8
Nesfield Gdns MID LS10 132 A8
Nesfield Garth MID LS10 132 A8
Nesfield Rd ILK LS29 38 B1
MID LS10 132 A8
Nesfield St BFD BD1 4 D3
Nesfield Vw ILK LS29 38 A2
MID LS10 132 B8
Nesfield Wk MID LS10 132 A8
Nessfield Dr HWTH BD22 2 B8
Nessfield Gv HWTH BD22 2 B8
Nessfield Rd HWTH BD22 2 B8
Nestfield Cl PONT WF8 180 F3
Nest La HBR HX7 143 M6
Neston Cl ROY/SHW OL2 229 M7
Neston Rd MILN OL16 228 E2
Neston Wy OSS WF5 * 174 F5
Netherby St BFDE BD3 5 M6
Nethercliffe Rd GSLY LS20 61 M4
Nether Cl HUDE HD5 193 G6
Nether Crs HUDE HD5 193 G6
Nethercroft DOD/DAR S75 260 A1
Netherdale Ct WBY LS22 30 C8
Netherend Rd MAR/SLWT HD7 212 B5
Netherfield Av HOR/CROF WF4 218 F1
Netherfield Cl CAS WF10 179 H1
KBTN HD8 216 B8
YEA LS19 62 D7
Netherfield Crs
HOR/CROF WF4 218 F1
Netherfield Dr GSLY LS20 61 M4
HOLM/MEL HD9 236 C7
Netherfield Pl CLECK BD19 150 A7
HOR/CROF WF4 196 F8
Netherfield Rd DEWS WF13 195 G1
GSLY LS20 61 M4
Nether Hall Av HUDE HD5 193 G6
Netherhall Rd BAIL BD17 82 F3
Nether House La
STKB/PEN S36 269 M7
Netherhouse Rd ROY/SHW OL2 229 J7
Netherhouses HOLM/MEL HD9 253 M1
Netherlands Av WBSY BD6 126 E7
Netherlands Sq WBSY BD6 126 F7
Nether La HOLM/MEL HD9 252 D3
Netherlea Dr HOLM/MEL HD9 236 B7
Netherley Dr MAR/SLWT HD7 233 G4
Netherly Brow OSS WF5 197 G3
Nether Moor Rd HUDS HD4 213 K6
Nether Moor Vw BGLY BD16 81 J3
Netheroyd FEA/AMT WF7 200 E1
Netheroyd Hill Rd HUDN HD2 192 B3
Netheroyd Pl HOR/CROF WF4 200 D3
Nether Rd DOD/DAR S75 259 J5
Nether St PDSY/CALV LS28 106 F2
Netherthong Rd
HOLM/MEL HD9 235 H6
Netherton Fold HUDS HD4 213 L8
Netherton Hall Dr
HOR/CROF WF4 196 F8
Netherton Hall Gdns
HOR/CROF WF4 197 G8
Netherton La HOR/CROF WF4 196 F8
Netherton Moor Rd HUDS HD4 213 M7
Netherwood Cl HUDN HD2 192 C3
Netley Av WHIT OL12 206 B3
Nettle Gv HIPP HX3 147 H5
Nettleton Av MIRF WF14 194 B1
Nettleton Cha OSS WF5 174 E5
Nettleton Cl BOW BD4 128 F4
Nettleton Ct MSTN/BAR LS15 111 M6
Nettleton Hill Rd
MAR/SLWT HD7 190 D8
Nettleton Rd HUDE HD5 193 J6
MIRF WF14 194 B1
Nettleton St EARD/LOFT WF3 155 K8
OSS WF5 174 E8
Neville Ap OSM LS9 110 E8
Neville Av BOW BD4 127 K5
BSLY S70 261 M7
OSM LS9 110 E8
Neville Cl BSLY S70 261 M7
HEM/SK/SE WF9 246 E3
OSM LS9 110 E8
Neville Crs BSLY S70 261 M7
OSM LS9 110 F6
Neville Garth OSM LS9 110 E8
Neville Gv HUDE HD5 215 H2
OSM LS9 110 E8
RTHW LS26 134 C4
Neville Mt OSM LS9 110 E8
Neville Pde OSM LS9 110 E8
Neville Pl OSM LS9 110 F7
Neville Rd BOW BD4 127 K2
MSTN/BAR LS15 111 G7
OSM LS9 110 F6
OT LS21 41 K7
WKFDW/WTN WF2 197 L1
Neville Rw OSM LS9 110 E8
Neville Sq OSM LS9 110 E7
Neville St BEE/HOL LS11 8 F2
CLECK BD19 150 A8
KGHY BD21 * 3 J3
NORM WF6 178 D5
SKP/WHF BD23 16 C2
WKFDE WF1 13 L7
Neville Ter OSM LS9 110 E8
Neville Vw OSM LS9 110 E8
Neville Wk OSM LS9 110 E8
Nevill Gv HTON BD9 103 M3
Nevins Rd DEWS WF13 172 F8
Nevison Av PONT WF8 181 G3
Nevis St ROCH OL11 228 C4
New Adel Av BHP/TINH LS16 86 C3
New Adel Gdns BHP/TINH LS16 86 C3
New Adel La BHP/TINH LS16 86 C3
Newall Av OT LS21 41 H5
Newall Carr Rd OT LS21 23 G8
Newall Cl ILK LS29 61 K1
OT LS21 41 H5
Newall Crs HEM/SK/SE WF9 223 H3
Newall Hall Pk OT LS21 41 J5
Newall St LIT OL15 185 K8
TOD OL14 163 J6
WBOW BD5 126 F2
New Ar HEM/SK/SE WF9 * 246 D4
Newark Cl DOD/DAR S75 242 D4
Newark Park Wy
ROY/SHW OL2 228 E8
Newark Rd BGLY BD16 81 G1
WHIT OL12 206 B3
Newark Sq WHIT OL12 206 B3
Newark St BOW BD4 5 K9
Newark V EARD/LOFT WF3 154 C3
New Augustus St BFD BD1 5 H7
New Av HUDE HD5 193 K5
New Bank HIPP HX3 11 K4
New Bank Ri BOW BD4 127 M3
New Bank St MOR LS27 152 D1
Newbarn Cl ROY/SHW OL2 229 J7
New Barn St ROCH OL11 228 C1
ROY/SHW OL2 229 J7
New Bath St COL BB8 74 A1
Newbold Moss MILN OL16 206 D7
Newbold St MILN OL16 206 E7
New Bond St HFAX HX1 10 F6
Newbridge Gv BSLYN/ROY S71 261 K3
New Bridge Rd
HOLM/MEL HD9 234 D4
New Briggate LDSU LS2 7 H8
New Brighton BGLY BD16 81 L8
New Broad La MILN OL16 228 E3
New Brook St ILK LS29 38 D1
New Brunswick St HFAX HX1 10 F5
WKFDE WF1 12 F6
New Buildings Pl MILN OL16 * 206 B6
Newburn Rd GTHN BD7 126 D1
Newbury Cl BAIL BD17 82 F2
Newbury Dr HEM/SK/SE WF9 247 J1
Newbury Rd BRIG HD6 170 B7
Newbury Wk HUDE HD5 193 L5
Newby Garth AL/HA/HU LS17 88 D1
Newby Rd AIRE BD20 34 F6
Newby St AIRE BD20 * 34 F7
Newcastle Cl BIRK/DRI BD11 150 F1
Newcastle Farm Ct KNOT WF11 159 J2
New Chapel Av STKB/PEN S36 270 E5
New Cl DOD/DAR S75 259 H6
SHPY BD18 81 M7
New Close Av AIRE BD20 * 36 A5
New Close La AWLS/ASK DN6 227 G7
MAR/SLWT HD7 211 K5
New Close Rd SHPY BD18 81 M7
New Clough Rd RPDN/SBR HX6 167 M4
Newcombe St ELL HX5 191 J1
New Craven Ga BEE/HOL LS11 9 H7
New Crs HORS LS18 85 K6
New Cft HORS LS18 85 K6
New Cross St LM/WK BD12 149 K1
WBOW BD5 127 G4
Newdale Av CUD/GR S72 262 C1
New Dales La AIRE BD20 16 E7
New Farmers Hl RTHW LS26 133 M7
Newfield Av BSLYN/ROY S71 261 M2
CAS WF10 158 A7
NORM WF6 178 E5
New Field Cl MILN OL16 206 D6
Newfield Cl NORM WF6 178 E5
Newfield Ct NORM WF6 178 E4
Newfield Crs GFTH/SHER LS25 135 K2
NORM WF6 178 E5
Newfield Dr GFTH/SHER LS25 135 K1
ILK LS29 61 J2
Newfield Head La MILN OL16 229 K1
Newfield La GFTH/SHER LS25 136 F6
Newfield Vw MILN OL16 207 J8
New Fold HOLM/MEL HD9 254 C2
WBSY BD6 126 A7
Newforth Gv WBOW BD5 * 126 E4
New Ga HOLM/MEL HD9 254 E5
Newgate MILN OL16 206 B7
MIRF WF14 194 C2
PONT WF8 180 E6
Newgate La HOLM/MEL HD9 235 G4
Newgate St BTLY WF17 174 B3
New Grove Dr HUDE HD5 193 G7
New Hall Ap HOR/CROF WF4 218 A2
Newhall Bank MID LS10 153 M1
Newhall Cha MID LS10 131 M8
New Hall Cl HOR/CROF WF4 220 A2
Newhall Cl MID LS10 131 M8
Newhall Crs MID LS10 131 M8
Newhall Cft MID LS10 131 M8
Newhall Dr WBSY BD6 127 H6
Newhall Gdns MID LS10 153 M1
Newhall Garth MID LS10 153 M1
Newhall Ga MID LS10 131 M7
Newhall Gn MID LS10 131 M8
New Hall La HOR/CROF WF4 218 B3
Newhall La MIRF WF14 194 D4
Newhall Mt MID LS10 153 M1
WBSY BD6 127 H6
Newhall Rd BOW BD4 * 127 K5
MID LS10 131 M8
New Hall Rd PONT WF8 181 G3
New Hall Wy HOR/CROF WF4 218 B3
New Hey Rd BOW BD4 127 J2
HUDW HD3 190 D5
HUDW HD3 191 K2
HUDW HD3 211 L2
Newhey Rd MILN OL16 229 J2
Newhill HEM/SK/SE WF9 246 D5
Newhill Rd BSLYN/ROY S71 261 J1
Newhold GFTH/SHER LS25 113 J6
New Holme Rd HWTH BD22 78 F8
Newhouse Cl WHIT OL12 184 E8
New House La CUL/QBY BD13 125 K6
Newhouse Pl HUD HD1 14 D5
New House Rd HUDN HD2 192 F2
Newill Cl WBOW BD5 127 H4
Newington Av CUD/GR S72 244 D6
New Inn St WOR/ARM LS12 108 C7
New John St BFD BD1 * 4 E6
New Kirkgate SHPY BD18 * 82 D6
New Laithe Cl HUDE HD5 214 E4
SKP/WHF BD23 16 D1
New Laithe Hl HUDS HD4 214 E4
New Laithe La HOLM/MEL HD9 254 D1
New Laithe Rd HUDE HD5 214 E4
HWTH BD22 77 G6
WBSY BD6 * 126 C5
Newlaithes Crs NORM WF6 178 E4
Newlaithes Gdns HORS LS18 85 K7
Newlaithes Garth HORS LS18 85 J8
Newlaithes Rd HORS LS18 85 K8
Newland Av CUD/GR S72 244 C8
Newland Ct HUDN HD2 14 C1
WKFDE WF1 199 G4
Newland La NORM WF6 178 A5
Newland Rd BSLYN/ROY S71 243 G7
HUDE HD5 193 J7
Newlands PDSY/CALV LS28 106 F4
YEA LS19 62 C6
Newlands Av AWLS/ASK DN6 249 G4
BFDE BD3 105 M5
HIPP HX3 147 J2
KBTN HD8 240 B4
RPDN/SBR HX6 167 G3
WHIT OL12 206 B3
YEA LS19 62 C7
Newlands Cl BRIG HD6 170 D5
WHIT OL12 206 B3
Newlands Crs MOR LS27 152 F2
Newlands Dr AIRE BD20 34 F7
BGLY BD16 81 G1
EARD/LOFT WF3 177 G1
HIPP HX3 147 J3
MOR LS27 152 F2
Newlands Gv HIPP HX3 147 J3
Newlands Pl BFDE BD3 5 K3
Newlands Ri YEA LS19 62 C7
Newlands Rd LUD/ILL HX2 145 K7
The Newlands RPDN/SBR HX6 167 G4
Newland St KNOT WF11 181 K1
WKFDE WF1 199 G4
Newlands Wk EARD/LOFT WF3 177 G1
Newland Vw NORM WF6 178 B4
New La AIRE BD20 35 H4
BEE/HOL LS11 8 F3
BOW BD4 105 M8
BOW BD4 128 D4
CLECK BD19 149 J8
COP/BISH YO23 51 M1
EARD/LOFT WF3 153 L6
GFTH/SHER LS25 115 M8
GFTH/SHER LS25 160 A3
GLE DN14 161 K8
HBR HX7 142 F3
HBR HX7 165 M2
HEM/SK/SE WF9 225 J8
HIPP HX3 168 D4
HOR/CROF WF4 198 A6
HUDW HD3 210 F2
KBTN HD8 239 K5
KNOT WF11 159 M3
LUD/ILL HX2 166 D1
MAR/SLWT HD7 190 D8
MAR/SLWT HD7 212 C3
MID LS10 153 K1
MOR LS27 129 J6
OT LS21 24 F6
New Lane Crs HEM/SK/SE WF9 225 J7
Newlay Cl IDLE BD10 84 A7
Newlay Gv HORS LS18 85 K8
Newlay La BRAM LS13 107 L2
HORS LS18 85 K7
Newlay Lane Pl BRAM LS13 107 L2
Newlay Wood Av HORS LS18 85 L7
Newlay Wood Cl HORS LS18 85 L7
Newlay Wood Crs HORS LS18 85 L7
Newlay Wood Dr HORS LS18 85 L7
Newlay Wood Gdns HORS LS18 * 85 L7
Newlay Wood Ri HORS LS18 85 K7
Newlay Wood Rd HORS LS18 85 K7
New Lennerton La
GFTH/SHER LS25 117 H7
Newley Av BTLY WF17 151 H6
Newley Mt HORS LS18 85 K8
New Line IDLE BD10 84 A7
New Lodge Crs
BSLYN/ROY S71 243 G7
New Longley La
RPDN/SBR HX6 167 J5
Newlyn Dr BSLYN/ROY S71 261 K3
WKFDW/WTN WF2 198 F4
Newlyn Rd AIRE BD20 58 C5
Newman Av BSLYN/ROY S71 243 L5
Newman St BOW BD4 127 K4
MILN OL16 206 E3
New Market OT LS21 41 J7
Newmarket Ap OSM LS9 132 D1
Newmarket La
EARD/LOFT WF3 155 L6
OSM LS9 132 D1
New Market Pl BFD BD1 4 F6
New Market St LDS LS1 9 H1
Newmarket St SKP/WHF BD23 16 C2
New Mill La BSPA/BRAM LS23 70 A1
New Mill Rd HOLM/MEL HD9 236 C2
HOLM/MEL HD9 236 D8
New Mill St LIT OL15 207 J1
New North Pde HUD HD1 14 E6
New North Rd HECK WF16 172 E1
HUD HD1 14 C4
MAR/SLWT HD7 212 C4
New Occupation La
PDSY/CALV LS28 106 E8
New Otley Rd BFDE BD3 5 J4
New Oxford St COL BB8 74 A1
New Park Av PDSY/CALV LS28 107 G3
New Park Cl PDSY/CALV LS28 107 G3
New Park Cft PDSY/CALV LS28 107 G3
New Park La OSS WF5 175 K6
New Park Pl PDSY/CALV LS28 107 G3
New Park Rd CUL/QBY BD13 124 F5
New Park St MOR LS27 152 B3
New Park V PDSY/CALV LS28 107 G3
New Park Vw PDSY/CALV LS28 106 F4
New Park Wk PDSY/CALV LS28 * 106 F3
New Park Wy PDSY/CALV LS28 107 G3
New Popplewell La
CLECK BD19 149 H6
Newport Av BRAM LS13 107 J4
Newport Crs HDGY LS6 108 F3
Newport Gdns HDGY LS6 108 F3
Newport Mt HDGY LS6 108 F3
Newport Pl GIR BD8 4 A3
Newport Rd GIR BD8 4 A2
Newport St PONT WF8 180 E5
Newport Vw HDGY LS6 * 108 F3
New Princess St BEE/HOL LS11 8 E5
New Pudsey Sq
PDSY/CALV LS28 106 E5
New Rd AIRE BD20 36 A5
AWLS/ASK DN6 227 J6
BSPA/BRAM LS23 69 M3
COP/BISH YO23 73 L4
CUL/QBY BD13 101 M6
DOD/DAR S75 240 D8
DOD/DAR S75 242 C4
EARD/LOFT WF3 154 F3
FEA/AMT WF7 178 F6
GFTH/SHER LS25 136 F4
GTL/HWG HX4 168 C7
GTL/HWG HX4 190 C5
HBR HX7 120 A8
HBR HX7 143 J3
HBR HX7 144 A6
HBR HX7 165 M5
HEM/SK/SE WF9 224 F4
HFAX HX1 11 H7
HOLM/MEL HD9 236 C7
HOR/CROF WF4 196 C7
HOR/CROF WF4 197 K5
HOR/CROF WF4 201 K5
HOR/CROF WF4 220 D8
HUDE HD5 193 K4
HUDW HD3 190 E4
KNOT WF11 181 J1
LIT OL15 207 G2
LUD/ILL HX2 144 F5
PONT WF8 204 E4
STKB/PEN S36 258 A5
TAD LS24 94 D1
TOD OL14 140 E1
TOD OL14 142 B6
TOD OL14 164 C2
YEA LS19 62 C8
New Rd East CLECK BD19 149 G6
Newroad End PONT WF8 204 D2
New Rd Side HORS LS18 85 J7
YEA LS19 84 D2
New Road Sq BRIG HD6 * 170 A8
New Rw COL BB8 74 E2
HOLM/MEL HD9 254 C1
HTON BD9 104 A4
WKFDW/WTN WF2 175 K4
New Row La STKB/PEN S36 257 G6
New Royd STKB/PEN S36 269 M3
Newroyd Rd WBOW BD5 127 G4
Newsam Ct MSTN/BAR LS15 * 111 J7
Newsam Dr MSTN/BAR LS15 111 G7
Newsam Green Rd
MSTN/BAR LS15 133 M4
RTHW LS26 134 A6
New Shaw La HBR HX7 142 B1
Newsholme La HOR/CROF WF4 198 B7
Newsholme New Rd
HWTH BD22 78 C2
New Smithy Av STKB/PEN S36 270 C2
New Smithy Dr STKB/PEN S36 270 C2
Newsome Av HUDS HD4 214 C5
Newsome Rd HUDS HD4 214 D2
Newsome Rd South HUDS HD4 214 C6
Newsome St DEWS WF13 173 K5
New Station St LDS LS1 8 F1
Newstead WHIT OL12 * 206 A6
Newstead Av HEM/SK/SE WF9 223 J3
HFAX HX1 146 A7
WKFDE WF1 176 C2
Newstead Crs HEM/SK/SE WF9 223 J2
Newstead Dr HEM/SK/SE WF9 223 J3
Newstead Gdns HFAX HX1 146 A7
Newstead Gv HEM/SK/SE WF9 223 J3
HFAX HX1 146 A7
Newstead Heath HFAX HX1 146 A7
Newstead La HOR/CROF WF4 223 G3
Newstead Pl HFAX HX1 146 A7
New Stead Ri AIRE BD20 58 D5
Newstead Rd BSLYN/ROY S71 243 G6
WKFDE WF1 12 D1
Newstead Ter HEM/SK/SE WF9 223 J3
HFAX HX1 146 A7
Newstead Vw HEM/SK/SE WF9 223 H3
Newstead Wk WBOW BD5 * 126 F2
New St AWLS/ASK DN6 249 M5
BOW BD4 127 K6
BRIG HD6 148 D7
BRIG HD6 170 F4
BSLY S70 261 H5
BSLYN/ROY S71 243 L3
BSLYN/ROY S71 262 A6
BTLY WF17 174 A3
CAS WF10 158 A6
CLECK BD19 150 B8
CUD/GR S72 222 F8
CUD/GR S72 245 J8
CUL/QBY BD13 101 M6
DOD/DAR S75 242 D5
DOD/DAR S75 260 B8
EARL WF12 174 B7
FEA/AMT WF7 224 B1
GFTH/SHER LS25 135 K5
GTL/HWG HX4 190 B3
HEM/SK/SE WF9 223 L4
HEM/SK/SE WF9 * 247 G3
HIPP HX3 169 J2
HOLM/MEL HD9 234 F4
HOLM/MEL HD9 236 B2
HOR/CROF WF4 197 K5
HORS LS18 85 K6
HUD HD1 14 A8
HUD HD1 14 F8
HUDE HD5 193 L6
HUDS HD4 213 L7
HUDW HD3 213 J2
HWTH BD22 78 E8
IDLE BD10 83 K6
KBTN HD8 239 J5
KBTN HD8 239 M5
LIT OL15 207 H2
LM/WK BD12 149 K1
LUD/ILL HX2 * 146 A6
MAR/SLWT HD7 212 C5
MAR/SLWT HD7 213 G2
MILN OL16 229 J1
OSS WF5 197 G1
PDSY/CALV LS28 106 F5
PDSY/CALV LS28 107 G8
TAD LS24 71 M3
WHIT OL12 206 A4
New Street Cl PDSY/CALV LS28 107 G8
New Street Gdns
PDSY/CALV LS28 107 G8
New Street Gv PDSY/CALV LS28 107 G8
New Sturton La
GFTH/SHER LS25 113 K7
New Tanhouse MIRF WF14 194 B1
New Temple Ga
MSTN/BAR LS15 111 J8
Newthorpe Rd AWLS/ASK DN6 227 L2
Newton Av WKFDE WF1 176 D4
Newton Cl AIRE BD20 35 M5
RTHW LS26 154 D2
WKFDE WF1 176 D5
Newton Ct RHAY LS8 88 E8
WKFDE WF1 176 D2
Newton Dr CAS WF10 158 D7
WKFDE WF1 176 D3
Newton Gdns WKFDE WF1 176 D5
Newton Garth CHAL LS7 110 A1
Newton Gn WKFDE WF1 176 D5
Newton Gv CHAL LS7 109 M2
TOD OL14 141 H7
Newton Hill Rd CHAL LS7 109 M1
Newton La CAS WF10 157 M2
WKFDE WF1 176 D3
Newton Lodge Cl CHAL LS7 109 L1
Newton Lodge Dr CHAL LS7 109 L1
Newton Pde CHAL LS7 109 M1
Newton Pk BRIG HD6 148 B8
Newton Park Ct CHAL LS7 * 110 A1
Newton Park Dr CHAL LS7 110 A1
Newton Park Vw CHAL LS7 110 A2
Newton Pl WBOW BD5 126 F2
Newton Rd CHAL LS7 110 A2
Newton St BSLY S70 260 F5
MILN OL16 228 C1
RPDN/SBR HX6 * 167 K2
WBOW BD5 127 G3
Newton Vw CHAL LS7 109 M1
Newton Vls CHAL LS7 * 87 L8
Newton Wk CHAL LS7 110 A2
Newton Wy BAIL BD17 * 82 E2
Newtown Av BSLYN/ROY S71 243 K2
CUD/GR S72 262 D1
New Town Ct HWTH BD22 2 D5
Newtown Gn CUD/GR S72 262 D1
Newtown St COL BB8 74 A2
ROY/SHW OL2 229 K8
New Wy BTLY WF17 173 L1
GSLY LS20 61 L5
New Wellgate CAS WF10 158 B8
New Wls WKFDE WF1 12 F4
New Wells Ter WKFDE WF1 * 12 F4
New Windsor Dr RTHW LS26 133 H8
New Works Rd LM/WK BD12 148 E1
New York La YEA LS19 84 F4
New York Rd LDSU LS2 7 J8
New York St LDSU LS2 9 H1
Nibshaw La CLECK BD19 150 C6
Nibshaw Rd CLECK BD19 150 C6
Nice Av RHAY LS8 110 B2
Nice St RHAY LS8 110 C2
Nice Vw RHAY LS8 110 B2
Nicholas Cl GTHN BD7 104 B7
Nicholas St BSLY S70 260 F5
Nichols Cl WBY LS22 47 L1
Nicholson Av DOD/DAR S75 260 A2
Nicholson Ct RHAY LS8 * 88 C8
Nicholson St CAS WF10 157 L7
ROCH OL11 228 B1
Nichols Wy WBY LS22 47 K1
Nickleby Rd OSM LS9 110 C6
Nicolsons Pl AIRE BD20 36 A5
Nidd Ap WBY LS22 29 M6
Nidd Ct AIRE BD20 36 A6
Nidderdale Cl GFTH/SHER LS25 135 K1
Nidderdale Wk BAIL BD17 83 G2
Nidd St BFDE BD3 5 M7
Nields Rd MAR/SLWT HD7 212 B6
Nigher Moss Av MILN OL16 206 E8
Nightingale Crest
WKFDW/WTN WF2 197 L2
Nightingale St KGHY BD21 * 3 H2
Nightingale Wk BGLY BD16 81 L2
Nijinsky Wy MID LS10 132 D5
Nile Crs HWTH BD22 2 A7
Nile Rd ILK LS29 38 D2
Nile St HUD HD1 14 D9
HWTH BD22 * 2 A7
HWTH BD22 79 G6
LDSU LS2 7 J8
MILN OL16 206 C6
Nina Rd GTHN BD7 126 B3
Ninelands La GFTH/SHER LS25 135 J1
Ninelands Sp GFTH/SHER LS25 113 H8
Ninelands Vw GFTH/SHER LS25 113 J7
Ninevah La CAS WF10 157 H1
HEM/SK/SE WF9 224 F3
Nineveh Gdns BEE/HOL LS11 8 D5
Nineveh Pde BEE/HOL LS11 8 D6
Nineveh Rd BEE/HOL LS11 8 C5
Ninth Av LVSG WF15 171 K1
Nippet La OSM LS9 7 M8
Nixon Av OSM LS9 110 D7
Nixon Cl EARL WF12 196 B5
Noble Ct HUDS HD4 213 M8
Noble Meadow WHIT OL12 * 206 F2
Noble St GTHN BD7 126 D1
Nog La HTON BD9 104 C2
Nook Farm Av WHIT OL12 206 B3
Nook Gdns MSTN/BAR LS15 90 B6
Nook Gn EARD/LOFT WF3 153 H7
EARL WF12 195 M4
The Nooking
WKFDW/WTN WF2 175 K3
Nook La HBR HX7 143 M2
RPDN/SBR HX6 166 B6
STKB/PEN S36 271 G5
Nook Rd MSTN/BAR LS15 90 B6
The Nooks MOR LS27 129 M7
The Nook AL/HA/HU LS17 87 M1
CLECK BD19 150 A6
EARD/LOFT WF3 153 G8
GFTH/SHER LS25 138 A2
RPDN/SBR HX6 167 K3
STKB/PEN S36 258 C8
Nook Wk DEWS WF13 173 H6
Noon Cl EARD/LOFT WF3 177 G1
Noon Sun St WHIT OL12 206 B5
Nopper Rd HUDS HD4 213 H7
Nora Pl BRAM LS13 107 J3
Nora Rd BRAM LS13 107 J3
Nora Ter BRAM LS13 107 J3
Norbeck Dr HWTH BD22 79 G6
Norbury Rd IDLE BD10 106 A1
Norbury St MILN OL16 * 228 D2
Norcliffe La HIPP HX3 147 J8
Norcroft BSLY S70 261 H8
Norcroft Brow GTHN BD7 4 C7
Norcroft La DOD/DAR S75 259 G3
Norcroft St BFD BD1 4 B6
Norcross Av HUDW HD3 191 J7
Nordale Cl ILK LS29 38 E1
Norfield HUDN HD2 192 C2
Norfolk Av BTLY WF17 173 K3
Norfolk Cl BSLYN/ROY S71 261 K2
CHAL LS7 87 M7
KNOT WF11 159 L6
LIT OL15 185 L6
ROY/SHW OL2 229 H7
RTHW LS26 155 M1
Norfolk Dr RTHW LS26 155 M1
Norfolk Gdns BFD BD1 4 F7
CHAL LS7 87 M7
RYKW YO26 32 B1
Norfolk Gn CHAL LS7 87 M7
Norfolk Mt CHAL LS7 87 M7
Norfolk Pl CHAL LS7 87 M7
HFAX HX1 10 D8
Norfolk St BGLY BD16 81 J3
BTLY WF17 173 K2
COL BB8 74 A1
HBR HX7 143 J4
ROCH OL11 206 A8
Norfolk Ter CHAL LS7 87 M7
Norfolk Vw CHAL LS7 87 M7
Norfolk Wk CHAL LS7 87 M7
Norgarth Cl BTLY WF17 174 B1
Norham Gv LM/WK BD12 148 F4
Norland Rd RPDN/SBR HX6 167 K3
Norland St GTHN BD7 126 B3
Norland Town Rd
RPDN/SBR HX6 167 M4
Norland Vw RPDN/SBR HX6 167 M2
Norman Av ECHL BD2 105 K1
ELL HX5 169 J8
Norman Cl BSLYN/ROY S71 261 L2
Norman Crs ECHL BD2 105 K1
Norman Dr MIRF WF14 172 B8
Norman Gv ECHL BD2 105 K1
ELL HX5 * 169 J8
KSTL LS5 108 C2
Norman La ECHL BD2 105 K1
Norman Mt ECHL BD2 105 K1
KSTL LS5 108 C2
Norman Pl RHAY LS8 88 C4
Norman Rd KBTN HD8 257 H1
MIRF WF14 172 B8
Norman Rw KSTL LS5 108 C2
Norman St BGLY BD16 * 81 J3
ELL HX5 169 J8
HFAX HX1 10 A9
KSTL LS5 108 C2
SHPY BD18 82 F7
Normans Wy
WKFDW/WTN WF2 199 H5
Norman Ter ECHL BD2 105 K1
ELL HX5 169 J8
RHAY LS8 88 C4
Normanton Gv BEE/HOL LS11 8 C7
Normanton Pl BEE/HOL LS11 8 D7
Normanton St BEE/HOL LS11 8 D8

HOR/CROF WF4 197 L6
Normanton Vw NORM WF6 178 D6
Norman Vw KSTL LS5 108 C2
Norreys St MILN OL16 206 C6
Norridge Bottom
HOLM/MEL HD9 254 C1
Norris Cl HUDE HD5 215 J2
Norristhorpe La LVSG WF15 172 C4
Nortech Cl CHAL LS7 7 K5
Northallerton Rd BFDE BD3 5 H2
North Ap TAD LS24 92 C2
North Av AIRE BD20 55 L2
CAS WF10 157 H7
HEM/SK/SE WF9 247 H4
HOR/CROF WF4 197 L5
HTON BD9 104 F3
OT LS21 41 J6
PONT WF8 180 C6
WKFDE WF1 176 E6
North Baileygate PONT WF8 180 F5
North Bank Rd BGLY BD16 103 J1
BTLY WF17 173 J1
HUDN HD2 14 C1
North Bolton LUD/ILL HX2 123 M7
North Br HIPP HX3 11 H4
North Bridge St HFAX HX1 11 H4
North Broadgate La HORS LS18 85 L5
Northbrook Cft CHAL LS7 * 87 M7
Northbrook Pl CHAL LS7 87 M7
North Brook St BFD BD1 5 G4
Northbrook St CHAL LS7 87 M7
North Byland LUD/ILL HX2 124 A7
North Carr HUDE HD5 193 G7
North Cliffe Av CUL/QBY BD13 103 H8
North Cliffe Cl CUL/QBY BD13 * 103 G8
North Cliffe Dr CUL/QBY BD13 103 G8
North Cliffe Gv CUL/QBY BD13 103 G7
North Cliffe La CUL/QBY BD13 103 H7
Northcliffe Rd SHPY BD18 82 C8
North Cl BSLYN/ROY S71 243 L3
FEA/AMT WF7 179 L5
RHAY LS8 88 F8
Northcote OSS WF5 174 E5
Northcote Crs BEE/HOL LS11 8 F7
Northcote Dr BEE/HOL LS11 8 E7
Northcote Fold WBY LS22 47 K4
Northcote Gn BEE/HOL LS11 8 F7
Northcote Rd ECHL BD2 105 K4
Northcote St PDSY/CALV LS28 106 F4
Northcote Ter DOD/DAR S75 260 E4
North Ct LDSU LS2 7 H8
North Court Gv WBY LS22 30 A8
North Crs GFTH/SHER LS25 116 A5
HEM/SK/SE WF9 247 K2
Northcroft HEM/SK/SE WF9 247 J3
North Cft ILK LS29 38 C2
Northcroft Av
HEM/SK/SE WF9 247 J3
Northcroft Ri HTON BD9 104 A5
North Cross Rd HUDN HD2 192 B4
North Cut BRIG HD6 170 A4
Northdale Av WBOW BD5 126 E4
Northdale Crs WBOW BD5 126 E4
Northdale Mt WBOW BD5 126 E4
Northdale Rd HTON BD9 104 D1
North Dean Av HWTH BD22 57 G7
North Dean Rd GTL/HWG HX4 168 B5
North Dene Rd AIRE BD20 36 A4
Northdowns Rd ROY/SHW OL2 229 H6
North Dr BHP/TINH LS16 64 B4
GFTH/SHER LS25 116 A5
MAR/SLWT HD7 213 G1
Northedge La HIPP HX3 147 M5
Northedge Meadow IDLE BD10 83 K8
Northedge Pk HIPP HX3 147 M6
Northern Cl GTHN BD7 126 B4
Northern St LDS LS1 8 D1
North Farm Rd RHAY LS8 110 D3
North Fld DOD/DAR S75 259 H6
Northfield Av HEM/SK/SE WF9 246 D3
KNOT WF11 182 B2
OSS WF5 174 F8
RTHW LS26 154 E2
Northfield Cl AWLS/ASK DN6 205 H3
ELL HX5 * 169 H8
Northfield Ct HEM/SK/SE WF9 246 E3
TAD LS24 94 F7
Northfield Crs BGLY BD16 81 J7
Northfield Dr PONT WF8 181 H5
Northfield Gdns WBOW BD5 126 E5
Northfield Gv HEM/SK/SE WF9 246 E3
HUD HD1 214 A2
WBSY BD6 126 E5
North Field La KBTN HD8 239 J4
Northfield La AWLS/ASK DN6 205 G2
GFTH/SHER LS25 137 M1
HEM/SK/SE WF9 246 D3
HOR/CROF WF4 197 L5
KBTN HD8 216 A6
KNOT WF11 182 F8
Northfield Pl DEWS WF13 173 K5
GIR BD8 4 B1
RTHW LS26 154 D2
WBY LS22 30 A8
North Field Rd AWLS/ASK DN6 248 A6
Northfield Rd DEWS WF13 173 K5
HOR/CROF WF4 200 D3
KNOT WF11 182 B2
OSS WF5 174 F8
WBSY BD6 126 D5
Northfields BSPA/BRAM LS23 49 J3
Northfields La TAD LS24 94 F6
Northfield St DEWS WF13 173 L5
HEM/SK/SE WF9 246 E3
Northfield Ter CUL/QBY BD13 125 J5
HOR/CROF WF4 * 197 L4
North Fold IDLE BD10 83 K6
North Ga MIRF WF14 193 M4
Northgate BAIL BD17 82 E2
BFD BD1 4 E5
CLECK BD19 150 A7
CUD/GR S72 223 G8
DEWS WF13 173 M6
DOD/DAR S75 260 E3
ELL HX5 169 H7
GTL/HWG HX4 190 D2
HBR HX7 143 H1
HECK WF16 172 E2
HFAX HX1 11 H5
HOLM/MEL HD9 236 C1
HOR/CROF WF4 197 J4
HUD HD1 15 G4
HUDE HD5 215 H3
PONT WF8 180 F5
RTHW LS26 133 L8
WKFDE WF1 176 D6
Northgate Cl PONT WF8 180 F5
Northgate La WBY LS22 47 J2
Northgate Ldg PONT WF8 180 F5
Northgate Ri WBY LS22 47 K4
Northgates WBY LS22 48 A1
North Grange Ms HDGY LS6 6 A1
North Grange Mt HDGY LS6 109 G1
North Grange Rd HDGY LS6 109 G2
North Gv WBY LS22 30 A8
North Grove Av WBY LS22 30 A7
North Grove Cl RHAY LS8 88 F8
North Grove Crs WBY LS22 30 A7
North Grove Dr RHAY LS8 88 F8
WBY LS22 30 A7
North Grove Mt WBY LS22 30 A8
North Grove Ri RHAY LS8 88 F8
North Grove Rd WBY LS22 30 A7
North Grove Wy WBY LS22 30 A7
North Hall Av IDLE BD10 83 J4
North Hl SCFT LS14 67 M6
North Hill Cl RHAY LS8 88 E8
North Hill Dr HUDE HD5 193 L6
North Hill Rd HDGY LS6 6 A1
North Holme St BFD BD1 4 F4
North King St BTLY WF17 173 M2
Northlands BSLYN/ROY S71 243 L2
North La MAR/SLWT HD7 211 M5
RHAY LS8 88 F8
RTHW LS26 133 L8
STKB/PEN S36 258 B4
WHIT OL12 206 B6
Northlea Av IDLE BD10 83 J5
North Lingwell Rd MID LS10 153 L1
North Lodge Fold DEWS WF13 173 H3
North Lodge La PONT WF8 204 B2
North Md BHP/TINH LS16 64 B4
North Moor La HUDE HD5 193 L4
Northolme Av BHP/TINH LS16 86 D7
Northolme Crs BHP/TINH LS16 86 D7
Northorpe Ct MIRF WF14 172 E7
Northorpe La MIRF WF14 172 E7
Northowram Gn HIPP HX3 147 J2
North Pde BFD BD1 4 E5
BHP/TINH LS16 86 C6
HFAX HX1 11 G5
ILK LS29 38 E2
ILK LS29 40 A4
MILN OL16 229 L2
OT LS21 41 J6
SKP/WHF BD23 16 C4
WIL/AL BD15 103 J4
North Park Av RHAY LS8 88 B6
North Park Gv RHAY LS8 88 C6
North Park La AWLS/ASK DN6 249 M3
North Park Rd HTON BD9 104 D3
RHAY LS8 88 C6
North Park St DEWS WF13 173 J5
North Park Ter HTON BD9 104 E4
North Pkwy SCFT LS14 111 G1
North Pl DOD/DAR S75 260 D3
MIRF WF14 172 C7
North Pollard St HIPP HX3 11 H4
North Queen St KGHY BD21 3 G4
North Ri HUDN HD2 192 E4
North Rd AIRE BD20 55 L1
BSLYN/ROY S71 243 M2
HORS LS18 85 K3
KBTN HD8 216 A7
KNOT WF11 159 J2
MIRF WF14 172 F8
MSTN/BAR LS15 111 L4
WBSY BD6 126 D6
North Road Ter WKFDE WF1 176 D7
Northrop Cl GIR BD8 104 C5
North Rw KBTN HD8 237 M6
North Royds Wd
BSLYN/ROY S71 243 H5
Northside Av GTHN BD7 104 C8
Northside Rd GTHN BD7 104 C8
Northside Ter GTHN BD7 104 B8
Northstead DEWS WF13 172 F8
North St AIRE BD20 34 F7
AIRE BD20 36 A4
AIRE BD20 55 M1
BFD BD1 5 H5
CAS WF10 157 L6
CAS WF10 158 E4
CHAL LS7 7 J5
DEWS WF13 173 L5
GTL/HWG HX4 168 F7
GTL/HWG HX4 190 D2
HECK WF16 172 F3
HEM/SK/SE WF9 246 D3
HUD HD1 213 M1
HWTH BD22 78 D7
IDLE BD10 83 K4
ILK LS29 19 J6
KGHY BD21 3 G5
LM/WK BD12 149 J2
MILN OL16 206 C6
MIRF WF14 194 B3
NORM WF6 178 C6
OT LS21 41 J6
PDSY/CALV LS28 107 G6
WBY LS22 48 A1
WMB/DAR S73 263 J8
YEA LS19 84 D2
North Sweeming Ct
GFTH/SHER LS25 117 J6
North Ter BTLY WF17 151 H5
MSTN/BAR LS15 * 111 L4
YEA LS19 62 D7
Northumberland St HUD HD1 14 F6
Northumberland Wy
BSLYN/ROY S71 262 B6
North Vale Ct BRIG HD6 148 D7
North Vw AIRE BD20 35 H8
EARL WF12 173 M8
KNOT WF11 182 A1
WIL/AL BD15 102 E1
WIL/AL BD15 103 J5
North View Rd BFDE BD3 105 H4
BOW BD4 128 C7
North View St AIRE BD20 57 K5
PDSY/CALV LS28 107 G4
North View Ter DEWS WF13 * 173 K4
HWTH BD22 78 E6
PDSY/CALV LS28 107 G4
North Wk BGLY BD16 80 C5
HEM/SK/SE WF9 223 M6
North Wy HUDN HD2 193 G2
RHAY LS8 88 F8
Northway MIRF WF14 172 B7
Northway Crs MIRF WF14 172 B7
Northway Gdns MIRF WF14 172 B6
Northwell Ga OT LS21 41 G5
North West Rd HDGY LS6 6 F3
North Wing BFDE BD3 5 H4
Northwood Cl PDSY/CALV LS28 129 H1
RTHW LS26 133 L7
Northwood Crs IDLE BD10 83 L7
Northwood Falls RTHW LS26 133 L7
Northwood Gdns
MSTN/BAR LS15 112 A7
Northwood Mt
PDSY/CALV LS28 129 H1
Northwood Pk KBTN HD8 216 A7
RTHW LS26 133 L7
Northwood Vw
PDSY/CALV LS28 129 H1
Norton Cl ELL HX5 191 H1
LUD/ILL HX2 145 K7
Norton Dr LUD/ILL HX2 145 K7
Norton Fold ECHL BD2 * 105 K1
Norton & Kirk Smeaton Rd
PONT WF8 226 F1
Norton Mill La AWLS/ASK DN6 227 L2
Norton Rd RHAY LS8 88 C3
WHIT OL12 206 B3
WKFDE WF1 176 F7
Norton St AIRE BD20 35 M5
ELL HX5 191 H1
WKFDE WF1 13 K7
Norton Tower LUD/ILL HX2 145 K7
Norton Wy MOR LS27 130 B8
Norville Crs WMB/DAR S73 263 K8
Norville Ter HDGY LS6 109 G2
Norwich Av MID LS10 131 M4
Norwich St ROCH OL11 228 C1
Norwood PONT WF8 203 J1
Norwood Av BIRK/DRI BD11 150 D2
ILK LS29 40 B5
SHPY BD18 82 D8
Norwood Bottom Rd OT LS21 23 H3
Norwood Cl ILK LS29 40 B5
ROY/SHW OL2 229 J6
Norwood Crs CLECK BD19 150 D2
PDSY/CALV LS28 107 H4
Norwood Dr BIRK/DRI BD11 150 D2
BTLY WF17 151 H6
CUD/GR S72 245 J3
DOD/DAR S75 260 A1
Norwood Green Hl HIPP HX3 148 B4
Norwood Gv BIRK/DRI BD11 150 D2
HDGY LS6 109 G3
Norwood La PBR HG3 24 D1
STKB/PEN S36 270 B1
Norwood Mt HDGY LS6 109 G3
Norwood Pk HUDW HD3 191 M5
ILK LS29 38 B2
Norwood Pl HDGY LS6 109 G3
SHPY BD18 82 D8
Nor Wood Rd HEM/SK/SE WF9 245 M1
Norwood Rd HDGY LS6 109 G3
HUDN HD2 192 A4
SHPY BD18 82 D8
Norwood St NORM WF6 178 F3
SHPY BD18 82 D8
WBOW BD5 126 F4
Norwood Ter HDGY LS6 109 G3
ILK LS29 40 B5
SHPY BD18 82 D8
Norwood Vw HDGY LS6 * 109 G3
Nostell Cl GIR BD8 4 C3
Nostell Fold DOD/DAR S75 260 B8
Nostell La HOR/CROF WF4 222 D4
Noster Gv BEE/HOL LS11 8 B9
Noster Hl BEE/HOL LS11 131 H3
Noster Pl BEE/HOL LS11 8 B9
Noster Rd BEE/HOL LS11 131 H3
Noster St BEE/HOL LS11 8 B9
Noster Ter BEE/HOL LS11 8 B9
Noster Vw BEE/HOL LS11 8 B9
Nottingham Cl BSLYN/ROY S71 262 C7
EARD/LOFT WF3 * 154 C3
Nottingham St BFDE BD3 106 A7
Notton La HOR/CROF WF4 221 L7
Nova La BTLY WF17 150 F4
Nowell Ap OSM LS9 110 D5
Nowell Av OSM LS9 110 D5
Nowell Cl OSM LS9 110 D5
Nowell Ct OSM LS9 110 D5
Nowell Crs OSM LS9 110 D5
Nowell End Rw OSM LS9 110 D5
Nowell Gdns OSM LS9 110 D5
Nowell Gv OSM LS9 110 D5
Nowell La OSM LS9 110 D5
Nowell Mt OSM LS9 110 D5
Nowell Pde OSM LS9 110 D5
Nowell Pl HUDE HD5 215 H2
OSM LS9 110 D5
Nowell St DEWS WF13 173 K5
OSM LS9 110 D5
Nowell's Yd DEWS WF13 173 K6
Nowell Ter OSM LS9 110 D5
Nowell Vw OSM LS9 * 110 D5
Nowell Wk OSM LS9 110 D5
Noyna Av COL BB8 52 A5
Noyna Vw COL BB8 52 A7
Nunburnholme Wk IDLE BD10 83 L8
Nunington Av WOR/ARM LS12 108 E6
Nunington St WOR/ARM LS12 108 E6
Nunington Ter WOR/ARM LS12 108 E6
Nunington Vw WOR/ARM LS12 108 E5
Nunlea Royd BRIG HD6 148 C8
Nunnery La BRIG HD6 169 M7
Nunns Av FEA/AMT WF7 201 L3
Nunn's Cl FEA/AMT WF7 201 L2
Nunns Ct FEA/AMT WF7 201 L3
Nunn's Cft FEA/AMT WF7 201 M2
Nunn's Gn FEA/AMT WF7 201 M2
Nunn's La FEA/AMT WF7 201 M2
Nunroyd HECK WF16 172 F1
Nunroyd Av GSLY LS20 62 B6
Nunroyd Gv AL/HA/HU LS17 87 M5
Nunroyd Lawn AL/HA/HU LS17 87 M5
Nunroyd Rd AL/HA/HU LS17 87 M5
Nunroyd Ter AL/HA/HU LS17 87 M5
Nunthorpe Rd BRAM LS13 107 H1
Nurser La WBOW BD5 126 E2
Nurser Pl WBOW BD5 126 E2
Nursery Av LUD/ILL HX2 146 B3
Nursery Cl AIRE BD20 57 J3
AL/HA/HU LS17 87 L2
BAIL BD17 * 82 A4
Nursery Gdns BSLY S70 262 A7
MILN OL16 * 206 E6
Nursery Garth WBY LS22 30 B8
Nursery Gv AL/HA/HU LS17 87 J2
EARL WF12 195 M2
LUD/ILL HX2 146 B3
Nursery La AL/HA/HU LS17 87 L2
HIPP HX3 146 B3
ILK LS29 19 J6
RPDN/SBR HX6 188 D3
Nursery Mt MID LS10 132 A5
Nursery Mount Rd MID LS10 132 A5
Nursery Rd GSLY LS20 61 M3
GTHN BD7 126 B4
Nursery St BSLY S70 261 G6
EARL WF12 195 L2
HUDN HD2 14 E1
Nursery Wy BSPA/BRAM LS23 48 D6
BSPA/BRAM LS23 69 M1
Nursery Wood Rd BTLY WF17 173 M4
Nussey Av BTLY WF17 151 G4
Nutclough Rd HBR HX7 143 K2
Nutfield St TOD OL14 141 K8
Nuthatch Ms WBSY BD6 125 L5
Nuttall Rd BFDE BD3 5 J5
Nutter La CLECK BD19 150 E4
Nutter St CLECK BD19 149 L7
Nutting Grove Ter
WOR/ARM LS12 130 A1
Nutwood Wk WBSY BD6 126 A8

O

Oak Av BGLY BD16 81 H5
COP/BISH YO23 73 L8
EARD/LOFT WF3 177 H2
GFTH/SHER LS25 113 H7
GIR BD8 104 E4
HOLM/MEL HD9 234 E3
HUDE HD5 215 G1
HUDW HD3 213 G1
ILK LS29 40 B6
MOR LS27 152 D3
NORM WF6 178 C6
ROY/SHW OL2 228 F8
RPDN/SBR HX6 167 K1
TOD OL14 141 J8
Oak Bank BGLY BD16 81 J4
SHPY BD18 104 F1
Oakbank Av HWTH BD22 2 A9
Oak Bank Broadway
HWTH BD22 79 H2
Oakbank Ct HWTH BD22 79 H2
Oakbank Crs HWTH BD22 79 H2
Oakbank Dr HWTH BD22 2 A9
Oakbank Gv HWTH BD22 2 B9
Oakbank La HWTH BD22 79 H2
Oakbank Mt HWTH BD22 79 H2
Oakburn Rd ILK LS29 38 C3
Oakcliffe Rd WHIT OL12 206 E2
Oak Crs GFTH/SHER LS25 113 H7
HOR/CROF WF4 222 D6
MSTN/BAR LS15 111 H7
Oakdale BGLY BD16 81 J1
Oakdale Av SHPY BD18 82 F8
WBSY BD6 126 D5
Oakdale Cl EARD/LOFT WF3 154 D8
HIPP HX3 146 C4
IDLE BD10 106 A3
Oakdale Crs HUDW HD3 191 J6
WBSY BD6 126 D5
Oakdale Dr IDLE BD10 106 A3
OT LS21 42 F8
SHPY BD18 83 G8
Oakdale Garth SCFT LS14 89 K5
Oakdale Gv SHPY BD18 83 G8
Oakdale Meadow SCFT LS14 89 K5
Oakdale Rd HEM/SK/SE WF9 223 K4
SHPY BD18 83 G8
Oakdale Ter WBSY BD6 126 D5
Oakdean HUDN HD2 192 C2
Oakdene Cl PDSY/CALV LS28 129 H1
Oakdene Ct AL/HA/HU LS17 88 C2
Oakdene Dr AL/HA/HU LS17 88 C2
HOR/CROF WF4 200 D6
Oakdene Gdns AL/HA/HU LS17 88 C2
Oakdene V AL/HA/HU LS17 88 C2
Oakdene Wy AL/HA/HU LS17 88 C2
Oak Dr GFTH/SHER LS25 113 H7
MAR/SLWT HD7 212 F3
Oakenshaw Ct LM/WK BD12 148 E4
Oakenshaw La CLECK BD19 149 J3
WKFDW/WTN WF2 199 J6
Oakenshaw St WKFDE WF1 13 L9
Oakes Av HOLM/MEL HD9 236 E5
Oakes Fold KBTN HD8 216 C3
Oakes La HOLM/MEL HD9 236 E4
Oakes Rd South HUDW HD3 191 K7
Oakes St WKFDW/WTN WF2 175 M8
Oakfield HDGY LS6 109 G1
Oakfield Av BGLY BD16 81 L4
RTHW LS26 * 133 G8
Oakfield Cl ELL HX5 169 G8
GFTH/SHER LS25 113 H8
ILK LS29 40 C8
Oakfield Ct DOD/DAR S75 * 242 C5
Oakfield Crs KNOT WF11 182 B3
Oakfield Dr BAIL BD17 82 F4
MIRF WF14 194 B3
Oakfield Gv HTON BD9 104 E4
KBTN HD8 239 J5
Oakfield Pk PONT WF8 225 K2
Oakfield Rd HUDN HD2 192 A5
KGHY BD21 79 J2
Oakfield Ter SHPY BD18 82 F7
Oakfield Wk DOD/DAR S75 260 D4
Oak Gv GFTH/SHER LS25 113 J7
HWTH BD22 79 J2
MOR LS27 152 D3
Oakhall Pk CUL/QBY BD13 102 F8
Oak Hall Pk HOR/CROF WF4 219 L2
Oakhall Park Av CUL/QBY BD13 102 F7
Oakham Pl DOD/DAR S75 260 E3
Oakhampton Ct RHAY LS8 88 E7
Oakham Wk BOW BD4 * 127 J2
Oakham Wy OSM LS9 110 D7
Oak Hl LIT OL15 207 H1
RPDN/SBR HX6 167 G6
Oak Hill Rd BRIG HD6 170 D3
Oakhill Rd BTLY WF17 151 J7
Oakhurst Av BEE/HOL LS11 131 H5
Oakhurst Gv BEE/HOL LS11 131 H5
Oakhurst Mt BEE/HOL LS11 131 H5
Oakhurst Rd BEE/HOL LS11 131 J5
Oakhurst St BEE/HOL LS11 131 J5
Oakland Ct KBTN HD8 216 B7
Oakland Dr HOR/CROF WF4 218 E1
Oakland Hills NORM WF6 178 E5
Oakland Rd HOR/CROF WF4 218 F1
WKFDE WF1 13 J9
Oaklands BRIG HD6 170 B5
EARD/LOFT WF3 154 C3
IDLE BD10 83 J6
ILK LS29 38 B4
SHPY BD18 81 M7
Oaklands Av BHP/TINH LS16 86 F3
BRAM LS13 107 G1
BSLYN/ROY S71 261 M2
HIPP HX3 147 J3
Oaklands Cl BHP/TINH LS16 86 F3
HOLM/MEL HD9 236 C7
Oaklands Cft
WKFDW/WTN WF2 199 K8
Oaklands Dr BHP/TINH LS16 86 F3
BTLY WF17 174 B1
HUDE HD5 215 H1
Oaklands Fold BHP/TINH LS16 86 F3
Oaklands Gv BHP/TINH LS16 86 F3
Oaklands Rd BRAM LS13 107 G1
Oakland St AIRE BD20 35 M5
Oak La GIR BD8 104 E4
HFAX HX1 10 C5
RPDN/SBR HX6 167 G6
Oaklea Cl DOD/DAR S75 242 D4
Oaklea Gdns BHP/TINH LS16 86 F4
Oaklea Hall Cl BHP/TINH LS16 86 F4
Oaklea Rd MSTN/BAR LS15 90 B8
Oak Leigh DOD/DAR S75 259 G2
Oakleigh Av CLAY BD14 125 K3
HIPP HX3 168 E3
WKFDW/WTN WF2 198 A1
Oakleigh Cl CLAY BD14 125 K2
HOR/CROF WF4 200 E2
Oakleigh Gdns CLAY BD14 * 125 K3
Oakleigh Gv CLAY BD14 125 K3
Oakleigh Rd CLAY BD14 125 K3
Oakleigh Ter CLAY BD14 125 K2
Oakleigh Vw BAIL BD17 82 D3
Oakley Gv BEE/HOL LS11 131 L3
Oakley St EARD/LOFT WF3 154 A5
Oakley Ter BEE/HOL LS11 131 L4
Oakley Vw BEE/HOL LS11 131 L4
Oakmont Cl NORM WF6 178 E5
Oak Mt GIR BD8 104 F4
HIPP HX3 * 148 A7
TOD OL14 141 K8
Oak Park Ri BSLY S70 261 J7
Oak Pl GFTH/SHER LS25 113 G7
HFAX HX1 10 B6
RPDN/SBR HX6 167 K1
Oak Rdg WBY LS22 47 L1
Oakridge Av ILK LS29 61 K2
Oakridge Ct BGLY BD16 81 J2
Oak Ri CLECK BD19 149 M4
Oak Rd CUD/GR S72 244 F4
GFTH/SHER LS25 113 G7
HUDN HD2 193 J1
MOR LS27 152 B4
MSTN/BAR LS15 111 H7
WBY LS22 30 F1
WOR/ARM LS12 109 G7
Oak Royd GFTH/SHER LS25 113 H7
Oakroyd RTHW LS26 155 H2
Oakroyd Av WBSY BD6 126 E6
Oakroyd Cl BIRK/DRI BD11 150 C1
BRIG HD6 170 D1
Oakroyd Dr BIRK/DRI BD11 150 C2
BRIG HD6 170 D1
Oakroyd Fold MOR LS27 * 130 E6
Oakroyd Mt PDSY/CALV LS28 107 G6
Oakroyd Rd WBSY BD6 126 E6
Oakroyd Ter BAIL BD17 82 F4
GIR BD8 104 F4
MOR LS27 * 130 E6
PDSY/CALV LS28 107 G6
Oakroyd Vls GIR BD8 104 F4
Oak Scar La HOLM/MEL HD9 254 F4
Oaks Crs BSLY S70 261 L6
Oaks Dr GIR BD8 103 L6
Oaks Farm Dr DOD/DAR S75 242 B6
Oaksfield RTHW LS26 156 F4
Oaks Fold KBTN HD8 * 216 C3
WBOW BD5 127 G3
Oaks Green Mt BRIG HD6 170 B7
Oaks La BSLY S70 261 L6
BSPA/BRAM LS23 48 F6
GIR BD8 103 M7
Oaks Rd BTLY WF17 174 A2
The Oaks HOR/CROF WF4 200 D2
MOR LS27 130 D7
Oak St BSLY S70 260 F5
CLAY BD14 125 K2
COL BB8 52 B8
CUD/GR S72 263 K1
ELL HX5 169 H8
HBR HX7 143 J3
HECK WF16 172 E2
HEM/SK/SE WF9 247 G5
HOR/CROF WF4 200 C7
HWTH BD22 78 F7
HWTH BD22 100 E3
LIT OL15 207 L1
MILN OL16 206 B7
MILN OL16 229 J3
MOR LS27 130 D7
PDSY/CALV LS28 106 E6
ROY/SHW OL2 229 L8
RPDN/SBR HX6 167 K1
TOD OL14 163 J2
WKFDE WF1 176 E2
Oaks Wood Dr DOD/DAR S75 242 C5
Oak Ter COL BB8 * 53 G8
HFAX HX1 * 10 C5
HUDN HD2 * 192 D5
LIT OL15 185 M4
Oak Tree Av CUD/GR S72 244 D7
KBTN HD8 215 M3
Oak Tree Cl DOD/DAR S75 241 M6
OSM LS9 110 E3
Oak Tree Ct AIRE BD20 35 M4
Oak Tree Crs OSM LS9 110 E3
Oak Tree Dr RHAY LS8 110 E3
Oak Tree Gv HEM/SK/SE WF9 224 B8
OSM LS9 110 E3
Oaktree La HEM/SK/SE WF9 224 E1
Oak Tree Meadow
WKFDW/WTN WF2 199 J8
Oak Tree Mt OSM LS9 110 E3
Oak Tree Pl OSM LS9 110 E3
Oak Tree Rd KBTN HD8 215 M3
Oak Tree Ter KBTN HD8 215 M3
Oak Tree Wk OSM LS9 110 E3
Oak Vw AIRE BD20 36 A4
Oak Vls GIR BD8 104 F4
Oakville Rd HBR HX7 142 F4
Oakway BIRK/DRI BD11 150 D2
Oakwell Av BTLY WF17 151 H8
PONT WF8 180 E8
RHAY LS8 88 C8
WOR/ARM LS12 108 F7
Oakwell Cl BIRK/DRI BD11 151 J1
GTHN BD7 126 D3
HEM/SK/SE WF9 223 J4
Oakwell Ct BRAM LS13 107 K3
Oakwell Crs RHAY LS8 88 C8
Oakwell Dr RHAY LS8 88 C8
Oakwell Gdns RHAY LS8 88 C8
Oakwell Gv BRAM LS13 107 K3
Oak Well La BSLY S70 261 J6
Oakwell Mt RHAY LS8 88 C8
Oakwell Ov RHAY LS8 88 C8
Oakwell Rd BIRK/DRI BD11 151 J1
Oakwell Ter BSLYN/ROY S71 261 J6
PDSY/CALV LS28 * 106 F3
Oakwell Vw BSLYN/ROY S71 261 K5
Oakwell Wy BTLY WF17 151 J3
Oakwood WKFDW/WTN WF2 * 197 M3
Oakwood Av BIRK/DRI BD11 150 C1
BSLYN/ROY S71 243 K2
ECHL BD2 104 F2
RHAY LS8 88 D8
WKFDW/WTN WF2 197 M1
Oakwood Boundary Rd
RHAY LS8 88 D8
Oakwood Cl NORM WF6 178 B2
TAD LS24 94 E8
Oakwood Ct GIR BD8 4 A4
RHAY LS8 88 E8
Oakwood Crs BSLYN/ROY S71 243 K3
Oakwood Dr BGLY BD16 81 H1
HEM/SK/SE WF9 246 B1
NORM WF6 178 B2
RHAY LS8 88 D8
RTHW LS26 132 F7
Oakwood Gdns
PDSY/CALV LS28 107 G8
RHAY LS8 88 D8
Oakwood Garth RHAY LS8 88 E8
Oakwood Gra RHAY LS8 88 E8
Oakwood Grange La RHAY LS8 88 E8
Oakwood Gn RHAY LS8 88 E8
Oakwood Gv GIR BD8 104 C5
HOR/CROF WF4 197 L5
RHAY LS8 88 D8
Oakwood La OSM LS9 110 F3
RHAY LS8 88 D8
Oakwood Mt RHAY LS8 88 D8
Oakwood Nook RHAY LS8 88 D8
Oakwood Pk RHAY LS8 110 E1
Oakwood Pl RHAY LS8 88 D8
Oakwood Ri RHAY LS8 88 E8
Oakwood Rd BSLYN/ROY S71 243 K2
BTLY WF17 174 A1
Oak Wood Rd WBY LS22 29 M7
Oakwood Sq DOD/DAR S75 241 K6
Oakwood Ter PDSY/CALV LS28 107 G8
Oakwood Vw RHAY LS8 * 88 E8
Oakwood Wk RHAY LS8 88 D8
Oakworth Cl DOD/DAR S75 260 D3

Oakworth Hall HWTH BD22 78 E4
Oakworth Rd HWTH BD22 79 H2
KGHY BD21 2 B9
Oasby Cft BOW BD4 128 A5
Oast House Cft
EARD/LOFT WF3 154 D3
Oastler Av HUD HD1 14 C7
Oastler Pl LM/WK BD12 126 F8
Oastler Rd PDSY/CALV LS28 84 D8
SHPY BD18 82 B6
Oastler St DEWS WF13 173 K6
Oates St DEWS WF13 173 M6
Oatland Cl CHAL LS7 7 H4
Oatland Ct CHAL LS7 7 H5
Oatland Dr CHAL LS7 7 H5
Oatland Gdns CHAL LS7 7 J5
Oatland Gn CHAL LS7 7 H4
Oatland Hts CHAL LS7 7 H5
Oatland La CHAL LS7 7 G4
Oatland Pl CHAL LS7 7 G3
Oatland Rd CHAL LS7 7 G4
Oatlands Dr OT LS21 41 H5
Oat St HWTH BD22 * 79 J2
Oban Cl EARD/LOFT WF3 152 F5
Oban Pl WOR/ARM LS12 108 D6
Oban St WOR/ARM LS12 108 D6
Oban Ter WOR/ARM LS12 108 D6
Oberon Crs WMB/DAR S73 263 H8
Oberon Wy BGLY BD16 81 K8
Occupation La BHP/TINH LS16 63 K3
DEWS WF13 173 H3
HOLM/MEL HD9 236 F5
HWTH BD22 79 H2
LUD/ILL HX2 124 A8
PDSY/CALV LS28 106 E8
TAD LS24 91 M2
Occupation Rd HUDN HD2 * 192 E3
HUDW HD3 191 K6
Ochrewell Av HUDN HD2 193 G3
Octagon Ter LUD/ILL HX2 168 A2
Odda La GSLY LS20 61 G5
Oddfellows' Ct BFD BD1 4 E7
Oddfellows St BRIG HD6 170 D3
CLECK BD19 149 H6
MIRF WF14 194 C1
Oddfellow St MOR LS27 152 C2
Oddy Fold HIPP HX3 10 F2
Oddy Pl WBSY BD6 126 D5
Oddy's Fold HDGY LS6 87 G6
Oddy St BOW BD4 128 A5
Odsal Pl WBSY BD6 126 F6
Odsal Rd WBSY BD6 126 F6
The Office Village OSS WF5 175 K8
Offley La HEM/SK/SE WF9 201 K8
Ogden Crs CUL/QBY BD13 101 M4
Ogden La BRIG HD6 170 B6
CUL/QBY BD13 101 M4
LUD/ILL HX2 123 M4
MILN OL16 229 M1
Ogden St RPDN/SBR HX6 167 J3
Ogden View Cl LUD/ILL HX2 123 M7
Ogilby Ct RTHW LS26 133 K7
Ogilby Ms RTHW LS26 133 K7
O'Grady Sq OSM LS9 110 B7
Old Allen Rd CUL/QBY BD13 102 C3
Old Anna La or Long La
STKB/PEN S36 270 C2
Old Bank HIPP HX3 11 K5
MAR/SLWT HD7 212 B6
Old Bank Fold HUDE HD5 * 15 L8
Old Bank Rd EARL WF12 174 A6
MIRF WF14 172 C7
Old Bar La HOLM/MEL HD9 255 K6
Old Barn Cl AL/HA/HU LS17 87 J1
Old Bell Ct HFAX HX1 * 11 G8
Old Bent La WHIT OL12 184 C7
Old Brandon La AL/HA/HU LS17 89 G8
Old Brewery Gdns TAD LS24 72 A2
Old Bridge Ri ILK LS29 38 C2
Old Brook Cl ROY/SHW OL2 229 M6
Old Brow La MILN OL16 206 E3
Old Canal Rd BFD BD1 4 F2
Old Cawsey RPDN/SBR HX6 167 L2
Old Church St OSS WF5 196 F1
Old Clay Dr WHIT OL12 206 F2
Old Cl BEE/HOL LS11 130 F6
Old Cock Yd HFAX HX1 * 11 H6
Old Corn Mill La GTHN BD7 * 126 C2
Old Crown Rd
WKFDW/WTN WF2 197 M3
Old Dalton La KGHY BD21 3 J4
Old Earth ELL HX5 169 K7
Oldfarm Ap BHP/TINH LS16 86 B6
Oldfarm Cl BHP/TINH LS16 86 C6
Old Farm Crs BOW BD4 * 127 K3
Oldfarm Cross BHP/TINH LS16 86 C6
Oldfarm Dr BHP/TINH LS16 86 C6
Oldfarm Garth BHP/TINH LS16 86 C6
Oldfarm Pde BHP/TINH LS16 86 C6
Oldfarm Wk BHP/TINH LS16 86 B6
Oldfield Av WOR/ARM LS12 108 E8
Oldfield Ct CHAL LS7 110 A1
Old Fieldhouse La HUDN HD2 192 F4
Oldfield La HECK WF16 172 F3
HWTH BD22 77 K7
HWTH BD22 78 C7
KBTN HD8 240 B4
WBY LS22 48 A5
WOR/ARM LS12 108 F8
Oldfield Rd HOLM/MEL HD9 236 A5
Oldfield St HIPP HX3 * 146 C2
HUDS HD4 214 A2
WOR/ARM LS12 108 E8
Old Forge Ms BHP/TINH LS16 63 M3
Old Garth Cft KNOT WF11 159 J2
Old Ga HBR HX7 143 J3
HOLM/MEL HD9 253 G7
Oldgate HUD HD1 15 G7
Oldgate La GFTH/SHER LS25 115 L2
Old Great North Rd KNOT WF11 159 K5
Old Gnd MAR/SLWT HD7 211 J6
Old Guy Rd CUL/QBY BD13 124 E4
Old Hall Cl AIRE BD20 34 D8
HWTH BD22 * 78 E8
Old Hall La KBTN HD8 240 A1
Old Hall Ms BTLY WF17 * 151 L7
Old Hall Rd AIRE BD20 34 D8
AWLS/ASK DN6 * 249 J5
BTLY WF17 151 L7
EARD/LOFT WF3 153 H6
Old Hall Wy AIRE BD20 34 C8
Oldham Rd MILN OL16 228 E5
ROCH OL11 228 C1
ROCH OL11 228 D6
RPDN/SBR HX6 210 A1
UPML OL3 230 C8
UPML OL3 230 E5
Oldham Wy MILN OL16 229 H5
ROY/SHW OL2 230 C4
UPML OL3 231 L3
Old Haworth La YEA LS19 62 D7
Old Hollings Hl BAIL BD17 61 L8
Old Laithe La HBR HX7 143 L1
Old La BEE/HOL LS11 131 H4
BHP/TINH LS16 63 J3
BIRK/DRI BD11 129 J7
BIRK/DRI BD11 150 D1
BRIG HD6 170 D3
BWCK/EAR BB18 52 B2
CUL/QBY BD13 79 M8
GSLY LS20 61 G6
HBR HX7 121 K6
HIPP HX3 10 E1
HIPP HX3 146 C3
HOLM/MEL HD9 252 E2
HUDN HD2 192 F2
HWTH BD22 54 E4
HWTH BD22 77 H7
ILK LS29 19 L8
ILK LS29 38 F3
LUD/ILL HX2 144 F5
MAR/SLWT HD7 211 M7
MAR/SLWT HD7 212 D1
RYKW YO26 33 J3
SEL YO8 139 L5
WHIT OL12 162 A8
Old Langley La BAIL BD17 82 F2
Old Lee Bank HIPP HX3 10 E2
Old Leeds Rd HUD HD1 15 H6
Old Lees Rd HBR HX7 143 J2
Old Lindley Rd HUDW HD3 190 E4
Old London Rd TAD LS24 71 J8
Old Main St BGLY BD16 81 H3
Old Manchester Rd
STKB/PEN S36 269 G6
Old Manor Dr STKB/PEN S36 271 K5
Old Manse Cft HWTH BD22 * 100 E3
Old Market HFAX HX1 11 H6
Old Marsh PDSY/CALV LS28 106 E7
Old Mill Cl HEM/SK/SE WF9 223 L7
ILK LS29 40 B4
Old Mill Dr COL BB8 74 B2
Old Mill La BSLY S70 261 G4
BSPA/BRAM LS23 70 A1
CHPT/GREN S35 271 M8
MID LS10 9 M8
Old Mill Rdg HBR HX7 143 L1
Old Mill Rd BAIL BD17 * 82 C6
Oldmill St WHIT OL12 206 B6
Old Mill Vw EARL WF12 195 K1
Old Mill Yd OSS WF5 * 196 E3
Old Moll Rd HOLM/MEL HD9 235 M1
Old Mount Farm
HOR/CROF WF4 220 C7
Old Mount Rd MAR/SLWT HD7 233 G3
Old Oak Cl BHP/TINH LS16 86 C7
Old Oak Dr BHP/TINH LS16 86 B7
Old Oak Garth BHP/TINH LS16 86 B7
Old Oak Lawn BHP/TINH LS16 86 C7
The Old Orch OT LS21 42 E7
Old Oxenhope La HWTH BD22 100 D1
Old Pack Horse Rd UPML OL3 231 K8
Old Park Rd IDLE BD10 83 L7
RHAY LS8 88 C7
Old Pool Bank BHP/TINH LS16 63 K2
Old Popplewell La CLECK BD19 149 G6
Old Power Wy ELL HX5 169 J6
Old Quarry La GFTH/SHER LS25 137 M5
Old Riding La LUD/ILL HX2 145 H3
Old Rd AL/HA/HU LS17 44 F4
BSLYN/ROY S71 261 J1
COP/BISH YO23 73 K5
CUL/QBY BD13 101 M6
CUL/QBY BD13 103 H8
GTHN BD7 126 A4
HBR HX7 121 J4
HOLM/MEL HD9 253 M3
HOR/CROF WF4 196 B8
MILN OL16 207 G2
MOR LS27 130 E6
Oldroyd Av CUD/GR S72 245 J8
Oldroyd Crs BEE/HOL LS11 131 G4
Oldroyd Rd TOD OL14 163 M1
Oldroyd Wy DEWS WF13 173 K6
Old Run Rd MID LS10 131 M4
Old Run Vw MID LS10 131 M6
The Old Sawmills
RPDN/SBR HX6 188 E4
Old School Ct CAS WF10 179 L1
DOD/DAR S75 260 A1
Old School La HUDE HD5 215 H3
Old School Ms MOR LS27 130 E6
Old Schools Gdns HIPP HX3 11 H2
Old Shaw La HBR HX7 142 B2
Old Side Ct AIRE BD20 59 G5
Old Souls Wy BGLY BD16 59 G8
Old South St HUD HD1 14 E7
Old Station Rd LUD/ILL HX2 144 F7
Old Station Wy ILK LS29 19 H6
Old Stone Brow
BWCK/EAR BB18 52 C2
Old Stone Trough La
BWCK/EAR BB18 52 C1
Old St AWLS/ASK DN6 248 B5
Old Town Mill La HBR HX7 143 K1
Old Vicarage Cl BGLY BD16 81 K8
Old Vicarage La
GFTH/SHER LS25 138 D6
Old Village St AWLS/ASK DN6 249 J2
Old Wakefield Rd HUDE HD5 15 L8
Old Well Head HFAX HX1 11 G8
Old Westgate EARL WF12 173 L6
Old Whack House La YEA LS19 62 B8
Old Wood La BGLY BD16 60 C4
The Old Woodyard
HOR/CROF WF4 218 E4
Old Yew La HOLM/MEL HD9 254 A4
Olicana Pk ILK LS29 38 C1
Olive Gv GIR BD8 104 A6
Oliver Cl LIT OL15 207 H1
RPDN/SBR HX6 166 F7
Oliver Gdns MIRF WF14 172 B7
Oliver Hl HORS LS18 85 L7
Oliver Mdw ELL HX5 169 J6
Oliver Rd HECK WF16 173 G1
Olivers Mt PONT WF8 181 G6
Oliver St BOW BD4 5 J9
Olive St HUD HD1 15 G1
Olive Ter MAR/SLWT HD7 * 211 L8
Ollerdale Av WIL/AL BD15 103 J3
Ollerdale Cl WIL/AL BD15 103 J4
Ollerton WHIT OL12 * 206 A6
Ollerton Rd BSLYN/ROY S71 243 H6
Olney ROCH OL11 * 206 A8
Olney St MAR/SLWT HD7 212 B5
Olympic Pk LM/WK BD12 149 G1
Omar St HECK WF16 172 E2
One Acre Garth SEL YO8 139 M4
One Ash Cl WHIT OL12 206 B4
Onslow Crs BOW BD4 127 K4
Ontario Pl CHAL LS7 87 M8
Opal St HWTH BD22 79 J2
Orange St BFDE BD3 105 L8
HFAX HX1 11 G5
Orange Ter HUD HD1 * 14 F3
Orange Tree Gv
EARD/LOFT WF3 153 L7
Orchan Rd TOD OL14 141 H7
Orchard Av EARD/LOFT WF3 177 H1
Orchard Cl AWLS/ASK DN6 227 M3
BSLYN/ROY S71 261 L1
DOD/DAR S75 242 D5
EARD/LOFT WF3 153 M8
GFTH/SHER LS25 138 A3
GFTH/SHER LS25 138 D6
HOLM/MEL HD9 235 H5
HOR/CROF WF4 197 J4
LUD/ILL HX2 145 M8
TAD LS24 115 M1
TAD LS24 116 A1
WKFDW/WTN WF2 176 A3
Orchard Ct BSPA/BRAM LS23 69 M4
HEM/SK/SE WF9 225 G4
HUDW HD3 191 H8
Orchard Cft DOD/DAR S75 260 C8
WKFDW/WTN WF2 176 A4
WKFDW/WTN WF2 199 J7
Orchard Dr AWLS/ASK DN6 227 M3
CUD/GR S72 222 F8
FEA/AMT WF7 224 C1
HOR/CROF WF4 198 B7
KNOT WF11 159 K1
SEL YO8 139 M4
WBY LS22 47 K3
Orchard Gdns HOR/CROF WF4 198 B7
Orchard Gv CAS WF10 179 H1
IDLE BD10 83 M7
ILK LS29 61 J2
ROY/SHW OL2 229 J7
Orchard Head Crs PONT WF8 181 G2
Orchard Head Dr PONT WF8 181 G3
Orchard Head La PONT WF8 181 G2
Orchard La ILK LS29 19 J6
PONT WF8 203 L2
TAD LS24 116 A2
Orchard Lees HUDE HD5 193 L6
Orchard Mt MSTN/BAR LS15 111 L4
Orchard Pl CUD/GR S72 262 E1
Orchard Ri RPDN/SBR HX6 167 H4
Orchard Rd HUDE HD5 193 L6
MSTN/BAR LS15 111 K4
WKFDW/WTN WF2 199 G5
Orchard Sq MSTN/BAR LS15 111 K4
The Orchards BGLY BD16 81 J1
CLECK BD19 150 E6
FEA/AMT WF7 202 D6
MSTN/BAR LS15 111 K4
RTHW LS26 156 E4
Orchard St EARL WF12 173 L8
HUDS HD4 214 C2
OT LS21 41 K7
Orchard St West HUDW HD3 213 J1
Orchard Ter DOD/DAR S75 259 H2
HUDS HD4 214 D2
The Orchard AWLS/ASK DN6 227 L6
FEA/AMT WF7 179 M5
HOR/CROF WF4 200 B5
KGHY BD21 58 B7
MIRF WF14 172 D7
NORM WF6 178 C6
OSS WF5 196 F1
PONT WF8 203 H1
WKFDW/WTN WF2 176 B3
Orchard Vw HEM/SK/SE WF9 * 246 E4
Orchard Wk BSLYN/ROY S71 * 261 H3
HBR HX7 144 B5
Orchard Wy BRIG HD6 170 C2
RTHW LS26 133 G8
Orchid Cl SHPY BD18 104 F1
Orchid Ct EARD/LOFT WF3 154 D4
Orchid Crest HEM/SK/SE WF9 225 J7
Orchid Vw WKFDW/WTN WF2 176 A6
Oriel St ROCH OL11 228 B1
Oriel Wy BSLYN/ROY S71 261 M3
Oriental St WOR/ARM LS12 108 E7
Orion Crs MID LS10 132 A7
Orion Dr MID LS10 132 A7
Orion Gdns MID LS10 132 B7
Orion Vw MID LS10 132 B7
Orion Wk MID LS10 132 B6
Orlando Cl MIRF WF14 172 B7
Orleans St WBSY BD6 126 B7
Ormonde Dr WIL/AL BD15 103 J6
Ormond Rd WBSY BD6 126 D6
Ormondroyd Av WBSY BD6 126 E6
Ormonde Pl GTHN BD7 126 C2
Orron St LIT OL15 207 J1
Orville Gdns HDGY LS6 109 G2
Orwell Cl CAS WF10 180 E1
Osborne Av HOR/CROF WF4 197 L3
Osborne Ms BSLY S70 * 261 J6
Osborne Pl TOD OL14 163 L1
Osborne Rd HUD HD1 14 D3
Osborne St BSLY S70 261 J6
HBR HX7 143 J3
HFAX HX1 10 B4
HUDE HD5 15 M8
ROCH OL11 228 A1
ROY/SHW OL2 229 K8
WBOW BD5 126 F1
Osbourne Ct BRAM LS13 107 M5
Osbourne Dr CUL/QBY BD13 125 G5
Osmondthorpe La OSM LS9 110 E7
Osmondthorpe Ter OSM LS9 110 D6
Osprey Cl AL/HA/HU LS17 88 B2
AWLS/ASK DN6 249 K8
WBY LS22 47 K5
Osprey Ct GIR BD8 * 103 L7
Osprey Dr HUDS HD4 214 A7
Osprey Gv AL/HA/HU LS17 88 B2
Osprey Meadow MOR LS27 152 F2
Ossett La EARL WF12 174 B7
Osterley Gv IDLE BD10 106 A1
Ostler Gv MIRF WF14 172 C8
Oswald Cl GSLY LS20 61 M5
Oswald St MILN OL16 206 C6
ROY/SHW OL2 229 L6
SHPY BD18 82 F7
Oswaldthorpe Av BFDE BD3 105 M5
Otley La YEA LS19 62 D7
Otley Mt AIRE BD20 * 58 F6
Otley Old Rd BHP/TINH LS16 86 B2
HORS LS18 63 J5
Otley Rd BAIL BD17 83 H3
BFDE BD3 5 H5
BGLY BD16 59 J5
BGLY BD16 60 B5
BHP/TINH LS16 64 D7
BHP/TINH LS16 86 D3
HDGY LS6 108 F1
ILK LS29 40 C6
ILK LS29 61 K1
OT LS21 44 C7
PBR HG3 25 K1
SHPY BD18 82 D8
SKP/WHF BD23 16 D2
Otley St HFAX HX1 10 A5
KGHY BD21 2 F7
SKP/WHF BD23 16 C2
Ottawa Pl CHAL LS7 87 M8
Otterburn Cl WBOW BD5 126 F1
Otterburn Gdns BHP/TINH LS16 86 D3
Otterburn St KGHY BD21 * 3 G1
Otter Lee La RPDN/SBR HX6 166 E6
Otters Holt HOR/CROF WF4 198 B7
Otterwood Bank WBY LS22 30 B7
Ouchthorpe La WKFDE WF1 176 E3
Ouldfield Cl MILN OL16 * 206 D8
Oulton Dr CUD/GR S72 244 E7
RTHW LS26 155 L3
Oulton La RTHW LS26 155 J1
Oulton Ter GTHN BD7 4 A9
Ounsworth St BOW BD4 127 K2
Ouse Dr WBY LS22 29 M6
Ouslethwaite Ct BSLY S70 261 G8
Ouson Gdns BSLYN/ROY S71 * 243 L5
Ouston Cl TAD LS24 72 A3
Ouston La TAD LS24 72 A3
Outcote Bank HUD HD1 14 E9
Outfield Cl HECK WF16 173 G2
Out Gang BRAM LS13 107 M3
Outgang La BRAM LS13 108 A3
Outlands Ri IDLE BD10 83 M6
Out La HOLM/MEL HD9 236 B6
KBTN HD8 217 L7
Outside La HWTH BD22 100 B4
Outwood Av HORS LS18 85 M7
Outwood Cha HORS LS18 85 M6
Outwood La HORS LS18 85 L7
TAD LS24 95 G3
Outwood Park Ct WKFDE WF1 176 D2
Outwood Wk HORS LS18 85 L7
Ouzelwell Crs EARL WF12 195 J3
Ouzelwell La EARL WF12 195 J3
Ouzelwell Rd EARL WF12 195 K2
Ouzlewell Gn EARD/LOFT WF3 154 F4
The Oval AWLS/ASK DN6 249 H8
BGLY BD16 81 K4
GIR BD8 104 A6
GLE DN14 183 H1
GSLY LS20 61 L6
HOLM/MEL HD9 236 B7
HOR/CROF WF4 221 K8
LVSG WF15 171 L1
MID LS10 9 K8
OT LS21 41 H5
RTHW LS26 155 H2
SCFT LS14 111 H4
SKP/WHF BD23 16 D3
Ovenden Av HIPP HX3 10 C1
Ovenden Cl HIPP HX3 * 10 D1
Ovenden Crs HIPP HX3 146 C4
Ovenden Gn HIPP HX3 146 B4
Ovenden Pk LUD/ILL HX2 * 146 B2
Ovenden Road Ter HIPP HX3 146 C4
Ovenden Ter HIPP HX3 146 C4
Ovenden Wy HIPP HX3 146 B4
Ovenden Wood Rd
LUD/ILL HX2 145 L4
Overburn Rd AIRE BD20 55 M2
Overdale RPDN/SBR HX6 167 G7
Overdale Av AL/HA/HU LS17 88 C1
BSLY S70 261 K8
Overdale Cl WBY LS22 29 M8
Overdale Ct SKP/WHF BD23 16 C1
Overdale Dr SHPY BD18 83 H5
Overdale Mt LUD/ILL HX2 167 M1
Overdale Ter HWTH BD22 * 78 E7
MSTN/BAR LS15 111 J6
Overfield Wy WHIT OL12 206 B4
Over Hall Cl MIRF WF14 172 D8
Over Hall Pk MIRF WF14 172 D8
Over Hall Rd MIRF WF14 172 D8
Overland Crs IDLE BD10 83 M6
Over La YEA LS19 84 E3
Overthorpe Av EARL WF12 195 M5
Overthorpe Rd EARL WF12 195 M4
Overton Dr WBSY BD6 125 M4
Overt St ROCH OL11 228 B1
Ovington Dr BOW BD4 128 A4
Owen Ct BGLY BD16 59 J8
Owlcotes Dr PDSY/CALV LS28 106 E6
Owlcotes Gdns
PDSY/CALV LS28 106 E6
Owlcotes Garth
PDSY/CALV LS28 106 D6
Owlcotes La PDSY/CALV LS28 106 E6
Owlcotes Rd PDSY/CALV LS28 106 D6
Owlcotes Ter PDSY/CALV LS28 106 E6
Owler Bars Rd HOLM/MEL HD9 234 E4
Owler Ings Rd BRIG HD6 170 C4
Owler La BTLY WF17 151 G3
Owler Mdw HECK WF16 172 E1
Owler Park Rd ILK LS29 20 B8
Owlers Cl HUDN HD2 193 H1
Owler's La HEM/SK/SE WF9 225 H2
Owlet Hurst La LVSG WF15 172 D4
Owlet Rd SHPY BD18 82 E7
Owlett Md EARD/LOFT WF3 154 A5
Owlett Mead Cl
EARD/LOFT WF3 154 A5
Owl La EARL WF12 174 C4
Owl Ms HUDE HD5 193 L8
Owl Rdg MOR LS27 152 E3
Owl St KGHY BD21 3 J3
Owston La AWLS/ASK DN6 249 M4
Owston Rd AWLS/ASK DN6 249 L6
Ox Close La WBY LS22 29 L1
Oxfield Ct HUDE HD5 193 J8
Oxford Av GSLY LS20 61 M5
Oxford Cl CLECK BD19 150 D6
CUL/QBY BD13 124 E7
Oxford Court Gdns CAS WF10 * 157 L7
Oxford Crs CLAY BD14 125 K2
HIPP HX3 168 F2
Oxford Dr CLECK BD19 150 D6
GFTH/SHER LS25 135 J5
Oxford La HIPP HX3 168 F2
Oxford Pl BAIL BD17 82 F4
BFDE BD3 5 H3
BSLYN/ROY S71 262 A6
HUD HD1 214 A3
LDS LS1 6 E8
MILN OL16 228 C1
PDSY/CALV LS28 107 G5
Oxford Rd BTLY WF17 151 G5
CHAL LS7 7 G3
CLECK BD19 150 D4
CUL/QBY BD13 * 124 E6
DEWS WF13 173 J5
ECHL BD2 105 J4
GSLY LS20 61 M5
HFAX HX1 11 G8
WKFDE WF1 176 D6
Oxford Rw LDS LS1 6 E8
Oxford St BSLY S70 261 J7
BSLYN/ROY S71 262 A6
BTLY WF17 173 K2
CLAY BD14 125 K2
COL BB8 74 A1
EARD/LOFT WF3 154 A6
FEA/AMT WF7 201 L1
GSLY LS20 62 A5
HBR HX7 143 H3
HEM/SK/SE WF9 247 H4
HUD HD1 14 F4
HWTH BD22 2 D6
NORM WF6 178 E3
ROY/SHW OL2 229 K7
RPDN/SBR HX6 167 M1
TOD OL14 163 K1
WKFDE WF1 13 J8
Oxford Ter BTLY WF17 173 M2
CLECK BD19 150 C6
Oxford Wk CLECK BD19 150 D6
Oxford Wy WHIT OL12 206 A4
Ox Hey La UPML OL3 230 F5
Ox Heys Mdw CUL/QBY BD13 103 J8
Ox Lee La HOLM/MEL HD9 255 G2
Oxley Gdns WBSY BD6 126 E7
Oxley Rd HUDN HD2 192 E2
Oxley St GIR BD8 4 B4
OSM LS9 110 B7
Oxmoor La GFTH/SHER LS25 117 L3
TAD LS24 95 J8
Oxspring La STKB/PEN S36 271 K3
Oxspring Rd STKB/PEN S36 270 F6
Oxton Dr TAD LS24 72 A3
Oxton La TAD LS24 72 A3
Oxton Mt OSM LS9 110 B6
Oxton Rd BSLYN/ROY S71 243 J6
Oxton Wy OSM LS9 110 B6
Oyster Cl MOR LS27 152 E3

P

Pacaholme Rd
WKFDW/WTN WF2 175 M6
Packer St MILN OL16 206 B7
Pack Horse Cl KBTN HD8 240 C2
Pack Horse Gn DOD/DAR S75 259 H6
Pack Horse Wk HUD HD1 15 G7
Padan St HIPP HX3 168 F2
Pad Cote La HWTH BD22 54 C6
Paddock HTON BD9 104 D2
Paddock Br WBY LS22 47 K5
Paddock Cl DOD/DAR S75 242 E5
GFTH/SHER LS25 113 J8
LM/WK BD12 148 E5
Paddock Dr BIRK/DRI BD11 151 G1
Paddock Foot HUD HD1 14 B9
Paddock Gn AL/HA/HU LS17 67 L1
Paddock Gv CUD/GR S72 244 E7
Paddock House La WBY LS22 46 C2
Paddock La BGLY BD16 59 M8
LUD/ILL HX2 145 L6
Paddock Rd DOD/DAR S75 242 E5
HIPP HX3 147 G1
KBTN HD8 216 C7
Paddocks Church BRIG HD6 171 G4
The Paddocks PBR HG3 28 A1
The Paddock AIRE BD20 36 A5
AL/HA/HU LS17 46 E8
AWLS/ASK DN6 249 L8
BAIL BD17 83 H2
CAS WF10 158 E8
CLECK BD19 * 149 H6
CUL/QBY BD13 79 M8
EARL WF12 174 B8
GFTH/SHER LS25 160 A2
HDGY LS6 87 H7
HOR/CROF WF4 220 C7
HUDE HD5 193 L6
ILK LS29 * 19 J5
KNOT WF11 182 B3
NORM WF6 178 D5
RTHW LS26 155 G1
SCFT LS14 90 B1
WKFDE WF1 * 176 C4
WMB/DAR S73 263 J8
Paddock Vw CAS WF10 158 D8
Paddy Bridge Rd HBR HX7 * 143 M5
Padgett Wy WKFDW/WTN WF2 175 M7
Padgum BAIL BD17 82 E2
Padley Cl DOD/DAR S75 260 A7
Padma Cl GTHN BD7 104 D7
Padstow Gdns MID LS10 153 J1
Page Hl LUD/ILL HX2 146 A4
Page St HUD HD1 15 G8
Paget Crs HUDN HD2 191 M5
Paget St KGHY BD21 2 D5
Pagewood Ct IDLE BD10 83 J5
Painter La SEL YO8 139 M3
Painthorpe La HOR/CROF WF4 220 B3
Paisley Gv WOR/ARM LS12 * 108 D6
Paisley Pl WOR/ARM LS12 * 108 D6
Paisley Rd WOR/ARM LS12 * 108 D6
Paisley St WOR/ARM LS12 108 D6
Paisley Ter WOR/ARM LS12 * 108 D6
Pakington St WBOW BD5 126 F2
Palace House Rd HBR HX7 143 J4
Palatine St MILN OL16 206 E7
Pale La SKP/WHF BD23 16 A6
Palermo Fold WMB/DAR S73 263 H8
Paleside La OSS WF5 174 F7
Palesides Av OSS WF5 174 F6
Palestine Rd HBR HX7 143 J2
Paley Rd BOW BD4 127 J2
Paley Ter BOW BD4 127 J2
Palin Av BFDE BD3 105 M5
Pall Ml BSLY S70 261 H5
Palma St TOD OL14 140 D5
Palm Cl WBSY BD6 126 D6
Palmer Cl STKB/PEN S36 270 E5
Palmer Rd BFDE BD3 5 M4
Palmer's Av HEM/SK/SE WF9 247 J4
Palmerston St ECHL BD2 * 105 K4
Palm St DOD/DAR S75 260 E3
HIPP HX3 146 D4
HUDS HD4 214 D2
Panelagh Av IDLE BD10 106 A1
Pannal Av PBR HG3 26 F3
WKFDE WF1 177 G6
Pannal Bank PBR HG3 26 F3
Pannal Gn PBR HG3 26 F2
Pannal Rd PBR HG3 27 J2
Pannal St GTHN BD7 126 C3
Panorama Dr ILK LS29 38 A4
The Parade BGLY BD16 81 J7
BRAM LS13 * 107 L4
BTLY WF17 * 151 H3
BTLY WF17 * 173 J2
HDGY LS6 108 F1
OSM LS9 9 L2
YEA LS19 * 62 B8
Paradise La LUD/ILL HX2 145 K8
TAD LS24 92 D1
Paradise Rd HTON BD9 * 104 B2
Paradise St BFD BD1 4 C5
HFAX HX1 10 F7
PDSY/CALV LS28 106 F3
Paragon Av WKFDE WF1 176 D4
Parish Ghyll Dr ILK LS29 38 B3
Parish Ghyll La ILK LS29 38 B3
Parish Ghyll Rd ILK LS29 * 38 C3
Parish Ghyll Wk ILK LS29 38 C3
Parish Wy BSLYN/ROY S71 261 M3
Paris Rd HOLM/MEL HD9 254 F3
Park Av AIRE BD20 55 M1
AWLS/ASK DN6 249 L6
BGLY BD16 81 H4
BIRK/DRI BD11 129 G8
BSLY S70 261 G5
BSLYN/ROY S71 243 H7
BSLYN/ROY S71 243 M3
CAS WF10 157 L2
CAS WF10 158 B7
CUD/GR S72 244 D7
CUD/GR S72 245 J6
CUD/GR S72 245 K3
DEWS WF13 173 K6
EARD/LOFT WF3 154 E7
ELL HX5 169 G8
GFTH/SHER LS25 115 M7
GFTH/SHER LS25 135 L5
HEM/SK/SE WF9 246 D4
HUD HD1 14 D6
HWTH BD22 78 F4
IDLE BD10 83 K4
KBTN HD8 238 C3
KBTN HD8 240 B3

KGHY BD21 2 E7
LVSG WF15 172 C4
MIRF WF14 194 D2
MOR LS27 152 B3
MSTN/BAR LS15 111 M4
NORM WF6 178 D4
PONT WF8 180 D6
PONT WF8 203 L1
RHAY LS8 88 D7
RTHW LS26 134 C5
SHPY BD18 82 C6
SKP/WHF BD23 * 16 B2
STKB/PEN S36 270 E3
WKFDE WF1 176 C2
WKFDE WF1 177 M7
WKFDW/WTN WF2 12 D6
WOR/ARM LS12 108 D6
YEA LS19 62 C7
Park Cliffe Rd ECHL BD2 105 J4
Park Cl BGLY BD16 81 J2
BIRK/DRI BD11 129 G8
BRAM LS13 107 L3
BTLY WF17 173 K3
CUL/QBY BD13 124 F5
DOD/DAR S75 242 E6
HIPP HX3 148 A7
HOR/CROF WF4 222 D5
IDLE BD10 105 L1
KBTN HD8 238 B3
KGHY BD21 3 G9
LUD/ILL HX2 145 K5
PONT WF8 203 L1
Park Copse HORS LS18 85 J5
Park Cottages ROY/SHW OL2 229 H6
Park Ct OSS WF5 197 H2
OT LS21 42 F8
Park Crs BFDE BD3 105 J4
BSLYN/ROY S71 243 M3
CAS WF10 158 E7
GSLY LS20 61 L6
HIPP HX3 10 C1
ILK LS29 19 J6
MOR LS27 129 M8
RHAY LS8 88 D5
RTHW LS26 133 J8
WOR/ARM LS12 108 D6
Park Crest HEM/SK/SE WF9 223 M8
Park Cft BTLY WF17 173 K2
DEWS WF13 173 J6
Parkcroft PDSY/CALV LS28 106 F4
Park Cross St LDS LS1 6 E9
Park Dl CAS WF10 158 E5
ILK LS29 61 J2
Parkdale Dr RPDN/SBR HX6 167 G7
Park Dene HFAX HX1 * 10 C7
Park Dr AIRE BD20 55 M1
AWLS/ASK DN6 227 M5
BGLY BD16 81 K1
BTLY WF17 151 J7
EARD/LOFT WF3 154 E7
HORS LS18 85 H6
HTON BD9 104 D2
HUD HD1 14 B5
KBTN HD8 238 B3
MIRF WF14 194 D2
Park Drive Rd KGHY BD21 3 G8
Park Dr South HUD HD1 14 B6
Park Edge Cl RHAY LS8 88 E7
Parker Av NORM WF6 178 A2
Parker La MIRF WF14 194 D1
Parker Rd EARL WF12 195 L3
HOR/CROF WF4 197 L5
Parkers La AIRE BD20 57 K3
Parker St AIRE BD20 34 F7
BSLY S70 260 F5
EARD/LOFT WF3 153 L7
HECK WF16 172 F2
Park Fld ILK LS29 61 J2
Parkfield Av BEE/HOL LS11 131 J3
ELL HX5 169 H8
MIRF WF14 194 E2
Parkfield Cl GFTH/SHER LS25 135 K4
PDSY/CALV LS28 106 F7
Parkfield Ct SCFT LS14 * 111 G3
Parkfield Crs MIRF WF14 194 D2
Parkfield Cft MIRF WF14 194 E2
Parkfield Dr BSPA/BRAM LS23 48 E6
CUL/QBY BD13 124 F5
RPDN/SBR HX6 167 J4
Parkfield Gv BEE/HOL LS11 131 J3
Parkfield La FEA/AMT WF7 179 L4
Parkfield Mt BEE/HOL LS11 131 H3
PDSY/CALV LS28 107 G7
Parkfield Pl BEE/HOL LS11 131 J3
Parkfield Rd BEE/HOL LS11 * 131 J3
GIR BD8 104 F4
SHPY BD18 82 A6
Parkfield Rw BEE/HOL LS11 131 J3
Park Flds LUD/ILL HX2 145 K4
Parkfield St BEE/HOL LS11 9 G6
ROCH OL11 228 D4
Parkfield Ter PDSY/CALV LS28 107 G5
Parkfield Vw BEE/HOL LS11 131 J3
OSS WF5 197 J1
Parkfield Wy MIRF WF14 194 D2
SCFT LS14 111 G3
Park Gdns KNOT WF11 159 M6
LUD/ILL HX2 167 M1
OSS WF5 197 H2
Park Ga BFDE BD3 5 H5
Parkgate HEM/SK/SE WF9 246 D5
HUDS HD4 214 B6
Parkgate Av WKFDE WF1 13 K2
Park Gate Cl HORS LS18 85 K6
Park Gate Rd MAR/SLWT HD7 211 K8
Park Ga West HIPP HX3 * 169 G4
Park Gn AIRE BD20 35 L5
NORM WF6 178 B5
Park Gv BSLY S70 261 G6
CUL/QBY BD13 124 F5
HDGY LS6 86 F8
HIPP HX3 147 H5
HOR/CROF WF4 197 H4
HORS LS18 85 H6
HTON BD9 104 E2
HUD HD1 14 D7
MIRF WF14 194 E2
MOR LS27 129 M8
RTHW LS26 134 D6
SHPY BD18 82 B6
YEA LS19 62 C7
Park Grove Rd
WKFDW/WTN WF2 12 A5
Parkhead Cl BSLYN/ROY S71 243 J2
Park Head La HOLM/MEL HD9 254 A2
KBTN HD8 256 B1
Park Hl DOD/DAR S75 241 K3
HUDN HD2 171 H8
Park Hill Cl GIR BD8 103 M5
Parkhill Crs WKFDE WF1 13 K2
Park Hill Dr GIR BD8 103 M5
Park Hill Gv WKFDE WF1 13 L3
Park Hill La WKFDE WF1 13 J3
Park Holme CHAL LS7 110 A2
Parkhome Est RTHW LS26 * 134 D5
Park House Cl LM/WK BD12 127 G7
Park House Ct STKB/PEN S36 257 G6
Park House Crs LM/WK BD12 127 G7
Park House Dr EARL WF12 195 M2
Park House Gn PBR HG3 28 F4
Park House Gv LM/WK BD12 * 127 G7
Park House Rd LM/WK BD12 126 F8
Park House Wk LM/WK BD12 127 G7
Parkin Hall La RPDN/SBR HX6 166 D4
Parkin House La STKB/PEN S36 269 M4
Parkin La IDLE BD10 84 B6
TOD OL14 140 F8
Parkinson Ap GFTH/SHER LS25 113 H6
Parkinson Cl WKFDE WF1 13 K1
Parkinson Rd CUL/QBY BD13 102 A6
Parkinson St WBOW BD5 126 F2
Parkin St LVSG WF15 171 L1
Parkland Av MOR LS27 152 A3
Parkland Crs HDGY LS6 87 J5
Parkland Dr HDGY LS6 87 J5
IDLE BD10 83 L7
TAD LS24 72 A2
Parkland Gdns HDGY LS6 87 J6
Park Lands PBR HG3 28 E4
Parklands BHP/TINH LS16 63 M3
CAS WF10 158 A7
ILK LS29 38 F2
OSS WF5 197 H2
ROY/SHW OL2 228 E8
ROY/SHW OL2 229 M6
Parklands Av HOR/CROF WF4 197 G5
Parklands Ct HOR/CROF WF4 197 G5
Parklands Crs BHP/TINH LS16 64 A3
HOR/CROF WF4 197 G5
Parklands Dr HOR/CROF WF4 197 G5
RPDN/SBR HX6 167 G5
Parklands Ga BHP/TINH LS16 64 A3
Parklands Wk KBTN HD8 238 B3
Parkland Ter HDGY LS6 87 H6
Parkland Vw BSLYN/ROY S71 262 B1
YEA LS19 62 D8
Park La AIRE BD20 55 M1
AWLS/ASK DN6 205 J3
BAIL BD17 83 H2
BVRD LS3 6 B8
CAS WF10 157 K1
CLAY BD14 125 K2
CUD/GR S72 263 K3
CUL/QBY BD13 125 H5
GFTH/SHER LS25 135 L6
GFTH/SHER LS25 136 E6
GSLY LS20 61 L7
GTL/HWG HX4 190 B5
HBR HX7 143 L6
HIPP HX3 169 G4
HOLM/MEL HD9 * 235 G4
HOR/CROF WF4 219 G7
HUDS HD4 214 C7
HWTH BD22 54 B4
KBTN HD8 239 J1
KBTN HD8 256 C1
KGHY BD21 3 H8
LDS LS1 6 C8
MAR/SLWT HD7 212 F2
MILN OL16 * 206 B6
PBR HG3 28 E4
PONT WF8 180 A5
RHAY LS8 88 D4
RTHW LS26 155 H1
RTHW LS26 156 C5
STKB/PEN S36 270 F3
STKB/PEN S36 271 J7
WBOW BD5 126 F2
WBY LS22 46 D1
Park Lane Ms AL/HA/HU LS17 88 D2
Park Lea HUDN HD2 171 J8
MID LS10 * 153 L1
Park Lodge Ct WKFDE WF1 13 J2
Park Lodge Crs WKFDE WF1 13 J2
Park Lodge Gv WKFDE WF1 13 H2
Park Lodge La WKFDE WF1 13 H2
Park Lodge Vw KBTN HD8 239 J5
Park Md IDLE BD10 83 K4
Parkmere Cl BOW BD4 127 K7
Park Ms OT LS21 42 F8
Park Mill La OSS WF5 175 J7
Park Mill Wy KBTN HD8 240 B3
Park Mt KSTL LS5 108 D2
OT LS21 63 K1
PBR HG3 28 E4
WOR/ARM LS12 108 C6
Park Mount Av BAIL BD17 83 G3
Park Pde DEWS WF13 173 K7
MOR LS27 * 152 B3
OSM LS9 110 C8
ROY/SHW OL2 229 L5
Park Pl HFAX HX1 * 10 C8
IDLE BD10 83 K4
LDS LS1 6 D9
PONT WF8 180 D6
Park Pl East HIPP HX3 148 A7
Park Pl West HIPP HX3 148 A7
Park Ri BRAM LS13 107 L2
CAS WF10 158 B7
Park Rd AIRE BD20 34 E7
BGLY BD16 81 J2
BRAM LS13 107 L3
BSLY S70 261 G7
BSPA/BRAM LS23 48 E6
BTLY WF17 173 M1
CAS WF10 180 C1
CUD/GR S72 245 J7
CUD/GR S72 245 K3
DEWS WF13 173 H8
EARL WF12 173 L8
ELL HX5 169 H6
GSLY LS20 61 M7
HECK WF16 172 F2
HFAX HX1 10 E7
HUDS HD4 214 A2
HWTH BD22 54 E3
IDLE BD10 83 K4
IDLE BD10 105 M1
ILK LS29 61 J2
KBTN HD8 240 B3
MSTN/BAR LS15 133 M1
PONT WF8 180 C3
RPDN/SBR HX6 167 L2
SHPY BD18 82 E7
TOD OL14 141 K8
WBOW BD5 127 G1
WBSY BD6 126 E7
WHIT OL12 206 D5
WOR/ARM LS12 108 C6
YEA LS19 62 C7
Park Rd West HUDS HD4 213 L2
Park Rw BRIG HD6 * 170 D4
LDS LS1 6 F9
PDSY/CALV LS28 107 G5
Park Side CLECK BD19 150 C7
HOLM/MEL HD9 255 G2
HOR/CROF WF4 217 L3
HORS LS18 85 J6
HUDE HD5 193 L5
Parkside BGLY BD16 81 K1
BSLYN/ROY S71 243 M5
CLECK BD19 149 M7
DOD/DAR S75 * 260 F2
HOR/CROF WF4 196 D8
Parkside Av CUL/QBY BD13 124 F5
HDGY LS6 87 H7
Park Side Av ROY/SHW OL2 229 L6
Parkside Cl HDGY LS6 87 H6
Parkside Ct HWTH BD22 79 G6
Parkside Crs HDGY LS6 87 H6
Parkside Gdns HDGY LS6 87 H7
Parkside Gn HDGY LS6 87 H7
Parkside Gv HTON BD9 104 C3
Parkside La BEE/HOL LS11 131 L4
EARD/LOFT WF3 177 G4
Parkside Lawns HDGY LS6 87 H7
Parkside Mt BEE/HOL LS11 131 J5
Parkside Pde BEE/HOL LS11 131 J5
Parkside Pl HDGY LS6 87 H6
Parkside Rd HDGY LS6 87 H6
PDSY/CALV LS28 106 F4
TOD OL14 140 D5
WBOW BD5 * 126 F3
Parkside Rw BEE/HOL LS11 131 J5
Parkside Ter CUL/QBY BD13 79 M8
Parkside Vw HDGY LS6 87 H6
Parkside Wk PDSY/CALV LS28 107 G4
Park Spring Gdns BRAM LS13 107 K5
Park Spring Ri BRAM LS13 107 K6
Park Spring Rd CUD/GR S72 245 H8
CUD/GR S72 263 K5
Park Sq EARD/LOFT WF3 154 E8
OSS WF5 197 H2
OT LS21 42 F8
WBSY BD6 126 B6
Park Sq East LDS LS1 6 E9
Park Sq North LDS LS1 6 E9
Park Sq South LDS LS1 6 E9
Park Sq West LDS LS1 6 E9
Parkstone HUDN HD2 171 H8
Parkstone Av BHP/TINH LS16 86 C5
Parkstone Dr IDLE BD10 105 L1
Parkstone Gn BHP/TINH LS16 86 C5
Parkstone Gv BHP/TINH LS16 86 C5
Parkstone Mt BHP/TINH LS16 86 C5
Parkstone Pl BHP/TINH LS16 * 86 C5
Park Stone Ri HIPP HX3 125 K8
Park St AIRE BD20 34 F7
BRIG HD6 170 D4
BSLY S70 261 G6
BTLY WF17 151 G6
CLECK BD19 149 K8
CLECK BD19 150 E6
DEWS WF13 173 M5
HECK WF16 172 F2
HOR/CROF WF4 197 J5
HWTH BD22 78 F7
LDS LS1 6 E8
MAR/SLWT HD7 190 E8
MILN OL16 206 B8
MOR LS27 130 E6
MSTN/BAR LS15 111 K6
OSS WF5 197 H2
ROY/SHW OL2 229 K8
RPDN/SBR HX6 167 L2
SHPY BD18 82 C6
SKP/WHF BD23 16 B2
WKFDE WF1 13 G4
WOR/ARM LS12 108 C6
YEA LS19 62 C7
Park Ter HDGY LS6 86 F8
HFAX HX1 * 10 C6
HIPP HX3 147 H5
KGHY BD21 3 K4
OT LS21 63 J1
SHPY BD18 82 C6
The Park DOD/DAR S75 259 G2
Park Top PDSY/CALV LS28 107 G5
The Park Towngate HIPP HX3 169 J3
Park Vw BEE/HOL LS11 131 J3
BRAM LS13 107 L3
BSLYN/ROY S71 243 M2
CAS WF10 158 E8
CLECK BD19 149 L6
CUD/GR S72 244 F4
CUD/GR S72 245 K3
DOD/DAR S75 260 B7
EARD/LOFT WF3 154 E8
EARL WF12 174 B6
HEM/SK/SE WF9 223 K5
HEM/SK/SE WF9 * 246 F3
HFAX HX1 10 C7
HOLM/MEL HD9 254 B1
LIT OL15 185 K8
MAR/SLWT HD7 * 233 J2
PDSY/CALV LS28 107 G7
RTHW LS26 134 C5
WKFDW/WTN WF2 * 176 A8
Park View Av HDGY LS6 108 F3
HIPP HX3 147 J5
HWTH BD22 79 G6
Parkview Ct RHAY LS8 88 D4
SHPY BD18 * 82 C7
Park View Crs RHAY LS8 88 D5
Park View Gv BULY LS4 108 F3
Park View Rd BULY LS4 108 F4
DOD/DAR S75 242 E5
HTON BD9 104 D4
Park View Ter HTON BD9 104 D3
YEA LS19 84 D2
Park Vls RHAY LS8 88 C5
Park Villas Dr PONT WF8 180 D5
Parkville Pl BRAM LS13 107 L3
Park Wy AWLS/ASK DN6 249 K8
BAIL BD17 82 B5
ILK LS29 61 J2
OT LS21 42 F8
Parkway AIRE BD20 35 L8
AIRE BD20 56 D1
CUL/QBY BD13 124 F5
HOR/CROF WF4 200 B4
KGHY BD21 3 G9
MOR LS27 129 L8
WBOW BD5 127 H5
Parkway Cl SCFT LS14 111 G2
Parkways RTHW LS26 133 K8
Parkways Av RTHW LS26 155 K1
Parkways Cl RTHW LS26 133 K8
Parkways Ct RTHW LS26 133 K8
Parkways Dr RTHW LS26 133 K8
Parkways Garth RTHW LS26 * 155 K1
Parkways Gv RTHW LS26 133 K8
Parkway V SCFT LS14 111 G3
Park West RTHW LS26 155 H1
Park Willow HIPP HX3 125 M8
Park Wood Av BEE/HOL LS11 131 H7
Parkwood Av RHAY LS8 88 C7
Parkwood Cl BEE/HOL LS11 131 H7
KBTN HD8 238 B3
Park Wood Cl SKP/WHF BD23 16 A1
Parkwood Ct RHAY LS8 88 C6
Park Wood Crs BEE/HOL LS11 131 H7
Park Wood Dr BEE/HOL LS11 131 H6
Parkwood Gdns
PDSY/CALV LS28 84 D8
RHAY LS8 88 C7
Parkwood Ri KGHY BD21 3 H7
Park Wood Rd BEE/HOL LS11 131 H7
Parkwood Rd MAR/SLWT HD7 191 G8
PDSY/CALV LS28 84 D8
SHPY BD18 82 B7
Parkwood St KGHY BD21 3 J6
Parkwood Vw RHAY LS8 88 C6
Parkwood Wy RHAY LS8 88 C7
Parliament Pl WOR/ARM LS12 108 F6
Parliament Rd
WOR/ARM LS12 108 F7
Parliament St
WKFDW/WTN WF2 12 C3
Parlington Ct MSTN/BAR LS15 91 G7
Parlington Dr GFTH/SHER LS25 92 A7
Parlington La GFTH/SHER LS25 113 J2
Parlington Meadow
MSTN/BAR LS15 91 G8
Parlington Vls GFTH/SHER LS25 92 A7
Parma St WBOW BD5 127 G1
Parnaby Av MID LS10 132 B5
Parnaby Rd MID LS10 132 B5
Parnaby St MID LS10 132 B5
Parnaby Ter MID LS10 132 B5
Parratt Rw BFDE BD3 105 M7
Parrock La HBR HX7 121 K8
Parrott St BOW BD4 127 M5
Parry Cl BGLY BD16 * 80 C5
Parry La BOW BD4 127 L1
Parsley Ms RTHW LS26 156 E3
Parsonage La BRIC HD6 170 C4
Parsonage Rd BOW BD4 127 M1
RTHW LS26 156 F3
WBOW BD5 127 G3
Parsonage St HIPP HX3 11 J2
Parsonage Wk MILN OL16 * 207 H7
Parson La HOR/CROF WF4 220 C7
Parsons Gn WBY LS22 48 B1
Parson's La ILK LS29 18 E6
Parsons Rd HTON BD9 104 C2
Parson St KGHY BD21 3 J3
Partons Pl EARD/LOFT WF3 154 E8
Partridge Cl MOR LS27 152 F2
Partridge Crs EARL WF12 196 B5
Partridge Dr WBSY BD6 125 L5
Paslew Ct AIRE BD20 58 D5
The Pass MILN OL16 206 C6
Pasture Av CHAL LS7 87 M7
GFTH/SHER LS25 116 C6
HWTH BD22 78 E5
Pasture Cl CLAY BD14 125 M2
SKP/WHF BD23 16 D1
Pasture Ct GFTH/SHER LS25 116 B7
Pasture Crs CHAL LS7 87 M7
Pasture Dr CAS WF10 157 J8
Pasture Fold ILK LS29 40 A4
Pasture Gv CHAL LS7 87 M7
Pasture La CHAL LS7 87 M7
CLAY BD14 125 M2
WBY LS22 46 A5
Pasture Mt WOR/ARM LS12 108 D6
Pasture Pde CHAL LS7 87 M7
Pasture Pl CHAL LS7 87 M7
Pasture Ri CLAY BD14 125 M2
Pasture Rd BAIL BD17 82 F4
RHAY LS8 110 A2
Pasture Side Ter East CLAY
BD14 125 M2
Pasture Side Ter West CLAY
BD14 125 L2
Pasture St CHAL LS7 * 87 M7
Pastures Wy MAR/SLWT HD7 212 F1
Pasture Ter CHAL LS7 87 M7
Pasture Vw GFTH/SHER LS25 116 B6
WOR/ARM LS12 108 D6
Pasture View Rd RTHW LS26 154 F1
Pasture Wk CLAY BD14 125 L2
Pasture Wy CAS WF10 157 J8
GFTH/SHER LS25 116 C6
Pateley Crs HUDN HD2 192 B4
Patent St HTON BD9 104 D4
Paternoster La GTHN BD7 126 C2
Paterson Av WKFDW/WTN WF2 12 B3
Patience La NORM WF6 178 A3
Patricia Gdns RPDN/SBR HX6 167 J1
RPDN/SBR HX6 * 168 B2
Patterdale Ap WBY LS22 47 K1
Patterdale Dr HUDE HD5 15 L6
Patterdale Rd EARL WF12 174 A4
Patte Roale Cl AWLS/ASK DN6 249 L5
Patterson Ct
WKFDW/WTN WF2 176 B3
Pattie St AIRE BD20 57 K5
Pauline Ter CAS WF10 157 L7
Paul La HOR/CROF WF4 216 E3
HUDE HD5 193 L1
Pavement La LUD/ILL HX2 124 A7
Pavilion Cl CUD/GR S72 245 J3
PDSY/CALV LS28 107 G4
WHIT OL12 206 B4
Pavilion Ct BOW BD4 127 L6
EARL WF12 174 C8
Pavilion Gdns PDSY/CALV LS28 107 G4
Pavilion Ms BULY LS4 108 E3
Pavilion Wy HOLM/MEL HD9 235 G3
PDSY/CALV LS28 106 F7
Paw Hill La STKB/PEN S36 269 L6
Paw La CUL/QBY BD13 125 H7
Pawson St BOW BD4 105 M8
EARD/LOFT WF3 154 A6
MOR LS27 152 A3
Paxton Av AWLS/ASK DN6 249 M5
Peabody St HIPP HX3 10 C1
Peace Hall Dr HUDE HD5 215 L1
Peace St BOW BD4 127 L1
Peach Tree Cl PONT WF8 * 180 D8
Peacock Av WKFDW/WTN WF2 176 B7
Peacock Ct YEA LS19 62 E8
Peacock Gn MOR LS27 152 E3
Peacock Gv WKFDW/WTN WF2 176 B7
Peak Rd BSLYN/ROY S71 * 243 J7
Peak Vw DEWS WF13 173 H4
Pearl St BTLY WF17 151 J8
HWTH BD22 79 J2
Pear Pl TOD OL14 140 C5
Pearson Av HDGY LS6 109 G3
Pearson Cl MILN OL16 207 H7
Pearson Gv HDGY LS6 109 G3
Pearson La HTON BD9 103 M5
Pearson Rd WBSY BD6 126 F6
Pearson Rw LM/WK BD12 148 F3
Pearson's La EARL WF12 195 H7
Pearson St BFDE BD3 105 L8
CLECK BD19 149 K8
MID LS10 9 J6
MILN OL16 206 E6
NORM WF6 178 C1
PDSY/CALV LS28 84 D7
Pearson Ter HDGY LS6 109 G3
Pear St HFAX HX1 10 A7
HUDS HD4 214 A2
HWTH BD22 79 J3
HWTH BD22 * 100 E4
Pear Tree Acre
BSPA/BRAM LS23 49 G5
Pear Tree Cl CUD/GR S72 263 M4
PONT WF8 180 D8
Pear Tree Ct AIRE BD20 36 A4
Peartree Field La PONT WF8 225 L2
Pear Tree Gdns MSTN/BAR LS15 91 G8
Pear Tree La HEM/SK/SE WF9 223 M7
Pear Tree Wk
WKFDW/WTN WF2 176 B6
Peasborough Vw ILK LS29 40 B7
Pease Cl PONT WF8 180 F8
Peasefold GFTH/SHER LS25 135 K5
Peasehill Cl BSLY S70 261 G6
YEA LS19 84 E2
Peasehill Pk YEA LS19 84 E2
Peaseland Av CLECK BD19 149 L7
Peaseland Cl CLECK BD19 149 M7
Peaseland Rd CLECK BD19 149 M7
Peat Ponds HUDW HD3 191 G5
Peckett Cl HUDW HD3 191 L7
Peckover Dr PDSY/CALV LS28 106 C6
Peckover St BFD BD1 5 H6
Pedler Brow La WHIT OL12 185 G8
Peebles Cl HUDW HD3 191 J5
Peel Av BTLY WF17 173 L1
Peel Cl BOW BD4 128 A1
HOR/CROF WF4 197 K5
Peel Cottage Rd TOD OL14 163 J5
Peel Cott St TOD OL14 163 J6
Peel Pde BSLY S70 261 G5
Peel Park Dr ECHL BD2 105 K4
Peel Park Ter ECHL BD2 105 J4
Peel Park Vw BFDE BD3 5 J1
Peel Pl BSLYN/ROY S71 261 J3
ILK LS29 40 A5
Peel Rw GTHN BD7 126 C3
Peel Sq BFD BD1 4 D4
BSLY S70 261 G5
Peel St BGLY BD16 81 K3
BSLY S70 261 C5
CUL/QBY BD13 102 F8
CUL/QBY BD13 125 H5
HECK WF16 172 E2
HOR/CROF WF4 197 K5
HUD HD1 14 F8
LIT OL15 207 K1
MAR/SLWT HD7 233 J3
MOR LS27 152 D2
RPDN/SBR HX6 * 167 K2
WHIT OL12 206 A6
WIL/AL BD15 102 E2
Peep Green Rd LVSG WF15 171 L3
Pegholme Dr OT LS21 40 F8
Pelham Ct ECHL BD2 105 K3
MID LS10 * 153 M3
Pelham Pl CHAL LS7 87 L7
Pelham Rd ECHL BD2 105 K3
Pell Ct HOLM/MEL HD9 236 E7
Pellentine Rd PBR HG3 28 A1
Pell La HOLM/MEL HD9 236 E8
Pellon La HFAX HX1 10 A3
Pellon New Rd LUD/ILL HX2 146 A6
Pellon St TOD OL14 163 H4
Pellon Ter IDLE BD10 83 K5
Pellon Wk IDLE BD10 83 K5
Pemberton Dr GTHN BD7 4 C8
Pemberton Rd CAS WF10 158 D6
Pemberton Wy ROY/SHW OL2 229 K6
Pembroke Cl MOR LS27 152 B1
Pembroke Ct HUDS HD4 213 K4
WHIT OL12 * 206 B5
Pembroke Ri GFTH/SHER LS25 135 L4
Pembroke Rd PDSY/CALV LS28 107 G6
Pembroke St LIT OL15 185 K8
SKP/WHF BD23 16 B3
WBOW BD5 127 G2
Pembury Mt MSTN/BAR LS15 112 B3
Penarth Av HEM/SK/SE WF9 225 J7
Penarth Rd MSTN/BAR LS15 111 K4
Penarth Ter HEM/SK/SE WF9 225 H7
Penda's Dr MSTN/BAR LS15 111 M4
Penda's Gv MSTN/BAR LS15 111 M3
Penda's Wk MSTN/BAR LS15 111 M4
Penda's Wy MSTN/BAR LS15 112 A4
Pendennis ROCH OL11 * 206 A8
Pendennis Av HEM/SK/SE WF9 247 G2
Pendil Cl MSTN/BAR LS15 111 L6
Pendle Ct CUL/QBY BD13 125 G7
Pendle Rd BGLY BD16 81 K3
Pendle Wy COL BB8 75 G1
COL BB8 75 L5
Pendragon ECHL BD2 * 105 J3
Pendragon La ECHL BD2 105 K3
Penfield Gv CLAY BD14 125 L2
Penfield Rd BIRK/DRI BD11 129 H8
Pengarth BGLY BD16 81 K1
Pengeston Rd STKB/PEN S36 270 D4
Penistone Av MILN OL16 206 E8
Penistone Boundary Wk
STKB/PEN S36 258 E6
STKB/PEN S36 269 K1
STKB/PEN S36 271 J1
Penistone Ct STKB/PEN S36 * 271 G3
Penistone Ms HWTH BD22 * 78 E7
Penistone Rd HOLM/MEL HD9 237 H8
HOLM/MEL HD9 255 G7
HUDE HD5 215 K1
KBTN HD8 215 M7
KBTN HD8 238 A8
KBTN HD8 238 B4
KBTN HD8 256 E4
Penlands Crs MSTN/BAR LS15 111 M7
Penlands Lawn MSTN/BAR LS15 111 M7
Penlands Wk MSTN/BAR LS15 111 M7
Penlington Cl HEM/SK/SE WF9 245 M1
Penmore Cl ROY/SHW OL2 229 L7
Penn Cl ECHL BD2 105 K3
Penn Dr CLECK BD19 149 M8
Penn Gv CLECK BD19 149 M8
Pennine Cl CUL/QBY BD13 124 F7
HOLM/MEL HD9 253 M1
WKFDW/WTN WF2 198 A4
Pennine Crs HUDW HD3 191 G6
Pennine Dr KBTN HD8 239 M4
MILN OL16 207 J8
WHIT OL12 184 E8
Pennine Gdns MAR/SLWT HD7 212 F5
Pennine Gv TOD OL14 141 L8
Pennine Ri KBTN HD8 239 M4
Pennine Rd EARL WF12 174 A6
Pennine V ROY/SHW OL2 229 L6
Pennine Vw BTLY WF17 151 J4
DOD/DAR S75 242 C4
HBR HX7 142 B2
HEM/SK/SE WF9 225 J6
HUDE HD5 193 L4
LIT OL15 185 M4
MAR/SLWT HD7 212 F5
Pennine Wy DOD/DAR S75 260 D4
GLSP SK13 264 D6
HBR HX7 119 M3
HBR HX7 120 D8
HBR HX7 142 F5
HEM/SK/SE WF9 224 B7
HUDW HD3 209 L8
HWTH BD22 76 F3
KBTN HD8 239 M4
LIT OL15 186 D7
MAR/SLWT HD7 251 L1
UPML OL3 231 M3
Pennington Gv HDGY LS6 6 D2
Pennington La RTHW LS26 155 K4
Pennington Pl HDGY LS6 6 D2
Pennington St HDGY LS6 6 D1
Pennington Ter HDGY LS6 6 D2
WBOW BD5 * 126 E2
Pennithorne Av BAIL BD17 82 E2
Penn St HFAX HX1 10 C4
MILN OL16 206 B6
Pennwell Fold SCFT LS14 112 A1
Pennwell Garth SCFT LS14 111 M1
Pennwell Gn SCFT LS14 111 M1
Pennwell Lawn SCFT LS14 111 M1
Pennyfield Cl HDGY LS6 87 H5
Pennygate BGLY BD16 59 M8

Penny Hill Dr CLAY BD14 125 M2
Penny La HUDE HD5 215 K1
Penny Lane Wy MID LS10 9 J8
Penny Spring HUDE HD5 215 G3
Pennythorne Ct YEA LS19 84 C1
Pennythorne Dr YEA LS19 84 C1
Penraevon Av CHAL LS7 7 G2
Penraevon St CHAL LS7 7 G2
Penrhyn Wk BSLYN/ROY S71 262 C6
Penrith Crs CAS WF10 159 G4
Penrith Gv BSLYN/ROY S71 262 B6
WOR/ARM LS12 108 E8
Penrith St ROCH OL11 228 B1
Penrose Beck Dr
FEA/AMT WF7 224 A1
Penrose Dr GTHN BD7 126 B3
Penrose Pl WKFDW/WTN WF2 220 B1
Penryn Av HUDE HD5 193 L6
Pentland Av CLAY BD14 125 M2
KNOT WF11 182 A2
Pentland Cl HWTH BD22 * 2 D6
Pentland Dr GFTH/SHER LS25 135 H1
Pentland Gv WKFDW/WTN WF2 198 A3
Pentland Rd EARL WF12 173 M8
The Pentlands ROY/SHW OL2 229 H6
Pentland Wy MOR LS27 152 C3
Penzance Ct GIR BD8 104 D6
Peplow Cl GFTH/SHER LS25 160 A3
Pepper Gdns BRAM LS13 108 A2
Pepper La BRAM LS13 107 M2
MID LS10 132 B3
Peppermint Cl MILN OL16 229 L2
Pepper Rd MID LS10 132 B4
Pepper Royd St DEWS WF13 173 M5
Percival Ct HUDW HD3 191 H8
Percival St BFDE BD3 5 K6
HUDW HD3 191 H8
LDSU LS2 6 F7
Percy St BGLY BD16 81 J3
COL BB8 52 A8
HEM/SK/SE WF9 246 D4
HUDN HD2 192 C5
KGHY BD21 79 K2
MILN OL16 228 D1
WHIT OL12 162 A8
WOR/ARM LS12 108 F8
Peregrine Av MOR LS27 152 F2
Peregrine Ct HUDS HD4 214 A7
Peregrine Wy WBSY BD6 125 L5
Peridot Fold HUDN HD2 192 E4
Per La LUD/ILL HX2 123 M7
Permain Ct HUDS HD4 214 D2
Perry Cl HWTH BD22 79 J3
Perseverance La GTHN BD7 126 C3
Perseverance Rd
CUL/QBY BD13 124 C3
Perseverance St BAIL BD17 * 82 F2
BSLY S70 260 F5
CAS WF10 157 L6
HUDS HD4 214 C3
LM/WK BD12 148 E2
PDSY/CALV LS28 106 E7
Perseverance Ter HFAX HX1 168 C1
RTHW LS26 155 G2
Perseverence St HUDS HD4 213 H3
Pershore WHIT OL12 206 A6
Perth Av ECHL BD2 105 G3
Perth Dr EARD/LOFT WF3 153 H6
Perth Mt HORS LS18 85 K2
Perth Rd ROCH OL11 228 D4
Peterborough Pl ECHL BD2 105 K3
Peterborough Rd ECHL BD2 105 K4
Peterborough Ter ECHL BD2 105 K3
Peterfoot Wy BSLYN/ROY S71 243 K5
Peter Hl BTLY WF17 173 M4
Peterhouse Dr OT LS21 41 L7
Peter La LUD/ILL HX2 145 K7
MOR LS27 152 F1
Petersfield Av MID LS10 132 A7
Peterson Rd WKFDE WF1 13 G3
Peter St COL BB8 * 74 A2
Pether Hl GTL/HWG HX4 190 B3
Petrel Cl WBSY BD6 125 L5
Petrel Wy MOR LS27 152 E3
Petrie Crs BRAM LS13 106 F1
Petrie Gv BFDE BD3 106 A7
Petrie Rd BFDE BD3 106 A7
Petrie St BRAM LS13 106 F1
WHIT OL12 * 206 B5
Petts Crs LIT OL15 185 J8
Petworth Cft BSLYN/ROY S71 243 K2
Petyt Gv SKP/WHF BD23 16 C2
Peverell Cl BOW BD4 128 A3
Peveril Crs BSLYN/ROY S71 243 J7
Peveril Mt ECHL BD2 105 L4
Pexwood Rd TOD OL14 163 H3
Pheasant Dr BTLY WF17 151 J3
Pheasant St KGHY BD21 3 J3
Philip Garth WKFDE WF1 176 D1
Philip La SEL YO8 139 L2
Philippa Wy WOR/ARM LS12 130 E3
Philip Rd BSLY S70 261 M7
Philip's Gv EARD/LOFT WF3 154 E8
Philip's La PONT WF8 203 L1
Philip St ROCH OL11 228 B1
Phillips St CAS WF10 157 K6
Phil May Ct WOR/ARM LS12 109 G7
Phoebe La HIPP HX3 168 F2
Phoenix Av KBTN HD8 217 M8
Phoenix Ct BTLY WF17 174 B1
TOD OL14 163 M1
WKFDW/WTN WF2 12 A3
Phoenix St BRIG HD6 170 D4
LIT OL15 185 K8
TOD OL14 141 M8
Phoenix Wy BOW BD4 106 A8
Piccadilly BFD BD1 4 F5
WKFDW/WTN WF2 12 C3
Pickard Bank HDGY LS6 109 H1
Pickard Ct MSTN/BAR LS15 111 L6
Pickard La AIRE BD20 36 A4
Pickard Wy DEWS WF13 173 K5
Pickering Av GFTH/SHER LS25 113 K6
Pickering Dr OSS WF5 174 E5
Pickering La OSS WF5 174 D5
Pickering Mt WOR/ARM LS12 108 F6
The Pickerings CUL/QBY BD13 125 G6
Pickering St WOR/ARM LS12 108 F6
Pickersgill St OSS WF5 174 E6
Pickford St HUDW HD3 213 J2
Pick Haven Garth GLE DN14 161 M8
Pick Hill Rd HOLM/MEL HD9 234 F3
Picklesfield DEWS WF13 173 K4
Pickles La GTHN BD7 126 B3
KBTN HD8 239 K5
Pickles St DEWS WF13 173 K4
KGHY BD21 2 F8
Pickrowfield La
GFTH/SHER LS25 117 G3
Pickthall Ter TOD OL14 163 M1
Pickup St MILN OL16 206 C7
Pickwood La RPDN/SBR HX6 168 A5
Picton St GIR BD8 4 C2
Picton Wy HUDE HD5 193 J7
Pictureville BFD BD1 4 E7
Piece Wood Rd BHP/TINH LS16 85 M3
Piethorne Cl MILN OL16 229 L2
Pigeon Cote Cl SCFT LS14 89 J8
Pigeon Cote Rd SCFT LS14 89 H8
Piggott St BRIG HD6 170 C3
Pighill Nook Rd
GFTH/SHER LS25 139 H7
Pighill Top La MAR/SLWT HD7 212 A4
Pike End Rd RPDN/SBR HX6 188 D6
Pike Law La MAR/SLWT HD7 212 D1
Pike Law Rd MAR/SLWT HD7 212 D1
Pike Lowe Gv DOD/DAR S75 242 F6
Pike St ROCH OL11 228 B1
Pildacre Brow OSS WF5 174 E8
Pildacre Cft OSS WF5 174 E8
Pildacre La EARL WF12 174 D8
Pilden La EARD/LOFT WF3 153 L7
Pilgrim Av DEWS WF13 173 H7
Pilgrim Crs DEWS WF13 173 H7
Pilgrim Dr DEWS WF13 173 H7
Pilgrim Wy PDSY/CALV LS28 107 J4
Pilkington St
WKFDW/WTN WF2 12 D8
Pilley Hl DOD/DAR S75 260 B8
Pilling La KBTN HD8 239 K4
Pilling Top La KBTN HD8 238 D2
Pill White La OT LS21 24 B8
Pilmer Ct WKFDW/WTN WF2 197 M2
Pilot St OSM LS9 7 L6
Pincheon St WKFDE WF1 * 13 G2
Pindar Oaks Cottages
BSLY S70 261 K6
Pindar Oaks St BSLY S70 261 J7
Pindar St BSLY S70 261 K6
Pinder Av WOR/ARM LS12 130 B2
Pinderfields Rd WKFDE WF1 176 E7
Pinder Gv WOR/ARM LS12 130 B1
Pinders Crs KNOT WF11 181 L1
Pinders Garth KNOT WF11 181 L1
Pinders Gn RTHW LS26 156 E5
Pinders Green Ct RTHW LS26 156 E5
Pinders Green Dr RTHW LS26 156 E5
Pinders Green Fold RTHW LS26 156 E5
Pinder's Gv WKFDE WF1 177 G6
Pinder St WOR/ARM LS12 130 B2
Pinebury Cl CUL/QBY BD13 124 E5
Pine Cl BSLY S70 261 L8
CAS WF10 158 A8
SKP/WHF BD23 16 A2
WBY LS22 30 A7
Pine Ct HUDS HD4 213 M8
LDSU LS2 9 H1
Pine Cft AIRE BD20 2 C1
Pinedale BGLY BD16 81 H1
Pinefield Pl HEM/SK/SE WF9 223 K4
Pine Gv BTLY WF17 173 K2
ROY/SHW OL2 228 F8
Pinehall Dr BSLYN/ROY S71 261 M2
Pine Rd TOD OL14 141 H7
Pines Gdns ILK LS29 38 B3
The Pines AL/HA/HU LS17 43 L3
EARL WF12 174 A8
ILK LS29 38 E3
Pine St BFD BD1 5 H5
HEM/SK/SE WF9 247 G5
HFAX HX1 11 G7
HUD HD1 15 H5
HWTH BD22 78 E8
LIT OL15 185 K8
MILN OL16 206 D7
MILN OL16 229 K3
Pine Tree Av BSPA/BRAM LS23 49 G6
PONT WF8 180 D8
Pine Tree La GFTH/SHER LS25 138 D8
Pinewood Av
WKFDW/WTN WF2 175 M8
Pinewood Cl CUD/GR S72 263 M3
ILK LS29 38 C3
Pinewood Gdns GTL/HWG HX4 190 D2
Pinewood Pl KNOT WF11 182 A3
Pinfold Av GFTH/SHER LS25 116 B6
Pinfold Cl BSLYN/ROY S71 262 A6
EARL WF12 196 A4
GFTH/SHER LS25 116 B6
GTL/HWG HX4 189 J1
HOR/CROF WF4 217 L4
KNOT WF11 181 L1
MIRF WF14 194 D1
WBY LS22 31 L5
Pinfold Ct GFTH/SHER LS25 116 B6
MSTN/BAR LS15 * 111 K6
Pinfold Cft CLAY BD14 125 L2
Pinfold Garth GFTH/SHER LS25 116 C6
Pinfold Gv MSTN/BAR LS15 111 J6
WKFDW/WTN WF2 198 F5
Pinfold Hl BSLY S70 261 J8
DEWS WF13 173 K7
MSTN/BAR LS15 111 K7
Pinfold La AWLS/ASK DN6 227 M3
BHP/TINH LS16 64 A8
BSLYN/ROY S71 243 L4
ELL HX5 169 M8
GFTH/SHER LS25 113 H7
HOR/CROF WF4 217 L4
HUDW HD3 211 L1
KBTN HD8 216 C3
MAR/SLWT HD7 212 C2
MIRF WF14 194 D1
MSTN/BAR LS15 111 J6
PONT WF8 226 F1
RPDN/SBR HX6 166 F2
RTHW LS26 157 G4
WKFDW/WTN WF2 199 G5
WOR/ARM LS12 108 D6
Pinfold Mt MSTN/BAR LS15 111 K7
Pinfold Ri GFTH/SHER LS25 92 B6
Pinfold Rd MSTN/BAR LS15 111 K7
Pinfold Sq MSTN/BAR LS15 111 J6
The Pinfold SKP/WHF BD23 16 B1
Pinfold Wy GFTH/SHER LS25 116 C6
Pingle Ri KBTN HD8 239 J7
Pinhaw Rd SKP/WHF BD23 16 C4
Pin Hill La LUD/ILL HX2 144 F5
Pink St HWTH BD22 78 E8
Pinnacle La HBR HX7 143 G5
Pinnacle Vw HWTH BD22 54 E3
Pinnar La HIPP HX3 169 H1
Pintail Av WBSY BD6 125 L5
Pioneer St EARL WF12 195 L3
LIT OL15 207 K1
ROCH OL11 206 C8
TOD OL14 * 163 J7
Pioneer Vls MILN OL16 * 230 A1
Pioneer Wy CAS WF10 179 H1
Pipe & Nook La
WOR/ARM LS12 108 B7
Pipercroft WBSY BD6 126 A8
Piper Hl KNOT WF11 159 J1
Piper La HWTH BD22 54 F5
OT LS21 41 H7
Piperwell Cl HECK WF16 172 F1
Piper Well La KBTN HD8 238 A8
Pipit Meadow MOR LS27 152 E3
Pippin's Ap NORM WF6 178 D3
Pippins Green Av
WKFDW/WTN WF2 175 K4
Pirie Cl ECHL BD2 105 H3
Pitchstone Ct WOR/ARM LS12 107 M7
Pitcliffe Wy BOW BD4 127 H1
Pitfall St LDS LS1 9 H2
Pit Field Rd EARD/LOFT WF3 154 F4
Pit Hl HIPP HX3 11 K8
Pit La CLECK BD19 150 D4
CUL/QBY BD13 101 L5
CUL/QBY BD13 124 E2
DEWS WF13 173 H4
GFTH/SHER LS25 136 A2
ROY/SHW OL2 228 F6
RTHW LS26 156 F3
Pits La CLECK BD19 149 G8
Pitt Hill La GTL/HWG HX4 189 L4
Pitt Rw LDS LS1 9 G2
Pitts St BOW BD4 127 M2
Pitt St BSLY S70 261 G5
KGHY BD21 3 J5
LVSG WF15 172 C4
TOD OL14 163 M1
WHIT OL12 206 B6
Pitt St West BSLY S70 260 F5
Pitty Beck Vw WIL/AL BD15 103 K7
Place's Rd OSM LS9 9 M2
Plaid Rw OSM LS9 7 M9
Plain La RPDN/SBR HX6 166 E4
Plains La ELL HX5 169 H5
MAR/SLWT HD7 233 J1
Plane Gn PONT WF8 181 H5
Plane St HUDS HD4 214 D3
TOD OL14 141 G7
Plane Tree Av AL/HA/HU LS17 88 B2
Plane Tree Cl AL/HA/HU LS17 88 B2
Plane Tree Cft AL/HA/HU LS17 88 B2
Plane Tree Gdns AL/HA/HU LS17 88 B2
Plane Tree Gv YEA LS19 62 F8
Plane Tree Nest La LUD/ILL HX2 146 A8
Plane Tree Ri AL/HA/HU LS17 * 88 B2
Plane Tree Rd RPDN/SBR HX6 167 K1
Plane Trees LUD/ILL HX2 145 M6
Plane Trees Cl CLECK BD19 149 M3
Planetrees Rd BFDE BD3 105 L8
Planetrees St WIL/AL BD15 103 J5
Plane Tree Vw AL/HA/HU LS17 88 B2
Planet Rd AWLS/ASK DN6 249 L7
Plantation Av AL/HA/HU LS17 88 C1
BSLYN/ROY S71 243 M3
MSTN/BAR LS15 111 H7
Plantation Dr HUDS HD4 214 C5
Plantation Gdns
AL/HA/HU LS17 88 D1
Plantation Pl BOW BD4 127 L2
Plantation Wy BAIL BD17 82 F3
Platt Cl MILN OL16 229 J1
Platting La ROCH OL11 228 C2
Platt La MAR/SLWT HD7 212 C5
Playfair Rd MID LS10 131 M4
Playground WOR/ARM LS12 * 129 M3
Playhouse Sq OSM LS9 7 K9
The Pleasance RTHW LS26 134 C5
Pleasant Ct HDGY LS6 6 C2
Pleasant Mt BEE/HOL LS11 8 C5
Pleasant Pl BEE/HOL LS11 8 C5
Pleasant St BEE/HOL LS11 8 B5
GTHN BD7 126 C2
Pleasant Ter BEE/HOL LS11 8 C5
Pleasant Vw CUD/GR S72 262 E2
Pledwick Crs
WKFDW/WTN WF2 198 F8
Pledwick Dr
WKFDW/WTN WF2 220 F1
Pledwick Gv
WKFDW/WTN WF2 220 E1
Pledwick La
WKFDW/WTN WF2 220 F1
Pledwick Ri
WKFDW/WTN WF2 198 F8
Plevna St MID LS10 132 C4
Plevna Ter BGLY BD16 81 H2
Plimsoll St BOW BD4 127 J2
HEM/SK/SE WF9 223 M7
Ploughcroft La HIPP HX3 146 D4
The Plough Garth GLE DN14 161 M8
Ploughmans Cft ECHL BD2 105 G2
Plover Dr BTLY WF17 173 H1
Plover Rd HUDW HD3 191 K6
Plover St KGHY BD21 3 H2
WBOW BD5 126 E3
Plover Wy MOR LS27 152 E3
Plumber St BSLY S70 260 F5
Plumpton Av ECHL BD2 83 H8
Plumpton Cl ECHL BD2 105 J1
Plumpton Dr SHPY BD18 83 H8
Plumpton End ECHL BD2 83 J8
Plumpton Gdns ECHL BD2 83 H8
Plumpton Lea ECHL BD2 83 H8
Plumpton Md ECHL BD2 83 H8
Plumpton Pk CUD/GR S72 244 E4
Plumpton Pl WKFDW/WTN WF2 12 B3
Plumpton Rd ROCH OL11 228 D6
WKFDW/WTN WF2 12 B3
Plumpton St GIR BD8 104 C6
WKFDW/WTN WF2 12 B3
Plumpton Ter
WKFDW/WTN WF2 12 B4
Plumpton Wk ECHL BD2 83 H8
Plum St HFAX HX1 10 B8
HWTH BD22 79 J3
Plum Tree Cl PONT WF8 180 D8
Plymouth Gv HFAX HX1 * 10 C3
Pochard Cl WBSY BD6 125 L5
Poet's Pl HORS LS18 85 L4
Pogmoor La DOD/DAR S75 260 C5
Pogmoor Rd DOD/DAR S75 260 D5
Pohlman St HFAX HX1 * 10 B9
Pole Ga HUDW HD3 211 M3
Pole Gate Branch HUDW HD3 211 M2
Pole Rd HWTH BD22 56 B6
Pollard Av BGLY BD16 81 K1
CLECK BD19 150 D5
Pollard Cl CLECK BD19 150 D5
Pollard Gv LIT OL15 185 L6
Pollard La BFDE BD3 5 M1
BRAM LS13 85 L8
Pollard's Flds KNOT WF11 181 K1
Pollard St BOW BD4 5 G9
EARD/LOFT WF3 176 E1
HUDN HD2 192 D4
TOD OL14 141 G7
Pollard St South HUDW HD3 213 K1
Pollard Wy CLECK BD19 150 D5
Pollit Av RPDN/SBR HX6 167 H3
Pollitt St DOD/DAR S75 260 F3
Pollyfox Wy DOD/DAR S75 260 A7
Polperro Cl NORM WF6 178 D3
Pomfret Pl GFTH/SHER LS25 113 K6
Pomona St ROCH OL11 228 B1
Pond Cl HUDS HD4 214 B4
Pond Common La
STKB/PEN S36 271 K8
Ponden La HWTH BD22 77 J8
Ponderosa Cl RHAY LS8 110 B3
Pondfields Cl GFTH/SHER LS25 135 K5
Pondfields Crest
GFTH/SHER LS25 135 K4
Pondfields Dr GFTH/SHER LS25 135 K4
Pondfields Ri GFTH/SHER LS25 135 K5
Pond La KBTN HD8 216 C4
Pond St BSLY S70 261 G6
KGHY BD21 3 H4
Ponker La KBTN HD8 239 G6
Ponker Nook La KBTN HD8 239 H5
Pontefract Av OSM LS9 110 B7
Pontefract La MSTN/BAR LS15 133 L4
OSM LS9 110 B7
OSM LS9 133 G2
Pontefract Lane Cl OSM LS9 110 B7
Pontefract Rd BSLYN/ROY S71 261 K5
CAS WF10 158 A7
CUD/GR S72 244 E5
FEA/AMT WF7 201 L2
FEA/AMT WF7 202 C6
HEM/SK/SE WF9 224 B5
HOR/CROF WF4 200 B4
MID LS10 132 C4
NORM WF6 178 F3
PONT WF8 181 J2
Pontefract St OSM LS9 110 B7
Pontefract Ter
HEM/SK/SE WF9 224 A8
Pontey Dr HUDE HD5 215 K1
Pontey Mt HUDE HD5 215 K1
Ponyfield Cl HUDN HD2 14 B1
Pool Bank Cl OT LS21 42 F7
Pool Bank Ct OT LS21 42 F8
Pool Bank New Rd
BHP/TINH LS16 63 K2
Pool Br OT LS21 42 E6
Pool Ct BFDE BD3 5 K4
Poole Crs MSTN/BAR LS15 111 K4
Poole La GFTH/SHER LS25 160 A3
Poole Mt MSTN/BAR LS15 111 K5
Poole Rd MSTN/BAR LS15 111 K5
Poole Sq MSTN/BAR LS15 111 K5
Pool Hill La KBTN HD8 257 L1
Pool Rd OT LS21 41 L6
Pools La BSLYN/ROY S71 244 A3
Pool St KGHY BD21 3 L1
Popeley Rd HECK WF16 150 E8
Pope St KGHY BD21 3 K3
NORM WF6 178 D1
Poplar Av CAS WF10 158 E7
CUD/GR S72 244 E4
GFTH/SHER LS25 113 G7
GTHN BD7 126 B4
HOLM/MEL HD9 236 E5
MSTN/BAR LS15 111 M4
RPDN/SBR HX6 167 K1
SHPY BD18 104 E1
TOD OL14 141 J7
WBY LS22 30 A7
WKFDW/WTN WF2 197 M1
Poplar Cl BRAM LS13 108 B6
ILK LS29 40 B6
Poplar Ct ELL HX5 * 169 H8
Poplar Crs EARD/LOFT WF3 152 E5
LUD/ILL HX2 124 B7
SHPY BD18 104 E1
Poplar Cft BRAM LS13 108 A6
Poplar Dr AIRE BD20 58 E7
HORS LS18 85 H5
NORM WF6 178 C1
SHPY BD18 104 E1
Poplar Gdns BRAM LS13 108 A6
Poplar Garth BRAM LS13 108 A6
Poplar Ga WOR/ARM LS12 108 A6
Poplar Gn PONT WF8 181 H5
Poplar Gv BGLY BD16 80 C5
BSLYN/ROY S71 262 A2
CLECK BD19 149 L8
GTHN BD7 126 B4
KNOT WF11 182 A4
PONT WF8 180 D6
SHPY BD18 104 E1
Poplar Ri BRAM LS13 108 A5
KBTN HD8 239 K5
Poplar Rd AWLS/ASK DN6 249 K5
GTHN BD7 126 C4
SHPY BD18 104 E1
Poplars Park Rd ECHL BD2 104 F2
Poplar Sq PDSY/CALV LS28 106 F4
Poplars Rd BSLY S70 261 K7
The Poplars AIRE BD20 55 L2
BHP/TINH LS16 64 B4
GSLY LS20 62 A4
HDGY LS6 109 G2
HIPP HX3 * 148 C4
KNOT WF11 182 D4
Poplar St CUD/GR S72 263 K1
EARD/LOFT WF3 154 E8
HIPP HX3 11 G3
HUDE HD5 15 K9
HUDN HD2 192 C5
Poplar Ter AIRE BD20 58 E7
BSLYN/ROY S71 243 M2
HEM/SK/SE WF9 247 J4
HUDE HD5 15 L8
Poplar Vw AL/HA/HU LS17 * 89 H3
BRAM LS13 108 A6
BRIG HD6 148 C8
GTHN BD7 126 A4
Poplar Wy BRAM LS13 108 A6
Poplarwood Gdns IDLE BD10 106 A1
Popley Dr HOLM/MEL HD9 234 F5
Popples Dr LUD/ILL HX2 124 B7
Poppleton Ct EARD/LOFT WF3 153 G5
Poppleton Dr EARD/LOFT WF3 153 G5
Poppleton Ri EARD/LOFT WF3 153 G6
Poppleton Rd EARD/LOFT WF3 153 G5
Poppleton Wy EARD/LOFT WF3 153 G6
Popple Wells La LUD/ILL HX2 145 H7
Poppy Ct WBSY BD6 * 126 B8
Porritt St CLECK BD19 * 149 M5
Portage Av MSTN/BAR LS15 111 H7
Portage Crs MSTN/BAR LS15 111 H7
Portal Crs MIRF WF14 172 C6
Portal Dr MIRF WF14 172 C6
Porter Av DOD/DAR S75 260 E4
Porter Ter DOD/DAR S75 260 D4
Portland Av PONT WF8 180 D5
Portland Cl HUDW HD3 * 191 L7
Portland Crs LDSU LS2 6 F7
Portland Ga LDSU LS2 6 F7
Portland Pl BGLY BD16 81 J4
HEM/SK/SE WF9 225 J7
HFAX HX1 11 H8
Portland Rd HIPP HX3 11 H3
WOR/ARM LS12 108 E8
Portland St BSLY S70 261 K6
COL BB8 74 B1
HFAX HX1 11 H5
HUD HD1 14 D6
HWTH BD22 78 F7
LDS LS1 6 E8
PDSY/CALV LS28 * 107 J7
WBOW BD5 4 F8
WKFDE WF1 13 M8
Portland Wy LDSU LS2 6 F7
Portman St PDSY/CALV LS28 84 D8
Portobello Gv
WKFDW/WTN WF2 13 G9
Portobello Rd WKFDE WF1 13 G9
Portsmouth Av BFDE BD3 5 H2
Portwood St HTON BD9 103 M4
Post Hill Ct WOR/ARM LS12 107 M7
Post Office Rd FEA/AMT WF7 201 M1
IDLE BD10 105 L1
Post Office St CLECK BD19 150 B8
Pothouse Rd WBSY BD6 126 D6
Pot La AIRE BD20 35 K8
Potovens La
WKFDW/WTN WF2 176 B3
Potter Av WKFDW/WTN WF2 198 A2
Potter Brow Rd BAIL BD17 60 E7
Potter Cl LM/WK BD12 149 G1
Potternewton Av CHAL LS7 87 K8
Potternewton Ct CHAL LS7 87 L8
Potternewton Crs CHAL LS7 109 K1
Potternewton Gdns CHAL LS7 * 87 L8
Potternewton Hts CHAL LS7 87 L8
Potternewton La CHAL LS7 87 J8
Potternewton Mt CHAL LS7 87 K8
Potternewton Vw CHAL LS7 * 87 K8
Potters Cft EARD/LOFT WF3 154 E8
Potters Wk MAR/SLWT HD7 213 G2
Potterton Br MSTN/BAR LS15 91 G5
Potterton Cl MSTN/BAR LS15 91 G6
Potterton La MSTN/BAR LS15 91 G7
Pottery La KNOT WF11 181 M1
RTHW LS26 133 M7
Pottery Rd MID LS10 9 J7
Pottery St CAS WF10 157 K6
HUDW HD3 191 G6
Potts' Ter NORM WF6 178 C6
Poulton Pl BEE/HOL LS11 9 H9
Poulton St BSLYN/ROY S71 243 M8
Poverty La RPDN/SBR HX6 166 C5
Powell Av WBOW BD5 126 E2
Powell Rd BGLY BD16 81 J3
SHPY BD18 104 F1
Powell St CAS WF10 157 M6
HECK WF16 172 F3
HEM/SK/SE WF9 246 F3
HFAX HX1 11 G6
Poxton Gv HEM/SK/SE WF9 247 G5
Prail Cl PONT WF8 181 H5
Pratt La MIRF WF14 172 C8
SHPY BD18 82 E8
Premiere Pk ILK LS29 38 A3
Premier Wy ELL HX5 169 J6
RTHW LS26 155 H6
Prescott St HFAX HX1 11 H8
MILN OL16 206 E4
Prescott Ter WIL/AL BD15 103 K5
Preston La LUD/ILL HX2 145 L4
RTHW LS26 135 G7
Preston Pde BEE/HOL LS11 131 J4
Preston Pl HFAX HX1 10 D6
Preston St BTLY WF17 173 L2
EARL WF12 174 A7
GTHN BD7 4 A5
Preston Vw RTHW LS26 134 D5
Preston Wy BSLYN/ROY S71 243 M8
Prestwich Dr HUDN HD2 192 B4
Prestwick Cl OT LS21 40 F8
Prestwick Fold OSS WF5 174 F7
Pretoria St CAS WF10 158 A7
FEA/AMT WF7 179 L8
MAR/SLWT HD7 212 B5
WKFDE WF1 13 H9
Priest Bank Rd AIRE BD20 35 G6
Priest Croft La BSLYN/ROY S71 263 H6
Priest Hill Gdns WBY LS22 29 M7
Priesthorpe Av
PDSY/CALV LS28 106 D4
Priesthorpe Ct
PDSY/CALV LS28 106 F2
Priesthorpe La
PDSY/CALV LS28 106 D3
Priesthorpe Rd
PDSY/CALV LS28 106 E2
Priest La RPDN/SBR HX6 189 G2
Priestley Av DOD/DAR S75 241 L6
HECK WF16 150 F8
WBSY BD6 126 D6
Priestley Cl PDSY/CALV LS28 107 H6
Priestley Ct PDSY/CALV LS28 107 H6
Priestley Dr PDSY/CALV LS28 107 H6
Priestley Gdns HECK WF16 172 E1
PDSY/CALV LS28 107 H6
Priestley Gv HUDS HD4 214 B5
Priestley Pl RPDN/SBR HX6 167 J3
Priestley Sq BTLY WF17 151 G4
Priestley St CUL/QBY BD13 102 F8
Priestley Ter WBSY BD6 126 E5
Priestley Vw PDSY/CALV LS28 107 H6
Priestley Wk PDSY/CALV LS28 107 H6
Priestley Wy ROY/SHW OL2 229 M7
Priestman Cl GIR BD8 4 A1
Priestman St GIR BD8 4 A2
Priest Royd DOD/DAR S75 242 C5
Priestthorpe Cl BGLY BD16 81 J2
Priestthorpe La BGLY BD16 81 J2
Priestthorpe Rd BGLY BD16 81 J3
Primitive St EARD/LOFT WF3 154 F3
HUD HD1 15 G6
Primley Gdns AL/HA/HU LS17 87 L2
Primley Park Av
AL/HA/HU LS17 87 L2
Primley Park Cl
AL/HA/HU LS17 87 M2
Primley Park Ct
AL/HA/HU LS17 87 L1
Primley Park Crs
AL/HA/HU LS17 87 L2
Primley Park Dr
AL/HA/HU LS17 87 L2
Primley Park Garth
AL/HA/HU LS17 87 M1
Primley Park Gn
AL/HA/HU LS17 87 M1
Primley Park La
AL/HA/HU LS17 87 M2
Primley Park Mt
AL/HA/HU LS17 87 M2
Primley Park Ri
AL/HA/HU LS17 87 M2
Primley Park Rd
AL/HA/HU LS17 87 L2
Primley Park Vw
AL/HA/HU LS17 87 L1
Primley Park Wk
AL/HA/HU LS17 87 M2
Primley Park Wy
AL/HA/HU LS17 87 L1
Primrose Av MSTN/BAR LS15 111 J5
RTHW LS26 134 D5
Primrose Bank BGLY BD16 81 K4
Primrose Cl MSTN/BAR LS15 111 J6
PONT WF8 180 F7
Primrose Ct AL/HA/HU LS17 * 87 M1
Primrose Crs MSTN/BAR LS15 111 J5
Primrose Dene KNOT WF11 159 M7
Primrose Dr BGLY BD16 81 L4
CAS WF10 158 D8
MSTN/BAR LS15 111 J6
Primrose Gdns BTLY WF17 152 A8
MSTN/BAR LS15 111 J5
Primrose Garth
MSTN/BAR LS15 111 H6
Primrose Gv HUDS HD4 214 C3
KGHY BD21 3 M4
Primrose Hl BTLY WF17 151 M8
KNOT WF11 182 C1
PDSY/CALV LS28 107 G5
SKP/WHF BD23 16 B2
Primrose Hill Cl RTHW LS26 134 D5
Primrose Hill Dr RTHW LS26 134 D5
Primrose Hill Gn RTHW LS26 134 D6
Primrose Hill Rd HUDS HD4 214 C2
Primrose La BEE/HOL LS11 9 H9
BGLY BD16 81 K5
BSPA/BRAM LS23 48 E7

ECHL BD2 ....104 F2
HOR/CROF WF4 ....197 M8
KBTN HD8 ....215 M6
LVSG WF15 ....172 K2
MIRF WF14 ....172 L7
MSTN/BAR LS15 ....111 J6
Primrose Rd MSTN/BAR LS15 ....111 J6
Primrose St GIR BD8 ....4 B3
HUDS HD2 ....214 C2
KGHY BD21 ....3 M4
Primrose V KNOT WF11 ....182 C2
Primrose Wk MOR LS27 ....130 E6
Primrose Wy HIPP HX3 ....125 M7
Prince Arthur St DOD/DAR S75 ....260 F4
Prince Edward Cr WOR/ARM LS12 ....130 C2
Prince Edward Rd WOR/ARM LS12 ....130 C2
Prince Henry Rd OT LS21 ....41 J5
Princeroyd Wy GTHN BD7 ....104 C7
Prince's Av RHAY LS8 ....88 D7
Princes Ct AL/HA/HU LS17 * 87 L5
Prince's Crs ECHL BD2 ....105 K3
SKP/WHF BD23 ....16 D2
Princes Dr SKP/WHF BD23 ....16 D2
Prince's Ga HIPP HX3 ....168 D2
Princes Gv WBOW BD5 ....108 F1
Princess Alexandra Wk HUD HD1 ....15 C1
Princess Av EARL WF12 ....174 C6
HEM/SK/SE WF9 ....247 H4
WHIT OL12 ....206 B2
Princess Cl EARL WF12 ....174 C6
Princess Ct AL/HA/HU LS17 ....87 M3
NORM WF6 ....178 E5
Princess Crs EARL WF12 ....174 C7
Princess Flds MSTN/BAR LS15 ....111 M8
Princess Ga HOR/CROF WF4 ....197 M4
Princess La EARL WF12 ....174 C6
Princes Rd LDS LS1 ....8 E2
Princess Rd EARL WF12 ....174 C6
ILK LS29 ....38 C3
MILN OL16 ....206 D7
ROY/SHW OL2 ....229 J8
Princess Royal Wy PBR HG3 ....26 F4
Princess St BRIG HD6 ....170 D4
BSLY S70 ....261 G5
BTLY WF17 ....151 J4
CAS WF10 ....158 A5
CUD/GR S72 ....245 J8
DOD/DAR S75 ....242 C5
EARL WF12 ....174 C6
GTL/HWG HX4 ....168 F7
HFAX HX1 ....11 H5
HUD HD1 ....14 B7
NORM WF6 ....178 D4
RPDN/SBR HX6 ....167 L2
WHIT OL12 ....206 B2
WKFDE WF1 ....198 F4
YEA LS19 ....84 C2
Princes St HECK WF16 ....173 G2
WBSY BD6 ....126 A4
WBSY BD6 ....126 D6
Prince St AIRE BD20 ....35 M5
BOW BD4 ....127 L5
BTLY WF17 * 151 L4
CAS WF10 ....135 G7
DEWS WF13 ....173 M6
HUDS HD4 ....214 D2
HWTH BD22 ....78 B8
MILN OL16 ....228 D1
Prince's Wy WBOW BD5 ....4 E7
Princeton Cl LUD/ILL HX2 ....146 E1
Princeville Dr GTHN BD7 ....104 C7
Princeville St GTHN BD7 ....104 C7
Prince Wood La HUDN HD2 ....191 L4
Priordale Rd FEA/AMT WF7 ....201 K2
Priors Ter GTL/HWG HX4 * 190 B2
Prior St KGHY BD21 ....3 K7
Priory Cl BGLY BD16 ....81 J2
MIRF WF14 ....172 A8
NORM WF6 ....178 D2
OSS WF5 ....196 F2
WBY LS22 ....30 E8
Priory Crs BSLYN/ROY S71 ....262 A3
Priory Est HEM/SK/SE WF9 ....247 K3
Priory Gv BGLY BD16 ....81 J2
Priory Ms EARD/LOFT WF3 ....155 H8
Priory Park Gv GFTH/SHER LS25 ....138 D6
HUDN HD2 ....191 G1
Priory Rdg HOR/CROF WF4 ....200 C6
Priory Rd BRIG HD6 ....170 E5
BSLYN/ROY S71 ....262 A3
FEA/AMT WF7 ....201 J2
Priory Rd or Hall La AWLS/ASK DN6 ....227 L1
Priory Sq WKFDW/WTN WF2 ....199 J3
Priory Wk MIRF WF14 ....172 A8
Priory Wy MIRF WF14 ....172 A8
Privilege St WOR/ARM LS12 ....108 D8
Proctor St BOW BD4 ....127 M5
Prod Ga BAIL BD17 * 82 A4
Prod La BAIL BD17 ....82 A4
Progress Av BGLY BD16 ....80 C5
Prospect Av BRAM LS13 ....107 J2
GFTH/SHER LS25 ....116 B7
LUD/ILL HX2 ....168 A4
NORM WF6 ....178 D3
PDSY/CALV LS28 ....106 C4
SHPY BD18 ....82 E7
Prospect Bank BSPA/BRAM LS23 ....69 M3
Prospect Cl LUD/ILL HX2 ....168 A4
SHPY BD18 ....82 E7
Prospect Ct LUD/ILL HX2 ....145 K6
TAD LS24 ....71 M2
Prospect Crs HWTH BD22 ....79 C1
MID LS10 ....131 M4
Prospect Dr HWTH BD22 ....79 C1
TAD LS24 ....71 M2
Prospect Gdns MSTN/BAR LS15 ....111 J6
Prospect Gv PDSY/CALV LS28 ....106 F6
SHPY BD18 ....82 E7
Prospect La BIRK/DRI BD11 ....150 D1
Prospect Mt HWTH BD22 ....79 C1
SHPY BD18 ....82 E7
Prospect Pl BRIG HD6 ....170 D4
EARD/LOFT WF3 ....154 D4
ECHL BD2 ....105 L4
HORS LS18 ....85 K6
HTON BD9 ....104 B5
LUD/ILL HX2 ....146 B3
RPDN/SBR HX6 * 166 F5
RTHW LS26 ....155 H2
SKP/WHF BD23 ....16 B2
Prospect Rd BFDE BD3 * 5 H5
BGLY BD16 ....81 L1
CLECK BD19 ....149 M6
HECK WF16 ....150 E8
HUDW HD3 ....191 H8
ILK LS29 ....40 B6
LVSG WF15 ....171 M4
OSS WF5 ....174 F8
Prospect Sq PDSY/CALV LS28 ....106 F4
Prospect St AIRE BD20 * 34 F7

BOW BD4 ....5 H9
BSLY S70 ....260 F5
BTLY WF17 * 151 J4
CLECK BD19 ....149 M7
CUL/QBY BD13 * 103 G8
HIPP HX3 ....11 J3
HOR/CROF WF4 ....197 L6
HUD HD1 ....14 B7
HWTH BD22 ....2 A7
HWTH BD22 ....78 B8
IDLE BD10 ....105 L1
LIT OL15 * 185 K8
PDSY/CALV LS28 * 107 G8
PDSY/CALV LS28 ....106 F3
ROCH OL11 ....228 A2
SHPY BD18 ....82 E7
WBSY BD6 ....126 B7
YEA LS19 ....84 E3
Prospect Ter BRAM LS13 ....107 J2
CLECK BD19 ....149 M6
GFTH/SHER LS25 ....114 C8
HBR HX7 * 143 G3
LVSG WF15 ....172 C2
WIL AL BD15 ....103 L5
Prospect Vw AWLS/ASK DN6 * 227 L3
BRAM LS13 ....107 L3
LVSG WF15 ....171 M4
Prospect Wk SHPY BD18 ....82 E7
Prospect Wy BRIG HD6 ....148 D7
Prosper St MID LS10 ....9 L7
Providence Av BAIL BD17 ....82 E2
HIPP HX3 ....6 D1
Providence Ct BSLY S70 ....261 G6
BAIL BD17 * 82 E2
Providence Crs HWTH BD22 ....78 E4
Providence Gn PONT WF8 ....181 D5
Providence La HWTH BD22 ....78 E4
Providence Pl BRIG HD6 * 170 E5
GFTH/SHER LS25 ....113 C2
MOR LS27 ....151 M2
PDSY/CALV LS28 * 107 G5
RTHW LS26 ....157 K3
Providence Rd HDGY LS6 ....6 C2
Providence Rw BAIL BD17 ....82 E2
LUD/ILL HX2 ....146 B3
Providence St BFD BD1 ....4 D6
BTLY WF17 ....173 L1
CLECK BD19 * 149 C6
CLECK BD19 * 150 A6
EARL WF12 ....174 B7
ELL HX5 ....169 H7
OSS WF5 ....9 M1
PDSY/CALV LS28 ....106 F4
WKFDE WF1 ....12 C3
Providence Ter CUL/QBY BD13 ....102 F8
LDSU LS2 ....6 D3
Providential St HOR/CROF WF4 ....217 K3
Provident St ROY/SHW OL2 * 229 K7
Prune Park La WIL/AL BD15 ....103 L3
Psalters Dr STKB/PEN S36 ....271 J3
Pudding La TOD OL14 ....140 E4
Pudsey Rd BRAM LS13 ....107 L6
TOD OL14 ....140 D5
Pugneys Rd WKFDW/WTN WF2 ....198 L4
Pule Green La HIPP HX3 ....146 D3
Pullan Av ECHL BD2 ....105 L2
Pullan Dr ECHL BD2 ....105 L2
Pullan Gv ECHL BD2 ....105 L2
Pullan La BAIL BD17 ....83 L1
Pullan St WBOW BD5 ....126 F1
Pullman St ROCH OL11 ....228 B1
Pumphouse La DEWS WF13 ....173 H6
Pump La DEWS WF13 ....173 H6
EARD/LOFT WF3 ....175 G1
KBTN HD8 ....216 E7
Punch Bowl Yd CLECK BD19 ....149 L7
Purbeck Ct BOW BD4 * 128 A4
Purbeck Gv GFTH/SHER LS25 ....113 H8
Purcell Dr AIRE BD20 ....35 M4
Purley Wk WBSY BD6 ....126 D6
Purlwell Av BTLY WF17 ....173 K5
Purlwell Crs BTLY WF17 ....173 K5
Purlwell Hall Rd BTLY WF17 ....173 K3
Purlwell La BTLY WF17 ....173 K3
Purprise La HBR HX7 ....121 J7
Purston La FEA/AMT WF7 ....201 L4
Purston Park Ct FEA/AMT WF7 ....201 M2
Pye Av DOD/DAR S75 ....242 C6
Pye Nest Av LUD/ILL HX2 ....167 M4
Pye Nest Ct LUD/ILL HX2 ....168 A2
Pye Nest Dr LUD/ILL HX2 ....168 A2
Pye Nest Gdns LUD/ILL HX2 ....167 M1
Pye Nest Gv LUD/ILL HX2 ....167 M1
Pye Nest Ri LUD/ILL HX2 ....168 A2
Pye Nest Rd RPDN/SBR HX6 ....167 M2
Pyenot Av CLECK BD19 ....150 A8
Pyenot Dr CLECK BD19 ....150 A8
Pyenot Gdns CLECK BD19 ....150 A8
Pyenot Hall La CLECK BD19 ....150 A7
Pymont Dr RTHW LS26 ....133 K7
Pymont Gv RTHW LS26 ....133 K7
Pymroyd La HUD HD4 ....213 J3
Pym St MID LS10 ....9 L6
Pynate Rd BTLY WF17 ....151 J8
Pyrah Rd LM/WK BD12 ....126 F7
Pyrah St DEWS WF13 ....173 L5
LM/WK BD12 ....148 F2

Q

Quail Av WBSY BD6 ....125 L5
Quail St KGHY BD21 ....3 J3
Quaker La BSLYN/ROY S71 ....262 C6
CLECK BD19 ....149 M8
HUD HD1 ....14 A9
LVSG WF15 ....171 M1
WBOW BD5 ....126 D3
Quakers La RPDN/SBR HX6 ....188 F4
Quarmby Cft HUDW HD3 ....191 J7
Quarmby Fold HUDW HD3 ....191 J7
Quarmby Rd HUDW HD3 ....191 K8
Quarrie Dene Ct CHAL LS7 * 87 L8
Quarry Av KNOT WF11 ....182 C3
Quarry Bank Cl CUD/GR S72 ....244 D8
Quarry Cl KSTL S75 ....86 B8
Quarry Cl DOD/DAR S75 ....241 M6
HOLM/MEL HD9 ....236 E4
Quarry Ct CAS WF10 ....157 M8
HUDW HD3 ....191 H7
Quarry Dene BHP/TINH LS16 ....86 E6
Quarry Dene Pk BHP/TINH LS16 ....86 E6
Quarry Dr HUDE HD5 ....193 K8
Quarry Farm Rd OT LS21 ....63 J1
Quarryfields WF14 ....172 D7
Quarry Gdns AL/HA/HU LS17 ....65 J8
HUDE HD5 ....215 K2
OSM LS9 ....7 K9
RPDN/SBR HX6 ....167 K3
RTHW LS26 ....133 J8

Quarry Hill La WBY LS22 ....29 M8
Quarry La BTLY WF17 ....151 H5
HEM/SK/SE WF9 ....225 J3
HUDE HD5 ....193 K8
HUDS HD4 ....213 C7
MOR LS27 ....152 C7
Quarry Mt HDGY LS6 ....109 J2
HOR/CROF WF4 ....222 D5
Quarry Mount St HDGY LS6 ....6 D1
Quarry Mount Ter HDGY LS6 ....6 D1
Quarry Pl ECHL BD2 ....105 K4
HDGY LS6 ....6 D1
MIRF WF14 ....149 L8
Quarry Rd CLECK BD19 ....149 L8
CLECK BD19 ....150 D7
DEWS WF13 ....173 K7
HIPP HX3 ....146 K4
HUD HD1 ....14 A6
HUDS HD4 ....213 K3
WF15 ....172 C2
OT LS21 ....63 J1
Quarryside Rd MIRF WF14 ....172 A8
Quarry St BSLY S70 ....261 H6
BSLYN/ROY S71 ....261 J6
CUD/GR S72 ....244 D7
FEA/AMT WF7 ....224 B1
HDGY LS6 ....6 D1
HTON BD9 ....104 C2
KGHY BD21 ....3 K5
WHIT OL12 ....184 A1
WHIT OL12 ....206 A5
The Quarry AL/HA/HU LS17 ....65 J8
Quarry Vw DEWS WF13 ....173 H5
Quayside BAIL BD17 ....82 D6
Quay St HUD HD1 ....15 G3
Quebec Rd HUDW HD3 ....212 A1
Quebec St ELL HX5 ....169 J8
KGHY BD21 ....2 F5
LDS LS1 ....6 E9
TOD OL14 ....163 J5
WKFDW/WTN WF2 ....12 C3
Queen Elizabeth Dr NORM WF6 ....178 C6
Queen Elizabeth Gdns HUD HD1 ....14 D6
Queen Elizabeth Gv WKFDE WF1 ....177 G7
Queen Elizabeth Rd WKFDE WF1 ....177 G7
Queen Elizabeth St WKFDE WF1 ....176 C2
Queen Margarets Av KNOT WF11 ....159 M6
Queen Margarets Cl KNOT WF11 ....159 M6
Queen Margaret's Dr KNOT WF11 ....159 M6
Queens Ar LDS LS1 ....7 G9
Queen's Av CUD/GR S72 ....263 M7
DOD/DAR S75 ....260 H4
ECHL BD2 ....105 H3
PONT WF8 ....180 C7
WHIT OL12 ....206 E2
Queensbury Av WKFDE WF1 ....176 E1
Queensbury Ct HIPP HX3 ....178 E5
Queensbury Rd HIPP HX3 ....146 D1
Queensbury Sq CUL/QBY BD13 * 125 G5
Queens Cl BGLY BD16 ....81 K4
CHAL LS7 ....87 L6
Queenscourt MOR LS27 ....152 C2
Queen's Crs HOR/CROF WF4 ....200 E2
OSS WF5 ....196 F1
Queen's Dr CUD/GR S72 ....244 D3
OSS WF5 ....196 F1
CUD/GR S72 ....244 E5
DOD/DAR S75 ....260 B7
EARD/LOFT WF3 ....154 F3
HIPP HX3 ....169 J2
ILK LS29 ....38 B5
OSS WF5 ....197 G2
PDSY/CALV LS28 ....106 F6
ROCH OL11 ....228 A3
WKFDW/WTN WF2 ....176 A5
Queens Drive Cl OSS WF5 ....197 H2
Queens Gdns DOD/DAR S75 ....260 E3
ILK LS29 ....38 C3
OSS WF5 ....196 F1
TAD LS24 ....71 L4
Queen's Ga HIPP HX3 ....168 D2
Queensgate BFD BD1 ....4 F9
Queensgate Dr ROY/SHW OL2 ....228 E8
Queensgate Market Ar HUD HD1 ....15 G8
Queens Gv KGHY BD21 ....2 E9
MOR LS27 ....152 C2
Queenshill Av AL/HA/HU LS17 ....87 L4
Queenshill Cl AL/HA/HU LS17 * 87 L4
Queenshill Ct AL/HA/HU LS17 * 87 L4
Queenshill Crs AL/HA/HU LS17 ....87 L4
Queenshill Dr AL/HA/HU LS17 ....87 L4
Queenshill Gdns AL/HA/HU LS17 ....87 K4
Queenshill Garth AL/HA/HU LS17 ....87 L4
Queenshill Rd AL/HA/HU LS17 ....87 L4
Queenshill Wk AL/HA/HU LS17 ....87 L4
Queenshill Wy AL/HA/HU LS17 ....87 L4
Queens Md HIPP HX3 * 147 J3
Queens Mill Rd HUD HD1 ....214 C2
Queens Park Cl CAS WF10 ....158 D6
Queen's Park Dr CAS WF10 ....158 D6
Queen's Pl MOR LS27 ....152 C2
OT LS21 ....41 J7
SHPY BD18 ....82 B6
Queen's Prom MOR LS27 ....152 C1
Queen Sq LDSU LS2 ....7 G7
Queen Square Ct LDSU LS2 ....6 F7
Queen's Rd AWLS/ASK DN6 ....249 L6
BGLY BD16 ....59 G8
BSLYN/ROY S71 ....261 H5
BSPA/BRAM LS23 ....48 E6
CAS WF10 ....158 C4
CUD/GR S72 ....244 E5
ECHL BD2 ....105 H3
HDGY LS6 ....6 B4
HFAX HX1 ....10 D5
HUDW HD3 ....14 B3
ILK LS29 ....38 C3
KGHY BD21 ....2 E9
LIT OL15 ....207 K1
MOR LS27 ....152 B3
PONT WF8 ....180 C7
SHPY BD18 ....82 B6
Queens Ter OSS WF5 ....196 F1
Queensthorpe Av BRAM LS13 ....108 A6
Queensthorpe Cl BRAM LS13 ....108 A6
Queensthorpe Ri BRAM LS13 ....107 M6
Queen St AIRE BD20 ....36 A5
AIRE BD20 ....56 D1

BAIL BD17 ....82 E5
BGLY BD16 ....81 H3
BSLY S70 ....261 H5
CAS WF10 ....158 A5
CLECK BD19 ....150 A8
DEWS WF13 ....173 G8
EARD/LOFT WF3 ....153 M6
EARD/LOFT WF3 ....154 F3
EARL WF12 ....174 C6
GTL/HWG HX4 ....168 E8
HBR HX7 * 5 G6
HECK WF16 ....172 E5
HEM/SK/SE WF9 ....247 H4
HOR/CROF WF4 ....197 J5
HUD HD1 ....15 G7
HWTH BD22 ....54 E5
IDLE BD10 ....83 M7
KBTN HD8 ....239 J4
LDS LS1 ....8 D1
LIT OL15 ....207 K1
MID OL16 ....132 C4
MIRF WF14 ....194 C2
MOR LS27 ....152 C2
NORM WF6 ....178 C4
OSS WF5 ....196 F1
PONT WF8 ....180 D6
ROY/SHW OL2 ....229 K8
RPDN/SBR HX6 ....167 G3
RTHW LS26 ....135 G8
STKB/PEN S36 ....271 G3
TOD OL14 ....163 K1
WBSY BD6 ....126 A7
WHIT OL12 ....206 B6
WIL/AL BD15 ....103 G2
WKFDE WF1 ....12 E5
WMB/DAR S73 ....263 K8
YEA LS19 ....84 D2
Queen St South HUD HD1 ....15 C9
Queens Vw LIT OL15 ....207 J3
SCFT LS14 * 111 K1
Queensway BGLY BD16 ....81 K4
BSLYN/ROY S71 ....243 L2
CUD/GR S72 ....245 J8
DOD/DAR S75 ....260 E5
GFTH/SHER LS25 ....112 F7
GSLY LS20 ....62 B5
HFAX HX1 ....10 A1
KBTN HD8 ....238 C1
MOR LS27 ....152 C2
MSTN/BAR LS15 ....111 J6
NORM WF6 ....178 C2
PONT WF8 ....181 H3
ROCH OL11 ....228 C2
RTHW LS26 ....133 C8
Queenswood Cl HDGY LS6 ....86 C7
Queenswood Ct HDGY LS6 ....86 D2
Queenswood Dr HDGY LS6 ....86 C8
Queenswood Gdns HDGY LS6 ....108 B2
Queenswood Gn HDGY LS6 ....86 C7
Queenswood Hts HDGY LS6 ....108 D1
Queenswood Mt HDGY LS6 ....108 B2
Queenswood Ri HDGY LS6 ....108 D1
Queenswood Rd HDGY LS6 ....108 D1
Queen Victoria Crs HIPP HX3 ....147 K5
Queen Victoria St ROCH OL11 ....228 C3
Quernmore Dr BWCK/EAR BB18 ....52 C1
Quern Wy WMB/DAR S73 ....263 J8
Quincy Cl ECHL BD2 ....105 L2
Quinton WHIT OL12 * 206 A6

R

Raby Av CHAL LS7 ....7 J2
Raby Pk WBY LS22 ....47 M1
Raby St CHAL LS7 ....7 J2
Raby Ter CHAL LS7 ....7 J2
Racca Av KNOT WF11 ....182 D2
Racca Gn KNOT WF11 ....182 C2
Race Common Av STKB/PEN S36 ....270 E6
Racecommon La BSLY S70 ....261 C7
Racecommon Rd BSLY S70 ....260 F6
Race Moor La HWTH BD22 ....78 D3
Race St BSLY S70 ....260 F6
Rachael St HOR/CROF WF4 ....197 H5
Racton St MAR/SLWT HD7 ....212 B5
Radcliffe Av ECHL BD2 ....105 J1
Radcliffe Gdns PDSY/CALV LS28 ....107 C7
Radcliffe La LUD/ILL HX2 ....144 E4
PDSY/CALV LS28 ....107 G7
Radcliffe Pl WKFDE WF1 ....12 E2
Radcliffe Rd BSLYN/ROY S71 ....243 H6
HUDW HD3 ....212 C5
MAR/SLWT HD7 ....212 C5
WKFDW/WTN WF2 ....197 K2
Radcliffe St KBTN HD8 ....239 H4
Radfield Dr WBSY BD6 ....127 G6
Radford Park Av HEM/SK/SE WF9 ....246 A1
Radnor St BFDE BD3 ....105 L7
WOR/ARM LS12 ....109 G8
Radwell Dr WBOW BD5 ....4 E9
Raeburn Dr WBSY BD6 ....126 C7
Rae Ct EARD/LOFT WF3 ....177 C1
Rae Rd SHPY BD18 ....82 C8
Ragdale Av HUDW HD3 ....191 G5
Raglan Av HWTH BD22 ....2 B6
Raglan Cl CAS WF10 ....157 K5
Raglan Ct HFAX HX1 ....10 C5
Raglan St BFDE BD3 ....105 M7
CUL/QBY BD13 ....125 C5
HFAX HX1 ....10 D5
HWTH BD22 ....2 B6
TOD OL14 ....163 K1
Raglan Ter BFDE BD3 ....106 A7
Raikes Av SKP/WHF BD23 ....16 B1
Raikes La BOW BD4 ....128 A7
BTLY WF17 ....151 G4
Raikes Rd SKP/WHF BD23 ....16 B1
Raikeswood Crs SKP/WHF BD23 ....16 A1
Raikes Wood Dr BOW BD4 ....128 A7
Raikeswood Dr SKP/WHF BD23 ....16 A1
Raikeswood Rd SKP/WHF BD23 ....16 A1
Railes Cl LUD/ILL HX2 ....144 F5
Railes La LUD/ILL HX2 ....144 F5
Railsfield Mt BRAM LS13 ....107 L4
Railsfield Ri BRAM LS13 ....107 L4
Railsfield Wy BRAM LS13 ....107 L4
Railway Av PONT WF8 ....180 L5
Railway Rd KBTN HD8 ....240 B3
Railway Rd IDLE BD10 ....83 L6
ILK LS29 ....38 D2
MSTN/BAR LS15 ....111 M4
Railway St BOW BD4 ....127 L5
BRIG HD6 ....170 D1
CLECK BD19 ....149 M7
DEWS WF13 ....173 H8
EARL WF12 ....173 M6

HECK WF16 ....172 F3
HUD HD1 ....14 F6
KCHY BD21 ....57 L5
LIT OL15 ....207 K1
MILN OL16 ....206 C8
MILN OL16 ....229 L2
OSM LS9 ....9 L1
TOD OL14 ....141 K8
Railway Ter EARD/LOFT WF3 ....153 L5
HEM/SK/SE WF9 ....223 J3
HIPP HX3 ....168 C4
ILK LS29 ....38 E2
Railway Vw CAS WF10 ....157 K7
ROY/SHW OL2 ....229 L6
Rainbow Ms WBSY BD6 * 126 B8
Raincliffe Gv OSM LS9 ....110 C6
Raincliffe Mt OSM LS9 * 110 C7
Raincliffe Rd OSM LS9 ....110 C6
Raincliffe St OSM LS9 ....110 C6
Raincliffe Ter OSM LS9 * 110 C7
Raines Crest MILN OL16 ....207 J8
Raines Dr AIRE BD20 ....34 E1
Rainford Dr BSLYN/ROY S71 ....243 M8
Rainsborough Av KNOT WF11 ....133 L3
Rainton Gv DOD/DAR S75 ....260 D3
Raistrick Wy SHPY BD18 ....82 F6
Rake HBR HX7 ....143 H6
Rake Head Barn La TOD OL14 ....163 J7
Rake Head Rd HOLM/MEL HD9 ....253 C2
Rakehill Rd MSTN/BAR LS15 ....90 B7
Rake Ter LIT OL15 ....185 L8
Rakewood Rd LIT OL15 ....207 K3
Raleigh Gdns LIT OL15 ....185 L5
Raleigh St HFAX HX1 * 10 B8
Raley St BSLY S70 ....260 F7
Ralph Garth RYKW YO26 ....32 C1
Ralph St WHIT OL12 ....206 C5
Rampart Rd HDGY LS6 ....6 C2
The Rampart COP/BISH YO23 ....73 J8
Ramsay Pl MILN OL16 ....206 C8
Ramsay St MILN OL16 ....206 C6
Ramsay Ter MILN OL16 ....206 C8
Ramsden Av GTHN BD7 ....126 A1
Ramsden Cl KNOT WF11 ....159 L6
Ramsden Ct GTHN BD7 ....126 C2
Ramsden La TOD OL14 ....163 H7
Ramsden Mill Bottom HUDW HD3 * 213 H3
Ramsden Mill La MAR/SLWT HD7 ....213 G3
Ramsden Pl CLAY BD14 ....125 K1
Ramsden Rd WHIT OL12 ....184 C2
Ramsden St CAS WF10 ....179 L1
GFTH/SHER LS25 ....135 H6
HIPP HX3 ....146 A4
HUD HD1 ....14 F8
MAR/SLWT HD7 ....213 G2
Ramsden Wood Rd TOD OL14 ....163 H7
Ramsey Crs HOR/CROF WF4 ....196 D7
Ramsey Rd HOR/CROF WF4 ....196 C7
Ramsey St WBOW BD5 ....126 F3
Ramsey Vw HOR/CROF WF4 ....196 C7
Ramsgate EARD/LOFT WF3 ....154 D5
Ramsgate Crs EARD/LOFT WF3 ....154 D5
Ramsgate St HFAX HX1 ....10 A5
Ramshaw Dr SKP/WHF BD23 ....16 C2
Ramshead Ap SCFT LS14 ....89 J8
Ramshead Cl SCFT LS14 ....89 J7
Ramshead Crs SCFT LS14 ....89 H7
Ramshead Dr SCFT LS14 ....89 H7
Ramshead Gdns SCFT LS14 ....89 H7
Ramshead Gv SCFT LS14 ....89 J8
Ramshead Hl SCFT LS14 ....89 J8
Ramshead Pl SCFT LS14 ....89 J8
Ramshead Vw SCFT LS14 ....89 J8
Randall Pl HTON BD9 ....104 C3
Randall Well St BFD BD1 ....4 E7
Randolph St BFDE BD3 ....106 A6
BRAM LS13 ....107 J4
HIPP HX3 ....11 J3
Random Cl HWTH BD22 ....2 A9
Rand Pl GTHN BD7 ....4 A9
Rand St GTHN BD7 ....4 A9
Ranelagh Av IDLE BD10 ....106 A1
Raneley Gv ROCH OL11 ....228 C4
Range Bank HIPP HX3 ....11 H2
Range Bank Top HIPP HX3 ....11 H1
Range Ct HIPP HX3 ....11 H2
Range Gdns HIPP HX3 ....11 H2
Range La HIPP HX3 ....11 H2
UPML OL3 ....230 F5
Range St HIPP HX3 ....11 G1
Rankin's Well Rd SKP/WHF BD23 ....16 D2
Ransdale Dr WBOW BD5 ....126 F3
Ransdale Gv WBOW BD5 ....126 F3
Ransdale Rd WBOW BD5 ....126 F3
Ranter's Fold HOR/CROF WF4 ....197 J5
Raper Vw GFTH/SHER LS25 ....92 A3
Rapes Hwy UPML OL3 ....231 J1
Rashcliffe Hill Rd HUD HD1 ....214 B2
Rastrick Common BRIG HD6 ....170 C6
Rathbone St MILN OL16 ....228 D1
Rathlin Rd EARL WF12 ....174 B4
Rathmell St WBOW BD5 ....126 F5
Ratten Rw DOD/DAR S75 ....260 A4
Ratten Row Rd RPDN/SBR HX6 ....166 F6
Raven Cl FEA/AMT WF7 ....179 K5
Ravenfield Dr BSLYN/ROY S71 ....243 J8
Raven La CUD/GR S72 ....222 C6
Raven Rd HDGY LS6 ....109 G2
Raven Royd BSLYN/ROY S71 ....243 H5
Ravens Av DEWS WF13 ....173 H5
HUDE HD5 ....215 C1
Ravenscar Av RHAY LS8 ....88 C8
Ravenscar Mt RHAY LS8 ....88 C8
Ravenscar Ter RHAY LS8 ....88 C8
Ravenscar Vw RHAY LS8 ....88 C8
Ravenscar Wk RHAY LS8 * 88 C8
Ravenscliffe Av IDLE BD10 ....106 A1
Ravenscliffe Cl HIPP HX3 ....168 E4
Ravenscliffe Rd PDSY/CALV LS28 ....84 A8
Ravens Cl DOD/DAR S75 ....242 D6
Ravens Crs DEWS WF13 ....173 H5
Ravensdeane HUDW HD3 ....191 M6
Ravensfield Rd DEWS WF13 ....173 H5
Ravens Gv DEWS WF13 ....173 H5
Ravenshaw Cl DOD/DAR S75 ....260 D3
Ravenshouse Rd DEWS WF13 ....173 H7
Ravensknowle Rd HUDE HD5 ....215 G1
Ravens Lodge Ter DEWS WF13 * 173 H7
Ravensmead FEA/AMT WF7 ....181 G4
Ravens Mt PDSY/CALV LS28 ....107 H7
Ravens St DEWS WF13 ....195 H1
Ravensthorpe Rd EARL WF12 ....195 H1
Ravenstone Gv GTL/HWG HX4 ....168 E8
Raven St BGLY BD16 ....81 H5
HFAX HX1 ....10 B5
KGHY BD21 ....2 F4
Ravens Vw AIRE BD20 * 55 M2
Ravensville AIRE BD20 ....35 C8
Ravens Wk DEWS WF13 ....173 J8
Ravens Wy HOLM/MEL HD9 ....255 C2
Ravenswharf Rd DEWS WF13 ....173 J8

Ravenswood GTL/HWG HX4 * ...168 B7
Ravensworth Cl
　MSTN/BAR LS15 ...112 B3
Ravensworth Wy
　MSTN/BAR LS15 ...112 B3
Raven Ter GIR BD8 ...103 L7
Rawden Hl OT LS21 ...44 A8
Rawdon Dr YEA LS19 ...84 D3
Rawdon Hall Dr YEA LS19 ...84 D3
Rawdon Rd HORS LS18 ...85 G5
　HWTH BD22 ...78 E7
Rawdon St HWTH BD22 ...2 C7
Raw End Rd LUD/ILL HX2 ...145 L6
Rawfield La GFTH/SHER LS25 ...137 L8
Rawfolds Av BTLY WF17 ...151 K4
Rawfolds Wy CLECK BD19 ...150 A8
Rawgate Av CAS WF10 ...157 K6
Raw Hl BRIG HD6 * ...170 B6
Raw La HBR HX7 ...143 M3
　LUD/ILL HX2 ...145 M1
　TAD LS24 ...94 A1
Rawling St KGHY BD21 ...2 E9
Rawling Wy HDGY LS6 ...109 H1
Raw Nook LM/WK BD12 ...149 H1
Raw Nook Rd HUDW HD3 ...191 G6
Rawroyds GTL/HWG HX4 ...190 F2
Rawson Av BFDE BD3 ...105 M6
　HIPP HX3 ...168 D3
Rawson Pl BFD BD1 ...4 E5
　RPDN/SBR HX6 ...167 J3
Rawson Rd BFD BD1 ...4 E5
Rawson Sq BFD BD1 ...4 E5
　IDLE BD10 ...83 K5
Rawson St HFAX HX1 ...11 G6
　LM/WK BD12 ...148 F2
Rawson St North HIPP HX3 ...10 E1
Rawson Ter BEE/HOL LS11 * ...131 L5
Rawtenstall Bank MARF HX7 ...143 G2
Rawthorpe Crs HUDE HD5 ...195 G2
Rawthorpe La HUDE HD5 ...15 M5
Rawthorpe Ter HUDE HD5 ...195 G2
Rayfield WKFDW/WTN WF2 ...198 B1
Ray Ga HBR HX7 ...122 B7
　HOLM/MEL HD9 ...236 F6
　HUDW HD3 ...190 F6
Raygill Cl AL/HA/HU LS17 ...88 D1
Raylands Cl MID LS10 ...132 B8
Raylands Ct MID LS10 ...132 B8
Raylands Fold MID LS10 ...132 B8
Raylands Garth MID LS10 ...132 B8
Raylands La MID LS10 ...132 B8
Raylands Pl MID LS10 ...132 B8
Raylands Rd MID LS10 ...132 B8
Raylands Wy MID LS10 ...154 B1
Rayleigh St BOW BD4 ...127 J2
Raymond Av CUD/GR S72 ...245 J8
Raymond Dr WBOW BD5 ...127 G4
Raymond Rd BSLY S70 ...261 M7
Raymond St WBOW BD5 ...127 H4
Raynbron Crs WBOW BD5 ...127 H4
Raynel Ap BHP/TINH LS16 ...86 B3
Raynel Cl BHP/TINH LS16 ...86 B2
Raynel Dr BHP/TINH LS16 ...86 B2
Raynel Gdns BHP/TINH LS16 ...86 C3
Raynel Garth BHP/TINH LS16 ...86 C3
Raynel Gn BHP/TINH LS16 ...86 C3
Raynel Mt BHP/TINH LS16 ...86 B2
Raynel Wy BHP/TINH LS16 ...86 B2
Rayner Av GIR BD8 ...104 B3
　HECK WF16 ...150 F8
Rayner Dr BRIG HD6 ...170 C2
Rayner Mt WIL/AL BD15 ...103 K6
Rayner Rd BRIG HD6 ...170 C2
Rayners Av LVSG WF15 ...171 J4
Rayner St HOR/CROF WF4 ...197 J5
Raynham Crs AIRE BD20 ...57 G6
Raynor Cl HUDW HD3 ...191 L7
Raynville Ap BRAM LS13 ...108 A3
Raynville Av BRAM LS13 ...108 A3
Raynville Crs WOR/ARM LS12 ...108 B4
Raynville Dr BRAM LS13 ...108 A3
Raynville Gn BRAM LS13 ...108 A4
Raynville Mt BRAM LS13 ...108 A3
Raynville Pl BRAM LS13 ...108 A3
Raynville Ri BRAM LS13 ...108 A4
Raynville Rd WOR/ARM LS12 ...108 A3
Raynville Ter BRAM LS13 ...108 A3
Raynville Wk BRAM LS13 ...108 A4
Ray St HUD HD1 ...15 G4
Raywood Cl YEA LS19 ...62 B7
Reap Hirst Rd HUDN HD2 ...191 M4
Reasbeck Ter BSLYN/ROY S71 ...261 H1
Rebecca Av BSLY S70 * ...261 H6
Rebecca Rd BSLY S70 ...261 H6
Rebecca St GIR BD8 ...4 C4
Recreation Av BEE/HOL LS11 * ...8 C7
Recreation Crs BEE/HOL LS11 ...8 C7
Recreation Gv BEE/HOL LS11 ...8 C7
Recreation La ELL HX5 ...169 G8
Recreation Mt BEE/HOL LS11 * ...8 B7
Recreation Pl BEE/HOL LS11 ...8 C7
Recreation Rd RPDN/SBR HX6 ...167 K2
Recreation Rw BEE/HOL LS11 ...8 B7
Recreation St BEE/HOL LS11 ...8 C7
Recreation Ter BEE/HOL LS11 * ...8 C7
Recreation Vw BEE/HOL LS11 ...8 C7
Rectory Cl BSLYN/ROY S71 ...243 M5
　COP/BISH YO23 ...73 J7
　GFTH/SHER LS25 ...113 H7
　MAR/SLWT HD7 ...233 H2
Rectory Dr BTLY WF17 ...151 J3
　HUDE HD5 ...193 K7
Rectory Gdn HUDN HD2 ...217 M7
Rectory La KBTN HD8 ...217 M7
　SKP/WHF BD23 ...16 C2
Rectory Wy KGHY BD21 ...2 D5
Rectory St CAS WF10 ...157 M6
　OSM LS9 ...7 M6
Rectory Vw EARL WF12 ...196 A4
Rectory Wy BSLYN/ROY S71 ...261 M1
Red Beck Rd HIPP HX3 ...147 H5
Red Beck V SHPY BD18 ...104 C1
Red Brink La RPDN/SBR HX6 ...166 D4
Redbrook Rd DOD/DAR S75 ...260 E2
Redbrook Vw DOD/DAR S75 ...260 E2
Redbrook Wk DOD/DAR S75 ...260 E2
Redburn Av SHPY BD18 ...104 C1
Redburn Dr SHPY BD18 ...104 C1
Redburn Rd SHPY BD18 ...104 C1
Redcar Av AIRE BD20 ...56 D4
Redcar Rd IDLE BD10 ...84 A8
Redcar St HFAX HX1 ...10 A6
　WHIT OL12 ...206 A6
Redcliffe Av KGHY BD21 ...2 D1
Redcliffe Cl DOD/DAR S75 ...260 D1
Redcliffe Gv KGHY BD21 ...2 D1
Redcote La BULY LS4 ...108 D5
Redcross St WHIT OL12 ...206 B6
Redcross St North
　WHIT OL12 * ...206 B6
Red Deer Park La EARL WF12 ...217 G1
Reddisher Rd MAR/SLWT HD7 ...233 G2
Red Doles La HUD HD1 ...192 E5
Red Doles Rd HUDN HD2 ...192 E4
Reddyshore TOD OL14 ...185 L2
Reddyshore Brow LIT OL15 ...185 M6

Reddyshore Scout Ga
　TOD OL14 ...185 K1
Redesdale Gdns BHP/TINH LS16 ...86 D3
Redfearn Av HECK WF16 ...172 F4
Redfearn St BSLYN/ROY S71 ...261 K4
Red Hall Ap SCFT LS14 ...89 J5
Red Hall Cha SCFT LS14 ...89 H5
Redhall Cl BEE/HOL LS11 ...131 G5
Redhall Crs BEE/HOL LS11 ...131 G5
Redhall Cft SCFT LS14 ...89 J6
Red Hall Gdns AL/HA/HU LS17 ...89 H5
Red Hall Garth SCFT LS14 ...89 H5
Redhall Gn SCFT LS14 ...89 J5
Red Hall La AL/HA/HU LS17 ...89 H5
　WKFDE WF1 ...176 D4
Red Hall Vw SCFT LS14 * ...89 J5
Red Hall Wk SCFT LS14 ...89 J5
Redhill Av BSLY S70 ...261 L7
　CAS WF10 ...158 B8
　EARD/LOFT WF3 ...175 G1
Redhill Cl BOW BD4 ...128 B6
　EARD/LOFT WF3 ...175 G1
Redhill Crs EARD/LOFT WF3 ...175 G1
Redhill Dr CAS WF10 ...158 C7
　EARD/LOFT WF3 ...175 G1
Redhill Gdns CAS WF10 ...158 C8
Red Hill La GFTH/SHER LS25 ...137 L5
Redhill Mt CAS WF10 ...158 C7
Redhill Rd CAS WF10 ...158 C7
Redhill Vw CAS WF10 ...158 C8
Redhill Wk CAS WF10 ...158 C8
Red House La AWLS/ASK DN6 ...248 A7
Red Laithes La DEWS WF13 ...173 G8
Redland Cl LIT OL15 ...185 K8
Redland Crs HEM/SK/SE WF9 ...223 K4
Redland Dr KBTN HD8 ...216 A2
Red La FEA/AMT WF7 ...201 G1
　HOLM/MEL HD9 ...234 D4
　PDSY/CALV LS28 ...106 E3
　WHIT OL12 ...206 D4
　WKFDE WF1 ...200 A1
Red Lodge Cl RHAY LS8 ...110 F7
Redman Garth HWTH BD22 ...78 A7
Redmayne Gv KNOT WF11 ...181 M2
Redmire Ct SCFT LS14 ...111 J2
Redmire Dr SCFT LS14 ...111 J2
Redmire St BFDE BD3 ...106 A7
Redmire Vw SCFT LS14 ...111 J2
Redpoll Wy WBSY BD6 ...125 L5
Redruth Dr NORM WF6 ...178 D5
Redshank Cl WBSY BD6 ...125 L5
Redshaw Rd WOR/ARM LS12 ...108 F8
Redthorne Wy CUD/GR S72 ...244 D3
Redthorpe Crest
　DOD/DAR S75 ...260 C2
Red V CLECK BD19 ...150 D4
Redvers Cl BHP/TINH LS16 ...86 C5
Redwald Dr GSLY LS20 ...61 L5
Redwing Crs HUDW HD3 ...213 H1
Redwood Av BSLYN/ROY S71 ...243 L3
　EARD/LOFT WF3 ...153 J6
Redwood Cl KGHY BD21 ...3 L8
　RTHW LS26 ...134 A8
Redwood Dr HUDN HD2 ...192 F1
Redwood Gv HOR/CROF WF4 ...200 A2
　HUDE HD5 ...15 L7
Redwood Wy YEA LS19 ...62 B7
Reed Hl MILN OL16 * ...206 B6
Reedling Dr MOR LS27 ...152 E3
Reed Rd WOR/ARM LS12 ...108 E8
Reedsdale Dr MOR LS27 ...129 L7
Reedsdale Gdns MOR LS27 ...129 L7
Reedshaw La HWTH BD22 ...54 B5
Reed St HUD HD1 ...191 M7
Rees Wy BFDE BD3 ...5 H3
Reeth Rd BRIG HD6 ...170 A6
Reevy Av WBSY BD6 ...126 B6
Reevy Crs WBSY BD6 ...126 B6
Reevy Dr WBSY BD6 ...126 C6
Reevylands Dr WBSY BD6 ...126 B6
Reevy Mt WBSY BD6 ...126 C6
Reevy Rd WBSY BD6 ...126 A6
Reevy Rd West WBSY BD6 ...126 A6
Reevy St WBSY BD6 ...126 C5
Reform St CLECK BD19 ...150 D5
　WHIT OL12 ...206 B6
Regal Av HUDE HD5 * ...15 M7
Regal Cl RPDN/SBR HX6 ...188 E5
Regal Ct EARL WF12 ...174 A6
Regal Dr RPDN/SBR HX6 ...188 E5
Regal Fold WHIT OL12 ...206 D2
Regency Ct GIR BD8 ...104 C6
Regency Gdns
　EARD/LOFT WF3 ...153 J6
Regency Park Gv
　PDSY/CALV LS28 ...129 G1
Regency Park Rd
　PDSY/CALV LS28 ...129 G1
Regency Rd MIRF WF14 ...194 C2
Regent Av COL BB8 ...52 A8
　HORS LS18 ...85 L7
Regent Cl BRIG HD6 ...170 A8
　HORS LS18 ...85 L7
Regent Ct HUD HD1 ...14 A4
　LDS LS1 * ...9 H1
Regent Crs BSLYN/ROY S71 ...243 H7
　CUD/GR S72 ...245 G1
　HORS LS18 ...85 K7
　SKP/WHF BD23 ...16 D1
Regent Dr SKP/WHF BD23 ...16 D1
Regent Gdns BSLY S70 ...261 G4
Regent Ms BTLY WF17 ...174 B2
Regent Pde RPDN/SBR HX6 * ...167 L2
Regent Park Av HDGY LS6 ...9 G1
Regent Park Cross HDGY LS6 ...9 G1
Regent Park Ter HDGY LS6 ...9 G1
Regent Pl HBR HX7 ...143 J3
　IDLE BD10 ...83 J3
　RPDN/SBR HX6 ...167 K1
Regent Rd HORS LS18 ...85 L7
　HUD HD1 ...14 A4
　HUDE HD5 ...193 L4
　ILK LS29 ...38 C2
Regents Pk WKFDE WF1 ...13 J3
Regent St BSLY S70 ...261 G4
　CAS WF10 ...157 L7
　CHAL LS7 ...87 L7
　CUD/GR S72 ...245 G1
　CUL/QBY BD13 ...125 H5
　FEA/AMT WF7 ...201 L1
　HBR HX7 ...143 J3
　HECK WF16 ...172 E3
　HEM/SK/SE WF9 ...223 L7
　HEM/SK/SE WF9 ...247 G3

　HFAX HX1 ...10 F7
　HOR/CROF WF4 ...197 H5
　IDLE BD10 ...83 J5
　LIT OL15 ...207 K1
　MIRF WF14 ...194 C3
　NORM WF6 ...178 C3
　OSM LS9 ...7 M7
　TOD OL14 * ...163 H5
　WHIT OL12 ...206 B5
　WKFDE WF1 ...13 K7
Regent St South BSLY S70 * ...261 H4
Regent Ter HDGY LS6 ...9 G1
Regina Crs CUD/GR S72 ...245 G5
　HOR/CROF WF4 ...222 E5
Regina Dr CHAL LS7 ...87 M8
Reginald Mt CHAL LS7 ...109 M2
Reginald Pl CHAL LS7 ...109 M2
Reginald Rd BSLY S70 ...261 M7
Reginald Rw CHAL LS7 ...109 M2
Reginald St CHAL LS7 ...109 M2
　WBOW BD5 ...126 F3
Reginald Ter CHAL LS7 ...109 M2
Reginald Vw CHAL LS7 ...109 M2
Reid Park Av HOR/CROF WF4 ...197 G5
Reighton Cft IDLE BD10 ...84 A8
Rein Closet GFTH/SHER LS25 ...92 A6
Rein Gdns EARD/LOFT WF3 ...152 E6
Rein Ms EARD/LOFT WF3 ...152 E6
Rein Rd BRAM LS13 ...108 E8
　EARD/LOFT WF3 ...152 E6
Reins Av BAIL BD17 ...82 D5
Reins Rd BRIG HD6 ...170 A6
Rein St MOR LS27 ...152 E5
The Rein SCFT LS14 ...89 H8
Reinwood Av HUDN HD2 ...191 K8
　RHAY LS8 ...110 F1
Rembrandt Av
　EARD/LOFT WF3 ...153 M6
Renaissance Dr MOR LS27 ...130 E6
Renald La STKB/PEN S36 ...258 A7
Renee Ct BOW BD4 ...127 L6
Renfield Gv NORM WF6 ...178 F3
Renshaw St IDLE BD10 ...83 K5
Renton Av GSLY LS20 ...61 M5
Renton Dr GSLY LS20 ...61 M6
Repton Rd AWLS/ASK DN6 ...249 K6
Reservoir Farm Ct
　HOR/CROF WF4 ...222 F4
Reservoir Pl CUL/QBY BD13 ...124 E4
Reservoir Rd HWTH BD22 ...78 A7
　LUD/ILL HX2 ...146 A6
Reservoir Side Rd
　MAR/SLWT HD7 ...213 G7
Reservoir St DEWS WF13 ...173 J5
　MILN OL16 ...206 F6
Reservoir Vw CUL/QBY BD13 ...102 F7
　KBTN HD8 ...239 C4
Restmore Av GSLY LS20 ...61 L6
Retford Av MILN OL16 ...228 D2
Retford Pl GTHN BD7 ...4 B9
Reuben St LVSG WF15 ...172 C1
Reva Cl BGLY BD16 ...81 K2
Reva Syke Rd CLAY BD14 ...125 K2
Revel Garth KBTN HD8 ...257 J1
Revie Rd BEE/HOL LS11 ...8 A9
Reyden Ms WOR/ARM LS12 ...108 E8
Reydon Wk WBSY BD6 ...126 B6
Reyner House Ms WBOW BD5 ...4 F9
Reynolds Av GTHN BD7 ...126 A1
Rhine St BOW BD4 ...127 J1
Rhodes Av HECK WF16 ...150 F8
Rhodes Crs PONT WF8 ...180 F8
　ROCH OL11 ...228 B5
Rhode's Hill La
　BSPA/BRAM LS23 ...70 A5
Rhodesia Av HIPP HX3 ...168 A5
　WIL/AL BD15 ...103 L6
Rhodesia St AIRE BD20 ...34 F8
Rhodes Pl SHPY BD18 ...82 D6
Rhodes St CAS WF10 ...157 L6
　HFAX HX1 ...10 E6
　LVSG WF15 ...172 E2
　SHPY BD18 ...82 C6
　WHIT OL12 ...206 D3
Rhodes Wy RHAY LS8 ...88 F8
Rhodesway GIR BD8 ...103 M7
Rhondda Pl HFAX HX1 ...146 A7
Rhum Cl WBSY BD6 ...126 B8
Rhyddings Av FEA/AMT WF7 ...224 B1
Rhyddings Gdns ILK LS29 ...38 D2
Rhylstone Mt GTHN BD7 ...4 A7
Rhyl St FEA/AMT WF7 ...179 M8
Ribble Av LIT OL15 ...185 H8
Ribblesdale Av
　GFTH/SHER LS25 ...113 K8
Ribble St KGHY BD21 ...3 M3
Ribbleton Gv BFDE BD3 ...5 J4
Ribbleton Av BSLYN/ROY S71 ...243 J7
Ribstone St HBR HX7 ...144 A5
Ribston Rd PBR HX3 ...29 C1
Riccall Nook IDLE BD10 ...83 M8
Rice St HUD HD1 ...15 G8
Richard Av BSLYN/ROY S71 ...243 J8
Richard Gossop Ct ILK LS29 * ...40 A3
Richard Rd BSLYN/ROY S71 ...243 J8
　DOD/DAR S75 ...241 M6
Richardshaw La
　PDSY/CALV LS28 ...107 G5
Richardshaw Rd PDSY/CALV LS28 ...107 H5
Richardson Av WBSY BD6 ...126 E6
Richardson Crs OSM LS9 ...110 D7
Richardson Rd OSM LS9 ...110 D7
Richardson Sq LM/WK BD12 ...149 J2
Richardson St LM/WK BD12 ...149 J2
Richard St BFDE BD3 ...5 J8
　BRIG HD6 ...170 C2
　BSLY S70 ...260 F5
　ROCH OL11 ...206 C8
　WKFDE WF1 * ...176 E7
Richard Thorpe Av MIRF WF14 ...194 D1
Rich Ga HOLM/MEL HD9 ...235 L7
Richmond Av DOD/DAR S75 ...241 M7
　HDGY LS6 ...109 G3
　HUDN HD2 ...192 C4
　KNOT WF11 ...181 K1
　RPDN/SBR HX6 ...167 K3
Richmond Cl BRAM LS13 ...107 J4
　HFAX HX1 ...10 F1
　MILN OL16 ...228 C3
　MOR LS27 ...152 C3
　RTHW LS26 ...133 H7
Richmond Cft OSM LS9 ...110 B7
Richmondfield Av
　MSTN/BAR LS15 ...91 G8
Richmondfield Cl
　MSTN/BAR LS15 ...91 G8
Richmondfield Crs
　MSTN/BAR LS15 ...91 G8
Richmondfield Cross
　MSTN/BAR LS15 ...91 G8

Richmondfield Dr
　MSTN/BAR LS15 ...91 G8
Richmondfield Garth
　MSTN/BAR LS15 ...91 G8
Richmondfield Gv
　MSTN/BAR LS15 ...91 G8
Richmondfield La
　MSTN/BAR LS15 ...91 G8
Richmondfield Mt
　MSTN/BAR LS15 ...91 G8
Richmondfield Wy
　MSTN/BAR LS15 ...91 G8
Richmond Flats HUD HD1 ...15 G5
Richmond Gdns
　PDSY/CALV LS28 ...107 J7
　RPDN/SBR HX6 ...167 H3
Richmond Garth OSS WF5 ...197 H2
Richmond Green St OSM LS9 ...9 M2
Richmond Hill Ap OSM LS9 ...9 M2
Richmond Hill Cl OSM LS9 ...9 M2
Richmond Lea MIRF WF14 ...172 C8
Richmond Ms SHPY BD18 ...82 B6
Richmond Mt HDGY LS6 ...109 G3
Richmond Park Av LVSG WF15 ...172 C3
Richmond Pl ILK LS29 ...38 C3
　SHPY BD18 ...82 B6
Richmond Rd CTHN BD7 ...4 B6
　HDGY LS6 ...109 G2
　HECK WF16 ...151 G4
　HEM/SK/SE WF9 ...225 K7
　HFAX HX1 ...10 F4
　KGHY BD21 ...2 F3
　PDSY/CALV LS28 ...106 F4
　SHPY BD18 ...82 B6
　WKFDE WF1 ...176 E5
Richmond St BSLY S70 * ...260 F5
　CLECK BD19 ...149 M7
　HFAX HX1 ...10 F4
　KGHY BD21 ...2 F3
　OSM LS9 ...9 L2
　TOD OL14 ...163 L1
Richmond Ter OT LS21 ...41 H7
　PDSY/CALV LS28 ...107 J7
Richmond Wy
　GFTH/SHER LS25 ...135 H1
Rickard St WOR/ARM LS12 ...8 A3
Ridding Ga OT LS21 ...41 J6
Riddings Cl HEM/SK/SE WF9 ...245 M1
　HUDN HD2 ...192 F3
Riddings Ri HUDN HD2 ...192 F3
Riddings Rd HUDN HD2 ...192 F3
　ILK LS29 ...38 C1
Riddlesden St AIRE BD20 * ...58 B5
Ridehalgh La BRFD/BLYE BB10 ...96 C5
Rider Rd HDGY LS6 ...6 F1
Rider St OSM LS9 ...7 L8
Ridge Av HOR/CROF WF4 ...196 C7
Ridge Bank TOD OL14 ...163 K1
Ridge Cl GSLY LS20 ...61 L6
　HUDS HD4 ...214 C3
　KBTN HD8 ...239 J5
Ridge Crs HOR/CROF WF4 ...196 C8
Ridgedale Mt PONT WF8 ...180 E2
Ridge Gv CHAL LS7 ...109 J2
Ridge La AIRE BD20 ...17 L7
Ridge Lea BRIG HD6 ...170 B5
Ridge Mt HDGY LS6 ...6 C1
Ridgemount Rd AIRE BD20 ...58 A4
Ridge Rd GFTH/SHER LS25 ...135 M4
　HDGY LS6 ...6 F1
　HOR/CROF WF4 ...196 C7
　TOD OL14 ...163 K1
Ridgestone Av
　HEM/SK/SE WF9 ...224 A8
Ridge St HUDS HD4 ...214 C3
Ridge Ter HDGY LS6 ...109 G1
The Ridge WBY LS22 ...47 K3
Ridge Vw BRAM LS13 ...107 L6
Ridge View Dr HUDN HD2 ...192 C4
Ridge View Gdns IDLE BD10 * ...83 L7
Ridge View Rd BRIG HD6 * ...170 B5
Ridgewalk Wy BSLY S70 ...261 H8
Ridge Wy RHAY LS8 ...88 F8
Ridgeway CUL/QBY BD13 ...125 H6
　GSLY LS20 ...61 K6
　HUDE HD5 ...193 G7
　SHPY BD18 ...83 G7
　SKP/WHF BD23 ...16 A1
Ridgeway Cl HUDE HD5 ...193 G7
　RHAY LS8 ...88 F8
Ridgeway Crs BSLYN/ROY S71 ...243 L5
Ridgeway Dr BTLY WF17 ...151 J5
Ridgeway Gdns BRIG HD6 ...170 A1
Ridgeway Mt HWTH BD22 ...2 A9
Ridgeway Sq KNOT WF11 ...182 B3
The Ridgeways
　MAR/SLWT HD7 ...212 F6
Ridgeway Ter HDGY LS6 * ...6 F1
The Ridgeways
　KNOT WF11 ...182 B3
Ridgewood Cl BAIL BD17 ...83 G3
Ridgill Av AWLS/ASK DN6 ...249 J5
Ridgway Av WMB/DAR S73 ...263 J8
Riding Head La LUD/ILL HX2 ...145 G5
Riding Hl HIPP HX3 ...126 A8
Riding La LUD/ILL HX2 ...145 L3
Ridings Cl EARD/LOFT WF3 ...261 K1
Ridings Ct EARD/LOFT WF3 ...154 D8
Ridings Flds HOLM/MEL HD9 ...236 E3
Ridings Gdns
　EARD/LOFT WF3 ...154 D8
Ridings La EARD/LOFT WF3 ...154 D8
　HOLM/MEL HD9 ...236 E2
　MAR/SLWT HD7 ...212 E2
Ridings Ms EARD/LOFT WF3 ...154 D8
Ridings Rd EARL WF12 ...173 M6
The Ridings BSLYN/ROY S71 ...261 L1
Riding St BTLY WF17 ...151 G8
Ridings Wy EARD/LOFT WF3 ...154 D8
　WBSY BD6 ...126 A6
Ridingwood Ri KBTN HD8 ...240 A4
Ridleys Fold ILK LS29 ...19 H6
Rievaulx Av GIR BD8 ...4 B3
Rievaulx Cl BSPA/BRAM LS23 ...48 E7
Riffa La OT LS21 ...41 K4
Rifle Flds HUD HD1 ...14 D7
Rifle St HUD HD1 ...15 G8
Rigg La FEA/AMT WF7 ...202 E1
Rightox Rd HOLM/MEL HD9 ...236 E3
Rigton Ap OSM LS9 ...7 M8
Rigton Bank AL/HA/HU LS17 ...67 M2
Rigton Cl OSM LS9 ...7 M8
Rigton Dr OSM LS9 ...7 M8
Rigton Gn AL/HA/HU LS17 ...68 A2
　OSM LS9 ...7 M8
Rigton Lawn OSM LS9 ...7 M8
Rigton Ms OSM LS9 ...7 M8
Rigton St WBOW BD5 ...126 F3
Riley La KBTN HD8 ...238 C2
　LUD/ILL HX2 ...124 B6
Riley Pk KBTN HD8 ...216 B8
Riley St WBOW BD5 ...214 D2
Rillbank La BVRD LS3 ...109 G5
Rillbank St BVRD LS3 ...109 G5
Rillington Md IDLE BD10 ...83 M8
Rillside KBTN HD8 ...238 B5

Rills Md OT LS21 ...41 J7
Rilston St GTHN BD7 ...104 D8
Rimswell Holt IDLE BD10 ...84 A8
Ringby Ter HIPP HX3 * ...146 D4
Ring Hay Rd BOW BD4 ...128 C5
Ring Lows La WHIT OL12 ...206 C2
Ring Road Beeston
　BEE/HOL LS11 ...131 G6
　WOR/ARM LS12 ...130 E3
Ring Road Beeston Pk
　BRAM LS13 ...131 H8
Ring Road Bramley
　BRAM LS13 ...107 M6
Ring Road Cross Gates
　MSTN/BAR LS15 ...111 L3
Ring Road Farnley
　WOR/ARM LS12 ...107 M7
Ring Road Farsley
　PDSY/CALV LS28 ...106 E3
Ring Road Halton
　MSTN/BAR LS15 ...111 L5
Ring Road Horsforth
　HORS LS18 ...86 A6
Ring Road Low Wortley
　WOR/ARM LS12 ...108 B8
Ring Road Meanwood
　BHP/TINH LS16 ...87 G4
Ring Road Middleton
　MID LS10 ...153 M1
Ring Road Moortown
　AL/HA/HU LS17 ...87 J4
　RHAY LS8 ...88 B3
Ring Road Seacroft SCFT LS14 ...89 J6
Ring Road Shadwell
　AL/HA/HU LS17 ...88 C4
Ring Road Weetwood
　BHP/TINH LS16 ...86 E5
Ring Road West Pk
　BHP/TINH LS16 ...86 C5
Ringstone GTL/HWG HX4 ...189 G5
Ringstone Gv CUD/GR S72 ...245 J3
Ringway GFTH/SHER LS25 ...112 F8
Ringwood Ct WKFDE WF1 * ...176 F1
Ringwood Crs SCFT LS14 ...89 J6
Ringwood Dr SCFT LS14 ...89 J6
Ringwood Edge GTL/HWG HX4 ...168 E8
Ringwood Gdns SCFT LS14 ...89 J6
Ringwood Mt SCFT LS14 ...89 J6
Ringwood Rd WBOW BD5 ...126 D3
Ringwood Wy
　HEM/SK/SE WF9 ...224 B7
Rink St BTLY WF17 ...173 M3
Riparian Wy AIRE BD20 ...35 G3
Ripley Ct NORM WF6 ...178 F4
Ripley Gv OSM LS9 ...7 L8
Ripley La GSLY LS20 ...62 A4
Ripley Rd BOW BD4 ...127 H2
　LVSG WF15 ...172 B2
Ripley St AIRE BD20 ...55 H2
　HIPP HX3 ...148 C7
　WBOW BD5 ...127 G2
　WIL/AL BD15 ...103 J4
Ripon Av HUDN HD2 ...192 C4
Ripon Rd EARL WF12 ...174 B6
Ripon St HFAX HX1 ...10 F1
Rippenden New Bank
　RPDN/SBR HX6 ...189 G2
Ripponden Old Bank
　RPDN/SBR HX6 ...189 G2
Ripponden Old La
　RPDN/SBR HX6 ...188 C3
Ripponden Rd LIT OL15 ...208 F8
　UPML OL3 ...230 F4
Risedale Av BTLY WF17 ...151 K4
Risedale Cl BTLY WF17 ...151 K4
Rise La TOD OL14 ...163 K1
The Rise HIPP HX3 ...147 J4
　KNOT WF11 ...159 L6
　KSTL LS5 ...108 C1
　PONT WF8 ...181 G7
Rishworth Av KBTN HD8 ...217 M8
Rishworth Cl
　WKFDW/WTN WF2 ...176 A4
Rishworth Hall Cl
　RPDN/SBR HX6 ...188 D5
Rishworthian Ct HIPP HX3 * ...168 C5
Rishworth Mill La
　RPDN/SBR HX6 ...188 F6
Rishworth New Rd
　RPDN/SBR HX6 ...188 D5
Rishworth Ri RPDN/SHW OL2 ...229 H5
Rishworth Rd EARL WF12 ...173 M6
　GTL/HWG HX4 ...189 J3
Rishworth St EARL WF12 ...173 M6
　HWTH BD22 ...2 B7
　WKFDE WF1 ...12 E1
Rivadale Vw ILK LS29 ...38 D2
Rivelin Rd CAS WF10 ...157 L8
River Bank Wy ILK LS29 ...169 K5
Riverdale GLE DN14 ...163 J7
　WBY LS22 ...48 B2
Riverdale Av EARD/LOFT WF3 ...177 H4
Riverdale Cl EARD/LOFT WF3 ...177 H4
Riverdale Crs EARD/LOFT WF3 ...177 H4
Riverdale Dr EARD/LOFT WF3 ...177 H4
Riverdale Gdns EARD/LOFT WF3 ...177 H4
　OT LS21 ...41 J6
Riverdale Rd EARD/LOFT WF3 ...177 H4
　OT LS21 ...41 J6
River Holme Vw
　HOLM/MEL HD9 ...236 E4
Rivermead MILN OL16 ...229 K3
　WKFDW/WTN WF2 ...13 G9
River Mt AIRE BD20 ...58 A4
River Pk HOLM/MEL HD9 ...236 B1
River Pl MILN OL16 * ...207 H8
Riverside KBTN HD8 ...240 A4
　KGHY BD21 ...3 L4
Riverside Cl OT LS21 ...41 K4
Riverside Crs OT LS21 ...41 K5
Riverside Ct CLECK BD19 ...149 M5
　MILN OL16 ...206 E4
　OT LS21 ...41 K4
Riverside Est BAIL BD17 ...82 C4
Riverside Pk OT LS21 ...41 K5
Riverside Vls WKFDW/WTN WF2 ...12 F9
River St BRIG HD6 ...170 C6
　COL BB8 ...74 E2
　HWTH BD22 ...2 D7
　KGHY BD21 ...3 L2
　MILN OL16 ...206 B7
　TOD OL14 ...163 L1
River Vw BSPA/BRAM LS23 ...49 H7
　ILK LS29 ...38 F1
　MIRF WF14 ...171 M8
River Wk BGLY BD16 ...81 H3
Riverwood Dr HIPP HX3 ...168 D4
Riviera Gdns CHAL LS7 ...87 L8
Rivington Dr ROY/SHW OL2 ...229 M7
Rivington St WHIT OL12 ...206 B5

Rivock Av AIRE BD20 35 M8
AIRE BD20 57 H3
Rivock Gv AIRE BD20 57 H4
Roach Grange Av
GFTH/SHER LS25 135 J3
Roach Pl MILN OL16 206 C6
Roach V MILN OL16 206 E4
Roads Ford Av MILN OL16 207 H7
Roaine Dr HOLM/MEL HD9 254 D3
Roans Brae IDLE BD10 84 A8
Robb Av BEE/HOL LS11 131 J5
Robbins Ter FEA/AMT WF7 179 M8
Robb St BEE/HOL LS11 131 J5
Roberson Ter CLECK BD19 150 C6
Robert Av BSLYN/ROY S71 261 M4
Robert La HOLM/MEL HD9 236 E7
Roberts Av OSM LS9 110 D4
Roberts Ct OSM LS9 110 D4
Robertsgate EARD/LOFT WF3 154 D5
Robertshaw Rd HBR HX7 143 H3
Robertson Av BRIG HD6 170 C6
Roberts Pl BFD BD1 4 D5
OSM LS9 110 D5
Robert's St CLECK BD19 149 L7
CUD/GR S72 * 244 D7
HWTH BD22 56 E8
PDSY/CALV LS28 106 F5
RTHW LS26 * 133 L8
Robert St BFDE BD3 5 J7
COL BB8 74 A1
HIPP HX3 146 C4
HWTH BD22 79 H6
Robert St North HIPP HX3 146 E4
Roberts Wy WKFDW/WTN WF2 199 H5
Roberttown La LVSG WF15 172 B4
Robin Cha PDSY/CALV LS28 107 H7
Robin Cl ECHL BD2 105 L2
PONT WF8 180 F3
Robin Dr AIRE BD20 35 K8
ECHL BD2 105 L2
Robin Hl BTLY WF17 151 J5
Robin Hood Av
BSLYN/ROY S71 243 M2
Robin Hood Crs
WKFDW/WTN WF2 197 M2
Robin Hood Gv HUDN HD2 192 E2
Robin Hood Hl HUDS HD4 214 B7
Robin Hood Rd HUDN HD2 192 E2
Robin Hood St CAS WF10 * 158 A7
Robin Hood Wy BRIG HD6 171 G4
Robinia Wk WKFDW/WTN WF2 176 B6
Robin La BSLYN/ROY S71 243 M2
DEWS WF13 173 H3
HEM/SK/SE WF9 245 J1
PDSY/CALV LS28 107 G7
Robin Rocks HOLM/MEL HD9 236 E4
Robin Royd Av MIRF WF14 172 C6
Robin Royd Cft MIRF WF14 172 C6
Robin Royd Dr MIRF WF14 172 C6
Robin Royd Garth MIRF WF14 * 172 C6
Robin Royd Gv MIRF WF14 * 172 C6
Robin Royd La MIRF WF14 172 C7
Robin's Gv RTHW LS26 155 H1
Robinson Ct GTHN BD7 104 B8
Robinson La GFTH/SHER LS25 135 K4
Robinson St CAS WF10 157 K3
HUD HD1 15 H8
MILN OL16 206 C7
PONT WF8 180 F5
The Robins ILK LS29 40 A6
Robin St HUD HD1 213 M1
WBOW BD5 * 126 E2
Robin Wk SHPY BD18 82 F8
Rob Royd DOD/DAR S75 260 B8
Rob Royd La BSLY S70 260 F8
Robson Cl PONT WF8 180 F8
Robsons Dr HUDE HD5 15 M6
Robsons Rd WKFDE WF1 * 12 D3
Rochdale Rd GTL/HWG HX4 168 A7
LUD/ILL HX2 167 M1
MILN OL16 206 F7
MILN OL16 229 G5
ROY/SHW OL2 228 E8
RPDN/SBR HX6 167 H4
RPDN/SBR HX6 187 H5
RPDN/SBR HX6 188 B3
TOD OL14 163 J3
TOD OL14 185 L2
UPML OL3 230 D3
Roche Cl BSLYN/ROY S71 261 K3
Rocheford Cl MID LS10 132 B3
Rocheford Gdns MID LS10 132 B3
Rocheford Gv MID LS10 132 B3
Rocheford Wk MID LS10 132 B3
Rochester Ct HOR/CROF WF4 197 L3
Rochester Dr HOR/CROF WF4 197 L3
Rochester Gdns BRAM LS13 107 H2
Rochester Pl ELL HX5 * 169 H8
Rochester Rd BSLYN/ROY S71 261 K2
BTLY WF17 151 G3
Rochester St BFDE BD3 105 L7
SHPY BD18 82 E8
Rochester Ter HDGY LS6 108 F2
Rochester Wynd
AL/HA/HU LS17 88 C2
Roch St MILN OL16 206 D5
Rockcliffe Av BAIL BD17 82 E5
Rock Edge LVSG WF15 172 C1
Rockery Cft HORS LS18 85 L4
Rockery Rd HORS LS18 85 L4
Rockfield Ter YEA LS19 62 E7
Rock Fold MAR/SLWT HD7 212 F2
Rock Hl CAS WF10 158 C8
Rockhill Cl BTLY WF17 151 H5
Rockhill La BOW BD4 127 J7
Rock House Dr DEWS WF13 173 L4
Rockingham Cl
MSTN/BAR LS15 112 B3
ROY/SHW OL2 229 G6
Rockingham Ct
BSLYN/ROY S71 261 J5
TAD LS24 93 M2
Rockingham La
HEM/SK/SE WF9 225 G1
Rockingham Rd
MSTN/BAR LS15 112 B3
Rockingham St
BSLYN/ROY S71 261 G2
CUD/GR S72 * 245 J7
HEM/SK/SE WF9 223 J3
Rockingham Wy
MSTN/BAR LS15 112 B3
Rockland Crs GTHN BD7 126 A1
Rocklands Av BAIL BD17 82 E2
Rocklands Pl BAIL BD17 82 E2
Rock La BRAM LS13 107 K2
CUL/QBY BD13 102 E6
MAR/SLWT HD7 212 C4
Rockley Cl HUDE HD5 215 G2
Rockley Dr WKFDW/WTN WF2 198 D8
Rockley Grange Gdns
GFTH/SHER LS25 134 F1
Rockley Mdw BSLY S70 260 E7
Rockley St EARL WF12 173 M6
Rockmill Rd HOLM/MEL HD9 236 E4
Rock Side Rd STKB/PEN S36 270 C3
Rocks La LUD/ILL HX2 123 M6
Rocks Rd HIPP HX3 168 C3
Rock St BRIG HD6 170 C3
BSLY S70 * 260 F4
HUDW HD3 * 191 G7
Rocks Vw LUD/ILL HX2 168 C2
Rock Ter CAS WF10 158 C8
CUL/QBY BD13 102 F8
EARL WF12 * 152 D8
GIR BD8 4 D1
HUDW HD3 191 K5
MOR LS27 152 D1
MSTN/BAR LS15 111 H7
The Rock MAR/SLWT HD7 * 213 G6
Rock Vw GTL/HWG HX4 190 E2
MAR/SLWT HD7 233 H3
Rockville Ter HFAX HX1 168 C1
Rockwell La IDLE BD10 83 L8
Rockwood Cl DOD/DAR S75 242 B6
HUDN HD2 171 G8
SKP/WHF BD23 16 A2
Rockwood Crs HOR/CROF WF4 197 M8
PDSY/CALV LS28 106 C3
Rockwood Dr SKP/WHF BD23 16 A1
Rockwood Gv PDSY/CALV LS28 106 D3
Rockwood Hill Ct
PDSY/CALV LS28 106 C4
Rockwood Ri KBTN HD8 239 J7
Rockwood Rd PDSY/CALV LS28 106 C4
Roderick St WOR/ARM LS12 108 D7
Rodger La WKFDW/WTN WF2 176 B4
Rodin Av GIR BD8 103 M7
Rodley La BRAM LS13 107 G1
KBTN HD8 217 M7
PDSY/CALV LS28 84 E8
Rodney Yd WKFDE WF1 12 F3
Rods Mills La MOR LS27 152 D3
Roebuck La OT LS21 41 J2
Roebuck St BTLY WF17 151 H5
Roeburn Cl DOD/DAR S75 242 C4
Roedhelm Rd AIRE BD20 58 D5
Roehampton Ri
BSLYN/ROY S71 262 B6
Roe La KNOT WF11 161 H2
Roger Ct ECHL BD2 5 M1
Roger Dr WKFDW/WTN WF2 198 F5
Roger Fold GFTH/SHER LS25 135 K5
Roger Ga HBR HX7 143 M6
Roger La HUDS HD4 214 D3
Roger Rd BSLYN/ROY S71 262 A4
Rogers Ct EARD/LOFT WF3 155 H8
Rogerson Sq BRIG HD6 170 C3
Rogers Pl PDSY/CALV LS28 107 H6
Roils Head Rd LUD/ILL HX2 145 K7
Rokeby Gdns HDGY LS6 108 E1
IDLE BD10 84 A8
Roker La PDSY/CALV LS28 129 H1
Rolleston Rd AWLS/ASK DN6 249 K6
Rolling Br TAD LS24 72 D1
Roman Av HUDW HD3 190 F5
RHAY LS8 88 D4
Romanby Shaw IDLE BD10 83 M8
Roman Cl HUDW HD3 190 F5
TAD LS24 71 M2
Roman Crs RHAY LS8 88 D4
Roman Dr HUDW HD3 190 F5
RHAY LS8 88 D4
Roman Gdns RHAY LS8 88 C4
Roman Gv RHAY LS8 88 C4
Roman Pl RHAY LS8 88 C4
Roman Rdg AWLS/ASK DN6 249 G7
Roman Ri PONT WF8 202 E1
Roman Rd BTLY WF17 151 H6
DOD/DAR S75 241 M7
Roman Ter RHAY LS8 88 C4
Roman Vw RHAY LS8 88 D4
Rombalds Av WOR/ARM LS12 108 E6
Rombalds Crs AIRE BD20 36 B6
WOR/ARM LS12 108 E5
Rombalds Dr BGLY BD16 81 K3
SKP/WHF BD23 16 C4
Rombalds Gv WOR/ARM LS12 108 E6
Rombalds La ILK LS29 39 G3
Rombalds Pl WOR/ARM LS12 108 E6
Rombalds St WOR/ARM LS12 108 E5
Rombalds Ter WOR/ARM LS12 108 E6
Rombald's Vw ILK LS29 38 F1
OT LS21 40 F4
WOR/ARM LS12 108 E5
Romford Av MOR LS27 152 C3
Romille St SKP/WHF BD23 16 B3
Romney Av ROCH OL11 228 A4
Romney Mt PDSY/CALV LS28 129 J1
Romsey WHIT OL12 * 206 A6
Romsey Cl HUDW HD3 191 H5
Romsey Gdns BOW BD4 127 M3
Romsey Ms BOW BD4 127 M3
Romwood Cl HEM/SK/SE WF9 223 K4
Rona Cft RTHW LS26 155 J1
Ronald Dr GTHN BD7 104 C7
Ronalds Cft YEA LS19 62 D7
Ron Lawton Crs ILK LS29 39 M6
Roods La HOLM/MEL HD9 253 J3
Rookdale Cl DOD/DAR S75 260 D2
Rookery La HIPP HX3 168 F3
Rookes Av WBSY BD6 126 E6
Rookes La HIPP HX3 148 C5
Rookhill Dr PONT WF8 181 G7
Rookhill Mt PONT WF8 181 G8
Rookhill Rd PONT WF8 181 H8
Rook La BOW BD4 127 K4
Rooks Av CLECK BD19 149 L6
Rooks Cl LM/WK BD12 148 F5
Rook's Nest Rd WKFDE WF1 176 E2
Rook St BGLY BD16 81 H3
HUD HD1 14 E5
Rookwith Pde IDLE BD10 83 M8
Rookwood Av
GFTH/SHER LS25 135 J6
OSM LS9 110 E6
Rookwood Crs OSM LS9 110 E6
Rookwood Gdns OSM LS9 110 E7
Rookwood Hl OSM LS9 110 E6
Rookwood Mt OSM LS9 110 E6
Rookwood Pde OSM LS9 110 F6
Rookwood Pl OSM LS9 110 E6
Rookwood Rd OSM LS9 110 E7
Rookwood Sq OSM LS9 110 F6
Rookwood St OSM LS9 110 E7
Rookwood Ter OSM LS9 110 E6
Rookwood V OSM LS9 110 E7
Rookwood Vw OSM LS9 110 E6
Rooley Av WBSY BD6 126 F6
Rooley Banks RPDN/SBR HX6 167 G3
Rooley Cl WBOW BD5 127 G5
Rooley Crs WBSY BD6 127 G6
Rooley Hts RPDN/SBR HX6 166 F3
Rooley La RPDN/SBR HX6 166 F4
WBOW BD5 126 F5
Roomfield St TOD OL14 163 K1
Rooms Fold MOR LS27 130 C8
Rooms La MOR LS27 130 B8
Ropefield Wy WHIT OL12 206 A3
Roper Av RHAY LS8 88 B6
Ropergate PONT WF8 180 E6
Ropergate Service Rd
PONT WF8 180 E6
Roper Gn LUD/ILL HX2 145 M2
Roper Gv RHAY LS8 88 B6
Roper La CUL/QBY BD13 124 D4
LUD/ILL HX2 124 B6
Rope St WHIT OL12 206 B6
Rope Wk KNOT WF11 182 C2
LUD/ILL HX2 123 H7
SKP/WHF BD23 16 C2
Roscoe St CHAL LS7 7 K4
Roseate Gn MOR LS27 152 E3
Rose Av GFTH/SHER LS25 116 A8
HEM/SK/SE WF9 225 H7
HORS LS18 85 J6
HUDS HD4 213 H3
HUDW HD3 191 L8
LIT OL15 207 H3
WMB/DAR S73 263 H7
Rose Bank GIR BD8 104 E4
ILK LS29 40 A6
LM/WK BD12 148 E2
Rosebank Crs HDGY LS6 6 A5
Rosebank Gdns BVRD LS3 6 A6
Rose Bank Pl GIR BD8 104 A7
Rosebank Rd BVRD LS3 6 A6
Rose Bank Rd TOD OL14 163 J2
Rosebank Rw BVRD LS3 6 A6
Rosebank St BTLY WF17 151 K8
Roseberry St HWTH BD22 78 F4
TOD OL14 140 D5
Rosebery Av HIPP HX3 168 F2
SHPY BD18 82 E7
Rosebery Mt SHPY BD18 82 E7
Rosebery Rd GIR BD8 104 E4
Rosebery St ELL HX5 169 H8
HUDN HD2 14 D1
PDSY/CALV LS28 106 E6
Rosebery Ter BSLY S70 261 H6
HFAX HX1 10 C3
PDSY/CALV LS28 107 H4
Rosebud Wk RHAY LS8 7 L4
Rosechapel Cl WBSY BD6 * 126 B8
Rosecliffe Mt BRAM LS13 107 L4
Rosecliffe Ter BRAM LS13 107 K4
Rose Cl HEM/SK/SE WF9 225 J7
Rose Ct GFTH/SHER LS25 113 J7
Rose Crs GFTH/SHER LS25 116 A8
Rose Cft AL/HA/HU LS17 46 E8
Rosedale PBR HG3 26 E2
RTHW LS26 133 H8
Rosedale Av HUDE HD5 15 M8
LVSG WF15 171 M4
WIL/AL BD15 103 H4
WKFDW/WTN WF2 199 G6
Rosedale Bank MID LS10 131 M5
Rosedale Cl BAIL BD17 82 C4
HEM/SK/SE WF9 225 K7
NORM WF6 178 F5
PBR HG3 26 E2
Rosedale Ct BOW BD4 128 A7
EARD/LOFT WF3 153 G8
Rosedale Gdns BSLY S70 260 E5
MID LS10 131 M5
Rosedale Gn MID LS10 131 M5
Rosedale Ri BSPA/BRAM LS23 48 E7
Rosedale Wk MID LS10 131 M5
Rose Farm Ap NORM WF6 178 B2
Rose Farm Cl NORM WF6 178 B1
Rose Farm Fold NORM WF6 178 B1
Rose Farm Ri NORM WF6 178 B1
Rosefield Crs MILN OL16 206 E7
Rose Garth HOR/CROF WF4 200 B5
ILK LS29 39 L7
Rosegarth Av HOLM/MEL HD9 236 E7
Rose Gv HBR HX7 144 A6
HEM/SK/SE WF9 225 J7
RPDN/SBR HX6 167 H1
RTHW LS26 132 F8
Rose Heath LUD/ILL HX2 123 M7
Rose Hl MAR/SLWT HD7 * 233 J2
Rosehill Av HEM/SK/SE WF9 223 L8
Rose Hill Cl STKB/PEN S36 270 F4
Rosehill Ct BSLY S70 261 G4
Rosehill Crs LM/WK BD12 148 E2
Rose Hill Dr DOD/DAR S75 260 B7
HUDW HD3 191 M5
Roseship Ri CLAY BD14 125 K3
Rose La FEA/AMT WF7 223 M2
TAD LS24 94 D8
Rose Lea Cl GFTH/SHER LS25 138 D8
Roselee Cl HIPP HX3 169 G3
Rosemary Av WOR/ARM LS12 108 F7
Rosemary Ct TAD LS24 71 M2
Rosemary Dr LIT OL15 185 H8
Rosemary La BRIG HD6 170 C6
HIPP HX3 169 G3
Rosemary Rw TAD LS24 71 M2
Rose Mdw HWTH BD22 79 G1
Rosemont Av BRAM LS13 * 107 L4
PDSY/CALV LS28 107 H6
Rosemont Dr PDSY/CALV LS28 107 H6
Rosemont Gv BRAM LS13 107 K4
Rosemont La BAIL BD17 82 F4
Rosemont Pl BRAM LS13 107 K4
Rosemont Rd BRAM LS13 107 L4
Rosemont St BRAM LS13 107 L4
PDSY/CALV LS28 107 H6
Rosemont Ter BRAM LS13 107 L4
PDSY/CALV LS28 107 H6
Rosemont Vw BRAM LS13 107 K4
Rosemont Wk BRAM LS13 107 L4
Rose Mt BOW BD4 * 128 C6
ECHL BD2 105 J3
HUDN HD2 191 M5
LUD/ILL HX2 * 168 C2
Rosemount Av ELL HX5 169 J8
Rosemount Cl KGHY BD21 * 2 F4
Rosemount Dr NORM WF6 178 F5
Rose Mount Pl WOR/ARM LS12 108 F8
Rosemount Wk KGHY BD21 * 2 F4
Roseneath Pl WOR/ARM LS12 108 F8
Roseneath St WOR/ARM LS12 108 F8
Roseneath Ter WOR/ARM LS12 108 F8
Rose Pl LUD/ILL HX2 167 G1
Rose St GIR BD8 104 D5
HFAX HX1 10 B6
HORS LS18 85 J6
KGHY BD21 58 B7
TOD OL14 163 K1
Rose Ter BTLY WF17 * 151 J4
HFAX HX1 10 C5
HUD HD1 * 15 G3
ILK LS29 19 H6
LUD/ILL HX2 * 168 C2
Rose Tree Av CUD/GR S72 244 D7
Rose Tree Ct CUD/GR S72 244 D7
Rosetta Dr GIR BD8 104 B7
Roseville Rd RHAY LS8 7 L5
Roseville St RHAY LS8 7 M4
Roseville Wy RHAY LS8 7 L5
Rosewood Av AIRE BD20 58 B5
GFTH/SHER LS25 135 H3
Rosewood Ct RTHW LS26 133 H7
Rosewood Gv BOW BD4 127 M1
Rosgill Dr SCFT LS14 111 H1
Rosgill Wk SCFT LS14 111 H1
Rosley Mt WBSY BD6 126 B8
Rosley St COL BB8 74 D1
Roslyn Av HUDS HD4 213 L7
Roslyn Pl GTHN BD7 104 D8
Rossall Gv RHAY LS8 * 110 B2
Rossall Rd RHAY LS8 110 B2
WHIT OL12 206 C4
Rossefield Ap BRAM LS13 107 M5
Rossefield Av BRAM LS13 107 M4
HUDN HD2 14 A1
Rossefield Cha BRAM LS13 107 M4
Rossefield Cl BRAM LS13 * 107 M4
Rossefield Dr BRAM LS13 107 M4
Rossefield Gv BRAM LS13 107 M4
Rossefield Lawn BRAM LS13 107 M4
Rossefield Pk HTON BD9 104 D2
Rossefield Pl BRAM LS13 107 M4
Rossefield Rd HTON BD9 104 C2
Rossefield Ter BRAM LS13 107 M4
Rossendale Cl ROY/SHW OL2 229 M7
Rossendale Pl SHPY BD18 82 C7
Rossendale Vw TOD OL14 164 C2
Rossendale Wy BCUP OL13 162 C7
WHIT OL12 184 C3
Rosse St GIR BD8 104 C7
SHPY BD18 82 D6
Rossett Green La HARS HG2 26 D1
Ross Gv BRAM LS13 107 K2
Rossington Gv RHAY LS8 7 M1
Rossington Pl RHAY LS8 7 M1
Rossington Rd RHAY LS8 110 C1
Rossington St LDSU LS2 6 F8
Rossiter Dr KNOT WF11 181 M3
Rosslyn Av FEA/AMT WF7 224 B1
Rosslyn Cl FEA/AMT WF7 224 B1
Rosslyn Ct EARL WF12 174 B7
FEA/AMT WF7 224 B1
Rosslyn Gv FEA/AMT WF7 224 B1
HWTH BD22 78 E8
Rossmore Dr WIL/AL BD15 103 L5
Rossyde AWLS/ASK DN6 * 227 M3
Rosy St HWTH BD22 79 H6
Rotcher La MAR/SLWT HD7 212 A6
Rotcher Rd HOLM/MEL HD9 254 C2
Rothbury Gdns BHP/TINH LS16 86 D3
Rotherham Rd BSLYN/ROY S71 243 J8
CUD/GR S72 263 M8
Rothery Ct HFAX HX1 * 10 D4
Rothesay Ter GTHN BD7 4 A9
MILN OL16 228 E2
Roth St HWTH BD22 79 G6
Rothwell La RTHW LS26 155 J1
Rothwell Mt HFAX HX1 10 E9
Rothwell Rd HFAX HX1 10 E9
Rothwell St HUDE HD5 193 G8
WHIT OL12 206 C5
Roughaw Cl SKP/WHF BD23 16 B4
Roughaw Rd SKP/WHF BD23 16 C4
Roughbirchworth La
STKB/PEN S36 271 K5
Rough Hall La LUD/ILL HX2 145 G1
Rough Hey Wk MILN OL16 206 D8
Rough Side La TOD OL14 163 L2
Round Close Rd
HOLM/MEL HD9 254 D8
Roundell Av BOW BD4 127 K6
Roundhay Av RHAY LS8 110 B1
Roundhay Crs RHAY LS8 110 B1
Roundhay Gdns RHAY LS8 * 110 B1
Roundhay Gv RHAY LS8 110 B1
Roundhay Mt RHAY LS8 110 B1
Roundhay Park La
AL/HA/HU LS17 88 D1
Roundhay Pl RHAY LS8 110 A2
Roundhay Rd CHAL LS7 7 K4
RHAY LS8 110 C2
Roundhay Vw RHAY LS8 * 110 B1
Roundhead Fold IDLE BD10 84 A6
Round Hl DOD/DAR S75 242 C5
LUD/ILL HX2 124 B8
Roundhill Av BGLY BD16 81 K7
Round Hill Cl CUL/QBY BD13 125 K4
Roundhill Mt BGLY BD16 81 K7
Roundhill Pl BFD BD1 4 D5
Roundhill Rd CAS WF10 157 M7
Roundhill St WBOW BD5 126 F2
Round Ings Rd HUDW HD3 190 B7
Round St WBOW BD5 127 G3
WKFDE WF1 13 K7
Round Thorn Pl GIR BD8 * 104 C6
Roundway HOLM/MEL HD9 236 B3
The Roundway MOR LS27 152 B2
Roundwell Rd LVSG WF15 171 L1
Roundwood SHPY BD18 82 A7
Round Wood Av HUDE HD5 193 J8
Roundwood Av BAIL BD17 83 H3
IDLE BD10 106 A1
Roundwood Crs
WKFDW/WTN WF2 197 L1
Roundwood Gln IDLE BD10 84 A8
Roundwood Ri
WKFDW/WTN WF2 197 M2
Roundwood Rd BAIL BD17 83 G3
OSS WF5 197 J2
Roundwood Vw IDLE BD10 84 A8
Rouse Fold BOW BD4 5 H9
Rouse Mill La BTLY WF17 173 M2
Rouse St LVSG WF15 172 C2
Rowan Av BFDE BD3 106 A7
HUDS HD4 213 M8
NORM WF6 178 C6
Rowan Avenue Ms HUDS HD4 213 M8
Rowanberry Cl ECHL BD2 105 K2
Rowan Cl BSLY S70 261 H7
BTLY WF17 151 J4
OT LS21 43 G8
Rowan Ct ECHL BD2 * 105 L5
RTHW LS26 134 A8
WKFDW/WTN WF2 176 B6
YEA LS19 84 D1
Rowan Dr BRIG HD6 170 E3
DOD/DAR S75 260 D3
Rowan Garth AIRE BD20 34 F8
Rowan Gn PONT WF8 181 H5
Rowan Pl GFTH/SHER LS25 113 K8
The Rowans BAIL BD17 82 B3
BHP/TINH LS16 64 B4
BRAM LS13 107 H3
Rowan St AIRE BD20 57 J4
Rowantree Av BAIL BD17 82 D2
Rowantree Dr IDLE BD10 83 L8
Rowanwood Gdns IDLE BD10 * 106 A1
Rowe Cl HEM/SK/SE WF9 247 J2
Row Ga KBTN HD8 237 M7
Rowgate KBTN HD8 238 C8
Rowland Ct MILN OL16 * 206 D8
Rowland La HBR HX7 143 L3
Rowland Pl BEE/HOL LS11 131 K3
Rowland Rd BEE/HOL LS11 131 K3
DOD/DAR S75 260 E3
Rowlands Av HEM/SK/SE WF9 225 J7
HUDE HD5 193 H8
Rowland St BSLYN/ROY S71 243 M2
MILN OL16 206 D8
SKP/WHF BD23 16 C3
Rowland Ter BEE/HOL LS11 131 L3
Row La MAR/SLWT HD7 211 L6
RPDN/SBR HX6 166 F3
Rowlestone Ri IDLE BD10 84 A8
Rowley Dr ILK LS29 39 H3
KBTN HD8 215 M3
Rowley La HEM/SK/SE WF9 247 J5
KBTN HD8 215 M4
Rowsley St KGHY BD21 3 J4
Row St HUDS HD4 214 A2
Rowton Thorpe IDLE BD10 84 A8
Roxburghe Dl NORM WF6 178 F5
Roxburgh Gv WIL/AL BD15 103 K6
Roxby Cl OSM LS9 7 M7
Roxby St WBOW BD5 126 F3
Roxholme Av CHAL LS7 110 A1
Roxholme Gv CHAL LS7 110 A1
Roxholme Pl CHAL LS7 110 A1
Roxholme Ter CHAL LS7 110 A1
Royal Birkdale Wy NORM WF6 178 F5
Royal Cl GTHN BD7 126 B3
MID LS10 131 M4
Royal Ct DOD/DAR S75 242 A8
MID LS10 131 M4
PONT WF8 202 D1
Royal Dr MID LS10 131 M4
Royal Gdns MID LS10 131 M4
Royal Park Av HDGY LS6 6 A4
Royal Park Gv HDGY LS6 6 A3
Royal Park Mt HDGY LS6 6 A3
Royal Park Rd HDGY LS6 109 G4
Royal Park Ter HDGY LS6 6 A3
Royal Park Vw HDGY LS6 6 A3
Royal Pl MID LS10 131 M4
Royal St BSLY S70 261 G5
MILN OL16 206 E4
Royal Ter BSPA/BRAM LS23 49 G6
HUDW HD3 213 J1
Royd Av BGLY BD16 81 K3
CUD/GR S72 244 D8
DOD/DAR S75 242 D5
HECK WF16 150 F8
HUDW HD3 191 J3
HUDW HD3 213 J1
STKB/PEN S36 269 M3
Royd Cl AIRE BD20 34 F8
Royd Crs HBR HX7 144 B5
HFAX HX1 * 10 A4
Royd Cft HUDW HD3 191 K8
Royden Gv HTON BD9 104 C4
Royd Field La STKB/PEN S36 270 F6
Roydfield St HUDN HD2 192 D4
Royd Head Farm OSS WF5 196 E1
Royd House Gv KGHY BD21 3 L8
Royd House La
MAR/SLWT HD7 212 F5
Royd House Rd KGHY BD21 3 M8
Royd House Wk KGHY BD21 3 M8
Royd House Wy KGHY BD21 3 L8
Royd Ings Av KGHY BD21 3 J1
Roydlands St HIPP HX3 147 M6
Royd La AIRE BD20 57 K5
DOD/DAR S75 259 M3
HIPP HX3 146 C3
HOLM/MEL HD9 254 A4
LUD/ILL HX2 124 A7
RPDN/SBR HX6 188 E1
STKB/PEN S36 269 M2
TOD OL14 141 K7
Royd Moor Ct STKB/PEN S36 270 C2
Royd Moor La HEM/SK/SE WF9 224 C5
Royd Moor Rd BOW BD4 128 B5
STKB/PEN S36 269 M1
Royd Mt HIPP HX3 146 E4
HOLM/MEL HD9 254 C2
Roydon Gv HTON BD9 104 C4
Royd Pl HIPP HX3 146 E4
Royd Rd HOLM/MEL HD9 235 G6
TOD OL14 141 J8
Royds Av BIRK/DRI BD11 150 D1
CAS WF10 158 E6
HOLM/MEL HD9 236 F8
HUDW HD3 191 K8
LM/WK BD12 148 D6
MAR/SLWT HD7 212 F4
OSS WF5 174 E6
Roydscliffe Dr HTON BD9 104 B2
Roydscliffe Rd HTON BD9 104 A3
Royds Cl HOLM/MEL HD9 236 F8
WOR/ARM LS12 130 E2
Royds Crs BRIG HD6 148 D7
Roydsdale Wy BOW BD4 127 J8
Royds Dr HOLM/MEL HD9 236 F8
Royds Farm Rd BEE/HOL LS11 130 E4
Royds Gv WKFDE WF1 176 E1
Royds Hall Av WBSY BD6 126 E6
Royds Hall La LM/WK BD12 148 C1
WBSY BD6 126 C8
Royds Hall Rd WOR/ARM LS12 130 E2
Royds La RTHW LS26 155 J2
WOR/ARM LS12 130 E3
Royds Pk KBTN HD8 239 J8
Royds Park Crs LM/WK BD12 148 F2
Royds Pl MILN OL16 228 C1
Royds St LIT OL15 207 L1
MAR/SLWT HD7 233 H3
MILN OL16 228 D1
MILN OL16 229 J1
Royds St West MILN OL16 228 C1
The Royds HOLM/MEL HD9 254 C1
KBTN HD8 240 C3
Roydstone Rd BFDE BD3 105 M6
Roydstone Ter BFDE BD3 105 M6
Royd St AIRE BD20 57 K4
BTLY WF17 174 A3
CUL/QBY BD13 102 E8
HUDW HD3 213 J1
HWTH BD22 54 E3
MAR/SLWT HD7 212 B5
TOD OL14 141 J8
WIL/AL BD15 102 E1
Royds Vw MAR/SLWT HD7 212 F5
Royd Ter HBR HX7 143 J3
Royd Vw HBR HX7 144 A5
Royd Vls HBR HX7 * 143 J3
Royd Wy KGHY BD21 3 H1
Royd Wls MIRF WF14 172 C8
Royd Wd CLECK BD19 149 M8
Roydwood Ter CUL/QBY BD13 79 M8
Roydwood Ter Back
CUL/QBY BD13 79 M8
Royle Fold HECK WF16 172 F2
Royles Cl HEM/SK/SE WF9 246 E4
Royles Head La HUDW HD3 191 G8
Roy Rd WBSY BD6 125 M5
Royston Cl EARD/LOFT WF3 153 M8
Royston Hl EARD/LOFT WF3 153 M8
Royston La BSLYN/ROY S71 243 M5
Royston Rd CUD/GR S72 244 C5
Ruby St BTLY WF17 151 J8
CHAL LS7 7 L6
HWTH BD22 79 J2
Rud Broom La STKB/PEN S36 270 D3
Rudding Av WIL/AL BD15 103 J5
Rudding Crs WIL/AL BD15 103 J5
Rudding Dr BTLY WF17 151 H8
Rudding La PBR HG3 26 A4
Rudding St HUDS HD4 213 M2
Rudd St GTHN BD7 126 C3
Rudgate RYKW YO26 31 L3
TAD LS24 49 L2
TAD LS24 70 F1
Rudgate Pk BSPA/BRAM LS23 49 J3
Rud La HBR HX7 165 H3
Rudstone Gv GFTH/SHER LS25 116 A6
Rudyard Gv ROCH OL11 228 B4
Ruffield Side LM/WK BD12 148 E1
Rufford Av BSLYN/ROY S71 243 J6
YEA LS19 62 D8
Rufford Bank YEA LS19 62 E8
Rufford Cl HOR/CROF WF4 222 C6
ROY/SHW OL2 229 H7

YEA LS19 ....62 E8
Rufford Crs YEA LS19 .....62 E8
Rufford Dr ILK LS29 ....62 E8
Rufford PI HFAX HX1 * 168 D2
Rufford Rdg YEA LS19 .....62 E8
Rufford Ri YEA LS19 ....62 D8
Rufford Rd ELL HX5 ....169 C8
HIPP HX3 ....168 D2
HUDW HD3 ....213 H1
Rufford St BFDE BD3 ....105 L7
Rufford Vis HIPP HX3 ....176 B8
Rufus St KGHY BD21 ....3 H2
WBOW BD5 ....126 D3
Rugby Av HIPP HX3 ....146 B3
Rugby Dr HIPP HX3 ....146 B3
Rugby Gdns HIPP HX3 ......146 B3
Rugby Mt HIPP HX3 ....146 B3
Rugby PI GTHN BD7 ....104 D8
Rugby Rd WHIT OL12 ....206 C5
Rugby Ter HIPP HX3 ....146 B3
Rumble Rd EARL WF12 ......174 B5
Rumbold Rd HUDW HD3 ....191 M7
Rumple Cft OT LS21 ....41 G4
Runswick Av BEE/HOL LS11 ....8 B6
Runswick Gv WBOW BD5 ...126 C5
Runswick PI BEE/HOL LS11 ....8 C6
Runswick St BEE/HOL LS11 ....8 B6
WBOW BD5 ....126 C5
Runswick Ter BEE/HOL LS11 ....8 C6
WBOW BD5 ....126 C5
Runtlings La OSS WF5 .....196 E2
The Runtlings OSS WF5 ....196 D1
Rupert Rd ILK LS29 ....38 C1
Rupert St HWTH BD22 ....79 H6
KGHY BD21 * 3 J2
Ruscombe PI BSLYN/ROY S71 ...243 L5
Rush Bank ROY/SHW OL2 ...229 H6
Rush Cft IDLE BD10 ....83 H5
Rushcroft Rd ROY/SHW OL2 ..229 H6
Rushdene Ct LM/WK BD12 ...148 E5
Rushfield V KBTN HD8 ....215 L2
Rushmoor Rd BOW BD4 ......127 M4
Rush Mt ROY/SHW OL2 ......229 H5
Rusholme Dr PDSY/CALV LS28 ...85 H6
Rushton Av HIPP HX3 ....168 A6
Rushton Hill CI LUD/ILL HX2 ...145 L5
Rushton Rd BFDE BD3 ....105 M6
Rushton St HIPP HX3 ....10 D1
PDSY/CALV LS28 ....84 D8
Rushton Ter BFDE BD3 ......106 A7
Rushworth CI DOD/DAR S75 ..241 L6
EARD/LOFT WF3 ....177 G1
Rushworth St HIPP HX3 * ...10 D1
WKFDE WF1 ....176 C1
Ruskin Av HTON BD9 ....103 M3
Ruskin CI CAS WF10 ....158 D6
Ruskin Ct WKFDE WF1 ......176 B4
Ruskin Crs CSLY LS20 ....62 E6
Ruskin Dr CAS WF10 ....158 D6
Ruskin Gv HUDN HD2 ....192 F3
Ruskin PI CAS WF10 ....158 D6
Ruskin Rd ROCH OL11 ....228 A4
Ruskin St PDSY/CALV LS28 ..106 C5
Ruskin Ter HIPP HX3 ....10 D1
Russell Av CUL/QBY BD13 ..125 C6
HOR/CROF WF4 ....220 B4
Russell CI BSLYN/ROY S71 ..261 K1
BTLY WF17 ....173 L1
HECK WF16 ....173 C3
Russell Hall La CUL/QBY BD13 ..125 G6
Russell Rd CUL/QBY BD13 ...124 F5
Russell St CUL/QBY BD13 ...125 C5
DEWS WF13 ....173 J5
HFAX HX1 ....11 H6
KGHY BD21 ....2 F7
LDS LS1 ....6 F9
SHPY BD18 ....104 E1
SKP/WHF BD23 ....16 C3
TOD OL14 ....163 L1
WBOW BD5 ....4 D9
WKFDE WF1 ....12 F6
Russell Wy BRIG HD6 ....170 D2
The Russets WKFDW/WTN WF2 ..199 G8
Russett Gv HUDS HD4 ....214 D3
The Russetts HIPP HX3 ....11 M8
Rustic Av HIPP HX3 ....169 J2
Rustless Av CLECK BD19 ....149 J8
Ruston Dr BSLYN/ROY S71 ..243 M1
Ruswarp Crs IDLE BD10 .....83 M8
Ruth St HUDS HD4 ....214 C4
Ruthven Vw RHAY LS8 ......110 C3
Rutland ROCH OL11 * 6 E9
Rutland Av PONT WF8 ....202 F1
WKFDW/WTN WF2 ....198 E4
Rutland CI GFTH/SHER LS25 ...135 K4
RTHW LS26 ....133 M8
Rutland Dr GFTH/SHER LS25 ..135 K4
HOR/CROF WF4 ....199 L3
Rutland Mt BVRD LS3 ....6 B8
Rutland Rd BTLY WF17 ......151 M8
HOR/CROF WF4 ....217 L3
WBOW BD5 ....213 H1
Rutland St BOW BD4 ....127 M4
COL BB8 ....74 E1
KGHY BD21 ....2 C8
LDS LS1 ....6 C8
Rutland Ter BVRD LS3 ....6 B8
Rutland Wy DOD/DAR S75 ..260 E3
ROY/SHW OL2 ....229 L6
Ryan Gv HWTH BD22 ....56 F6
Ryan PI RHAY LS8 ....110 C2
Ryan St WBOW BD5 ....126 E3
Ryburn Ct HFAX HX1 ....189 C1
Ryburn La RPDN/SBR HX6 ..189 G1
Ryburn PI WKFDW/WTN WF2 ..12 C6
Ryburn Rd HUDW HD3 ......191 K7
Ryburn Ter HFAX HX1 ....10 B5
Ryburn Vw LUD/ILL HX2 ....168 A1
RPDN/SBR HX6 ....188 E3
Rycroft Av BGLY BD16 ....81 J8
BRAM LS13 ....107 J5
Rycroft CI BRAM LS13 ....107 K5
Rycroft Dr BRAM LS13 ......107 K5
Rycroft Gdns BRAM LS13 ...107 K5
Rycroft St SHPY BD18 ....104 F1
Rycroft Towers BRAM LS13 ..107 J5
Rydal Av GFTH/SHER LS25 ..113 C8
HTON BD9 ....104 E2
ROY/SHW OL2 ....228 E6
Rydal Crs MOR LS27 ....152 F1
WKFDW/WTN WF2 ....176 A7
Rydal Dr HUDE HD5 ....15 L6
MOR LS27 ....152 F1
WKFDW/WTN WF2 ....176 A7
Rydal Gv OSS WF5 ....196 F2
Rydale Ms OSS WF5 ....196 F2
Rydal Gv LVSG WF15 ....172 C5
Rydal PI BEE/HOL LS11 ....8 B6
Rydal Ri BEE/HOL LS11 ....8 B6
Rydal PI COL BB8 ....74 C1
Rydal Rd AWLS/ASK DN6 ...249 L5
HWTH BD22 ....2 A1
Rydal Ter BSLYN/ROY S71 ..261 J5
Ryder CI PONT WF8 ....180 D6

Ryder Gdns RHAY LS8 ....88 C3
Rydings Av BRIG HD6 ....170 C3
Rydings CI BRIG HD6 ....170 C3
Rydings Dr BRIG HD6 ....170 B3
Rydings Rd WHIT OL12 ......184 C8
Rydings Rd WHIT OL12 ......206 D2
Ryebank HOLM/MEL HD9 ...254 D2
Ryebread CAS WF10 ....158 A5
Rye Close La HOLM/MEL HD9 ...252 F2
Ryecroft BGLY BD16 ....80 B5
Rye Cft BSLYN/ROY S71 .....243 J8
LUD/ILL HX2 ....124 D8
Ryecroft Av AWLS/ASK DN6 ..227 L3
HOR/CROF WF4 ....220 A5
Ryecroft CI WKFDE WF1 ....176 D1
Ryecroft Crs LUD/ILL HX2 ..145 M5
Ryecroft Dr HUDW HD3 .....191 H3
Ryecroft Farm CI CUD/GR S72 ..222 F7
Ryecroft La HOLM/MEL HD9 ..254 D2
LUD/ILL HX2 ....145 M6
Ryecroft Rd AIRE BD20 ....34 D7
AWLS/ASK DN6 ....227 L3
BGLY BD16 ....79 M4
Ryecroft St OSS WF5 ....174 E8
Ryecroft Ter LUD/ILL HX2 ...145 M5
Ryecroft Wy AIRE BD20 ......34 C8
Ryedale HUD5 ....193 K4
WOR/ARM LS12 ....130 D2
Ryedale Av KNOT WF11 .....182 K4
WOR/ARM LS12 ....130 D2
Ryedale CI NORM WF6 * 178 C1
TAD LS24 ....94 F2
Ryedale Ct SCFT LS14 ....111 H1
Ryedale Holt WOR/ARM LS12 ..130 D1
Ryedale PK ILK LS29 ....38 F3
Ryedale PI NORM WF6 ....178 C1
Ryedale Wy EARD/LOFT WF3 ..153 C2
WIL/AL BD15 ....103 J4
Ryefield AV CLAY BD14 ......125 K1
Rye Field La HUDW HD3 ....189 H8
Rye Field La West HUDW HD3 ..189 H8
Ryefields HOLM/MEL HD9 ...254 D2
Ryefields Av HUDW HD3 ....191 J7
Ryefields Rd MAR/SLWT HD7 ..213 C5
Rye Garth WBY LS22 ....29 M6
Ryeland CI MILN OL16 ....228 D2
Ryelands Gv HTON BD9 ......103 M2
Ryeland St AIRE BD20 ....34 F8
Rye La LUD/ILL HX2 ....145 L5
Rye PI SCFT LS14 ....111 H5
Rye St HWTH BD22 ....79 K2
Ryhill Pits La HOR/CROF WF4 ..221 M5
Rylands Av BGLY BD16 ....81 K3
Rylands Meadow HWTH BD22 ..79 C6
Rylstone Gdns BFDE BD3 .....5 K1
Rylstone Gv WKFDE WF1 ...177 G6
Rylstone Rd BAIL BD17 ....82 B2
Rylstone St KGHY BD21 ....3 K2
Rylstone Wk BSLY S70 ....261 M8
Ryndleside HUDW HD3 ......191 H5
Ryshworth Av BGLY BD16 ....58 F7
Ryton DI IDLE BD10 ....84 A8

S

Sable Crest ECHL BD2 ....105 H2
Sackup La DOD/DAR S75 .....242 B3
Sackville Ap CHAL LS7 ....7 H5
Sackville CI ROY/SHW OL2 ..229 H5
Sackville Rd AIRE BD20 ....36 A4
Sackville St BFD BD1 ....4 E6
BSLY S70 ....260 F4
CHAL LS7 ....7 H3
DEWS WF13 ....173 G8
HBR HX7 ....143 J3
SKP/WHF BD23 ....16 C5
TOD OL14 ....163 L1
Saddlers Cft CAS WF10 ......158 D8
ILK LS29 ....38 C2
Saddlers Gv HEM/SK/SE WF9 ..225 C3
Saddlers La KNOT WF11 .....159 L5
Saddler St LM/WK BD12 .....148 E2
Saddlers Wy RYKW YO26 .....33 J3
Saddleworth Rd
GTL/HWC HX4 ....169 G7
GTL/HWC HX4 ....189 K1
HUDW HD3 ....210 E3
Sadler Cl BHP/TINH LS16 .....86 E2
Sadler Copse BHP/TINH LS16 ..86 E2
Sadler Ga BSLY S70 ....261 C4
Sadler Wy BHP/TINH LS16 ...86 E2
Saffron CI WKFDW/WTN WF2 ..176 A6
Saffron Dr WIL/AL BD15 .....103 J5
Sagar La TOD OL14 ....140 F4
Sagar PI HDGY LS6 ....108 F2
Sagar St CAS WF10 ....157 M6
Sage St WBOW BD5 ....126 D8
Sahara Ct CIR BD8 ....104 H4
St Abbs CI WBSY BD6 ....126 E7
St Abbs Dr WBSY BD6 ....126 E7
St Abbs Fold WBSY BD6 .....126 E7
St Abbs Ga WBSY BD6 ....126 E7
St Abbs Wk WBSY BD6 ......126 E7
St Abbs Wy WBSY BD6 ......126 E7
St Aidan's Rd BAIL BD17 ......82 F4
RTHW LS26 ....135 G6
St Aiden's Wk OSS WF5 .....197 J2
St Alban Ap OSM LS9 ....110 E5
St Alban CI OSM LS9 ....110 E5
St Alban Crs OSM LS9 ....110 E5
St Alban Crs OSM LS9 * 110 E5
St Alban Mt OSM LS9 ....110 E5
St Alban Rd OSM LS9 ....110 E5
St Alban's Av HIPP HX3 .....168 E3
HUDW HD3 ....191 J3
St Albans Cft HIPP HX3 .....168 E3
St Albans PI LDSU LS2 ....7 H7
St Alban's Rd HIPP HX3 .....168 E3
St Alban's Wk ROCH OL11 * ..206 A8
St Alban Vw OSM LS9 ....110 E5
St Andrew's AV MOR LS27 ..152 A3
MOR LS27 ....152 A3
WHIT OL12 ....207 D2
YEA LS19 ....62 E7
St Andrews Ct BVRD LS3 ......6 B6
St Andrew's CI BRAM LS13 ..107 C1
St Andrews Cft AL/HA/HU LS17 ..87 K2
St Andrews Dr AL/HA/HU LS17 ..87 K2
BRIG HD6 ....170 C2
DOD/DAR S75 ....242 C5
FEA/AMT WF7 ....193 K6
HUDE HD5 ....195 K6
KNOT WF11 ....181 J1
GTHN BD7 ....4 A7
St Andrew's Gv MOR LS27 ..152 A3
St Andrew's PI BVRD LS3 .....6 B6
St Andrews Rd CAS WF10 ...158 E5
HUD HD1 ....15 J7
YEA LS19 ....62 E7
St Andrew's St BVRD LS3 .....6 B6
St Andrew's VIs GTHN BD7 ...4 A6

St Andrews Wk
AL/HA/HU LS17 ....87 L2
St Andrews Wy
BSLYN/ROY S71 ....262 C7
St Anne's Dr BSLYN/ROY S71 ..243 M7
St Anne's Rd HDGY LS6 .....108 E1
BULY LS4 ....108 E2
St Anne's Gn BULY LS4 ......108 E2
HIPP HX3 ....168 E4
St Anne's Rd HOR/CROF WF4 ..222 D5
St Ann's CI BULY LS4 ....108 E2
LDS LS1 ....6 F8
St Ann's Av BULY LS4 ....108 E2
St Ann's CI BULY LS4 ....108 E2
St Ann's Gdns BULY LS4 ....108 E2
St Ann's La KSTL LS5 ....108 E2
St Ann's Mt BULY LS4 ....108 F3
St Ann's Ri BULY LS4 ....108 E3
St Ann's Rd MILN OL16 ......206 E6
St Ann's Sq BULY LS4 ....108 E3
OSM LS9 * 7 L9
RPDN/SBR HX6 ....167 L2
St Ann's Wy BULY LS4 ....108 E3
St Anthony's Dr BEE/HOL LS11 ..131 H4
St Anthony's Rd BEE/HOL LS11 ..131 G4
St Anuil GIR BD8 * 104 D5
St Augustine's Ter BFDE BD3 ...5 J2
HFAX HX1 ....10 C1
St Austell Dr WBSY BD6 .....260 A2
St Barnabas Rd BEE/HOL LS11 ..8 F4
LVSG WF15 ....171 L1
St Barnabas's Dr LIT OL15 ..185 J8
St Bartholomew's CI 108 E7
St Bartholomews Ct
WKFDW/WTN WF2 ....197 L2
St Barts Ter BSLY S70 * 261 H6
St Benedicts Cha BRAM LS13 ..107 M1
St Benedicts Dr BRAM LS13 ..107 M1
St Bernard's Av PONT WF8 ..180 D6
St Bevan's Rd HIPP HX3 ....168 D6
St Blaise Ct WBOW BD5 ....4 F8
St Blaise Wy BFD BD1 ....4 F4
St Boltophs CI KNOT WF11 * ..182 C2
St Catherine's Crs BRAM LS13 ..107 M2
St Catherine's Dr BRAM LS13 ..107 M2
St Catherine's Gn BRAM LS13 ..107 M2
St Catherine's HI BRAM LS13 ..107 M2
St Catherine St WKFDE WF1 ..13 K8
St Catherine's VIs WKFDE WF1 ..13 M8
St Catherine's Wk RHAY LS8 ..88 C8
St Catherines Wy
DOD/DAR S75 ....260 D4
HDGY LS6 ....86 B8
St Chad's Av BRIG HD6 * 170 A1
HDGY LS6 ....86 B7
St Chads CI MILN OL16 * 206 B7
St Chad's Dr HDGY LS6 ......86 B7
St Chad's Ri HDGY LS6 ....86 B7
St Chad's Rd GIR BD8 ....104 D5
HDGY LS6 ....86 B7
St Chad's Vw HDGY LS6 ....108 D1
St Christopher's Av
RTHW LS26 ....155 H1
St Christophers CI
BSLYN/ROY S71 ....262 C7
St Christophers Dr ILK LS29 ..19 H7
St Clair Gn WKFDW/WTN WF2 ..175 M6
St Clair Rd OT LS21 ....41 K6
St Clair St OT LS21 ....41 K6
WKFDE WF1 ....13 C3
St Clare's Av ECHL BD2 .....105 M4
St Clements Av RTHW LS26 ..155 G1
St Clements CI BSLYN/ROY S71 ..262 C7
RTHW LS26 ....154 F2
St Clements Ri RTHW LS26 ..154 F2
St Cuthbert's La FEA/AMT WF7 * ..202 C6
St Cyprians Gdns OSM LS9 * ..110 D4
St Davids CI EARD/LOFT WF3 ..154 D4
St Davids Dr BSLYN/ROY S71 ..262 B6
St Davids Garth
EARD/LOFT WF3 ....154 D4
St Davids Rd EARD/LOFT WF3 ..154 D4
OT LS21 ....41 C4
St Edmunds CI CAS WF10 ...158 E6
St Edwards Ct KNOT WF11 ..160 N1
St Eloi Av BAIL BD17 ....82 C2
St Elmo Gv OSM LS9 ....110 C6
St Enoch's Rd WBSY BD6 ...126 D5
St Francis Bvd BSLYN/ROY S71 ..243 M7
St Francis Gdns HUDN HD2 ...7 B2
St Francis PI BEE/HOL LS11 ...8 E3
St George's Av HUDW HD3 ..191 J5
RTHW LS26 ....132 E7
St Georges Ct HOR/CROF WF4 ..222 E4
St George's Crs HFAX HX1 ..10 D3
RTHW LS26 ....132 E7
St Georges Ms
WKFDW/WTN WF2 ....220 C1
St George's PI WBOW BD5 ....4 E9
St George's Rd BSLY S70 ...261 G5
HIPP HX3 ....168 D7
HOLM/MEL HD9 ....254 F2
LDS LS1 ....6 E7
WKFDW/WTN WF2 ....197 M3
St George's Sq HBR HX7 * ..143 J3
HUD HD1 ....14 F7
St George's Wk
WKFDW/WTN WF2 ....198 E8
St Giles Av PONT WF8 ....180 D6
St Giles CI BRIG HD6 ....170 A1
St Giles Garth BHP/TINH LS16 ..63 M3
St Giles Rd HIPP HX3 ....148 A8
St Helena St WBSY BD6 ......126 D5
St Helens Av BHP/TINH LS16 ..86 F3
BSLYN/ROY S71 ....261 K1
HEM/SK/SE WF9 ....223 L7
St Helens Bvd BSLYN/ROY S71 ..243 K8
St Helens CI BHP/TINH LS16 ..86 F3
St Helens Cft BHP/TINH LS16 ..86 F3
St Helen's Dr GFTH/SHER LS25 ..114 D6
St Helens Fld HUDS HD4 ....213 J8
St Helens Gdns BHP/TINH LS16 ..86 E3
St Helens Ga BHP/TINH LS16 ..215 J4
St Helens Gv BHP/TINH LS16 ..86 D3
St Helen's La BHP/TINH LS16 ..86 D3
St Helens PI MID LS10 ....9 K6
St Helens St MID LS10 * 9 K6
St Helens Wy BHP/TINH LS16 ..86 F3
BSLYN/ROY S71 ....261 M1
St Helier Gv BAIL BD17 ....82 F2
St Helier Dr DOD/DAR S75 ..260 D4
St Hilda Av BSLY S70 ....260 E5
St Hilda's Av OSM LS9 ....110 D8
St Hilda's Crs OSM LS9 ......110 D8
St Hilda's Mt OSM LS9 ....110 D8
St Hilda's PI OSM LS9 ....110 D8
St Hilda's Rd OSM LS9 ....110 D8
St Hilda's Ter BFDE BD3 .....106 A6
St Ians Cft ILK LS29 ....19 H7
St Ives CI PONT WF8 ....180 D7
St Ives Crs CAS WF10 ....180 E1

St Ive's Gdns HIPP HX3 * ...168 E3
WOR/ARM LS12 ....108 C6
St Ives Mt WOR/ARM LS12 ..108 C6
St Ives PI BGLY BD16 ....80 E4
St Ives Rd BGLY BD16 ....80 E4
HIPP HX3 ....168 D3
St James Ap SCFT LS14 .....111 J2
St James Av HORS LS18 .....85 L5
St James's CI MILN OL16 ....228 E6
WOR/ARM LS12 ....108 A6
St James Cr HFAX HX1 * 11 G5
HOR/CROF WF4 ....222 E4
SKP/WHF BD23 ....16 A4
St James Crs PDSY/CALV LS28 ..106 D7
St James Dr HORS LS18 ......85 M5
St James Ms WOR/ARM LS12 ..108 B6
St James Ri HFAX HX1 * 11 C5
ILK LS29 ....38 C3
St James's Ct RHAY LS8 .....9 M4
St James's Mt HORS LS18 ...85 M5
St James Wk HORS LS18 ....85 M5
St James's Pk WKFDE WF1 ..13 L8
St John Pde DEWS WF13 ...173 K6
St Johns STKB/PEN S36 .....258 D8
HDGY LS6 ....6 E9
HUDE HD4 ....193 K5
HUDS HD4 ....214 C4
ILK LS29 ....38 C3
OSS WF5 ....197 J1
St John's Cha WKFDE WF1 ..176 D6
St Johns CI CLECK BD19 * ..150 A7
DEWS WF13 ....173 K6
DOD/DAR S75 ....260 A8
GFTH/SHER LS25 ....92 A5
HBR HX7 ....143 J3
HDGY LS6 ....6 E9
OSS WF5 ....197 J1
RPDN/SBR HX6 ....188 E5
STKB/PEN S36 ....270 E4
St John's CE BAIL BD17 ......83 G4
KBTN HD8 * 216 B3
MILN OL16 ....206 D8
SCFT LS14 * 90 B1
SKP/WHF BD23 ....16 C2
TAD LS24 ....94 F1
WKFDE WF1 ....176 D7
YEA LS19 ....62 C8
St John's Crs GIR BD8 ....104 A6
HUD HD1 ....14 E3
NORM WF6 ....178 C7
OSS WF5 ....197 J1
St John's Ct WKFDE WF1 ...176 C7
HUD HD1 ....14 E3
MILN OL16 ....206 D8
St John's Dr AL/HA/HU LS17 ..25 M7
HUD HD1 ....14 E3
St John's Garth
GFTH/SHER LS25 ....92 A6
St John's Gv HDGY LS6 ....6 A6
WKFDE WF1 ....176 E6
St John's La HFAX HX1 ....11 G8
St Johns Ms WKFDE WF1 * ..176 D6
St John's North WKFDE WF1 ..176 D7
St John's Pk ILK LS29 ....61 H1
St John's PI BIRK/DRI BD11 * ..128 C8
HFAX HX1 * 11 G8
St John's Rd AIRE BD20 ....57 J4
BSLY S70 ....261 G6
BSPA/BRAM LS23 ....48 F8
BVRD LS3 ....6 A6
CUD/GR S72 ....244 D6
HUDE HD1 ....14 E2
HUDE HD5 ....193 L5
ILK LS29 ....39 C2
YEA LS19 ....62 C8
St John's Sq WKFDE WF1 ...176 D7
St John's St AIRE BD20 ....34 B4
AIRE BD20 ....36 A1
HOR/CROF WF4 ....197 C5
RTHW LS26 ....155 L1
St Johns Ter HDGY LS6 ....6 B5
DEWS WF13 ....173 K6
St Johns Vw CUD/GR S72 * ..244 D6
St John's WK BSLYN/ROY S71 ..243 M3
St John Wk DEWS WF13 ....173 K6
St Josephs Ct GFTH/SHER LS25 ..113 G7
St Josephs Gdns BSLY S70 ..261 K6
St Joseph's Mt PONT WF8 ..180 D7
St Joseph's St TAD LS24 ......71 L3
St Jude's PI GIR BD8 ....4 C3
St Jude's St BFD BD1 ....4 C3
HFAX HX1 ....168 D1
St Julien's Mt DOD/DAR S75 ..259 G2
St Julien's Wy DOD/DAR S75 ..259 G2
St Laurence CI
PDSY/CALV LS28 ....106 F8
St Lawrence CI
AWLS/ASK DN6 ....249 J8
St Lawrence Md
PDSY/CALV LS28 ....106 F8
St Lawrence Ter
PDSY/CALV LS28 ....107 C3
St Leonards Ct ILK LS29 ......19 H7
St Leonards Gv GIR BD8 ....104 D5
St Leonard's Rd GIR BD8 ....104 D5
St Leonard's Wy
BSLYN/ROY S71 ....262 C7
St Lucius's CI HUDW HD3 ...215 G8
St Luke's CI BSPA/BRAM LS23 ..69 M1
St Luke's Crs BEE/HOL LS11 ...8 E4
St Luke's Gn BEE/HOL LS11 ...8 E4
St Luke's Rd BEE/HOL LS11 ...8 E4
St Luke's St BEE/HOL LS11 ...8 E4
St Luke St ROCH OL11 ......228 B1
St Luke's Vw BEE/HOL LS11 ...8 E4
St Margaret's Av BOW BD4 ..127 M4
HORS LS18 ....85 K4
RHAY LS8 ....88 C3
St Helier Dr DOD/DAR S75 * ..261 M1

St Margaret's CI HORS LS18 ...85 K4
St Margarets Ct
HEM/SK/SE WF9 ....225 K8
St Margaret's Dr HORS LS18 ..85 K4
RHAY LS8 ....88 C2
St Margaret's Gv RHAY LS8 ...88 C3
St Margaret's PI GTHN BD7 ..104 D3
HORS LS18 ....85 K4
RTHW LS26 ....155 F3
St Margaret's Rd GTHN BD7 ..104 D3
HORS LS18 ....85 K4
St Margaret's Ter CTHN BD7 ..126 D1
ILK LS29 ....38 D3
St Margaret's Vw RHAY LS8 ..88 C3
St Mark's Av LDSU LS2 ....6 E1
LM/WK BD12 ....148 E1
St Mark's Rd HUDW HD3 ....191 H3
LDSU LS2 ....6 E4
WKFDE WF1 ....176 F6
St Mark's St LM/WK BD12 ...148 E1
St Mark's Vw HUDW HD3 ....109 L1
St Martin's Av CHAL LS7 .....109 L1
GTHN BD7 ....4 A3
OT LS21 ....41 H4
St Martins CI DOD/DAR S75 ..260 D4
FEA/AMT WF7 ....201 L2
St Martins Ct EARD/LOFT WF3 ..154 D4
St Martin's Crs CHAL LS7 ...109 M1
St Martin's Dr CHAL LS7 * ...87 M8
St Martins Fold
EARD/LOFT WF3 ....154 D4
St Martin's Gdns CHAL LS7 ..109 L1
St Martin's Gv CAS WF10 ....157 K8
CHAL LS7 ....109 M1
St Martin's Rd CHAL LS7 ....109 M1
St Martin's Ter CHAL LS7 * ..109 M1
St Martin's Vw BRIG HD6 ....170 C3
CHAL LS7 ....109 M1
St Mary Magdalenes CI
GIR BD8 * 4 B3
St Mary's Av BTLY WF17 ....173 J3
HOLM/MEL HD9 ....236 B6
LM/WK BD12 ....148 E4
MIRF WF14 ....172 E8
NORM WF6 ....178 B2
RTHW LS26 ....134 C5
St Mary's CI CHAL LS7 ......109 M1
EARD/LOFT WF3 ....152 E7
GFTH/SHER LS25 ....113 H8
ILK LS29 ....38 C2
LM/WK BD12 ....148 D4
MILN OL16 ....228 D2
WOR/ARM LS12 ....108 B6
St Mary's Ct CAS WF10 * 157 K8
CHAL LS7 ....109 M1
St Mary's Crs HOLM/MEL HD9 ..236 B6
LM/WK BD12 ....148 D5
St Mary's Dr LM/WK BD12 ..148 E4
St Mary's Gdns LM/WK BD12 ..148 E4
St Mary's Garth AL/HA/HU LS17 ..67 K1
St Mary's Ga BSLY S70 ......261 G4
ELL HX5 ....169 H7
ROY/SHW OL2 * 229 K7
WHIT OL12 ....206 A3
St Mary's La HUDE HD5 .....193 L7
OSM LS9 ....7 L8
St Mary's Mt LM/WK BD12 ..148 D4
St Mary's Park Ap
WOR/ARM LS12 ....108 B6
St Mary's Park Ct
WOR/ARM LS12 ....108 B6
St Mary's Park Crs
WOR/ARM LS12 ....108 B6
St Mary's Park Gn
WOR/ARM LS12 ....108 B6
St Mary's PI BSLY S70 ....261 G4
EARL WF12 ....176 F1
St Mary's Ri HOLM/MEL HD9 ..236 B6
St Mary's Rd AIRE BD20 ......127 M1
BOW BD4 ....109 M1
CHAL LS7 ....109 M1
HOLM/MEL HD9 ....236 B1
HTON BD9 ....104 E4
NORM WF6 ....178 B2
St Mary's Sq HOLM/MEL HD9 ..236 B1
LM/WK BD12 ....148 D4
MOR LS27 * 152 C2
St Mary's St BSPA/BRAM LS23 ..48 F8
OSM LS9 ....7 K8
STKB/PEN S36 ....270 E3
St Mary St HFAX HX1 ....10 D1
St Mary's Wk GFTH/SHER LS25 ..114 B7
MIRF WF14 ....172 E8
St Mary's Wy HOLM/MEL HD9 ..236 B6
St Matthew Rd DEWS WF13 ..173 K8
St Matthew's CI WIL/AL BD15 ..102 D2
St Matthew's Dr HIPP HX3 ..147 J3
St Matthew's Gv WIL/AL BD15 ..102 D2
St Matthew's St BEE/HOL LS11 ..8 E5
St Matthew's Wk CHAL LS7 ..87 L6
St Matthews Wy
BSLYN/ROY S71 ....261 L3
St Matthias Ct BULY LS4 ....108 F4
St Matthias PI BULY LS4 .....108 F4
St Matthias Ter BULY LS4 ...108 F4
St Merrion Crs HIPP HX3 .....11 M9
St Michael's Av
BSLYN/ROY S71 ....243 M7
PONT WF8 ....180 D6
St Michael's CI CAS WF10 ..180 D6
EARL WF12 ....196 M4
KBTN HD8 * 217 M7
WKFDW/WTN WF2 ....12 A1
St Michael's Crs HDGY LS6 ..108 F2
St Michael's Gdns KBTN HD8 ..217 L7
St Michaels Gn NORM WF6 ..178 B3
St Michael's Gv HDGY LS6 ..108 F2
St Michael's La HDGY LS6 ..108 F2
St Michael's Mt EARL WF12 ..196 M4
St Michael's Rd GIR BD8 ......4 A3
HDGY LS6 ....108 F2
St Michaels Ter HDGY LS6 ..108 F2
St Michaels VIs HDGY LS6 ..108 F2
St Michaels Wy ILK LS29 .....19 H6
ILK LS29 ....40 B6
St Nicholas Rd ILK LS29 ......38 C1
St Nicholas St CAS WF10 ...157 M7
St Oswald Av PONT WF8 ....180 D6
St Oswald Rd
WKFDW/WTN WF2 ....197 L1
St Oswalds Garth GSLY LS20 ..62 M5
St Oswalds PI OSS WF5 .....173 G7
St Owens Dr DOD/DAR S75 ..260 D4
St Paulinus CI DEWS WF13 ..173 K6
St Paul's Av BIRK/DRI BD11 ..130 D6
WBSY BD6 ....126 D6
St Pauls CI GIR BD8 * 4 B8
HEM/SK/SE WF9 * 225 M6
St Pauls Ct PONT WF8 ....181 G3
St Paul's Dr WKFDW/WTN WF2 ..175 M6
St Paul's Gv ILK LS29 ....38 C2
WBSY BD6 ....126 D6
St Paul's Pde BSLYN/ROY S71 ..262 B6
St Paul's PI LDS LS1 * 6 E9
St Pauls Ri ILK LS29 ....19 H7

St Paul's Rd BIRK/DRI BD11 150 C1
DOD/DAR S75 260 E3
GIR BD8 104 E4
HFAX HX1 10 A9
HUDE HD5 193 K6
KGHY BD21 3 J6
MIRF WF14 194 C2
SHPY BD18 82 C7
WBSY BD6 126 D6
St Paul's St HUD HD1 15 G9
LDS LS1 6 D9
MOR LS27 * 152 C3
St Paul's Ter MIRF WF14 194 C2
St Paul's Wk WKFDW/WTN WF2 175 M6
St Peg Cl CLECK BD19 150 A7
St Peg La CLECK BD19 150 A7
St Peter's Av RPDN/SBR HX6 167 H3
RTHW LS26 155 H1
St Peter's Cl BTLY WF17 150 F5
MIRF WF14 * 194 B1
St Peters Ct BEE/HOL LS11 9 G8
BRAM LS13 107 M3
HOR/CROF WF4 197 J4
ILK LS29 19 H7
St Peter's Crs EARD/LOFT WF3 155 K8
HUDE HD5 193 K6
MOR LS27 130 C8
St Peter's Gdns BRAM LS13 107 L3
St Peter's Garth SCFT LS14 68 C8
St Peters Ga OSS WF5 174 F7
St Peter's Gv HOR/CROF WF4 * 197 K5
St Peter's Mt BRAM LS13 107 L4
St Peter's Sq OSM LS9 7 K9
St Peter's St HUD HD1 15 G6
LDSU LS2 7 J9
MILN OL16 206 D8
St Peter's Ter BSLY S70 * 261 J6
St Peter's Wy ILK LS29 61 H2
St Philip's Av MID LS10 153 K1
St Philip's Cl DEWS WF13 * 173 M5
ILK LS29 40 B6
MID LS10 153 L1
St Philips Ct HUDW HD3 191 K4
St Philip's Dr ILK LS29 40 B6
St Philip's Wy ILK LS29 40 B5
St Phillips Ct GIR BD8 104 B5
St Richards Rd OT LS21 41 H4
St Stephen's Cl SKP/WHF BD23 16 B2
St Stephen's Ct AIRE BD20 35 L8
HIPP HX3 * 168 C4
OSM LS9 * 110 B6
St Stephen's Rd AIRE BD20 56 E1
HUD HD1 * 214 B2
OSM LS9 110 B6
PDSY/CALV LS28 84 C7
WBOW BD5 126 F3
St Stephen's St HIPP HX3 168 C4
St Stephen's Ter WBOW BD5 * 127 G3
St Stephen's Wy COL BB8 74 B1
Saint St GTHN BD7 126 C2
St Swithins Dr
EARD/LOFT WF3 177 H4
St Swithins Gv
EARD/LOFT WF3 * 177 H4
St Thomas Gdns HUDN HD2 171 H8
St Thomas Rd FEA/AMT WF7 201 M1
St Thomas Rw LDSU LS2 7 J7
St Thomas's Rd DOD/DAR S75 260 C2
St Vincent Av AWLS/ASK DN6 249 H8
St Vincent Rd PDSY/CALV LS28 107 G8
St Wilfred's St PDSY/CALV LS28 84 D7
St Wilfrid's Av RHAY LS8 110 D3
St Wilfrid's Circ RHAY LS8 110 D3
St Wilfrid's Cl GTHN BD7 126 B1
St Wilfrid's Crs GTHN BD7 126 B1
RHAY LS8 110 D2
St Wilfrid's Dr RHAY LS8 110 C2
St Wilfrid's Garth RHAY LS8 110 D3
St Wilfrid's Gv RHAY LS8 110 D2
St Wilfrid's Rd GTHN BD7 126 B1
St Winifred's Cl LUD/ILL HX2 * 145 M1
Salcombe Cl DOD/DAR S75 242 E6
Salcombe Pl BOW BD4 128 A4
Salem Pl GFTH/SHER LS25 113 G7
MID LS10 9 H3
Salem St BFD BD1 4 E5
CUL/QBY BD13 124 F5
HBR HX7 143 J3
Salerno Wy WMB/DAR S73 263 G8
Sale St LIT OL15 185 K8
Salford Wy TOD OL14 163 J2
Salik Gdns ROCH OL11 228 B1
Salisbury Av BAIL BD17 82 E3
WOR/ARM LS12 108 E6
Salisbury Cl EARL WF12 174 B6
NORM WF6 178 D3
Salisbury Gv WOR/ARM LS12 108 E6
Salisbury Ms HORS LS18 85 M5
Salisbury Pl HIPP HX3 10 F1
PDSY/CALV LS28 84 C8
Salisbury Rd CLECK BD19 149 H6
HTON BD9 104 E1
HWTH BD22 2 D7
LM/WK BD12 126 E8
WOR/ARM LS12 108 E6
Salisbury St DOD/DAR S75 260 F3
PDSY/CALV LS28 84 C8
ROY/SHW OL2 229 H6
RPDN/SBR HX6 167 J3
SKP/WHF BD23 16 A2
YEA LS19 84 D2
Salisbury Ter HIPP HX3 10 F1
WOR/ARM LS12 108 E6
Salisbury Vw WOR/ARM LS12 108 E6
Salkeld St ROCH OL11 228 B1
Salmon Crs HORS LS18 85 L5
Sal Nook Cl LM/WK BD12 126 F7
Sal Royd Rd LM/WK BD12 149 G1
Saltaire Rd BGLY BD16 59 M8
SHPY BD18 82 C6
Saltburn Pl HTON BD9 104 B4
Saltburn St HFAX HX1 10 A5
Salt Drake RPDN/SBR HX6 166 D6
Salterhebble Hl HIPP HX3 168 F4
Salter Hill La STKB/PEN S36 271 G8
Salterlee HIPP HX3 147 G4
Salter Oak Cft BSLYN/ROY S71 243 L5
Salter Rake Ga TOD OL14 163 K6
Salter Rw PONT WF8 180 F6
Saltersbrook Rd
WMB/DAR S73 263 H7
Saltersgate Av KNOT WF11 182 A1
Salter St DEWS WF13 173 K4
Salter's Wy STKB/PEN S36 270 F4
Salt Horn Cl LM/WK BD12 149 H1
Saltonstall La LUD/ILL HX2 144 F1
Salt Pie Aly WKFDW/WTN WF2 12 C4
Salts Dr LIT OL15 185 J8
Salts Mill Rd BAIL BD17 82 D6
Salts St ROY/SHW OL2 229 K7
Salt St GIR BD8 4 A2
HFAX HX1 10 C4
Samlesbury Cl ROY/SHW OL2 229 H7
Sampson St LVSG WF15 172 D2
Samson St MILN OL16 206 E6
Samuel Dr EARD/LOFT WF3 177 G1
Samuel La ROY/SHW OL2 229 G6
Samuel Rd DOD/DAR S75 260 D3
Samuel Sq DOD/DAR S75 260 D3
Samuel St KGHY BD21 * 3 G4
Sandal Av WKFDW/WTN WF2 199 G5
Sandal Cliff WKFDW/WTN WF2 199 G6
Sandale Wk WBSY BD6 126 B7
Sandal Hall Cl
WKFDW/WTN WF2 199 H6
Sandal Hall Ms
WKFDW/WTN WF2 199 G5
Sandall Cl GFTH/SHER LS25 135 K4
Sandall Magna WBSY BD6 126 A7
Sandal Ri PONT WF8 225 J1
Sandals Rd BAIL BD17 82 E4
Sandal Wy BTLY WF17 151 H5
Sandbeck Cl BSLYN/ROY S71 261 H3
Sandbeck La WBY LS22 30 C6
Sandbeck Pk WBY LS22 30 B7
Sandbeck Wy WBY LS22 30 B7
Sandbed Ct MSTN/BAR LS15 111 M3
Sandbed La MSTN/BAR LS15 111 M3
Sand Beds CUL/QBY BD13 125 G5
Sandbeds HOLM/MEL HD9 214 B8
Sandbeds Crs LUD/ILL HX2 146 A5
Sandbeds Rd LUD/ILL HX2 146 A6
Sandbeds Ter LUD/ILL HX2 146 A5
Sandbrook Pk ROCH OL11 * 228 A2
Sandbrook Wy ROCH OL11 228 A2
Sandene Av HUDS HD4 213 L4
Sandene Dr HUDS HD4 213 L4
Sanderling Ct GIR BD8 * 103 L7
Sanderling Garth MID LS10 153 M1
Sanderling Wy MID LS10 153 M1
Sanderson Av NORM WF6 178 C5
WBSY BD6 126 E5
Sanderson La RTHW LS26 155 J4
Sanderson St WKFDE WF1 13 H3
Sandfield Av HDGY LS6 87 G8
Sandfield Garth HDGY LS6 87 G8
Sandfield Rd IDLE BD10 83 K8
MILN OL16 228 D1
Sandfield Ter TAD LS24 72 A2
Sandfield Vw HDGY LS6 87 G8
Sandford Ct BSLY S70 260 F6
Sandford Pl KSTL LS5 108 C2
Sandford Rd BFDE BD3 105 L7
HEM/SK/SE WF9 247 J1
KSTL LS5 108 D3
Sandforth Av HIPP HX3 146 E4
Sandgate Dr GFTH/SHER LS25 135 K4
Sandgate La GFTH/SHER LS25 135 L5
Sandgate Ri GFTH/SHER LS25 135 L4
Sandgate Ter GFTH/SHER LS25 135 L5
Sandhall Av LUD/ILL HX2 145 M7
Sandhall Dr LUD/ILL HX2 145 M7
Sandhall Gn LUD/ILL HX2 145 M6
Sandhall La LUD/ILL HX2 145 M7
Sandhill Cl PONT WF8 180 F2
Sandhill Crs AL/HA/HU LS17 88 A2
Sandhill Dr AL/HA/HU LS17 88 A2
Sandhill Fold IDLE BD10 83 J7
Sandhill Gv AL/HA/HU LS17 88 A1
CUD/GR S72 245 J5
Sand Hill La AL/HA/HU LS17 87 M3
Sandhill Lawn PONT WF8 180 E7
Sand Hill Lawns AL/HA/HU LS17 87 M3
Sandhill Mt AL/HA/HU LS17 87 M1
IDLE BD10 83 K8
Sandhill Ov AL/HA/HU LS17 88 A1
Sandhill Ri PONT WF8 180 F3
Sand Hole La ROCH OL11 228 B5
Sandholme Crs HIPP HX3 147 M7
Sandholme Dr IDLE BD10 83 L8
ILK LS29 40 B7
OSS WF5 196 F1
Sandhurst Av RHAY LS8 110 C2
Sandhurst Gv RHAY LS8 110 C3
Sandhurst Pl RHAY LS8 110 C3
Sandhurst Rd RHAY LS8 110 C3
Sandhurst St PDSY/CALV LS28 84 C7
Sandhurst Ter RHAY LS8 110 C2
Sandiford Cl MSTN/BAR LS15 111 M3
Sandiford Ter MSTN/BAR LS15 111 M3
Sandiway Bank EARL WF12 195 M3
Sand La GFTH/SHER LS25 138 A3
Sandleas Wy MSTN/BAR LS15 112 B4
Sandlewood Cl BEE/HOL LS11 8 D6
Sandlewood Ct HDGY LS6 87 H5
Sandlewood Crs HDGY LS6 87 H5
Sandlewood Gn BEE/HOL LS11 8 D6
Sandmead Cl BOW BD4 128 A3
MOR LS27 130 C8
Sandmead Cft MOR LS27 130 C8
Sandmead Wy MOR LS27 130 C8
Sandmoor Av AL/HA/HU LS17 65 M8
Sandmoor Cha AL/HA/HU LS17 87 M1
Sandmoor Cl AL/HA/HU LS17 87 M1
CUL/QBY BD13 103 G8
Sandmoor Dr AL/HA/HU LS17 65 M8
HUDW HD3 191 J5
Sandmoor Gdns HIPP HX3 147 K2
Sandmoor Garth IDLE BD10 83 K5
Sandmoor Gn AL/HA/HU LS17 65 L8
Sandmoor La AL/HA/HU LS17 65 M8
Sandmoor Ms AL/HA/HU LS17 87 M1
Sandon Gv MID LS10 * 132 A4
Sandon Mt MID LS10 132 A4
Sandown Av HOR/CROF WF4 200 B5
LUD/ILL HX2 146 A2
Sandown Rd LUD/ILL HX2 146 A2
Sandpiper Ap MOR LS27 152 E3
Sandpiper Ms GIR BD8 103 L7
Sandringham HUDN HD2 193 G1
Sandringham Ap
AL/HA/HU LS17 88 A3
Sandringham Av KNOT WF11 181 L2
Sandringham Cl CLAY BD14 * 125 M1
MOR LS27 152 E1
PONT WF8 202 E1
STKB/PEN S36 270 C2
Sandringham Ct CLAY BD14 125 M1
Sandringham Crs
AL/HA/HU LS17 87 M3
PDSY/CALV LS28 107 G8
Sandringham Dr
AL/HA/HU LS17 87 M3
MILN OL16 207 J8
Sandringham Gdns
AL/HA/HU LS17 87 M3
Sandringham Gn
AL/HA/HU LS17 * 88 A3
Sandringham Mt
AL/HA/HU LS17 88 A2
Sandringham Rd CLAY BD14 125 M1
KNOT WF11 159 M7
WBY LS22 30 A8
Sandringham Wy
AL/HA/HU LS17 87 M3
ROY/SHW OL2 228 E8
Sandrock Rd PONT WF8 181 G4
Sandsend Cl HTON BD9 103 M3
Sands House La HUDS HD4 213 K5
Sandside Cl WBOW BD5 127 H4
Sands La EARL WF12 173 M7
HUDE HD5 194 B8
MIRF WF14 194 F3
Sands Rd EARL WF12 174 A8
Sands Ter HUDN HD2 * 193 G4
Sandstone Cl HOLM/MEL HD9 236 B3
Sandstone Dr WOR/ARM LS12 107 L7
Sandstone La HUDS HD4 213 K3
Sandstone Rd MILN OL16 207 H7
Sand St HUD HD1 15 H8
HWTH BD22 78 E8
KGHY BD21 3 G3
Sandwath La TAD LS24 94 D7
Sandway MSTN/BAR LS15 111 K4
Sandway Gdns MSTN/BAR LS15 111 K4
Sandway Gv MSTN/BAR LS15 111 K4
Sandwell St MAR/SLWT HD7 212 B5
Sandwich Crs HUDN HD2 192 B3
Sandyacres RTHW LS26 133 H8
Sandyacres Crs RTHW LS26 133 H8
Sandyacres Dr RTHW LS26 133 H8
Sandy Bank ROY/SHW OL2 229 H6
Sandy Bank Av RTHW LS26 133 H8
Sandy Banks BGLY BD16 80 D6
Sandy Beck WIL/AL BD15 103 J3
Sandybridge La CUD/GR S72 244 D2
Sandy Dyke La RPDN/SBR HX6 167 G6
Sandyfields Vw
AWLS/ASK DN6 249 K5
Sandyfoot GTL/HWG HX4 189 K2
Sandyforth La HWTH BD22 53 M4
Sandy Ga AIRE BD20 2 C2
AL/HA/HU LS17 44 F7
HBR HX7 143 K3
HOLM/MEL HD9 254 E2
Sandy Gate La FEA/AMT WF7 202 E3
Sandygate La HEM/SK/SE WF9 223 L7
Sandygate Ter BOW BD4 127 M1
Sandy Gv RTHW LS26 133 H8
Sandylands HUDS HD4 213 M8
Sandy La HOR/CROF WF4 196 D7
HUDS HD4 213 J7
Sandy Lobby OT LS21 42 E8
Sandymoor WIL/AL BD15 103 J2
Sandy Wk BHP/TINH LS16 64 B4
WKFDE WF1 12 C1
Sandy Wy YEA LS19 62 D7
Sandywood St KGHY BD21 3 G3
Sangster Wy WBOW BD5 127 J5
Santa Monica Crs IDLE BD10 83 J7
Santa Monica Gv IDLE BD10 83 J7
Santa Monica Rd IDLE BD10 83 J7
Santingley La HOR/CROF WF4 200 C8
Sanworth St TOD OL14 163 L1
Sapgate La CUL/QBY BD13 103 G8
Saplin St GIR BD8 104 D5
Sapphire Ct BTLY WF17 151 J8
Sarah Butterworth Ct
MILN OL16 * 206 D7
Sarah Butterworth St
MILN OL16 206 D8
Sarah St EARD/LOFT WF3 153 M6
ROCH OL11 206 B8
Sardinia St MID LS10 9 J6
Saunders Cl HUDW HD3 191 L7
Saunderson Rd STKB/PEN S36 270 D2
Saunters Wy NORM WF6 178 C2
Savile Av CHAL LS7 7 J2
IDLE BD10 83 L8
KBTN HD8 217 M7
Savile Cl BRIG HD6 170 F3
Savile Ct MIRF WF14 * 172 C8
Savile Crs HFAX HX1 10 F8
Savile Dr CHAL LS7 7 J2
HFAX HX1 10 E9
HOR/CROF WF4 197 J4
Savile Gln HFAX HX1 10 F8
Savile Gn HFAX HX1 11 G8
Savile Gv EARL WF12 173 L7
Savile La BRIG HD6 170 F3
Savile Lea HFAX HX1 10 F8
Savile Ms EARL WF12 195 L1
Savile Mt CHAL LS7 7 J2
Savile Pde HFAX HX1 168 D1
Savile Pk HFAX HX1 168 C1
Savile Park Gdns HFAX HX1 168 D1
Savile Park Rd CLECK BD19 149 M3
HFAX HX1 10 F8
Savile Park St HFAX HX1 168 C1
Savile Park Ter HFAX HX1 * 168 C1
Savile Pit La EARL WF12 174 C5
Savile Pl CHAL LS7 7 J2
MIRF WF14 172 C8
Savile Rd CAS WF10 157 L6
CHAL LS7 7 J2
EARL WF12 195 L1
ELL HX5 169 H8
HBR HX7 143 G3
HFAX HX1 10 F8
HUDW HD3 191 L6
RTHW LS26 156 F3
Savile Royd HFAX HX1 10 E9
Savile St CLECK BD19 149 M5
DEWS WF13 173 L4
HUDW HD3 213 J1
KBTN HD8 217 M7
Savile Ter HFAX HX1 10 D9
Savile Wk CUD/GR S72 245 K3
Savile Wy ELL HX5 169 J6
Saville Cl EARD/LOFT WF3 154 E5
Saville Ct OT LS21 41 H7
Saville Hall La DOD/DAR S75 260 B8
Saville La STKB/PEN S36 270 B3
Saville Pk OSS WF5 197 H2
Saville Park Rd HFAX HX1 10 E9
Saville Rd DOD/DAR S75 260 C8
KBTN HD8 239 J4
Saville St CUD/GR S72 244 D7
KBTN HD8 * 239 M5
OSS WF5 197 H2
WKFDE WF1 176 E7
Saville Ter BSLY S70 * 261 G6
Savins Mill Wy KSTL LS5 108 C2
Sawley Av LIT OL15 185 J7
Sawley Cl WKFDE WF1 177 G6
Sawley St KGHY BD21 2 E7
Saw Mill La ILK LS29 19 J6
Saw Mill St BEE/HOL LS11 8 E3
Sawood La HWTH BD22 101 H6
Sawrey Pl WBOW BD5 4 D8
Saw Wells La TAD LS24 116 A2
Saw Yd WKFDE WF1 12 E3
Sawyers Garth ILK LS29 19 J6
Sawyer St WHIT OL12 206 B5
Saxilby Rd AIRE BD20 58 D5
Saxon Av HEM/SK/SE WF9 246 B4
Saxon Cl HEM/SK/SE WF9 226 A7
KBTN HD8 217 L8
Saxon Ga AL/HA/HU LS17 87 K4
Saxon Gn AL/HA/HU LS17 87 J4
Saxon Gv AL/HA/HU LS17 87 J4
HEM/SK/SE WF9 246 C5
Saxon Mt AL/HA/HU LS17 87 K3
HEM/SK/SE WF9 246 B4
Saxon Rd AL/HA/HU LS17 87 J4
Saxon St CUD/GR S72 244 D8
GIR BD8 4 A4
HFAX HX1 10 A5
TOD OL14 163 J5
Saxon Wy CAS WF10 158 C6
Saxstead Ri WOR/ARM LS12 108 E8
Saxton Av WBSY BD6 126 B5
Saxton Ct GFTH/SHER LS25 113 H6
TAD LS24 93 K7
Saxton Gdns OSM LS9 * 9 L1
Saxton La OSM LS9 9 K1
TAD LS24 93 K8
Saxton Pl HUDE HD5 215 J2
Saxton St LVSG WF15 172 E1
Sayers Cl KSTL LS5 108 D2
Sayle Av BOW BD4 127 K6
Sayner La MID LS10 9 K4
Sayner Rd MID LS10 9 J4
Scalebor Park Cl ILK LS29 39 M5
Scalebor Sq ILK LS29 39 M6
Scale Hl HUDN HD2 192 C4
OT LS21 42 D3
Scaley St BFDE BD3 105 M7
Scaly Ga HOLM/MEL HD9 255 J1
Scammonden Rd
GTL/HWG HX4 189 H7
RPDN/SBR HX6 167 J8
Scape Vw MAR/SLWT HD7 213 G2
Scarboro Mdw MIRF WF14 * 194 C1
Scarborough Gv SHPY BD18 82 C7
Scarborough La
EARD/LOFT WF3 152 F6
Scarborough Rd SHPY BD18 82 C7
Scarborough St
EARD/LOFT WF3 152 F5
EARL WF12 173 M8
Scarborough Ter EARL WF12 173 M8
Scar Bottom La GTL/HWG HX4 168 B7
Scarbro' Jct BRAM LS13 107 M5
Scarcroft Ct SCFT LS14 67 M6
Scarfield Cl BSLYN/ROY S71 262 B6
Scarfold HOLM/MEL HD9 254 C1
Scargill Cl OSM LS9 110 B5
Scargill Gra OSM LS9 110 B6
Scar Gv HUDS HD4 214 B4
Scar Head Rd RPDN/SBR HX6 167 K4
Scar Hole La HOLM/MEL HD9 255 J2
Scarhouse La MAR/SLWT HD7 213 G2
Scar La BSLYN/ROY S71 262 B6
HUDW HD3 213 H2
Scarlet Hts CUL/QBY BD13 125 H5
Scarr Bottom Rd LUD/ILL HX2 168 B2
Scarr Dr WHIT OL12 206 B4
Scarr End La DEWS WF13 173 H4
EARL WF12 196 B1
Scarr End Vw DEWS WF13 173 H4
Scarr La ROY/SHW OL2 229 L7
Scarsdale La AL/HA/HU LS17 47 G8
Scarsdale Rdg AL/HA/HU LS17 47 G8
Scarth Av OSM LS9 110 C4
Scarthingwell Crs TAD LS24 93 K7
Scarthingwell La TAD LS24 93 M7
Scarth Ter EARD/LOFT WF3 155 K8
Scar Top GTL/HWG HX4 * 168 B7
Scar Top La HUDS HD4 213 M8
Scar Top Rd HWTH BD22 77 H7
Scarwood Cl BGLY BD16 81 J2
Scatcherd Gv MOR LS27 152 B2
Scatcherd La MOR LS27 152 B3
Scatcherd Park Av MOR LS27 152 C1
Scawthorpe Cl PONT WF8 181 H5
Sceptone Gv CUD/GR S72 244 E3
Schofield Ct MOR LS27 * 152 C2
Schofield Dr WMB/DAR S73 263 J8
Schofield Hall Rd LIT OL15 207 M5
Schofield La HUDE HD5 15 L7
Schofield Pl WMB/DAR S73 263 J8
Schofield Rd WMB/DAR S73 263 H8
Schofield St LIT OL15 185 L8
LIT OL15 185 M4
MILN OL16 229 J1
ROCH OL11 228 C2
Scholars Wk ECHL BD2 105 K3
Scholars Wy AIRE BD20 58 B4
Schole Av STKB/PEN S36 270 E3
Scholebrook La BOW BD4 128 E3
Schole Hill La STKB/PEN S36 270 D4
Scholemoor Av GTHN BD7 126 A1
Scholemoor La GTHN BD7 126 A1
Scholemoor Rd GTHN BD7 126 B1
Scholes La CLECK BD19 149 H7
GTL/HWG HX4 168 C5
HWTH BD22 78 B5
MSTN/BAR LS15 90 A6
Scholes Moor Rd
HOLM/MEL HD9 254 E5
Scholes Rd CAS WF10 158 F5
HOLM/MEL HD9 255 G2
HUDN HD2 192 C4
Scholes St WBOW BD5 126 F4
Scholey Av BRIG HD6 170 C6
Scholey Rd BRIG HD6 170 C6
Scholfield St TOD OL14 141 K8
School Av DEWS WF13 173 H5
School Cl HOR/CROF WF4 200 D2
LUD/ILL HX2 124 B7
RPDN/SBR HX6 189 G2
WOR/ARM LS12 129 M3
School Cote Brow HIPP HX3 124 D8
School Crs DEWS WF13 173 H5
LUD/ILL HX2 124 B7
WKFDW/WTN WF2 197 M2
School Cft KNOT WF11 159 L6
RTHW LS26 133 G8
School Dr KNOT WF11 181 L1
Schoolgate MSTN/BAR LS15 91 G7
School Gn BHP/TINH LS16 64 A4
BRIG HD6 170 C6
CUL/QBY BD13 103 J8
School Green Av
CUL/QBY BD13 103 H8
School Gv DEWS WF13 173 H5
School Hl CUD/GR S72 244 D7
HUDS HD4 213 J7
KBTN HD8 216 B8
WKFDW/WTN WF2 220 D2
School House Fold AIRE BD20 58 B4
School Land La HBR HX7 120 B8
School La AL/HA/HU LS17 66 D6
AL/HA/HU LS17 67 L1
BSPA/BRAM LS23 49 H2
CAS WF10 158 B8
CHAL LS7 87 L7
COL BB8 53 G8
DEWS WF13 173 H5
GFTH/SHER LS25 92 A7
GFTH/SHER LS25 138 A3
HDGY LS6 87 G8
HIPP HX3 169 J3
HOR/CROF WF4 197 J5
HOR/CROF WF4 222 D5
HUD HD1 14 A9
HUDE HD5 193 K7
HUDS HD4 214 B6
ILK LS29 19 G6
KBTN HD8 217 M7
KBTN HD8 239 J8
LUD/ILL HX2 124 B6
LVSG WF15 171 M4
MAR/SLWT HD7 190 D8
MAR/SLWT HD7 211 L8
MILN OL16 206 B7
MSTN/BAR LS15 111 J6
MSTN/BAR LS15 112 A7
PBR HG3 28 E3
TOD OL14 163 K1
WBY LS22 47 K6
WKFDW/WTN WF2 176 A4
WKFDW/WTN WF2 199 J7
School Ms MILN OL16 * 229 K2
WOR/ARM LS12 108 E7
School Pl LM/WK BD12 * 148 E2
School Rd HWTH BD22 2 A5
MAR/SLWT HD7 190 D8
PONT WF8 181 G7
WBY LS22 30 B8
WKFDW/WTN WF2 197 M3
School Sq BFDE BD3 105 M7
School St AIRE BD20 56 E1
AIRE BD20 57 J4
BGLY BD16 81 K7
BOW BD4 127 K6
BOW BD4 127 L3
BSLY S70 261 M6
BTLY WF17 151 H5
CAS WF10 157 L6
CAS WF10 158 A5
CLAY BD14 125 K2
CLECK BD19 149 L8
CUD/GR S72 244 D6
CUD/GR S72 263 M4
CUL/QBY BD13 79 M8
CUL/QBY BD13 102 A6
DEWS WF13 194 F1
DOD/DAR S75 242 A5
DOD/DAR S75 242 E5
DOD/DAR S75 260 F3
EARD/LOFT WF3 174 F1
EARL WF12 173 L6
EARL WF12 174 D6
GTL/HWG HX4 168 D6
HBR HX7 143 J3
HEM/SK/SE WF9 225 M6
HFAX HX1 11 J7
HOLM/MEL HD9 236 B1
HOLM/MEL HD9 236 B6
HOLM/MEL HD9 254 C1
HUDE HD5 15 M8
LIT OL15 207 G1
LM/WK BD12 126 E8
LM/WK BD12 149 J2
LVSG WF15 172 A4
LVSG WF15 172 D4
MOR LS27 130 E6
MOR LS27 152 D2
OSS WF5 174 E5
PDSY/CALV LS28 106 F3
PDSY/CALV LS28 106 F8
WHIT OL12 * 206 B6
WIL/AL BD15 102 E1
WMB/DAR S73 263 K8
School St West HUDW HD3 191 K6
School Vw HDGY LS6 109 G3
School Wk HWTH BD22 2 B5
School Yd SKP/WHF BD23 * 16 C2
School Yard Vw HIPP HX3 * 11 H2
Sconce La BAIL BD17 60 C6
Scopsley Gn EARL WF12 195 G6
Scopsley La EARL WF12 194 F5
Scorcher Hills La
AWLS/ASK DN6 249 H2
Score Cft KBTN HD8 239 J4
Score Hl HIPP HX3 147 J2
Scoresby St BFD BD1 5 H6
Scotchman Cl MOR LS27 152 B4
Scotchman La MOR LS27 152 A6
Scotchman Rd HTON BD9 104 B4
Scotgate Rd HOLM/MEL HD9 235 M2
Scotland Cl HORS LS18 85 K3
Scotland La HORS LS18 63 J7
Scotland Mill La BHP/TINH LS16 87 H4
Scotland St CLECK BD19 150 E5
Scotland Wy HORS LS18 85 J2
Scotland Wood Rd
AL/HA/HU LS17 87 H4
Scott Av HECK WF16 150 F8
Scott Cl AIRE BD20 55 M1
HECK WF16 * 173 G2
RTHW LS26 134 C5
Scott Dr HOR/CROF WF4 200 C6
Scott Gn MOR LS27 129 K6
Scott Green Crs MOR LS27 129 K6
Scott Green Dr MOR LS27 129 K6
Scott Green Gv MOR LS27 * 129 L6
Scott Green Mt MOR LS27 129 K6
Scott Green Vw MOR LS27 129 L6
Scott Hall Av CHAL LS7 109 L2
Scott Hall Dr CHAL LS7 7 H2
Scott Hall Gn CHAL LS7 109 L1
Scott Hall Gv CHAL LS7 109 L1
Scott Hall Pl CHAL LS7 109 L1
Scott Hall Rd CHAL LS7 109 L1
Scott Hall Rw CHAL LS7 7 J1
Scott Hall Sq CHAL LS7 109 L1
Scott Hall St CHAL LS7 7 G1
Scott Hall Ter CHAL LS7 109 L1
Scott Hall Wk CHAL LS7 109 L2
Scott Hall Wy CHAL LS7 87 L8
Scott Hl KBTN HD8 240 B3
Scott La AIRE BD20 58 A4
CLECK BD19 149 M6
CLECK BD19 150 D5
MOR LS27 152 A3
WBY LS22 48 A1
Scott La West AIRE BD20 57 M4
Scott Ms WBY LS22 48 A1
Scotts Hill Cl SCFT LS14 90 B1
Scott St KGHY BD21 2 F4
PDSY/CALV LS28 107 H8
TOD OL14 163 J6
Scott V HUDN HD2 192 F3
Scott Wood La CHAL LS7 109 L2
Scotty Bank BRIG HD6 * 170 C4
Scotty Croft La BRIG HD6 170 C5
Scout Bottom La HBR HX7 144 B6
Scout Cl HBR HX7 144 B6
Scout Hill Rd DEWS WF13 173 J8
Scout La MAR/SLWT HD7 211 K5
Scout Rd HBR HX7 144 A6
Scowcroft La ROY/SHW OL2 229 J8
Scrapers La TOD OL14 141 K6
Scriftain La WBY LS22 30 A5
Seacroft Av SCFT LS14 111 K1
Seacroft Cl SCFT LS14 111 K1
Seacroft Crs SCFT LS14 111 K1
Seacroft Ga SCFT LS14 * 111 K1
Seaforth Av OSM LS9 110 C3
Seaforth Gv OSM LS9 110 C3
Seaforth Mt OSM LS9 110 C3
Seaforth Pl RHAY LS8 110 C3
Seaforth Rd OSM LS9 110 C3
Seaforth Ter RHAY LS8 110 C3
Seagrave Rd HUDS HD4 213 L3
Seaton St BFDE BD3 5 L5
Seckar La HOR/CROF WF4 220 C6
Secker St WKFDW/WTN WF2 12 D8
Second Av AL/HA/HU LS17 68 A1
BFDE BD3 105 L5
HEM/SK/SE WF9 223 J2
HEM/SK/SE WF9 225 J6
HEM/SK/SE WF9 246 B5
HIPP HX3 168 D2
HOR/CROF WF4 197 H5
HUDE HD5 193 H7
KGHY BD21 2 E7
LVSG WF15 171 K2
RTHW LS26 133 H7
WBY LS22 48 B1
WKFDE WF1 176 D4
WOR/ARM LS12 109 G7

YEA LS19 ....84 E1
Second St *LM/WK* BD12 ....127 G8
Sedan St *HFAX* HX1 * 11 G7
Sedbergh Cl *MSTN/BAR* LS15 ....110 F7
Sedbergh Dr *ILK* LS29 ....38 E3
Sedbergh Pk *ILK* LS29 ....38 E3
Sedburgh Rd HX3 ....11 J9
Sedgegarth *SCFT* LS14 ....68 G3
Sedge Gv *HWTH* BD22 ....78 E6
Sedgefield Ter *BFD* BD1 ....4 C5
Sedgley Av *MILN* OL16 ....228 D2
Sedgwick Cl *GIR* BD8 ....4 C4
Seedhill Ter *AIRE* BD20 ....56 E1
Seed Hill Ter *LUD/ILL* HX2 ....123 L8
Seed Rw *BOW* BD4 ....127 K6
Seed St *LM/WK* BD12 ....126 F8
Sefton Av *BEE/HOL* LS11 ....131 J3
  BRIG 170 B1
Sefton Ct *HDGY* LS6 ....86 B1
Sefton Crs *BRIG* HD6 ....170 B1
Sefton Dr *BRIG* HD6 ....170 B1
  ILK LS29 ....38 D3
Sefton Gv *ECHL* BD2 ....105 K3
Sefton La *HOLM/MEL* HD9 ....234 K3
Sefton Pl *KGHY* BD21 ....3 G3
Sefton Ri *EARL* WF12 ....195 M2
Sefton St *BEE/HOL* LS11 ....131 K3
  COL BB8 ....74 B1
  HFAX HX1 ....10 D4
  KGHY BD21 ....3 G3
  ROCH OL11 ....228 A1
Sefton Ter *BEE/HOL* LS11 ....131 J3
  HFAX HX1 ....10 D4
Selbourne Gv *HTON* BD9 ....100 D3
  KGHY BD21 ....2 D8
Selborne Mt *HTON* BD9 ....104 C4
Selborne Ter *HTON* BD9 ....104 C4
  SHPY BD18 ....82 D8
Selborne Vis *CLAY* BD14 ....125 J3
  HTON BD9 ....104 C4
Selbourne Av *EARL* WF12 ....173 J6
Selbourne Cl *DOD/DAR* WF5 ....260 A1
Selbourne Dr *EARL* WF12 ....195 L1
Selbourne Rd *EARL* WF12 ....195 L1
Selby Av *OSM* LS9 ....111 G6
Selby Cl *MILN* OL16 ....207 G8
Selby Rd *BSLYN/ROY* S71 * 243 H7
  GFTH/SHER LS25 ....134 F1
  MSTN/BAR LS15 ....111 K6
Selby St *MILN* OL16 ....206 D6
  WKFDE WF1 ....176 E7
Seldon St *WBOW* BD5 ....126 D3
Selene Cl *CLECK* BD19 ....150 E4
Sellars Fold *GTHN* BD7 * 126 C2
Sellerdale Av *LM/WK* BD12 ....148 F4
Sellerdale Dr *LM/WK* BD12 ....148 F4
Sellerdale Ri *LM/WK* BD12 ....148 F4
Sellerdale Wy *LM/WK* BD12 ....148 G5
Selso Rd *EARL* WF12 ....174 B5
Seminary St *LDSU* LS2 ....6 D6
Semon Av *ECHL* BD2 ....105 H1
Senior St *DEWS* WF13 ....173 K7
  HUDE HD5 ....15 M8
Senior Wy *WBOW* BD5 ....4 E8
Sennen Cft *BSLYN/ROY* S71 ....261 K5
Sentry *HOLM/MEL* HD9 ....236 B1
Sergeantson St *HUD* HD1 ....14 F7
Serpentine Rd *CLECK* BD19 ....149 M6
Servia Dr *CHAL* LS7 ....6 F1
Servia Gdns *CHAL* LS7 ....7 G3
Servia Hl *CHAL* LS7 ....6 F3
Servia Rd *HDGY* LS7 ....6 F3
Sessions House Yd *PONT* WF8 ....180 E5
Seth Ter *BSLY* S70 ....261 J6
Sevenoaks Md *WIL/AL* BD15 ....103 K5
Seventh Av *LVSG* WF15 ....171 K1
  RTHW LS26 ....133 J8
Severn Dr *GFTH/SHER* LS25 ....115 J1
  MILN OL16 ....207 J8
Severn Rd *ECHL* BD2 ....105 J4
Severn Wy *MID* LS10 ....132 B2
Sewell Rd *BFDE* BD3 ....5 M7
Sewerbridge La *FEA/AMT* WF7 ....179 H5
Seymour Gv *MILN* OL16 ....228 D3
Seymour St *BFDE* BD3 ....5 K1
  WKFDW/WTN WF2 ....12 E7
Seymour Wk *HOLM/MEL* HD9 ....235 G4
Shackleton St *TOD* OL14 ....140 E5
Shackleton Vw *STKB/PEN* S36 ....270 F4
Shade St *TOD* OL14 ....163 J3
Shadwell La *AL/HA/HU* LS17 ....87 M4
Shadwell Park Av
  AL/HA/HU LS17 ....88 E1
Shadwell Park Cl
  AL/HA/HU LS17 ....88 E1
Shadwell Park Ct
  AL/HA/HU LS17 ....88 E1
Shadwell Park Dr
  AL/HA/HU LS17 ....88 E2
Shadwell Park Gdns
  AL/HA/HU LS17 ....88 E1
Shadwell Park Gv
  AL/HA/HU LS17 ....88 E2
Shadwell Wk *AL/HA/HU* LS17 ....88 A3
Shady La *AIRE* BD20 ....34 B3
Shaftesbury Av *BRIG* HD6 ....170 A4
  GLE DN14 ....183 H1
  HTON BD9 ....103 M4
  LIT OL15 ....207 J4
  RHAY LS8 ....88 C5
  SHPY BD18 ....82 E7
Shaftesbury Dr *WHIT* OL12 ....184 F8
Shaftesbury Pde *OSM* LS9 * 110 E5
Shaftesbury Rd *RHAY* LS8 ....88 C4
Shaftesbury St *BSLY* S70 ....261 M6
Shafton Hall Dr *CUD/GR* S72 ....244 D3
Shafton La *BEE/HOL* LS11 ....8 B6
Shafton Pl *BEE/HOL* LS11 ....8 B6
Shafton St *BEE/HOL* LS11 ....8 C6
Shafton Vw *BEE/HOL* LS11 ....8 B6
Shakespeare Av
  AWLS/ASK DN6 ....227 C4
  NORM WF6 ....178 C7
  OSM LS9 ....110 B5
  TOD OL14 ....141 M8
Shakespeare Cl *BFDE* BD3 * 5 K4
  LIT OL15 ....185 L1
  OSM LS9 ....110 B5
Shakespeare Ct *OSM* LS9 ....110 B5
Shakespeare Crs *CAS* WF10 ....180 F1
Shakespeare Gdns *OSM* LS9 ....110 B5
Shakespeare Gra *OSM* LS9 ....110 B5
Shakespeare Lawn *OSM* LS9 ....110 B5
Shakespeare Rd *SHPY* BD18 ....62 A6
Shakespeare St *HFAX* HX1 ....11 H7
  OSM LS9 ....110 B4
Shakespeare Towers *OSM* LS9 ....110 B4
Shalimar St *HFAX* HX1 ....10 A5
Shambles St *BSLY* S70 ....261 G5
The Shambles *WBY* LS22 ....48 A1
Shancara St *EARD/LOFT* WF3 ....153 G5
Shann Av *AIRE* BD20 ....2 B3
Shann Crs *AIRE* BD20 ....2 B3
Shann La *AIRE* BD20 ....2 B3
Shannon Cl *BRIG* HD6 ....170 A7

ILK LS29 ....38 B3
Shannon Dr *HUDW* HD3 ....190 F5
Shannon Rd *BRIG* HD6 ....170 A7
  OSM LS9 ....7 M9
Shann St *OSM* LS9 ....7 L9
Shapla Cl *HWTH* BD22 ....2 C6
Share Hl *MAR/SLWT* HD7 ....212 E1
Sharp Av *WBSY* BD6 ....126 E6
Sharpe St *HECK* WF16 ....172 F3
  WBOW BD5 ....6 E8
Sharphaw Av *SKP/WHF* BD23 ....7 G7
Sharp House Rd *MID* LS10 ....154 A2
Sharp La *HUDS* HD4 ....215 H5
  MID LS10 ....154 A2
Sharp Ms *HDGY* LS6 ....109 H1
Sharp Rd *HUDE* HD5 ....215 J1
Sharp Rw *PDSY/CALV* LS28 ....107 H8
Sharp St *DEWS* WF13 ....173 M6
  WBSY BD6 ....126 E5
Shaw Av *NORM* WF6 ....178 E4
Shaw Barn Cft *WBY* LS22 ....47 L1
Shaw Barn La *WBY* LS22 ....47 L1
Shaw Booth La *LUD/ILL* HX2 ....145 H2
Shaw Cl *GFTH/SHER* LS25 ....135 J1
  GTL/HWG HX4 ....190 D2
  HEM/SK/SE WF9 ....247 J2
  NORM WF6 ....178 E4
Shawfield Av *HOLM/MEL* HD9 ....253 M2
Shawfield Rd *BSLYN/ROY* S71 ....243 L8
Shaw Fields La
  MAR/SLWT HD7 ....211 L6
Shaw Fold *WKFDW/WTN* WF2 ....199 G5
Shaw Ga *MAR/SLWT* HD7 ....213 A8
Shaw Hl *HFAX* HX1 ....11 J9
Shaw Hill La *HIPP* HX3 ....11 J9
Shaw La *BSLY* S70 ....260 E5
  BSLYN/ROY S71 ....243 M6
  DOD/DAR S75 ....242 D2
  ELL HX5 ....169 L7
  GSLY LS20 ....62 B5
  GTL/HWG HX4 ....190 D2
  HDGY LS6 ....86 F1
  HIPP HX3 ....125 H8
  HIPP HX3 ....168 M2
  HOLM/MEL HD9 ....253 K2
  HUDW HD3 ....213 K2
  KGHY BD21 ....79 M3
  MAR/SLWT HD7 ....211 J6
  OL16 ....207 H5
  PBR HG3 ....25 J4
  PBR HG3 ....28 D2
  RPDN/SBR HX6 ....167 L5
  RPDN/SBR HX6 ....188 E4
  TOD OL14 ....140 D3
Shaw Lane Gdns *GSLY* LS20 ....62 B6
Shaw Leys *YEA* LS19 ....59 J7
Shaw Ms *NORM* WF6 ....178 E4
Shaw Rd *MILN* OL16 ....228 E6
  MILN OL16 ....229 K3
Shaw Royd *YEA* LS19 ....62 G6
Shaws La *MSTN/BAR* LS15 ....90 E8
  RPDN/SBR HX6 ....166 E4
Shaw St *BSLY* S70 ....260 F6
  CLECK BD19 * 149 K7
  GTL/HWG HX4 ....190 E2
  LM/WK BD12 ....148 C8
  WHIT OL12 ....194 C1
Shaw Wood Rd *TOD* OL14 ....142 B8
Shay Cl *HTON* BD9 ....104 A2
Shay Crs *HTON* BD9 ....104 A2
Shay Dr *HTON* BD9 ....104 A2
Shayfield La *EARD/LOFT* WF3 ....154 F3
Shay Fold *HTON* BD9 ....104 A2
Shay Gap Rd *HWTH* BD22 * 56 E7
Shay Ga *WIL/AL* BD15 * 105 G2
Shay Gra *HTON* BD9 ....104 A1
Shay La *HOLM/MEL* HD9 ....253 G3
  HOR/CROF WF4 ....199 M6
  HTON BD9 ....104 A2
  LUD/ILL HX2 ....146 C2
  WIL/AL BD15 ....103 G2
Shay St *LDSU* LS3 ....6 B3
Shay Syke *HFAX* HX1 ....11 J8
Sheaf Ct *BSLY* S70 ....261 M7
Sheaf St *MID* LS10 ....9 J3
Shearbridge Gn *GTHN* BD7 ....4 B9
Shearbridge Rd *GTHN* BD7 ....4 A7
Shearbridge Ter *GTHN* BD7 ....4 B9
Shearing Cross Gdns *HUD* 15 G1
Shed St *KGHY* BD21 ....3 G4
Sheep Hill La *CUL/QBY* BD13 ....125 K4
Sheepridge Gv *HUDN* HD2 ....192 E3
Sheepridge Rd *HUDN* HD2 ....192 E3
Sheepscar Gv *CHAL* LS7 ....7 J2
Sheepscar St North *CHAL* LS7 ....7 H2
Sheepscar St South *CHAL* LS7 ....7 K5
Sheepscar Wy *CHAL* LS7 ....7 J1
Sheep St *SKP/WHF* BD23 ....16 B2
Sheepwalk La *CAS* WF10 ....158 F8
  HEM/SK/SE WF9 ....226 A6
Sheerien Cl *BSLYN/ROY* S71 ....243 G6
Sheffield Rd *BSLY* S70 ....261 H6
  HOLM/MEL HD9 ....255 G1
  STKB/PEN S36 ....271 H4
Sheila Henry Dr *WBSY* BD6 ....125 L5
Sheldon Rdg *BOW* BD4 ....127 K7
Sheldrake Av *GIR* BD8 ....103 L7
Sheldrake Rd *CAS* WF10 ....157 M8
Shelf Hall La *HIPP* HX3 ....147 K1
Shelfield La *BRFD/BLYE* BD7 ....74 A7
Shelf Moor Rd *HIPP* HX3 ....125 L7
Shelf Moor Rd *HIPP* HX3 ....125 L7
Shelldrake Dr *MID* LS10 ....153 M1
Shelley Av *HECK* WF16 * 173 G4
Shelley Cl *RTHW* LS26 ....155 L5
Shelley Dr *BSLYN/ROY* S71 ....261 K3
  KNOT WF11 ....181 K2
Shelley Gv *GIR* BD8 ....104 A6
Shelley La *KBTN* HD8 ....238 C1
Shelley Woodhouse La
  KBTN HD8 ....238 F4
Shelton Ct *CUL/QBY* BD13 ....102 A5
Shepcote Crs *BHP/TINH* LS16 ....86 B5
Shepcote Ter *BSLY* S70 * 261 M6
Shepherds Gv *HUDN* HD2 ....193 G3
  RHAY LS8 ....7 M1
Shepherd's La *CHAL* LS7 ....110 A2
  RHAY LS8 ....7 M1
Shepherd's Pl *RHAY* LS8 * 7 M1
Shepherds Thorn La
  HUDN HD2 ....170 B8
Shepherds St *WHIT* OL12 * 206 B6
Shepherds Wy *MILN* OL16 ....229 G1
Shepley Mt *MIRF* WF14 ....172 D7
Shepley Rd *HUDS* HD4 ....237 L4

Shepley St *WKFDE* WF1 ....13 J2
Shepstye Rd *HOR/CROF* WF4 ....197 J6
Sherborne Dr *HWTH* BD22 ....79 G1
Sherborne Rd *GTHN* BD7 ....4 C7
  IDLE BD10 ....83 K5
Sherbourne Dr *HDGY* LS6 ....87 G5
Sherbrooke Av
  MSTN/BAR LS15 ....111 H7
Sherburn Cl *SCFT* LS14 ....89 J3
Sherburn Dr *AWLS/ASK* DN6 ....249 G4
  BIRK/DRI BD11 ....128 D8
Sherburn Ct *SCFT* LS14 ....89 J3
Sherburn Gv *BIRK/DRI* BD11 ....128 D8
Sherburn Pl *SCFT* LS14 ....89 J3
Sherburn Rd *BRIG* HD6 ....169 M6
  BSLYN/ROY S71 ....243 G7
  SCFT LS14 ....89 J3
Sherburn Rd North *SCFT* LS14 ....89 K6
Sheridan Cl *PDSY/CALV* LS28 ....107 H8
Sheridan Ct *BSLYN/ROY* S71 ....261 K3
  PDSY/CALV LS28 * 107 H8
Sheridan St *BOW* BD4 ....127 J2
  WKFDE WF1 ....176 F1
Sheriff La *BGLY* BD16 ....81 L2
Sheriff St *WHIT* OL12 ....206 M6
Sherwell Gv *WIL/AL* BD15 ....103 L5
Sherwell Ri *WIL/AL* BD15 ....103 L5
Sherwood Av *CLECK* BD19 ....150 D6
  HUDN HD2 ....193 H1
Sherwood Cl *AWLS/ASK* DN6 ....249 J2
  BGLY BD16 ....81 L1
  CLECK BD19 * 150 D6
  DEWS WF13 ....173 H5
Sherwood Dr *AWLS/ASK* DN6 ....249 G4
Sherwood Gdns
  EARD/LOFT WF3 * 154 D4
Sherwood Gn *EARD/LOFT* WF3 ....154 D4
  WKFDW/WTN WF2 ....197 M2
Sherwood Pl *ECHL* BD2 ....105 K4
Sherwood Rd *BRIG* HD6 ....170 E4
Sherwood St *BSLYN/ROY* S71 ....261 H5
Sherwood Wy *CUD/GR* S72 ....244 D5
  ROY/SHW OL2 ....229 G6
Shetcliffe La *BOW* BD4 ....127 M5
Shetcliffe Rd *BOW* BD4 ....127 K6
Shetland Cl *ECHL* BD2 ....105 H2
Shibden Br *BTLY* WF17 ....151 G8
Shibden Garth *HIPP* HX3 ....147 H5
Shibden Grange Dr *HIPP* HX3 ....147 H5
Shibden Hall Cft *HIPP* HX3 ....147 H6
Shibden Hall Rd *HIPP* HX3 ....147 H6
Shibden Head La *CUL/QBY* BD13 ....124 E2
Shibden Vw *CUL/QBY* BD13 ....124 F7
Shield Cl *MSTN/BAR* LS15 ....112 A3
Shield Hall La *RPDN/SBR* HX6 ....166 E2
Shill Bank Av *MIRF* WF14 ....172 E1
Shill Bank La *MIRF* WF14 ....172 E1
Shillbank Vw *MIRF* WF14 ....172 E1
Shilling St *WKFDE* WF1 ....176 F7
Shinwell Dr *HEM/SK/SE* WF9 ....225 M6
Shipley Airedale Rd *BFDE* BD3 ....5 L5
Shipley Fields Rd *SHPY* BD18 ....104 F4
Ship St *BRIG* HD6 ....170 C4
Shipton Ms *MOR* LS27 ....152 D3
Ship Yd *WKFDE* WF1 * 13 G4
Shirburn *ROCH* OL11 * 206 A8
Shire Gv *MOR* LS27 ....152 C5
Shire Oak Rd *HDGY* LS6 ....109 G1
Shire Oak St *HDGY* LS6 ....108 F1
Shire Rd *MOR* LS27 ....152 D5
Shires Gv *EARD/LOFT* WF3 ....177 H1
Shire St *HUD* HD1 ....13 B9
Shirland Av *BSLYN/ROY* S71 ....243 J8
Shirley Av *BTLY* WF17 ....150 F4
  CLECK BD19 ....150 D6
  LM/WK BD12 ....148 G5
Shirley Crs *LM/WK* BD12 ....148 G5
Shirley Dr *BRAM* LS13 ....107 L2
Shirley Gv *CLECK* BD19 ....150 D6
Shirley Pl *CLECK* BD19 ....150 D6
  LM/WK BD12 ....148 G5
Shirley Mt *CLECK* BD19 ....150 D6
Shirley Pde *CLECK* BD19 ....150 D6
Shirley Rd *CLECK* BD19 ....150 D6
  GTHN BD7 ....104 D8
Shirley St *CLECK* BD19 ....150 D7
  SHPY BD18 ....83 K2
Shirley Ter *CLECK* BD19 ....150 D6
Shirley Wk *CLECK* BD19 ....150 D6
Shoebridge Av *AIRE* BD20 ....35 H8
Shoebroad La *TOD* OL14 ....163 K2
Shoe Market *PONT* WF8 ....180 E6
Sholebroke Av *CHAL* LS7 ....109 M2
Sholebroke Mt *CHAL* LS7 ....109 L2
Sholebroke Pl *CHAL* LS7 ....109 M2
Sholebroke St *CHAL* LS7 ....109 M1
Sholebroke Ter *CHAL* LS7 ....109 M1
Sholebroke Vw *CHAL* LS7 ....109 M2
Shone Ct *MOR* LS27 ....152 D4
Shoolaboards La *PONT* WF8 ....181 H6
Shop La *EARD/LOFT* WF3 ....154 D6
  HUDE HD5 ....193 L5
  HWTH BD22 ....54 D1
Shore Av *ROY/SHW* OL2 ....229 L5
Shore End La *HRBR* HX7 ....122 C7
Shorefield Cl *MILN* OL16 ....207 H7
Shore Fold *LIT* OL15 ....185 H8
Shore Gn *TOD* OL14 ....140 E4
Shore Hall La *STKB/PEN* S36 ....270 A4
Shoreham Rd *WOR/ARM* LS12 ....108 B8
Shore Hl *LIT* OL15 ....185 L8
Shore Lea *LIT* OL15 ....185 H8
Shore Mt *LIT* OL15 ....185 H8
Shore New Rd *TOD* OL14 ....140 D4
Shore St *MILN* OL16 ....228 D6
Shore St *HIPP* HX3 ....207 H8
Shortbank Cl *SKP/WHF* BD23 ....16 E5
Shortbank Rd *SKP/WHF* BD23 ....16 E5
Short Cl *LM/WK* BD12 ....148 D2
Shortfield Ct *BSLYN/ROY* S71 ....243 G6
Short La *CHAL* LS7 * 87 L7
Short St *EARL* WF12 ....174 C7
  FEA/AMT WF7 ....201 L1
Shortway *CUL/QBY* BD13 ....103 J3
  PDSY/CALV LS28 ....106 C5
Shottwood Fold *LIT* OL15 ....185 L8
Showfield Cl *GTHN* BD7 ....104 D7
Shrewsbury Ct *GFTH/SHER* LS25 ....115 M6
Shrewsbury Rd *STKB/PEN* S36 ....270 F4
Shrewsbury St *STKB/PEN* S36 ....270 F4
Shrike Cl *WBSY* BD6 ....125 L5
Shroggs Head Cl
  WMB/DAR S73 ....263 K8
Shroggs Rd *HFAX* HX1 ....10 B1
Shroggs Rd *HFAX* HX1 ....10 C1
Shroggs Vue Ter *HFAX* HX1 ....10 B1

Shuttocks Fold
  GFTH/SHER LS25 ....135 K3
Shutts La HX3 ....148 K4
The Shutt *HOR/CROF* WF4 ....197 K6
Sickleholme Ct *HUDN* HD2 ....193 D1
Sickle St *CLECK* BD19 ....150 A6
Sicklinghall Rd *WBY* LS22 ....47 K1
Sidcop Rd *CUD/GR* S72 ....244 D6
Siddal Gv *HIPP* HX3 ....168 F2
Siddal La *HIPP* HX3 ....168 F3
Siddal St *BEE/HOL* LS11 ....8 E4
  ROY/SHW OL2 ....229 K7
Siddal New Rd *HIPP* HX3 ....168 F2
Siddal St *HIPP* HX3 ....169 G3
Siddal Top La *HIPP* HX3 ....169 G3
Siddon Dr *HUDE* HD5 ....215 J3
Side Copse *OT* LS21 ....41 G6
Side La *HUDW* HD3 ....191 H8
Sides Rd *PONT* WF8 ....180 D5
Sidgwick Ct *SKP/WHF* BD23 ....16 E3
The Sidings *EARL* WF12 ....173 L8
  GSLY LS20 ....61 M5
  SHPY BD18 * 82 C6
Sidney St *LDS* LS1 ....7 H9
Siegen Cl *MOR* LS27 ....152 C2
Siena Cl *WMB/DAR* S73 ....263 G8
Siggett La *TOD* OL14 ....141 H8
Sigott St *HUDW* HD3 ....191 H8
Sike Cl *DOD/DAR* S75 ....241 L5
Sike La *HOLM/MEL* HD9 ....254 F1
  WKFDW/WTN WF2 ....221 K1
Sikes Cl *HUDE* HD5 ....215 H3
Silcoates Av *WKFDW/WTN* WF2 ....176 A6
Silcoates Ct *WKFDW/WTN* WF2 ....176 A6
Silcoates Dr *WKFDW/WTN* WF2 ....176 A5
Silcoates St *WKFDW/WTN* WF2 ....175 M5
Silcoates Wy *WKFDW/WTN* WF2 ....176 B2
Silk Mill Ap *BHP/TINH* LS16 ....86 A4
Silk Mill Bank *BHP/TINH* LS16 ....85 M4
Silk Mill Cl *BHP/TINH* LS16 ....85 M4
Silk Mill Dr *BHP/TINH* LS16 ....85 M4
Silk Mill Gdns *BHP/TINH* LS16 ....85 M4
Silk Mill Gn *BHP/TINH* LS16 ....85 M4
Silk Mill Ms *BHP/TINH* LS16 ....85 M4
Silk Mill Rd *BHP/TINH* LS16 ....85 L4
Silk Mill Wy *BHP/TINH* LS16 ....86 A4
Silkstone Cl *GFTH/SHER* LS25 ....113 K5
Silkstone Ct *MSTN/BAR* LS15 ....111 L5
Silkstone Crs *NORM* WF6 * 178 B2
  WKFDW/WTN WF2 ....198 B2
Silkstone La *DOD/DAR* S75 ....259 H4
Silkstone Wy *MSTN/BAR* LS15 ....111 L5
Silk St *HTON* BD9 ....104 C5
Silsden Br *AIRE* BD20 ....35 M7
Silsden House Gdns *AIRE* BD20 ....35 L5
Silsden Rd *AIRE* BD20 ....58 B2
  AIRE BD20 ....58 B2
  ILK LS29 ....18 D7
Silson La *BAIL* BD17 ....83 G2
Silver Birch Av *LM/WK* BD12 ....148 F4
Silver Birch Cl *LM/WK* BD12 ....148 F4
Silver Birch Dr *LM/WK* BD12 ....148 F4
Silver Birch Gv *LM/WK* BD12 ....148 F4
Silverdale Av *AIRE* BD20 ....58 A5
  AL/HA/HU LS17 ....88 C1
  GSLY LS20 ....62 A6
Silverdale Cl *GSLY* LS20 ....62 A7
Silverdale Dr *BSLYN/ROY* S71 ....261 J5
  GSLY LS20 ....62 A7
Silverdale Gra *GSLY* LS20 ....62 A7
Silverdale Gra *GSLY* LS20 ....61 M7
Silverdale Mt *GSLY* LS20 ....62 A7
Silverdale Rd *GSLY* LS20 ....61 M7
  WBOW BD5 ....127 G4
Silver Hl *MILN* OL16 ....207 H8
Silverhill Dr *BFDE* BD3 ....105 M6
Silverhill Rd *BFDE* BD3 ....105 L6
Silver La *YEA* LS19 ....59 J7
Silver Mill Hl *OT* LS21 ....41 K8
Silver Royd Av *WOR/ARM* LS12 ....108 B8
Silver Royd Cl *WOR/ARM* LS12 ....108 B8
Silver Royd Garth
  WOR/ARM LS12 ....108 B8
Silver Royd Gv *WOR/ARM* LS12 ....108 B8
Silver Royd Hl *WOR/ARM* LS12 ....108 B8
Silver Royd Pl *WOR/ARM* LS12 ....108 B8
Silver Royd Rd *WOR/ARM* LS12 ....108 B8
Silver Royd St *WOR/ARM* LS12 ....108 B8
Silver Royd Ter *WOR/ARM* LS12 ....108 B8
Silverstone Av *CUD/GR* S72 ....244 E7
Silver St *BEE/HOL* LS11 ....8 B1
  BSLY S70 ....261 G6
  DOD/DAR S75 ....260 B3
  GIR BD8 ....104 D5
  HFAX HX1 ....11 G5
  HUD HD1 ....15 M8
  KNOT WF11 ....159 J4
  TOD OL14 ....163 J7
  WKFDE WF1 ....12 E5
Silver St East *HUD* HD1 ....15 K8
Silver St West *HUD* HD1 ....15 J8
Silverwood Ct *LUD/ILL* HX2 ....145 K5
Silverwood Wy
  HEM/SK/SE WF9 ....223 M4
Silwood Dr *ECHL* BD2 ....105 L3
Simbach Cl *SKP/WHF* BD23 ....16 D3
Simeon St *TOD* OL14 ....163 J6
Simes St *BFD* BD1 ....4 D3
Simm Carr La *HIPP* HX3 ....146 F2
Simmonds La *HFAX* HX1 ....11 G7
Simmons Wy *RHAY* LS8 ....110 D3
Simms Dene *WIL/AL* BD15 ....103 J2
Simon Cl *BOW* BD4 ....128 B4
Simon Green Rd
  MAR/SLWT HD7 ....212 D3
Simon Gv *IDLE* BD10 ....83 L5
  WOR/ARM LS12 ....108 F7
Simpson Rd *HBR* HX7 ....143 M5
  HEM/SK/SE WF9 ....247 M2
Simpsons La *KNOT* WF11 ....181 M3
Simpson St *EARD/LOFT* WF3 ....154 A6
  HIPP HX3 ....146 D2
  KGHY BD21 ....3 H6
Sim Royd La *STKB/PEN* S36 ....257 M2
Sinclair Garth
  WKFDW/WTN WF2 ....199 G6
Sinclair Rd *ECHL* BD2 ....105 H1
Sinden Ms *IDLE* BD10 ....83 K4
Singleton St *BFD* BD1 ....5 G5
Sion Hl *HIPP* HX3 ....169 G3
Sir George Martin Dr
  BHP/TINH LS16 ....86 F1
Sir Isaac Holden Pl *GTHN* BD7 ....104 D7
Sir John's La *GFTH/SHER* LS25 ....115 M6
Sir Karl Cohen Sq
  WOR/ARM LS12 ....108 D7
Siskin Cl *MOR* LS27 ....152 D3
Siskin Dr *WBSY* BD6 ....125 L6
Sisley St *MOR* LS27 ....164 C2
Sissons Av *MID* LS10 ....153 K2
Sissons Dr *MID* LS10 ....153 K2
Sissons Gn *MID* LS10 ....153 K2
Sissons Gv *MID* LS10 ....153 K2

Sissons Mt *MID* LS10 ....153 J3
Sissons Pl *MID* LS10 ....153 K2
Sissons Rd *MID* LS10 ....153 J2
Sissons Rw *MID* LS10 ....153 K2
Sissons Ter *MID* LS10 ....153 K2
Sissons Vw *MID* LS10 ....153 J3
Sitka Cl *BSLYN/ROY* S71 ....243 K4
Siward St *HEM/SK/SE* WF9 ....247 G1
Sixroad La *AWLS/ASK* DN6 ....249 J1
Sixth Av *BFDE* BD3 ....105 L6
  LVSG WF15 ....171 K1
  RTHW LS26 ....133 J7
Sizers Ct *YEA* LS19 ....84 C1
Skelbrooke Dr *PONT* WF8 ....202 F1
Skelda Ri *ILK* LS29 ....38 D3
Skelf St *TAD* LS24 ....95 G5
Skellow Hall Gdns
  AWLS/ASK DN6 ....249 H5
Skellow Rd *AWLS/ASK* DN6 ....249 J5
  OSM LS9 ....110 D6
Skelton Crs *HUDS* HD4 ....213 K3
  OSM LS9 ....110 D6
Skelton Grange Rd *MID* LS10 ....132 D4
Skelton Mt *OSM* LS9 ....110 D6
Skelton Pl *OSM* LS9 ....110 D6
Skelton Rd *OSM* LS9 ....110 D6
Skelton St *COL* BB8 ....74 A1
Skelton La *MSTN/BAR* LS14 ....89 K5
Skelton St *COL* BB8 ....74 A1
Skelton Ter *OSM* LS9 ....110 D6
Skelton Wk *IDLE* BD10 ....83 M7
Skelwith Ap *SCFT* LS14 ....111 J4
Skibeden Ct *SKP/WHF* BD23 * 16 D1
Skinner La *GIR* BD8 ....104 E4
  LDSU LS2 ....7 K6
  PONT WF8 ....180 F5
Skinner St *LDS* LS1 ....6 C9
Skinpit La *STKB/PEN* S36 ....258 D8
Skipton Av *HUDN* HD2 ....192 D4
Skipton Old Rd *COL* BB8 ....52 A4
Skipton Ri *GFTH/SHER* LS25 ....113 K7
Skipton Rd *AIRE* BD20 ....34 B3
  AIRE BD20 ....57 H3
  COL BB8 ....74 D3
  ILK LS29 ....18 F5
  ILK LS29 ....37 M1
  KGHY BD21 ....3 G1
  SKP/WHF BD23 ....16 G1
Skipton St *BTLY* WF17 ....173 L4
Skircoat Gn *HIPP* HX3 ....168 E4
Skircoat Green Rd *HIPP* HX3 ....168 E3
Skircoat Moor Cl *LUD/ILL* HX2 ....168 C2
Skircoat Moor Rd *LUD/ILL* HX2 ....168 C2
Skircoat Rd *HFAX* HX1 ....11 H9
Skirrow St *BGLY* BD16 ....81 K8
Skye Vw *RTHW* LS26 ....155 H1
Slack Bottom Rd *WBSY* BD6 ....126 C6
Slackcote La *UPML* OL3 ....230 E7
Slack Ga *WHIT* OL12 ....184 A6
Slack Gate La *UPML* OL3 ....230 F6
Slack House La *HBR* HX7 ....121 K8
Slack La *CUD/GR* S72 ....244 D1
  GTL/HWG HX4 ....190 D1
  HBR HX7 ....144 D2
  HOLM/MEL HD9 ....200 B6
  HOR/CROF WF4 ....200 B6
  HUDW HD3 ....190 D6
  HWTH BD22 ....78 D3
  RPDN/SBR HX6 ....166 B5
  UPML OL3 ....230 F8
  WBSY BD6 ....220 D2
Slacks La *MAR/SLWT* HD7 ....211 J6
  MAR/SLWT HD7 ....234 A1
  STK ST *MILN* OL16 ....206 C7
Slack Top La *HOLM/MEL* HD9 ....253 L5
Sladdin Rw *CUL/QBY* BD13 ....124 E6
Slade Cl *BSPA/BRAM* LS23 ....48 F5
Slade La *BRIG* HD6 ....170 B8
Sladen St *KGHY* BD21 ....3 G5
  WHIT OL12 ....206 M1
Slades La *HOLM/MEL* HD9 ....235 G2
Slades Rd *MAR/SLWT* HD7 ....212 D6
Slade Wk *BTLY* WF17 ....151 H5
Slaithburn Cl *MILN* OL16 ....229 H1
Slaithwaite Av *EARL* WF12 ....173 G4
Slaithwaite Cl *EARL* WF12 ....195 M2
Slaithwaite Ga *MAR/SLWT* HD7 ....212 C3
  HOLM/MEL HD9 ....234 D7
Slant Ga *KBTN* HD8 ....216 A7
  MAR/SLWT HD7 ....213 G4
  STKB/PEN S36 ....269 A2
Slant La *TOD* OL14 ....141 M8
Slater Av *HBR* HX7 ....143 J2
Slater Ing La *HBR* HX7 ....142 E1
Slaters Rd *PDSY/CALV* LS28 ....107 G5
Slates La *ILK* LS29 ....20 D7
Slaymaker La *HWTH* BD22 ....78 E3
Slead Av *BRIG* HD6 ....170 B1
Slead Ct *BRIG* HD6 ....170 B1
Slead Crs *BRIG* HD6 ....170 B1
Slead Gv *BRIG* HD6 ....170 B1
Slead Royd *BRIG* HD6 ....170 B2
Sledbrook Crs *STKB/PEN* S36 ....255 L8
Sledgate La *MAR/SLWT* HD7 ....234 A1
Sledge Ga *HUDW* HD3 ....211 H8
Sledmere Cft *SCFT* LS14 ....89 L8
Sledmere Garth *SCFT* LS14 ....89 L8
Sledmere Pl *SCFT* LS14 ....89 L8
Sledmere Sq *SCFT* LS14 ....89 L8
Sleep Hill La *HEM/SK/SE* WF9 ....226 A7
Sleights La *AL/HA/HU* LS17 ....45 K8
The Sleights *AL/HA/HU* LS17 ....43 M7
Sleningford Gv *SHPY* BD18 ....82 A6
Sleningford Rd *BGLY* BD16 ....81 H1
  SHPY BD18 ....82 A6
Slice La *TAD* LS24 ....72 D5
Slingsby Cl *IDLE* BD10 ....83 M6
Slipper La *MIRF* WF14 ....172 A6
Slippery Ford La *HWTH* BD22 ....55 K2
Slippy La *LUD/ILL* HX2 ....145 L1
Sloan Sq *GIR* BD8 ....104 D6
Slutwell La *PONT* WF8 ....180 D6
Smalewell Cl *PDSY/CALV* LS28 ....106 C5
Smalewell Dr *PDSY/CALV* LS28 ....106 C5
Smalewell Gdns *PDSY/CALV* LS28 ....106 C5
Smalewell Gn *PDSY/CALV* LS28 ....106 D5
Smalewell Rd *PDSY/CALV* LS28 ....106 B5
Smallbrook La *PDSY/CALV* LS28 ....106 B5
Small La *MAR/SLWT* HD7 ....212 F2
Small Lees Rd *RPDN/SBR* HX6 ....188 E5
Small Page Fold
  CUL/QBY BD13 * 125 G5
Smallpage Yd *WKFDE* WF1 ....12 F2
Small Shaw La *HBR* HX7 ....121 H5
Smallwood Gdns *EARL* WF12 ....174 C3
Smallwood Rd *EARL* WF12 ....174 C4
Smawell La *KNOT* WF11 ....182 A1
Smawthorne Av *CAS* WF10 ....157 M7
Smawthorne Gv *CAS* WF10 ....157 M7

Smawthorne La *CAS* WF10 ....157 M7
Smeatley's La *PONT* WF8..............205 G7
Smeaton Ap *MSTN/BAR* LS15 ......112 A3
Smeaton Gv *RTHW* LS26.............134 C4
Smeaton Rd *HEM/SK/SE* WF9.....225 M6
Smiddles La *WBOW* BD5..............126 E4
Smiddy Hl *BSPA/BRAM* LS23 ....49 J2
Smirthwaite St *WKFDE* WF1 ....176 E6
Smirthwaite Vw *NORM* WF6..........178 C5
Smith Av *WBSY* BD6 ....126 E6
Smith Crs *BRIG* HD6 ....170 A6
Smitherds St *KGHY* BD21 ....2 F7
Smithfield Av *HIPP* HX3 ....147 L6
Smith Hl *MILN* OL16......................207 H8
Smith House Crs *BRIG* HD6 ....170 B1
Smith House Gv *BRIG* HD6............170 C1
Smith House La *BRIG* HD6 ....170 C1
Smithies La *BSLYN/ROY* S71 ....261 G2
BTLY WF17 ....151 G6
LVSG WF15 ....172 E4
Smithies Moor Crs *BTLY* WF17 ....151 H6
Smithies Moor La *BTLY* WF17 ......151 G7
Smithies Moor Ri *BTLY* WF17 ....151 H6
Smithies St *BSLYN/ROY* S71..........261 G2
Smith La *HTON* BD9.......................104 A4
Smith Rd *DEWS* WF13....................173 H5
GTHN BD7 ....126 D3
Smiths Av *HUDW* HD3...................191 M7
Smithson Av *CAS* WF10 ....158 D8
Smithson St *RTHW* LS26...............155 H2
Smith's Ter *HIPP* HX3 ....146 C3
Smith St *BGLY* BD16 ....81 K8
BOW BD4 ....127 K6
CAS WF10 ....158 B5
CAS WF10 ....158 E3
GTHN BD7...4 C6
KGHY BD21 ....2 D3
LIT OL15..207 K1
LVSG WF15 ....172 D3
MILN OL16.....................................206 B7
Smithville *AIRE* BD20 ....58 B5
Smith Wk *HEM/SK/SE* WF9 ....247 J2
Smith Wy *OSS* WF5 ....175 G8
Smithwell La *HBR* HX7 ....143 G1
Smithybridge Rd *LIT* OL15............207 G2
Smithy Bridge Rd *LIT* OL15 ....207 J4
Smithy Brook La *EARL* WF12.........196 B5
Smithy Carr La *BRIG* HD6..............170 C2
Smithy Cl *HOR/CROF* WF4 ....200 B6
KBTN HD8 ....239 J5
Smithy Clough La
RPDN/SBR HX6 ....188 C3
Smithy Hl *CUL/QBY* BD13.............102 A8
KBTN HD8 ....257 H3
WBSY BD6.....................................126 E5
Smithy La *AL/HA/HU* LS17 ....67 L4
BHP/TINH LS16...............................64 A8
EARD/LOFT WF3...........................153 H6
GTL/HWG HX4..............................188 F7
HBR HX7 ....142 C1
HOLM/MEL HD9 ....253 L4
HOR/CROF WF4 ....218 B2
HUDE HD5.......................................15 K8
ILK LS29..21 K5
ILK LS29..40 A6
KBTN HD8 ....239 J5
TAD LS24 ....95 G1
WIL/AL BD15...................................80 E8
Smithy Mills La *BHP/TINH* LS16.......86 F4
Smithy Pde *EARL* WF12 ....196 B5
Smithy Place La
HOLM/MEL HD9 ....236 D4
Smithy St *HFAX* HX1 ....11 J5
Smithy Wk *EARL* WF12..................196 B5
Smithy Wood La
DOD/DAR S75...............................260 B8
Smyth St *WKFDE* WF1.....................12 D3
Snail La *HBR* HX7 ....143 K6
Snailsden Wy *DOD/DAR* S75 ....242 F6
Snaith Wood Dr *YEA* LS19 ....84 E5
Snaith Wood Ms *YEA* LS19.............84 E5
Snape Dr *GTHN* BD7 ....125 M4
Snapes Fold *HUDE* HD5 ....215 H2
Snape St *KGHY* BD21......................79 L2
Snapethorpe Crs
WKFDW/WTN WF2.........................197 M2
Snapethorpe Ga
WKFDW/WTN WF2.........................197 L2
Snapethorpe Rd
WKFDW/WTN WF2.........................197 M2
Snell Gv *COL* BB8 ....52 B8
Snelsins La *CLECK* BD19 ....149 L5
Snelsins Rd *CLECK* BD19...............149 L5
Snetterton Cl *CUD/GR* S72...........244 E7
Snittle Rd *HOLM/MEL* HD9...........254 D7
Snowden Ap *BRAM* LS13..............108 A3
Snowden Carr Rd *OT* LS21.............22 E5
Snowden Cl *BRAM* LS13...............107 M4
Snowden Crs *BRAM* LS13..............107 M4
Snowden Fold *BRAM* LS13............107 M4
Snowden Gv *BRAM* LS13 ....107 M4
Snowden Lawn *BRAM* LS13...........107 M4
Snowden Rd *SHPY* BD18 ....82 F8
Snowden Royd *BRAM* LS13...........107 M4
Snowden St *BFD* BD1 ....4 E4
Snowdens Wk *CLAY* BD14 ....125 M2
Snowden V *BRAM* LS13 ....107 M4
Snowdon Av *KNOT* WF11 ....181 L2
Snowdon St *BTLY* WF17...............173 K2
ROCH OL11 ....228 C4
Snowdrop Ms *WIL/AL* BD15...........103 K6
Snow Hill Cl *WKFDE* WF1 *...........176 C5
Snow Hill Ri *WKFDE* WF1 ....176 C5
Snow Hill Vw *WKFDE* WF1 *.........176 D6
Snug La *HOLM/MEL* HD9...............255 J5
Snydale Av *NORM* WF6 ....178 E5
Snydale Cl *NORM* WF6 ....178 E5
Snydale Ct *NORM* WF6.................178 E5
Snydale Gv *NORM* WF6 ....178 E5
Snydale Rd *CUD/GR* S72 ....244 D7
NORM WF6.....................................178 D4
Soaper House La *HIPP* HX3 ....147 L4
Soaper La *HIPP* HX3 ....125 M7
Society St *ROY/SHW* OL2 *...........229 K7
Sod House Gn *HIPP* HX3...............146 C3
Soho Gv *WKFDW/WTN* WF2 ....12 A3
Soho St *BFD* BD1 ....4 D6
HFAX HX1 ....10 B6
Solid *HUDS* HD4 ....214 B4
Solomon Hl *LUD/ILL* HX2 ....144 F5
Solway Rd *BTLY* WF17 ....174 B1
Somerdale Cl *BRAM* LS13 ....107 M5
Somerdale Gdns *BRAM* LS13.........107 M5
Somerdale Gv *BRAM* LS13 ....107 M5
Somerdale Wk *BRAM* LS13 ....107 M5
Somerset Av *BAIL* BD17 ....82 D2
BRIG HD6 ....170 D7
ROY/SHW OL2 ....229 H7
Somerset Crs *HUD* HD1 ....15 J8
Somerset Rd *HUD* HD1....................15 J8
PDSY/CALV LS28...........................107 G6
Somerset St *CUD/GR* S72.............244 D8
Somers Pl *LDS* LS1 *........................6 D9
Somers St *LDS* LS1..........................6 D9
Somerton Dr *BOW* BD4 ....127 M4
Somerville Av *SCFT* LS14 ....111 H4
WBSY BD6......................................126 D7
Somerville Dr *SCFT* LS14...............111 H4
Somerville Gn *SCFT* LS14 ....111 H4
Somerville Gv *SCFT* LS14 ....111 H3
Somerville Mt *SCFT* LS14 ....111 H4
Somerville Pk *WBSY* BD6 ....126 D7
Somerville Vw *SCFT* LS14..............111 H4
Sonning Rd *WIL/AL* BD15..............103 K6
Soothill La *BTLY* WF17 ....174 B1
Sorbus Wy *KBTN* HD8 ....216 A3
Sorrel Cl *PONT* WF8......................180 F7
Sorrel Dr *LIT* OL15 ....185 H8
Sorrell Wy *BAIL* BD17 ....83 H2
Sorrento Wy *WMB/DAR* S73 ....263 H8
Sorrin Cl *IDLE* BD10 ....83 J7
Sotheron Cft *PONT* WF8...............203 L1
Soureby Cross Wy *BOW* BD4.........128 B7
Sourhall Ct *TOD* OL14 ....140 F8
Sourhall Rd *TOD* OL14 ....162 F1
South Accommodation Rd
MID LS10..9 K5
Southampton St *BFDE* BD3.............5 H2
South Ap *BSPA/BRAM* LS23 ....69 H6
GFTH/SHER LS25 ....92 A4
TAD LS24 ....92 C3
South Av *CAS* WF10.......................157 H7
HEM/SK/SE WF9 ....247 G4
HOR/CROF WF4 ....197 L5
HUDS HD4.....................................213 H3
PONT WF8.....................................180 C7
South Baileygate *PONT* WF8.........181 G5
South Bank *AL/HA/HU* LS17.............46 E8
CUL/QBY BD13 ....125 H5
South Bank Rd *BTLY* WF17 ....151 J8
South Bolton *LUD/ILL* HX2...........123 M7
South Brook Ter *GTHN* BD7 * 4 D7
South Cliffe *CUL/QBY* BD13...........102 F8
Southcliffe *HIPP* HX3 ....11 M9
Southcliffe Dr *BAIL* BD17 ....82 D5
Southcliffe Wy *BAIL* BD17 ....82 E5
South Cl *BSLYN/ROY* S71 ....243 L4
GSLY LS20 ....61 K6
South Clough Head *LUD/ILL* HX2..145 J7
Southcote Pl *IDLE* BD10...................83 K6
Southcote St *PDSY/CALV* LS28 ....106 F4
South Crs *DOD/DAR* S75...............260 B7
South Cft *CUD/GR* S72 ....244 E3
KBTN HD8 ....257 H3
South Croft Av *BIRK/DRI* BD11 ...128 C8
South Croft Dr *BIRK/DRI* BD11 ...128 C7
South Croft Ga *BIRK/DRI* BD11 ...128 C8
South Cross Rd *HUDN* HD2 ....192 B4
Southdale Gdns *OSS* WF5 ....196 F1
Southdale Rd *OSS* WF5 ....196 F2
Southdown Cl *HTON* BD9...............104 A4
Southdown Rd *BAIL* BD17 ....82 D5
Southdowns Cl *ROY/SHW* OL2 .....229 H8
South Dr *BSLYN/ROY* S71 ....243 L4
GSLY LS20 ....61 K6
PDSY/CALV LS28............................106 F3
WKFDW/WTN WF2........................198 F5
South Drive Farm
AWLS/ASK DN6..............................249 J5
South Edge *AIRE* BD20 ....2 C3
SHPY BD18 ....82 A7
Southedge Cl *HIPP* HX3 ....147 L7
South End Av *BRAM* LS13 ....107 M5
South End Gv *BRAM* LS13 ....107 M5
South End Mt *BRAM* LS13 ....107 M5
South End Ter *BRAM* LS13 ....108 A5
Southern Rd *HUDS* HD4 ....213 J3
Southey Cl *LIT* OL15 ....207 H4
Southey St *SKP/WHF* BD23 ....16 C3
South Farm Crs *OSM* LS9..............110 E4
South Farm Rd *OSM* LS9 ....110 E4
Southfield *BHP/TINH* LS16..............64 B4
HBR HX7 ....143 H2
Southfield Av *AIRE* BD20 ....58 B4
AL/HA/HU LS17 ....88 A4
FEA/AMT WF7 ....201 K2
WBSY BD6......................................126 E6
Southfield Cl *HOR/CROF* WF4 ....197 K5
WKFDW/WTN WF2.........................176 A5
Southfield Ct *KBTN* HD8...............216 B7
Southfield Dr *AIRE* BD20 ....58 C4
AL/HA/HU LS17 ....88 A4
Southfield Fold
HOR/CROF WF4 ....197 K6
Southfield La *CLE* DN14................183 M3
GTHN BD7 ....126 C3
HOR/CROF WF4 ....197 K6
ILK LS29..19 H6
South Field La *RYKW* YO26 ....32 A3
Southfield Mt *AIRE* BD20 ....58 C4
WOR/ARM LS12 ....108 E7
Southfield Rd *BGLY* BD16 ....81 J5
CUD/GR S72 ....262 E2
HOR/CROF WF4 ....197 K6
HUDE HD5.....................................215 J2
ILK LS29..19 H6
ILK LS29..40 A5
KNOT WF11.....................................182 B3
WBOW BD5 ....126 E3
Southfield Sq *GIR* BD8 ....4 B2
Southfield St *WOR/ARM* LS12 ....108 E7
Southfields Vw
HOR/CROF WF4 ....218 F1
Southfield Ter *BIRK/DRI* BD11.......128 C8
HIPP HX3.......................................147 L5
ILK LS29 *.......................................19 H6
SKP/WHF BD23 ....16 B3
Southfield Wy *AIRE* BD20 ....58 C4
Southgate *BFD* BD1 ....4 E7
CUD/GR S72 ....223 G8
CUD/GR S72 ....244 F4
DOD/DAR S75................................260 E3
EARL WF12 ....173 L6
ELL HX5 ....169 H7
GSLY LS20 ....61 K7
HFAX HX1 ....11 H6
HOLM/MEL HD9 ....236 B2
HUD HD1 ....15 G6
PONT WF8......................................180 F6
RTHW LS26 ....133 L8
STKB/PEN S36 ....271 G4
WKFDE WF1 ....12 F3
South Gv *BRIG* HD6........................169 M1
SHPY BD18 ....81 M7
South Hawksworth St *ILK* LS29 ....38 D2
South Hill Cl *MID* LS10 ....132 B7
South Hill Cft *MID* LS10 * 132 B7
South Hill Dr *BGLY* BD16................81 K3
South Hill Gdns *MID* LS10.............132 B7
South Hill Ri *MID* LS10 ....132 B7
South Hill Wy *MID* LS10 ....132 B7
Southlands *BAIL* BD17 ....82 D5
HUDE HD5......................................193 K5
LUD/ILL HX2 ....124 B5
Southlands Av *AIRE* BD20 ....58 C5
AL/HA/HU LS17 ....87 L6
BGLY BD16 ....81 J5
CUL/QBY BD13 ....103 L8
YEA LS19 ....84 F4
Southlands Cl *GFTH/SHER* LS25 ..138 B3
HEM/SK/SE WF9 ....225 G4
Southlands Crs *AL/HA/HU* LS17 ....87 L6
Southlands Dr *AIRE* BD20 * 58 C5
AL/HA/HU LS17 ....87 L6
HUDN HD2 ....192 C3
Southlands Gv *AIRE* BD20 ....58 C5
BGLY BD16 ....81 H5
CUL/QBY BD13 ....103 K8
Southlands Gv West *AIRE* BD20 ....58 C4
Southlands Mt *AIRE* BD20 ....58 C5
Southlands Rd *AIRE* BD20 ....58 C4
South La *DOD/DAR* S75 ....258 D5
ELL HX5 ....191 H2
HIPP HX3.......................................125 K7
HOLM/MEL HD9 ....254 C1
HOR/CROF WF4 ....218 F2
South Lane Gdns *ELL* HX5 ....191 H1
South Lea *EARD/LOFT* WF3 * 153 H5
Southlea Av *HWTH* BD22 ....79 G4
Southlea Cl *LM/WK* BD12..............149 J1
South Lee *HORS* LS18 ....85 K5
Southleigh Av *BEE/HOL* LS11 ....131 J6
Southleigh Crs *BEE/HOL* LS11 ......131 J6
Southleigh Cft *BEE/HOL* LS11 ......131 K6
Southleigh Dr *BEE/HOL* LS11........131 J6
Southleigh Gdns *BEE/HOL* LS11 ..131 J6
Southleigh Gra *BEE/HOL* LS11.......131 K6
Southleigh Gv *BEE/HOL* LS11 ....131 J6
Southleigh Rd *BEE/HOL* LS11 ....131 J6
Southleigh Vw *BEE/HOL* LS11.......131 J6
South Md *BHP/TINH* LS16 ....64 B4
Southmere Av *GTHN* BD7 ....126 C3
Southmere Crs *GTHN* BD7 ....126 C3
Southmere Dr *GTHN* BD7..............126 C3
Southmere Gv *GTHN* BD7 ....126 C3
Southmere Ov *GTHN* BD7 ....126 B4
Southmere Rd *GTHN* BD7 ....126 C3
Southmere Ter *GTHN* BD7 ....126 C3
Southmoor La *KNOT* WF11 ....182 E4
Southmoor Rd *CUD/GR* S72 ....245 M4
South Mt *AL/HA/HU* LS17................46 D8
South Nelson St *MOR* LS27 ....152 D1
Southolme Cl *KSTL* LS5.................108 B1
Southowram Bank *HIPP* HX3 ....11 L6
South Pde *CLECK* BD19.................149 L6
ELL HX5 ....191 H1
GIR BD8..4 D2
GTL/HWG HX4...............................190 B3
HDGY LS6 ....108 F1
HFAX HX1 ....11 J8
ILK LS29..38 C2
LDS LS1 ....6 F9
MILN OL16.....................................206 B7
MOR LS27......................................152 D2
OSS WF5 ....197 J2
PDSY/CALV LS28...........................107 G8
WKFDE WF1 ....12 E3
South Parade Cl
PDSY/CALV LS28............................106 F8
South Pkwy *SCFT* LS14.................111 G3
South Park Wy
WKFDW/WTN WF2.........................176 B2
South Parkway Ap *OSM* LS9 ....111 G3
South Pl *DOD/DAR* S75................260 D3
South Point *MID* LS10 *...................9 L5
South Queen St *MOR* LS27 ....152 D3
South Rdg *GFTH/SHER* LS25 ....135 J5
South Rd *CUL/QBY* BD13 ....101 M1
DOD/DAR S75...............................260 B6
HTON BD9......................................104 E2
OSM LS9 ....132 E3
South Royd *HUDE* HD5 ....215 J2
South Royde Av *HIPP* HX3.............168 E3
Southroyd Ri *PDSY/CALV* LS28 ....129 G1
South Sq *CUL/QBY* BD13 ....102 F8
South St *BRIG* HD6 ....170 C3
BSLY S70 ....260 E5
CUL/QBY BD13 ....101 M6
CUL/QBY BD13 ....102 F7
DOD/DAR S75................................260 B8
EARL WF12 ....173 L6
HEM/SK/SE WF9 ....224 A8
HFAX HX1 ....10 F7
HOLM/MEL HD9 ....236 E8
HOR/CROF WF4 ....222 F5
HUD HD1 ....213 M1
HUDS HD4.....................................213 M8
KGHY BD21 ....79 K2
LM/WK BD12 ....149 J2
LVSG WF15 ....172 D2
MILN OL16.....................................206 C6
MIRF WF14 ....194 B3
MOR LS27......................................152 D2
NORM WF6 ....178 C7
OSS WF5 ....196 F2
WBOW BD5 ....126 E3
WKFDE WF1 ....13 H4
South Ter *OSS* WF5 ....197 G3
South Terrace Ct *MILN* OL16 ....228 C1
South Vw *AIRE* BD20 ....34 F6
AIRE BD20.......................................58 D5
BAIL BD17 ....82 E3
CAS WF10 ....158 E4
CAS WF10 ....180 A1
FEA/AMT WF7 ....179 M8
HIPP HX3.......................................169 J2
HOLM/MEL HD9 ....255 H3
HUD HD1 ....213 M1
HWTH BD22 ....78 E7
IDLE BD10 ....83 M7
ILK LS29..38 D3
ILK LS29..61 J3
PDSY/CALV LS28...........................106 E5
PDSY/CALV LS28...........................107 H7
RTHW LS26 ....132 F8
TAD LS24 ....51 J3
WBY LS22 ....30 A6
YEA LS19 ....62 B7
South View Cl *BOW* BD4 ....128 A7
YEA LS19 ....62 B7
South View Ct *HIPP* HX3 ....147 M8
South View Dr *BOW* BD4 ....128 B7
South View Gdns *PONT* WF8..........181 H6
South View Gv *CLECK* BD19 * 150 D6
South View Rd *BOW* BD4...............128 B7
MID LS10 ....132 A5
MILN OL16......................................207 G3
YEA LS19 ....62 B7
South View St *TOD* OL14 ....140 E5
South View Ter *AIRE* BD20...............35 M5
BAIL BD17 * 82 E3
HFAX HX1 ....10 B4
HOR/CROF WF4 ....217 G2
MILN OL16......................................206 D2
YEA LS19 ....62 E8
Southwaite La *SCFT* LS14..............111 H2
Southwaite Pl *SCFT* LS14..............111 H2
South Wk *BGLY* BD16 ....80 C5
South Wy *BOW* BD4 ....128 A7
SHPY BD18 ....81 M7
Southway *BGLY* BD16.......................81 L1
GSLY LS20 ....61 K6
HORS LS18 ....85 J3
HUDW HD3 ....191 L5
ILK LS29..38 F3
MIRF WF14 ....172 B7
Southwell Av *HUDW* HD3...............191 K7
Southwell La *HOR/CROF* WF4 ......197 J6
Southwell St *DOD/DAR* S75 ....260 F4
Southwood Av
HOLM/MEL HD9.............................236 D1
Southwood Cl *SCFT* LS14 ....111 L2
Southwood Crs *SCFT* LS14.............111 L2
Southwood Ga *MSTN/BAR* LS15 ..111 L2
Southwood Rd *SCFT* LS14 ....111 L2
Sovereign Cl *BTLY* WF17 ....151 H5
Sovereign Ct *AL/HA/HU* LS17 ....66 A8
Sovereign Gdns *NORM* WF6 ....178 C4
Sovereign Pk *BAIL* BD17...................83 G2
Sovereign Quay *LDS* LS1 * 9 H2
Sovereign St *HFAX* HX1 * 10 F6
LDS LS1 ....8 F2
Sovereign's Wy *EARL* WF12............195 K3
Sowden Buildings *ECHL* BD2 ....105 K4
Sowden Gra *CUL/QBY* BD13 ....102 F8
Sowden Rd *HTON* BD9 ....103 M3
Sowden St *GTHN* BD7 * 126 D3
Sowden's Yd *HDGY* LS6 *.................86 F8
Sowerby Croft La
RPDN/SBR HX6 ....167 K3
Sowerby La *LUD/ILL* HX2 ....144 D8
Sowerby New Rd
RPDN/SBR HX6 ....167 G3
Sowerby St *RPDN/SBR* HX6...........167 K3
Sowgate La *PONT* WF8..................181 J3
Sowood Av *OSS* WF5 ....197 G3
Sowood Ct *OSS* WF5.....................197 H3
Sowood Gdns *OSS* WF5.................197 H2
Sowood Gra *OSS* WF5 ....197 G3
Sowood La *EARL* WF12..................195 K7
OSS WF5 ....197 H3
Sowood St *BULY* LS4.....................108 E4
Sowood Vw *OSS* WF5...................197 H2
Soyland Town Rd
RPDN/SBR HX6 ....166 F8
Spa Bottom *HUDE* HD5 ....215 L1
Spa Croft Rd *OSS* WF5 ....197 J2
Spa Flds *MAR/SLWT* HD7 ....212 D5
Spa Gv *WKFDW/WTN* WF2 ....198 A3
Spaines Rd *HUDN* HD2 ....192 C5
Spa La *BGLY* BD16 ....81 J1
BSPA/BRAM LS23 ....49 G7
MAR/SLWT HD7 ....212 D5
OSS WF5 ....197 J3
Spa Ms *BSPA/BRAM* LS23 ....49 G7
Sparable La *WKFDE* WF1 ....13 J9
Sparkfields *DOD/DAR* S75 ....242 D6
Spark House La
RPDN/SBR HX6 ....167 L3
Spark La *DOD/DAR* S75.................242 D7
Sparks Rd *HUDW* HD3...................191 K7
Spark St *HUDW* HD3 ....191 G8
Sparrow Hl *MILN* OL16..................206 A7
Spartal La *GFTH/SHER* LS25.........136 A6
Spartan Rd *LM/WK* BD12...............148 F1
Sparthfield Av *ROCH* OL11 ....228 A1
Spartha La *HOLM/MEL* HD9...........253 K2
Spa St *BTLY* WF17 ....173 L1
OSS WF5 ....197 K2
Spawd Bone La *KNOT* WF11 ....182 A3
Spa Well Gv *CUD/GR* S72 ....245 J3
Speak Cl *WKFDE* WF1 ....177 H6
Speakers Ct *DEWS* WF13 ....173 K6
Spear Fir *AL/HA/HU* LS17 ....67 J4
Spearhead Wy *KGHY* BD21 ....3 H3
Speedwell Mt *HDGY* LS6..................6 F2
Speedwell Rd *CAS* WF10 ....157 G8
Speedwell St *HUD* HD1 * 213 M1
Speeton Av *GTHN* BD7 ....126 A4
Speeton Gv *GTHN* BD7 ....125 M4
Spen Ap *BHP/TINH* LS16.................86 B7
Spen Bank *BHP/TINH* LS16..............86 B7
CLECK BD19 ....150 B7
Spence La *WOR/ARM* LS12..............8 A3
Spenceley St *LDSU* LS2...................6 D4
Spencer Av *AIRE* BD20 ....36 A4
GTHN BD7 ....126 C1
MOR LS27......................................152 C4
Spencer Cl *AIRE* BD20.....................35 G7
Spencer La *HBR* HX7 ....143 J5
Spencer Mt *RHAY* LS8 ....7 M2
Spencer Pl *RHAY* LS8........................7 M3
Spencer Rd *GSLY* LS20 ....62 B6
GTHN BD7 ....126 B1
Spencer St *AIRE* BD20......................55 M1
BSLY S70 ....261 G6
KBTN HD8 ....239 J4
KGHY BD21 ....2 D4
MIRF WF14 ....194 C3
Spencer Wk *SKP/WHF* BD23 ....16 E3
Spen Cl *BOW* BD4 ....127 K7
Spen Common La *TAD* LS24.............70 A8
Spen Crs *BHP/TINH* LS16 ....86 B7
Spen Dr *BHP/TINH* LS16 ....86 C6
Spenfield Ct *LVSG* WF15...............172 C4
Spen Fold *LIT* OL15 ....207 J2
Spen Gdns *BHP/TINH* LS16.............86 D6
Speng La *RYKW* YO26 ....33 L7
Spen Gn *BHP/TINH* LS16.................86 B7
Spen La *CLECK* BD19 ....150 B6
HDGY LS6 ....86 C8
Spen Ms *BHP/TINH* LS16.................86 C7
Spennithorne Av
BHP/TINH LS16...............................86 C5
Spennithorne Dr
BHP/TINH LS16...............................86 C5
Spennithorne Rd
AWLS/ASK DN6..............................249 G4
Spen Rd *BHP/TINH* LS16..................86 D6
Spenser Ri *GSLY* LS20 ....62 B6
Spenser Rd *GSLY* LS20 ....62 B6
Spenslea Gv *MOR* LS27 ....152 C4
Spen Vale St *HECK* WF16 ....172 F3
Spen Valley Heritage Trail
BIRK/DRI BD11 ....128 A8
CLECK BD19 ....150 A4
Spen Valley Rd *DEWS* WF13 ....173 G8
Spen Vw *DEWS* WF13 ....173 H5
Spen View La *BOW* BD4 ....127 K7
Spen Wk *BHP/TINH* LS16 ....86 B7
Spenwood Rd *LIT* OL15 ....207 H1
Spey Cl *DOD/DAR* S75...................242 E7
Spibey Crs *RTHW* LS26 ....132 F7
Spibey La *RTHW* LS26 ....132 F7
Spicer House La *STKB/PEN* S36 ...256 D7
Spicer St *WBOW* BD5 * 126 E3
Spiers Garth *WBSY* BD6 ....126 F5
The Spindles *MID* LS10..................131 M6
Spindle St *LUD/ILL* HX2..................146 C1
Spinkfield Rd *HUDN* HD2 ....14 C3
Spink La *PONT* WF8.......................180 F5
Spinks Gdns *SCFT* LS14..................111 K2
Spink St *GIR* BD8 ....4 B4
Spink Well La *EARD/LOFT* WF3 ....153 H5
Spinkwell Rd *DEWS* WF13 ....173 L5
Spinners Cha *PDSY/CALV* LS28 ....107 G7
Spinners Ct *SKP/WHF* BD23.............16 C3
Spinners Gdns *WHIT* OL12 ....206 E2
Spinners Gn *WHIT* OL12 ....206 B4
The Spinners *HWTH* BD22 ....78 E8
Spinners Wy *CLECK* BD19..............149 H6
MIRF WF14 ....194 C3
Spinneyfield *HUDN* HD2................192 C3
Spinneyfield Ct *OSM* LS9 ....9 M2
Spinney Ri *BOW* BD4 ....128 B5
The Spinney *AL/HA/HU* LS17 ....88 A4
BRIG HD6 ....170 C1
HBR HX7 * 143 K4
IDLE BD10 ....84 C4
OSM LS9 ....9 M2
SKP/WHF BD23 ....17 M1
WBY LS22 ....29 M8
WKFDW/WTN WF2..........................199 G8
Spinning Mill Ct *SHPY* BD18...........82 A6
Spire Ct *HUD* HD1 ....14 A4
Spitalgap La *PONT* WF8.................181 K7
Spitfire Wy *GFTH/SHER* LS25........116 D7
Spittal Hardwick La *CAS* WF10 ....180 E1
Spittlerush La *PONT* WF8..............227 J2
Spofforth Hl *WBY* LS22...................29 L8
Spofforth La *PBR* HG3 ....28 A1
WBY LS22 ....29 J2
Spofforth Wk *GFTH/SHER* LS25 ..113 K7
Spokeshave Wy *MILN* OL16 ....206 E4
Spout Fold *WKFDW/WTN* WF2 .....175 M8
Spout Hl *BRIG* HD6 ....170 A8
Spout House La *BRIG* HD6............148 A8
Spring Av *KGHY* BD21 ....3 M7
MOR LS27.......................................129 L6
Spring Bank *HUD* HD1 * 14 D5
LUD/ILL HX2 ....145 G6
Springbank *YEA* LS19 ....84 C2
Springbank Av *MOR* LS27 ....129 L7
PDSY/CALV LS28............................107 G2
Springbank Cl *BSLYN/ROY* S71 ....243 L6
PDSY/CALV LS28............................107 G3
Spring Bank Crs *HDGY* LS6............109 G2
Springbank Crs
GFTH/SHER LS25 ....112 E8
HUD HD1 ....15 L1
MOR LS27.......................................129 L6
Spring Bank Cft
HOLM/MEL HD9 ....253 M2
Spring Bank Dr *LVSG* WF15 ....172 D4
Springbank Dr
PDSY/CALV LS28............................107 G3
Springbank Gv
PDSY/CALV LS28............................107 G3
Springbank Ms
HOLM/MEL HD9 * 236 D3
Spring Bank Pl *GIR* BD8 ....4 C1
Spring Bank Ri *KGHY* BD21 ....79 L2
Springbank Ri *PDSY/CALV* LS28....107 G3
Springbank Rd *HUD* HD1 ....15 L1
MOR LS27.......................................129 L6
PDSY/CALV LS28............................106 F3
Springcliffe *GIR* BD8 ....104 D5
Springcliffe St *GIR* BD8 ....104 D5
Spring Cl *BGLY* BD16 ....81 K4
GFTH/SHER LS25 ....113 J6
GFTH/SHER LS25 ....113 K8
HEM/SK/SE WF9 ....223 K4
KGHY BD21 ....3 M7
MOR LS27.......................................130 C7
Spring Close Av *OSM* LS9 ....9 M3
Spring Close Gdns *OSM* LS9.........110 B8
Spring Close St *OSM* LS9 ....9 M3
Spring Close Wk *OSM* LS9 ....110 B8
Spring Ct *WIL/AL* BD15 *...............103 J3
Spring Dl *HOLM/MEL* HD9 ....236 B1
Springdale Crs *IDLE* BD10 ....83 K6
Springdale St *HUD* HD1 ....214 B2
Spring Dr *KGHY* BD21 ....3 M7
Spring Edge North *HFAX* HX1 ....10 C9
Spring Edge South *HFAX* HX1 ......168 C1
Spring Edge West *HFAX* HX1.........168 B1
Spring End Rd *OSS* WF5 ....197 K3
Spring Farm *HOR/CROF* WF4 ....221 J8
Spring Farm La *BGLY* BD16 ....80 C5
Spring Farm Ms *WIL/AL* BD15 ....102 E1
Springfield *BSPA/BRAM* LS23 ....48 E6
BSPA/BRAM LS23.............................69 M1
HUDW HD3 ....190 D6
RPDN/SBR HX6 ....167 J3
Springfield Av *BTLY* WF17 ....173 K1
GTHN BD7 ....126 B1
HEM/SK/SE WF9 ....224 A8
HOLM/MEL HD9.............................236 B3
ILK LS29..38 E2
KBTN HD8 ....240 A4
LIT OL15..185 J7
MAR/SLWT HD7 ....212 A7
MOR LS27......................................130 C8
PONT WF8......................................181 G5
Springfield Cl *HORS* LS18 ....85 M5
KBTN HD8 ....240 A4
Springfield Ct *AIRE* BD20 ....2 C2
GFTH/SHER LS25 ....116 B5
Springfield Crs *MOR* LS27 ....130 C8
PONT WF8......................................227 G1
Springfield Dr *KBTN* HD8 ....256 C2
LVSG WF15 ....171 L1
Springfield Gdns *AIRE* BD20 ....2 D2
HORS LS18 ....85 M5
Springfield Gra
WKFDW/WTN WF2.........................175 M8
Springfield Gn *MID* LS10 *............132 A4
Springfield Gv *BGLY* BD16 ....81 H2
BRIG HD6 ....170 C2
Springfield La *BOW* BD4...............129 H5
KBTN HD8 ....216 A7
LVSG WF15 ....172 A1
MILN OL16.....................................206 F3
MOR LS27......................................130 C8
ROY/SHW OL2 ....228 E7
Springfield Mt
HEM/SK/SE WF9 ....247 G5
HORS LS18 ....85 M5
ILK LS29..19 H5
LDSU LS2 ....6 C6
WOR/ARM LS12 *..........................108 C7
Springfield Pk *MIRF* WF14............194 D1
Springfield Pl *BSLY* S70 ....260 F5
GFTH/SHER LS25 ....112 E8
GIR BD8...4 D3
MID LS10.......................................132 A4
Springfield Ri *HORS* LS18...............85 M5
RTHW LS26 ....155 H2
Springfield Rd *AIRE* BD20 ....2 C2
BAIL BD17 ....82 D2
CUD/GR S72 ....222 D8
ELL HX5 ....169 K7
GFTH/SHER LS25 ....116 B6
GSLY LS20 ....62 A6
GSLY LS20 ....62 B6
MOR LS27......................................130 C8
Springfields *DOD/DAR* S75 ....260 C2
KNOT WF11.....................................182 D3
SKP/WHF BD23 ....16 D2
Springfields Av *KNOT* WF11..........182 D2
Springfield St *BSLY* S70 ....260 E5
CUL/QBY BD13 ....103 G8
GIR BD8...4 B3
RTHW LS26 ....155 H2
Springfield Ter *CLECK* BD19..........149 H5
DEWS WF13 ....173 L5
GIR BD8 * 4 B3
GSLY LS20 ....62 A5
PDSY/CALV LS28...........................106 F5
Spring Gdns *AL/HA/HU* LS17 ....45 J7
BFD BD1 ....4 D3
BIRK/DRI BD11 ....129 H8
BRIG HD6 * 170 C2
BSLYN/ROY S71 ....261 L2
BTLY WF17 * 173 K1
HOLM/MEL HD9..............................254 A1
MOR LS27......................................130 E7
Spring Gardens La *AIRE* BD20 ....2 E1
Spring Gardens Mt *AIRE* BD20 ....2 E1
Spring Gardens Rd *HTON* BD9 ......104 C3
Spring Garden St
CUL/QBY BD13 ....125 G5
Spring Gv *COL* BB8 ....52 E8
HBR HX7 ....143 J2
HFAX HX1 ....146 A7
Spring Grove St *HUD* HD1 ....14 E8

Spring Grove Vw HDGY LS6 109 G4
Spring Grove Wk HDGY LS6 * 109 G4
Spring Hall Cl HIPP HX3 147 K1
Spring Hall Ct HFAX HX1 146 A6
Spring Hall Dr LUD/ILL HX2 146 A8
Spring Hall Gdns LUD/ILL HX2 146 A7
Spring Hall Gv LUD/ILL HX2 146 A7
Spring Hall La HFAX HX1 146 A8
Spring Hall Pl HFAX HX1 146 A7
Spring Head La MAR/SLWT HD7 233 H1
Spring Head Rd CUL/QBY BD13 103 G8
HWTH BD22 78 E6
Springhead Rd RTHW LS26 133 J8
Spring Hl BAIL BD17 82 B3
BHP/TINH LS16 87 G2
CHAL LS7 7 G1
SHPY BD18 83 G7
Springhill Av HOR/CROF WF4 200 C5
Springhill Cl WKFDE WF1 176 C1
Springhill Ct TAD LS24 71 M2
Springhill Dr HOR/CROF WF4 200 C5
Springhill Gv HOR/CROF WF4 200 C5
Springhill Mt HOR/CROF WF4 200 C6
Springhills WKFDE WF1 176 C1
Spring Hill Ter HDGY LS6 87 G8
Spring Holes La CUL/QBY BD13 102 E7
Springhurst Rd SHPY BD18 82 C7
Spring La BGLY BD16 59 M8
BSLYN/ROY S71 243 L6
BTLY WF17 151 K7
DOD/DAR S75 242 E2
GTL/HWG HX4 168 C7
HOLM/MEL HD9 253 M4
HOLM/MEL HD9 255 G1
HOR/CROF WF4 200 D7
PBR HG3 26 E2
PBR HG3 45 H2
RYKW YO26 33 K4
WBY LS22 48 E1
Springlodge Pl GIR BD8 4 D2
Springmead Dr
GFTH/SHER LS25 113 H8
Spring Mill La OSS WF5 175 H8
Spring Mill St WBOW BD5 127 G1
Spring Mill Wk MILN OL16 206 E4
Spring Mt KGHY BD21 3 M8
Spring Park Rd WIL/AL BD15 102 E1
Spring Pl GTHN BD7 4 B9
KGHY BD21 3 M8
Spring Ri KGHY BD21 3 M7
ROY/SHW OL2 229 J5
SKP/WHF BD23 17 M1
Spring Rd HDGY LS6 108 F2
Spring Rw BGLY BD16 80 D5
COL BB8 * 52 E8
KGHY BD21 2 F7
Springroyd Ter GIR BD8 104 B6
Spring Side Ri MAR/SLWT HD7 212 F1
Springs La BSPA/BRAM LS23 31 H8
ILK LS29 38 D2
Springs Pavement ILK LS29 * 38 D2
Springs Rd BAIL BD17 84 A1
HOLM/MEL HD9 252 D3
The Springs WKFDE WF1 12 F2
Springstone Av
HEM/SK/SE WF9 224 A7
OSS WF5 174 F7
Spring St BRIG HD6 170 C4
BSLY S70 261 G6
DEWS WF13 173 L5
HUD HD1 14 D7
IDLE BD10 83 K8
KGHY BD21 3 H2
LVSG WF15 172 D2
MAR/SLWT HD7 212 B6
MAR/SLWT HD7 233 H3
RPDN/SBR HX6 188 F2
TOD OL14 140 E5
Springswood Av SHPY BD18 82 C7
Springswood Pl SHPY BD18 82 C7
Springswood Rd SHPY BD18 82 C7
Spring Ter HIPP HX3 11 J4
KGHY BD21 3 M6
MILN OL16 * 229 K3
RPDN/SBR HX6 167 L4
Springvale Cl HOR/CROF WF4 200 D3
Springvale Gv STKB/PEN S36 271 G3
Springvale Ri HEM/SK/SE WF9 223 M6
Springvale Rd CUD/GR S72 263 H1
Spring Vale Rd
HEM/SK/SE WF9 246 E3
Spring Vale Ter LIT OL15 207 K1
Spring Va PDSY/CALV LS28 107 G5
Spring Valley Av BRAM LS13 107 L5
Spring Valley Cl BRAM LS13 107 L5
Spring Valley Crs BRAM LS13 107 L5
Spring Valley Cft BRAM LS13 107 L5
Spring Valley Dr BRAM LS13 107 L5
Spring Valley St LVSG WF15 172 C1
Spring Valley Vw BRAM LS13 107 L5
Spring Valley Wk BRAM LS13 107 L5
Spring Vw MOR LS27 129 M6
OSS WF5 175 H8
Spring Vls TOD OL14 140 D5
Springville Gdns
HEM/SK/SE WF9 225 K7
Spring Wy KGHY BD21 3 M7
Springwell Av RTHW LS26 134 C5
Springwell Cl HWTH BD22 54 F3
YEA LS19 62 E8
Springwell Ct BEE/HOL LS11 8 B3
EARD/LOFT WF3 153 G5
Springwell Dr WBOW BD5 127 G2
Springwell Rd RTHW LS26 134 C5
WOR/ARM LS12 8 B3
Springwell St BEE/HOL LS11 8 B3
Springwell Vw BEE/HOL LS11 8 C4
Spring Wood Av HIPP HX3 168 D4
Springwood Av HUD HD1 14 C8
WBOW BD5 127 H3
Spring Wood Dr HIPP HX3 168 D4
Spring Wood Gdns HIPP HX3 * 168 D5
WBOW BD5 127 H4
Springwood Gdns RHAY LS8 88 D8
Springwood Gv RHAY LS8 88 E8
Springwood Hall Gdns
HUD HD1 14 C8
Springwood Rd
HOLM/MEL HD9 236 E6
RHAY LS8 88 D8
YEA LS19 84 C3
Springwood Sq HUD HD1 * 14 E7
Springwood St HUD HD1 14 E8
Springwood Ter ECHL BD2 105 G4
Springwood Vw
STKB/PEN S36 271 H4
Sprinkwell Cl BFDE BD3 5 G2
Spruce Av BSLYN/ROY S71 243 K3
Spruce Ct WKFDW/WTN WF2 198 C4
Spruce Dr HUDS HD4 213 M8
Spruce Drive Ms HUDS HD4 213 M8
Spruce Hts BRIG HD6 148 C8
Spruce St KGHY BD21 3 J3
Sprutts La HBR HX7 121 K7
Spur Dr MSTN/BAR LS15 112 A3
Spurr Gv WKFDW/WTN WF2 199 K8
Spurrier's Av KNOT WF11 181 L3
Spurr St BTLY WF17 173 M2
Square Rd HFAX HX1 11 J6
TOD OL14 163 J6
Square St BOW BD4 127 J1
The Square BSLY S70 260 F6
BSPA/BRAM LS23 49 G7
CAS WF10 158 E7
CUD/GR S72 245 K8
GFTH/SHER LS25 135 J5
GIR BD8 103 L7
KBTN HD8 * 238 A6
KNOT WF11 159 L8
TAD LS24 72 A2
Squire Gn GIR BD8 104 B5
Squire La HTON BD9 104 B5
Squirrel Cl DEWS WF13 173 J3
Squirrel Ct HUDN HD2 191 L4
Squirrel Ditch HUDS HD4 214 E3
Squirrel Hall Dr DEWS WF13 173 H3
Squirrel La CUL/QBY BD13 124 D1
Squirrels Drey
HOR/CROF WF4 198 B7
Squirrel Wk DEWS WF13 173 H3
Squirrel Wy AL/HA/HU LS17 88 B2
Stable Fold LM/WK BD12 148 F4
Stableford Gdns HUDN HD2 191 M4
Stableford Mnr MAR/SLWT HD7 213 G1
Stable La HIPP HX3 10 E2
Stablers Wk NORM WF6 178 C2
Stables La BSPA/BRAM LS23 49 G7
The Stables WKFDW/WTN WF2 199 J7
Stacey Crs CUD/GR S72 245 H7
Stackgarth BRIG HD6 170 C6
Stackhills Rd TOD OL14 163 L1
Stacks La HBR HX7 166 B1
Stadium Rd WBSY BD6 126 F6
Stadium Wy BEE/HOL LS11 131 G3
HEM/SK/SE WF9 247 K1
HUDE HD5 15 J4
Stafford Av HIPP HX3 168 E2
Stafford Hill La HUDE HD5 193 L6
Stafford Pde HIPP HX3 168 E3
Stafford Rd HIPP HX3 168 E3
Stafford Sq HIPP HX3 168 F3
Stafford St BOW BD4 127 K2
CAS WF10 157 K6
MID LS10 9 L7
Stafford Ter
WKFDW/WTN WF2 176 B8
Stainbeck Av CHAL LS7 87 H8
Stainbeck Cnr CHAL LS7 87 L7
Stainbeck Gdns CHAL LS7 87 K8
WBSY BD6 125 M6
Stainbeck La CHAL LS7 87 J7
Stainbeck Rd CHAL LS7 87 J8
Stainbeck Wk CHAL LS7 87 K8
Stainborough Cl DOD/DAR S75 260 B8
Stainborough Rd
DOD/DAR S75 260 B8
Stainburn Av AL/HA/HU LS17 88 A5
CAS WF10 180 C1
Stainburn Cl OT LS21 42 C4
Stainburn Crs AL/HA/HU LS17 87 M5
Stainburn Dr AL/HA/HU LS17 87 M5
Stainburn Gdns AL/HA/HU LS17 88 A5
Stainburn La OT LS21 42 C4
Stainburn Mt AL/HA/HU LS17 88 A6
Stainburn Rd AL/HA/HU LS17 87 M6
Stainburn Ter AL/HA/HU LS17 87 M6
Stainburn Vw AL/HA/HU LS17 88 A5
Staincliffe Cl DEWS WF13 173 H6
Staincliffe Crs DEWS WF13 173 H4
Staincliffe Hall Rd BTLY WF17 173 H3
Staincliffe Mill Yd
DEWS WF13 * 173 J3
Staincliffe Rd DEWS WF13 173 H4
Staincross Common
DOD/DAR S75 242 D4
Stainecross Av HUDS HD4 213 L4
Staines Cft HUDE HD5 193 G8
Stainland Dean GTL/HWG HX4 189 M5
Stainland Rd GTL/HWG HX4 168 E8
GTL/HWG HX4 189 J2
GTL/HWG HX4 190 B3
HUDW HD3 190 C6
Stainley Cl DOD/DAR S75 260 D2
Stainmore Cl DOD/DAR S75 259 H6
SCFT LS14 111 J3
Stainmore Pl SCFT LS14 111 J3
Stainton Cl BSLYN/ROY S71 243 G8
WBSY BD6 126 A6
Stainton La EARD/LOFT WF3 154 F2
Stair Case La OT LS21 63 M1
Stairfoot Cl BHP/TINH LS16 86 F1
Stair Foot La BHP/TINH LS16 86 F1
Stairfoot Vw BHP/TINH LS16 86 F1
Staithe Av MID LS10 153 M1
Staithe Cl MID LS10 153 M1
Staithe Gdns MID LS10 153 M1
Staithgate La WBSY BD6 127 H6
Stake La Bank HOLM/MEL HD9 254 D1
Stallabrass St GIR BD8 4 B4
Stalley Royd La
HOLM/MEL HD9 255 H3
Stamford Av CAS WF10 157 J8
Stamford St BOW BD4 5 L9
MILN OL16 206 D8
Stamford Wy DOD/DAR S75 242 D4
Stammergate La WBY LS22 47 K4
Stamp Hill Cl ILK LS29 18 F6
Stanacre Pl BFDE BD3 5 H2
Stanage La HIPP HX3 125 L7
Stanbury Cl DOD/DAR S75 260 D3
Stancliffe Wy HUDE HD5 193 K5
Standale Av PDSY/CALV LS28 106 F6
Standale Crs PDSY/CALV LS28 106 F6
Standale Ri PDSY/CALV LS28 106 F6
Standard Dr HUDS HD4 213 K4
Standbridge Cl
WKFDW/WTN WF2 220 C1
Stand Bridge Garth
HOR/CROF WF4 198 B8
Standbridge La
WKFDW/WTN WF2 198 E7
Standedge Foot Rd
UPML OL3 231 M7
Standedge Trail
MAR/SLWT HD7 232 C5
UPML OL3 231 M7
Standhill Crs BSLYN/ROY S71 243 G7
Standiforth La HUDE HD5 193 G7
Standiforth Rd HUDE HD5 15 M7
Standish Crs HEM/SK/SE WF9 246 E2
Standroyd Dr COL BB8 74 C1
Standroyd Rd COL BB8 74 C1
Stanhall Av PDSY/CALV LS28 106 F5
Stanhope Av DOD/DAR S75 259 H1
HORS LS18 85 L4
Stanhope Cl HORS LS18 85 L4
Stanhope Dr HORS LS18 85 L6
Stanhope Gdns DOD/DAR S75 260 E3
EARD/LOFT WF3 154 A5
Stanhope Gv EARD/LOFT WF3 154 A5
Stanhope St BSLY S70 260 F5
KBTN HD8 239 M5
ROCH OL11 228 B1
Stanks Ap SCFT LS14 111 M2
Stanks Av SCFT LS14 111 M2
Stanks Cl SCFT LS14 112 A2
Stanks Cross SCFT LS14 111 M2
Stanks Dr SCFT LS14 89 L8
Stanks Gdns SCFT LS14 111 M1
Stanks Garth MSTN/BAR LS15 111 M2
Stanks Gn SCFT LS14 112 A2
Stanks Gv SCFT LS14 111 M2
Stanks La North SCFT LS14 89 L8
Stanks La South SCFT LS14 111 M2
Stanks Pde SCFT LS14 111 M2
Stanks Ri SCFT LS14 112 A2
Stanks Rd SCFT LS14 111 M2
Stanks Wy SCFT LS14 111 M2
Stanleigh Cft HBR HX7 143 J3
Stanley Av RHAY LS8 110 B4
Stanley Cottages NORM WF6 178 C4
Stanley Dr RHAY LS8 88 D4
Stanley Garth HECK WF16 * 173 G2
Stanley La GTL/HWG HX4 190 B3
LVSG WF15 172 C1
WKFDE WF1 176 F2
Stanley Pl BTLY WF17 173 M1
OSM LS9 110 C4
WHIT OL12 206 A6
Stanley Rd BSLY S70 262 A6
CHAL LS7 7 H2
ECHL BD2 104 F2
HFAX HX1 10 A8
HUDW HD3 191 J2
HWTH BD22 79 J2
LVSG WF15 172 C4
RHAY LS8 110 B4
WKFDE WF1 176 F7
Stanley St BGLY BD16 81 J3
BRIG HD6 170 D3
BSLY S70 260 F5
CAS WF10 158 A6
CLECK BD19 149 M6
CUD/GR S72 262 E1
FEA/AMT WF7 179 M7
HUDS HD4 214 A3
HWTH BD22 79 G6
IDLE BD10 83 K6
KGHY BD21 * 2 F3
RPDN/SBR HX6 167 L2
SHPY BD18 104 E1
WHIT OL12 206 A5
WKFDE WF1 13 H2
Stanley Ter OSM LS9 110 C4
WOR/ARM LS12 108 D7
Stanley Vw WOR/ARM LS12 108 E7
Stanmoor Dr EARD/LOFT WF3 155 G8
Stanmore Av BULY LS4 108 E3
Stanmore Crs BULY LS4 108 E3
Stanmore Gv BULY LS4 108 E3
Stanmore Hl BULY LS4 108 F3
Stanmore Mt BULY LS4 108 E3
Stanmore Pl BULY LS4 108 E3
GTHN BD7 126 C1
Stanmore Rd BULY LS4 108 E3
Stanmore St BULY LS4 108 E3
Stanmore Ter BULY LS4 108 E3
Stanmore Vw BULY LS4 108 E3
Stannard Well Dr
HOR/CROF WF4 197 K4
Stannard Well La
HOR/CROF WF4 197 K4
Stannary Pl HFAX HX1 10 F4
Stannery End La HBR HX7 144 B7
Stanneybrook Cl MILN OL16 206 D6
Stanney Cl MILN OL16 229 G1
Stanney Rd MILN OL16 206 D6
Stannigley Field Cl
BRAM LS13 107 J5
Stanningley Av LUD/ILL HX2 145 K1
Stanningley By-Pass
BRAM LS13 107 M6
PDSY/CALV LS28 106 E5
Stanningley Dr LUD/ILL HX2 145 K1
Stanningley Gv HECK WF16 172 F3
Stanningley Rd LUD/ILL HX2 145 K1
PDSY/CALV LS28 107 J4
WOR/ARM LS12 108 B5
Stansfield Cl CAS WF10 158 D5
HFAX HX1 10 D5
Stansfield Ct RPDN/SBR HX6 167 K3
Stansfield Dr CAS WF10 158 E6
Stansfield Hall LIT OL15 185 L5
Stansfield Hall Rd TOD OL14 141 K8
Stansfield Mill La
RPDN/SBR HX6 167 H5
Stansfield Rd CAS WF10 158 D6
TOD OL14 163 K1
Stansfield St TOD OL14 141 K8
Stan Va PONT WF8 205 G8
Stanwell Av HUDW HD3 191 M5
Stapper Gn WIL/AL BD15 80 D8
Starbeck Rd WKFDE WF1 177 G6
Starfield Av LIT OL15 207 H4
Starkey La AIRE BD20 34 F5
Starkie St KGHY BD21 2 F6
Star La BSLY S70 261 G5
Starmire HWTH BD22 54 D2
Starring La LIT OL15 207 G1
Starring Rd WHIT OL12 207 G1
Starring Wy LIT OL15 207 H1
Star St WBOW BD5 126 E3
Starwort Cl PONT WF8 180 F7
Station Ap HOLM/MEL HD9 236 D1
ILK LS29 40 A6
TOD OL14 163 K1
Station Av BRAM LS13 107 K4
Station Ct GSLY LS20 * 61 M5
KBTN HD8 240 B3
Station Crs WOR/ARM LS12 108 D7
Stationers Entry MILN OL16 206 B7
Station Est TAD LS24 * 71 L3
Station Flds GFTH/SHER LS25 113 H7
Station Gv AIRE BD20 34 F7
Station La BIRK/DRI BD11 128 D8
EARD/LOFT WF3 153 G5
EARD/LOFT WF3 153 M5
FEA/AMT WF7 201 L1
HUDS HD4 214 B6
KBTN HD8 238 B5
LVSG WF15 172 E4
MAR/SLWT HD7 212 F3
PONT WF8 180 F6
RTHW LS26 133 M7
SCFT LS14 68 B8
WBY LS22 47 K5
Station Mt BRAM LS13 107 L4
Station Pde KSTL LS5 108 C2
TOD OL14 140 C5
Station Pl BRAM LS13 107 L4
Station Rd AIRE BD20 34 F7
AIRE BD20 35 M8
AWLS/ASK DN6 205 J4
AWLS/ASK DN6 249 M6
BAIL BD17 61 K8
BAIL BD17 82 F3
BIRK/DRI BD11 129 G8
BRIG HD6 170 E4
BSLY S70 260 F4
BSLYN/ROY S71 243 L2
BSLYN/ROY S71 262 B1
BTLY WF17 173 M2
CAS WF10 157 L2
CAS WF10 157 M6
CLAY BD14 125 L2
CUL/QBY BD13 79 L8
CUL/QBY BD13 102 A6
CUL/QBY BD13 125 G5
DOD/DAR S75 242 A5
DOD/DAR S75 260 A7
EARL WF12 174 B8
EARL WF12 195 L1
FEA/AMT WF7 202 C7
GFTH/SHER LS25 135 H6
GSLY LS20 61 M5
GTL/HWG HX4 190 D2
HBR HX7 143 J4
HECK WF16 172 F3
HEM/SK/SE WF9 224 A7
HEM/SK/SE WF9 247 J3
HIPP HX3 147 L7
HIPP HX3 148 C4
HOLM/MEL HD9 235 G4
HOLM/MEL HD9 236 C1
HOLM/MEL HD9 254 C1
HOR/CROF WF4 222 C5
HORS LS18 85 L4
HUDN HD2 193 J1
HUDS HD4 237 L4
HWTH BD22 78 E7
HWTH BD22 78 F4
HWTH BD22 100 E4
ILK LS29 38 D2
ILK LS29 40 A6
ILK LS29 61 J2
KBTN HD8 215 L3
KBTN HD8 238 B5
KBTN HD8 239 J2
KNOT WF11 * 181 L1
LIT OL15 207 K1
LM/WK BD12 149 G1
LUD/ILL HX2 144 F7
MAR/SLWT HD7 212 B5
MAR/SLWT HD7 212 F2
MAR/SLWT HD7 233 H2
MILN OL16 229 H1
MIRF WF14 194 C2
MOR LS27 152 C1
MSTN/BAR LS15 90 B7
MSTN/BAR LS15 111 L4
NORM WF6 178 B3
OSS WF5 196 F1
OSS WF5 197 G2
OT LS21 41 J7
OT LS21 64 B1
PBR HG3 26 F2
ROCH OL11 206 B8
RPDN/SBR HX6 167 L3
RTHW LS26 156 E3
SHPY BD18 82 D6
TAD LS24 71 L3
TAD LS24 94 E8
TOD OL14 140 E5
WIL/AL BD15 102 B3
WOR/ARM LS12 108 D7
Station St HOLM/MEL HD9 234 F4
HUD HD1 14 F6
PDSY/CALV LS28 106 F8
WKFDE WF1 199 G4
Station Ter BRAM LS13 107 L4
CAS WF10 157 L2
Station to Station Wk LIT OL15 207 M7
MAR/SLWT HD7 231 L1
Station Vw AIRE BD20 56 F1
HWTH BD22 100 E3
MSTN/BAR LS15 111 L5
Station Wy WOR/ARM LS12 108 D7
Staups La HBR HX7 142 B4
HIPP HX3 147 H5
Staveley Cl ROY/SHW OL2 229 M8
Staveley Dr SHPY BD18 81 M7
Staveley Gv HWTH BD22 79 J3
Staveley Ms BGLY BD16 * 81 J2
Staveley Rd BGLY BD16 81 H2
GTHN BD7 104 D8
HWTH BD22 79 J3
SHPY BD18 81 M6
Staveley Wy HWTH BD22 79 J2
Stavely Ms BGLY BD16 * 81 J2
Staverton Gv CUL/QBY BD13 103 G7
Staverton St LUD/ILL HX2 146 A7
Stavordale WHIT OL12 * 206 A6
Staybrite Av BGLY BD16 81 J7
Staygate Gn WBSY BD6 127 G5
Staynton Crs HUDN HD2 193 H1
Stead Ga KBTN HD8 238 F4
Stead Hill Wy IDLE BD10 83 H5
Steadings Wy HWTH BD22 79 G1
Stead La HUDE HD5 193 K6
ILK LS29 39 K6
SCFT LS14 90 C1
Steadman St BFDE BD3 5 M7
Steadman Ter BFDE BD3 5 M7
Stead Rd BOW BD4 128 A6
Stead St HFAX HX1 * 10 F6
SHPY BD18 82 D6
Stead's Yd HORS LS18 85 L4
Steanard La MIRF WF14 194 E3
Steander OSM LS9 9 K2
Steele La GTL/HWG HX4 189 L5
Steeplands HUDN HD2 171 H8
Steep La HBR HX7 166 C2
STKB/PEN S36 271 H2
Steeple Av HOR/CROF WF4 217 G2
Steep Riding HOLM/MEL HD9 236 E3
Steeton Gv AIRE BD20 35 L8
Steeton Hall Gdns AIRE BD20 35 L8
Steeton Wy GFTH/SHER LS25 137 L3
Steincroft Rd GFTH/SHER LS25 138 B3
Stella Gdns PONT WF8 181 H4
Stell Hl HWTH BD22 78 F1
Stennard Island WKFDE WF1 13 H5
Stephen Cl HIPP HX3 147 J5
Stephen Crs ECHL BD2 105 G3
Stephen Rd GTHN BD7 126 B4
Stephenson Cl EARL WF12 174 A5
Stephenson Dr
WOR/ARM LS12 129 M3
Stephenson Rd WIL/AL BD15 102 F4
Stephenson St GTHN BD7 126 D3
Stephenson Wy
WKFDW/WTN WF2 176 B1
WOR/ARM LS12 129 M3
Stepping Stones AIRE BD20 59 G6
Steps La RPDN/SBR HX6 167 L1
Steps Meadow WHIT OL12 206 E2
Sterling Ct EARD/LOFT WF3 153 G4
Sterling Wy EARD/LOFT WF3 152 F4
Sterne Hl LUD/ILL HX2 168 B2
Stevenson Av CAS WF10 180 E1
Stevenson Dr DOD/DAR S75 260 A2
Stewart Cl ECHL BD2 105 L1
MSTN/BAR LS15 111 L7
Stewart Pl BEE/HOL LS11 * 8 D9
Stewart Royd HECK WF16 * 173 G2
Stewart St HWTH BD22 79 G6
MILN OL16 229 K3
Sticker La BOW BD4 127 L3
Stile Common Rd HUDS HD4 214 D3
Stile Hill Wy MSTN/BAR LS15 112 B7
Stilemoor Ri TOD OL14 141 J7
Stile Rd TOD OL14 141 J7
Stillwell Dr WKFDW/WTN WF2 199 G6
Stillwell Garth
WKFDW/WTN WF2 199 G6
Stillwell Gv WKFDW/WTN WF2 199 G6
Stirling Crs BOW BD4 128 A3
HORS LS18 85 J2
Stirling Rd ILK LS29 39 M5
Stirling St AIRE BD20 36 A4
HFAX HX1 10 E7
Stirling Wy GFTH/SHER LS25 113 K7
Stirrup Gv ECHL BD2 105 H2
Stirton St WBOW BD5 126 F3
Stithy St OSS WF5 174 E6
Stiups La MILN OL16 228 E2
Stock Cl WHIT OL12 206 A4
Stockeld La WBY LS22 28 F8
Stockeld Rd ILK LS29 38 C2
Stockeld Wy ILK LS29 38 C1
Stockerhead La
MAR/SLWT HD7 212 C6
Stock Gv MILN OL16 207 H7
Stockheld La MSTN/BAR LS15 90 B5
Stock Hey La TOD OL14 142 D8
Stockhill Fold IDLE BD10 83 M6
Stockhill Rd IDLE BD10 83 M7
Stockhill St DEWS WF13 173 J6
Stockingate HEM/SK/SE WF9 246 E4
Stockinger La ILK LS29 19 H6
Stocking La GFTH/SHER LS25 92 C8
GFTH/SHER LS25 138 E8
KNOT WF11 182 E2
SEL YO8 139 L5
Stock La LUD/ILL HX2 145 K8
Stocks Ap SCFT LS14 111 K2
Stocks Av HBR HX7 143 M6
Stocksbank Dr MIRF WF14 171 M8
Stocks Bank Rd MIRF WF14 171 M7
Stocks Crs HBR HX7 143 M6
Stocks Dr KBTN HD8 237 M6
Stocksfield Vw CUL/QBY BD13 125 K5
Stocks Gdns HBR HX7 143 M6
Stocks Hl BEE/HOL LS11 8 C5
ILK LS29 61 H2
WOR/ARM LS12 108 E6
Stocks Hill Cl AIRE BD20 * 58 F5
Stocks La BTLY WF17 173 L1
DOD/DAR S75 260 F4
HBR HX7 143 M6
HUDS HD4 237 K5
LUD/ILL HX2 145 G5
RPDN/SBR HX6 167 G3
WBSY BD6 125 K5
Stocksmoor Rd
HOR/CROF WF4 218 E4
Stocks Moor Rd HUDS HD4 237 K4
Stocks Ri SCFT LS14 111 K2
Stocks Rd SCFT LS14 111 K2
Stocks St CHAL LS7 7 G2
Stocks Wk HUDE HD5 215 H3
Stocks Wy KBTN HD8 237 M6
Stockton St LIT OL15 207 J1
Stockwell Dr BTLY WF17 151 M8
Stockwell Hl HUDS HD4 214 B6
Stod Fold LUD/ILL HX2 123 L6
Stoke St MILN OL16 206 D8
Stone Acre Hts
HOLM/MEL HD9 * 235 H5
Stone Arches WBOW BD5 127 G2
Stonebridge Ap
WOR/ARM LS12 * 108 A8
Stonebridge Av
WOR/ARM LS12 108 B8
Stonebridge Gv
WOR/ARM LS12 108 A8
Stonebridge La
WOR/ARM LS12 108 B8
Stonebridge Wk KBTN HD8 238 B5
Stone Brig Gn RTHW LS26 154 F2
Stone Brig La RTHW LS26 155 G2
Stonechat Ri MOR LS27 152 E2
Stonecliffe LUD/ILL HX2 168 C2
Stonecliffe Crs
WOR/ARM LS12 108 A8
Stonecliffe Dr HOR/CROF WF4 196 D7
WOR/ARM LS12 107 M8
Stonecliffe Garth
WOR/ARM LS12 108 A8
Stonecliffe Gv WOR/ARM LS12 107 M8
Stonecliffe Mt WOR/ARM LS12 108 A8
Stonecliffe Ter WOR/ARM LS12 107 M8
Stonecliffe Wy WOR/ARM LS12 129 M1
Stone Ct AIRE BD20 58 F6
CUD/GR S72 245 G1
Stonecroft EARD/LOFT WF3 177 G1
ECHL BD2 105 L2
Stonecroft Gdns KBTN HD8 238 A6
Stonecroft Mt LUD/ILL HX2 145 L8
Stonedale Cl OT LS21 43 G8
Stonedene HDGY LS6 87 H6
Stonedene Pk WBY LS22 30 A8
Stonefield SCFT LS14 67 M6
Stonefield Av HUDS HD4 213 K3
Stonefield Cl IDLE BD10 105 K1
Stonefield Pl BTLY WF17 151 H5
Stonefield Rd HUDS HD4 213 K3
Stonefield St CLECK BD19 149 J8
DEWS WF13 173 L5
MILN OL16 229 H1
Stonefleece Ct
HOLM/MEL HD9 236 B3
Stonegarth Cl CUD/GR S72 244 D8
Stonegate BGLY BD16 81 J1
CHAL LS7 7 H2
OSS WF5 197 G3
Stonegate Ap CHAL LS7 87 H8
Stonegate Cha CHAL LS7 87 H7
Stonegate Cl AL/HA/HU LS17 87 M3
Stonegate Crs CHAL LS7 87 J7
Stonegate Dr PONT WF8 180 E8
Stonegate Farm Cl CHAL LS7 87 H7
Stonegate Gdns CHAL LS7 87 H7
Stonegate Gn CHAL LS7 87 H8
Stonegate La CHAL LS7 87 H7
FEA/AMT WF7 224 A1
Stonegate Ms CHAL LS7 87 H8
Stonegate Pl CHAL LS7 * 87 H8
Stonegate Rd AL/HA/HU LS17 87 M4
IDLE BD10 83 L8
Stonegate Wk CHAL LS7 87 J8
Stone Gv AIRE BD20 56 E1
Stone Hall Rd ECHL BD2 105 K2
Stone Head La HWTH BD22 53 M2
Stone Hl BGLY BD16 81 K2
Stonehill Ri CUD/GR S72 244 D8
STKB/PEN S36 270 E5
Stonehouse Dr CUL/QBY BD13 124 E6
Stonehurst MSTN/BAR LS15 111 M2
Stonehurst Rd MIRF WF14 172 C8
Stonehyrst Av DEWS WF13 173 M5
Stone La HWTH BD22 100 D4
Stonelea GTL/HWG HX4 189 J1
Stonelea Cl DOD/DAR S75 259 H6
Stonelea Ct CHAL LS7 87 J7
HDGY LS6 108 F1
Stone Lea Gv
HEM/SK/SE WF9 * 247 J4
Stoneleigh CUL/QBY BD13 125 H5
Stoneleigh Av AL/HA/HU LS17 88 B2
Stoneleigh Cl AL/HA/HU LS17 88 B2
Stoneleigh Ct CLECK BD19 149 G5
KBTN HD8 238 C3
Stoneleigh Cft BSLY S70 * 261 H7
Stoneleigh La AL/HA/HU LS17 88 B3

Stonely Dr TOD OL14 ...163 J7
Stone Mill Ap HDGY LS6 ...87 G7
Stone Mill Ct HDGY LS6 ...87 G7
Stone Mill Wy HDGY LS6 ...87 G7
Stone Pits La MOR LS27 ...151 M1
Stoneroyd HOR/CROF WF4 ...217 G1
Stones Dr RPDN/SBR HX6 ...188 D4
Stones Hey Ga HBR HX7 ...120 E8
Stones La MAR/SLWT HD7 ...212 E6
  MAR/SLWT HD7 ...212 F3
  TOD OL14 ...163 G2
Stones Rd TOD OL14 ...163 H2
Stones Ter TOD OL14 * ...163 J4
Stone Ter BAIL BD17 ...83 C4
  BFD BD1 ...4 F5
  BSLN/ROY S71 ...261 G2
  WIL/AL BD15 ...103 J3
Stone Vls FEA/AMT WF7 * ...224 A1
  HDCY LS6 ...86 F8
Stone Wood La KBTN HD8 ...237 L5
Stoney Back La HUDS HD4 ...214 A6
Stoney Bank HOR/CROF WF4 * ...197 H5
Stoney Bank La
  HOLM/MEL HD9 ...236 F6
Stoney Bank St DEWS WF13 ...173 J8
Stoney Battery HIPP HX3 ...11 K9
Stoney Battery Rd
  HUDW HD3 ...213 M2
Stonebrook Cl
  HOR/CROF WF4 ...219 H6
Stoney Cft CLECK BD19 ...150 D7
Stoneycroft HORS LS18 ...85 K6
Stoneycroft La AIRE BD20 ...57 K4
Stoney Cross St HUDS HD4 ...214 A4
Stoney Ford La HUDE HD5 ...193 K5
Stoney Hl BRIG HD6 ...170 C4
Stoneyhurst Sq BOW BD4 ...128 A3
Stoney La AL/HA/HU LS17 ...89 J1
  BTLY WF17 ...151 M8
  COL BB8 ...52 A5
  HIPP HX3 ...146 C3
  HIPP HX3 ...148 C7
  HOR/CROF WF4 ...220 B3
  HUDW HD3 ...191 H8
  ILK LS29 ...39 L8
  UPML OL3 ...230 F7
  WKFDW/WTN WF2 ...175 M1
Stoney Ridge Av WIL/AL BD15 ...103 K2
Stoney Ridge Rd BGLY BD16 ...103 L1
Stoney Ri HORS LS18 ...85 K6
Stoney Rock Ct OSM LS9 ...110 B5
Stoney Rock La OSM LS9 ...110 B5
Stoney Rock La OSM LS9 ...110 B5
Stoney Royd BSLN/ROY S71 ...243 G5
Stoney Royd La TOD OL14 ...141 M6
Stoney Royd Ter HIPP HX3 ...168 F2
Stoneys WIL/AL BD15 ...80 D8
Stoney St AIRE BD20 ...57 K4
Stoneythorpe HIPP HX3 ...85 K6
Stonie Heyes Av WHIT OL12 ...206 D4
Stony Croft La AWLS/ASK DN6 ...249 J2
  GTL/HWG HX4 ...189 K2
Stony Ga HOLM/MEL HD9 ...254 A4
Stony La ECHL BD2 ...105 L1
  GTL/HWG HX4 ...168 C4
  HBR HX7 ...142 F4
  HIPP HX3 ...169 L2
  HOLM/MEL HD9 ...236 B2
  RPDN/SBR HX6 ...188 F1
  TOD OL14 ...141 C5
  WIL/AL BD15 ...103 H4
Stony Royd PDSY/CALV LS28 ...106 C3
Stony Royd La HBR HX7 ...165 J2
Stoodley Cl TOD OL14 ...164 C1
Stoodley Gra TOD OL14 * ...164 C1
Stoodley La TOD OL14 ...142 C7
Stoodley Ter HUDW HX2 ...146 A8
Stopford Av LIT OL15 ...207 G2
  WKFDW/WTN WF2 ...199 G6
Stopford Garth
  WKFDW/WTN WF2 ...199 G6
Store St ROY/SHW OL2 ...229 L6
Storey Pl SCFT LS14 ...111 G5
Storey Stones BGLY BD16 ...81 M1
Storie Crs WKFDW/WTN WF2 ...198 A2
Stormer Hill La RPDN/SBR HX6 ...167 M4
Storr Hl LM/WK BD12 ...148 E2
Storr Hill Ter LM/WK BD12 ...148 E2
Storrs Av STKB/PEN S36 ...197 M2
Storrs La BSLN/ROY S71 ...263 G4
Storrs Mill La BSLN/ROY S71 ...263 G4
Storrs Wood Vw CUD/GR S72 ...262 F2
Storth Av HUDS HD4 ...213 H3
Storthes Hall La KBTN HD8 ...237 K1
Storth Pl HUDN HD2 ...14 C1
Storths Rd HUDN HD2 ...14 C1
Stottercliffe Rd STKB/PEN S36 ...270 E3
Stott Hl BFD BD1 ...5 C5
Stott Rd HDCY LS6 * ...109 G3
Stott St MILN OL16 ...206 F2
  MILN OL16 ...229 H2
  WHIT OL12 ...206 B5
  WOR/ARM LS12 ...108 F7
Stott Ter ECHL BD2 ...105 M2
Stourton St BGLY BD16 ...38 B1
Stowe Gv OSM LS9 ...110 E6
Stowell Mill St WBOW BD5 ...126 C4
Stradbroke Wy WOR/ARM LS12 ...108 E6
Stradmore Rd CUL/QBY BD13 ...101 M6
Strafford Av BSLY S70 ...261 J8
Strafford Rd DOD/DAR S75 ...241 L6
Strafford Wk IDLE BD10 ...84 A6
Straightacres La IDLE BD10 ...105 M1
Straight La AWLS/ASK DN6 ...248 D2
  ILK LS29 ...36 F1
  LUD/ILL HX2 ...145 M1
Strait La AL/HA/HU LS17 ...43 L2
Straits BAIL BD17 ...82 E2
Strauss St BTLY WF17 ...151 L8
Strands Ct HOR/CROF WF4 ...197 G8
The Strand ROCH OL11 ...228 B4
Strangford St IDLE BD10 ...83 M6
Stranglands La KNOT WF11 ...159 J3
Stratford Av BEE/HOL LS11 ...131 K3
  ROCH OL11 ...228 A1
Stratford Cl MAR/SLWT HD7 ...213 G1
Stratford Rd CTHN BD7 ...126 D1
Stratford St BEE/HOL LS11 ...131 L3
Stratford Ter BEE/HOL LS11 ...131 K3
Strathallan Dr BAIL BD17 ...82 F3
Stratheden Rd
  WKFDW/WTN WF2 ...12 B1
Strathmore Av OSM LS9 ...110 C4
Strathmore Dr BAIL BD17 ...82 D3
  OSM LS9 ...110 C4
Strathmore Gdns
  HEM/SK/SE WF9 ...247 G3
Strathmore Rd ILK LS29 ...39 G2
Strathmore St OSM LS9 ...110 C4
Strathmore Vw OSM LS9 ...110 C4
Stratton Cl BRIG HD6 ...170 D5
Stratton Pk BRIG HD6 ...170 D5
Stratton Rd BRIG HD6 ...170 D5
Stratton Vw BOW BD4 ...128 A2
Stratus Cl FEA/AMT WF7 ...224 A1
Strawberry Av
  GFTH/SHER LS25 ...113 G8
  LVSG WF15 ...172 C2

Strawberry Bank LVSG WF15 ...172 C2
Strawberry Flds KGHY BD21 ...3 G3
Strawberry Gdns
  BSLN/ROY S71 ...243 L2
Strawberry La WOR/ARM LS12 ...108 E7
Strawberry La WOR/ARM LS12 ...108 E7
Strawberry St AIRE BD20 ...35 M5
  KGHY BD21 ...3 G3
Straw Vw IDLE BD10 ...83 H6
Stream Head Rd
  CUL/QBY BD13 ...102 D4
Streamside HDGY LS6 ...87 G8
Streamside Fold HBR HX7 * ...144 A6
Street 1 BSPA/BRAM LS23 ...49 J6
Street 2 BSPA/BRAM LS23 ...49 K5
Street 3 BSPA/BRAM LS23 ...49 K5
Street 5 BSPA/BRAM LS23 ...49 K4
Street 6 BSPA/BRAM LS23 ...49 K3
Street 7 BSPA/BRAM LS23 ...49 K3
Street 8 BSPA/BRAM LS23 ...49 K3
Street Furlong La PONT WF8 ...181 K7
Street Hall HFAX HX1 ...7 J6
Street Head La HWTH BD22 ...78 A5
Street La AIRE BD20 ...58 D3
  MOR LS27 ...129 L8
The Street ILK LS29 ...18 F6
Strelley Rd BSLN/ROY S71 ...243 G6
Stretchgate La LUD/ILL HX2 ...146 A6
Stretton Av HDGY LS6 ...87 G5
Stretton Cl FEA/AMT WF7 ...179 J5
Stretton Rd BSLN/ROY S71 ...261 J1
Strickland Av AL/HA/HU LS17 ...89 H1
Strickland Cl AL/HA/HU LS17 ...89 H2
Strickland Crs AL/HA/HU LS17 ...89 H2
Strickland Rd HEM/SK/SE WF9 ...225 M6
Strikes La AIRE BD20 ...56 A3
Strines Moor Rd
  HOLM/MEL HD9 ...254 E7
Strines St TOD OL14 ...163 J7
Stringer Cl BOW BD4 ...127 K6
Stringer House La KBTN HD8 ...237 J7
Stringer La HOR/CROF WF4 ...197 K5
Strong Close Gv KGHY BD21 ...3 L4
Strong Close Rd KGHY BD21 ...3 L4
Strong Close Wy KGHY BD21 ...3 L4
Stuart Gv MAR/SLWT HD7 ...212 C6
Stuart Pl HUDN HD2 ...193 H1
Stuart Rd PONT WF8 ...180 E5
Stuart St CAS WF10 ...179 M8
  MILN OL16 ...206 D8
  PONT WF8 ...180 E5
Stubbin Fold HOLM/MEL HD9 ...253 J8
Stubbing Brink HBR HX7 ...143 G3
Stubbing Dr HBR HX7 ...143 G3
Stubbing Holme Rd HBR HX7 ...143 H3
Stubbing La GTL/HWG HX4 ...190 A1
  RPDN/SBR HX6 ...167 G6
Stubbings Cl HBR HX7 ...144 A6
Stubbings Ri BAIL BD17 ...82 B4
Stubbings St HBR HX7 ...144 A6
Stubbings Wy HBR HX7 ...82 E8
Stubbin La HOLM/MEL HD9 ...253 L3
  KBTN HD8 ...239 K8
Stubbs La MAR/SLWT HD7 ...233 K2
Stubbs La AWLS/ASK DN6 ...227 M1
  EARD/LOFT WF3 ...154 A7
  KNOT WF11 ...182 C7
Stubbs Br PONT WF8 ...227 J1
Stubham Ri ILK LS29 ...38 C1
Stubley Farm Rd HECK WF16 ...150 E8
Stubley Gdns LIT OL15 ...207 J1
Stubley Holme TOD OL14 ...140 C5
Stubley La LIT OL15 ...207 H2
  TOD OL14 ...140 C5
Stubley Mill Rd LIT OL15 ...207 G2
Stubley Rd HECK WF16 ...150 E8
Stubley St WKFDE WF1 * ...12 D3
Stubs Beck La CLECK BD19 ...149 L4
Stubsdol Vw SCFT LS14 ...111 J3
Studio Rd BVRD LS3 ...109 G5
Studley Av WBSY BD6 ...148 B7
Studley Cl AIRE BD20 ...58 F5
Studley Crs BGLY BD16 ...81 K3
Studley Rd ECHL BD2 ...105 H4
Stump Cross HIPP HX3 ...147 H5
Stumpcross Ct PONT WF8 ...181 J4
Stumpcross La PONT WF8 ...181 J3
Stumpcross Mdw PONT WF8 ...181 H4
Stumpcross PONT WF8 ...181 J3
Stunstead Rd COLK BB8 ...74 E3
Stunsteds Rd CLECK BD19 ...149 M6
Sturges Gv ECHL BD2 ...105 K4
Sturton Av GFTH/SHER LS25 ...113 J6
Sturton Grange La
  GFTH/SHER LS25 ...113 K7
Sturton La LUD/ILL HX2 ...124 A7
Sturton La GFTH/SHER LS25 ...113 J6
  LUD/ILL HX2 ...124 A8
Stutely Gv HUDN HD2 ...193 G1
Stutton Rd TAD LS24 ...71 M4
Styes La LUD/ILL HX2 ...166 F2
Stygate La AWLS/ASK DN6 ...227 L4
Sty La BGLY BD16 ...59 H8
Styveton Wy AIRE BD20 ...35 K8
Sude Hl HOLM/MEL HD9 ...237 H8
Sude Hill Ter HOLM/MEL HD9 ...237 H8
Sudforth La GLE DN14 ...183 J1
Sudlow St MILN OL16 ...206 D4
Suffield Crs MOR LS27 ...129 K6
Suffield Dr MOR LS27 ...129 K6
Suffield Rd MOR LS27 ...129 K6
Suffolk Av BTLY WF17 ...173 J3
Suffolk Ct YEA LS19 ...62 D7
Suffolk Pl ECHL BD2 ...105 K2
Suffolk St BTLY WF17 ...173 K2
  ROCH OL11 ...29 H2
Sufton St HUDN HD2 ...14 D1
Sugar Hill Cl RTHW LS26 ...155 L3
Sugar La EARL WF12 ...174 A6
  WKFDE WF1 ...13 J7
Sugar Well Ap CHAL LS7 ...109 J1
Sugar Well Ct CHAL LS7 * ...109 K2
Sugar Well Mt CHAL LS7 ...109 J1
Sugar Well Rd CHAL LS7 ...109 J1
Sugden Cl BRIG HD6 ...170 C6
Sugden St BFD BD1 ...4 B5
  LM/WK BD12 ...149 H2
Sulby Gv BSLY S70 ...261 M8
  IDLE BD10 ...84 A8
Sullivan Cl HUDS HD4 ...213 M3
Sullivan St HEM/SK/SE WF9 ...246 D5
Summerbank Cl BIRK/DRI BD11 ...129 H7
Summerbridge Cl BTLY WF17 ...151 J8
Summerbridge Crs
  CLECK BD19 ...150 D4
  IDLE BD10 ...105 M1
Summerbridge Dr IDLE BD10 ...105 M1
Summer Castle MILN OL16 * ...206 D7
Summerdale CLECK BD19 ...150 D4
Summerdale Rd CUD/GR S72 ...262 C4
Summerfield Av BRAM LS13 ...107 J3
  BRIG HD6 ...148 D8
Summerfield Cl BAIL BD17 ...82 C3

KNOT WF11 ...160 A6
Summerfield Dr BAIL BD17 ...82 D3
  BRAM LS13 ...107 J3
  KNOT WF11 ...159 M6
Summerfield Gdns BRAM LS13 ...107 J3
Summerfield Gn BAIL BD17 ...82 D3
  BRAM LS13 ...107 J3
  KBTN HD8 ...215 M4
Summerfield Pk BAIL BD17 ...82 D3
Summerfield Pl BRAM LS13 ...107 J3
Summerfield Rd BRAM LS13 ...107 H3
  IDLE BD10 ...83 L8
  TOD OL14 ...163 L8
Summergate Pl HFAX HX1 ...10 A8
Summergate St HFAX HX1 ...10 B9
Summerhall Ing LM/WK BD12 ...148 D2
Summerhill Av AIRE BD20 ...35 M8
Summerhill Dr AIRE BD20 ...35 M8
Summerhill Gdns RHAY LS8 ...88 D3
Summerhill Gv
  GFTH/SHER LS25 ...112 F8
Summerhill La AIRE BD20 ...35 M8
Summerhill Pl RHAY LS8 ...88 D3
Summerhill Rd
  GFTH/SHER LS25 ...112 F7
Summer Hill Rd RTHW LS26 ...156 F3
Summer Hill St GTHN BD7 ...126 C1
Summer Hill Vw UPML OL3 ...230 F7
Summerlands Gv WBOW BD5 ...127 J4
Summer La BSLN/ROY S71 ...243 K2
  DOD/DAR S75 ...260 E4
  KBTN HD8 ...217 M8
Summer Lea IDLE BD10 ...83 J6
Summerley Ct IDLE BD10 ...83 K7
Summer Meadow PONT WF8 * ...180 E7
Summer Rd BSLN/ROY S71 ...243 K2
Summerscale St HFAX HX1 * ...10 C4
Summerseat Pl GTHN BD7 ...126 D1
Summer St BSLY S70 ...260 F4
  HIPP HX3 ...10 B9
  HUD HD1 * ...214 B2
  HUDS HD4 ...213 M8
  MILN OL16 ...206 C7
Summervale HOLM/MEL HD9 ...236 C8
Summerville Rd GTHN BD7 ...4 B4
  PDSY/CALV LS28 ...106 E4
Summit St KGHY BD21 * ...2 F1
Sunbeam Av BEE/HOL LS11 ...131 K3
Sunbeam Gv BEE/HOL LS11 ...131 K3
Sunbeam Pl BEE/HOL LS11 ...131 K3
Sunbeam Ter BEE/HOL LS11 ...131 K3
  EARD/LOFT WF3 * ...153 G5
Sunbridge Rd BFD BD1 ...4 B4
Sunbury Gv HUDE HD5 ...193 G8
Sun Ct FEA/AMT WF7 ...179 L5
Sunderland Ct BRIG HD6 ...170 C3
Sunderland Rd AIRE BD20 ...34 F1
  HTON BD9 ...104 D4
Sunderland St HFAX HX1 ...10 F6
  HWTH BD22 ...79 H6
  KGHY BD21 ...2 F7
Sunderland Ter BSLY S70 ...261 J6
Sundown Av GTHN BD7 ...126 A2
Sun Fld PDSY/CALV LS28 ...106 C5
Sunfield Dr PDSY/CALV LS28 ...106 F4
Sunfield Gdns PDSY/CALV LS28 ...106 F4
Sunfield Pl PDSY/CALV LS28 ...106 F5
Sun Fold HFAX HX1 ...11 J8
Sunhill Cl MILN OL16 ...228 D4
Sun Hill Dr BAIL BD17 ...82 A3
Sunhurst Cl HWTH BD22 ...78 E3
Sunhurst Dr HWTH BD22 ...78 E3
Sun La HWTH BD22 ...78 E4
  ILK LS29 ...39 M5
  WKFDE WF1 ...13 G3
Sunmoor Dr SKP/WHF WF23 ...16 D2
Sunningdale GFTH/SHER LS25 ...114 B7
  GIR BD8 ...103 M6
Sunningdale Av AL/HA/HU LS17 ...87 J2
  DOD/DAR S75 ...242 C5
Sunningdale Crs
  CUL/QBY BD13 ...102 A1
Sunningdale Cft HUDN HD2 ...192 B3
Sunningdale Dr
  AL/HA/HU LS17 ...87 J2
  CUD/GR S72 ...244 E5
Sunningdale Gn
  AL/HA/HU LS17 ...87 J2
Sunningdale Rd HUDS HD4 ...213 M3
Sunningdales NORM WF6 ...178 F5
Sunny Av HEM/SK/SE WF9 ...225 J7
  HEM/SK/SE WF9 ...247 K4
Sunny Bank CHAL LS7 ...110 B1
  HBR HX7 ...144 A5
  HEM/SK/SE WF9 ...223 J2
  HOR/CROF WF4 ...222 C5
  KNOT WF11 ...182 D2
  MOR LS27 ...130 E6
  NORM WF6 ...178 C6
  SHPY BD18 ...82 D7
Sunny Bank Av BTLY WF17 ...151 M7
  HBR HX7 ...165 L2
  HIPP HX3 ...147 K8
Sunnybank La BFDE BD3 ...5 H1
  GTL/HWG HX4 ...168 C2
Sunny Bank Pde MIRF WF14 ...172 B6
Sunny Bank Rd AIRE BD20 ...170 B3
  BRIG HD6 ...170 B3
  BTLY WF17 ...151 M8
  DOD/DAR S75 ...259 H6
  HOLM/MEL HD9 ...234 E4
  LUD/ILL HX2 ...145 K1
  MAR/SLWT HD7 ...212 D4
  MIRF WF14 ...172 C6
  WBOW BD5 ...127 J3
Sunnybank Rd
  GFTH/SHER LS25 ...114 D8
  GTL/HWG HX4 ...168 C2
  HORS LS18 ...85 K7
  HUDW HD3 ...191 M6
Sunnybank St OSS WF5 ...196 F5
Sunny Bank Ter HIPP HX3 ...11 C2
  TOD OL14 ...140 D5
Sunny Bank Vw RHAY LS8 ...110 B1
Sunny Bank Wk MIRF WF14 ...172 C6
Sunnybank Woods BTLY WF17 ...151 M8
Sunnybrae Crs BGLY BD16 ...81 K4
Sunny Brow HUDS HD4 ...214 B6
Sunny Brow La HTON BD9 ...103 M4
Sunnycliffe AIRE BD20 ...58 F6

Sunnydale Av BRIG HD6 ...170 C6
Sunnydale Ct OT LS21 ...40 F8
Sunnydale Cft OSS WF5 * ...197 G1
Sunnydale Gv KGHY BD21 ...58 B8
Sunnydale Pk AIRE BD20 ...59 G5
  OSS WF5 ...197 G1
Sunnydale Rdg OT LS21 ...40 F8
Sunnydale Rd OSS WF5 ...197 G1
Sunnydale Ter OSS WF5 ...197 G1
Sunnydene SCFT LS14 ...111 H5
Sunnyfield EARD/LOFT WF3 ...153 L8
Sunnyfield Dr
  HEM/SK/SE WF9 ...223 J7
Sunny Heys Rd
  HOLM/MEL HD9 ...234 F3
Sunny Heys West
  HOLM/MEL HD9 ...234 F3
Sunny Hill WKFDW/WTN WF2 ...175 M5
Sunnyhill Av HUDE HD5 ...193 K4
Sunny Hill Av HWTH BD22 ...2 B8
Sunny Hill Cl
  WKFDW/WTN WF2 * ...176 A4
Sunnyhill Crs
  WKFDW/WTN WF2 ...175 M5
Sunnyhill Cft
  WKFDW/WTN WF2 * ...175 M5
Sunny Hill Gv HWTH BD22 ...2 B8
Sunny Lea MAR/SLWT HD7 * ...233 J2
Sunny Lea Ter WBSY BD6 * ...126 F8
Sunnylee Est OT LS21 * ...41 J6
Sunny Md HUDE HD5 ...193 J8
Sunnymead KBTN HD8 ...239 M4
Sunny Mt BGLY BD16 ...58 E7
  BGLY BD16 ...80 D5
  KGHY BD21 ...36 C3
Sunnymount HWTH BD22 ...56 F6
Sunnyridge Av PDSY/CALV LS28 ...106 D7
Sunnyside BRIG HD6 ...170 F6
  GTL/HWG HX4 ...190 B5
  HECK WF16 ...172 F3
  HUDW HD3 ...14 A3
  TOD OL14 ...163 J7
Sunnyside Av EARD/LOFT WF3 ...152 F6
  LVSG WF15 ...172 B4
Sunnyside La BFDE BD3 ...5 H1
Sunnyside Rd BRAM LS13 ...107 K5
Sunny Side St HIPP HX3 ...11 H1
Sunnyvale HEM/SK/SE WF9 * ...247 G3
Sunnyvale Av EARD/LOFT WF3 ...152 L7
Sunnyview Av BEE/HOL LS11 ...131 H5
Sunnyview Gdns BEE/HOL LS11 ...131 H5
Sunny View Crs HUDN HD2 ...192 F3
Sunnyview Ter BEE/HOL LS11 ...131 H5
Sunny View Ter CUL/QBY BD13 ...124 E6
Sunroyd Av HOR/CROF WF4 ...197 K4
Sunroyd Hl HOR/CROF WF4 ...197 K4
Sunset Av HDGY LS6 ...87 G6
Sunset Dr HDGY LS6 ...87 G6
  ILK LS29 ...38 F1
Sunset Hilltop HDGY LS6 ...87 G6
Sunset Mt HDGY LS6 ...87 G6
Sunset Rd HDGY LS6 ...87 G6
Sunset Ter ILK LS29 ...39 G1
Sunset Vw HDGY LS6 ...87 G6
Sunshine Ct WBSY BD6 ...126 B7
Sun St AIRE BD20 ...56 C1
  BFDE BD3 ...5 H4
  COL BB8 ...74 A1
  HWTH BD22 ...54 E3
  KGHY BD21 ...3 G6
  PDSY/CALV LS28 ...107 G5
  YEA LS19 ...62 E7
Sun Ter TOD OL14 * ...140 D5
Sun Vale Av TOD OL14 ...140 D5
Sun Wy HIPP HX3 ...169 H1
Sunways MIRF WF14 ...172 A7
Sun Wood Av HIPP HX3 ...147 K2
Surat Rd MAR/SLWT HD7 ...212 B4
Suresnes Rd KGHY BD21 ...2 C5
Surgery St HWTH BD22 ...78 E8
Surma Cl MILN OL16 ...228 D1
Surrey Av ROY/SHW OL2 ...229 H7
Surrey Cl BSLY S70 ...261 H7
Surrey Gv PDSY/CALV LS28 ...107 G6
  WBOW BD5 ...127 G2
Surrey Park Cl ROY/SHW OL2 * ...229 K6
Surrey Rd PDSY/CALV LS28 ...107 G6
Surrey St BTLY WF17 ...173 M1
  HFAX HX1 ...146 A3
  KGHY BD21 ...3 L2
  TOD OL14 ...141 K8
Sussex Av HORS LS18 ...85 L5
  MID LS10 ...132 B3
Sussex Cl HEM/SK/SE WF9 ...223 M6
Sussex Crs CAS WF10 ...159 G7
Sussex Gdns MID LS10 ...132 B3
Sussex Gn MID LS10 ...132 B3
Sussex Pl MID LS10 ...132 B3
Sussex St BTLY WF17 ...173 M1
  KGHY BD21 ...3 L2
  OSM LS9 ...9 M2
  ROCH OL11 * ...206 B8
Sutcliffe St LIT OL15 ...185 K8
  LUD/ILL HX2 ...146 A6
Sutcliffe Wood La HIPP HX3 ...147 L8
Sutherland Av RHAY LS8 ...88 C5
Sutherland Crs RHAY LS8 ...88 C5
Sutherland Dr HUDS HD4 ...213 L5
Sutherland Mt OSM LS9 ...110 C4
Sutherland Rd HIPP HX3 ...148 A6
  OSM LS9 ...110 C4
Sutherland St WOR/ARM LS12 * ...109 G8
Sutherland Ter OSM LS9 ...110 C4
Sutton Ap SCFT LS14 ...111 L8
Sutton Av BSLN/ROY S71 ...243 H6
  ECHL BD2 ...105 H1
  HUDE HD5 ...193 J6
Sutton Crs BOW BD4 ...128 A2
  SCFT LS14 ...111 G5
Sutton Dr CUL/QBY BD13 ...101 M1
Sutton Gv BOW BD4 ...128 A1
  MOR LS27 ...152 C3
Sutton La AIRE BD20 ...56 A1
  KNOT WF11 ...159 M7
Sutton Rd AWLS/ASK DN6 ...227 L6
  BOW BD4 ...128 A1
Sutton St WOR/ARM LS12 ...108 E8
Suzanne Crs HEM/SK/SE WF9 ...247 G5
Swadford St SKP/WHF WF23 ...16 B2
Swaindrod La LIT OL15 ...186 A7
Swaine Hill Crs YEA LS19 ...62 C7
Swaine Hill St YEA LS19 ...62 C7
Swaine Hill Ter YEA LS19 ...62 C7
Swain House Crs ECHL BD2 ...105 J1
Swain House Rd ECHL BD2 ...105 J1
Swain Mt ECHL BD2 ...105 J1
Swain St WHIT OL12 * ...206 A5
Swale Ap NORM WF6 ...178 F5
Swale Crs GFTH/SHER LS25 ...113 K6
Swales Moor Rd HIPP HX3 ...146 F1
Swales' Yd PONT WF8 ...180 E4
Swallow Av WOR/ARM LS12 ...108 C3
Swallow Cl AL/HA/HU LS17 ...88 B2
  DOD/DAR S75 ...242 F8
  OT LS21 ...42 F8
Swallow Crs WOR/ARM LS12 ...108 C3
Swallow Dr AL/HA/HU LS17 ...88 B2

OT LS21 ...42 F8
Swallow Fold GIR BD8 ...103 L7
Swallow Garth
  WKFDW/WTN WF2 ...220 F1
Swallow Gv HUDS HD4 ...214 A8
Swallow Hl BTLY WF17 ...151 J5
Swallow Hill Rd DOD/DAR S75 ...242 C7
Swallow La MAR/SLWT HD7 ...212 E1
Swallow Mt WOR/ARM LS12 ...108 C3
Swallow St HECK WF16 ...172 E3
  HUD HD1 ...14 E8
  KGHY BD21 ...3 J3
Swallow V MOR LS27 ...152 F2
Swan Av BGLY BD16 ...81 L3
Swan Bank Ct HOLM/MEL HD9 ...254 C2
Swan Bank La HIPP HX3 ...11 K9
Swan Ct ROY/SHW OL2 * ...229 K8
Swanee Rd BSLY S70 ...261 K8
Swanhill La PONT WF8 ...180 F7
Swan La HUDS HD4 ...214 A3
  WHIT OL12 ...190 D5
Swan V YEA LS19 ...4 D9
Swarcliffe Ap SCFT LS14 ...111 L2
Swarcliffe Av SCFT LS14 ...111 L2
Swarcliffe Bank SCFT LS14 ...111 L2
Swarcliffe Dr SCFT LS14 ...111 L2
Swarcliffe Dr East
  MSTN/BAR LS15 ...111 M2
Swarcliffe Gn SCFT LS14 ...111 M2
Swarcliffe Rd SCFT LS14 ...111 L1
Swarcliffe La AIRE BD20 ...111 L2
Swardale Gn SCFT LS14 ...111 L2
Swardale Rd SCFT LS14 ...111 L2
Swarland Gv WBOW BD5 ...127 G1
Swartha La AIRE BD20 ...36 C3
Sweeming La GFTH/SHER LS25 ...117 G3
Sweetbriar Cl ROY/SHW OL2 ...229 K7
Sweet Briar Cl WHIT OL12 ...206 A4
Sweet Briar La WHIT OL12 ...206 A4
Sweet St BEE/HOL LS11 ...8 F4
Sweet St West BEE/HOL LS11 ...8 D4
Swift Dr WBSY BD6 ...125 L5
Swift's Fold HOLM/MEL HD9 ...236 B1
  LVSG WF15 ...172 B4
Swift St DOD/DAR S75 ...260 E4
Swift Wy WKFDW/WTN WF2 ...220 E1
Swillington La RTHW LS26 ...134 B5
Swinburne Av YEA LS19 ...62 D7
Swincliffe Cl CLECK BD19 ...150 C2
Swincliffe Crs CLECK BD19 ...150 C3
Swincroft OSS WF5 ...197 G1
Swindon La PBR HC3 ...26 E6
Swindon Rd DEWS WF13 ...173 L6
Swinegate LDS LS1 ...9 J8
Swine La AIRE BD20 ...58 D6
  HOR/CROF WF4 ...201 G8
  HOR/CROF WF4 ...222 E3
Swine Lane Br AIRE BD20 ...58 D6
Swine Market La HBR HX7 ...165 J2
Swineshead La TOD OL14 ...163 K3
Swineshead Rd TOD OL14 ...163 J3
Swinnow Av BRAM LS13 ...107 J5
Swinnow Cl BRAM LS13 ...107 J5
Swinnow Crs PDSY/CALV LS28 ...107 J5
Swinnow Dr BRAM LS13 ...107 J5
Swinnow Gdns BRAM LS13 ...107 J5
Swinnow Garth
  PDSY/CALV LS28 ...107 J6
Swinnow Gn PDSY/CALV LS28 ...107 H6
Swinnow Gv BRAM LS13 ...107 J5
Swinnow La PDSY/CALV LS28 ...107 J4
Swinnow Rd PDSY/CALV LS28 ...107 J5
Swinnow Vw BRAM LS13 ...107 J5
Swinnow Wk BRAM LS13 ...107 J5
Swinton Pl GTHN BD7 ...126 D1
Swinton Ter HFAX HX1 ...10 A8
Swires La AIRE BD20 ...34 B1
Swires Rd ECHL BD2 ...5 L1
  HFAX HX1 ...10 F8
Swires Ter HFAX HX1 ...10 F8
Swiss St CAS WF10 ...158 A5
Swithenbank Av OSS WF5 ...174 E6
Swithen Hl DOD/DAR S75 ...241 K2
Swithens Ct RTHW LS26 ...155 G2
Swithens Dr RTHW LS26 ...155 G2
Swithens Gv RTHW LS26 ...155 G2
Swithens La RTHW LS26 ...155 H1
Swithen's St RTHW LS26 ...155 H2
Swordfish Wy
  GFTH/SHER LS25 ...116 D7
Sybil St LIT OL15 ...185 J8
  CUD/GR S72 ...244 D7
  CUD/GR S72 ...263 K1
  GFTH/SHER LS25 ...135 M4
  GTHN BD7 ...104 B7
  HOLM/MEL HD9 ...234 F5
  HUDW HD3 ...213 H1
  KNOT WF11 ...181 M3
  MILN OL16 ...181 M3
  MSTN/BAR LS15 ...111 J6
  RHAY LS8 ...110 B1
  TOD OL14 ...141 J7
  WKFDW/WTN WF2 * ...176 B4
Sycamore Cha
  PDSY/CALV LS28 ...107 H7
Sycamore Cl BFDE BD3 ...5 J3
  BHP/TINH LS16 ...64 B5
  CHAL LS7 ...6 C1
  HDGY LS6 ...6 C1
  KBTN HD8 ...216 B3
  KNOT WF11 ...181 M4
  WKFDW/WTN WF2 ...207 H1
Sycamore Copse
  WKFDW/WTN WF2 ...198 B1
Sycamore Ct KBTN HD8 ...216 B1
  PONT WF8 ...181 H5
Sycamore Cft BEE/HOL LS11 ...8 E4
Sycamore Dr BRIG HD6 ...148 C8
  BSLN/ROY S71 ...243 K3
  CLECK BD19 ...168 F8
  ELL HX5 ...168 F8
  ILK LS29 ...19 J6
Sycamore Fold BEE/HOL LS11 ...8 E4
  PONT WF8 ...181 H5
Sycamore Gv AIRE BD20 ...56 B1
  NORM WF6 ...178 C6
  WKFDW/WTN WF2 ...176 B7
Sycamore La AL/HA/HU LS17 ...46 F6
Sycamore Ri HOLM/MEL HD9 ...236 F6
Sycamore Rd HEM/SK/SE WF9 ...223 L8
Sycamore Rw BRAM LS13 ...107 J2
The Sycamores BHP/TINH LS16 ...64 B5
  DEWS WF13 ...173 K4
  GSLY LS20 ...62 A4
  HOR/CROF WF4 ...197 G5
  WIL/AL BD15 * ...102 E2
Sycamore St DOD/DAR S75 ...260 E4
  WKFDE WF1 ...13 K7
Sycamore Vw BRIG HD6 ...170 B3
  HWTH BD22 ...2 B7
Sycamore Wk PDSY/CALV LS28 ...106 C3
  STKB/PEN S36 ...271 G6
Sycamore Wy BTLY WF17 ...151 H5
  FEA/AMT WF7 ...179 M8
Sydenham Pl BFDE BD3 ...105 J4
Sydenham Rd BEE/HOL LS11 ...8 A4

Sydenham St BEE/HOL LS11 .....8 A4
Sydney Gdns LIT OL15 .....185 L5
Sydney St BGLY BD16 .....81 J3
　LVSG WF15 .....172 D5
　PDSY/CALV LS28 .....106 F4
　RTHW LS26 .....133 M8
Syke Av EARD/LOFT WF3 * 152 E7
　EARL WF12 .....174 B6
Syke Cl EARD/LOFT WF3 .....152 E7
Syke Cft BSLYN/ROY S71 .....243 L1
Syke Gdns EARD/LOFT WF3 .....152 E7
Syke Gn SCFT LS14 .....67 L6
Syke Gv EARL WF12 .....174 B6
Syke House La GTL/HWG HX4 .....168 B8
Syke Ing Cl EARL WF12 .....174 C7
Syke La CUL/OBY BD13 .....125 C7
　EARL WF12 .....174 B7
　HIPP HX3 .....148 A5
　LUD/ILL HX2 .....123 M4
　RPDN/SBR HX6 .....167 J3
　SCFT LS14 .....67 J6
　WHIT OL12 .....206 B2
Syke Pde EARD/LOFT WF3 * 152 E6
Syke Rd EARD/LOFT WF3 * 152 E7
　EARL WF12 .....174 B6
　HTON BD9 .....104 C3
　LIT OL15 .....207 L4
　WBY LS22 .....48 C1
　WHIT OL12 .....206 C3
Sykes Av DOD/DAR S75 .....260 F4
　MIRF WF14 .....172 E8
Sykes Cl BTLY WF17 .....152 A8
Sykes Ct MILN OL16 * 206 D8
Sykes Ga HBR HX7 .....165 K7
Syke Side WBOW BD5 .....57 K4
Sykes La AIRE BD20 .....35 M6
　EARL WF12 .....174 C2
　HWTH BD22 .....78 F3
　LM/WK BD12 .....149 J2
Sykes Rd BTLY WF17 .....152 A8
Sykes St BSLY S70 .....260 F7
　CAS WF10 .....157 M6
　CLECK BD19 .....149 M7
　MILN OL16 .....206 D8
　MILN OL16 .....229 J2
Syke St EARL WF12 .....174 B6
Syke Ter EARD/LOFT WF3 * 152 E7
Syke Vw EARL WF12 .....174 B6
Sylhet Cl BFD BD1 .....4 D4
Sylvan Av CUL/OBY BD13 .....124 F6
Sylvester Av NORM WF6 .....178 B9
Symons St WKFDW/WTN WF2 .....12 D6
Syringa Av WIL/AL BD15 .....103 J2
Syringa St HUDW HD3 .....191 M7

T

Tabbs Ct CLECK BD19 .....149 H5
Tabbs La CLECK BD19 .....149 G5
Tadman St WKFDE WF1 .....12 F6
Tagore Ct BOW BD4 .....105 M8
Talbot Av AL/HA/HU LS17 .....88 A4
　BULY LS4 .....108 E3
　HUDW HD3 .....191 L6
Talbot Ct RHAY LS8 .....88 B5
Talbot Crs RHAY LS8 .....88 B4
Talbot Fold RHAY LS8 .....88 B5
Talbot Gdns RHAY LS8 .....88 B4
Talbot Mt BULY LS4 .....108 E3
Talbot Rd RHAY LS8 .....88 B4
Talbot Rd RHAY LS8 .....88 B4
　STKB/PEN S36 .....270 E3
Talbot Rw BTLY WF17 .....173 M1
Talbot St BTLY WF17 .....173 L2
　GTHN BD7 .....104 D7
　KGHY BD21 .....2 C5
　NORM WF6 .....178 C4
　ROCH OL11 .....206 B8
Talbot Ter BULY LS4 .....108 E5
　RTHW LS26 .....155 G2
Talbot Vw BULY LS4 .....108 E3
Tallow Ms KBTN HD8 .....239 J5
Tall Trees AL/HA/HU LS17 .....87 L3
Tall Trees Dr FEA/AMT WF7 .....179 M6
Tamar Cl DOD/DAR S75 .....260 A3
Tamar St WBOW BD5 .....126 C2
Tam Ct ILK LS29 .....38 E3
Tame Barn Cl MILN OL16 * 207 J4
Tame La UPML OL3 .....230 E7
Tammy Hall St WKFDE WF1 * 12 E2
Tamworth St BOW BD4 .....106 A8
Tandem Wy HUDE HD5 .....193 K8
Tandle Hill Rd ROY/SHW OL2 .....228 D8
Tanfield Cl BSLYN/ROY S71 .....243 J2
Tanfield Dr ILK LS29 .....40 A4
Tanfield Rd HUD HD1 .....14 D2
Tanglewood BEE/HOL LS11 .....131 J7
Tanglewood Ct WBSY BD6 .....126 C5
Tanhouse Hl HIPP HX3 .....147 L7
　HORS LS18 .....86 A6
Tarn House La FEA/AMT WF7 .....202 D7
　HIPP HX3 .....147 J2
　WIL/AL BD15 .....80 D8
Tanhouse La MIRF WF14 .....194 D3
Tanhouse Pk HIPP HX3 .....147 L7
Tanhouse St DEWS WF13 .....173 H8
Tanhouse Vw HIPP HX3 * 147 L7
Tank Rw BSLY S70 .....261 M5
Tan La BOW BD4 .....127 K8
Tannerbrook Cl CLAY BD14 .....125 M2
Tanner Hill Rd GTHN BD7 .....126 A3
Tanners MAR/SLWT HD7 .....212 B7
Tanner St LVSG WF15 .....171 K1
Tannery Ct IDLE BD10 .....83 M6
　PDSY/CALV LS28 * 107 H7
Tannery Sq HDGY LS6 .....87 G2
Tanpit La AWLS/ASK DN6 .....227 M1
Tanpits HBR HX7 * 143 J3
Tanshelf Dr PONT WF8 .....180 E6
Tanton Crs CLAY BD14 .....125 M2
Tanton Wk CLAY BD14 .....125 M2
Tanyard Av HUDW HD3 .....191 H7
Tanyard Fold HOR/CROF WF4 .....220 C2
Tanyard Rd HUDW HD3 .....191 J7
Tarn BAIL BD17 * 83 J2
Tarn Cl CAS WF10 .....159 G5
Tarn Ct HWTH BD22 * 2 A2
　WKFDE WF1 .....176 D3
Tarnhill Ms WBOW BD5 .....127 G4
Tarn Hows Wk FEA/AMT WF7 .....202 A8
Tarn La AL/HA/HU LS17 .....66 F7
　HWTH BD22 .....56 E6
Tarn Rd FEA/AMT WF7 .....202 A2
Tarnside Cl MILN OL16 .....206 E5
Tarnside Dr SCFT LS14 .....111 H3
Tarn View Rd YEA LS19 .....62 F7
Tarn Vis ILK LS29 .....38 E2
Tatefield Gv GFTH/SHER LS25 .....135 J6
Tatefield Pl GFTH/SHER LS25 .....135 J6
Tateley Cl OSS WF5 .....174 F5
Tateley La OSS WF5 .....174 E5

Tate Naylor St DEWS WF13 * 173 K4
Tatham St MILN OL16 .....206 C7
Tatham Wy RHAY LS8 .....88 B3
Tatton St WKFDE WF1 .....13 L8
Tatton St SHPY BD18 .....82 C6
Taunton St WKFDE WF1 .....13 H4
Tavern St WKFDE WF1 .....13 H4
Tavistock Cl WOR/ARM LS12 .....108 A3
Tavistock Ms WOR/ARM LS12 .....108 B3
Tavistock Pk WOR/ARM LS12 .....108 B3
Tavistock Rd ROCH OL11 .....228 B3
Tavistock Wy
　WKFDW/WTN WF2 .....220 B1
　WOR/ARM LS12 .....108 B3
Tavora St WKFDE WF1 .....176 E7
Tavy Cl DOD/DAR S75 .....260 A1
Tawny Beck WOR/ARM LS12 .....107 L2
Tawny Cl BOW BD4 .....128 A5
　MOR LS27 .....152 F2
Tay Cl DOD/DAR S75 .....242 E7
Taylor Av AIRE BD20 .....35 M5
Taylor Cl OSS WF5 .....197 H2
Taylor Crs CUD/GR S72 .....263 J5
　OSS WF5 .....197 H2
Taylor Dr OSS WF5 .....197 H2
Taylor Gv RTHW LS26 .....157 G3
Taylor Hall La MIRF WF14 .....172 A5
Taylor Hill Rd HUDS HD4 .....214 A5
Taylor La LUD/ILL HX2 .....124 C4
　MAR/SLWT HD7 .....212 D1
　MSTN/BAR LS15 .....90 D8
Taylor Rw BSLY S70 .....261 H6
Taylors Cl SCFT LS14 .....111 K2
Taylor St BTLY WF17 .....173 L2
　CLECK BD19 .....149 L7
　MAR/SLWT HD7 .....213 G1
　WHIT OL12 .....206 B5
Taylor Wy WHIT OL12 * 206 B5
Tealby Cl BHP/TINH LS16 .....86 A4
Teal Cl CAS WF10 .....157 M8
Teal Ct MOR LS27 .....152 F2
Teale Dr CHAL LS7 .....10 A1
Teall Ct OSS WF5 .....197 J1
Teall St OSS WF5 .....197 J2
　WKFDE WF1 .....12 F1
Teal Ms MID LS10 .....153 M1
Teal St WKFDE WF1 .....12 F2
Teasdale St BOW BD4 .....127 K3
Teasel Cl LM/WK BD12 .....149 J2
Tebbet Pl HECK WF16 * 173 G2
Technology Dr BTLY WF17 .....174 A2
Teddington Av HUDE HD5 .....193 H6
Tees St MILN OL16 * 206 D8
　WBOW BD5 .....126 E3
Telephone Pl CHAL LS7 .....7 K6
Telford Cl AIRE BD20 .....36 B6
　CAS WF10 .....157 K7
　MID LS10 .....132 A4
Telford Pl MID LS10 .....132 A4
Telford Ter MID LS10 * 132 A5
Telford Wy ROCH OL11 .....228 C4
　WKFDW/WTN WF2 .....176 A1
Telscombe Dr BOW BD4 .....127 M4
Temperance Flds CLECK BD19 .....149 H6
Temperance St
　PDSY/CALV LS28 * 107 G5
Tempest Av WMB/DAR S73 .....263 J4
Tempest Pl BEE/HOL LS11 .....8 D3
Tempest Rd HEM/SK/SE WF9 .....246 E2
Templar La LDSU LS2 .....7 J3
　MSTN/BAR LS15 .....111 M2
Templar Pl LDSU LS2 * 7 J3
Templars Cl GTL/HWG HX4 .....168 C2
Templar St LDSU LS2 .....7 J3
　WKFDE WF1 .....13 M8
Templars Wy GFTH/SHER LS25 .....113 H8
　GIR BD8 .....104 A6
Temple Av MSTN/BAR LS15 .....111 J8
　RTHW LS26 .....133 H7
Temple Cl HUD HD1 .....14 F6
　MSTN/BAR LS15 .....111 J8
Temple Crs BEE/HOL LS11 .....8 C9
Temple Gdns NORM WF6 .....178 B2
Temple Gate Dr
　MSTN/BAR LS15 .....111 J7
Templegate Av
　MSTN/BAR LS15 .....111 J8
Templegate Cl
　MSTN/BAR LS15 .....111 K7
Templegate Crs
　MSTN/BAR LS15 .....111 K8
Templegate Gn
　MSTN/BAR LS15 .....111 J7
Templegate Ri
　MSTN/BAR LS15 .....111 J8
Templegate Rd
　MSTN/BAR LS15 .....111 K8
Templegate Vw
　MSTN/BAR LS15 .....111 J8
Templegate Wk
　MSTN/BAR LS15 .....111 J8
Templegate Wy
　MSTN/BAR LS15 .....111 K8
Temple Gn RTHW LS26 .....133 J7
Temple Gv MSTN/BAR LS15 .....111 J7
Temple La LIT OL15 .....185 L5
　MSTN/BAR LS15 .....111 J7
Temple Lea MSTN/BAR LS15 .....111 J7
Temple Moor MSTN/BAR LS15 * 111 J7
Templenewsam Rd
　MSTN/BAR LS15 .....111 H7
Templenewsam Vw
　MSTN/BAR LS15 .....111 H8
Temple Park Cl
　MSTN/BAR LS15 .....111 J7
Temple Park Gdns
　MSTN/BAR LS15 .....111 J7
Temple Park Gn
　MSTN/BAR LS15 .....111 J7
Temple Rhydding Dr
　BAIL BD17 .....82 E4
Temple Ri MSTN/BAR LS15 .....111 J8
Temple Rd DEWS WF13 .....173 J7
Temple Row Cl
　MSTN/BAR LS15 .....112 A8
Templestowe Crs
　MSTN/BAR LS15 .....111 L5
Templestowe Dr
　MSTN/BAR LS15 .....111 L6
Templestowe Gdns
　MSTN/BAR LS15 .....111 K6
Templestowe Hl
　MSTN/BAR LS15 .....111 K5
Temple St CAS WF10 .....157 L7
　COL BB8 .....52 A8
　HTON BD9 .....104 C3
　HUDW HD3 .....191 K5
　KGHY BD21 .....2 F5
Temple Vw EARD/LOFT WF3 .....154 C3
Temple View Gv OSM LS9 .....110 D8
Temple View Pl OSM LS9 .....110 D8
Temple View Rd OSM LS9 .....110 D8
Temple View Ter OSM LS9 .....110 D8

Temple Vue HDGY LS6 .....86 F8
Temple Wy BSLYN/ROY S71 .....261 M3
Temple Wy MSTN/BAR LS15 .....111 K6
Tenbury Fold BOW BD4 .....128 A5
Tenby Ter HFAX HX1 * 10 B4
Ten Lands La HOR/CROF WF4 .....222 B7
Tennis Av BOW BD4 .....128 A5
Tennis Wy BAIL BD17 .....82 C5
Tennyson Av AWLS/ASK DN6 .....227 L5
　EARD/LOFT WF3 .....155 G8
　RPDN/SBR HX6 .....167 H3
　TOD OL14 .....141 M8
Tennyson Cl PDSY/CALV LS28 .....107 H8
　STKB/PEN S36 .....270 F2
Tennyson Pl BFDE BD3 .....5 L3
　CLECK BD19 .....149 M6
Tennyson Rd BSLYN/ROY S71 .....261 K2
　WBSY BD6 .....126 D6
Tennyson St GSLY LS20 .....62 B6
　HIPP HX3 .....10 D1
　KGHY BD21 .....2 B7
　MOR LS27 .....152 D2
　PDSY/CALV LS28 .....106 F4
　ROCH OL11 .....228 C1
Tennyson Ter MOR LS27 * 152 D2
Tennyson Wy PONT WF8 .....180 F5
Tenterden Cl BTLY WF17 * 152 A8
　KBTN HD8 .....239 J4
Tentercroft WHIT OL12 * 206 A7
Tentercroft Ct DEWS WF13 * 173 M5
Tenterden Wy MSTN/BAR LS15 .....112 B3
Tenterfield Ri HIPP HX3 .....147 J5
Tenterfield Rd OSS WF5 .....197 G1
Tenterfields IDLE BD10 .....84 A6
　LUD/ILL HX2 .....167 G1
Tenter Hl BSPA/BRAM LS23 .....69 K4
　CLAY BD14 .....125 M2
　HOLM/MEL HD9 .....255 H2
　STKB/PEN S36 .....270 C2
Tenter Hill La HUDN HD2 .....192 F2
Tenter La STKB/PEN S36 .....271 J8
Tenters Cl KNOT WF11 .....181 L1
Tenters Gv HUDN HD2 .....192 E3
Tenth Av LVSG WF15 .....171 K1
Ten Yards La CUL/OBY BD13 .....102 B5
Terminus Pde
　MSTN/BAR LS15 * 111 L4
Tern Pk WBY LS22 .....47 K5
Tern St WBOW BD5 .....126 E5
Terrace Gdns HIPP HX3 .....10 E2
The Terrace PDSY/CALV LS28 .....129 C2
Terracotta Dr WIL/AL BD15 .....103 J6
Terrington Crest CLAY BD14 .....125 M2
Terry Rd LM/WK BD12 .....149 J2
Tetley Dr BIRK/DRI BD11 .....150 D2
Tetley La HIPP HX3 .....147 J4
Tetley Pl ECHL BD2 .....105 H3
Tetley St BFD BD1 .....4 D6
Teville Ct BOW BD4 .....127 J2
Tewit Cl LUD/ILL HX2 .....124 B7
Tewit Gn LUD/ILL HX2 .....124 B7
Tewit Hall Gdns LUD/ILL HX2 .....124 B8
Tewit Hall Rd BFDE BD3 .....105 L6
Tewit La LUD/ILL HX2 .....124 B7
Tewitt Cl AIRE BD20 .....35 K8
Tewitt La BGLY BD16 .....59 K8
　CUL/OBY BD13 .....102 C4
Tew St WKFDW/WTN WF2 .....12 E6
Texas St MOR LS27 .....152 D4
Thackeray Gv HUDS HD4 .....213 M3
Thackeray Rd IDLE BD10 .....105 M2
Thacker Gate Rd HBR HX7 .....166 D2
Thackley Av IDLE BD10 .....84 B3
Thackley Ct SHPY BD18 .....82 F6
Thackley Old Rd SHPY BD18 .....82 F6
Thackley Rd IDLE BD10 .....83 J4
Thackley Vw IDLE BD10 .....83 J4
Thackray Av HECK WF16 .....173 G5
Thackray La PONT WF8 .....180 F5
Thackray St LUD/ILL HX2 .....145 M7
　MOR LS27 .....152 C3
Thames Dr GFTH/SHER LS25 .....113 J8
Thames Rd MILN OL16 .....207 J8
Thanes Cl HUDN HD2 .....192 A4
Thanet Garth AIRE BD20 .....36 B6
Thane Wy MSTN/BAR LS15 .....112 A3
Thatchers Wy CLECK BD19 .....150 C5
Theaker La WOR/ARM LS12 .....108 E6
Theakston Md CLAY BD14 .....125 L1
Thealby Cl OSM LS9 .....7 L8
Thealby Lawn OSM LS9 .....7 L7
Thealby Pl OSM LS9 .....7 L7
Thearne Gn CLAY BD14 .....125 M2
The Meadow NORM WF6 .....178 C2
Theodore St BEE/HOL LS11 .....131 H5
Thetford WHIT OL12 * 206 A4
Thewlis La HUDS HD4 .....213 H4
Thickett La STKB/PEN S36 .....271 G4
Thick Hollins Dr
　HOLM/MEL HD9 .....235 H5
Thick Hollins Rd
　HOLM/MEL HD9 .....235 H6
Thimble Cl WHIT OL12 .....206 F2
The Thimbles WHIT OL12 .....206 F2
Third Av BFDE BD3 .....105 L5
　HEM/SK/SE WF9 .....225 A5
　HIPP HX3 .....168 D2
　KGHY BD21 .....2 B7
　LVSG WF15 .....171 K1
　RTHW LS26 .....133 H7
　WBY LS22 .....48 B1
　WKFDE WF1 .....176 A4
　WOR/ARM LS12 .....108 F6
Third St LM/WK BD12 .....127 G8
Thirkleby Royd CLAY BD14 .....125 L2
Thirlmere Av COL BB8 .....52 B8
Thirlmere Cl BEE/HOL LS11 .....131 G5
Thirlmere Dr CAS WF10 .....158 F7
　EARD/LOFT WF3 .....153 A6
　WBY LS22 .....48 B1
Thirlmere Gdns BEE/HOL LS11 .....131 G6
　ECHL BD2 .....105 K4
Thirlmere Gv ROY/SHW OL2 .....228 F8
Thirlmere Rd BSLYN/ROY S71 .....261 J5
　EARL WF12 .....174 A8
　WKFDW/WTN WF2 .....176 A8
Thirsk Dr GFTH/SHER LS25 .....135 J4
Thirsk Gra CLAY BD14 .....125 L2
Thirsk Rw LDS LS1 .....8 A7
Thirstin Rd HOLM/MEL HD9 .....236 A1
Thirteenth Av LVSG WF15 .....171 J1
Thistle Cl HUDN HD2 .....192 A4
Thistle Dr HEM/SK/SE WF9 .....225 H7
Thistle Hill Av HUDE HD5 .....215 L1
Thistle St HUD HD1 .....15 H1
　MOR LS27 .....151 M7
Thistlewood Rd
　WKFDE WF1 .....176 F1
Thistleyfields MILN OL16 * 207 H3
Thomas Ct WBSY BD6 .....126 C5
Thomas St BRIG HD6 .....170 C5
　BSLY S70 .....261 G4
　BTLY WF17 .....151 K8
　CAS WF10 .....158 A5
　ELL HX5 .....169 J8
　HDGY LS6 .....6 D2
　HEM/SK/SE WF9 .....224 A8
　HFAX HX1 .....11 H6
　HUD HD1 .....214 A2
　HUDW HD3 .....191 J5
　HWTH BD22 .....78 F8
　MILN OL16 .....206 C6
　ROY/SHW OL2 .....229 L8
　TOD OL14 .....140 E5
Thomas St South HFAX HX1 .....10 B7
Thomas St West HFAX HX1 .....168 C1
Thomas Wy HEM/SK/SE WF9 .....247 J2
Thompson Av CAS WF10 .....159 G8
　ECHL BD2 .....105 H1
Thompson Dr
　WKFDW/WTN WF2 .....176 B3
Thompson Gn BAIL BD17 .....82 C4
Thompson La BAIL BD17 .....82 C5
Thompson St SHPY BD18 .....82 C6
Thompson's Yd WKFDE WF1 * 12 D2
Thong La HOLM/MEL HD9 .....236 C6
Thoresby Av BSLYN/ROY S71 .....261 K2
Thoresby Dr CLECK BD19 .....150 D8
Thoresby Gv GTHN BD7 .....126 A3
Thoresby Rd IDLE BD10 * 84 A7
Thornaby Dr CLAY BD14 .....125 M1
Thornacre Crs SHPY BD18 .....83 G8
Thornacre Rd SHPY BD18 .....83 G7
Thorn Av EARL WF12 .....195 L5
　HTON BD9 .....103 L2
Thorn Bank Av HWTH BD22 .....79 G2
Thornberry Dr LVSG WF15 .....171 K1
Thornbridge Ms ECHL BD2 .....105 K2
Thornbury ROCH OL11 * 206 A8
　BHP/TINH LS16 .....86 E7
Thornbury Crs BFDE BD3 .....105 M6
Thornbury Dr BFDE BD3 .....105 M6
Thornbury Gv BFDE BD3 .....105 M6
Thornbury Pk
　WKFDW/WTN WF2 .....198 B2
Thornbury Rd BFDE BD3 .....105 M7
　WKFDW/WTN WF2 .....198 B2
Thornbush BFDE BD3 .....105 M7
Thornbush Wy MILN OL16 .....206 E8
Thorncliffe Av ROY/SHW OL2 .....228 E8
Thorncliffe Est BTLY WF17 .....173 J3
Thorncliffe Pk ROY/SHW OL2 .....228 E7
Thorncliffe Rd BTLY WF17 .....173 J3
　GIR BD8 .....83 G8
　HWTH BD22 .....79 G1
Thorncliffe St HUDW HD3 .....191 K5
Thorne Cl BSLYN/ROY S71 .....243 G7
Thorne End Rd DOD/DAR S75 .....242 D4
Thornefield Crs EARD/LOFT WF3 .....152 F6
Thorne Gv RTHW LS26 .....133 H8
Thornely Av DOD/DAR S75 .....260 B6
Thorner Gv AIRE BD20 .....36 A4
Thorner La BSPA/BRAM LS23 .....48 E7
　SCFT LS14 .....67 M6
Thorne Rd HUD HD1 .....214 A2
Thorner Rd BSPA/BRAM LS23 .....68 F6
Thornes Lane Whrf WKFDE WF1 .....13 G6
Thornes Moor Av
　WKFDW/WTN WF2 .....12 A9
Thornes Moor Cl
　WKFDW/WTN WF2 .....12 A8
Thornes Moor Dr
　WKFDW/WTN WF2 .....12 A8
Thornes Moor Rd
　WKFDW/WTN WF2 .....12 A9
Thornes Pk BRIG HD6 .....170 C5
　ECHL BD2 .....104 F1
Thornes Park Ct
　WKFDW/WTN WF2 .....12 C8
Thornes Rd WKFDW/WTN WF2 .....12 C8
Thorne St GTL/HWG HX4 .....190 C2
Thorneycroft Rd AIRE BD20 .....58 D5
Thorney La LUD/ILL HX2 .....144 F4
Thornfield BGLY BD16 .....81 G5
Thornfield Av HUDS HD4 .....214 A3
　PDSY/CALV LS28 .....106 E3
　WBSY BD6 .....126 B5
Thornfield Ct MSTN/BAR LS15 .....111 K4
Thornfield Dr MSTN/BAR LS15 .....111 K4
Thornfield Ms BGLY BD16 .....59 G7
　MSTN/BAR LS15 .....111 K4
Thornfield Pl ECHL BD2 .....105 L3
Thornfield Ri GTL/HWG HX4 .....168 D7
Thornfield Rd BHP/TINH LS16 .....86 D6
　WBY LS22 .....48 B1
　WKFDE WF1 .....176 A4
　WOR/ARM LS12 .....108 B3
Thornfield Sq CLECK BD19 .....149 L8
Thornfield Wy MSTN/BAR LS15 .....111 K4
Thorn Garth AIRE BD20 .....57 J5
　CLECK BD19 .....149 L8
Thorn Gv COL BB8 .....52 B8
　HTON BD9 .....103 M2
　RHAY LS8 .....110 D3
Thornham Ct MILN OL16 .....228 E6
Thornham La ROY/SHW OL2 .....228 E6
Thornham New Rd ROCH OL11 .....228 C5
Thornham Old Rd ROY/SHW OL2 .....228 C7
Thornhill Ct WOR/ARM LS12 .....108 D8
Thornhill Cft WKFDW/WTN WF2 .....12 D8
　WOR/ARM LS12 .....108 D8
Thornhill Dr PDSY/CALV LS28 .....84 D8
　SHPY BD18 .....83 G6
　WKFDW/WTN WF2 .....199 J7
Thornhill Gv AIRE BD20 .....35 K8
　PDSY/CALV LS28 .....84 D7
　SHPY BD18 .....83 G6
Thornhill Hey GTL/HWG HX4 .....190 B4
Thornhill Park Av EARL WF12 .....195 M2
Thornhill Pl BFDE BD3 .....106 A6
　WOR/ARM LS12 .....108 D8

Thornhill Rd AIRE BD20 .....35 K8
　BRIG HD6 .....170 A8
　CAS WF10 .....158 A8
　EARL WF12 .....173 K8
　EARL WF12 .....196 C5
　HUDW HD3 .....191 J8
　WOR/ARM LS12 .....108 D8
Thornhills Beck La BRIG HD6 .....170 D2
Thornhills La BRIG HD6 .....170 D3
Thornhill St EARL WF12 .....173 M8
　PDSY/CALV LS28 .....84 D8
　WKFDE WF1 .....12 F3
　WOR/ARM LS12 .....108 D8
Thornhill St Bungalows
　WKFDE WF1 .....12 F4
Thornhill Ter BFDE BD3 .....105 M6
Thornie Bank EARL WF12 * 173 M8
Thorn La HTON BD9 .....103 M2
　RHAY LS8 .....88 B2
Thornlea Cl YEA LS19 .....63 J3
Thornleigh EARL WF12 .....173 M8
Thornleigh Av
　WKFDW/WTN WF2 .....12 F7
Thornleigh Crs
　WKFDW/WTN WF2 .....12 E7
Thornleigh Cft
　WKFDW/WTN WF2 .....12 F7
Thornleigh Dr LVSG WF15 .....172 D1
　WKFDW/WTN WF2 .....12 F7
Thornleigh Gdns OSM LS9 * 110 B8
Thornleigh Garth
　WKFDW/WTN WF2 .....12 F8
Thornleigh Gv OSM LS9 .....110 B8
　WKFDW/WTN WF2 .....12 E8
Thornleigh Mt OSM LS9 .....110 B8
Thornleigh Rd HUDS HD4 .....213 K8
　WKFDW/WTN WF2 .....12 E7
Thornleigh St OSM LS9 .....110 B8
Thornleigh Vw OSM LS9 .....110 B8
Thornmead Rd BAIL BD17 .....82 F4
Thorn Mt RHAY LS8 .....110 D3
Thorn Rd EARL WF12 .....195 L5
Thorn Royd Dr BOW BD4 .....128 B4
Thornsgill Av BOW BD4 .....127 L3
Thorn St BTLY WF17 * 151 G5
　GIR BD8 .....104 B5
　HWTH BD22 .....79 G6
Thorn Ter RHAY LS8 .....110 D3
Thornton Av WOR/ARM LS12 .....108 C7
Thornton Cl BTLY WF17 .....151 H5
　HEM/SK/SE WF9 .....245 M1
Thornton Gdns
　WOR/ARM LS12 .....108 C7
Thornton Gv WOR/ARM LS12 .....108 C7
Thornton La WBOW BD5 .....126 E3
Thornton Lodge Rd HUD HD1 .....214 A4
Thornton Moor Rd
　HWTH BD22 .....101 J7
Thornton Old Rd GIR BD8 .....103 J7
Thornton Rd BRIG HD6 .....170 A6
　BSLY S70 .....261 L7
　CUL/OBY BD13 .....103 H8
　CUL/OBY BD13 .....124 B1
　EARL WF12 .....195 K2
　GIR BD8 .....104 D6
Thorntons Ar LDS LS1 * 7 G9
Thorntons Dl HORS LS18 .....85 K9
Thornton St BFD BD1 .....4 B5
　CLECK BD19 .....149 J8
　DEWS WF13 .....150 B7
　HFAX HX1 .....173 K7
　ILK LS29 .....40 A9
　ROCH OL11 .....228 A6
Thornton Ter BSLY S70 .....261 L7
Thornton View Rd CLAY BD14 .....125 L2
Thorntonville CLECK BD19 .....150 B9
Thorntree Av HOR/CROF WF4 .....200 A5
Thorntree Ct PONT WF8 .....203 M2
Thorntree La HOR/CROF WF4 .....200 A5
Thorntree Rd DOD/DAR S75 .....260 F3
Thorn Tree St HFAX HX1 .....10 B9
Thorn Vw HBR HX7 .....144 A6
　HIPP HX3 .....148 A1
　RHAY LS8 .....110 D3
Thornville MOR LS27 .....130 D7
Thornville Cl HDGY LS6 .....109 G4
Thornville Ct HDGY LS6 * 109 G3
Thornville Crs HDGY LS6 .....109 G3
Thornville Gv HDGY LS6 .....109 G3
Thornville Mt DEWS WF13 .....173 J8
　HDGY LS6 .....109 G3
Thornville Pl DEWS WF13 * 173 J8
　HDGY LS6 .....109 G3
Thornville Rd HDGY LS6 .....109 G4
Thornville Row HDGY LS6 .....109 G4
Thornville St DEWS WF13 * 173 J8
　HDGY LS6 .....109 G4
Thornville Ter DEWS WF13 * 173 J8
　HDGY LS6 .....109 G3
Thornville Vw HDGY LS6 .....109 G4
Thornville Wk DEWS WF13 .....173 J8
Thorn Wk RHAY LS8 .....110 E3
Thornwell Gv CUD/GR S72 .....244 C8
Thorp Arch Pk
　BSPA/BRAM LS23 .....49 G6
Thorp Av HOLM/MEL HD9 .....254 D2
Thorpe Av CUL/OBY BD13 .....103 J8
Thorpe Cl GSLY LS20 .....61 K6
Thorpe Ct MID LS10 .....153 K3
Thorpe Crs MID LS10 .....153 K3
Thorpe Dr GSLY LS20 .....61 K5
Thorpe Gdns MID LS10 .....153 K3
Thorpe Garth MID LS10 .....153 K3
Thorpe Green Dr HUDW HD3 .....191 G8
Thorpe Gv CUL/OBY BD13 .....103 K8
　MID LS10 .....153 L2
Thorpe La EARD/LOFT WF3 .....155 G5
　GSLY LS20 .....61 J6
　HEM/SK/SE WF9 .....225 H3
　HUDE HD5 .....215 J2
Thorpe Lower La
　EARD/LOFT WF3 .....154 C3
Thorpe Mill Ct
　RPDN/SBR HX6 * 167 G7
Thorpe Mt MID LS10 .....153 K3
Thorpe Rd CUL/OBY BD13 .....103 J8
　EARD/LOFT WF3 .....153 M7
　MID LS10 .....153 L2
　PDSY/CALV LS28 .....106 F6
Thorpes Av IDLE BD10 .....83 K7
Thorpes Crs KBTN HD8 .....239 J5
Thorpe Sq MID LS10 .....153 M3
Thorpe St HIPP HX3 .....146 A1
　KGHY BD21 .....3 G2
　MID LS10 .....153 L2
　MSTN/BAR LS15 .....111 L7
　OSS WF5 .....197 H3
　WKFDW/WTN WF2 .....176 B8
Thorp Garth IDLE BD10 .....83 K7
Thorverton Dr BOW BD4 .....128 A6
Thorverton Gv BOW BD4 .....128 A6
Threadneedle St HUD HD1 .....14 F7
Threap Cft LUD/ILL HX2 .....124 B7
Three Nooks La CUD/GR S72 .....244 D4

Three Sisters Sq HUD HD1 14 F2
Threshfield Crs BIRK/DRI BD11 128 C8
Thrice Fold IDLE BD10 83 H5
Thrift Wy BGLY BD16 81 H4
Throstle Av MID LS10 153 K3
Throstle Bank LUD/ILL HX2 168 B1
Throstle Crest FEA/AMT WF7 179 J6
Throstle Dr MID LS10 153 J3
Throstle Hl MID LS10 153 K3
Throstle La MID LS10 153 L3
Throstle Mt LUD/ILL HX2 167 H1
MID LS10 153 K3
Throstle Nest BTLY WF17 173 J2
Throstle Nest Cl OT LS21 40 F4
Throstle Nest Rd AIRE BD20 * 35 M4
Throstle Nest Vw HORS LS18 85 L7
Throstle Pde MID LS10 153 J4
Throstle Pl MID LS10 153 K3
Throstle Rd MID LS10 153 L3
Throstle Rw MID LS10 153 K3
Throstle Sq MID LS10 153 M2
Throstle St MID LS10 153 K3
Throstle Ter MID LS10 153 M3
Throstle Vw MID LS10 153 M3
Throstle Wk MID LS10 153 K3
Throxenby Wy CLAY BD14 125 L2
Thrum Hall Cl HFAX HX1 146 A7
Thrum Hall Dr HFAX HX1 10 A5
Thrum Hall La HFAX HX1 10 A5
WHIT OL12 206 A3
Thrumpton Rd BSLYN/ROY S71 243 H5
Thrush Hill Rd HBR HX7 143 M6
Thrush St KGHY BD21 3 J2
Thruxton Cl CUD/GR S72 244 E6
Thryberg St BFDE BD3 5 K7
Thunder Bridge La KBTN HD8 237 M3
Thunderhead Rdg CAS WF10 180 A1
Thunderton La RPDN/SBR HX6 166 D4
Thurgoland Bank
STKB/PEN S36 271 M6
Thurgory Ga KBTN HD8 215 M3
Thurgory La KBTN HD8 216 B2
Thurlestone Ct AIRE BD20 58 D6
Thurley Dr BOW BD4 127 K4
Thurley Rd BOW BD4 127 K4
Thurlstone Rd STKB/PEN S36 270 D2
Thurnscoe Rd BFD BD1 4 D3
Thurrish La HBR HX7 121 K1
Thursby St BFDE BD3 5 L6
Thurston Gdns WIL/AL BD15 103 K6
Thurstonland Bank Rd
HOLM/MEL HD9 236 F5
Thurstonland Rd HUDS HD4 237 G1
Thwaite Ga MID LS10 132 B3
Thwaite La MID LS10 132 C3
Thwaites Av ILK LS29 38 E2
Thwaites Br KGHY BD21 3 M4
Thwaites Brow Rd KGHY BD21 58 B7
Thwaites La KGHY BD21 3 M4
Tib Garth WBY LS22 47 K3
Tichborne Rd WBOW BD5 * 127 G3
Tichborne Rd West WBOW BD5 127 G3
Tichborne St LVSG WF15 172 A2
Tichbourne St BTLY WF17 173 H2
Tickhill St BFDE BD3 5 L7
Tiding Field La MAR/SLWT HD7 211 M4
Tidswell St HECK WF16 173 G2
Tiflis St WHIT OL12 206 A6
Tilbury Av BEE/HOL LS11 8 B8
Tilbury Gv BEE/HOL LS11 8 B8
Tilbury Mt BEE/HOL LS11 8 B8
Tilbury Pde BEE/HOL LS11 8 B8
Tilbury Rd BEE/HOL LS11 8 B7
Tilbury Rw BEE/HOL LS11 8 A8
Tilbury Ter BEE/HOL LS11 8 B8
Tilbury Vw BEE/HOL LS11 * 8 B8
Tile Cl SKP/WHF BD23 16 D3
Tile La BHP/TINH LS16 86 F3
Tile St GIR BD8 104 D5
Tiley Sq WBOW BD5 127 G2
Till Carr La HIPP HX3 148 C7
Tillotson Av RPDN/SBR HX6 167 J3
Tillotsons Ct AIRE BD20 * 34 C4
Tillotson St AIRE BD20 * 35 M4
Timber St ELL HX5 169 H8
KGHY BD21 * 3 L3
Timberwood KBTN HD8 237 M2
Timble Dr BGLY BD16 81 K2
Tim La HWTH BD22 78 D5
Timmey La RPDN/SBR HX6 167 J1
Timothy La BTLY WF17 151 M7
Tinderley Gv HUDE HD5 215 G2
Tingley Av EARD/LOFT WF3 153 G5
Tingley Common MOR LS27 152 D5
Tingley Crs EARD/LOFT WF3 152 E5
Tinker La HOLM/MEL HD9 234 F5
KBTN HD8 216 C4
Tinkingfield La WBY LS22 31 L5
Tinkler's La KNOT WF11 161 J3
Tinkler Stile IDLE BD10 83 H6
Tinsel Rd EARL WF12 174 B5
Tinshill Av BHP/TINH LS16 86 A3
Tinshill Cl BHP/TINH LS16 86 A3
Tinshill Crs BHP/TINH LS16 86 A2
Tinshill Dr BHP/TINH LS16 86 A2
Tinshill Garth BHP/TINH LS16 86 A2
Tinshill Gv BHP/TINH LS16 86 A2
Tinshill La BHP/TINH LS16 85 M3
Tinshill Mt BHP/TINH LS16 86 A2
Tinshill Rd BHP/TINH LS16 85 M3
Tinshill Vw BHP/TINH LS16 86 A2
Tinsworth Rd
WKFDW/WTN WF2 220 C2
Tintagel Ct NORM WF6 178 D3
Tintern Av GIR BD8 103 M7
HUDW HD3 213 H1
LIT OL15 185 J7
WHIT OL12 206 A4
Tippaty La KNOT WF11 160 C7
Tipping La KBTN HD8 217 M7
Tippit La CUD/GR S72 262 E1
Tisma Dr BOW BD4 127 L6
Tithe Barn Cl WHIT OL12 * 206 F2
Tithe Barn La AL/HA/HU LS17 67 K4
Tithe Barn Rd KNOT WF11 182 C2
Tithe Barn St EARL WF12 173 M6
HOR/CROF WF4 197 J5
Tithe Barn Vw BRIG HD6 170 E6
Tithe House Wy HUDN HD2 171 G8
Titus La KBTN HD8 216 F8
Titus St SHPY BD18 82 B6
Tivoli Pl ILK LS29 38 E3
WBOW BD5 126 E3
Tivy Dl DOD/DAR S75 259 G2
Tivy Dale Cl DOD/DAR S75 259 G2
Tivydale Dr DOD/DAR S75 242 A7
Tivy Dale Dr DOD/DAR S75 259 G2
Toad Carr TOD OL14 * 141 J8
Toad La MILN OL16 206 B6
Toby La GTHN BD7 126 C1
Toby Wood La KBTN HD8 256 F1
Tockwith La RYKW YO26 32 C2
Tockwith Rd RYKW YO26 32 E1
RYKW YO26 33 J3
Todd St MILN OL16 206 C7
Todd Ter GTHN BD7 * 126 D2
Todley Hall Rd HWTH BD22 56 B8
Todmorden Rd LIT OL15 185 L8
TOD OL14 162 B2
Todwell La WBOW BD5 126 E3
Toft La HUDS HD4 215 H8
Tofts Av LM/WK BD12 148 E4
Tofts Gv BRIG HD6 170 B7
Tofts Grove Gdns BRIG HD6 170 B7
Toftshaw Fold BOW BD4 127 M6
Toftshaw La BOW BD4 128 A6
Toftshaw New Rd BOW BD4 127 M6
Tofts House Cl
PDSY/CALV LS28 107 G7
Tofts La HUDS HD4 * 215 H8
PBR HG3 28 A1
Tofts Rd CLECK BD19 149 M7
PDSY/CALV LS28 106 F7
Toft St WOR/ARM LS12 108 F8
Toll Bar Cl SEL YO8 139 M4
Tollbar Cl STKB/PEN S36 271 K6
Toll Bar La WKFDW/WTN WF2 175 M5
Toll Bar Rd CAS WF10 157 H7
Toll Bar Wy TAD LS24 72 B1
Toller Dr HTON BD9 104 A3
Toller Gv HTON BD9 104 B3
Toller La HTON BD9 104 B3
Toller Pk HTON BD9 104 B3
Tollgate Cl CUD/GR S72 244 F4
Tollgate Wy MILN OL16 206 E6
Tolson Crs HUDE HD5 193 J7
Tolson St DEWS WF13 * 173 L5
OSS WF5 174 D6
Tolsons Yd HUDE HD5 15 L8
Tolworth Fold WIL/AL BD15 103 J6
Tomahawk Trail CAS WF10 180 B1
Tombridge Crs
HEM/SK/SE WF9 223 J5
Tom Cat La WBY LS22 31 L5
Tom Dando Cl NORM WF6 179 G4
Tom La HUDS HD4 213 K3
HWTH BD22 53 L1
Tomling Cote La AIRE BD20 36 C6
Tomlinson Wy GFTH/SHER LS25 115 M7
Tomlinson Yd HUD HD1 15 G6
Tommy La MAR/SLWT HD7 213 G5
Tom Wood Ash La
HEM/SK/SE WF9 225 M7
Tonbridge Cl WBSY BD6 126 B6
Tonbridge St LDS LS1 6 D6
Tong Ap WOR/ARM LS12 107 M8
Tong Dr WOR/ARM LS12 107 M7
Tonge St ROCH OL11 * 206 C8
Tong Ga WOR/ARM LS12 107 M7
Tong Gn WOR/ARM LS12 107 M7
Tong La BOW BD4 128 E6
Tong Rd WOR/ARM LS12 129 K2
Tong St BOW BD4 127 M5
Tongue La HDGY LS6 87 H5
Tong Wy WOR/ARM LS12 107 M7
Tootal St WKFDE WF1 13 G6
Toothill Av BRIG HD6 170 C7
Toothill Bank BRIG HD6 170 C7
Toothill La BRIG HD6 170 C8
Toot Hill La RPDN/SBR HX6 166 D4
Toothill La South HUDN HD2 192 B1
Topaz Cl HUDN HD2 192 E4
Topcliffe Av MOR LS27 152 F2
Topcliffe Cl EARD/LOFT WF3 152 F4
Topcliffe Garth MOR LS27 152 F2
Topcliffe Gv MOR LS27 152 E4
Topcliffe La EARD/LOFT WF3 152 F4
Topcliffe Md MOR LS27 152 F2
Topcliffe Rd BSLYN/ROY S71 261 J1
Topfield Fold MOR LS27 152 E4
Top Fold BSLYN/ROY S71 * 262 C6
KNOT WF11 159 J2
Top House Farm Ms
KNOT WF11 * 159 J2
Top La COL BB8 74 E2
HOR/CROF WF4 218 F5
OT LS21 23 J2
Top Meadow MIRF WF14 194 B4
Top Moor Side BEE/HOL LS11 8 C6
Top of The Hl HUDS HD4 237 G4
Top Orch HOR/CROF WF4 222 D5
Top O' Th' Bank HUDS HD4 237 G5
Top O' Th' Close Rd TOD OL14 163 K8
Top O' Th' Hill Rd TOD OL14 163 J5
Top Rd KBTN HD8 239 G7
Top Rw BSLYN/ROY S71 * 262 C6
Top Stone Cl GFTH/SHER LS25 160 A3
Top St HEM/SK/SE WF9 223 L7
Tor Av LM/WK BD12 148 E5
Tor Cl BSLYN/ROY S71 261 K1
Torcote Crs HUDN HD2 192 E1
Tordoff Av GTHN BD7 126 A1
Tordoff Gn WBSY BD6 126 D6
Tordoff Rd LM/WK BD12 127 G8
Tordoff Ter KSTL LS5 * 108 C2
Toronto Pl CHAL LS7 87 M8
Torre Cl OSM LS9 110 C6
Torre Crs OSM LS9 110 D5
WBSY BD6 125 M5
Torre Dr OSM LS9 110 C5
Torre Gv OSM LS9 110 C5
WBSY BD6 125 M5
Torre Hl OSM LS9 110 D6
Torre La OSM LS9 110 D6
Torre Mt OSM LS9 110 C5
Torre Pl OSM LS9 110 C6
Torre Rd OSM LS9 110 B6
WBSY BD6 125 M5
Torre Sq OSM LS9 110 D5
Torre Vw OSM LS9 110 D5
Torre Wk OSM LS9 110 D5
Torridon Crs WBSY BD6 126 A8
Torridon Rd EARL WF12 174 A4
Tor Vw HOLM/MEL HD9 236 E4
Totley Cl BSLYN/ROY S71 243 K7
Totties La HOLM/MEL HD9 254 F1
Toulston La TAD LS24 70 B4
Tower Av HEM/SK/SE WF9 225 J6
Tower Cswy TOD OL14 140 D6
Tower Crs TAD LS24 71 K2
The Tower Dr OT LS21 43 G8
Tower Gdns LUD/ILL HX2 168 B2
Tower Gv WOR/ARM LS12 108 C6
Tower Hl RPDN/SBR HX6 167 K2
Tower House St LDSU LS2 7 G7
Tower La WOR/ARM LS12 108 B6
Tower Pl WOR/ARM LS12 108 B6
Tower Rd SHPY BD18 82 A6
Towers Cl HOR/CROF WF4 200 B6
Towers La HOR/CROF WF4 200 D5
Towers Paddock CAS WF10 158 C7
Towers Sq HDGY LS6 87 J6
The Towers WOR/ARM LS12 108 C6
Tower St BSLY S70 261 G7
ECHL BD2 105 K4
TOD OL14 140 C5
Towers Wy HDGY LS6 87 J6
Tower Vw HFAX HX1 168 A1
Towlerton La
WKFDW/WTN WF2 176 A4
Town Av HUD HD1 15 J3
Town Cl HORS LS18 85 K5
Townclose Vw
GFTH/SHER LS25 135 H6
Town Crs HUD HD1 15 J2
Town End GFTH/SHER LS25 113 G6
GTHN BD7 126 C2
HUDE HD5 215 G2
MAR/SLWT HD7 212 F2
MOR LS27 129 M7
OSS WF5 196 F1
Town End Av FEA/AMT WF7 202 E7
HOLM/MEL HD9 236 E8
Town End Cl AIRE BD20 * 34 E8
Town End Crs HOLM/MEL HD9 236 E8
Town End La KBTN HD8 216 C2
Townend Pl AIRE BD20 34 E8
PDSY/CALV LS28 107 H6
Town End Rd CLAY BD14 125 K1
HOLM/MEL HD9 236 D8
Townend Rd WOR/ARM LS12 130 D1
Town End Vw HOLM/MEL HD9 236 D8
Townfield WIL/AL BD15 102 E1
Townfield La HBR HX7 143 H1
Town Fields Rd ELL HX5 169 G8
Townfold OSS WF5 175 G8
Town Ga CLECK BD19 149 H6
GSLY LS20 62 A5
HBR HX7 143 H1
HIPP HX3 147 J3
HOLM/MEL HD9 236 B6
HOLM/MEL HD9 253 M1
HOLM/MEL HD9 254 C1
HOLM/MEL HD9 255 G4
KBTN HD8 216 A6
KBTN HD8 216 C2
LUD/ILL HX2 144 D5
MAR/SLWT HD7 233 H2
PDSY/CALV LS28 84 D7
RPDN/SBR HX6 166 F3
Towngate BRIG HD6 170 F3
BRIG HD6 171 G4
DOD/DAR S75 242 D5
DOD/DAR S75 259 H6
HIPP HX3 147 L6
HIPP HX3 169 J2
HUDS HD4 214 C4
KGHY BD21 * 3 G4
LM/WK BD12 148 E4
MIRF WF14 172 D8
OSS WF5 197 G1
SHPY BD18 82 F7
STKB/PEN S36 270 C2
Towngate Av BRIG HD6 170 F3
Town Gate Cl GSLY LS20 62 A5
Towngate Gv MIRF WF14 194 D1
Towngate Rd BTLY WF17 173 J1
Town Hall Sq YEA LS19 62 D7
Town Hall St ELL HX5 169 H8
HOLM/MEL HD9 254 C1
KGHY BD21 3 G5
MIRF WF14 * 194 C2
RPDN/SBR HX6 167 K3
Town Hall St East HFAX HX1 * 11 H5
Town Hall Wy EARL WF12 * 173 M6
Townhead Fold ILK LS29 19 G6
Town Hl BSPA/BRAM LS23 69 M4
Town Hill St BGLY BD16 * 81 K8
Town House Rd LIT OL15 185 K8
Town La IDLE BD10 83 K6
Townley Av HIPP HX3 169 J2
Townley Rd MILN OL16 207 H8
WKFDW/WTN WF2 197 M1
Townley St COL BB8 74 A1
Town Mdw MILN OL16 206 A7
Town Mill Brow WHIT OL12 * 206 A7
Town Moor HUDS HD4 237 H4
Town Pl HUD HD1 15 J3
Town Rd HUDE HD5 193 L5
Town St BEE/HOL LS11 131 H4
BIRK/DRI BD11 128 C8
BRAM LS13 107 H1
CHAL LS7 87 M7
DEWS WF13 173 L4
EARD/LOFT WF3 154 F3
EARL WF12 174 B7
GSLY LS20 62 A5
HEM/SK/SE WF9 223 L7
HORS LS18 85 K6
MID LS10 153 L1
MOR LS27 129 M7
PDSY/CALV LS28 106 F4
WOR/ARM LS12 108 C6
YEA LS19 62 D7
YEA LS19 84 F3
Town Street Ms CHAL LS7 87 M7
Town Street Wk CHAL LS7 87 M7
Town Ter HUD HD1 15 J3
The Town EARL WF12 195 M4
Town Wells Dr PDSY/CALV LS28 84 D8
Towton Dr CAS WF10 157 J8
Track Mt BTLY WF17 173 K4
Track Rd BTLY WF17 173 K4
Trackside LM/WK BD12 149 H1
Trafalgar Cl HUDN HD2 192 D2
Trafalgar Gdns MOR LS27 152 C3
Trafalgar Rd DEWS WF13 173 K5
ILK LS29 38 D2
Trafalgar Sq HFAX HX1 10 C9
Trafalgar St AWLS/ASK DN6 249 L5
BFD BD1 4 E4
BTLY WF17 173 J1
HFAX HX1 * 10 C9
LDSU LS2 7 J8
MILN OL16 206 C6
Trafford Av OSM LS9 110 D4
Trafford Gv OSM LS9 110 C3
Trafford Rd AWLS/ASK DN6 227 M3
Trafford St ROCH OL11 228 A1
Trafford Ter OSM LS9 110 D4
Traith Ct BTLY WF17 * 151 G8
Tramways LM/WK BD12 149 H1
Tranbeck Rd GSLY LS20 61 K5
Tranfield Av GSLY LS20 61 L5
Tranfield Cl GSLY LS20 61 L5
Tranfield Gdns GSLY LS20 61 L5
Tranmere Ct GSLY LS20 61 L5
Tranmere Dr GSLY LS20 61 K5
Tranquility MSTN/BAR LS15 111 L4
Tranquillity Ct MSTN/BAR LS15 111 L4
Trans Pennine Trail
BSLYN/ROY S71 244 A7
EARD/LOFT WF3 177 J1
MID LS10 9 K2
RTHW LS26 134 A7
WKFDE WF1 199 J2
Transperience Wy
LM/WK BD12 127 H8
Transvaal Ter BTLY WF17 151 K7
Trans Wk TAD LS24 95 G5
Tranter Gv BOW BD4 128 A1
Tranter Pl MSTN/BAR LS15 111 G6
Travis St MILN OL16 229 K2
ROY/SHW OL2 229 K7
Trawden Rd COL BB8 74 D2
Tredgold Av BHP/TINH LS16 64 A4
Tredgold Cl BHP/TINH LS16 64 A4
Tredgold Crs BHP/TINH LS16 64 A4
Tredgold Garth BHP/TINH LS16 64 A4
Tredis Cl BSLYN/ROY S71 261 K3
Treecrest Ri DOD/DAR S75 261 G2
Treelands DOD/DAR S75 260 D3
Tree La LUD/ILL HX2 145 H1
Trees St GIR BD8 4 A1
Tree Tops Ct RHAY LS8 88 E7
Tree Top Vw CUL/QBY BD13 124 E4
Trefoil Wy LIT OL15 185 H8
Trelawn Av HDGY LS6 108 F1
Trelawn Pl HDGY LS6 108 F1
Trelawn St HDGY LS6 108 F1
Trelawn Ter HDGY LS6 108 F1
Tremont Gdns MID LS10 132 A4
Trenam Park Dr IDLE BD10 83 J4
Trenance Dr SHPY BD18 82 B7
Trenance Gdns GTL/HWG HX4 168 C8
Trenholme Av LM/WK BD12 126 D8
Trenic Crs HDGY LS6 108 F3
Trenic Dr HDGY LS6 108 F3
Trent Av GFTH/SHER LS25 135 J1
MILN OL16 207 J8
NORM WF6 178 C2
Trentham Av BEE/HOL LS11 131 K4
Trentham Gv BEE/HOL LS11 131 K4
Trentham Pl BEE/HOL LS11 131 K4
Trentham Rw BEE/HOL LS11 131 K4
Trentham St BEE/HOL LS11 131 K4
Trenton Dr GIR BD8 4 B2
Trenton Rd EARL WF12 174 B4
Trent Rd OSM LS9 110 B6
ROY/SHW OL2 229 J6
Trent St BEE/HOL LS11 8 E5
MILN OL16 206 D8
Trescoe Av WOR/ARM LS12 108 A5
Tresham Ct EARL WF12 174 B4
Trevelyan Sq LDS LS1 * 9 G1
Trevelyan St BRIG HD6 170 C1
HUDE HD5 15 M8
Trewan Ct BSLYN/ROY S71 261 K3
The Triangle HUD HD1 14 B9
Triath Ct BTLY WF17 151 G8
Trilby St WKFDE WF1 13 G1
Trimmingham La LUD/ILL HX2 145 M8
Trimmingham Rd LUD/ILL HX2 145 M8
Trimmingham Vls
LUD/ILL HX2 * 146 A8
Trinity Church Ga WKFDE WF1 12 F3
Trinity Cl LUD/ILL HX2 124 C8
Trinity Ct HEM/SK/SE WF9 247 J2
HOLM/MEL HD9 236 B2
Trinity Dr KBTN HD8 257 H1
Trinity Fold HFAX HX1 * 11 G7
Trinity Gv BRIG HD6 * 170 C2
Trinity Mt DEWS WF13 * 173 L4
Trinity Pl BGLY BD16 81 J4
HFAX HX1 11 G7
Trinity Ri OT LS21 41 K7
Trinity Rd HFAX HX1 11 G7
WBOW BD5 4 C9
Trinity St BTLY WF17 173 L4
HBR HX7 143 H3
HFAX HX1 11 G7
HUD HD1 14 B5
KGHY BD21 3 H2
LDS LS1 7 G9
MIRF WF14 194 C2
PONT WF8 180 F5
WKFDE WF1 13 L8
Trinity Ter BTLY WF17 150 F5
Trinity Vw HIPP HX3 11 K8
LM/WK BD12 127 G7
OSS WF5 174 F7
Trinity Wk HEM/SK/SE WF9 247 J2
LM/WK BD12 127 G7
Trip Garth WBY LS22 47 K4
Trip La WBY LS22 47 H4
Tristram Av WBOW BD5 127 J4
Triumph Cl BEE/HOL LS11 8 C4
Troon Cl NORM WF6 178 F5
Troon Dr HUDN HD2 192 B3
Troon Wy WKFDW/WTN WF2 198 C4
Trooper La HIPP HX3 11 K8
Trooper Ter HIPP HX3 11 K8
Trough La HEM/SK/SE WF9 247 L3
HWTH BD22 101 J5
Troughton Pl PDSY/CALV LS28 129 H1
Trough Well La
WKFDW/WTN WF2 176 A3
Trowell Wy BSLYN/ROY S71 243 H6
Troydale Gdns PDSY/CALV LS28 129 K1
Troydale Gv PDSY/CALV LS28 129 K1
Troydale La PDSY/CALV LS28 107 J8
Troy Hl MOR LS27 * 152 C1
Troy Ri MOR LS27 152 D1
Troy Rd HORS LS18 85 L4
MOR LS27 152 C2
Trueman Av HECK WF16 173 G2
Trueman Ct LM/WK BD12 127 G8
Trueman Ter BSLYN/ROY S71 262 A4
Trueman Wy HEM/SK/SE WF9 247 J2
Truncliffe WBSY BD6 126 F5
Trundles La KNOT WF11 182 D2
Truro Ct BSLYN/ROY S71 261 K3
Truro Dr NORM WF6 178 D3
Truro St WOR/ARM LS12 108 E6
Truro Wk NORM WF6 178 D3
Trust Fold GFTH/SHER LS25 159 M3
Tubby La HUDN HD2 192 D5
Tudor Barn Ct SHPY BD18 82 F7
Tudor Cl PDSY/CALV LS28 106 E4
PONT WF8 202 E1
Tudor Ct HEM/SK/SE WF9 247 H3
WHIT OL12 * 206 D5
Tudor Cft HUDN HD2 193 H1
Tudor Gdns BEE/HOL LS11 131 G4
Tudor Lawns RHAY LS8 88 D7
WKFDW/WTN WF2 176 A1
Tudor St MAR/SLWT HD7 212 C6
ROY/SHW OL2 229 K7
WBOW BD5 126 F2
Tudor Wy EARL WF12 195 K3
Tuel La RPDN/SBR HX6 167 L2
Tufton Pl SKP/WHF BD23 16 B3
Tufton St AIRE BD20 35 M4
Tuke Gv WKFDE WF1 176 F6
Tulip Gv WHIT OL12 206 A3
Tulip St HWTH BD22 78 E8
Tumbling Cl OSS WF5 175 G8
Tumbling Hl PONT WF8 203 J1
Tumbling Hill St GTHN BD7 4 C7
Tumbling La BSLYN/ROY S71 244 B8
Tune St BSLY S70 261 J6
Tun La CUD/GR S72 222 F8
Tunnacliffe Rd HUDS HD4 214 D3
Tunnel St CUL/QBY BD13 101 M6
HUDS HD4 213 L7
Tunnicliffe Pl AIRE BD20 35 M5
Tunshill La LIT OL15 208 A7
MILN OL16 207 L7
Tunstall Gn BOW BD4 128 A3
Tunstall Rd BEE/HOL LS11 131 L3
Tunwell La ECHL BD2 105 L2
Tunwell St ECHL BD2 105 L2
Tup La HOR/CROF WF4 222 E6
Turbary Av PDSY/CALV LS28 107 G4
Turbary Wk MILN OL16 206 F8
Turbid La HUDS HD4 213 J8
Turbury La GTL/HWG HX4 168 A6
Turf Ct CUL/QBY BD13 101 L1
Turf Hill Rd MILN OL16 228 D2
Turf House Cl LIT OL15 * 185 H7
Turf La CUL/QBY BD13 79 L8
Turf Ter LIT OL15 185 J8
Turgate La RPDN/SBR HX6 166 B5
Turley Cote La HUDW HD3 190 E5
Turlow Ct OSM LS9 9 K2
Turnberry Av AL/HA/HU LS17 87 K2
Turnberry Cl AL/HA/HU LS17 87 K2
Turnberry Ct AIRE BD20 57 J3
NORM WF6 178 F5
Turnberry Dr AL/HA/HU LS17 87 K2
EARD/LOFT WF3 152 F6
Turnberry Fold AL/HA/HU LS17 87 K2
Turnberry Gdns
EARD/LOFT WF3 152 F6
Turnberry Gv AL/HA/HU LS17 87 K2
CUD/GR S72 * 244 E5
Turnberry Pl AL/HA/HU LS17 87 K2
Turnberry Ri AL/HA/HU LS17 87 K2
Turnberry Vw AL/HA/HU LS17 87 K2
Turnbridge Rd HUDE HD5 15 J6
Turner Av BTLY WF17 * 173 L1
GTHN BD7 126 B1
Turner Av North LUD/ILL HX2 145 M1
Turner Av South LUD/ILL HX2 146 A2
Turner Cl EARD/LOFT WF3 153 G6
Turner Crs OT LS21 41 J5
Turner Dr EARD/LOFT WF3 153 G6
Turner La HIPP HX3 11 K2
ILK LS29 18 E6
Turner Pl GTHN BD7 126 D1
LUD/ILL HX2 146 A2
Turner's Ct HIPP HX3 146 D4
Turner's Pl WHIT OL12 206 A3
Turner St WHIT OL12 206 A5
Turners Yd PDSY/CALV LS28 106 F3
Turner Vw LUD/ILL HX2 146 A2
Turner Wy WKFDW/WTN WF2 12 E5
Turney St HIPP HX3 146 C4
Turnfield Cl MILN OL16 206 F3
Turnhill Rd MILN OL16 228 D3
Turnip La EARL WF12 195 M5
Turn O'The Nook OSS WF5 174 E8
Turnough Rd MILN OL16 207 H7
Turnpike La WBY LS22 31 L5
Turnpike Rd TAD LS24 72 B1
Turnpike St ELL HX5 169 J7
Turnshaw Rd KBTN HD8 216 C8
Turnshaws Av KBTN HD8 216 C7
Turnshaws Cl KBTN HD8 216 C7
Turnsteads Av CLECK BD19 149 K6
Turnsteads Cl CLECK BD19 149 L6
Turnsteads Crs CLECK BD19 149 L6
Turnsteads Dr CLECK BD19 149 L6
Turnsteads Mt CLECK BD19 149 L6
Turnstone Ct MID LS10 153 M1
The Turnways HDGY LS6 108 E2
Turpin La GFTH/SHER LS25 138 D3
Turret Hall Rd HBR HX7 142 E4
Turret Royd Rd HBR HX7 142 E4
Turton Gn MOR LS27 129 M7
Turton St WKFDE WF1 13 G3
Turton V MOR LS27 129 M8
Turver's La KNOT WF11 183 H3
Turvin Rd RPDN/SBR HX6 186 F4
Tuscany Wy NORM WF6 156 D8
Tuxford Crs BSLYN/ROY S71 261 M4
Twain Crs CAS WF10 180 E1
Tweedale Gdns DEWS WF13 173 K6
Tweedale St DEWS WF13 * 173 K6
ROCH OL11 228 A1
Tweed Cl BTLY WF17 151 J5
Tweedy St WIL/AL BD15 102 E1
Twelfth Av LVSG WF15 171 K1
Twibell St BSLYN/ROY S71 261 J3
Twickenham Ct GIR BD8 104 F4
Twinegate WHIT OL12 206 A3
Twitch Hl HOR/CROF WF4 197 K5
Twivey St CAS WF10 157 L7
Two Acre Dr ROY/SHW OL2 229 H6
Two Bridges Rd MILN OL16 229 K3
Two Laws Rd HWTH BD22 76 E5
Tyas Gv OSM LS9 110 D7
Tyas La MAR/SLWT HD7 211 K4
Tyburn La KBTN HD8 217 K8
Tydeman Wk MILN OL16 * 229 J1
Tyersal Av BOW BD4 106 B7
Tyersal Cl BOW BD4 106 B7
Tyersal Ct BOW BD4 106 B8
Tyersal Crs BOW BD4 106 B8
Tyersal Dr BOW BD4 106 B8
Tyersal Garth BOW BD4 106 B8
Tyersal Gn BOW BD4 106 B8
Tyersal Gv BOW BD4 106 B7
Tyersal La BOW BD4 128 A2
PDSY/CALV LS28 106 E8
Tyersal Pk BOW BD4 106 B8
Tyersal Rd BOW BD4 106 B8
Tyersal Ter BOW BD4 106 A8
Tyersal Vw BOW BD4 106 A8
Tyersal Wk BOW BD4 106 B8
Tyler Cl NORM WF6 179 G4
Tyndale Av HOR/CROF WF4 197 L4
Tyndale Wk BTLY WF17 173 G1
Tynedale Ct CHAL LS7 87 J8
Tyne St BFDE BD3 5 H4
KGHY BD21 3 K5
Tynwald Cl AL/HA/HU LS17 * 87 J4
Tynwald Dr AL/HA/HU LS17 87 J3
Tynwald Gn AL/HA/HU LS17 87 J3
Tynwald Hl AL/HA/HU LS17 87 J4
Tynwald Mt AL/HA/HU LS17 87 J3
Tynwald Rd AL/HA/HU LS17 87 J4
Tyrrell Ct WKFDW/WTN WF2 175 M7
Tyrrel St BFD BD1 4 F6
Tyson St HFAX HX1 146 A8

U

Ulla Gn TAD LS24 95 G5
Ullesthorpe WHIT OL12 * 206 A6
Ullswater Av EARL WF12 174 A3
ROY/SHW OL2 228 F8
Ullswater Cl EARL WF12 174 A3
ELL HX5 169 K7
Ullswater Crs MSTN/BAR LS15 111 G8
RTHW LS26 133 L8
Ullswater Dr WBSY BD6 126 B8
WBY LS22 29 L8
Ullswater Ri WBY LS22 29 L8
Ullswater Rd BSLYN/ROY S71 262 D6
EARL WF12 174 A4
Ulster Av ROCH OL11 228 A1
Una Pl HUDN HD2 14 B2
Uncouth Rd MILN OL16 207 G7
Underbank Av TOD OL14 142 D5
Underbank Old Rd
HOLM/MEL HD9 254 D3
Undercliffe La BFDE BD3 5 J2
Undercliffe Old Rd ECHL BD2 5 L1
Undercliffe Ri ILK LS29 39 G4
Undercliffe Rd ECHL BD2 105 K3
Undercliffe St BFDE BD3 5 L2
Underwood WHIT OL12 * 206 A7
Underwood Av BSLY S70 261 K8
Underwood Dr YEA LS19 84 D5
Underwood Wy ROY/SHW OL2 229 M6
Union Bank Yd HUD HD1 * 14 F7
Union Ct BSLY S70 261 H6
Union Gv LVSG WF15 172 D3
Union House La CLAY BD14 125 L4

Union La *LUD/ILL* HX2 .....123 M5
Union Pl *BEE/HOL* LS11 .....8 D4
Union Rd *GTHN* BD7 .....126 D1
　LVSG WF15 .....172 Q3
　WBSY BD6 .....126 E7
　WHIT OL12 .....207 M8
Union Sq *WKFDE* WF1 .....12 F5
Union St *BAIL* BD17 .....82 F4
　BGLY BD16 .....59 G7
　BSLY S70 .....261 H6
　BTLY WF17 .....151 L4
　COL BB8 .....74 A1
　CUL/QBY BD13 * 125 C5
　DEWS WF13 .....173 M6
　GTL/HWG HX4 .....168 F7
　HEM/SK/SE WF9 .....224 A8
　HFAX HX1 .....11 H7
　HUD HD1 .....15 G5
　HUDW HD3 .....191 K6
　LDSU LS2 .....7 H9
　LVSG WF15 .....172 E3
　MAR/SLWT HD7 .....212 B5
　MOR LS27 * 130 E6
　OSS WF5 .....174 F8
　OT LS21 .....41 H7
　RPDN/SBR HX6 .....167 G5
　RPDN/SBR HX6 .....167 L1
　WHIT OL12 .....206 B6
　WKFDE WF1 .....12 F2
Union St South *HFAX* HX1 * 11 H8
　TOD OL14 .....163 K1
Union Ter *CHAL* LS7 .....
　SKP/WHF BD23 * 16 B3
Union Yd *IDLE* BD10 .....83 K6
Unity Cl *HDGY* LS6 .....6 E1
Unity Ct *DEWS* WF13 .....173 K6
Unity St *AIRE* BD20 .....58 B4
　EARD/LOFT WF3 .....154 F3
　HBR HX7 .....143 J2
　TOD OL14 .....163 J6
Unity St North *BGLY* BD16 .....81 H4
Unity St South *BGLY* BD16 .....81 H4
Unity Ter *HFAX* HX1 .....
University Rd *LDSU* LS2 .....6 C5
University St *CAS* WF10 .....157 M7
Unwin Crs *STKB/PEN* S36 .....270 A4
Unwin Pl *HTON* BD9 .....104 A4
Unwin St *STKB/PEN* S36 .....270 A4
Upland Crs *RHAY* LS8 .....110 C1
Upland Gdns *RHAY* LS8 .....110 C1
Upland Gv *RHAY* LS8 .....110 C1
Upland Rd *RHAY* LS8 .....110 C2
Uplands *AIRE* BD20 .....57 J5
　HUDN HD2 .....192 A5
　SKP/WHF BD23 .....16 D7
Uplands Av *CUL/QBY* BD13 .....125 K4
　DOD/DAR S75 .....241 M6
Uplands Crs *CUL/QBY* BD13 .....125 K4
Uplands Dr *MIRF* WF14 .....172 C8
Uplands Gv *CUL/QBY* BD13 .....125 K4
The Uplands *PONT* WF8 .....180 E7
Upper Accommodation Rd
　OSM LS9 .....9 M1
Upper Ada St *SHPY* BD18 .....82 B6
Upper Addison St *BOW* BD4 .....5 H9
Upper Allerton La *WIL/AL* BD15 .....105 G6
Upper Ash Gv *HEM/SK/SE* WF9 .....247 J3
Upper Ashley La *SHPY* BD18 * 82 D6
Upper Bank End Rd
　HOLM/MEL HD9 .....254 D8
Upper Barker St *LVSG* WF15 .....172 C2
Upper Basinghall St *LDS* LS1 .....6 F9
Upper Batley La *BTLY* WF17 .....151 K6
Upper Batley Low La
　BTLY WF17 .....151 K4
Upper Battye St *HECK* WF16 .....172 F1
Upper Bell Cft *HIPP* HX3 .....169 J2
Upper Bell Hall *HFAX* HX1 .....168 C1
Upper Bolton Brow
　RPDN/SBR HX6 .....167 M1
Upper Bonegate *BRIG* HD6 .....170 D3
Upper Brig Royd
　RPDN/SBR HX6 .....188 F2
Upper Brow Rd *HUDW* HD3 .....213 M1
Upper Butts *CLECK* BD19 .....149 M7
Upper Camroyd St *DEWS* WF13 .....173 M5
Upper Carr La *PDSY/CALV* LS28 .....86 F4
Upper Carr St *LVSG* WF15 .....172 C1
Upper Castle *WBOW* BD5 .....127 G4
Upper Chelsea St *BFD* BD1 .....2 E8
Upper Cliffe Rd *DOD/DAR* S75 .....260 A6
Upper Cliff Hl *ROY/SHW* OL2 .....229 L5
Upper Clough Rd
　MAR/SLWT HD7 .....212 E6
Upper Commercial St
　BTLY WF17 .....173 L1
Upper Common La *KBTN* HD8 .....240 B6
Upper Croft Rd *BTLY* WF17 .....173 K2
Upper Cross St *DEWS* WF13 * 173 L5
Upper Ellistones Ct
　GTL/HWG HX4 .....168 C8
Upper Ferndown Gn
　WIL/AL BD15 * 103 J5
Upperfield Dr *MAR/SLWT* HD7 .....212 F6
Upper Field House La
　RPDN/SBR HX6 .....166 F4
Upper Field La *DOD/DAR* S75 .....240 F5
Upper Folderings
　DOD/DAR S75 .....260 B7
Upper Forest Rd
　BSLYN/ROY S71 .....243 H4
Upper Forge *HFAX* HX1 .....11 G6
Upper Fountaine St *LDS* LS1 .....6 F8
Upper Fountain St
　RPDN/SBR HX6 .....167 K2
Upper Fyfe La *BAIL* BD17 .....83 G3
Upper Ga *HOLM/MEL* HD9 .....255 G4
Upper George St *HECK* WF16 .....172 F2
　HUD HD1 .....14 D7
　WBSY BD6 * 126 D5
　WHIT OL12 .....206 B6
Upper Grange Av *WIL/AL* BD15 .....103 K6
Upper Green Av *CLECK* BD19 * 149 H6
Upper Green Dr
　EARD/LOFT WF3 .....152 F7
Upper Green La *BRIG* HD6 .....170 A1
Upper Green Wy
　EARD/LOFT WF3 .....152 F7
Upper Hagg Rd
　HOLM/MEL HD9 .....236 D5
Upper Hall Fold *GTL/HWG* HX4 .....189 K2
Upper Hall Vw *HIPP* HX3 .....147 J3
Upper Hatfield Pl
　HOR/CROF WF4 .....222 D7
Upper Haugh Shaw *HFAX* HX1 .....10 D9
Upper Hayes Ct *MILN* OL16 .....206 M4
Upper Headley
　CUL/QBY BD13 * 124 F1
Upperhead Rw *HUD* HD1 * 14 C7
Upper Heaton La *HUDE* HD5 .....193 M4
Upper Heights Rd
　CUL/QBY BD13 .....102 E6
Upper High Royds
　DOD/DAR S75 .....242 C6
Upper House La *LVSG* WF15 .....171 L2
Upper House Rd
　HOLM/MEL HD9 .....254 E6

Upper House St *BOW* BD4 .....127 K1
Upper Kirkgate *HFAX* HX1 .....11 J6
Upper La *CLECK* BD19 .....150 D7
　HIPP HX3 .....147 H2
　HOR/CROF WF4 .....218 G2
　KBTN HD8 .....217 M8
　TOD OL14 .....141 M5
Upper Langwith *WBY* LS22 .....47 G6
Upper Lombard St *YEA* LS19 .....84 C2
Upper Lumb La *HBR* HX7 .....165 L2
Upper Lunns Cl *BSLYN/ROY* S71 .....244 A3
Upper Marsh *HIPP* HX3 .....169 H1
Upper Marsh La *HWTH* BD22 .....100 B1
Upper Martin Gn *GTL/HWG* HX4 .....168 C7
Upper Mary St *SHPY* BD18 .....82 B6
Upper May Day Green Ar
　BSLY S70 * 261 H5
Upper Maythorn La
　HOLM/MEL HD9 .....255 M6
Upper Mdw *CUL/QBY* BD13 .....125 G6
　HOLM/MEL HD9 .....253 M1
Uppermoor *PDSY/CALV* LS28 .....106 E7
Uppermoor Cl *PDSY/CALV* LS28 .....106 F8
Upper Mosscar St *BFDE* BD3 .....5 K6
Upper Mount St *BTLY* WF17 .....173 L3
　HUD HD1 .....214 B2
Upper New St *BSLY* S70 * 261 H6
Upper Nidd St *BFDE* BD3 .....5 M7
Upper North St *BTLY* WF17 .....173 K2
Upper Parish Ghyll La *ILK* LS29 .....38 B3
Upper Park Ga *BFDE* BD3 .....5 H5
Upper Peel St *DEWS* WF13 * 173 L5
Upper Piccadilly *BFD* BD1 * 4 E5
Upper Quarry Rd *HUDN* HD2 .....171 J8
Upper Raglan St *TOD* OL14 * 141 M4
Upper Range *HIPP* HX3 .....11 H1
Upper Rd *DEWS* WF13 .....173 K4
Upper Royd *HIPP* HX3 .....147 L6
Upper Rushton Rd *BFDE* BD3 .....105 M5
Upper Sackville St
　SKP/WHF BD23 .....16 C3
Upper School St *AIRE* BD20 .....56 E1
Upper Seymour St *MILN* OL16 .....206 D8
Upper Sheffield Rd *BSLY* S70 .....261 J7
Upper South St *DEWS* WF13 * 173 L5
Upper Stone Dr *MILN* OL16 .....206 F8
Upper St *EARD/LOFT* WF3 * 153 H5
Upper Sutherland Rd
　HIPP HX3 .....148 A6
Upperthong La
　HOLM/MEL HD9 .....254 B1
Upper Town St *BRAM* LS13 .....107 L3
Upper Union St
　SKP/WHF BD23 .....16 B3
Upper Warrengate
　WKFDE WF1 .....13 G2
Upper Washer La *LUD/ILL* HX2 .....168 B1
Upper Wellhouse Rd
　MAR/SLWT HD7 .....212 E3
Upper West St *BTLY* WF17 * 174 A1
Upper Willow Hall *LUD/ILL* HX2 .....145 M8
Upperwood Hall
　WMB/DAR S73 * 263 H8
Upper Woodlands Rd *GIR* BD8 .....104 C5
Upperwood Rd *WMB/DAR* S73 .....263 G8
Upper Woodview Pl
　BEE/HOL LS11 * 131 K4
Upper Wortley Ct
　WOR/ARM LS12 .....108 D7
Upper Wortley Dr
　WOR/ARM LS12 * 108 D7
Upper Wortley Rd
　WOR/ARM LS12 .....108 D7
Upper York St *WKFDE* WF1 .....12 E1
Upton *ROCH* OL11 .....206 A8
Upton St *BTLY* WF17 .....151 K8
Upwood La *AIRE* BD20 .....58 F4
Ure Crs *GIR* BD8 .....4 B3
Ure Gv *WBY* LS22 .....29 M6
Usher St *BOW* BD4 .....127 H1
Uttley St *HIPP* HX3 * 146 D4

V

Vaal St *BSLY* S70 .....261 K6
Vale Av *KNOT* WF11 .....181 M2
　RHAY LS8 .....88 C3
Vale Cl *HUDE* HD5 .....215 H1
Vale Cottages *LIT* OL15 .....207 J1
Vale Crs *KNOT* WF11 .....181 M2
Vale Crest *KNOT* WF11 .....181 M2
Vale Gv *AIRE* BD20 .....35 M5
　CUL/QBY BD13 .....125 H6
Vale Head Gv *KNOT* WF11 .....181 M2
Vale Head Mt *KNOT* WF11 .....181 M2
Vale Mill La *HWTH* BD22 .....78 F5
Valentine Ct *CUL/QBY* BD13 .....103 C3
Valentine Ms *EARD/LOFT* WF3 .....154 L6
Vale Rd *HEM/SK/SE* WF9 .....223 K5
　ROY/SHW OL2 .....229 M8
Valestone Av *HEM/SK/SE* WF9 .....224 A7
Vale St *BRIC* HD6 .....170 C3
The Vale *HDGY* LS6 .....109 H1
　WBY LS22 .....47 J6
Vale Vw *FEA/AMT* WF7 .....202 D7
Valley Av *HEM/SK/SE* WF9 .....247 K3
　HIPP HX3 .....148 B6
Valley Cl *AL/HA/HU* LS17 .....87 J1
Valley Ct *BFD* BD1 * 4 F1
　CAS WF10 .....179 J1
　CHAL LS7 .....87 M6
Valley Dr *EARL* WF12 .....196 B6
　ILK LS29 .....38 F2
　MSTN/BAR LS15 .....111 K5
Valley Fold *CUL/QBY* BD13 .....125 G6
Valley Gdns *CHAL* LS7 .....87 G6
　PONT WF8 .....204 A2
Valley Gv *PDSY/CALV* LS28 .....107 H8
Valley Gv *BSLYN/ROY* S71 .....262 B3
　LUD/ILL HX2 .....124 B7
　PDSY/CALV LS28 .....107 H8
Valley Head *HUDW* HD3 .....191 L4
Valley Hts *CUL/QBY* BD13 .....101 M5
Valley Mt *BRAM* LS13 .....107 J6
　ILK LS29 .....38 F1
Valley Pde *GIR* BD8 .....4 E1
Valley Rdg *GFTH/SHER* LS25 .....135 H4
Valley Ri *BRAM* LS13 .....107 L1
　ROY/SHW OL2 .....229 J5
Valley Rd *BFD* BD1 .....4 F1
　BRAM LS13 .....107 L1
　CLECK BD19 .....150 A6
　DOD/DAR S75 .....242 D5
　EARL WF12 .....196 B5
　GFTH/SHER LS25 .....135 H3
　HBR HX7 .....143 J1
　ILK LS29 .....38 B2
　KGHY BD21 .....3 H2
　LVSG WF15 .....172 C1

　MOR LS27 .....152 D1
　OSS WF5 .....196 F2
　PDSY/CALV LS28 .....107 H8
　PONT WF8 .....204 A2
　ROCH OL11 .....228 A2
　SHPY BD18 .....82 D8
　YEA LS19 .....62 F7
Valley Sq *PDSY/CALV* LS28 .....107 H8
Valley St *HEM/SK/SE* WF9 .....247 H4
Valley Ter *AL/HA/HU* LS17 .....88 B3
The Valley *AL/HA/HU* LS17 .....65 J8
Valley Vw *AIRE* BD20 .....34 E7
　BAIL BD17 .....82 D5
　BGLY BD16 .....80 C5
　HEM/SK/SE WF9 .....247 K3
　LUD/ILL HX2 .....124 B7
Valley View Cl *HWTH* BD22 .....79 G3
Valley View Gdns *HWTH* BD22 * 79 G6
Valley View Gv *ECHL* BD2 .....105 J4
Valley View Rd *HBR* HX7 .....143 H2
Vancouver Pl *CHAL* LS7 .....88 A3
Varley Rd *MAR/SLWT* HD7 .....212 B8
Varley St *COL* BB8 .....52 A8
Vaughan Rd *AWLS/ASK* DN6 .....227 M5
　DOD/DAR S75 .....260 D3
Vaughan St *BFD* BD1 .....4 C5
　HFAX HX1 .....10 A9
Vavasour Ct *MILN* OL16 * 206 D8
Vavasour St *MILN* OL16 .....206 D8
Vaynor *WHIT* OL12 .....206 A6
Velvet Wood Cl *DOD/DAR* S75 .....260 C5
Venables Av *COL* BB8 .....52 B8
Ventnor Cl *CLECK* BD19 .....150 D4
　ROCH OL11 .....228 B1
Ventnor Dr *OSS* WF5 .....196 F1
Ventnor St *BFDE* BD3 .....5 K6
　ROCH OL11 .....228 B1
Ventnor Ter *HFAX* HX1 * 10 C5
Ventnor Wy *OSS* WF5 .....196 F1
Vento Cl *WBSY* BD6 .....125 M8
Vermont Wy *MILN* OL16 .....228 E3
Verdun Rd *WBSY* BD6 .....126 C6
Vere Sq *WBOW* BD5 .....127 Q2
Verity Sp *SCFT* LS14 .....111 C6
Verity St *BOW* BD4 .....128 B7
Verity Vw *SCFT* LS14 .....111 C6
Vermont St *BRAM* LS13 .....107 J4
Verner St *FEA/AMT* WF7 .....201 L2
Vernon Av *HUD* HD1 .....14 D4
　YEA LS19 .....62 C7
Vernon Cl *BSLY* S70 .....261 H7
Vernon Ct *KGHY* BD21 .....2 F5
Vernon Pl *ECHL* BD2 .....105 K4
　PDSY/CALV LS28 .....107 J2
　WKFDW/WTN WF2 .....12 D8
Vernon Rd *COL* BB8 .....52 F8
　LDS LS1 .....6 E6
　LVSG WF15 .....172 D2
Vernon St *BSLYN/ROY* S71 .....261 H4
　HWTH BD22 .....79 H6
　LDSU LS2 .....6 F7
　TOD OL14 .....163 J3
Vernon St North
　BSLYN/ROY S71 .....261 H4
Vernon Wy *DOD/DAR* S75 .....260 D3
Vesper Cl *KSTL* LS5 .....86 B9
Vesper Ct *KSTL* LS5 .....86 A8
Vesper Gdns *KSTL* LS5 .....108 B1
Vesper Gate Crs *KSTL* LS5 .....86 A9
Vesper Gate Dr *KSTL* LS5 .....86 A9
Vesper Gate Mt *KSTL* LS5 .....86 B8
Vesper Gv *KSTL* LS5 .....108 C2
Vesper La *KSTL* LS5 .....108 C2
Vesper Mt *KSTL* LS5 .....108 C2
Vesper Pl *KSTL* LS5 .....86 A9
Vesper Ri *KSTL* LS5 .....86 B8
Vesper Rd *KSTL* LS5 .....86 A8
Vesper Ter *KSTL* LS5 .....108 A2
Vesper Wk *KSTL* LS5 .....85 M8
Vesper Wy *KSTL* LS5 .....86 A8
Vestry St *BOW* BD4 .....127 K3
Viaduct Rd *WOR/ARM* LS12 .....108 B5
Viaduct St *HUD* HD1 .....14 F5
　MAR/SLWT HD7 .....212 C5
Vicarage Av *KSTL* LS5 .....108 D2
Vicarage Cl *HEM/SK/SE* WF9 .....246 E3
　LM/WK BD12 .....148 E4
　WKFDE WF1 .....176 D1
Vicarage Ct *CLECK* BD19 .....149 M6
Vicarage Dr *HOLM/MEL* HD9 .....234 F5
　MILN OL16 .....206 E3
　PDSY/CALV LS28 .....107 G2
Vicarage Gdns *BIRK/DRI* BD11 .....150 C1
　BRIG HD6 .....170 B6
　FEA/AMT WF7 .....179 M6
　OT LS21 .....41 J7
Vicarage La *BSLYN/ROY* S71 .....243 L5
　BSPA/BRAM LS23 .....69 M4
　FEA/AMT WF7 .....201 M7
Vicarage Meadow *MIRF* WF14 .....194 E1
Vicarage Rd *EARL* WF12 .....195 L1
　HDGY LS6 .....6 A4
　HUDW HD3 .....191 J8
　SHPY BD18 .....83 G6
Vicarage St *KSTL* LS5 .....108 D2
　ROY/SHW OL2 .....229 K7
Vicarage St North *WKFDE* WF1 .....13 G1
Vicarage St South *WKFDE* WF1 .....13 G2
Vicarage Vw *KSTL* LS5 .....108 D2
Vicarage Wk *STKB/PEN* S36 .....270 F3
Vicar La *BSLYN/ROY* S71 .....243 L5
　LDS LS1 .....7 H9
　OSS WF5 .....197 G3
Vicar Park Dr *LUD/ILL* HX2 .....145 K6
Vicar's Dr *MILN* OL16 .....206 B7
Vicar's Ga *MILN* OL16 .....206 A7
Vicars Rd *RHAY* LS8 .....110 B2
Vicar St *CAS* WF10 .....157 K2
　RHAY LS8 * 110 B2
Vickerman Crs *HUDS* HD4 .....214 B5
Vickerman St *HFAX* HX1 .....10 B8
Vickers Av *HEM/SK/SE* WF9 .....247 G5
　KSTL LS5 .....108 B3
Vickersdale *PDSY/CALV* LS28 .....107 G4
Vickers St *CAS* WF10 .....157 M7
　MOR LS27 .....152 B4
Victor Dr *GSLY* LS20 .....62 A6
Victoria Av *BRIG* HD6 .....170 E3
　BTLY WF17 .....173 L1
　CLECK BD19 * 149 M7
　ECHL BD2 .....105 M2
　ELL HX5 .....169 M3
　HFAX HX1 .....10 A8
　HIPP HX3 .....148 B6
　HWTH BD22 .....78 D4
　ILK LS29 .....38 B2
　KGHY BD21 .....3 H2
　KSTL LS5 .....108 C2
　LUD/ILL HX2 .....167 G1
　MAR/SLWT HD7 * 233 J1
　OSM LS9 .....110 C7
　RPDN/SBR HX6 .....167 L3
　RTHW LS26 .....155 G2
　SHPY BD18 .....82 B6
　WKFDW/WTN WF2 .....12 A2

　YEA LS19 .....62 F7
Victoria Cha *BRIG* HD6 .....148 D6
Victoria Cl *CAS* WF10 .....157 K2
　HORS LS18 .....85 J7
　ILK LS29 .....38 B2
　YEA LS19 .....62 F7
Victoria Ct *KGHY* BD21 2
Victoria Court Ms *HDGY* LS6 * 109 G5
Victoria Crs *BSLY* S70 .....260 F4
　DEWS WF13 .....173 J5
　ELL HX5 .....169 H8
　HORS LS18 .....85 J7
　PDSY/CALV LS28 .....106 E7
Victoria Crs West
　DOD/DAR S75 .....260 F4
Victoria Dr *EARL* WF12 .....195 L2
　ECHL BD2 .....105 M2
　HIPP HX3 .....147 K3
　HORS LS18 .....85 J7
　ILK LS29 .....38 B2
　MOR LS27 .....130 D8
Victoria Gdns *HORS* LS18 .....85 K7
　ILK LS29 .....38 B2
　PDSY/CALV LS28 .....106 E7
　ROY/SHW OL2 * 229 K7
Victoria Grange Dr *MOR* LS27 .....152 C1
　DOD/DAR S75 .....260 D3
Victoria Gv *HORS* LS18 .....85 K7
　ILK LS29 .....38 B2
　OSM LS9 .....110 D8
Victoria Ms *ELL* HX5 * 169 H8
　HORS LS18 .....85 J7
　KGHY BD21 .....2 D1
　MOR LS27 .....152 C1
Victoria Mt *HORS* LS18 .....85 J7
　SHPY BD18 .....82 B7
Victoria Park Av *BRAM* LS13 .....108 A3
Victoria Park Gv *BRAM* LS13 .....108 B3
Victoria Park St *KGHY* BD21 .....3 J3
Victoria Pk *HFAX* HX1 * 10 C5
　SHPY BD18 .....82 B7
Victoria Ri *PDSY/CALV* LS28 .....106 E7
Victoria Rd *AIRE* BD20 .....34 E8
　AWLS/ASK DN6 .....249 M8
　BEE/HOL LS11 .....6 D9
　BRIG HD6 .....148 D7
　BSLY S70 .....260 F4
　CLECK BD19 .....150 E6
　DEWS WF13 .....173 L5
　EARL WF12 .....195 L2
　ECHL BD2 .....105 L2
　ELL HX5 .....169 G8
　GSLY LS20 .....61 M6
　HBR HX7 .....143 J2
　HDGY LS6 .....109 G3
　HIPP HX3 .....147 M7
　HUDW HD3 .....191 J6
　HWTH BD22 .....54 F3
　HWTH BD22 .....78 F4
　ILK LS29 .....38 B2
　KGHY BD21 2
　KSTL LS5 .....108 C2
　LVSG WF15 .....172 C3
　MOR LS27 .....152 C1
　PDSY/CALV LS28 .....106 E7
　RPDN/SBR HX6 .....167 H3
　RTHW LS26 .....132 F8
　SCFT LS14 .....89 K7
　SHPY BD18 .....82 B7
　TOD OL14 .....141 K8
　WBSY BD6 .....126 C6
Victoria Springs
　HOLM/MEL HD9 .....254 A2
Victoria Sq *LDS* LS1 .....7 H9
Victoria St *AIRE* BD20 .....55 M1
　BAIL BD17 .....82 E5
　BFD BD1 .....5 G5
　BRIC HD6 .....170 D5
　BSLY S70 .....261 G4
　BSLY S70 .....261 M6
　BTLY WF17 .....151 H5
　BTLY WF17 .....151 K8
　BVRD LS3 .....6 B7
　CAS WF10 .....157 K2
　CAS WF10 .....157 L2
　CLAY BD14 .....5 K2
　CLECK BD19 .....149 M6
　CUD/GR S72 .....244 D7
　CUL/QBY BD13 .....80 A8
　CUL/QBY BD13 .....125 H5
　DEWS WF13 .....173 G8
　ECHL BD2 .....105 L4
　FEA/AMT WF7 .....201 M1
　FEA/AMT WF7 .....223 M1
　GTL/HWG HX4 .....168 F7
　HECK WF16 .....172 F2
　HEM/SK/SE WF9 .....224 A8
　HFAX HX1 .....11 G5
　HOLM/MEL HD9 .....254 C1
　HOR/CROF WF4 .....197 H5
　HUD HD1 .....214 D2
　HUDE HD5 .....15 M8
　HUDW HD3 .....193 G3
　IDLE BD10 .....83 K4
　KBTN HD8 .....240 A4
　LIT OL15 .....207 L1
　MAR/SLWT HD7 .....233 J1
　MID LS10 .....9 K4
　MOR LS27 .....152 B1
　PDSY/CALV LS28 .....84 C8
　PONT WF8 .....180 G5
　ROY/SHW OL2 .....229 K7
　RPDN/SBR HX6 .....167 K3
　SKP/WHF BD23 .....16 B2
　STKB/PEN S36 .....270 F3
　TOD OL14 .....140 C5
　WBY LS22 .....48 A1
　WHIT OL12 .....206 B2
　WIL/AL BD15 .....102 E2
　WKFDE WF1 .....176 D2
　WKFDW/WTN WF2 .....12 A2
　WMB/DAR S73 .....263 K6
Victoria Ter *BSLY* S70 .....261 J6
　BVRD LS3 .....6 B7
　CLECK BD19 .....149 L6
　HDGY LS6 .....109 G3
　HIPP HX3 .....148 B6
　KGHY BD21 .....3 J3
　KSTL LS5 .....108 C2
　LUD/ILL HX2 .....167 G1
　MAR/SLWT HD7 * 233 J1
　PDSY/CALV LS28 .....107 H8
　SKP/WHF BD23 .....16 B2
Victoria Wk *HORS* LS18 .....85 J7

Victoria Wy *WKFDE* WF1 .....176 D3
Victor Rd *HEM/SK/SE* WF9 .....246 E4
　HTON BD9 .....104 D4
Victor St *AWLS/ASK* DN6 .....249 K6
　BFDE BD3 .....106 A7
　BTLY WF17 .....173 M1
　CAS WF10 .....179 L1
　HEM/SK/SE WF9 .....247 H4
　HTON BD9 .....104 D4
Victor Ter *BSLY* S70 .....261 J6
　HFAX HX1 .....10 C3
　HTON BD9 .....104 D4
Victory Av *HUDW* HD3 .....213 K1
Victory La *EARD/LOFT* WF3 .....177 J4
Victory Rd *ILK* LS29 .....38 C3
View Croft Rd *BAIL* BD17 .....82 D6
Viewland Cl *CUD/GR* S72 .....262 E1
Viewlands *HUDN* HD2 .....192 C2
Viewlands Cl *STKB/PEN* S36 .....270 F1
Viewlands Mt *ILK* LS29 .....61 M1
Viewlands Ri *ILK* LS29 .....61 M2
View Rd *AIRE* BD20 .....22 D2
　STKB/PEN S36 .....270 C2
View St *HUDE* HD5 .....15 M8
　RHAY LS8 .....88 B6
Vignola Ter *CLAY* BD14 .....125 L1
Viking Av *KBTN* HD8 .....217 M8
Viking Rd *PONT* WF8 .....181 G6
Villa Cl *FEA/AMT* WF7 .....202 D6
Village Av *BULY* LS4 .....108 F4
Village Farm Cl *CLE* DN14 .....161 K7
Village Farm Ct *CLE* DN14 .....161 K7
Village Ms *WIL/AL* BD15 * 102 E1
Village Pl *BULY* LS4 .....108 F4
Village Rd *BHP/TINH* LS16 .....65 H4
Village St *AWLS/ASK* DN6 .....249 K8
　HIPP HX3 .....148 B4
The Village *BULY* LS4 .....108 F4
The Village *BULY* LS4 .....108 F4
The Village *BSPA/BRAM* LS23 .....49 G5
　HUDS HD4 .....215 H8
　HUDS HD4 .....237 G5
Villa Gv *BGLY* BD16 .....81 J3
Villa St *RPDN/SBR* HX6 .....167 L2
Villa Vw *BGLY* BD16 .....81 J3
Villier Ct *WIL/AL* BD15 .....103 K5
Vincent Av *AIRE* BD20 .....56 C1
Vincent Rd *BSLYN/ROY* S71 .....262 A3
Vincent St *BFD* BD1 * 4 D6
　COL BB8 .....74 A1
　HFAX HX1 .....10 B7
　MILN OL16 .....228 C1
Vine Av *BRIC* HD6 .....149 L6
Vine Cl *BRIG* HD6 .....170 E4
　BSLYN/ROY S71 .....261 L2
　ROY/SHW OL2 .....229 K7
Vine Ct *BRIG* HD6 .....170 F4
　MILN OL16 .....206 D8
Vine Crs *CLECK* BD19 .....149 L6
Vine Garth *BRIG* HD6 .....170 F4
Vine Gv *BRIG* HD6 .....170 F4
Vine Pl *ROCH* OL11 .....228 B1
Vinery Av *OSM* LS9 .....110 C6
Vinery Cl *KBTN* HD8 .....240 D4
Vinery Ct *OSM* LS9 .....110 C6
Vinery Gv *OSM* LS9 .....110 C6
Vinery Mt *OSM* LS9 .....110 C7
Vinery Pl *OSM* LS9 .....110 C7
Vinery Rd *BULY* LS4 .....108 F4
Vinery St *OSM* LS9 .....110 C6
Vinery Ter *OSM* LS9 .....110 C7
Vinery Vw *OSM* LS9 .....110 C7
Vine St *CLECK* BD19 .....149 M6
　GTHN BD7 .....126 D1
　HUD HD1 .....15 H2
Vine Ter *CUL/QBY* BD13 .....102 F8
Vine Ter East *GIR* BD8 .....104 A6
Vine Ter West *GIR* BD8 .....104 A6
Vineyard Cl *WHIT* OL12 .....184 E7
Violet St *HFAX* HX1 .....10 C5
　HWTH BD22 .....78 D3
Violet St North *HFAX* HX1 .....10 C4
Virginia Cl *EARD/LOFT* WF3 .....154 C4
Virginia Ct *EARD/LOFT* WF3 .....154 C4
Virginia Dr *EARD/LOFT* WF3 .....154 C4
Virginia Gdns *EARD/LOFT* WF3 .....154 C4
Virginia Rd *HUDW* HD3 .....191 L7
Virginia St *CLAY* BD14 .....125 L2
　ROCH OL11 * 228 A2
Vissett Cl *HEM/SK/SE* WF9 .....223 K8
Vissett La *HEM/SK/SE* WF9 .....223 J8
Vivian Pl *GTHN* BD7 .....126 C3
Vivian St *ROCH* OL11 .....228 A1
Vivien Rd *GIR* BD8 .....103 L6
Vollan's Ct *SCFT* LS14 .....111 J1
Vulcan Cl *DEWS* WF13 .....173 L6
Vulcan Gdns *DEWS* WF13 .....173 L6
Vulcan Rd *DEWS* WF13 .....173 L6
Vulcan St *BOW* BD4 .....127 M5
　BRIG HD6 .....170 C5
　TOD OL14 .....163 J5

W

Waarburton *KBTN* HD8 .....217 L8
Waddington Fold *MILN* OL16 .....228 E4
Waddington Rd *DOD/DAR* S75 .....260 D4
Waddington St *KGHY* BD21 * 2
Wade House Av *HIPP* HX3 .....125 L8
Wade House Rd *HIPP* HX3 .....147 L1
Wade La *LDSU* LS2 .....7 G7
Wade St *BFD* BD1 * 4 E7
　DOD/DAR S75 .....260 D4
　HFAX HX1 .....11 J5
　PDSY/CALV LS28 .....106 C3
Wadhouse La *HOR/CROF* WF4 .....198 B6
Wadlands Cl *PDSY/CALV* LS28 .....106 C2
Wadlands Dr *PDSY/CALV* LS28 .....106 C2
Wadlands Gv *PDSY/CALV* LS28 .....106 C2
Wadlands Ri *PDSY/CALV* LS28 .....106 C3
Wadman Rd *HOLM/MEL* HD9 .....254 F3
Wadsworth La *HBR* HX7 .....143 H5
Wadsworth St *HFAX* HX1 .....10 A8
Waggon La *HEM/SK/SE* WF9 .....225 K7
Wagon La *BGLY* BD16 .....81 J5
Wagtail Cl *WBSY* BD6 .....125 L5
Wain Brow *HUDS* HD4 .....214 B6
Waincliffe Crs *BEE/HOL* LS11 .....131 H5
Waincliffe Dr *BEE/HOL* LS11 .....131 H5
Waincliffe Garth *BEE/HOL* LS11 .....131 J6
Waincliffe Mt *BEE/HOL* LS11 .....131 H6
Waincliffe Pl *BEE/HOL* LS11 .....131 H5
Waincliffe Ter *BEE/HOL* LS11 * 131 H6
Wain Cl *GFTH/SHER* LS25 .....137 M3
Waindale Cl *LUD/ILL* HX2 .....145 L3
Waindale Crs *LUD/ILL* HX2 .....145 J3
Waindyke Wy *NORM* WF6 .....178 F4
Waingap Ri *WHIT* OL12 .....206 B2
Waingate *MAR/SLWT* HD7 .....212 F6
Waingate Pk *MAR/SLWT* HD7 .....212 F6
Wainhouse Rd *HFAX* HX1 .....10 A9
Wainman's Cl *HWTH* BD22 .....54 F3

Wainman St BAIL BD17 ....82 D6
BAIL BD17 ....82 F2
HFAX HX1 ....10 C5
Wain Pk HUDS HD4 ....214 B6
Wainscot Pl AWLS/ASK DN6 ....249 J4
Wainscott Cl HBR HX7 ....121 K8
Wainsgate HBR HX7 ....121 K8
Wainsgate La HBR HX7 ....121 K8
Wainstalls La LUD/ILL HX2 ....145 G1
Wainstalls Lodge La
LUD/ILL HX2 ....145 G1
Wainstalls Rd WKFDW/WTN WF2 * 123 H8
Waite St WKFDW/WTN WF2 ....176 A8
Waithlands Rd MILN OL16 ....206 D8
Wakefield Av SCFT LS14 ....111 H5
Wakefield Crs EARL WF12 ....174 B6
Wakefield La LUD/ILL HX2 ....168 B2
Wakefield Old Rd EARL WF12 * 173 M6
Wakefield Rd BFD BD1 ....5 H8
BIRK/DRI BD11 ....151 J1
BOW BD4 ....5 K9
BRIG HD6 ....170 E4
BSLY/ROY S71 ....243 H7
DOD/DAR S75 ....242 F5
EARL WF12 ....173 M6
FEA/AMT WF7 ....200 F2
GFTH/SHER LS25 ....112 F7
HEM/SK/SE WF9 ....223 K4
HIPP HX3 ....148 B7
HOR/CROF WF4 ....197 L4
HUDE HD5 ....15 L8
KBTN HD8 ....216 D3
KBTN HD8 ....195 G3
KBTN HD8 ....257 C1
LVSG WF15 ....172 D2
MID LS10 ....132 B4
NORM WF6 ....178 C5
OSS WF5 ....175 H7
PONT WF8 ....180 D7
RPDN/SBR HX6 ....167 M2
RTHW LS26 ....134 C5
RTHW LS26 ....154 D1
RTHW LS26 ....155 L3
Walden Dr HTON BD9 ....103 L3
Walden St CAS WF10 ....157 M7
Walden Stubbs Rd
AWLS/ASK DN6 ....227 M2
Waldorf Wy WKFDW/WTN WF2 * 12 D4
Walesby Ct BHP/TINH LS16 ....86 A4
Walford Av OSM LS9 ....110 C6
Walford Gv OSM LS9 ....110 C6
Walford Mt OSM LS9 ....110 C6
Walford Rd OSM LS9 ....110 C6
Walford Ter OSM LS9 ....110 C6
Walkden St WHIT OL12 * 6 D7
Walken Av GTHN BD7 ....126 A1
WKFDW/WTN WF2 ....176 D7
Walker Cl AIRE BD20 ....34 D8
Walker Dr GIR BD8 ....104 C6
Walkergate OT LS21 ....41 J7
PONT WF8 ....181 G5
Walker Gn EARL WF12 ....196 A5
Walker La HBR HX7 ....143 L1
HOR/CROF WF4 ....197 K5
RPDN/SBR HX6 ....167 M2
Walker Pl MOR LS27 * 130 D7
SHPY BD18 ....82 E6
Walker Rd HORS LS18 ....85 K5
LM/WK BD12 ....149 H2
Walkers Av WOR/ARM LS12 ....130 C2
Walker's La AIRE BD20 ....17 M7
WOR/ARM LS12 ....130 C2
Walkers Mt BTLY WF17 ....173 L3
HDGY LS6 ....109 H1
Walker's Pl AIRE BD20 ....36 A6
Walkers Rw YEA LS19 ....62 C8
Walker's Ter WKFDE WF1 * 12 C1
Walker St BOW BD4 ....127 K6
CLECK BD19 ....149 H5
CLECK BD19 ....149 M6
DEWS WF13 ....194 F2
EARL WF12 ....195 M2
MILN OL16 ....206 C7
Walker Ter BOW BD4 ....127 J2
CUL/QBY BD13 ....101 M1
Walker Wd BAIL BD17 ....82 B4
Walkley Av HECK WF16 ....172 F4
Walkley Gv HECK WF16 ....172 F5
Walkley La HECK WF16 ....173 C4
Walkley Ter HECK WF16 ....173 G4
Walk Mill La WHIT OL12 ....206 F2
Walk Royd Hl DOD/DAR S75 ....241 K4
The Walk KGHY BD21 ....3 H6
MILN OL16 ....206 B7
PDSY/CALV LS28 ....106 E4
Wallace Gdns EARD/LOFT WF3 ....154 D8
Wallace St HFAX HX1 ....10 A7
Wallbank Dr SHPY BD18 ....82 E8
Waller Clough Rd
MAR/SLWT HD7 ....212 B2
Wallhead Rd MILN OL16 ....206 F7
Wallingford Mt WIL/AL BD15 ....103 K7
Wallis St GIR BD8 ....104 C7
RPDN/SBR HX6 ....167 K2
Wall Nook La KBTN HD8 ....237 M8
Wallroyds KBTN HD8 ....257 G1
Wall St BSLY S70 ....261 G6
HWTH BD22 ....2 B7
Walmer Gv PDSY/CALV LS28 ....129 H1
Walmer Vls GIR BD8 ....4 C1
Walmsley Av LIT OL15 ....207 H3
Walmsley Dr HEM/SK/SE WF9 ....223 K7
Walmsley Rd HDGY LS6 ....109 G3
Walney Fold BSLY/ROY S71 ....243 M8
Walnut Av EARL WF12 ....174 C7
WKFDW/WTN WF2 ....176 B7
Walnut Cl BSLY S70 * 261 K7
EARL WF12 ....174 C8
SCFT LS14 ....89 L6
TAD LS24 ....93 K8
Walnut Crs EARL WF12 ....174 C8
WKFDW/WTN WF2 ....176 B7
Walnut Dr EARL WF12 ....174 C7
NORM WF6 ....178 D8
PONT WF8 ....180 D8
Walnut Gv EARL WF12 ....174 C8
Walnut La EARL WF12 ....174 C8
Walnut Pl EARL WF12 ....174 C7
Walnut Rd EARL WF12 ....174 C8
Walnut St BFDE BD3 ....105 L8
HEM/SK/SE WF9 ....247 H5
HFAX HX1 ....10 C6
KGHY BD21 ....79 K2
Walpole Rd HUDS HD4 ....213 M3
Walsden St MILN OL16 ....206 C7
Walsham Rd HDGY LS6 ....191 G5
Walshaw La HBR HX7 ....120 F3
Walshaw St GTHN BD7 ....4 B9
Walsh La BGLY BD16 ....59 H8
HIPP HX3 ....148 D5
WOR/ARM LS12 ....129 L4
Walsh Sq HFAX HX1 * 168 C1
Walsh St HFAX HX1 ....10 B5
Walter Clough La HIPP HX3 ....169 K1
Walter Crs OSM LS9 ....110 C7
Walter St BULY LS4 ....108 F5
ECHL BD2 ....104 F2
IDLE BD10 ....83 K6

Waltham Dr AWLS/ASK DN6 ....249 G4
Waltham St BSLY S70 ....261 H6
Waltin Rd HOLM/MEL HD9 ....254 D5
Walton Av PBR HG3 ....27 G3
Walton Cha BSPA/BRAM LS23 ....49 H3
Walton Cft HUDE HD5 ....193 G8
Walton Dr BIRK/DRI BD11 ....151 H1
Walton Garth BIRK/DRI BD11 ....151 H1
Walton Head La PBR HG3 ....26 F6
Walton La BRIG HD6 ....171 G6
WKFDW/WTN WF2 ....199 H6
Walton Locks
WKFDW/WTN WF2 ....199 J7
Walton Pk PBR HG3 ....27 G3
Walton Pl PBR HG3 ....26 F3
Walton Rd BSPA/BRAM LS23 ....48 F2
HEM/SK/SE WF9 ....225 M6
Walton Station La
WKFDW/WTN WF2 ....199 H7
Walton St BEE/HOL LS11 ....8 E4
BOW BD4 ....5 L8
DEWS WF13 ....260 E3
HWTH BD22 ....54 E3
MID LS10 ....9 L8
RPDN/SBR HX6 ....167 K2
SKP/WHF BD23 ....16 B5
Walton St North DOD/DAR S75 ....260 D3
Waltroyd Rd CLECK BD19 ....149 L7
Wansfell Ter BSLY/ROY S71 ....261 J5
Wansford Cl BOW BD4 ....128 A4
Wanstead Crs WIL/AL BD15 ....103 K6
Wapping Nick La HUDE HD5 ....193 G5
Wapping Rd BFDE BD3 ....5 G3
Ward Bank Rd HOLM/MEL HD9 ....254 D1
Ward Fall HOR/CROF WF4 ....220 B3
Ward La EARD/LOFT WF3 ....177 J4
MID LS10 ....131 M5
Wardle Crs HWTH BD22 ....2 B3
Wardle Edge WHIT OL12 ....206 A6
Wardle Fold WHIT OL12 ....184 E7
Wardle Gdns WHIT OL12 ....206 E3
Wardle Rd WHIT OL12 ....206 A6
Wardle St LIT OL15 * 185 J8
Wardman St KGHY BD21 ....3 L1
Ward Place La HOLM/MEL HD9 ....254 B3
Ward's End HFAX HX1 ....11 H7
Wards Hi BTLY WF17 ....173 L1
Wards Hill Ct BTLY WF17 * 173 L1
Ward Sq HUD HD1 * 14 E7
Ward St DEWS WF13 ....173 M5
GTHN BD7 ....126 C3
KGHY BD21 ....2 E7
MID LS10 ....9 J5
SKP/WHF BD23 ....16 C2
SKP/PEN S36 ....270 F4
Wareham Cnr BOW BD4 ....128 A4
Wareham Gv DOD/DAR S75 ....260 C6
Warehouse Hill Rd
MAR/SLWT HD7 ....233 H2
Warehouse St BTLY WF17 ....173 M2
Wareings Yd ROCH OL11 ....228 C2
War Field La WBY LS22 ....31 G2
Warhurst Rd ELL HX5 ....169 J6
Waring Wy EARL WF12 ....174 A5
Warlbeck ILK LS29 ....38 B2
Warley Av BFDE BD3 ....105 M6
Warley Dene LUD/ILL HX2 ....145 K8
Warley Dr BFDE BD3 ....105 M6
Warley Edge La LUD/ILL HX2 ....145 K7
Warley Gv BFDE BD3 ....105 M6
LUD/ILL HX2 ....145 M7
Warley Rd LUD/ILL HX2 ....145 M8
Warley St HFAX HX1 ....10 C7
LIT OL15 ....185 K8
Warley Town La LUD/ILL HX2 ....145 J7
Warley Vw LUD/ILL HX2 ....145 M7
Warley Wise La COL BB8 ....53 J5
Warley Wood Av LUD/ILL HX2 ....167 H1
Warley Wood La LUD/ILL HX2 ....145 G8
Warmfield La WKFDE WF1 ....178 A7
Warmfield Vw WKFDE WF1 ....178 A7
Warm La YEA LS19 ....84 C1
Warmleigh Pk CUL/QBY BD13 ....124 D5
Warneford Av OSS WF5 ....174 F1
Warneford Ri HUDS HD4 ....213 J2
Warneford Rd HUDS HD4 ....213 J2
Warner Av DOD/DAR S75 ....260 D4
Warner Pl DOD/DAR S75 ....260 D4
Warner Rd DOD/DAR S75 ....260 D4
Warrel's Av BRAM LS13 ....107 L4
Warrel's Ct BRAM LS13 ....107 L4
Warrel's Mt BRAM LS13 ....107 L4
Warrel's Pl BRAM LS13 ....107 L4
Warrel's Rd BRAM LS13 ....107 L3
Warrel's Rw BRAM LS13 * 107 L4
Warrel's St BRAM LS13 ....107 L4
Warrel's Ter BRAM LS13 ....107 L4
Warren Av BGLY BD16 ....81 K1
KNOT WF11 ....181 M3
WKFDW/WTN WF2 ....198 F4
Warren Cl BSLYN/ROY S71 ....243 M1
Warren Crs BSLY S70 ....261 H7
Warren Ct WKFDE WF1 * 13 H2
Warren Crs BSLY S70 ....261 H7
Warren Dr BGLY BD16 ....81 K2
FEA/AMT WF7 ....179 J6
Warrenfield Ct HUDN HD2 ....192 F3
Warren House La HUDN HD3 ....191 J3
YEA LS19 ....62 F5
Warren La BGLY BD16 ....81 K2
DOD/DAR S75 ....242 E2
OT LS21 ....43 J7
Warren Pk BRIG HD6 ....148 A8
Warren Park Cl BRIG HD6 ....170 A1
Warren Pl BSLY S70 ....261 H6
Warren Quarry La BSLY S70 ....261 H6
Warren Rd FEA/AMT WF7 ....201 K1
Warrenside HUDN HD3 ....193 G2
Warrens La BIRK/DRI BD11 ....150 F3
Warren St EARL WF12 * 173 M1
Warrenton Pl GTHN BD7 * 126 C1
Warren Vw BSLY S70 ....261 H6
Warrington Ter
MAR/SLWT HD7 * 233 G2
Warsop Rd BSLYN/ROY S71 ....243 H6
Warton Av BOW BD4 ....127 K5
Warwick Av MAR/SLWT HD7 ....213 G2
Warwick Cl BOW BD4 ....127 K2
HFAX HX1 * 168 D1
ROY/SHW OL2 ....229 H7
Warwick Dr BOW BD4 ....127 K2
Warwick Rd BOW BD4 ....127 K2
BSLYN/ROY S71 ....243 M1
BTLY WF17 ....173 L1
Warwick St WHIT OL12 ....206 D4
WKFDE WF1 ....13 L9
Wasdale Crs
WKFDW/WTN WF2 ....176 A7
Wasdale Rd
WKFDW/WTN WF2 ....176 A7
Washburn Ct WBY LS22 ....29 M6
Washburn Dr AIRE BD20 ....34 E8
Washer La LUD/ILL HX2 ....168 A3
Washfold Rd HBR HX7 ....165 J7
Washington Pl BRAM LS13 ....107 J6
Washington St BRAM LS13 ....107 J6

BVRD LS3 ....109 G6
GIR BD8 ....104 B5
HIPP HX3 ....10 D1
Washington Ter BRAM LS13 ....107 J6
Washpit New Rd
HOLM/MEL HD9 ....254 C4
Wasp Av ROCH OL11 ....228 C3
Wasp Nest Rd HUDN HD2 ....14 F1
Waste La HBR HX7 ....121 J1
HUDE HD5 ....215 G3
MIRF WF14 ....194 C3
Wastwater Dr WBSY BD6 ....126 B8
Watchit Hole La PONT WF8 ....225 L2
Watercock St BOW BD4 ....5 L4
Watercroft HUDE HD5 ....215 H3
Waterfall Fold PONT WF8 ....181 G5
Waterfall Pl BSLYN/ROY S71 ....262 A6
Waterfront Ms IDLE BD10 ....84 A6
Watergate HIPP HX3 ....147 L7
HUD HD1 ....15 H6
PONT WF8 ....180 E6
RTHW LS26 ....156 D5
Watergate Rd DEWS WF13 ....173 K7
Waterhall La STKB/PEN S36 ....270 F2
Waterhall Vw STKB/PEN S36 ....270 F2
Water Hill La RPDN/SBR HX6 ....167 J1
Waterhouse Cl WHIT OL16 ....206 E1
Waterhouse Gv
WKFDW/WTN WF2 ....12 B3
Waterhouse St HFAX HX1 ....11 G4
KGHY BD21 ....2 F6
WHIT OL12 ....206 B6
Watering Place Rd
STKB/PEN S36 ....270 C3
Water La BEE/HOL LS11 ....8 C5
BFD BD1 ....4 C5
EARD/LOFT WF3 ....177 K2
EARL WF12 ....174 C7
EARL WF12 ....174 C3
GFTH/SHER LS25 ....138 D6
HEM/SK/SE WF9 ....246 B2
HFAX HX1 ....11 J8
HOR/CROF WF4 ....196 H6
HOR/CROF WF4 ....220 C6
HORS LS18 ....85 C5
KGHY BD21 ....2 F6
MILN OL16 ....229 J1
PDSY/CALV LS28 ....106 F3
PONT WF8 ....181 H3
PONT WF8 ....202 F4
PONT WF8 ....205 G8
WOR/ARM LS12 ....107 M7
Water Lane Cl HOR/CROF WF4 ....196 H6
Waterloo Cl CAS WF10 ....179 H1
Waterloo Crs BRAM LS13 ....107 M3
IDLE BD10 ....84 B6
Waterloo Fold LM/WK BD12 ....148 F4
Waterloo Gv PDSY/CALV LS28 ....106 D7
Waterloo La BRAM LS13 ....107 M3
Waterloo Mt PDSY/CALV LS28 ....106 D6
Waterloo Ri HUDE HD5 ....215 J4
Waterloo Rd BGLY BD16 ....81 H5
BRIG HD6 ....170 C3
BSLY S70 ....260 F5
HUDE HD5 ....193 M8
PDSY/CALV LS28 ....107 H3
Waterloo St MID LS10 ....9 H2
WKFDE WF1 * 13 G6
Waterloo Ter LUD/ILL HX2 ....145 L8
Waterloo Wy BRAM LS13 ....107 M3
Waterman Vw MILN OL16 * 206 E6
Watermill La MILN OL16 ....206 F8
Water Rw HOLM/MEL HD9 ....237 G8
Water Royd Av MIRF WF14 ....172 C8
Water Royd Crs MIRF WF14 ....172 C8
Water Royd Dr DOD/DAR S75 ....260 B7
MIRF WF14 ....172 C8
Water Royd La MIRF WF14 ....172 C8
Waterside AIRE BD20 ....36 B6
BGLY BD16 ....80 F1
HIPP HX3 ....11 J8
HUD HD1 ....14 B9
HUDS HD4 ....214 B4
HWTH BD22 ....100 E4
SKP/WHF BD23 ....16 B4
Waterside Fold HBR HX7 ....143 J4
Waterside La MILN OL16 ....206 D6
Waterside Rd MID LS10 ....132 D4
Waterside Wk HUDE HD5 ....193 M1
Waters Rd MAR/SLWT HD7 ....232 E1
Water Stalls Rd
RPDN/SBR HX6 ....166 A6
Water St BRIG HD6 ....170 D3
HOLM/MEL HD9 ....253 M5
HUD HD1 ....14 D1
KBTN HD8 ....239 M5
MILN OL16 ....206 C7
RPDN/SBR HX6 ....167 K3
SKP/WHF BD23 ....16 B2
Waterton Cl HEM/SK/SE WF9 ....246 F3
WKFDW/WTN WF2 ....199 J8
Waterton Gv
WKFDW/WTN WF2 ....198 B1
Waterton Rd
WKFDW/WTN WF2 ....197 M2
Water Vw CAS WF10 ....157 M6
Waterview Cl MIRF WF14 ....229 K3
Waterwheel Ri HUDS HD4 ....213 M4
Waterwood Cl
EARD/LOFT WF3 ....153 H7
Waterworks Rd BTLY WF17 ....173 H2
UPML OL3 ....251 J8
Watery La HOLM/MEL HD9 ....253 H6
Watford Av HIPP HX3 ....148 B3
Wath La TAD LS24 ....94 F2
Watkin Av CUL/QBY BD13 ....103 H8
Watkinson Av LUD/ILL HX2 ....146 B2
Watkinson Dr LUD/ILL HX2 ....146 B2
Watkinson Rd LUD/ILL HX2 ....146 B2
Watkin St WD LS16 ....228 C2
Watling Rd CAS WF10 ....158 C5
Watmough St GTHN BD7 ....126 C3
Watnall Rd BSLYN/ROY S71 ....243 H6
Watroyd La MAR/SLWT HD7 ....212 D3
Watson Av EARL WF12 ....174 D6
Watson Crs WKFDE WF1 ....177 G2
Watson Mill La RPDN/SBR HX6 ....167 K3
Watson Rd SCFT LS14 ....111 H5
Watson's Houses
SKP/WHF BD23 * 16 B2
Watson's La TAD LS24 ....70 F1
Watson St MOR LS27 ....152 B3
NORM WF6 ....178 C4
Wattle Syke WBY LS22 ....47 M5
Watts St CLAY BD14 ....125 K2
WHIT OL12 ....206 D6
Watt St BOW BD4 ....127 M1
Watty Hall Av WBSY BD6 ....126 C4
Watty Hall La WBSY BD6 ....126 C4
Watty Hall Rd WBSY BD6 ....126 C4
Watty La TOD OL14 ....163 H3
Wauchope St
WKFDW/WTN WF2 ....12 D6
Wauds Gates BAIL BD17 ....82 E5
Waulkmill Cl HEM/SK/SE WF9 ....225 J7
Wavell Garth
WKFDW/WTN WF2 ....199 H7
Wavell Gv WKFDW/WTN WF2 ....199 G7

Waveney Dr DOD/DAR S75 ....260 A3
Waveney Rd ROY/SHW OL2 ....229 J6
WOR/ARM LS12 ....108 E8
Waverley Av WHIT OL12 * 206 A6
Waverley Av AIRE BD20 ....58 D6
GTHN BD7 ....126 D1
Waverley Crs HIPP HX3 ....147 L7
Waverley Garth BEE/HOL LS11 ....8 E8
Waverley Pl GTHN BD7 ....126 D1
Waverley Rd ELL HX5 ....191 H1
GTHN BD7 ....126 D1
HUD HD1 ....14 D5
Waverley St EARL WF12 ....173 L4
MAR/SLWT HD7 ....212 B5
Waverley Ter GTHN BD7 ....126 D1
HUD HD1 ....191 M7
Waverton Gn WBSY BD6 ....126 A7
Wavertree Park Gdns
LM/WK BD12 ....148 E2
Waycliffe BSLYN/ROY S71 ....261 L3
Wayland Ap BHP/TINH LS16 ....86 F2
Wayland Dr BHP/TINH LS16 ....86 F2
Wayne Cl BTLY WF17 ....151 L8
Wayside Av SCFT LS14 ....67 M5
Wayside Crs SCFT LS14 ....57 J4
Wayside Mt SCFT LS14 ....67 M4
Wayside Ter AL/HA/HU LS17 ....43 M3
Weardale Cl BOW BD4 ....127 L5
Weardley La AL/HA/HU LS17 ....44 D8
Weatherall Pl AWLS/ASK DN6 ....249 H4
Weatherhead Pl AIRE BD20 ....36 B5
Weatherhill Rd HUDN HD3 ....191 J4
Weather Hill La HBR HX7 ....166 A1
HOLM/MEL HD9 ....254 A6
Weather Hill Rd HUDW HD3 ....191 J3
Weatherhouse Ter
LUD/ILL HX2 ....145 M5
Weaver Cl DOD/DAR S75 ....260 A3
Weaver Gdns MOR LS27 ....152 F3
Weavers Cha
WKFDW/WTN WF2 ....175 M7
Weavers Ct HOLM/MEL HD9 ....235 H4
LUD/ILL HX2 ....145 L8
SKP/WHF BD23 ....16 B3
WOR/ARM LS12 ....108 D7
Weavers Cft CLECK BD19 ....150 B8
IDLE BD10 ....83 J4
PDSY/CALV LS28 ....107 H8
Weavers Gra GSLY LS20 ....62 A5
Weavers Hl HWTH BD22 ....78 E8
Weavers La CUL/QBY BD13 ....79 M8
Weavers Rd PONT WF8 ....181 G5
Weavers Rw PDSY/CALV LS28 ....107 H8
Weaver St BULY LS4 ....108 F5
Weavers Wk AIRE BD20 ....36 A4
Weaverthorpe Rd BOW BD4 ....128 A4
Weaving La EARL WF12 ....173 K8
Webb Dr ECHL BD2 ....105 J4
Webb's Ter HIPP HX3 ....11 K3
Weber Ct BFDE BD3 * 105 L7
Webster Hl EARL WF12 ....173 L6
Webster Pl NORM WF6 ....178 C4
Webster Rw WOR/ARM LS12 ....108 D8
Webster St BFDE BD3 ....5 L4
DEWS WF13 * 173 L6
Wedgemoor Cl LM/WK BD12 ....148 E2
Wedgewood Dr RHAY LS8 ....88 C5
Wedgewood Gv RHAY LS8 ....88 C5
Weedling Ga TAD LS24 ....71 K6
Weedon St MILN OL16 ....206 D6
Weeland Av HOR/CROF WF4 ....200 D3
Weeland Ct KNOT WF11 ....182 C2
Weeland Crs HOR/CROF WF4 ....200 E3
Weeland Dr HOR/CROF WF4 ....200 D3
Weeland Rd HOR/CROF WF4 ....200 E2
KNOT WF11 ....183 G2
Weetlands Cl GFTH/SHER LS25 ....135 K4
Weeton Av AL/HA/HU LS17 ....43 M3
Weet Shaw La CUD/GR S72 ....244 C5
Weetwood Av BHP/TINH LS16 ....86 D6
Weetwood Crs BHP/TINH LS16 ....86 F6
Weetwood Grange Gv
BHP/TINH LS16 ....86 D6
Weetwood House Ct
BHP/TINH LS16 ....86 D6
Weetwood La BHP/TINH LS16 ....86 E6
Weetwood Mill La
BHP/TINH LS16 ....86 F6
Weetwood Park Dr
BHP/TINH LS16 ....86 D6
Weetwood Rd BHP/TINH LS16 ....86 D6
GIR BD8 ....104 C6
Weetwood Wk BHP/TINH LS16 ....86 E7
Weetworth Av CAS WF10 ....158 A8
Weetworth Pk CAS WF10 ....158 A8
Weir Rd MILN OL16 ....207 G7
Weir Side MAR/SLWT HD7 * 233 H2
Weir St TOD OL14 ....163 J3
Weir Vw CAS WF10 ....157 M6
Welbeck Av LIT OL15 ....185 J8
Welbeck Cl MILN OL16 ....207 G8
Welbeck Dr GTHN BD7 ....126 A2
Welbeck Ri GTHN BD7 ....125 M2
Welbeck Rd BTLY WF17 ....151 H4
MILN OL16 ....228 D2
OSM LS9 ....110 C7
Welbeck St CAS WF10 * 157 M6
WKFDE WF1 ....13 H8
Welburn Av BHP/TINH LS16 ....86 D7
HIPP HX3 ....147 M7
Welburn Cl WKFDW/WTN WF2 ....199 H5
Welburn Dr BHP/TINH LS16 ....86 D7
Welburn Gv BHP/TINH LS16 ....86 D7
Welburn Mt WBSY BD6 ....126 A6
Welbury Dr GIR BD8 ....104 E4
Weldon Ct BOW BD4 ....128 A2
Weldon Dr HUDW HD3 ....190 C6
Welfare Av MSTN/BAR LS15 ....91 J3
Welham Wk BFDE BD3 ....5 J3
Welland Ct DOD/DAR S75 ....260 A3
Welland Dr GFTH/SHER LS25 ....113 J8
Welland Rd ROY/SHW OL2 ....229 J6
Wellands Ga CLECK BD19 ....149 K7
Wellands La CLECK BD19 ....149 H6
Wellands Ter BFDE BD3 ....105 L7
Well Cl RTHW LS26 ....135 G6
YEA LS19 ....84 E5
Well Close Rd LDSU LS2 ....9 K1
Well Close St BRIG HD6 ....170 C3
Well Croft CLAY BD14 ....125 J3
WHIT OL12 ....206 D6
Well Cft SHPY BD18 ....82 C7
Wellcroft Gdns HIPP HX3 ....147 L6
Wellcroft Gv EARD/LOFT WF3 ....153 H7
Wellesley Gn WKFDW/WTN WF2 ....176 A1
Wellesley Rd HEM/SK/SE WF9 ....146 A7
Wellfield Av HOR/CROF WF4 ....217 G1
Wellfield Cl HOR/CROF WF4 ....217 G1
Wellfield Gv
MAR/SLWT HD7 ....213 G4
Wellfield Gv STKB/PEN S36 ....270 F1
Wellfield La ILK LS29 ....40 A4
Wellfield Pl ROCH OL11 ....228 C1
Wellfield Rd DOD/DAR S75 ....260 F3
HUDW HD3 ....191 J4

Wellfield St ROCH OL11 ....228 C1
Wellfield Ter TOD OL14 ....163 K2
Wellgarth HFAX HX1 ....10 F9
Well Garth Bank BRAM LS13 ....107 L4
Well Garth Mt MSTN/BAR LS15 ....111 L4
Wellgarth Rd FEA/AMT WF7 ....202 A2
Well Garth Vw BRAM LS13 ....107 L4
Wellgate CAS WF10 ....158 B8
DOD/DAR S75 ....242 D5
GTL/HWG HX4 ....168 E6
MAR/SLWT HD7 ....212 D3
Well Green Gdns
HOLM/MEL HD9 ....236 B7
Well Green La BRIG HD6 ....170 B1
Well Gv BRIG HD6 ....170 B1
HUDN HD2 ....192 E3
Wellhead Cl BHP/TINH LS16 ....86 E2
Well Head Dr HFAX HX1 ....11 G8
Well Head La HFAX HX1 ....11 G8
RPDN/SBR HX6 ....166 E4
Well Heads CUL/QBY BD13 ....102 C8
Well Hl HOLM/MEL HD9 ....236 B2
OT LS21 ....41 H7
YEA LS19 ....62 D7
Well Hill Gv BSLYN/ROY S71 ....243 L2
Well Hill Rd HOLM/MEL HD9 ....254 D2
Wellholme BRIG HD6 ....170 D3
Well Holme Md
HOLM/MEL HD9 ....130 A3
Wellhouse Av MIRF WF14 ....172 D7
Wellhouse Cl MIRF WF14 ....172 C7
Well House Crs RHAY LS8 ....110 C1
Well House Dr RHAY LS8 ....110 C1
Well House Gdns RHAY LS8 ....110 C1
Wellhouse La HUDE HD5 ....193 G6
MIRF WF14 ....172 D7
Well House La STKB/PEN S36 ....257 K8
Well House Rd RHAY LS8 ....110 C1
Wellhouse Wy STKB/PEN S36 ....270 F1
Wellington Ar BRIG HD6 * 170 C4
Wellington Br WOR/ARM LS12 ....8 A2
HUDN HD2 ....192 E3
Wellington Bridge St BVRD LS3 ....8 B1
LDS LS1 ....8 B1
Wellington Ct BIRK/DRI BD11 ....128 C8
BTLY WF17 * 173 K1
LUD/ILL HX2 ....146 A5
Wellington Gra SHPY BD18 ....82 C7
Wellington Gdns BRAM LS13 ....107 M3
Wellington Garth BRAM LS13 ....107 M3
Wellington Gn GTHN BD7 ....126 B2
ECHL BD2 ....105 K4
PDSY/CALV LS28 ....106 E7
Wellington Hl SCFT LS14 ....89 J4
Wellingtonia Dr AWLS/ASK DN6 ....227 L3
Wellington Mt BRAM LS13 ....107 M3
Wellington Pl BSLY S70 ....260 F5
KNOT WF11 ....181 M2
LDS LS1 ....8 B1
MILN OL16 ....206 C6
Wellington Rd EARL WF12 ....173 L6
DEWS WF13 * 173 L6
ECHL BD2 ....105 K3
ILK LS29 ....38 D2
KGHY BD21 ....3 G3
TOD OL14 ....163 K1
WIL/AL BD15 ....102 E2
WOR/ARM LS12 ....8 B1
Wellington Rd East
DEWS WF13 * 173 L6
Wellington St BFD BD1 * 5 G6
BGLY BD16 ....81 H3
BOW BD4 ....105 M8
BSLY S70 ....261 G5
BVRD LS3 ....8 B9
CAS WF10 ....6 B9
CUL/QBY BD13 ....125 H5
DEWS WF13 ....173 K3
ECHL BD2 ....105 K3
IDLE BD10 ....83 K7
LDS LS1 ....8 D1
LVSG WF15 ....172 D3
MILN OL16 ....206 C6
MOR LS27 ....152 C3
SKP/WHF BD23 ....206 B5
WHIT OL12 ....103 L5
WKFDW/WTN WF2 ....12 D7
Wellington St South HFAX HX1 ....11 J7
Wellington St West HFAX HX1 ....10 E8
Wellington Ter BRAM LS13 ....107 M2
MAR/SLWT HD7 * 233 J2
Well I' Th' La ROCH OL11 ....228 C1
Well La BRIG HD6 ....171 G4
BSLYN/ROY S71 ....261 L1
BTLY WF17 ....173 M1
CHAL LS7 ....87 G3
DEWS WF13 ....173 H6
GFTH/SHER LS25 ....135 J5
GFTH/SHER LS25 ....138 A2
GSLY LS20 ....62 D7
HFAX HX1 ....11 J5
YEA LS19 ....62 D8
Wells Ct CUD/GR S72 ....244 D8
DOD/DAR S75 ....242 A6
The Wells LUD/ILL HX2 ....168 A1
LUD/ILL HX2 ....168 A1
Wellstone Av BRAM LS13 ....107 K6
Wellstone Dr BRAM LS13 ....107 K6
Wellstone Gdns BRAM LS13 ....107 K6
Wellstone Garth BRAM LS13 ....107 K5
Wellstone Gn BRAM LS13 ....107 K6
Wellstone Ri BRAM LS13 ....107 K6
Wellstone Rd BRAM LS13 ....107 K6
Wellstone Wy BRAM LS13 ....107 K6
Well St BFD BD1 ....5 G6
BSLY S70 ....260 F5
CUL/QBY BD13 ....101 M6
EARL WF12 ....174 A6
GTL/HWG HX4 ....190 D2
HUD HD1 ....14 C9
KGHY BD21 ....2 F4
LVSG WF15 ....172 C1
ROCH OL11 ....228 C1
TOD OL14 ....163 K2
Well Ter GSLY LS20 ....62 A5
Wellthorne La STKB/PEN S36 ....256 F5
Welton Av HDGY LS6 ....109 G3
Weltondown Gdns ROY/SHW OL2 ....229 H6
Welton Gv HDGY LS6 ....109 G3
Welton Mt HDGY LS6 ....109 G3
Welton Pl HDGY LS6 ....109 G3
Welton Rd HDGY LS6 ....109 G3

Welwyn Av BTLY WF17 151 H8
SHPY BD18 83 H7
Welwyn Dr BAIL BD17 82 E4
SHPY BD18 83 H7
Welwyn Rd EARL WF12 174 B3
Wembly Av CUL/QBY BD13 103 H8
Wenborough La BOW BD4 128 B3
Wendel Av MSTN/BAR LS15 90 F7
Wendron Cl LVSG WF15 172 B5
Wendron Wy IDLE BD10 83 K7
Wenlock St BFDE BD3 5 J7
Wenning St KGHY BD21 3 M3
Wensley Av CHAL LS7 87 L7
SHPY BD18 82 C7
Wensley Bank CUL/QBY BD13 102 E8
Wensley Bank Ter
CUL/QBY BD13 102 E8
Wensley Bank West
CUL/QBY BD13 102 E8
Wensley Crs CHAL LS7 87 L7
Wensleydale Av
SKP/WHF BD23 16 D2
WOR/ARM LS12 108 B4
Wensleydale Crs
WOR/ARM LS12 108 B4
Wensleydale Dr
WOR/ARM LS12 108 B4
Wensleydale Ms
WOR/ARM LS12 108 B4
Wensleydale Ri BAIL BD17 83 G2
WOR/ARM LS12 * 108 B4
Wensleydale Rd BFDE BD3 106 A7
Wensley Dr CHAL LS7 87 L7
PONT WF8 181 G8
Wensley Gn CHAL LS7 87 K7
Wensley Gv BRIG HD6 170 A6
Wensley Lawn MID LS10 153 L2
Wensley Rd BSLYN/ROY S71 243 G7
CHAL LS7 87 K6
Wensley St East
HOR/CROF WF4 197 H5
Wensley Vw CHAL LS7 87 L7
Wensley Wy MILN OL16 206 D8
Went Av FEA/AMT WF7 201 L3
Wentbridge La PONT WF8 203 L8
Wentbridge Rd FEA/AMT WF7 202 A2
Wentcliffe Rd KNOT WF11 181 K2
Went Cft PONT WF8 202 F1
Wentdale PONT WF8 205 G8
Went-Dale Rd PONT WF8 202 E1
Went Edge Rd PONT WF8 203 M8
Went Fold PONT WF8 202 F1
Went Garth PONT WF8 202 E1
Went Gv FEA/AMT WF7 201 L2
Went Hill Cl FEA/AMT WF7 202 C6
Went La HOR/CROF WF4 201 J8
Went Vw PONT WF8 225 J1
Went View Ct PONT WF8 * 203 H7
Wentwell Rd FEA/AMT WF7 200 E1
Wentworth Av AL/HA/HU LS17 87 K2
KBTN HD8 217 L8
Wentworth Cl HOR/CROF WF4 220 B7
ILK LS29 61 J2
Wentworth Ct BRIG HD6 170 B7
Wentworth Crs
AL/HA/HU LS17 87 L2
DOD/DAR S75 242 E6
STKB/PEN S36 270 F3
Wentworth Dr DOD/DAR S75 * 242 E6
HEM/SK/SE WF9 246 E3
HOR/CROF WF4 200 C6
KBTN HD8 217 L8
LUD/ILL HX2 124 B7
Wentworth Ga WBY LS22 29 K8
Wentworth Gv LUD/ILL HX2 124 B7
Wentworth Mdw
STKB/PEN S36 270 E2
Wentworth Ms STKB/PEN S36 270 F3
Wentworth Park Ri PONT WF8 203 M1
Wentworth Rd DOD/DAR S75 241 L6
DOD/DAR S75 242 E6
FEA/AMT WF7 201 K2
STKB/PEN S36 270 E2
Wentworth St BSLYN/ROY S71 261 G3
HUD HD1 14 D5
WKFDE WF1 176 D6
Wentworth Ter
HEM/SK/SE WF9 223 K3
WKFDE WF1 * 176 D7
Wentworth Wy AL/HA/HU LS17 87 L2
DOD/DAR S75 260 B8
WKFDW/WTN WF2 199 G5
Wepener Mt OSM LS9 110 D5
Wepener Pl OSM LS9 110 D5
Wescoe Hill La AL/HA/HU LS17 43 M4
Wesleyan Ter BOW BD4 * 127 L3
Wesley Ap BEE/HOL LS11 131 H4
Wesley Av LM/WK BD12 126 F7
WOR/ARM LS12 108 E7
Wesley Av South LM/WK BD12 127 G8
Wesley Cl BTLY WF17 151 G5
WHIT OL12 206 D4
Wesley Ct BEE/HOL LS11 131 H4
HDGY LS6 6 D2
HFAX HX1 * 11 H5
OSS WF5 174 E8
Wesley Cft BEE/HOL LS11 8 A9
Wesley Dr LM/WK BD12 127 G7
Wesley Garth BEE/HOL LS11 131 H3
Wesley Gn BEE/HOL LS11 131 H4
Wesley Gv IDLE BD10 83 L5
Wesley Hall Ct
EARD/LOFT WF3 * 177 H4
Wesley Pl AIRE BD20 36 A5
DEWS WF13 * 173 L6
FEA/AMT WF7 201 M2
KGHY BD21 79 K3
OSM LS9 9 M1
WOR/ARM LS12 108 E7
Wesley Rd PDSY/CALV LS28 106 E5
WOR/ARM LS12 108 E7
Wesley Rw PDSY/CALV LS28 * 107 G6
Wesley Sq PDSY/CALV LS28 107 G6
Wesley St BEE/HOL LS11 131 G3
BRAM LS13 107 H1
BSLY S70 261 H5
CAS WF10 179 L1
CLECK BD19 149 M6
HEM/SK/SE WF9 247 G4
MILN OL16 207 G8
MOR LS27 152 C2
OSS WF5 174 E8
OT LS21 41 J6
PDSY/CALV LS28 106 F3
WHIT OL12 * 206 D3
WKFDE WF1 13 K8
Wesley Ter BRAM LS13 107 H1
BRAM LS13 107 M3
KBTN HD8 239 H8
PDSY/CALV LS28 107 G6
Wesley Vw BRAM LS13 * 107 H1
PDSY/CALV LS28 107 G7
Wessenden Cl DOD/DAR S75 260 C5
Wessenden Head Rd
HOLM/MEL HD9 234 E5
Wessenden Rd MAR/SLWT HD7 233 J6
Wessex Park Cl ROY/SHW OL2 229 K6
West Acres KNOT WF11 159 M6
STKB/PEN S36 271 G3
West Av BAIL BD17 82 E2
BSPA/BRAM LS23 48 E6
HEM/SK/SE WF9 225 J7
HIPP HX3 148 C7
HIPP HX3 168 D2
HOLM/MEL HD9 236 A2
HOR/CROF WF4 197 L5
HUDW HD3 191 L5
PONT WF8 180 C6
RHAY LS8 88 E6
West Bank HWTH BD22 2 B3
LUD/ILL HX2 145 M2
West Bank Cl HWTH BD22 2 A3
West Bank Gv AIRE BD20 58 A4
West Bank Ri HWTH BD22 2 A3
West Bank Rd AIRE BD20 57 M4
SKP/WHF BD23 16 A2
West Bolton LUD/ILL HX2 123 M7
Westborough Dr LUD/ILL HX2 145 M7
Westbourne Av BEE/HOL LS11 131 K3
GFTH/SHER LS25 112 F8
PONT WF8 180 D7
Westbourne Cl OT LS21 41 G8
WKFDW/WTN WF2 198 E8
Westbourne Crs
GFTH/SHER LS25 112 F8
HIPP HX3 168 F3
PONT WF8 180 D7
Westbourne Dr
GFTH/SHER LS25 112 F8
GSLY LS20 61 L5
ILK LS29 61 J1
Westbourne Gdns
GFTH/SHER LS25 112 F8
Westbourne Gv DOD/DAR S75 260 F3
GFTH/SHER LS25 112 F8
HIPP HX3 168 F3
OT LS21 41 G7
Westbourne Mt BEE/HOL LS11 131 K3
PONT WF8 180 E7
Westbourne Pl BEE/HOL LS11 131 K3
PDSY/CALV LS28 106 F5
Westbourne Rd GIR BD8 * 104 D4
HUD HD1 191 M7
PONT WF8 180 E7
Westbourne St BEE/HOL LS11 131 K3
Westbourne Ter BSLY S70 260 E5
GFTH/SHER LS25 112 E8
HIPP HX3 168 F3
Westbrook Cl HORS LS18 85 K4
West Brook Ct HFAX HX1 10 F4
Westbrook Dr HUDE HD5 193 K8
Westbrook La HORS LS18 85 K4
West Buck La OT LS21 40 F8
Westburn Av HWTH BD22 2 A8
Westburn Crs HWTH BD22 2 A8
Westburn Gv HWTH BD22 2 B8
Westburn Wy HWTH BD22 2 A8
Westbury Cl BOW BD4 127 M1
DOD/DAR S75 260 D2
Westbury Gv MID LS10 132 B4
Westbury Mt RTHW LS26 132 B5
Westbury Pl HFAX HX1 146 A8
Westbury Pl North MID LS10 132 B4
Westbury Pl South RTHW LS26 132 B5
Westbury Rd WBSY BD6 125 M5
Westbury St BOW BD4 127 M1
ELL HX5 169 J7
MID LS10 132 B5
Westbury Ter HFAX HX1 146 A8
RTHW LS26 132 B5
West Byland LUD/ILL HX2 123 M7
West Carr La HUDW HD3 211 G4
West Chevin Rd OT LS21 61 M1
Westcliffe Av BAIL BD17 82 D2
Westcliffe Dr LUD/ILL HX2 145 M7
Westcliffe Ri CLECK BD19 149 L7
Westcliffe Rd CLECK BD19 149 L6
SHPY BD18 82 D7
West Cl HUDN HD2 192 D4
NORM WF6 178 C4
PONT WF8 203 G1
Westcombe Av RHAY LS8 88 C4
Westcombe Ct LM/WK BD12 148 E2
West Cote Dr IDLE BD10 83 H5
West Ct RHAY LS8 88 E7
West Crs STKB/PEN S36 271 J4
West Cft AIRE BD20 55 L2
ILK LS29 19 H6
LM/WK BD12 148 E3
Westcroft HOLM/MEL HD9 236 A2
Westcroft Av HIPP HX3 147 K2
Westcroft Dr OSS WF5 174 E5
Westcroft La SEL YO8 139 M5
Westcroft Rd GTHN BD7 126 C2
HEM/SK/SE WF9 223 M7
West Dl BSPA/BRAM LS23 48 E5
Westdale Dr PDSY/CALV LS28 106 F6
Westdale Gdns
PDSY/CALV LS28 106 F6
Westdale Gv PDSY/CALV LS28 106 F6
Westdale Ri PDSY/CALV LS28 106 F6
Westdale Rd PDSY/CALV LS28 106 F6
West Dene AIRE BD20 36 A4
AL/HA/HU LS17 88 B1
West Dr HWTH BD22 100 E3
PONT WF8 181 G7
West Edge Rd PONT WF8 204 A8
West End BSPA/BRAM LS23 48 E6
CUL/QBY BD13 124 F6
HFAX HX1 * 146 A8
HOLM/MEL HD9 236 B6
MOR LS27 129 L7
WOR/ARM LS12 129 M3
West End Ap MOR LS27 151 M3
TAD LS24 94 F1
West End Av BSLYN/ROY S71 243 J3
FEA/AMT WF7 179 J6
HOLM/MEL HD9 236 E8
STKB/PEN S36 269 M3
West End Cl HORS LS18 85 H5
West End Crs BSLYN/ROY S71 243 J3
West End Dr CLECK BD19 149 K8
HORS LS18 85 J5
West End Gv HORS LS18 85 H5
West End La HORS LS18 85 H4
West End Pl BEE/HOL LS11 8 C5
West End Ri HORS LS18 85 H5
West End Rd AWLS/ASK DN6 227 L3
HFAX HX1 146 A8
MAR/SLWT HD7 212 E2
PDSY/CALV LS28 84 D8
Westend St BFD BD1 4 D5
West End Ter ECHL BD2 105 K1
GSLY LS20 61 L5
HBR HX7 144 A5
SHPY BD18 82 C6
Westercroft La HIPP HX3 147 K3
Westercroft Vw HIPP HX3 147 K3
Westerley Cl KBTN HD8 238 C3
Westerley Crs AIRE BD20 35 L5
Westerley La KBTN HD8 238 C3
Westerly Cft WOR/ARM LS12 108 E6
Westerly Ri WOR/ARM LS12 108 E6
Westerly Wy KBTN HD8 238 C3
Westerman Cl FEA/AMT WF7 * 179 M8
Westerman St WKFDE WF1 13 K9
Western Av AIRE BD20 57 M3
BTLY WF17 151 J5
PONT WF8 181 H5
Western Ct PONT WF8 181 H5
Western Gales Wy NORM WF6 178 F5
Western Gv WOR/ARM LS12 130 D1
Western Mt WOR/ARM LS12 130 D1
Western Pl CUL/QBY BD13 125 K5
Western Rd HUDS HD4 213 J2
SKP/WHF BD23 16 D3
WOR/ARM LS12 130 D1
Western St BSLY S70 261 G4
WOR/ARM LS12 130 D1
Western Wy WBSY BD6 126 C7
Westerton Cl EARD/LOFT WF3 153 K7
Westerton Ct LM/WK BD12 149 K1
Westerton Rd
EARD/LOFT WF3 152 F7
Westerton Wk
EARD/LOFT WF3 153 K6
West Farm Av MID LS10 153 K1
Westfell Cl HWTH BD22 2 B7
Westfell Rd HWTH BD22 2 B7
Westfell Wy HWTH BD22 2 B7
Westfield CUL/QBY BD13 103 J8
HBR HX7 143 L1
PDSY/CALV LS28 106 F5
Westfield Av CAS WF10 157 J1
CAS WF10 179 L2
EARL WF12 174 C6
GFTH/SHER LS25 135 J4
HIPP HX3 147 M7
HOLM/MEL HD9 234 E3
HUDW HD3 191 K7
KBTN HD8 239 H5
KNOT WF11 182 B3
PONT WF8 180 E8
STKB/PEN S36 270 C2
WOR/ARM LS12 108 B6
YEA LS19 62 B8
Westfield Cl GFTH/SHER LS25 137 M3
HECK WF16 * 172 E1
RTHW LS26 154 E2
YEA LS19 62 B8
Westfield Ct GFTH/SHER LS25 138 B2
HOR/CROF WF4 197 H4
HUDE HD5 15 M6
MIRF WF14 194 C1
RTHW LS26 154 E2
WOR/ARM LS12 130 D1
Westfield Crs AIRE BD20 58 B4
ECHL BD2 5 L1
HDGY LS6 6 A5
HOR/CROF WF4 222 C5
OSS WF5 196 E1
SHPY BD18 83 G8
TAD LS24 71 L3
WKFDW/WTN WF2 175 K4
Westfield Dr AIRE BD20 58 B5
HIPP HX3 147 M7
KBTN HD8 239 H5
OSS WF5 196 E1
YEA LS19 62 A8
Westfield Farm OSS WF5 174 E8
Westfield Gdns
GFTH/SHER LS25 135 H4
HIPP HX3 147 M7
Westfield Gn RYKW YO26 32 A1
Westfield Gv CAS WF10 135 J8
CAS WF10 179 L2
DEWS WF13 173 H6
FEA/AMT WF7 202 D6
IDLE BD10 83 J6
SHPY BD18 * 83 G8
WKFDE WF1 176 E6
West Field La HOLM/MEL HD9 236 E8
Westfield La GFTH/SHER LS25 135 H4
GFTH/SHER LS25 137 J4
HEM/SK/SE WF9 247 H5
KBTN HD8 217 G6
LM/WK BD12 148 F5
PONT WF8 203 L3
PONT WF8 227 G3
SHPY BD18 83 H7
STKB/PEN S36 270 C2
Westfield Mt YEA LS19 62 A8
Westfield Ov YEA LS19 62 A8
Westfield Pk WKFDE WF1 176 E6
Westfield Pl CLECK BD19 149 G5
HFAX HX1 10 C8
WKFDW/WTN WF2 175 K4
Westfield Rd AIRE BD20 58 B5
BVRD LS3 6 A6
CLAY BD14 125 K2
HECK WF16 172 E1
HEM/SK/SE WF9 223 M7
HOR/CROF WF4 197 H4
HTON BD9 104 C4
KNOT WF11 182 B3
MOR LS27 * 152 C2
RTHW LS26 154 E2
RYKW YO26 32 A1
WKFDE WF1 176 D6
Westfields BSLYN/ROY S71 243 J2
CAS WF10 179 L1
Westfields Av MIRF WF14 194 C1
Westfield Sq TAD LS24 71 L2
Westfields Rd MIRF WF14 194 C1
Westfield St BSLY S70 * 260 F5
HECK WF16 172 E1
HFAX HX1 10 E7
OSS WF5 196 E1
Westfield Ter BAIL BD17 82 E2
BVRD LS3 6 A6
CAS WF10 157 J1
CLAY BD14 125 K2
ECHL BD2 5 L1
HFAX HX1 10 C3
TAD LS24 71 L2
WKFDE WF1 176 E6
Westfield Vw WKFDE WF1 176 E5
West Garth TAD LS24 94 F1
Westgarth WBY LS22 47 K3
West Garth Ms BAIL BD17 82 D4
West Ga WBY LS22 48 A1
Westgate BAIL BD17 82 E2
BRIG HD6 171 G4
BSLY S70 261 G5
BSLYN/ROY S71 261 K2
CLECK BD19 149 L7
EARL WF12 173 M6
ECHL BD2 105 L2
ELL HX5 169 H7
GIR BD8 4 C4
GSLY LS20 61 K6
HEM/SK/SE WF9 223 L8
HFAX HX1 11 H6
HOLM/MEL HD9 234 F4
HOLM/MEL HD9 236 B2
HUD HD1 14 F7
HUDE HD5 215 H4
LDS LS1 6 C9
LVSG WF15 172 E2
OT LS21 41 H7
SHPY BD18 82 D6
SKP/WHF BD23 * 16 B2
STKB/PEN S36 270 F4
TAD LS24 71 L3
WKFDE WF1 12 E2
Westgate Cl EARD/LOFT WF3 154 D6
Westgate Ct EARD/LOFT WF3 154 E6
Westgate End
WKFDW/WTN WF2 12 B4
Westgate Gdns KGHY BD21 2 F6
Westgate Gv EARD/LOFT WF3 154 E6
Westgate Hill St BOW BD4 128 C6
Westgate La EARD/LOFT WF3 154 D6
Westgate Market HFAX HX1 11 H6
Westgate Ter BOW BD4 128 C6
West Grange Cl MID LS10 131 M5
West Grange Dr MID LS10 131 M5
West Grange Fold MID LS10 131 M5
West Grange Gdns MID LS10 131 M5
West Grange Garth MID LS10 131 M5
West Grange Rd MID LS10 131 M5
West Grange Wk MID LS10 131 M5
West Gv BAIL BD17 82 E2
BSLYN/ROY S71 243 J2
West Grove Av HUDE HD5 15 M6
Westgrove Ct CLECK BD19 149 L6
West Grove St
PDSY/CALV LS28 * 106 F5
West Grove Ter HFAX HX1 10 E6
West Hall La ILK LS29 19 J4
Westhaven CUD/GR S72 * 262 E1
West Hl ROCH OL11 * 206 A8
West Hill Av CHAL LS7 87 L7
Westhill Av CUL/QBY BD13 102 A1
West Hill St HFAX HX1 10 D6
Westholme Rd HFAX HX1 10 A6
Westholme St BFD BD1 4 D7
West Ings Ct KNOT WF11 182 D1
West Ings Crs KNOT WF11 182 D1
West Ings La KNOT WF11 182 D1
West Ings Ms KNOT WF11 182 D1
West Ings Wy KNOT WF11 182 D1
Westland Cl AIRE BD20 35 G8
Westland Rd BEE/HOL LS11 131 J5
Westlands RYKW YO26 32 D5
Westlands Dr WIL/AL BD15 103 K5
Westlands Gv WIL/AL BD15 103 L5
Westland Sq BEE/HOL LS11 131 K6
West La AIRE BD20 34 B3
AIRE BD20 34 E1
AIRE BD20 55 L3
BAIL BD17 82 C4
BSPA/BRAM LS23 48 E5
CLECK BD19 150 D5
CUL/QBY BD13 102 F8
HIPP HX3 169 H3
HOR/CROF WF4 200 D5
HWTH BD22 2 A3
HWTH BD22 78 D7
OT LS21 40 A1
Westlea Av AIRE BD20 58 B5
West Lea Cl AL/HA/HU LS17 87 K5
West Lea Crs EARD/LOFT WF3 152 F7
YEA LS19 62 B8
West Lea Dr AL/HA/HU LS17 87 K5
EARD/LOFT WF3 152 F7
West Lea Gdns AL/HA/HU LS17 87 K5
West Lea Garth AL/HA/HU LS17 87 K5
West Lea Gv YEA LS19 62 B8
West Leeds St HWTH BD22 2 D5
Westleigh BGLY BD16 81 J2
Westleigh Cl BAIL BD17 * 82 C4
Westleigh Dr BAIL BD17 82 C4
Westleigh Rd BAIL BD17 82 C3
Westleigh Wy BAIL BD17 82 B4
Westley Av HOLM/MEL HD9 236 B6
Westlock Av OSM LS9 110 C5
West Ldg ILK LS29 * 40 A6
West Lodge Crs HUDW HD3 191 K2
West Lodge Gdns CHAL LS7 87 L8
West Md CAS WF10 158 C7
Westminister Cl ROY/SHW OL2 229 K6
Westminster Av CLAY BD14 125 J2
ROY/SHW OL2 228 E8
Westminster Cl BRAM LS13 107 H2
Westminster Crs CLAY BD14 125 J2
MSTN/BAR LS15 111 G8
PBR HG3 26 E3
Westminster Cft BRAM LS13 * 107 H2
Westminster Dr BRAM LS13 107 H2
CLAY BD14 125 J2
PBR HG3 26 E2
Westminster Gdns CLAY BD14 125 J2
Westminster Ga PBR HG3 26 E2
Westminster Gv PBR HG3 26 E2
Westminster Pl BFDE BD3 5 H2
Westminster Ri PBR HG3 26 E3
Westminster Rd BFDE BD3 5 H2
HIPP HX3 147 M8
PBR HG3 26 D2
Westminster Ter BFDE BD3 5 H3
Westmoor Av BAIL BD17 82 D2
Westmoor Cl BAIL BD17 * 82 D2
West Moor Crs DOD/DAR S75 260 C5
West Moorlands Av
DEWS WF13 * 173 K5
Westmoor Pl BRAM LS13 107 K3
Westmoor Ri BRAM LS13 107 K3
West Moor Rd
HEM/SK/SE WF9 223 J4
Westmoor St BRAM LS13 107 K3
Westmoreland Mt
BRAM LS13 * 107 M2
Westmoreland St
SKP/WHF BD23 16 C3
Westmorland Dr WHIT OL12 184 F8
Westmorland St WKFDE WF1 12 F2
West Mt TAD LS24 71 K4
West Mount Pl HFAX HX1 10 C4
West Mount St BEE/HOL LS11 * 8 D9
Westmount St PONT WF8 180 E6
Westoff La CUD/GR S72 222 E7
Weston Av CUL/QBY BD13 124 F6
MILN OL16 228 D2
Weston Crs OT LS21 41 G5
Weston Dr OT LS21 40 F4
Weston La OT LS21 40 F5
Weston Moor Rd OT LS21 22 E6
Weston Park Vw OT LS21 40 F4
Weston Rdg OT LS21 41 G4
Weston Rd ILK LS29 38 D2
Weston St HWTH BD22 2 A9
MILN OL16 207 H8
Weston Vale Rd
CUL/QBY BD13 124 E6
Westover Gdns
PDSY/CALV LS28 106 E7
Westover Gn BRAM LS13 * 107 L3
Westover Gv BRAM LS13 * 107 L3
Westover Mt BRAM LS13 * 107 L3
Westover Rd BRAM LS13 107 L3
Westover St BRAM LS13 107 L3
Westover Ter BRAM LS13 107 L3
Westover Vw BRAM LS13 107 L3
West Pde BHP/TINH LS16 86 C6
HFAX HX1 10 E7
ILK LS29 38 E2
RPDN/SBR HX6 167 M2
RTHW LS26 155 H1
WKFDE WF1 12 F3
West Parade Ct WKFDE WF1 12 E4
West Parade Flats HFAX HX1 10 F7
West Parade St WKFDE WF1 12 E4
West Pk BHP/TINH LS16 86 C6
GSLY LS20 61 L4
West Park Av RHAY LS8 88 D3
West Park Cl RHAY LS8 88 C3
West Park Crs RHAY LS8 88 D3
West Park Dr BHP/TINH LS16 86 C6
PONT WF8 203 M4
West Park Dr East RHAY LS8 88 C3
West Park Dr West RHAY LS8 88 B3
West Park Gv BTLY WF17 173 J1
RHAY LS8 88 C3
West Park Pl RHAY LS8 88 D4
West Park Rd BTLY WF17 173 H2
GIR BD8 104 B6
RHAY LS8 88 D4
West Parks PDSY/CALV LS28 106 F7
West Park St BRIG HD6 170 D4
DEWS WF13 173 K5
West Park Ter BTLY WF17 173 J1
GIR BD8 * 104 B6
West Pasture Cl HORS LS18 85 H5
West Pinfold BSLYN/ROY S71 243 L3
West Pl HUDE HD5 15 M6
Westridge Dr HUDS HD4 213 L5
West Rd DOD/DAR S75 260 D4
Westroyd PDSY/CALV LS28 106 E8
West Royd WIL/AL BD15 102 E1
West Royd Av ECHL BD2 * 105 K2
HFAX HX1 10 B9
MIRF WF14 194 C1
SHPY BD18 82 F6
Westroyd Av CLECK BD19 149 M3
PDSY/CALV LS28 106 E8
West Royd Cl HFAX HX1 10 C9
SHPY BD18 82 F6
Westroyd Crs PDSY/CALV LS28 106 E8
West Royd Crs SHPY BD18 83 G6
West Royd Dr MIRF WF14 172 C8
SHPY BD18 83 G6
Westroyd Gdns
PDSY/CALV LS28 106 E8
West Royd Gv MIRF WF14 172 C8
SHPY BD18 83 G6
West Royd Mt SHPY BD18 83 G6
West Royd Pk MIRF WF14 172 C8
West Royd Rd SHPY BD18 83 G6
West Royd Ter SHPY BD18 83 G6
West Royd Vls HFAX HX1 10 C9
West Royd Wk SHPY BD18 83 G6
West Scausby Pk LUD/ILL HX2 124 A7
West Shaw La HWTH BD22 100 C3
West Side Ct GIR BD8 104 B5
West Slaithwaite Rd
MAR/SLWT HD7 211 L7
West St BAIL BD17 82 E2
BFD BD1 5 G7
BIRK/DRI BD11 151 G1
BRIG HD6 148 D7
BRIG HD6 170 C3
BSLYN/ROY S71 243 M2
BTLY WF17 173 M1
BVRD LS3 6 B9
CAS WF10 157 L6
CLECK BD19 149 M7
CLECK BD19 150 D5
COL BB8 74 A2
CUD/GR S72 245 G1
EARL WF12 173 L7
ECHL BD2 105 K3
GTL/HWG HX4 190 D2
HEM/SK/SE WF9 223 L7
HEM/SK/SE WF9 246 B4
HEM/SK/SE WF9 247 K2
HFAX HX1 10 C5
HIPP HX3 147 K2
HOR/CROF WF4 222 E5
HUDW HD3 191 J5
ILK LS29 38 D2
LIT OL15 207 K1
MILN OL16 206 C6
MILN OL16 206 F7
MOR LS27 152 D3
NORM WF6 178 C4
PDSY/CALV LS28 107 G6
RPDN/SBR HX6 167 K3
WKFDW/WTN WF2 198 B1
West V WOR/ARM LS12 131 G1
Westvale Ms BRAM LS13 108 A5
West Vw AIRE BD20 36 A4
BEE/HOL LS11 8 D9
BOW BD4 127 J2
BSLY S70 261 G7
CUD/GR S72 262 E1
DEWS WF13 173 K4
FEA/AMT WF7 223 M1
GFTH/SHER LS25 114 D8
GFTH/SHER LS25 116 A8
GFTH/SHER LS25 135 K4
GTL/HWG HX4 190 C2
HIPP HX3 146 D4
HUD HD1 213 M1
LIT OL15 207 L1
NORM WF6 178 B1
OT LS21 41 K6
OT LS21 43 H8
RTHW LS26 155 L1
SKP/WHF BD23 17 M1
WBY LS22 29 K2
WKFDW/WTN WF2 175 K4
YEA LS19 62 B7
Westview Av AIRE BD20 2 E2
West View Av CAS WF10 158 C7
ILK LS29 40 A5
LUD/ILL HX2 146 A7
SHPY BD18 83 G7
Westview Cl AIRE BD20 34 E1
West View Cl SHPY BD18 83 G7
Westview Ct AIRE BD20 2 D2
West View Ct YEA LS19 * 62 B7
West View Crs LUD/ILL HX2 146 A8
West View Dr LUD/ILL HX2 145 M7
Westview Gv AIRE BD20 2 D2
West View Ri HUD HD1 213 M1
West View Rd HIPP HX3 * 146 D4
ILK LS29 40 A5
West View Ter GIR BD8 * 104 A7
LUD/ILL HX2 * 146 A6
Westview Wy AIRE BD20 2 E2
West Villa Rd GSLY LS20 62 A5
Westville Av ILK LS29 38 C2
Westville Cl ILK LS29 38 C2
Westville Rd DOD/DAR S75 260 F3
ILK LS29 38 C2
Westville Wy
CUL/QBY BD13 102 F8
Westward Cft HUDW HD3 191 L4
Westward Ho HIPP HX3 146 C2
MILN OL16 207 H8
West Wy BSLY S70 261 G5
SHPY BD18 81 M7
Westway AIRE BD20 2 B1
BTLY WF17 174 B3
GFTH/SHER LS25 112 F8
GSLY LS20 61 K6
HTON BD9 103 L4
MIRF WF14 172 B7
PDSY/CALV LS28 106 E3
ROY/SHW OL2 229 K8
Westways WKFDW/WTN WF2 176 B3
Westways Cl
WKFDW/WTN WF2 176 B4
Westways Dr RHAY LS8 88 E7

Westways Ri
WKFDW/WTN WF2 * 176 B4
West Wells Crs OSS WF5 196 E1
West Wells Rd OSS WF5 196 E1
West Winds ILK LS29 61 G1
Westwinn Garth SCFT LS14 89 L6
Westwinn Vw SCFT LS14 89 L5
Westwood Av ECHL BD2 105 K1
HOLM/MEL HD9 236 E2
Westwood Cl FEA/AMT WF7 179 M7
MOR LS27 130 D8
Westwood Ct BSLY S70 261 G4
West Wood Ct MID LS10 153 J1
Westwood Crs BGLY BD16 81 J6
Westwood Dr ILK LS29 38 B4
Westwood Edge Rd
MAR/SLWT HD7 212 C3
Westwood Fold
MAR/SLWT HD7 212 D4
Westwood Gv ECHL BD2 105 K1
Westwood Ri ILK LS29 38 B4
MOR LS27 130 C8
West Wood Rd MOR LS27 153 H2
Westwood Rd CAS WF10 179 K1
OSS WF5 197 H1
Westwood Side MOR LS27 130 D7
Westwood St HUDN HD2 * 171 J8
Westwood Wy
BSPA/BRAM LS23 48 F7
Wetherby Grange Pk
WBY LS22 * 48 C3
Wetherby Gv BULY LS4 108 E4
Wetherby La WBY LS22 30 C1
Wetherby Pl BULY LS4 108 F4
Wetherby Rd AL/HA/HU LS17 67 M2
BSPA/BRAM LS23 49 G2
BSPA/BRAM LS23 69 L3
RHAY LS8 88 D7
RYKW YO26 32 B5
RYKW YO26 33 J3
SCFT LS14 89 H5
TAD LS24 71 L3
WBY LS22 30 A6
WBY LS22 46 F1
WBY LS22 47 M5
Wetherby Ter BULY LS4 108 E4
Wetherhill St BTLY WF17 173 K1
Wetlands Rd HOLM/MEL HD9 235 G5
Wetton Ct BFDE BD3 105 M7
Weydale Av HUDW HD3 191 J6
Weyhill Dr WIL/AL BD15 103 K6
Weymouth Av HUDW HD3 191 K7
WIL/AL BD15 103 J6
Whack House Cl YEA LS19 62 C8
Whales La GLE DN14 183 M1
Whaley Rd DOD/DAR S75 260 B1
Whalley Av LIT OL15 185 J8
Whalley Cl MILN OL16 * 207 G8
Whalley La CUL/QBY BD13 101 M4
Wham La UPML OL3 230 F5
Whams Rd STKB/PEN S36 269 G4
Wharfe Bank WBY LS22 47 G6
Wharfe Cl BHP/TINH LS16 86 F2
Wharfe Ct AIRE BD20 36 A5
Wharfe Crs OT LS21 42 F7
Wharfedale Av CHAL LS7 109 K2
Wharfedale Cl SKP/WHF BD23 16 D2
Wharfedale Ct OT LS21 41 K6
SCFT LS14 111 H1
Wharfedale Crs
GFTH/SHER LS25 135 H1
KBTN HD8 239 K5
Wharfedale Dr ILK LS29 38 E3
NORM WF6 178 C2
Wharfedale Gdns BAIL BD17 83 G2
Wharfedale Gv HDGY LS6 6 E1
Wharfedale Lawns WBY LS22 48 A1
Wharfedale Ms OT LS21 41 K6
Wharfedale Mt HIPP HX3 125 K8
Wharfedale Pl HDGY LS6 6 E1
Wharfedale Ri EARD/LOFT WF3 152 F7
HTON BD9 103 L4
Wharfedale Rd BOW BD4 127 J7
DOD/DAR S75 260 C3
Wharfedale St HDGY LS6 6 E1
Wharfedale Vw HDGY LS6 109 K2
ILK LS29 19 G6
ILK LS29 61 J2
Wharfe Gra WBY LS22 47 M1
Wharfe Gv WBY LS22 47 M1
Wharfe La WBY LS22 45 L4
Wharfe Ms ILK LS29 * 61 K2
WBY LS22 * 48 A1
Wharfe Pk ILK LS29 19 J6
Wharfe Rein WBY LS22 47 G6
Wharfeside La ILK LS29 38 E1
Wharfe St OT LS21 41 K6
Wharfe Vw PBR HG3 27 K7
WBY LS22 47 M1
Wharfe View Rd ILK LS29 38 D2
Wharf St BAIL BD17 82 D6
BFDE BD3 5 G4
BRIG HD6 170 D4
BSLYN/ROY S71 261 J3
EARL WF12 173 M7
LDSU LS2 9 J1
RPDN/SBR HX6 167 L2
TOD OL14 163 J5
Wharncliffe DOD/DAR S75 260 C8
Wharncliffe Crs ECHL BD2 105 M2
Wharncliffe Dr ECHL BD2 105 M2
Wharncliffe Gv ECHL BD2 105 M2
SHPY BD18 82 D8
Wharncliffe Rd SHPY BD18 104 D1
WKFDW/WTN WF2 220 C2
Wharncliffe St BSLY S70 260 F5
BSLYN/ROY S71 243 M6
The Whartons OT LS21 41 J4
Wharton St LVSG WF15 172 D2
Wheat Cl DEWS WF13 173 H6
HOLM/MEL HD9 253 K4
Wheatcroft CAS WF10 158 D8
Wheatcroft Av BTLY WF17 173 L2
Wheatdale Rd TAD LS24 94 F2
Wheater Rd GTHN BD7 * 126 C1
Wheat Field Av HUDW HD3 191 J7
Wheatfield Ct PDSY/CALV LS28 106 F8
Wheathead Crs HWTH BD22 79 G1
Wheat Head Dr HWTH BD22 2 A8
Wheathead La HWTH BD22 2 A8
Wheathill St ROCH OL11 228 C2
Wheathouse Rd HUDN HD2 14 D1
Wheathouse Ter HUDN HD2 14 D1
The Wheatings OSS WF5 197 H1
Wheatlands ILK LS29 38 E2
PDSY/CALV LS28 106 E3
Wheatlands Av AIRE BD20 34 E7
HTON BD9 104 A4
Wheatlands Crs HTON BD9 104 A4
Wheatlands Dr HTON BD9 104 A4
LVSG WF15 * 172 B4
Wheatlands Gv HTON BD9 104 A4
Wheatlands La AIRE BD20 34 E7
Wheatlands Sq HTON BD9 104 A4
Wheatley Av ILK LS29 39 G3
NORM WF6 178 D5
Wheatley City HIPP HX3 146 A4
Wheatley Cl BSLYN/ROY S71 261 H2
HIPP HX3 * 10 C1
Wheatley Dr MIRF WF14 194 C3
Wheatley Gdns ILK LS29 39 G3
Wheatley Gv ILK LS29 39 G3
Wheatley Hill La KBTN HD8 240 A6
Wheatley La HIPP HX3 10 C1
ILK LS29 39 G3
Wheatley Ri DOD/DAR S75 242 D4
ILK LS29 39 G3
Wheatley Rd BSLY S70 262 A7
HIPP HX3 146 B4
ILK LS29 38 E3
Wheaton Av MSTN/BAR LS15 111 J6
Wheatroyd Crs OSS WF5 196 F3
Wheatroyd La HUDE HD5 215 G4
Wheat St HWTH BD22 79 J2
Wheelwright Av
WOR/ARM LS12 130 C1
Wheelwright Cl
WOR/ARM LS12 130 C1
Wheelwright Dr DEWS WF13 173 K4
MILN OL16 206 E3
Wheelwright St EARL WF12 * 173 L6
Wheldale La CAS WF10 159 G4
Wheldon Rd CAS WF10 158 A6
CAS WF10 158 F3
Whernside Mt GTHN BD7 126 A4
Whernside Wy LUD/ILL HX2 145 J3
Wherwell Rd BRIG HD6 170 D5
Whetley Cl GIR BD8 4 A3
Whetley Gv GIR BD8 104 C5
Whetley Hl GIR BD8 104 D5
Whetley La GIR BD8 104 C6
Whetley Ter GIR BD8 4 B3
Whewell St BTLY WF17 151 G5
Whiddon Cft ILK LS29 61 H1
Whimbrel Cl GIR BD8 103 L7
Whimbrel Ms MOR LS27 152 E3
Whinbeck Av NORM WF6 178 F5
Whinberry Pl BTLY WF17 151 H3
Whinbrook Crs
AL/HA/HU LS17 87 L5
Whinbrook Gdns
AL/HA/HU LS17 87 L5
Whinbrook Gv AL/HA/HU LS17 87 L5
Whinby Cft DOD/DAR S75 260 B7
Whinby Rd DOD/DAR S75 259 M6
Whin Cl HEM/SK/SE WF9 245 M1
Whincop Av CAS WF10 157 J7
Whincover Cl WOR/ARM LS12 130 B1
Whincover Cross
WOR/ARM LS12 130 B1
Whincover Dr WOR/ARM LS12 130 B1
Whincover Gdns
WOR/ARM LS12 130 B1
Whincover Gv WOR/ARM LS12 130 B1
Whincover Hl WOR/ARM LS12 130 B1
Whincover Mt WOR/ARM LS12 130 B1
Whincover Rd WOR/ARM LS12 130 A1
Whincover Vw WOR/ARM LS12 130 B1
Whinfell Cl AWLS/ASK DN6 249 K8
Whinfield BHP/TINH LS16 86 D2
ILK LS29 38 A3
Whinfield Av HWTH BD22 57 G6
Whinfield Cl HWTH BD22 2 A3
Whinfield Ct SKP/WHF BD23 16 B3
Whinfield Dr HWTH BD22 57 G6
Whingate WOR/ARM LS12 108 C6
Whingate Av WOR/ARM LS12 108 C7
Whingate Cl WOR/ARM LS12 108 C7
Whingate Gn WOR/ARM LS12 108 C7
Whingate Gv WOR/ARM LS12 108 C7
Whingate Rd WOR/ARM LS12 108 C7
Whingrove Av HOLM/MEL HD9 234 E5
Whin Knoll Av KGHY BD21 2 B3
Whin La GFTH/SHER LS25 137 J3
Whinmoor Cl DOD/DAR S75 259 H5
Whinmoor Ct SCFT LS14 89 J5
Whinmoor Crs SCFT LS14 89 J5
Whinmoor Dr DOD/DAR S75 259 H5
KBTN HD8 240 C2
Whinmoor Gdns SCFT LS14 89 H5
Whin Moor La DOD/DAR S75 258 E6
Whinmoor Vw DOD/DAR S75 259 H5
Whinmoor Wy DOD/DAR S75 259 H6
SCFT LS14 89 L7
Whinmore Gdns CLECK BD19 150 D7
Whin Mt NORM WF6 178 E6
Whinney Brow IDLE BD10 83 H6
Whinney Cl FEA/AMT WF7 200 F1
Whinney Hill Pk BRIG HD6 170 C1
Whinney La FEA/AMT WF7 200 F1
Whinney Moor Av
WKFDW/WTN WF2 197 M3
Whinney Royd La HIPP HX3 147 J1
Whinn Moor La AL/HA/HU LS17 89 G3
Whinny Gill Rd SKP/WHF BD23 16 D3
Whins La BSPA/BRAM LS23 49 H5
PBR HG3 28 E6
Whin St HWTH BD22 2 C4
Whirlaw Av TOD OL14 141 J7
Whirlaw La TOD OL14 141 K6
Whiskers La HIPP HX3 147 G3
Whisperwood Cl WKFDE WF1 * 176 F1
Whisperwood Rd WKFDE WF1 176 F1
Whistler Dr CAS WF10 180 A2
Whitacre Cl HUDN HD2 193 G3
Whitacre St HUDN HD2 193 G3
Whitaker Av ECHL BD2 105 L3
Whitaker Cl ECHL BD2 105 L3
Whitaker St BTLY WF17 173 M2
PDSY/CALV LS28 106 F4
Whitaker Wk HWTH BD22 * 100 E4
Whitbourne Cl BSLYN/ROY S71 261 H1
Whitby Av HUDN HD2 192 C4
Whitby Crs EARL WF12 174 B6
Whitby Rd GIR BD8 104 C5
Whitby St ROCH OL11 228 C1
Whitby Ter GIR BD8 104 C5
Whitcliffe Rd CLECK BD19 149 L6
Whitcliffe Sq CLECK BD19 149 M6
White Abbey Rd GIR BD8 4 B3
White Apron St
HEM/SK/SE WF9 246 D4
Whitebeam Cl MILN OL16 229 J3
Whitebeam Gn PONT WF8 181 H5
Whitebeam La MID LS10 131 M6
Whitebeam Pk HUDN HD2 191 M4
White Birch Ter HIPP HX3 146 B4
Whitebridge Av
MSTN/BAR LS15 111 G6
Whitebridge Crs OSM LS9 111 G5
Whitebridge Sp SCFT LS14 111 G5
Whitebridge Vw OSM LS9 111 G5
White Castle Ct CUL/QBY BD13 124 D4
Whitechapel Cl RHAY LS8 88 D8
Whitechapel Gv CLECK BD19 149 J5
Whitechapel Rd CLECK BD19 149 J6
Whitechapel Wy RHAY LS8 88 D8
Whitecliffe Crs RTHW LS26 134 C4
Whitecliffe Dr RTHW LS26 134 C4
Whitecliffe Ri RTHW LS26 134 C4
Whitecote Gdns BRAM LS13 107 K2
Whitecote Hl BRAM LS13 107 K2
Whitecote La BRAM LS13 107 K1
GFTH/SHER LS25 137 K2
Whitecote Ri BRAM LS13 107 K2
White Ct HOR/CROF WF4 200 C6
Whitecroft Av ROY/SHW OL2 229 M7
White Cross HUDN HD2 193 G1
White Cross Av CUD/GR S72 262 D1
White Cross Ct CUD/GR S72 262 D1
White Cross Gdns CUD/GR S72 222 F8
White Cross Mt CUD/GR S72 262 E1
White Cross Rd CUD/GR S72 262 D1
EARL WF12 174 A5
Whitefield La GLE DN14 183 M5
White Field La HBR HX7 143 L6
Whitefield Pl GIR BD8 104 C6
White Ga HOLM/MEL HD9 236 B1
LUD/ILL HX2 123 M7
Whitegate AL/HA/HU LS17 46 E8
HIPP HX3 168 F2
LIT OL15 207 G2
Whitegate Dr HIPP HX3 168 F2
Whitegate Hl PONT WF8 203 G6
Whitegate La PONT WF8 203 G7
White Gate Rd
HOLM/MEL HD9 253 M5
Whitegate Rd HIPP HX3 168 F1
HUDS HD4 214 D2
Whitegates Cl
WKFDW/WTN WF2 176 B5
Whitegates Gv KBTN HD8 215 M4
Whitegate Ter HIPP HX3 168 F2
Whitegate Top HIPP HX3 169 G2
White Gv RHAY LS8 88 C6
Whitehall Av LM/WK BD12 148 E5
MIRF WF14 172 C7
WKFDE WF1 176 C5
Whitehall Crs WKFDE WF1 176 C5
Whitehall Cft RTHW LS26 155 H1
Whitehall Est
WOR/ARM LS12 * 130 B2
Whitehall Fold HBR HX7 * 143 H1
Whitehall Gv BIRK/DRI BD11 128 F8
BIRK/DRI BD11 150 D1
Whitehall Quay LDS LS1 8 E1
Whitehall Ri WKFDE WF1 176 C6
Whitehall Rd BIRK/DRI BD11 129 H7
LM/WK BD12 149 G5
MAR/SLWT HD7 212 E6
WOR/ARM LS12 8 B3
Whitehall Rd East
BIRK/DRI BD11 150 D1
Whitehall Rd West
CLECK BD19 149 M4
Whitehall St HIPP HX3 147 M6
WHIT OL12 206 B6
WKFDW/WTN WF2 176 B8
Whitehall Wy DEWS WF13 173 M6
White Hart Dr HUDS HD4 214 C3
White Hart Fold
HEM/SK/SE WF9 225 K8
RPDN/SBR HX6 188 E3
Whitehaven Cl WBSY BD6 126 B7
Whitehead Gv ECHL BD2 105 L5
Whitehead La HOLM/MEL HD9 213 H8
HUDS HD4 214 B3
Whitehead Pl ECHL BD2 105 L4
Whitehead's Ter HFAX HX1 * 10 B5
Whitehead St BFDE BD3 5 M7
MILN OL16 * 207 G8
MILN OL16 229 M2
ROY/SHW OL2 229 H6
White Hl MAR/SLWT HD7 211 L7
White Hill Av BSLY S70 260 C5
Whitehill Crs LUD/ILL HX2 146 A1
Whitehill Dr LUD/ILL HX2 124 A8
Whitehill Gn LUD/ILL HX2 124 B8
White Hill Gv BSLY S70 * 260 D5
Whitehill Rd HWTH BD22 77 L1
LUD/ILL HX2 146 A1
White Hill Ter BSLY S70 * 260 C5
White Holme Dr OT LS21 43 G8
White Horse Cl BTLY WF17 151 K4
White Horse Fold CAS WF10 158 A1
White Horse Mdw MILN OL16 * 228 E4
White Horse Ms PBR HG3 28 E4
White Horse Yd WKFDE WF1 12 E3
Whitehouse Av RTHW LS26 134 F6
Whitehouse Crs RTHW LS26 135 G6
Whitehouse Dr RTHW LS26 134 F6
Whitehouse La RTHW LS26 134 E3
YEA LS19 63 H6
Whitehouse St MID LS10 9 K6
White Laith Av SCFT LS14 89 K6
White Laithe Ap SCFT LS14 89 K6
White Laithe Cl SCFT LS14 89 K6
White Laithe Cft SCFT LS14 89 K6
White Laithe Gdns SCFT LS14 * 89 L6
White Laithe Garth SCFT LS14 89 K5
White Laithe Gn SCFT LS14 89 L6
White Laithe Gv SCFT LS14 89 L6
White Laithe Rd SCFT LS14 89 K6
White Laithe Wk SCFT LS14 89 L6
White Lands YEA LS19 84 C2
Whitelands Crs BAIL BD17 82 F3
Whitelands Rd BAIL BD17 82 F3
White La HWTH BD22 78 B4
WBSY BD6 126 F6
White Lee Av COL BB8 74 E4
White Lee Cl BTLY WF17 151 G8
White Lee Gdns HBR HX7 144 B5
White Lee Rd BTLY WF17 151 G8
White Lee Side HECK WF16 151 G8
Whitelees Rd LIT OL15 207 J1
Whiteley Av RPDN/SBR HX6 167 H3
White Ley Bank
HOLM/MEL HD9 237 J7
Whiteley Cft OT LS21 41 J7
Whiteley Croft Ri OT LS21 41 J7
Whiteley Croft Rd OT LS21 41 J7
White Ley Rd AWLS/ASK DN6 227 G5
Whiteley St FEA/AMT WF7 201 L1
HFAX HX1 10 F7
HUDW HD3 213 K2
Whitelock St CHAL LS7 7 J6
Whitely Croft Garth OT LS21 41 H7
Whitemoor Wy CUL/QBY BD13 102 A8
White Moss Cl FEA/AMT WF7 202 B8
Whiteplatts St TOD OL14 141 K8
White Rose Av
GFTH/SHER LS25 113 H7
HUDE HD5 193 H7
Whiterose Md
GFTH/SHER LS25 * 113 J7
White Rose Wy
GFTH/SHER LS25 113 J7
White Slack Ga TOD OL14 163 H8
White's Rd WKFDE WF1 13 G2
White's Ter GIR BD8 104 D5
Whitestone Crs YEA LS19 62 D7
Whitestone Dr AIRE BD20 58 F5
Whitestone La HUD HD1 15 G2
White St RTHW LS26 133 L8
White's Vw GIR BD8 104 D6
White Walls La
HOLM/MEL HD9 253 H3
Whiteways ECHL BD2 105 G3
Whitewell Cl MILN OL16 206 E6
Whitewell Green La ELL HX5 169 K7
White Wells Gdns
HOLM/MEL HD9 254 F3
White Wells Rd
HOLM/MEL HD9 254 F3
Whitewood Cl
BSLYN/ROY S71 243 K3
Whitfield Av MID LS10 9 L8
Whitfield Crs MILN OL16 229 K3
Whitfield Dr MILN OL16 229 G1
Whitfield Gdns MID LS10 * 9 L8
Whitfield Pl MID LS10 9 L8
Whitfield Ri ROY/SHW OL2 229 J5
Whitfield Sq MID LS10 9 L8
Whitfield St CLECK BD19 149 M6
RHAY LS8 110 B3
Whitfield Wy MID LS10 9 L7
Whitham Cl BSPA/BRAM LS23 48 F6
Whitkirk Cl MSTN/BAR LS15 112 A6
Whitkirk La MSTN/BAR LS15 111 M6
Whitlam St SHPY BD18 82 B6
Whitley Dr LUD/ILL HX2 124 B8
Whitley Gdns RHAY LS8 7 M3
Whitley La HIPP HX3 169 J1
Whitley Pl CAS WF10 157 K2
Whitley Rd EARL WF12 195 G6
KGHY BD21 2 C8
STKB/PEN S36 256 B8
Whitley Spring Crs OSS WF5 175 H8
Whitley Spring Rd OSS WF5 175 H8
Whitley St BFDE BD3 5 J6
BGLY BD16 81 H3
Whitley Wy HOR/CROF WF4 217 G1
Whittaker Dr LIT OL15 207 H4
Whittaker Fold LIT OL15 * 208 A1
Whittaker La LIT OL15 207 M2
Whitteron Cl HUDW HD3 * 191 K5
Whittle Crs CLAY BD14 125 K1
Whittle Dr ROY/SHW OL2 229 M6
Whittle St LIT OL15 207 H1
Whitty La LUD/ILL HX2 145 K8
Whitwell Av ELL HX5 169 K7
Whitwell Dr ELL HX5 169 K7
Whitwell Gv ELL HX5 169 K7
Whitwell St BOW BD4 127 J1
Whitwood Common La
CAS WF10 179 G1
Whitwood La CAS WF10 157 G8
CLECK BD19 148 E7
Whitworth Rd DEWS WF13 * 173 K7
WHIT OL12 206 B4
Whitworth St MILN OL16 * 206 E4
MILN OL16 207 H8
Wholestone Ga
MAR/SLWT HD7 212 D1
Whytecote End LM/WK BD12 148 E2
Wibsey Bank WBSY BD6 126 F5
Wibsey Park Av WBSY BD6 126 C5
Wicken Cl IDLE BD10 83 L8
Wicken La CUL/QBY BD13 102 E7
Wickets Cl WBSY BD6 126 F6
The Wickets BTLY WF17 173 K4
HDGY LS6 87 H7
MSTN/BAR LS15 112 A7
WKFDW/WTN WF2 * 199 G6
Wickham Av BSPA/BRAM LS23 48 E6
WBSY BD6 * 126 E6
Wickham Cl BSPA/BRAM LS23 48 E6
Wickham St BEE/HOL LS11 8 D9
CLECK BD19 149 H5
Wicking La RPDN/SBR HX6 166 C6
Wickins La HOLM/MEL HD9 235 M8
Wickleden Ga HOLM/MEL HD9 254 F3
Wickliffe Pl ROCH OL11 206 B8
Widdop Rd HBR HX7 120 E7
Wide La HWTH BD22 78 C3
MOR LS27 152 F2
Wigan St BFD BD1 4 D5
Wigeon Ap MOR LS27 152 E2
Wiggan La HUDN HD2 192 F3
Wighill Garth TAD LS24 71 M2
Wighill La BSPA/BRAM LS23 49 L4
TAD LS24 50 D7
TAD LS24 51 G1
Wighill St AIRE BD20 55 M1
Wightman St BFDE BD3 105 J4
Wignall St AIRE BD20 57 K5
Wigton Cha AL/HA/HU LS17 88 C1
Wigton Ga AL/HA/HU LS17 66 A8
Wigton Gn AL/HA/HU LS17 66 B8
Wigton Gv AL/HA/HU LS17 66 A8
Wigton La AL/HA/HU LS17 66 A8
Wigton Park Cl AL/HA/HU LS17 66 B8
Wike La AL/HA/HU LS17 66 D3
Wike Ridge Av AL/HA/HU LS17 88 C1
Wike Ridge Cl AL/HA/HU LS17 66 C8
Wike Ridge Ct AL/HA/HU LS17 66 D8
Wike Ridge Fold AL/HA/HU LS17 66 C8
Wike Ridge Gv AL/HA/HU LS17 88 D1
Wike Ridge La AL/HA/HU LS17 88 D1
Wike Ridge Ms AL/HA/HU LS17 88 D1
Wike Ridge Mt AL/HA/HU LS17 88 D1
Wike Ridge Vw AL/HA/HU LS17 88 C1
Wike Rd BSLYN/ROY S71 262 A4
Wilbrook Ri DOD/DAR S75 260 C2
Wilby La BSLY S70 261 J6
Wilcock La AIRE BD20 35 H2
Wild Gv PDSY/CALV LS28 106 C7
Wildhouse La LIT OL15 207 H5
Wildspur Gv HOLM/MEL HD9 255 G2
Wild St ROY/SHW OL2 229 L8
Wild's Yd WKFDE WF1 12 F4
Wilford Rd BSLYN/ROY S71 243 G5
Wilfred Av MSTN/BAR LS15 111 K6
Wilfred St CLAY BD14 125 M2
MSTN/BAR LS15 111 K6
Wilfrid Ter WOR/ARM LS12 130 C2
Wilkinson Fold LM/WK BD12 * 148 E4
Wilkinson St BSLY S70 261 H6
Wilkinson Ter GTHN BD7 104 B8
Wilkinson Wy OT LS21 41 G5
Wilkin St KGHY BD21 2 F4
Willans Av RTHW LS26 133 G7
Willan's Rd DEWS WF13 173 L6
Willerton Cl EARL WF12 174 D3
William Av MSTN/BAR LS15 * 111 G6
William Fison Ride ILK LS29 39 M6
William Foster Wy ILK LS29 39 M6
William Henry St BRIG HD6 * 170 C3
ROCH OL11 228 C2
SHPY BD18 * 82 B6
William Hey Ct OSM LS9 * 110 D4
William Horsfall St HUDS HD4 213 L3
William Prince Gv WKFDE WF1 13 K7
William Ri MSTN/BAR LS15 111 G6
William Royd La HECK WF16 173 G1
Williams Dr AIRE BD20 56 D1
Williamson St HFAX HX1 10 C4
Williams Rd AIRE BD20 56 D1
William St BOW BD4 127 M1
BOW BD4 127 M5
BRIG HD6 170 C5
CAS WF10 157 M5
CAS WF10 158 E4
COL BB8 74 A2
CUL/QBY BD13 101 M5
DEWS WF13 173 H3
DEWS WF13 195 G1
EARL WF12 * 174 A5
HDGY LS6 109 G3
HUD HD1 15 G5
HUDS HD4 213 L2
LIT OL15 207 J1
LVSG WF15 172 C2
MILN OL16 206 F2
MOR LS27 130 E6
PDSY/CALV LS28 106 F5
ROCH OL11 206 B8
WBOW BD5 4 E8
WBSY BD6 126 B7
WKFDE WF1 13 G4
William Vw MSTN/BAR LS15 111 G6
Willington Rd AWLS/ASK DN6 249 J5
Willis St OSM LS9 9 M2
Willman Rd BSLYN/ROY S71 262 B3
Willoughby Ter BEE/HOL LS11 8 B6
Willow Ap BULY LS4 109 G5
Willow Av BSPA/BRAM LS23 48 F8
BULY LS4 109 G5
ECHL BD2 83 J8
Willow Bank BSLYN/ROY S71 260 F2
HFAX HX1 10 C9
HUDW HD3 * 191 M6
TOD OL14 141 K8
Willow Bank Cl WIL/AL BD15 103 K7
Willow Bank Dr PONT WF8 181 G4
Willowbank Gv HUDE HD5 193 K5
Willow Beck HOR/CROF WF4 221 J7
Willowbridge Cl CAS WF10 179 J1
Willowbridge La CAS WF10 157 H8
Willowbridge Rd
AWLS/ASK DN6 205 J7
Willowbridge Wy CAS WF10 157 H8
Willowbrook AWLS/ASK DN6 249 H4
Willow Brook HIPP HX3 146 A4
Willow Brook Rd DOD/DAR S75 242 C6
Willow Cl BULY LS4 109 G5
CLECK BD19 150 D7
CUD/GR S72 244 D7
ILK LS29 40 A5
KBTN HD8 239 H5
LUD/ILL HX2 145 M8
WBSY BD6 126 E7
Willow Clough RPDN/SBR HX6 188 F4
Willow Ct BTLY WF17 151 L8
FEA/AMT WF7 179 L5
OT LS21 42 F8
WKFDW/WTN WF2 175 M7
Willow Crs BSPA/BRAM LS23 48 F8
ECHL BD2 83 J8
MSTN/BAR LS15 111 H7
NORM WF6 178 C6
RPDN/SBR HX6 167 L1
Willow Cft CLECK BD19 149 L7
Willow Dene Av LUD/ILL HX2 167 M1
Willowdene La PONT WF8 180 F3
Willow Dene Rd CUD/GR S72 245 J7
Willow Dr HEM/SK/SE WF9 245 L1
HOR/CROF WF4 222 D6
LUD/ILL HX2 145 M8
WBSY BD6 126 E7
WKFDE WF1 13 J9
Willowfield Av LUD/ILL HX2 167 M1
Willowfield Cl LUD/ILL HX2 145 M8
Willowfield Crs IDLE BD10 83 J8
LUD/ILL HX2 145 M8
Willowfield Dr LUD/ILL HX2 167 M1
Willowfield Rd LUD/ILL HX2 167 M1
Willow Flds KBTN HD8 216 C3
Willowfield St GTHN BD7 104 D8
Willowfield Ter LUD/ILL HX2 168 A1
Willowfield Vw LUD/ILL HX2 145 M8
Willow Gdns CAS WF10 158 F8
ECHL BD2 83 J8
GSLY LS20 62 A5
WKFDW/WTN WF2 175 M7
Willow Garth FEA/AMT WF7 179 L5
HEM/SK/SE WF9 247 K4
Willow Garth Av AIRE BD20 34 F6
Willowgarth Cl
HOR/CROF WF4 222 C6
Willow Gld BSPA/BRAM LS23 69 M1
Willow Gn WKFDE WF1 176 D3
Willow Gv BSPA/BRAM LS23 48 F8
ECHL BD2 83 J8
GFTH/SHER LS25 135 H3
MAR/SLWT HD7 213 G1
OSS WF5 197 G2
WKFDE WF1 13 J9
Willow Hall Dr RPDN/SBR HX6 167 L1
Willow Hall La RPDN/SBR HX6 167 L1
Willow La BSPA/BRAM LS23 48 F8
FEA/AMT WF7 179 L5
HUD HD1 14 E2
NORM WF6 177 M7
WKFDW/WTN WF2 175 M7
Willow La East FEA/AMT WF7 179 L5
HUD HD1 15 G2
Willow Ms WKFDW/WTN WF2 175 M7
Willow Mt WKFDW/WTN WF2 175 M7
Willow Pk PONT WF8 181 H6
WKFDE WF1 176 D4
Willow Ri LIT OL15 207 H3
LUD/ILL HX2 145 M8
TAD LS24 71 K4
Willow Rd AWLS/ASK DN6 227 M5
BTLY WF17 174 A2
BULY LS4 109 G5
CAS WF10 157 M8
KNOT WF11 182 C1
PDSY/CALV LS28 106 E4
WKFDW/WTN WF2 175 M7
Willows La MILN OL16 206 F8
The Willows AL/HA/HU LS17 87 L4
BGLY BD16 80 D5
HOR/CROF WF4 197 J5
LUD/ILL HX2 124 A7
SEL YO8 139 M4
Willow St BSLY S70 260 F6
CLECK BD19 149 M5
GIR BD8 104 C6
HFAX HX1 10 C6
RPDN/SBR HX6 167 L2
Willow Terrace Rd LDSU LS2 6 D6
Willow Tree Cl KGHY BD21 3 K8
Willow Tree Gdns BGLY BD16 81 L1
ILK LS29 40 B5
Willow V WBY LS22 29 M7
Willow Vls IDLE BD10 83 J8
Willow Wk HEM/SK/SE WF9 223 K4
LVSG WF15 172 C3
Willow Well Rd
MSTN/BAR LS15 111 H6
Wills Gill GSLY LS20 62 B5
Willwood Av HUDW HD3 191 K7
Wilman Dr OSS WF5 174 E8
Wilman Post OSS WF5 174 E8
Wilmer Dr HTON BD9 104 C2
Wilmer Rd HTON BD9 104 C3
Wilmington Gv CHAL LS7 7 H3
Wilmington St CHAL LS7 7 J4
Wilmington Ter CHAL LS7 7 H4
Wilmot Rd ILK LS29 38 E2
Wilsden Gv DOD/DAR S75 260 D2
Wilsden Hill Rd WIL/AL BD15 102 D1
Wilsden Old Rd BGLY BD16 80 D5
Wilsden Rd BGLY BD16 80 D5
WIL/AL BD15 103 G3
Wilshaw Mill Rd
HOLM/MEL HD9 235 J6
Wilshaw Rd HOLM/MEL HD9 235 J6
Wilson Av AIRE BD20 35 K8
MIRF WF14 194 B1
OSS WF5 197 J2
STKB/PEN S36 270 F4
Wilson Cl TOD OL14 141 J7

Wilson Ct WKFDE WF1 176 E2
Wilson Dr WKFDE WF1 176 D2
Wilson Gv BSLYN/ROY S71 262 A2
Wilson Rd BGLY BD16 81 H2
HFAX HX1 10 A9
LM/WK BD12 148 F2
MIRF WF14 194 B1
Wilson St AIRE BD20 56 A1
CAS WF10 157 L6
FEA/AMT WF7 201 L1
GIR BD8 * 4 B1
PONT WF8 * 180 F5
WHIT OL12 206 B6
Wilsons Yd PDSY/CALV LS28 106 F5
Wilson Ter MIRF WF14 194 B1
Wilson Wood St BTLY WF17 173 K3
Wilthorpe Av DOD/DAR S75 260 E2
Wilthorpe Crs DOD/DAR S75 260 E2
Wilthorpe Farm Rd
DOD/DAR S75 260 E2
Wilthorpe Gn DOD/DAR S75 260 E2
Wilthorpe La DOD/DAR S75 260 D2
Wilthorpe Rd DOD/DAR S75 260 C2
Wilton Av HUDN HD2 171 G8
Wilton Gv HDGY LS6 87 G8
Wilton Rd ILK LS29 38 C3
Wilton St BRIG HD6 170 B3
EARL WF12 173 M7
GTHN BD7 4 D8
Wilton Ter CLECK BD19 149 M7
WHIT OL12 206 A6
Wimborne Dr HWTH BD22 57 G6
WIL/AL BD15 103 L5
Winbrooke Ter WBSY BD6 126 C5
Winburg Rd GTHN BD7 126 C1
Winchester Cl
WKFDW/WTN WF2 175 M5
Winchester Gdns BOW BD4 127 M2
Winchester St WOR/ARM LS12 108 F7
Winchester Wy
BSLYN/ROY S71 262 C7
HEM/SK/SE WF9 247 J2
Winden Cl HOR/CROF WF4 197 M8
WKFDE WF1 176 E1
Winden Gv WKFDE WF1 * 176 D1
Windermere Av COL BB8 52 B8
ILK LS29 40 C8
Windermere Cl AWLS/ASK DN6 249 J5
Windermere Dr AL/HA/HU LS17 65 H8
GFTH/SHER LS25 113 H8
KNOT WF11 182 A4
Windermere Ri BRIG HD6 148 D8
Windermere Rd
BSLYN/ROY S71 * 261 J5
CAS WF10 158 F7
EARL WF12 174 A3
GTHN BD7 126 A3
ROY/SHW OL2 228 F7
STKB/PEN S36 270 F2
WKFDW/WTN WF2 176 A7
Windermere Ter GTHN BD7 126 A3
Winders Dl MOR LS27 130 B8
Windgate AIRE BD20 36 B6
Windham Cl BSLYN/ROY S71 261 H3
Windham St MILN OL16 206 E3
Windhill Av DOD/DAR S75 242 C3
Windhill Ct WKFDE WF1 177 G6
Windhill Crs DOD/DAR S75 242 C3
WKFDE WF1 177 G6
Windhill Dr DOD/DAR S75 242 C3
Windhill La DOD/DAR S75 242 C3
Windhill Mt DOD/DAR S75 242 B3
Windhill Old Rd IDLE BD10 83 H4
Windhill Rd WKFDE WF1 177 G6
Windhill Vw WKFDE WF1 176 F7
Winding Rd HFAX HX1 11 H5
Winding Wy AL/HA/HU LS17 87 K1
Windle Edge STKB/PEN S36 267 J8
STKB/PEN S36 267 M5
Windle La AIRE BD20 34 C5
Windle Royd La LUD/ILL HX2 145 L7
Windmill Ap MID LS10 132 A6
Windmill Av CUD/GR S72 245 J5
Windmill Cha RTHW LS26 155 G2
Windmill Cl MID LS10 132 A7
Windmill Ct MILN OL16 * 206 D8
SCFT LS14 89 K8
Windmill Crs HIPP HX3 147 J4
KBTN HD8 239 K5
Windmill Dr HIPP HX3 147 H4
Windmill Field Rd RTHW LS26 155 G2
Windmill Gdns MSTN/BAR LS15 111 M7
Windmill Gn RTHW LS26 155 G2
Windmill Gv CLECK BD19 150 D8
TAD LS24 71 K4
Windmill Hl PDSY/CALV LS28 106 E8
WBSY BD6 126 C5
Windmill Hill La KBTN HD8 217 H6
Windmill La AWLS/ASK DN6 227 K4
BTLY WF17 151 J5
ILK LS29 61 M2
KBTN HD8 255 M3
RTHW LS26 155 G2
Wind Mill La STKB/PEN S36 270 C3
Windmill La WBSY BD6 126 E5
YEA LS19 62 E8
Windmill Meadow
AWLS/ASK DN6 227 L3
Windmill Ri GFTH/SHER LS25 92 A8
TAD LS24 71 K5
Windmill Rd BSPA/BRAM LS23 70 A3
MID LS10 132 A6
Windmill St MILN OL16 206 D8
Windmill Vw HOLM/MEL HD9 254 E3
Windross Cl NORM WF6 178 C2
Windsor Av AIRE BD20 35 M5
DOD/DAR S75 241 L6
FEA/AMT WF7 202 E7
MSTN/BAR LS15 111 K6
SKP/WHF BD23 16 C2
STKB/PEN S36 270 C2
Windsor Cl EARL WF12 174 D3
GFTH/SHER LS25 135 J4
NORM WF6 178 E5
Windsor Crs BSLYN/ROY S71 261 K3
CUD/GR S72 263 M7
HWTH BD22 78 D4
LUD/ILL HX2 146 A5
RTHW LS26 133 G8
WKFDE WF1 176 B5
Windsor Dr DOD/DAR S75 * 260 B7
HUDE HD5 193 J8
KBTN HD8 239 K5
KNOT WF11 181 K1
LVSG WF15 172 D4
Windsor Gdns EARL WF12 174 D3
Windsor Gn GFTH/SHER LS25 113 K7
Windsor Gv CUL/QBY BD13 102 F8
HWTH BD22 78 D4
Windsor Mt MSTN/BAR LS15 111 K6
Windsor Pl HUDN HD2 193 G1
Windsor Ri PONT WF8 202 D1
Windsor Rd BTLY WF17 151 J5
EARL WF12 174 C4
HBR HX7 143 J2
HEM/SK/SE WF9 224 B8
HUDS HD4 213 H3
HWTH BD22 78 D4
SHPY BD18 * 82 D6
TOD OL14 141 J8
WKFDE WF1 176 B4
Windsor St BOW BD4 5 J9
COL BB8 74 A1
HEM/SK/SE WF9 247 J4
HFAX HX1 11 G8
ROCH OL11 228 C1
WKFDE WF1 13 K3
Windsor Ter MILN OL16 206 E7
MILN OL16 207 G8
Windsor Vw EARL WF12 174 C4
HBR HX7 143 J2
Windsor Wk BRIG HD6 148 C8
Windy Bank COL BB8 74 A1
Windy Bank La HIPP HX3 124 D8
LVSG WF15 171 K2
Windy Gv WIL/AL BD15 102 F3
Windy Harbour La TOD OL14 141 K5
Windyridge St HOR/CROF WF4 197 H5
Wine St LDS LS1 6 F9
Wine Tavern La
RPDN/SBR HX6 166 D3
Winewall La COL BB8 74 E1
Winfield Dr HUDW HD3 191 H6
Winfield Gv LDSU LS2 * 6 F4
Winfield Pl LDSU LS2 6 F4
Winfield Rd BIRK/DRI BD11 128 A8
Winfield Ter LDSU LS2 6 F4
Wingate Av HWTH BD22 2 B7
Wingate Cft WKFDW/WTN WF2 199 H6
Wingate Gv WKFDW/WTN WF2 199 G6
Wingate Wy HWTH BD22 2 B6
Winget Av HUDS HD4 213 H3
Wingfield Ct BGLY BD16 81 J2
Wingfield Mt BFDE BD3 5 L3
Wingfield Rd BSLYN/ROY S71 243 J8
Wingfield St BFDE BD3 5 L4
Winnard Rw WBOW BD5 * 127 H3
Winney Bank La
HOLM/MEL HD9 254 D1
Winnipeg Pl CHAL LS7 87 M8
Winnow La BSPA/BRAM LS23 48 D7
Winrose Ap MID LS10 132 A7
Winrose Av MID LS10 131 M6
Winrose Cl LM/WK BD12 148 E2
Winrose Crs MID LS10 131 M6
Winrose Dr MID LS10 131 M6
Winrose Garth MID LS10 131 M6
Winrose Gv MID LS10 132 A6
Winrose Hl MID LS10 132 A5
Winsford Dr HUDE HD5 193 K7
Winslow Rd IDLE BD10 106 A2
Winstanley Ter HDGY LS6 109 G3
Winston Av AIRE BD20 35 G7
Winston Gdns HDGY LS6 108 E1
Winston Mt HDGY LS6 108 E1
Winston Ter GTHN BD7 126 C1
Winter Av BSLYN/ROY S71 243 L1
DOD/DAR S75 260 E4
Winterbourne Av MOR LS27 130 D8
Winterburn La LUD/ILL HX2 145 J8
Winterburn St KGHY BD21 * 3 G2
Winterbutlee Gv TOD OL14 163 J5
Winterbutlee Rd TOD OL14 163 J5
Winter Ct WIL/AL BD15 103 J3
Winter Hl HUDW HD3 * 190 C7
Winter Rd DOD/DAR S75 260 E4
Wintersett La HOR/CROF WF4 222 C2
Winter's La HBR HX7 142 E4
Winter St HFAX HX1 10 B9
Winter Ter DOD/DAR S75 260 E4
Winterton Dr LM/WK BD12 148 E1
Winthorpe Av EARD/LOFT WF3 153 M3
Winthorpe Crs
EARD/LOFT WF3 153 M4
Winton Cl BSLY S70 * 261 J7
Winton St HUD HD1 214 A3
LIT OL15 207 K1
Wintoun St CHAL LS7 7 J6
Wiston Dr PONT WF8 181 G3
Wistons La ELL HX5 169 J7
Witchfield Hl HIPP HX3 125 M8
Witham Ct DOD/DAR S75 260 A3
Witham Rd SHPY BD18 82 A6
Witham Wy GFTH/SHER LS25 113 J8
Withens Ct DOD/DAR S75 242 C5
Withens End La GTL/HWG HX4 189 G7
Withens Hill Cft LUD/ILL HX2 123 M7
Withens La GTL/HWG HX4 189 H6
HBR HX7 165 H3
Withens New Rd HBR HX7 164 F4
Withens Rd BTLY WF17 151 G4
LUD/ILL HX2 123 H4
Withinfield Ct HIPP HX3 169 J2
Within Flds HIPP HX3 169 J2
Withins Cl WBOW BD5 126 D4
Withyside KBTN HD8 239 J8
Witley Rd MILN OL16 206 D7
Witmore St HEM/SK/SE WF9 247 J3
Witton St WKFDE WF1 12 F1
Woburn Cl MILN OL16 207 G8
Woburn Dr HUDE HD5 193 K8
Woburn Pl DOD/DAR S75 260 B8
Woburn Ter CLAY BD14 125 K2
Woburn Wy NORM WF6 178 F5
Wold Cl CUL/QBY BD13 102 F8
Wolfstones Rd HOLM/MEL HD9 235 L8
Wollaton Cl BSLYN/ROY S71 243 G6
Wolley Av WOR/ARM LS12 129 M3
Wolley Ct WOR/ARM LS12 129 M3
Wolley Dr WOR/ARM LS12 129 M3
Wolley Gdns WOR/ARM LS12 129 M3
Wolseley Rd BULY LS4 108 F5
Wolseley St CLAY BD14 125 L1
MILN OL16 229 K2
Wolseley Ter HFAX HX1 10 B4
Wolsey Av PONT WF8 180 D6
Wolsey Cl GFTH/SHER LS25 116 B6
Wolsey Cft GFTH/SHER LS25 116 B6
Wolsey Gdns GFTH/SHER LS25 116 B6
Wolston Cl BOW BD4 128 A4
Wolvesey ROCH OL11 * 206 A8
Wombwell La BSLY S70 262 B7
Womersley Park Gdns
AWLS/ASK DN6 205 J4
Womersley Pl PDSY/CALV LS28 106 F8
Womersley Rd KNOT WF11 182 C3
Womersley St HFAX HX1 10 B5
Wonder St WKFDE WF1 13 G4
Woodacre Crs AL/HA/HU LS17 67 L3
Woodacre Gn AL/HA/HU LS17 67 L2
Woodacre La AL/HA/HU LS17 67 L2
Wood Acres DOD/DAR S75 260 C2
Woodale Av HTON BD9 103 M3
Wood Av HECK WF16 172 F1
Wood Bank Rd LIT OL15 207 J3
Woodbine Av PONT WF8 180 E6
Woodbine Gv IDLE BD10 83 K7
Woodbine Rd HUDN HD2 215 G1
Woodbine St BFDE BD3 5 J5
HFAX HX1 * 10 C9
MILN OL16 228 C1
OSS WF5 174 F7
Woodbine St East MILN OL16 228 D1
Woodbine Ter BRAM LS13 * 107 L3
HDGY LS6 87 G8
HFAX HX1 * 10 C9
IDLE BD10 83 K7
TOD OL14 140 D5
Wood Bottom La BRIG HD6 170 A1
Wood Bottom Rd HUDS HD4 235 K1
Woodbourne Av
AL/HA/HU LS17 87 L5
Woodbridge Av
GFTH/SHER LS25 113 L6
Woodbridge Cl HDGY LS6 108 D1
WKFDE WF1 13 K3
Woodbridge Crs HDGY LS6 86 C8
Woodbridge Fold KSTL LS5 108 C1
Woodbridge Gdns HDGY LS6 86 C8
Woodbridge Garth HDGY LS6 108 D1
Woodbridge Gn HDGY LS6 108 C1
Woodbridge Lawn HDGY LS6 108 C1
Woodbridge Pl HDGY LS6 108 C1
Woodbridge Rd HDGY LS6 108 C1
Woodbridge V HDGY LS6 108 C1
Woodbrook Av LUD/ILL HX2 145 L1
Woodbrook Cl LUD/ILL HX2 145 L1
Woodbrook Pl LUD/ILL HX2 145 L1
Woodbrook Rd LUD/ILL HX2 145 L1
Woodburn Av EARL WF12 196 B1
Woodbury Rd GIR BD8 104 D4
Woodchurch Vw
HOLM/MEL HD9 236 D6
Wood Cl AIRE BD20 34 E1
BAIL BD17 82 D4
BHP/TINH LS16 86 F3
CHAL LS7 87 L7
HEM/SK/SE WF9 223 J4
NORM WF6 178 A3
RTHW LS26 132 F8
SKP/WHF BD23 16 A1
Woodcock Cl PBR HG3 26 E2
Woodcock St WKFDE WF1 13 H8
Woodcock Wy AWLS/ASK DN6 249 K7
HEM/SK/SE WF9 247 J2
Woodcot Av BAIL BD17 82 F4
Wood Crs RTHW LS26 132 F8
Wood Cft BRIG HD6 170 B5
RPDN/SBR HX6 167 G3
Woodcroft WKFDW/WTN WF2 199 G5
Woodcross MOR LS27 130 C8
Woodcross End MOR LS27 130 C7
Woodcross Fold MOR LS27 130 C8
Woodcross Gdns MOR LS27 130 C8
Woodcross Garth MOR LS27 130 C7
Wood Dr RTHW LS26 132 E8
Woodedge Av HUDE HD5 193 J8
Wood End HUDS HD4 214 B3
Woodend CAS WF10 135 H8
ROY/SHW OL2 229 L5
Wood End Av STKB/PEN S36 270 E5
Wood End Cl HIPP HX3 168 D3
Woodend Ct WBOW BD5 127 H4
Woodend Crs CAS WF10 157 H1
Wood End Crs SHPY BD18 82 E5
Wood End La KBTN HD8 237 L7
Woodend La WHIT OL12 184 F8
Wood End Rd HUDS HD4 214 A6
Woodend Rd MIRF WF14 194 B2
Woodeson Ct BRAM LS13 107 H1
Wood Farm La
HOLM/MEL HD9 236 E4
Woodfield Av BTLY WF17 173 J2
GTL/HWG HX4 168 D7
WHIT OL12 * 206 A4
Woodfield Cl IDLE BD10 83 K6
WMB/DAR S73 263 J8
Woodfield Ct HUDN HD2 14 C3
Woodfield Dr AIRE BD20 34 E1
GTL/HWG HX4 168 D8
Woodfield Pk
WKFDW/WTN WF2 199 J8
Woodfield Rd AWLS/ASK DN6 227 K4
CUL/QBY BD13 80 A7
Woodford Av HIPP HX3 168 F2
ROY/SHW OL2 229 M7
Woodford Cl WIL/AL BD15 103 J6
Woodford Dr HUDE HD5 193 J7
Woodgarth Ct AWLS/ASK DN6 227 L8
Woodgarth Gdns BOW BD4 128 B3
Woodgate La AL/HA/HU LS17 43 M2
Wood Gn CAS WF10 179 H1
Wood Gv OSS WF5 174 F6
WOR/ARM LS12 107 M7
Woodhall Av BFDE BD3 106 A6
KSTL LS5 86 A8
Woodhall Cl HOR/CROF WF4 196 C8
PDSY/CALV LS28 106 C4
WMB/DAR S73 263 J8
Woodhall Ct MSTN/BAR LS15 111 M8
PDSY/CALV LS28 106 C1
Woodhall Cft PDSY/CALV LS28 106 C4
Woodhall Dr BTLY WF17 173 J2
FEA/AMT WF7 202 B8
KSTL LS5 86 A8
Woodhall Gv RTHW LS26 156 F3
Woodhall La AWLS/ASK DN6 205 J3
PDSY/CALV LS28 106 C3
Woodhall Park Av
PDSY/CALV LS28 106 C4
Woodhall Park Crs
West PDSY/CALV LS28 106 C5
Woodhall Park Cft
PDSY/CALV LS28 * 106 D5
Woodhall Park Dr
PDSY/CALV LS28 106 C5
Woodhall Park Gv
PDSY/CALV LS28 106 C5
Woodhall Park Mt
PDSY/CALV LS28 106 C4
Woodhall Pl BFDE BD3 106 A5
Woodhall Rd BFDE BD3 106 A6
PDSY/CALV LS28 106 A3
Woodhall Ter BFDE BD3 106 A6
Woodhall Vw BFDE BD3 106 B5
Woodhead Cl HUDN HD2 192 E3
Woodhead La BRIG HD6 171 G5
MOR LS27 129 L7
Woodhead Rd BTLY WF17 151 K3
GTHN BD7 104 D8
HOLM/MEL HD9 236 C3
HOLM/MEL HD9 265 M1
Woodhead St CLECK BD19 150 A8
LUD/ILL HX2 146 A6
Wood Hey Gv WHIT OL12 206 B2
Wood Hey La HBR HX7 143 K5
Woodheys Rd LIT OL15 207 J4
Wood Hl RTHW LS26 132 F8
Wood Hill Ct BHP/TINH LS16 85 M2
Wood Hill Crs BHP/TINH LS16 85 M3
Wood Hill Gdns BHP/TINH LS16 85 M2
Wood Hill Ri BHP/TINH LS16 85 M2
Woodhill Ri IDLE BD10 84 A6
Wood Hill Rd BHP/TINH LS16 85 M2
Woodhill Vw WBY LS22 30 A8
Woodhouse Av HUDN HD2 192 E4
KGHY BD21 3 H9
Woodhouse Cliff HDGY LS6 6 D2
Woodhouse Cl
EARD/LOFT WF3 153 K8
KGHY BD21 3 H9
Woodhouse Crs NORM WF6 178 D6
Woodhouse Dr KGHY BD21 79 L2
Woodhouse Gdns BRIG HD6 170 E6
Woodhouse Gv HUDN HD2 192 D4
KGHY BD21 3 G9
TOD OL14 163 M1
Woodhouse Hall Rd HUDN HD2 192 E4
Woodhouse Hl HUDN HD2 192 E4
Woodhouse Hill Av MID LS10 * 132 A4
Woodhouse Hill Gv MID LS10 * 132 A4
Woodhouse Hill Pl MID LS10 132 A4
Woodhouse Hill Rd MID LS10 132 A4
Woodhouse Hill Ter MID LS10 * 132 A4
Woodhouse La BRIG HD6 170 E6
DOD/DAR S75 242 D1
HDGY LS6 6 C2
HIPP HX3 168 C3
HOLM/MEL HD9 253 M5
KBTN HD8 218 B7
WKFDW/WTN WF2 175 J3
Woodhouse Mt NORM WF6 178 C6
Woodhouse Rd KGHY BD21 79 L2
ROY/SHW OL2 229 L6
TOD OL14 164 A1
WKFDE WF1 13 J2
Woodhouse Sq BVRD LS3 6 D8
Woodhouse St HDGY LS6 6 C2
Woodhouse Ter WBSY BD6 126 F6
Woodhouse Wk KGHY BD21 3 H9
Woodhouse Wy KGHY BD21 3 H9
Woodkirk Av EARD/LOFT WF3 152 E6
Woodkirk Gdns EARL WF12 174 D1
Woodkirk Gv EARD/LOFT WF3 152 F6
LM/WK BD12 148 E5
Woodland Av RTHW LS26 134 B5
WKFDE WF1 177 L7
Woodland Cl HOR/CROF WF4 220 B4
HTON BD9 103 L2
MSTN/BAR LS15 111 L6
Woodland Ct BGLY BD16 80 F1
RHAY LS8 110 B1
Woodland Crs BGLY BD16 103 K2
RTHW LS26 132 F7
RTHW LS26 134 C5
Woodland Dr BRIG HD6 170 B3
BSLY S70 260 D6
CHAL LS7 87 M7
KBTN HD8 239 K5
LUD/ILL HX2 167 M1
RTHW LS26 134 B5
WKFDW/WTN WF2 198 F8
Woodland Gv CHAL LS7 110 A2
DEWS WF13 173 H6
FEA/AMT WF7 202 C5
HTON BD9 103 L1
RTHW LS26 134 B5
Woodland Hl MSTN/BAR LS15 111 K6
Woodland La CHAL LS7 87 M7
Woodland Meadow KBTN HD8 216 B7
Woodland Mt CHAL LS7 * 110 A2
Woodland Pk ROY/SHW OL2 228 D8
RTHW LS26 155 L1
Woodland Park Rd HDGY LS6 109 G1
Woodland Ri MSTN/BAR LS15 111 L6
WKFDW/WTN WF2 197 M1
Woodland Rd HUDN HD2 193 H4
MSTN/BAR LS15 111 K6
WKFDW/WTN WF2 175 M8
Woodlands BAIL BD17 * 83 G2
EARD/LOFT WF3 153 L7
HOR/CROF WF4 197 L4
HOR/CROF WF4 200 A5
HWTH BD22 * 78 E4
ILK LS29 38 F2
OSS WF5 174 F7
RPDN/SBR HX6 167 H4
Woodlands Av CAS WF10 158 E8
CLECK BD19 150 C5
HIPP HX3 11 G1
HOLM/MEL HD9 236 E6
PDSY/CALV LS28 106 E5
TAD LS24 71 J4
TOD OL14 141 K8
Woodlands Cl EARD/LOFT WF3 153 L7
GFTH/SHER LS25 138 A2
HUDN HD2 171 J8
IDLE BD10 84 B5
ILK LS29 38 A2
KBTN HD8 239 J8
SCFT LS14 67 L6
Woodlands Ct BHP/TINH LS16 86 D5
Woodlands Crs CLECK BD19 150 C6
HEM/SK/SE WF9 224 A6
Woodlands Cft
GFTH/SHER LS25 135 K6
Woodlands Dr CLECK BD19 150 C5
EARD/LOFT WF3 153 K7
GFTH/SHER LS25 113 K8
IDLE BD10 84 C4
MOR LS27 130 B8
SKP/WHF BD23 16 A1
Woodlands Fold BIRK/DRI BD11 150 D1
Woodlands Gv BAIL BD17 82 B4
BGLY BD16 81 K7
CUL/QBY BD13 125 J5
GFTH/SHER LS25 135 L6
HIPP HX3 11 G1
ILK LS29 38 A2
PDSY/CALV LS28 106 E5
Woodlands La DEWS WF13 173 H6
GFTH/SHER LS25 160 F1
Woodlands Mt HIPP HX3 146 E4
Woodlands Pk CLECK BD19 149 K3
SCFT LS14 67 L6
Woodlands Park Rd
PDSY/CALV LS28 128 F1
Woodland Sq BRIG HD6 * 170 E5
WOR/ARM LS12 108 B6
Woodlands Ri AWLS/ASK DN6 227 L5
HWTH BD22 78 E8
ILK LS29 38 A2
Woodlands Rd BGLY BD16 81 L2
BTLY WF17 151 J6
CLECK BD19 150 C5
CUL/QBY BD13 125 J5
ELL HX5 169 H6
GIR BD8 * 104 C5
HIPP HX3 11 G1
KBTN HD8 216 A3
MILN OL16 229 G1
PDSY/CALV LS28 106 E5
Woodlands Rd East KBTN HD8 215 M3
Woodlands St GIR BD8 4 B4
Woodlands Ter
PDSY/CALV LS28 106 E5
The Woodlands HBR HX7 143 J4
PONT WF8 181 G8
RTHW LS26 * 155 L1
Woodland St HWTH BD22 54 E3
WHIT OL12 206 C4
Woodlands Vw AL/HA/HU LS17 88 C3
GFTH/SHER LS25 135 L6
HIPP HX3 11 G2
MILN OL16 206 E6
TAD LS24 71 K4
Woodlands Wk SKP/WHF BD23 16 A1
Woodland Ter CHAL LS7 87 J7
CUD/GR S72 263 K1
Woodland Vw CUD/GR S72 262 D1
HEM/SK/SE WF9 * 247 G3
PDSY/CALV LS28 84 C7
PONT WF8 181 G8
Woodland Vls CUD/GR S72 * 245 K8
Wood La AL/HA/HU LS17 67 M3
BRAM LS13 107 L2
BRAM LS13 107 M6
BSLYN/ROY S71 243 L5
BSPA/BRAM LS23 49 G3
CAS WF10 179 H1
CHAL LS7 87 L7
DEWS WF13 173 L4
DOD/DAR S75 243 G4
EARL WF12 195 L6
ECHL BD2 105 H1
HBR HX7 122 D8
HDGY LS6 109 G1
HIPP HX3 147 K5
HIPP HX3 169 M4
HOLM/MEL HD9 236 C8
HOR/CROF WF4 220 C3
HORS LS18 85 M6
HUDE HD5 193 M2
HUDS HD4 214 E3
HUDS HD4 237 K2
KBTN HD8 239 G8
KNOT WF11 161 K3
LUD/ILL HX2 145 M5
MAR/SLWT HD7 234 B1
MSTN/BAR LS15 90 A8
PDSY/CALV LS28 84 D7
RPDN/SBR HX6 167 G2
RTHW LS26 132 F8
RTHW LS26 133 G8
RTHW LS26 135 G8
WOR/ARM LS12 130 C3
Wood Lane Ct HDGY LS6 109 G1
Woodlark Cl WBSY BD6 125 M5
Woodlea BSPA/BRAM LS23 48 F6
Wood Lea KNOT WF11 159 M6
TOD OL14 141 G6
Woodlea Ap HDGY LS6 87 H5
YEA LS19 62 B8
Woodlea Av HUDW HD3 191 L8
Woodlea Cha HDGY LS6 87 H6
Woodlea Cl YEA LS19 84 B1
Woodlea Ct HDGY LS6 87 H6
Woodlea Cft HDGY LS6 87 H5
Woodlea Dr HDGY LS6 87 H5
YEA LS19 84 B1
Woodlea Fold HDGY LS6 87 H6
Woodlea Gdns HDGY LS6 87 H5
Woodlea Garth HDGY LS6 87 H5
Woodlea Ga HDGY LS6 87 H5
Woodlea Gn HDGY LS6 87 H5
Woodlea Gv BEE/HOL LS11 * 131 H3
HDGY LS6 87 H6
YEA LS19 62 B8
Woodlea Holt HDGY LS6 87 H5
Woodlea La HDGY LS6 87 H5
Woodlea Lawn HDGY LS6 87 H5
Woodlea Mt BEE/HOL LS11 131 H3
YEA LS19 62 B8
Woodlea Pk HDGY LS6 87 H6
Woodlea Pl BEE/HOL LS11 131 H3
Woodlea Rd YEA LS19 62 B8
Woodlea Sq HDGY LS6 * 87 H6
Woodlea St BEE/HOL LS11 131 H3
Woodlea Vw HDGY LS6 87 H6
Woodleigh EARL WF12 * 195 M4
Woodleigh Av GFTH/SHER LS25 113 G7
WBOW BD5 127 G5
Woodleigh Crs FEA/AMT WF7 202 B8
Woodleigh Hall Vw YEA LS19 * 85 G5
Woodlesford Crs LUD/ILL HX2 145 K4
Woodliegh Gv HUDS HD4 * 213 L5
Woodliffe Ct CHAL LS7 87 L7
Woodliffe Dr CHAL LS7 87 L7
Woodman Av ELL HX5 191 H1
HUDN HD2 193 H1
Woodman Ct WBSY BD6 126 A8
Woodman St MSTN/BAR LS15 111 J6
Woodmoor Cl HOR/CROF WF4 219 M2
Woodmoor Dr HOR/CROF WF4 219 M2
Woodmoor Ri HOR/CROF WF4 219 M1
Wood Moor Rd
HEM/SK/SE WF9 224 B7
Woodmoor Rd
WKFDW/WTN WF2 220 C1
Woodmoor St BSLYN/ROY S71 243 M6
Wood Mt HOR/CROF WF4 196 B8
RTHW LS26 132 E8
Woodnook Cl BHP/TINH LS16 85 M4
Woodnook Dr BHP/TINH LS16 85 M4
Woodnook Garth
BHP/TINH LS16 85 M4
Wood Nook La HOLM/MEL HD9 235 K4
RPDN/SBR HX6 167 L1
Woodnook Rd BHP/TINH LS16 85 M3
Wood Nook Ter
PDSY/CALV LS28 106 E5
Woodpecker Cl WIL/AL BD15 103 K7
Woodpecker Rd ILK LS29 39 M4
Wood Pl BEE/HOL LS11 * 8 D9
GIR BD8 4 B3
Wood Rd HTON BD9 104 E2
WBOW BD5 127 G2
Wood Rw RTHW LS26 156 D3
Woodrow Crs RTHW LS26 156 C3
Woodrow Dr LM/WK BD12 149 G1
Woodroyd MAR/SLWT HD7 212 E1
Woodroyd Av BSLYN/ROY S71 243 L5
HOLM/MEL HD9 236 D1
WBOW BD5 * 127 H4
Woodroyd Cl BSLYN/ROY S71 243 L5
Woodroyd Dr HIPP HX3 146 A4
Woodroyd Gdns ILK LS29 39 H3
RPDN/SBR HX6 167 H1
Wood Royd Hill La
HOLM/MEL HD9 255 K7
Woodroyd Rd WBOW BD5 127 G4
Woodroyd Ter WBOW BD5 127 H3
Woodside AIRE BD20 57 J5
CAS WF10 158 E6
KBTN HD8 239 J8
MILN OL16 229 L1
ROY/SHW OL2 229 M6
SHPY BD18 82 F6
WKFDW/WTN WF2 176 A4
Woodside Av BGLY BD16 81 H7
BULY LS4 108 E4
CHAL LS7 87 H7
HOR/CROF WF4 200 E3
SHPY BD18 82 A6
WKFDW/WTN WF2 176 A4
Woodside Cl MOR LS27 130 C8
Woodside Ct CUL/QBY BD13 79 M8
HORS LS18 86 A6
ILK LS29 20 C8
Woodside Crs BGLY BD16 81 H7
BTLY WF17 173 J2
HIPP HX3 10 F2
HOR/CROF WF4 200 D2
Woodside Dr BGLY BD16 81 H7
MOR LS27 130 C7
WKFDW/WTN WF2 176 A4
Woodside Gdns MOR LS27 130 C7
Woodside Gv CAS WF10 135 H8
GTL/HWG HX4 168 E8
HIPP HX3 11 G2
Woodside Hill Cl HORS LS18 85 M6
Woodside La AIRE BD20 34 B2
HUDN HD2 192 D2
MOR LS27 130 C7
Woodside Ldg HUDS HD4 215 K8
Woodside Ms CHAL LS7 87 H7

Woodside Mt HIPP HX3 ....10 F3
Woodside Park Av HORS LS18 ...85 M6
Woodside Park Dr HORS LS18....85 M6
　HIPP HX3 ....10 F2
Woodside Rd AIRE BD20 ......35 L5
　BSPA/BRAM LS23 ....48 D7
　HIPP HX3................10 F3
　HUDS HD4 ....213 M5
　LM/WK BD12 ....148 E2
Woodside St CAS WF10 ....135 H4
Woodside Ter BULY LS4........108 L4
　HIPP HX3.................10 F2
Woodside Veiw HUDS HD4 .....213 H3
Woodside Vw BGLY BD16 ....81 H7
　BULY LS4 ....108 L4
　HIPP HX3................10 F2
　HOLM/MEL HD9 ....253 M2
Woodsley Gn HDGY LS6 ....6 A5
Woodsley Rd BVRD LS3........109 G5
　HDGY LS6 ....6 A6
　IDLE BD10 ....83 J8
Woodsley Ter HDGY LS6........6 C6
Woodsome Av MIRF WF14.....172 A4
Woodsome Dr HUDS HD8.......215 M4
　MIRF WF14 ....172 B8
Woodsome Hall La KBTN HD8 ..215 L5
Woodsome Lees La KBTN HD8 ..215 M7
Woodsome Pk KBTN HD8 ......215 M4
Woodsome Rd HUDS HD4 ......215 H7
Woods Sq HIPP HX3 ....146 D4
Wood's Rw PDSY/CALV LS28 ...107 G5
Woodstock Ct BHP/TINH LS16...86 F5
Woodstock Crs HUDS HD4 .....191 K6
Woodstock Gdns DOD/DAR S75..260 F2
Woodstock Rd DOD/DAR S75 ...260 F2
Woodstock Wk WBOW BD5 * ...127 G1
Wood St AIRE BD20 ....56 E1
　BAIL BD17 ....82 E5
　BGLY BD16 ....59 G8
　BRIG HD6 ....170 D4
　BSLY S70 ....261 H6
　BTLY WF17 ....173 L2
　CAS WF10 ....157 L6
　CLECK BD19 ....149 L7
　COL BB8 ....74 A2
　CUD/GR S72 ....223 G8
　DEWS WF13 ....173 M5
　EARD/LOFT WF3..........153 M6
　ELL HX5 ....169 J8
　HOR/CROF WF4 ....200 D2
　HUD HD1 ....14 F4
　HUDE HD5 ....15 L7
　HUDW HD3 ....191 H8
　KBTN HD8 ....239 H4
　KBTN HD8 ....239 M5
　KGHY BD21 ....3 H7
　LIT OL15 ....207 K1
　MAR/SLWT HD7 ....212 B5
　MILN OL16 ....229 L2
　MOR LS27 ....152 B1
　OSS WF5 ....174 F7
　ROCH OL11 ....206 D8
　ROY/SHW OL2 ....229 C7
　WIL/AL BD15 ....103 L5
　WKFDE WF1 ....12 E2
Wood St North HIPP HX3 * 146 D4
Wood Syke DOD/DAR S75 .....260 C2
Wood Ter HUDS HD4...........214 C3
Woodthorne Cft
　AL/HA/HU LS17 ....88 B2
Woodthorpe Cl
　WKFDW/WTN WF2 ....199 G7
Woodthorpe Dr
　WKFDW/WTN WF2 ....199 G7
Woodthorpe Glades
　WKFDW/WTN WF2 ....198 F7
Woodthorpe La
　WKFDW/WTN WF2 ....198 F7
Woodthorpe Park Dr
　WKFDW/WTN WF2 ....198 F7
Woodthorpe Ter HUD HD1 .....14 C8
Wood Top BRIG HD6............170 A1
Wood Top Rd HBR HX7 ....143 K4
Woodvale Cl BOW BD4 ....128 A1
Woodvale Crs BGLY BD16 ......81 J1
Woodvale Gv GTHN BD7 ....126 A1
Woodvale Rd BRIG HD6 ....170 D3
Woodvale Wy CLAY BD14.......126 A1
Woodview BIRK/DRI BD11 ......128 F7
Wood Vw HUDN HD2 ....191 M4
　HWTH BD22 * 79 H2
　MOR LS27 ....130 E6
Woodview Av BAIL BD17 ....83 H2
Wood View Av CAS WF10 ......157 M4
Wood View Cl WF10 ....157 J7
Woodview Cl HORS LS18........85 L4
Wood View Crs WF10 ....157 M6
Wood View Dr ECHL BD2 ......105 L4
Woodview Gv BEE/HOL LS11 ...131 K4

Wood View Gv BRIG HD6.......170 B2
　HUDE HD5................215 H3
　LVSG WF15 ....172 E3
Woodview La DOD/DAR S75 ...260 D3
Woodview Mt BEE/HOL LS11 ..131 K4
Woodview Rd BEE/HOL LS11 ..131 K4
　HWTH BD22 ....79 H2
Woodview St BEE/HOL LS11 ...131 K4
Wood View Ter KGHY BD21 .....79 K2
Woodville Av HORS LS18.......85 M5
　MAR/SLWT HD7 * 213 G2
Woodville Ct RHAY LS8.........88 D5
　WKFDW/WTN WF2 ....198 E4
Woodville Crs HORS LS18 ......85 M5
Woodville Gv HORS LS18.......85 M6
　HWTH BD22 ....79 H6
　MID LS10 * 132 A5
Woodville Pl HORS LS18.......86 A5
　HTON BD9 ....104 B2
　HUDN HD2 ....171 G8
Woodville Rd AIRE BD20 ....2 B2
　EARL WF12 ....173 M6
Woodville Sq MID LS10........132 A5
Woodville St HIPP HX3 ....10 D1
　HORS LS18 ....86 A5
　SHPY BD18 ....82 F6
Woodville Ter HORS LS18 ......85 M5
　WBOW BD5 ....4 D9
Wood Vine Rd PDSY/CALV LS28..106 E5
Wood Wk BSLY/ROY S71 ......243 L1
Woodward Ct MIRF WF14......172 D7
Woodway BGLY BD16 ....81 H7
　HORS LS18 ....85 L7
Woodway Dr HORS LS18 ....85 L7
Woodworth Gv KGHY BD21 .....79 K3
Woolcomb Ct HTON BD9 ....104 C4
Woolcroft Dr HOLM/MEL HD9 ..236 B8
Wooldale Cliff Rd
　HOLM/MEL HD9 ....236 D8
Wooldale Rd HOLM/MEL HD9 ..236 E5
Wooler Av BEE/HOL LS11......131 K1
Wooler Dr BEE/HOL LS11 ......131 J4
Wooler Gv BEE/HOL LS11 .....131 J4
Wooler Pl BEE/HOL LS11 ......131 J4
Wooler Rd BEE/HOL LS11 * ...131 H4
Wooler St BEE/HOL LS11 ......131 H4
The Wool Ex BFD BD1..........4 F6
Woolford Wy EARD/LOFT WF3 ..154 F8
Woolgreaves Av
　WKFDW/WTN WF2 ....198 F8
Woolgreaves Cl
　WKFDW/WTN WF2 ....198 F7
Woolgreaves Cft
　WKFDW/WTN WF2 ....198 F8
Woolgreaves Dr
　WKFDW/WTN WF2 ....198 F8
Woolgreaves Garth
　WKFDW/WTN WF2 ....198 F8
Wooller Rd LM/WK BD12 ......148 F1
Woolley Colliery Rd
　DOD/DAR S75 ....242 A4
Woolley Edge La
　DOD/DAR S75 ....242 A1
Woolley Low Moor La
　HOR/CROF WF4 ....219 M4
Woolley Park Gdns
　HOR/CROF WF4 ....220 C7
Woolley Vw HOR/CROF WF4 ..220 B4
Woollin Av EARD/LOFT WF3....175 G1
Woollin Crs EARD/LOFT WF3 ..153 G8
Woolmarket PONT WF8........180 F6
Woolpack's Yd WKFDE WF1 ....12 C2
Woolrow La BRIG HD6 ....148 E8
Wool Row La KBTN HD8........238 L1
Wool Royd MAR/SLWT HD7 ....211 L4
Woolshops Sq KNOT WF11.....11 H6
Woolstock La DOD/DAR S75 ...258 F3
Wootton St HECK WF16 ....172 E5
Wootton St WBOW BD5 ....126 E7
Worcester Av MID LS10 ....154 B2
Worcester Cl EARD/LOFT WF3 ..153 L5
Worcester Dr MID LS10........154 B2
Worcester Gv HUDS HD4 ......214 D3
Worcester Pl BOW BD4 ....127 J2
Worcester St ROCH OL11 .....228 A2
Worden Gv CLAY BD14.........126 A2
Wordsworth Ap PONT WF8.....180 F4
Wordsworth Av
　AWLS/ASK DN6 ....227 L5
　STKB/PEN S36 ....270 E4
Wordsworth Ct RTHW LS26 ....155 L3
Wordsworth Crs LIT OL15 .....207 H4
Wordsworth Dr KNOT WF11 ...181 K2
　WKSE LS26 ....155 L3
Wordsworth Gv
　EARD/LOFT WF3..........177 G1
Wordsworth Rd
　BSLYN/ROY S71 ....261 K2
Work Bank La STKB/PEN S36 ..270 E2
Workhouse La CTL/HWG HX4 ..168 F8
　LUD/ILL HX2 ....145 J7
Wormald Rw LDS LS1 ....7 G8

Wormald St DEWS WF13.......173 L6
　HUDE HD5................215 H3
Wormalds Vw EARL WF12 .....173 K8
Worral Cl BSLY S70 ....261 H6
Worrall Rd WKFDW/WTN WF2 ..220 C2
Worrall St MOR LS27..........152 B3
Worsley Cl BSLY S70 ....261 H4
Worsley Pl AWLS/ASK DN6....249 H4
　MILN OL16...............229 L6
　ROY/SHW OL2 ....229 J8
Worsnop Buildings
　LM/WK BD12 ....148 E2
Worsnop St LM/WK BD12......126 F8
Worstead Rd HWTH BD22......79 H6
Worth Av KGHY BD21..........3 M1
Worth Bridge Rd KGHY BD21 ...3 L3
Worthing Head Cl LM/WK BD12..148 F3
Worthing Head Rd
　LM/WK BD12 ....148 E3
Worthing St LM/WK BD12 .....148 F3
Worthington St GIR BD8 ....4 B4
Worthville Cl KGHY BD21.......3 H9
Worth Wy HWTH BD22 ....79 J6
　HWTH BD22 ....100 F2
　KGHY BD21 ....3 G7
Wortley Hts WOR/ARM LS12...108 F8
Wortley La WOR/ARM LS12 .....8 A4
Wortley Moor La
　WOR/ARM LS12 ....108 D8
Wortley Moor Rd
　WOR/ARM LS12 ....108 C7
Wortley Pk WOR/ARM LS12 ...109 G8
Wortley Rd WOR/ARM LS12 ...108 D7
Wortley St BGLY BD16 ....81 K3
　BSLY S70 ....261 G5
Worts Hill La HUDW HD3......211 K5
Worts Hill Side HUDW HD3 ...211 L2
Wrangbrook La
　HEM/SK/SE WF9 ....225 L8
Wrangbrook Rd
　HEM/SK/SE WF9 ....225 M6
Wrangthorn Av HDGY LS6 .....6 A3
Wrangthorn Pl HDGY LS6 ......6 A3
Wrangthorn Ter HDGY LS6 ....6 A3
Wray Pl MILN OL16 ....206 E8
Wray's Buildings
　HOR/CROF WF4 ....197 J5
Wrelton Cl BSLYN/ROY S71 ...243 K3
Wren Av GTHN BD7............126 A1
Wrenbeck Av OT LS21 ....41 J4
Wrenbeck Cl OT LS21 ....41 J4
Wrenbeck Dr OT LS21 ....41 K4
Wrenbury Av BHP/TINH LS16 ..85 M1
Wrenbury Crs BHP/TINH LS16 ..85 M1
Wrenbury Gv BHP/TINH LS16 ...86 A1
Wren Cft PONT WF8 ....180 F3
Wren Dr MOR LS27............152 F3
Wren Garth WKFDW/WTN WF2..220 E1
Wren Gn MILN OL16 ....206 D8
Wren Hl BTLY WF17 ....151 J6
Wren's Nest Av ROY/SHW OL2 ..229 L6
Wren St HUD HD1 ....213 M1
　KGHY BD21 ....3 H5
Wrenthorpe La
　WKFDW/WTN WF2 ....175 L5
Wrenthorpe Rd
　WKFDW/WTN WF2 ....176 B5
Wrexhall Rd EARL WF12 ......174 A4
Wrexham Rd ILK LS29 ....39 M5
Wright Av HWTH BD22 ....78 F3
Wrights La KNOT WF11........182 F7
Wright St AIRE BD20 ....55 M1
　HWTH BD22 ....100 F2
Wrigley Av BOW BD4 ....127 K5
Wrigley Hl LUD/ILL HX2 ......124 A8
Wrigley Pl LIT OL15 ....207 H3
Wroe Crs LM/WK BD12 ....148 E3
Wroe Pl LM/WK BD12 ....148 E3
Wroe St DEWS WF13 ....173 H5
Wrose Av ECHL BD2 ....105 J1
　SHPY BD18 ....82 F8
Wrose Brow Rd SHPY BD18 ...82 F6
Wroseclife Gv SHPY BD18 .....83 H6
Wrose Dr SHPY BD18 ....83 H8
Wrose Gv ECHL BD2 ....83 J8
　SHPY BD18 ....82 F8
Wrose Hill Pl ECHL BD2.......104 F1
Wrose Mt SHPY BD18 ....83 G8
Wrose Rd ECHL BD2 ....83 J8
　SHPY BD18 ....82 F8
Wrose Vw SHPY BD18 ....82 F8
Wuerdle Cl MILN OL16........207 G3
Wuerdle Farm Wy MILN OL16 ..207 G2
Wuerdle Pl MILN OL16........207 G2
Wuerdle St MILN OL16 ....207 G2
Wycliffe Cl BRAM LS13 ....106 F1

Wycliffe Dr AL/HA/HU LS17 ....87 M4
Wycliffe Gdns SHPY BD18.....82 C6
Wycliffe Rd SHPY BD18 ....82 C6
Wycliffe St OSS WF5 ....174 E7
Wycollier Cl LM/WK BD12 .....148 E2
Wycombe Gn BOW BD4 ....128 A3
Wycombe Sq BSLYN/ROY S71 ..262 A4
Wykebeck Av OSM LS9 ....110 F9
Wykebeck Crs OSM LS9 ....110 F6
Wykebeck Gdns OSM LS9 .....110 F6
Wykebeck Mt OSM LS9........110 F6
Wykebeck Pl OSM LS9.........111 G6
Wykebeck Rd OSM LS9 ....110 F6
Wykebeck Sq OSM LS9 ....110 F6
Wykebeck St OSM LS9 ....110 F6
Wykebeck Ter OSM LS9.......110 F6
Wykebeck Valley Rd OSM LS9 ..110 F6
Wykebeck Vw OSM LS9 ....110 F6
Wyke Crs LM/WK BD12 ....148 F4
Wyke La LM/WK BD12.........148 F4
Wykelea Cl LM/WK BD12 .....148 F4
Wyke Old La BRIG HD6 ....148 D7
Wyncliffe Gdns AL/HA/HU LS17..87 M4
Wyncroft Gv BHP/TINH LS16 ...86 C5
Wyncroft Ri SHPY BD18 ......104 F1
Wyndham Av ECHL BD2.......105 H3
Wynford Av BHP/TINH LS16 ...86 C5
Wynford Dr HEM/SK/SE WF9 ..247 J3
Wynford Gv BHP/TINH LS16 ...86 C5
Wynford Mt BHP/TINH LS16 ...86 C5
Wynford Ri BHP/TINH LS16 ....86 C5
Wynford Ter BHP/TINH LS16 ...86 C5
Wynford Wy WBSY BD6 ......127 G6
Wynmore Av BHP/TINH LS16 ..64 B4
Wynmore Crs BHP/TINH LS16 ..64 B4
Wynmore Dr BHP/TINH LS16 ..64 B4
　HUDW HD3 ....191 H5
Wynne St GIR BD8 ....4 C4
Wynthorpe Rd
　HOR/CROF WF4 ....197 K5
Wynyard Dr MOR LS27 ....152 B2
Wyther Dr KSTL LS5 ....108 C3
Wyther La KSTL LS5 ....108 B3
Wyther Park Av
　WOR/ARM LS12 ....108 B5
Wyther Park Cl
　WOR/ARM LS12 ....108 B5
Wyther Park Crs
　WOR/ARM LS12 ....108 B5
Wyther Park Gv
　WOR/ARM LS12 ....108 B5
Wyther Park Hl
　WOR/ARM LS12 ....108 B4
Wyther Park Pl
　WOR/ARM LS12 ....108 B4
Wyther Park Rd BRAM LS13 ..108 A5
Wyther Park Sq
　WOR/ARM LS12 ....108 A4
Wyther Park St
　WOR/ARM LS12 ....108 B5
Wyther Park Ter
　WOR/ARM LS12 ....108 A5
Wyther Park Vw
　WOR/ARM LS12 ....108 B4
Wyvern Av HUDW HD3........191 L8
Wyvern Cl BTLY WF17 ....151 L8
Wyverne Rd MAR/SLWT HD7 ..213 G2
Wyvern Pl LUD/ILL HX2 ......146 A6
Wyvern Ter LUD/ILL HX2 .....146 A6
Wyvil Crs ILK LS29 ....39 G2
Wyvil Rd ILK LS29 ....39 G1

Yewdall Wy IDLE BD10 ....83 L8
Yew Green Av HUDS HD4 .....214 A3
Yew Green Rd HUDS HD4......214 A3
Yew Gv HUDS HD4 ....213 H3
Yew La GFTH/SHER LS25......113 K8
Yews Hill Rd HUDS HD4 ......214 A3
Yews La HUDS HD4 ....261 K8
Yews Mt HUD HD1............261 K7
Yews Pl BTLY WF17 ....14 L1
Yew St HUDN HD2 ....14 E1
Yew Tree Av GIR BD8 ....103 M5
Yew Tree Cl AIRE BD20 ....16 D8
　HARS HG2 ....26 D1
　SHPY BD18 ....82 E8
Yew Tree Ct AWLS/ASK DN6 ..227 L6
Yew Tree Crs GIR BD8 ....104 A5
Yew Tree Dr RTHW LS26 .....134 A2
Yew Tree La HOLM/MEL HD9 ..253 L3
　HUDS HD4 ....213 H3
　MAR/SLWT HD7 ....212 B6
　MSTN/BAR LS15 ....112 A7
　WIL/AL BD15 ....103 G6
Yew Tree Rd HUDW HD3 .....191 J4
　KBTN HD8 ....238 B5
Yew Trees Av HUDS HD4 .....147 J3
Yew Trees Cft LUD/ILL HX2 ...144 D5
Yew Tree St WKFDE WF1 .....13 K7
Yew Tree Ter WHIT OL12 * ...162 A4
York Av HUDN HD2 ....192 C4
York Ct BTLY WF17 ....151 L8
York Crs BCLY BD16 * 81 J4
York Dr BTLY WF17...........151 M8
　HECK WF16 ....150 F8
York Ga OT LS21 ....62 A2
　OT LS21 ....62 E2
York Gv BTLY WF17 ....151 L8
York Pl CLECK BD19 ....149 M6
　FEA/AMT WF7 ....202 D7
　LDS LS1 ....6 E9
　TOD OL14 ....163 K1
　WBY LS22 ....30 A8
York Rd BTLY WF17 ....151 L8
　EARL WF12 ....178 B5
　ILK LS29 ....40 B5
　MIRF WF14 ....194 B1
　OSM LS9 ....7 M9
　RYKW YO26 ....33 K2
　SCFT LS14 ....111 K1
　SCFT LS14 ....111 K3
　TAD LS24 ....51 K2
　TAD LS24 ....72 A2
　WBY LS22 ....30 E7
　WBY LS22 ....31 K5
Yorkshire St MILN OL16 ......206 C6
Yorkshire Wy GTHN BD7 .....126 D3
Yorkstone HUDS HD4.........213 K3
York St AIRE BD20 * 34 F7
　BGLY BD16 ....81 J4
　BRIG HD6 ....170 C5
　BSLY S70 ....261 G5
　CAS WF10 ....158 A6
　COL BB8 ....74 B1
　CUD/GR S72 ....244 C8
　GIR BD8 ....125 G5
　HBR HX7 ....143 J4
　HEM/SK/SE WF9 ....246 A1
　HFAX HX1................10 F7
　MILN OL16 ....206 D8
　NORM WF6 * 178 B3
　OSM LS9 ....9 K1
　TOD OL14 ....141 K8
York Ter HIPP HX3 ....10 F1
York Vls NORM WF6 ....178 D4
Young's Ct GFTH/SHER LS25 ..92 A3
Young St GIR BD8 ....104 B7

Y

Yarborough Cft HIPP HX3 .....147 J2
Yard Four BTLY WF17 ....151 H5
Yardley Wy LM/WK BD12......127 G8
Yarn St MID LS10 ....9 M6
Yarrow Cl ROCH OL11 ....228 B1
Yarwood Av GTHN BD7 ....126 A3
Yarwood Gv GTHN BD7 ....126 A3
Yate La HWTH BD22 ....100 E3
Yates Flat SHPY BD18 ....104 F1
Yates La HUDW HD3 ....213 J2
Yeadon Dr HIPP HX3..........169 J2
Yeadon Moor Rd YEA LS19 ...63 G8
Yea Fold MILN OL16 ....207 G3
Yealand Cl AWLS/ASK DN6 ...249 K8
Ye Farre Cl BRIG HD6 ....170 B2
Yeoman's Cl MILN OL16 .....207 H7
Yewbank Cl ILK LS29 ....38 C2
Yewbank Ter ILK LS29 ....38 C2
Yewdall Rd BRAM LS13 ......106 F1

Z

Zealand St BOW BD4 ....127 M2
Zedburgh WHIT OL12 * 206 A6
Zermatt Gv CHAL LS7 ....87 L8
Zermatt Mt CHAL LS7 * 87 L8
Zermatt St CHAL LS7 ....87 M8
Zermatt Ter CHAL LS7 ....87 M8
Zetland Pl RHAY LS8 ....110 B3
Zetland St HUD HD1 ....15 G8
　WKFDE WF1 ....12 F2
Zion Cl HUDW HD3 ....191 K5
Zion Dr DOD/DAR S75 ....242 D5
Zion Ter HBR HX7 ....144 A5
Zoar St MOR LS27 ....152 C2

Index - featured places

A1 Business Park
　KNOT WF11 ....181 L3
Abbey Grange CE High School
　BHP/TINH LS16 ....86 B6
Abbey House Museum
　KSTL LS5 ....108 B1
Abbey Park Primary School
　LUD/ILL HX2 ....123 M8
Aberford CE Primary School
　GFTH/SHER LS25 ....92 A7
Abraham Ormerod Day
　Hospital TOD OL14 ......163 K1
Ackton Pastures Primary
　School CAS WF10 ....157 J8
Ackworth Business Park
　FEA/AMT WF7 ....202 A5
Ackworth Howard CE
　J & I School FEA/AMT WF7 ..202 C7
Ackworth School
　FEA/AMT WF7 ....202 C7
Acorn Business Park
　AIRE BD20 ....16 C7
　SCFT LS14 ....111 G5
Acorn Park Industrial Estate
　BAIL BD17 ....83 G4
Addingham CC
　ILK LS29 ....19 G6
Addingham Primary School
　ILK LS29 ....19 H5
Adel Primary School
　BHP/TINH LS16 ....87 G3
Adel St John the Baptist CE
　Primary School
　BHP/TINH LS16 ....86 E2
Adwalton CC
　BIRK/DRI BD11 ....151 L4
Adwalton Moor Business Park
　BOW BD4 ....128 D7
Agnes Stewart CE High School
　OSM LS9 ....7 L8

Ainley Industrial Estate
　ELL HX5 ....191 J1
Aireborough Leisure Centre
　GSLY LS20 ....62 A5
The Aire & Calder Industrial
　Park CAS WF10 ....157 M5
Airedale Business Centre
　AIRE BD20 ....16 C7
Airedale Centre
　KGHY BD21 ....3 G5
Airedale Clinic
　CAS WF10 ....158 E7
Airedale Community
　Business Centre
　CAS WF10 ....158 D6
Airedale Community Campus
　CAS WF10 ....158 F7
Airedale General Hospital
　AIRE BD20 ....35 J8
Airedale High School
　Performing Arts College
　CAS WF10 ....158 E7
Airedale Infant School
　CAS WF10 ....158 E7
Aireside Business Centre
　LDS LS1 ....8 E1
Aireside Retail Park
　LDS LS1 ....8 D1
Aire Valley Business Centre
　KGHY BD21 ....3 G3
Aire Valley Clinic
　AIRE BD20 ....56 L1
Aireview Business Centre
　BAIL BD17 ....82 C6
Aire View Infant School
　AIRE BD20 ....35 M5
Aireview Primary School
　BRAM LS13 ....107 G2
Albion Mills Retail Park
　WKFDW/WTN WF2 ....12 C3

The Alcuin School
　CHAL LS7 ....87 M7
Alder House Hotel
　BTLY WF17 ....173 J1
The Alhambra Shopping
　Centre BSLY S70 ....261 H5
Alhambra Theatre
　BFD BD1 ....4 E7
Alice Ingham RC Primary
　School MILN OL16.......206 E4
Allerton Bywater Business
　Park CAS WF10 ....157 M2
Allerton Bywater Infant School
　CAS WF10 ....157 K2
Allerton Bywater Primary
　School CAS WF10 ....157 K1
Allerton Clinic
　WIL/AL BD15 ....103 K6
Allerton Grange School
　AL/HA/HU LS17 ....88 C4
Allerton High School
　AL/HA/HU LS17 ....87 K2
Allerton Primary School
　WIL/AL BD15 ....103 K5
All Saints CE Infants School
　NORM WF6 ....178 D4
All Saints CE J & I School
　FEA/AMT WF7 ....179 L5
All Saints CE Primary School
　HIPP HX3 ....168 E4
　ILK LS29 ....38 D1
　OT LS21 ....41 L7
　WBOW BD5 ....126 E2
　WOR/ARM LS12 ....108 E6
All Saints CE School
　PBR WF8.5 ....27 J7
All Saints Industrial Estate
　PONT WF8 ....181 G5
All Saints Infant School
　PONT WF8 ....181 G5

All Saints RC High School
　HUDN HD2 ....192 E1
Alma Industrial Estate
　WHIT OL12 ....206 B5
Almondbury High School
　HUDE HD5 ....215 H2
Almondbury Infant School
　HUDE HD5 ....215 G4
Almondbury Junior
　School
　HUDE HD5 ....215 J2
Alston Retail Park
　KGHY BD21 ....3 K1
Altofts Junior School
　NORM WF6 ....178 B3
Altofts Sports Club
　NORM WF6 ....178 C1
Alwoodley Golf Club
　AL/HA/HU LS17 ....66 A8
Alwoodley Primary School
　AL/HA/HU LS17 ....87 J3
AMF Bowling
　LDSU LS2 ....7 G7
Anglers Country Park
　HOR/CROF WF4 ....222 B1
Apex Business Centre
　BEE/HOL LS11 ....9 G5
Apex Business Park
　BEE/HOL LS11 ....9 G5
Aragon Hotel
　CHAL LS7 ....87 J7
Archbishop Cranmer CE
　Primary School
　AL/HA/HU LS17 ....87 K3
Ardsley House Hotel
　BSLYN/ROY S71 ....262 C6
Arlington Business Centre
　MOR LS27 ....130 F6
Armley Clinic
　WOR/ARM LS12 ....108 E6

Armley Gaol
　WOR/ARM LS12 ....109 G7
Armley Link Trading Estate
　WOR/ARM LS12 ....108 F6
Armley Primary School
　WOR/ARM LS12 ....108 E6
Armley Sports & Leisure
　Centre WOR/ARM LS12 ..108 D7
Armytage Road Industrial
　Estate BRIC HD6 ....170 E4
Arndale Centre
　HDGY LS6 ....108 F1
Arndale Shopping Centre
　SHPY BD18 ....82 D7
ASBS Sports Club
　FEA/AMT WF7 ....201 L1
Ashbrow Junior School
　HUDN HD2 ....192 D3
Ashfield Medical Centre
　MSTN/BAR LS15 ....111 L4
Ashfield Primary School
　OT LS21 ....41 G5
Ashfield Valley Primary School
　ROCH OL11 ....228 A2
Ash Green Primary School
　LUD/ILL HX2 ....145 L1
Ashlands Primary School
　ILK LS29 ....38 E1
Ashley Business Centre
　LDSU LS2 ....7 J8
Ashley Industrial Estate
　CHAL LS7 ....7 H3
　HUDN HD2 ....193 J1
　OSS WF5 ....175 G7
Ashmount Industrial Park
　HEM/SK/SE WF9 ....223 K4
Ashton Road Industrial Estate
　RHAY LS8 ....110 C3
Ashton View Medical Centre
　RHAY LS8 ....110 B4

Ashville Medical Centre
BSLY S70 ....261 M6
Askwith Community Primary
School *OT* LS21 ....40 C1
Asquith Primary School
MOR LS27 ....130 B8
Astley Lane Industrial Estate
RTHW LS26 ....134 D6
Astra Business Park
BEE/HOL LS11 ....131 L4
Athelstan Primary School
GFTH/SHER LS25 ....116 A8
Athersley North Primary
School *BSLYN/ROY* S71 ..243 G6
Athersley South Primary
School *BSLYN/ROY* S71 ..243 H7
Atlas Community Primary
School *GIR* BD8 ....4 A2
A to Z Business Park
DOD/DAR S75 ....242 C5
Austhorpe Primary School
MSTN/BAR LS15 ....112 A4
Automobilia Transport
Museum *HBR* HX7 ....143 L1
Aylesham Industrial Estate
LM/WK BD12 ....126 F3
Badsworth CE J & I School
HEM/SK/SE WF9 ....225 G4
Bagden Hall Hotel
KBTN HD8 ....239 M6
Bagshaw Museum
BTLY WF17 ....151 K6
Baildon CE Primary School
BAIL BD17 ....83 J2
Baildon Golf Club
BAIL BD17 ....82 E1
Baildon Recreation Centre
BAIL BD17 ....82 D5
Baileygate Industrial Estate
PONT WF8 ....181 G5
Bailiff Bridge J & I School
BRIG HD6 ....148 D7
Baillie Street Health Centre
MILN OL16 ....206 B6
Balderstone Technology
College *ROCH* OL11 ......228 C3
Balm Road Industrial Estate
MID LS10 ....9 K9
Bankfield Museum
HIPP HX3 ....11 G2
Bankfoot Primary School
WBOW BD5 ....126 F4
Bardsey Primary School
AL/HA/HU LS17 ....67 L2
Barkerend Primary School
BFDE BD3 ....5 K4
Barkisland CC
GTL/HWG HX4 ....189 J2
Barkisland CE Primary School
GTL/HWG HX4 ....189 J1
Barkston Ash Catholic Primary
TAD LS24 ....115 M1
Barnsley Business Innovation
Centre *CUD/GR* S72 ......244 D7
Barnsley College
BSLY S70 ....261 G4
STKB/PEN S36 ....270 F3
Barnsley College (Belle Vue)
DOD/DAR S75 ....261 G3
Barnsley County Court
BSLY S70 ....261 G4
Barnsley District General
Hospital *DOD/DAR* S75 ..260 E4
Barnsley FC (Oakwell Stadium)
BSLYN/ROY S71 ....261 J5
Barnsley Magistrates Court
BSLY S70 ....261 G4
Barnsley Municipal Golf Club
DOD/DAR S75 ....242 E4
Barnsley Private Clinic
DOD/DAR S75 ....260 F3
Barplas Industrial Park
WBOW BD5 ....127 G4
Barras Garth Industrial Estate
WOR/ARM LS12 ....108 D8
Barugh Green Primary School
DOD/DAR S75 ....259 M2
Barwick In Elmet CE Primary
School *MSTN/BAR* LS15 ..91 G7
The Base
BSLY S70 ....261 H5
Batley Baths & Recreation
Centre *BTLY* WF17 ......173 L1
Batley Bulldogs RLFC
BTLY WF17 ....173 L2
Batley Business Centre
BTLY WF17 ....151 K8
Batley Business & Enterprise
College *BTLY* WF17 ......151 L7
Batley Business & Technology
Centre *BTLY* WF17 ......174 A1
Batley Bus Station
BTLY WF17 ....173 L1
Batley Grammar School
BTLY WF17 ....151 K7
Batley Parish CE (A) J I & N
School *BTLY* WF17 ......151 K8
Batley Sports Centre
BTLY WF17 ....151 K5
Battyeford CE Primary School
MIRF WF14 ....172 A8
Batty Street School
HECK WF16 ....172 F2
BBC North
OSM LS9 ....7 K9
BBC North Studios
BFD BD1 ....4 F7
LDSU LS2 ....6 F6
Beacon Business Centre
HIPP HX3 ....11 L8
The Beaconsfield Centre
HIPP HX3 ....11 L9
Beal Vale Primary School
ROY/SHW OL2 ....229 K7
Beckett Park Athletics Centre
HDGY LS6 ....86 C8
Beckett Park Campus
HDGY LS6 ....108 D1
Beckett Park Primary School
HDGY LS6 ....108 D1
Beckfoot Grammar School
BGLY BD16 ....81 J5
Beech County J & I School
MAR/SLWT HD7 ....213 G1
Beech Hill Primary School
HFAX HX1 ....10 E4
Beech House School
ROCH OL11 ....228 A1
Beechwood Primary School
SCFT LS14 ....111 J1
Beecroft Primary School
BULY LS4 ....108 D3
Beeston Hill St Lukes CE
Primary School
BEE/HOL LS11 ....8 E7
Beeston Primary School
BEE/HOL LS11 ....131 G4
Beeston Royds Industrial
Estate *BEE/HOL* LS11 ..130 E3

Beetles Gallery Restaurant
& Hotel *BAIL* BD17 ......82 B5
Beevor Industrial Estate
BSLYN/ROY S71 ....261 K4
Belfield Community Primary
School *MILN* OL16 ......206 E6
Belfield Trading Estate
MILN OL16 ....206 F5
Belle Isle Medical Centre
RTHW LS26 ....132 B6
Belle Vue Boys Upper School
HTON BD9 ....103 M2
Belle Vue Girls School
BGLY BD16 ....103 L1
Bell Lane Primary School
FEA/AMT WF7 ....224 B1
Ben Rhydding CE Primary
School *ILK* LS29 ....39 H4
Ben Rhydding Primary School
ILK LS29 ....38 F2
Ben Rhydding Sports Club
ILK LS29 ....39 J1
Bent Ley Industrial Estate
HOLM/MEL HD9 ....234 F5
Bentley Primary School
HDGY LS6 ....87 H8
Benton Park School
YEA LS19 ....84 D1
Bero Bu School
LDSU LS2 ....7 G6
Berry Brow Infant School
HUDS HD4 ....214 B6
Bewley's Hotel
GIR BD8 ....4 A4
Bilton Medical Centre
GIR BD8 ....4 A4
Bingley Grammar School
BGLY BD16 ....81 G2
Bingley Health Centre
BGLY BD16 ....81 G3
Bingley Hospital
BGLY BD16 ....81 K3
Bingley Little Theatre
BGLY BD16 ....81 H1
Bingley St Ives Golf Club
BGLY BD16 ....80 E3
Birchfield Primary School
MOR LS27 ....129 L8
Birchinley Manor
Showground
MILN OL16 ....207 H6
Birch Lane Medical Centre
WBOW BD5 ....127 G3
Birdsedge First School
KBTN HD8 ....256 C2
Birkby Infant School
HUD HD1 ....14 D3
Birkby Junior School
HUD HD1 ....14 F1
Birkdale High School
DEWS WF13 ....173 J4
Birkenshaw CE First School
BIRK/DRI BD11 ....128 C8
Birkenshaw Health Centre
BIRK/DRI BD11 ....128 C8
Birkenshaw Middle School
BIRK/DRI BD11 ....150 D2
Birksland Industrial Estate
BOW BD4 ....5 M9
Birkwood Primary School
CUD/GR S72 ....262 E1
Birstall CC
BTLY WF17 ....151 J5
Birstall Primary School
BTLY WF17 ....151 H5
Blackburn Industrial Estate
GFTH/SHER LS25 ....116 D6
Blackgates Primary School
EARD/LOFT WF3 ....153 H6
Blakehill Primary School
IDLE BD10 ....83 J8
Blenheim Primary School
LDSU LS2 ....6 F5
BMK Industrial Estate
LVSG WF15 ....172 D2
Bolling Hall
BOW BD4 ....127 J3
Bolling Special School
BOW BD4 ....127 K3
Bolton Brow Primary School
RPDN/SBR HX6 ....167 M2
Bolton Villas CC
IDLE BD10 ....83 J8
Bondgate Industrial Estate
PONT WF8 ....181 G5
Borough Market
HFAX HX1 ....11 H6
Boston Spa School
BSPA/BRAM LS23 ......48 D7
Bowers Mill Industrial Estate
GTL/HWG HX4 ....189 M1
Bowling Community College &
Swimming Pool
BOW BD4 ....127 J3
Bowling Court
Industrial Estate
BOW BD4 ....105 L8
Bowling Green Primary School
GTL/HWG HX4 ....190 B3
Bowling Park Primary School
WBOW BD5 ....127 H3
Bracken Edge Primary School
CHAL LS7 ....110 A1
Bracken Ghyll Golf Club
ILK LS29 ....18 F5
Brackenhill Primary School
GTHN BD7 ....126 B2
Bradford & Bingley RFC
BGLY BD16 ....81 K5
Bradford Bulls RLFC
(Odsal Stadium)
WBSY BD6 ....127 G6
Bradford Business Park
BFDE BD3 ....4 F2
Bradford Cathedral Community
College
BOW BD4 ....127 K3
Bradford Christian School
SHPY BD18 ....104 F1
Bradford City FC
(Bradford & Bingley Stadium)
GIR BD8 ....4 D1
Bradford College
BFD BD1 ....4 D6
BFD BD1 ....4 D7
Bradford College
(McMillan Campus)
WBOW BD5 ....4 C9
Bradford Girls Grammar School
GIR BD8 ....104 A5
Bradford Golf Club
GSLY LS20 ....61 J7
Bradford Grammar School
HTON BD9 ....104 E2
Bradford & Ilkley Community
College *GTHN* BD7 ......4 B8
Bradford Industrial Museum
& Horses at Work
ECHL BD2 ....105 L3

Bradford Moor Community
Primary School
BFDE BD3 ....105 L6
Bradford Royal Infirmary
HTON BD9 ....104 B4
Bradford Royal Infirmary
Remedial Unit
HTON BD9 ....104 A4
Bradford Salem RFC
HTON BD9 ....104 A2
Bradford University
PDSY/CALV LS28 ....106 C5
Bradley CE J & I School
HUDN HD2 ....193 H1
Bradley Junction Industrial
Estate *HUDN* HD2 ......193 H2
Bradley Mills Cricket & Bowling
Club *HUD* HD1 ....15 J1
Bradley Park Golf Club
HUDN HD2 ....170 F8
Bradleys Both Community
Primary School
AIRE BD20 ....16 E8
Braishaw Primary School
LUD/ILL HX2 ....124 B5
Braim Wood Boys High School
RHAY LS8 ....88 F7
Bramall Business Park
WBOW BD5 ....127 G2
Bramham Park
BSPA/BRAM LS23 ......69 H6
Bramham Primary School
BSPA/BRAM LS23 ......69 M2
Bramhope Primary School
BHP/TINH LS16 ....64 A4
Bramley Business Centre
BRAM LS13 ....107 K4
Bramley Grange College
SCFT LS14 ....89 L5
Bramley Health Centre
BRAM LS13 ....107 L3
Bramley RUFC
BRAM LS13 ....107 L3
Bramley St Peters CE Primary
School *BRAM* LS13 ......107 L4
The Branch Christian School
HECK WF16 ....172 F3
Brandon Golf Club
AL/HA/HU LS17 ....88 F1
Branshaw Golf Club
HWTH BD22 ....78 F3
Branshaw Special School
HWTH BD22 ....2 D6
Branxholme Industrial Estate
BRIG HD6 ....148 E7
Brathwaite Special School
BRIG HD6 ....57 G6
Bretton Country Park
HOR/CROF WF4 ....219 H8
Bretton Hall College
WKFDE WF1 ....13 H9
Bridge Court Business Park
BEE/HOL LS11 ....8 C5
Bridge Theatre
HBR HX7 ....121 H7
Brierley CE Primary School
CUD/GR S72 ....245 J3
Brighouse High School
BRIG HD6 ....170 B1
Brighouse Sports Centre
BRIG HD6 ....170 B1
Brighouse Sports Club
BRIG HD6 ....170 D3
Brighouse Swimming Pool
BRIG HD6 ....170 D4
Brigshaw High School
CAS WF10 ....135 H7
Britannia Business Enterprise
Centre *EARL* WF12 ......174 A1
Britannia Mills Trading Estate
HUDW HD3 ....213 H1
The British Library Document
Supply Centre
BSPA/BRAM LS23 ......49 K3
Broadfield Industrial Estate
HUD HD1 ....214 B3
Broadfield Primary School
MILN OL16 ....206 B7
Broadgate Primary School
HORS LS18 ....85 L5
Broad Lane Business Centre
HEM/SK/SE WF9 ....247 H5
Broad Oak Cricket & Athletic
Club *MAR/SLWT* HD7 ..213 G4
Broadway (due to open 2007)
BFD BD1 ....5 G6
Broadwood School
LUD/ILL HX2 ....145 M5
Brockholes CE School
HOLM/MEL HD9 ....236 E3
Brockholes Industrial Park
HOLM/MEL HD9 ....236 D4
Brodetsky Primary School
AL/HA/HU LS17 ....87 L2
Bronte House School
IDLE BD10 ....84 B4
Brontë Parsonage Museum
HWTH BD22 ....78 D7
Brookfoot Industrial Estate
BRIG HD6 ....170 B4
Brooklands Community
Special School
SKP/WHF BD23 ....16 A4
The Brooksbank School
ELL HX5 ....191 G1
Brookwoods Industrial Estate
GTL/HWG HX4 ....190 E1
Brotherton & Byram CP
School *KNOT* WF11 ......159 L6
Brownhill Infant School
BTLY WF17 ....151 J5
Brownhill Primary School
OSM LS9 ....110 C5
Brownhill Special School
WHIT OL12 ....206 A5
Brow Quarry Industrial Estate
HIPP HX3 ....147 M8
Brudenell Primary School
HDGY LS6 ....109 G3
Brunswick Industrial Estate
HFAX HX1 ....10 E8
Bruntcliffe High School
MOR LS27 ....152 A2
Buckley Road Industrial Estate
WHIT OL12 ....206 D4
Buckstones Primary School
ROY/SHW OL2 ....229 M6
Bull Royd Industrial Estate
GIR BD8 ....104 A6
Burley FC
KSTL LS5 ....86 B8
Burley Hill Trading Estate
BULY LS4 ....108 E3
Burley Oaks Primary School
ILK LS29 ....40 B6
Burley Park Medical Centre
BULY LS4 ....108 F4
Burley St Matthias CE Primary
School *BULY* LS4 ....108 F4

Burley & Woodhead CE Primary
School
ILK LS29 ....40 B6
Burmantofts Health Centre
OSM LS9 ....7 M7
Burnley Road Primary School
HBR HX7 ....143 M5
Burntwood J & I School
HEM/SK/SE WF9 ....246 E4
Burntwood Sports &
Leisure Centre *CUD/GR* S72 ..245 L4
Burton Road Business Park
BSLYN/ROY S71 ....262 A1
Burton Road Primary School
BSLYN/ROY S71 ....261 J3
Burton Salmon Primary School
GFTH/SHER LS25 ....160 A2
Business Enterprise Centre
BFD BD1 ....5 G5
Business & Innovation Barnsley
Centre
DOD/DAR S75 ....260 D2
Butterfield Industrial Estate
BAIL BD17 ....82 F5
Buttershaw High School
WBSY BD6 ....126 B6
Buttershaw Primary School
WBSY BD6 ....126 A7
Byram Industrial Park
KNOT WF11 ....159 M6
Byron Primary School
BFDE BD3 ....5 M4
Bywell CE Junior School
EARL WF12 ....174 B4
Calderdale Business Centre
LUD/ILL HX2 ....10 B6
Calderdale Business Park
LUD/ILL HX2 ....146 B3
Calderdale College
BRIG HD6 ....170 B5
HFAX HX1 ....10 D7
Calderdale College (Princess
Mary Centre) *HFAX* HX1 ..10 C7
Calderdale Industrial
Museum
HFAX HX1 ....11 G8
The Calderdale Royal Hospital
HIPP HX3 ....168 E3
The Calder High School
HBR HX7 ....144 B5
Calder Industrial Estate
BRIG HD6 ....148 D8
Calder Trading Estate
HUDN HD2 ....171 J8
RPDN/SBR HX6 ....167 L3
Calverley CE Primary School
PDSY/CALV LS28 ....84 D7
Calverley Golf Club
PDSY/CALV LS28 ....106 C3
Calverley Medical Centre
PDSY/CALV LS28 ....84 C8
Calverley Parkside Primary
School *PDSY/CALV* LS28 ..84 C8
Campanile Hotel
WKFDW/WTN WF2 ......198 C4
Campsall Country Park
AWLS/ASK DN6 ....227 M6
Campsmount School
AWLS/ASK DN6 ....227 K4
Canalside Industrial Estate
MILN OL16 ....228 D1
Cannon Hall Country Park
DOD/DAR S75 ....258 C5
Cannon Hall Museum
DOD/DAR S75 ....258 C1
Cape Industrial Estate
PDSY/CALV LS28 ....107 G3
Carcroft Health Centre
AWLS/ASK DN6 ....249 L6
Carcroft Industrial Estate
AWLS/ASK DN6 ....249 M7
Cardigan Trading Estate
BULY LS4 ....108 F5
Cardinal Heenan RC High
School *HDGY* LS6 ....87 H5
Carleton Business Park
SKP/WHF BD23 ....16 A3
Carleton High School
PONT WF8 ....203 G1
Carleton Park J & I School
PONT WF8 ....180 F8
Carlinghow Princess Royal
School *BTLY* WF17 ......151 J7
Carlisle Mills Business Centre
GIR BD8 ....4 A1
Carlton Bolling College
BFDE BD3 ....5 K2
Carlton CC
EARD/LOFT WF3 ....154 F4
Carlton Industrial Estate
BSLYN/ROY S71 ....243 L6
Carlton J & I School
DEWS WF13 ....173 K4
HEM/SK/SE WF9 ....247 H3
Carlton Lanes Shopping Area
CAS WF10 ....157 M6
Carlton Mills Trading Estate
WOR/ARM LS12 ....108 F6
Carlton Northfield AFC
EARD/LOFT WF3 ....154 F4
Carlton Primary School
BSLYN/ROY S71 ....243 M6
EARD/LOFT WF3 ....154 F3
Carr Gate Hospital
WKFDW/WTN WF2 ......176 A1
Carr Green J & I School
BRIG HD6 ....170 B5
Carr Manor High School
AL/HA/HU LS17 ....87 J6
Carr Manor Primary School
AL/HA/HU LS17 ....87 J6
Carr Wood Industrial Estate
CAS WF10 ....180 B1
Carrwood Primary School
BOW BD4 ....128 B2
Cartwright Hall Art Gallery
HTON BD9 ....104 E3
Castlefields Industrial Estate
BGLY BD16 ....80 F7
Castlefields Infant School
BRIG HD6 ....170 B5
Castleford Health Centre
CAS WF10 ....157 M6
Castleford High School
CAS WF10 ....158 A6
Castleford RUFC
CAS WF10 ....179 H1
Castleford Swimming Pool
CAS WF10 ....157 K8
Castleford Tigers RLFC
(The Jungle) *CAS* WF10 ..158 B5
Castle Grove Infant School
WKFDW/WTN WF2 ......199 G4
Castle Hall School
MIRF WF14 ....194 D1
Castle Hill J & I School
TOD OL14 ....141 M8
Castleton Primary School
WOR/ARM LS12 ....108 F7

Cathedral Retail Park
WKFDW/WTN WF2 ......12 D5
The Cathedral School
WKFDW/WTN WF2 ......12 A9
Cavendish Primary School
IDLE BD10 ....105 L1
Cawley J & I School
HECK WF16 ....173 G2
Cawthorne CE Primary School
DOD/DAR S75 ....259 G2
Cawthorne Victoria Jubilee
Museum *DOD/DAR* S75 ..259 G1
Cedar Court Hotel
HOR/CROF WF4 ....197 M7
HUDW HD3 ....191 J3
Central Leisure Centre
MILN OL16 ....206 C7
Central Library, Museum &
Art Gallery *LDS* LS1 ....6 F8
Central Street Infant School
HBR HX7 ....143 H3
Centre 27 Business Park
BTLY WF17 ....151 K3
Challenge College
HTON BD9 ....104 E3
Chantry Bridge Industrial
Estate *WKFDE* WF1 ....12 F5
Chapel Allerton Hospital
CHAL LS7 ....110 A1
Chapel Allerton Medical Centre
CHAL LS7 ....87 M8
Chapel Allerton Primary School
CHAL LS7 ....87 L8
Chapel Grange Special School
GIR BD8 ....103 L6
Chapeltown Business Centre
CHAL LS7 ....7 K1
Chapeltown Health Centre
CHAL LS7 ....7 L3
Chel House Business Centre
CHAL LS7 ....7 K4
Chequerfield Infant School
PONT WF8 ....181 H7
Chesney Park Industrial Estate
MID LS10 ....9 J8
Chevet Business Centre
KNOT WF11 ....181 L3
Chevin Country Park Hotel
OT LS21 ....62 E2
Chevin Forest Park
OT LS21 ....62 F1
Chichester Business Centre
MILN OL16 ....206 C7
Chickenley Community J &
I School *EARL* WF12 ....174 C7
Chickenley Medical Clinic &
Health Centre
EARL WF12 ....174 C7
Chohan Medical Centre
WBOW BD5 ....126 F2
Christ Church CE Junior School
RPDN/SBR HX6 ....167 L1
Christ Church CE Primary
School *COL* BB8 ....74 D1
LUD/ILL HX2 ....145 M6
SKP/WHF BD23 ....16 B3
UPML OL3 ....230 F4
Christ Church Upper Armley CE
Primary School
WOR/ARM LS12 ....108 D6
Christchurch Woodhouse J &
I School *HUDN* HD2 ....192 F2
Christ the King RC Primary
School *BRAM* LS13 ......108 A5
Churwell Primary School
MOR LS27 ....130 D7
Cineworld
BFD BD1 ....5 G6
WKFDW/WTN WF2 ......12 C5
City Art Gallery
LDS LS1 ....6 F8
City Link Industrial Park
BOW BD4 ....106 A7
City of Leeds School
HDGY LS6 ....109 J2
City of Wakefield Golf Club
WKFDW/WTN WF2 ......198 A4
City Park Industrial Estate
WOR/ARM LS12 ....130 E3
City Tennis Club
BEE/HOL LS11 ....131 J4
City Varieties Music Hall
LDS LS1 ....7 G9
Civic Theatre
BSLY S70 ....261 H5
DEWS WF13 ....173 L4
HFAX HX1 ....11 G7
Clapgate Primary School
MID LS10 ....154 B1
Clark's Brewery
WKFDW/WTN WF2 ......12 C3
Claycliffe Business Park
DOD/DAR S75 ....260 A1
Clayton Cemetery
CLAY BD14 ....125 M1
Clayton CE Primary School
CLAY BD14 ....125 L2
Clayton Golf Club
CLAY BD14 ....125 L3
Clayton Hospital
WKFDE WF1 ....176 D7
Clayton Village Primary School
CLAY BD14 ....125 L2
Cleckheaton & District Golf
Club *CLECK* BD19 ......149 K4
Cleckheaton Sports Club
CLECK BD19 ....149 L4
Clevedon House School
ILK LS29 ....39 J4
Cliffe Castle Museum & Gallery
AIRE BD20 ....34 D1
Cliffe Commercial Business
Park *HUD* HD1 ....14 B9
Cliffe Hill Primary School
HIPP HX3 ....148 B8
Clifton Cemetery
BRIG HD6 ....171 G4
Clifton Forge Business Park
KNOT WF11 ....182 A2
Clifton Infant School
HOR/CROF WF4 ....197 H3
Clough Head J & I School
MAR/SLWT HD7 ....212 C2
Cobblers Lane Junior School
PONT WF8 ....181 J6
Cobden Primary School
WOR/ARM LS12 ....130 B2
Cockburn High School
BEE/HOL LS11 ....131 G4
Cocksford Golf Club
TAD LS24 ....93 J2
Colden Primary School
HBR HX7 ....142 C1
College of Technology
LDSU LS2 ....6 F7
College of Technology (Annexe)
OSM LS9 ....9 L2
College of the Resurrection
MIRF WF14 ....171 M8

The College
WKFDE WF1 ....176 E7
Collingham Lady Elizabeth
Hastings CE Primary School
WBY LS22 ....47 J5
Colne CC
COL BB8 ....74 C1
Colne Golf Club
COL BB8 ....52 D7
Colne Side Business Park
HUDW HD3 ....213 K1
Colne Valley Business Park
MAR/SLWT HD7 ....212 F5
Colne Valley High School
MAR/SLWT HD7 ....213 F5
Colne Valley Leisure Centre
MAR/SLWT HD7 ....212 C5
Colne Valley Museum
MAR/SLWT HD7 ....212 E2
The Colour Museum
BFD BD1 ....4 D4
Colton Primary School
MSTN/BAR LS15 ....112 A8
Colton Retail Park
MSTN/BAR LS15 ....112 A7
Common Road Industrial
Estate *LM/WK* BD12 ....126 F8
Common Road Infant School
HEM/SK/SE WF9 ....246 C5
The Community Science
College at Thornhill
EARL WF12 ....196 A3
Cononley Business Park
AIRE BD20 ....34 D4
Cononley Primary School
AIRE BD20 ....34 C3
Conway Medical Centre
RHAY LS8 ....110 C3
Cookridge Hall Golf &
Country Club
BHP/TINH LS16 ....64 B8
Cookridge Hospital
BHP/TINH LS16 ....86 A3
Cookridge Primary School
BHP/TINH LS16 ....86 A2
Co-operative Museum
WHIT OL12 ....206 A6
Coper Lane Primary School
WBSY BD6 ....125 L5
Copley Hill Trading Estate
WOR/ARM LS12 ....131 G1
Copley Primary School
HIPP HX3 ....168 D5
Copthorne Primary School
GTHN BD7 ....4 A4
Copwood Mental Health Clinic
BOW BD4 ....128 A2
Cornholme J & I School
TOD OL14 ....140 C5
Coronation Business Centre
KGHY BD21 ....3 J1
Coronation Hospital
ILK LS29 ....38 E3
Corpus Christi Catholic College
OSM LS9 ....110 F6
Corpus Christi Primary School
OSM LS9 ....110 F7
Cottage Road Picture House
HDGY LS6 ....86 E8
Cottingley Clinic
BGLY BD16 ....81 J7
Cottingley Community Health
Centre *BEE/HOL* LS11 ....130 F5
Cottingley Hall Crematorium
BEE/HOL LS11 ....130 F4
Cottingley Primary School
BEE/HOL LS11 ....130 C5
Cottingley Village Primary
School *BGLY* BD16 ....81 K8
The Coulthurst Craven Sports
Centre *SKP/WHF* BD23 ....16 A1
Courtyard by Marriott
BOW BD4 ....129 G4
Cowlersley Primary School
HUDS HD4 ....213 H3
Cowling Primary School
HWTH BD22 ....54 D3
Cragg Vale Primary School
HBR HX7 ....165 L3
The Craiglands Hotel
ILK LS29 ....38 E3
Craven Clinic
SKP/WHF BD23 ....16 B2
Craven College
SKP/WHF BD23 ....16 B2
Craven Road Medical Centre
HDGY LS6 ....6 F2
Crawshaw School
PDSY/CALV LS28 ....107 H7
The Crescent Hotel
ILK LS29 ....38 D2
Crigglestone Sports Club
HOR/CROF WF4 ....220 B2
Crofton Health Centre
HOR/CROF WF4 ....200 B5
Crofton High School
HOR/CROF WF4 ....200 B6
Crofton Infant School
HOR/CROF WF4 ....200 C6
Crofton Junior School
HOR/CROF WF4 ....200 C6
Crompton CC
ROY/SHW OL2 ....229 K6
Crompton Health Centre
ROY/SHW OL2 ....229 K8
Crompton House CE School
ROY/SHW OL2 ....229 H7
Crompton Primary School
ROY/SHW OL2 ....229 J8
Crompton Swimming Pool
ROY/SHW OL2 ....229 K8
Crosland Heath Golf Club
HUDS HD4 ....213 J5
Crosland Moor County Junior
School *HUDS* HD4 ....213 L8
Crosland Road Industrial
Estate *HUDS* HD4 ....235 K1
Crossflatts CC
BGLY BD16 ....58 F8
Cross Flatts Park Primary
School *BEE/HOL* LS11 ....131 J4
Crossflatts Primary School
BGLY BD16 ....59 G8
The Crossgates Centre
MSTN/BAR LS15 ....111 L4
Crossgates Primary School
MILN OL16 ....207 J7
Cross Gates Retail Park
SCFT LS14 ....111 J4
Cross Green Light Industrial
Estate *OSM* LS9 ....132 C1
Cross Hall Junior School
MOR LS27 ....152 B3
Cross Lane Business Park
LVSG WF15 ....172 C2
Cross Lane Industrial Estate
LVSG WF15 ....172 C2
Cross Lane Primary School
ELL HX5 ....191 G1

Crossley Fields J & I School
MIRF WF14 ....172 D7
Crossley Hall Primary School
GIR BD8 ....104 A7
The Crossley Heath School
HFAX HX1 ....168 C2
Crossley Retail Park
HFAX HX1 ....10 E4
Crossley Street Primary School
WBY LS22 ....30 A8
Crow Lane J & I School
HUDW HD3 ....213 J1
Crown Point Retail Park
MID LS10 ....9 H4
Cuckoo Nest Industrial Estate
GTHN BD7 ....4 B6
Cudworth Churchfield Primary
School *CUD/GR* S72 ....244 D7
Cudworth Pontefract Road
Primary School
CUD/GR S72 ....244 D6
Cullingworth Medical Centre
CUL/QBY BD13 ....79 M8
Cullingworth Primary School
CUL/QBY BD13 ....79 M8
Cumberworth CE (A) First
School *KBTN* HD8 ....238 D8
Dale Lane Industrial Estate
HEM/SK/SE WF9 ....247 K1
Dalesgate Hotel
AIRE BD20 ....57 J4
Dalton School J & I School
HUDE HD5 ....193 H8
Dane Royd J & I School
HOR/CROF WF4 ....220 B4
Dansk Way
ILK LS29 ....38 C1
Darfield CC
WMB/DAR S73 ....263 K6
Darfield Upperwood J & I
School *WMB/DAR* S73 ....263 K6
Darrington CE J & I School
PONT WF8 ....203 M1
Darton High School
DOD/DAR S75 ....241 K6
Darton Primary School
DOD/DAR S75 ....242 B5
Days Inn Hotel
BRIG HD6 ....171 H1
Dearne Valley Health Centre
KBTN HD8 ....239 M5
Deeplish Primary School
ROCH OL11 ....228 C1
Deighton Gates Primary
School *WBY* LS22 ....30 A6
Denby Dale Industrial Park
KBTN HD8 ....239 H8
Denby First School
KBTN HD8 ....257 G3
Denholme Clinic
CUL/QBY BD13 ....101 M5
Denholme Primary School
CUL/QBY BD13 ....101 M5
Dental Institute
LDSU LS2 ....6 D7
De Vere Oulton Hall Hotel
RTHW LS26 ....155 K2
De Vere Village Hotel
BHP/TINH LS16 ....86 E6
Dewsbury Bus Station
EARL WF12 ....173 L7
Dewsbury Cemetery
DEWS WF13 ....173 J7
Dewsbury College
DEWS WF13 ....173 K5
Dewsbury College Batley
School of Art & Design
DEWS WF13 ....173 J4
Dewsbury District Golf Club
MIRF WF14 ....194 F3
Dewsbury & District Hospital
DEWS WF13 ....173 J4
Dewsbury Moor Crematorium
DEWS WF13 ....173 H5
Dewsbury Museum & Art
Gallery *DEWS* WF13 ....173 J7
Dewsbury Sports Centre
EARL WF12 ....173 M6
Dimplewell Infant School
OSS WF5 ....196 F2
District Archives Office
WKFDE WF1 ....12 C1
Dixon Lane Medical Centre
WOR/ARM LS12 ....130 C2
Dixons City Technology College
WBOW BD5 ....127 G2
Dockfield Industrial Estate
BAIL BD17 ....82 E6
Dodworth Business Park
DOD/DAR S75 ....259 M6
Dodworth CE School
DOD/DAR S75 ....260 A8
Dodworth Health Centre
DOD/DAR S75 ....260 B1
Dodworth Keresforth Road
Primary School
ROY/SHW OL2 ....260 C8
Dodworth Primary School
DOD/DAR S75 ....260 B7
Domestic Street Industrial
Estate *BEE/HOL* LS11 ....8 A4
Dominion Industrial Park
HIPP HX3 ....147 L6
Doncaster Road Primary
School *BSLYN/ROY* S71 ....261 J5
Dorothy Hyman Stadium
CUD/GR S72 ....244 B8
Drakes Industrial Estate
LUD/ILL HX2 ....146 B2
Drighlington Primary School
BIRK/DRI BD11 ....129 G8
Drug Addiction Clinic
LDSU LS2 ....6 C1
Drummond Trading Estate
GIR BD8 ....4 D3
Dryclough Infant School
HUDS HD4 ....213 L3
Durn Street Industrial
Estate
LIT OL15 ....185 L8
Eagles Yard Business Park
WKFDE WF1 ....12 F1
Earlsheaton High School
EARL WF12 ....174 A6
Earlsheaton Infant School
EARL WF12 ....174 B7
East Ardsley High School
EARD/LOFT WF3 ....153 L7
East Ardsley Infant School
EARD/LOFT WF3 ....153 M6
East Ardsley Primary School
EARD/LOFT WF3 ....153 M6
East Ardsley United CC
EARD/LOFT WF3 ....153 L8
East Bierley CC
BOW BD4 ....128 A7
East Bierley First School
BIRK/DRI BD11 ....128 B7

East Bierley Golf Club
BOW BD4 ....128 A7
Eastborough J I & N School
EARL WF12 ....173 M6
Eastburn J & I School
AIRE BD20 ....35 H8
East Crompton St Georges
CE Primary School
ROY/SHW OL2 ....229 L7
East Crompton St James CE
Primary School
ROY/SHW OL2 ....229 K7
East Garforth Primary School
GFTH/SHER LS25 ....113 K6
East Leeds Clinic
OSM LS9 ....110 D5
East Leeds Leisure Centre
MSTN/BAR LS15 ....111 G7
Eastmoor Health Centre
WKFDE WF1 ....177 H6
East Morton CE Primary
School *AIRE* BD20 ....58 E6
Eastwood Primary School
KGHY BD21 ....3 J2
Ebor Gardens Primary School
OSM LS9 ....110 B6
Eccleshill CC
IDLE BD10 ....105 M1
Eccleshill Clinic & Health
Centre *IDLE* BD10 ....83 M8
Eccleshill United Sports Club
IDLE BD10 ....83 H7
Edgerton Cemetery
HUD HD1 ....14 C3
Edward Sheerien Secondary
School *BSLYN/ROY* S71 ....243 K8
Eldwick Primary School
BGLY BD16 ....81 L2
Elizabeth Industrial Estate
HFAX HX1 ....10 D3
Elland CE J & I School
ELL HX5 ....169 H7
Elland Road Industrial Park
BEE/HOL LS11 ....130 F3
Ellar Carr School
IDLE BD10 ....83 L5
Ellen Royde Health Centre
ELL HX5 ....169 G7
Elmete Wood School
RHAY LS8 ....88 F6
Elmfield Business Park
GFTH/SHER LS25 ....113 J6
Elmwood Health Centre
HOLM/MEL HD9 ....236 C7
Emley First School
KBTN HD8 ....217 M7
Emley Moor Business Park
KBTN HD8 ....217 K8
Emmanuel Trading Estate
WOR/ARM LS12 ....8 B3
Empire Business Centre
LUD/ILL HX2 ....146 C2
England Lane J & I School
KNOT WF11 ....182 C3
English Martyrs RC Primary
School *WKFDW/WTN* WF2 ....197 M1
Enterprise Park Industrial
Estate *BEE/HOL* LS11 ....131 H5
Environmental Business
Centre *MOR* LS27 ....152 C2
Ermysteds Grammar School
SKP/WHF BD23 ....16 B1
Esholt & Aire Bronians
Sports Club *BAIL* BD17 ....83 K1
Esplanade Arts & Heritage
Centre *MILN* OL16 ....206 A7
Essex Park Industrial Estate
BFDE BD3 ....5 J8
Eureka! The Museum for
Children *HIPP* HX3 ....11 J7
Euroway Trading Estate
BOW BD4 ....127 J8
Fagley Primary School
ECHL BD2 ....105 M4
Fairburn Community School
KNOT WF11 ....159 J2
Fairburn Sports & Recreation
Centre *KNOT* WF11 ....159 J2
Fairfield School
HECK WF16 ....173 G1
Fairway Industrial Estate
MOR LS27 ....151 H4
Fall Bank Industrial Estate
DOD/DAR S75 ....259 M7
Fardew Golf Club
AIRE BD20 ....58 E6
Farfield Primary School
PDSY/CALV LS28 ....106 D4
Farnham Primary School
GTHN BD7 ....126 D1
Farnley CE Primary School
OT LS21 ....41 L1
Farnley Park High School
WOR/ARM LS12 ....130 A2
Farnley Tyas CE First School
HUDS HD4 ....215 G8
Farrowdale House School
ROY/SHW OL2 ....229 K8
Farrow Medical Centre
BFDE BD3 ....5 H3
Farsley Celtic AFC
PDSY/CALV LS28 ....107 G4
Farsley Community Clinic
PDSY/CALV LS28 ....106 E3
Fartown Health Centre
HUDN HD2 ....192 C5
Fartown High School
HUDN HD2 ....192 E4
Fearnville Primary School
BOW BD4 ....127 M1
Fearnville Sports Centre
RHAY LS8 ....110 F2
Featherbank Infant School
HORS LS18 ....85 K6
Featherstone Cemetery
FEA/AMT WF7 ....179 K4
Featherstone High School
FEA/AMT WF7 ....202 B1
Featherstone Sports
Centre
FEA/AMT WF7 ....202 B2
The Felkirk School
CUD/GR S72 ....222 E8
Felnex Trading Estate
OSM LS9 ....110 E8
Fentham Industrial Estate
BRIG HD6 ....170 C5
Fernandes Brewery
WKFDE WF1 ....13 G3
Fernbank School
AWLS/ASK DN6 ....249 L8
Ferney Lee Primary School
TOD OL14 ....141 J8
Fernley Green Industrial
Estate *KNOT* WF11 ....182 D2
Ferrybridge Infant School
KNOT WF11 ....181 L1
Fieldhead Carr Primary
School *SCFT* LS14 ....89 K5

Field Head Hospital
WKFDE WF1 ....176 F4
Fieldhead J & I School
BTLY WF17 ....151 H3
Fieldhouse Industrial Estate
WHIT OL12 ....206 B4
Field Lane J & I School
BTLY WF17 ....173 M2
Field Lane Primary School
BRIC HD6 ....170 A7
Firbank Primary School
ROY/SHW OL2 ....228 F7
Firgrove Business Park
MILN OL16 ....206 F6
First Avenue Industrial Estate
PDSY/CALV LS28 ....107 G6
Fir Tree Primary School
AL/HA/HU LS17 ....87 M3
Fitzwilliam Primary School
HEM/SK/SE WF9 ....223 K2
Five Lanes Primary School
WOR/ARM LS12 ....108 D3
Five Rivers Project
BEE/HOL LS11 ....8 E7
Fixby J & I School
HUDN HD2 ....192 C2
Flanshaw J & I School
WKFDW/WTN WF2 ....176 B7
Flockton CE School
HOR/CROF WF4 ....217 L3
Flushdyke Primary School
OSS WF5 ....175 H7
Forster Square Retail Park
BFD BD1 ....4 E3
Foundry Industrial Estate
KNOT WF11 ....181 L1
PDSY/CALV LS28 ....106 F5
The Fountain Medical Centre
MOR LS27 ....152 C3
Four Gates End
HBR HX7 ....119 K8
Four Lanes Business Park
GIR BD8 ....104 B7
Fowler Street Industrial
Estate *BOW* BD4 ....127 K1
Foxhill Primary School
CUL/QBY BD13 ....124 F4
The Freeston College of
Business Enterprise
NORM WF6 ....178 D5
Friars Industrial Estate
IDLE BD10 ....83 K7
Frizinghall Medical Centre
HTON BD9 ....104 D2
Frizinghall Primary School
HTON BD9 ....104 E1
The Froebelian School
HORS LS18 ....85 K7
Frost Hill Business Park
LVSG WF15 ....172 D2
Fulford Grange Hospital
YEA LS19 ....84 D7
Fulneck Golf Club
PDSY/CALV LS28 ....128 F2
Fulneck School
PDSY/CALV LS28 ....129 G2
Garforth Clinic
GFTH/SHER LS25 ....113 G8
Garforth Community College
GFTH/SHER LS25 ....113 G8
Garforth Golf Club
GFTH/SHER LS25 ....113 G3
Garforth Leisure Centre
GFTH/SHER LS25 ....113 J7
Garforth Medical Centre
GFTH/SHER LS25 ....113 G7
Gascoigne Wood Mine
GFTH/SHER LS25 ....139 G2
Gateways School
AL/HA/HU LS17 ....45 J8
Gawber Primary School
DOD/DAR S75 ....260 C3
Gawthorpe Primary School
OSS WF5 ....174 E5
Gelderd Trading Estate
WOR/ARM LS12 ....131 G1
Gemini Business Park
CHAL LS7 ....7 J3
Ghyll Royd School
MOR LS27 ....39 M3
Gildersome Primary School
MOR LS27 ....129 L7
Gillott Industrial Estate
BSLY S70 ....260 F5
Gilthwaites First School
KBTN HD8 ....239 J7
Girlington Industrial Centre
GIR BD8 ....104 B6
Girlington Primary School
GIR BD8 ....104 C6
Girls High School
SKP/WHF BD23 ....16 A2
Glasshoughton Infant School
CAS WF10 ....158 A7
Glebe House School
MILN OL16 ....206 A8
The Gleddings School
HIPP HX3 ....168 C3
Gledholt Business Park
HUD HD1 ....14 A8
Gledhow Primary School
RHAY LS8 ....88 B6
Glenaire Primary School
BAIL BD17 ....82 C4
Glen Cable Tramway
BAIL BD17 ....82 B4
Glenfield Caravan Park
AL/HA/HU LS17 ....67 H5
Glusburn Community Primary
School *AIRE* BD20 ....34 E8
Goicar J & I School
MAR/SLWT HD7 ....212 F1
Golden Acre Park & Gardens
BHP/TINH LS16 ....64 D6
Golden Lion Hotel
LDS LS1 ....9 G2
Gomersal CE Middle School
CLECK BD19 ....150 E9
Gomersal First School
CLECK BD19 ....150 D5
Gomersal Lodge Hotel
CLECK BD19 ....150 B6
Gomersal Park Hotel
CLECK BD19 ....150 E3
The Good Health Centre
RHAY LS8 ....88 C4
Gorrells Industrial Estate
ROCH OL11 ....228 A8
Gotts Park Golf Club
WOR/ARM LS12 ....108 C5
Grafton School
HDGY LS6 ....6 F2
Grand Theatre & Opera House
LDSU LS2 ....7 G4
Grangefield Industrial
Estate
PDSY/CALV LS28 ....107 H5
Grange Gate Junior School
BSLYN/ROY S71 ....262 A4

Grange Lane Industrial Estate
BSLYN/ROY S71 ....262 A6
The Grange Medical Centre
SCFT LS14 ....111 K1
Grange Road Business Park
BTLY WF17 ....174 A3
Grange Road Industrial Estate
BTLY WF17 ....174 A2
Grange Road Primary School
GTHN BD7 ....126 C1
The Grange Technology
College *WBOW* BD5 ....126 D4
Grasmere School
BSLYN/ROY S71 ....262 A6
Great Horton Industrial Estate
WBSY BD6 ....125 M4
Great & Little Preston CE
Infants School *RTHW* LS26 ....135 G7
Great & Little Preston Junior
School *RTHW* LS26 ....135 G7
Great Northern Retail Park
HUD HD1 ....15 H4
Greatwood Community
Primary School
SKP/WHF BD23 ....16 C3
Greenacre School
BSLY S70 ....260 E7
Greenbank Primary School
WHIT OL12 ....206 B5
Greenfield Primary School
GFTH/SHER LS25 ....135 J4
Greenfield Special School
IDLE BD10 ....83 J5
Greengates Primary School
IDLE BD10 ....84 A7
Greenhead Athletics Track
AIRE BD20 ....57 K5
Greenhead College
HUD HD1 ....14 C7
Greenhead High School
AIRE BD20 ....57 K4
Greenhill CP School
BRAM LS13 ....107 M6
Greenhill Industrial Estate
HBR HX7 ....144 A6
Greenhill J & I School
WKFDE WF1 ....13 H1
Green Lane Industrial Estate
FEA/AMT WF7 ....179 J8
Green Lane Primary School
GFTH/SHER LS25 ....113 K8
GIR BD8 ....4 B2
Green Meadows School
CSLY LS20 ....61 L5
Greenmount Primary School
BEE/HOL LS11 ....8 E9
Green Mount Retail Park
HFAX HX1 ....10 E5
Greenside Infant School
HUDE HD5 ....215 H2
Greenside Primary School
PDSY/CALV LS28 ....106 C3
Greenwood Primary School
BEE/HOL LS11 ....8 F8
Greetland Cricket & Bowling
Club *GTL/HWG* HX4 ....168 E7
Greetland Primary School
GTL/HWG HX4 ....168 C7
Gresley Road Industrial Estate
KGHY BD21 ....3 H5
Grimethorpe Hall
CUD/GR S72 ....245 H6
Grimethorpe Ladywood
Primary School
CUD/GR S72 ....245 K4
Grove House Primary School
ECHL BD2 ....105 J2
Grove Lea Primary School
HEM/SK/SE WF9 ....223 M7
Grove Mills Industrial Estate
ELL HX5 ....169 J7
Grove Street Primary School
BSLYN/ROY S71 ....261 J5
Guard House Primary School
HWTH BD22 ....2 A5
Guide Post Hotel
LM/WK BD12 ....126 F8
Guiseley AFC
CSLY LS20 ....61 L5
Guiseley Cemetery
CSLY LS20 ....61 L3
Guiseley Infant School
CSLY LS20 ....62 C3
Guiseley School
CSLY LS20 ....61 M6
Gulsyke Medical Centre
MSTN/BAR LS15 ....111 J7
Gunthwaite Hall
STKB/PEN S36 ....257 K4
Hade Edge J & I School
HOLM/MEL HD9 ....254 C6
Haggs Business Park
PBR HG3 ....27 M3
Haigh Hall Medical Centre
IDLE BD10 ....83 M7
Haigh Road Infant School
RTHW LS26 ....133 G8
Haley's Hotel & Restaurant
HDGY LS6 ....109 G1
Half Acres J & I School
CAS WF10 ....157 L7
Halfpenny Bridge Industrial
Estate *MILN* OL16 ....206 C8
Halfpenny Lane J & I School
PONT WF8 ....180 D6
Halifax Blue Sox RLFC
(The Shay Stadium) *HFAX* HX1 ..11 H9
Halifax Bradley Hall Golf Club
GTL/HWG HX4 ....190 C1
Halifax Building Society
HFAX HX1 ....11 G7
Halifax Cricket Ground
HFAX HX1 ....146 A7
Halifax Golf Club
LUD/ILL HX2 ....123 C5
Halifax High School
HFAX HX1 ....11 G8
The Halifax High School
HFAX HX1 ....168 C1
Halifax Industrial Centre
HFAX HX1 ....10 D4
Halifax Leisure Centre
HFAX HX1 ....11 H7
Halifax RUFC
LUD/ILL HX2 ....146 B2
Halifax Ski Centre
HIPP HX3 ....146 E3
Halifax Swimming Pool
HFAX HX1 ....11 H8
Halifax Town FC
(The Shay Stadium) *HFAX* HX1 ..11 H9
Halifax West End Golf Club
LUD/ILL HX2 ....145 L6
Hall Bower Athletic Club
HUDS HD4 ....214 D5
Hall Bower CC
HUDS HD4 ....214 D5
Hall Park CC
HORS LS18 ....85 J6

Hamer County Community Primary School *WHIT* OL12 ....206 D4
Hanging Heaton CE J & I School *BTLY* WF17 ....174 B3
Hanging Heaton Golf Club *EARL* WF12 ....174 A4
Hanson Upper School *ECHL* BD2 ....105 H2
Harden Primary School *BGLY* BD16 ....80 C5
Harehills Middle School *RHAY* LS8 ....110 B3
Harehills Primary School *RHAY* LS8 ....110 C3
Harewood CE Primary School *AL/HA/HU* LS17 ....45 J7
Harewood House & Bird Garden *AL/HA/HU* LS17 ....45 H7
Hartshead J & I School *LVSG* WF15 ....171 J4
Hartshead Moor Special School *CLECK* BD19 ....149 H8
Hatfield Hall Golf Club *EARD/LOFT* WF3 ....177 C3
Havercroft Health Centre *HOR/CROF* WF4 ....222 D6
Havercroft J & I School *HOR/CROF* WF4 ....222 D6
Hawkins Clinic *MILN* OL16 ....206 D4
Hawksworth CE Primary School *OSLY* LS20 ....61 G6
Hawksworth Wood Primary School *KSTL* LS5 ....86 A7
Haycliffe Special School *WBOW* BD5 ....126 C6
Hazlewood Castle Hotel *TAD* LS24 ....92 D2
Headfield CE Junior School *EARL* WF12 ....195 L1
Headingley Golf Club *BHP/TINH* LS16 ....86 F1
Headingley Primary School *HDGY* LS6 ....108 F1
Headlands CE J & I School *LVSG* WF15 ....172 C2
Headley Golf Club *CUL/QBY* BD13 ....124 F1
Headrow Shopping Centre *LDS* LS1 ....7 G9
Headway Business Park *WKFDW/WTN* WF2 ....12 B1
Heady Fields Golf Club *HOLM/MEL* HD9 ....235 J6
Healds Hall Hotel *LVSG* WF15 ....172 D1
Healey J & I School *BTLY* WF17 ....173 H1
Healey Primary School *WHIT* OL12 ....206 A3
Heath Cottage Hotel *EARL* WF12 ....174 B6
Heathfield Industrial Estate *ELL* HX5 ....169 J8
Heathfield-Rishworth School *RPDN/SBR* HX6 ....188 E4
Heathfield School *RPDN/SBR* HX6 ....188 E4
Heath View Community School *WKFDE* WF1 ....13 M1
Heaton Avenue First School *CLECK* BD19 ....149 L7
Heaton Primary School *HTON* BD9 ....103 M2
Heaton Royds Hospital *HTON* BD9 ....103 M1
Heaton Royds Special School *SHPY* BD18 ....104 B1
Heaton St Barnabas Aided CE Primary School *HTON* BD9 ....104 C2
Hebble Brook Business Park *LUD/ILL* HX2 ....123 L7
Hebden Bridge Cinema *HBR* HX7 ....143 J3
Hebden Bridge Golf Club *HBR* HX7 ....143 H3
Hebden Bridge Health Centre *HBR* HX7 ....143 J3
Hebden Royd Primary School *HBR* HX7 ....143 G2
Heckmondwike Grammar School *HECK* WF16 ....172 F2
Heckmondwike Sports Club *HECK* WF16 ....172 F2
Helme CE J & I School *HOLM/MEL* HD9 ....234 F2
Hemsworth Art & Community College *HEM/SK/SE* WF9 ....224 A7
Hemsworth RUFC *HEM/SK/SE* WF9 ....224 B7
Hemsworth Sports Complex *HEM/SK/SE* WF9 ....246 A1
Hemsworth Water Park & Playworld *HEM/SK/SE* WF9 ....223 L5
Hendal Primary School *WKFDW/WTN* WF2 ....220 D1
Henry Moore Clinic *CAS* WF10 ....157 M7
Heptonstall CP School *HBR* HX7 ....143 H1
Hepworth J & I School *HOLM/MEL* HD9 ....255 G5
Herriott's Hotel, Bar & Dining Room *SKP/WHF* BD23 ....16 A2
Heybrook Primary School *WHIT* OL12 ....206 C5
Hey Green Country House Hotel *MAR/SLWT* HD7 ....232 D1
High Bank First School *LVSG* WF15 ....171 K1
Highburton CE (C) First School *KBTN* HD8 ....216 A6
Highbury Special School *BRIG* HD6 ....170 A7
Highcliffe Industrial Estate *MOR* LS27 ....152 B1
High Crags Primary School *SHPY* BD18 ....82 E8
High Fernley Primary School *LM/WK* BD12 ....148 E3
Highfield Primary School *AL/HA/HU* LS17 ....88 A2
Highfield School *OSS* WF5 ....174 F5
The Highfields Medical Centre *BRAM* LS13 ....107 M4
Highfields Special School *HUD* HD1 ....14 D4
Highlander Sports Club *KBTN* HD8 ....216 D3
High Royds Hospital *ILK* LS29 ....61 K4
Hightown First School *LVSG* WF15 ....171 L1
High Trees School *BSPA/BRAM* LS23 ....49 G8
Hillcrest Primary School *CHAL* LS7 ....7 M1

Hillside Primary School *BEE/HOL* LS11 ....8 E8
Hillside Works Industrial Estate *CLECK* BD19 ....149 M4
Hill Top CE Primary School *ECHL* BD2 ....126 E8
Hill Top Community Primary School *ROCH* OL11 ....228 C5
Hillcliffe Primary School *EARD/LOFT* WF3 ....174 F1
Hinchliffe Mill J & I School *HOLM/MEL* HD9 ....253 L4
Hipperholme Clinic *HIPP* HX3 ....147 M6
Hipperholme Grammar School *HIPP* HX3 ....147 L6
Hipperholme & Lightcliffe High School & Sports College *HIPP* HX3 ....148 B7
HM Prison *BSPA/BRAM* LS23 ....49 J4
WKFDW/WTN WF2 ....12 B2
HM Prison Service College *WKFDW/WTN* WF2 ....12 B2
HM Young Offender Institution *WBY* LS22 ....30 D7
Hockney Road Industrial Estate *GIR* BD8 ....104 C6
IDLE BD10 ....105 K1
Holdsworth House Hotel *LUD/ILL* HX2 ....124 C7
Holgate Secondary School *BSLY* S70 ....260 E5
Hollingwood Primary School *GTHN* BD7 ....125 M3
Hollingworth High School *MILN* OL16 ....207 J8
Hollingworth Lake Activity Centre *LIT* OL15 ....207 J4
Hollingworth Lake Caravan Park *LIT* OL15 ....207 L5
Hollingworth Lake Country Park *LIT* OL15 ....207 L4
Holly Bank School *MIRF* WF14 ....172 A6
Hollywood Bowl *BULY* LS4 ....108 F5
Holme J & I School *HOLM/MEL* HD9 ....253 G5
Holme Mills Industrial Estate *HUDW* HD3 ....213 H2
Holme Valley Business Park *HUDS* HD4 ....214 B6
Holme Valley Clinic *BOW* BD4 ....236 B1
Holme Wood Health Centre *BOW* BD4 ....128 A3
Holmfield Industrial Estate *LUD/ILL* HX2 ....124 C7
Holmfirth Craft Market *HOLM/MEL* HD9 ....254 B1
Holmfirth High School *HOLM/MEL* HD9 ....236 E6
Holmfirth J & I School *HOLM/MEL* HD9 ....254 C2
Holmfirth Swimming Pool *HOLM/MEL* HD9 ....236 D7
Holt Park Shopping Centre *BHP/TINH* LS16 ....86 B1
Holybrook Primary School *IDLE* BD10 ....83 M8
Holycroft Primary School *KGHY* BD21 ....2 E7
Holy Cross Deanery CE Primary School *BSLY/ROY* S71 ....243 K8
Holy Family RC Primary School *ROCH* OL11 ....228 C3
Holy Family RC School *AIRE* BD20 ....2 E1
Holy Family & St Michaels RC Primary School *PONT* WF8 ....181 J5
Holylandswaine Primary School *STKB/PEN* S36 ....258 B7
Holy Name RC Primary School *BHP/TINH* LS16 ....86 B3
Holy Rood Catholic Primary School *BSLY* S70 ....260 F6
Holy Rosary & St Annes RC Primary School *CHAL* LS7 ....7 K3
Holy Spirit RC Primary School *HECK* WF16 ....172 F2
Holy Trinity CE J & I School *OSS* WF5 ....174 F8
Holy Trinity CE Primary School *BHP/TINH* LS16 ....85 M1
HFAX HX1 ....10 E8
LIT OL15 ....207 K1
Holy Trinity CE Senior School *LUD/ILL* HX2 ....124 C8
Holywell Green Primary School *GTL/HWG* HX4 ....190 D2
Homestead Clinic *WKFDW/WTN* WF2 ....176 B8
Honley Business Centre *HOLM/MEL* HD9 ....236 C2
Honley CE Infant School *HOLM/MEL* HD9 ....236 B2
Honley CE Junior School *HOLM/MEL* HD9 ....236 B2
Honley High School & College *HOLM/MEL* HD9 ....236 C1
Hopton J & I School *MIRF* WF14 ....194 B2
Horbury Bridge CE J & I School *HOR/CROF* WF4 ....196 F5
Horbury Junction Industrial Estate *HOR/CROF* WF4 ....197 L1
Horbury Junior School *HOR/CROF* WF4 ....197 K5
The Horsefair Centre *WBY* LS22 ....48 A1
Horsfall Stadium *WBSY* BD6 ....126 D7
Horsforth CC *HORS* LS18 ....85 K3
Horsforth Golf Club *HORS* LS18 ....85 H3
Horsforth Newlaithes Junior School *HORS* LS18 ....85 J8
Horsforth School *HORS* LS18 ....85 K4
Horsforth Village Museum *HORS* LS18 ....85 J6
Horsforth Woodside CE Primary School *HORS* LS18 ....85 M5
Horton Park Primary School *WBOW* BD5 ....126 D2
Hotel Ibis *BAIL* BD17 ....82 D6
The Hotel Metropole *LDS* LS1 ....6 E9
Hotel St Pierre *WKFDW/WTN* WF2 ....220 D3
Hothfield Street Junior School *AIRE* BD20 ....35 M5

Hot Shots Ten Pin Bowl & Bar *HUD* HD1 ....14 E9
Hovingham Primary School *RHAY* LS8 ....110 C2
Howden Clough Girls High School *BTLY* WF17 ....151 K5
Howden Clough Industrial Estate *BTLY* WF17 ....151 K5
Howland Centre *EARL* WF12 ....173 L6
Howley Hall Golf Club *MOR* LS27 ....152 A7
Howley Park Trading Estate *MOR* LS27 ....152 C4
Hoyers Industrial Estate *HUD* HD1 ....192 F5
Hoyle Court Primary School *BAIL* BD17 ....83 G3
Hoyle Head Mills Industrial Estate *EARL* WF12 ....174 B7
Huddersfield Amateurs FC *ELL* HX5 ....169 K6
Huddersfield Art Gallery *HUD* HD1 ....15 G8
Huddersfield Concert Hall *HUD* HD1 ....14 F8
Huddersfield Crematorium *HUDN* HD2 ....170 C8
Huddersfield Giants RLFC *HUDE* HD5 ....15 K4
Huddersfield Golf Club (Fixby Hall) *HUDN* HD2 ....192 A3
Huddersfield Lawn Tennis & Squash Club *HUD* HD1 ....14 C4
Huddersfield New College *HUD3* HD3 ....191 H6
Huddersfield Royal Infirmary *HUDW* HD3 ....191 L6
Huddersfield RUFC *HUDS* HD4 ....214 A4
Huddersfield School of Theatre *HUDS* HD4 ....214 A6
Huddersfield Sports Centre *HUD* HD1 ....15 H6
Huddersfield Technical College *HOLM/MEL* HD9 ....236 C8
HUD HD1 ....14 E6
HUDN HD2 ....192 F4
HUDS HD4 ....214 B4
Huddersfield Town FC (The Galpharm Stadium) *HUDE* HD5 ....15 K3
Huddersfield University *HUD* HD1 ....15 G6
Hugh Gaitskell Primary School *BEE/HOL* LS11 ....131 G4
Hungate Primary School *GFTH/SHER* LS25 ....116 A6
Hunningley Primary School *BSLY* S70 ....262 A7
Hunslet Business Park *MID* LS10 ....9 L6
Hunslet Carr Primary School *MID* LS10 ....132 A4
Hunslet Hall Shopping Centre *BEE/HOL* LS11 ....8 F7
Hunslet Health Centre *MID* LS10 ....9 M8
Hunslet Moor Primary School *BEE/HOL* LS11 ....9 G9
Hunslet St Marys CE Primary School *MID* LS10 ....9 G9
Hunslet Trading Estate *MID* LS10 ....132 B3
Hyde Park Picture House *HDGY* LS6 ....109 G3
Hyrstmount Junior School *BTLY* WF17 ....173 L3
Ida & Robert Arthington Hospital *BHP/TINH* LS16 ....86 A4
Idle CE Primary School *IDLE* BD10 ....83 J3
Idle CC *IDLE* BD10 ....83 L7
Idle Medical Centre *IDLE* BD10 ....83 K6
IKEA Store Leeds *BTLY* WF17 ....151 J2
Ilkley Golf Club *ILK* LS29 ....20 B8
Ilkley Grammar School *ILK* LS29 ....38 E3
Ilkley Health Centre *ILK* LS29 ....38 E3
Ilkley Swimming Baths *ILK* LS29 ....38 D1
Immaculate Heart of Mary Primary School *AL/HA/HU* LS17 ....87 M5
Immanuel CE Community School *IDLE* BD10 ....83 K5
Imperial Crown Hotel *HFAX* HX1 ....11 J7
Ingfield Business Centre *HUDN* HD2 ....193 G3
Inglebrook School *PONT* WF8 ....180 F5
Ingram Road Primary School *BEE/HOL* LS11 ....8 A6
Ingrow Primary School *HWTH* BD22 ....79 J2
Inland Revenue Office *BFD* BD1 ....4 F5
Innkeeper's Lodge *ILK* LS29 ....39 G4
KBTN HD8 ....215 M7
KCHY BD21 ....3 K2
MOR LS27 ....151 M2
Institute of Islamic Education *EARL* WF12 ....173 L8
Intake High School Arts College *BRAM* LS13 ....107 H2
IQRA Community Primary School *GIR* BD8 ....4 A2
Ireland Wood Primary School *BHP/TINH* LS16 ....86 C2
Islamia Girls High School *HUD* HD1 ....214 A2
Iveson Primary School *BHP/TINH* LS16 ....86 C4
Jacksons Estate *OSS* WF5 ....175 G2
Jawbone Industrial Estate *RTHW* LS26 ....132 D7
Jerry Clay Lane J & I School *WKFDW/WTN* WF2 ....176 A4
Joe Dean Recreation Centre *WOR/ARM* LS12 ....108 B7
John Jamieson School *RHAY* LS8 ....110 E1
John O'Gaunts Trading Estate *RTHW* LS26 ....133 G7
John Smeaton Community High School *MSTN/BAR* LS15 ....112 A3
John Smeaton Sports Centre *MSTN/BAR* LS15 ....112 A2
Joseph Priestley College *MOR* LS27 ....152 C2

Joseph Priestly College *MOR* LS27 ....152 D2
Junction 1 Retail Park *BEE/HOL* LS11 ....130 F4
Junction 25 Business Park *MIRF* WF14 ....194 B1
Junction 32 Outlet Shopping Village *CAS* WF10 ....180 B1
Jurys Inn *MID* LS10 ....9 J2
Kayes First School *KBTN* HD8 ....240 D4
Keelham Primary School *CUL/QBY* BD13 ....124 B1
Keighley Business Centre *KGHY* BD21 ....2 E7
Keighley College *KGHY* BD21 ....3 G4
KGHY BD21 ....3 K3
Keighley CC *KGHY* BD21 ....3 H1
Keighley Crematorium *HWTH* BD22 ....78 C3
Keighley Golf Club *AIRE* BD20 ....57 K2
Keighley Industrial Park *KGHY* BD21 ....57 L5
Keighley Leisure Centre *KGHY* BD21 ....3 J2
Keighley Retail Park *KGHY* BD21 ....3 H1
Keighley RUFC *AIRE* BD20 ....57 J9
Keighley and Worth Valley Railway *HWTH* BD22 ....78 D3
MILN OL16 ....3 G8
Kelbrook Primary School *BWCK/EAR* BB18 ....52 C1
Kendray Hospital *BSLY* S70 ....261 L6
Kendray Infant School *BSLY* S70 ....261 K7
Kendray Primary School *BSLY* S70 ....261 L7
Kensington Street Health Centre *GIR* BD8 ....104 C6
Kentmere Primary School *WHIT* OL12 ....206 D3
Kents Sports Club *ECHL* BD2 ....105 K2
Kerr Mackie Primary School *RHAY* LS8 ....88 C7
Kershaw Drive Health Centre *LUD/ILL* HX2 ....144 F7
Kettlethorpe High School *WKFDW/WTN* WF2 ....198 B3
Kexbrough Primary School *DOD/DAR* S75 ....241 K6
Kildwick CE Primary School *AIRE* BD20 ....35 G5
Killingbeck Retail Park *SCFT* LS14 ....111 H4
Killinghall Primary School *BFDE* BD3 ....105 L5
Kiln Hill Industrial Estate *MAR/SLWT* HD7 ....212 C6
King James School *HUDS* HD4 ....215 J4
Kingsgate Shopping Centre *HUD* HD1 ....15 G7
Kings High School *PONT* WF8 ....180 E7
Kingsland Primary School *EARD/LOFT* WF3 ....155 K3
The Kingstone School *BSLY* S70 ....260 D6
Kingsway Retail Park *MILN* OL16 ....206 F7
Kingsway West Business Park *MILN* OL16 ....228 D1
Kinsley Industrial Estate *HEM/SK/SE* WF9 ....223 L5
Kinsley Primary School *HEM/SK/SE* WF9 ....223 K5
Kippax Ashtree Primary School *GFTH/SHER* LS25 ....135 K5
Kippax Health Centre *GFTH/SHER* LS25 ....135 K4
Kippax Infant School *GFTH/SHER* LS25 ....135 J5
Kippax Leisure Centre *GFTH/SHER* LS25 ....135 H5
Kippax North Primary School *GFTH/SHER* LS25 ....135 L1
Kirkburton CE First School *KBTN* HD8 ....216 B8
Kirkburton CC *KBTN* HD8 ....216 B8
Kirkburton Middle School *KBTN* HD8 ....216 C7
Kirk Fenton Primary School *TAD* LS24 ....94 E7
Kirkfields Business Centre *YEA* LS19 ....62 C7
Kirkgate Business Centre *WKFDE* WF1 ....13 H5
Kirkgate Market *LDSU* LS2 ....7 H9
Kirkgate Shopping Centre & Market *BFD* BD1 ....4 E6
Kirkhamgate Primary School *WKFDW/WTN* WF2 ....175 M4
Kirkheaton Cricket & Bowling Club *HUDE* HD5 ....193 K5
Kirkheaton Primary School *HUDE* HD5 ....193 K4
Kirklees Light Railway *KBTN* HD8 ....239 K4
Kirkroyd Infant School *HOLM/MEL* HD9 ....236 F7
Kirk Smeaton CE Primary School *PONT* WF8 ....204 F8
Kirkstall Abbey (remains of) *KSTL* LS5 ....108 B1
Kirkstall Health Clinic *KSTL* LS5 ....108 C2
Kirkstall Industrial Park *KSTL* LS5 ....108 F5
Kirkstall Leisure Centre *KSTL* LS5 ....108 C2
Kirkstall Valley Primary School *BULY* LS4 ....108 E4
Knottingley CE (C) J & I School *KNOT* WF11 ....182 C2
Knottingley Vale J & I School *KNOT* WF11 ....181 M2
Knowle Hill Infant School *DEWS* WF13 ....173 H4
Knowle Spring Industrial Estate *KGHY* BD21 ....2 F9
Knowlestwood Primary School *BOW* BD4 ....127 M3
LA Bowl *BEE/HOL* LS11 ....8 E5
Lady Anne Business Park *BTLY* WF17 ....151 M8
Lady E Hastings CE Primary School *BSPA/BRAM* LS23 ....49 G5

Lady Lane Park School *BGLY* BD16 ....81 J1
Lady Royd Junior School *GIR* BD8 ....104 A5
Laisterdyke Clinic *BFDE* BD3 ....105 M7
Laisterdyke High School *BFDE* BD3 ....105 M7
Lakeside Industrial Estate *WOR/ARM* LS12 ....108 A7
Laneshawbridge Primary School *COL* BB8 ....52 F8
Langdale Primary School *RTHW* LS26 ....133 K7
Langthwaite Grange Industrial Estate *HEM/SK/SE* WF9 ....246 F3
Lapage Primary School *BFDE* BD3 ....105 L6
La Pergola Hotel *UPML* OL3 ....230 D3
Larks Hill Primary School *PONT* WF8 ....180 D8
Lascelles Hall CC *HUDE* HD5 ....215 L1
Last of the Summer Wine Exhibition *HOLM/MEL* HD9 ....254 B1
Latchmore Industrial Park *WOR/ARM* LS12 ....130 E3
WOR/ARM LS12 ....131 G2
Laura Mitchell Health Centre *HFAX* HX1 ....11 G5
Lawefield First School *WKFDW/WTN* WF2 ....12 B4
Lawns Park Primary School *WOR/ARM* LS12 ....130 A1
Lawnswood Business Park *BHP/TINH* LS16 ....86 C5
Lawns Wood Cemetery *BHP/TINH* LS16 ....86 D3
Lawns Wood Crematorium *BHP/TINH* LS16 ....86 D3
Lawnswood School *BHP/TINH* LS16 ....86 D6
Lawrence Batley Theatre *HUD* HD1 ....15 G7
Laycock Primary School *HWTH* BD22 ....56 E7
Lee Bridge Industrial Estate *HFAX* HX1 ....10 D3
Lee Brigg Infant School *NORM* WF6 ....178 A3
Leeds 27 Industrial Estate *MOR* LS27 ....151 M2
Leeds Bradford Airport Industrial Estate *YEA* LS19 ....63 G5
Leeds Bradford International Airport *YEA* LS19 ....63 H7
The Leeds Business Centre *MOR* LS27 ....152 A2
Leeds College of Art & Design *LDSU* LS2 ....6 E4
LDSU LS2 ....6 F7
Leeds College of Building *LDSU* LS2 ....6 F5
Leeds College of Music *OSM* LS9 ....7 K9
Leeds College of Technology *BEE/HOL* LS11 ....131 J6
Leeds General Infirmary *LDSU* LS2 ....6 D7
Leeds Girls High School *HDGY* LS6 ....6 A1
Leeds Golf Centre *AL/HA/HU* LS17 ....66 E5
Leeds Golf Club *RHAY* LS8 ....88 F6
Leeds Grammar School *AL/HA/HU* LS17 ....66 B7
Leeds & Hull Business Centre *LDSU* LS2 ....6 E5
Leeds Industrial Museum at Armley Mills *BULY* LS4 ....108 F5
Leeds International Swimming Pool *LDS* LS1 ....6 D9
Leeds Marriott Hotel *LDS* LS1 ....6 F8
Leeds Menorah School *AL/HA/HU* LS17 ....87 M3
Leeds Metropolitan University *HDGY* LS6 ....86 D8
KSTL LS5 ....108 B2
LDS LS1 ....6 E7
Leeds Rhinos RLFC (Headingley Stadium) *BULY* LS4 ....108 E2
Leeds Road Hospital *BFDE* BD3 ....5 L6
Leeds Road Retail Park *HUD* HD1 ....15 L2
Leeds Shopping Plaza *LDS* LS1 ....6 G1
Leeds Tykes RFC (Headingley Stadium) *BULY* LS4 ....108 E2
Leeds United AFC (Elland Road) *BEE/HOL* LS11 ....131 G3
Leeds University *LDSU* LS2 ....6 C5
Leeds University Business School *HDGY* LS6 ....6 B5
Lee Mills Industrial Estate *HFAX* HX1 ....10 E3
HOLM/MEL HD9 ....254 F1
Lee Mount Primary School *HIPP* HX3 ....10 C2
Leeside J & I School *HECK* WF16 ....151 G8
Lees Primary School *HWTH* BD22 ....79 G6
Leisure Exchange *BFD* BD1 ....5 H7
Leopold Primary School *CHAL* LS7 ....7 L3
Lepton CE J & I School *KBTN* HD8 ....215 M3
Ley Top Primary School *WIL/AL* BD15 ....103 K6
Library Headquarters *WKFDW/WTN* WF2 ....12 B1
Lidget Green Primary School *GTHN* BD7 ....104 B8
Lightcliffe CE J & I School *HIPP* HX3 ....148 A7
Lightcliffe Golf Club *HIPP* HX3 ....148 A6
Lightcliffe Preparatory School *HIPP* HX3 ....147 M6
Light Waves Sports Centre *WKFDE* WF1 ....12 F1
Lilycroft Primary School *HTON* BD9 ....104 D4
Limestone Trail *BRFD/BLYE* BB10 ....118 A8
Lindley Junior School *HUDW* HD3 ....191 K5
Linfit Brewery *MAR/SLWT* HD7 ....213 G5

Ling Bob Primary School
LUD/ILL HX2 ....145 M6
Linthwaite Ardron Memorial CE
Primary School
MAR/SLWT HD7 ....213 G5
Linthwaite Business Centre
MAR/SLWT HD7 ....212 F5
Linthwaite Clough J & I School
MAR/SLWT HD7 ....212 G5
Lister Lane School
ECHL BD2 ....105 J3
Littleborough CC
LIT OL15 ....185 K8
Littleborough Primary School
LIT OL15 ....185 K7
Little London CP School
CHAL LS7 ....7 H4
Littlemoor Primary School
YEA LS19 ....84 E2
Littleroyd Mills Business Park
HUD HD1 ....214 C2
Little Theatre
HBR HX7 ....143 J3
SKP/WHF BD23 ....16 B3
Littletown J & I School
CLECK BD19 ....172 C1
Liversedge CC
LVSG WF15 ....172 B4
Lobden Golf Club
WHIT OL12 ....184 A2
The Lodge Hotel
HUDN HD2 ....14 C2
Lofthousegate J & I School
EARD/LOFT WF3 ....154 F4
Lofthouse Hill Golf Club
EARD/LOFT WF3 ....154 F2
Longcar Primary School
BSLY S70 ....260 E6
Longclose Industrial Estate
OSM LS9 ....7 M5
Longlands Trading Estate
OSS WF5 ....175 G8
Long Lee Primary School
KGHY BD21 ....3 L7
Longley Park Golf Club
HUD HD1 ....15 J9
Longley School
HUDE HD5 ....214 E2
Longley Tennis Club
HUDE HD5 ....214 F2
Long Marston CE Primary
School *RYKW* YO26 ....33 J3
Longroyde Junior School
BRIG HD6 ....170 B5
Lotherton Hall
GFTH/SHER LS25 ....114 E1
Lounge Cinema
HDGY LS6 ....108 F1
Low Ash Primary School
SHPY BD18 ....82 F8
Lower Fields Primary School
BOW BD4 ....127 L2
Lower Grange Medical Centre
GIR BD8 ....103 L7
Lowerhouses CE J & I School
HUDE HD5 ....214 F3
Lowerplace Primary School
MILN OL16 ....228 D1
Lower Wortley Primary School
WOR/ARM LS12 ....130 C2
Lowfields Business Park
ELL HX5 ....169 K5
Low Laithes Golf Club
OSS WF5 ....175 K6
Low Mills Industrial Estate
DEWS WF13 ....194 F2
Low Moor Business Park
LM/WK BD12 ....127 C8
Low Moor CE Primary School
LM/WK BD12 ....126 F8
Low Road Primary School
MID LS10 ....9 M8
Lowtown Primary School
PDSY/CALV LS28 ....107 H7
Luddenden Dene CE J & I
School *LUD/ILL* HX2 ....145 G6
Luddendenfoot Primary
School *LUD/ILL* HX2 ....167 G1
Lund's Tower
HWTH BD22 ....55 H4
Lupset Hall (Club House)
WKFDW/WTN WF2 ....198 B4
Lydgate J & I School
BTLY WF17 ....174 B1
Lydgate Special School
HOLM/MEL HD9 ....236 F7
Lynfield Mount Hospital
HTON BD9 ....103 M4
M1 Industrial Estate
MID LS10 ....9 L8
Mackie Hill J & I School
HOR/CROF WF4 ....219 M2
Madni Muslim Girls High School
EARL WF12 ....173 L6
Magdale Industrial Park
HUDS HD4 ....214 B8
Magistrates Courts
DEWS WF13 ....173 L6
Magnet Sports Club
TAD LS24 ....71 L4
Malsis School
AIRE BD20 ....34 B8
Manningham Baths & Sports
Centre *GIR* BD8 ....104 D5
Manningham Clinic
GIR BD8 ....4 C1
Manorfield Infant School
BTLY WF17 ....173 J2
Manor House Gallery &
Museum *ILK* LS29 ....38 C1
Manor Leisure Centre
YEA LS19 ....62 C7
Manor Park Industrial Estate
BIRK/DRI BD11 ....129 G2
Manor Street Industrial Estate
CHAL LS7 ....7 L4
Manston Primary School
MSTN/BAR LS15 ....111 L3
Manston St James CE Primary
School *MSTN/BAR* LS15 ...111 M3
Mantra House Business Centre
KGHY BD21 ....2 F6
Manywells Brow
Industrial Estate
CUL/QBY BD13 ....101 M1
Maple Industrial Estate
DOD/DAR S75 ....242 F6
Mapplewell Health Centre
DOD/DAR S75 ....242 D6
Mapplewell Primary School
DOD/DAR S75 ....242 E5
Margram Business Centre
HFAX HX1 ....10 E5
Marley Mills Industrial Estate
KGHY BD21 ....3 G6
Marriott Hollins Hall Hotel
GSLY LS20 ....61 J8
Marsden County Junior School
MAR/SLWT HD7 ....233 J2

Marsden Health Centre
MAR/SLWT HD7 ....233 H2
Marsden Infant School
MAR/SLWT HD7 ....233 J2
Marshfield Primary School
WBOW BD5 ....126 E4
Martin Frobisher Infant School
NORM WF6 ....178 B2
Maybrook Industrial Park
WOR/ARM LS12 ....8 A1
Meadowfield Primary School
OSM LS9 ....110 F6
Meanwood CE Primary School
HDGY LS6 ....87 G7
Meanwood Health Centre
HDGY LS6 ....87 H8
Meanwood Park Hospital
HDGY LS6 ....87 G5
Meltham CE J & I School
HOLM/MEL HD9 ....235 G5
Meltham Cricket & Athletic
Club *HOLM/MEL* HD9 ....235 G3
Meltham Golf Club
HOLM/MEL HD9 ....235 H5
Meltham Mills Industrial
Estate *HOLM/MEL* HD9 ....235 H4
Meltham Moor Primary
School *HOLM/MEL* HD9 ....234 E3
Menston CC
ILK LS29 ....61 K1
Menston Primary School
ILK LS29 ....61 H2
The Merrion Hotel
LDSU LS2 ....7 G7
Merrion Shopping Centre
LDSU LS2 ....7 G7
Methley Park Hospital
RTHW LS26 ....156 C3
Methley Primary School
RTHW LS26 ....157 G3
Methley Road Industrial Park
CAS WF10 ....157 K7
Metrodome Sports & Leisure
Complex *BSLYN/ROY* S71 ..261 J4
Metropolitan Shopping Centre
BSLY S70 ....261 H5
Micklefield CE Primary School
GFTH/SHER LS25 ....114 C7
Middlestown Health Centre
HOR/CROF WF4 ....196 D7
Middlestown J & I School
HOR/CROF WF4 ....196 C8
Middleton Park High School
MID LS10 ....153 M2
Middleton Park Leisure Centre
MID LS10 ....153 M1
Middleton Park Municipal
Golf Club *MID* LS10 ....153 J1
Middleton Primary School
MID LS10 ....153 K2
Middleton Railway
MID LS10 ....131 L5
Middleton St Marys CE
Primary School *MID* LS10 .153 L1
Midgley Primary School
LUD/ILL HX2 ....144 E5
Midland Hotel
BFD BD1 ....4 F5
Mid Point Business Park
PDSY/CALV LS28 ....106 A6
Mid Yorkshire Golf Club
PONT WF8 ....204 A1
Mid Yorkshire Nuffield
Hospital *HORS* LS18 ....85 M6
Milefield Primary School
CUD/GR S72 ....245 H7
Miles Hill Primary School
CHAL LS7 ....87 J7
Milford Hotel
GFTH/SHER LS25 ....136 F2
Milford RUFC
KSTL LS5 ....108 C2
Millbridge J & I School
LVSG WF15 ....172 D2
Mill Dam J & I School
FEA/AMT WF7 ....202 C8
Millennium Business Park
AIRE BD20 ....35 L8
Mill Hill Community Health
Centre *HUDE* HD5 ....193 J7
Millhouse Primary School
STKB/PEN S36 ....269 M3
Mill Lane J & I School
BTLY WF17 ....173 M3
Millshaw Park Trading Estate
MOR LS27 ....131 G6
Mill Trading Estate
BSLYN/ROY S71 ....261 K5
Milnrow CC
MILN OL16 ....229 H1
Milnrow Health Centre
MILN OL16 ....229 H1
Milnrow Parish CE Primary
School *MILN* OL16 ....207 H8
Minerva Industrial Estate
RTHW LS26 ....134 A7
Minsthorpe Community
College *HEM/SK/SE* WF9 ...247 J1
Minsthorpe Swimming Pool
HEM/SK/SE WF9 ....247 J2
Mirfield Free Grammar School
& Sixth Form Centre
MIRF WF14 ....172 D7
Mirfield Parish CC
MIRF WF14 ....172 D8
Miriam Lord Community
Primary School *GIR* BD8 ..104 D5
Mixenden Clinic
LUD/ILL HX2 ....145 M2
Mixenden Community
Primary School
LUD/ILL HX2 ....123 K8
Moderna Business Park
HBR HX7 ....144 D3
Moldgreen Community
Primary School
HUDE HD5 ....15 L8
Monckton Road Industrial
Estate *WKFDW/WTN* WF2 ..198 C4
Monk Bretton Health Centre
BSLYN/ROY S71 ....261 L2
Monk Bretton Priory
BSLYN/ROY S71 ....262 A4
Monk Fryston CE Primary
School *GFTH/SHER* LS25 ..138 D6
Monk Fryston Hall Hotel
GFTH/SHER LS25 ....138 D6
Moor Allerton Golf Club
AL/HA/HU LS17 ....67 G6
Moor Allerton Hall Primary
School *AL/HA/HU* LS17 .....88 B5
Moorend CE First School
CLECK BD19 ....149 L5
Moorfield Business Park
YEA LS19 ....62 F6
Moorfield School for Girls
ILK LS29 ....38 E3
Moorfield Shopping Centre
HUDS HD4 ....213 M2

Moorhouse Primary School
MILN OL16 ....207 G8
Moorlands School
BHP/TINH LS16 ....86 F5
Moorlands Small Business
Centre *CLECK* BD19 ....149 M5
Moor Lane Trading Estate
GFTH/SHER LS25 ....116 D7
Moor Lodge Park
AL/HA/HU LS17 ....67 J3
Moor Park Business Centre
WKFDW/WTN WF2 ....12 B9
Moorside Community Primary
School *LUD/ILL* HX2 ....146 B2
The Moors Shopping Centre
ILK LS29 ....38 C2
Moorthorpe Primary School
HEM/SK/SE WF9 ....247 G3
Moortown Golf Club
AL/HA/HU LS17 ....87 M1
Moortown Primary School
AL/HA/HU LS17 ....87 M4
Moortown RUFC
AL/HA/HU LS17 ....87 J1
Moorview Business Park
IDLE BD10 ....83 J5
Morley Elmfield Infant School
MOR LS27 ....152 C4
Morley High School
MOR LS27 ....152 B3
Morley Leisure Centre
MOR LS27 ....152 C2
Morley Newlands Primary
School *MOR* LS27 ....152 F2
Morley Victoria Primary
School *MOR* LS27 ....152 C1
Moslem School
BTLY WF17 ....173 K2
Moss Industrial Estate
CLECK BD19 ....228 D1
Mountjoy House School
HUD HD1 ....14 C5
The Mount J & I School
WKFDW/WTN WF2 ....198 B3
Mount Osborne Industrial
Park *BSLYN/ROY* S71 ....261 K5
Mount Pellon J & I School
HFAX HX1 ....10 A4
Mount Pleasant J & I School
HUDS HD4 ....214 D3
Mount St Marys Catholic
High School *OSM* LS9 ....9 M2
Mount St Marys RC Primary
School *OSM* LS9 ....110 C6
Mount Vernon Hospital
BSLY S70 ....261 J8
Municipal Baths
BRIG HD6 ....170 D4
Myrtle Park Primary School
BGLY BD16 ....81 H4
Mytholmroyd Health Centre
HBR HX7 ....144 A5
Nab Wood Cemetery
SHPY BD18 ....81 M6
Nab Wood Crematorium
SHPY BD18 ....81 M6
Nab Wood School
BGLY BD16 ....81 L7
Napoleon Business Park
BOW BD4 ....127 K1
National Coal Mining Museum
for England
HOR/CROF WF4 ....217 M1
National Film Theatre North
LDS LS1 ....9 H2
National Museum of
Photography, Film & Television
WBOW BD5 ....4 E8
Neil Hunt Memorial Ground &
RFC *BOW* BD4 ....127 L1
Nessfield Primary School
HWTH BD22 ....2 B8
Netherfield Industrial Estate
DEWS WF13 ....195 G1
Netherlands Avenue Special
School *WBSY* BD6 ....126 F7
Netherleigh & Rossefield
School *HTON* BD9 ....104 C2
Netherleigh School
HTON BD9 ....104 B4
Netherthong J & I School
HOLM/MEL HD9 ....236 C6
Netherton Infant School
HUDS HD4 ....213 M7
Netherton J & I School
HOR/CROF WF4 ....197 G8
Newbridge Industrial Estate
KGHY BD21 ....3 J5
Newby Primary School
WBOW BD5 ....126 F3
New College
PONT WF8 ....180 D5
New Cross Street Health
Centre *WBOW* BD5 ....126 F3
Newhall Park Primary School
WBOW BD5 ....127 J5
Newhaven Business Park
HUDW HD3 ....213 J1
Newhey Community Primary
School *MILN* OL16 ....229 J2
New Hold Industrial Estate
GFTH/SHER LS25 ....113 J6
New Horizon Community
School *CHAL* LS7 ....87 M8
Newlands Industrial Estate
SHPY BD18 ....82 E6
Newlands Primary School
NORM WF6 ....178 C6
New Line Clinic
IDLE BD10 ....84 A7
Newmillerdam Country Park
WKFDW/WTN WF2 ....220 E4
New Park Spring
CUD/GR S72 ....263 K2
New Road Primary School
RPDN/SBR HX6 ....167 J3
Newsome High School
HUDS HD4 ....214 B5
Newsome Junior School
HUDS HD4 ....214 C5
Newspaper Office
BFD BD1 ....5 G6
New Street Health Centre
BSLY S70 ....261 G6
Newton Hill J & I School
WKFDE WF1 ....176 A4
New Wortley Holy Family RC
Primary School
WOR/ARM LS12 ....108 F7
Nields Primary School
MAR/SLWT HD7 ....212 B6
Ninelands Lane Primary
School *GFTH/SHER* LS25 ..113 J8
Norcroft Industrial Estate
BFD BD1 ....4 B6
Norland CE Primary School
RPDN/SBR HX6 ....167 M4
Normanton Common Primary
School *NORM* WF6 ....178 E2

Normanton Health Centre
NORM WF6 ....178 C5
Normanton Industrial Estate
NORM WF6 ....179 G3
Normanton Junior School
NORM WF6 ....178 C5
Norquest Industrial Park
BTLY WF17 ....151 J3
Norristhorpe Primary School
LVSG WF15 ....172 D4
North Bridge Leisure Centre
HFAX HX1 ....11 H4
Northcliffe Golf Club
SHPY BD18 ....82 A8
North Dean Business Park
GTL/HWC HX4 ....168 E5
North Dean RFC
GTL/HWC HX4 ....168 F7
Northern Ballet Theatre
BHP/TINH LS16 ....86 C7
Northern School of
Contemporary Dance
CHAL LS7 ....7 J2
North Featherstone J & I
School *FEA/AMT* WF7 ......180 A3
Northfield J & I School
HEM/SK/SE WF9 ....246 E6
The North Halifax Grammar
School *LUD/ILL* HX2 ....124 B8
North Leeds CC
RHAY LS8 ....88 C6
Northowram Hall Hospital
HIPP HX3 ....147 J3
Northowram Primary School
HIPP HX3 ....147 J3
Northside Business Park
CHAL LS7 ....7 J4
Northside Retail Park
BTLY WF17 ....87 H7
Northwest Business Park
HDGY LS6 ....6 F3
Norton Junior School
AWLS/ASK DN6 ....227 L3
Norton Thorpe Hall School
HUD HD1 ....14 E5
Nortonthorpe Hall Special
School *KBTN* HD8 ....239 M5
Nortonthorpe Industrial
Estate *KBTN* HD8 ....239 M5
Norwood Business Park
LM/WK BD12 ....148 D4
Nostell Priory (NT)
HOR/CROF WF4 ....201 G7
Notre Dame Catholic Sixth
Form College *LDSU* LS2 .....6 E3
Nova Scotia Medical Centre
CAS WF10 ....157 J1
Novotel
BOW BD4 ....127 J8
LDS LS1 ....8 D1
Nuffield Hospital
LDSU LS2 ....6 D8
Nuffield Institute for Health
LDSU LS2 ....6 B6
Oakbank School
HWTH BD22 ....79 H2
Oakfield Park Special School
FEA/AMT WF7 ....224 B2
Oakhill Primary School
BSLY S70 ....262 A6
Oaks Business Park
BSLY S70 ....261 M5
Oaktree Business Park
BSLYN/ROY S71 ....89 J7
Oakwell Business Centre
BSLYN/ROY S71 ....261 K5
Oakwell Hall
BTLY WF17 ....150 F3
Oakwell Hall Country Park
BTLY WF17 ....150 E3
Oakwell Industrial Park
BTLY WF17 ....151 H2
Oakwood Primary School
RHAY LS8 ....110 D3
Oakworth Health Centre
HWTH BD22 ....78 E5
Oakworth Primary School
HWTH BD22 ....78 E4
Oastler Centre
BFD BD1 ....4 E5
Odeon Cinema
BFD BD1 ....4 E7
BFDE BD3 ....106 A1
BSLY S70 ....261 H4
ROCH OL11 ....228 A2
Old Bank J & I School
MIRF WF14 ....172 C7
Old Bear Brewery
KGHY BD21 ....3 J5
Old Bridge Hotel
HOLM/MEL HD9 ....254 C2
Old College of Technology
BSLY S70 ....261 G4
Old Earth CE Primary School
ELL HX5 ....169 K7
Oldfield Primary School
HWTH BD22 ....77 L6
The Old Golf House Hotel
HUDW HD3 ....190 C6
Old Mill Business Park
MID LS10 ....132 B2
Old Otliensians RUFC
OT LS21 ....41 L6
Old Rishworthians RUFC
HIPP HX3 ....168 C4
Old Roundhegians RUFC
AL/HA/HU LS17 ....88 A4
Old Town Primary School
HWTH BD22 ....143 L1
The Old Vicarage Hotel
MOR LS27 ....152 A3
Old White Lion Hotel
HWTH BD22 ....78 E7
Open College of the Arts
DOD/DAR S75 ....260 D2
Open University
LDS LS1 ....9 G1
Optimax Eye Clinic
LDS LS1 ....6 E8
Orchard Business Park
HBR HX7 ....144 A6
Orchard Croft Medical Centre
HOR/CROF WF4 ....197 K5
Orchard Head Primary School
PONT WF8 ....181 G2
Ossett Brewery
OSS WF5 ....196 E3
Ossett Cricket & Athletic Club
OSS WF5 ....196 F3
Ossett Health Centre
OSS WF5 ....196 F1
Ossett School
OSS WF5 ....196 F3
Otley Golf Club
OT LS21 ....40 E8
Otley RUFC
OT LS21 ....41 K6
Otley Town FC
OT LS21 ....41 L6

Oulton Health Centre
RTHW LS26 ....133 L8
Oulton Park Golf Club
RTHW LS26 ....155 K2
Oulton Primary School
RTHW LS26 ....133 K8
Our Lady of Good Counsel RC
Primary School
SCFT LS14 ....89 J8
Our Lady of Lourdes
CP School
HUDN HD2 ....192 E2
Our Lady of Victories RC
Primary School *HWTH* BD22 ..2 B4
Our Lady & St Brendans RC
Primary School
IDLE BD10 ....83 M8
Outlane Golf Club
HUDW HD3 ....190 C7
Outlane Junior School
HUDW HD3 ....190 F5
Outwood Grange College
WKFDE WF1 ....176 C2
Outwood Ledger Lane J & I
School *WKFDE* WF1 ....176 D2
Overland Industrial Estate
MOR LS27 ....151 L1
Overthorpe CE J & I School
EARL WF12 ....195 L4
The Owlcotes Centre
PDSY/CALV LS28 ....106 F5
Owston Park Golf Club
AWLS/ASK DN6 ....249 L4
Owston Park Primary School
AWLS/ASK DN6 ....249 K4
Oxenhope CE Primary School
HWTH BD22 ....100 D3
Oxspring Primary School
STKB/PEN S36 ....271 K5
Oyster Park Infant School
CAS WF10 ....158 F5
Oyster Park Middle School
CAS WF10 ....158 F6
Packhorse Shopping Centre
HFAX HX1 ....14 F7
Paddock Cricket & Bowling
Club *HUD* HD1 ....213 L1
Paddock J & I School
HUD HD1 ....213 M1
The Paddock Surgery
EARL WF12 ....195 M4
Painthorpe House Golf &
Country Club
HOR/CROF WF4 ....219 M2
Pannal Golf Club
PBR HG3 ....27 G3
Pannal Primary School
PBR HG3 ....26 F2
Paradise Primary School
EARL WF12 ....173 M8
Paragon Industrial Estate
LIT OL15 ....207 H3
Park High School
COL BB8 ....52 B8
Parkhouse Industrial Estate
LM/WK BD12 ....127 G8
Parkinson Lane Community
Primary School
HFAX HX1 ....10 C8
Park Junior School
CAS WF10 ....158 A7
Parkland Primary School
IDLE BD10 ....83 M7
Parklands CP School
SCFT LS14 ....111 J2
Parklands Girls High School
SCFT LS14 ....111 K2
Park Lane College
BVRD LS3 ....6 C3
HORS LS18 ....85 H7
LDSU LS2 ....7 H8
PDSY/CALV LS28 ....107 G6
Park Lane College of Further
Education
CHAL LS7 ....110 A1
Park Plaza Hotel
LDS LS1 ....8 F1
Park Primary School
COL BB8 ....74 B1
Park Road J & N School
BTLY WF17 ....173 M1
Park Road Medical Centre
WBOW BD5 ....127 G1
Park Road Retail Park
PONT WF8 ....180 E4
Parkside Industrial Estate
BEE/HOL LS11 ....131 L5
Parkside School
CUL/QBY BD13 ....80 A8
Park Spring CP School
BRAM LS13 ....107 L2
Park Wood Crematorium
ELL HX5 ....169 H5
Parkwood First School
KGHY BD21 ....3 J6
Parkwood Primary School
KGHY BD21 ....3 J6
Parkwood Street Industrial
Estate *KGHY* BD21 ....3 M4
Pathways School
CAS WF10 ....158 E7
Pavilion Business Centre
PDSY/CALV LS28 ....107 H4
Pavilion Business Park
WOR/ARM LS12 ....130 E3
Pecket Well College
HBR HX7 ....121 K7
Pecketwell College
HFAX HX1 ....10 F5
Peel Mill Business Centre
MOR LS27 ....152 D2
Pellon Industrial Estate
HFAX HX1 ....10 B4
Penistone Grammar School
STKB/PEN S36 ....270 E1
Penistone Hill
HWTH BD22 ....78 C8
Penistone St John the Baptist
CE Infant School
STKB/PEN S36 ....270 E4
Penistone St John the Baptist
CE Junior School
STKB/PEN S36 ....270 E4
Penistone Sports Centre
STKB/PEN S36 ....270 E2
Penistone Springvale Primary
School *STKB/PEN* S36 ......271 H3
Pennine Industrial Estate
WOR/ARM LS12 ....108 D7
Pennine Industrial Park
HBR HX7 ....143 J3
Pennine Manor Hotel
MAR/SLWT HD7 ....190 D8
Penny Field School
HDGY LS6 ....87 H5
Penraevon Industrial Estate
CHAL LS7 ....7 H3
Pentland Infant School
EARL WF12 ....195 M1

Index - featured places 335

Pentland Road Clinic
EARL WF12 ...... 173 M8
Peter Laycock Industrial Estate
CHAL LS7 ...... 7 H3
Phoebe Lane Industrial Estate
HIPP HX3 ...... 168 F2
Phoenix Works Estate
HOR/CROF WF4 ...... 197 G5
Pickup Business Park
PDSY/CALV LS28 ...... 107 G6
Picturedrome Cinema & Museum *HOLM/MEL* HD9 ...... 254 B1
Picture House Cinema
CHAL LS7 ...... 7 K5
KGHY BD21 ...... 3 G4
NORM WF6 ...... 178 E4
WKFDE WF1 ...... 13 G1
WKFDE WF1 ...... 176 F7
Pictureville Cinema
BFD BD1 ...... 4 E8
Piece Hall
HFAX HX1 ...... 11 J6
Pilot Theatre
CAS WF10 ...... 158 B8
Pinderfields General Hospital
WKFDE WF1 ...... 176 F5
Pinderfields Hospital School (Wrenthorpe Centre)
WKFDW/WTN WF2 ...... 176 F6
Pinders Primary School
WKFDE WF1 ...... 176 F6
Pioneer Business Park
WKFDE WF10 ...... 179 H2
Pitt Street Business Centre
KGHY BD21 ...... 3 K5
Playhouse & Film Theatre
BFD BD1 ...... 5 H7
Playhouse Theatre
HFAX HX1 ...... 10 F6
The Point Retail Park
MILN OL16 ...... 206 C4
Police Sports Ground
RHAY LS8 ...... 88 D7
Pollard Park Health Centre
BFDE BD3 ...... 5 J3
Pontefract Castle
PONT WF8 ...... 180 F5
Pontefract Crematorium
PONT WF8 ...... 180 C8
Pontefract & District Golf Club
PONT WF8 ...... 180 C4
Pontefract General Infirmary
PONT WF8 ...... 180 E5
Pontefract Museum
PONT WF8 ...... 180 E5
Pontefract Racecourse
PONT WF8 ...... 180 C5
Pontefract RFC
PONT WF8 ...... 203 H2
Pontefract Squash & Leisure Centre *PONT* WF8 ...... 180 E5
Pontefract Swimming Pool
PONT WF8 ...... 180 E5
Pool CE Primary School
OT LS21 ...... 42 F7
Poplars Farm Primary School
ECHL BD2 ...... 105 G2
Potternewton Primary School
CHAL LS7 ...... 109 K1
Powerhouse Showcase Theatre *WKFDE* WF1 ...... 12 D3
Premier Travel Inn
AIRE BD20 ...... 58 E7
BEE/HOL LS11 ...... 130 F3
BIRK/DRI BD11 ...... 151 J1
BVRD LS3 ...... 6 B9
CAS WF10 ...... 179 H1
CLECK BD19 ...... 149 J5
HIPP HX3 ...... 168 F4
HUDN HD2 ...... 171 H6
HUDW HD3 ...... 191 K2
KNOT WF11 ...... 181 L3
MILN OL16 ...... 229 J2
MSTN/BAR LS15 ...... 111 L6
PONT WF8 ...... 203 M2
WKFDW/WTN WF2 ...... 12 C7
YEA LS19 ...... 62 F8
Priestley Centre
BFD BD1 ...... 5 H6
Priestthorpe Medical Centre
BGLY BD16 ...... 81 L7
Priestthorpe Primary School
BGLY BD16 ...... 81 J3
Priestthorpe School
PDSY/CALV LS28 ...... 106 C4
Primrose High School
OSM LS9 ...... 7 M5
Primrose Hill Primary School
PDSY/CALV LS28 ...... 106 F5
Primrose Lane Primary School
BSPA/BRAM LS23 ...... 48 F7
Prince Henrys Grammar School
OT LS21 ...... 41 J5
Prince of Wales Business Park
BRIG HD6 ...... 170 C4
Princess Mary Stadium
CLECK BD19 ...... 172 B1
Princess Royal Health Centre
HUD HD1 ...... 14 D7
Princeville Primary School
GTHN BD7 ...... 104 D7
Princeville Road Industrial Estate *GIR* BD8 ...... 104 C7
Priory Business Park
HEM/SK/SE WF9 ...... 223 K2
Priory School & Sports College
BSLYN/ROY S71 ...... 261 M4
Prospect Business Centre
HUD HD1 ...... 14 E9
Public Health Laboratory Service Seacroft Hospital
SCFT LS14 ...... 111 H4
Pudsey Bolton Royd Primary School *PDSY/CALV* LS28 ...... 106 C6
Pudsey Business Centre
PDSY/CALV LS28 ...... 107 H7
Pudsey Grangefield School
PDSY/CALV LS28 ...... 107 G6
Pudsey Leisure Centre
PDSY/CALV LS28 ...... 107 G2
Pudsey St Lawrence CC
PDSY/CALV LS28 ...... 106 F7
Pugneys Country Park
WKFDW/WTN WF2 ...... 198 D5
Purlwell Infant School
BTLY WF17 ...... 173 H1
Purston Infant School
FEA/AMT WF7 ...... 201 L2
Python Industrial Estate
LIT OL15 ...... 185 L8
OBM Business Park
BTLY WF17 ...... 151 H4
QF Industrial Estate
BOW BD4 ...... 127 K2
Quarry Hill Industrial Estate
HOR/CROF WF4 ...... 197 G5
Quarry House
OSM LS9 ...... 7 K9

Quarry Mount Primary School
HDGY LS6 ...... 6 D1
Quebecs Hotel
LDS LS1 ...... 8 F1
Queen Elizabeth Grammar School *WKFDE* WF1 ...... 176 E7
Queensbury Golf Club
CUL/QBY BD13 ...... 125 H6
Queensbury Health Centre
CUL/QBY BD13 ...... 124 F6
Queensbury School
CUL/QBY BD13 ...... 125 G6
Queensgate Market
HUD HD1 ...... 15 G8
Queens Hotel
LDS LS1 ...... 8 F1
Queens Mill Business Centre
HUD HD1 ...... 214 C2
Queens Mill Industrial Estate
HUD HD1 ...... 214 C2
Queens Road Clinic
BSLYN/ROY S71 ...... 261 H5
Queens Road School
HFAX HX1 ...... 10 A5
Queens Sports Club
HFAX HX1 ...... 10 A5
Queen Street J & I School
NORM WF6 ...... 178 D4
Queensway Primary School
GSLY LS20 ...... 62 C6
ROCH OL11 ...... 228 A3
Radisson Sas Hotel
LDS LS1 ...... 6 F8
Raglan Industrial Estate
CAS WF10 ...... 157 K6
Railwaymens Sports Club
BSLYN/ROY S71 ...... 244 A2
Ralph Thoresby High School
BHP/TINH LS16 ...... 86 B2
Ralph Williams Clinic
WHIT OL12 ...... 206 E3
Ramada Hotel
BGLY BD16 ...... 81 L6
BHP/TINH LS16 ...... 64 D7
SCFT LS14 ...... 111 K1
Ramada Wetherby Hotel
WBY LS22 ...... 48 A3
Ramgarhia Sikh Sports Centre
CHAL LS7 ...... 7 J4
Rastrick High School
BRIG HD6 ...... 170 B5
Rastrick Preparatory & Nursery School
BRIG HD6 ...... 170 B6
Rastrick Squash Centre
BRIG HD6 ...... 170 C5
Ravensbridge Industrial Estate
DEWS WF13 ...... 173 H8
Ravenscliffe First School
IDLE BD10 ...... 106 A2
Ravenscliffe High Special School *HIPP* HX3 ...... 168 D4
Ravenshall Special School
EARL WF12 ...... 195 J2
Ravensthorpe CE Junior School
DEWS WF13 ...... 194 F1
Ravensthorpe Infant School
DEWS WF13 ...... 172 F8
Rawdon CC
YEA LS19 ...... 84 E2
Rawdon CE Primary School
YEA LS19 ...... 84 F7
Rawdon Golf & Lawn Tennis Club *YEA* LS19 ...... 84 C3
Rawfolds Industrial Estate
CLECK BD19 ...... 150 B8
Rawson J & I School
WBSY BD6 ...... 146 D4
Rawson Market
BFD BD1 ...... 4 D5
Rawthorpe CE Infant School
HUDE HD5 ...... 15 M3
Rawthorpe High School
HUDE HD5 ...... 193 G6
Rawthorpe Junior School
HUDE HD5 ...... 15 M4
Raynville Primary School
BRAM LS13 ...... 108 A4
Redbrook Business Park
DOD/DAR S75 ...... 260 D1
Red Doles Industrial Estate
HUD HD1 ...... 192 E5
Redhill Infant School
CAS WF10 ...... 158 E6
Red House
CLECK BD19 ...... 150 D5
Red Ledge Business Centre
HOLM/MEL HD9 ...... 236 D6
Reevy Hill Primary School
WBSY BD6 ...... 126 B5
Reinwood Infant School
HUDW HD3 ...... 191 K7
Revival Industrial Estate
BOW BD4 ...... 5 J9
Rex Cinema
ELL HX5 ...... 169 H8
Rhodesway School
GIR BD8 ...... 103 L6
Richard Dunn Sports Centre
WBOW BD5 ...... 126 F5
Richard Newman Primary School
BSLYN/ROY S71 ...... 243 H7
Richard Oastler School
BULY LS4 ...... 108 F4
Richmond Hill Primary School
OSM LS9 ...... 110 B8
Richmond House School
BHP/TINH LS16 ...... 86 E7
Riddlesden Golf Club
AIRE BD20 ...... 57 K2
Riddlesden St Marys CE Primary School
AIRE BD20 ...... 58 A5
Ridings Business Park
HFAX HX1 ...... 10 A7
The Ridings School
LUD/ILL HX2 ...... 146 B3
Ridings Shopping Centre
WKFDE WF1 ...... 12 F3
Riffa Business Park
OT LS21 ...... 43 H4
Rifle Range
UPML OL3 ...... 250 C1
Rigton CE Primary School
AL/HA/HU LS17 ...... 26 A7
Ringway Industrial Estate
WKFDE WF1 ...... 14 F3
Ripponden J & I School
RPDN/SBR HX6 ...... 189 G1
Riverhead Brewery
MAR/SLWT HD7 ...... 233 H7
Riverside Business Park
BAIL BD17 ...... 82 E6
ILK LS29 ...... 38 E1
KBTN HD8 ...... 239 M4
Riverside Industrial Estate
EARL WF12 ...... 173 L7
HOR/CROF WF4 ...... 197 G6

Riverside Junior School
HBR HX7 ...... 143 J3
Riverside Medical Centre
CAS WF10 ...... 157 L6
Riverside Primary School
LS24 ...... 71 L2
RM Grylls Middle School
LS24 ...... 171 K2
Robertown CE J & I School
LVSG WF15 ...... 171 M4
Robin Hood Golf Club
AWLS/ASK DN6 ...... 249 M3
Robin Hood Primary School
EARD/LOFT WF3 ...... 154 C4
Rochdale Curtain Theatre
ROCH OL11 ...... 206 A8
Rochdale Healthcare
WHIT OL12 ...... 206 F1
Rochdale Infirmary
WHIT OL12 ...... 206 A5
Rock Hill Sports Club
WHIT OL12 ...... 158 C8
The Rock Inn & Hotel
GTL/HWG HX4 ...... 190 E2
Rodillian School Performing Arts College
EARD/LOFT WF3 ...... 154 D5
Rodley Primary School
BRAM LS13 ...... 107 H1
Rogerthorpe Manor Hotel
HEM/SK/SE WF9 ...... 225 H3
Rombalds Hotel
ILK LS29 ...... 38 D3
The Rookeries Carleton J & I School *PONT* WF8 ...... 181 H8
Rooks Nest Primary School
WKFDE WF1 ...... 176 E2
Rosebank Primary School
BVRD LS3 ...... 6 A7
The Rose Hill Crematorium
BSLYN/ROY S71 ...... 262 C7
Roseneade School
HUDE HD5 ...... 215 G1
Roseville Business Park
RHAY LS8 ...... 7 M4
Rossett Business Park
BRAM LS13 ...... 107 K2
Rotherham Road Medical Centre *BSLYN/ROY* S71 ...... 243 J8
Rothwell CE Primary School
RTHW LS26 ...... 133 G8
Rothwell Health Centre
RTHW LS26 ...... 155 G1
Rothwell Primary School
RTHW LS26 ...... 155 G2
Rothwell Sports Centre
RTHW LS26 ...... 155 L2
Rothwell West Junior School
RTHW LS26 ...... 154 F2
Roundhay Golf Club
RHAY LS8 ...... 88 E4
Roundhay St Johns Primary School *RHAY* LS8 ...... 88 B3
Roundhay School
RHAY LS8 ...... 88 C7
Roundhill Junior School
KNOT WF11 ...... 181 K1
Roundhouse Business Park
WOR/ARM LS12 ...... 8 B2
Roundwood Industrial Estate
OSS WF5 ...... 197 K1
Rowley Lane J & I School
KBTN HD8 ...... 216 A1
Royal Armouries Museum
MID LS10 ...... 9 K3
Royal Halifax Infirmary
HFAX HX1 ...... 168 D1
Royal Industrial Park
HFAX HX1 ...... 10 E6
The Royal London Industrial Estate *BEE/HOL* LS11 ...... 131 H5
Royd Mill Business Park
BRIG HD6 ...... 170 D4
Royds Hall High School
HUDW HD3 ...... 191 L8
Royds School
RTHW LS26 ...... 155 K4
Royston Clinic
BSLYN/ROY S71 ...... 243 L3
Royston High School
BSLYN/ROY S71 ...... 243 L3
Royston Meadstead Primary School *BSLYN/ROY* S71 ...... 243 K3
Royston Parkside Primary School *BSLYN/ROY* S71 ...... 243 L2
Royston Summerfields Primary School *BSLYN/ROY* S71 ...... 243 L2
RSPB Nature Reserve (Fairburn Ings) *CAS* WF10 ...... 158 D3
Rudgate Business Park
RYKW YO26 ...... 31 L1
Rufford Park Primary School
YEA LS19 ...... 62 D8
Rushcroft Primary School
ROY/SHW OL2 ...... 229 K6
Russell Hall Primary School
CUL/QBY BD13 ...... 125 G5
Rutland Industrial Estate
WKFDE WF1 ...... 13 G6
Ryburn Brewery
RPDN/SBR HX6 ...... 167 M3
Ryburn Golf Club
RPDN/SBR HX6 ...... 167 L5
Ryburn Valley High School
RPDN/SBR HX6 ...... 167 H3
Rydings Special School
WHIT OL12 ...... 206 D2
Ryecroft Primary School
BOW BD4 ...... 128 B4
WOR/ARM LS12 ...... 108 A4
Ryhill Industrial Estate
HOR/CROF WF4 ...... 222 C5
Ryhill J & I School
HOR/CROF WF4 ...... 222 C4
Sacred Heart Catholic Primary School *BULY* LS4 ...... 108 C4
The Sacred Heart Primary School *ILK* LS29 ...... 38 E1
Sacred Heart J & I School
MILN OL16 ...... 206 E8
Sacred Heart RC Primary School *MILN* OL16 ...... 167 J3
Sai Medical Centre
GIR BD8 ...... 104 C4
St Agnes PNEU School
HDGY LS6 ...... 86 F8
St Aidans CE First School
KBTN HD8 ...... 239 J5
St Andrews CE Infant School
BRIG HD6 ...... 170 C4
St Andrews CE Junior School
BRIG HD6 ...... 170 C4
St Andrew's CE Primary School *WHIT* OL12 ...... 207 J4
St Andrews Primary School
HWTH BD22 ...... 2 D5
St Annes Cathedral
LDSU LS2 ...... 6 F8

St Annes RC Primary School
KGHY BD21 ...... 2 E3
St Anthonys RC Primary School
BEE/HOL LS11 ...... 131 H4
CLAY BD14 ...... 125 M1
IDLE BD10 ...... 83 H6
St Augustines CE Community Primary School *BFDE* BD3 ...... 5 G1
St Augustines CE Primary School *HFAX* HX1 ...... 10 C4
St Augustines RC Primary School *RHAY* LS8 ...... 110 C3
St Austins Catholic Primary School *WKFDE* WF1 ...... 176 F7
St Bartholomews CE Primary School *WOR/ARM* LS12 ...... 108 E7
St Bedes Catholic Grammar School *HTON* BD9 ...... 104 C3
St Benedicts RC Primary School *GFTH/SHER* LS25 ...... 113 H7
St Catherines Business Complex *BRAM* LS13 ...... 107 M2
St Catherines Catholic High School *LUD/ILL* HX2 ...... 124 C8
St Chads CE Primary School
BHP/TINH LS16 ...... 86 C7
BRIG HD6 ...... 170 A1
St Clares RC Primary School
ECHL BD2 ...... 105 L4
St Columbas Catholic Primary School *BOW* BD4 ...... 127 M4
St Cuthberts RC High School
MILN OL16 ...... 228 D5
St Cuthberts & The First Martyrs Primary School *HTON* BD9 ...... 104 C4
St Edwards RC Primary School *BSPA/BRAM* LS23 ...... 48 E6
St Francis of Assisi RC Primary School *BEE/HOL* LS11 ...... 8 F7
St Francis RC Primary School
ECHL BD2 ...... 105 J2
MOR LS27 ...... 152 B2
St George's Hall
BFD BD1 ...... 5 G5
St Giles CE (VA) Primary School *PONT* WF8 ...... 180 F5
St Gregorys CE Primary School *SCFT* LS14 ...... 111 M1
St Helena's Caravan Park
BHP/TINH LS16 ...... 63 L5
St Helens CE Aided J & I School *HEM/SK/SE* WF9 ...... 223 H3
St Helens Primary School
BSLYN/ROY S71 ...... 261 M1
St Hildas School
HOR/CROF WF4 ...... 197 J4
St Ignatius RC Primary School
OSS WF5 ...... 196 F3
St James Business Park
BFD BD1 ...... 5 H7
St James CE J & I School
HOR/CROF WF4 ...... 198 A8
St James CE Primary School
WBY LS22 ...... 30 B8
St James C E Primary School
WHIT OL12 ...... 184 B8
St James Church Primary School *WIL/AL* BD15 ...... 103 J7
St James School
BFDE BD3 ...... 5 J8
St James's University Hospital
OSM LS9 ...... 110 B4
St John Baptist CE (VA) Primary School *BSLYN/ROY* S71 ...... 243 L3
St John Fisher Catholic High School *DEWS* WF13 ...... 173 J5
St John RC Primary School
ROCH OL11 ...... 206 B8
St Johns Catholic School
BSPA/BRAM LS23 ...... 48 F7
St Johns CE Infant School
DEWS WF13 ...... 173 J6
St Johns CE J & I School
WKFDE WF1 ...... 176 D6
St Johns CE Primary School
BOW BD4 ...... 127 L5
BRIG HD6 ...... 171 G4
MDTN M24 ...... 228 A8
RPDN/SBR HX6 ...... 188 E5
St Johns Health Centre
HFAX HX1 ...... 10 C5
St Johns Shopping Centre
LDSU LS2 ...... 7 G8
St John the Baptist Catholic Primary School *NORM* WF6 ...... 178 D4
St John the Evangelist RC Primary School *WBSY* BD6 ...... 126 A5
St John with St Michael Primary School *WHIT* OL12 ...... 184 A1
St Josephs Catholic College
HTON BD9 ...... 104 E3
St Joseph's Catholic Primary School *HEM/SK/SE* WF9 ...... 247 G3
St Josephs Catholic Primary School *MID* LS10 ...... 9 L7
OT LS21 ...... 41 H6
WBY LS22 ...... 30 A8
St Josephs Catholic School
BRIG HD6 ...... 170 D1
St Joseph's Primary School
TOD OL14 ...... 163 K1
St Josephs RC Primary School
BGLY BD16 ...... 81 J3
CAS WF10 ...... 158 A6
DEWS WF13 ...... 173 J4
HIPP HX3 ...... 11 J3
HUDE HD5 ...... 193 H8
KGHY BD21 ...... 2 E7
PDSY/CALV LS28 ...... 107 H6
PONT WF8 ...... 180 E5
TAD LS24 ...... 71 J2
TOD OL14 ...... 141 J8
WBOW BD5 ...... 126 F2
St Lukes CE First School
CLECK BD19 ...... 149 K7
St Lukes CE Primary School
ECHL BD2 ...... 105 M2
St Lukes Hospital
HUDS HD4 ...... 213 M3
WBOW BD5 ...... 126 F2
St Malachys RC Primary School *LUD/ILL* HX2 ...... 146 A2
St Margarets CE Primary School *HORS* LS18 ...... 85 L3
St Marys Catholic Comprehensive School *ILK* LS29 ...... 61 G3
St Marys Catholic Primary School *HFAX* HX1 ...... 10 C4
St Marys CE (A) First School
CLECK BD19 ...... 150 D6
St Marys CE J & I School
WKFDE WF1 ...... 13 H3

St Mary's CE Primary School
DOD/DAR S75 ...... 260 E4
ROCH OL11 ...... 228 C2
St Marys CE School
ROY/SHW OL2 ...... 229 H6
St Marys CE School
BSPA/BRAM LS23 ...... 48 F7
St Marys CE (VC) J & I School
RPDN/SBR HX6 ...... 166 E7
St Marys Hospital
WOR/ARM LS12 ...... 108 B6
St Marys RC J I & N School
BTLY WF17 ...... 173 K1
St Marys RC Primary School
BFD BD1 ...... 5 G5
HORS LS18 ...... 85 L5
St Mary's RC Primary School
LIT OL15 ...... 207 J1
St Marys RC Primary School
RTHW LS26 ...... 155 H2
St Matthews Catholic Primary School *WIL/AL* BD15 ...... 103 K6
St Matthews CE Primary School *CHAL* LS7 ...... 87 L7
WBOW BD5 ...... 127 G4
St Matthews Infant School
DOD/DAR S75 ...... 260 E4
St Michaels & All Angels CE Primary School
COL BB8 ...... 52 A6
HIPP HX3 ...... 125 M8
St Michaels Catholic College
LDSU LS2 ...... 6 B6
St Michaels C & CE High School
BSLYN/ROY S71 ...... 243 L7
St Michaels CE Primary School
HDGY LS6 ...... 109 G1
WKFDW/WTN WF2 ...... 176 A8
St Nicholas RC Primary School
OSM LS9 ...... 110 F3
St Oswalds CE Junior School
GSLY LS20 ...... 62 A6
St Oswalds CE Primary School
GTHN BD7 ...... 126 C2
St Patricks Catholic Primary School *GTL/HWG* HX4 ...... 168 F3
HUDW HD3 ...... 14 A2
HUDW HD3 ...... 191 H6
St Patricks RC Primary School
BTLY WF17 ...... 151 G4
St Patricks VA RC Primary School *WHIT* OL12 ...... 110 C6
St Patricks VA RC Primary School *WHIT* OL12 ...... 206 C5
St Paulinus Catholic Primary School *DEWS* WF13 ...... 173 J7
St Pauls CE Primary School
WBSY BD6 ...... 126 D6
St Pauls J & I CE School
WKFDW/WTN WF2 ...... 175 M6
St Pauls RC Primary School
AL/HA/HU LS17 ...... 87 J2
St Peter & St Paul RC Primary School *YEA* LS19 ...... 62 B8
St Peters Cathedral
BFD BD1 ...... 5 G5
St Peters CE J & I School
BTLY WF17 ...... 151 G4
St Peters CE Junior School
HOR/CROF WF4 ...... 197 L5
St Peters CE Primary School
OSM LS9 ...... 7 K8
St Peters RC Primary School
BFDE BD3 ...... 5 M6
St Peters VC CE Primary School *MILN* OL16 ...... 228 D1
St Philips CE First School
GIR BD8 ...... 104 B6
St Philip's CE Primary School
GIR BD8 ...... 104 C5
St Philips RC Primary School
MID LS10 ...... 153 K1
St Saviours CE Junior School
BTLY WF17 ...... 151 J5
St Stephens CE Primary School *KSTL* LS5 ...... 108 C2
WBOW BD5 ...... 127 G3
St Stephens RC Primary School *SKP/WHF* BD20 ...... 16 B2
St Theresas C Primary School *MSTN/BAR* LS15 ...... 111 L3
St Thomas A Becket Catholic Comprehensive School *WKFDW/WTN* WF2 ...... 199 G5
St Thomas CE Junior School
FEA/AMT WF7 ...... 201 L1
St Thomas CE Primary School *MILN* OL16 ...... 229 K2
St Urbans RC Primary School
HDGY LS6 ...... 87 J5
St Walburgas CP School
SHPY BD18 ...... 82 B6
St Wilfrids Catholic High School *FEA/AMT* WF7 ...... 175 K5
St Williams Catholic Primary School *GIR* BD8 ...... 104 C6
St Winefrides RC Primary School *WBSY* BD6 ...... 126 D6
Salendine Nook High School
HUDW HD3 ...... 191 H7
Salford Industrial Estate
TOD OL14 ...... 163 J1
Saltaire Medical Centre
SHPY BD18 ...... 82 B6
Saltaire Primary School
SHPY BD18 ...... 82 B6
Salterhebble J & I School
HIPP HX3 ...... 168 F3
Salterlee Primary School
HIPP HX3 ...... 147 H4
Salt Grammar School
BAIL BD17 ...... 82 B4
Sandal Castle
WKFDW/WTN WF2 ...... 198 F5
Sandal Endowed CE Junior School *WKFDW/WTN* WF2 ...... 199 G6
Sandal Magna J & I School
WKFDE WF1 ...... 199 H6
Sandal Medical Centre
WKFDW/WTN WF2 ...... 198 E7
Sandal Primary School
BAIL BD17 ...... 82 D3
Sandal RUFC
WKFDW/WTN WF2 ...... 198 F7
Sandbeck Industrial Estate
WBY LS22 ...... 30 B7
Sandbeck Park Industrial Estate *WBY* LS22 ...... 30 B7
Sandbeds Trading Estate
OSS WF5 ...... 174 F7
Sandhill Golf Club
CUD/CR S72 ...... 263 M6
Sand Moor Golf Club
AL/HA/HU LS17 ...... 65 L8
Sandylands Business Centre
SKP/WHF BD20 ...... 16 A3
Sandy Lane Primary School
WIL/AL BD15 ...... 103 J2
Savile Business Centre
EARL WF12 ...... 173 M7

Savile Centre
EARL WF12 ....195 M4
Savile Town CE Infant School &
Nursery School
EARL WF12 ....173 L7
Savoy Squash Club
KBTN HD8 ....239 J4
Saxon Hall Leisure Centre
MILN OL16 ....206 E6
Saxton CE Primary School
TAD LS24 ....93 J8
Scammonden Sailing Club
HUDW HD3 ....211 J4
Scapegoat Hill Primary School
MAR/SLWT HD7 ....190 D8
Scarcroft Golf Club
SCFT LS14 ....67 K6
Scarthingwell Golf Club
TAD LS24 ....94 A7
Scholemoor Cemetery
GTHN BD7 ....104 A8
Scholemoor Crematorium
GTHN BD7 ....104 A8
Scholes CC
HOLM/MEL HD9 ....254 F3
Scholes (Elmete) Primary School
MSTN/BAR LS15 ....90 A4
Scholes First School
CLECK BD19 ....149 G5
Scholes Primary School
HOLM/MEL HD9 ....254 F3
School Lane Health Centre
DEWS WF13 ....173 H5
School of Art Architecture &
Design (Leeds Metropolitan
University)
LDSU LS2 ....7 G7
School of Education & Prof
Studies *HDCY* LS6 ....86 C8
School of Teacher Education
Studies *HDCY* LS6 ....86 C8
Schreiber Business Centre
WKFDE WF1 ....13 H5
Scissett CE First School
KBTN HD8 ....239 M4
Scissett Middle School
KBTN HD8 ....239 M4
Scissett Swimming Baths
KBTN HD8 ....240 A4
Scotch Park Trading Estate
WOR/ARM LS12 ....108 F6
Scout Road Primary School
HBR HX7 ....144 B6
SDH Industrial Estate
RPDN/SBR HX6 ....167 K4
Seacroft Clinic
SCFT LS14 ....111 K1
Seacroft Industrial Estate
SCFT LS14 ....89 K7
Seemore Shopping Centre
OSS WF5 ....174 F8
Selby College
LDS LS24 ....71 M3
WBY LS22 ....48 B1
Selby College
(Sherburn Cyber Centre)
GFTH/SHER LS25 ....116 A6
Seven Hills Primary School
MOR LS27 ....152 D2
Shade Primary School
TOD OL14 ....163 J3
Shadwell CP School
AL/HA/HU LS17 ....89 H2
Shadwell Medical Centre
AL/HA/HU LS17 ....88 A3
Shafton Primary School
CUD/GR S72 ....244 F4
Shakespeare Primary School
OSM LS9 ....110 B5
Sharlston Community School
HOR/CROF WF4 ....200 D2
Sharma Park Industrial Estate
RHAY LS8 ....7 L5
Sharp Lane Primary School
MID LS10 ....154 A1
Shaw Business Park
HUDE HD5 ....15 K7
Shawclough Community
Primary School
WHIT OL12 ....206 A3
Shawcross Business Park
EARL WF12 ....174 B4
Shaw Cross Health Centre
EARL WF12 ....174 C3
Shaw Cross Infant School
EARL WF12 ....174 C3
Shaw House School
HTON BD9 ....104 C3
Shay Lane Infant School
HOR/CROF WF4 ....200 A5
Sheibarg Industrial Estate
BOW BD4 ....127 M2
Shelf Health Centre
HIPP HX3 ....125 L8
Shelf Primary School
HIPP HX3 ....147 K1
Shelley College
KBTN HD8 ....239 G4
Shelley First School
KBTN HD8 ....238 C3
Shepley First School
KBTN HD8 ....238 A6
Sherburn High School
GFTH/SHER LS25 ....116 A8
Sherburn-in-Elmet
Aerodrome
GFTH/SHER LS25 ....116 F8
Sherwood Industrial Estate
EARD/LOFT WF3 ....154 D3
Shibden Hall & Folk Museum
HIPP HX3 ....147 H6
Shibden Head Primary School
CUL/QBY BD13 ....124 F6
Shipley Baths
SHPY BD18 ....82 C7
Shipley CE Primary School
SHPY BD18 ....82 D8
Shipley College
SHPY BD18 ....82 C6
Shipley Golf Club
BGLY BD16 ....81 H5
Shipley Health Centre
SHPY BD18 ....82 D7
Shipley Hospital
SHPY BD18 ....82 C7
Shires Business Park
GTHN BD7 ....126 C3
Shirley Manor Primary School
LM/WK BD12 ....148 E5
Showcase Cinemas
BTLY WF17 ....151 K2
Sicklinghall Primary School
WBY LS22 ....46 D1
Siddal Primary School
HIPP HX3 ....168 F3
Sikh Leisure Centre
HUD HD1 ....14 E8
Silcoates School
WKFDW/WTN WF2 ....176 A5

Silkstone Golf Club
DOD/DAR S75 ....259 L6
Silkstone Primary School
DOD/DAR S75 ....259 H6
Silsden CC
AIRE BD20 ....35 M6
Silsden Golf Club
AIRE BD20 ....36 C5
Silsden Health Centre
AIRE BD20 ....35 M5
Silver Blades Ice Rink
BFD 4 E8
Silver Court Industrial Estate
HUD HD1 ....15 K8
Silverwood School
DOD/DAR S75 ....259 H6
Simpsons Lane J & I School
KNOT WF11 ....181 M3
Sirdar Business Park
WKFDW/WTN WF2 ....176 A7
Skelmanthorpe Business Park
KBTN HD8 ....239 J4
Skelmanthorpe First School
KBTN HD8 ....239 K4
Skipton Castle
SKP/WHF BD23 ....16 C2
Skipton General Hospital
SKP/WHF BD23 ....16 B3
Skipton Girls High School
SKP/WHF BD23 ....16 A1
Skipton Hospital
SKP/WHF BD23 ....16 A3
Skipton Lm Sports Club
SKP/WHF BD23 ....16 A3
Skipton Parish CE Primary
School *SKP/WHF* BD23 ....16 C3
Slaithwaite CE Primary School
MAR/SLWT HD7 ....212 A6
Slaithwaite Health Centre
MAR/SLWT HD7 ....212 C5
Slaithwaite Swimming Baths
MAR/SLWT HD7 ....212 C5
Smallbridge Health Centre
WHIT OL12 ....206 E3
Smallbridge Industrial Park
MILN OL16 ....206 D4
Smawthorne Henry Moore
Primary School
CAS WF10 ....157 M8
Smeaton Industrial Estate
PONT WF8 ....227 G1
Smithy Bridge Primary School
LIT OL15 ....207 H3
Snapethorpe Primary School
WKFDW/WTN WF2 ....197 L2
Snaygill Industrial Estate
SKP/WHF BD23 ....16 B5
Soothill CC
BTLY WF17 ....174 A1
South Bradford Golf Club
WBSY BD6 ....127 G6
South Craven School
AIRE BD20 ....34 F8
South Crosland Junior School
HUDS HD4 ....213 M7
Southdale CE Junior School
OSS WF5 ....197 G1
South Elmsall Ash Grove J &
I School *HEM/SK/SE* WF9 ....247 J2
South Elmsall Health Centre
HEM/SK/SE WF9 ....247 H3
South Halifax High School
HIPP HX3 ....169 G5
South Hiendley J & I School
CUD/GR S72 ....222 F8
South Leeds Art College
MID LS10 ....132 A6
South Leeds Business Park
MID LS10 ....9 J7
South Leeds Golf Club
BEE/HOL LS11 ....131 J7
South Leeds High School
BEE/HOL LS11 ....8 A7
South Leeds Sports Centre
BEE/HOL LS11 ....8 F6
South Leeds Stadium
BEE/HOL LS11 ....131 L6
Southmere Primary School
GTHN BD7 ....126 C7
South Milford Primary School
GFTH/SHER LS25 ....138 A3
South Ossett Infant School
OSS WF5 ....197 G2
South Parade Primary School
OSS WF5 ....197 H1
Southroyd Primary School
PDSY/CALV LS28 ....107 G8
South Side Aviation Centre
YEA LS19 ....63 G7
South View Business Centre
GSLY LS20 ....62 A4
Southview Business Park
GSLY LS20 ....62 A4
GSLY LS20 ....62 A7
South Yorkshire (Redbrook)
Industrial Estate
DOD/DAR S75 ....260 C1
Sovereign Business Centre
HUDS HD4 ....214 B3
Sovereign Business Park
MID LS10 ....9 H5
Sowerby Bridge Clinic
RPDN/SBR HX6 ....167 L3
Sowerby Bridge CC
RPDN/SBR HX6 ....167 K2
Sowerby Bridge High School
RPDN/SBR HX6 ....167 L1
Sowerby Village Primary
School
RPDN/SBR HX6 ....167 G4
Spa Baths
BSPA/BRAM LS23 ....49 G6
Spa Fields Industrial Estate
MAR/SLWT HD7 ....212 D5
Spenborough Industrial Estate
LVSG WF15 ....172 E3
Spen Trading Estate
CLECK BD19 ....150 B7
Spen Valley High School
LVSG WF15 ....172 C3
Spen Valley Industrial Park
LVSG WF15 ....150 A8
Spen Victoria Cricket
Bowling & Athletic Club
CLECK BD19 ....150 B4
Spofforth Castle
PBR HG3 ....28 D3
Spofforth CE Primary School
PBR HG3 ....28 E4
Spring Bank Industrial Estate
RPDN/SBR HX6 ....167 J4
Springbank Junior School
PDSY/CALV LS28 ....106 F3
Spring Bank Primary School
HDGY LS6 ....108 F2
Spring Grove Primary School
HUD HD1 ....14 D8
Springhill High School
MILN OL16 ....228 V4

Spring Ram Business Park
BTLY WF17 ....151 J2
DOD/DAR S75 ....241 L4
Springwell Health Clinic
WKFDW/WTN WF2 ....199 G4
Springwood Primary School
GIR BD8 ....4 B3
Stafford Hall Education
Resource *HIPP* HX3 ....146 D4
Staincliffe CE Junior School
BTLY WF17 ....173 J3
Stairfoot Health Centre
BSLY S70 ....261 M7
Stairfoot Industrial Estate
BSLY S70 ....262 B6
Stanbury Village School
HWTH BD22 ....77 M8
Standard Industrial Estate
ECHL BD2 ....105 J3
Standbridge Primary School
WKFDW/WTN WF2 ....220 C1
Standedge Experience
MAR/SLWT HD7 ....232 F2
Stanley Grove J & I School
EARD/LOFT WF3 ....177 H3
Stanley Health Centre
EARD/LOFT WF3 ....177 G1
Stanley Mills Business Park
HUDW HD3 ....213 H2
Stanley Royal Hospital
WKFDE WF1 ....176 F6
Stanley St Peters CE Primary
School *EARD/LOFT* WF3 ....177 H1
Stanley Sports & Social Club
EARD/LOFT WF3 ....155 H8
Stanningley Industrial Centre
PDSY/CALV LS28 ....106 F5
Stanningley Primary School
PDSY/CALV LS28 ....107 H4
Stanningley RLFC
PDSY/CALV LS28 ....107 J4
Stansfield Hall CE Free Primary
School *LIT* OL15 ....185 L6
Station Approach Business
Estate *ROCH* OL11 ....206 B8
Station Industrial Park
LUD/ILL HX2 ....144 F7
Station Road Industrial Estate
GFTH/SHER LS25 ....135 H7
Station Works Industrial Park
KGHY BD21 ....3 L4
Steed Court Business Park
HEM/SK/SE WF9 ....225 L6
Steeton Hall (Gatehouse)
GFTH/SHER LS25 ....137 L3
Steeton Health Centre
AIRE BD20 ....56 E1
Steeton Primary School
AIRE BD20 ....56 F1
Steps Industrial Park
HOLM/MEL HD9 ....214 C8
Sterling Industrial Park
CAS WF10 ....158 B8
Stile Common Infant School
HUDS HD4 ....214 D3
Stile Common Junior School
HUDS HD4 ....214 D3
Stockingate Junior School
HEM/SK/SE WF9 ....246 C5
Stocks Lane Primary School
CUL/QBY BD13 ....125 K5
Stoney Ridge Hospital
BGLY BD16 ....103 L1
Stoney Royd Cemetery
HIPP HX3 ....168 F1
Stoodley Pike Monument
HBR HX7 ....164 E1
The Strand Medical Centre
ROCH OL11 ....228 B4
Strawberry Fields Primary
School *GFTH/SHER* LS25 ....113 G8
Streethouse J & I School
FEA/AMT WF7 ....200 E1
Sues Health Centre
BSLYN/ROY S71 ....225 J6
Summerfield Primary School
BRAM LS13 ....107 H3
Summer Lane Primary School
DOD/DAR S75 ....260 E4
Sunfield Medical Centre
PDSY/CALV LS28 ....106 F5
Sunny Hill House School
WKFDW/WTN WF2 ....176 A5
Sutton in Craven CE Primary
School *AIRE* BD20 ....55 M1
Sutton in Craven Community
Primary School
AIRE BD20 ....55 M1
Swain House Primary School
ECHL BD2 ....105 J2
Swillington Primary School
RTHW LS26 ....134 C4
Swinnow Primary School
PDSY/CALV LS28 ....107 J6
Swinnow Shopping Centre
BRAM LS13 ....107 J6
Sycamore Industrial Estate
HECK WF16 ....172 F4
Tadcaster Albion FC
TAD LS24 ....71 M3
Tadcaster CC
TAD LS24 ....71 L3
Tadcaster East Primary School
TAD LS24 ....72 A2
Tadcaster Grammar School
TAD LS24 ....70 F4
Tadcaster Sports & Leisure
Centre *TAD* LS24 ....71 L3
Tainton Park Trading Estate
WOR/ARM LS12 ....109 G8
Taison Industrial Park
BTLY WF17 ....151 J3
Takaiani Dance Theatre
RHAY LS8 ....110 E2
Talbot Primary School
RHAY LS8 ....88 B5
Tandem Industrial Estate
HUDE HD5 ....193 K8
Tandle Hill Country Park
ROY/SHW OL2 ....228 C8
The Tandy Trading Estate
BULY LS4 ....108 E5
Tannery Business Park
HIPP HX3 ....147 J3
Tanshelf Industrial Estate
PONT WF8 ....180 E5
Tanyard Industrial Estate
HUD HD3 ....213 K2
Temple Bank Special School
HTON BD9 ....104 A4
Temple Moor High School
MSTN/BAR LS15 ....111 K7
Temple Newsam Country Park
MSTN/BAR LS15 ....111 K8
Temple Newsam Golf Club
MSTN/BAR LS15 ....111 H8
Temple Newsam Halton
Primary School
MSTN/BAR LS15 ....111 J6

Temple Newsam House
MSTN/BAR LS15 ....133 K1
Tenterfields Business Park
LUD/ILL HX2 ....167 G1
Tetley's Brewery
MID LS10 ....9 H3
Thackley AFC
IDLE BD10 ....83 J4
Thackley CC
IDLE BD10 ....83 K4
Thackley Primary School
IDLE BD10 ....83 K4
Thackray Museum
RHAY LS8 ....110 E3
Thomas Danby College
CHAL LS7 ....7 K4
Thongsbridge Cricket &
Bowling Club
HOLM/MEL HD9 ....236 D6
Thongsbridge Tennis Club
HOLM/MEL HD9 ....236 D6
Thornbury Primary School
BFDE BD3 ....106 A7
Thorncliffe Park Industrial
Estate *GIR* BD8 ....4 D1
Thorncliffe Square Industrial
Estate *GIR* BD8 ....4 C1
Thorner CE Primary School
SCFT LS14 ....90 C1
Thornes Industrial Estate
WKFDE WF1 ....12 F6
Thornes Park Athletics Stadium
WKFDW/WTN WF2 ....12 A6
Thornham St James CE Primary
School
ROY/SHW OL2 ....228 F6
Thornhill Cricket & Bowling
Club *EARL* WF12 ....196 B3
Thornhill J & I School
EARL WF12 ....195 M5
Thornhill Lees CE Infant
School *EARL* WF12 ....195 L6
Thorn Park School & Service
for Deaf & Hearing
HTON BD9 ....103 M2
Thornton Baths
CUL/QBY BD13 ....103 C8
Thornton Grammar School
CUL/QBY BD13 ....103 K8
Thornton Lodge Health Centre
HUD HD1 ....214 B2
Thornton Medical Centre
CUL/QBY BD13 ....103 C8
Thornton Primary School
CUL/QBY BD13 ....102 E8
Thorp Arch Trading Estate
BSPA/BRAM LS23 ....49 J3
Thorpe Park Hotel
MSTN/BAR LS15 ....112 B7
Thorpe Primary School
EARD/LOFT WF3 ....154 A4
IDLE BD10 ....83 K6
Three Lane Ends Business
Centre *CAS* WF10 ....157 J6
Three Lane Ends J & I School
CAS W10 ....157 J7
Throstle Farm J & I School
KNOT WF11 ....182 B4
Thrum Hall Industrial Park
LUD/ILL HX2 ....146 A7
Thurlstone Primary School
STKB/PEN S36 ....270 C2
Thurstonland Endowed
Primary School
HUDS HD4 ....237 H4
Thwaite Mills Watermill
OSM LS9 ....132 D3
Tockwith CE Primary School
RYKW YO26 ....32 B1
Todmorden CC
TOD OL14 ....141 J8
Todmorden Community
College *TOD* OL14 ....163 K1
Todmorden Golf Club
TOD OL14 ....141 L8
Todmorden Health Centre
TOD OL14 ....163 K1
Todmorden High School
TOD OL14 ....141 H7
Tolson Memorial Museum
HUDE HD5 ....215 G1
Tong Sports Centre
BOW BD4 ....128 C6
Top Rank Theatre
HFAX HX1 ....11 G3
Towngate Primary School
OSS WF5 ....175 G7
Tranmere Park Primary School
GSLY LS20 ....61 K6
Travelodge
BFDE BD3 ....106 B6
BSLYN/ROY S71 ....262 A6
HIPP HX3 ....10 F3
HOR/CROF WF4 ....219 K6
HOR/CROF WF4 ....219 L5
KNOT WF11 ....181 M4
LDS LS1 ....9 G2
MIRF WF14 ....171 L7
MSTN/BAR LS15 ....112 B7
PONT WF8 ....226 D4
YEA LS19 ....63 H6
Trawden Forest Primary School
COL BB8 ....74 D4
Treefield Industrial Estate
MOR LS27 ....151 M1
Trent Industrial Estate
ROY/SHW OL2 ....229 K6
Triangle Business Park
BTLY WF17 ....151 J3
Triangle CE Primary School
RPDN/SBR HX6 ....167 G5
Trinity All Saints CE Primary
School *BGLY* BD16 ....81 J4
Trinity & All Saints College
HORS LS18 ....85 J3
Trinity Business Centre
WKFDE WF1 ....13 H4
Trinity Business Park
WKFDE WF1 ....12 F5
Trinity Medical Centre
WKFDE WF1 ....12 F3
Tropical World
RHAY LS8 ....88 D5
Tuel Lane Infant School
RPDN/SBR HX6 ....167 L2
Tulip Street Retail Park
MID LS10 ....131 M3
Tunshill Golf Club
MILN OL16 ....207 L8
Turkey Inn
HWTH BD22 ....56 D8
Turnshaws Special School
KBTN HD8 ....216 C8
Tyersal Family Clinic
BOW BD4 ....106 B8
Tyersal Primary School
BOW BD4 ....106 B8

UCI Cinema
HUDE HD5 ....15 K3
Undercliffe CC
ECHL BD2 ....105 L4
Undercliffe Cemetery
BFDE BD3 ....5 K1
Undercliffe Primary School
ECHL BD2 ....105 J4
Union Business Centre
ECHL BD2 ....105 M2
University of Bradford
GTHN BD7 ....4 B8
WBOW BD5 ....126 F1
University of Bradford Sports
Centre *GTHN* BD7 ....4 B8
LDSU LS2 ....6 D6
University of Huddersfield
HUD HD1 ....15 G6
HUD HD1 ....15 G8
HUDW HD3 ....191 L5
KBTN HD8 ....215 L8
University of Huddersfield
Annexe *HUD* HD1 ....14 D5
University of Leeds
BHP/TINH LS16 ....86 E5
HDGY LS6 ....6 C4
HDGY LS6 ....109 H2
LDSU LS2 ....6 D6
University of Leeds
(Bretton Hall Campus)
HOR/CROF WF4 ....219 G8
University Sports Centre
LDSU LS2 ....6 D6
Upper Abrigg Special School
HOLM/MEL HD9 ....236 F8
Upperthong J & I School
HOLM/MEL HD9 ....254 A2
Upper Whitley J & I School
HOR/CROF WF4 ....217 G2
Upton ARLFC
HEM/SK/SE WF9 ....225 K6
Upton Clinic
HEM/SK/SE WF9 ....225 M6
Upton Primary School
HEM/SK/SE WF9 ....225 L6
Usher Street Primary School
BOW BD4 ....127 J1
Valley Medical Centre
HBR HX7 ....143 J3
Valley Mills Industrial Estate
IDLE BD10 ....84 A6
Valley Road Business Park
LVSG WF15 ....172 C2
Vehicle Testing Centre
BSPA/BRAM LS23 ....49 J2
Venio Industrial Centre
BOW BD4 ....127 L4
Victoria Baths
ELL HX5 ....169 J8
Victoria Centre
EARL WF12 ....173 L6
Victoria Industrial Estate
ECHL BD2 ....105 L2
Victoria Industrial Park
SCFT LS14 ....89 K6
Victoria Junior School
RTHW LS26 ....132 F8
Victoria Park School
BRAM LS13 ....108 A3
Victoria Primary School
KGHY BD21 ....2 D4
OSM LS9 ....110 D6
Victoria Spring Business Park
LVSG WF15 ....172 B1
The Victoria Theatre
HFAX HX1 ....11 G6
Village Medical Centre
LIT OL15 ....207 K1
Vine Industrial Estate
BRIG HD6 ....170 B3
Vintage Railway Carriage
Museum *HWTH* BD22 ....78 E7
VUE Cinema
BULY LS4 ....108 E5
Wainman's Pinnacle
AIRE BD20 ....55 J3
Wainstalls J & I School
LUD/ILL HX2 ....145 H1
Wakefield 41 Industrial Park
EARD/LOFT WF3 ....176 B1
Wakefield Art Gallery
WKFDE WF1 ....176 D7
Wakefield Cathedral
WKFDE WF1 ....12 F2
Wakefield City Baths
WKFDE WF1 ....13 G2
Wakefield City High School
WKFDE WF1 ....177 H7
Wakefield College
CAS WF10 ....157 K8
FEA/AMT WF7 ....201 M1
HEM/SK/SE WF9 ....224 F2
WKFDE WF1 ....12 C1
Wakefield College (Thornes
Park Campus)
WKFDW/WTN WF2 ....12 A7
Wakefield Crematorium
WKFDW/WTN WF2 ....198 C8
Wakefield Girls High School
WKFDE WF1 ....176 D7
Wakefield Girls High School
(Mulberry House)
WKFDE WF1 ....176 D7
Wakefield Girls High School
(Senior Girls)
WKFDE WF1 ....12 D1
Wakefield Golf Club
WKFDW/WTN WF2 ....198 F8
Wakefield Independent Junior
School *HOR/CROF* WF4 ....201 H8
Wakefield Methodist J & I School
WKFDW/WTN WF2 ....12 A7
Wakefield Museum
WKFDE WF1 ....12 E2
Wakefield RUFC
WKFDE WF1 ....176 E6
Wakefield Superbowl 2000
WKFDE WF1 ....13 L8
Wakefield Theatre Royal & Opera
House
WKFDE WF1 ....12 C2
Wakefield Trinity Wildcats
RLFC (Belle Vue)
WKFDE WF1 ....13 K8
Wakefield Tutorial
Preparatory School
MOR LS27 ....152 C2
Walnut Business Centre
HFAX HX1 ....10 C6
Walsden CC
TOD OL14 ....163 J6
Walsden CE (VC) Infant School
TOD OL14 ....163 K5
Walsden Industrial Estate
TOD OL14 ....163 J5
Walton Grove Infant School
WKFDW/WTN WF2 ....199 K7

Walton Junior School
  WKFDW/WTN WF2 ....199 J7
Waltonways Cemetery
  SKP/WHF BD23 ....16 A5
Waltonways Crematorium
  SKP/WHF BD23 ....16 A4
Wardle High School
  WHIT OL12 ....206 F1
Warley Road Primary School
  LUD/ILL HX2 ....146 A8
Warley Town Primary School
  LUD/ILL HX2 ....145 J8
Warwick Road J & I School
  BTLY WF17 ....173 L3
The Watergate Clinic
  MILN OL16 ....206 B7
Waterloo Primary School
  PDSY/CALV LS28 ....106 E7
Waterside Industrial Estate
  COL BB8 ....74 A4
Waterside Industrial Park
  OSM LS9 ....132 D3
Water Street Primary School
  SKP/WHF BD23 ....16 B2
Waterton J & I School
  WKFDW/WTN WF2 ....197 M2
Waterton Park Golf Club
  WKFDW/WTN WF2 ....199 K8
Waterton Park Hotel
  WKFDW/WTN WF2 ....221 L1
Weavers Restaurant & Hotel
  HWTH BD22 ....78 D6
Wedgwood Special School
  BOW BD4 ....128 B4
Weetwood Primary School
  BHP/TINH LS16 ....86 F7
Wellgate Primary School
  DOD/DAR S75 ....242 D5
Wellhouse J & I School
  MAR/SLWT HD7 ....212 F4
Wellhouse Middle School
  MIRF WF14 ....172 D7
Wellington Business Centre
  ELL HX5 ....169 J7
Wellington Primary School
  ECHL BD2 ....105 K3
Wellington Road Industrial
  Estate *WOR/ARM* LS12 ....6 B9
Wellington Shopping Arcade
  BRIG HD6 ....170 C4
Wellington Street Business
  Park *CAS* WF10 ....157 L6
Well Lane Business Centre
  BTLY WF17 ....173 L1
Wellwoman Clinic
  HFAX HX1 ....11 G7
Wentbridge House Hotel
  PONT WF8 ....203 M7
Westborough High School
  DEWS WF13 ....173 J6
Westbourne Primary School
  GIR BD8 ....104 D4
West Bowling Golf Club
  WBOW BD5 ....127 J5
West Bradford Golf Club
  HTON BD9 ....103 K3
West Bretton Primary School
  HOR/CROF WF4 ....219 H6
Westbrook Lane Primary
  School *HORS* LS18 ....85 J3
Westcliffe Medical Centre
  SHPY BD18 ....82 C7

West End Industrial Estate
  MOR LS27 ....151 M3
West End Middle School
  CLECK BD19 ....149 K7
West End Primary School
  HEM/SK/SE WF9 ....223 L7
  HORS LS18 ....85 H4
Westerton Primary School
  EARD/LOFT WF3 ....152 F7
Westfield Industrial Estate
  YEA LS19 ....62 C8
Westfield Junior School
  YEA LS19 ....62 B8
Westfield Medical Centre
  CHAL LS7 ....109 M1
Westgate Hill First School
  BOW BD4 ....128 C7
Westgate Primary School
  OT LS21 ....41 G7
Westgate Retail & Leisure Park
  WOR/ARM LS12 ....12 C4
West Leeds High School
  WOR/ARM LS12 ....108 B7
Westmoor Junior School
  DEWS WF13 ....173 H5
West Oaks School
  BSPA/BRAM LS23 ....48 E7
West Oaks School Oakwood
  RHAY LS8 ....110 F2
West Park Bramhope RUFC
  BHP/TINH LS16 ....64 C5
West Riding Magistrates Court
  BTLY WF17 ....151 G5
Westroyd Infant School
  PDSY/CALV LS28 ....106 F4
West Side Retail Park
  GSLY LS20 ....62 B7
West Specialist Inclusive
  Learning Centre
  BRAM LS13 ....108 A3
West Vale Primary School
  GTL/HWG HX4 ....168 F7
Westville House School
  ILK LS29 ....20 F7
Westwood Park
  Primary School
  HIPP HX3 ....125 M6
Westwood Primary School
  MID LS10 ....153 J2
West Yorkshire College of
  Health Studies
  WKFDE WF1 ....177 G5
West Yorkshire Industrial Estate
  BOW BD4 ....127 M5
West Yorkshire Playhouse
  OSM LS9 ....7 K9
West Yorkshire Police
  Headquarters *WKFDE* WF1 ....12 D1
West Yorkshire Retail Park
  BTLY WF17 ....151 K2
Wetherby Business Park
  WBY LS22 ....30 B8
Wetherby Golf Club
  WBY LS22 ....47 L2
Wetherby High School
  WBY LS22 ....48 B1
Wetherby Leisure Centre
  WBY LS22 ....48 A2
Wetherby Racecourse
  WBY LS22 ....30 E8
Wharfebank Business Centre
  OT LS21 ....41 G7

Wharfedale Business Park
  BOW BD4 ....127 M5
Wharfedale General Hospital
  OT LS21 ....41 H4
The Whartons Primary School
  OT LS21 ....41 J4
Wheatsheaf Shopping Centre
  MILN OL16 ....206 B6
Wheldon Infant School
  CAS WF10 ....158 A6
Whetley Primary School
  GIR BD8 ....104 C6
Whingate Business Park
  WOR/ARM LS12 ....108 D7
Whingate Primary School
  WOR/ARM LS12 ....108 C7
The Whitcliffe Hotel
  CLECK BD19 ....149 M7
Whitcliffe Mount School
  CLECK BD19 ....149 K6
Whitcliffe Road First School
  CLECK BD19 ....149 M6
Whitechapel Middle School
  CLECK BD19 ....149 K5
Whitecote Primary School
  BRAM LS13 ....107 M2
Whitehall Industrial Estate
  WOR/ARM LS12 ....130 B2
Whitehall Primary School
  LUD/ILL HX2 ....124 A8
Whitehall Trading Estate
  WOR/ARM LS12 ....130 A2
White Horse Leisure Centre
  WKFDE WF1 ....12 D3
White Laith Primary School
  SCFT LS14 ....89 L7
White Rose House
  WKFDE WF1 ....12 F4
White Rose Shopping Centre
  MOR LS27 ....131 G7
Whitkirk Medical Centre
  MSTN/BAR LS15 ....111 M6
Whitkirk Primary School
  MSTN/BAR LS15 ....111 K7
Whittaker Golf Club
  LIT OL15 ....207 M2
Whitwood Business Centre
  CAS WF10 ....157 J6
Whitwood Golf Club
  CAS WF10 ....157 G8
Wiggan Lane Trading Estate
  HUDN HD2 ....192 F2
Wigton Moor Primary School
  AL/HA/HU LS17 ....88 B1
Wilberlee J & I School
  MAR/SLWT HD7 ....211 M4
The William Henry Smith
  School *BRIG* HD6 ....169 M6
Willow Industrial Complex
  RPDN/SBR HX6 ....167 K3
The Willows Medical Centre
  CUL/QBY BD13 ....125 G5
Willow Park Junior School
  PONT WF8 ....181 H6
Willow Valley Golf & Country
  Club *BRIG* HD6 ....171 G1
Wilsden Primary School
  WIL/AL BD15 ....102 E1
Wilthorpe Infant School
  DOD/DAR S75 ....260 E2
Wilthorpe Junior School
  DOD/DAR S75 ....260 E2

Windhill CC
  SHPY BD18 ....82 F5
Windhill CE Primary School
  SHPY BD18 ....82 F6
Windhill Green Medical Centre
  SHPY BD18 ....82 E6
Windmill Primary School
  MID LS10 ....132 A6
Windsor Medical Centre
  EARL WF12 ....174 A6
Wira Business Park
  BHP/TINH LS16 ....86 B5
Withinfields Primary School
  HIPP HX3 ....169 H1
Womersley CE Primary School
  AWLS/ASK DN6 ....205 H3
Woodbank Special School
  HDGY LS6 ....6 F3
Woodhall Hills Golf Club
  PDSY/CALV LS28 ....106 B2
Wood Hall Hotel
  WBY LS22 ....46 F4
Woodhouse Business Centre
  NORM WF6 ....178 C5
Woodhouse CC
  CHAL LS7 ....87 H8
Woodhouse Grove School
  IDLE BD10 ....84 B5
Woodhouse Health Centre
  HDGY LS6 ....6 F3
Woodhouse Primary School
  BRIG HD6 ....170 D6
Woodkirk High School
  EARD/LOFT WF3 ....152 E5
Woodland Glade Leisure
  Centre *HUDN* HD2 ....192 F1
Woodlands CE Primary
  School *LM/WK* BD12 ....149 J1
Woodlands CC
  LM/WK BD12 ....149 H1
Woodlands Primary School
  OSM LS9 ....110 D3
Woodlesford Primary School
  RTHW LS26 ....133 M7
Woodroyd Industrial Estate
  LM/WK BD12 ....149 G1
Woodside Clinic
  WBSY BD6 ....126 C8
Woodside Primary School
  WBSY BD6 ....126 C8
Woodside Trading Estate
  HORS LS18 ....86 A5
Woodsley Health Centre
  HDGY LS6 ....6 A5
Woodsome Hall Golf Club
  KBTN HD8 ....215 K5
Wooldale Junior School
  HOLM/MEL HD9 ....236 F7
Woolley Hall College
  HOR/CROF WF4 ....220 D7
Woolshops Shopping Centre
  HFAX HX1 ....11 H6
Worsbrough Bank End Primary
  School *BSLY* S70 ....261 L8
Worsbrough Common Primary
  School *BSLY* S70 ....261 H8
Worthinghead Primary School
  LM/WK BD12 ....148 F3
Worth Valley Primary School
  HWTH BD22 ....79 J3
Wortley High School
  WOR/ARM LS12 ....108 B8

Wortley Moor Lane Trading
  Estate *WOR/ARM* LS12 ....108 D8
WRCC Clinic
  MAR/SLWT HD7 ....212 F5
Wrenthorpe Health Centre
  WKFDW/WTN WF2 ....176 A4
Wrenthorpe Primary School
  WKFDW/WTN WF2 ....176 B4
Wrenthorpe Sports Club
  WKFDW/WTN WF2 ....176 B3
Wrose Health Centre
  ECHL BD2 ....105 H1
Wycliffe CE Primary School
  SHPY BD18 ....82 C6
Wykebeck Infant School
  OSM LS9 ....110 F4
Wykebeck Primary School
  OSM LS9 ....110 F4
Wyke Manor Upper School
  LM/WK BD12 ....148 F3
Wyther Lane Industrial Estate
  KSTL LS5 ....108 C3
XSCAPE & XSITE Arena
  HORS LS18 ....180 B2
Yarnbury RUFC
  HORS LS18 ....85 J3
Yeadon Airport Industrial
  Estate *YEA* LS19 ....63 G5
Yeadon Cemetery
  YEA LS19 ....62 E6
Yeadon CC
  YEA LS19 ....62 E7
Yeadon Health Centre
  YEA LS19 ....62 D7
Yeadon Westfield Infant School
  YEA LS19 ....62 B8
York Road Industrial Estate
  WBY LS22 ....30 B8
Yorkshire Amateurs FC
  CHAL LS7 ....88 B8
Yorkshire Bank Sports Ground
  AL/HA/HU LS17 ....87 M4
Yorkshire CCC (Headingley
  Cricket Ground) *HDGY* LS6 ....108 F2
Yorkshire Clinic
  BGLY BD16 ....81 L7
Yorkshire College of Music &
  Drama *HDGY* LS6 ....109 G1
Yorkshire Martyrs Catholic
  College Sports College
  BOW BD4 ....128 C6
Yorkshire Post Offices
  LDS LS1 ....8 C1
Yorkshire Post Sports Club
  BHP/TINH LS16 ....86 E7
Yorkshire Sculpture Park
  HOR/CROF WF4 ....219 C7
Yorkshire Television Studios
  BVRD LS3 ....109 G5
Young Street Industrial Estate
  GIR BD8 ....104 B6
Zakaria Muslim Girls High
  School *BTLY* WF17 ....173 M3

Acknowledgements

The Post Office is a registered trademark of Post Office Ltd. in the UK and other countries.

Schools address data provided by Education Direct.

Petrol station information supplied by Johnsons

One-way street data provided by © Tele Atlas N.V. Tele Atlas

Garden centre information provided by

Garden Centre Association   Britains best garden centres

Wyevale Garden Centres

The statement on the front cover of this atlas is sourced, selected and quoted from a reader comment and feedback form received in 2004

Notes

 **Street by Street** QUESTIONNAIRE

Dear Atlas User
Your comments, opinions and recommendations are very important to us.
So please help us to improve our street atlases by taking a few minutes to
complete this simple questionnaire.

You do not need a stamp (unless posted outside the UK). If you do not want to remove this page from your street atlas, then photocopy it or write your answers on a plain sheet of paper.

Send to: The Editor, AA Street by Street, FREEPOST SCE 4598,
Basingstoke RG21 4GY

ABOUT THE ATLAS...

Which city/town/county did you buy?

_____

Are there any features of the atlas or mapping that you find particularly useful?

_____
_____
_____

Is there anything we could have done better?

_____
_____
_____

Why did you choose an AA Street by Street atlas?

_____
_____
_____

Did it meet your expectations?

Exceeded ☐   **Met all** ☐   **Met most** ☐   **Fell below** ☐

Please give your reasons

_____
_____
_____
_____
_____

MX16y

continued overleaf

Where did you buy it?

For what purpose? (please tick all applicable)

To use in your own local area ☐ **To use on business or at work** ☐

Visiting a strange place ☐ **In the car** ☐ **On foot** ☐

Other (please state)

LOCAL KNOWLEDGE...

Local knowledge is invaluable. Whilst every attempt has been made to make the information contained in this atlas as accurate as possible, should you notice any inaccuracies, please detail them below (if necessary, use a blank piece of paper) or e-mail us at *streetbystreet@theAA.com*

ABOUT YOU...

Name (Mr/Mrs/Ms)

Address

Postcode

Daytime tel no **Mobile tel no**

E-mail address

Please only give us your e-mail address and mobile phone number if you wish to hear from us about other products and services from the AA and partners by e-mail or text or mms.

Which age group are you in?

Under 25 ☐ **25-34** ☐ **35-44** ☐ **45-54** ☐ **55-64** ☐ **65+** ☐

Are you an AA member? **YES** ☐ **NO** ☐

Do you have Internet access? **YES** ☐ **NO** ☐

The information we hold about you will be used to provide the product(s) and service(s) requested and for identification, account administration, analysis, and fraud/loss prevention purposes. More details about how that information is used is in our Privacy Statement, which you will find under the heading "Personal information" in our Terms and Conditions and on our website. Copies are available from us by post, by contacting our Data Protection Manager at AA, Fanum House, Basing View, Hampshire, Basingstoke RG21 4EA.
We may want to contact you about other products and services provided by us or our partners but please tick the box if you DO NOT wish to hear about such products and services from us by mail or telephone. ☐

Thank you for taking the time to complete this questionnaire. Please send it to us as soon as possible, and remember, you do not need a stamp (unless posted outside the UK).

MX16y